The Insider's Guide to the Colleges

36th Edition

2 0 1 0

Compiled and Edited
by the Staff of
The Yale Daily News

St. Martin's Griffin
New York

Readers with comments or questions should address them to Editors, *The Insider's Guide to the Colleges*, c/o *The Yale Daily News*, 202 York Street, New Haven, CT 06511-4804.

Visit *The Insider's Guide to the Colleges* Web site at www.yaledailynews.com/books.

The editors have sought to ensure that the information in this book is accurate as of press time. Because policies, costs, and statistics do change from time to time, readers should verify important information with the colleges.

ISBN-13: 978-0-312-57029-3
ISBN-10: 0-312-57029-5

First Edition: July 2009

10 9 8 7 6 5 4 3 2 1

Contents

Preface

Welcome to the 2010 edition of *The Insider's Guide to the Colleges*! The college application process may seem overwhelming, but you are beginning your search on the right foot simply by picking up this book. In this 36th edition of the *Guide*, we provide you with an accurate picture of what day-to-day life is like for college students at the schools featured. For each college profile, we rely on hours of personal interviews with actual college students to give you a true sense of the school and its student body.

We tell you what we wanted to know when we were in your shoes. College is going to be one of the most exciting and rewarding experiences of your life. It's all about opening yourself up to new experiences, haphazardly putting together something edible in the dining hall when the lines are long and the food is bad, and making the kinds of friends who will skip class to give you a hand when you need it. It's about pulling all-nighters on papers due the next morning or talking to your roommates until the sun comes up. It's about driving halfway across the country to see your football team win, walking onto a team for a sport you've never played before, or volunteering at the local elementary school when you still have 300 pages of reading to do. College is gallons of coffee, stress and laughter.

But first you need to choose a school. Among the thousands of colleges that span the continent, you can apply to no more than a handful. Maybe you have a vague idea of what you are looking for, but how do you begin to narrow your choices?

That's where the *Insider's Guide* comes in. For this 36th edition, we've revamped our entire book to ensure that it provides an accurate portrayal of life at each of the more than 300 colleges and universities in the United States and Canada we feature. We give you the inside scoop directly from the students who attend these institutions. We research each school by interviewing friends, friends of friends, and a random selection of student leaders at each school. These students' unique perspectives give us insights that you won't find on the glossy pages of admissions brochures or by browsing schools' Web sites. It also means that we are only as accurate as our sources. Although we have worked hard to make each article factually correct and current, the college experience is unique for every individual—after all, one student's closet-sized dorm room might be another student's palace.

In addition to articles on each college, the *Insider's Guide* includes a number of special features to help you in your search. "The College Finder" gives you a rundown on various schools according to key attributes. "Getting In" takes you step-by-step through the intricacies of the admissions process. In "The College Spectrum," we discuss some of the most important factors to consider when choosing between schools, as well as giving you a look at current trends in college life. "Introduction for International Students" provides some tips on applying to American schools if you live outside of the United States, while "Students with Disabilities" informs students with learning or physical disabilities about issues they should be aware of when applying to college. "Study Abroad" gives you a peek at the overseas adventures of college students. We have also included "Terms You Should Know," a glossary to help you decode confusing college slang.

We have revised our "Insider's Packing List" and our "Insider's Quiz." Our editors have also added to the ever-popular "Editors' Choice" feature, a ranking of schools in categories ranging from ugliest school colors to biggest rivalries. These lists are based on research, statistics and student interviews as well as our own assessments. Our hope is that this feature will offer you a new perspective or introduce you to a school you might not have considered.

We know how stressful the college selection process is. After all the hard work of preparing and applying, acceptances often appear to have been offered at random. It may sound difficult, but try not to worry. The majority of students love college. In part, this is because they chose schools that were right for them. But remember, every single college will provide you with new people to meet, new freedoms to explore, and new experiences to enjoy and learn from. Wherever you end up, remember: those four years fly by, so make the most of them!—*Kimberly Chow*

Acknowledgments

We would like to give particular thanks to Matt Martz, our editor at St. Martin's Press. Without his organizational and creative vision, the 2010 *Guide* would never have been published. To Emad Haerizadeh, we give considerable thanks for his time and patience at *The Yale Daily News*. We would also like to thank all the interviewees who were gracious enough to give us a peek into their lives and their colleges: Without you, this book would not have been possible. Finally, we are especially thankful to those Yalies who 40 years ago decided to devote their time and energy toward creating a helpful guide for high schoolers about to go to college. We hope you enjoy the book!

Sunceti Agrawal
Josh Allen
Nicole Alvarado
Graham Anderson
Jourdan Aromin
Joe Babarsky
Ashley Barber
Kevin Baremore
Colleen Bartman
Katie Bartolotta
Danny Berring
Caroline Berson
Jennifer Bieznak
Kyle Boylan
Abby Cable
Laura Cambruzzi
Steve Carmody
Erica Carpenter
Johanna Chong
Lindsay Clements
Kate Comaskey
Brad Cox
Will Cullen
Richard Dang
Jonathan Patrick DeWeese
Lauren Drozd
Asa Eisenhardt
Dylan Elder
Jacob Eller
Maria Endsley
Kelly England
Ashkon Farmand
Michael Fennel
Marissa Ferber
Noam Finkelstein
Matt Foley
Martin Freres
Jessica Frey
Cassandra Garcia
Christopher Golden
Ethan Greenspan
Betsy Grether

David Grometer
Daniel Hauben
Amy Hernandez
Lauren Hofmayer
John Holland
Grace Hong
Arian Jalali
Danny Jimenez
Bree Ann Johnson
David Johnson
Jaleesa Joy
Danny Karp
Dan Kaufman
Roxanne Kierne
Hugo Klaers
Brianna Kohr
Caroline Lartz
Kara Lauko
Karissa Le
Marissa Lee
Erica Leslie
Andy Levine
Leigh Ann Lilly
Janet Lin
Tiffany Ling
Madison Lipton
Boris Lipvetsky
Alice Lou
Stephen Ma
Emanuel Magana
Samantha Mangel
Rochelle McConkie
Andrew McCreary
Joe McDonald
Crystal Mckenzie
Maggie Melchiorre
Alisa Miller
Amy Mokris
Molly Moody
Jenny Morrow
James Mulligan
Becky Murphy

Chelsea Murphy
Simon Neely
Zackery O'Connor
John Officer
Krzysztof Pakula
Dearon Panossian
Bennett Parmington
Amanda Perez
Cat Pien
Anna Pitoniak
Claire Psarouthakis
Andrea Rectenwald
Samantha Rose
Kenny Ryan
Elias Saber-Khiabani
McKinley Sayre
Sara Schilling
Eli Schmitt
Bing Shao
Ryan Sigurdson
Maninder Singh
Justin Smith
Kathryn Steinhubl
Kyle Stokes
Mike Stutes
Casey Super
Matthew Sutter
Esteban Tapetillo
Sarah Thurston
Rebecca Turkington
Tim Vogeler
Kelly Walsh
Katy Weaver
Alexandra Weiss
Wendy Wilde
Rhett Williamson
Chui-Hung Wong
Grace Wong
Lisa Woo
KaaBao Yang
Alfred Young

How to Use This Book

How We Select the Colleges

One of the most difficult questions we wrestle with here at *The Insider's Guide* is which schools to include in the upcoming edition. From more than 2,000 four-year institutions nationwide, we only cover slightly over 300 colleges. We examine a number of criteria in deciding which colleges to select, but our first priority is always the quality of academics offered by the institution. Another key factor in our decisions is the desire to offer a diversity of options in *The Insider's Guide*. Thus we have included schools from all 50 states as well as top institutions in Canada. In deciding which schools to include, we also take into account the range of extracurricular options available to students, including student publications, teams and ethnic organizations. Each year we review our list of schools, research potential additions, and try to include new schools that we have not had the space to write about before to insure you're getting the most comprehensive insider information that is to be had.

We have made a point to review the largest state-affiliated institutions because of the significant number of students who apply to and matriculate at their states' schools. These universities tend to offer an especially wide range of opportunities. We have also made every effort to include a broad cross-section of the smaller colleges because of the unique kind of education they offer. Many of these small schools are top liberal arts colleges, generally clustered in the Northeast, offering a broad but personalized education. To add to the diversity of schools reviewed by *The Insider's Guide*, we have also included selections from the most prominent technical schools and creative and performing arts schools. These schools provide a more specialized education that combines general knowledge with a concentration in a particular field. The sampling of schools in this category is by no means comprehensive, and we encourage students interested in specialized institutions to explore their options more deeply through additional research.

In sum, this book covers the colleges we believe to be among the most noteworthy in both the United States and Canada. This selection does not imply in any way that you cannot get a good education at a school not listed in the *Guide*. We strongly encourage students to use strategies discussed within this book to explore the wide variety of schools that we did not have space to include here, including community colleges, state schools, international schools and professional schools. In addition, it's not guaranteed that you will have a blissful four years if you attend one of the schools we feature! Rather, we believe that every school in the *Guide* offers students the raw materials for constructing an excellent education.

It's All Up to You

Now that you have picked up a copy of *The Insider's Guide*, it's up to you how to use it. A few dedicated readers scrutinize the book from start to finish, determined to gain the most complete understanding of the college process and the schools that are out there. Others flip through the *Guide* for only a few minutes to look at **FYIs** from schools that interest them, or to read funny quotes taken from nearby colleges. Another good strategy is to use the **College Finder**, **Editors' Choice lists**, and statistics that begin each article to learn more about colleges that you may not have heard of before. It might be worthwhile to read up on colleges that you wouldn't initially consider—you just may find yourself intrigued by the student perspectives. Take advantage of the opening features of the book—they are designed to help you zero in on schools that meet your search criteria. You can also explore these beginning sections to learn what is unique and important about schools you are already considering. We encourage all these approaches. Above all, we hope that the *Guide* is fun to read, educational, and a useful aid in helping to make the college selection process less stressful.

While our **Editors' Choice lists** use a mix of statistics and subjectivity to provide an alternative perspective on the schools we include, we have avoided the temptation to pigeon-hole the colleges with some kind of catch-all rating system, or worse, to numerically rank them from first to last. Our reason is that the "best" college for one person may come near the bottom of the list for another. Each student has his or her own particular set of wants and needs, so it would be impossible for us to objectively rank the schools from "best" to "worst." Whereas most rankings focus solely on academic factors, the college experience is a balance of academics, social life, extracurricular activities and much more.

Even so, some may wonder why we don't rate the colleges solely on the basis of academic quality. We think that attempting to come up with such a ranking is both impossible and undesirable. There are too many variables—from the many factors that contribute to the quality of a department and school as a whole to the articulateness and accessibility of the professor who happens to be your academic advisor. Furthermore, it's useless to try to compare a college of 2,000 students with a university of 10,000 (or a university of 10,000 with a state school of 40,000 for that matter) on any basis other than individual preference. Despite these reasons not to, some reportedly reputable sources such as national magazines often insist on publishing numerical rankings of colleges. We advise you not to take these lists too seriously. Oftentimes the determining factor in the rankings is a statistic such as "percent of alumni who donate money," something that means very little to most college applicants.

For over 35 years, *The Insider's Guide* has been dedicated to the belief that the best rankers of schools are students themselves, not magazine writers. Our goal, therefore, is to help you train your eye so you can select the college that is best for you. Remember, we may describe, explain, interpret and report—but in the end, the choice is always yours.

Getting In

Applying to college can seem as intimidating as the thickness of this book, but neither should be a chore. In the spring of your sophomore year of high school your Aunt Doris, whom you have not seen in seven years, pinches your cheek and asks you where you are going to college. How the heck should I know? you think to yourself. That fall, your mom tells you that the girl down the street with the 4.0 grade point average is taking the SAT prep course for the fifth time to see if she can get a perfect score and win thousands in scholarship money. You reply that you are late for school. You keep ducking the subject, but the hints come with increasing regularity. Not only has dinnertime become your family's "let's talk about Lauren's college options" hour, but friends at school are already beginning to leaf through college catalogs. Soon you find the guidance counselor's office crowded with your wide-eyed peers, and it's clear they aren't asking for love advice. Panicking, you decide to make an appointment with the counselor yourself.

When you first talk to your counselor, preferably in the early part of your junior year, you may have just begun to feel comfortable in high school, let alone prepared to think about college. The entire prospect seems far away, but choosing the right school for you takes a good amount of thought and organization—and a visit to your counselor is a solid start. You may even be wondering if college is the path you want to take after high school. And you're not alone. A good number of people choose to take a year or two off to work or travel before pursuing a college education.

One important resource in making a decision about any post-graduation plans is your counselor. College counselors have a wealth of information and experience from which to draw, and they can help you lay out a plan for whatever direction you wish to take. If you decide that college is your next step, you will have a lot of options. Although many schools are surveyed in this book, we have not included professional schools or community colleges, all of which also offer a wide variety of opportunities. With research of your own and the aid of your counselor, you should be able to find a school that will give you what you're looking for.

In your hunt for the best college, it is wise to do a little exploring of your own before sitting down with your counselor. Counselors can be invaluable advisors and confidants throughout the college admissions process, but sometimes counselors inadvertently limit your search by only recommending noncompetitive schools, or, conversely, by assuring you that you'll get into whichever school you want. A few may even try to dissuade you from applying to colleges that you are seriously considering. These cases aren't common, but they do happen. Regardless of your counselor's perspective, it is best if you already have an idea of what you are looking for, as it will help both you and your advisor sort out all the options. You can refer back to these initial goals as you learn more. In the end, always follow your instincts.

As you begin to wade through the piles of brochures, ask yourself questions. What factors about a school make a difference to you? What do you want in a college? A strong science department? A Californian landscape? A small student body? A great social life? Although each college is a mix of different features, it is wise to place your academic needs first. Check out the general academic quality of the school, as well as what kind of programs they offer. Please note: since many students change their majors repeatedly before finally settling down, it's a good idea to look for schools with programs in a number of areas that interest you.

Of course, it's impossible to think of all the angles from which you should approach your college search. You can't predict what your interests will be three or four years from now, or what things will prove most important to you at the college you attend. After all, those realizations are a big part of what the college experience is all about. But by taking a hard look at yourself now, and proceeding thoughtfully, you can be confident that you are investigating the right colleges for the right reasons.

As you begin the search, schools will start to seek you out as well. In the early winter of your junior year, you'll receive your PSAT scores, and unless you request otherwise, your mailbox will soon become inundated with letters from colleges around the country. The College Search Service of the College Board provides these schools with the names and addresses of students who show promise, and the schools crank out thousands of form letters to send, often to students who they feel are underrepresented in their student population.

While sorting through these masses of glossy brochures, you'll probably notice that most of them contain lofty quotes and pictures of a diverse, frolicking student body. One of the best ways to find out if these ideals are actually truths is to visit the college. But before that, you can verify some of what you read by comparing it to nationally published articles and statistics. You will probably find the colleges that most interest you through your own research, and the majority of these schools wait for you to contact them before they send information. In that case, create a form letter that briefly expresses your interest in the college and requests materials. You'll get your name on their mailing lists and they'll appreciate the fact that you took the initiative.

Throughout this process, make sure to listen to those who know you well and often have sound advice to share—namely, your parents and elder siblings. Besides having some ideas of schools you might enjoy attending, your parents also have great insight into how your education can and will be financed. If you come to an early understanding with your family about prospective colleges and financial concerns, things will move much more smoothly down the road. But be warned—the college search can be one of the most trying times in any parent-child relationship, and some parents become more or less involved in the process than students want. The best advice we can give is to remember that calm, patient discussions are a better tactic than yelling matches.

When consulting others about your college search, it is helpful to keep a few things in mind. Every piece of advice you receive will be a reflection of someone's own life experiences, and it is likely to be highly subjective. Most adults will suggest schools located in regions they know or colleges they have visited or attended themselves. Also, opinions are often based on stereotypes that can be false, outdated, or just misleading. Still, the more people you talk to, the better perspective you will gain on the colleges you are considering. Once you have a few outside ideas, this book can give you some inside information. If you like what you have heard about a particular school, follow up with some research and find out if it's still a place that calls to you.

As you approach the time when your final

college list must be made, you will probably have visited college fairs and attended various college nights. Real-life representatives from the schools are always good to meet. Talking to current college students is an even more important step, as is visiting the schools that make it to your last list. During these encounters, ask the questions that are on your mind. Be critical and observant. When it's time for the final leg of the college selection process, you'll be calm and satisfied if you know you've really looked hard into yourself and all your options.

Visit

Whether your list of schools has been set for months or fluctuates on a daily basis, college visits are a great way to narrow down your choices and prioritize your list of options. Try to plan campus visits so you'll be finished by the fall of your senior year, especially if you are considering early application programs. Additionally, aim to see as many schools that interest you as possible—there's no better way to get a feel for where you'd like to spend the next four years of your life.

When you visit a campus, try to keep in mind why you are there. You have probably already seen the college viewbook with glossy pictures of green lawns and diverse groups of students in seminar-size classes. Now is the time to find out what the campus is really like. Is the student population truly that diverse? Do people really gather and play Frisbee on plush green lawns? What do the dorms actually look like? And most importantly, do you feel comfortable there?

If you are visiting a campus for an interview, make sure you schedule one in advance. Making the decision not to interview on campus may be a good one, however. While some schools require an on-campus interview, some insiders recommend that you request an alumni interview instead. Alumni interviews tend to be more convenient and less grueling than on-campus interviews. In any case, make sure you check a school's policy regarding interviews before you arrive, and schedule your visit accordingly.

While some prefer to visit colleges over summer vacation, we think the best time to visit is during the academic year, when regular classes are in session. During the summer months very few students are on campus, so it will be much more difficult to get a feel for the student culture and vibrancy (or lack thereof). Times of unusually high stress also will not give you a good idea of what ordinary life is like. For this reason, you'll also want to avoid exam periods and vacations. During the academic year, your questions about the campus are much more likely to be answered. You'll get a feel for the type of people at the school, and you'll get an idea of what it is like to be a student living on campus. It's important to get a good sense of what your daily life will be like if you end up attending the school.

Before you look at any college, take a little time to prepare. Perhaps you will want to come up with some kind of system to evaluate the schools you will visit. Putting together a list of characteristics that are important to you will make it easier to compare one school to the next, whether they be academics, the size of the campus, or the surrounding area's vibrancy and atmosphere. Make sure you jot down some notes on the schools during and after your trips. Although colleges may seem easy to differentiate at the time, your impressions of each may blur together when you are back at home, sitting in front of 10 seemingly identical applications.

An overnight stay with undergraduates can provide you with a more inside look at campus life. Most admissions offices have students on call who are happy to show you around campus, take you to some classes and parties, and let you crash in their dorms. If you have friends there, they are good resources as well. Either way, staying with students will help you see what an undergraduate's academic and social life is really like. One student said, "I found that it didn't matter much if I stayed over or not, as long as I got to talk to students. But if you do stay over, Thursday or Friday night is the best time." Sometimes it is hard to connect with students during a single day when everybody is rushing around to classes. Try to spend a night late in the week when students will have more time for you and the nightlife will be more vibrant. It is always possible that you will end up with hosts that are difficult to relate to or socially withdrawn. Don't let a bad hosting experience completely dictate your feelings about the college—just do everything you can to get out into the student body and explore what the school has to offer.

Keep in mind that college life doesn't consist entirely of classes. Sample the food, which is, after all, a necessity of life. Check out the dorms. Take the campus tour. Although you are sure to be inundated with obscure facts about the college that may not interest you, it can be useful to have a knowledgeable guide to show you the buildings themselves and the campus as a whole. If you have any questions, do not hesitate to ask. Tour guides are often students, and are a great resource for any information you want about the school.

Should you bring your parents along? Maybe. Some students prefer to leave them at home. Although parents don't mean any harm, they can sometimes get in the way. Your discomfort at having them around when you're trying to get along with new students may cloud your opinion of a school. However, most students do bring along at least one family member. If you go this route, don't completely discount the advice or opinions they may have about the school. Parents can be great resources to bounce ideas off of, particularly regarding the pros and cons of the various colleges you have seen. You might want to take the campus tour with them, and then break away to explore the campus on your own and talk with students one-on-one. When you enter college your parents will not be there with you, so it's a good idea to get a feel for what that will actually be like.

Most importantly, keep in mind your sense of the campus atmosphere. How does it feel to walk across the main quad? Does the mood seem intellectual or laid-back? Do T-shirts read "Earth Day Every Day" or "Coed Naked Beer Games"? Look for postings of events; some campuses are alive and vibrant while others seem pretty dead. Check your comfort level. Imagine yourself on the campus for the next four years and see how that makes you feel. Focus on these characteristics while you are on campus—you can read about the distribution requirements when you get back home. Most of all, enjoy yourself! The campus visit is an exciting peek into a world that will soon be your own.

The Interview

Just about every college applicant dreads the interview. It can be the most nerve-wracking part of the college application process. But relax—despite the horror stories you might have heard, the interview will rarely make or break your application. If you are a strong candidate, don't be overly self-assured; if your application makes you look like a hermit, be lively and personable. Usually the interview can only help you, and at some schools it is nothing more than informational. "I was constantly surprised at how many questions they let me ask," one applicant reported.

Consider the interview your chance to highlight the best parts of your application and explain the weaker parts without being whiny or making excuses. Are your SAT scores on the low side? Does your extracurricular section seem a little thin? An interview gives you the opportunity to call attention to your successes in classes despite your scores, or explain that of the three clubs you listed, you founded two and were president of the third.

There are a few keys to a successful interview.

1. The first and most important is to stand out from the crowd. Keep in mind that the interviewer probably sees half a dozen or more students every day, month after month. If you can make your interviewer laugh, interest him or her in something unusual you have done, or somehow spice up the same old questions and answers, you have had a great interview. Don't just say that you were the president of something; be able to back up your titles with interesting and genuine stories. On the other hand, don't go overboard—shocking your interviewer with spring break stories, for example. That will most likely work against you.

2. Do not try to be something you are not. Tell the truth and give the interviewer a feel for who you really are—your passions, your strengths and your challenges. By doing so, you will be more relaxed and confident. Even if you feel that the "real you" isn't that interesting or amazing, take time to reflect on your high school experience—the stories that surface in your mind may just surprise you.

3. A few days before the actual interview, think about some of the questions you might be asked. Some admissions officers begin every interview by asking, "Why do you want to go to this school, and why should we let you?" You should not have memorized speeches for every answer, but try not to get caught off guard. Make sure you really know why you want to attend this college. Even if you are not sure, think of a few plausible reasons and be prepared to give them. Students often make the mistake of giving a canned answer, which is okay since most answers are similar, but admissions officers look to admit students who want to take advantage of all that is available at their school. Your answer must include the

three essential elements of a good reply: your interests, whether academic or extracurricular; what you believe the school will provide; and how and why you are excited about the opportunity to take advantage of them. Other common questions include those about your most important activities, what you did with your summers, and what vision you may have for your future.

4. A note of caution: If your interview takes place after you have submitted your application, the interviewer might ask you questions about some of the things you included. One student wrote on his application that he read *Newsweek* religiously. During his interview, the admissions officer asked the student about a story in a recent issue of the magazine. The student had no idea what the interviewer was talking about. He was not accepted. While this was only one in many factors that the admissions officer had to consider, it is still important. So be ready to back up your claims. It is always an excellent idea to indicate that you have a special interest in something, but make sure the interest is genuine—you may wind up in an hour-long conversation on the topic. Do not start talking about how you love learning about philosophy if you have only dabbled in it once. An open, thoughtful manner can do as much as anything else to impress your interviewer, although an overly negative attitude will make just as much of an impression.

5. Being spontaneous in a contrived situation usually amounts to having a successful interview. If you are nervous, that's okay. Said one applicant, "I felt sick and I didn't eat for a day before the interview." The most common misconception is that admissions officers are looking for totally confident individuals who know everything and have their entire future planned out. Almost the opposite is true. An admissions officer at a selective private college said, "We do not expect imitation adults to walk through the door. We expect to see people in their last year or two of high school with the customary apprehensions, habits and characteristics of that time of life." Admissions officers know students get nervous. They understand. If everything in your life is not perfect, do not be afraid to say so when appropriate. For example, if the conversation comes around to your high school, there is no need to cover up if problems do exist. It is

okay to say you did not think your chemistry lab was well equipped. An honest, realistic critique of your school or just about anything else will make a better impression than false praise ever could.

6. If something you say does not come out quite right, try to react as you would with a friend. If the interviewer asks about your career plans, it is all right to say that you are undecided. As a high school student, no one expects you to have all the answers—that is why you are going to college. Above all, remember that the admissions officer is a person interested in getting to know you as an individual. A person who may be a parent to someone, a friend of someone's, a sibling of someone's. They empathize. As one interviewer explained, "I'm not there to judge the applicants as scholars. I'm just there to get a sense of them as people."

7. Do not get so worried about saying all the right things that you forget to listen carefully to the interviewer. The purpose of the interview is not to grill you, but to match you with the school in the best interest of both. Sometimes the interviewer will tell you, either during the interview or in a follow-up letter, that you have little chance of getting in. If she says so or implies it, know that such remarks are not made lightly. On the other hand, if she is sincerely encouraging, listen to that, too. If an interviewer suggests other schools for you to look into, remember that she is a professional and take note. Besides, many interviewers appreciate a student's ability to listen as well as to talk.

8. Your interviewer might ask you whether you have a first choice, particularly if her college is often seen as a backup. If the school is really not your first choice, feel free to sidestep that question as gracefully as possible. Not only is it more than likely that you haven't made up your mind, but your first choice is your business, not theirs. If the school really is your first choice, though, feel free to say so, and give a good reason why. A genuine interest can be a real plug on your behalf.

9. Also know that you can direct the conversation. Do not worry about occasional lapses as some interviewers wait to see how you will react to a potentially awkward situation. Take advantage of the pause to ask a question or bring up a relevant topic that really interests you. It is your job to present the parts of you and your background that you want noted.

10. Selective colleges need reasons to accept you. Being qualified on paper is not always enough. Think of the interviewer's position: "Why should we accept you instead of thousands of other qualified applicants?" The answer to that question should be evident in every response you give. Use the interview to play up and accentuate your most memorable qualities. Show flashes of the playful sense of humor that your English teacher cites in his recommendation; impress the interviewer with the astute eye for politics about which your history teacher raves.

11. Too many applicants are afraid to talk confidently about their accomplishments. If the interviewer is impressed by something, do not insist that it was not much, or he might believe you. If he is not impressed by something you think is important, tactfully let him know that he should be. But do not, under any circumstances, act like you are too good for the college. One well-qualified applicant to a leading college was turned down when the interviewer wrote, "It obviously isn't going to be the end of his world if he doesn't get in. And it won't be the end of our world, either." If there is any quality you want to convey, it is a sincere interest in the school.

12. Almost all interviewers will eventually ask, "Do you have any questions about our school?" Come to the interview armed with a couple good questions, and not ones whose answers are easily found in the college's viewbook or on the school Web site. Do not ask if they have an economics department, for example—ask the average class size in introductory economics courses. It may help to do some extra preparation ahead of time. Are you interested in studying abroad? If so, know what kind of programs the school offers and ask a few questions about them. If you are excited to learn more about the school and have already done some homework, it goes a long way in the eyes of the interviewer. Also, if the interviewer is an alumnus, a good question is to ask what they would have done differently during their time at the college. You can be sure that they will need a moment of reflection, and you'll have time to relax!

13. You will probably wonder what to wear. This is no life or death decision, but remember that your appearance is one of the first things the interviewer will notice about you. Wear something you will be comfortable in—a jacket and a tie or a

nice dress is fine. Do not, however, be too casual. Faded jeans and a T-shirt will give the impression that you are taking the interview too lightly. But, if your interview is at Starbucks as opposed to someone's office building, take their choice in location as a cue for dress.

14. One crucial point: Keep your parents a thousand feet and preferably a thousand miles away from the interview session. It will be harder to relax and be genuine with an additional set of eyes on you, and you might hold back some interesting information. When parents sit in, interviews tend to be short, boring, and, worst of all, useless. If the interviewer feels you cannot handle an hour without your parents, she might be concerned about your ability to survive the pressures of college life. Take the risk of hurting your parents' feelings and ask them to wait outside.

Once the interview is over, it is perfectly all right for your parents to ask any questions they may have if the interviewer walks with you back to the waiting room. Even if this makes you uncomfortable, do not let it show. Admissions officers can learn as much about you by the way you treat your parents as they do in the interview. The interviewer is not judging your parents. As long as you conduct yourself calmly and maturely, you have nothing to worry about.

15. It is a good idea to send a thank you note after the interview. It doesn't need to be extensive, just let the interviewer know that you appreciate the time she or he spent with you and that you enjoyed learning more about the school. While it doesn't seem like much, a simple note can leave a lasting impression. Be sure to say something specific to your interview. If you shared a laugh or if the interviewer mentioned something about his or her job, try to slip something personal into the note. All of this advice applies for interviews given by alumni as well as those conducted by admissions staff. Alumni interviewers sometimes carry slightly less weight with the admissions office, but they are valuable contacts with the schools and should not be taken lightly. Expect on-campus interviews to be a bit more formal than alumni interviews.

What if you do not have an interview at all? Perhaps you live too far away, and you cannot get to the school itself. Or, perhaps you feel that your lack of poise is serious enough that it would work against you in any interview you had. Talk it over with your guidance counselor. In general, geographic isolation is a valid excuse for not having an interview, and most colleges will not hold it against you. Ask if they will allow a phone interview instead. Yet, if the college is fairly close and makes it clear that applicants should have an on-campus interview if at all possible, make the effort to go. Otherwise, the college will assume that for some reason you were afraid to interview, or worse, that you simply did not care enough to have one. If the prospect is genuinely terrifying, schedule your first interview for a safety school, or ask your guidance counselor to grant you a practice interview. You might discover that the process is not as horrible as you originally thought.

The Tests

Whether you are an Olympic hopeful, a musical prodigy, or a third-generation legacy, it doesn't matter. You cannot avoid taking standardized tests if you want to go to college. Approximately 90 percent of all four-year institutions now require some type of admissions test. Certainly tests do not tell the whole story—grades, recommendations, extracurricular activities, the application essays and personal interviews round out the picture. However, standardized test scores are often the only uniform criteria available to admissions committees. They are meant to indicate the level of education you have had in the past, as well as your potential to succeed in the future. Unfortunately, while they aren't perfect, they are a necessary evil.

Virtually all of the nation's colleges require applicants to submit SAT I or ACT scores. In addition, some colleges will ask their applicants for SAT Subject Test scores. If you are an international student with a native language other than English (or recently moved from an education system using a foreign language), you may be required to take the TOEFL as well. If you take AP tests or are in an International Baccalaureate IB program, your scores could help you earn college credit if they agree with the score requirements of the college you are applying to. Does all this seem overwhelming to you? Read this section and hopefully we can help you understand each test a little better.

The Scholastic Aptitude Test (SAT) is the most widely chosen admissions test by college applicants. Administered by the Educational Testing Service (ETS) and created by the College Board, the SAT Reasoning Test currently has a math section, a critical reading section, and a writing section. A nearly four-hour test, there are a total of 10 sections; three are writing, three are verbal, three are math, and there is an unscored variable section (math or critical reading) thrown in somewhere to try out new question formats. The new math section has been upgraded to include material up through Geometry and Algebra II, and, to your benefit, you are allowed to use calculators. It has five-choice multiple-choice questions and questions where you produce the answer yourself. In the critical reading section, you will find sentence completions and short and long passages with reading comprehension questions.

The SAT scores the math, critical reading, and writing sections separately on a 200 to 800 scale. Therefore, your combined score can be a minimum of 600 and a maximum of 2400. One disadvantage with the SAT is that you are penalized for wrong answers, so avoid guessing haphazardly. However, if you can eliminate a few answer choices, it is often better to guess than to leave the question blank. The average score for each section is a 500 based on the recentered scale that the ETS implemented starting in 1995. When the SAT was originally calibrated, it was done so that the average score for the math and verbal sections would each be 500. Over several decades, the average dropped—some say as a result of the declining American education system. However, others argue that the perceived "decrease" is not surprising considering that today's over two million SAT-takers are much more representative of American education as a whole than the 10,000 primarily affluent prep-school students who took the test when it was implemented in 1941. As a result, the scoring was recentered in 1995 in order to redistribute scores more evenly along the 200 to 800 scale. All colleges and scholarship institutions are aware of this new scoring calibration, so even though it may be easier to get that rare 800 section score, your percentile rank among other students who took the exam will not change.

There are five ways to register for the SAT. The two most common methods are to complete an online registration at www.collegeboard.com or mail in a registration form, which you can get from your high school counselor's office. If you've registered for an SAT Program test before, you can complete the registration over the phone. For those students living outside of the United States, U.S. territories, and Puerto Rico, there is an option to fax in your registration. International students have the option of registering through a representative found in the International Edition of the SAT Registration Bulletin. The SAT is administered seven times a year in the domestic areas, and six times a year overseas.

Before you take the test, be sure to take advantage of two services offered by the College Board upon registration. The first is called the Student Search Service. It allows universities, colleges and scholarship programs to get general information about you, as well as what range your score falls into. You will receive a flood of information about different schools and scholarship programs in the mail in addition to information regarding financial aid opportunities. While you'll begin to see most of these letters as junk mail, some of them will help you come up with the list of colleges to which you intend to apply. As a second service the College Board will mail your test scores to a maximum of four specified schools or scholarship programs for free. You can send additional score reports for a fee. Be aware that if you have taken the SAT more than once, all of your previous scores will be sent when reporting to schools and scholarship programs. If you have second thoughts and want to cancel your scores, you must do so by the Wednesday following your exam via e-mail, fax, or mail.

The American College Test (ACT) was required mostly by colleges in the southern and western regions of the country, but is now accepted by most colleges across the nation. The exam covers English, reading, mathematics and science reasoning in the format of 215 multiple-choice questions. It also offers an optional writing component. One distinguishing feature of the ACT is that it measures what you have learned in the high school curriculum rather than your aptitude.

The ACT, unlike the SAT, does not deduct any points for incorrect answers, so be sure to fill in every bubble. You will receive a score on a scale of 1 to 36 for each of the four subject areas; your Composite score is just an average of the four scores rounded to the nearest whole number. Based on the over 1.3 million students who choose to take the test, the average Composite score is around 21. Registration is much like the SAT, with a mail-in option, online registration at www.act.org, or telephone preregistration. There is a stand-by registration option for those who forget to register. As far as score reporting goes, you can choose up to six schools or scholarship programs on your registration to have the scores sent to for free. The great thing about the ACT is that you can choose to send just one testing date's scores instead of having your whole history of scores sent, as is done with the SAT.

Many of the more selective colleges also require up to three SAT Subject Tests, formerly called SAT IIs. Available subjects include English, a variety of foreign languages, math, history, and several of the sciences. Due to the changes in the SAT Reasoning Test, there is no longer a writing exam available. One thing about the SAT Subject Tests is that you don't have to choose which tests you want to take until you're at the test center on the test date. The scores are reported on a 200 to 800 scale, but Score Choice is no longer an option. Score Choice had allowed students to put their subject tests on hold until they had decided which scores to send to universities, colleges and scholarship agencies. It posed problems in giving those who could pay for more tests an unfair advantage and also in that students would often forget to send their scores later on. The College Board abandoned this option in 2002; now all SAT Subject Test scores are reported, but only your highest in each subject will be taken into consideration.

The Test of English as a Foreign Language (TOEFL) is an English proficiency test provided for international students who want to study in the United States, Canada, or other English-speaking countries. It is administered on the computer or by paper-and-pencil depending on the location you choose. The scale for your total score is from 0 to 300 along with a score of 0 to 6 for the essay, which is scored separately. The TOEFL will test your listening, structured writing, and reading skills—giving a better picture of your English to the schools you apply to.

Advanced Placement (AP) exams are another animal altogether since their purpose is not only to get you into college, but also to earn you credits once you get there. Administered in May, each test covers a specific subject area and scores your performance from 1 to 5. Different schools require different scores for granting college credit. Some will offer credit but still require you to take classes in a subject that you aced on the AP exams. Since the tests require in-depth knowledge of specific subjects, do not put off studying for them. The general practice is to take the exam in a particular subject the May right after you have finished (or are in the midst of finishing) a course in that area. Not only can you get college credit with a high score, but you can also help your college applications with AP exams taken before your senior year.

If you attend an International Baccalaureate (IB) school, you might be able to receive college credit for your coursework depending on your score. A score of 4 or 5 are the required minimum by a college for credit and/or placement, but many institutions require a higher score of 6 or 7. Although not as popularly embraced by colleges and universities across the nation for giving college credit, they will definitely recognize you for the rigorous work you have completed in the program.

You may have already taken the PSAT/NMSQT, which is usually administered to sophomores or juniors through their high school. This is a great practice exam for the SAT Reasoning Test because it has a lot of the same type of questions. It is also a good way to qualify for merit scholarships if you get a high score. The PSAT changed its format in the fall of 2004 to complement the new SAT in 2005.

The most reliable way to keep up-to-date on test dates, sites and registration deadlines is through your high school guidance office. After the PSAT, you will be on your own about when and where you take the tests. Find out way ahead of time which ones are required by the colleges you are interested in; deadlines have a way of sneaking up on you. It is a good idea to begin taking the tests by the spring of your junior year. If you take the SAT I in March or May of your junior year and do not do as well as you think you should, you will have a couple of other opportunities to improve your score. The required SAT Subject Tests should be taken by June of your junior year so that if you decide to apply to an early-action or early-decision program, you will have completed the required testing.

Avoid postponing required testing until November, December, or January of your senior year. One new college student, who put off his exams until the last minute, recalled his college freshman faculty advisor saying to him, "I just don't understand it . . . you went to one of the best high schools in Chicago and did very well. How could your SAT scores have been so low?" He told her how lucky he felt just getting into college; he had contracted a nasty flu and thrown up before, during and after the test! On the other hand, do not repeat tests over and over. The ETS reports that students can gain an average of 25 points on both the math and verbal sections of the SAT I if they take the test a second time. Two or three shots at the SATs should be sufficient. If you've got the time and money, you may want to consider taking a prep course given by a professional test-preparation service. National test-prep companies like Kaplan and the Princeton Review, as well as dozens of local companies, attempt to give helpful tips on how to take tests for those willing to shell out hundreds of dollars. If you do decide to take a prep course, take it seriously. You may have six or seven high school classes to worry about, but you cannot hope to get your money's worth if you do not attend all of the sessions and complete the homework in these prep courses.

Many people choose not to take practice courses. A good student who is confident about taking tests can probably do just as well studying on his or her own. Practice exams are available online and in commercially marketed practice books. Get acquainted with the tests you plan to take beforehand; you should not have to waste time during your exam re-reading instructions and trying to figure out what to do. It's a good idea to even simulate an actual test by timing yourself with no interruptions on a real test that was previously administered.

The College Board puts out a book called *10 Real SATs* that proves to be one of the most effective ways to prepare for the SAT I. True to its title, the book has official SATs from the past, along with hints, test-taking strategies and exercises to help you improve your test score. The ACT has a similar book called *Getting into the ACT* with two complete exams plus ACT's own analyses and explanations designed to help you with the test. Getting the chance to practice exams in a real test-like situation (no phones, family or friends to distract you) will help you to get a keener sense of the overall structure of the test and help you work faster during the actual exam. It might also help you calm down!

Do not cram the night before the exam. Get plenty of sleep and relax. "My teacher encouraged us to go out and have a good time the day before," recalled one first-year college student. "So I went to the movies as a distraction. I think it worked!" On the day of the test, eat a full breakfast that isn't too heavy, dress comfortably, and do not forget to bring two pieces of ID, a calculator, a couple of number two pencils and a pencil sharpener. Make sure you are up early and know where you will be taking the test as well as how to get there. The test center may be overcrowded, there may be no air-conditioning or heat, and a hundred construction workers may be drilling outside

the nearest window—be prepared for anything!

The key to success on any of these exams is to keep calm. During the exam, keep track of how many problems there are and allot time accordingly. Read and attempt to answer every question since you do not get more credit for the hard ones than the easy ones. If you are stuck on a question, try to eliminate as many answers as possible and select from the remaining choices. Only if you really have no clue about the question should you leave it blank on the SAT.

A word of warning: Do not even think about cheating. It is not worth it, and your chances of getting caught and blackballed from college are high. To weed out cheaters, the ETS uses the mysterious K-index, a statistical tool that measures the chance of two students selecting the same answers. If your K-index is suspect, a form letter goes out to the colleges you are interested in, delaying your score until you retake the exam or prove your innocence. Know that looking at another person's test is not the only activity that the ETS considers cheating. Going back to finish work on a previous section is also against the rules. Do not tempt fate—a low score is better than no score at all.

At the beginning of this section, we stressed that standardized tests are important. How important? It varies depending on the school you are applying to. At many state schools, admission depends almost entirely on test scores and grades; if you score above the cutoffs, you are in. With the more selective schools, scores are usually only one of many important factors in the admissions process. According to the dean of admissions at Harvard University, "If scores are in the high 500 to low 700 range, they probably have a fairly small impact on our decisions." Each of the schools in this book lists a mean score range for the SAT. Remember that there are students who score below this range and above this range that were accepted to that college. Unless you score far below or far above the mean of your desired college, most likely your SAT I score will not make or break your chances of getting in. If you attended an inner-city school or a school in an area of the country where education standards are below the norm, your apparent deficit might, in fact, indicate a strength—as long as you are above the minimum levels.

Many students mistakenly believe that the SAT is the only test that "really matters" in competitive college admissions. In fact, SAT Subject Test scores taken as a whole are usually of equal importance. Colleges will often view these scores as a more accurate predictor of future performance than the SAT Reasoning Test. Aside from tests, it is important to remember that your high school record is weighed heavily. If you bomb your admissions tests, but have decent grades, there's a chance that your high school performance can outweigh the bad test scores. However, a poor GPA is hard to overlook, even if your scores are high. Remember that your admissions test scores are just a portion of the whole picture you present to the colleges. So try your best to make it advantageous for you and don't worry if you don't get a perfect score!

The Application

It's the fall of your senior year of high school. You've done your research, and found a few schools that you're interested in. You've taken the standardized tests, you've visited the campuses, and you may even have had some on-campus interviews. You still have one major hurdle ahead of you, however: The Application. Although the piles of paperwork may seem daunting, with some advance planning you can make the application process as painless as possible. As you go through the often challenging process, keep in mind that it's all worth it in light of your ultimate goal: acceptance.

First, you have to decide where you want to apply. You should have this done no later than the first few weeks of your senior year. After talking to students and visiting campuses, try to narrow down your original list of colleges to somewhere between five and 15. Applying to any more schools than this is probably overkill. Not only is it a waste of time to apply to more schools than necessary, it is also a waste of money to apply to any school you won't be happy attending—application processing fees can be pricey. However, you want to apply to enough schools that you'll be sure to get accepted somewhere.

It's also important to think about the selectivity of the schools you apply to. Don't be scared to apply to your dream school even if your SAT score or GPA is a bit low. On the other hand, make sure to apply to at least one or two "safety schools," where you'll be both happy and stand an excellent chance of getting accepted. A good rule of thumb is to apply to at least one "reach" school, a school that may be a long-shot to get into, but one where you'd love to go, at least one "safety school," and a few "good fit" schools in between.

After you've listed the schools where you'll apply, get the applications and figure out when each of them is due. It may be a good idea to make a list of deadlines, both early and regular, and hang it somewhere in your room. Many schools allow you to download their applications from their Web sites. Others send them to you in the mail; if this is the case, make sure you request the application in plenty of time to fill it out carefully and send it in. Whatever you do, make sure you get your applications in on time. Many schools won't even look at applications they receive late, so make deadlines a priority.

Different schools accept applications in a variety of ways. A brief description of the major types of applications follows:

- *Rolling Admissions:* Most large public schools and many less-selective colleges accept "rolling applications," which means they process applications continuously, in the order they receive them. You hear back from the school a few weeks after you send in your application. Though these schools often accept applications into the spring, it is important to send in your application early because admittance often becomes more challenging as these schools accept more and more students. Try to send in applications to schools with rolling deadlines as early as you can.

- *Regular Decision:* Colleges that don't offer rolling admissions typically require all your application materials to be sent by a specific date, usually in December or early January. The applications are processed and evaluated all at the same time, so while it is still a good idea to send in your application materials early, there is no automatic advantage to applying as soon as you can, as there is with rolling admissions. Whereas with rolling admissions, you'll hear back from the college within a few weeks, with regular decision all applicants hear back from the school at the same time. Many schools have separate parts of the application with different deadlines, so be prepared to organize your calendar so as not to miss any deadlines. Acceptances and rejections get mailed in late March or early April.

- *Early Decision:* Some schools offer an "early decision" option as part of their regular decision program. However, a recent push by presidents of several top universities (including Harvard, Stanford, Yale and others) is working to erode this option since it may hurt economically disadvantaged students who would need to compare financial aid packages in making their decision. Typically available at more selective colleges, the early-decision program allows you to apply to one school by mid-October or November. The school will then respond by mid-December either with an acceptance, rejection or deferral. An acceptance to a school under an early decision program is binding. This means that when you apply early decision, you sign a contract stating that you absolutely commit to attending that school if you are accepted. Failure to comply with the agreement can lead to unpleasant consequences like being blackballed from other schools. Rejections are final. A deferral means that the admissions committee will wait to make a decision about your application until they see what the regular pool of applicants is like. If you are deferred from an early decision acceptance but are accepted with the regular pool, the contract is no longer binding, and you may choose to attend a different school.

Early decision does have some advantages. By expressing a clear interest in one school, you may gain some advantage in admissions, and if accepted you'll already know where you're going to school in December. However, by no means feel that you need to apply to a school under an early decision commitment. You should not apply to a school early decision unless you are totally, completely, positively sure that the school is your first choice, and you should not apply early decision if you feel like your credentials will improve significantly during your first semester of your senior year. Rejections under early decision are final, so if you think your application will be stronger after another semester, you should wait until you can provide the best application possible.

- *Early Action:* Early action has become an increasingly common option at schools across the country. Like early decision, early action offers applicants a chance to find out in December if they've been admitted. However, the acceptance is not binding; if you get accepted to another school in April that you would prefer to attend, you're welcome to do so. This provides a convenient alternative for students who want to hear back from a school as soon as possible, but aren't ready to commit to attending a particular

school right away. Some institutions, such as Stanford and Yale, now offer single-choice early action programs. Under these plans acceptance is still non-binding, but students may not submit an early application (early action or early decision) to any other institution. This allows early applicants to compare financial aid packages from the regular round of admissions before making a decision.

Once you know when your applications will be due, it's time to start filling out the paperwork, either on actual paper or online. The latter is becoming increasingly common. There are a few general guidelines to follow. First, read the entire application carefully before you begin. Plan what you are going to say in each section before you write anything. It is a great idea to make a photocopy of the application to "practice" on before you fill out the official form, although applying online means you can go back and change your answers before the final submission. Always fill out or type the application yourself. If you're going to handwrite the application, try to use the same pen for the entire thing, to remain consistent in ink color and thickness. If you're going to use a printer, use a standard font like Times New Roman or Arial, and use the best printer you can find. Presentation and neatness count. If the application specifically suggests that you handwrite anything, be sure to do so, but draft exactly what you're going to write on scrap paper so that you don't have to make any corrections on the actual application.

More and more colleges nationwide are coming to accept the Common Application in lieu of applications specifically tailored for their schools. With a standard format and several general essays, you can fill out this application—online or on paper—once and submit to any of the participating schools. It makes the application process somewhat less burdensome and time-consuming, although you may still want to consider tweaking essays to better fit the demands of each individual college.

Applications are usually divided up into several sections. All of them are important, and you should use all of them to your advantage. The following explanations of the application sections include some things you should remember when filling out your application:

- *Personal Information:* This section is fairly straightforward. It asks for general information about you, your school, and your family. Since all applications will ask for pretty much the same information, it's a good idea to keep it all on an index card so that you can easily reference it whenever you need to. This section often includes a question about race. Although this question is optional, you can go ahead and answer it; it won't hurt you, and the answer could help you. If you do answer, don't try to stretch the truth; answer it the way you would on a census form. Legal debates about affirmative action have gotten a lot of attention in recent years, but you still should not worry about answering this question.

- *Standardized Tests:* This is another relatively easy section to fill out. Most applications require you to fill in your test scores here, but also require you to have copies of your scores sent from the testing companies to the admissions offices. Make sure you do this in enough time for the test scores to arrive at the admissions office well before applications are due. Also, be sure you pay attention to which tests are required by your school. Some schools don't require test scores at all, others require either SAT and SAT II or ACT scores, and still others specify which they want. Be sure your school receives all of the scores that it needs.

- *Extracurricular Activities:* This is the first section where your personality and accomplishments can shine through; be sure to make the most of it. Your extracurriculars allow the admissions office to see what you do when you're not studying. Sports, clubs, publications, student government, jobs and volunteer positions are examples of some of the activities that fall into this category. Make sure to follow directions carefully when filling out this section. Some schools want you to write your activities directly on the form; others allow you to attach a typed list to the application instead. If you have the option to type a list it's a good idea to do so, even if the rest of your application is handwritten. It looks neater, you'll have more space for all your activities, and you can just print out a copy of the list for each school that requests it. Just make sure to adapt the list to the particular requirements of the school. If the application instructs you to list your activities in chronological order, do so. Otherwise it is best to list activities in order of their importance to you.

A few final words about extracurriculars—quality is more impor-

tant than quantity. It is infinitely better to have long-term involvement and leadership positions in a few activities than it is to join a thousand groups to which you devoted only an hour a month. Admissions officers can tell when you're just trying to pad your résumé with activities. They look more highly on passion and commitment to a few activities that reflect who you are and what interests you. You're also more likely to stand out to admissions officers if you have dedicated your time to an activity or subject that few others have explored. Admissions officers come across countless tennis captains and student-body presidents, but few national kayaking champions.

- *Transcript:* Your transcript is a window into your academic history. Admissions officers look at your grades and class rank, along with the types of classes you've taken. A high GPA is important, but so is the number of AP or Honors courses you've had. Colleges look for students who challenge themselves. At this point you can't go back and fix that C you got in freshman biology, but you can do a few things to make your transcript look as good as possible. First, make sure everything is accurate. Check that your grades are correct, and that every honors class you have taken is listed as such. Second, remember that colleges will see your grades from senior year. Don't pad your schedule with blow-off courses; make sure to continue to take challenging classes. Try not to let yourself develop a serious case of "senioritis," because admissions committees will think that you don't take academics seriously. Also, if you received a poor grade in a particular class because of a certain situation, or you struggled all of sophomore year because someone you loved passed away, feel free to write an additional essay explaining any vast discrepancies. Lastly, request transcripts from your school as soon as you can. They can take a while to print, and you don't want your application to be late because you did not get your transcript in time.

- Recommendations: Many schools request letters of recommendation from teachers, coaches, or other adults who know you well. These letters let the admissions officers see how others view you and your potential. Most people will be happy to write a good recommendation for you. If a teacher doesn't feel comfortable recommending you, he or she will most likely not agree to write a letter for you. So don't worry about a teacher trashing you behind your back; it probably won't happen.

Do think carefully about whom you choose to write these letters, though. You want to choose teachers whom know you personally and with whom you have a good relationship. It's a good idea to choose teachers in your strong subjects, but it's also important to demonstrate some diversity of interest. For example, it is better to have your English teacher and your physics teacher write recommendations than it is to have two math teachers write them. Whomever you choose, make sure to provide them with plenty of time to write and revise a strong recommendation. You may even want to contact them before the summer of your senior year and let them know you'd like them to write on your behalf. That will give them ample time to write a shining letter! Many colleges want your teachers to send recommendations in separate from the rest of your application. If so, don't forget to give teachers a stamped and addressed envelope in which to send it. Be assertive; there's nothing wrong with reminding your teachers about the recommendation, and asking before the deadline if they'd gotten it done. Most teachers are careful about these deadlines, but it does not hurt to make sure. And don't forget to to thank the people who have done such a big favor for you!

Additionally, most recommendation forms have a line asking you to waive your right to see the recommendation. You should probably sign it. Signing the waiver shows confidence that your teachers respect you and gives the recommendation more credibility. Finally, though most schools only require two recommendations from teachers, some allow you to send additional recommendations from others who know you well. Though by no means required or necessary, this is a good opportunity for students with significant activities outside of school-affiliated activities to get people like coaches, art tutors, or employers to say something helpful. Don't go overboard on these though; one extra recommendation is more than enough. Content is more important than the person who writes it. It's not impressive to get your state senator to write a recommendation for you if he's never met you before.

- *The Essay:* The college essay strikes fear in the hearts of high school seniors every fall, but you should not think about it as something scary. Instead, consider it an opportunity to show your wonderful, special, unique personality while telling the admissions officers a bit about yourself. If you give yourself plenty of time and have some fun with it, it can actually be the most enjoyable part of your application.

Think about your topic carefully, but do not kill yourself trying to come up with a topic that you think an admissions officer will like. It's always a good idea to write about something that is meaningful to you. If you feel strongly about the topic it will show through in your writing, and that will catch an admissions officer's attention. Too many students write about a class project or winning the state championship—try to describe any experiences that are less common. You want your personality and your passion to shine through. Though it might seem obvious, it's worth restating that you should be sure to answer whatever question the application asks. Sometimes you can reuse an essay for more than one school, but don't try to make an essay fit a topic just so you don't have to write another one. And be prepared to write several different essays if you're applying to a lot of schools.

Once your topic is chosen, give yourself enough time to write a good rough draft. It's sometimes intimidating to begin writing, but just put your pen to paper and start. It doesn't matter what your draft looks like at first; you'll have plenty of time to correct and edit it later. Since the essay is the part of the application where you can be yourself, write in a way that feels natural to you, whether that's humorous or serious or something completely different. Your essay should give colleges an idea of who you really are. Being honest with yourself and schools makes it more likely you'll end up somewhere that is a good fit. You should never submit a first draft to a college. Revise your essay a few times, both for style and for content. If the application gives you a word limit, stick to it.

Once you feel confident about the essay, it's a good idea to have a teacher, parent, older sibling or counselor look over it for you. They can both help you find technical mistakes in spelling and grammar, and can point out places where you could be more clear in your content. By all means have others help you out with your essay in these ways, but under no circumstances should you ever, ever let anyone else write your essay for you. Not only is this dishonest, admissions officers read thousands of essays every year and have a good eye for essays that do not seem to be written by a particular student. While they probably won't be able to pinpoint why they're uncomfortable with a particular essay, they could be left with a negative feeling about your application. Once your essay has been drafted, revised, edited and perfected, you can either handwrite it on the application form, or, if the school allows, you can attach a typed version to the form.

Once your application is complete, put a stamp on the envelope and pat yourself on the back. Your application was honest, well-thought-out, neat, and will show the admissions committee who you are. Although you might want to call the admissions office in a week or so to make sure they've received all your materials, there is not much left to stress out about. Once the application is in the mail it's out of your hands, so kick back, relax, and enjoy the end of your senior year. After all that work you deserve it.

The Wait

There is probably nothing anybody can say to you at this point to make you feel secure and confident regarding your applications. Your worries of the last few months about application deadlines and teacher recommendations are now petty concerns, replaced with the general unease that comes with the uncertain ground of your fate resting in somebody else's hands. Your applications are in the mail (and by now they have arrived at various admissions offices across the state and country.) You hope they did, anyway. You are finished with the applications, but have only just begun the long road of anxiety.

Well, all is not lost. While it is nearly impossible to distract you from the near-constant pressure of the uncertainty regarding your future, we can at least let you know a little more about what is going on in the office.

Your application will arrive and most likely be put into an anonymous-looking, plain envelope. It will then be given to the admission officer who is in charge of your district or school. In some larger schools, you will not get much individual attention: There are often grade and SAT/ACT score cutoffs that they use to determine who gets admitted. With limitations on resources and thousands of applications pouring in, this is usually the only way they can manage the process in the given time frame. In smaller, private schools that can afford it, your application will be considered much more closely. Generally, your application will be read by up to three or four officers. Some schools use a numbering system to rate your academic record, your standardized test scores, and your extracurricular activities. There are some "bonus points" that you may end up with for uncontrollable variables such as your economic or racial background, or your relationship to an alumnus of the school.

Mostly, your application will speak for itself. While some schools weigh academics over extracurriculars, others might want to see high levels of community involvement or strong standardized test scores. This is where things are entirely out of your control. Each school is looking for a diverse group of students. The schools keep their academic standards relatively high, while looking for people from every possible background with every possible interest. If there happen to be 20 other students just like you from Houston, Texas, with 2100 SATs, a 3.5 GPA, roles in several school plays, and playing time on the varsity basketball team, all 20 will probably not be accepted. Likewise, if you happen to be the only student applying with an 1740 SAT, 2.8 GPA, and founded a nonprofit organization to help teach English to needy children in Africa, you would probably look more unique and attractive to the admissions officer. It is fantastically frustrating, but in the end much of this process is out of your control. You are not only competing to be good enough for a school, but you are competing against everybody else who is applying to the school. Admissions officers are quick to admit that they turn away an incredible number of qualified applicants every year; enough, in fact, to more than fill two separate classes of equal strength. The decision process, therefore, often seems arbitrary. You may end up on the wait list of one of your safety schools, and find yourself accepted at the strongest school you applied to. You simply cannot know what is going to happen until you receive the letters. Most schools are constantly adjusting their criteria in order to admit what they see as the most accomplished and vibrant student body possible.

When the decision has been made, the myth is generally true: Big, thick envelopes often have big admit letters inside. The thin ones often bring bad news. You will probably be receiving a mix of these, so don't let a poor first response get you down. You may end up knowing the decision before the envelope ever reaches your mailbox. Each year, more schools are letting students find out their acceptance status online.

The good news is that thin envelopes sometimes bring news of a place on the wait list. The last thing you want to do in this situation is anger the admissions office. Surely, a place on the wait list is disappointing. There are only two things that can help you get off, however. First and foremost, the best you can hope for is a lot of luck. Your eventual admission depends a lot on how many people reject their offers of admission. The second factor is how you act: Admissions offices like to see people eager to attend their school. A simple letter stating your excitement about the school and your eagerness to attend may help nudge things in your direction. Anything pestering or negative directed at the admissions office will ensure you a rejection letter. In the end, you should choose the school where you feel most comfortable. The best advice we can offer you is to follow your instincts. If you get some kind of feeling about a school, go with it! There is no better reason out there to make a decision. For now, sit back and relax. It's your senior year, your very last semester in high school. While you can't start failing your classes now, there is plenty of room left for you to chill out. Do what you can to forget about your applications (and stress about work) and instead think about how you can make the most out of your last couple months of high school. Be proud that your applications are finished and go out and have some fun!

The Money

Best case scenario: you get into the college of your dreams. But what if you get into the college of your dreams only to realize you cannot pay for it. With many of the nation's most expensive colleges quickly passing the $35,000 annual tuition mark, adding up to $140,000+ for a four-year education, it is no wonder that many students are talking as much about finances as they are about SAT scores. Although few families can afford this expensive price tag, especially if there is more than one member of the family attending college, there are many resources to aid families in paying for college. You should never hesitate to apply to a college simply because of its "sticker price." Many colleges meet most, if not all, of a family's financial need with a combination of scholarships, grants, loans, and work-study programs.

The most important step you can take as a student is to openly discuss your family's financial situation at the outset of your college search. Talk about how much your family is able to pay for college, how much your parents are willing to take out in loans, and other financial topics. By initiating this discussion with your family, you are showing them that you are both responsible and sensitive to your family's financial situation.

Your biggest advantage in the financial aid game is to be organized. As you will find out, there are many forms that you must fill out in order to even begin applying for financial aid. Getting organized helps you to see exactly where you stand in the financial aid process. The money is not going to land on your doorstep, so you have to be proactive in looking for it. There are plenty of resources available to you, but you have to know where to look for them.

A good place to start is with your college guidance counselor. Counselors have knowledge and experience in helping students like yourself get into college and pay for college. Oftentimes, they receive information from colleges regarding scholarships and will post them around the school. Take note of these announcements and fill out the applications as soon as possible. The applications can be time-consuming, but if you are well-organized, there should be no problem. The following Web sites also provide useful information for students seeking financial aid: www.finaid.org and www.fastweb.com. The more persistent and diligent you are in your search, the better your chances will be for finding the resources you need.

The best sources for financial aid are the colleges themselves. Colleges oftentimes earmark large sums of money specifically for financial aid. Many colleges also receive money from federal and private sources for financial aid purposes. Scholarships come in a variety of forms, including need-based, and merit or achievement awards. You will need to look at what types of financial aid the schools that you are considering offer. Be aware of which colleges offer only need-based financial aid packages and which colleges offer merit and/or achievement scholarships. The policies and practices at each school can vary significantly, so it is important that you have the information you need.

Carefully read the bulletins provided by the colleges you are considering. If you have any questions, e-mail or call the admissions office or financial aid office right away. Find out what the colleges' admissions policies are regarding financial aid applicants. Some of the nation's wealthier schools have need-blind admissions, which means that you are considered for admission without taking into account your family's ability to pay. However, at some schools, financial need may play a part in the final admission decision, especially in borderline cases where preference may be given to those with the ability to pay. Even if you do not think you can afford it, apply to the school and for the financial aid. Then, just wait and see. You might be pleasantly surprised. Sometimes it is cheaper to attend a more expensive college because they often provide superior aid packages. Of course this is not always the case, but it does prove that you should never decide against a school because of money until you have a financial aid offer (or rejection) in your hand.

As a financial aid applicant, you will soon notice all that paperwork involved. Most schools require you to file a standardized need analysis form to determine an expected family contribution (EFC). Depending on the school, the form will either be the College Board's Profile form or the U.S. Department of Education's Free Application for Federal Student Aid (FAFSA), or in some cases, both. The school will also have its own financial form for you to fill out, which you have to send along with the family's income tax forms for verification. The school will determine a reasonable family contribution for one year. (The student is also usually expected to contribute at least $1,000 from summer earnings.) To come up with an estimate, a formula established by Congress is used. The formula takes into account family income, expenses, assets, liabilities, savings accounts and other data. The cost of attendance minus this expected family contribution yields an approximate financial need. The school then designs a financial aid package that may consist of a low-interest, federally guaranteed loan, a work-study job, and a combination of different types of grants. This would lead one to believe that all packages would be similar, yet this is not always the case. Even though all schools receive the same input data, they do not all use the same formula. The family contribution will thus vary slightly, but there should not be a big difference. The difference in aid packages comes mainly from the way the school issues money. Some schools may require you to get more loans, or they might give you more money.

Some schools will always make better offers than others. Some wealthier schools guarantee to meet the full "demonstrated" need of every applicant that they accept. At other colleges, however, the financial aid package may leave an "unmet" need that

you will have to cover on your own. In unfortunate cases like these, students can bear the extra financial burden or choose a college that gives them a better offer.

There are a few things that you can do to improve your chances of receiving an adequate financial aid package from a school. First of all, be efficient in getting all of the forms in as early as possible. Some schools have a limited supply of funds available for financial aid, and the earlier they look at your application, the better your chance of receiving a larger share. Getting your forms in early shows a good-faith effort on your part, and schools are more likely to be cooperative with you if they feel you are being cooperative with them. Another thing you can do is write a letter to the financial aid office explaining any special family circumstances that are not reflected on the financial aid forms. These can include a recent death in the family or the need to support an aging relative. If you do not let the school know about such situations, there is no way they can take them into account.

If a school offers you a financial aid package that you consider inadequate despite your best efforts to let them know about your family situation, all is still not lost. After you have been accepted at the school, make a polite call to the school's financial aid office. If you noted any special circumstances either on the financial aid form or in a separate letter, ask if they took them into account when determining the award. Sometimes letters or comments get overlooked in the haste to get the aid awards out on time. If they say they took the circumstances into account, or if you did not mention any, tell them you would really like to attend the school but do not think it will be possible without more aid. If another school has offered you more aid, mention that, especially if the school is a competitor of the one you're talking to. Calling may not help, but they are not going to withdraw your acceptance once you are in.

If you are eligible for money on the basis of need, then the school may list some federal government assistance. The first of the types of federal government assistance are grants. Grants do not have to be paid back, unlike loans, but they are also harder to obtain. The federal government offers two grants: the Federal Pell Grant and the Federal Supplemental Education Opportunity Grants. You have to demonstrate "exceptional" financial need for either, but the latter is harder to obtain since the government does not guarantee as much. A Pell Grant is as high as $4,050, and the FSEOG is as high as $4,000 annually.

The federal government also offers lower-interest loans. If you demonstrate "exceptional" financial need, you may be eligible for a Perkins Loan, which can be loaned at 5 percent interest up to a maximum of $4,000. There are two types of Stafford Loans, one subsidized and the other unsubsidized. The subsidized Stafford Loan is only for people who demonstrate financial need, and it has a fixed rate of 6.80 percent interest. The government pays for the interest while you are in school and during the grace period after you graduate. The unsubsidized loan is for those who do not demonstrate financial need, and they have to pay interest the whole time. There is also a new loan called the Federal Direct Student Loan which is just like the Stafford except that the lender is the federal government and not a bank.

There is also a federal government sponsored loan for parents called the PLUS loan. It is particularly valuable for those who qualify for little or no financial aid. Each year, parents are allowed to borrow the full amount of tuition less any financial aid the student receives. The loan requires good credit, repayment while the child is still in school, and interest rates that are not far from market rates. Still, it can help to ease the burden on middle-class families.

You will also probably be required to take a job through the federal work-study program. Many applicants worry that working part-time will detract from studying or, equally important, playtime. Yet, if you work on campus, you certainly will not be the only one: Most colleges report that about half of their students hold term-time jobs. It is possible to take a full load of courses, participate in extracurricular activities, and work 10 or 15 hours per week, all while maintaining a good grade point average. Although freshmen tend to get the least exciting jobs on campus, in later years you may well find yourself working on interesting research, in a lab, or in a library job.

Many private colleges also provide scholarships based on academic, athletic or artistic ability. As competition among colleges for the best students intensifies, more and more colleges are offering lucrative merit awards to well-qualified students. There are many excellent schools, including many state universities, that offer merit scholarships in ever-increasing numbers. The best sources for information are your high school counselor and state Department of Education.

Be sure not to overlook the millions of dollars of aid available from private sources. Organizations ranging from General Motors to the Knights of Columbus offer money for college, often as prizes to assist students from your community. Sometimes large companies offer scholarships to children of their employees, so have your parents find out if their employers have such programs. There are also several scholarships out there related to specific majors, religions or even ethnic heritage. Or if you scored very high on the PSAT, you could be in the running for a National Merit Scholarship. There is often a catch to merit-based awards, however: If you qualify for awards from private sources, your school will often deduct some or all of the amount from any need-based aid you receive.

In the past two decades there has also been a revival of interest in ROTC (Reserve Officers Training Corps) programs. These scholarships from the four branches of the armed forces help pay for tuition, books, and room and board during college. When you graduate, you are committed to anywhere between four and eight years of reserve or active duty, depending on the program. As the supply of financial aid declines and the cost of college education continues to climb, more and more students are coming to see ROTC scholarships as worthwhile. However, be very thorough when investigating ROTC programs at different schools. Some colleges tend to be more anti-military, and you may find yourself part of a controversial program. Even so, the benefits of the program can be substantial for a student who joins after careful consideration and research.

More and more, federal aid is being reserved exclusively for the very needy. Many families with incomes over $35,000 who qualify for PLUS loans must now pass a needs test to get Stafford Loans. Yet, if you play your cards right, your family should not have to undergo severe financial hardship to put you through school.

Advice for Transfers

If you are already in college and are thinking about transferring to another school, the preceding advice is mostly old news to you. Theoretically you know what to do now, but there are actually a number of new considerations that all potential transfers should keep in mind.

There are plenty of reasons students cite for transferring. Perhaps you don't feel comfortable in the social or political environment at your school. Maybe your academic interests have changed, and the programs available at your current college are not extensive enough. It could also be an issue of being too far from or close to home. Whatever the reason, it's important to figure out what it is about your college experience that doesn't work, so you can find one that does.

You're about to embark on a daunting and sometimes disappointing process, so be sure to think it through beforehand. It can be easy to blame your school if you are unhappy. But issues with the college experience itself, such as roommate problems or work overload, may be the real source of your dissatisfaction. If so, you may be able to work out these troubles without transferring.

Don't assume that you'll necessarily be happy at another university. One student left Stanford in search of "greener pastures." Instead, she found New England "cold, gray, and without pastures at all." According to another student, "It's a big risk. You have to really want to leave where you are or really want to go where you will be." There are no guarantees that you will be better off at another school, and the process itself may make things even less satisfactory for you. You might want to take a semester or two off to reevaluate your situation, or think about giving a more wholehearted effort at making your current situation work.

Most schools accept transfer students who have up to two years of credit at another university. It may be safer, however, to transfer after your first year, because your old university will be more likely to take you back if you change your mind. One student advised that it is better to take a leave of absence from your original school than to withdraw completely.

The application process is also slightly different for transfer students. Be aware that colleges tend to consider a transfer student in a different light from a high school senior. To your advantage, admissions officers tend to look upon transfer applicants as mature and motivated candidates who have the potential to make a significant impact on campus. However, few students tend to leave top private universities, so the acceptance rate for transfers at top schools is much, much lower than that for first-time applicants. The situation can be different at larger state schools.

Each school looks for different students, but grades, recommendations, and the essay that explains why you want to transfer are usually the three most important parts of the application. Make sure that you find classes with professors who will be able to write you good recommendations. Standardized test scores and extracurriculars are less important. One exception to this may be if you decide to take time off and do something exceptional during your time away from school. Keep in mind that your college transcript is incredibly important. As much as you might want to leave your school, do not ease up on your academics. If staying an extra semester will help boost your academic record, you may want to consider holding off on your move.

Because colleges will expect you to prove that you have developed during your first year or two of college and to show why you absolutely cannot stay at your old school, your essay (and interview if you can arrange one) is critical. Be definite and clear about your reasons for transferring and what you expect to find in a new environment. Academic reasons are best; personal ones are only as convincing as you can make them. It also helps if the department in which you want to major is under-subscribed at the new school.

Make sure you know a lot about the school you are applying to. Not only will this show through in your application, but you will also be much more prepared for the experience ahead. If what you need is an active, social campus in which to get involved, then make sure that you will be guaranteed on-campus housing. If you are going to need financial aid, check and see that it will be available for transfer students. Also, be sure you look into how your credits will transfer at the new school. Will you get credit toward a major, or only toward graduation? If you don't have a major already picked out, it can be very difficult to graduate in four years.

Before submitting the paperwork, make sure that you are confident in your decision to transfer, and be ready for anything. It's important to have a backup plan for the upcoming year in case you don't get accepted. Come up with a plan for what you would do with a year off, or be prepared to make another run at getting the most out of your school. If everything does work out for you, make sure you have covered all of the bases before you commit to the new school. Making the decision to transfer is not a walk in the park, but you shouldn't let this deter you. If you are truly unhappy with your current situation, it can be a very rewarding and worthwhile route.

The College Spectrum

Current Trends and Comparing Colleges

At first glance, the sheer number of colleges included in this book might seem a bit overwhelming—clearly you would never consider applying to over 300 schools. Since colleges and their student bodies vary in so many ways, it can be difficult to identify schools at which you would feel comfortable. One piece of advice is to be aware of the general social, political and academic trends many schools are currently experiencing. Issues such as affirmative action, the fairness of standardized testing, expanding financial aid and early application programs have become heated topics of discussion on countless college campuses. It can be helpful to figure out where certain schools stand in terms of these trends. Another way to get some perspective on different colleges is to identify where they stand in terms of various criteria—to figure out where they fall on a continuum that we call the College Spectrum. Most importantly, it is not our place to judge which types of schools are best, but instead to present a variety of perspectives and observations that can help you with the decision-making process. Here are some of the many areas you can consider in comparing different schools.

Size

The total undergraduate enrollments of the schools in this book range from 26 at California's Deep Springs College to nearly 40,000 at Ohio State University. Considering the size of the campus you want to attend is helpful in the initial narrowing-down process; the feel of a school can be very dependent on the number of students around. There are two main parts of your experience that will be affected by the size of the school you choose: academics and social life.

Academically, class size and the accessibility of senior faculty are two important areas of comparison that tend to vary between large and small schools. In this case, smaller colleges decidedly have the advantage simply because a smaller population usually translates into smaller classes. Students at small schools have great opportunities for one-on-one student-faculty interaction. At large schools, students are more likely to complain of impersonal instruction and "being treated as a Social Security number."

To make up for this apparent disadvantage, many larger schools offer special programs intended to create a more intimate sense of community among professors and students. Different universities have different approaches. Some offer honors programs for a limited number of students, and some house all the students who are in special programs together. Generally, students in such programs all take the same or similar courses—most of which are small, discussion-oriented classes. Bear in mind that many honors and special programs are highly selective; do your best to make a realistic assessment of your chances to be accepted. Additionally, don't be taken in by the glossy pictures in admissions booklets: If you are considering a large university, take a close look at the quality of its special programs. If you are seriously considering one of these programs, try to speak with an undergraduate currently participating in the program—he or she may be able to paint a more accurate picture of what it is like. Another important factor to remember is that no matter how large a school is, not all of the classes it offers will be huge and overcrowded, and some of the bigger classes will break into smaller discussion groups. Thus, although most schools do have some very large classes, you can almost always find small ones of interest. But in this case, it is important to remember that in bigger schools, it is often difficult to get into small classes as an underclassman.

Also, pay attention to who teaches the classes. At most liberal arts colleges, only professors do. Many large universities pad their student-faculty ratios by including graduate students, or they advertise discussion classes that turn out to be taught by people who are still working toward a Ph.D. By reading guides such as this one and by talking to students, you can find out roughly how many graduate students teach and whether or not senior professors teach undergraduates at all. Keep in mind that having younger, less experienced professors teach is not always a bad thing. Many times, courses taught by graduate students allow for a rapport between teachers and students that does not develop with some of the stodgier old professors. However, if graduate students appear to dominate the teaching, even if only for the freshman year, you should definitely consider this as you make your decision. These facts will also give you a sense of how much personal attention the typical undergraduate student receives from the administration.

For highly specialized fields that require extensive facilities, the resources at small schools are generally limited. Larger universities usually have the funding to sponsor more expensive research facilities and to draw renowned professors to their specialized programs. For facilities not associated with academics, such as the gym or the library, size and showiness are not nearly as important as accessibility. You will not care how many racquetball courts the gym has as long as one is available when you want to play and it's not a three-mile walk away. Instead of asking how many volumes there are in the library, find out whether everyone has full access to all its resources, and if the library holds long hours. Since they cater to so many students with diverse interests, large universities most often offer a wide range of facilities.

Social life, too, is affected by the size of the school. Consider carefully what kind of social life you plan to have and which type of school would be more conducive to your interests. The setup of freshman housing will play a significant role in your social experience; your first-year roommates and hall-mates often become some of your closest friends. It's likely that the people you associate with will also be determined by your extracurricular interests—a sports team, a student newspaper, or student government. This tends to be especially true for universities that do not provide more than one year of campus housing.

The key is finding your own comfortable niche within any school. While there are usually more niches to be discovered in large colleges, finding yours may require some initiative. The larger the school, the more subgroups there are likely to be within the student body. Frats and sororities tend to be more abundant and popular on bigger campuses. An advantage to being a member of a very large community is that the supply of new faces never runs out. If you get tired of one circle of friends, you can always find another. But it is also important to keep in mind that when you are on your own in the midst of all those unfamiliar people, it is also possible to feel very lonely. On the other hand, small environments can be more welcoming and friendly. Small schools often have a greater sense of community and people can find that making friends is easier. But some students find that small schools can be a little too small, because "everybody knows everybody else's business." If the overall size of the school is closer to that of your high school than you feel comfortable with, you may want to consider studying at a school where you won't necessarily know everyone's name.

One common misconception about smaller schools is that they are inevitably more homogenous and have less school pride or spirit. On the contrary, many of them, especially the more selective ones, have just as many different types of people as do most large universities, only in smaller numbers. Although larger schools, especially those with a big emphasis on athletics, may have tremendous school spirit, smaller ones foster their own brand of pride, usually stemming from rich tradition and a strong sense of community.

Schools come in all different sizes. No matter how big or small a school is, make sure it prioritizes what is important to you. Be sure to keep in mind both academic and social consequences of the size of your school: Both have the potential to drastically change your college experience.

Location

At some point, if not right away, you will find yourself thinking about the towns in which each of your college choices is located. Can you see yourself living there for four years? What sounds more appealing to you—a college where your dorm is surrounded by towering oak trees, or a college with easy access to shops and malls? Before you answer these questions, be sure you really understand the difference between urban and rural settings, and more importantly, how this difference will impact your college experience.

Often, what some students perceive to be "city life," "suburban life," or "life on the farm" is not the reality of what living at a college in one of these areas would be like. Many factors need to be considered in order to get an accurate idea of how location will affect your whole college experience.

Whether you've found your way through corn fields for 18 years, or you've wandered around Times Square by yourself since you were 10, going away to college, while exciting and rewarding, can also be an intimidating experience. Many people arrive at school the very first day completely oblivious to the opportunities and the challenges of being out of their town, their state or their region. If you are from a rural area and are considering the big move to the city, expect adjustment (to noise, traffic, people, crime, the hectic pace), but try not to make or accept any assumptions about "the horrors" of city life. If you are from an urban area and are considering the peace and quiet of a smaller school tucked in the woods somewhere, also expect adjustment (to relatively silent nights, no movie theater or department store, the slower pace), but also try not to make or accept any assumptions about "life with the cows." Your thoughts about the location of the school should be balanced by the fact that every school will inherently have some sort of community; is this community, along with the city the school is located in, right for you?

College is a great time to try new things, including a new location—a new city, a new state, maybe a whole new region of the United States or beyond. In general, you do need to be aware of certain broad characteristics of each type of campus. At a campus in a big city, for example, there is a greater chance that on-campus nightlife will be nonexistent, as everyone will head to clubs and bars to relax. Yet after a week of academic work, extracurricular activities, dorm parties, visiting speakers, football games, and the multitude of other school-sponsored events, being in an urban environment means there is still the option of seeing a Broadway show or going to a world-renowned museum. As for a campus in a smaller town, the exact opposite may be true. Without anything to do around town, students will have all of their activities and create all of their own nightlife on campus. While you may sometimes wish you did have the major clubs and bars, the tight-knit community that forms among students at the school may very well more than compensate for those longings. Whichever setting you do end up choosing should depend on your own reflections on how you would feel in those surroundings.

Another point to consider is how comfortable you would be living so close to or so far away from home. Does leaving the Pacific Ocean for the Atlantic Ocean sound like a real adventure, or does being even two hours away from your family make your hands start to tremble? Are you at a point in your life where you still want to be with all of your friends going to the same school near your hometown, or can you not wait for all of your new friends and your "whole new life" far from home? Distance is one of those factors that require thinking about everything in context. Your life will change in college, whether you pack your bags to travel far away or keep your room at home. Anywhere you end up, even if you do stay close to home, your old relationships will change at least a little bit. Make sure you are honest with yourself about your reasons for choosing a particular school. It may be helpful to talk to current students at the school to get a sense of where they came from and what they think about the location. It may also be helpful to come up with a list of positive and negative aspects of the school's location. Include everything that will affect your life: the weather, the people, the travel expenses, and the homesickness, without forgetting to take into account the school's own community. Life at college will require at least some adjustment, but it may be that exact adjustment which completes your college experience.

Private vs. Public

The question of whether to attend a public or private school is best answered through a cost-benefit approach. Don't worry, we know you haven't had Econ 101, so consider this a free lesson. Let's first divide the universities in the United States into three categories: large private, public, and small private.

The most obvious distinction between a private and a public university is the price tag. As the cost of a private school education continues to climb, public school is becoming an increasingly attractive option. However, in recent years the tuition gap has significantly diminished for those who are eligible for financial aid, as private schools have allocated increasingly more funds to aid packages. These packages are almost always a combination of loans and grants, meaning that they do not always diminish the cost of college, but simply postpone it to a future date.

Most top-tier private institutions have adopted need-blind admissions policies which mean that they admit regardless of your ability to pay and then work with you to create a financial aid package that will allow you to attend. Princeton led the pack in this respect by announcing that it would replace loans with outright grants; soon many other colleges followed suit.

Smaller private schools, however, do not have the high-powered endowments necessary to fund such need-blind policies. In this area, public universities definitely have an advantage. Subsidized by state taxpayers, they offer an outstanding education at a fraction of its actual cost—everyone is basically a financial aid recipient.

If you do decide to break the bank and attend a private school, you will often be rewarded with smaller class sizes and greater student-teacher interaction. There is, however, a not-so-obvious advantage to small private colleges. At larger private or state universities much of the teaching duty has been increasingly placed on the shoulders of teaching assistants (graduate students). Additionally, at large private universities, professors must often devote a significant amount of time to research in order to stay ahead in their field. Small private colleges offer teaching environments in which the professors are not burdened with this dictum of publish or perish; they can devote all their time to teaching the material instead of contributing to it.

At college you will learn as much from your fellow students as you will from your professors, so it's important to consider the quality and diversity of the student body. This is an important consideration because at any good college, public or private, much of the valuable learning takes place outside of the classroom.

When deciding which type of school to attend, make sure you look beyond its label as either public or private. While some applicants consider attending a state university second-best when compared to an elite private school, others make a public institution their first choice. It is important to consider department-specific academic strengths along with the overall reputation of the university as whole. Public schools such as UC Berkeley, UCLA, and University of Michigan rank among some of the top academic institutions, public or private, in the country. In the end, you should never be swayed too much by a school's private or public designation. Instead, try to choose the school that's best suited to you.

Coed or Single-Sex?

Since coeducation became the norm at American universities in the 1960s, the number of single-sex schools in the nation has dropped significantly. There are only four men's colleges remaining in this book: Deep Springs College, Hampden-Sydney College, Morehouse College, and Wabash College. The students here chose to attend mainly because of their belief that the absence of the opposite sex allows greater dedication to academics and a friendlier, more fraternal atmosphere. Tradition prevail at these all-male institutions, and men that work best in these atmospheres find themselves very content.

Women's colleges have similar reasons for existence as all-male colleges, but with a few twists. There are many more women's colleges, as the whole movement for women's education came later and is still firmly rooted in feminist beliefs. The most famous all-female schools are the Seven Sisters, a group of seven Northeastern colleges that self-organized in 1927 to promote single-sex education. The seven sisters—Barnard, Bryn Mawr, Mount Holyoke, Radcliffe (now folded into Harvard), Smith, Vassar (now coed), and Wellesley—hoped to compete with the image of the Ivy League schools.

Most women who attend single-sex colleges cite the supportive, nurturing environment as their college's greatest asset. In an arguably male-dominated culture, women's schools provide a learning environment where there is support for developing one's female identity, no academic competition with men, and numerous leadership opportunities. Women's colleges are usually very liberal, with focus on current events and debates on different points of view.

There is no debate, however, about the fact that life at a single-sex institution is very different from life at a coed one. Because single-sex schools tend to be smaller, there are often fewer academic programs and resources than at larger coed colleges. Also, the atmosphere is somewhat contrived, since one of the sexes is missing. There are always outlets through which students can find the opposite sex, such as "brother universities," but the social life and vivacity of the campus is usually at a much "calmer" level than coed schools. For students who want the best of both worlds, there are a few colleges that are part of coed consortia.

Women at Mount Holyoke and Smith can take classes at the neighboring Amherst and Hampshire Colleges and the University of Massachusetts; the women at Barnard are paired with the coed Columbia University; and Bryn Mawr allows its female students to explore academic offerings at Haverford and Swarthmore Colleges.

Besides the actual experience, another thing to keep in mind is a certain stigma attached to many single-sex schools. Since the majority of these schools are extremely liberal, they are generally known for strong activism in women's and gay rights. This reputation exists despite the more conservative nature of some of the top academic single-sex schools. Whether accurate or not, this is another factor to consider in your choice.

Single-sex atmospheres can be ideal for some students, but not everyone seeks out such a college experience. Most college-bound seniors end up enrolling in coeducational schools, an environment that requires little adjustment. Issues of coed bathrooms and dormitories may concern you, but there are many different housing options, including single-sex floors and Greek houses, and administrators work to make you comfortable. Most campuses also feature organizations that encourage members of the same sex to bond with each other, including fraternities and sororities as well as advocacy groups (usually female). So after choosing whether a single-sex or coed college is right for you, wait for your institution to send you information on handling all the details.

Advising and Tutoring

The first few weeks of college can be confusing. There are placement tests to take, forms to fill out, questions about AP credits to ask, and parents to kiss goodbye. Many freshmen are often unaccustomed to the breadth of courses from which to choose. Also, it's hard to plan your academic year when you're in the midst of meeting new friends, moving into your dorm room, trying to go to as many parties as possible, and asking out that cute girl from pre-orientation. However, do not be daunted.

Almost all colleges provide students with faculty advisors for at least the first year. Their function is twofold: they can both rubber-stamp your schedule and be used as reference for everything from course selection to general questions about the college. Though most students agree that faculty advisors are usually only good for placing their John Hancocks on your schedule, there are a few who are adamant that faculty advisors do have some value. If you do not know what you want to major in from day one, don't worry, your advisor can help you plan your schedule and think things through.

If you still have unanswered questions, ask upperclassmen (often the best source of good, quick information). They can point you toward interesting classes, often-overlooked majors and talented professors—but remember their advice is very much based on their personal experience. For more detailed, department-specific questions about graduation/major requirements, ask a faculty member in that department.

Once you have chosen your classes, remember that this is only half the battle! Fortunately, most colleges and universities offer tutoring resources free of charge to help you succeed. If you find yourself in a large class with a professor who rushes through the most important points in the last five minutes of lecture or have a nervous or unhelpful TA, you should consider getting a tutor. Professors' office hours are usually insufficient for detailed explanations. Even the brightest students can benefit from going over the subject matter now and again.

Many times tutors are graduate students or particularly advanced undergraduates proficient in that specific academic discipline. Having recently learned the material, they can often make it more accessible than a professor who had taught it for decades. When exam time rolls around, look to upperclassmen for old study guides and more general insight into acing specific courses.

A Minority Perspective

As a minority student or a person of color, there might well be some additional factors to consider in your decision. You may, for example, be searching for a school with a high population of students from a particular background or for a school with high overall diversity. A school with a large minority population may prove to be more supportive and even more comfortable. Regardless of size, a strong minority community can be helpful during the next four years and can even help reduce ignorance on some campuses.

Another factor to consider is the general attitude of both the administration and the student body. Unfortunately, racism still exists in many parts of society, but do not assume a defensive attitude while visiting schools. Instead, be aware of possible situations and attitudes that may make you feel excluded and uncomfortable. What might have seemed like a diverse college in the brochures may not seem so open-minded after all. Take note of how integrated the minority community is, and what the school does to recognize and support other cultures. Some schools may foster a pressure to conform; if the school has a large population of a certain race, there may be a distinct sense of separatism. For some this may provide a stronger sense of belonging, while for others it will only increase the stress of college life.

To determine the true attitude of the administration, look at how it attempts to support the minority communities. Some schools assign ethnic counselors to help minority students adjust to college life. Some students appreciate this; others resent it. One student reported that her school was doing so much to accommodate her minority status she felt separated rather than integrated. Many students, however, get used to the idea of special resources and ultimately find them supportive. Another thing to look at is the extracurricular life. What kinds of organizations are there for specific minority groups or minority students in general? The school may have cultural centers and politically oriented associations that focus on the traditional arts and dances of their culture. Examples of popular organizations that foster a sense of community among minority students include Movimiento Estudiantil *Chicano* de Aztlán (MEChA) for Chicano students; Native American Student Associations at campuses around the country; and Asian American Student Associations.

Besides cultural centers and politically oriented associations, many schools have Greek organizations centered around celebration of heritage. This category includes the predominantly Jewish fraternity Alpha Epsilon Pi, the Asian sorority Sigma Phi Omega, and African-American fraternity Alpha Phi Alpha. Other minority students choose to organize themselves around professional aspirations (National Association of Black Journalists) or religion (Asian American Christian Fellowship).

For African-American students, an important decision may be whether to attend a predominantly black college over another school. Despite the improving financial situations of most private black colleges, you are likely to find better facilities and larger academic departments at other schools. Unfortunately, the continuing decline of federal funding is likely to exacerbate this situation, since black colleges rely heavily on such resources. Nevertheless, many students choose to attend a predominantly black college for many of the same reasons other students choose to attend a single-sex school. Some black students find them a more congenial and accepting community that is more conducive to personal growth. Likewise, students often have a better chance to attain key leadership positions at a college where they do not have minority status. At a predominantly black school, the African-American experience is one of the central issues on campus. What does it mean to be a black person in 21st century America? Of what importance is African-American heritage? At predominantly black schools, these questions are addressed in a manner and with a commitment unrivaled by other institutions.

In this book, we include reports on five of the best-known predominantly black schools in the United States: Howard University in Washington, D.C.; Spelman and Morehouse Colleges in Georgia; Florida A&M University; and Tuskegee University in Alabama. For a more complete listing, we suggest you consult *The Black Student's Guide to Colleges*, written by Barry Beckham and published by Beckham House. Another school with an ethnic majority is the University of Hawaii, which is predominantly made up of Asian students.

Ultimately, you have to decide where you will feel most comfortable. Whatever your choice, it is important to remember that your ethnicity is an integral part of yourself and is not something you should have to compromise in choosing a school.

Sexual Minorities

The first question that a gay, lesbian, bisexual, or transgender student should ask when considering a college is the same one that straight students ask: where will I be the happiest and most comfortable for four years? Students planning on being openly gay at college will want to choose a campus where they can come out to their roommates, friends and even professors without worrying about the consequences. But how can you tell after one or two trips to a college whether or not you'll get a positive reception?

The good news is that, as one transfer student put it, "there are sensitive people everywhere—at large schools and small ones." Another student said she sought out a campus with diversity, guessing that a diverse population "would create more understanding." But beyond these general guidelines, there are other aspects of campus life to observe. Check out a school's listing of organizations, for instance. A school with several gay alliances and clubs, for example, probably has a more accepting environment, even if you don't think you'll end up being active in any of them. One student pointed out that the surrounding community can be just as important. "Knowing that there were gay bars and events in the town made me more comfortable in my choice." The more town-gown interaction there is, the more important it is that a prospective student feels comfortable being gay in that city.

In looking for a school, all students search for a place with unlimited options. As a gay or lesbian student, the best college is going to be one where your opportunities are not constrained by your sexual orientation. As one gay member of a fraternity pointed out, "I wanted to join a frat in college, so it was important that I found a place where my sexuality wouldn't be as big a deal…." In other words, there are countless schools where gay and lesbian students participate in every aspect of campus life—and fortunately it isn't too hard to track them down. This is not to say life for gay students is always perfect; gay students do risk running up against prejudices, but it is reassuring to know that gay and lesbian students at large and small schools, public and private, have managed to find their niche, be active members of the undergraduate community, and simply have a good time.

Politics

The level of political activism on a campus may affect how comfortable you are there. You will find that many schools have clubs of all alignments, and political journals of all bents as well, from the left-wing liberals to the Green Party to the ultra-conservatives. Generally these partisan organizations are most active in presidential election years. If this is what interests you, you will have no trouble finding your political niche.

Forty years ago, political activism permeated college campuses. Today, the number of students strongly involved in politics on campus is generally a minority. One student remarked that a majority of her fellow students stay away from politics for social reasons: many people at her university look down on those with strong convictions because they assume them to be closed-minded. Instead of joining political organizations, many students channel their activism into volunteer programs that confront specific problems such as urban blight or environmental destruction. Usually, small liberal arts schools are the most politicized colleges. "At my school, you don't just put your name on name tags, you put your cause, your oppressor, your god, and your sexual orientation," said one student. Before selecting a school, you may want to see if it has a political forum that brings in outside speakers and organizes discussions and lectures.

While only a few years ago campus activism was moving toward being institutionalized and domesticated, recent events, such as the September 11 attacks, the war in Iraq, and the presidential election, have provoked an increasing amount of activity on behalf of students. Student protests, petitions, and marches have garnered much support as well as media recognition. Additionally certain incidents and issues, particularly those involving racism and sexuality, receive community-wide attention. The gay- and lesbian-rights activists at some schools sponsor a kiss-in where same-sex couples cluster around the campus' central promenade and make out. Gay rights, AIDS awareness, and race-related issues are commonly on the collegiate slate of activist causes. Today, to be politically correct (PC)— manifested by a tolerance for others' ideas and political affiliations and an attempt to be inoffensive to any and all groups in speech as well as in print—is something of a secondary issue. Although PC was a hot topic on campuses in the nineties, the debates on the spelling of "woman" and whether your roommate is disabled or "differently abled" seem to have faded.

However, the PC movement's focus on the implications of language has pushed people—particularly educators—to reconsider the lens through which academic disciplines are typically approached. Many schools now require students to take courses that focus on non-Western cultures, or courses aimed at raising sensitivity to minority issues and concerns. More and more schools have started classifying "Women and Gender Studies" as a major, as well as "Latin-American Studies" and "African-American Studies." Courses and programs exploring Native American Studies have also begun to emerge.

By visiting a college you can quickly pick up on how important politics are to the student body. Read posters and skim student newspapers to gauge whether or not the political climate on that campus is right for you. The best schools may be those that can absorb all viewpoints, so that no matter what you think, there will be others who will embrace your thoughts, challenge them, or respect your decision not to vocalize them.

Preprofessionalism vs. Liberal Arts

Preprofessionalism is a term you will see repeated throughout this book. Not all curriculums are the same, and whether you will receive either a preprofessional or liberal arts education is determined both by the school you attend and the major you choose there.

Majors that do not lead directly to a specific career fall into the liberal arts category. Even if a student plans to be an accountant, for example, he or she might get a liberal arts degree in philosophy or English, and then go on to study accounting at the appropriate professional school. The goal of a liberal arts education is to teach students how to think creatively and analytically, preparing them to pursue any career.

There are pros and cons to both tracks. Some argue that a liberal arts education is the key to a solid education and to becoming a well-rounded individual. Others believe that a liberal arts degree can be a waste of four years and thousands of dollars for those who already have their career plans mapped out. Students from a liberal arts background may also have a more difficult time securing a job immediately after graduating, as they tend to lack both experience and specific skills. Many preprofessional programs require students to take general education courses in liberal arts departments. In fact, almost all colleges insist that you take some courses outside your chosen field.

If you don't yet know your interests well enough to decide now which option is for you, you may be pleased to learn that the largest colleges and universities have both liberal arts and preprofessional students.

The University of Michigan, for example, has a strong undergraduate school of business; many students in Michigan's liberal arts school also plan to go into business eventually but are pursuing a B.A. in a more general field first. The case is similar with Cornell.

If you do know what you want from a school in terms of career preparation, then you may prefer to attend a preprofessional institution. But keep in mind that getting a liberal arts education and getting a good job are not mutually exclusive. Moreover many report that the learning environment at a preprofessional university is more competitive, and would therefore not be as enjoyable to a student who enjoys the intellectual exchange more common to liberal arts campuses.

Greek Life and Other Social Options

When choosing a college, you are choosing a place in which to live and learn. In this way the social life at colleges becomes a large factor in choosing your school and many people claim that when they visited colleges, the people they met made them love or hate the campus more than any other aspect. You will find that sometimes you just click with the students at a particular school. Although most schools are large enough to ensure you will find your social niche, it is also important to consider how the overall social atmosphere will affect you while you are there.

Collegiate life in the United States often conjures images of a social scene dominated exclusively by fraternities and sororities. While this is true of some schools, there are many schools where Greek life is either non-existent or less central to college life than some would believe. Greek life can run the gamut from a dominating institution to a relatively unknown and tame element of college life. It is also true that while many fraternities and sororities have high levels of membership, some of the numbers are dropping across the country. This is due mostly to increasingly strict policies on campuses to curb hazing as well as alcohol abuse that has made Greek life so infamous in today's media.

Although the most widely publicized side of Greek organizations has to do with their partying habits, belonging to a Greek organization is not just for those who like to party.

In fact, many organizations have reformed their policies to reduce or eliminate such practices as pledge hazing and many require that Greeks be dry at official functions (although that does not mean they cannot party together outside of meetings).

Beyond being a social group, Greek organizations offer many advantages to students including a nationwide network of alumni, community service opportunities and housing (which is often very difficult to find for upperclassmen). The emphasis on community service is particularly important to most Greek organizations and most chapters have an office dedicated specifically to organizing the chapter to participate in local charitable activities. On some campuses, the fraternities and sororities are the most active social-service organizations.

In terms of housing considerations, most organizations are on campus and thus are financially supported by the school, national chapter and students. Because of this, Greek houses are some of the nicest housing available, often as free-standing buildings with manicured lawns and beautifully decorated interiors. However, an increasing trend among colleges is to kick Greek organizations off campus. This trend is especially marked among fraternities that gain the reputation of being unkempt and raucous. Without campus funding, many of the organizations lose large amounts of their financial support and thus cannot run as well as those that are on campus.

Whether Greek life appeals to you or not, it is essential to know just how influential the Greek organizations are at each school you are considering. At some campuses, not rushing could seriously limit your social options. On the other hand, there are many schools where fraternities and sororities are most certainly not part of campus life and are regarded as conformist. There are also schools, especially among the Ivy League, where although Greek life is present, there is a strong residence system that fills many of the social functions that Greek organizations occupy elsewhere. As a rule of thumb, Greek life is more dominant at the largest schools where practical concerns keep the organizations strong and smallest at the most specialized schools where campus life is intimate enough that smaller social organizations may prove stifling.

However, even at the most Greek-dominated campuses, there are always other social outlets. Your interests will largely determine who your friends are. Therefore, you should choose a school that has groups that represent your interests. Greek organizations, athletics, cultural organizations, or theater groups can all be part of your college experience. The people you meet in these organizations often become some of your closest friends. Ultimately, the best way to tell if a school's social scene is right for you is to visit the campus or talk to friends who go there. Most college applicants worry that they will not find people like themselves when they get to college, but when they get there realize that making friends was much easier than expected. Find what you think will be the right combination of organizations, Greek or otherwise, and you will meet the right people.

Security

Students are in college to learn and to take advantage of what their schools have to offer, and campus security efforts are one reflection of schools' commitment to making that possible. Crime in general is increasing on campuses across the country, from recent tragedies that made students question the safety of their own classrooms to the rising number of sexual assaults. In response to this trend, federal legislation has made it mandatory for all colleges receiving federal aid (which is almost every one) to publish crime statistics in several categories. At your request, the appropriate office (usually the public relations or admissions offices) at any college or university should release to you the crime count for the last calendar year. Many colleges have also taken measures to beef up security. If you visit a campus and notice very stringent security measures (at the University of Pennsylvania, for example, you have to show your ID just to get into the quadrangle), remember that this means two things: there is a need for security measures, and the administration is responding to this need.

There are a number of features that any safety-conscious campus should have. Doors to individual dorm rooms and to the building entrances should be equipped with locks. All walkways should have bright lights, not only so that you can see, but so friends and classmates would be able to see you from a distance in case of danger. Another important security measure is a safety phone system with one-touch access to an emergency line. Each safety phone should have a distinct light to make it easily recognizable at night.

Ideally, there should be enough units so that you are never more than half a block from a phone. For getting around campus late at night, colleges should provide bus service or student safety escorts, free of charge. At least one of these services should be available 24 hours a day and should travel to every possible destination on campus. Every school should employ some type of security guard, whether unarmed monitors in or near the dorms or full-time police officers responsive solely to students and the affairs of the college. At the beginning of the year, make sure you enter these phone numbers into your cell, although they should be clearly posted as well.

Security problems are not limited to urban campuses. Some rural schools have crime rates as high as the urban ones. The sad truth is that most non-violent crimes are committed by other students, not outsiders. Why is campus crime such an issue now? College students are ideal targets—they keep expensive stereo and computer equipment in poorly guarded areas, and they often walk alone across dark, seemingly safe campuses.

It is important to understand that you cannot judge the safety of a campus simply by eyeing it from the safe confines of a brochure. Yet, by using a little common sense and preventive measures, the security problems of a given school should not prevent you from attending. By making yourself aware of potential problems and following the school's security guidelines, you can improve your chances of enjoying a safe four years.

Computers

Whether you are an art major, a computer science major or an expert procrastinator, computers will be an important part of your college experience. Looking up information for that research paper due in 12 hours, searching for your classmate's e-mail address in the online directory, and downloading the next problem set from the class Web site are just a few examples of the countless ways that computers are a part of everyday life on campus. With that in mind, here are a few things to look for when evaluating a college's computing facilities:

24-Hour Computer Clusters: Make sure that there are at least a few accessible computer clusters to rely on when your computer or printer stops cooperating once you finally sit down to start your homework.

Many people also like to work on their papers in computer clusters to get away from the distractions of their own room. Easily accessible clusters with numerous, fast computers are always a plus.

Macs vs. PCs: Although compatibility issues are largely a thing of the past, the networks at some schools may be preferentially built for Macs or PCs. If you are looking into bringing your computer, double-check that your school provides adequate support for your machine.

Support Staff: Another important thing to consider is the availability of technical assistance. Many schools hire students or other staff to troubleshoot the problems you may encounter with networking, hardware, or software licensed by the school. This can be especially helpful at the beginning of each semester when you have to register your computers with the school network and install the necessary software.

Internet and E-mail Access: Nearly every school now provides Ethernet access from dorm rooms and e-mail accounts that you can use during both the semester and your breaks. Another feature to look for is the availability of wireless Internet access at your school, which is also becoming more and more universal. In addition to getting rid of an extra wire on your desk, it also allows you to check your e-mail or chat with your roommate from anywhere on campus, including common rooms, labs, classrooms and nearby coffee shops. But make sure you don't get too caught up in reading the New York Times online when you should be taking notes in lecture!

Academic Usage of the Internet: Professors at most schools now use the Internet (in some form) as an important resource for their classes. Being able to find class notes, handouts, homework assignments, or even taped lectures posted on a Web site can be worth considering when choosing a class or a school. Although not every professor at every school is willing to put extensive course information online, finding a school where it is more common will help make your life slightly easier over the next four years.

A Final Note About Quality of Life

If you started at the first page and you've read up to here, you are probably thinking there are just way too many things to think about in choosing a college! Certainly, you already have many reasons why, right off the bat, you would add a college to, or eliminate a college from, your list. Perhaps the school has the best zoology program in the nation. Or maybe you have always wanted to be in the stands cheering as your school's basketball team wins the championship game. Either way, a final but crucial criterion for your decision is the overall quality of life you can expect to have at college.

Everyone goes to college to learn more, right? Yes, of course. Continuing your academic education will provide you with even more ways of thinking as well as more opportunities after graduation. You have to remember, though, college is someplace you will be for three or more years of your life. Academics are the most important reason to go to college, but when it comes down to everyday life, the college you choose will basically be your new world. Everything from extracurricular activities to housing, social life, and even weather will affect the way you eat, dress, study and relax. Don't consider UMass if you can't stand the cold; and don't go to Florida State if the heat makes you miserable. Have you always thought about joining a fraternity or a sorority, and there just aren't any on campus? Or perhaps your favorite weekend activity is to curl up on a chair in a coffee shop; is the college in such a small town that there is no coffee shop? What about the housing situation? Could you see yourself coming "home" every day to that closet-sized room you share with three other students? Speaking of the other students, would you be comfortable being around them—or any of the people walking down the street? All of these factors can and will make a difference in how you feel about a school. The best

way to really get an idea of what it would be like to be a student at the college is to visit the school, maybe stay over for a night or two, talk to the students around you, and browse through the student newspaper. Do you like what you see and how it feels to be there?

As you figure out what you like about a college, you may also want to check that those aspects of the school will still be there when you enroll. When the economy is doing poorly, an increasing number of schools, both public and private, face a shortage of funds; administrations at the schools have no choice but to make budget cuts. Without adequate funding, programs or even entire departments may be eliminated, the number of tenured professors may be reduced, campus renovations and additions may be delayed, extracurricular activities and sports teams may be cut, or worse yet, a combination of all of these possibilities may take place. If you are the star of your high school's varsity swimming team and want to continue swimming in college, check with the coach or the current swimmers to make sure the team is not rumored to be next on the list of programs to be cancelled. If you know that you want to major in biomedical engineering, make sure the department is big enough so that it is not one of the smaller and less popular departments that would be first to go. As recent newspaper headlines will tell you, even the best-endowed schools are tightening their purse strings.

We hope that we have given you a stronger sense as to what to think about and what to focus on as you continue to search for the college that's right for you. Just remember, in the end you are the one who will be attending the college, so you should be the one who is happy. Best of luck!

Introduction for International Students

International students looking to apply to colleges in the United States may discover a daunting and unfamiliar path ahead of them. More so than in many other countries, admission to U.S. colleges depends not only on grades and scores, but on the whole package: what you have done outside of school-work, what your teachers have to say about you, and what you have to say about yourself. In addition to the typical trials of the application process, students from abroad may also have to deal with linguistic and cultural differences, scarce resources, and communication delays that their American counterparts do not. Yet you should not let yourself be deterred by these challenges—some basic planning can eliminate many potential obstacles and pave the way to a unique and rewarding college experience.

An "international student" formally refers to anyone who is applying to American universities from an address outside of the United States. This means U.S. citizens and permanent residents applying from abroad are still placed in the international category. Many colleges review this applicant pool differently from the domestic applicants—admissions committees might place less emphasis on SAT scores, for example. Many schools also look for geographical and cultural diversity, which could work in your favor if only a few students are applying from your country, or against you if there are many other applicants.

With these advantages and disadvantages in mind, here are some tips about the application process that might be especially helpful. You should also read the **Getting In** section of this book for more general information. The best advice is: get started early. Deadlines for American universities can be as early as October for fall admissions. As one student said, "make sure you take care of everything well ahead of time—last minute surprises are harder to deal with abroad."

Pre-Application Preparations

If you decide that you want to go to an American university, start getting involved. While extracurricular activities are not considered in the admissions processes for schools in many countries, American universities place emphasis on what you achieve outside of the classroom. Extracurricular experiences can include a variety of activities such as taking piano lessons, writing for the newspaper, doing volunteer work or working part-time. These activities might highlight your leadership, talent or determination. If your school does not offer many extracurricular activities, look for opportunities to get involved in the community or take the initiative to organize something yourself. When application time rolls around, be sure to list everything to which you have devoted your time.

Academically, international students might want to think about taking Advanced Placement (AP) tests and courses related to them if they are not already following the International Baccalaureate (IB) program. Although not required for college admission, AP exams measure the level of your knowledge in the subject as compared to American high school students. As an added bonus, high scores might let you bypass some classes in college or accelerate and graduate early. Arranging to take an AP test internationally might be difficult since testing sites are less ubiquitous than in the States; try to see if an American school in your area will arrange it. If you can take it and you have recently completed a course corresponding to one of the tests, it would be a risk-free way to increase your chances at admission—students can choose whether to report individual AP scores. Students studying under the IB system, and even students who do not take either of these tests, might be able to negotiate for acceleration in their first year of college. Acceleration policies, however, vary greatly from college to college.

Deciding that you want to go to college in the United States and figuring out where to apply might be a rocky starting point for many international students because of the relative lack of information. But research is an essential part of the college application process and what many internationals said they wished they had spent more time doing. The United States is a huge country, and it will make a difference whether you are in

California or Massachusetts, whether you are in a city or a rural area. There are also many schools with excellent programs, beyond the names that people outside of the United States would recognize. If you have a college guidance counselor in your school who is knowledgeable about admissions to U.S. schools, take advantage of the resource. However, many advisors are not. One international student, now a senior, warned, "don't trust your high school counselors too much; they probably don't know as much about the schools you're applying to as you might assume they do—including application deadlines."

If your advisor is unable to offer you the help you need, seek out a counselor outside of the school. You might also want to speak with someone who has recently gone through a similar decision-making process, or talk to an American expatriate. Libraries and the Internet are prime sources of information. College Web sites provide accurate, up-to-date information, and sometimes feature special application guidelines for international students. If possible, try to visit the colleges. It could make a big difference in your opinions.

You may also want to consider the size of the international population at the schools you are deciding between. Colleges with a larger number of students from abroad tend to have more organizations and activities geared toward international students. These schools will likely have more extensive resources available for you at the administrative level as well. However this may not be an important factor in your decision, and it all depends on what kind of college environment you are looking for.

Testing

Most American colleges require international students to take the SAT Reasoning Test, a selection of SAT Subject Tests, and the TOEFL. The Educational Testing Service (ETS) has many international test sites, although the tests might still be hard to come by in certain countries. Students from such diverse countries as Israel, Japan, and Guatemala all said signing up was easy, particularly with online registration. However, some people might have to travel hours out of the way to get to the testing center. To avoid any unnecessary travel, register for these tests early before popular testing centers fill their seats. To find out where the nearest testing center is located, write to ETS or visit their Web site, www.ets.org.

Many colleges require the TOEFL (Test of English as a Foreign Language) if English is not your first language or the language of instruction in your high school. While taking another test might seem like a hassle, TOEFL is easier than the SAT and could work to your advantage since many schools will substitute a TOEFL score for the SAT Verbal score. If you are satisfied with your SAT Verbal scores, you should probably not bother taking TOEFL—although a near perfect score could never hurt. The more recently instituted SAT Essay section will pose a further hurdle to non-native English speakers, and while colleges are likely to take your native abilities into account when making admissions decisions, the essay will most likely require more test preparation on the part of such students.

Application Package

In getting teachers to write recommendations for you, be sure to approach those who not only know your work but know you and are willing to write enthusiastically about you. International teachers tend to be more reluctant to award superlatives or write a personalized recommendation than their American counterparts. If you attended a school taught in a non-English language, you can ask the teachers to write you recommendations in English, have them translated, or send them to the colleges to have them translated. It is often better to have the recommendations translated in your own country than to send them to colleges to be translated by someone there. You might offer to work with your teacher to translate the letter into English, especially if you have a higher level of proficiency.

The essay is a personal reflection of yourself and an opportunity to have the different parts of your application come together. Think of what will be interesting to the admissions officers reading the essay, and allow for more creativity than might be acceptable in college applications in your own country. Many internationals choose to write about living in different countries or experiencing cultural differences, which might be more interesting than the fact that you won a national academic award—the latter point can be listed elsewhere in the application. You want to give the admissions officers a strong sense of who you are and how you will add to the college community.

Financial Aid and Visas

While some large and wealthy colleges can afford to be need-blind in their admission of international students, the consensus is that there is very little financial aid available for non-U.S. citizens and residents. If you will definitely need aid, you should research the financial aid policy of each college before applying. Depending on which country you are from, you might be able to look to sources in your home country for financial support. If, on the other hand, you are an American citizen applying from abroad, the financial aid process is the same as for any other American student.

As soon as you mail that final college application, most of your hard work will be over. Although regulations differ from country to country, you shouldn't have any problems obtaining a student visa once you are accepted to a U.S. school. The visa will allow you to work inside the university, but be forewarned that finding an outside job will be very difficult.

International students face a number of challenges when applying to U.S. universities, but some advance research and planning can help make the process as painless as possible. There are numerous benefits to pursuing an American education—you'll have a vast array of academic options, enjoy access to high-tech facilities, and be exposed to students with backgrounds quite different from your own. Attending a U.S. college is a chance to expand your horizons, and you shouldn't let the application obstacles hold you back. One international student summed it up by saying, "Although it is an endless process, it is worth it!"

Students with Disabilities

The college search process is a difficult one, but it can be even more so for students with disabilities. Whether the disability is physical or learning-related, the need for special resources means that, on top of evaluating academics and social life, students need to be certain that a school will help them learn and live as comfortably as any other student. Early preparation, along with careful planning for the transition from high school to college, will make life at college much easier.

Planning Is Key

Above all, students should choose a school for its merits. The director of the Resource Office on Disabilities at Yale said that her most important advice was to "check out the school first, but also consider the disability services office, as a second choice, very important." Even a high quality of services cannot remedy a school at which the student is unhappy—but weak or nonexistent disability services can be very detrimental to one's college experience.

High schools must accommodate students as fully as possible under the Individuals with Disabilities Education Act. However, colleges are classed under the Americans with Disabilities Act, which mandates that they provide "reasonable accommodations" for those in need; the definition of "reasonable" will vary from school to school. The best place to figure out what a school offers as "reasonable accommodation" is at the school's designated office for students with disabilities; the people there will be able to tell you what they have on hand and can arrange.

Before visiting the school, be sure to alert the admissions office. They can usually work with the disabilities office to make sure, for instance, that your tour has a sign interpreter or that it only visits wheelchair-accessible sites. When you visit, you will see how good a fit the school is for you in terms of accommodations. If at all possible, make time to visit the disabilities office while you are there. Have an honest discussion with the staff about the accommodations that are necessary for your disability; and get a feel from them about what they believe can be provided.

During the applications process, you can disclose or not disclose your disability at your discretion; admissions officers from multiple selective schools have made clear that "when we learn of an applicant with a disability, we check to make sure that our school has the resources available to accommodate the individual before we ask the traditional questions: Have they made the most of their high school career? Would they contribute to the school's community? And so on."

As soon as you decide on a school, you should contact the people at the school's disabilities office immediately, mid-May at the latest. The first thing they will need is documentation of the disability, and they will work from there. They will work with the housing department to provide necessary living accommodations, such as ground-floor rooms or flashing fire alarms. Often, the people in the disabilities office will ask more questions over the summer than you do to find out what you need and what other resources you can use. Don't be afraid to check back with them over the summer; working closely with the office will make it more likely that you're comfortable at the school in the fall.

Before coming to college, you should prepare yourself for the transition. Make sure that everything you need has been set up ahead of time. The first few weeks of college are such a whirlwind that dealing with small problems like malfunctioning hearing aids or mislaid walking sticks will take away from the experience of your new life away from home. And if things do not go as planned, the disabilities office will be one of your best resources for handling the unexpected.

If You Have a Physical Disability

For physical disabilities, the actual layout of the campus may matter most. If you are blind, you will want to make sure that the campus is easy to familiarize yourself with, and that there are multiple ways available to orient yourself. If you are in a wheelchair, you will need to know which buildings are accessible for you, including dorms, classroom buildings and administrative buildings. Older campuses, especially those built in the 18th or 19th centuries, will need to be examined more thoroughly and it may be necessary to ask the disabilities office to make sure that classes you have preregistered for are located in accessible buildings. One student pointed out that "schools that are truly committed to making their campuses accessible for wheelchair users will not only have many ramps available, but those ramps will be attractive and blend in naturally with the immediate environment." Elevators should be available when necessary. Many campuses will also provide special shuttle transport services for disabled students.

If You Have a Learning Disability

For learning disabilities, providing documentation starts with a diagnosis. If you don't have a formal diagnosis, check to see if the school of your choice offers diagnostic services; some even offer those services free. Given that information, the school will often work directly with the professors to make sure that those disabilities are accommodated. This might include extended testing time, typing rather than writing, or a private room for testing. These accommodations may also be available for students with temporary disabilities, such as severe recurrent migraine headaches or short-term injuries. The specific accommodations depend on the circumstances.

It is common for schools to offer alternate methods for course reading. Blind students might need the texts in Braille, while dyslexic students might prefer the text as an audio recording.

Note-taking services are offered at nearly every school. Because lectures can be fast-paced and seminars can be intensive, it may make more sense for students to receive notes from another person in the class. This option is also offered for those experiencing minor injuries: if a right-handed student breaks her right wrist, she will need a note-taker until she can write again.

Final Thoughts

Social life is an area in which students tend to be more independent: having a sign interpreter in class is common, but having a sign interpreter outside the academic sphere usually does not fall under "reasonable accommodation." Check, however, to see whether your school provides escort services if you are blind, or whether they will provide personal care assistants if you have a severe mobility disability; in that case, they may work with Vocational Rehabilitation services in your home state to help pay for those accommodations.

Usually, you will not have to pay for these services since they fall under "reasonable accommodations" mandated by the state. For specialized services, it will vary by school. Remember, it is entirely your decision whether or not to disclose your disability up front. Above all, you should find a school that is best suited to you individually, and *then* make sure that the school can help you and provide you with resources to be a successful student.

Essay: Study Abroad

Three students, three countries, and three unique and unforgettable experiences! The following students recount their time abroad in different parts of the globe.

Name: Elisabeth Wang Forsman

University/college: Mount Holyoke College

Major: English & Asian Studies Minor

Year of college you studied abroad: Junior (2008)

Place you studied abroad: Kunming, China

Subject/field studied: Chinese Language & Culture

Program name: Duke Study in China

Extremely random thing you most enjoyed about your experience: Chasing around monkeys in the mountains of southwestern China.

Upon deciding to go to China I realized that I didn't want to go to one of the major cities. I am of the opinion that all major cities are alike, only the language changes. Therefore, I travelled to Kunming, a city located in the mountains of Western China, with Duke University. Kunming is known as the "City of Eternal Spring" because of its consistently pleasant climate. The city has a population of five million people and is home to much of China's ethnic minority population.

Kunming may be a "smaller" city, with a laid-back atmosphere, but it is definitely not lacking in spirit. Given a food allowance of 350 Renminbi a week by the program, the equivalent of $50 at the time, my classmates and I were allowed to find our own way through the city. The majority of us were immediately drawn to the foreigners' district, just 10 minutes away from campus, where we would dine, shop and go dancing with foreigners and locals alike, and have regular run-ins with a wandering pig that we named Wu Tongchin after two of our classmates. Rarely did we spend more than what we were given. At Green Lake Park or Cui Hu we would lounge around, watching as people practiced t'ai chi or formed performing groups complete with instrumental sections.

For a two week period the program went on spring break. For the first week we all got onto a bus and travelled throughout Yunnan Province. We spent a week hiking, biking, horseback riding, teaching English to elementary school students, looking for monkeys and going out to the clubs. At night we stayed everywhere from Buddhist Temples and the homes of rural villagers to four-star hotels. We ate the strangest foods, like one dish made entirely of pig fat. For the second week we were given free rein. A group of us went to Beijing, Shanghai and Xi'an, even taking the 19-hour train from Shanghai to Xi'an, which was an experience in itself. Not at all like in the states.

As a part of the intensive total language immersion program we lived with Chinese roommates, spent two afternoons a week with a language tutor and every other weekend we would individually spend a day at the home of a local family. On other weekends we would take field trips to various locations outside of the city. At first it was tough to handle the workload and the requirement to speak only Chinese but over time we became well acclimated to it. The individualized attention was fantastic. My knowledge of Chinese increased exponentially. I came to China barely able to string phrases together and left being able to discuss even political issues with ease.

Name: Thi Ho

University/college: Brown University

Major: Literatures and Cultures in English

Year of college you studied abroad: Junior (2008)

Place you studied abroad: Paris, France

Subject/field studied: Literature, Art History, History

Program name: Brown in France, La Sorbonne

Extremely random thing you most enjoyed about your experience: I enjoyed Perle de Lait's coconut yogurt so much that I tried to have them ship it to me in the U.S. It didn't work.

Paris, commonly perceived as the city of lights and love, regularly lives up to the hype. It is a gorgeous city. From major monuments like the Eiffel Tower to the Arc de Triomphe, Paris does not fail to impress you with the amount of beauty and history it possesses. I would definitely recommend visiting all the major tourist attractions, but this can be done in a day or two, depending on how fast you can walk and your tolerance for the crowds and sky-high prices. Personally, I preferred getting to know the city by simply strolling through the streets of the Latin Quarter and Montmartre, or by visiting the less well-known museums, like the Rodin Museum or the stunning St. Chapelle Cathedral.

Nevertheless, I have many conflicting opinions of Paris. For one, I studied abroad at a time when the exchange rate forced me to pay nearly twice as much for everything and I also lived alone in a tiny one-room studio with an oftentimes occupied and foul toilet down the hall. Still, I maintain that my experience in Paris was enlightening and enjoyable. Though prices were high, there are ways to budget, like going to the numerous open-air markets. The Bastille Market on the weekends stretches an entire street and has fresh ingredients and even jewelry. Bread, wine and chocolate can sometimes be cheaper than bottled water and of great quality. Monoprix, the French equivalent of Target, was my second home and has everything you need, from food to clothes to makeup. If you want a cheap meal, the bakeries on every block offer sandwiches and quiches with fresh-baked bread and fine cheese at very cheap prices. My personal favorite was the crepe stand across from the metro stop, Cluny-la-Sorbonne, which sold the cheapest crepes I found in the city.

One of the factors to consider before choosing Paris is whether city life is what you want for your study abroad experience. Cities can represent an extreme microcosm of the country as a whole, which can be a lot to take on all at once. Life is inevitably quicker and more expensive. It can also be eye-opening in many positive ways, like in familiarizing you with public transportation and life on a budget.

Name: Molly Moody
University/college: University of California, Los Angeles
Major: Political Science, Minor: Spanish
Year of college you studied abroad: Junior (2007)

Place you studied abroad: Granada, Spain
Subject/field studied: Political Science, History, Spanish
Program name: Universidad de Granada, Centro de Lenguas Modernas
Extremely random thing you most enjoyed about your experience: Taking a weekly "movemiento" (aerobics) class with an overly-enthusiastic and overly-sculpted male instructor.

Southern Spain has one of the most hospitable cultures in the entire world—and I was lucky enough to experience this on a daily basis with my incredible Spanish family. One of the most loving individuals I have ever met, my Spanish mom, Conchi, became like a second mother to me. She would spend hours sitting talking to me in Spanish, teaching me about Granada's extraordinary culture, explaining her difficult experiences as a woman during the Franco era, exposing me to Spanish art, and making me some of the best authentic Spanish food imaginable.

Every day, I would wind through Granada's intricate cobblestone streets, in the shadows of the majestic Alhambra, on my way to the University of Granada. I took classes ranging from the Art History of Spain to the Politics of the European Union—and loved them all. Although all of my classes were in Spanish, I never felt overwhelmed by the language barrier. The enthusiastic professors were sensitive to the fact that their students were from different areas of the world who spoke Spanish as a second or even third language.

Granada is also an incredibly lively city at night with plenty of places to meet some of the 70,000 local and international students. There are discotecas underneath the "Plaza de Toros" where local Spaniards love to dance and bars where you feel like you are right back at home in the United States.

My experience abroad turned out to be one of the most defining times of my entire life, where every day presented a new challenge—be it understanding my host father's thick Andalucían accent, avoiding the Moroccan water on my excursion to Africa, or trying to plan a trip to Barcelona and Paris for less than 50 Euro. However, I grew more as an individual in this incredible country than I could have ever imagined. I learned to speak Spanish, I learned to be independent, I learned to be away from everything familiar—and I truly believe that I am a better person because of this magical city.

Terms You Should Know

Advanced Placement (AP)—College credit earned by students while still in high school. Many high schools offer specially designed AP courses that prepare students for the College Board's AP Exams. Administered in May, they can qualify students who score well for advanced standing when they enroll at certain colleges.

all-nighter—As in, "pulling an all-nighter." The process by which students attempt to learn a semester's worth of course material or crank out a paper of considerable length in a short period, often 24 to 48 hours. Soda, coffee, and/or caffeine pills are the staples of most all-night cramming sessions.

American College Test (ACT)—Test administered to high school juniors and seniors by the American College Testing Program. Traditionally it has been used as an admissions criterion primarily by Midwestern schools. Some Southern and Western schools use it as well.

American College Testing Program (ACTP)—The organization that produces the American College Test (ACT) and the Family Financial Statement (FFS). Many Midwestern universities use the ACT and the FFS in admissions instead of the SAT and the Financial-Aid Form (FAF). (See also "Family Financial Statement" and "Financial-Aid Form").

arts and sciences (also called liberal arts)—A broad term that encompasses most traditional courses of study, including the humanities, social sciences, natural sciences, mathematics, and foreign languages. A liberal arts college is also a college of arts and sciences. (See also "humanities" and "social sciences").

beer pong—A party game usually played with Solo cups and cheap beer. The 10 cups on each side of the table are arranged in a triangular formation, and attempts are made by the teams to direct ping pong balls into the other team's cups, either by a perfected toss or with a ping pong paddle. When the other team's ball lands in your cup, you must drink the contents. A frat house staple.

candidate's reply date—The May 1 deadline, observed by most selective colleges, by which the applicant must respond to an offer of admission, usually with a nonrefundable deposit of several hundred dollars. Colleges that require students to respond by May 1 in almost all cases notify them of their acceptance on or before April 15.

College Board—The organization that sponsors the SAT, the SAT Subject Tests, the Advanced Placement tests and the Financial-Aid Form (FAF). College Board admissions tests are developed and administered by the Educational Testing Service (ETS). (See also "Advanced Placement" and "Financial-Aid Form").

Common Application—A form produced by a consortium of over 300 colleges that may be filled out and sent to member colleges in lieu of each school's individual application. Colleges often require that a supplemental application specific to the particular school be submitted as well.

comprehensive exams (comps)—Also known as "generals," these tests, administered by some colleges (usually during the senior year) are designed to measure knowledge gained over a student's entire college career. Schools that give comps usually require students to pass the test in their major field in order to graduate.

computing assistant (CA)—A university employee, often an undergraduate, who helps students with all varieties of computing problems, from using a word processor to downloading games from the network.

consortium—A group of colleges affiliated in some way. The extent of the association can vary widely. Some consortiums—usually among colleges in close proximity—offer a range of joint programs that may include cross-registration, interlibrary loans, residential exchanges, and coordinated social, cultural and athletic events.

co-op job—A paid internship, arranged for a student by his or her college, that provides on-the-job training, usually in an occupation closely related to the student's major.

core curriculum—A group of courses all students in a college must take in order to graduate. Core curricula are becoming widespread.

crew (rowing)—A sport, more familiar to those who live on or near either coast than to those from the South and Midwest, in which teams of two, four, or eight oarsmen or oarswomen race in long, narrow boats, usually on inland waterways. Crew is very "Ivy," quite popular at many schools, and usually requires no high school experience.

deferral—A college's postponement of the decision to accept or reject an early admissions applicant. The applicant's file is entered in with those of regular-action candidates in the spring and is reviewed once again, this time for a final decision.

discussion section—A smaller group of students who meet regularly with the guidance of a teaching assistant to discuss the material covered in a large lecture. Designed to make sure students do not get lost in large classes. The teaching assistant answers questions, fosters discussion, and usually grades assignments.

distribution requirements—Requirements stipulating that students take courses in a variety of broad subject areas in order to graduate. The number and definition of subject areas and the number of courses required in each varies from school to school. Typical categories include the humanities, social sciences, fine arts, natural sciences, foreign languages and mathematics. Unlike a core curriculum, distribution requirements do not usually mandate specific courses that students must take. (See also "humanities," "social sciences," and "core curriculum").

drunk dial—To make a phone call to an old boyfriend or girlfriend, former hook-up (see below), or current love interest in an inebriated state.

dry—as in "dry campus." A school that does not allow alcohol for any students in its dorms or other campus facilities.

early action—A program that gives students early notification of a college's admissions decision. Unlike early decision, it does not require a prior commitment to enroll if accepted. Early action has become increasingly popular and is now available at many colleges covered in this book. Some institutions, including Stanford and Yale, offer "single-choice"

early action programs. These plans work the same way as regular early action, except that students cannot apply early anywhere else. Deadlines for both types of early-action applications are usually in late fall, with notification in December, January or February. An applicant accepted under early action usually has until May 1, the candidate's reply date, to respond to the offer of admission. (See also "early decision" and "candidate's reply date").

early decision—A program under which a student receives early notification of a college's admissions decision if the student agrees in advance to enroll if accepted. Students may apply early decision to only one college; it should be a clear first choice. Application deadlines for early decision are usually in November, with decision letters mailed by mid-December.

Ethernet—A direct, high-speed means of access to the Internet, as well as a way to keep in touch with friends via e-mail. Most campuses are "wired" with Ethernet.

Facebook—An online directory launched in 2004 that connects individuals through high school, college and residential networks. Invaluable tool for procrastinators.

Facebookstalk—The process of "researching" the likes of a crush, former high school sweetheart, or ex-boyfriend's girlfriend through Facebook (See Facebook).

family contribution—The amount of money that a family can "reasonably" be expected to pay toward a student's education, as determined by one of the two standardized needs-analysis forms. (See also "Financial-Aid Form" and "Family Financial Statement").

Family Financial Statement (FFS)—The financial-needs analysis form submitted to the American College Testing Program (ACTP), which, like the FAF, determines the expected family contribution. Colleges that use the American College Test (ACT) for admissions purposes usually require a copy of the FFS report from students applying for financial aid. (See also "American College Testing Program," "family contribution," and "Financial-Aid Form").

fee waiver—Permission, often granted upon request, for needy students to apply for college admission without having to pay the application fee.

Financial-Aid Form (FAF)—The financial-needs analysis form submitted to the College Board by students applying for financial aid. Like the Family Financial Statement (FFS), it yields the expected family contribution. Colleges that require the Scholastic Assessment Test (SAT) for admission typically use the FAF as the basis for financial-aid awards. (See also "Family Financial Statement," "family contribution," and "College Board").

financial-aid package—The combination of loans, grants and a work-study job that a school puts together for a student receiving financial aid.

five-year plan—The practice of completing a four-year degree program over a five-year period.

flex dollars—Miscellaneous credit, usually part of a purchased meal plan, that can be used at campus stores and sometimes restaurants on and off campus, rather than cash. Especially convenient for late-night snacking and study breaks.

four-one-four—An academic calendar consisting of two regular four-month semesters with a short "winter" or "January" term in between. Variations include four-four-one and three-three-two. In most cases, these numbers refer to the number of courses a student is expected to complete in each segment of the year, although at some schools they refer to the number of months in each segment.

freshman 15—A reference to the number of pounds students often gain during the freshman year. Usually caused by a combination of too little exercise, unlimited helpings in the dining hall, too many late-night runs for pizza and overconsumption of alcoholic beverages.

gap year—The option of taking a year off between high school and college. Usually spent traveling, working or volunteering.

government aid—Money that federal or state governments make available to students, most of which is administered through the colleges on the basis of need. Government aid can come in the form of grants, loans, and work-study jobs. Stafford Loans (formerly Guaranteed Student Loans) and PLUS parent loans are made available through commercial lending institutions. For further information on government aid programs, contact the state and federal departments of education.

grade inflation—A situation in which average work is consistently awarded a higher letter grade than it would normally earn. At most schools, the grade for average work is about B–/C+. But in classes or entire colleges with grade inflation, it can be as high as B or even B+.

Greek system—The fraternities and sororities on a particular campus. They are called "Greek" because most take their names from combinations of letters in the Greek alphabet.

gut—A course widely known to be very easy, often with enrollments well into the hundreds. Guts are traditionally favorites among second-semester seniors, but they can also help to balance a term that includes very difficult courses.

hipster—a member of the student body who appears to be more artsy, literary, emotionally attuned, and/or nicotine-addicted than the rest of the class. Known to sport vintage and/or ill-fitting clothing.

hook up—To enjoy a person's nonplatonic company, often used in reference to a one-night event. A very vague term that can range from an innocent kiss to sex, depending on usage.

humanities—Subjects in which the primary focus is on human culture. Examples include philosophy, language and literature. (See also "social sciences").

independent study—A course, usually in a student's major field, in which he or she studies independently and meets one-on-one with a professor on a topic of the student's choosing. Some colleges require an independent study essay or research paper for graduation.

interdisciplinary major—A major that combines two complementary subjects from different fields, such as biology and psychology. Students completing these majors take courses in each area as well as courses that explicitly join the two.

International Baccalaureate (IB)—A high school program found across the world which, like AP courses, can earn a student advanced standing upon college enrollment.

intramurals—Athletic leagues informally organized within a college. Students are free from the burden of tryouts and play with and against fellow classmates.

jungle juice—A potent mix of liquor (often grain alcohol) and juice served at college parties out of a large watercooler or punchbowl. Freshmen who underestimate the juice's power due to its fruity taste, inevitably regret consumption the morning after.

language requirement—A rule at many colleges that requires students to study a foreign language before graduation. Two years on the college level are usually required, although credit from Advanced Placement or SAT Subject Tests often allows students to bypass the requirement.

legacy—An applicant whose mother or father is a graduate of a particular school. On occasion, students with legacy status are given extra consideration in admissions.

merit scholarship—A financial grant for some part of college costs, usually awarded for academic achievement or special skill in an extracurricular activity and not based on need. Private corporations and many colleges offer merit scholarships.

Natty Light—Cheap beer, a staple of college parties, sometimes referred to by its brand name, Natural Light. Often accompanied by its comrade "The Beast" (Milwaukee's Best), as well as a variety of inexpensive hard liquors.

need-based aid—Money awarded solely on the basis of need, usually administered through the colleges. Some schools agree to pay the difference between their total fees and the expected family contribution; others pay only part of it, leaving some "unmet" need. Most financial-aid packages consist of some combination of three components: grants, loans and work-study jobs. Some of the money comes from the college's own resources, although part is financed by federal and state governments. (See also "government aid").

need-blind admissions—A policy in which the applicant's ability to pay does not affect the college's consideration of his or her application. Some schools with need-blind admissions

also guarantee to meet the full demonstrated financial need of all accepted applicants as determined by one of the two standardized needs-analysis forms; others do not. (See also "family contribution," "Family Financial Statement," and "Financial-Aid Form").

office hours—A period during which a professor agrees to be available in his or her office for the purpose of talking with students about their coursework. Professors are not always required by their colleges to have office hours, but most do regardless.

open admissions—A policy under which any applicant with a high school diploma is accepted. State universities that have this policy usually limit open admission to state residents.

parietals—Regulations that govern the times when students of one sex may visit dorms or floors housing the opposite sex. Now usually found only at the most conservative schools.

pass/fail or CR/F or CR/D/F—An option offered by some schools in certain classes. A student may enroll in a class and simply receive credit or failure (or a D in "CR/D/F") for it on his or her transcript instead of a specific grade. While students often are not allowed to take required classes CR/D/F, the option allows them to take classes out of their comfort range without the fear of being punished with a bad grade for experimenting.

Phi Beta Kappa—An academic honor society to which students with the best grade point average in each class are elected. Less than the top 10 percent of a class, and usually far fewer, receive this honor.

PLUS parent loans—A component of the Stafford Loan, for parents. (See also "government aid").

pre-frosh—A visiting high school student, potential college recruit or admitted student who has yet to enroll.

pregame—To prepare for a party, bar, show, or another event by imbibing beforehand. Saves time and money.

problem set—An annoying weekly assignment that is usually inevitable in science or quantitative classes. This thankless task will keep you up till 2 a.m. Sunday nights but can count for anywhere between 1/50 of your grade or one-half. Previously known as homework.

quad—An abbreviation for "quadrangle"; many dorm complexes are built in squares (quadrangles) with a courtyard in the middle. Quad can also refer to a suite of dormitory rooms in which four students live together.

quarter system—An academic calendar dividing the school year into four quarters, three of which constitute a full academic year. Less common than the semester system, it is most often used by large universities with extensive programs in agricultural and technical fields.

resident advisor/assistant (RA)—A student, usually an upperclassman, who lives in a dorm and helps to maintain regulations and enforce school policy, as well as offering advice and support to dorm residents. RAs receive compensation from the school for their services, usually in the form of free room and board.

rolling admissions—A policy under which a college considers applications almost immediately after receiving them. Decision letters are mailed within a month after the application is filed. Colleges with rolling admissions continue to accept applications only until the class is filled, so it is best to apply early.

Scholastic Assessment Test (SAT)—Test administered to high school juniors and seniors by the College Board of the Educational Testing Service, with math, verbal, and written-language sections. Used as an admissions criterion at most colleges nationwide.

section all-star—A member of a discussion section who distinguishes him or herself by volunteering contributions in an excessively obnoxious or earnest manner. Sometimes encouraged by the TA, always reviled by other section members. Known for quoting from the original Greek and becoming belligerent during debates.

senior project—Many majors at many colleges require seniors to complete a special project during their senior year. This could involve a thesis (anywhere from 15 to 100 pages), a research project, some sort of internship, or all of the above. Some colleges offer seniors a choice between taking comps or doing a project. (See also "comps").

sexile—There are two people in the bedroom you share with your roommate, and you are not one of them. If you are lucky, you have a common room with a comfortable couch.

social sciences—Subjects that deal systematically with the institutions of human society, most notably economics and political science. The behavioral sciences, which include psychology, sociology and anthropology, are often included in this group as well.

Sophomore Slump—A period, usually the first semester of sophomore year, when students experience unprecedented levels of stress and angst. Often results from the disillusionment and increased workload following freshman year.

study break—An institutionalized form of procrastination involving food and talk. Often informally arranged—"I'm sick of calculus, let's take a study break at—(insert name of local hangout)"—but can be sponsored by RAs, cultural groups, or even school administrators. Some nights, study breaks can take more of your time than the actual studying.

teaching assistant (TA)—A graduate student who assists a professor in the presentation of a course. Usually the professor gives two to four lectures a week for all the students in the class; the TAs hold smaller weekly discussion sections.

three-two program (3–2)—A program that allows students to study for three years at one school, followed by two at another, more specialized school. Upon completion, many of these programs award both the bachelor's and the master's degrees.

town-gown relations—The contact between a college (students, employees, buildings) and its host town (citizens, businesses, local government) and the set of issues around which this contact revolves. Such issues include taxes, traffic, local employment practices and government services such as road maintenance, sewage, and trash collection.

townie—A resident of a college town or city who is not enrolled in the college, but who might sit beside you at the local pub. Often involves a them-versus-us mentality.

trimesters—An academic calendar that divides the school year into three terms of approximately equal length. Schools on the trimester system generally have one term before the winter break and two after.

tutorial major (also self-designed or special major)—A program offered by many schools in which a student can plan his or her own major, combining the offerings of two or more traditional majors, usually in consultation with a faculty member. An example is Medieval studies, in which the student might study the history, literature, philosophy and art of the period, taking courses from a number of departments. (See also "interdisciplinary major").

waiting list—A list of students who are not initially accepted to a certain school, but who may be admitted later, depending on the number of accepted students who enroll. Most colleges ultimately accept only a fraction of the students on the waiting list, who are notified during the summer.

work-study—Campus jobs, for financial-aid recipients, that are subsidized by the federal government. Work-study jobs are a component of most need-based financial-aid packages. Students typically work 10 to 20 hours a week to help finance their education.

Editors' Choice

Biggest Jock Schools

University of Florida
University of Notre Dame
Ohio State University
Michigan State University
University of California/Los Angeles
Stanford University
University of Texas
University of Connecticut
Pennsylvania State University
University of North Carolina

"Sports are vital to the University because the teams bring in millions of dollars a year and create a sense of pride and tradition. The jocks get treated like the second coming of Christ."—Alexandria Butler, University of Connecticut

Easiest Course Load

Arizona State University
Seton Hall University
Hofstra University
University of Hawaii
Salve Regina University
Hampshire College
University of Alaska/Fairbanks
Texas Tech University
Benedict College
University of California/Santa Cruz

"Hampshire is full of self-motivated kids with extraordinarily high goals. Hampshire does not have majors; you choose what to take. This creates a lot of pressure to choose the 'right' thing. We do have requirements, but they are just broader and include areas like multicultural perspectives and community service."—Jill Erwich, Hampshire College

Most Blondes

University of Southern California
University of Mississippi
Southern Methodist University
Pepperdine University
Arizona State University
University of California/Santa Barbara
Vanderbilt University
University of Notre Dame
Baylor University
Auburn University

Most difficult requirements

Columbia University
Claremont McKenna College
Stanford University
United States Air Force Academy
Colorado School of Mines
United States Military Academy
Marquette University
United States Naval Academy
Reed College
United States Coast Guard Academy

"I think it's completely true. Reed is ridiculously hard and truly belongs with the Harvards and Yales of the world. Going to Reed is like the Bataan Death March except we're not in the Philippines and the march never ends."—Alex Gersovitz, Reed College

Schools that never sleep

New York University
Arizona State University
University of Southern California
Hunter College
University of Miami
Tulane University
Yale University
Denver University

University of Chicago
Parsons School of Design

"Contrary to popular belief, New York City sleeps . . . everywhere. Try taking the F train at 8 a.m.: it's all suits and snores. However, there's always a bunch of stuff you can busy yourself with so you can return home with pretty incredible stories for your friends stuck on those 'campus' things."—Jenna Rosenberg, New York University

Happiest students

Stanford University
Whitman College
Yale University
University of Colorado
Clemson University
Bowdoin College
The College of New Jersey
Pomona College
St. Johns College
Brigham Young University

Most Behind the Times

College of William and Mary
Oral Roberts University
Bob Jones University
University of North Dakota
Union College
George Mason University
Davidson College
Brigham Young University
Washington and Lee University
Princeton University

"Princeton's attempt to spearhead a grade-deflation policy has received no followers among the Ivy League, which single-handedly puts us behind the times. Also, the obsession with both traditions and the creation of a Fitzgerald-era class of elitism and exclusivity definitely acts counter to the diversification efforts of most other institutions."—Ota Amaize, Princeton University

Strongest Undergraduate Focus

Princeton University
Carleton College
Grinnell College
Williams College
Yale University
Amherst College
Swarthmore College
California Institute of Technology
Occidental College
Stanford University

"Our professors are always available for office hours and spend significantly more time actually teaching than many others in the Ivy League. In addition, Yale has significant resources geared toward making undergraduate life as smooth and exciting as possible."—Ayibitari Owi, Yale University

Most Millionaire Graduates

Harvard University
University of Pennsylvania
Yale University
Massachusetts Institute of Technology
University of Southern California
Princeton University
Stanford University
Northwestern University
Duke University
Brown University

Best Study Abroad Programs

University of Virginia
Baylor University
New York University
American University
Michigan State University
Florida State University
Middlebury College
University of Dallas
Bates College
DePauw University

"There are a bunch of study abroad locations. I plan on going to Ghana junior year because I've heard some pretty wonderful things from upperclassmen. I'm excited for the great artist community and the food is supposed to be pretty incredible."—Jenna Rosenberg, New York University

Biggest Rivalries

Duke University–University of North
  Carolina
West Point–United States Naval Academy
Harvard University–Yale University
Stanford University–University of
  California/Berkeley
University of Florida–Florida State
  University
University of Alabama–Auburn University
University of Texas/Austin–Texas A&M
  University
Ohio State University–University of
  Michigan
University of Southern California–University
  of California/Los Angeles
University of South Carolina–Clemson
  University

"Our rivalry with UNC is a great part of the Duke experience and quantifies the passion we bring to everything. There are some students that really bleed blue as they sleep in tents outside of Cameron Indoor Stadium for weeks on end in order to reserve seats for the big game."—Rajhai Wilson, Duke University

Place Most Likely to Find Your Spouse

Middlebury College
Connecticut College
Williams College
Princeton University
Brigham Young University
Clemson University
Florida State University
Wheaton College (Illinois)
University of Southern California
University of Mississippi

Best College Town

University of California/Berkeley (Berkeley)
University of Michigan (Ann Arbor)
University of Wisconsin (Madison)
Florida State University (Tallahassee)
Indiana University (Bloomington)
University of Florida (Gainesville)
North Carolina State (Raleigh)
University of Texas (Austin)
University of Miami (Oxford)
Boston College (Chestnut Hill)

"Chestnut Hill is a great college town because it combines the benefits of a big city with the feel of a suburban college campus. Just be sure to bring money, because Boston is expensive."—Gordon Bell, Boston College

Best Local Restaurants

Columbia University
New York University
Georgetown University
Tulane University
University of California/Los Angeles
Boston University
University of Texas/Austin
Harvard University
Yale University
University of Chicago

"New Haven's restaurants are fantastic. Even though it's a small city, New Haven possesses the diverse cuisines of a metropolis 10 times its size, including Japanese, Thai, Cuban, Italian, French, vegetarian, and even vegan."—JonPaul McBride, Yale University

Ugliest school colors

Clemson University (Burnt Orange and
  Purple)
University of Oregon (Green and Yellow)
Bowling Green State University (Brown and
  Orange)
Rice University (Blue and Gray)
University of Washington (Purple and Gold)

Florida State University (Maroon and Dark Gold)

Rowan University (Brown and Yellow)

University of Tennessee (Bright Orange and White)

University of Wyoming (Brown and Gold)

Auburn University (Burnt Orange and Navy Blue)

Craziest mascot

Xavier University (Blue Blob)

Syracuse University (Orangemen)

University of Maryland (Terrapins)

University of California/Irvine (Anteaters)

University of California/Santa Cruz (Banana Slugs)

North Carolina School of the Arts (Fighting Pickles)

Ohio Wesleyan University (Battling Bishops)

Whittier College (Poets)

University of Hawaii (Rainbow Warriors)

Connecticut College (Camels)

"An anteater is definitely a strange mascot because most people want a mascot to be intimidating. Instead, we have an anteater. At the same time, I guess it's cool because we always know that no one else will."

College Finder 2010

Regions

New England:
Connecticut
Maine
Massachusetts
New Hampshire
Rhode Island
Vermont
Eastern Canada

Mid-Atlantic:
Delaware
District of Columbia
Maryland
New Jersey
New York
Pennsylvania
West Virginia

Midwest:
Illinois
Indiana
Iowa
Kansas
Kentucky
Michigan
Minnesota
Missouri
Nebraska
North Dakota
Ohio
South Dakota
Wisconsin

Southeast:
Alabama
Arkansas
Florida
Georgia
Louisiana
Mississippi
South Carolina
North Carolina
Tennessee
Virginia

West:
Alaska
Arizona
California
Colorado
Hawaii
Idaho
Montana
New Mexico
Nevada
Oklahoma
Oregon
Texas
Utah
Washington
Wyoming
Western Canada

Schools with Fewer than 1500 Undergraduates

New England:
College of the Atlantic
Marlboro College
Bennington College
United States Coast Guard Academy
Hampshire College
Bard College

Mid-Atlantic:
St. John's College
Trinity College
Haverford College
Bryn Mawr College
Swarthmore College
Goucher College
The Cooper Union for the
    Advancement of Science and Art
Sarah Lawrence College
The Juilliard School

Midwest:
Wabash College
Centre College
Cornell College
Earlham College
Knox College
Kalamazoo College
Alma College
Beloit College
Lake Forest College
St. Mary's College
Lawrence University
Principia College

Southeast:
New College of Florida
Randolph College
Sweet Briar College
Hollins University
Agnes Scott College
Milsaps College
Hampden-Sydney College
Wofford College
Birmingham-Southern College

West:
Deep Springs College
Harvey Mudd College
Mills College
California Institute of the Arts
Scripps College
California Institute of Technology
Pitzer College
Claremont McKenna College
Whitman College
Reed College
University of Dallas
Hendrix College
Whittier College

1500–5000 Undergrads

New England:
Amherst College
Babson College
Bates College
Bowdoin College
Clark University
Colby College
Connecticut College
College of the Holy Cross
Middlebury College
Mount Holyoke College
Rhode Island School of Design
Salve Regina University
Simmons College
Smith College
Trinity College
Wellesley
Wesleyan
Wheaton College
Williams College
Worcester Polytechnic Institute

Mid-Atlantic:
Alfred University
Allegheny College
Barnard College
Catholic University

Clarkson University
Colgate University
Dickinson College
Drew University
Franklin and Marshall College
Gettysburg College
Hamilton College
Hobart and William Smith Colleges
Lafayette College
Manhattanville College
Muhlenberg College
Skidmore College
St. Bonaventure University
St. Lawrence University
St. Mary's College of Maryland
Stevens Institute of Technology
Susquehanna University
Union College
Ursinus College
Vassar College

Midwest:
Albion College
Carleton College
College of Wooster
Denison University
DePauw University
Grinnell College
Gustavus Adolphus College
Kenyon College
Macalester College
Oberlin College
Ohio Wesleyan University
Rose-Hulman Institute of Technology
St. Olaf College
Wheaton College
Wittenberg University

Southeast:
Florida Southern University
Florida Institute of Technology
Furman University
Morehouse College
Rhodes College
Rollins College
Spelman College
Stetson University
Tuskegee University
University of Richmond
Washington and Lee University

West:
Colorado College
Colorado School of Mines
Lewis and Clark College
Occidental College
Pepperdine University
Pomona College
Rice University

St. Mary's University
Trinity University
University of Puget Sound
University of Redlands
University of Tulsa
Willamette University

Over 20,000 undergrads

New England:
University of Toronto
University of Massachusetts/Amherst

Mid-Atlantic:
University of Maryland/College Park
Temple University
Penn State University

Midwest:
Indiana University
Iowa State University
Michigan State University
Ohio State University
Purdue University
University of Illinois/Urbana-Champaign
University of Iowa
University of Kansas
University of Michigan
University of Minnesota
University of Missouri/Columbia
University of Wisconsin/Madison

Southeast:
Florida State University
Louisiana State University
North Carolina State University
University of Florida
University of Georgia
University of South Florida
University of Tennessee/Knoxville
Virginia Polytechnic Institute

West:
Arizona State University
Brigham Young University
Texas A&M University
Texas Institute of Technology University
University of Arizona
University of California/Berkeley
University of California/Davis
University of California/Los Angeles
University of California/San Diego
University of Colorado/Boulder
University of Houston
University of Texas/Austin

University of Washington
University of Western Ontario

Single Sex Schools

Female:
Mills College
Scripps College
Agnes Scott College
St. Mary's College
Mount Holyoke College
Spelman College
Barnard College
Smith College
Wellesley College
Trinity College (D.C.)
Bryn Mawr
Sweet Briar College
Hollins University
Simmons College
Wells College

Male:
Deep Springs College
Wabash College
Hampden-Sydney College
Morehouse College

Predominantly Male Schools (>66%)

California Institute of Technology
Clarkson University
Colorado School of Mines
Florida Institute of Technology
Georgia Institute of Technology
Harvey Mudd College
Michigan Technological Institute
Rensselaer Polytechnic Institute
Rochester Institute of Technology
Rose-Hulman Institute of Technology
Stevens Institute of Technology
United States Military Academy
United States Naval Academy
United States Air Force Academy
United States Coast Guard Academy
Worcester Polytechnic Institute

Predominantly Female Schools (>66%)

Adelphi University
Bennington College
College of the Atlantic
Drew University
Eugene Lang College of The New
   School University
Goucher College
Howard University
Hunter College
Manhattanville College
Parsons The New School for Design
Rhode Island School of Design
Salve Regina University
Sarah Lawrence College
St. Mary's University
Wells College

High Minority Enrollment (>35%)

New England:
Amherst College
Babson College
College of the Atlantic
Dartmouth College
Harvard University
Massachusetts Institute of Technology
Mount Holyoke College
Rhode Island School of Design
Smith College
Trinity College (CT)
Wellesley College
Wesleyan University
Yale University

Mid-Atlantic
Adelphi University
American University
City University of New York/City College
City University of New York/Queens College
Columbia University
The Cooper Union for the Advancement of
   Science and Art
Cornell University
Howard University
Hunter College
Johns Hopkins University
New York University
Princeton University
Rutgers/The State University of New Jersey
State University of New York/Stony Brook

Trinity University
University of Maryland/College Park

Midwest
DePaul University
Loyola University
University of Chicago
University of Illinois/Chicago

Southeast
Florida A & M University
Morehouse College
Spelman College
Tuskegee University
University of Miami
University of South Florida
University of Tampa

West
California State University/Fresno
California Institute of Technology
Claremont McKenna College
New Mexico State University
Occidental College
Pepperdine University
Rice University
Scripps College
St. Mary's College of California
University of California/Riverside
University of California/Irvine
University of California/Los Angeles
University of California/Berkeley
Stanford University
University of California/Davis
University of California/San Diego
University of Alaska/Fairbanks
University of Hawaii/Manoa
University of Houston
University of New Mexico
University of Texas/Austin
University of Washington
University of Southern California
Whittier College

Schools Accepting <25% of applicants

The Juilliard School
Yale University
United States Naval Academy
Harvard University
United States Military Academy
The Cooper Union for the Advancement of
   Science and Art
Stanford University
Princeton University

Columbia University
United States Air Force Academy
California Institute of the Arts
Massachusetts Institute of Technology
Brown University
Dartmouth College
Amherst College
Williams College
Pomona College
California Institute of Technology
University of Pennsylvania
Duke University
Washington University in St. Louis
Rice University
Claremont McKenna College
Georgetown University
United States Coast Guard Academy
University of California/Los Angeles
Middlebury College
Bowdoin College

Schools Accepting 25–40% of Applicants

University of California/Berkeley
Swarthmore College
University of South Carolina
Pepperdine University
Barnard College
Wesleyan College
Tufts University
Haverford College
Cornell University
Carleton College
Vassar College
Hunter College
Northwestern University
University of Notre Dame
Washington and Lee
Bates College
Boston College
Colgate University
Hamilton College
Bucknell College
Rhode Island School of Design
College of William and Mary
Connecticut College
Johns Hopkins University
New York University
Vanderbilt University
Oberlin College
Emory University
Trinity College
Bard College
Colby College
Wellesley College

Babson College
University of Virginia
Harvey Mudd College
California Polytechnic State University/
    San Luis Obispo
George Washington University
Kenyon College
Pitzer College
Macalester College
Brandeis University
University of Chicago
University of Richmond
Lehigh University
Carnegie Mellon University
City University of New York/Queens College
University of California/San Diego
University of Miami
Northeastern University
Elon University
State University of New York/Binghamton
Denison University
Colorado College
University of Tennessee, Knoxville
College of the Holy Cross
Sarah Lawrence College
Franklin and Marshall College
Reed College
Occidental College
Tulane University
University of Delaware
Wheaton College
Muhlenberg College
Gettysburg College
Spelman College
Howard University
Bryn Mawr College
Wake Forest University
Union College
University of Rochester
The College of New Jersey
Skidmore College
Kansas State University
Stevens Institute of Technology
Scripps College
Wabash College
University of Pittsburg
Dickinson College
Rhodes College
University of Maryland/College Park
Fordham University
University of Connecticut
Whitman College
State University of New York/Stony Brook

Large Fraternity/ Sorority Systems (More than 30%)

Albion College
Birmingham-Southern College
Bucknell College
Case Western Reserve University
Centre College
Colgate University
Cornell College
Dartmouth College
Denison University
DePauw University
Emory University
Franklin and Marshall College
Furman College
Gettysburg College
Hamilton College
Hampden-Sydney College
Lehigh University
Millsaps College
Massachusetts Institute of Technology
Northwestern University
Ohio Wesleyan University
Rensselaer Polytechnic Institute
Rhodes College
Rollins College
Rose-Hulman Institute of Technology
Stevens Institute of Technology
Texas Christian University
Tulane University
University of Richmond
University of the South/Sewanee
University of Virginia
Ursinus College
Vanderbilt University
Wabash College
Wake Forest University
Washington and Lee University
Whitman College
Willamette University
College of William and Mary
Wofford College

Schools with no Fraternities or Sororities

Agnes Scott College
Alfred College
Amherst College
Antioch College
Bennington College

Boston College
Bowdoin College
Brandeis University
Brigham Young University
Bryn Mawr College
California Institute of Technology
California Institute of the Arts
Carleton College
Claremont McKenna College
Clark University
Colby College
College of the Atlantic
Connecticut College
Deep Springs College
DePaul University
Drew University
Earlham College
Eugene Lang College of The New School
    University
Evergreen State University
Fairfield University
Fordham University
Georgetown University
Goucher College
Hampshire College
Harvey Mudd College
Haverford College
Ithaca College
Lewis and Clark College
Macalester College
Marlboro College
Mills College
New College of South Florida
Pitzer College
Principia College
Rice University
Rhode Island School of Design
Sarah Lawrence College
Scripps College
Seton Hall University
Simmons College
Skidmore
Smith College
St. Bonaventure University
St. John's University/College of St. Benedict
St. Mary's College
St. Olaf College
Sweet Briar College
Trinity University
United States Air Force Academy
United States Coast Guard Academy
United States Military Academy
United States Naval Academy
University of Dallas
University of North Carolina/Chapel Hill
University of Notre Dame
University of Washington
Vassar College
Wellesley College

Wells College
Williams College

Schools with very high four-year graduation rates (>85%)

Amherst College
Bates College
Bucknell College
Carleton College
Claremont McKenna College
Columbia University
Dartmouth College
Davidson College
Duke University
Georgetown University
Harvard University
Haverford College
College of Holy Cross
Johns Hopkins University
Lafayette College
Middlebury College
Muhlenberg College
Oberlin College
Oxford University
Pomona College
Princeton University
Principia College
St. Olaf College
Swarthmore College
Tufts University
University of Pennsylvania
United States Naval Academy
University of Notre Dame
United States Air Force Academy
United States Coast Guard Academy
University of Chicago
University of Michigan
University of Virginia
Vanderbilt University
Vassar College
Villanova University
Wake Forest University
Washington and Lee University
Washington University in St. Louis
Wellesley College
Whitman College
College of William and Mary
Williams College
Yale University

Under $10,000 (Out of State)

Brigham Young University
City University of New York/City College
Deep Springs College
Michigan State University
Millsaps College
Mississippi State University
New Mexico State University
Ohio University
Queen's University
Rutgers/The State University of New Jersey
United States Military Academy
United States Naval Academy
University of Arizona
University of Kansas
University of Michigan
University of Minnesota
University of South Alabama
University of South Dakota
University of Utah
University of Virginia
University of Waterloo
University of Western Ontario
United States Air Force Academy
United States Coast Guard Academy
West Virginia University
College of William and Mary

Under $10,000 (In State)

Arizona State University
Auburn University
Bowling Green State University
California Polytechnic State University/
    San Luis Obispo
California State University/Chico
California State University/Fresno
City University of New York/City College
Clemson University
Colorado School of Mines
Evergreen State University
Florida A & M University
Florida State University
George Mason University
Hunter College
Illinois State University
Indiana University, Bloomington
Iowa State University
Kansas State University
Louisiana State University
Marshall University

McGill University
Mississippi State University
New College of South Florida
New Mexico State University
Ohio State University
Oklahoma State University
Oregon State University
Southern Illinois University/Carbondale
State University of New York/Albany
State University of New York/Binghamton
State University of New York/Buffalo
State University of New York/Stony Brook
Texas A&M University
Texas Tech University
University of Connecticut
University of Massachusetts/Amherst
United States Military Academy
United States Naval Academy
University of California/Berkeley
University of California/Davis
University of California/Irvine
University of California/Los Angeles
University of California/Riverside
University of California/San Diego
University of California/Santa Barbara
University of California/Santa Cruz
University of North Carolina/Chapel Hill
University of Illinois/Urbana-Champaign
University of Alabama
University of Alaska/Fairbanks
University of Arkansas
University of Cincinnati
University of Colorado/Boulder
University of Delaware
University of Florida
University of Georgia
University of Hawaii/Manoa
University of Houston
University of Idaho
University of Illinois/Chicago
University of Iowa
University of Kansas
University of Kentucky
University of Maine/Orono
University of Maryland/College Park
University of Mississippi
University of Missouri/Columbia
University of Missouri/Kansas City
University of Montana
University of Nebraska/Lincoln
University of Nevada/Reno
University of New Mexico
University of North Dakota
University of Oklahoma
University of Oregon
University of Rhode Island
University of South Alabama
University of South Carolina
University of South Dakota

University of Tennessee/Knoxville
University of Texas/Austin
University of Washington
University of Wisconsin/Madison
University of Wyoming
United States Air Force Academy
United States Coast Guard Academy
Virginia Polytechnic University
Washington State
West Virginia University

Over $35,000

Amherst College
Bard College
Barnard College
Bennington College
Boston College
Boston University
Bowdoin College
Brandeis University
Brown University
Bucknell University
Carnegie Mellon University
Claremont McKenna College
Colgate University
Columbia University
Dickinson College
Franklin and Marshall College
George Washington University
Georgetown University
Hamilton College
Hampshire College
Haverford College
Kenyon College
Middlebury College
New York University
Pitzer College
Reed College
Sarah Lawrence College
Scripps College
St. John's University
St. Lawrence University
St. Olaf College
Stevens Institute of Technology
Swarthmore College
Trinity College
Tufts University
Tulane University
University of Pennsylvania
University of Richmond
Vassar College
Wheaton College
Whitman College

Insider's Quiz

What kind of college is right for you?

Which high school stereotype would best describe you?
- a. Athlete
- b. Intellectual
- c. Hipster
- d. Prepster
- e. Emo or granola-loving Hippie

Which of the following statements do you best relate to?
- a. I want everyone to have heard of my college!
- b. It's okay if people haven't heard of my college before. I know it's a great school.
- c. In college I want to have the big city at my fingertips!
- d. I want my classmates to dress like me—classic and colorful with collars always up.
- e. I can't wait to go to school with people who understand me!

You wouldn't like a college that:
- a. Is too far away from home.
- b. Isn't in the quintessential college town.
- c. Isn't in a big city.
- d. Has too many students who don't summer in Nantucket or Martha's Vineyard.
- e. Doesn't care about political issues.

What do you expect walks to class will be like in college?
- a. I'll see lots of people that I have never met before.
- b. I'll see half my friends on the way and know almost all the people I see who are in my year.
- c. I'll be surrounded by the noises, people, and cars that fill a busy, buzzing city.
- d. It will look like a Ralph Lauren fashion show.
- e. I'll be almost too busy reading all the posters about political activism events that are going on around campus to walk!

You imagine that varsity athletics at your dream school will be:
- a. A huge draw.
- b. Not as popular as intramural sports.
- c. Not as well attended as the professional athletic events in the city.
- d. Important depending on the sport—lacrosse and crew will be bigger than football and basketball.
- e. What do you mean by varsity athletics?

Where do you see yourself meeting up with your college friends?
- a. At the student center, the hub of campus activity.
- b. On the quad, where people are hanging out on the lawn.
- c. At one of the zillion Starbucks that are on every corner.
- d. The squash court.
- e. At social activism meetings.

When you run into your professor outside of class, what do you think you'll discuss?
- a. Whether he/she saw the big game this weekend.
- b. The intense argument about Kant that took place between the 10 students who make up the class.
- c. Recommended local concert venues.
- d. The best conditions for yachting.
- e. Whether we could all just sit in a circle on the floor in the classroom and not at the desks.

You're running late to class, so you pull your tried-and-true wardrobe staple out of the closet:
- a. Your school sweatshirt.
- b. A sweater you permanently borrowed from your best friend.
- c. Skinny jeans.
- d. A Polo shirt.
- e. A hand-dyed scarf obtained in an obscure country.

What will your dream job be like?
- a. I'll be working at a big company with a dynamic atmosphere.
- b. I'll work at a smaller company where I can have a big influence.
- c. I'm not sure, but I know it will be in a big city.

d. I'll either be a high-power consultant or a trophy wife/husband.

e. Who knows? I don't plan for the future. I just go with the flow.

What will you be doing in your free time 10 years after college graduation?

a. Cheering on my alma mater at home games.

b. Reading books in the local coffee shop.

c. Going to museums and cultural events during the day and clubbing at night.

d. Relaxing at my getaway home, sailing, and gossiping about my old classmates.

e. Going to rallies and protests.

Results

What kind of college is right for you?

If you answered mostly a's, a Big State School like University of Florida or Ohio State University.

If you answered mostly b's, a Small Liberal Arts school like Williams College or Vassar College.

If you answered mostly c's, an Urban School like New York University or Georgetown University.

If you answered mostly d's, a Preppy School like Washington and Lee University or Hamilton College.

If you answered mostly e's, an Alternative School like Wesleyan University or Reed College.

Insider's Packing List

Recreational

___Twister
___Deck of cards
___Dice
___A white T-shirt to write on
___Shot glass
___Magnetic poetry
___Board games
___Fan
___Feather boa
___Cowboy hat
___Picnic blanket
___Cute Facebook photo
___Bottle opener
___Corkscrew
___Water guns
___Water balloons
___Sexy underwear
___Bathing suit
___US Weekly subscription
___Hookah
___Frisbee
___DVDs
___A pair of aviators
___Volleyball/Basketball/Baseball (pretty much anything you can throw)
___Body paint
___Wig
___Game Console (preferably a Nintendo Wii)

Practical

___Red cups
___Clorox wipes
___Airborne
___Shower shoes
___Febreze
___Tool kit
___iPod
___Duct tape
___Iron
___Layers
___Compact umbrella
___Brita
___Cough drops

___ATM card
___Checkbook
___Stamps
___Stationery
___Homemade cookies
___Sweatshirt blanket
___bleach pen
___Energy-saving light bulbs
___Hand sanitizer
___Thai bowls
___Microwaveable mac & cheese
___One pair of shoes that you don't mind ruining
___One pair of shoes that you'd hate to ruin
___At least one nice outfit
___Social Security number (memorized)
___Best high school friends' e-mails and school addresses
___Markers
___Organized jewelry holder
___Lots of towels
___Hair straightener
___Plastic utensils
___Day planner
___Mirror
___Punch bowl
___Nalgene water bottle
___North Face Fleece
___Ethernet cord
___Alarm clock
___Overnight bag
___As many pairs of socks and underwear as possible (to put off laundry day)
___Hangers
___Scissors
___Digital camera
___Rechargeable batteries

Academic

___Laptop
___USB flash drive
___1-subject notebooks
___Index cards
___An endless supply of pens, highlighters, No. 2 pencils, etc.

Decorative

___Photos of your family
___Photos of your high school friends
___Christmas lights
___Sticky tack (for posters)
___Throw pillows
___Plastic hooks
___Corkboard
___Whiteboard

Things to Leave at Home

___Varsity jackets
___High school yearbooks
___Pleasure reading
___More than two stuffed animals
___A high school sweetheart
___SAT scores
___Trophies
___Stamp/baseball card/Absolut ad
    collections
___Overly descriptive Away messages
___Dry-clean-only clothes
___College T-shirts

A Word About Statistics

Do you want to narrow your search, size up a school quickly, or check out your chances of getting admitted? Statistics are a useful place to start when you are browsing colleges, and they are also helpful in creating that perfect list of reach, mid-range, and safety schools to which you will apply. A statistical profile precedes every college in The Insider's Guide. The colleges themselves typically provide the data. The letters "NA" (not available) either represent data that the school did not report, or those that could not be found on the school's Web site. For the most up-to-date information, as well as for all data not included in The Insider's Guide, you should contact the colleges directly.

As a rule, the statistics provided are from the most recent year for which the college has information. In most cases, this means either the 2007–2008 or the 2008-2009 academic year. In general, percentages have been rounded to the nearest whole-number percent. Statistically speaking, there is no significant difference between an acceptance rate of 30 percent and 30.4 percent; in fact, even a difference of 3 to 5 percent would hardly be noticeable.

Below the name of each school the **address,** undergraduate **admissions phone number,** and undergraduate **admissions e-mail** address are listed; this is the contact information that a school's admissions office prefers applicants to use when corresponding.

A **Web site URL** is listed for each school, which we recommend you visit to get a quick sense of the school online.

Founded is the year that the school first accepted students.

The designation **private or public** refers to private schools versus publicly funded state schools. Tuition is often lower for public schools, especially for in-state students. This label cannot in any way be applied to refer to the quality of education.

Religious affiliation indicates whether a school is affiliated in any way with a particular religious establishment. This affiliation may vary—simply being a part of the school's history to being the religion predominantly practiced on campus.

Location describes the setting of the college, which is either rural, suburban, in a small city, or urban. This description gives only a general idea of the surroundings, and remember, like the rest of the statistics, it is given by the school itself.

The **application deadline** is the final deadline for completed applications (except for second-term grade reports and late admissions tests) for freshman students. Early decision and early action programs have different deadlines, and rolling admissions may have priority deadlines after which an application is at a disadvantage. Transfer student applications usually are due one or two months after freshman applications. Nevertheless, submitting your application early gives the admissions committee more time to become familiar with your application and increases your chance of getting in.

Number of applicants is the number of completed first-year undergraduate applications received by the university.

The **percent accepted** figure is the number of applicants accepted for the most recent entering freshman class (in this case, usually the class of 2012) divided by the total number of applicants. This is an imperfect measure of a college's selectivity, and does not necessarily reflect academic quality, since many factors can influence acceptance rates. One example of this is that some schools with reputations for being easy after admission tend to attract larger numbers of applicants. For another example, public schools offer lower tuition to in-state residents, which is an attractive incentive for those applicants. Even winning sports teams can increase application numbers. There are many other factors that can influence the quality and size of the applicant pool even from year to year. Despite these caveats, the percent accepted figure is a revealing statistic. Colleges that accept relatively small numbers of applicants are usually in the best position to maintain high academic standards. When the acceptance rate is less than one-third, you can be assured that the school is one of the best around.

Percent accepted who enroll is the number of students who enroll divided by the number of students accepted. This figure, commonly called the "yield" by the admissions offices, is another way to assess how well a school attracts qualified applicants.

Since many applicants have to decide between several schools, the yield is a good indicator of which schools are first-choice and which are "safety" schools. The latter usually have yields below 40 percent. The main use of yields is to compare colleges that have similar applicant pools. State universities tend to have high yields because some applicants are in-state students who do not apply elsewhere.

Entering class includes the number of first-years and transfers on campus at the beginning of the year.

Transfers reports the number of students who were accepted for transfer to that institution each year. The transfers accepted is a better indication of an applicant's chances of gaining admission than the actual number of transfers matriculated, since often the number of transfers accepted is large compared to the number of matriculating transfer students. Keep in mind that "NA" here does not mean that there were no transfers, only that the schools did not report a number. Of course, not every school accepts transfer students, but those that do may restrict the number or have as many students leaving as transferring. Many big state schools are known for accepting lots of transfers from local community colleges. For these reasons, the number of transfers is not a good measure of a school's popularity.

The **average SAT** is the mean SAT score for the most recent entering class. Some schools choose to express this value separately for the Math, Verbal and Writing sections, while some will give an overall average, out of 2400. The new SAT essay section was implemented in the spring of 2005, but some schools still did not offer statistical information based on the new range available. Therefore, some of the average scores may be out of only 1600.

The College Board prefers schools to use the **middle 50% SAT** range when discussing scores. This represents the range in which half of a particular school's new freshman students' scores fell. A mathematics range of 550 to 650 would mean that half the incoming freshmen had SAT mathematics scores between 550 and 650. The middle 50 percent range are the numbers between the twenty-fifth and seventy-fifth percentile boundaries; someone whose SAT score falls on the seventy-fifth percentile scored higher than 75 percent of the people who took that particular test. The same applies for someone whose score falls on the twenty-fifth percentile; the median is a score at the fiftieth percentile. Therefore, if your SAT score falls within the middle 50 percent range, you are on par with the SAT scores of last year's successful applicants. This does not mean that you have a 50–50 chance of getting in. Instead, view this figure as an indication of your own competitiveness against the overall applicant pool that the school evaluates.

Schools in the South and Midwest often prefer the American College Test (ACT). We report both the **average ACT** and the **middle 50% ACT** range as well as the SAT for this reason. The scale for this test is 1 to 36, and the middle 50 percent range for this test means the same as it does for the SAT.

Early decision or **early action acceptance rate** is a recent addition to *The Insider's Guide*. There has been a growing population of students applying early to college to demonstrate commitment or to increase chances of admission. A school's policy for early admission may include "early action" (EA) or "early decision" (ED). Both programs have application due dates far in advance of regular admission, so check with the school to make sure your application will arrive on time. Remember that while early action is advance acceptance with the option of applying and matriculating elsewhere, early decision requires a commitment to matriculate and to rescind all outstanding applications to other schools. The fact that these programs exist should not exert any pressure on an applicant to commit to an institution early, and many institutions in fact prefer to use regular or rolling admissions.

Undergraduate enrollment is the number of full-time undergraduate students for the most recent year available at the time of publication, whereas **Total enrollment** gives the total number of students, including part-time and full-time undergraduates, graduate students, and professional students. Often the ratio of undergraduate to graduate students gives an indication of the relative emphasis an institution places on each.

Percent male/female (M/F) gives the percentage of undergraduates of each sex.

Percent minority is the percentage of enrolled students who indicated on their applications that they consider themselves members of a minority group. This figure is broken down by percentages of students in four broad minority groups—**African-American, Asian/Pacific Islander, Hispanic, and Native-American**—to give a measure of the ethnic diversity of the school. **Other** includes any student who is a member of a minority group but not one of the four listed above. Many students of different ethnicities, such as international students and biracial students, are not included in this section. You may want to contact the college directly for more specific information.

Percent in-state/out-of-state is the percentage of enrolled undergraduates who are residents of the state in which the school is located. For Canadian schools, the percentage is that of students from within Canada. This figure gives an approximation of the regional diversity of the school. Obviously, the in-state numbers will usually be much higher for public schools than for private schools, although in most cases, states provide incentives for private schools to take in-state students.

Percent from public HS is, of course, the percentage of students whose secondary education took place in a public school.

The **Retention rate** is the percentage of first-year students who remain enrolled at a given institution for their second (sophomore) year. This statistic is an indicator of the quality of life, resources, and general satisfaction of the students at a particular college. Like the statistics on percent accepted who enroll, these numbers are most useful in comparisons between schools of the similar academic caliber, size and student body.

The **Graduation rate** represents the percentage of students who graduate successfully over a certain time period. Schools were asked for both their **four-year** and **six-year** graduation rates. Many students take at least five years to obtain their bachelor's degree, and in this case the six-year graduation rate would be higher than the four-year rate. Contact a school directly to find out how long the average student takes to complete the requirements for his or her degree. Generally students are more likely to take over four years to graduate in public schools than private schools.

On-campus housing gives the percentage of students living in school-controlled housing. Some smaller schools guarantee on-campus housing for all students if they choose to remain on campus. At most institutions, a large percentage of the freshman class lives on campus, while most of the rest of the student body lives off campus. There are often opportunities for upperclassmen to live on campus if they choose to do so, as Resident Assistants (RAs) or in other student leader positions. Be prepared to seek off-campus housing arrangements early if a school's housing percentage is less than 90 percent or if no figure is listed.

The figures for **Greek life** represent the approximate percentage of male students joining fraternities and female students joining sororities, as reported by the administration. Some schools have divided the statistics by gender. Fraternity and sorority enrollment over 25 or 30 percent usually indicates a strong Greek system. Note that fraternity and sorority figures do not include non-Greek exclusive clubs or secret societies.

Varsity or club athletes represents the percentage of students who play a varsity or club sports at the college. Some schools keep track only of the varsity numbers, and some record both. Like the fraternity and sorority figures, this statistic helps to give an impression of the general composition of the student body and campus life.

The **Extracurricular organizations** figure represents the number of official (recognized by the school) organized extracurricular organizations. This is just another indicator of what student life is like outside of classes.

Most popular majors lists the top three majors among the seniors in the most recent graduating class for which the college has data. Remember, though, that popularity is not necessarily a measure of quality. Also, the exact number of students majoring in any given field can vary widely from year to year. Certain schools, however, are well-known for specific programs (e.g., criminology, biomedical engineering, government, journalism).

The **Student/Faculty** ratio indicates how many students there are in comparison to professors. While this statistic certainly varies by department, and has no real implication in the possibility of faculty-student interactions, many people like to know it. A more useful statistic is the **Average class size** for undergraduate classes, but beware, as often this includes small classes or sections not taught by a professor.

Percent grad school represents the percentage of students going on to graduate or professional school after graduation. Schools vary on whether this number represents those who go immediately after graduation, or after a few years. If you are interested in a particular graduate or professional degree, you may want to check with individual schools as to preparation programs they offer.

Tuition and fees and **Room and board** figures are given for the most recent year available. In cases where costs differ for in-state and out-of-state students, both figures are listed. Also, many public schools charge tuition that varies with the course load taken. Remember that these figures are meant as an estimate of the cost for a year at a given institution, and do not include travel, books and personal expenses. These figures tend to increase every year. Use these figures as a relative index of how expensive one college is compared to another. For Canadian schools, these figures are reported in Canadian dollars.

The **application fee** is the processing fee for an application and is due at the same time as the other application materials. Check with individual schools to see if the application fee can be waived for economic reasons or for in-state applicants.

For **financial aid, first-year** figures, schools are asked to report the percentage of the entering class receiving need-based financial assistance from the institution out of those applying for aid. This does not in-clude students receiving only merit-based scholarships, federal loans not given out by the institution, and students who did not apply for aid. These figures are most relevant for comparing similar institutions. Questions about schools' particular financial aid programs should be addressed directly to their financial aid offices.

Finally, **Canadian schools** report their statistical information in a very different manner from American schools, so some statistics such as average SAT scores are not reported. Most schools in Canada also report their deadlines and statistics by individual program of study rather than for the college or university as a whole. Furthermore, admissions procedures, competitiveness, and tuition fees are often very different based on whether the student is a Canadian or international citizen. Our advice is to visit the schools' Web sites for detailed statistical information on the specific programs.

A Note About Some Statistics We Do Not Include

Previous editions of the *Insider's Guide* included a percentage of international students. Since the international student percentage was generally under 9 percent, the figure was dropped in favor of others that would better serve the audience. International students should not feel slighted by this.

Mean SAT and ACT numbers were also eliminated, as not enough schools reported the numbers to warrant their inclusion. The trend seems to be to list the middle 50 percent range of scores to give an idea of the broader composition of the student body.

Other statistics an applicant might wish to research independently are the percentage of students involved in community service, the average loan debt of a typical graduate, the number of transfers from a community college at your state university, and the percentage of graduates who continue their education within five years of graduation.

Alabama

Address: Quad Center
  Auburn, AL 36849
Phone: 800-282-8769
E-mail address:
  admissions@auburn.edu
Web site URL:
  www.auburn.edu
Year Founded: 1856
Private or Public: Public
Religious Affiliation: None
Location: Suburban
Number of Applicants:
  17,798
Percent Accepted: 69%
Percent Accepted who
  enroll: 34%
Number Entering: 4,160
Number of Transfers
  Accepted each Year: 1,980
Middle 50% SAT range:
  M: 520–630, **CR:**
  500–610, **Wr:** Unreported
Middle 50% ACT range:
  22–27
Early admission program
  EA/ED/None: None

Percentage accepted
  through EA or ED: NA
EA and ED deadline: NA
Regular Deadline: Rolling
Application Fee: $40
Full time Undergraduate
  enrollment: 19,812
Total enrollment: 23,187
Percent Male: 52%
Percent Female: 48%
Total Percent Minority or
  Unreported: 15%
Percent African-American:
  9%
Percent Asian/Pacific
  Islander: 2%
Percent Hispanic: 2%
Percent Native-American:
  <1%
Percent International: 1%
Percent in-state/out of
  state: 69%/31%
Percent from Public HS: 86%
Retention Rate: 86%
Graduation Rate 4-year:
  34%

Graduation Rate 6-year:
  62%
Percent Undergraduates
  in On-campus housing:
  14%
Number of official organized
  extracurricular
  organizations: 300
3 Most popular majors:
  Business, Education,
  Engineering
Student/Faculty ratio: 18:1
Average Class Size: 25
Percent of students going to
  grad school: 35%
Tuition and Fees: $18,260
In State Tuition and Fees if
  different: $6,500
Cost for Room and Board:
  $8,260
Percent receiving financial
  aid out of those who apply,
  first year: 64%
Percent receiving financial
  aid among all students:
  54%

L ess than an hour's drive east of Montgomery, the plains of Alabama give rise to Auburn University. The school, whose athletics department has produced stars like Charles Barkley and Bo Jackson, boasts some of the region's top veterinary and engineering programs. But it is the student body that will most likely catch the eye of a passerby, especially if he or she hails from more northern lands. "Southern hospitality is alive and well here," students declare, and this charm mixed with fun and academics keeps Auburn students smiling.

Bed and Breakfast (and Lunch and Dinner)

Auburn students electing to live on campus can choose from four clusters of residence halls, but the housing is not guaranteed to anyone, even freshmen. The more popular living areas are the Hill and the Quad, and dorms are either women-only or coed by floor. Many in-state students and upperclassmen choose to live off campus in one of the several apartment complexes near campus. Since many students opt not to live in dorms, Auburn provides an apartment guide and some helpful tips for students shopping the off-campus market. Tiger Transit is available to get students from point A to point B, and the Off Campus Association "gets you a good deal on utilities."

There is no shortage of food options on campus. The two main dining areas, Terrell Dining Hall and War Eagle Food Court, are located at the southern and northern ends of the campus, respectively. Both have an assortment of fast food and local restaurants that cater to students on the go. Auburn offers a variety of meal plans to meet a wide range of needs, and the Tiger Card can be used "like a debit card" at local eateries and grocery stores. Students deposit funds into the account and use the swipes until the balance dwindles down again.

Students choosing to eat on campus can get all the basic sandwiches and burgers, or they can go for a smoothie at Chillers in War Eagle Court. The town of Auburn offers the traditional fare of Ruby Tuesday and family dining along with some establishments appealing to the younger crowd. Students frequent the Mellow Mushroom for a more gourmet pizza and head to Moe's for "the best burritos in town."

Cracking the Books

Auburn University was the first land-grant college in the Southeast (a result of the Morrill Act), and to this day its engineering and agriculture departments remain strong. But the University has become more diverse in its faculty and currently offers undergraduate degrees in 12 schools—agriculture, architecture, business, education, engineering, forestry and wildlife, human sciences, liberal arts, nursing, pharmacy, science and mathematics and veterinary medicine. Moreover, the University recently began a Bachelor of Wireless Engineering program which represents the first degree of this type in the nation. Students select their majors at the end of the second year, but changing majors is not difficult with the help of Auburn's advising system.

> "Most professors are more than willing to help you out. All you have to do is ask."

The University offers plenty of options for study abroad. Auburn itself has a growing number of distinct programs, or students can participate in approved programs from other universities. One student who returned from a summer in Florence, a popular destination for art students, said "transferring credits was really easy."

While Auburn students put in their time in Draughton Library (open 24 hours a day during finals), they do not often complain of being tremendously overworked. "Some students skip classes and don't work that hard," but workload largely depends on the course of study. If an Auburn Tiger is having some difficulties in the classroom, he or she can usually find plenty of support. "Most professors are more than willing to help you out. All you have to do is ask."

Auburn professors have earned a reputation for being accessible and invested in their students' educations, but the same cannot always be said about teaching assistants, especially in math and science courses. Students said some TAs have problems speaking clear English, which can make learning more difficult.

In preparation for life after graduation, Auburn provides advice and information for students interested in graduate or professional school. A senior in the College of Sciences and Mathematics said her adviser has helped her not only navigate Auburn's undergraduate curriculum, but also apply to graduate schools. The University brings in representatives from schools throughout the region to speak to students about opportunities after graduation.

Frivolity, Fraternities and Football

The social scene is alive and well at Auburn no matter what time of year, but students have different preferences for the seasons. During the fall, students don their best orange and blue to support their Tigers on the field at Jordan-Hare Stadium. The on-campus stadium is regularly filled to capacity of over 85,000 raucous fans screaming "War Eagle," and the surrounding areas are teeming with tailgates for each home game. Don't be surprised to see Auburn students dressed up for this Saturday afternoon affair. The game is a place to be seen as well as show school spirit. The fun continues, especially after a win, at Toomers Corner after the final snap.

The stadium is bursting at the seams when in-state rival the University of Alabama comes to town the Saturday before Thanksgiving for the Iron Bowl. Students must make sure they get their tickets early if they want a seat at this perennially sold-out event.

Many students hit the fraternity parties Friday and Saturday nights. A significant chunk of the student body is Greek, but "parties are open for the most part." In contrast to most other SEC schools, there are no sorority houses at Auburn. The sisterhoods have halls in dorms, mostly populated with sophomore members, and a chapter room. Greek organizations maintain a lively party environment with formal dances and band parties.

The Auburn police are usually present at larger organized events, but there is not a visible crackdown on underage drinking as long as students act responsibly. The police are strict on drunk driving. Since most students at Auburn come with cars and many live off campus, there is a volunteer designated-driver program to make sure every student makes it home safely.

In the spring semester, students focus their revelry on off-campus locales—apartments or downtown bars. College Park Apartments usually has something going on during the weekends. For good drink deals, of-age students head to Buffalo's for a brew and then to Quixote's, where "there is always a good band playing." While the town restaurants might let things slide, bars have no problem carding, and they can be quite difficult to get into at times.

Apart from the night life, students engage in many social activities and student groups on campus. Students can try their hand at radio broadcasting on WEGL, do community service through Habitat for Humanity or Kiwanis Club, partake in theater and singing groups, and do just about anything else that might be of interest.

Getting Your Bearings

Two important landmarks on campus for new students are the Foy Student Union and the Haley Center. These two buildings are the hubs of student life on campus. Foy contains the War Eagle Food Court, a CD and game store, study lounges, student organization offices, an ATM and a mail drop. The Haley Center houses a cafeteria, lecture halls and the campus bookstore. The one thing these buildings don't have is parking, which can be a "nightmare" on campus. Since most students are in-state or from surrounding areas, they drive to school from home, and having a car is "a big plus on the weekends for road trips to the beach."

Go to one football game, and it's easy to see the tradition that pervades the Auburn campus. Some students are third- or fourth-generation Tigers, but that should not scare away newcomers to the South. With pleasant weather and people, it is easy to understand why Auburn is one of the most popular universities in the region.—*Adam Weber*

FYI
If you come to Auburn, you'd better bring "your country music collection."
What's the typical weekend schedule? "Drink, drink, drink, go to a football game, drink, drink, and pass out."
If I could change one thing about Auburn, I'd "move it to a more metropolitan area."
Three things every Auburn student should do before graduating are "get every single flavor of milkshake at Cheeburger Cheeburger, participate in the cheesy 'Hey Day,' and run in the Cake Race."

Birmingham-Southern College

Address: 900 Arkadelphia Road Birmingham, AL 35254
Phone: 800-523-5793
E-mail address: admission@bsc.edu
Web site URL: www.bsc.edu
Year Founded: 1856
Private or Public: Private
Religious Affiliation: United Methodist
Location: Urban
Number of Applicants: 2,227
Percent Accepted: 60%
Percent Accepted who enroll: 23%
Number Entering: 292
Number of Transfers Accepted each Year: 101
Middle 50% SAT range: M: 520–650, CR: 520–640, Wr: Unreported
Middle 50% ACT range: 22–28
Early admission program EA/ED/None: None

Percentage accepted through EA or ED: NA
EA and ED deadline: NA
Regular Deadline: Rolling
Application Fee: $40
Full time Undergraduate enrollment: 1,339
Total enrollment: 1,389
Percent Male: 59%
Percent Female: 41%
Total Percent Minority or Unreported: 16%
Percent African-American: 9%
Percent Asian/Pacific Islander: 2%
Percent Hispanic: 2%
Percent Native-American: <1%
Percent International: Unreported
Percent in-state/out of state: 67%/33%
Percent from Public HS: 65%
Retention Rate: 86%
Graduation Rate 4-year: 60%

Graduation Rate 6-year: 69%
Percent Undergraduates in On-campus housing: 77%
Number of official organized extracurricular organizations: 70
3 Most popular majors: Business Administration/Management, Health/Medical Preparatory Programs, Pre-Law Studies
Student/Faculty ratio: 10:1
Average Class Size: 15
Percent of students going to grad school: 50%
Tuition and Fees: $25,586
In State Tuition and Fees if different: No difference
Cost for Room and Board: $8,595
Percent receiving financial aid out of those who apply, first year: 80%
Percent receiving financial aid among all students: 46%

Birmingham-Southern College prides itself on its reputation as a top-notch university, and the students here work hard to live up to BSC's expectations. Students manage the intense workload and credit the "loads of personal attention" to their success and survival.

"Life-long Learners"

As a four-year liberal arts college, Birmingham-Southern seeks to send out well-rounded, well-educated, and cultured leaders. As such, the academic requirements cover a broad range of subjects and interests. Freshmen have to take three "First-Year Foundations" courses in order to acclimate themselves to the college environment as well as to take their first steps as "life-long learners." Over the course of four years, students at BSC must accumulate at least one unit each of art, lab science, history, literature, a non-native language, humanities, philosophy and religion, writing, math, and social science. After fulfilling these core courses, students must take two additional credits in humanities and one additional

credit in math or science. Although there are no pre-professional majors, many take a difficult course load aimed at medical or law school. English, Business, and Education are, not surprisingly, extremely popular majors. Math and Science majors are rarer but remain a presence on campus. A highly selective honors program is also available to the most motivated and qualified students at BSC. The program offers accelerated courses and small seminars with an interdisciplinary approach. Those interested in the program are encouraged to apply as early as spring of their senior year in high school.

BSC requires its students to go even farther above and beyond the minimal requirements, and make use of its unique "interim term." The interim term, the "1" portion of Birmingham-Southern's 4-1-4 year, is a month-long period between the school's two four-month semesters in which students are free to explore one specific interest. One student used one of her four interim terms to design a course as a teaching assistant in an urban school environment. The student explained, "I decided how long I was in the classroom, what types of activities I would do, how I would be graded . . . all of that." Although some students think the interim term can be a "pain," many say it also provides the opportunity to travel abroad without worrying about falling off a four-year track.

With all that Birmingham-Southern requires, "the workload can be tough"; however, students have advisors at their disposal and a strong support system. Professors are generally described as "great" and "absolutely approachable." Classes with good reputations may be tricky to obtain for freshmen (it's not easy getting that first-choice class), but amazing classes are definitely available. "[My professor] set up a fake crime scene . . . roped it off, had a chalk outline of the body, fake blood everywhere . . ." said a student about his Forensic Science course. "We had to walk around, take it apart . . . all the way to conviction." The bottom line remains: people at BSC take academics pretty seriously, and as one student affirmed, "people do what they've got to do."

Outside the Classroom—Like Wonder Bread?

Despite the high academic expectations, BSC students know how to balance the books with some much-needed down time. With Birmingham in their backyard and a variety of clubs and activities to choose from, students have a wide array of weekend options. Prospective students should be aware, however, that Birmingham-Southern has a definite Greek feel. "The frat scene is definitely the dominant social scene here . . . the rush process starts during the summer," a freshman explained, "but the formal rush doesn't happen until the third week of school or so." The downside of having such a close-knit and supporting Greek system is that "what Greek organization you belong to has a large impact on who you're going to be friends with." As one student remarked, "It's sad in my opinion that in the cafeteria, people still sit at certain tables based on what fraternity, sorority or sports team he/she is on." Still, students are quick to point out that the Greek life isn't for everybody at BSC— and that's okay. The Student Government Association sponsors movie-nights out, for example, and clubs such as "Chaos" and "Platinum" are a short drive away. And as most students have cars on campus—"if you don't, you can always mooch off someone else," according to one student— transportation is usually not a huge issue.

Big annual activities include the Greek-sponsored "Philanthropy Party" as well as the Entertainment Festivals (E-Fest in BSC vernacular) where local talents are showcased each semester. Students also note attempts by administration and other students to broaden the cultural offerings on campus. Although diversity at Birmingham-Southern may prove a disappointment to some (minority enrollment has been documented at around 20 percent, but students generally deemed geographic and class diversity to be somewhat lacking), clubs such as the BSC Step Team are giving a different feel to the pervasive—as one student termed it, "Wonderbread—white and rich"—culture of the school.

> "We know how to do things—be it academics, partying, or whatever— right here."

Another extracurricular option is intramurals, also known as IMs. Flag football, inner tube water polo, and dodgeball are just a few examples of available intramural activities. "People play [IMs] and they can get pretty competitive, but everybody realizes it's just IMs and we're all out of shape," one BSC student said. In addition to IMs, students can cheer for their school's teams. While Birmingham-Southern does not have a football team, they "live vicariously through [University of] Alabama and Auburn [University]." The basketball and baseball games are well-attended, and "it's a face-painted, T-shirt-wearing, screaming, jumping good time." One student summed it up saying, "We know how to do things—be it academics, partying, or whatever—right here."

Living and Dining

"Dorms are . . . well, dorms" one junior explained, "you can't expect too much." Freshmen guys live in New Men's, while freshmen girls live in either Cullen Daniel or Margaret Daniel. A student revealed that "New Men's is pretty nasty, but it's a cool experience." The freshmen dorms have two people to a room and communal bathrooms. Other options include a four room–four person suite, a four room–eight person suite, or two doubles connected by a bathroom. Housing situations improve with both seniority and GPA—those with seniority and higher GPAs pick first. Residential Advisors (RAs) are on each floor of the freshmen dorms, ready to help with any problems. However, RAs are also meant to enforce the rules: "Level of strictness varies from person to person . . . they're there to enforce the rules through fines mostly." Students sometimes choose to forgo dorm life for student apartments on campus or the Sorority Townhouses and Fraternity Row. Other notable buildings and locations on campus include the science building (which was remodeled in 2003), the humanities building, and the United Methodist Center. The Center recently built a new facility on the former Frat Row. "The [Frats] are a hangout area . . . as well as the Caf, and the Cellar." The Cellar, a coffee house, is a popular place for both relaxing and studying. The cafeteria, or "Caf" as BSC students call it, was recently revamped and is "a definite improvement" over the old cafeteria, and now boasts a Subway, a KFC, a soul food bar, a grille and a salad stand. Students living on campus have to purchase a meal plan; the choices range from light, medium, and hearty, which differ in numbers of meals provided.

Coming to Birmingham-Southern is coming into a great tradition of excellence. With its mixture of Division I sports, academics, and bridges into the business world, Birmingham promises to provide not only an unforgettable college experience, but connections for life. "We produce the best and the brightest—but not only that, once you're a part of the BSC family, those ties never die. [That] sounds so sappy, but it's true."—*Melody Pak*

FYI
If you come to BSC, you'd better bring "your leg muscles, it's hilly."
The typical weekend schedule includes: "Friday: some sort of party Friday night, Saturday: football games, sports, party on Saturday night, Sunday: really low key."
If I could change one thing about BSC, I'd "bring more diversity."
Three things every student at BSC should do before graduating are "spend half of your day trying to figure out what you did the night before, make love, and still pass with a 3.5 or higher."

Tuskegee University

Address: 120 Old Administration Building Tuskegee, AL 36088
Phone: 334-727-8500
E-mail address: adm@tuskegee.edu
Web site URL: www.tuskegee.edu
Year Founded: 1881
Private or Public: Private
Religious Affiliation: None
Location: Rural
Number of Applicants: Unreported
Percent Accepted: 58%
Percent Accepted who enroll: Unreported
Number Entering: 795
Number of Transfers Accepted each Year: 378
Middle 50% SAT range: M: 380–490, CR: 390–500, Wr:** Unreported
Middle 50% ACT range: 16–21
Early admission program EA/ED/None: None

Percentage accepted through EA or ED: NA
EA and ED deadline: NA
Regular Deadline: 15-Jul
Application Fee: $25
Full time Undergraduate enrollment: 2,514
Total enrollment: 2,701
Percent Male: 44%
Percent Female: 56%
Total Percent Minority or Unreported: 99%
Percent African-American: 86%
Percent Asian/Pacific Islander: <1%
Percent Hispanic: <1%
Percent Native-American: <1%
Percent International: Unreported
Percent in-state/out of state: 30%70%
Percent from Public HS: Unreported
Retention Rate: Unreported
Graduation Rate 4-year: 25%

Graduation Rate 6-year: 50%
Percent Undergraduates in On-campus housing: 55%
Number of official organized extracurricular organizations: 36
3 Most popular majors: Electrical, Electronics and Communications Engineering, Veterinary Medicine
Student/Faculty ratio: 12:1
Average Class Size: Unreported
Percent of students going to grad school: 23%
Tuition and Fees: $15,450
In State Tuition and Fees if different: No difference
Cost for Room and Board: $7,130
Percent receiving financial aid out of those who apply, first year: 72%
Percent receiving financial aid among all students: Unreported

Tuskegee University has historically been home to many generations of African-American men and women searching for an outstanding academic experience in addition to a unique cultural enrichment. Tuskegee's close-knit student community lives and studies in one of the country's most historic African-American universities.

Changing Tradition

Tuskegee affords its undergraduates the opportunity to pursue a true liberal arts education through the College of Liberal Arts and Education. Although it was founded with the intention of giving African-Americans a more technical, career-specific education to give them an edge in specific job markets, the curriculum has gradually changed to ally Tuskegee with other liberal arts schools. Still, some traditions remain: all freshmen are required to take an orientation course, which consists of University history, including the mandatory reading of Booker T. Washington's *Up from Slavery*, and advice for adapting to college life. Freshmen will also discover that their other basic requirements include physical education and English courses.

The University includes five colleges in total: the College of Agriculture, Environmental and Natural Sciences; the College of Business and Information Science; the College of Engineering, Architecture and Physical Sciences; the College of Veterinary Medicine, Nursing and Allied Health; and the College of Liberal Arts and Education. Thus, despite the shift toward a more liberal arts–oriented academic environment, many Tuskegee students are engineering or science majors. The school often receives acclaim for its pre-vet, pre-med and nursing programs, and students confirm high numbers of enrollees in each of these disciplines. Lower level lectures tend to enroll between 40 and 50 students, but the average class size overall ranges from 10 to 20 students. Students like the class sizes, and report that "whatever class size you prefer, you can usually pick accordingly." The smaller class sizes and minimal use of TAs keep student-faculty interaction high. Students generally give Tuskegee's academics a high rating. There were those who disagreed, remarking that "it can be easy to feel lost in the larger classes that don't have TAs," but on the whole, many agreed that the school is "demanding but rewarding." Tuskegee's history is clearly visible around

its campus. A senior commented that "It's very cool, some of the brick buildings were built by students when the school was founded."

Still Living in the Past

The residential life on campus is one of students' more frequent complaints. In addition to being "ancient" and "without much furniture," dorms are not coed and students are required to live on campus both freshman and sophomore years. The older dorm buildings have a reputation for being in poor physical condition, and one student called the dorms "older than rocks." "You had better bring things that make you feel at home," said one undergrad, because "there's no real cozy feeling." The on-campus apartment situation is slightly better; the Commons apartments offer students the amenities of a kitchen in addition to rooms that they can make their own with decorations. Students' biggest problem, however, is with the University housing regulations. Because of the school's conservative nature, men's and women's dorms are separated by a 10-minute walk to prevent students from visiting those of the opposite gender. The University staff also keeps a close eye on dorms; students are not allowed to be on the "wrong" side of campus after 11 p.m. and, if caught, face punishment.

> "The town of Tuskegee offers nothing except seclusion from the modern world, but you learn a lot trapped in the wilderness."

Many upperclassmen choose to move off campus. One student said of the coed policies, "I love my campus, but I had to leave it because of the rules." Students tend to meet in the student union, which contains a movie theater, a grill, a game room and offices for student organizations. The student cafeteria is another popular meeting place, and serves as a place where Tuskegee's many clubs and organizations can meet to bring students together. Some of the biggest clubs are the state clubs, which unite students hailing from the same state to plan activities relating to their home turf. African-American groups like the National Society of Black Engineers and several prominent fraternities and sororities are also present on campus. There is an active chapter of ROTC, which helps some students to fund their education. Students are active in community service, and the nearby hospital employs a number of Tuskegee students.

Football and basketball games generate great excitement at Tuskegee. In particular, the rivalries with Morehouse College and Alabama State University tend to draw the largest crowds to sporting events. Homecoming is one of the biggest social events of the year. The weeklong tradition incorporates performances by student groups, the Miss Tuskegee Gala and a number of pep rallies to boost school spirit. In the spring, the school hosts "Springfest," an event drawing many students together for shows, concerts and a dance.

The Typical Tuskegee Student

While the Greek system is a visible presence on campus, students report that they do not feel an urge to rush. There is little animosity between the fraternities, but they reportedly have a "friendly rivalry." Officially, alcohol is prohibited on campus and students who are caught with it face fines or other penalties.

As a result, drinking generally tends to occur off campus. Students said they considered the town of Tuskegee "slow," but most agree that it has most of the things necessary for college life. And, as one student put it, "Tuskegee has a lot of potential to grow," adding, "but you come for the school, not the town." Tuskegee students also added that their campus is safe, with a large body of security officers and a closely monitored electronic keycard system.

Tuskegee is more than just an academic college experience; it is also one of cultural and historical enrichment. The school's fundamental mission remains an avid part of why students attend, and the school's community and tradition are enough to overcome some of its more conservative and comparatively strict policies. The experience tends to bind people in a lasting way. As one student said, "There are a lot of good people here and you can meet a lot of great minds—not to mention we're friends for life. People might complain about things here, but in the end, you don't want to leave."—*Melissa Chan and Staff*

FYI
If you come to Tuskegee, you'd better bring "a car to survive here because the nearest mall is 20 minutes away. The town of Tuskegee offers nothing except seclusion from the modern world, but you learn a lot trapped in the wilderness."
What's the typical weekend schedule? "Go to a football game if we're playing at home and then party at a fraternity at night."
If I could change one thing about Tuskegee I'd "change the administration. It seems to have no respect or regard for the students, the registration process takes three days, and the dorms are really run-down."
The three things every student should do before graduating from Tuskegee are "try the food at the Chicken Coop, go to Homecoming, and visit the George Washington Carver Museum on campus."

University of Alabama

Address: Box 870132
  Tuscaloosa, AL 35487-0132
Phone: 205-348-5666
E-mail address:
  admissions@ua.edu
Web site URL: www.ua.edu
Year Founded: 1831
Private or Public: Public
Religious Affiliation: None
Location: Suburban
Number of Applicants:
  18,500
Percent Accepted: 60%
**Percent Accepted who
  enroll:** 45%
Number Entering: 5,034
**Number of Transfers
  Accepted each Year:** 2,006
Middle 50% SAT range:
  M: 500–610, CR:
  490–600, Wr:** Unreported
Middle 50% ACT range:
  21–27
**Early admission program
  EA/ED/None:** None

**Percentage accepted
  through EA or ED:** NA
EA and ED deadline: NA
Regular Deadline: 1-Feb
Application Fee: $35
**Full time Undergraduate
  enrollment:** 22,341
Total enrollment: 26,318
Percent Male: 48%
Percent Female: 52%
**Total Percent Minority or
  Unreported:** 16%
Percent African-American:
  11%
**Percent Asian/Pacific
  Islander:** 1%
Percent Hispanic: 2%
Percent Native-American:
  <1%
Percent International: 1%
**Percent in-state/out of
  state:** 73%/27%
Percent from Public HS: 90%
Retention Rate: 86%
Graduation Rate 4-year: 35%

Graduation Rate 6-year:
  62%
**Percent Undergraduates in
  On-campus housing:** 30%
**Number of official organized
  extracurricular
  organizations:** 294
3 Most popular majors:
  Elementary Education,
  Finance, Nursing
Student/Faculty ratio: 20:1
Average Class Size: 10 to 19
**Percent of students going to
  grad school:** 24%
Tuition and Fees: $18,000
**In State Tuition and Fees if
  different:** $6,400
Cost for Room and Board:
  $6,430
**Percent receiving financial
  aid out of those who apply,
  first year:** 64%
**Percent receiving financial
  aid among all students:**
  61%

With four buildings that survived the Civil War (Gorgas House, Maxwell Hall, the Little Round House, and the President's Mansion), the graceful architecture and serene campus might be awe-inspiring to a new freshman arriving at Alabama. As one student said, "The campus is just so beautiful, it really can be a very peaceful place." But before you can say the words "Roll Tide," the semester propels forward into football season, with the first games taking place in the month of September.

You would have to try really hard to leave "Bama" without knowing the significance of the Iron Bowl, "Bear" Bryant, and why Alabama must always beat Auburn in any competition. But students agree that athletic traditions and rivalries hardly define the UA experience: "It's just a great school in so many different ways."

Academics

Overall, students at Alabama seem pretty satisfied with the academic opportunities. "There's pretty much any major you could ever want" and a fair amount of minor op-

tions too. In addition to completing the requirements for each individual major, students must also complete the core curriculum requirements for graduation. These requirements force students to take courses in a variety of areas, such as humanities and fine arts, history, social/behavioral sciences, natural science and mathematics, foreign languages or computers, and writing. "The requirements actually aren't that hard to fill," says one student. "By the time you've taken all the classes that look interesting to you, you realize that you're really knocking out the core requirements."

But for those not satisfied with Alabama's offerings, the interdisciplinary New College program, though "relatively small and relatively new," allows admitted students to design their own majors and minors. The program is considered "pretty intense," requiring, in addition to the University requirements for graduation, extra language classes, New College seminars, and independent study. The program boasts that it promotes more independent thinking and allows a student a closer relationship with his or her advisor.

Another option for Alabama students who desire "more of a challenge" in their academic pursuits is the Honors College, which is divided up into three programs: the Computer-Based Honors Program, the International Honors Program, and the University Honors Program. The trailblazing Computer-Based Honors Program accepts about 40 students each year and allows undergraduates of any major the opportunity to work one-on-one with faculty members in computer-oriented research. The students "really jump in" with an intense course freshmen year in computing concepts. The International Honors Program helps students incorporate an international flair into their major, grooming the students for a study-abroad experience. The University Honors Program is the largest of the programs, with approximately 10 percent of the undergraduate population taking part. The program seeks to provide a higher level of education to Alabama students; admission is primarily based on ACT or SAT scores, and honors students are required to maintain their GPAs throughout college.

Bama Life

Students agree that the housing available on campus is adequate, but not luxurious by any means, and most will say that the primary motivating factor for living on campus is convenience. They say that it is "very easy for walking to class," while off-campus students complain that "it's hard to decide which is worse, traffic or parking." Students who choose to live off campus generally do so either to live in their Greek houses or to have more independence in an apartment or house. One student commented that "guys are more inclined to get houses" because "there's not really a nice guys dorm."

Beginning in fall 2006, all students were required to spend their first year on campus. One student wholeheartedly endorsed this change, saying "it's a great way to meet new people. A lot of Alabama kids already come here with friends from home, so if you want to branch out, the dorms are a way to do it." Ask current students for the lowdown on which dorms are the best, but right now the new Riverside Residential Complex seems to be the hottest ticket on campus. The dorm complex primarily houses honors college students and freshmen, and includes two- and four-bedroom suites, which each have a kitchenette and a living room. Students say that it is "unbelievably nice" and

even has an Einstein Bros. Bagel place, a small grocery store, and a pool.

Students on campus most often dine at the Ferguson Center, where they can choose from fast-food options like Blimpie, Burger King, and Chick-Fil-A, or a variety of pizza, soups, sandwiches, sushi, salads, and other hot dishes. Other on-campus dining locations include a coffee shop in the Gorgas Library (a favorite study spot), and quick eateries in Tutwiler, Burke, Paty halls, and the Riverside Residential Complex. Students on the whole seem to be satisfied with the options overall—"You can always find something different"—though one student remarked that the offerings can get boring. "You get tired of having the same stuff all the time, but that's just what it's like at every college. The nice thing is that if you want to go out to eat, you always can."

All freshmen are required to participate in the freshman meal plan. First-year students can choose from one of three meal plans, and then are also charged $300 a semester in Dining Dollars. After freshman year, students are allowed more flexibility in which meal plan they choose, with four different meal options available. Dining Dollars can be used at all on-campus dining locations, at all vending machines, and at off-campus locations like Domino's, Buffalo Phil's, and Crimson Cafe. Students seem to think the dining system a fair one: "The good thing is that you don't lose your Dining Dollars if you don't spend them all in a semester." At the end of the year, students can request a refund for any remaining Dining Dollars. After the rush season, many students also choose to dine at their fraternity or sorority houses, and there is a meal plan that accommodates that change.

The Diversity Question

Students today seem to be more or less divided over the current state of race relations at Bama, but one doesn't have to look far into the past to see that the University has come a long way. On June 11, 1963, Alabama Governor George Wallace made his infamous "stand at the schoolhouse door" in an attempt to prevent desegregation of the University. Federal marshals had to be called in, and the two African-American students were ultimately admitted.

Though students say that "all people are welcome at Alabama" and that they have "never seen any signs of racial discrimination on campus," students will also admit that the "social life can be segregated." One place that this de facto segregation is most apparent is in the Greek system. The fraternities and sororities at Alabama are "mostly homogeneous," and the Greek systems for whites and for minorities are even managed by different organizations. But these divisions, too, seem to be breaking down with time, as one student noted that "Greek life at Alabama is becoming more and more diverse every day."

In Their Free Time

By far the most prevalent extracurricular activity for students is the Greek system, with over 20 percent belonging to a University-recognized fraternity or sorority. There are three different governing bodies for the Greek system, each with its own timeline for rush. The Interfraternity Council oversees some 29 fraternities in their rush, which takes place in the first weeks of freshman year. The Alabama Panhellenic Association governs the women's sororities and holds rush in August before the start of classes. The National Pan-Hellenic Council, which oversees the seven minority-dominated fraternities and sororities, begins its rush season after the first semester of school.

Students generally disagree over how large the divide between Greeks and "independents" (non-Greeks) is, and it seems to depend on the individual character of each person. "Some people have lots of independent friends, but I just don't have any," one student said. Students agree, though, that while the Greek system may have seemed super-important freshman year, by senior year it is not that big of a deal. "As you get older, the distance between people in fraternities and sororities and people not in them lessens."

Other activities that students take part in are intramural sports ("even that competition can get pretty intense"); the school newspaper, *The Crimson White*; and "countless community service opportunities." While Alabama is "not considered a very political campus per se," there are some activist options for students who are more politically minded.

Fun and Games

In the fall semester, football more or less dominates the weekend social scenes, with games most weekends and tons of parties surrounding each game. The highlights of the season are definitely the two most important games: homecoming and the Iron Bowl. "Homecoming is a crazy experience" at the University of Alabama. "You have to see it to believe it." The event is met with droves of alumni and fans, a huge bonfire the night before the game, music, food, fireworks, and parties. "You might even say the spectacle is more important than who wins the game." That is, unless Alabama is playing against Auburn University. Auburn, located just a few hours away, is Alabama's biggest rival. "You learn in your first days here that you're not supposed to like Auburn," said one student. The two teams match off every year in the "Iron Bowl," an annual game that has been played since 1893. The competition even extends beyond football, into community service areas with competitions like the "Beat Auburn Beat Hunger" food drive.

> "You learn in your first days here that you're not supposed to like Auburn"

Off campus, students find Tuscaloosa to be a "nice, medium-sized town," with "everything you need," but "not big enough for you to get lost." The Jupiter is the "best place to see concerts" in town, and students often frequent the "fun, run-down little bars" surrounding campus. For the first years of college, it seems that the fraternity houses, which often invite bands to play for their parties, are social hubs, but "as students get older, they tend to prefer to go to bars over the frats."

But, as one student put it, "the best part of the social scene is just in the everyday, individual interactions." Whether it's in their classwork, extracurricular activities, or in the football stadium, Bama students really seem to enjoy what they do. "Coming here was one of the best decisions I've ever made. It's just a really fun place to be."—*Susanna Moore*

FYI
If you come to Alabama, you'd better bring "a red-and-white shaker for the football games."
What is the typical weekend schedule? "Band party Friday, game Saturday, rest on Sunday."
If I could change one thing about Alabama, I'd "improve campus parking."
Three things every student at Alabama should do before graduating are "go to the Paul 'Bear' Bryant Museum, go to the homecoming bonfire, get involved with a community-service activity."

University of South Alabama

Address: 307 University Boulevard North Mobile, AL 36688-0002
Phone: 251 460-6101
E-mail address: admiss@usouthal.edu
Web site URL: www.southalabama.edu
Year Founded: 1963
Private or Public: Public
Religious Affiliation: None
Location: Suburban
Number of Applicants: 3,089
Percent Accepted: 88%
Percent Accepted who enroll: 53%
Number Entering: 1,457
Number of Transfers Accepted each Year: 1,750
Middle 50% SAT range: M: 460–580, CR: 440–570, Wr: Unreported
Middle 50% ACT range: 19–24
Early admission program EA/ED/None: None

Percentage accepted through EA or ED: NA
EA and ED deadline: NA
Regular Deadline: 10-Sep
Application Fee: $35
Full time Undergraduate enrollment: 10,690
Total enrollment: 13,500
Percent Male: 45%
Percent Female: 55%
Total Percent Minority or Unreported: 3%
Percent African-American: 18%
Percent Asian/Pacific Islander: 4%
Percent Hispanic: 2%
Percent Native-American: 1%
Percent International: 5%
Percent in-state/out of state: Unreported
Percent from Public HS: 92%
Retention Rate: 70%
Graduation Rate 4-year: 13%
Graduation Rate 6-year: 31%

Percent Undergraduates in On-campus housing: 16%
Number of official organized extracurricular organizations: 185
3 Most popular majors: Health Professions, Business/Marketing, Education
Student/Faculty ratio: Unreported
Average Class Size: Unreported
Percent of students going to grad school: Unreported
Tuition and Fees: $9,922
In State Tuition and Fees if different: $5,512
Cost for Room and Board: $5,308
Percent receiving financial aid out of those who apply, first year: Unreported
Percent receiving financial aid among all students: Unreported

L ocated in Mobile, Alabama; the University of South Alabama—"USA" or "South" to students—combines the conservative hospitality of the South with the warm sunny climate of the Gulf Coast. Mobile itself is a historic port city and boasts wildlife-rich deltas and estuaries, antebellum homes with hanging Spanish moss, its own popular Mardi Gras celebration and of course, 21 golf courses and a variety of nearby beaches. The University, located in the heart of the city, caters to both traditional and non-traditional students alike and offers a variety of degree options for adults of any age returning to earn their bachelors' degrees.

Academics: Something for Everyone

The University of South Alabama offers a variety of special programs to accommodate the diverse groups that comprise its student body. Those maintaining at least a 3.5 GPA in high school can apply for the university Honors Program, which includes participation in small honors seminars and the completion of an Honors Senior Project. Each honor student is assigned a faculty mentor from the department of his or her major; these mentors offer advice on everything from course selection to future careers within the field, and both mentor and student participate in group community service projects. New students jump into college life through USA's First Year Experience Program, in which all freshmen living in the dorms are required to participate. The program includes a mandatory freshman seminar designed to teach "effective study skills, exam preparation, college level research skills, writing effectively and student health issues," among other topics, as well as providing tutors, a campus meal plan, and access to student RAs who can offer advice and counsel about campus life. In addition, many USA courses in a variety of disciplines are offered online, allowing students to attend class from home and submit homework in their pajamas.

A branch campus of the University in Fairhope, Alabama, located in Baldwin County—USABC—also offers undergraduate, graduate, and non-degree courses and opportunities for public service involvement for students who, for a variety of reasons, might prefer a different location. This branch campus primarily supports undergraduate majors in business, both elementary and secondary education, nursing and adult interdisciplinary studies. USABC is not a residential campus—students enrolling here generally commute from their homes in Baldwin County—and boasts its own computer lab and performance center but shares the libraries and other research resources with the main University campus across Mobile Bay.

> **"The university, located in the heart of the city, caters to both traditional and non-traditional students alike."**

All students must fulfill the core curriculum before graduation, which requires taking several courses in each of the major academic disciplines—humanities and fine arts; natural sciences and mathematics; and history, social and behavioral sciences—as well as two classes in written composition. South is divided into nine different colleges encompassing a variety of fields of study. Those related to healthcare—the Colleges of Medicine, Nursing and Allied Health Professions—are considered to be particularly strong and rigorous. The joint BS/MS degree programs in these majors are popular, but to gain admission, students must have GPAs in the 3.8 range and apply during their junior year.

BYOB

South's architecture is fairly nondescript like many college campuses built in the late twentieth century. One student described it as "nothing fancy . . . built to last, not to look pretty." Few students live in the dorms all four years, but for those who do, it can be a rewarding experience and provide the opportunity to meet many new friends quickly. "Living in dorms is a terrific way to meet people," enthused one junior. "Most of the people I hang out with now I met freshman year in dorms." The residence halls offer various rooming options in the form of suites and apartments; for first-time students, the most popular options are the Epsilon and Delta two-person suites with private baths. All students living on campus are required

to purchase a meal plan, but limited weekend operating hours for the on-campus eateries can reportedly cause frustration. USA also offers married students housing in the form of unfurnished single-family houses in the neighborhood of Hillsdale Heights.

Most of South's 11,000 undergraduate students come from nearby cities and towns in Alabama, making the University primarily a commuter school in which much of the student body drives to class every day. Many clubs, for example, hold meetings in the afternoons to accommodate members who leave campus in the evening. Because of this, the campus activities and night life can be somewhat lacking; as one student complained, "there is no campus life at South!" However, the University is taking steps to correct this problem, and programs such as the Freshman Year Experience help new students to make friends and connections. The RAs in each dorm occasionally sponsor activities to foster a community spirit, and interested students can join intramural sports and other organizations to stay involved.

The social scene that does exist at USA revolves around the Greek system, and most events that take place on campus are sponsored by one of the college's eight sororities and eight fraternities. Although total membership is not huge, the Greeks have a strong presence on campus, due mainly to their widespread involvement in other clubs and organizations. Because South's campus is officially dry (although, as one student put it, this is true "in name only"), the frats do not usually supply alcohol at their parties, so Greek and non-Greek partiers alike are encouraged to bring their own beverages.

The Jaguar Life

The University recently approved the addition of a football team to the school's athletic offerings; it is scheduled to start play in the fall of 2009. In the past, many students have lamented the lack of school spirit that results from not having a football team. In the sport's absence, the crowd-pleasing sports to watch are men's and women's varsity basketball; die-hard Jaguar fans can also watch these games live via Internet streaming. Students can also indulge their competitive sides in an assortment of intramural sports based out of USA's state-of-the-art Intramural Field Complex, including inner tube water polo, soccer, flag football, basketball, volleyball and softball. The Student

Recreation Center is home to two basketball courts, a weight-lifting room, a track and a game room containing table tennis and a pool table as well as free SouthFit aerobics and dance classes. The University has also recently announced plans to build a brand-new recreation center with additional facilities.

South also boasts a sizeable Student Center that hosts lounge areas, a computer lab, office space for student groups, a big-screen TV, a variety of small eateries located in the Market area, and a large ball room that can be reserved for student use. Jaguar Productions, the Student Activities Board, meets here as well, and provides a relatively popular way for students to become involved with the university and help to plan campus-wide concerts, film screenings, lectures, vacation trips and more. About 185 clubs and organizations also offer a chance to meet fellow students and include everything from pre-professional organizations to groups for sports, music, meteorology, and video gaming enthusiasts. Jag TV, USA's student-run television station, is broadcast in all of the residence halls and other buildings throughout the campus.

The University of South Alabama offers numerous benefits to its many students, from its location in the welcoming Deep South city of Mobile to its variety of special degree and enrichment programs. Non-traditional students especially find its continuing education programs to be accommodating and flexible, while those living in the residential dorms appreciate the social atmosphere and the friendly RAs. The University's shortcomings, most notably a lack of school spirit, can be overcome through a determination to stay involved, and South's recent efforts to this end have made strides in improving the sense of community.—*Kristin Knox*

FYI
If you come to USA, you better bring "a desire to get involved and make the most of the college experience."
What is the typical weekend schedule? "Go to a frat party at night, catch up on work during the day."
If I could change one thing about USA, it would be "the lack of a football team."
Three things every student at USA should do before graduating are "play oozeball (volleyball in a knee-deep mud pit), go to an event in the Mitchell Center, and take advantage of the fine-arts offerings."

Alaska

University of Alaska/Fairbanks

Address: PO Box 757480
Fairbanks, AK 99775-7480
Phone: 907-474-7500
E-mail address:
admissions@uaf.edu
Web site URL: www.uaf.edu
Year Founded: 1917
Private or Public: Public
Religious Affiliation: None
Location: Suburban
Number of Applicants:
1,758
Percent Accepted: 78%
**Percent Accepted who
enroll:** 58%
Number Entering: 793
**Number of Transfers
Accepted each Year:** 667
Middle 50% SAT range:
M: 450–590, CR:
450–600, Wr: Unreported
Middle 50% ACT range:
18–25
**Early admission program
EA/ED/None:** None

**Percentage accepted
through EA or ED:** NA
EA and ED deadline: NA
Regular Deadline: 1-Aug
Application Fee: $40
**Full time Undergraduate
enrollment:** 7,568
Total enrollment: 8,627
Percent Male: 42%
Percent Female: 58%
**Total Percent Minority or
Unreported:** 40%
Percent African-American:
3%
**Percent Asian/Pacific
Islander:** 3%
Percent Hispanic: 3%
Percent Native-American:
20.0%
Percent International: 2%
**Percent in-state/out of
state:** 87%/13%
Percent from Public HS:
Unreported
Retention Rate: 74%

Graduation Rate 4-year: 8%
Graduation Rate 6-year: 30%
**Percent Undergraduates in
On-campus housing:** 31%
**Number of official organized
extracurricular
organizations:** 93
3 Most popular majors:
Biology, Business,
Psychology
Student/Faculty ratio: 10:1
Average Class Size: 10 to 19
**Percent of students going to
grad school:** Unreported
Tuition and Fees: $14,248
**In State Tuition and Fees if
different:** $4,828
Cost for Room and Board:
$7,190
**Percent receiving financial
aid out of those who apply,
first year:** 44%
**Percent receiving financial
aid among all students:**
55%

Originating as a federal Agricultural and Forestry Experiment Station in the northernmost frontier of the United States, the University of Alaska at Fairbanks today continues its legacy of cutting-edge research in a unique arctic environment. Through the gradual accumulation of government grants and support, Alaska's largest university has developed into an institution that prides itself on its ability to teach specialized skills to students in a very distinctive setting.

Scientific Significance
Since its founding in 1917, the University of Alaska at Fairbanks has acquired an array of resources from the government in order to further its progress in the world of research. After its humble beginnings as a land-grant institute, UAF eventually gained sea-grant

and space-grant status—signs of the importance of its scientific polar research. Additionally, its unique location in the middle of Alaska led Congress in 1946 to establish the Geophysical Institute, which is renowned for its studies of the geological world in polar regions and which also maintains the Poker Flat Research Range, the world's largest land-based rocket range. Indeed, for the brave souls that can withstand the bitterly cold winters in this harsh arctic tundra, UAF provides excellent opportunities for students to interact with the exceptional environment surrounding them.

Arctic Adventures
One of the main factors that differentiates UAF from other schools is its setting just 200 miles south of the Arctic Circle. UAF does not joke when it boasts about its

"360-million-acre classroom." Many of the majors that are offered make use of the University's vast environmental resources: Geophysics majors may find themselves measuring tectonic plate motions in Denali National Park; Oceanography majors might conduct research on the R/V *Alpha Helix*, one of the Seward Marine Center's research vessels; a Natural Resources Management student could end up developing and promoting Alaska's reindeer industry—the list goes on. Above this, one of the most unique opportunities students have is the ability to work right alongside the world's brightest scientists at any of the top-notch research institutes that call UAF home. In fact, many professors are "from all over the country, including Ivy League schools, since the research here is not available in science programs elsewhere."

The educational route that students take is in large part framed by the Baccalaureate Core, which requires a range of credits in six different areas: communication, perspectives on the human condition, mathematics, natural sciences, library and information research, and upper-division communication. Although most students agree that the Core provides the foundation upon which students begin to build their knowledge, some find it a little bit strict (38–39 core credits are needed). The classes can get quite large, and sometimes it is hard to get into your first-choice course. In the end, though, UAF's eight schools and colleges—Engineering and Mines, Liberal Arts, Natural Science and Mathematics, Rural and Community Development, Education, Fisheries and Ocean Sciences, Management, Natural Resources and Agricultural Sciences—still manage to provide flexibility by covering a broad spectrum of fields, offering 167 degrees and 28 certificates in over 122 disciplines. The professors will assist students "as long as you communicate with them one on one."

All Bundled Up

The most obvious shared trait evident amongst the student body is their similar taste in fashion: everyone wears winter hats, scarves, and jackets. Although one student opined that the culture is "very bad because we're always late to get all the latest trends in clothing and music," another countered that at least all the students have the latest in winter-weather clothing. The typical student can be as variable as the arctic weather. On one hand, there are a handful of traditional party-types, who scour the campus

for the liveliest events. One student believes that "because it is dark most of the winter, a lot of people drink more than usual." On the other hand, "a lot of people [at UAF] do not drink—but instead are outdoorsy and down-to-earth." The drinking that does occur usually takes place in the many student apartments on campus. Freshmen are required to live in dorms for their first year.

> **"The characteristic student can be as variable as the arctic weather."**

Though UAF was founded in the 20th century, it already has a number of traditions that continue their legacy each year. "Starvation Gulch," started in 1923 by the founding president, Charles Bunnell, involves a ceremony with the building of very large bonfires—"some of the piles the size of a small house"—that signify the "passing of knowledge" from upperclassmen to the incoming freshmen. Many campus groups fight over the possession and control of the "Tradition Stone," a block of concrete with a sign that was placed on a pile of beer bottles in defiance of an alcohol ban instituted in the 50s.

Close-knit Community

Though many of the campus buildings may be aesthetically unappealing, one student quaintly characterizes the campus as "90s meets Gotham." Filled with a mix of "square/blah" and more-modern buildings, the tight layout of the campus—one student posits that it might be to "increase the 'warmth' of the community"—contains a number of wonderful structures. The Elmer E. Rasmuson Library now holds more than 1.75 million volumes and contains a specialized collection of "Alaska and Polar Regions" materials. The Wood Campus Center, created "as a solution to cabin fever," serves as the center of the student community. Housing a ballroom, adjoining conference rooms, an eight-lane bowling alley ("Polar Alley"), and a number of eateries, the facility is frequented by many students. Pizza Piazza, in particular, is a popular hangout spot for students. Additionally, the Upper Campus views of the stunning Brookes Mountain Range more than make up for any lack of architectural beauty.

Polar Pastimes

Though the thermometer can hit extremely low readings during the winter, students try to take advantage of what they can. Within heated buildings, the Alaska Gravity Works juggling club spends time "throwing things in the air and periodically letting them hit the ground." The Space and Robotics clubs cater toward the many students that have a passion for science. Students can also participate in a video game tournament sponsored by the VICE Club. In the great Alaskan outdoors, students take advantage of the ski slopes and trails, which the University Trails Club maintains.

Athletes make the most of the fairly limited varsity-level athletic offerings. The UAF "Nanooks" (polar bears) have had particular success in cold-weather sports such as skiing and hockey. Even the more traditional basketball team has had its successes: it won the Division I Top of the World Classic in 2002. Alone in national prominence, however, is the Nanook rifle team, which dominates the national circuit with 10 NCAA titles in the past 15 years. As a testament to the team's success, UAF hosted the 2007 NCAA Championships for the first time ever. Most students, however, rally around the hockey team as they compete each season. Of course, for those looking for a more leisurely experience, the UAF intramurals program offers 19 sports ranging from two-person volleyball to hoop shooting to the IM classic, broomball.

Northern Nuance

The single-most important factor that UAF students emphasize is Alaska's beautiful arctic landscape and natural resources. With gorgeous summer days filled with 24 hours of sunshine, and winter nights dazzled by the flashing of the Aurora Borealis in the sky, UAF's setting in rural Alaska provides its students with an outstanding learning environment. The biggest complaint one might have of the University of Alaska at Fairbanks, however, is the extreme cold and harsh winters. At times, the thermometer readings can hit as low as −65. But as one student declared, "Don't let that scare you out of the experience, because it's sure to be one you'll never forget." Indeed, UAF students take the climate in stride; it is a testament to the hearty character of the student body that you can always find a scantily clad student posing alongside a time/temperature sign that flashes 40 below zero.—*Wookie Kim*

FYI

If you come to UAF, you'd better bring "lots of entertainment and no clothing; the only quality winter clothes are sold here."

What's the typical weekend schedule? "Each night starts out with calling or MySpacing friends to see where the parties are. Bowling, sledding, bonfires, cabin parties, clubbing, concerts, drag shows . . ."

If I could change one thing about UAF, I'd "make it less cold!"

Three things every student at the University of Alaska at Fairbanks should do before graduating are "sled at midnight under the Northern Lights, eat moose meat, and join the 40-below club."

Arizona

Arizona State University

Address: PO Box 870112
Tempe, AZ 85287
Phone: 480-965-7788
E-mail address:
ugradinq@asu.edu
Web site URL: www.asu.edu
Year Founded: 1885
Private or Public: Public
Religious Affiliation: None
Location: Suburban
Number of Applicants:
27,089
Percent Accepted: 95%
Percent Accepted who
enroll: 35%
Number Entering: 8,458
Number of Transfers
Accepted each Year:
5,258
Middle 50% SAT range:
M: 480–610, CR:
470–600, Wr: Unreported
Middle 50% ACT range:
20–26
Early admission program
EA/ED/None: None

Percentage accepted
through EA or ED: NA
EA and ED deadline: NA
Regular Deadline: Rolling
Application Fee: $25
Full time Undergraduate
enrollment: 53,298
Total enrollment: 65,804
Percent Male: 48%
Percent Female: 52%
Total Percent Minority or
Unreported: 35%
Percent African-American:
5%
Percent Asian/Pacific
Islander: 6%
Percent Hispanic: 15%
Percent Native-American:
2.28%
Percent International: 2%
Percent in-state/out of
state: 78%/22%
Percent from Public HS:
Unreported
Retention Rate: 80%
Graduation Rate 4-year: 29%

Graduation Rate 6-year:
54%
Percent Undergraduates
in On-campus housing:
78%
Number of official organized
extracurricular
organizations: 512
3 Most popular majors:
Journalism, Multidisciplinary
Studies, Psychology
Student/Faculty ratio: 22:1
Average Class Size: 15
Percent of students going to
grad school: Unreported
Tuition and Fees: $17,949
In State Tuition and Fees if
different: $5,661
Cost for Room and Board:
$8,790
Percent receiving financial
aid out of those who apply,
first year: 70%
Percent receiving financial
aid among all students:
66%

W ith four campuses and a projected enrollment of 100,000 students by 2020, Arizona State University is one of the nation's fastest growing universities. The school's focus on research has bolstered Arizona State's academic reputation in recent years, while President Michael Crow's crackdown on partying and underage drinking has taken ASU out of the country's top-ten party schools. But those seeking a big party school atmosphere still have plenty to look forward to at ASU.

Decisions, Decisions

Arizona State's academic menu boasts over 250 undergraduate programs and majors at its four campuses, presenting a unique op-portunity for students. "Anything you could possibly imagine there's probably a major for it, or at least a class or club," one undergraduate revealed. Most freshmen declare a major during orientation and are then given a "Major Map" that charts out their required courses for the next four years, though it is possible to change majors later on. Although some find this system rigid, students have plenty of opportunities to double major, minor or take elective courses. Business and Communications are two of the most popular majors, while the Department of Engineering has the reputation of being the most difficult in terms of requirements and course work.

With over 53,000 undergraduates at ASU, it is not difficult for individuals to slip "under the radar" academically. "It's easy to feel like you're just a piece on the assembly line," one student commented. But for those who show interest, there are plenty of opportunities to interact with professors via e-mail or in person at office hours. And professors love it when students do: "professors get really excited if you come in during office hours," another student said.

Class size varies although most students take mainly large lecture classes at the beginning and later move on to smaller seminar-style classes. And because classes are so mapped out, students do not generally consider online registration a major hassle.

> **"Anything you could possibly imagine there's probably a major for it, or at least a class or club."**

The University further insures that students not fall through the cracks with a five-week course called ASU 101. The class is, as one freshman described it, "basically 'how to be successful at ASU.' It makes sure that everyone is on the same page going in." Taught by faculty members "whenever possible" (though graduate students, academic advisors and even undergraduates have been known to lead a section), the required course instructs new students how to use the resources available at a place that, for many, has the potential to be overwhelming. Students are encouraged to take the course through their own colleges as each school adds its own content. But while some find it helpful, most students view the course simply as a dull rite of passage to get through as painlessly as possible.

Arizona State University is home to a number of highly esteemed schools and departments. The Walter Cronkite School of Journalism (located at the new Downtown Phoenix Campus, which students can access via the newly constructed Lightrail), the W. P. Carey School of Business and the College of Design are also well known. Donald Johanson, the paleoanthropologist who discovered the world-famous 3.2-million-year-old "Lucy" skeleton, is the director of ASU's Institute of Human Origins. ASU is also home to the pioneering School of Sustainability. Opened in 2007, the school is the first degree-granting institution of sustainability in the country with its first graduate in fall of 2008. Meanwhile, students in the well-established Barrett Honors College, who are required to take about a third of their classes through the competitive program, have the singular opportunity of learning in an intimate, academic community while having access to the resources of the larger university.

Friends and Fraternities

Students agree that making friends is no problem at ASU. One of the benefits of attending such a large school is that the diversity of students makes it easy to find those with common interests. "The vastness is good because there is such a variety of people," one freshman said.

Once students find their friends, it's time to party. If they want to, that is. "Thirsty Thursday" is the big party night at ASU. Students flock to gatherings just off campus to drink, smoke (almost exclusively pot) and unwind. Dorm parties rarely exceed more than five or six people as the school maintains a strict no-alcohol policy in the on-campus dormitories. With over 50 campus fraternities and sororities, Greek life is a large component of Arizona State's social life. But, as one student put it, "the Greek scene is pretty influential but you don't have to be in a fraternity to have a social life."

Although many have cars (even though parking is expensive and a hassle), students tend to hang out near the campus on the weekends. And while one sophomore insisted that "pretty much everyone drinks," there is plenty to do for students who abstain. Attending cultural events at architect Frank Lloyd Wright's Gammage Auditorium, wandering around the shops, clubs and restaurants on Mill Avenue, or venturing to Tempe Marketplace, a huge shopping center that was recently built nearby, are all popular weekend activities.

Sun Devil Dwellings

On-campus housing at Arizona State can be anything from a dream come true to a freshman's worst nightmare. As one student put it, "ASU dorms come in two flavors: extremely crappy or extremely nice." The quality of living conditions depends on when the building was constructed. While the newer dorms are "really nice and spacious," the old housing leaves much to be desired. But students who are unsatisfied with their living arrangements freshman year shouldn't be too concerned. Most Sun Devils choose to live off campus starting their sophomore year, opting for the affordable apartments and houses located near the school.

Once admitted, incoming students apply for housing online. On the Tempe campus, there are several options, including old-fashioned dormitories, on-campus apartments and residential colleges. The residential colleges, similar to the "themed housing" found at other schools, range from academic-interest-based to substance-free living to the Global Village, which houses primarily international students. Students may choose their own roommates or ask to be randomly assigned.

Starting in fall 2009, students enrolled at the Barrett Honors College will have the option of living in a brand new complex built exclusively for honors students. The complex will encourage the students at Barrett to live on campus all four years and will have its own dining, fitness and computer facilities.

Sun Devil Pride

Sports are a big deal at Arizona State. No, really. "I had to buy my [football] season tickets in June," one student revealed. Football and basketball reliably draw large crowds, and tailgating is a highly-anticipated event. Thousands of students, alumni and fans bedecked in maroon and gold traditionally gather to sip or chug from red cups before each football game. But recently the campus police department has become stricter about underage drinking at tailgates, much to the chagrin of many of ASU's younger students.

The biggest sporting event of the year is the football game against the University of Arizona. The big game, which is also known as the "Territorial Cup" or the "Duel in the Desert," takes place the Saturday after Thanksgiving and dates back to 1899 (Arizona State won). Every year, the Student Alumni Association organizes the guarding of the giant gold "A" on a nearby mountain from U of A students trying to paint over it.

And in one of ASU's newest traditions—appropriately termed the "Undie Run"—students participate in a uniquely fashioned clothing drive. Donors don all the clothing they intend to give, and then remove the articles down to their underwear at the donation site. They then proceed to run around campus, spawning countless Facebook albums.

For students wishing to show their school spirit in ways beyond varsity athletics and strip charity, there are over 500 registered student clubs and organizations at Arizona State. From the Hip Hop Coalition to the Kazakhstan Student Association to the Arizona Outing Club, there is an organization for just about everyone. Undergraduate organizations are especially important at ASU because, as one freshman put it, "you need small breakdowns of the population to meet people because there are just so many." The Student Organization Resource Center (SORC), which provides funding for clubs and acts as an organizing body for all registered groups, is housed in the Memorial Union, the community center on campus. The "MU" is a central meeting point for students, a crossroads of humanity that houses restaurants like Jamba Juice and Taco Bell, a bank and ATM, a bowling alley called Sparkey's Den and meeting spaces. Most students with meal plans choose to forgo the mediocre dining halls in favor of the fast food options and university restaurants at the MU.

While it may be overwhelming at times, students willing to put in the time and effort can obtain a "surprisingly good" education at Arizona State University. With limitless opportunities and resources, vibrant party scene and intense school sprit, ASU, as one student said, "gives everybody a chance at a higher education."—*Lauren Motzkin*

FYIs
If you come to Arizona State University you'd better bring a bike and a red cup.
What the typical weekend schedule? "Party on Thursday night, sleep Friday until you have to go to class in the afternoon, party on Friday night, go to work on Saturday, hang out with friends on Saturday night, and then relax and do homework on Sunday."
If I could change one thing about Arizona State University I would "make it so there was less pressure to choose a major right away."
Three things every student at Arizona State University should do before graduating are "light the A on 'A Mountain' on fire for Homecoming, join a club and go to a giant party."

University of Arizona

Address: PO Box 210040
Tucson, AZ 85721-0040
Phone: 520-621-3237
E-mail address:
appinfo@arizona.edu
Web site URL:
www.arizona.edu
Year Founded: 1885
Private or Public: Public
Religious Affiliation: None
Location: Urban
Number of Applicants:
25,449
Percent Accepted: 77%
Percent Accepted who
enroll: 43%
Number Entering: 8,426
Number of Transfers
Accepted each Year: 2,846
Middle 50% SAT range:
M: 500–630, CR:
490–600, Wr: Unreported
Middle 50% ACT range:
20–26
Early admission program
EA/ED/None: None

Percentage accepted
through EA or ED: NA
EA and ED deadline: NA
Regular Deadline: 1-May
Application Fee: $50
Full time Undergraduate
enrollment: 29,070
Total enrollment: 35,940
Percent Male: 46%
Percent Female: 54%
Total Percent Minority or
Unreported: 32%
Percent African-American:
3%
Percent Asian/Pacific
Islander: 6%
Percent Hispanic: 17%
Percent Native-American:
4.0%
Percent International: 3%
Percent in-state/out of
state: 69%/31%
Percent from Public HS: 90%
Retention Rate: 80%
Graduation Rate 4-year:
Unreported

Graduation Rate 6-year:
Unreported
Percent Undergraduates in
On-campus housing: 20%
Number of official organized
extracurricular
organizations: 504
3 Most popular majors:
Cellular and Molecular
Biology, Political Science and
Government, Psychology
Student/Faculty ratio: 18:1
Average Class Size: 10 to 19
Percent of students going to
grad school: 42%
Tuition and Fees: $16,058
In State Tuition and Fees if
different: $4,824
Cost for Room and Board:
$7,812
Percent receiving financial
aid out of those who apply,
first year: 60%
Percent receiving financial
aid among all students:
35%

T he University of Arizona Wildcats spend their four years living the ideal of "fun in the sun." Located in the desert oasis of Tucson, Arizona (an hour from the Mexican border), students bask in 300 days of sunshine as they scurry between sporting events and classes. Quality academics and a large student body provide for nearly every degree and extracurricular interest.

If You Want It, You Got It
A student would be hard pressed to find something he or she didn't love among the more than 150 undergraduate degree programs offered at Arizona. Majors like accounting, theatre arts, and Wildlife, Watershed and Rangeland Resources provide a mere glimpse at the incredible variety of academic options available to Wildcats. Taming the freedom of the student body is the notorious "Gen. Ed." requirement. Gen. Ed. is made up of three tiers of classes, including Traditions and Cultures, Individuals and Societies, and the feared Natural Sciences. Gen. Ed. classes can be annoying and

packed with 150 to 300 students, but students say that they fulfill the requirements with minimal discomfort.

Psychology, communications, political science and business are the most popular majors. Students wishing to take a more rigorous academic route subscribe to the engineering department's five-year program. One student warned, however, that "as a general rule it seems that all of the hard science classes and engineering courses are the toughest on campus."

Arizona boasts one of the nation's top business schools, the Eller College of Management. One student proudly stated, "The Eller School is one of the most well-known departments in the country and is perennially one of the top business schools in the country." Brainy Wildcats enjoy a special Honors College that demands no lower than a 3.5 GPA. Competition for admission is fierce, but the select few enjoy smaller classes, a support structure of 90 advisors and 11 staff members, private residence halls, and $40,000 annually for student research projects. Although for the majority of

Wildcats the classes can be large and the student-teacher ratio overwhelming, students agree that, "grading is done fairly and the professors are always willing to listen if you have a question."

Going Greek
Outside of the classroom, most Wildcats spend time at the restaurants and bars located on University and Fourth Avenue. Students report that they value their fake IDs, but those without still have ample opportunity for underage drinking at Tucson house parties and along Frat Row.

Arizona administrators can be tough, however, on those caught drinking, as one student revealed. "There is no tolerance for underage drinking on campus, and if caught there is a mandatory program that all students must attend." Worse still is the Red Tag Policy, which declares that for six months post party-breakup students must hang a red tag in the window and limit visitors to the number of housemates. Luckily, students report that "the Student Senate is currently trying to amend the situation" and Wildcats have plenty of opportunities for good clean fun.

Greek life is "the dominant social scene on campus," consisting of 24 sororities and 30 fraternities. Undergrad Greeks agree that Arizona Greek life offers members a support system, a community service group, and a post-grad network system, not to mention a full calendar of mixers and socials. Nearly 1,500 men and women rush, and getting a bid can be stressful. Yet, as one sorority girl advised, "Don't worry about everything. If it's right, it will happen."

Where'd Everybody Go?
With all that sunshine, students freely frolic about the entire campus. But the most popular spot is the student union. "The union is the main place people go if they have time. There are restaurants and rooms for people to sit and study or sleep." The newly built Student Union Memorial Center on the west side of campus is a $60 million dollar, 450,000 square feet structure, with amenities including a bookstore, a post office, and even an arcade. Although everyone frequents the unions, University Drive, "a street right next to campus with restaurants, bars and shopping," is another hot spot for student activity. The campus is safe and full of friendly Wildcats, but students are warned to retain common sense as they travel around.

Dorms at Arizona vary significantly from "some really nice ones to some really bad dorms." The housing system offers students coed dorms, women-only dorms, sorority and fraternity housing, apartments for single students, special housing for disabled students, and even special housing for international students. For the adventurous, the Coronado dorm is "the biggest dorm on campus and every year it leads all the other dorms in evictions." The RAs at Arizona are described as "cool." "Their major role," one student explained, "is to make sure nothing horrible happens . . . and they usually organize activities to let everyone get to know each other."

Although the insides of dorms vary, students report that the architecture is exactly the same: "everywhere you go, brick red buildings, everywhere." The most famous building on campus is the Old Main, built upon the University's founding in 1885. But one student noted that, "there is always construction of some kind on campus and new buildings are always popping up," leaving hope for a campus mini-makeover in the near future.

In terms of food, students can choose from a variety of meal plans offering fast food and restaurant fare. When describing student union food, one student reported that, "there are several different meal plans to choose from, but the food generally stinks." In response to whether the dining hall is better or worse than other schools, a student offered, "There is only one. So there isn't much choice in the matter."

> **"A big city, Tucson can still be looked at as a college town."**

Perhaps the bad dining is the reason "there is a huge off-campus life." "The majority of upper classmen live in the neighborhoods surrounding campus," one student explained. Whatever the reason, students are well received by the nearby towns. "The University is one of the largest employers in town, and it seems that the population supports the university as much as it can. . . . A big city, Tucson can still be looked at as a college town."

Wildcat Fever
Sports rule at the University of Arizona, and basketball is king. One student reported that, "Yesterday, there was a basketball game against North Carolina. The game started at 11, and there were students lining up at 10

the night before to get in." But all those denied basketball tickets have football, baseball and softball games, not to mention numerous intramurals, to attend. Wildcats are an active bunch, so if they're not outside enjoying the sun, they're sweating it out at the student recreation center, which one student said is "nice, but it is always packed." In true Arizona fashion, plans to expand the popular rec center are already in progress.

The University of Arizona offers every student opportunities for academics, extracurricular activities, and socializing. School spirit permeates every aspect of life—school pride, sports, student organizations and popular events like Spring Fling and Homecoming make life at Arizona unforgettable. With so much to offer, a wise Wildcat advised, "Make the most of your time here."—*Eliza Crawford*

FYI

If you come to Arizona, you'd better bring "suntan lotion."

What is the typical weekend schedule? "Friday nights you usually go out [and party], Saturdays are sporting events and more partying, and Sundays are usually recovery days [when] you get all your work for the week done."

If I could change one thing about Arizona, I'd "lower the faculty to student ratio; some of the lower-level class sizes are pretty big."

Three things every student at Arizona should do before graduating are "attend a Wildcat basketball game, sunbathe in January, make the most of your time here."

Arkansas

Hendrix College

Address: 1600 Washington Avenue Conway, AR 72032
Phone: 501-450-1362
E-mail address: adm@hendrix.edu
Web site URL: www.hendrix.edu
Year Founded: 1876
Private or Public: Private
Religious Affiliation: Methodist
Location: Rural
Number of Applicants: 1,420
Percent Accepted: 94%
Percent Accepted who enroll: 32%
Number Entering: 433
Number of Transfers Accepted each Year: 41
Middle 50% SAT range: M: 550–660, CR: 580–690, Wr:, Unreported
Middle 50% ACT range: 25–31
Early admission program EA/ED/None: Priority

Percentage accepted through EA or ED: Unreported
EA and ED deadline: 1-Feb
Regular Deadline: 1-Aug
Application Fee: $40
Full time Undergraduate enrollment: 1,342
Total enrollment: 1,342
Percent Male: 45%
Percent Female: 55%
Total Percent Minority or Unreported: 6%
Percent African-American: 4%
Percent Asian/Pacific Islander: 3%
Percent Hispanic: 4%
Percent Native-American: <1%
Percent International: 2%
Percent in-state/out of state: 49%/51%
Percent from Public HS: 71%
Retention Rate: 85%
Graduation Rate 4-year: 62%

Graduation Rate 6-year: 68%
Percent Undergraduates in On-campus housing: 84%
Number of official organized extracurricular organizations: 80
3 Most popular majors: Biology/Biological Sciences, General English Language and Literature, General Psychology
Student/Faculty ratio: 12:1
Average Class Size: 10 to 19
Percent of students going to grad school: 92%
Tuition and Fees: $25,780
In State Tuition and Fees if different: No difference
Cost for Room and Board: $7,950
Percent receiving financial aid out of those who apply, first year: 100%
Percent receiving financial aid among all students: 100%

Located in Conway, Arkansas, Hendrix College is a tiny, Methodist-affiliated liberal arts school with an openly liberal student body. Yet despite the elitism you might expect at an "oasis of liberalness" in the middle of conservative Arkansas, Hendrix is a down-to-earth college where "the atmosphere is just awesome, and the people are so friendly." Don't pass over this Southern school without a closer look—the outstanding academics and intimate size make Hendrix a perfect fit for many.

Journeys and Explorations

Universally, students are delighted with the quality of Hendrix academics, the hallmark of which is the faculty-student interaction permitted by its small student body (about 1,350 undergraduates and no graduate school). "The academic life," one sophomore said, "is by far my favorite aspect of Hendrix. I'm a pretty big fan of the faculty. I haven't had a bad teacher yet, and I've had some amazing ones."

A small college, of course, means that there are fewer majors available (31) and fewer course options. Yet students are satisfied with the trade-off, reporting that their classes are intimate (the average class size being 17) and they know their professors well. One sophomore said that her classes have been evenly split between lectures and seminars, but that even her lectures are no larger than 30 students. In all classes, active student participation is emphasized. "One of the things I've noticed about my classes," a freshman said, "is that there's a lot more open discussion than in what most people would consider a college environment."

Though there are no noticeably weak academic programs here, Hendrix's strong suits are traditional fields such as English, politics, and biology, with pre-med being a popular choice. Hendrix has many core requirements that it believes constitute a broad liberal arts education. But as one sophomore said, "While a lot of students at other schools dread core requirements, students often have fun here taking core classes no matter how unrelated to their major they are. I'm currently in a natural history lab where we take fun field trips to forests." Plus, because the school is so small, many upper-level courses are available to freshmen and sophomores.

Hendrix places heavy emphasis on integrating freshmen into the social and academic life of the college immediately upon arrival. A mandatory course for all freshmen, "Journeys," introduces students to important works by Plato, Confucius and other philosophers all in one year. Less popular is the required orientation "Explorations," which focuses on introducing freshmen to the campus by creating small groups led by a faculty member and a sophomore guide.

The college welcomes freshmen to Hendrix life in more ways than just academics. Every student participates in an orientation trip before even arriving on campus; one freshman described his trip up to the Buffalo River, where his group went canoeing for two days with upperclassmen, who "kind of showed us the ropes." Indeed, because Hendrix is so small, college life thrives on interaction between upperclassmen and freshmen.

"Hippies and Gays"?

One junior described a "weird kind of dual stereotype" about the Hendrix student body. On the one hand, he said, Hendrix is the most academically challenging school in the state and the object of many Arkansans' aspirations, but on the other, "there is the image of Hendrix as an out-of-control party school with hippies and gays running rampant." Students say neither stereotype is truly accurate, though they do agree that many diverse opinions and beliefs are expressed openly on the Hendrix campus.

The school's Methodist background and religious life play an important part in many students' lives at Hendrix. One freshman described "countless religious groups at Hendrix, lots of Catholics and other religions who have their organizations on campus."

And though political leanings here are "predominantly liberal," one student assures that "you'll find your conservatives and socialists and other groups there too."

Still, there isn't much geographic diversity, and students who are from out-of-state sometimes find themselves isolated. "There's a lot of southerners, a fair amount from Little Rock and Arkansas," a sophomore said. "All the non-southern people sort of clump together. It's a very regional school in that sense."

Partying Under Strict Scrutiny

Hendrix may have a miniscule student body and lack fraternities or sororities, but students repeatedly emphasized that they still manage to have a bustling social life. Residential dorm parties are the major attraction on weekend nights. Each dorm has its own personality and reputation, and in a fake rush week every year they mimic fraternities and pretend to recruit new "taps." "There's definitely one spot—Martin Hall, one of the dorms—where every Wednesday, Friday and Saturday you can pretty much guarantee there will be people drinking," one student said.

Students frequently complain about the way the Hendrix administration deals with partying. "In recent years, there's been a very notable and organized effort by the administration to crack down on parties," one student said. As part of its efforts, the administration has attempted to cloister all student partying in one house, the Cottage, or in the Brick Pit, an open space in the middle of campus where college police can easily manage students. Other Hendrix-approved social events including a dance competition called Shirttails Serenade at the end of the first week of school, for which all the male freshmen "do this sort of dance, usually a little raunchy, where they're just wearing their boxer shorts and an Oxford shirt. They perform it in front of these judges, and the winners get a pizza party."

The insularity and closeness of Hendrix social life—and the jumping through hoops required to throw parties on campus—lead a number of students to escape campus on the weekends, usually to Little Rock, the closest major city. Conway offers up a few movie theatres and restaurants near campus, and Hendrix puts on some concerts and theatrical productions throughout the year, but partying seems to be the central focus of student social lives.

Beyond complaints about the administration's alcohol policies, students also cited inflexible and difficult housing regulations and poor access to health services as further problems. In fact, a number of students mentioned the uncaring administration as their biggest gripe with Hendrix. "I was lucky, and housing flowed for me," a sophomore said, "but there's a Facebook group about getting screwed over by the administration." "The president is highly unpopular, as well as the new dean of students," another sophomore noted. "The students aren't afraid to speak up and try to do something about it, but it is very hard to get pro-student laws passed as the board of trustees is a bunch of conservative Methodists."

An Unusual School Spirit

Although extracurricular involvement varies widely among students, there are several influential organizations on campus. The Student Senate deals with campus issues and gives students a voice. "They struggle with the administration every once in a while," a freshman said. But despite occasional problems, they "really do care about the students and try to get stuff done."

Another popular activity is writing for and editing the student newspaper, *The Profile*, which has a regular staff of 50 and an editorial staff of 10–15. For a small school, Hendrix boasts an impressive array of other extracurricular options, from political groups such as the Young Democrats and the Progressive Student Alliance to musical ensembles such as the jazz band, pep band, and wind ensemble.

At Hendrix, approximately 200 students are athletes, on nine men's teams and 10 women's teams. Students say that they show a great deal of school spirit, but winning is not necessarily important to Hendrix culture. "We're not going to be real upset if the basketball team doesn't do that well this year. We care because our friends might be on it, but we don't care because we want Hendrix to win—we care about the people and not about the competition," one student said. Describing the easygoing nature of Hendrix athletics, one junior said, "We're probably best known for our Ultimate Frisbee team, the Flying Squirrels."

A Close Community

The sense that every Hendrix student knows everyone else constitutes a great deal of the school's appeal, but also its drawbacks. Several students said they felt claustrophobic after being on campus a year. "Last year, I found that a lot of my friends, one way or another, thought about leaving," a sophomore said. "But the feeling is that this year, my friends are more settled in. It's just anxiety over change."

> "Whatever bias or opinions or preconceived notions you have about anything will be challenged at Hendrix."

Many students come to Hendrix for financial reasons, citing its strong financial aid package as a major appeal. But once they've arrived on campus and have gotten over some of its problems, most thrive in its intimate atmosphere. "I don't think twice when I meet new people," a sophomore said. "I almost think, well, they're at Hendrix, they have to be good people."

Above all, Hendrix prizes an active academic life and personal, social, and academic development. As one student put it, "Whatever bias or opinions or preconceived notions you have about anything will be challenged at Hendrix."—*Yotam Barkai*

FYI
If you come to Hendrix, you'd better bring "flip-flops, a Ryan Adams CD, and a healthy appreciation for mob flicks."
What is the typical weekend schedule? "Friday, there's usually some sort of party going on, and the campus usually tries to have some other activity going on (a play at the theater or a movie). Saturdays are pretty much up in the air—unless there's a soccer game, there's usually not that much on campus. We do a lot of studying."
If I could change one thing about Hendrix, I'd "loosen the rules regarding partying and social life and alcohol."
Three things every student at Hendrix should do before graduating are "break into the greenhouse, check out the Ozarks, and get thrown into the fountain for your birthday."

University of Arkansas

Address: 232 Silas Hunt Hall
Fayetteville, AR 72701
Phone: 479-575-5346
E-mail address:
uofa@uark.edu
Web site URL: www.uark.edu
Year Founded: 1871
Private or Public: Public
Religious Affiliation: None
Location: Urban
Number of Applicants:
12,045
Percent Accepted: 58%
**Percent Accepted who
enroll:** 43%
Number Entering: 2,979
**Number of Transfers
Accepted each Year:**
1,686
Middle 50% SAT range:
M: 520–650, CR:
510–630, Wr: Unreported
Middle 50% ACT range:
23–29
**Early admission program
EA/ED/None:** EA

**Percentage accepted
through EA or ED:**
Unreported
EA and ED deadline: 15-Nov
Regular Deadline: 15-Aug
Application Fee: $40
**Full time Undergraduate
enrollment:** 14,948
Total enrollment: 18,245
Percent Male: 50%
Percent Female: 50%
**Total Percent Minority or
Unreported:** 15%
Percent African-American:
5%
**Percent Asian/Pacific
Islander:** 3%
Percent Hispanic: 3%
Percent Native-American:
2.0%
Percent International: 3%
**Percent in-state/out of
state:** 67%/33%
Percent from Public HS: 84%
Retention Rate: 83%
Graduation Rate 4-year: 32%

Graduation Rate 6-year:
56%
**Percent Undergraduates in
On-campus housing:** 29%
**Number of official organized
extracurricular
organizations:** 238
3 Most popular majors:
Finance, Journalism,
Marketing/Marketing
Management
Student/Faculty ratio: 17:1
Average Class Size: 20 to 29
**Percent of students going to
grad school:** Unreported
Tuition and Fees: $15,279
**In State Tuition and Fees if
different:** $6,399
Cost for Room and Board:
$7,422
**Percent receiving financial
aid out of those who apply,
first year:** 62%
**Percent receiving financial
aid among all students:**
71%

F or it's A-A-A-R-K-A-N-S-A-S for Arkansas! Fight! Fight! Fi-i-i-ght!" Don't even think about setting foot in Fayetteville, Arkansas, without knowing the words to the Razorback fight song. Athletics aren't just for the jocks at this Southern university. If you are looking for a community with school pride, are unsure if you want to rush Pi Beta Phi or just go to their parties, and are interested in anything from engineering to agriculture, the University of Arkansas is calling your name.

Welcome to Fayetteville

Located in the Ozark Mountains, Fayetteville is the home of 345 acres of University of Arkansas campus. The city has a population of nearly 70,000 people for now, but Northwest Arkansas is considered the sixth-fastest-growing region in the United States, according to the U.S. Census.

Upon arrival in Fayetteville, freshmen are introduced to their academic advisers, who "really know what they're doing," according to one senior. During orientation period, freshmen are clued in to all university poli-

cies and academic requirements. "It's hard to fall through the cracks freshman year," students said. "There are advisers and older students who really take pride in helping the younger ones." Make sure you ask about Advanced Placement status in classes, or how to "CLEP-out" of the University's second-language requirement by taking proficiency tests or foreign language classes. Oftentimes high school AP credits can cut down your "core" course load. The completion of core classes is required for graduation, and according to a senior, the readily accessible advisers are helpful in "letting us know exactly what we need" in order to graduate on time.

By sophomore year undergrads are usually enrolled in a specific college at the University of Arkansas. Students may choose between the Dale Bumpers College of Agricultural, Food & Life Sciences, the School of Architecture, the Fulbright College of Arts & Sciences, the Sam M. Walton College of Business, the College of Education and Health Professions, and the College of Engineering, depending on the student's academic interests. With over 200 academic degree programs, UA covers virtually all academic bases.

Most students are quick to say that the professors are all easy to reach, and hold convenient office hours, often meeting students for coffee on campus. However, as the freshmen core courses (such as Chemistry and Communications) are usually numbered at around 300 or 400 students, they are mostly taught by Teaching Assistants, not actual professors. One senior business major explained, "Once you get more into your major by junior and senior year, you get more of the professors, and people who actually wrote the books you are reading."

Deemed the hardest major at Arkansas by a number of students, engineering is only a hair less harrowing than molecular biology. Nonetheless, students claim that the difficulty of the subjects really shouldn't deter any undergrads from taking them. "Help is really just around the corner," one sophomore said. "I have tutors in a few subjects, and they are really flexible, and helpful around midterms and finals especially."

Life as a Razorback

While students are required to live on campus their freshman year, this is certainly not viewed as a bad thing. The dorms are described as "traditional" and "spacious" but beware: they are not all created equal. Humphreys (aka "the Hump-Dump") is coed and in the middle of campus. However, it has no air-conditioning and is "miserable" at the beginning of school because "it can get pretty hot here in Arkansas." A better dorm is Pomfret, which "everyone who lives there loves" and "they have a lot of fun." Its location isn't as convenient, however, as it sits at the "very bottom of a great big hill." (Don't come to Fayetteville without good walking shoes; students say "we have a ton of huge hills!")

By sophomore year many students choose to live off campus in any of Fayetteville's many apartment complexes. The city is "overflowing" with them, and the crowding in the city has also created a huge parking problem. Students call the city parking "awful" and "downright impossible." Luckily for future classes, the city just built the biggest parking deck in the state of Arkansas, which holds 550 automobiles.

Greeks and Non-Greeks

Sophomore year is also the first year that students who choose to "Go Greek" can live in their fraternity and sorority houses. While Greek life is a large part of the Arkansas social scene, it is certainly not something that students feel pressured to join. "If you do it, great, but if you don't want to do it, that's great too," one Razorback senior commented. Greek or not, students can still attend frat parties, where the serving of alcohol to minors is reportedly "not a problem whatsoever." Students who live in off-campus apartments and houses often open up their houses for parties and keggers, and offer a stress-free night for students who are underage.

The Greek houses are also all on campus, making party-hopping very convenient. With Sorority Row on Maple Street and Fraternity Row on Stadium Drive, undergrads don't have to look far for a "typical huge, beautiful, southern-style Greek house" offering plenty of cold beer and Southern hospitality.

Students are quick to add that there are no lines drawn between dorm-dwellers and off-campus renters. UA offers over $100 million of financial aid each year, and many students receive this in the form of free room and board. The cafeterias received mixed reviews from Razorback undergrads. While some students lived on campus for four years and "never got tired of it" others don't think they will "step foot into a dining hall" for a whole year, even if they live in the dorms.

On campus or off, students mix and mingle the nights away on Fayetteville's Dickson Street. Running straight through campus, the street offers so many bars and clubs that "it's hard to keep up with the new names and owners," explains one seasoned senior. Go to George's Majestic Lounge and rub elbows with University of Arkansas alums recounting the nights they spent at the waterhole 50 years ago. Gypsy, Alligator Ray's and Grubb's are just a few of the places that shouldn't be missed during an educational stint in Razorback Country. Even underage students can party with the rest of them on certain nights. Clubs and bars often offer 18-and-over nights, and on big weekends (think Homecoming Weekend versus South Carolina, or 'Bama and Texas games) the whole street is closed off.

"Suuuey, Hogs"

A University of Arkansas education is incomplete without the inclusion of Arkansas athletics. Their unstoppable track program, which has won 17 consecutive indoor titles, and their powerhouse football and basketball teams, are just a few examples of nationally dominant Razorbacks sports. "The weekends are all about sporting events," students explain. "You have to get real geared up for the game, and no matter what, you MUST know the fight songs."

> "Arkansas sporting events are huge, women's or men's, it's just a culture."

With no professional sports teams to root for in the area, the entire Fayetteville community supports their hogs on game day. From the parquet in the Bud Walton Arena to the green grass of the Donald W. Reynolds Razorback Stadium, the thrill of victory (and the stench of keg beer) lingers in the sweet Southern air. Arkansas sports aren't simple weekend entertainment for UA Students. Students reported that "Arkansas sporting events are huge. Women's or men's, it's just a culture."

If a Division I athletic career isn't a personal option, undergrads can still quench their competitive spirits within the confines of HPER (the UA Health, Physical Education, and Recreation building). The $14 million facility is the largest in the area and features 10 racquetball courts, four basketball gyms, an indoor track, an Olympic-size swimming pool, a climbing wall, men's and women's saunas, a computer lab, thousands of lockers, and a human performance lab.

Greek or non-Greek, on campus or off, athlete or academic, Razorbacks are all about one thing: having one hell of a time. If you are looking for a school with tons of school pride nestled in a true Southern college city, then University of Arkansas is the place to be. When you are leaving home, don't forget to pack your Razorback football jersey. You won't regret it.—*Meredith Hudson*

FYI

If you come to Arkansas, you'd better bring "your car or enough money to buy one."

What's the typical weekend schedule? "Friday: hit up a frat party; Saturday: go crazy at the football game, head to the bars at night; Sunday: sleep in, catch up on studying."

If I could change one thing about the University of Arkansas, I would "send more funds to the science department instead of to athletics. Sometimes we lack a sufficient amount of chemicals to perform chemistry experiments."

Three things every student should do before graduating are "attend a Razorback football game and 'call the hogs,' take a class that is taught in Old Main, and eat at Herman's restaurant."

California

California Institute of Technology

Address: 1200 East California Boulevard Pasadena, CA 91125
Phone: 626-395-6341
E-mail address: ugadmissions@caltech.edu
Web site URL: www.caltech.edu
Year Founded: 1891
Private or Public: Private
Religious Affiliation: None
Location: Urban
Number of Applicants: 3,597
Percent Accepted: 16.9%
Percent Accepted who enroll: 38%
Number Entering: 231
Number of Transfers Accepted each Year: 11
Middle 50% SAT range: M: 770–800, CR: 700–780, Wr: 680–770
Middle 50% ACT range: 32–35
Early admission program EA/ED/None: EA

Percentage accepted through EA or ED: Unreported
EA and ED deadline: 1-Nov
Regular Deadline: 1-Jan
Application Fee: $60
Full time Undergraduate enrollment: 913
Total enrollment: 2,126
Percent Male: 59%
Percent Female: 41%
Total Percent Minority or Unreported: 44%
Percent African-American: 1%
Percent Asian/Pacific Islander: 38%
Percent Hispanic: 5%
Percent Native-American: <1%
Percent International: 9%
Percent in-state/out of state: 35%/65%
Percent from Public HS: Unreported
Retention Rate: 98%
Graduation Rate 4-year: 80.0%

Graduation Rate 6-year: 87.0%
Percent Undergraduates in On-campus housing: 90%
Number of official organized extracurricular organizations: 148
3 Most popular majors: Mathematics, Mechanical Engineering, Physics
Student/Faculty ratio: 3:1
Average Class Size: Unreported
Percent of students going to grad school: Unreported
Tuition and Fees: $31,437
In State Tuition and Fees if different: No difference
Cost for Room and Board: $10,146
Percent receiving financial aid out of those who apply, first year: 60%
Percent receiving financial aid among all students: 60%

Many people across the nation just think of football and New Year's parades when they think of Pasadena, but this sunny Southern California suburb is home to more than just the Rose Bowl. For those who are familiar with science, they know that Caltech is home to one of the world's premier research institutions. And for students who are serious about math and science, and looking for opportunities for world-class research, they'll find what they're looking for in the small, close-knit community of Caltech. At this school, students take their education seriously, but they also have fun in an off-beat way, all while sharing the campus with Nobel Prize winners and professors who are the leaders in their fields.

Not for the Faint of Heart

To be blunt, Caltech is not for everyone, and students don't pretend otherwise. Caltech students say that the academics are rigorous and a love for learning and science is definitely necessary. The core curriculum required of all students includes five terms each of math and physics, in addition to classes in chemistry and biology. But don't think students can get through without taking any English classes—although Caltech places an obvious emphasis on math and science, it also requires students to take 12 courses in the humanities and social sciences. For many, making the transition from high school to Caltech's level of academics may be a bit challenging; students describe classes as especially hard. Luckily, students take all classes pass/fail for their first two terms to help them transition and, beyond freshman year, collaboration is always a big part of Caltech life. People typically work in small groups for homework, and exchange answers between groups. "You wouldn't pass if you didn't work with other people," one sophomore said.

Students say most of the work involves lots of problem-solving as opposed to just plug-and-chug with numbers. One student described freshman classes as very intellectual—calculus is proof-based and chemistry classes go beyond the typical high school approach. "I expected that I would be one of the people left behind, since there are so many smart people, but everyone really starts off in the same place," one freshman said. "Most people haven't seen the new material covered since we basically start from scratch—it's much more of a theoretical approach."

Students admit that Caltech's academics can get overwhelming, but that help is readily available for those who seek it, whether it's from friends, classmates, RAs, or free tutors. "You can get help in whatever class you need and if you're sick and can't finish a set, you can get an extension from the health department," one student said. "People are glad to help and it's mutual because even if you're one of the few people who know how to do a problem, you're going to need help on other ones."

A big part of Caltech's academic community is the honor code, which in effect makes almost all exams take-home and trusts undergraduates to time themselves and be honest. One student said, "Undergrads are given a lot of free range and people take it pretty seriously." Students say the honor code is designed not to punish, but to eliminate unfair advantage. "I really like the honor code because it goes into all aspects of Caltech life," said one freshman, who hadn't had any proctored tests yet. "There are open kitchens, and you can leave your door unlocked because people won't steal your stuff unless it's for a prank, but then you'll get it back." And it's exactly this kind of trust that builds a small, close-knit undergraduate community.

Ditching the Books for the Stacks

Sleep deprivation due to late-night problem sets is a regular part of Caltech culture, but don't think that Caltech students skip out on fun. Pranks are very much a part of Caltech culture, and they happen very often. But these go beyond your typical college pranks. A classic example of Caltech fun is the annual Pumpkin Drop, where students use liquid nitrogen to freeze pumpkins and drop them off the tallest building on campus. One of the most popular days on campus is Ditch Day, when school essentially stops—professors even extend set deadlines so that everyone can participate in the fun. The senior class plays hooky for a day, and in order to prevent underclassmen from ransacking their rooms, they block their doors with "stacks." Originally, these were physical blocks made of plywood and concrete intended to prevent anyone from entering, but they've since become complex sets of puzzles planned months or years in advance, intended to occupy the underclassmen's attentions while the seniors are away.

> "It's a lot of hard work, in not very much time, but it's fun."

Students say that Ditch Day consists of people running around solving problems—essentially high-tech, brainy scavenger hunts. "Last year, I worked on a stack that involved rearranging electrical circuits," one sophomore said. "There was one stack where undergrads were given a reprogrammed T1-83 to plug in numbers and get clues to run around campus."

Houses Are Where the Heart Is

Caltech's social scene is dominated by houses, which students describe as a cross between frats and dorms. All students go through Rotation during their first days at Caltech, a process when every freshman eats a meal in each of the eight houses. After getting a feel for the houses, which each have different personalities, the freshmen rank their top three choices and get assigned to the house where they will live for the rest of their time at Caltech. Students say they meet many if not most of their friends through their houses—living in the same dorm and having family-style dinners every day creates a strong bond. "The house system is great because it gives you an instant sense of connection," one student said. "It's not so great for people who don't like the houses they're in, but it works for almost everyone, and you can switch house affiliation."

And at the heart of the housing system are the students of Caltech. Although students admit Caltech has a much higher density of nerds and geeks than your typical school, and that there is an uneven mix of genders, they say that the students make the close-knit community very comfortable. "It's an exceptional group of students," one sophomore said. "People are really interested in science, but you can typically talk to people about any topic and they'll be knowledgeable." Students say there are a certain number of students who stay in their rooms and study all day, but that most people are very outgoing and willing to help out with house events. In response to the stereotype of awkward nerds, one freshman said, "If anything, that helps us bond better, because if there's someone just like you, you're more likely to bond." Even if they're working, most students will leave their doors open and many leave messages on dry-erase whiteboards, keeping the small community connected.

Under Construction

"Our idea of fun is definitely different from most colleges," one freshman said. Students say that partying in the typical college sense of the word isn't very prevalent on campus, but when Caltech students party, they go all out—in an off-beat way, of course. Students don't just go to the local store for red Solo cups; they go to Home Depot to buy two-by-fours for major construction. For all large parties, the houses spend two to three weeks building elaborate structures in their courtyards. One freshman described her house's courtyard: "We built a dance floor about five feet off the floor, and then flooded the entire courtyard two to three feet. We also had fountains and waterfalls." For

Interhouse, one of the biggest parties of the year, all the south houses build similarly elaborate structures in their courtyard, and if students aren't happy with one party, they can hop on over to another party close by. On other days of the year, there are camping trips and pool games and even margarita Mondays.

But despite the fun, students are brought back by the reality of the demands of school. Students point out the high rate of 5–6 year graduations, dropouts and transfers, and say that students need to be able to perform under high pressure. "Even if you're the best, you can still not do well here," one sophomore said. "Being smart and working hard don't guarantee success, and you can't let that drag you down." But if students can get beyond the challenges of hard classes, they'll find a rewarding experience and will have some fun along the way. In fact, they may become one of the many famous physicists, engineers or scientists who have graduated from Caltech and gone on to make a name for themselves in science-related fields, whether in academia, industry or research. Students have the opportunity sample the big leagues as part of professors' research projects, or by getting hands-on experience at the famous Jet Propulsion Laboratory, which Caltech operates for NASA.

Summing up the Caltech experience, one sophomore said, "It's a lot of hard work, in not very much time, but it's fun." This sunny Southern California school may not be for everyone, but if you're dedicated to math and science, willing to work really hard, and can persevere with a sense of humor, then this just might be the school for you. Caltech is a unique experience and, upon graduation, students enjoy the unique benefit of a world-class education and the respect of anyone familiar with the fields of math and science. One student said, "It's not for everyone, but anyone can come here and be accepted, no matter who you are."—*Della Fox*

FYI

If you come to Caltech, you'd better realize "it's not so much what you bring, but what you take out, and how you stay through in the middle."

What's the typical weekend schedule? "Saturday is typically relaxed—playing Frisbee and maybe catching up on sleep a bit. Sunday you work until midnight when you order pizza, and then you work more."

If I could change one thing about Caltech, I'd "make the classes easier so we would have more time to engage in extracurricular activities. And make pass/fail last longer than two terms."

Three things every student at Caltech should do before graduating are "participate in Ditch Day, do SURF (Summer Undergraduate Research Fellowship), and explore the tunnels underneath the campus, which help you get into buildings you wouldn't normally be able to get into."

California Institute of the Arts

Address: 24700 McBean Parkway Valencia, CA 91355
Phone: 661-255-1050
E-mail address: admiss@calarts.edu
Web site URL: www.calarts.edu
Year Founded: 1961
Private or Public: Private
Religious Affiliation: None
Location: Suburban
Number of Applicants: Unreported
Percent Accepted: 32.0%
Percent Accepted who enroll: Unreported
Number Entering: Unreported
Number of Transfers Accepted each Year: Unreported
Middle 50% SAT range: Unreported
Middle 50% ACT range: Unreported
Early admission program EA/ED/None: None

Percentage accepted through EA or ED: NA
EA and ED deadline: NA
Regular Deadline: 4-Jan
Application Fee: $70
Full time Undergraduate enrollment: 820
Total enrollment: 1,317
Percent Male: 54%
Percent Female: 46%
Total Percent Minority or Unreported: 30%
Percent African-American: 9%
Percent Asian/Pacific Islander: 9%
Percent Hispanic: 12%
Percent Native-American: <1%
Percent International: 8%
Percent in-state/out of state: 66%/44%
Percent from Public HS: Unreported
Retention Rate: Unreported
Graduation Rate 4-year: 57.0%

Graduation Rate 6-year: unreported
Percent Undergraduates in On-campus housing: 40%
Number of official organized extracurricular organizations: 5
3 Most popular majors: Acting; Film, Video and Photographic Arts; Visual Performing Arts
Student/Faculty ratio: 7:1
Average Class Size: 12
Percent of students going to grad school: Unreported
Tuition and Fees: $32,860
In State Tuition and Fees if different: No difference
Cost for Room and Board: $3,663
Percent receiving financial aid out of those who apply, first year: Unreported
Percent receiving financial aid among all students: 38%

California Institute of the Arts, a school self-contained in a single building, was supposed to be a haven for artists in the middle of nowhere. Besides the fact that a strip-mall town grew up around it, Cal Arts is pretty much just that: a place for artists to gather and work on their skills. Students who go to Cal Arts love it, but more importantly, they love what they do, making the focused nature of the school perfect for self-motivated artists.

Math and Science? Not really . . .

The 863 undergraduates enrolled in Cal Arts are members of one of six schools, in a range of highly selective BFA programs. One student said that the music technology program accepts around six to eight students each year. Cal Arts only has Bachelor of Fine Arts and Master of Fine Arts programs. To graduate, students not only need to take a certain number of classes within their "métier," what the students interviewed called their discipline, but also need to complete a Critical Studies requirement. Critical Studies are academic subjects, spread over a number of distributional requirements. There are also core classes required of students: a Writing Arts course, which discusses the relationship between art and society, and Foundation courses, which could be on a number of topics. The Foundation courses are geared specifically toward a certain discipline. One photography and media major said that the Foundation course required of all fine arts majors entitled "What Makes it Art," was "kind of a lame class," and featured the only teacher he did not like.

The categories for distributional requirements, the Breadth requirements, include humanities, social sciences, cultural studies, natural sciences, quantitative, métier studies in the student's métier and métier studies in a separate métier. Yes, there is even a quantitative requirement. "But it's art school math, so it's pretty friendly," one student said. Even in the Critical Studies classes, which students take on Wednesdays, there is usually an art bent, the same student said. She said that her paper topic for her philosophy class was to pick three pieces of art and "philosophize about them." Another student said Critical Studies is "kind of the fun way to do something that is out of your métier."

While the classes within the métiers are usually capped around eight to 10 students, Critical Studies classes can have up to about 30. Despite this, students said that there are no 800-student lectures, and all classes are taught with students sitting "in a round," emphasizing student participation. One student, who transferred to Cal Arts from NYU's Tisch School of the Arts, said she preferred the Critical Studies classes at Cal Arts as opposed to the distributional requirements at NYU. The student, who is in the School of Theater's BFA Acting program, said that it was hard to be in classes at NYU with majors in non-art subjects. "The academics are set up for artists and they are very artist friendly," she said. That being said, students agreed that the Critical Studies classes are not particularly challenging. "I can definitely say it is not as challenging as it could be and sometimes I do find myself a little bored," one student said.

"You have to love what you do, because that is basically all you do."

For students at Cal Arts, most of their time, both inside and outside of the classroom is spent concentrating on their métier. "I'm a violin performance major and for my major all I do is focus on music," one student said. Most students interviewed said that the classes within their métier are challenging and require a lot of work outside the classroom. One student stressed that to succeed in métier classes one has to be self-motivated. "The department classes are going to be challenging," the student in the acting program said. "You are going to work really hard. It's easy to sit back, but the kids who do that don't last very long."

Each student is given a mentor in his or her field, and, since the student body is relatively small, that professor only has a small number of students he or she is mentoring, which makes relationships quite casual. Students always call their instructors by their first names. Students praise the instructors, who for the most part are all working professionals. "They have great insight," one student in the dance program said. "It's really different than having someone who has sort have had their career that is sort of over and is teaching. Another student said he liked the fact that while you are showing a teacher your work, that teacher will often turn around and show you theirs as well.

No ABCs

Students at Cal Arts are graded on a pass/fail basis. Upon finishing a course students receive a mark of High Pass, Pass, Low Pass, No Credit or "NX" (incomplete). No credit is essentially the equivalent of failing. If a student chooses to take the class in which he or she received a No Credit again, the previous class will go off their record. Additionally, if a student receives an "Incomplete," he or she is required to finish that class at some point in time. One student, who came to Cal Arts from a high-stress level private school said she appreciates the system of grading. "I take so much more pride in my work because I feel like I am getting positive feedback as opposed to feeling like there is someone out to get me in the grading."

Let's put on a show!

Students at Cal Arts in the performing arts are required to be involved in performances outside of their classroom work, and the facilities are state of the art. The student in the acting program raved about the Disney Modular Theater. The theater—there is only one other like it in the entire world–can transform into anything a production wants it to be. The stage can be raised if that is necessary, or a production can even have a waterfall, like one recent show did. There are also smaller and more casual ways for students to perform. Most students interviewed mentioned the Coffee House, which puts on performances that are student-run, directed, produced and performed. At Cal Arts students interviewed said the focus is interdisciplinary. One student described an instance in which a student in the world music program helped out his friend who is a dance major.

An artists' commune in a conservative town

There are two dorm complexes, one for undergraduates and one for grad students. In Ahmanson, the dorm for graduate students, most of the residents are older, and many have families. Every freshman is required to have a meal plan, but some students end up cooking in their dorm rooms. Since there is no guaranteed housing for undergraduates, many students live off campus. But that doesn't mean they spend a lot of time in Valencia. While students love the Cal Arts campus, the surrounding town of Valencia receives less than rave reviews. "The town of Valencia is like one giant strip mall," one student said. "Basically everything is a chain." She added that students go to Abbey Lane Café, one of the few restaurants that is not a chain in the neighborhood. Cal Arts remains isolated from the town. "The town never knows what is going on," another student said. "It's like the house on the hill in 'Edward Scissorhands.'"

> **"All of the action happens at Cal Arts. It's like the Vatican."**

Despite the fact that Valencia is a suburb of Los Angeles, one student said he does not get the opportunity to go there often since transportation is difficult. There is no easy form of public transportation to get to the city, and once there it is hard to get around without a car. While some students have cars, others who don't often don't want to feel like they are begging rides off of them. "If you don't have a car you can feel like you are in a bubble," he said. "All of the action happens at Cal Arts," another student said. "It's like the Vatican."

The Red Cup Rule

Even though there are not a lot of the big parties that come with Greek life, there is a fair amount of alcohol and drug use on and off campus among students. Most students interviewed agreed that school policy on drug and alcohol use is fairly lax. One student mentioned what she knows as the "red cup rule." The "red cup rule" is an unspoken rule between school security and students. The rule implies that as long as the liquid is protected in a plastic red cup, students can drink anything. "If a security guard sees you with a red cup they can't tell you to throw it away," she said. Another student said, "there is obviously a lot of pot." While there is a lot of pot, harder drugs are rare, although one student said you will hear about the isolated instances of a student going to rehab.

While most students socialized with others in their métier, art gallery openings on Thursdays are a chance for all students to get together. At the gallery openings there is wine and beer for students over 21 years old, and sometimes live music or a DJ. There are also a few famed parties that most students at the school attend, such as the Halloween party. Despite the popularity of the art gallery openings and the Halloween party, one student said that most of the "hardcore parties" are off-campus.

The place for artists

Most students interviewed had trouble finding things to complain about at Cal Arts. For students who really care about their art and want to pursue it as their career, Cal Arts seems to be the perfect place. While there are so many opportunities for artists that one student said a "workaholic" tendency can take over, she emphasized that "it's a really good school if you are self-motivated."—*Esther Zuckerman*

FYIs
If you come to Cal Arts, you'd better bring "receptivity, a willingness to work. If you aren't willing to do the work then you are not going to do very well."
What is the typical weekend schedule? "If I were in a show there would be rehearsal on Saturday and rehearsal on Friday night. Sundays would be off and your free time is your free time. I'd rehearse at some point for a scene in my acting class. At night it's a social hour or its work."
If I could change one thing about Cal Arts, I'd "have online class sign-ups. Everyone just runs for it."
Three things every student at Cal Arts should do before graduating are "put on your own show, live in the dorms for one year and make sure to chill on the hill a lot."

California State University System

The California State system boasts that it comprises the largest and most diverse universities in America. It offers the chance to study everything from marine navigation and technology to mathematics and engineering among its 23 campuses. Geographically too, the University spans from San Diego State—just 18 miles from the Mexican border, to Humboldt State, 774 miles north in Eureka, Calif.

Founded in 1960 and administered by a governor-appointed 25-member Board of Trustees, the CSU system coexists with the University of California system and California Community Colleges to form a trifecta of higher education in the Golden State.

Where to go

With so many options in regards to location, the third-largest state may seem a bit intimidating. To help out, www.csumentor.com eases the application and decision process for prospective undergrads. Each campus offers different programs and has different sized student bodies. Along with the UCs and Community Colleges, the three systems allow a place for every California resident to pursue a degree. Financing an education is easy too—tuition ranges from $4,000 to $21,000 depending on living situation and campus and financial aid opportunities are plentiful.

The wide array of campuses, along with their geographical differences offers prospective students enough choice to satisfy even the most fickle of tastes.

In the Classroom

Though the UC system retains the spotlight, Cal States are no slouch in academics. The system maintains a focus on undergraduate education, as opposed to the larger universities' research-oriented approach.

California Polytechnic—San Luis Obispo's College of Engineering, for example, was ranked No. 1 by U.S. News and World Report for public undergrad engineering schools. One of the first Cal State universities, San Francisco State, offers a world-class cinema department. Cal-Maritime Academy offers the opportunity to study Coast Guard and Naval operations without the requirement of military service.

The Cal State system offers a variety of academic opportunities boasting, "We prepare graduates who go on to make a difference in the workforce."

Sunshine and Sports

All 23 campuses, except CSU–Channel Islands, have either a Division I or Division II, sports program. Cal State Dominguez Hills sent their No. 9 ranked men's soccer team to the national semifinals before the Toros' championship run was cut short in a 3-2 double overtime defeat to Tampa. CSU–Northridge, affectionately known as cee-sun, boasts a long sports tradition. The Matadors men's basketball squad finished second in the Big West to UC–Santa Barbara.

Many CSU schools compete in the Big West league while six campuses participate in the Mountain Pacific Sports Federation. With the sun shining year-round, IM and club sports are also popular.

With the draw of a diverse student body, numerous options in location and academic course of study, the California State University system retains a vital role to California's higher education.—*Brittany Golob*

California Polytechnic State / San Luis Obispo

Address: Admissions Office
San Luis Obispo, CA 93407
Phone: 805-756-2311
E-mail address:
admissions@calpoly.edu
Web site URL:
www.calpoly.edu
Year Founded: 1901
Private or Public: Public
Religious Affiliation: None
Location: Suburban
Number of Applicants:
33,352
Percent Accepted: 33.5%
**Percent Accepted who
enroll:** 31%
Number Entering: 3,501
**Number of Transfers
Accepted each Year:**
1,623
Middle 50% SAT range:
M: 570–680, CR:
530–630, Wr:** Unreported
Middle 50% ACT range:
24–29
**Early admission program
EA/ED/None:** ED

**Percentage accepted
through EA or ED:**
Unreported
EA and ED deadline: 31-Oct
Regular Deadline: 30-Nov
Application Fee: $55
**Full time Undergraduate
enrollment:** 18,516
Total enrollment: 19,777
Percent Male: 56%
Percent Female: 44%
**Total Percent Minority or
Unreported:** 24%
Percent African-American:
1%
**Percent Asian/Pacific
Islander:** 11%
Percent Hispanic: 11%
Percent Native-American:
<1%
Percent International: 1%
**Percent in-state/out of
state:** 96%/4%
Percent from Public HS:
Unreported
Retention Rate: 90%
Graduation Rate 4-year: 23%

Graduation Rate 6-year:
70.0%
**Percent Undergraduates in
On-campus housing:**
29%
**Number of official organized
extracurricular
organizations:** 375
3 Most popular majors:
Engineering, Business,
Agriculture
Student/Faculty ratio: 19:1
Average Class Size:
Unreported
**Percent of students going to
grad school:** 20%
Tuition and Fees: $15,213
**In State Tuition and Fees if
different:** $5,043
Cost for Room and Board:
$9,369
**Percent receiving financial
aid out of those who apply,
first year:** 43%
**Percent receiving financial
aid among all students:**
Unreported

A manageable distance from both San Francisco and Los Angeles, California Polytechnic State University San Luis Obispo (often known as Cal Poly) can be said to have the best of all worlds: Northern and Southern California, many academic and extracurricular options, and a balance between urban and suburban environments.

Out of the Classroom and Beyond Four Years

One of the best parts of Cal Poly's academic program is its emphasis on engaging students with real-world experience. Cal Poly's official motto is "Learn by doing," and students often find themselves doing just that at school. Notable projects have included the business plans for Jamba Juice, the San Luis Obispo public transportation system and urbandictionary.com, and many courses involve hands-on projects that require implementation in the community or field at large. One student described a final project he did for a marketing class, which involved surveying several hundred people and writing a detailed marketing proposal for a local company.

At the same time, several students complained about the difficulty of getting into courses required for graduation, particularly general education classes. In addition to their major-related courses, students are required to take general education classes distributed across communication, science and technology, arts and humanities, social, political, economic institutions, life understanding and technology. The administration's effort to keep overall course sizes lower has made getting into these classes more difficult, but this often forces students to choose between sacrificing summers to take supplementary coursework or remaining at Cal Poly for a fifth year to finish remaining requirements.

Students apply to Cal Poly with an academic major in mind, and enrolled students say that this has helped to shape their college experience. "People are really focused on what they want to do, and that helped me to make connections right away," one third-year student raved. Some of the stronger academic programs students described were the engineering, accounting, and business majors; one senior also named the architecture and construction management programs as being very strong. Students from different disciplines describe the academic experience at Cal Poly very differently, with some students complaining of "more schoolwork than I ever could have imagined" and others describing their classes as "ridiculously easy." Some of the easier college majors identified were the recreation administration and marketing programs.

Building a Beautiful Campus

"They're doing all kinds of construction," said one student of the Cal Poly campus. The aerospace department recently received a new building, and current projects include the expansion of the recreation center. Popular student hangout areas include the business building and the University Union. Students convene at the student union on Thursdays at 11 a.m. for "UU Hour," during which most students do not have class and the student union sponsors bands.

Like at many public universities, the school only guarantees housing freshman year, although there are separate facilities for transfer students and a set of on-campus apartments for second years. Students may select to be in dorms based on major if they choose, and buildings change in personality each year. One student described the mixed dorm FYC (First Year Connection) as being the most fun, but acknowledged that the major-affiliated dorms can provide valuable connections. Cal Poly is a dry campus, and alcohol is prohibited in the dorms; one student described RAs as "strict, but can be cool about rules if you get to know them."

Students living in dormitories must purchase a meal plan, and students may eat at a number of on-campus dining facilities, including the Garden Grille, which serves restaurant-like options. However be warned, as one student described campus food as being "among the top 10 worst in the country." Nearby off-campus eating options include J.D. Boones Smokehouse and Woodstock's pizza, both of which are frequented by students. The vast majority of students are quick to move off campus after freshman year, and the city of San Luis Obispo provides a number of reasonably priced housing options. Many of them are farther away, though, and can make owning a car to get to class a necessity.

Close to the Beach and the Mountains

When not studying, many Cal Poly students were quick to name the beach as a frequent destination. With Pismo and Avila beaches short distances away and a reasonably warm temperature year-round, sand and surf time is a regular extracurricular activity.

Unlike at many public schools, the Cal Poly student body is not engulfed in its sports teams. "Football games are free and we have a tiny stadium," remarked one student, and, although the Mustangs have several NCAA Division I teams, most students express little or no interest in attending collegiate sports events. Instead, the social scene is largely dominated by clubs. One notable club is the Central Pacific Ski Club, known to take three to four hundred students skiing several times a year. Other club options include Poly Escapes, which takes students on trips all over the state, the Rose Bowl Float Building Club, which devotes its time to producing a float for the Rose Bowl, and a number of popular professional clubs sponsored by the school. The student body also rallies around "Open House," a weekend-long event put on for prospective students including a tractor pull, parade and rodeo.

> "People are really focused on what they want to do, and that helped me to make connections right away."

Students say differing things about Cal Poly's student body. One student described the student body as having a lot less diversity than he anticipated when enrolling at Cal Poly. "Sometimes it feels like just a lot of rich white kids," said one graduating senior, while another student remarked that the relaxed and diverse student environment was her favorite part about Cal Poly.

Cal Poly has a Greek community, but it's not prominent, and "the University has been cracking down on the frats, bigtime," kicking several of the larger fraternities off campus and threatening the same to others. Alternatively on weekend nights, students go to off-campus parties and bars. Popular bars include Bulls, McCarthy's (known for being the biggest purchaser of Jameson's whiskey in the country) and the Frog and Peach Pub (formerly owned by Scott and Lacey Peterson). Each Thursday night, downtown is blocked off for the weekly Farmer's Market, which many students attend to enjoy good food and inexpensive drinks.

Cal Poly offers its students a valuable way to spend four (or five) exciting years in a beautiful California environment, and prospective students can also look forward to taking advantage of the many academic, social, and local opportunities the college provides.—*Stephanie Teng*

FYI

If you come to Cal Poly, you'd better bring "a swimsuit or a surfboard."

If I could change one thing about Cal Poly, I'd "change the locals' perception of Cal Poly students."

What's the typical weekend schedule? "Friday: hit the bars and clubs and then off campus parties; Saturday: beach during the day and then fraternity parties at night; Sunday: Frank's Famous Hot Dogs for breakfast burritos, do some homework and then barbecue for the rest of the day or night."

Three things every student should do before graduating are "a bulls sweat on their birthday, see sunrise at Pismo Beach, and hike Bishop's Peak."

California State University / Chico

Address: 400 West First Street Chico, CA 95929-0722
Phone: 530-898-4428
E-mail address: INFO@csuchico.edu
Web site URL: www.csuchico.edu
Year Founded: 1887
Private or Public: Public
Religious Affiliation: None
Location: Urban
Number of Applicants: 15,069
Percent Accepted: 87.4%
Percent Accepted who enroll: 21%
Number Entering: 2,765
Number of Transfers Accepted each Year: 3,082
Middle 50% SAT range: M: 460–570, CR: 450–550, Wr: Unreported
Middle 50% ACT range: 19–24
Early admission program EA/ED/None: None

Percentage accepted through EA or ED: NA
EA and ED deadline: NA
Regular Deadline: 30-Nov
Application Fee: $55
Full time Undergraduate enrollment: 15,804
Total enrollment: 17,034
Percent Male: 48%
Percent Female: 51%
Total Percent Minority or Unreported: 22%
Percent African-American: 2%
Percent Asian/Pacific Islander: 6%
Percent Hispanic: 13%
Percent Native-American: 1.0%
Percent International: 2%
Percent in-state/out of state: 98%/2%
Percent from Public HS: Unreported
Retention Rate: 79%
Graduation Rate 4-year: 15%

Graduation Rate 6-year: 52.0%
Percent Undergraduates in On-campus housing: 1%
Number of official organized extracurricular organizations: 192
3 Most popular majors: Business Administration, Liberal Arts, Psychology
Student/Faculty ratio: 22:1
Average Class Size: 23
Percent of students going to grad school: Unreported
Tuition and Fees: $14,178
In State Tuition and Fees if different: $4,008
Cost for Room and Board: $8,718
Percent receiving financial aid out of those who apply, first year: 88%
Percent receiving financial aid among all students: 87%

For students who want to experience the relaxed yet festive atmosphere of a true "college town," California State University at Chico may be the ideal school. The University is located in the northern part of California in a city that can best be described as "a small town located in the middle of nowhere." However, what Chico State lacks in location, it makes up for in the friendliness of the students and faculty and the type of open welcome that only a small town can provide.

Personable Academics

CSU Chico offers 66 undergraduate majors in a number of distinct colleges, including Agriculture; Behavioral and Social Sciences; Business; Communication and Education; Engineering; Computer Science and Construction Management; Humanities and Fine Arts; and Natural Sciences. Students must fulfill a number of general education courses in order to graduate. These requirements include 12 units of Area A, or "Skills," 27 units of Areas B–E, or "Breadth," and nine units of upper division courses. The comprehensive GEs reveal that CSU isn't all about social life; in fact, the curriculum can be quite challenging. One student was quick to point out that "Chico has recently become a lot tougher academically."

> **"Most faculty members are very close with their students. It's a great benefit."**

However the administration at Chico makes a concerted effort to create an enjoyable academic experience, and it shows in CSU's comparatively high retention rate. One of the most impressive facets of the academic system is student-professor relationships. One student boasted that "most faculty members are very close with students. It's a great benefit." This type of relationship is made possible thanks to small class sizes, the average class being only 27 students. Another benefit is the ease with which students are able to select classes they want—registration takes place through personal Portal accounts. Another option for the high-achieving Chico student is the honors program. This program is made available to incoming freshman with a 3.5 GPA or higher. If admitted into the program students receive academic luxuries like individual attention from professors, small classes, and off-campus Honors Houses. For those students just looking for an easy A, Chico has obliged them with classes like "American Sports in Film" and "Lifetime Fitness."

Middle of Nowhere . . . So What?

Students don't really seem to mind the isolated location; instead they take advantage of being set among the foothills of the beautiful Sierra Nevada Mountains. Most are more than pleased with their scenic surroundings—"It's really picturesque!" one student exclaimed.

Chico boasts a plethora of clubs and organizations, many that reap the benefits from its surrounding areas. The "Chico Snow Club is a bunch of people who party and go snowboarding," and the Adventure Outings organization is a university-sponsored program that promotes outdoor expeditions. Expeditions like white-water rafting and hiking trips are among the most popular. Along with being near the sixth-largest waterfall in the country, Chico students pride themselves on their annual tubing event along the Sacramento River. Though the Labor Day event is quite dangerous and can lead to arrests, some still brave the adventure.

One Big Slumber Party

The largest freshman dorm is also the tallest building in all of Chico. Whitney Hall is nine stories high and houses both lots of first-years and the only dining hall. Students can also use their meal cards at eateries around campus, such as the recently revamped Bell Memorial Union. The housing department is planning to add a new dining center as well as additional residence space. Reviews of the existing dorms are better than average. Most students are assigned doubles and the rest live in triples and are happy with their living situation. Both alcohol rules and security are reportedly tight. Moreover, when entering the dorm, students must check in themselves and any visitors they may have. Since it is a dry campus, students are not allowed to bring alcohol into their rooms. Officials look through any bags the student is carrying to ensure the rules are not broken. To further enforce the strict alcohol rules, two RAs live on each floor. Upperclassmen usually move off campus into apartments or houses. One student noted that "compared to many other colleges, off-campus housing in Chico is dirt-cheap."

Go Wildcats!

Chico students have a strong sense of pride in their athletic teams, and with good reason—in a recent year, 10 of their 13 athletic teams saw postseason playoffs. The basketball and baseball games are among the most popular and well-attended. Most student attention is focused on intramural competition, and the two most popular and competitive IMs are flag football and soccer. The gym facilities are only decent, so most students opt for an off-campus gym membership. For those who enjoy outdoor activities, Bidwell Park is a popular destination. The park offers a number of swimming holes as well as trails for biking, jogging and hiking.

In 2005, students passed a referendum to build a state-of-the-art recreation center, which is scheduled to open in 2009. A new Student Services Center opened in the summer of 2008. For those who enjoy the arts, BMU auditorium and Chico Performances attract many top acts.

Parties Done Right

If there is one thing a Chico student knows how to do, it is how to party. Just check the local liquor store on any given Tuesday, Thursday, Friday or Saturday; there is often a line that winds its way out into the street. Ivy Street is also made popular by all the Greek Houses located within close proximity. The Greek system is the predominant force in the Chico social scene. However, the Greeks aren't the only ones having a good time. There are plenty of other party options like house parties or downtown bars to keep the students entertained.

A perfect end to a long night of fiestas is Franky's Pizza; another late-night food option is Tacos de Acapulco, which is "the best Mexican food in Chico, but it only tastes good when you are drunk!" While Chico students party on regular days, they go out for holidays as well—including Labor Day's "tubing" and Halloween. In the end, Chico students enjoy a vibrant social life, vast academic options, and close personal attention from professors, all in the picturesque setting of Northern California.—*Kelly Cooper*

FYI
If you come to Chico State, you'd better bring "a spirit for the outdoors."
What's the typical weekend schedule? "Friday: bars; Saturday: party, hiking; Sunday: relax."
If I could change one thing about Chico State, I'd "make the drinking rules more lenient."
Three things every student at Chico State should do before graduating are "float down the river, go to the Farmer's Market, and participate in an Adventure Outing."

California State University / Fresno

Address: 5150 North Maple Ave. M/S JA 57 Fresno, CA 93740-8026
Phone: 559-278-2261
E-mail address: admissions@csufresno.edu
Web site URL: www.csufresno.edu
Year Founded: 1911
Private or Public: Public
Religious Affiliation: None
Location: Urban
Number of Applicants: 14,537
Percent Accepted: 70.1%
Percent Accepted who enroll: 27%
Number Entering: 2,823
Number of Transfers Accepted each Year: 2,798
Middle 50% SAT range: M: 410–540, CR: 400–510, Wr: Unreported
Middle 50% ACT range: 16–22
Early admission program EA/ED/None: None

Percentage accepted through EA or ED: NA
EA and ED deadline: NA
Regular Deadline: 1-Feb
Application Fee: $55
Full time Undergraduate enrollment: 19,245
Total enrollment: 21,728
Percent Male: 43%
Percent Female: 57%
Total Percent Minority or Unreported: 56%
Percent African-American: 6%
Percent Asian/Pacific Islander: 16%
Percent Hispanic: 34%
Percent Native-American: <1%
Percent International: 1%
Percent in-state/out of state: Unreported
Percent from Public HS: 99.0%
Retention Rate: 82%
Graduation Rate 4-year: 15.0%

Graduation Rate 6-year: 46.0%
Percent Undergraduates in On-campus housing: 6%
Number of official organized extracurricular organizations: 250
3 Most popular majors: Health Sciences, Liberal Arts and Sciences
Student/Faculty ratio: Unreported
Average Class Size: Unreported
Percent of students going to grad school: Unreported
Tuition and Fees: $13,857
In State Tuition and Fees if different: $3,687
Cost for Room and Board: $8,590
Percent receiving financial aid out of those who apply, first year: 80%
Percent receiving financial aid among all students: Unreported

If you come to the city of Fresno on a typical Saturday afternoon, you might be engulfed in a sea of red. "The whole town comes out" for University tailgates and football games, taking over the campus and celebrating their successful team. But California State University, Fresno, or "Fresno State," has even more to offer than great athletics. The student body invests pride in not only its strong agriculture programs, but a wide range of popular academic offerings, ranging from criminology and education to preparation for jobs in the health profession. Students looking for a state school that provides diversity, a "laid-back but ambitious" atmosphere, and plenty of opportunities for involvement in the heart of California should give Fresno State a closer look.

Not Just an Ag School

Students at Fresno State are required to take a wide range of specific classes over their first two years to fulfill their General Education credits. These courses, which are classified as Foundation, Breadth, Integration and Multicultural/International, are designed to give undergraduates a broad base of knowledge along with their specialized areas of study. Foundation covers oral and written communication, critical thinking, and quantitative reasoning; Breadth includes physical and life sciences and arts and humanities. Integration courses are upper-division versions of these offerings, and the Multicultural/International requirements provide insights into international relations and countries around the world. Some students say that, as far as GE classes are concerned, "If you show up and do your work, you'll be fine," but others complain that the requirements "are a real pain—I feel like I'm wasting my time taking so many of these courses when I would rather have more focus on my interests."

Students feel that Fresno State offers a good liberal arts background—the most popular majors include teaching and business. On the other hand, one senior griped that "the sciences are not well developed or taken care of—the humanities are more straightforward." One of the school's most distinguishing features is its agriculture program; Fresno is perfectly situated in the richly cultivated San Joaquin Valley and includes a 1,022-acre University Farm. In particular, students mention the viticulture program, which teaches participants about winemaking in the school's very own vineyard. Overall students report that, while grading is fair and

people don't do much work on the weekends, "A lot of people get really stressed out around midterms and finals, maybe because they skip classes during the semester."

Underclassmen also complained about being able to sign up for their courses, saying that "seniors are given top priority, and freshmen are last, which can really make it difficult getting into some of the courses you want." However, few had problems with inordinately large class sizes, since many classes are capped at 30, and the occasional large lecture class has around 200 members. Students praised their professors for being "helpful and available," although many feel people don't take as much advantage of office hours as they should. One senior stated, "My professor was really surprised when I came to his office—apparently, it doesn't happen that often." The school also offers many tutoring options, such as a writing lab, that struggling students use to keep their grades up.

Variety of Social Options

A great deal of Fresno's social scene centers around the football team. Weekend games are elaborate events that entail rowdy tailgates in the campus parking lots, cheering yourself hoarse in the stands, and usually after-parties in the frats. The frats and sororities have a "pretty big presence on campus, and their parties are popular." They often have themed parties, such as "Pimps and Hos" and toga parties. In general, "the police don't shut them down unless things are really out of control."

Another big party sector at Fresno State is present in the apartments near campus, where many students choose to live. One freshman girl who lives in the apartments said that "on the weekends, no one sleeps." Students say that, in general, "everyone drinks—from what I've seen, maybe two people don't," and smoking is not uncommon, but anything harder than that is rare. There have been a few binge-drinking incidents, but "people are usually just social drinkers, not drinking to get hammered."

There are "tons of places around campus to eat or go shopping—I think every major store or restaurant on the West Coast is present here," a junior girl said. Some students venture farther off campus to areas like the Tower District, which offers a more unique experience with its thrift stores and clubs, even though it "isn't as advertised as it should be."

Fresno State's University Student Union (USU) also provides students with entertainment a little closer to home, including a food court, a post office, a lounge, and a recreation center complete with bowling, billiards, video games, and more. The University also puts on a number of events throughout the year. The new Save Mart Center often hosts concerts, counting Prince and Britney Spears among its recent attractions. Big annual events include Vintage Days, when the University invites local bands and offers activities like wine tasting, and the Top Dog Alumni Awards, when students are recognized for contributions to the school and community. However, "the sad thing is that few students really care that much about these events. The school needs to step it up and get better attractions if they want a lot of people to come."

While "it's difficult to describe a typical Fresno student because there's so much diversity," many people are from the Fresno County area, and nearly everyone is from California. Guys are "usually into sports" and girls are a "happy medium between really fashionable and laid-back." In general, "people here are really cool and chill," and there aren't problems with making friends. Students feel that there is a very strong feeling of diversity on campus, in part because it has a large Hispanic population, as well as many Asian-Americans and African-Americans.

Living in Fresno

Students who choose to live in the dorms can decide between the community and the suite options. In the community-style dorms, there is a guys' side and a girls' side to each floor, separated by a common lounge area, with two bathrooms and two RAs. In the suites, six people share a common room and a bathroom. All the rooms are doubles, often with bunk beds. The dorms are dry, and "the RAs are very strict if they catch you with alcohol." On the other hand, "they will take care of you if you're in bad shape after a night of partying, so you shouldn't be afraid of going to them for help." People "spend a lot of time hanging out in the dorms," where "they leave their doors open and people can just walk in and talk if they want to." But, if you want on-campus housing, you'd better be on top of the applications, because "they fill up very quickly—in fact, some people are still living in a hotel because there were more people who wanted to live in the dorms than the school anticipated."

A lot of students choose to move off campus into apartments, which are plentiful, close to campus and affordable. One girl said enthusiastically that "it gives me more freedom, plus the social scene out here is

great." However, students caution against discounting the dorms right away, since that's where many of them met their friends. It's also easy to move off campus into Greek housing, which is another popular option.

A meal plan is not required, but there are quite a few options if you choose to purchase one. There is one central dining hall, the Residence Dining Facility, which some students not-so-affectionately nickname "RD-Barf." However, others say the food "isn't that bad—I was expecting much worse, but I eat the same thing every day." Meal plans can include flex points which students use to buy food at the Student Union restaurants, which include Panda Express, Subway and Taco Bell.

The dominant theme of the campus architecture is "old and brick," but there are new buildings scattered around as well. Students say proudly that "a lot goes into campus maintenance," resulting in picturesque lawns and greenery. Fresno State has been undergoing a lot of renovation recently, including the expansion of the Henry Madden Library.

Students say that "just about everyone has a car, and if you don't have one, you're probably getting one next semester." A lot of people make weekend trips to Cal Poly San Luis Obispo, which is about an hour and a half away, and others even drive north to the Bay Area or south to Los Angeles, since Fresno is directly in-between the two locations. Cars are also useful since a sizeable portion of the student body (students estimate as much as 25 percent) commute from their homes in the Fresno area. While it doesn't mean that the campus is dead on the weekends, "it can get kind of quiet sometimes." Fresno State offers a good opportunity for students looking for an education close to home.

"Fresno State is the city of Fresno!"

All in all, "Fresno State *is* the city of Fresno," since both have developed together. The school is such a dominant presence in the area, providing jobs and opportunities for the community, that "although Fresno is not really a college town, the city really does a lot to make things nicer for college kids." Students report feeling safe walking around campus and the surrounding area, as well as enjoying the support of the many local businesses, which "always have Fresno State posters and paraphernalia up."

Go Bulldogs

If you haven't noticed already, "Sports are huge here!" The football team's successes have "really boosted school spirit," encouraging the school and "what seems like everyone who lives in Fresno County" to come out to the games and support the Bulldogs. Other popular sports are basketball and baseball. The school supports its athletic teams with stunning facilities, such as the new Save Mart Center, two gyms, and a new two-story fitness center that includes an indoor track and pool. You don't have to be a stellar athlete to get in on the action, though, because "intramural sports are also really popular," encouraging many students to play everything from inner-tube water polo to ultimate Frisbee.

Fresno State also boasts a large number of student organizations, which range from the Bulldogger Rodeo Club to the Meat Science Club. Some of the most popular include the Campus Crusade for Christ, the Salsa Club, and various cultural organizations. Generally, "people are very committed to their extracurricular activities, and there are a ton to choose from!" In addition, "almost everyone has a job because so many of us are paying our own college tuition." Competition for on-campus jobs can be tough, but there are so many businesses in the surrounding area that "if you want a job, you'll be able to find one somewhere." Students don't report much of a problem balancing their jobs with schoolwork on the whole.

If you're a California student looking for a school not too far from home that will offer myriad opportunities for your next four years, Fresno State may be the perfect school for you. Along with its strong agricultural tradition, Fresno also provides its students with good preparation in other disciplines, giving them a wide field of experience with which to face the world after college. Just don't forget your Bulldog spirit!—*Kimberly Chow*

FYI
If you come to Fresno State, you'd better bring "all of your red clothing to show your Bulldog spirit!"
What's the typical weekend schedule? "College Night on Thursday, going to bars, a football or basketball game, chilling."
If I could change one thing about Fresno State, I'd "make the nightlife better—there isn't a lot for people under 21, and frat parties get old."
Three things every student at Fresno should do before graduating are: "Go to a football game, go to the Tower District, and go snowboarding or tubing at Sierra Summit."

The Claremont Colleges

The Claremont Colleges are a cluster of five small liberal arts colleges and two graduate schools nestled in a suburban valley about 35 miles east of Los Angeles. The member colleges are Claremont McKenna, Harvey Mudd, Pitzer, Pomona and Scripps, as well as Claremont Graduate University and Keck Graduate Institute, both of which are separate from the undergraduate colleges. Each college is independent, with its own faculty, campus and academic focus. However, the schools' proximity to one another gives their respective students the best of both worlds: the feel of a small institution with the resources of a large university.

Academic Integration

Cross-registration of classes between the colleges is easy and commonplace. The five campuses make up about 12 blocks total, so commuting is not a problem. Since each college has a particular academic focus and expertise, students can take advantage of specialized instruction in almost every subject. Claremont McKenna offers over 25 majors with strengths in economics, government and international relations. Harvey Mudd specializes in science and engineering with the option of a five-year master's program. Pitzer offers liberal arts majors with an emphasis on social and behavioral sciences. Pomona offers a variety of majors in arts, humanities, and social and natural sciences with a paraprofessional bent. Scripps is a liberal arts college for women. All the libraries are integrated as is the campus bookstore.

Campus-wide Activities

The Claremont Colleges are also linked through athletic, social and extracurricular activities. Pitzer and Pomona together comprise a NCAA Division III team, while Claremont McKenna, Harvey Mudd and Scripps make up another. However, most athletic competition usually occurs between the schools. Parties thrown in one college draw people from the other colleges. And there are several all-college parties thrown throughout the year. Many student organizations are composed of undergrads from all the colleges, including *The Collage*, the student daily newspaper; the Claremont Colleges Model U.N., and the Claremont Shades,

an a cappella group. The Claremont Center is the hub for social groups, organizations, and administrations on each campus, and orchestrates the activities of all five schools.

As integrated as the five colleges are, they still retain distinct characteristics, and prospective students should look to find the right fit. As one student summed it up, "It's really a matter of your academic interests as well as your personality. There is something for everyone at each of the colleges, but one college will definitely be the best fit."—*Seung Lee*

Claremont McKenna College

Address: 890 Columbia Avenue Claremont, CA 91711
Phone: 909-621-8088
E-mail address: admission@claremontmckenna.edu
Web site URL: www.claremontmckenna.edu
Year Founded: 1946
Private or Public: Private
Religious Affiliation: None
Location: Suburban
Number of Applicants: 3,670
Percent Accepted: 21.8%
Percent Accepted who enroll: 40%
Number Entering: 320
Number of Transfers Accepted each Year: 86
Middle 50% SAT range: M: 660–750, CR: 630–740, Wr: Unreported
Middle 50% ACT range: Unreported

Early admission program EA/ED/None: ED
Percentage accepted through EA or ED: 28%
EA and ED deadline: 15-Nov
Regular Deadline: 2-Jan
Application Fee: $60
Full time Undergraduate enrollment: 1,211
Total enrollment: 1,211
Percent Male: 54%
Percent Female: 46%
Total Percent Minority or Unreported: 28%
Percent African-American: 4%
Percent Asian/Pacific Islander: 12%
Percent Hispanic: 11%
Percent Native-American: <1%
Percent International: 6%
Percent in-state/out of state: 46%/54%
Percent from Public HS: Unreported

Retention Rate: 97%
Graduation Rate 4-year: 90%
Graduation Rate 6-year: 94%
Percent Undergraduates in On-campus housing: 98%
Number of official organized extracurricular organizations: 280
3 Most popular majors: Economics, International Relations, Political Science
Student/Faculty ratio: 8:1
Average Class Size: 16.8
Percent of students going to grad school: Unreported
Tuition and Fees: $37,060
In State Tuition and Fees if different: No difference
Cost for Room and Board: $11,930
Percent receiving financial aid out of those who apply, first year: 45%
Percent receiving financial aid among all students: 51%

For any student who wishes they could have the nurturing, close-knit environment of many liberal arts schools on the East Coast but balks at the thought of New England weather, Claremont McKenna College offers the best of both coasts. Located at the foot of the San Gabriel Mountains in the suburban town of Claremont, California, the College is roughly three hours from Las Vegas and less than an hour

away from Los Angeles. Somewhat closer, however, are the four other schools that comprise the Claremont consortium. This close proximity to other colleges gives Claremont McKenna the feel of a larger university, despite its relatively small undergraduate enrollment of just over 1,200 students. In addition, students have the chance to utilize the resources—from dining halls to parties—of their neighboring institutions. Whether to take advantage of that larger community or to remain within the cozy campus of Claremont McKenna is the personal choice of each student; every "CMC-er" can attend a college that is truly whatever size they wish.

Academics on Lockdown

Claremont McKenna's academic requirements, on the other hand, are somewhat less fluid. Students must fulfill eleven General Education (GE) requirements that include taking required classes in four disciplines—including science and mathematics, literature, social sciences and humanities—as well as show proficiency in a foreign language and satisfy a physical education requirement. The nine or ten additional requirements for each major leave underclassmen with relatively little freedom of choice when it comes to their course loads. One freshman lamented, "It's stricter than I'd like it to be. As a freshman, you're pretty much locked in because you have to get these requirements out of the way. It's frustrating not being able to take some of the really good courses that you know are out there."

The upside to the broad range of mandated classes, however, is that by the end of their sophomore year, when it is recommended that GE requirements be completed, CMC students have a rich educational base from which to select their major. "They really emphasize a liberal arts education here. They want you to be grounded in a wide range of things before you decide what you want to study. You really have to test everything out," said one student who is a fan of the broad range of requirements. The college is known for its exceptional programs in government, international relations, and economics. According to one student, the government professors are "the most well-known on campus," while another added that "the economics professors are notoriously the most difficult." The strength of those three programs also leads to a semiserious stereotype among the students at the Claremont Colleges that Claremont McKennans are "capitalist, conservative, power-hungry maniacs."

"We aren't so big in the sciences," remarked one student. "At least half the people I know are majoring in econ." Nonetheless, students who pursue the premed course of study still perform well above the national average; recently, 70% of them were accepted to medical school. Other programs have a strong pre-professional focus; the newspaper editor-in-chief remarked that

"It's a school-wide event when top consulting and investment banker firms come in for recruitment."

Before students can choose a major or a career, however, they must register for classes. The process is still done manually and can seem fairly arbitrary, with students being assigned a time to register for classes and sometimes finding themselves at the mercy of their scheduled time slot. "The people who get the times earlier in the day definitely benefit from that," one student said. "Class sizes are also kept small, which can be a problem." Yet perseverance, combined with the friendly atmosphere for which the school is known, can often overcome the inconvenience of registration. "If you really want to take a class, you can," one freshman said. "I just showed up to all the classes I wanted to take and the professors were willing to let me in."

Additionally, students may take advantage of programs, classes and majors offered at the other four Colleges. Undergraduates have the ability to cross-register for off-campus courses, and if they choose an off-campus major from another school's department they may submit their required senior thesis to the sponsoring college's department in lieu of writing their CMC thesis.

While cross-registering can give Claremont McKenna the feel of a larger college, students agree that the school's small size usually makes for a decidedly intimate and personal classroom experience. "My largest class has 20 students, and we're really on a family member basis with our teachers. We go to dinner with them pretty often," said one student. In addition to forming friendships outside the classroom, faculty members and students have generally good academic relationships. One freshman observed that while much of the grading for his classes is done on a curve, his teachers are not unreasonable when it comes to distribution of A's. "The teachers really want you to do well. No one is out to trick you, but there also are no easy teachers. It's really up to the student." Professors really work to make themselves accessible beyond their standard office hours, with some even handing out their cell phone numbers.

No Frats? Who Cares?

While CMC's lack of Greek life sets it apart from many other college campuses, the social scene hardly suffers as a result. In fact, with four other schools close by, students say that people who are eager to go out are never at a loss for a party—in fact, they have five different campus party scenes to choose from. "When one campus is hosting an especially big or good party, everyone else from the Five C's will go there too. There's a lot of interaction between schools," said one student.

"Every Thursday, there's a huge themed party," explained another. "We've had a resort theme, rock star night, a black and white party. Harvey Mudd even threw a foam party—and they made their own foam." These theme parties are organized by the upperclassmen in individual dorms but are usually held outside. Dorms even have funds earmarked for buying alcohol for such events, a practice that is indicative of the administration's view towards alcohol on campus. One student says, "The alcohol policy is very, very lax. Officially the school doesn't condone it, but it's certainly very lax. The school provides a keg to anyone over the age of 21 who wants to host a party, and they are then responsible for carding at parties. But that rarely happens."

The general consensus on campus is that the campus security staff is primarily there to protect students rather than break up parties or arrest anyone who's underage and imbibing. In fact, the campus has what is known as "a red cup policy"—as long as students carry their alcohol around campus in a cup rather than a bottle, they run into very few problems with the administration. While students feel that "the social scene does center around drinking," Claremont McKenna makes an extra effort to plan social events like movie nights for non-drinkers. "There's an entire committee set up on campus that plans weekly sober activities. I mean, drinking is a big part of being at CMC. But if you don't, it's no big deal."

Sticking to "The Five C's"
In general, the school's social scene extends only as far as the campuses of the other Five C's; students report trips to Claremont, or "the Village," as relatively rare—especially for anyone looking to go out. "We don't really go to bars in Claremont. I don't know if there are any bars here," one student commented.

While the relations between town residents and students are thought to range from "non-existent" to "fine," students sometimes spot "townies" or "drunk Claremont high school kids" at campus parties. In general, however, students have limited but cordial contact with Claremont residents and choose to stick close to home; this sentiment is supported by the overwhelming majority of students, about 97 percent, who opt to live on campus all four years.

Despite the popularity of campus living arrangements, not every student is as enthusiastic about the campus itself. As one student said, "Everything is in really good shape, but I just can't stand the architecture. It's all stucco, and the campus is made up of all these one- or two-story buildings. It's really different in that regard from East Coast Schools."

Even so, many students are content to stay on campus as much as possible, though one student deemed a car (or at least a friend with one) as "definitely a necessity." This campus-centric outlook applies to many aspects of student life. Rather than eat at restaurants in Claremont itself, most students opt to swipe at one of any of the five colleges' dining halls—Harvey Mudd has Steak Night every Sunday, "the best dining halls are at Scripps and Pomona," and free snacks are served each night at 10:30 p.m. While the student center, ironically called "The Hub," is not a very popular gathering spot, many students enjoy hanging out on the school's social North Quad, which is also home to dorms. "People spend a lot of time out there, which makes life for people that live there kind of tough." In comparison, Mid Quad dorms are known as the slightly more subdued social areas and South Quad, comprised of three towers, is "generally pretty quiet." Students who do not drink have the option to live in a substance-free dorm, Stark Hall. One upperclassman shared a very unusual fact: "Although CMC offers a cleaning service, it is by no means conventional. Many students developing lasting relationships with those staff, as with all other branches of service work at the school. CMC is a community for not only students, but also faculty and staff on every level."

For those nights when the standard dining hall fare becomes bland, the Athenaeum is a viable option. Every weeknight, there will be "a distinguished speaker who gives a presentation over a gourmet meal. Recent Athenaeum speakers include Salman Rushdie, Justice Antonin Scalia, and Anderson Cooper. However, speakers are not limited to the big names. From artists to historians, student debated panels to top political analysts, the Athenaeum is a true incarnation of the liberal arts experience," said a former Student Government participant.

Dorms are assigned via a lottery system, with some students having the option to retain their room from year to year. Each year, the Dean of Students chooses seniors to live in each dormitory as a resident assistant. While students did not report having especially close relationships with these RAs, they are generally well-liked by their advisees. "They're cool people," one freshman said. "We don't really hang out with them, but it's not like they pop in to our rooms every few hours to make sure we aren't doing anything bad."

"We're the frat boys with no frats, according to the kids at the other Five C's."

Claremont McKenna students often branch out from their dorms and make the trip "literally across the street" to their neighboring schools for social events like the aforementioned foam party. "It's really like one huge campus. If your school is too small for you, you can always expand it to include any of the others."

"Our football team sucks," as an upperclassman put it. Pomona College is Claremont McKenna's main rival, which often leads to the sentiment that the competition can be extreme at times due to proximity.

Indeed, even students who claim to see a lack of diversity in their student body had a difficult time identifying the "stereotypical" Claremont McKenna student. "We're the frat boys with no frats, according to kids at the other Five C's," one student ultimately decided. "And the stereotypical CMC girl? Well, we don't know. We don't date the girls from CMC." Ultimately, whatever their background, Claremont McKenna students have come to their school to take part in world-class academics while also reaping the benefits of a vibrant party scene. And the California sunshine doesn't hurt either.—*Angelica Baker*

FYI

If you come to CMC, you'd better bring "an air-conditioning unit, a red cup, and a skateboard—that seems to be the preferred method of transportation on-campus."

The typical weekend schedule includes "a theme party on Thursday night, studying on Friday, going to whatever 5C is hosting the main party for the night, and spend Sunday recovering and studying."

If I could change one thing about CMC, I'd "make it a little bit bigger. The campus can get small really quickly."

Three things every student at CMC should do before graduating are "get thrown in 'the pond' on your birthday, win a beer pong tournament, and learn how to skateboard."

Harvey Mudd College

Address: 301 Platt Boulevard Claremont, CA 91711
Phone: 909-621-8011
E-mail address: admission@hmc.edu
Web site URL: www.hmc.edu
Year Founded: 1955
Private or Public: Private
Religious Affiliation: None
Location: Suburban
Number of Applicants: 2,493
Percent Accepted: 28%
Percent Accepted who enroll: 31%
Number Entering: 219
Number of Transfers Accepted each Year: 5
Middle 50% SAT range: M: 740–820, CR: 690–760, Wr: 680–760
Middle 50% ACT range: Unreported
Early admission program EA/ED/None: ED

Percentage accepted through EA or ED: 21%
EA and ED deadline: 15-Nov
Regular Deadline: 2-Jan
Application Fee: $60
Full time Undergraduate enrollment: 735
Total enrollment: 735
Percent Male: 66%
Percent Female: 33%
Total Percent Minority or Unreported: 50%
Percent African-American: 1%
Percent Asian/Pacific Islander: 21%
Percent Hispanic: 8%
Percent Native-American: 1%
Percent International: 4%
Percent in-state/out of state: 50%/50%
Percent from Public HS: 74%
Retention Rate: 96%
Graduation Rate 4-year: 83%
Graduation Rate 6-year: 89%

Percent Undergraduates in On-campus housing: 99%
Number of official organized extracurricular organizations: 109
3 Most popular majors: Computer Science, Engineering, Math
Student/Faculty ratio: 8:1
Average Class Size: 18
Percent of students going to grad school: 43%
Tuition and Fees: $36,635
In State Tuition and Fees if different: No difference
Cost for Room and Board: $11,971
Percent receiving financial aid out of those who apply, first year: 83%
Percent receiving financial aid among all students: 59%

Harvey Mudd College is one of the five prestigious Claremont Colleges located in sunny southern California. Although many may not have heard of this small college, which only enrolls about 200 students per class, Harvey Mudd is one of the best math, science, and engineering colleges in the nation—all while maintaining its identity as a liberal arts college. Harvey Mudd is home to some of the brightest and quirkiest students in the country.

The List of Majors: Short and Sweet

At Harvey Mudd, there are only nine majors: biology, biology/chemistry, chemistry, computer science, engineering, mathematics, mathematics/computer science, mathematical biology and physics. In addition, there is the Independent Program of Study and the Off-Campus Major. The limited number of majors demonstrates how serious Harvey Mudd is in its commitment to teaching math, science, and engineering, but the students there do not find themselves restricted. Students at Harvey Mudd are free to take humanities classes either at Harvey Mudd or at any of the other four Claremont colleges.

The core requirements required of all Harvey Mudd students are eight math classes, three semesters of physics, two semesters of physics lab, two semesters of chemistry and chemistry lab, an engineering course, a biology class and a computer science class.

Since there really is no such thing as a gut class at Harvey Mudd, no particular major is considered harder than the others. Getting into classes for one's major is quite easy; one student noted, "I have never *not* gotten into a class I wanted to be enrolled in." Just as the list of majors is short, classes are likewise very small. Classes are at the most 200 students for freshmen core lecture classes, and upper division classes tend to be around 30 students at the most. An engineering major said, "Upper division classes tend to weed people out and have smaller class sizes." In fact, there are certain engineering classes known as "weed-out" classes, intended to determine which students *really* want to major in that field.

Once students get through these most difficult courses, however, they are rewarded. Mudd offers a Clinic program, which gives upperclassmen the opportunity to work on real-world industrial projects in teams of four or five under the guidance of a student team leader, a faculty advisor, and a liaison from a sponsoring organization. While other schools have engineering senior projects, Mudd "actually gets companies to pay something like $40,000 to have a few Mudd students do a project for them, so it's cool to get that real world experience before graduating."

A Liberal Arts/Math and Science School

On top of the core science requirements and classes required for their major, Mudd students are required to take 11 humanities and social sciences classes, which students fondly call "hum/soc classes" (pronounced hum-sock). They must also pick a concentration in the humanities as well, which ensures that Harvey Mudd students aren't knowledgeable only about numbers and equations. Even though they are at a math and science school, students tend to be quite well rounded. A sophomore said, "We get to take a lot of really cool humanities classes from the other Claremont colleges."

Students agree that, although Harvey Mudd is the best of the five Claremont Colleges, it is definitely nice to have the other colleges around. With four other colleges in such close proximity, students are offered countless opportunities. One student listed the classes he took outside of Harvey Mudd: "I've taken voice lessons, music theory and Chinese at some of the other colleges."

All My Professors Know My Name

Because classes tend to be so small, students are usually very close to their professors and professors are very involved in their students' academic pursuits and personal lives. Professors want students to achieve academic excellence, but at the same time believe in personal development. First-semester freshmen do not have grades for their classes but receive either high pass, pass or fail marks. If a freshmen "high passes" all or too many of their classes, they are promptly sent a good-natured letter from their dean: "We are very happy with your academic achievement but, please, get a life!" The Dean's words are humorous, but true. Professors and deans truly want their students to be happy and have fun—Mudd throws famous annual parties funded by the school such as "Tequila Night."

In addition, professors are provided with a financial fund to take students out for

lunch or dinner. One student noted that her professor was "in competition" with another professor to see who could take out the most students for a meal. Opportunities like these encourage interaction and foster relationships between students and professors outside of the classroom. Students say professors tend to be "down to earth" and very accessible for help or questions. Students agree that professors truly want to help their students and will often seek out those who are not doing well in their classes to help them. Nonetheless, even though professors are kind and good-natured, they still are hard graders. One student said, "Getting A's is hard and there is definitely grade deflation at our school."

So What Do You Do Outside of Studying?

Outside of studying and doing endless problems for their five or more classes, Mudd students play as hard as they study. They may be some of the brightest students in the nation, but Mudd students do many of the same things any college student would do: "hang out with people, play guitar, procrastinate." The people that Mudd students tend to hang out with are determined on proximity—the dorms that Mudd students are assigned to often function as their social circles as well. Because dorms are considered "extremely spacious," pretty much everyone lives on campus, even as upperclassmen.

Dorm life is exciting and packed with personality. North dorm folk, or "Northies," know how to party and will often have a game or two of beer pong going. The school is strict on underage drinking, but often "turns a blind eye" and cares more about their students' well-being. West dorm folk have their own traditions: "Their courtyard often has broken electronics, appliances, who-knows-what lying around, and often a fire going on at night." East dorm is quieter and composed mainly of CS majors, and one can always join them for a competitive video game or two. The South dorm is also considered quieter, although they are quite a musical bunch; one can often find a few Southies in the courtyard playing guitar together. Across the street from Mudd is Scripps College, which is a small, all-girls liberal arts college. Students comment that there is definitely a lot of interaction between the schools, "enough to make the Mudd girls jealous sometimes."

Mudd also throws some pretty wicked parties which are kindly funded by the school. Parties that all students must attend at least once include the LTG (Long Tall Glasses), a formal party hosted in the North dorms. Suds is another popular party open to all the Claremont colleges involving foam generating machines and a lot of partying.

Besides partying, Mudd students are very active and involved in their extracurricular activities. For those who are artistically inclined there is a jam society that maintains a jam room with a drum set and other musical equipment. There is also a Mudd art club which exhibits a lot of student artwork. Mudd students can also join organizations at other Claremont colleges as well. For the physically active, there is the "Foster's Run," which is an annual nine-mile unicycle ride to a local donut shop which gives students free strawberry donuts "which are quite tasty." Overall, Mudd students are a diverse and involved group of people who seem to find their niche in the school pretty quickly.

The Joke's on You

Harvey Mudd may not have a Greek scene or a football team, but it does have some of the nation's best pranksters. Pranks play a huge role on campus and myths are passed on from upperclassmen to underclassmen about past accomplishments. However, there are rules to pulling a prank such as the "24-hour reverse rule" in which the prank must be reversible in 24 hours. Therefore, a student fondly noted, "you can't shave off someone's eyebrows while they're sleeping because it won't grow back in 24 hours."

Individuals enjoy pranking each other, but there is also a rivalry between Mudd, Caltech and MIT. Mudd was the first college to steal Caltech's campus cannon, followed by MIT. Perhaps due to the nature of their pranks, Mudd students are not allowed to prank other Claremont colleges. Despite the prankster nature of students, the administration trusts students and there is a school-wide honor code. Students are given 24-hour access to the academic buildings, including labs and machine shops. The campus is filled with unlocked bikes, skateboards and scooters because students respect each other's property and well-being.

> **"Although school and work can get hard, it's good to know that everyone's working as hard as you. Everyone is doing something amazing."**

Mudd students all learn to accept the fact that they are nerds. In fact, they are proud of it. A sophomore remarked that her physics professor "quacks when he's lecturing" because he uses penguins to describe special relativity. Professors and students alike are quirky, but friendly. Freshmen are encouraged to find their interests immediately on campus and dorm with upperclassmen, who often help them integrate into the campus. Students agree that "although school and work can get hard, it's good to know that everyone's working as hard as you. Everyone is doing something amazing."—*Emily Chen*

FYI
If you come to Harvey Mudd, you'd better bring "a Brita water filter, since the tap water isn't too good to drink."
What is the typical weekend schedule? "Slack off as much as possible on Friday and Saturday, and then do pretty much all my weekend work on Sunday. It seems to work pretty well. I think many manage to not even have classes on Friday, so their weekend probably starts a bit earlier."
If I could change one thing about Harvey Mudd, I'd "make studying abroad easier."
Three things every student at Harvey Mudd should do before graduating are "learn to unicycle, explore the random basements in the academic buildings, and pull a prank on someone."

Pitzer College

Address: 1050 North Mills Avenue Claremont, CA 91711
Phone: 909-621-8129
E-mail address: admission@pitzer.edu
Web site URL: www.pitzer.edu
Year Founded: 1963
Private or Public: Private
Religious Affiliation: None
Location: Suburban
Number of Applicants: 4,031
Percent Accepted: 22%
Percent Accepted who enroll: 29%
Number Entering: 268
Number of Transfers Accepted each Year: 20
Middle 50% SAT range: Unreported
Middle 50% ACT range: Unreported
Early admission program EA/ED/None: ED
Percentage accepted through EA or ED: Unreported

EA and ED deadline: 15-Nov
Regular Deadline: 1-Jan
Application Fee: $50
Full time Undergraduate enrollment: 1,025
Total enrollment: 1,025
Percent Male: 41%
Percent Female: 59%
Total Percent Minority or Unreported: 59%
Percent African-American: 6%
Percent Asian/Pacific Islander: 11%
Percent Hispanic: 15%
Percent Native-American: <1%
Percent International: Unreported
Percent in-state/out of state: 48%/52%
Percent from Public HS: Unreported
Retention Rate: 92%
Graduation Rate 4-year: 74%

Graduation Rate 6-year: Unreported
Percent Undergraduates in On-campus housing: 65%
Number of official organized extracurricular organizations: 120
3 Most popular majors: Psychology, Media Studies, Sociology
Student/Faculty ratio: Unreported
Average Class Size: Unreported
Percent of students going to grad school: Unreported
Tuition and Fees: $37,870
In State Tuition and Fees if different: No difference
Cost for Room and Board: $10,930
Percent receiving financial aid out of those who apply, first year: 77%
Percent receiving financial aid among all students: 42%

I n the unique setting of the Claremont Colleges is Pitzer College, reputedly "the most carefree" and "the most liberal" of the five. The number one thing you should know about Pitzer, according to its students, is that stereotypes are not always correct. Whether you've heard that Pitzer students are actively concerned about social justice, pot smokers or laid-back hippies, they caution that, for the most part, people who come to Pitzer are surprised by how it differs from its various reputations. The bottom line is that "things at Pitzer are changing a lot," and while students may complain about the surprising level of apathy or protest the hippie stereotype, "Pitzer is designed to be a place free of restrictions so, if you have the initiative, you can basically do whatever you want to follow your dreams."

Lots of Freedom

Pitzer's academic requirements, simply known as "Objectives," are composed of two courses in the humanities, two in the social and behavioral sciences, one in the natural sciences and one in mathematics, with a community service, or "social responsibility," and an interdisciplinary requirement. In other words, "you get a tremendous amount of freedom to explore your own interests due to the lack of structured curriculum." In fact, students say that "one of Pitzer's greatest attractions is that it lets you pursue subjects outside the norm." A very popular option among students is the ability to create your own major, which in the past has led to majors such as "Political Psychology," "Social Responsibility and the Arts," and "Nature, Meditation, and Healing."

Most students at Pitzer major in the humanities, with political science, psychology and sociology being three of the most popular choices, but "a lot of people choose the good environmental studies program" as well. The sciences are reputedly "pretty rigorous," and the joint science program that Pitzer shares with Claremont McKenna and Scripps gets high marks. The workload is "very manageable if you had a good college preparatory experience," and some classes, particularly some of the Freshman Seminars, are dismissed as being "much too easy," a phenomenon that is described as "weird, because it's not an easy school to get into."

The small class sizes are a big draw for the Claremont schools, with classes usually capped at around 30 students and most classes enrolling fewer. A student marveled, "Even Introduction to Biology, a traditionally huge class at other schools, only had 40 people in it." However, a common complaint is that the low cap causes classes to fill up quickly, a problem especially for the freshmen, who enroll last. One junior lamented, "It can get very competitive when it comes time to sign up for classes—I've been trying to get in this one class for three years and haven't been able to." On the other hand, students pointed out that it's also not difficult to go to the class after the semester has started and talk to the professor: "Most of the time, they'll let you into the classes you want."

One of the best aspects of Pitzer, students say, is its place in the community of the Claremont Colleges. Students are encouraged to cross-register at Pomona, Claremont McKenna, Harvey Mudd, and Scripps, giving them a wide range of options that Pitzer doesn't offer by itself. It's only a 15-minute walk from one side of the Claremont Colleges campus to the other, so access to the other colleges is convenient and rewarding. A freshman said that "you can find a class in pretty much anything you're interested in somewhere in the five colleges." Even with this added benefit, however, a freshman girl still felt that "the classes that Pitzer offers are more creative and original compared to the other Claremonts."

Tearing Down the Stereotypes

One student claimed, "Everyone here is always bashing Bush and smoking weed." Another defended Pitzer as a typical college environment, saying, "there is substance abuse here just like you'll find at pretty much every other college in the nation." Students agree that marijuana and alcohol are very present on campus, but opinions differ on whether it is more than anywhere else or if Pitzer is just the victim of an exaggerated reputation. It's true that sometimes "hundreds of students from the 5-C's, but mostly Pitzer," are present at "Smoke Force" gatherings on Wednesday nights, when students gather to flip a coin on a map of the Claremont Colleges, then smoke weed where the coin lands.

The school has taken steps to address the problem of drinking on campus with forums about its abuse, but for the most part, Pitzer's policies are "ambivalent" about substances. A senior said that "the official rules are that there is no drinking under 21 and no illegal drug use, but the actual rules are that it's a closed-door policy: if there's no noise or smell, then the RA can't intrude. There's no policing." One student cautioned against getting the wrong impression of the school, though, saying that "as long as you're well-adjusted and come in with the knowledge that there will be these temptations, you won't be any more affected than you would at another college."

The social scene is "very laid-back" at Pitzer, and few students leave the Claremont campus often because "there's always something to do at one of the 5-C's." At least once a weekend, events range from music, which is "more pop and hip-hop at the other colleges than at Pitzer, which has a relaxed, coffeehouse vibe," to "occasional laser-tag at Claremont McKenna." "A lot of partying goes on in people's rooms and suites in the dorms," while "the few people who live in off-campus apartments throw larger-scale parties," said a sophomore. Few people have cars because "you definitely don't need one to get around campus" and "most people don't usually go into L.A. because there's so much to do here."

Pitzer "definitely has a very liberal feel—there might be five conservatives here out of a thousand students," but more right-leaning students can find others who share their beliefs in the other 5-C colleges. While most students are from California and are mostly white or Latino, they found difficulty characterizing the typical Pitzer student, and many expressed dissatisfaction at this inability. One girl remarked ruefully that "the school claims to be socially active and progressive, but the people I've met here don't fulfill that image, and neither does the school." Others speculated that "Pitzer is trying to increase its endowment by getting wealthier, more mainstream students who just don't fit its traditional image." One student expressed frustration at "the general lack of motivation and commitment to Pitzer's ideals." A senior summed it up by saying, "You really should come to Pitzer with a strong sense of initiative and social justice, which are very important here if you have goals and want to make a difference in the world, but I've been both disillusioned and happy with the activist community here."

Living in Claremont

Pitzer offers dorms of the long-hallway design, with every two double rooms connected by a bathroom, as well as suite-style living accommodations. The doubles "are pretty standard size-wise for college" and feature fast Internet connections and enough room for a microwave, a fridge, lofted beds, a sink, and a medicine cabinet. In Mead, the rooms are suites for either four or eight people, and any suite above the first floor has a balcony, sometimes with a view of the mountains. In 2007, three new "green" dorms were opened as part of Pitzer's Residential Life Project. Atherton, Pitzer and Sanborn halls are the first in the nation to fulfill certain environmental sustainability and low-energy standards, and as a senior put it, "We talk so much about the environment and social justice that it would be hypocritical not to meet these standards." Other environmental sustainability projects on campus include the Green Bike Program, which allows raffle winners to borrow a bike to get around campus for the year, and bottle redemption and recycling programs.

Within the residence halls, students can elect to stay in HUSH Hall in Holden, which features 24 hours of quiet, the substance-free hall, where the students do not drink or smoke, or the Involvement Tower, where the students are especially involved in the school or the community. One senior even described how he and his friends created a Game Hall one year with the theme hall charters that Pitzer offers—it was designated for people to play anything from tag to Monopoly.

Students who live on campus are required to have a meal plan, and reviews of Pitzer's dining hall, McConnell, vary. Some praise the variety of vegetarian fare, and others complain that "it's okay, but always the same," but everyone agrees that "if you don't like it, you can go to any of the other five dining halls on campus, as well as the seven different on-campus restaurants." Meal plans vary, so students can elect to have fewer meals and more flex dollars to use at places like Pitzer's Grove House, which is a popular place to grab a bite at the café, meet with clubs, or just hang out. Other popular places to have a quiet moment to yourself or talk with friends include Pitzer's Arboretum, the orange grove, and "the Mounds," which are "hilly lawns."

The city of Claremont, where the 5-C's are located, is "very wealthy" and "definitely not oriented towards a college crowd, since everything closes early and the town sleeps." It offers some nice restaurants, but they're on the pricey side. The result is that "some kids never leave campus," instead participating in the myriad activities and events that the colleges offer. "Many good speakers come to the 5-C's," said a sophomore, describing the recent visit of a documentary filmmaker who held open forums and panels to discuss his work, among other guests.

> "The only things holding me back at Pitzer are my own level of passion and commitment—no one's going to stop me."

The most heralded Pitzer event every year is Kohoutek, a multiple-day music and arts festival that originated in the 70's when the community gathered with a lot of hype to watch the Kohoutek comet, which turned out to be indiscernible in the sky. Pitzer continues the tradition today as "a tongue-in-cheek way to make fun of ourselves and of science for trying to make predictions," said a senior. It draws bands like The Roots and OAR. The Bob Marley festival every fall is also a big attraction for the Pitzer community.

Concerned Students

"Pitzer's philosophy of freedom extends to extracurriculars as well as academics," commented a senior. "There's a club for every interest and the school will give you money to start something if you aren't already represented." Students at Pitzer are "not really into sports at all, since we share a team with Pomona and most of the training and coaching goes on there." The Women's Center and the Arts Collective have large followings, as well as the Student Activities Committee and the Student Senate. Many students have jobs, mostly on campus, which range from working in the admission office to the Grove House. Many students are also involved in protesting the destruction of the Bernard Field Station, activism that has even led to students "chaining themselves to the building." A member of the Eco Club and other environmental activism groups complained that "it's the same seven or eight people in all of my clubs—I feel like a lot of people here just are too apathetic to fit the traditional image of Pitzer's concerned students." He summed up his view of the activist's plight at Pitzer by saying, "You can do or accomplish anything here—you just have to take charge, but it's hard to get people to help you."

"The warm, friendly people here and the degree of freedom that Pitzer offers really make it worth staying," said a freshman. Whether Pitzer's changing image is simply due to unstoppable nationwide trends or whether it's time for a new generation of students to revive the "Vietnam War-protesting, environmentally conscious hippie" stereotype of the 1960's and 70's, there's a lot that this unique school has to offer. As a freshman put it, "The only things holding me back at Pitzer are my own level of passion and commitment—no one's going to stop me."—*Kimberly Chow*

FYI

If you come to Pitzer, you'd better bring "a sense of initiative so you can take control of your own education and ideals."

What's the typical weekend schedule? "Parties at the other 5-C's on Thursday and Friday nights, a musical event, playing Frisbee, maybe going into L.A., and studying on Sunday."

If I could change one thing about Pitzer, I would change "the level of student apathy—I really wish the average student would care more about the environment and stop sinking into the Southern California lifestyle."

Three things every student at Pitzer should do before graduating are: "Go to the hot springs, have an internship with a social justice group in L.A., and go on a Pitzer Outdoor Adventures trip."

Pomona College

Address: 333 N College Way Claremont, CA 91711
Phone: 909-621-8134
E-mail address: admissions@pomona.edu
Web site URL: www.pomona.edu
Year Founded: 1887
Private or Public: Private
Religious Affiliation: None
Location: Suburban
Number of Applicants: 6,293
Percent Accepted: 15.60%
Percent Accepted who enroll: 38.90%
Number Entering: 396
Number of Transfers Accepted each Year: Unreported
Middle 50% SAT range: M: 690–780, CR: 700–780, Wr: 680–770
Middle 50% ACT range: 30–34
Early admission program EA/ED/None: ED

Percentage accepted through EA or ED: 29%
EA and ED deadline: 1-Nov, 28-Dec
Regular Deadline: 2-Jan
Application Fee: $65
Full time Undergraduate enrollment: 1,532
Total enrollment: 1,532
Percent Male: 49%
Percent Female: 51%
Total Percent Minority or Unreported: 39%
Percent African-American: 8%
Percent Asian/Pacific Islander: 18%
Percent Hispanic: 11%
Percent Native-American: 1%
Percent International: Unreported
Percent in-state/out of state: 33 %/67%
Percent from Public HS: 69%
Retention Rate: 97%

Graduation Rate 4-year: 90%
Graduation Rate 6-year: 95%
Percent Undergraduates in On-campus housing: 98%
Number of official organized extracurricular organizations: 227
3 Most popular majors: Economics, English, Politics
Student/Faculty ratio: 8:1
Average Class Size: 14
Percent of students going to grad school: 80%
Tuition and Fees: $35,318
In State Tuition and Fees if different: No difference
Cost for Room and Board: $12,220
Percent receiving financial aid out of those who apply, first year: 81%
Percent receiving financial aid among all students: 52%

Pomona College might not be the most recognizable of names outside the state, but it has an appeal all its own. This small liberal arts college tucked into Southern California boasts "very curious and passionate" students and a location that's "one hour from snow, one hour from the beach, and one hour from Disneyland." As one of the members of the Claremont College Consortium, the college is able to have the benefits of an undergraduate focus without sacrificing the resources of a large research university. Combining strong academics, an idyllic setting, and an intimate atmosphere, Pomona boasts some of the happiest students in the country. One student summed up Pomona's unique appeal: "Pomona gives you a liberal arts education as good as anything on the East Coast, but I think the people here are a lot more cheerful, a lot friendlier, and just really happy."

A Truly Liberal Education

Students at Pomona say their classes are "demanding," but that they ultimately have a lot of freedom to design their own educations. To graduate, Pomona requires all students to take thirty-two courses and fulfill the Breadth of Study Requirements, which one junior described as "take five classes you like and then, done." Every student takes at least one course in each of five disciplines: Creative Expression; Social Institutions and Human Behavior; History, Values, Ethics and Cultural Studies; Physical and Biological Sciences; and Mathematical Reasoning. In addition, students have to participate in physical education and take an intermediate language class or its equivalent. While upperclassmen can pick any of forty-five different majors to concentrate in, freshmen start out by taking a required first-year seminar. These Critical Inquiry classes, with unique topics ranging from "Facebook, Fairness, and Forgery" to "The Heart of a Doctor," have a capped enrollment of 15 students and are "writing-intensive."

Although the most popular majors at Pomona are said to be in the social sciences and humanities, especially politics and economics, many students focus on the natural sciences, which are notoriously difficult. "It's a big jump place for medical school, and there are lots of premeds," said one freshman. But non-science majors need not fear; Pomona offers a variety of science courses that are relatively easier and more interdisciplinary, such as geology classes and "Physics and Music." In general, students are interested in a range of areas and are easily able to find classes to fulfill their requirements: "Here, you can really like religious studies even if you're a chemistry major," one senior said.

Students at Pomona frequently mentioned having casual meals with their professors, getting advanced research opportunities as underclassmen, and learning about their professors' quirkier sides. "Classes are small enough that you get to know your professors as people," a junior said. In addition to having accessible professors, Pomona students can take advantage of small discussion-based classes that are taught seminar-style. According to one student, a "big" class consists of thirty students, and "most of them are small enough that they can be definitely interactive." While upperclassmen have priority in picking classes, a freshman said that he hadn't had problems registering for the courses he wanted.

One of Pomona's most distinctive features is its membership in the Claremont Colleges consortium (Pomona even shares athletic teams and a mascot, the Sagehen, with Pitzer College), which gives Pomona students the option of registering in courses offered by the other colleges—Claremont McKenna, Harvey Mudd, Pitzer and Scripps. Many students sample the rigorous science courses at Harvey Mudd, the media studies program at Pitzer, and the business program at Claremont McKenna. "If it were just Pomona, I would feel a little limited by class options," said one girl. However, freshmen aren't allowed to cross-register, and even upperclassmen must take at least two courses at Pomona every semester. Popular courses at Pomona itself include the English seminar "Obscure and Eclectic Fiction" and "The U.S. Congress," in which students participate in simulations of the U.S. legislature along with other Claremont students. In general, students say the workload is intense but "open-ended," with much more collaboration than competition. "It's definitely challenging, but it's never too much. You get a lot of collaboration here," said one. Another added, "There's almost nonexistent competition between students here. Individually, they are really high-achieving, they are motivated, they have goals in life, and they work really hard, but it's not like if you get an A, I can't get an A."

Surfing, Skiing, and Partying

"The smart and personable people you will meet at Pomona and love for the rest of your life—that's really the best thing about it," declared a senior. Students say Pomona does an excellent job of welcoming its freshmen right from the beginning and continues to support them for the rest of their undergraduate years. Before classes start, freshmen go on student-led Orientation Adventure trips throughout California. Freshmen say they "really start to bond" with their classmates over four days of hiking around Yosemite, surfing in Santa Barbara, or just exploring Southern California while doing community service. But one of the most praised features of freshman year is the sponsor group program, in which freshmen are divided into groups of ten to twenty. Guided and mentored by two sophomores who are "like their brothers and sisters," these groups live in the same hall together and become "like family."

The consortium system offers Pomona students not only academic options, but also a variety of social scenes. "There definitely is a big party scene, but there are basically no frats," said a freshman. "Parties are usually inside the rooms, or there's always a big party at the other colleges." In addition, Pomona students receive a daily "student digester e-mail" listing all of the day's events and activities, including official college-sponsored parties, shows, movie screenings, and even "politics talks," in which politics professors and students gather to drink wine, eat cheese, and discuss current events. Although "the alcohol scene is definitely present," and "pretty much everyone" drinks, students have the option of choosing substance-free housing. A sophomore said, "I've generally found that there are more non-drinkers than one would think and it's not hard to find stuff to do without drinking heavily."

Pomona's alcohol policy is considered "not super-rigid." Drinks are allowed everywhere on campus; however, no hard liquor is allowed on South Campus, where underclassmen live. RAs are known to be stricter on South Campus, but are mostly there to make sure students understand how to handle alcohol responsibly, and "if there's an emergency they'd know how to respond to it."

The college often sponsors parties, and when it comes to big annual events, "the administration treats students like royalty." These events are a large part of Pomona's quirky culture and lore, or "Pomoniana." Along with traditional parties like the "screw your roommate dance," in which students set up their roommates on blind dates, Pomona organizes an annual "Death by Chocolate" event on the last day of classes before fall semester finals. "Basically, they just fill one of our auditorium rooms with chocolate—fondue, cocoa, cake, everything," explained a junior. On Snow Day, another pre-finals event, the college hires a snow machine to fill the quad with snow, so students can enjoy snowball fights and snowmen in the middle of Southern California. Of course, ski resorts aren't that far from Pomona, and one of the college's most beloved traditions is Ski-Beach Day: "In the morning, Pomona pays for us to go skiing and snowboarding in the mountains, and in the afternoon, we drive down to the beach and hang out in the sun." Despite its closeness to both beaches and mountains—not to mention that it's just an hour away from L.A.—most students stay on campus. That's because there's plenty to do at Pomona itself, students say, but for those who would like to venture off campus, there's a Metrolink station a few blocks away, and "people will drive or ride up to go see games and concerts."

Students say that hall life is very social, with residents keeping their doors open most of the time. "The students here are pretty easygoing and pretty content and smiley," said a junior. "People will go out all the time and do homework in the sun on the lawn or on the 'beach,' which is this sandy area with a beach volleyball court." While some students praised the feel of a small, intimate community—"everyone knows everyone else, everyone knows where everyone else lives"—one freshman said he already felt that the community was "too small." Even in this small community, students have a wide variety of passions and come from a variety of ethnic backgrounds and states. However, most students are considered "really liberal" and middle- to upper-class.

A Sagehen's Habitat

Housing at Pomona is guaranteed for all four years, and only a few seniors live off-campus. About two-thirds of freshmen are in doubles, and the rest are in singles. Most underclassmen live on South Campus in hall-style dorms, but housing improves with seniority. North Campus, where upperclassmen live, has many two-room doubles, which are two singles connected by a small entryway and a door. Juniors and seniors generally have singles or even suites, and "one of our nicest dorms has fireplaces and balconies, with really spacious rooms."

In addition, students can also choose to live in a few themed dorms, including substance-free housing, and "Unity Dorm," which consists of one floor of students who "really actively want to be engaged in their dorm, so they do barbecues and field trips and stuff together." Students who want to immerse themselves in a foreign language can live in one of six special language halls in Oldenborg, the language center. For example, if you live in the Spanish hall, "you don't have to talk in Spanish all the time, but if you're doing Spanish work there's always someone to help you," a junior explained. Oldenborg's dining hall—one of three at Pomona—offers language tables where students can practice conversing over lunch.

Since meal plans can be used at any of the other Claremont campuses' dining halls, students have a total of eight dining halls to choose from. The different meal plans offer either a set number of meals per week or meals plus "flex dollars," which are accepted at the "Coop Fountain," a student-run snack and smoothie shop and convenience store. For a nicer, sit-down meal, students can visit the Sagehen Café. One of Pomona's most popular dining features is "Snack," a weeknight study break, in which the dining halls reopen at 10:30 p.m. and students can enjoy free snacks. "We come at the end of the day to just kind of run into each other, sum up our days, relax, eat, and talk. It's great because I always get hungry at night," said a junior. In general, students say they are really satisfied with the food.

The meal plan's flex dollars can't be applied off-campus, but Pomona does offer a "Claremont Cash" card, which works like a debit card at campus stores and about half of the stores in "the Village," which is what students call the surrounding town of Claremont. The Village "is a little bit on the small side" and "a little sleepy," with not much nightlife, according to students. About a third of the town's population consists of retirees, and students describe it as "such a safe, nice, quaint little town; we feel completely comfortable walking around, even at night."

Pomoniana and More

Activities outside the classroom aren't just limited to exploring the Village. Pomona students can join clubs not just on their own campus, but also those at any of the other campuses. One of Pomona's most popular clubs is "On the Loose," which rents out outdoors equipment, sponsors several outdoors trips every week and trains students to lead trips. Favorite destinations include Death Valley and Joshua Tree.

Also, "it's really easy to get a job if you want a job. Students mentioned jobs at the libraries and other campus facilities, as well as positions as volunteer coordinators and interns in the Pomona College internship program. Under this program, students can take normally unpaid internships in the L.A. area, but still receive wages from Pomona.

Although Pomona fields a variety of Division III teams, athletics don't dominate other campus activities. "I wouldn't say our school is the greatest on athletic spirit," said one student. The Pitzer-Pomona Sagehens' biggest rivals are the neighboring Claremont McKenna-Scripps-Harvey Mudd teams, especially in basketball, which can get "pretty heated." Coaches at Pomona understand that students' focus is on academics, so "it's nice for people who want to continue playing sports in college, but not dedicate their lives to sports," said a sophomore.

> **"The smart and personable people you will meet at Pomona and love for the rest of your life—that's really the best thing about it."**

In keeping with Pomona's sunny, carefree atmosphere, campus traditions are often more quirky and fun than steeped in history and legend. All of the fountains on campus are chlorinated because on students' birthdays, "it's a tradition to dump them into the fountains." Possibly the oddest bit of Pomona lore is the campus' fascination with the number 47. From Pomona's highway exit (47) to the founding date of Claremont McKenna (1947) to the number of students in Pomona's first graduating class (47), the number seems to be everywhere, and one student even wrote a thesis on all the different places 47 occurs in nature. Alum Joe Menosky '79, a writer and co-producer for Star Trek, has also inserted the number into episode after episode of the series.

With academic rigor and opportunities comparable to that of any liberal arts college and a relaxed, intimate atmosphere, Pomona is home to happy students, caring faculty, and a sunny "California attitude." As one senior said, "I feel like we are on the one hand selecting bright students, but they're not just smart students who study a lot; we choose people who are really decent. There are so many instances where I've had a conversation with someone and they've surprised me in so many ways and made me realize how good people can be."—*Vivian Yee*

FYIs

If you come to Pomona College, you'd better bring "sunblock and sunglasses, innovativeness and inventiveness."

What is the typical weekend schedule? "Get out of class on Friday, do a little work or go into town, play a game of basketball or volleyball, go to a dorm party at one of the 5-Cs, sleep in Saturday, work and hang out, go to events or concerts or lectures, go out to dinner in the village and party again. Sunday, people work."

If I could change one thing about Pomona, I'd "expand the college a little—it's too small."

Three things every student at Pomona should do before graduating are "break into the pool after hours, watch the sun set at Joshua Tree National Park, and leave with a really great group of friends."

Scripps College

Address: 1030 N. Columbia Avenue Claremont, CA 91711
Phone: 909-621-8149
E-mail address: admission@scrippscollege.edu
Web site URL: www.scrippscollege.edu
Year Founded: 1926
Private or Public: Private
Religious Affiliation: None
Location: Suburban
Number of Applicants: 1,931
Percent Accepted: 43%
Percent Accepted who enroll: 30%
Number Entering: 260
Number of Transfers Accepted each Year: 55
Middle 50% SAT range: M: 620–710, CR: 640–730, Wr: 650–730
Middle 50% ACT range: 28–32
Early admission program EA/ED/None: ED

Percentage accepted through EA or ED: 15%
EA and ED deadline: 1-Nov, 1-Jan
Regular Deadline: 1-Jan
Application Fee: $50
Full time Undergraduate enrollment: 944
Total enrollment: 944
Percent Male: 0%
Percent Female: 100%
Total Percent Minority or Unreported: 25%
Percent African-American: 4%
Percent Asian/Pacific Islander: 13%
Percent Hispanic: 7%
Percent Native-American: 1%
Percent International: Unreported
Percent in-state/out of state: 41%/59%
Percent from Public HS: 59%
Retention Rate: 95%
Graduation Rate 4-year: 74%

Graduation Rate 6-year: 80%
Percent Undergraduates in On-campus housing: 96%
Number of official organized extracurricular organizations: 50
3 Most popular majors: Psychology, Politics and International Relations, Media Studies
Student/Faculty ratio: 11:1
Average Class Size: 15
Percent of students going to grad school: 60%
Tuition and Fees: $37,950
In State Tuition and Fees if different: No difference
Cost for Room and Board: $11,500
Percent receiving financial aid out of those who apply, first year: 70%
Percent receiving financial aid among all students: 11%

One of the first things that come to students' minds when describing Scripps College is its intimate community, coupled with a great location outside of Los Angeles. Scripps is the only single-sex school among the Claremont Colleges, offering a highly reputable education to about 950 female students. Although, students are quick to point out that they chose Scripps because of the great education and numerous opportunities it offers, not because of its all-female student body. So if you want to spend four years in a college that has perfect weather, Mediterranean architecture, a proximity to a large city and reputable academics, maybe take a closer look at Scripps.

An All-Female School

One of the advantages of going to an all-female school is its "very warm, friendly atmosphere." According to one student, "A lot of kids here went to high schools with as many or even more people. That's why we didn't feel at the beginning that college life was so overwhelming." Her sentiments are echoed by other members of the student population. "The small student body makes it a great and really close community," added one.

Despite the small enrollment, however, Scripps is located right next to the other four Claremont Colleges, all of which are coeducational. As a result, being an all-female school does not mean that there is no interaction with male students. In fact, since students often register for classes in the other colleges, there are plenty of opportunities to make friends with people in the other colleges, both male and female. "Scripps is like part of a much larger campus. You get to go to other colleges all the time, so you don't have to worry about Scripps being an all-female college," said a student. One undergrad pointed out that, as a single-sex school, Scripps receives "differing, condescending attitudes from other colleges in the consortium," but most people agree that the consortium system works very well for Scripps' social atmosphere.

The City of Trees and PhDs

As an upscale suburb of Los Angeles, Claremont is also known as the "City of Trees and PhDs," thanks to a high concentration of professors working in the city's universities. The older neighborhoods of Claremont take pride in their shade-covered streets, making Scripps "a delightful place to live in."

The primary shopping center is at the Village, a collection of small shops and restaurants located at walking distance of the Claremont Colleges. Some students complain about the overpriced shopping, but they generally agree that, "the Village is indispensable for college life." Whenever they crave a little more excitement than the Village, students can jump on a train and visit Los Angeles. Although downtown Los Angeles is still about 30 miles away, it only takes ten minutes for Scripps students to walk to the MetroLink station, a railway system that connects directly to Los Angeles Union Station.

Within the Claremont Colleges, Scripps' own campus is very small. It extends over about three blocks and is only built around one single quad, the Jaqua Quadrangle. Nevertheless, the small campus adds even more to the College's intimacy, and according to the students, "the Mediterranean Revival architecture that dominates the campus feels very welcoming to us."

Sharing is Fun!

Scripps is generally ranked among the top 30 liberal arts colleges by *US News and World Report*. It is a relatively selective college, accepting less than 50 percent of the applicant pool. "Above all else, people come to Scripps because it has a strong academic program," said a student.

By sharing facilities with the other colleges of the consortium, Scripps, despite its small size, offers its students the level of resources and opportunities of a large university. "The departments here are often interrelated to the same departments of the other colleges," said one junior. "For example, Scripps College has a Joint Science Department with Pitzer and Claremont McKenna." This close relationship between the colleges maximizes the resources of the consortium, letting the students explore a greater number of opportunities.

Just like most other liberal arts colleges, Scripps has an interdisciplinary Core Program, which focuses on critical thinking. The Core is divided into three different courses. Core I teaches the students about the relationship between knowledge and cultures. Core II lets the students choose between different courses that offer in-depth studies of topics introduced in Core I. Core III focuses on innovation and requires the students to come up with a self-designed project as part of the course. According to a student, "Core I is important. It builds the foundations for future undergraduate work. Core II is not as beneficial, as it is too narrow. My section, at least, did not seem to end up anywhere. Core III is a wonderful experience. It makes one feel potent and encourages applying what you've learned."

In addition, the students are also required to fulfill the general requirements, which include one class each in fine arts, letters, writing, natural science, social science, race and ethnic studies and mathematics. Students also have to take three semesters of a foreign language. These rather extensive requirements enable the students to acquire knowledge and skills in a variety of fields, an important goal of the College.

Scripps' classes are generally small, having less than 20 students, which lets students interact frequently with their professors. Since there are no teaching assistants, the professors devote a significant part of their time to office hours in order to help their students. "I interact a lot with professors outside of class," one undergrad explained. "I go to office hours frequently, have done an internship with one professor, and have gone to conferences with some others."

Kicking it with the Consortium

Scripps provides its students with great dorm rooms. "The average dorm room is spacious, elegantly furnished, and clean." Each dorm also has a browsing room, a small quiet library that forbids male entrance.

> "During Friday and Saturday, there are generally several parties going on in different colleges, but if you just restrict yourself to Scripps, you might not find anything interesting during the weekends."

Scripps athletes participate in competitions with Claremont McKenna and Harvey Mudd as one single team. Scripps does have its own clubs, but many larger organizations draw members from the entire consortium.

The weekend life is similarly conjoined with that of the other colleges. Students usually go to parties in any of the Claremont Colleges, since Scripps' small size usually does not make for extremely exciting parties. According to one student, "During Friday and Saturday, there are generally several parties going on in different colleges, but if you just restrict yourself to Scripps, you might not find anything interesting during the weekends." But lack of social life said, one student still cited the biggest disadvantage of being at Scripps as being that "they make you leave after four years."—*Xiaohang Liu*

FYI

What is the typical weekend schedule? "Friday: party. Saturday: party, L.A. Sunday: work, work, and work."

If you come to Scripps, you'd better bring "a stapler!"

If I could change one thing about Scripps, I'd "have more diversity."

Three things every student at Scripps should do before graduating are "to play glow-in-the-dark Frisbee on the lawn at midnight, attend candlelight dinners, and participate in the Humanities Institute"

Deep Springs College

Address: HC 72, Box 45001 Dyer, NV 89010-9803

Phone: 760-872-2000

E-mail address: apcom@deepsprings.edu

Web site URL: www.deepsprings.edu

Year Founded: 1917

Private or Public: Private

Religious Affiliation: None

Location: Rural

Number of Applicants: 186

Percent Accepted: 7%

Percent Accepted who enroll: 92%

Number Entering: 12

Number of Transfers Accepted each Year: Unreported

Middle 50% SAT range: M: 700–800, Cr: 750–800, Wr: 750–780

Middle 50% ACT range: Unreported

Early admission program EA/ED/None: None

Percentage accepted through EA or ED: NA

EA and ED deadline: NA

Regular Deadline: 15-Nov

Application Fee: $0

Full time Undergraduate enrollment: 26

Total enrollment: 26

Percent Male: 100%

Percent Female: 0%

Total Percent Minority or Unreported: Unreported

Percent African-American: Unreported

Percent Asian/Pacific Islander: Unreported

Percent Hispanic: Unreported

Percent Native-American: Unreported

Percent International: Unreported

Percent in-state/out of state: 20%/80%

Percent from Public HS: 50%

Retention Rate: 100%

Graduation Rate 4-year: Unreported

Graduation Rate 6-year: Unreported

Percent Undergraduates in On-campus housing: Unreported

Number of official organized extracurricular organizations: Unreported

3 Most popular majors: Liberal Arts and Sciences, General Studies and Humanities

Student/Faculty ratio: 4:1

Average Class Size: 2 to 9

Percent of students going to grad school: 96%

Tuition and Fees: $0

In State Tuition and Fees if different: No difference

Cost for Room and Board: $0

Percent receiving financial aid out of those who apply, first year: NA

Percent receiving financial aid among all students: NA

Deep Springs College is absolutely unique. Founded in 1917, this two-year, all-male, tuition-free, 26-student educational institution remains an anachronism in the landscape of higher education. Whether it's because of Deep Springs' precious isolation, its drug and alcohol-free student body, its commitment to training young men for lives of service, or the fact that it's situated on a working farm and cattle ranch, every Deep Springer will agree that there is no college like it. Students at Deep Springs give up the amenities and resources of a normal college campus to live, study and work hard in an isolated desert valley in Eastern California. While graduates from other universities may reminisce about their time in college, there's a reason why Deep Springs' alumni always refer back to their "Deep Springs experience."

Don't Let Me Out!

The first thing any visitor to Deep Springs will notice is its isolation. An hour's drive from the closest town (Bishop, CA) and five hours from the closest cities (Las Vegas and Los Angeles), Deep Springs is a little speck of green in the middle of a high desert valley. This isolation is made even more intense by the students' self-imposed "isolation policy" which states that students cannot leave the valley or have visitors while school is in session. It may seem excessive, but this policy does have its benefits. "We never meet new people at Deep Springs, but we meet the same people over and over again, each time with more intensity and understanding," one second-year student commented. The students also uphold a policy against the use of drugs and alcohol during term which, like the isolation policy, is self-imposed and self-regulated. These rules are a part of the Self-Governance process which allows the students to effectively own and run the college while they are enrolled. "Students hold each other accountable for upholding rules, completing all of their tasks, and generally running the college," one recent graduate explained. "Rarely are young people given so much responsibility and so many opportunities."

Each student at Deep Springs sits on a committee (Applications, Curriculum, Communications, or Review and Reinvitation Committee) and each committee is responsible for running a part of the college. Whether they're reading essays and accepting the incoming class, interviewing and hiring faculty, or writing and publishing the college brochure, every student has a hand in making the place run. The student body also gathers every Friday night for a collective meeting where committees give reports, legislation is discussed, and issues are debated. During the winter these meetings are held in the dorm or the boarding house, though in the summer students often drive out to remote spots in the desert to meet around a campfire, under the stars. Meetings often run late into the night, only ending when all the business has been completed, or when the cows need to be milked.

The Self-Governance process is also a way for students to hold positions of responsibility. Some of the positions include: student body president, labor commissioner, secretary, annual giving representative and committee chair. "You are a political member before you are a social member of this community," one first-year student noted, and most students do hold an elected position in the Self-Governance process before they graduate.

Home On the (Gas) Range

At the same time that students at Deep Springs run the administrative side of the college, they also provide nearly all the labor for the school, farm and cattle ranch. Though they pay no tuition, students are required to work an average of 20 to 30 hours per week in various jobs. Labor positions are assigned by the student Labor Commissioner and change often, so students get to experience a lot of different kinds of work before they graduate. "One term you might be cooking dinner for the community every night, and the next you're building fences or herding cows." The one job that every Deep Springer is required to do is BH duty, which includes washing dishes, mopping floors, and cleaning up after meals. Other labor positions include butcher, gardener, farm assistant and dairy boy.

Many students enjoy the labor program because of the practical skills that they learn, like cooking, carpentry or welding, but even the work they'll probably never do again, like slaughtering or milking cows, has its benefits. "Deep Springs is first and foremost about learning to put the needs of the community and of the farm and ranch on which you live above yourself, and coming to cherish yourself as a piece in the puzzle," said one second-year student. Deep Springers also use the time during work to talk or think about intellectual issues. Four hours of painting a wall or digging post-holes in the desert is a good amount of time to think about an upcoming paper or discuss a reading with another student. Most students come to appreciate the labor program as an important part of their education, and not as a distraction from academics. "With so much physical work to do all the time, academic work begins to seem like a privilege and a kind of relaxation. It really makes you appreciate your education."

Will This Class Ever End?

Classes at Deep Springs are comparable to courses at top level institutions, except that you'll never have to sit in a lecture hall with 300 other students. Most classes have enrollments between four and 10 students, and nearly all of them are seminars. The only two required courses are composition and public speaking, the latter taken every semester. Class discussions can get very intense, since the students all know each other perhaps too well. "Classes here are intense, and students often expect more of each other than professors are able to expect of students in other, more traditional environments," said one second-year student. "At Deep Springs, if a peer doesn't prepare well and class discussion suffers as a result, you have both a right and a responsibility to confront him about it." Though this kind of intensity can be daunting for new students straight out of high school, the general atmosphere in class is one of deep concern and engagement with issues. "Classes at Deep Springs are like a cross between a big family meal and a trial in court: personal, rigorous, intense, and deeply enjoyable."

Since students and their professors live within a few steps of each other, classroom discussions often continue after class is over. It's not uncommon for students to continue debating an issue in the dining hall at lunch and through their afternoon work. "I don't think that 'the way people think' could be more important at another school than Deep Springs," as students are always engaging each other's beliefs and though processes inside and outside of class. Professors often open their homes to students at night to continue discussions, help edit papers, or just to have coffee. "The most common social activity is talking. Simply talking," and Deep Springers certainly do a lot of it: with their professors, each other, and the families and kids that make up the community.

The majority of the courses at Deep Springs are in the humanities or literary arts,

though a number of math and science courses are always offered. To keep the curriculum balanced, Deep Springs employs three long-term professors in Humanities, Social Sciences, and Math and Natural Sciences. Along with these three, the student body hires a handful of visiting professors each semester to teach anything from "Figure Drawing" to "Wittgenstein's *Philosophical Investigations*."

Dance It Off

Whatever diversity Deep Springs may lack in its small and somewhat homogeneous student body, it makes up for in the larger campus community. Though only around 50 people live in the valley, they range in age from very young to very old, and come from all over the country and the world. Professors often bring their spouses and kids along, and everyone takes part in the greater community of Deep Springs. The one obvious thing lacking is female students, though the issue is formally debated every year and is a constant topic of discussion. "Most students' feelings about going to a single-sex school change radically, in all kinds of directions, once they've actually been at Deep Springs," said a recent graduate. But the lack of girls doesn't stop the boys from having their fun. "Of course we dance (boogie)," explained a second-year. "An hour of heavy boogie-ing provides enough exercise and catharsis to last a week or so."

"Students who are looking for a challenging academic environment should look into Deep Springs."

The valley provides great opportunities for hiking, running and climbing, and even though Deep Springs has no sports program, students will often organize games of soccer or basketball in the free half-hour before dinner. But as any Deep Springer will tell you, free time is hard to come by. Often weekends are filled with extra work projects, slaughters, cattle drives or music practice. "There isn't much free time, but dance parties, shooting guns, making paintings, and reading groups occupy the little that there is." Often, because of the amount of work and responsibility every student must take on, relaxation feels just like procrastination. But then again, every student signed on to push themselves and take on a challenge. One graduate summed it up nicely: "Attending Deep Springs is like running a marathon. While you're in it you can only think about how hard it is, but once it's over you can look back and see what an amazing thing you just did."—*Jesse Bradford*

FYIs

If you come to Deep Springs, you'd better bring "a toothbrush. Almost everything else you need can be found in the bonepile (communal clothing stockpile)."

What is a typical weekend schedule? "Cooking a meal for the community, preparing for a Heidegger reading group, doing committee work, a game of soccer, working on a couple essays, a quick boogie, then a few hours of solid reading."

If I could change one thing about Deep Springs, "I'd add a couple of hours to each day."

Before graduating, every Deep Springer should "cook an elaborate meal without enough help, stay up all night writing a paper then go for a swim in the upper reservoir at dawn, and punch a charging bull in the face."

Mills College

Address: 500 MacArthur Boulevard Oakland, CA 94613
Phone: 510-430-2135
E-mail address: admission@mills.edu
Web site URL: www.mills.edu
Year Founded: 1852
Private or Public: Private
Religious Affiliation: None
Location: Suburban
Number of Applicants: 1,416
Percent Accepted: 85%
Percent Accepted who enroll: 26%
Number Entering: 205
Number of Transfers Accepted each Year: 207
Middle 50% SAT range: M: 490–590, CR: 520–650, Wr: 520–620
Middle 50% ACT range: 20–27
Early admission program EA/ED/None: EA
Percentage accepted through EA or ED: 67%

EA and ED deadline: 15-Nov
Regular Deadline: 1-Aug
Application Fee: $50
Full time Undergraduate enrollment: 930
Total enrollment: 1454
Percent Male: 0%
Percent Female: 100%
Total Percent Minority or Unreported: 57%
Percent African-American: 9%
Percent Asian/Pacific Islander: 8%
Percent Hispanic: 14%
Percent Native-American: <1%
Percent International: 3%
Percent in-state/out of state: 80%/20%
Percent from Public HS: 80%
Retention Rate: 74%
Graduation Rate 4-year: 54%

Graduation Rate 6-year: 60%
Percent Undergraduates in On-campus housing: 56%
Number of official organized extracurricular organizations: 47
3 Most popular majors: English, Political Science, Psychology
Student/Faculty ratio: 11:1
Average Class Size: 10 to 19
Percent of students going to grad school: 20%
Tuition and Fees: $35,190
In State Tuition and Fees if different: No difference
Cost for Room and Board: $10,550
Percent receiving financial aid out of those who apply, first year: 86%
Percent receiving financial aid among all students: 72%

Mills College, an all-female liberal arts college in Oakland, California, has been committed to women's education for over 150 years. In fact, Mills made news in 1990 when the board of trustees voted to admit males to the undergraduate program. Students, outraged, immediately adopted the slogan "Better Dead than Coed." They mounted protests, officially shutting down the campus, and they refused to resume their normal lives until the board of trustees reversed their decision. Eventually, the trustees conceded, and Mills reinforced its position as a school dedicated to women's education. That take-charge spirit is characteristic of Mills students, who remain a group of empowered women committed to making the most of their education.

Blaze Your Own Trail

Historically, Mills has been a school of "firsts": the first women's college to the west of the Rockies, the first women's college to offer a computer science major and a 4+1 MBA degree, and even one of the first liberal arts colleges to offer a modern dance degree. Mills students agree that their academic experience is completely "what you make of it." One student noted that it's possible to "slack" through a semester with easy classes, but said that it is equally possible to have a hard semester by taking classes from hard professors—it's all up to the individual.

The general education requirement at Mills consists of 36 credits in what the school calls three "outcome categories": skills, perspectives, and disciplinary experiences. The skills category includes classes in written communication, quantitative reasoning, and information technology skills. Perspectives courses include women and gender, multicultural, and interdisciplinary studies. Classes in arts criticism, historical perspectives, natural sciences, and human behavior comprise the disciplinary exercises category. Despite the variety of academic requirements at Mills, many students complain about the lack of diversity in the choice of classes, saying they wish there were "more fun and random classes." Fortunately, for those seeking classes outside the box, UC Berkeley and other Bay Area schools welcome Mills students to cross-register in some of their programs.

Some of the most popular Mills majors are English, psychology, and Political, Legal, and Economic Analysis. Several students complained about the school's recent loss of the theater major. "The theater department was dropped because there weren't enough people majoring in it," one student explained. And although there's still a theater club on campus, those looking to major in theater arts may be disappointed. For those Mills women anxious to get a head start on advanced degrees, the school has seven dual degree programs, in which students can get master's degrees in Business Administration, Public Policy, Infant Mental Health, Interdisciplinary Computer Science, Engineering, Mathematics, or they can get a Credential in Teacher Education. Another specialized degree program at Mills is its Nursing Leadership Program, which consists of two years of liberal arts followed by two years of nursing school.

The Hills of Mills

Living at Mills is like, as one student put it, living in a "gorgeous oasis" with "beautiful architecture." The campus has recently completed a significant amount of renovations, such as a new environmentally friendly "green" science building. Mills women agree that their dorms are "very nice." Freshmen live in singles or doubles in two residences right in the middle of campus, and their housing is not too shabby. "One of our buildings, Orchard Meadow, is considered one of the nicest dorms on campus," one freshman boasted. There are a total of five residence halls at Mills. Upperclass women can choose among on-campus apartments, townhouses, or house co-ops.

The main dining hall at Mills is called Founders Commons, and it is set atop a hill. Students generally agree that the food is "fairly good for a college." The cafeterias are independently owned, and, to the relief of many Californians, "there are always vegetarian and vegan options." In addition to dining halls, Mills has a teashop that serves hot breakfast and "quick meals like hamburgers," along with a popular coffee shop, Café Susie's.

> "Most Mills women are usually feminists and interested in women's rights—or at least, they become so after four years here!"

Unfortunately, Oakland has no real "college-town feel." In fact, some students even go so far as to say that, "the area around campus does not feel very safe." Nonetheless, Mills has its own shuttle system and even a bus stop outside its front gate, making it easy to get on and off campus. There are several restaurants and shops off campus that are popular with Mills women, especially the Italian favorite, La Fiesta Pizza. And, for those looking to escape from Oakland entirely, San Francisco and all its distractions are just a car or shuttle ride away.

Friendly Feminists

Outside of the classroom, Mills women are famous for being friendly and sociable. One freshman enthused that, "On the first day of college, I sat down at tables at the cafeteria where I didn't know anyone, and was warmly welcomed!" The student body of Mills is notoriously diverse, both ethnically and culturally. One Caucasian woman even went so far as to joke that "sometimes I feel like a minority."

The women of Mills also have their own unique take on age diversity: 24 percent of the undergraduate population is made up of "resumers," or students over the age of 23. Resumers are usually students who have taken time off from their studies to pursue careers or raise families. Resumers have their own apartments on campus that welcome spouses and children. Yet, far from being secluded from the rest of the population, students universally proclaim that there is no real division on campus between resumers and regular undergraduates. Friendships form between women of all ages.

The integration of resumers into the community is just one aspect of Mills' openness and tolerance of differences. These include sexual orientation as well. "There is a lesbian stereotype," one student said, "but although there are many lesbians on campus, it is often hard to tell whose toast is buttered which way." No matter one's sexual preference, "most Mills women are usually feminists and interested in women's rights—or at least, they become so after four years here!"

Partying Without Guys?

Mills women agree that their school is not, by any means, a party school. Most students go out on weekend nights, and because many students don't have classes on Fridays, weekends tend to include Thursdays. There are a few popular campus-wide parties, including the Fetish Ball, which discourages clothing. Alcohol has little presence on campus. One freshman noted that she has seen "very little drinking in the freshman dorms." Even once you hit the age of 21, "even then it has to be done behind closed doors," one student explained. Students do note that drugs, mostly pot, are a lot more prevalent on campus than alcohol.

Be warned, Mills women don't often get a chance to mingle with members of the opposite sex. In fact, most couples around the school are female-female. Mills allows men to stay overnight in the dorms for up to seven nights each month, which is good news for students with boyfriends at other schools. Mills' graduate school, on the other hand, *is* coed, and Berkeley and Stanford are not too far away, so students say that if you're really looking for men, they're not too hard to find if you're willing to make a small trek.

Fun and Games

Athletics are admittedly not Mills' main focus, and, not surprisingly, the school doesn't have a football team. However, as a Division III school, Mills has seven varsity sports: cross country, crew, soccer, swimming, tennis, volleyball, and track and field. Students generally seem happy that more inexperienced athletes are allowed to participate since some of the pressure is off. As one Mills woman put it, "We take pride in what we've got." If varsity sports aren't your thing, you can get a workout by playing club sports, or by taking yoga and swimming classes at the gym.

Off the field, there are a plethora of student clubs and organizations, some favorites of which are the Animé Club, Horror Movie Club, Superhero Club, and the Gay/Lesbian Alliance. Mills women say that there is definitely something for everybody to be involved in, and if not, students are encouraged to start new organizations. Many students also get on-campus jobs, like serving food in the campus cafeteria.

A Tradition of Empowerment

In a school rooted in tradition, Mills students say that one of their favorite rites of passage is Paint Night. Students assign a color to each class, and on Paint Night—which takes place in the spring—seniors storm the campus and paint surfaces the color of their class. This tradition, fun and silly as it is, ties into Mills' continual emphasis on fostering strong women, ready to use their education to make a difference in the world around them. Still stubbornly single-sex, Mills continues to be a place where students and administration both remain believers in the power of all-women's schools.—*Becky Bicks*

FYI
If you come to Mills you'd better bring "an open mind."
What's the typical weekend schedule? "Enjoying weekend brunch, relaxing during free time, and evening on-campus activities."
If I could change one thing about Mills, I'd "make the campus more accessible, offering a shuttle to and from the airport at break time."
Three things every student at Mills should do before graduating are "explore the whole campus, get an on-campus job, eat the dining hall waffles for breakfast."

Occidental College

Address: 1600 Campus Road
Los Angeles, CA 90041
Phone: 800-825-5262
E-mail address:
admission@oxy.edu
Web site URL: www.oxy.edu
Year Founded: 1887
Private or Public: Private
Religious Affiliation: None
Location: Urban
Number of Applicants: 5,790
Percent Accepted: 39%
**Percent Accepted who
enroll:** 21%
Number Entering: 519
**Number of Transfers
Accepted each Year:** 60
Middle 50% SAT range:
M: 590–680, CR:
590–690, Wr: 590–690
Middle 50% ACT range: 26–30
**Early admission program
EA/ED/None:** ED
**Percentage accepted
through EA or ED:** 11%

EA and ED deadline: 15-Nov
Regular Deadline: 10-Jan
Application Fee: $60
**Full time Undergraduate
enrollment:** 1,846
Total enrollment: 1,868
Percent Male: 44%
Percent Female: 56%
**Total Percent Minority or
Unreported:** 36%
Percent African-American:
6%
**Percent Asian/Pacific
Islander:** 15%
Percent Hispanic: 14%
Percent Native-American:
1.20%
Percent International:
Unreported
**Percent in-state/out of
state:** 49%/51%
Percent from Public HS:
60%
Retention Rate: 94%
Graduation Rate 4-year: 82%

Graduation Rate 6-year:
86%
**Percent Undergraduates in
On-campus housing:** 80%
**Number of official organized
extracurricular
organizations:** 104
3 Most popular majors:
Economics, Diplomacy and
World Affairs, Psychology
Student/Faculty ratio: 10:1
Average Class Size: 17
**Percent of students going to
grad school:** Unreported
Tuition and Fees: $37,071
**In State Tuition and Fees if
different:** No difference
Cost for Room and Board:
$10,270
**Percent receiving financial
aid out of those who apply,
first year:** 76%
**Percent receiving financial
aid among all students:**
27%

I f living on a hilltop close to mountains, deserts, and beaches sounds like a pretty good deal, Occidental College in Los Angeles might be the perfect fit for you. This small school boasts a population of only 1,846 students who are both high achievers and very laid-back, in a climate that couldn't be much nicer. Oxy, as it is more commonly known, was one of the first schools to include the word "diverse" in its mission statement, and the community lives up to that goal. Although it is a very small school, Oxy provides diversity not only in the student body, but also in the breadth of academic options, the expansive extracurricular opportunities, and the great resources of Los Angeles that make the school unique.

The Core of it All

The school may be small, but the educational requirements certainly are not. The distributional core at Oxy requires all students to take three courses in math and lab sciences, study two out of four time periods and world areas, achieve the 102 level of a foreign language, and take two art credits. Although students are generally expected to have completed these core courses by the end of sophomore year, "that isn't strictly enforced." The freshman year Cultural Studies Program (CSP) is another part of Oxy's dedication to bringing students a well-rounded educational experience, and it takes advantage of all the resources Los Angeles has to offer. One freshman said that her CSP took her around to concerts in LA in addition to on campus, which allowed her to get off campus while bonding with members of her class. For the most ambitious students, the Oxy Honors Program requires a certain GPA within a given department, "usually around 3.5," and also mandates a more complex senior project than the ones that are required for the rest of the student body.

The school definitely does not skimp on the academics, and students say that small classes play a large role in the effectiveness of the classes at Oxy. While one student said that class size "depends on the department and class level," he also noted that his classes this semester "range from four to 10 people." Even introductory science courses, which at larger schools can fill auditoriums, only have about 20 to 30 students each at Oxy. The small size gives great access to all professors, whom one student said are "very flexible and accommodating." A sophomore said that he has "gotten together with professors over lunch, sometimes to discuss class-related issues, and sometimes just to get to know them better." This relaxed relationship between students and professors contributes a great deal to the learning environment at Oxy, and it allows for students to learn not from imposing figures, but from "actual human beings."

Living and Breathing Oxy

Despite the "beastly, steep hill" that divides the campus into upper and lower components, students say that "most of the stuff you need" is fairly conveniently located on the small campus, including two dining halls. Because classroom buildings are on lower campus, students do not need to go to upper campus often. In fact, "unless you can fly," the amount of stairs makes it a pretty big commitment to go up there. Still, upper campus houses some of the nicest dorms as well as Keck Theater, where performances occur all the time. Lower campus is still the center of community life, as the two all-freshman dorms are located there along with two housing all upperclassman. Students agree that most of the dorms are essentially the same, but they disagree about the nicest. One freshman mentioned that "Haines has all four years and a really nice porch," while a sophomore highlighted the brand new Rangeview Hall, which is "very fancy. All the rooms have private bathrooms, there's a weight room, and a bunch of posh lounges. The only problem is that it's pretty far away." Another particularly distinctive dorm is Pauley, which "places a special emphasis on bringing together students of different cultures," although the student added, "really, that could be said of any dorm." Wherever they happen to live, generally it is on campus. Although "a few upperclassmen live in houses within walking distance from campus," the vast majority live in dorms and "very few commute by car."

The Ins-N-Outs of Oxy Social Life

"People mostly stay on campus during the weekends. If they leave, it's usually just during the day to go to the beach or late night In-N-Out runs or concerts." With a location that makes it "hard to get off campus without a car," Oxy encourages students to stay on the hill and make the most of the college. There is "a good sushi place within walking distance" as well as the rest of the Eagle Rock community that directly surrounds the college. Students describe the partying as "low key" and "not very organized," especially since there is very little Greek presence on campus. Although students admit that the party scene is "mostly centered on drinking," they are quick to point out that "it's unfair to lump all drinkers together. Many people are very reasonable" and do not overdo the partying. Oxy students also have excellent access to concerts and performances, both on campus and in the LA area. One student noted that there is little pressure to go out at all. "There is a little kitchen in the dorm and you can stay in, bake a cake, and watch a movie—it all depends on who you hang out with." Even within such a small community, there are many different options for the levels of partying students feel comfortable with, but it is certainly "small scale." One student summed it up well by saying, "If partying is your scene, you can definitely find it, but people also spend a lot of time just hanging out with small groups of close friends."

Fun in the Sun

During the day, there are "lots of clubs" which are "really easy to get involved in." Extracurriculars are a main focus of most students, and there are plenty to choose from even though the school itself is small. Students clearly find plenty of activities to suit any interest, as one student mentioned "yoga and political groups" as some of the most popular clubs on campus, whereas another student emphasized orchestra, a cappella, Glee Club, and Dance Production as big draws on campus, both for people involved and for the students who "show up to their shows in big numbers." Though students may find their niche in very different places, one sophomore said that "Oxy's a small enough community that there isn't really one main social scene; they all kind of overlap."

> "Professors make themselves available to students both during and outside of class. Many times I have gotten together with professors over lunch, sometimes to discuss class-related issues and sometimes just to get to know them better."

In addition to the student clubs, "lots of people have on-campus jobs." Students emphasize that Oxy is very good at supplying these jobs and making them available for anyone. Popular jobs include working at the Cooler, which is one of the dining halls, driving the Oxy Bus, which transports students around campus, researching, doing grounds work, and helping in the financial aid office. The countless opportunities for work and play at Oxy really set it apart from other colleges of its size.

Oxy-gen Bonds

"The Oxy community is really open and friendly," said one freshman, and a sophomore added, "It's a small enough community that even with total strangers you're almost guaranteed to have mutual friends, and there's a lot of overlapping in social circles." Although with such a small school, students are likely to "see a lot of the same people," the students generally appreciate the closeness of the campus and the comfortable environment that creates. "Students are very vocal" and they are "very accepting of what other people have to say." In addition to the niceness of the students, the environment itself is conducive to a pleasant experience. When asked about the climate, one student paused before saying, "well . . . it rained twice, and forest fires made my asthma go to town. Otherwise it's sunny." With LA in their backyard and a small community of open, happy students, it's no surprise that "people love Oxy."—*Hannah Jacobson*

FYI
If you come to Occidental, you'd better bring "sunscreen!"
What is the typical weekend schedule? "Thursday night is the beginning of the weekend, but most people just stay up late and do some low-key hanging out and sleeping in, then go to Stewie Hall, the party dorm, on Friday and Saturday nights."
If I could change one thing about Occidental, I'd "make it easier to leave large musical instruments on upper campus rather than having to lock them in a broom closet."
Three things every student at Occidental should do before graduating are "take a class with Simeon Pillich, go to an a cappella and orchestra concert, and find the Taco Truck at three in the morning."

Pepperdine University

Address: 24255 Pacific Coast Highway Malibu, CA 90263
Phone: 310-506-4392
E-mail address: admission-seaver@pepperdine.edu
Web site URL: www.pepperdine.edu
Year Founded: 1937
Private or Public: Private
Religious Affiliation: Church of Christ
Location: Suburban
Number of Applicants: 6,661
Percent Accepted: 35%
Percent Accepted who enroll: 33%
Number Entering: 753
Number of Transfers Accepted each Year: Unreported
Middle 50% SAT range: M: 570–680, CR: 560–670, Wr: 560–670
Middle 50% ACT range: 24–29
Early admission program EA/ED/None: None

Percentage accepted through EA or ED: NA
EA and ED deadline: NA
Regular Deadline: 15-Nov, 15-Jan
Application Fee: $65
Full time Undergraduate enrollment: 3,398
Total enrollment: 6,877
Percent Male: 45%
Percent Female: 55%
Total Percent Minority or Unreported: 41%
Percent African-American: 7%
Percent Asian/Pacific Islander: 10%
Percent Hispanic: 10%
Percent Native-American: 1%
Percent International: 7%
Percent in-state/out of state: 50%/50%
Percent from Public HS: Unreported
Retention Rate: 88%
Graduation Rate 4-year: 72%

Graduation Rate 6-year: Unreported
Percent Undergraduates in On-campus housing: 67%
Number of official organized extracurricular organizations: 50
3 Most popular majors: Business, Communication, Social Sciences
Student/Faculty ratio: 13:1
Average Class Size: Unreported
Percent of students going to grad school: 53%
Tuition and Fees: $36,770
In State Tuition and Fees if different: No difference
Cost for Room and Board: $10,480
Percent receiving financial aid out of those who apply, first year: 57%
Percent receiving financial aid among all students: 35%

Located in scenic Malibu, California, Pepperdine University bills itself as a Christian university committed to the highest standards of academic excellence and Christian values. Combining ethical ideals of the Christian faith with high academic standards, Pepperdine's mission rests on its belief that spiritual commitment demands the highest standards of academic excellence. With its emphasis on international perspective, broad education, religious devotion, and high standards of academic excellence, Pepperdine seeks to create individuals with a solid grasp of both their duties to the world and their duties to themselves.

Spiritual and Academic Commitment

George Pepperdine, who founded the university in 1937, was a devout member of the Church of Christ, and thus constructed a college that would teach students to lead lives of purpose, service, and leadership. Accepting students from all faiths and races, the University seeks to extend its ideals to all students.

Pepperdine University enrolls 8,300 students and is comprised of five colleges and schools. Originally, George Pepperdine had a vision of a small, primarily undergraduate university. Seaver College, the undergraduate residential college of letters, arts, and sciences, is the embodiment of that vision. Every year, it matriculates 3,000 of Pepperdine's students.

In 1971, Pepperdine became a university with the addition of the School of Law. Shortly following this development, a grant by Mrs. Frank Seaver allowed the university to move from its location in south-central Los Angeles to its current 830-acre campus in Malibu.

Pepperdine's academic reputation and its beautiful campus has been the subject of much acclaim, and as a result, its selectivity has been significantly rising over the past few years. In 2005, Seaver experienced one of its largest applicant pools ever, with 7,800 applicants and 837 freshmen and transfer students enrolled. "I think Pepperdine is getting more and more academically ambitious students," one senior said. "Good thing for the reputation, maybe not so much for the people who have to compete with them!"

The bachelor's degree is offered in 38 fields of study, and high-achieving students are given the opportunity to study for a master's degree in one of seven areas. In addi-

tion to focusing on a particular major, the university encourages students to develop as broadly educated persons and take classes in unfamiliar terrains. In keeping with George Pepperdine's original goals, it also requires that students take three terms of religious classes. "The religious classes are pretty much what you would expect," one student said. "Not exactly the most exciting things in the world." Other students, however, said that the classes are "pretty interesting."

> "Be smart. Be religious. Be conservative. Be good looking. You'll fit in."

Aside from the larger general education lectures, classes are usually small. "That's probably Pepperdine's biggest weakness and greatest strength." While students maintain close relationships with professors, one junior complained, "Sometimes you get a little sick of seeing the same people over and over again . . . after a few years, I actually want my lectures back!"

In addition, the small class structure works extremely well if the professor is engaging, but if he or she is not, then the class becomes disproportionately unbearable. As one student stated, "I think the small classes are hit or miss, because if you like your class, then you love it, and if you don't like it, then you *really* don't like it."

Location, Location, Location

Students rarely, if ever, complain about their on-campus housing. "I never thought I'd say this, but the dorms are absolutely beautiful," admitted one student. Even during freshman year, when other universities tend to give their freshmen sub-par housing, Pepperdine pampers its students. It houses four freshmen in a suite of two bedrooms, each suite filled with such amenities as a common area and a regularly cleaned bathroom. Despite these amenities, however, many students do choose to move off campus after freshman year. "It's about having the space and the freedom to move around," said one off-campus student.

As beautiful as the view is, many students claim that Pepperdine's student body can rival it. "We have the best-looking student population in the entire United States!" one student boasted enthusiastically. This confidence can be shown by the fact that many wear little more than a bathing suit while tanning on or nearby campus.

But although "Malibu is beautiful," "it isn't a college town. Sure, we live in great dorms with a great view of the ocean, but if you don't love the beach, you'll definitely need a car." With Santa Monica, Westwood, and Los Angeles about half an hour away, students are often tempted with an easy escape on weekends. However, Southern California's terrible traffic often puts a damper on students' impromptu getaways. Because the getaways might take an hour to reach, students tend to stay on campus and go to parties which "aren't too difficult to find."

International Perspective

Many students agree that Pepperdine's study abroad program sets it apart from other Christian universities. Seaver College students are offered year-round residential programs in Germany, England, Italy, Argentina, and various other countries. Having established its study abroad program in 1963, Pepperdine has worked hard to expand and enhance its students' experiences abroad. Pepperdine believes that by encouraging students to study abroad and by making the transfer process painless, students will be more likely to venture out and gain an international perspective. If students decide not to study abroad during the school year, they may study abroad during the summer. Additionally, students are encouraged to partake in language programs at Pepperdine over the summer to complete their language requirements. According to the school's center for international programs, over half of all Seaver College students go overseas during their college career. "International programs and study abroad opportunities are Pepperdine's greatest strength. I went to South America and Asia and didn't have to worry about credits or anything. They take really good care of you."

Political Activism

Students claim that there isn't much political activism in either direction. While some Democratic or Republican organizations may hang a banner here and there, students do not often discuss politics. One female student stated, "I often protest Pepperdine's conservatism. As a liberal arts education, you'd expect them to be more liberal about homosexuality and women's rights. But they aren't." Another student noted that the College Republicans are much more popular than the Young Democrats, though neither of the two draw much support, which he felt was indicative of Pepperdine's apolitical nature.

Despite this, however, Pepperdine has a strong history of community service. For example, it had the top acceptance rates in its region for the selective Teach for America program. While the program only accepts 30 percent of its students, over 50 percent of Pepperdine applicants were accepted.

Of course, Pepperdine isn't above having a good joke now and then. Pepperdine won the NCAA National Collegiate Men's Volleyball Championship last year, beating the UCLA Bruins at an away tournament. This scored them a visit to the White House, where they proceeded to present President Bush with an honorary surfboard.—*Danny Friedman*

FYI
If you come to Pepperdine, you'd better bring "your best Gucci sunglasses."
What's the typical weekend schedule? "The usual—partying, studying, taking advantage of the beach."
If I could change one thing about Pepperdine, I'd "get rid of the hugely conservative atmosphere! C'mon, people, we need a little diversity now and then."
Three things every student at Pepperdine should do before graduating are "One, get a great tan; two, go abroad; three, take advantage of being on the most beautiful campus in the world!"

St. Mary's College of California

Address: 1928 Saint Mary's Road Moraga, CA 94556
Phone: 925-631-4224
E-mail address: smcadmit@stmarys_ca.edu
Web site URL: www.stmarys-ca.edu
Year Founded: 1863
Private or Public: Private
Religious Affiliation: Roman Catholic
Location: Suburban
Number of Applicants: 3,929
Percent Accepted: 82%
Percent Accepted who enroll: 19%
Number Entering: 611
Number of Transfers Accepted each Year: 293
Middle 50% SAT range: M: 480–590, CR: 480–590, Wr: Unreported
Middle 50% ACT range: Unreported
Early admission program EA/ED/None: EA

Percentage accepted through EA or ED: Unreported
EA and ED deadline: 15-Nov
Regular Deadline: 1-Feb
Application Fee: $55
Full time Undergraduate enrollment: 2,402
Total enrollment: 2,685
Percent Male: 39%
Percent Female: 61%
Total Percent Minority or Unreported: 42%
Percent African-American: 5%
Percent Asian/Pacific Islander: 11%
Percent Hispanic: 21%
Percent Native-American: 1%
Percent International: 2%
Percent in-state/out of state: 85%/15%
Percent from Public HS: 58%
Retention Rate: 77%
Graduation Rate 4-year: 53%

Graduation Rate 6-year: 61%
Percent Undergraduates in On-campus housing: 58%
Number of official organized extracurricular organizations: 42
3 Most popular majors: Business Administration, Management and Operations, Other Communication and Media Studies
Student/Faculty ratio: 11:1
Average Class Size: 20 to 29
Percent of students going to grad school: 48%
Tuition and Fees: $33,250
In State Tuition and Fees if different: No difference
Cost for Room and Board: $11,680
Percent receiving financial aid out of those who apply, first year: 72%
Percent receiving financial aid among all students: 69%

A t St. Mary's, students won't hesitate to tell you that their location is "perfect." This small Catholic college, located in a picturesque valley sheltered from the metropolises of Berkeley and San Francisco, also offers easy access to these cities at any time. Along with the cosmopolitan experience, St. Mary's offers a tradition of solid academics and athletics, as well as a supportive environment that encourages its students to seek out new ways of learning and helping the community—all principles rooted firmly in the philosophy of its founding Christian Brothers.

The Big Picture

St. Mary's boasts a number of strong programs. Applicants can choose to study in the following schools: The School of Liberal Arts, the School of Science, the School of Economics and Business Administration, the School of Education, or the School of Intercollegiate Nursing. Within these programs, except for the School of Nursing, students pick from a variety of different majors, the most popular of which are business, communications and social sciences. However, students point out other interesting choices, such as the undergraduate teacher's preparation program that gives students their teaching credentials and a Masters of Education in five years. Some students believe that St. Mary's most unique opportunity is the Integral Program of liberal arts. While only a handful of students enroll in the program, it allows them to spend all four years in rigorous and well-rounded classes taught in small seminar and tutorial settings with "discussions around round tables." Academics are truly an area in which the small size of St. Mary's becomes especially valuable. The average class size is 21 students, and professors are usually known on a first-name basis. One student even boasted, "We all exchanged phone numbers in my class, and my professor called me at home to make sure I was okay when I was sick."

St. Mary's seeks to develop the whole student, a sentiment reflected in the college's General Requirements, which asks that all students take 12 classes from three distinct groups: Religious Studies, Collegiate Seminars, and the Area Requirements in humanities, empirical science and the social sciences. There are also requirements in language proficiency, diversity and writing. Within the broad spectrum of courses offered, students say that in general, it's easy to fulfill the various requirements. One senior explained, "I took two music theory classes, which counted for the General Requirements. It wasn't my area of study, but I like listening to music, so it was enjoyable and fulfilled an area." On the other hand, other students pointed out that the number of required courses makes it difficult to change from one major to another. Another senior admitted that she must spend an extra semester taking courses after her class has graduated because she changed majors in her junior year.

> "We all exchanged phone numbers in my class, and my professor called me at home to make sure I was okay when I was sick."

"Jan-term," or the January Term, is a distinctive aspect of St. Mary's academic calendar. St. Mary's operates on a 4-1-4 system. This means that students take four course credits in both the fall and spring terms, but have four weeks in between to explore subjects outside of their majors in one full-credit class. It's a time that "pretty much everyone looks forward to" and students have the opportunity to study abroad, pursue a unique on-campus class, take a course from another 4-1-4 college, or participate in an independent study project. Some choices the college offers for on-campus courses include "The Semiotics of Buffy the Vampire Slayer (and other Female Heroes)," "The Sixties through Film," and "Chocolate, Waffles, and Other Belgian Passions." One student raved that she got to "spend 10 days at the Sundance Film Festival" as part of her Jan-term course, as well as take field trips to Buddhist temples around the Bay Area as part of her "What is Buddhism?" course.

Living in Moraga

St. Mary's guarantees housing only to freshmen and sophomores, while juniors and seniors must enter a lottery if they want housing. Even so, students say "people who want it generally get it." Freshmen live in doubles or triples that are "a little cramped" with sinks in the rooms and a bathroom down the hall. Sophomores live in suites with combinations of doubles and singles and a common room with a "nice bathroom." Upperclassmen who luck out in the lottery are provided with on-campus townhouses that include bathrooms, kitchens and living rooms.

Freshmen dorms are single-sex by floor, and for underclassmen, there is a Resident Advisor or a Resident Director on every floor; upperclassmen have one per building. "They vary in terms of strictness," but policies often get more lenient as the students get older. One student explained that the policy for the townhouses is more like "see no evil, smell no evil, as long as you're being legal and safe," while for the freshmen, they crack down harder for alcohol violations or having the opposite sex in the rooms past 2 a.m.

There is one dining hall on campus, where students classify the food as "not great" and "pretty standard for college food, although people tend to complain a lot." One student confessed that "during sophomore year, when I had to have a meal plan, I ate in the dining hall about three times the whole year." While the dining hall may not receive the best reviews, there are other on-campus options, including "The Brickpile," which has burgers and fries, and a café, at which it is possible to redeem "flex dollars." Flex dollars are part of some meal plans and allow students to purchase à la carte. Students living on campus are required to purchase a meal plan but the plans vary by the number of meals per week and amount of flex dollars.

Some students choose to move off campus into apartments in downtown Moraga, while others find housing in the neighboring towns of Lafayette and Walnut Creek. However, these options can be a lot pricier, although comfortable and convenient. Student housing discounts are available and make it easier for students to afford a slightly more vibrant setting. Moraga in itself is "not the most exciting place," but students find it pretty easy to make the short trips to have dinner and see shows in San Francisco and Berkeley or go shopping in Walnut Creek. These excursions range from 10 to 45 minutes away by car or the Bay Area Rapid Transit train system. In Moraga, the nearest grocery stores and restaurants to campus are five to 10 minutes away by car. Many students also choose to take the bus, which stops by the campus regularly and is free with a St. Mary's ID card. But one girl complained that "I feel a bit isolated because the bus makes it harder to go places at night."

Relaxing Between Activities

Students classify St. Mary's as "not a party school . . . but people have fun here." There are no fraternities or sororities, so most of the social scene is in the dorms, especially the townhouses, which are "where the party's at" for upperclassmen. The freshman dorms are dry, and alcohol is strictly off-limits for everyone under 21, so freshmen usually hang out in each other's rooms and watch movies. Regardless, students feel that "many people drink, although there's not a lot of pressure to join in." The school also hosts many events, ranging from concerts to various speakers, and everyone is invited to attend, most often in the Soda Center, at the center of campus. The most attended dance every year is Oasis, a Hawaiian-themed party held on the quad. There are other dances too, like the Halloween Dance, but "mostly freshmen go to them."

St. Mary's students pride themselves on a diversity of political opinion and thought, saying that while "the Liberals are more vocal, the Republican club is definitely growing." However, other students said that they haven't noticed much socioeconomic diversity around the campus, seeing mostly white, middle-class students from around the Bay Area. Students speculated that "the average St. Mary's girl is blonde, rich and perky," while guys are "more geeky and outgoing," but hasten to add that there are many exceptions. One student proudly cited the college's efforts to increase the diversity of the school by making it easier for lower-income students to attend, referring to the LaSallian Catholic Brothers' mission of teaching and serving the disadvantaged.

In general, "people are really friendly here," and it's not uncommon to see students relaxing on the quad or talking at the picnic tables on warm California days. People meet many friends in their dorms, but "people in the same clubs tend to hang out together," such as those who work on *The Collegian*, the college newspaper, or those who play on sports teams. Overall, the atmosphere is easygoing, explained a senior,

saying, "Classes tend to intermix a lot, and it's really easy to meet people" in other grades. In addition, people don't feel that the Catholic presence at St. Mary's is overbearing at all; in fact, one student feels that "the school's greatest untapped resource is its network of Brothers."

Go Gaels!

Any St. Mary's student will tell you that the school is fiercely proud of its sports teams, even though the football program was recently canceled. St. Mary's boasts NCAA Division I teams in 15 sports, including baseball, basketball and soccer, and the school works hard to recruit talented athletes from California and around the country. St. Mary's has seen action at March Madness and at the Sweet Sixteen of the NCAA tournament with its strong men's basketball and women's volleyball teams. Many students come out to support these up-and-coming teams by joining the "Gael-Force," the school's pep squad, which has a special section reserved at every home game so that the legions of loyal fans can cheer on their teams.

The school also offers myriad club and intramural sports, which "can sometimes get pretty intense, but are a lot of fun." While students don't hesitate to step out on the fields, some students feel that the gym, weight room, the fields and some of the other athletics facilities could use a facelift. Overall, "it's really hard to find a student who's just involved in class," as the groups present on campus range from the school newspaper and the Intervarsity Christian Fellowship to Best Buddies, which pairs students with disabled kids from the community, to Italian club. Many students also join clubs affiliated with their particular majors. In addition, a lot of students at St. Mary's spend time working. The college offers various on-campus jobs, but many students venture into the surrounding area. Babysitting is one of the most popular jobs for girls, due to the rich suburban atmosphere of Moraga and neighboring Orinda and Lafayette.

There is a strong sense of tradition and serenity as you walk across the St. Mary's campus among the mission-style buildings bathed in the California sunshine. At St. Mary's, students can find a refreshing blend of an intimate, liberal arts education and the Catholic mission of developing the many parts of an individual.—*Kimberly Chow*

FYI

If you come to St. Mary's, you better bring "a good attitude towards the small Catholic school atmosphere."

What is the typical weekend schedule? "Hang out with your roommates and have dinner and watch a movie on Friday; on Saturday, go to Berkeley or San Francisco; and on Sunday, relax, do homework and laundry.

If I could change one thing about St. Mary's, I'd "make it easier for students who don't have cars, because the bus is inadequate for really going out at night and on the weekends."

Three things every student should do before graduating from St. Mary's are "hike up to the cross at midnight, sneak into the catacombs, and get to know a Brother."

Stanford University

Address: 355 Galvez Street Stanford, CA 94305-6106
Phone: 650-723-2091
E-mail address: admission@stanford.edu
Web site URL: www.stanford.edu
Year Founded: 1885
Private or Public: Private
Religious Affiliation: None
Location: Suburban
Number of Applicants: 23,958
Percent Accepted: 10%
Percent Accepted who enroll: 70%
Number Entering: 1,722
Number of Transfers Accepted each Year: 23
Middle 50% SAT range: M: 680–790 CR: 660–760 Wr: 660–760
Middle 50% ACT range: 29–33
Early admission program EA/ED/None: EA

Percentage accepted through EA or ED: 16%
EA and ED deadline: 1-Nov
Regular Deadline: 1-Jan
Application Fee: $75
Full time Undergraduate enrollment: 6,532
Total enrollment: 16,812
Percent Male: 49%
Percent Female: 51%
Total Percent Minority or Unreported: 52%
Percent African-American: 8%
Percent Asian/Pacific Islander: 25%
Percent Hispanic: 13%
Percent Native-American: 2%
Percent International: 6%
Percent in-state/out of state: 44%/56%
Percent from Public HS: 60%
Retention Rate: 98%
Graduation Rate 4-year: 79%

Graduation Rate 6-year: 93%
Percent Undergraduates in On-campus housing: 88%
Number of official organized extracurricular organizations: 600
3 Most popular majors: Biology/Biological Sciences, General Economics, General Political Science and Government
Student/Faculty ratio: 6:1
Average Class Size: 10 to 19
Percent of students going to grad school: 52%
Tuition and Fees: $36,030
In State Tuition and Fees if different: No difference
Cost for Room and Board: $11,182
Percent receiving financial aid out of those who apply, first year: 75%
Percent receiving financial aid among all students: 78%

Whether they're running madly from fountain to fountain, participating in a campus-wide makeout session during the first full moon of the year, or enjoying the mild California weather, Stanford students will tell you they know how to have fun. But they still find time in their busy schedules to fit in demanding course loads, community service, sports and music, all while maintaining a social life. An hour away from San Francisco in the affluent dot-com community of Palo Alto, some of the nation's top students have found a school that will support their interests and goals,

however quirky or lofty they may be. Beneath this laid-back, West Coast "summer camp" atmosphere, lies the university's strong commitment to balancing a prominent research institution with a strong undergraduate academic experience.

Balancing Act

To fulfill the 180 units required for graduation, which includes requirements for the major, writing and rhetoric, humanities, science, math, culture studies and a year of foreign language, Stanford students generally take four or five units per quarter. The

Stanford year is divided into quarters, which makes for three marking periods during the academic year and the fourth one during the summer. Because of this arrangement, students said they often find that their midterm period extends from "the second week of classes until dead week [the week before finals]." But many said they enjoy the quarter system, in part because it allows them both to explore more classes and be done quickly with classes they dislike. Although IHUM, the humanities requirement for freshmen and sophomores, got mixed reviews due to occasional "overambitious" or "irrelevant" subject matters, most agreed that they benefited from PWR, the writing and rhetoric requirement. Overall, students said the general requirements, or "GERs," are very flexible and often fulfill themselves; in fact, one sophomore said his history class fulfilled four at once.

> "If someone told you they never get stressed they'd be lying to you."

Freshman classes are generally large, ranging from 100 to 200 students, but there are always discussions sections, as well as opportunities for more specialized seminars. Although academic concentrations are categorized as either "fuzzy" (the humanities) or "techie" (science and math), students said they love that Stanford is so evenly divided among different disciplines. Some of the most popular disciplines include human biology, economics and psychology. Among the renowned faculty, Robert Sapolsky attracts many undergrads to his neurology courses. Students touted the small introductory seminars as particularly engaging, especially when they offer the opportunity to get to know "ridiculously important and famous" experts in the field. Opportunities to interface with professors are not difficult to find if you make an effort, one junior explained, and developing a relationship can lead to research positions or simply the chance to discuss your studies with a world specialist. One biology major confessed that what he likes most about Stanford is its ability to be "an amazing research institution, while simultaneously giving a lot of emphasis to teaching."

"If someone told you they never get stressed they'd be lying to you here," a sophomore said. "It's a way of life, but it's definitely a manageable level of stress, and it makes it that much more enticing to blow off steam on weekends." Most Stanford students appear to have found the balance between work and play that allows them to take advantage of their many academic resources, as well as the pleasant weather. And they agree that people usually collaborate when studying; one girl emphasized that she had "never met anyone who wouldn't give you their full help right when you asked."

Camp Stanford

Many upperclassmen describe their freshman year as "Camp Stanford." "It's basically an amazing time the whole year, doing crazy things with your dorm like scavenger hunts in San Francisco and Secret Snowflake, when you dare each other to do things like lick the RA's toes," one male student said. "I tried on a $3,000 dress at Neiman Marcus." While it's not uncommon for freshmen to go out en masse to frat parties and campus events, upperclassmen said they usually go out in smaller groups of their close friends and meet up with residents of other buildings. But the more the merrier for Full Moon on the Quad, the time of year when the freshmen and seniors rush out at midnight to swap spit (and probably mono, one student commented). A good number of students in all grades drink, and in freshman dorms it can run to excess when "people don't know what their limits are since they just studied all through high school." Pot is less common, and hard drugs are "just about nonexistent, at least as far as I've seen." The 15 frats and 11 sororities on campus often host parties, but "you definitely don't need to join in order to have fun," one girl said. "They're there if you want them, but there's no pressure at all."

Some students said they were surprised at "how normal people are" at Stanford. "Instead of being totally awkward like I was expecting, people are very well-rounded and have good social networks of close friends and acquaintances," a junior commented. Most seem to have found a healthy balance between intense studying and having fun. "People are very focused on work, but they can still relax and go out to parties," a girl said. "People will do well in school, but they won't talk about it too much, like they won't bring up academics in conversation but they'll flow with it if it comes up and have interesting ideas." While the student body is perceived as being mostly upper-middle class, there is an impressive amount of diversity. Undergraduates hail from 68 foreign countries and minorities are well-represented. Politically, the campus is less stratified; students tend to lean towards the left, and one of the most recent campus protests occurred when President George W. Bush visited campus.

Among the Palm Trees

The attractive, sprawling campus boasts predominantly Spanish-style architecture and landscaping, featuring red tiles, adobe, and palm trees—lots of palm trees. But underneath its uniform exterior, Stanford seems to offer every housing option imaginable, including "all-frosh, freshman-sophomore, and four-class" residence halls for first years, then upperclassmen dorms that include small houses, mid-sized dorms, apartments, and suites. After freshman year, students enter the "Draw," in which they form groups of friends and enter the lottery, hoping to get a good number so they have a better chance of getting the living situation they desire. Out of the three years, two are "preferred" in the lottery while one year is "un-preferred," and students automatically receive a worse draw number. There is a lot of "Draw-ma" when it comes to forming groups or when the housing students receive is too far away or doesn't have a good social scene, but "people tend to be pretty happy, or at least neutral, about where they end up." One sophomore raved about the open kitchen and chef in her house on "The Row," the nice strip of houses, fraternities, and sororities on one end of campus, while one junior said his four-class dorm wasn't nearly as exciting as his freshman residence, which was "wild and chaotic 24-7."

A more controversial element of the housing system is the "theme house" option, through which students choose a house based on language, culture, or academic interest. In Casa Zapata, the Chicano/Latino theme house, for example, 50 percent of residents are of that particular ethnic heritage, while the other 50 percent are not. While some students have said the theme houses are a great chance to live with those who share their cultures, others have protested that the houses both divide the undergraduate population and oblige the half of the house that aren't of that heritage to "live with people who didn't necessarily choose to live with them."

Dorms often play host to consumption of alcohol, although not usually in a raucous party setting, and "the RAs are usually very cool about it, even letting you have kegs, although some houses are stricter than others and you aren't allowed to bring anything into the hall." Campus police will sometimes enforce the rule of no open containers outside the dorms. The dining hall food—which students eat when living in the dorms—gets pretty good reviews for being generally tasty and including many vegetarian and vegan options, but "you can definitely get tired of it after a few weeks because it doesn't change much," one freshman lamented. Students can also apply their meal plans to a variety of on-campus eateries, including CoHo coffeehouse, Subway and the Treehouse. Stanford attracts many speakers, in the past few years featuring the Dali Lama, Elie Wiesel, and Cameron Diaz, among others.

Stanford is often called a "bubble" because of its self-sufficiency—it even has its own zip code. Palo Alto doesn't get high marks as a college town, although most students don't seem to mind since "everything you need in terms of entertainment is on campus." But the quiet, predominantly-wealthy city does offer an array of Asian restaurants, the sandwich chain Pluto's, and the Cheesecake Factory, as well as bowling and ice skating. Once in a while, students take the local Caltrain for about an hour to get to San Francisco. This metropolis offers a wealth of entertainment and culture, from concerts in small nightclubs to browsing through tie-dye shirts and used books in the legendary Haight-Ashbury district.

Find Your Passion

"A lot of us used to be athletes in high school," one sophomore said. "And even though only the very best go on to play for Stanford, it's a very active campus on the whole." When they aren't playing intramurals—the most popular of which are Frisbee, volleyball, and basketball—you can find Cardinals working out at the new Arrillaga gym or running outside. But they're not afraid to take to the sidelines, and "people often spend their Saturdays cheering on their friends at their sports events." Much of the campus comes out for football and basketball games; some fanatical male supporters have even been known to paint the Stanford letters on their chests and get the outlines sunburned on their skin. The combined excellence of Stanford's Division I programs has earned it the Director's Cup for success in college athletics for the past 14 years in a row, out of the 15 the award has been offered.

When they aren't at the gym making the "athletic, attractive campus" even more so, Stanford students get involved in "as many activities as you could imagine." "There is every kind of dance group, publication, a cappella, cultural, religious, or club sport organization there is," a political science major said. Community service groups are particularly popular, allowing undergraduates the opportunity to venture off campus and tutor in underprivileged neighborhoods or work with the homeless. Undergrads can even stay on campus and help Stanford employees with their English skills in a program called Habla la Noche.

"Everyone here has something they really care about," one Cardinal reflected. And it seems to be true. You have your world-class athletes, community service movers and shakers, dedicated researchers, and political activists, and yet, "this amazing person is just the kid down the hall from you who you can have late-night conversations with and who got dared to do something outrageous during Secret Snowflake." The opportunities that Stanford students enthusiastically enumerated featured not only the challenging academics and fine research facilities; but they also praised their fellow undergrads: "The caliber of people here, not necessarily just the professors, but also the students, is amazing," a sophomore said. "You learn so much from the people around you."—*Kimberly Chow*

FYI

If you come to Stanford, you'd better bring "a more laid-back attitude, but a desire to do something meaningful."

What's the typical weekend schedule? "Friday go out to dinner in Palo Alto, then go to a frat or hang out with friends in one of the houses; Saturday morning sleep in, then go to a sports event or do community service, then go to a room party; Sunday hit the books during the day, but if you have time, go to FLICKS at 10PM to watch a movie and throw paper at each other."

If I could change one thing about Stanford, "I'd make Palo Alto more of a college town; even though staying on campus is fine, it would be nice if places stayed open later and there was more to do."

Three things every student at Stanford should do before graduating are "Go fountain-hopping, when you run from fountain to fountain on campus with a group of your friends or dorm and get really wet; get to know a big-name professor; do Sophomore College, when you come a few weeks early for your second year and either take a small class you're interested in or travel to locations like the Galápagos Islands."

University of California System

Students from California undoubtedly will have heard of the University of California, the state's leading public university system for high-achieving high school students. But the UC system stands out not only in California, but across the country, and even the world. A model for public institutions across the United States, eight of its undergraduate campuses rank in the top 100, six in the top 50, and two in the top 25 universities in the country. With more than 191,000 students, 1,340,000 living alumni and an overall endowment of $9.6 billion as of 2007, students looking to enter the UC system will be joining good company. Counting 32 Nobel laureates and 254 members of the National Academy of Sciences within their faculty, UC students are able to get a world-class education without the hefty price tag that comes with private colleges.

So Many Choices

The UC system counts nine campuses among its members, along with a tenth school, San Francisco, which is limited to graduate study in the health sciences. As the charter campus, Berkeley is still regarded by some as the system's flagship school, leading the other campuses with its tradition of academic excellence. But the University of California, Los Angeles, and UC San Diego are not far behind. UCLA's admission rate is comparable to Berkeley's in competitiveness—both hover around 20 percent—and UCSD has already made a name for itself both in the U.S. and abroad for its excellence in the sciences. Irvine boasts an ideal campus location in sunny Orange County, just miles from the beach, not to mention its technological and scientific instruction. Davis is a leading university known for its premier agricultural research as well as strengths in math and sciences. Santa Barbara is quickly proving itself as a rising star in the academic world for its active research, which includes 11 national research centers. Santa Cruz can find pride in its physics, math and astronomy programs, as well its political science and art departments, not to mention its convenient location right outside beautiful Monterey Bay, just a short trip away from San Francisco and San Jose. Back down south near the greater Los Angeles area, Riverside maintains its reputation for pioneering citrus research and entomology, as well as well-known programs in science fiction and photography. Finally, last but not least, is Merced, founded in 2005 as the newest addition to the UC family. Although it is located in a rural area associated with agriculture (it's just miles from Yosemite National Park), it emphasizes cutting edge research in the fields of natural science, math, and engineering.

Something for Everyone

While each school handles its admissions separately, students only need to use one application for all the UC's, thereby simplifying the process for students. All eligible students from California are guaranteed a spot in the UC system, though admissions to their top choice of campuses is not necessarily guaranteed. Through statewide admissions, the UC system automatically accepts students among the top eighth of California public school graduates, as well as the top four percent of any given high school. If eligible students are not granted admissions to their top choices, they are then referred to other UC campuses which still have open space. Because several UC campuses have fairly competitive admissions policies, some students will inevitably be disappointed, but even those who end up at their second, third or even fourth choice colleges generally find themselves satisfied with their experience. As one student said about UC Irvine, "The people that come to this school are friendly and the atmosphere is welcoming and comfortable. This was not my first choice school, but when I came here, I grew to like it a lot."

The UC system no longer uses affirmative action policies after the passing in 1996 of California's Proposition 209, which prohibits public institutions such as the UC schools from considering race, sex and ethnicity in their selection processes. As a result, underrepresented minorities and students from underprivileged backgrounds have had a more difficult time enrolling at UC schools, especially those in the proverbial top tier. As such, issues of racial imbalance have arisen, but the UC system has named representing California's diversity in its schools as one of its priorities. Riverside itself can boast of a student body that draws its strength from diversity—the school has topped national rankings in ethnic and socioeconomic diversity, third and fifteenth in the nation, respectively.

All in all, the University of California offers a variety of opportunities among its many campuses and within each campus, the benefits of a huge array of strong academic departments. Students who are looking for a quality education but don't want to graduate with significant debt will certainly be able to find the rewarding experience they seek in the UC system. With so many campuses and a wide range of strengths in research and departments, the UC system is bound to have something for everyone.
—*Della Fok*

University of California / Berkeley

Address: 110 Sproul Hall, #5800 Berkeley, CA 94720-5800
Phone: 510-642-3175
E-mail address: NA
Web site URL: www.berkeley.edu
Year Founded: 1868
Private or Public: Public
Religious Affiliation: None
Location: Urban
Number of Applicants: 43,983
Percent Accepted: 23%
Percent Accepted who enroll: 41%
Number Entering: 4,204
Number of Transfers Accepted each Year: 3,311
Middle 50% SAT range: M: 630–760, CR: 590–710, Wr: 600–720
Middle 50% ACT range: Unreported
Early admission program EA/ED/None: None

Percentage accepted through EA or ED: NA
EA and ED deadline: NA
Regular Deadline: 30-Nov
Application Fee: $60
Full time Undergraduate enrollment: 24,636
Total enrollment: 33,903
Percent Male: 45%
Percent Female: 55%
Total Percent Minority or Unreported: 70%
Percent African-American: 3%
Percent Asian/Pacific Islander: 45%
Percent Hispanic: 12%
Percent Native-American: <1%
Percent International: 3%
Percent in-state/out of state: 90%/10%
Percent from Public HS: 85%
Retention Rate: 97%
Graduation Rate 4-year: 60%

Graduation Rate 6-year: Unreported
Percent Undergraduates in On-campus housing: 35%
Number of official organized extracurricular organizations: 300
3 Most popular majors: Computer Engineering, English Language and Literature, Political Science and Government
Student/Faculty ratio: 15:1
Average Class Size: 2 to 9
Percent of students going to grad school: Unreported
Tuition and Fees: $28,264
In State Tuition and Fees if different: $7,656
Cost for Room and Board: $14,494
Percent receiving financial aid out of those who apply, first year: 63%
Percent receiving financial aid among all students: 49%

The University of California, Berkeley is a long name for a college, so the lucky students who do manage to land a spot here affectionately call it "Cal." Sprawling over 1,232 acres that overlook the San Francisco Bay, Berkeley is home to over 24,500 undergraduates and boasts a long history of preeminent scholars and academic breakthroughs. It is no wonder that Berkeley is consistently named among one of the top public universities in the nation.

Let There Be Light—and A's

First chartered in 1868, Berkeley was the founding campus of the University of California system. Now, it offers more than 100 majors, each of which belongs to one of the six undergraduate colleges and schools scattered across the campus. The six undergraduate colleges consist of the College of Chemistry, College of Engineering, College of Environmental Design, College of Letters and Science, College of Natural Resources and the Haas School of Business. The College of Letters and Science boasts more than 70 majors from Peace & Conflict Studies to Scandinavian. On the other hand, those wishing to be in the Haas School of Business will find that the enrollment is capped at 700, and only sophomores may apply for the two-year program. Freshmen must first enroll at the College of Letters and Science and declare their major as "pre-business administration." In addition, some majors, like economics, are called "impacted majors," and require an application for admittance.

Requirements vary according to college and major. However, there are three University requirements that all students must take to receive a bachelor's degree—Entry Level Writing, American History and American Institutions. The latter two requirements are to ensure that all students "have a basic understanding of U.S. history and governmental institutions." All University requirements can be satisfied with high-school classes.

Class sizes vary from the very small to the extremely large. One student recalled her Astronomy 10 experience, which included 700 students. However, that doesn't mean that individualized attention isn't possible. She remembered, "All of my professors have strongly-encouraged students to come visit them in office hours, including my astronomy professor who would remember the names of students who had visited him as he called on them amongst 699 other students during lectures."

"Anyone who says they are in the schools of chemistry or engineering is sort of automatically-deemed very smart," a third-year student said. Lower-level science courses are often called "weed classes" because they seem designed to weed out students who may not be so committed to the scientific path.

Students seem to agree that grading at Berkeley is hard, but fair. "We have one professor who wrote the textbook and is known to give difficult exams where the mean is failing," one student said. 'I do believe that grading at Berkeley is fair. It's not hard to get a B . . . The curve never hurts you." But as another student explained, "It's difficult for everyone to do well because there are so many smart people." His peer agreed: "I think science midterms are hard as hell, but as long as you're doing better than most of the class, you'll at least get a B."

Living in the Bay

Berkeley now guarantees housing for students for two years, instead of just one. Undergraduates have a variety of housing options. All students may apply for residence halls, which mostly consist of doubles and triples. Unit 1, Unit 2, Unit 3 and the Clark Kerr Campus together house about 4,800 students. Those wishing to live in single-sex dorms can choose either the Bowles for male students or Stern for females. Freeborn Hall is a substance-free dorm. In addition, within this system there are six themed residence halls such as African-American or Women in Science & Engineering. In addition, juniors, seniors and new transfers may apply for one of the two university apartment complexes, Channing Bowditch or Yoritada Wada.

Most students agree that living in the dorms is a great experience, if only for the social aspect. One first-year who lived in the Units said, "My dorm is more social . . . People who are in Clark Kerr/Foothill/Stern are in a quieter environment, they're not as socially focused as the people in the Units."

Despite the new change in housing guarantees, most upperclassmen do move off-campus. Many students find that housing co-ops are the easiest way to go. There are 20 co-ops in Berkeley—17 houses and four apartments—and the costs are very reasonable. About $3,000 a semester will snag you a room with food, utilities and furniture included. A downside to the co-op is that all members are expected to contribute 5 hours per week to the upkeep of the buildings, including chores like mopping and cooking. Students can also find their own houses and apartments around the Berkeley area, although affordable housing can be run-down. All in all, for most Berkeley students, moving off campus isn't as big a deal as it may be for students in other colleges. "Distance-wise, it's pretty much the same thing," one third-year said.

The Berkeley meal plan system is based on points. Standard meal plans are included in room and board and offer a certain number of points a semester; with the option to purchase more points at any time. Even though the city of Berkeley itself offers a myriad of restaurant choices, the dining hall system seems lackluster. One student put it frankly when he explained that, "the dining halls are not the best. Students don't rave about them."

Blue and Gold Weekends

Berkeley students definitely do not lack things to do on the weekends. "On the weekends, many undergrads go to football games (and many don't), study in cafés or at the library, go out to clubs in Berkeley or San Francisco, or to house, co-op, or frat parties," said one Peace and Conflict Studies major. "Frat parties seem to dominate the social scene," commented another student, "but there is the occasional house party." Dorm parties are not all that frequent, mainly due to the presence of the RA's and security monitors. Upperclassmen frequent bars and clubs around the area, like Blake's.

There are also plenty of social opportunities for those who do not drink, such as theater, musical performances, talks and lectures, cheap movies and even speed-dating. The city of San Francisco also provides a great source of entertainment.

Although alcohol doesn't seem like a big deal on campus, drugs, especially pot, are prevalent. "Come on, it's Berkeley," one student said. "People smoke weed on the streets." Another student noted wryly that "a co-op got headlines for sending 12 people to the hospital because they ate too many special brownies."

Extracurricular activities also take up a lot of students' time. There are over 350 registered student organizations on campus, with the majority of them falling in the academic, professional and service sectors. "The Greek life and athletic program are thriving here, but so are political activism, theater and dance, and the Rubber Band Club," a student said.

Approximately 3,000 students—12 percent of the Berkeley population—goes Greek. There are three councils that govern the 55 fraternities and sororities, with an additional 12 multicultural Greek organizations that do not belong to a council. However, Greek life isn't the be-all-end-all. The overwhelming majority seems to agree that "Greek life is pretty popular, but you don't have to pledge to be let in the party scene."

The Times Are A-Changin'?

Berkeley has two great reputations—its academic prowess and its student activism. Students differ in their opinions of whether the academic competitiveness helps the overall college atmosphere. As one student said, "Everyone sees everyone else as competition." However, another disagreed, stating that the academic environment actually helps the college: "It's great to know people that like other things and think differently."

The 1960s, especially the Free Speech Movement, garnered Berkeley a reputation for being the academic haven for student activism. Even though times have changed, politics has only done so to a small extent. Student activism is still alive and well. "Yesterday there was a two-hour rally—with press—called 'Save the Oaks.' It is exactly what it is, saving the beautiful oaks on campus," one student recalled.

Although most students identify themselves as liberal or "middle of the road," that doesn't mean that there is not a vocal minority. One third-year noted that, "one of the largest groups, surprising to many, is Berkeley College Republicans."

The shift in political beliefs might be gradual, but the ethnic makeup of Berkeley has changed drastically from the 1960s. Now, Asians make up the largest group, comprising more than 45 percent of the population. Some students deride Proposition 209, which ended affirmative action, for the lack of underrepresented minorities. "It is especially frustrating that the student demographics are not at all representative of the popula-

tion of the state of California," said one third-year. "When you walk around campus it's hard to not notice that the majority of students are Asian," another student explained. Others also complain that there aren't a lot of out-of-state students, which is hardly surprising given the fact that non-residents are accepted at about half the rate of residents. Nevertheless, one out-of-state student said that, "Adjusting isn't too difficult. The weather's really nice—we just had a blizzard in my hometown!"

Golden Bear Is Ever Watching

Berkeley sponsors 27 sports, including crew, cross-country and women's volleyball, and it has claimed 62 national championships to date. Berkeley students truly redefine the term "student-athlete," as 48% of them hold a GPA above 3.0.

Berkeley's main athletic rival is Stanford, which can be evidenced in its fight song, in which the Golden Bear "fiercely growls" at the "lowly Stanford Red." The Stanford-Berkeley football game is easily the biggest athletic event of the year, and is simply referred to as the "Big Game." The Big Game stretches all the way back to 1892, when former U.S. President Herbert Hoover was team manager for Stanford. The 1910 Big Game saw the first ever "card stunt," which depicted the Stanford Axe and a big C on a white background. Nowadays, 10 different card stunts are performed per year, with computer technology aiding in the process.

> "Berkeley is a tough school. Be prepared."

The Stanford Axe is another Big Game tradition, but it actually stems from an 1899 baseball game between Stanford and Berkeley. On the eve of this game, Stanford students used an axe to chop up a straw man in blue and gold. However, the very next day, Berkeley pulled a stunning upset over their rival and managed to steal the axe. In 1933, both schools agreed that the Stanford Axe should be mounted on a plaque and given as a trophy to the winner of the Big Game.

Nobel Laureates ONLY!

Visiting Berkeley, one might notice that there are certain parking spots marked "NL Parking Only." These are actually spots reserved for Nobel Laureates, and they are well-needed—Berkeley has the sixth largest number of Nobel Laureates out of all the universities in the world.

In the world of public universities, Berkeley's rich history, academic reputation, and social opportunities are truly unparalleled. The availability of such resources can be equally part of Berkeley's allure as it is part of its challenge. As one student said, "Berkeley is a tough school. Be prepared." Another student reflected, "Berkeley has opened me up and helped me learn about myself. I'm thankful I got in and am thoroughly enjoying my time here." But perhaps one molecular biology and economics double-major summed it up the best: "I love Berkeley, with all its bad and good things."—*Janet Xu*

FYI

If you come to Berkeley, you'd better bring "something blue and gold!"

What is the typical weekend schedule? "Go to a frat party or a bar on Thursday and Friday night, go to the city or see a game on Saturday, and study all day Sunday."

If I could change one thing about Berkeley, I'd "get rid of the unpredictable and sometimes annoying weather . . . and if they can form an inner tube water polo team I'd be satisfied."

Three things every student should do before graduating from Berkeley are: "Live in the dorms, nap on the Glade, and eat in as many restaurants as possible."

University of California / Davis

Address: 178 Mrak Hall, One Shields Avenue Davis, CA 95616
Phone: 530-752-2971
E-mail address: undergraduateadmissions@ucdavis.edu
Web site URL: www.ucdavis.edu
Year Founded: 1905
Private or Public: Public
Religious Affiliation: None
Location: Suburban
Number of Applicants: 35,148
Percent Accepted: 59%
Percent Accepted who enroll: 24%
Number Entering: 4,955
Number of Transfers Accepted each Year: 5,466
Middle 50% SAT range: M: 540–660, CR: 490–630, Wr: 500–630
Middle 50% ACT range: 20–27

Early admission program EA/ED/None: None
Percentage accepted through EA or ED: NA
EA and ED deadline: NA
Regular Deadline: 30-Nov
Application Fee: $60
Full time Undergraduate enrollment: 23,499
Total enrollment: 27,593
Percent Male: 44%
Percent Female: 56%
Total Percent Minority or Unreported: 65%
Percent African-American: 3%
Percent Asian/Pacific Islander: 41%
Percent Hispanic: 12%
Percent Native-American: 1%
Percent International: 2%
Percent in-state/out of state: 97%/3%
Percent from Public HS: 84%
Retention Rate: 90%

Graduation Rate 4-year: 42%
Graduation Rate 6-year: 80%
Percent Undergraduates in On-campus housing: 81%
Number of official organized extracurricular organizations: 364
3 Most popular majors: Biology, Economics, Psychology
Student/Faculty ratio: 19:1
Average Class Size: 20 to 29
Percent of students going to grad school: 40%
Tuition and Fees: $29,243
In State Tuition and Fees if different: $8,635
Cost for Room and Board: $11,978
Percent receiving financial aid out of those who apply, first year: 58%
Percent receiving financial aid among all students: 75%

Just minutes away from Sacramento and San Francisco Bay, UC Davis is cozily set in the lush green surroundings of California's Central Valley. The school continues its legacy as a top-notch public research institution and maintains its commitment to excellence through rigorous liberal arts academic programs, research experience, and diverse extracurricular activities. With over 700 athletes in 26 varsity sports and over $500 million in research funding, the largest UC campus creates an atmosphere of achievement and opportunity.

Size Matters

UC Davis is one of the larger public schools in the country, a fact with both positive and negative impacts on student life. With over 100 undergraduate majors, 86 graduate programs, and more than 30,000 enrolled students, UC Davis provides unparalleled variety for study. Despite its large size, students say it is relatively easy to get into their desired courses. While upperclassmen do seem to have priority in choosing some of the more popular and entertaining classes, there are no complaints most of the time. As one student explained, "Classes aren't really large, but they aren't so small as to not be able to accommodate people's requirements for their majors."

Introductory courses are taught in lecture hall settings with PowerPoint slides as a primary tool for professors. Such classes meet in small sections of 10–20 students with teaching assistants as instructors. During such discussion sections, students are encouraged to ask for clarifications and help on material that they are having difficulties with. A few students claim that it is occasionally hard to understand TAs whose first language is not English, but most students find it beneficial to attend sections, even if they are not mandatory. Regardless of the size of lecture, most professors are easily accessible either after class or during office hours and are eager to converse with students.

UC Davis is composed of three colleges that differ in general coursework and interdisciplinary resources: Agricultural and Environmental Sciences, Biological Sciences, Letters and Science, and Engineering. The College of Letters and Science is the largest and most diverse of the four colleges, including instruction in the natural sciences, social sciences, humanities, arts, and cultural studies. Potential undergraduates apply to specific college programs when applying to Davis, each with unique general requirements. Although students are allowed to change majors after the first quarter, some find it tedious switching to another college.

The school year at Davis runs on a quarter system, which is made up of three quarters during the traditional academic year and one during the summer. This is similar to that of most high schools, so most students have little problem in the transition process. The quarter system induces a fast-paced learning environment in which work for classes is concentrated. One freshman stated that "there is no time to slack off since it is difficult to anticipate upcoming exams." As an upside, she said, "Students can get out of a class they dislike in as short as nine to 10 weeks."

Luxurious Living

All incoming freshmen are guaranteed spots in on-campus residence halls, and approximately 90 percent of them end up in on-campus housing. Consequently, on-campus housing is mostly occupied by freshmen. There are a wide variety of options including single-sex, coed, and theme housing. Floor plans illustrate single room arrangements, double room arrangements, cluster-style four-person arrangements, and suite-style four-person arrangements. The three undergraduate residence locations on campus are Segundo, Tercero, and Cuarto. All these residence halls have certain features in common: high-speed internet, cable television, study space, laundry rooms, kitchenettes, and lounges.

Dining commons are present at all four residence halls, and students are free to eat at any one. Students select one of 12 meal plans, each with a number of "points," with one point swiped per meal. The dining halls put on theme dinner nights throughout the year, so there is no need to worry about eating the same foods everyday. The Segundo dorm has a relatively new dining commons, and an overwhelmingly high proportion of students compliment it. One Cuarto resident said, "In general, the dining hall in Segundo provides more variety and food of better quality." Midnight snackers may add "late-night points" to purchase pizza, cookies, and snack foods sold in the commons until midnight each night.

Sophomores also have the choice to live in dorms, but most decide to live off campus since they receive lowest priority in housing. Students described the process of finding off-campus housing as very easy, with "a lot of beautiful neighborhoods to choose from" and a "very tight relationship between Davis and the community." From apartments to townhouses to condos, the city of Davis has options to match any lifestyle. People moving in from large metropolises experience pleasant surprises from the affordability of off-campus arrangements. Generally, off-campus housing is more than significantly cheaper than on-campus housing. Average rental rates for unfurnished apartments range from $867/month for a one-bedroom to $2738/month for a five-bedroom. Living prices are major factors to consider for some people who are somewhat dissatisfied with their current living arrangements. But, as one freshman complained, "a negative side to on-campus housing is that students are randomly assigned rooms inside their resident halls, and everyone pays the same price regardless of room size."

The Davis campus offers a number of facilities, such as the popular MU Games Area, which features old-time favorites like bowling, pool, and air hockey. One student said, "The MU arcade is a nice place to relax, especially during events where iPods are given away." Other students enjoy spending time at the Quad in their spare time, where various extracurricular organizations congregate and advertise. Davis also recently constructed the Activities and Recreation Center (REC), a large, modern gym. A student who is currently taking a Pilates class in the REC praises it for the diversity of activities that are offered, such as yoga and the "*300* Spartan Training Class," a program teaching warrior-like philosophy and exercises to its participants. Professional academic and leadership coordinators are on-hand at each of the housing areas to work with residents individually or through programs and events.

Campus Culture

Thursday, Friday, and Saturday nights represent the zenith of undergraduate social life, as fraternities and sororities frequently throw parties. Responsible drinking is expected of students. University alcohol permits can be easily attained as long as event coordinators demonstrate good judgment. To reduce binge drinking, the university has implemented a "0–3" campaign in an effort to limit student alcohol to three drinks or fewer.

As parties aren't frequent on campus, the Moldavi Center provides an alternative way to enjoy the weekend through exploration of the full range of performing arts. Students may come to Moldavi to enjoy international music, dance, and theater. The university hosts events like Picnic Day and Open House for Davis, designed to showcase recreational activities and the achievements of UC Davis students and alumni. People come to wander through the more than 150 events throughout the day, sampling delicious food and grabbing informational pamphlets along the way.

Whether you're a spectator or competitor, UC Davis won't disappoint your athletic needs. With 26 varsity sports, 30 club sports, and 36 intramural sports ranging from ultimate Frisbee to water polo, there will be plenty to cheer for and play in. With UC Davis's entrance into NCAA Division I comes phenomenal new recreational facilities including the Activities and Recreation Center, Equestrian Center, Hockey Pool, Recreation Fields, and Rec Pool. One student noted, "While athletics aren't as large as they are at Berkeley or UCLA, school spirit is large and obvious—you can always spot someone in a school sweatshirt."

> "While athletics aren't as large as they are at Berkeley or UCLA, school spirit is large and obvious—you can always spot someone in a school sweatshirt."

The city of Davis is a great small city, devoid of cinderblock superstores like Walmart and Target. But those looking for a "small town" feel need not panic. As one student remarked, the Target still takes a 15-minute bike ride away from central campus. Davis is also quite strict about its recycling policies, which keeps the area green and lush. Cleanliness makes the town a perfect location for a sunny afternoon snack at Fuji Café's sushi buffet or a $4 movie screening at the local theater. Downtown Davis features student hangouts like Ciocalate, a great place to study while soaking in the sun and enjoying a cup of tea. Sophia's Thai Restaurant features a casual dining environment and includes a Thai room where one has the option of sitting on the floor in traditional Thai style. This is also the place to get enough free refills of Thai tea to satisfy anyone's appetite.

No matter where you go in Davis, you'll find something to enjoy. One freshman summed up her experience: "Davis is a welcoming community. Everyone always smiles and everyone is accepting. I feel like I belong. I feel like I can get to know people better. There's a feeling of innocence. Davis is a home away from home."—*Bing Han*

FYI
If you come to UC Davis, you'd better bring "a bicycle with locks, because that's the most efficient way to get around."
The typical weekend schedule at UC Davis "involves a combination of doing homework, spending time with friends, and occasional partying."
If I could change one thing about UC Davis, I'd "construct a Chinatown in its vicinity, so that there would be better Chinese food."
Three things every UC Davis student should do before graduating are "get a free tire fill-up at the Bike Barn located in the Silo Student Union, join the Aggie Pack in support of the athletic department's 75 percent home winning record, and check out the Cross Cultural Center."

University of California / Irvine

Address: 204 Aldrich Hall Irvine, CA 92697-1075
Phone: 949-824-6703
E-mail address: admissions@uci.edu
Web site URL: www.uci.edu
Year Founded: 1965
Private or Public: Public
Religious Affiliation: None
Location: Suburban
Number of Applicants: 34,531
Percent Accepted: 60%
Percent Accepted who enroll: 21%
Number Entering: 4,314
Number of Transfers Accepted each Year: 5,939
Middle 50% SAT range: M: 570–680, CR: 540–630, Wr: Unrepoted
Middle 50% ACT range: Unreported
Early admission program EA/ED/None: None

Percentage accepted through EA or ED: NA
EA and ED deadline: NA
Regular Deadline: 30-Nov
Application Fee: $60
Full time Undergraduate enrollment: 19,930
Total enrollment: 24,283
Percent Male: 50%
Percent Female: 50%
Total Percent Minority or Unreported: 74%
Percent African-American: 2%
Percent Asian/Pacific Islander: 49%
Percent Hispanic: 12%
Percent Native-American: <1%
Percent International: 2%
Percent in-state/out of state: 97%/3%
Percent from Public HS: Unreported
Retention Rate: 93%
Graduation Rate 4-year: 57%

Graduation Rate 6-year: 79%
Percent Undergraduates in On-campus housing: 82%
Number of official organized extracurricular organizations: 378
3 Most popular majors: Biology, Computer and Information Sciences, Economics
Student/Faculty ratio: 19:1
Average Class Size: 20 to 29
Percent of students going to grad school: 30%
Tuition and Fees: $28,654
In State Tuition and Fees if different: $8,046
Cost for Room and Board: $10,527
Percent receiving financial aid out of those who apply, first year: 44%
Percent receiving financial aid among all students: 64%

Halfway between Los Angeles and San Diego lies the sunny campus of UC Irvine. With beaches, restaurants and shopping destinations within close reach, students at this school can enjoy strong academics without a stressful atmosphere. Taking a peek at this low-key campus will reveal college staples such as supportive freshman dorms, as well as the bonuses of great meal options and a budding hip hop scene.

Break out those calculators
At UC Irvine, math and science are kings. Students agreed that their school is more math, science and engineering based and stronger in these fields than in the humanities. This is reflected in the popular majors on campus—biology (in which the school has a very strong department), chemistry, and engineering; psychology and social sciences are also popular. Despite the science-leaning tendencies of the school, UC Irvine makes sure that its students get a well-rounded education through the Breadth Requirements, which require students to take classes across a variety of academic disciplines including social sciences, humanities and math.

On the whole, classes at UC Irvine tend to be on the large size, though "it depends on your major and the class you're taking," one junior explained. Writing or art classes typically have a max of 20–30 students, while lower-division bio classes can have up to 450 students. A psychology major said, "In the classes I have been in, the average number is about 150 to 200 students." Students said classes begin to get smaller in upper-division courses specifically in the major. To get into classes, students register according to how many units they have completed, so upperclassmen have first dibs. Students said certain classes—writing classes, labs, popular major/minor classes, and GE's—are hard to get into because so many are competing for the same spots. However, students in the Campus-Wide Honors Program are one of the first to register for classes regardless of units-taken, which is one of the major perks of the program. First-years get accepted into this program while they are still in high school (no additional application necessary), but current and transfer students must apply.

Grading at UC Irvine varies, depending on the professor's choice or the department. The more competitive classes such as biology, chemistry and mathematics are curved down so that a certain amount of A's, B's, C's, D's, and F's are set in advance. For other classes such as language courses, they are curved in the sense that only the maximum amount of students that can receive A's is 15 percent and the rest receive a B+ and lower. One junior explained, "It is definitely possible to get A's, but there are those teachers that make it hard to get them. The older professors are usually the ones that don't curve in their classes." But despite the occasional competitive curve and difficulty in getting into popular courses, "the academic life is very rewarding due to the prominent and notable professors that teach here," a Social Ecology major said.

Living in Irvine

For incoming freshman, there are three main housing options—Middle Earth, Mesa Court, and Arroyo Vista. The first two are dorming communities, whereas students who live in Arroyo Vista need to take a shuttle to get to class since it is located off of the main campus. The application for first-year housing is very specific on helping students find the right people to live with, and according to upperclassmen, the freshman dorms are very comfortable and fit the needs of students living away from their parents for the

first time. "It's recommended for first-years. You meet a lot of new people and learn a lot about each other," one student said.

The dorm community is composed of a variety of small buildings, each with specific themes that fit the students' interests, though some dorm rooms are nicer than others, depending which hall you get. The general rule is, "The newer the hall, the bigger your room," as one junior put it. UC Irvine guarantees two years of on-campus housing, and most people move into on-campus apartments their second year after living in dorms as freshmen. In their third year, students move off-campus to the many apartments near campus.

Each hall in the dorms has its own RA, but students say that they usually aren't that strict about policies because they are students themselves and thus, more lenient. In addition, a senior commented, "RA's for the dorms are really nice people and they act as mentors, friends, and teachers for freshmen—they help make living on campus fun and easy." Students praised Irvine for its safety, overwhelmingly citing Irvine as "one of the safest cities to live in" and being known as "the safest city in California."

As for food, there is a plethora of options in restaurants and restaurants, both on- and off-campus. Even among the dining halls, there are distinctions—Mesa Court has one dining hall while Middle Earth has two. Students living in Mesa Court or Middle Earth have three meal plans to choose from, and one junior advised, "People usually never finish their meals so it's better to choose the cheapest one." She added, "The food seems to be getting better every quarter, and you can even choose from organic foods." In addition to dorm dining halls, there is also an on-campus food court which offers a variety of choices, including Chinese food, pasta, Quizno's, and Wendy's. For those who need their caffeine fix, there are two coffee shops on campus—Starbucks and Cyber A Cafe. UC Irvine also has its own pub and three other "restaurants" on different parts of the campus. Meal options include the option of flex dollars, which is money you can use at any of these places. Of course, the Southern California experience wouldn't be complete without In-N-Out, the quintessential California fast-food chain that serves fresh burgers and fries. Students can find one literally on their doorstep, as there is one right across the street from campus at the University Town Center, which also features a Yogurtland. In addition, you can find sandwiches,

Mexican food and Japanese food, just to mention a few.

Feel the Beat

UC Irvine offers many clubs that fit specific interests and culture. One student noted, "Clubs are run by very enthusiastic members who are willing to give the time to making the club prosper and letting students feel comfortable." But another student added, "How much a person commits to their club/organization really depends on the person." Many people are involved in culture clubs such as Chinese Association, Korean-American Student Association, and Tomo No Kai (Japanese Club), to name a few. Due to the school's student population, which students describe as not very diverse, these culture clubs tend to be Asian-American-oriented.

A school in the suburbs of Orange County with a majority of Asian students may not seem like it would have this reputation, but the campus features prominent hip-hop dance teams. "A lot of people know UCI as the 'hip hop dance' university," a junior said. The school has four hip hop teams, the most famous of which is Kaba Modern, which was featured on MTV's "America's Best Dance Crew." As a result, "a lot of hip hoppers want to go to UCI," a student explained.

Students say there are many social scenes on campus, including the aforementioned cultural clubs and dance teams, in addition to academic clubs, a cappella groups, and sports teams. But fraternities and sororities are by far the most dominant, students say. During the first two weeks or so of every quarter, the Greek society takes over the campus to promote their fraternities and sororities. One junior described the experience: "At the beginning of the school year, there will be booths set up at the club fair, as well as on Ring Road. You will get bombarded with flyers to rush for their fraternity/sorority. Panhellenic frats and sororities have a different rushing process than Asian fraternities and sororities." Thursdays are usually when fraternities and sororities have clubbing events, and conveniently, there are usually buses taking people to the club so they don't have to worry about drinking and driving. Students say that not everybody drinks ("Those who go to parties usually drink; those who don't go to parties don't drink."), but alcohol, hookah and pot are popular around campus. Dorm policies are the same as anywhere else—Students can't get drunk in the dorms (no alcohol or drugs are allowed in the dorms), but students can be drunk in the dorms. One student added, "I would say that the people who drink the most are those who are involved in sorority and frat events."

On other nights, students say they usually just hang out at each other's apartments or dorm rooms, or attend club events and meetings. Other low-key weekend options include going out to eat and shopping at Fashion Island in Newport Beach or South Coast Plaza and the Irvine Spectrum, which are popular malls nearby. In addition, students said many people have Disneyland passes and sometimes hang out and eat at Downtown Disney or go watch fireworks at night. One student said, "On the weekends, a lot of people stay or go home every other weekend, but usually, on the weekends there isn't really much to do in Irvine." One the whole, though, a junior summed up social life at UC Irvine as "It's what you make of it."

> **"A lot of hip hoppers want to go to UCI."**

Students who end up at Irvine can expect to dress to impress, even to class. A Film and Media Studies major said, "People at school are definitely into fashion, and our school is good on keeping up with the latest fashion trends." However, he added, "There are also a lot of people who have their own style/attitude. Unlike high school, it's okay to dress the way you want and not be judged for it."

UC Irvine may not be as high-profile as its counterparts in Berkeley or Los Angeles, but the experience can be just as positive. As one senior reflected, "The people that come to this school are friendly and the atmosphere is welcoming and comfortable."—*Della Fok*

FYI
If you come to UC Irvine, "you'd better bring money and a swimsuit."
What's the typical weekend schedule? "Most SoCal people leave on the weekends, which leaves all the NorCal people alone in Irvine."
If I could change one thing about UC Irvine, "I'd put on campus apartments within walking distance of class. Why are off campus apartments closer to classes than on campus apartments?"
Three things every student at UC Irvine should do before graduating are: "make a lot of friends, join a club, and learn the area because there are so many restaurants around campus!"

University of California / Los Angeles

Address: 1147 Murphy Hall, Box 951436 Los Angeles, CA 90095-1436
Phone: 310-825-3101
E-mail address: ugadm@saonet.ucla.edu
Web site URL: www.ucla.edu
Year Founded: 1919
Private or Public: Public
Religious Affiliation: None
Location: Urban
Number of Applicants: 50,755
Percent Accepted: 24%
Percent Accepted who enroll: 38%
Number Entering: 4,515
Number of Transfers Accepted each Year: 5,330
Middle 50% SAT range: M: 700–760, CR: 660–720, Wr: 670–720
Middle 50% ACT range: 28–31
Early admission program EA/ED/None: None

Percentage accepted through EA or ED: NA
EA and ED deadline: NA
Regular Deadline: 30-Nov
Application Fee: $60
Full time Undergraduate enrollment: 25,928
Total enrollment: 36,899
Percent Male: 45%
Percent Female: 55%
Total Percent Minority or Unreported: 66%
Percent African-American: 3%
Percent Asian/Pacific Islander: 38%
Percent Hispanic: 15%
Percent Native-American: <1%
Percent International: 4%
Percent in-state/out of state: 96%/4%
Percent from Public HS: 78%
Retention Rate: 97%
Graduation Rate 4-year: 64%

Graduation Rate 6-year: 87%
Percent Undergraduates in On-campus housing: 92%
Number of official organized extracurricular organizations: 774
3 Most popular majors: Biology, Political Science and Government, Psychology
Student/Faculty ratio: 16:1
Average Class Size: 10 to 19
Percent of students going to grad school: Unreported
Tuition and Fees: $28,162
In State Tuition and Fees if different: $7,551
Cost for Room and Board: $12,891
Percent receiving financial aid out of those who apply, first year: 49%
Percent receiving financial aid among all students: 82%

Strolling on UCLA's sunlit Bruin Walk in the middle of the day, one is surrounded by faces representing countless different nationalities, races, academic inclinations, and extracurricular interests. But one thing is for certain on this Southern California public school campus in a city that advertises 329 days of sun per year: the Bruin spirit courses through its large, diverse student body, making them proud of their nationally renowned sports, academics, and West Coast culture.

Studying among the Stars

UCLA is situated on 419 acres in the picturesque Los Angeles district of Westwood, bordering Beverly Hills and Bel-Air. But the school's proximity to the glamour of Hollywood doesn't mean the students don't put in their work. The schools open to undergraduate enrollment are the College of Letters and Science, the School of the Arts and Architecture, the Henry Samueli School of Engineering and Applied Science, the School of Nursing, and the School of Theater, Film, and Television. Students in the College of Letters and Science must fulfill General Education requirements in three foundational areas: three courses in the arts and humanities, three in society and culture, and four in scientific inquiry. Possible subgroups of these areas include visual and performance arts analysis and practice, historical analysis, and physical sciences. In addition, there are writing, quantitative reasoning, and foreign language requirements, but these can be fulfilled with test scores or high school credit. Students say that the GE requirements aren't too much of a pain; in fact, there is the option of taking a GE cluster, which is a group of classes across disciplines that allows them to get several GEs out of the way in one fell swoop.

UCLA is on the quarter system, meaning that there are three segments during the academic year and one in the summer. While one female student said that this system lets her finish courses she dislikes fairly quickly, she complained that "it's midterm season all the time!" Classes are geographically split, for the most part, between South Campus—the sciences—and North Campus—humanities—with rare crossover. Although some students pointed to a psychological divide between the two, saying that there is often mutual distrust or the feeling that one side is more challenging than the other, a junior said that "at the end of the day, it's not going to stop you being friends with people from the other side." Students did generally agree that the atmosphere on South Campus is "more cutthroat," especially since more and more freshmen are coming to UCLA intending to be pre-med. Recent additions to scientific research and health buildings on campus reflect this growing trend.

Besides biology and other sciences, popular majors at UCLA include psychology, political science, economics, and communications. South Campus grading is more curve-based because the classes are larger, while North Campus grading is reportedly more subjective, but less stressful. The system by which students sign up for classes, while "imperfect and sometimes more stressful than it should be" because of the high demand for many classes, seems to be working for now. Signups occur online, and the order is determined by class year and honors status. Students generally take three or four courses per quarter, ranging from 13 to 19 units per quarter, with 180 units needed to graduate. Most students are able to graduate within four years, but if you choose your major late, it's less likely that you'll be able to pull the credits together, at least without summer school. But the academic offerings are impressive: professors include Nobel laureates, Rhodes scholars, and countless other famous researchers. But somehow, the focus on undergraduate education is maintained, even in this large public university. Students report developing close relationships with professors—one sophomore gushed about a seminar leader she invited to her sorority's professor dinner.

Luckily, studying isn't all about work. Every finals week, on Wednesday at midnight, students run through campus to Royce Hall, doing the UCLA cheers, and jump in the fountain—in their underwear. "Undie Run is one of those experiences that makes a big school smaller," a junior said.

Living in LaLa Land

Living accommodations earn mixed reviews, but with more than 25,000 undergraduates crammed into housing, that's to be expected. The four high-rise residence halls in which freshmen are housed are Dykstra, Hedrick, Rieber, and Sproul. These are "typical college dorms," with between 100 and 200 students per coed floor. A girl explained that, on her floor, 50 girls shared a bathroom, and most people were in one-room triples with bunk beds. The "res halls" are currently being renovated one at a time, but the plazas are less than five years old, featuring triples as well but with the convenience of sharing a bathroom between only two rooms. The suites have private bathrooms and two-bedrooms, each with two or three people living in them. While the latter two options may be less hectic and cramped, most students recommended living in the res halls because of the social component. Those who choose to live off campus can move into their sororities and fraternities or rent apartments in Westwood close to campus. The rent is expensive in the area, getting cheaper farther away from the University, but a junior said that "it's worth it to have a nice apartment."

The food gets stellar reviews. Students are given a certain amount of "swipes" for the quarter, which they can use at various times of the day at the four main dining halls—Covel, De Neve, Hedrick, and Rieber—and at the three cafes: Bruin, Crossroads, and Puzzles. "Compared to the average dining hall experience, UCLA is excellent," a history major said. "Everyone who moves out of the dorms always tries to bribe people into giving them a swipe," commented a junior political science major, going on to describe the variety of cuisines available at the main dining facilities, including Italian, American, Thai, and just plain healthy.

The striking campus features a variety of architectural styles, predominantly brick and Spanish Mediterranean, and sometimes Gothic. When they venture into the surrounding area, Bruins find themselves with a wealth of opportunities for play, and even work. The bus system easily (and inexpensively) takes them around the city, from the beach at Santa Monica to downtown Hollywood. Cars, which are off-limits for first-years, are more difficult to manage simply because the parking is "limited and inconvenient," but those who have jobs and internships elsewhere in the city find them worth the effort. Just walking down to the shops in Westwood opens up a variety of shopping, eating, and bar-hopping possibilities. Even trips to Las Vegas or Mexico are not unusual.

A perk, according to one sophomore, is

the University's proximity to Hollywood. Many directors who want to screen their films before releasing them to wider audiences gives sneak previews to UCLA students, she said.

Socializing in the Sun

An awareness that has arisen over the past few years at many UC campuses, UCLA in particular, is that the student body is becoming more diverse—or is that less so? It's true that Asian-American students make up nearly 40 percent of the student body, while black students account for less than three percent. As the stereotype of "University of Caucasians Lost among Asians" becomes increasingly pervasive, the school's administration is working hard establishing initiatives that will supposedly ensure that the sense of diversity is maintained. Keeping with the Southern California feel, though, there is a significant Latino presence.

Students' geographical origins may be likewise deceptively diverse—all 50 states and more than 100 countries are represented, although only two percent of the student body is from outside California—but politics, while heavily weighted toward liberal viewpoints, are by no means homogenous. The Bruin Republicans are reported to be "pretty vocal." People come from "every background imaginable," because of the University's public school availability, though the upper-middle class is well-represented. The relatively casual nature of the campus, with many simply sporting sweatpants or semi-preppy outfits, contributes to the laid-back feel.

Fraternities and sororities are a big part of social life on campus, whether you belong to a Greek organization or not. The houses host many events, although non-Greek girls have an easier time gaining access than their male counterparts. For those who belong, the array of date parties, formals, theme parties, and spirit events means there is no lack of a social life. But for those who are reluctant to join the 13 percent of students who go Greek, fear not: "It's just another outlet—some people choose it, and some people don't," a non-Greek junior explained. "It's not necessarily exclusive." "If you aren't in it, there are plenty of other ways to fit in on campus," added a sorority girl, who indicated the superior housing as a reason she chose to pledge.

Superfluous Spirit

There are countless ways to get involved at UCLA. More than 700 registered organizations attract the motivated each year, from Unicamp, through which Bruins volunteer to hold a summer camp for underprivileged LA kids, to *The Daily Bruin*, the student newspaper. Some of the most visible groups on campus include the Student Alumni Organization, which organizes some of the biggest events each year, the Undergraduate Students Association Council, and Tours, the tour guide group. The SAA puts on Spring Sing and Homecoming Week events, among others. Welcome Week, held each year on the Sunday before the first week of class, kicks off with BruinBash, usually featuring a star-studded concert. Previous performers include T.I. and Rooney. The annual Dance Marathon raises money for the Elizabeth Glaser Pediatric AIDS Foundation—over the past seven years, the event has raised almost a million dollars for the cause.

> "Our athletics are unparalleled, and our school spirit definitely shows it."

Although school spirit is evident in these activities, it is truly apparent when Bruins are backing their sports teams—especially when they come head-to-head with the crosstown rival, University of Southern California. "Our athletics are unparalleled, and our school spirit definitely shows it," said a sophomore, pointing out UCLA's consistently strong showing in the NCAA Division 1-A Pac-10 conference. As of 2007, UCLA had racked up 121 national championships across the many teams it fields, including 11 NCAA championships, exceeding the totals of all other universities. The Rose Bowl and Pauley Pavilion are usually packed for competitions, and tailgates are especially intense, with full body paint a common sighting. The school has ticket packages for the football and basketball seasons, and many loyal fans take them up on the offer.

And it's not only the students who are feeling the draw of the vibrant, involved campus. "To say celebrities like to get involved at UCLA is an understatement," a political science major said, rattling off a list of recent visitors that included Bill Clinton, Al Gore, Stevie Wonder, Julie Andrews, and Oprah. The students may not ever get used to bumping into the rich and famous as they walk their dogs or jog in Westwood, but the shock of the large university setting does wear off, as most can attest to. "I thought I'd get lost here, but not a day goes by where I don't see someone I know every 10 seconds," a sophomore said. "By joining different clubs and organizations, you create communities within communities." Don't let the six campus pools and plentiful opportunities for sunbathing fool you—Bruins take their academics as seriously as their leisure. A junior put it succinctly:

"Everyone here is really good at having fun, but also getting stuff done." If you think the LA mentality might be for you, or if you're good at focusing on your studies even when the weather is beautiful year-round, you might find that four years in Southern California are right for you.—*Kimberly Chow*

FYI

If you come to UCLA, you'd better bring "face paint and your jersey; the spirit here on campus is awesome."

What is the typical weekend schedule? "On Saturday, sleep in, then go head to the pool or a football game or hang out in Westwood with friends, then at night go to parties in the apartments or the frats. Sunday, have brunch in Westwood, do some reading, and have club meetings at night."

If I could change one thing about UCLA, I'd "have more counseling and more of an ability to contact academic advisors so you can figure out classes."

Three things every student at UCLA should do before graduating are "spot a celebrity in Westwood, do Undie Run, and go to a basketball game in Pauley Pavilion and sit in the Den."

University of California / Riverside

Address: 1120 Hinderaker Hall Riverside, CA 92521
Phone: 951-827-3411
E-mail address: discover@ucr.edu
Web site URL: www.ucr.edu
Year Founded: 1954
Private or Public: Public
Religious Affiliation: None
Location: Suburban
Number of Applicants: 20,126
Percent Accepted: 82%
Percent Accepted who enroll: 22%
Number Entering: 3,701
Number of Transfers Accepted each Year: 4,086
Middle 50% SAT range: M: 470–610, CR: 450–560, Wr: 450–560
Middle 50% ACT range: 18–23
Early admission program EA/ED/None: None

Percentage accepted through EA or ED: NA
EA and ED deadline: NA
Regular Deadline: 30-Nov
Application Fee: $60
Full time Undergraduate enrollment: 14,973
Total enrollment: 17,138
Percent Male: 48%
Percent Female: 52%
Total Percent Minority or Unreported: 82%
Percent African-American: 7%
Percent Asian/Pacific Islander: 42%
Percent Hispanic: 26%
Percent Native-American: <1%
Percent International: 2%
Percent in-state/out of state: 99%/1%
Percent from Public HS: 88%
Retention Rate: 83%
Graduation Rate 4-year: 39%

Graduation Rate 6-year: 63%
Percent Undergraduates in On-campus housing: 71%
Number of official organized extracurricular organizations: 251
3 Most popular majors: Biology, Business, Psychology
Student/Faculty ratio: 18:1
Average Class Size: 20 to 29
Percent of students going to grad school: Unreported
Tuition and Fees: $28,453
In State Tuition and Fees if different: $7,846
Cost for Room and Board: $10,850
Percent receiving financial aid out of those who apply, first year: 63%
Percent receiving financial aid among all students: 80%

W hile sometimes overshadowed by the other University of California schools, UC Riverside is known for its convenient location, diverse academics, and its vibrant student population. UC

Riverside offers a wide array of majors ranging from Global Studies and Entomology to Dance and Creative Writing.

As its name suggests, the campus is in the large city of Riverside and near the famous forests and mountains of Southern California. This allows students many getaways to shopping centers, movie theaters and various other distractions located conveniently near campus, as well as giving nature-lovers the opportunity to explore right in the backyard of their dormitories.

Higher Education's Little Asia

When asked about the typical student activities at UC Riverside, all students, no matter of what background, come up with the same response—"of course, the ethnic organizations! The Chinese, Vietnamese, Japanese and Korean-Student Associations are all very strong in both numbers and influence over the entire campus atmosphere." UC Riverside is one of the few American colleges where the Asian population claims the absolute majority. Although most of the Asian population is second, third, or even fourth generation Asian-American, and for many, English is their first language, their connections with their Asian heritages have yet to wane. However, they are more than willing to share their cultural heritage with the rest of the school. As one Caucasian student pointed out, "compared to the other colleges in America, the students of Riverside know much more about Asia, its people, its customs and its society. That comes from the existence of the large Asian population on the campus."

> **"It's good everybody in my suite is gone for the weekend, it's finally quiet and I can get down to studying."**

Because of the abundant Asian population, activities relating to Asian life have exploded near UC Riverside. For example, large numbers of Asian restaurants flourish near the campus, driven by student demand. One Caucasian student noticed, "because of all the Asian stuff near the campus, it feels like all the non-Asian people at UC Riverside became more and more Asian, and you know, once we graduate, it's going to feel like we automatically graduate with a degree in Asian Studies."

Of course, the University offers options not involving Asian cultures. Athletic clubs, scientific and political organizations are abundant, and Greek life is very influential. There are also many newspapers and magazines on campus; journalism is one of the most popular majors at UC Riverside. As one senior male student said, "The student life here is so vibrant, and the professors are really nice; I really feel like I can fit in really well in the school no matter what my background is."

Although UCR is not accorded national, academic renown, students often find the coursework more challenging than it first appears. One student complained, "You know, I thought since it was so easy getting into this school, it was going to be easy to get A's in all of my classes. But I was deceived! I am having a hard time in my classes, not because the material is hard, but because the curves in the classes are working against me because the average of the classes is driven up so much by really studious people, meaning that there is so little grade inflation." The competitive nature of Riverside academics is disproportionate to its high admission rate.

L.A.? Not L.A.?

Riverside is located east of Los Angeles, within the driving distance of its downtown, yet it is known for its quietness and proximity to a natural environment. The San Bernardino Mountains are just east of the town and the Los Angeles National Forest is north and west of the campus. Other than shops and eateries, there are relatively few man-made attractions to be noted in the city itself. The surrounding wilderness, however, offers plenty for students to explore. To get away from campus, students can camp out in the woods (assuming that it is not closed due to wildfire) or take skiing and snowboarding lessons. As one Colorado student remarked, "San Bernardino Mountains are great! I don't even have to go back home to snowboard, it really reminds me of home. Plus, it is a great way to show off my skills because most of the people in Southern California can't even ski or snowboard at all."

Many Riverside students own cars. This is especially true for the many students who commute daily to the campus from as far as northern San Diego County. Cars allow students to visit Los Angeles as often as possible, for its shopping, parks and beaches. Also many live within the confines of the city.

But living next to Los Angeles and the natural environment has its downside as well. The foul industrial and automobile smog from Los Angeles, America's second-largest urban center, constantly floods the UC Riverside campus. Also, the frequent wildfires in the nearby forests bring large amounts of flying ash into the campus, darkening the sky from sunny to "cloudy." As a result of the poor air quality and proximity to home, students drive away from the campus almost every weekend, leaving one student to remark, "The campus is almost 50 percent empty every weekend; people are mostly going home, some are in L.A." Nonetheless, the people remaining on campus are generally not bothered by the mass exodus. As one student eagerly said, "It's good everybody in my suite is gone for the weekend, it's finally quiet and I can get down to studying." After all, academics are what really matters in all colleges, including UC Riverside.—*Xiaochen Su*

FYI

If you come to UCR, you better bring "summer clothes (because you'll need them until the middle of November) and a car!"

The typical weekend schedule at UCR is "going home because all of my friends do."

If I could change one thing about UCR, I would change "the poor air quality."

The three things you have to do before graduating from UCR are "go to L.A., learn to ski, and learn about Asia from practical experience."

University of California / San Diego

Address: 9500 Gilman Drive, 0021 La Jolla, CA 92093-0021
Phone: 858-534-4831
E-mail address: admissionsinfo@ucsd.edu
Web site URL: www.ucsd.edu
Year Founded: 1959
Private or Public: Public
Religious Affiliation: None
Location: Suburban
Number of Applicants: 45,073
Percent Accepted: 43%
Percent Accepted who enroll: 22%
Number Entering: 4,141
Number of Transfers Accepted each Year: 6,408
Middle 50% SAT range: M: 590–700, CR: 540–660, Wr: 550–670
Middle 50% ACT range: 23–29
Early admission program EA/ED/None: None

Percentage accepted through EA or ED: NA
EA and ED deadline: NA
Regular Deadline: 30-Nov
Application Fee: $60
Full time Undergraduate enrollment: 22,048
Total enrollment: 22,048
Percent Male: 48%
Percent Female: 52%
Total Percent Minority or Unreported: 72%
Percent African-American: 1%
Percent Asian/Pacific Islander: 43%
Percent Hispanic: 12%
Percent Native-American: <1%
Percent International: 3%
Percent in-state/out of state: 97%/3%
Percent from Public HS: Unreported
Retention Rate: 95%
Graduation Rate 4-year: 55%

Graduation Rate 6-year: 83%
Percent Undergraduates in On-campus housing: 92%
Number of official organized extracurricular organizations: 405
3 Most popular majors: Economics, Microbiology, Political Science and Government
Student/Faculty ratio: 19:1
Average Class Size: 10 to 19
Percent of students going to grad school: 30%
Tuition and Fees: $28,670
In State Tuition and Fees if different: $8,062
Cost for Room and Board: $10,787
Percent receiving financial aid out of those who apply, first year: 49%
Percent receiving financial aid among all students: 69%

The University of California, San Diego, is one of 10 colleges in the University of California system and is located in La Jolla, California. The school was founded in 1960 as a science and engineering research institution in hopes of becoming the next CalTech. Today, UCSD is ranked one of the top public universities in America, known for excellence not only in scientific research but also in undergraduate academics and student life.

Get the GE out of the way!

The undergraduate program at UCSD is separated into five divisions. These include the Arts and Humanities, Biological Sciences,

Physical Sciences, Social Sciences and the Jacobs School of Engineering. Students may take classes from any of these divisions, provided they complete their General Education (GE) Requirements. Depending on the residential college into which you are placed, your GE requirements can vary greatly. Some find the GE requirement a way to explore areas of interests outside of their major, while others find it a nuisance. One junior International Studies Majors complains, "I'm in Revelle which has the most GE requirements. I've had three quarters of chem, one of bio and physics, while other colleges have less!" There are six of these colleges and on top of designating your GE requirements they also serve as residential halls. Muir College is known to have very loose requirements and the most recently established Sixth College has requirements focusing on culture, art and technology. When applying, each student indicates which colleges they would like to study and live in, and for the most part "you end up where you're supposed to," said one senior.

Classes tend to be larger during freshman and sophomore years—many have up to 500 students in one lecture hall, with alternate times offered during the day. Upper division classes taken during the junior and senior years tend to be smaller and more intellectually stimulating. However, UCSD also offers Freshman Seminars to freshmen who miss the intimacy of high school classrooms. The offerings are unique, from French New Wave Cinema to Psychology of Humor.

Studying is a must and UCSD students make it a major priority. Students say that in general they take academics very seriously and many classes at UCSD are very competitive, in particular the science and engineering courses. "If one does not keep up with their work, they will lag behind for sure," said one junior. Another factor that makes academics fast-paced and intense for students is the quarter system. Rather than switching classes in the middle of the year like most colleges, UCSD adopted the unconventional quarter system. Most students claim to enjoy this rapid turnover "because you get to take a variety of subjects during one year."

The Jewel

While school takes up a majority of time for the UCSD kids, they still manage to get involved on campus, partake in festivities and kick back and relax. The name of the city La Jolla comes from the Spanish "la joya"

meaning "jewel," and most students would agree that it's a gem of a city. It is primarily a suburban area known for its high-class neighborhoods and expensive rent. One student says of La Jolla, "The area is definitely pretty, the beach is right there, the air is clean, and we're so close to Sea World and the San Diego Zoo." However, the high cost of living and lack of parking space for cars can be a problem for students. But another junior claims, "Despite what others may say, there is a lot to do in La Jolla [without spending money]. My advice is . . . go on random adventures!" A senior in Warren College says, "I love La Jolla because of the climate. You can't beat sunny, high 60, low 50, every day of the year!"

> **"You can't beat sunny, high 60, low 50 every day of the year!"**

During the weekend, when they aren't studying, UCSD students can find a plethora of activities to engage in. The going-out crowd is rather small at UCSD and many of those that go out on the weekends are involved in Greek life. There are 11 fraternities and eight sororities on campus and some are known for throwing "insane" parties. Those who choose not to go Greek still have weekend options. San Diego and La Jolla have nightclubs and the campus is close to other college-populated towns at Mission Beach and Pacific Beach. An experienced senior added, "Also, it's only a 30-minute drive to Mexico where hundreds of underage students go to party."

Campus Traditions

While normal weekends are usually pretty tame, students go crazy during the annual Sun God festival, named for one of a dozen public art pieces on campus which together comprise the Stuart Collection. The Sun God is a winged structure by the artist Niki de Saint Phalle located near the Faculty Club. But the Sun God is also an all-day extravaganza with concerts, games, and "a lot of drinking." Although music aficionados complain that "they don't get very good performers or big names often," the majority agree that "it's great. You get to see all of your friends from all the colleges, enjoy a fun night with a free concert, and then head over to OVT (a late night café) and grab a midnight snack."

Another anticipated campus tradition is the Pumpkin Drop in the fall and the Watermelon

Drop during the spring. The Watermelon Drop comes from a physics exam question in 1965 involving the velocity of a dropped object. The event today involves the dropping of a large watermelon from the top floor of Revelle College's Urey Hall and a beauty pageant resulting in a Watermelon King and Queen. One student cites this event as the "weirdest thing I've seen on campus." The Pumpkin Drop is similar but involves a large pumpkin filled with candy instead of a watermelon.

College Spirit?

Student life on campus is defined also by the various extracurricular activities that UCSD-ers take part in. Due to the high percentage of Asian-Americans on campus, there are many cultural and political groups for various Asian-American interests such as the Japanese American Student Organization. Also, student run papers are widely circulated. *The Koala*, a somewhat controversial, satirical humor paper, and the *UCSD Guardian*, the campus newspaper, are both read exten-sively on campus. Such enthusiasm is not universal, however. Despite UCSD's 28 varsity sports teams, most students agree that there isn't much support for the Titans. "I wouldn't say UCSD is very school spirited. The lack of a football team probably makes it worse. I myself haven't been to any sports games" said one junior.

The aforementioned residential college system is by far the most significant aspect of student life at UCSD. "I personally like the college system," one junior in Muir College remarked. "It gives you that small campus feel within a larger university. I didn't understand the benefit of it going into school, but now it's one of my favorite features of UCSD. It allows you to meet more people and gives you a much more accessible administrative office and faculty." In fact, the college system is so ingrained into the students that some feel they have more spirit and pride toward their residential college than to the University itself. "I'm from Muir, the best college EVER!" exclaimed one senior.—*Lee Komeda*

FYI
If you come to UCSD, you'd better bring "a surfboard, a bike to get around the huge campus, and a willingness to find a club that interests you.
What's the typical weekend schedule? "Usually, I have to put some time away for studying since UCSD is a quarter system and it moves quickly. We usually play a little beer pong, go out to eat, relax from the school week and just meet up with friends and socialize."
If I could change one thing about USCD, I'd "add more parking spaces. Parking on campus SUCKS!"
Three things every student at UCSD should do before graduating are "visit the cliffs of Black's Beach on a full moon, spray paint the stairwell at Mandeville and experience Mexico (the overrated-ness of Tijuana)."

University of California / Santa Barbara

Address: 1210 Cheadle Hall
Santa Barbara, CA
93106-2014
Phone: 805-893-2881
E-mail address:
admissions@sa.ucsb.edu
Web site URL: www.ucsb.edu
Year Founded: 1909
Private or Public: Public
Religious Affiliation: None
Location: Suburban
Number of Applicants:
40,933
Percent Accepted: 54%
**Percent Accepted who
enroll:** 19%
Number Entering: 4,324
**Number of Transfers
Accepted each Year:** 5,622
Middle 50% SAT range:
M: 540–660, CR:
530–650, Wr: 530–650
Middle 50% ACT range: 23–29
**Early admission program
EA/ED/None:** None

**Percentage accepted
through EA or ED:** NA
EA and ED deadline: NA
Regular Deadline: 30-Nov
Application Fee: $60
**Full time Undergraduate
enrollment:** 18,415
Total enrollment: 21,410
Percent Male: 45%
Percent Female: 55%
**Total Percent Minority or
Unreported:** 47%
Percent African-American:
3%
**Percent Asian/Pacific
Islander:** 16%
Percent Hispanic: 19%
Percent Native-American:
1%
Percent International: 1%
**Percent in-state/out of
state:** 96%/4%
Percent from Public HS: 86%
Retention Rate: 91%
Graduation Rate 4-year: 62%

Graduation Rate 6-year:
81%
**Percent Undergraduates in
On-campus housing:** 94%
**Number of official organized
extracurricular
organizations:** 508
3 Most popular majors:
Biology, Economics,
Psychology
Student/Faculty ratio: 17:1
Average Class Size: 2 to 9
**Percent of students going to
grad school:** Unreported
Tuition and Fees: $28,994
**In State Tuition and Fees if
different:** $8,386
Cost for Room and Board:
$12,485
**Percent receiving financial
aid out of those who apply,
first year:** 46%
**Percent receiving financial
aid among all students:**
68%

S et against the backdrop of the golden Santa Ynez Mountains, overlooking the blue Pacific Ocean, and surrounded by fresh green palm fronds that ripple gently in the sea breeze, the University of California, Santa Barbara always stuns its visitors with its spectacular natural beauty. Students take advantage of their seaside location as they whiz along to class on the vast network of campus bike trails or enjoy a bonfire on the beach before heading out to parties in Isla Vista. Although students enjoy a notoriously thriving social life that has led some to refer to the school as the "University of Casual Sex and Beer" (UCSB), the University offers much more, including a stellar faculty, plentiful research opportunities and a relaxed atmosphere that allows for academics to be challenging without being super-competitive.

Yes, We Do Study Sometimes

"The academics are really strong here," said one student. "More than people give it credit for." Students are divided into three main schools: the College of Letters and Science, the College of Engineering, and the College of Creative Studies. There are a lot of "pretty broad" requirements that all students regardless of major must fulfill, in areas such as writing, language, western culture, non-western culture and science. Top choices for majors include biology (particularly marine biology), philosophy, engineering (one of the hardest majors) and global studies. The school boasts several Nobel Prize-winning faculty and other professors who are highly-distinguished in their fields.

Competition within classes varies according to major, and is probably most intense in the sciences where a large number of pre-meds are all vying for the top grades. According to one student, "I love the laid-back atmosphere. I don't feel that it's overly-competitive; it never gets to the point you hear about at other schools where people are stealing each other's binders." Another student disagreed, saying that students "sometimes bring materials into closed-book tests and don't get caught, which makes the atmosphere unnecessarily competitive. I wish the school regulated that kind of thing more effectively." Competition to get into classes can be tricky, especially for the more popular majors, but students say it helps to come in with extra credits from high school in order to gain a higher standing in the course selection process. •

As at most colleges, introductory level classes have hundreds of students, while higher-level classes are smaller. "Because classes are so big, you really have to make an effort to get to know your professors," commented one junior. All professors and TAs have office hours, though students generally agree that not a lot of people take advantage of this system. The workload varies between classes and majors, but one student estimated that to get Bs, people must study about two hours for each day of classes. Said one sophomore, "I feel like I always have work to do and it's never-ending! But some people seem to get it all done quickly and then go out and party every night. It really depends on the classes and the students."

California Nights
Everyone overwhelmingly agrees that UCSB is a notorious party school. "That's probably because we're all crammed into one place," said one student, in reference to Isla Vista. "I.V.," a party zone often referred to as the "most densely populated square mile west of the Mississippi" is a little close-knit community right off campus where student apartments are packed up next to each other. House parties are probably the most common kind of party, particularly along Del Playa; frats also host parties, but it's often difficult for guys to get in if they don't already know someone in the fraternity. Some people prefer to hang out in small groups with friends in their rooms, drinking, watching movies, or just winding down after a long week of classes.

For non-drinkers, the school's Alternative Program Board arranges dances, movie nights by the lagoon, concerts and other musical events, such as debuting new freshman bands. The Magic Lantern also screens movies in one of the nearby theatres, and even though there are not often a lot of drama events that people attend, there is a well-liked improv comedy group that performs on Friday nights. One sophomore reported, "The dance teams and clubs get together and put on performances for benefits or other activities. And one of the frats puts on a huge show every year. There are

definitely other things to do—you don't have to come here and party, though it's certainly an option!"

The alcohol policy on campus is similar to most schools, but regulations are rarely enforced. Recently, USCB has been trying to gain more jurisdiction over what goes on in Isla Vista, but "people are fighting it, because this is where we live!" one junior said, "Everyone knows what's going on. Professors plan exams around Halloween weekend so that 'people don't come in hung-over,' and they always throw a lot of beer jokes into their lectures." Another student noted that there have been some new policies regarding the usual Halloween craziness, such as the rule that all kegs and music must now be indoors. Since about a quarter of I.V. is home to families, older residents and others, the administration tries to work to achieve a healthy relationship between the various factions of the Isla Vista community.

In addition to Halloween, special annual parties include a large and raucous St. Patrick's Day celebration, summertime Fiesta and Fight Night at one of the frats, where students box in the basketball arena. Each of the residence halls also holds an annual All-Hall Ball, where students go to a formal dance held at one of the nearby hotels. Generally speaking, there will always be something going on at UCSB, whether alcohol-related or not, and students have a wide array of activities to choose from when deciding upon their weekend plans.

Surfer Guys and O.C. Girls
When asked to describe the general population of UCSB, most students respond with one word: "surfer." The guys especially are part of the "surfer crowd—you know, like cargo shorts, t-shirts, sunglasses, maybe a hooded sweatshirt if the weather is cool." Girls have been described as walking "right out of the O.C, complete with highlighted hair, huge sunglasses, short skirts and Uggs. "When popped collars were popular, absolutely everyone had a popped collar," said one student. "And people are very fashion-conscious . . . Abercrombie, Gucci, Chanel, you name it." While this kind of culture is the norm for many students, some find it rather troubling. "It's definitely a high-income school," one freshman noted. "That's probably why the Greek life is so popular here, because so many people can afford it. It does make me feel uncomfortable once in a while."

Still, everyone agrees that the students are all very friendly, welcoming people. With such a large student population and large classes, however, sometimes it can be hard to meet people. According to one student, "TAs try to promote interaction among the students in discussion sections, but even so, it can be really hard to meet other kids if you're not involved in an extracurricular activity." Many recommend the freshman summer program as a way to meet people. The dating scene is typical of most colleges, where "dating" doesn't really exist since most romantic interactions take the form of one of two extremes: either random hookups or long-term relationships.

The school is not typically described as being diverse. Students say that their school is known for being a basically Caucasian campus. "There are a lot of culturally/ethnically-based clubs and organizations," said one student. "But the actual diversity here is pretty low." In terms of geography, most students are from California. "I've only ever met three people who are from outside the state," one junior commented.

Life Along The Beach

The majority of freshmen opt to live in the dorms for at least their first year (often moving out to I.V. for their second or third year) because everyone tends to feel that dorm life is an essential part of the college experience and it's an easy way to meet people. "The dorms are kind of small, but the quality is good, and the food isn't bad," one freshman said. The Santa Cruz dorms are located closest to the beach and are usually considered to be the "most fun." Students who move to I.V. in later years love it, saying that "there are always people coming and going, and it's not as loud as you'd think it would be."

When asked to describe the campus itself, one student observed that it is "very spread out. There are a lot of empty green spaces." The campus is slowly renovating its older buildings, particularly those in the science and engineering departments. The Marine Biology building is especially beautiful, with one side of the building designed to look like a lighthouse and a room at the top with windows that offer a 360-degree view of the surrounding area. The backdrop of the campus is the beautiful blue Pacific Ocean, and many of the dorms look out over the water. Several students also commented on the horseshoe-shaped lagoon, a quiet area where people can read, study, have picnics and watch the wildlife. The student population is very active, so there are often runners taking a jog around the lagoon and down along the beach. Other favorite places on campus include the University Center, which is a great central meeting place right next to the bookstore with computers, restaurants and a corner store for snacks, as well as the strip, the library and the rec center. Most students agree that the campus is pretty safe at night, and members of the campus security team are always around to escort students back to their dorms if they feel anxious about walking back alone.

In the neighborhood immediately surrounding the campus, students can take advantage of off-campus eateries such as the famous Freebirds (open 24 hours) for delicious burritos and nachos, Pita Pit, Starbucks, Chili's, Borders, a Japanese restaurant and more. "Some places are a little far, and if you don't want to walk, we have a free bus system," one sophomore explained. There is also a convenient cab system from downtown Santa Barbara to I.V.

Get Involved

Varsity sports do not enjoy a huge following on campus (USCB does not have a football team), although the soccer team is "pretty good." The biggest (and sometimes the only) sports fans are the members of Gauchos Locos, a club that goes to every sporting event and tries to spark more school spirit. Although students may not watch the games, they do often participate in sports through intramurals. Soccer, softball, volleyball and lacrosse are always popular. Students may also stay active in the Rec Center, which boasts a field with artificial grass, several outdoor pools, two weight rooms for non-athletes, racquetball courts, a climbing wall and a roller hockey arena. Some unique club sports include kayaking, snorkeling, scuba diving, sailing, surfing and skiing.

"Not a lot of campuses are located on a beach, and where else can you have surfing and skiing within such a close distance?"

There are a number of other clubs and organizations on campus where students can pursue individual interests and meet people with similar passions. One of the more prominent is the Community Affairs Board, a service-based organization. Many people in dorms participate in the Hall Council, a group that throws events for the dorms. Sororities and fraternities are popular, as are ethnic clubs and some religious organizations. People also enjoy a break-dancing club, a swing and ballroom dance club, shows put on by a Filipino urban dance group and performances by a cappella groups, who usually perform at fund-raisers and variety shows.

California Dreamin'

Students say that they enjoy the closeness of the community at UCSB, particularly in I.V., and that the entire campus is permeated by a "warm, homey, kick-back kind of feeling." One student reported, "One of the most unique aspects of our school is the location.

Not a lot of campuses are located on a beach, and where else can you have surfing and skiing within such a close distance?" Many people say that they are pleasantly surprised when they arrive at USCB to discover that there is more to the school than wild, drunken parties at beachfront apartments (although the party scene is definitely dynamic). When asked if she would choose USCB again if she had to do it all over, a senior responded, "Yeah, I think I would. It's pretty cool here. It's a closer-knit community and a smaller town than UCLA with all the benefits of a California setting, so really, why not?"—*Lindsay Starck*

FYI
If you come to UCSB, you'd better bring "a pair of Rainbow sandals, a bike, and a swimsuit."
What's the typical weekend schedule? "Friday night party or see a movie, Saturday go to the beach and then go to I.V., and Sunday get work done."
If I could change one thing about UCSB, "I'd reduce the emphasis on drinking—even the professors are almost encouraging it! It kind of makes you feel dumb if you don't party as much as everyone else."
Three things every UCSB student should do before graduating are "have a bonfire on the beach, try a Freebirds burrito, party in I.V. on Halloween."

University of California / Santa Cruz

Address: Cook House, 1156 High Street Santa Cruz, CA 95064
Phone: 831-459-4008
E-mail address: admissions@ucsc.edu
Web site URL: www.ucsc.edu
Year Founded: 1965
Private or Public: Public
Religious Affiliation: None
Location: Suburban
Number of Applicants: 24,453
Percent Accepted: 82%
Percent Accepted who enroll: 19%
Number Entering: 3,717
Number of Transfers Accepted each Year: 3,374
Middle 50% SAT range: M: 520–630, CR: 500–620, Wr: 500–620
Middle 50% ACT range: 21–29
Early admission program EA/ED/None: None

Percentage accepted through EA or ED: NA
EA and ED deadline: NA
Regular Deadline: 30-Nov
Application Fee: $60
Full time Undergraduate enrollment: 14,403
Total enrollment: 15,825
Percent Male: 47%
Percent Female: 53%
Total Percent Minority or Unreported: 49%
Percent African-American: 3%
Percent Asian/Pacific Islander: 21%
Percent Hispanic: 16%
Percent Native-American: 1%
Percent International: 1%
Percent in-state/out of state: 97%/3%
Percent from Public HS: 85%
Retention Rate: Unreported

Graduation Rate 4-year: 45%
Graduation Rate 6-year: 66%
Percent Undergraduates in On-campus housing: 99%
Number of official organized extracurricular organizations: 141
3 Most popular majors: Art, Business, English
Student/Faculty ratio: 19:1
Average Class Size: 20 to 29
Percent of students going to grad school: Unreported
Tuition and Fees: $28,808
In State Tuition and Fees if different: $8,200
Cost for Room and Board: $13,038
Percent receiving financial aid out of those who apply, first year: 47%
Percent receiving financial aid among all students: 67%

Though it is known among Californian high school students as one of the easier University of California campuses to be admitted to, UCSC nonetheless offers one of the best educations of all public universities in the country. A school of almost 15,000 people located in a small coastal town directly south of San Francisco and San Jose, UCSC offers students a liberal arts-oriented education along with a quiet and picturesque, yet friendly environment.

UCSC models its system after other, earlier UC schools. With its large freshman class of more than 3,000, 63 majors and the quarter system unique to the UC schools, UCSC allows its students to pursue exactly what they wish with extensive support from faculty and fellow students.

A Relaxing Experience in Education

The most famous aspect of the UCSC education was once its pass/fail grading system. The only difference between an A+ and a D− were the words in the evaluations of the students written by professors. But the evaluations were usually not accessible to potential employers and the graduate school admission officers, so the system was finally revamped and replaced by the A through F used in most schools.

However, the impact of the pass/fail system continues. Students can take up to one-quarter of their classes pass/fail. At the same time, UCSC is known for its minimal course requirements, allowing students to take most of their classes in their fields of interest. Also, almost all incoming freshmen receive large amounts of UCSC course credits for almost all of their AP scores above three, allowing many freshmen to enter UCSC as sophomores in their first year. Therefore, as one freshman pointed out, the amount of courses in which students actually have to try hard is at UCSC "next to nothing, so I can do extracurricular activities for hours, even during weekdays."

As a result of such a relaxing academic atmosphere, it is not difficult to find some of the most carefree students in the entire University of California system at UCSC. Because the Core classes of a UCSC education consist of writing-focused large lecture classes of more than 100 students and unbelievably-favorable curves, some students find classes a little less challenging than they'd like. As one freshman remarked, "People just fall asleep in the back of the lecture hall as soon as the professor starts talk-ing; no worries, the professor doesn't see them."

However, once students choose majors, the classes can become fairly-small in size and very competitive. Students can also get a personal touch from the professors in these small, often seminar-like classes. One freshman remarked on her class atmosphere, "The people are all pretty friendly and the RAs [equivalent to Teaching Assistants] are very cool." It is a common feeling that the personal academic feel of UCSC increases as the time of study increases.

Real Definition of Coed

UCSC's campus consists of many residential colleges, each consisting of several large dorm buildings. In each of the residential/academic colleges, there are several hundred students and separate facilities such as gym/exercise area and dining halls. It is said that there are large differences in the quality of facilities from college to college, especially in terms of dining hall food. As one girl pointed out, "The food at my college (Crown) is pretty good but there are other places that are best avoided." Also, each college has their own education principle and emphasizes different subjects. Thus, the Core classes in different colleges all have different themes and thus are taught differently.

> "People just fall asleep in the back of the lecture hall as soon as the professor starts talking; no worries, the professor doesn't see them."

It should be noted that even with such great dorms, UCSC students do not usually just live within the bubble that is the University itself. With its closeness to the city of Santa Cruz and its relatively-relaxing academic atmosphere, UCSC students find large amounts of time to explore the city of which they are a part. One freshman said, "I haven't gone downtown very often, but it seems neat." Most students have cars, and even though it is difficult to get a parking permit on campus, it is also not uncommon for students to leave UCSC and Santa Cruz altogether on weekends and long holiday breaks for trips to such places as Golden Gate Bridge in San Francisco and Yosemite National Park. Students find great pleasure in exploring all the tourist spots in and around Santa Cruz or Northern California in general.

"Go Banana Slugs?"

Students complain sometimes that there is relatively little to do on campus, even on the weekends. According to many students, one of the great drawbacks of UCSC is its lack of a football team. "We are just missing out on college football!" one male student said with dismay. "There is so little school spirit here, because we have no decent sports teams!" another student noted with sorrow. For those who enjoy tailgating sports teams, UCSC is not the choice.

Greek life is also close to nonexistent in UCSC; sororities and fraternities do not have their own houses. There is no obvious "rush" for sororities and fraternities and not many students join the few choices that are available. When asked why UCSC students do not care about Greek life, one student responded, "What's the point? The parties are not good without hot girls, and there are no good-looking girls here." Another student in-

terjected, "Haven't you heard of the saying? 'Nine of ten Californian girls are hot, the tenth goes to UCSC.'" Apparently, female beauty is not prevalent at UCSC. The male students describe the typical female students at UCSC as lacking. But the female students returned the favor with equally negative terms to describe the typical UCSC guy.

Also, even though clubs and organizations of any kind and any interests are available to students, participation is usually sporadic and the presence of the majority of the campus organizations is not obvious enough to be known among the majority of the student body. This is why so many UCSC students typically spend weekends outside of campus in the city or driving through Northern California. As one student remarked, "what's the point of staying on campus on the weekend? The parties are lame, the clubs are dead and the homework is done."—*Xiaochen Su*

FYI
If you come to UCSC, you better bring "a warm jacket, an open mind, and a pair of walking shoes."
What's the typical weekend schedule? "Sleeping, eating, homework, hanging out with people."
If you could change one thing about UCSC, I'd have "slightly larger shower stalls."
Three things every student at UCSC should do before graduating are "satisfy all the requirements, not suck at life and have a major."

University of Redlands

Address: 1200 East Colton Avenue Redlands, CA 92373-0999
Phone: 909 748-8074
E-mail address: admissions@redlands.edu
Web site URL: www.redlands.edu
Year Founded: 1886
Private or Public: Private
Religious Affiliation: None
Location: Suburban
Number of Applicants: 3,757
Percent Accepted: 67%
Percent Accepted who enroll: 25%
Number Entering: 604
Number of Transfers Accepted each Year: 230
Middle 50% SAT range: M: 540–620, CR: 520–620, Wr: Unreported
Middle 50% ACT range: 21–27
Early admission program EA/ED/None: None

Percentage accepted through EA or ED: NA
EA and ED deadline: NA
Regular Deadline: 1-Apr
Application Fee: $45
Full time Undergraduate enrollment: 2,354
Total enrollment: 4,269
Percent Male: 45%
Percent Female: 55%
Total Percent Minority or Unreported: 17%
Percent African-American: 3%
Percent Asian/Pacific Islander: 5%
Percent Hispanic: 12%
Percent Native-American: <1%
Percent International: 1%
Percent in-state/out of state: 61%/39%
Percent from Public HS: Unreported
Retention Rate: 86%
Graduation Rate 4-year: 54%

Graduation Rate 6-year: 66%
Percent Undergraduates in On-campus housing: 72%
Number of official organized extracurricular organizations: 106
3 Most popular majors: Liberal Arts, Business/Marketing, Social Sciences
Student/Faculty ratio: 12:1
Average Class Size: 19
Percent of students going to grad school: 15%
Tuition and Fees: $32,294
In State Tuition and Fees if different: No difference
Cost for Room and Board: $10,122
Percent receiving financial aid out of those who apply, first year: 80%
Percent receiving financial aid among all students: 63%

Boasting an enviable location in the midst of Southern California, the Univeristy of Redlands lays at the base of the magnificent San Bernardino Mountains. The desert landscape is indicative of the great weather year-round, but also serves as a reminder that a Redlands experience without a car can quickly turn into a very isolated one. Most students find a way to get around the small city and many say they appreciate the college's small size, citing the 600-student entering class size and the 12:1 student-faculty ratio as proof that they are more than just numbers here. "Coming from a small high school, I feel like Redlands has helped make the transition a very smooth one," said one junior. "Almost all of my professors know my name and I often see them outside of class." With a beautiful campus, small classes, and professors who are interested in teaching, Redlands seems to offer a good deal; that is if you're willing to pick up the tab.

When Nature Calls—Being Aware of Your Surroundings

The Redlands campus has been used as a set for recent films such as "Rules of Attraction" and "Joy Ride," but even if the college grounds are attractive, it's the surroundings that stand out the most, for they offer great opportunities for students to interact with nature. Students recognize their surroundings as full of opportunities for wildlife observation, rock climbing, hiking, mountain biking, photography or just camping out. To this end, Redlands helps organize "Outdoor Programs" which may last from as short as a weekend afternoon to a month during the summer. "Going out on the hot air balloon was the coolest experience ever!" recalled one student. Other available excursions include bungee jumping, skiing, snowboarding, skydiving and surfing.

For those who wish to take their own initiative, Redlands has everything the casual outdoorsman needs: tents, sleeping bags, backpacks and rain gear are all available to students for free. Although a credit card is required as deposit, students generally agree that the rental shop is very accessible. "As long as you plan a few days in advance, you can usually get what you need."

Unfortunately, while its surroundings may be a paradise for the outward bound, the small city of Redlands (population approximately 60,000) does not have much to offer. The town is a little far from central campus, but almost everyone either owns a car or knows someone who does. The trolley system that operates during the mornings and afternoons doesn't run during the nights, but it's usually easy to catch a ride. Downtown Redlands boasts many of the most popular fast food shops, as well as some fancier Italian restaurants and coffee shops, which students and townspeople frequent. Besides going downtown, students use their cars to "catch a late-night snack or go shopping at the nearby outlet malls." One student agreed that "Redlands will definitely get dull very quickly if you don't get out often." He commented that he and his friends often go into downtown Los Angeles or San Diego, which are only about an hour away. Some upperclassmen also go to Las Vegas—about five hours away.

Making Service a Way of Life

Although students often reveal their concern for the lack of economic diversity at Redlands, one thing that can be said about the kids here is that they know how to get their hands dirty to serve others. Community service is integrated into the curriculum and students must complete a combination of service instruction and outreach requirements. While some students serve at the local high schools, others use their summers or May terms to go as far as Africa. One senior recalled her experience with helping victims of Hurricane Katrina as "one of the most enriching experiences of my entire life." She added, "I felt like I was really making a difference in people's lives and I really want to go back." The same student agreed that Redlands seems to attract a more service-oriented crowd, "but it's not like a huge deal for everyone."

A Bold Academic Experiment

The flagship of the Redlands academic experience is the Johnston Center for Integrative Studies. Requiring a supplemental application, the center admits a limited number of the incoming freshman class. Students in the Johnston Center have unparalleled control over their education. Students may create their own major and choose their own courses. They are also allowed to write contracts for individual courses, leaving it to the students to decide how they will go about meeting their educational needs and which requirements they will fulfill. Quizzes may be substituted for longer tests or papers, and vice-versa. It's also possible to increase or decrease the credits for many courses by contracting to do more or less work.

> **Redlands has everything the casual outdoorsman needs . . . for free.**

However, as is true of many things, there's a catch: each contract must be negotiated between the student and the professor, and complete academic freedom is more of an aspiration than a reality. All Redlands students are also expected to graduate with sufficient "depth" and "breadth" in their studies. "The distributional requirements are complex and pretty burdensome," a freshman pointed out. "I think it's a little easier for the Johnston kids because they don't have to take any particular courses, but for those in the LAF [Liberal Arts Foundation], there's not that much freedom because you have to be worrying about your requirements so much."

Unlike large research universities, Redlands is focused on teaching. Students express a lot of respect for their faculty and really like the individualized attention. "My expectations have been surpassed over and over again," said one student. Another student added: "Having such small classes helps me keep motivated. I feel like I know my professors and my professors know me. I also know who I'm working with and that makes me feel much more comfortable. I don't think I'd be as motivated if I were taking larger classes at a bigger school." Most people refer to their peers as "competent" or "smart," but generally agree that the school "does not attract the biggest minds. Most kids care about their classes and study, but their interest rarely goes beyond the classes they're taking. This is not the kind of place where you'll find people discussing philosophy all day, although politics seem to be a common dinner table topic."

One aspect of Redlands that is appreciated by almost everyone in the community is the strong emphasis that is placed on study abroad. Although the focus is often on

European countries to the exclusion of other regions of the world, there are ample opportunities for Redlands students to study a semester or a whole year abroad through a university-approved program. The most popular study abroad destination is Salzburg, Germany. Credit and financial aid are easily transferable. Students hoping to spend less time abroad may also opt to take one of the courses during the "May term." The May term refers to one month of intensive study, usually undertaken abroad. Courses during the May term include "Japanese Gardens" and "Economics in Buenos Aires."

Housing for All Tastes

Redlands doesn't approach housing in a "one-size-fits-all" fashion. While all undergraduates are guaranteed a room on-campus, every year, students can choose to live in one of the dozen or so different halls. Each of these housing complexes has its own perks and advantages. Some of them, like East Hall, are for freshmen only, while Cortner Hall and Melrose Hall tend to have more upperclassmen. Melrose, with its extended quiet hours, is also seen as a good fit for the more studious. On the other hand there's North Hall, the closest to the gymnasium and thereby host to many of Redlands' jocks. Some of the halls are same-sex, but most are coed.

"Most people seem to be happy with their living conditions," one junior said. "The most common complaint about housing is that some halls are not air-conditioned and it can get extremely hot during the summer." Students are advised to bring a fan—or several. "It was pretty bad the first few weeks of the fall semester," noted a freshman. "However, for most of the year the weather was just perfect." Still, those who hail from colder weather may often be less excited. SNOW (Students in Need of Winter) is a student group that brings together all those who are interested in following the ski season in the nearby Rockies.

Besides the regular housing options, students may also elect to live at one of the fraternity or sorority houses. Although there are several Greek organizations around campus, they don't seem to dominate the social scene. "Generally, there are a few guys who are really into it, but Greek life just isn't as big as you would expect." Students estimate that less than 10 percent of their peers have donned Greek letters.

It's Not Just About the Academics

Redlands offers a fairly wide variety of extracurricular activities and student groups. Opportunities for giving back to the community are plentiful through volunteer groups and there are many student-run religious and cultural organizations as well. The University also has an outstanding debate society, often placing among the top in the country. In fact, debate is valued so much at Redlands that the University offers merit scholarships for outstanding debaters.

Everyone has an opportunity to play sports—at some level—at Redlands. "It's fairly easy to be a walk-on at Redlands if you played in high school," said one junior who plays for the basketball team. "Some kids certainly get recruited, but some sports membership may be almost half walk-ons." The most popular club sports include golf, lacrosse, ultimate Frisbee and ice hockey. There is also an equestrian club.

While many find Redlands too small by the end of their four years, most enjoy the tight-knit community it affords. Within that community, some complain of "a total lack of diversity," and one student remarked that the stereotypical Redlands student was "your average intellectual rich white kid from the West Coast." This does seem to be changing, as Redlands has been recruiting more widely and applications have been increasing significantly in recent years. For all its insularity, Redlands seems to be about unexpected surprises. Whether students enjoy uncovering these hidden treasures will dictate whether they survive their four years out in the oasis of the Californian desert.—*Gerardo Giacoman*

FYI

If you come to Redlands, you'd better bring: "a car or a friend who has one; also, bring a fan—or several in case your housing unit is not air-conditioned."

What's the typical weekend schedule? "Fraternity parties are prevalent during the weekends, but with the recent crackdown on alcohol consumption, weekend nights usually involve hanging out with friends, or getting out of Redlands to find a real party."

If I could change one thing about Redlands, I'd "move it closer to Las Vegas and fight the formation of social cliques."

Three things that every student should do before graduating are: "attend the festival of lights, make a 2 a.m. Del Taco run, drive to Mexico for Spring Break."

University of Southern California

Address: 700 Childs Way
Los Angeles, CA
90089-0911
Phone: 213 740-2311
E-mail address:
admitusc@usc.edu
Web site URL:
www.usc.edu
Year Founded: 1880
Private or Public: Private
Religious Affiliation: None
Location: Suburban
Number of Applicants:
33,760
Percent Accepted: 25%
**Percent Accepted who
enroll:** 35%
Number Entering: 2,963
**Number of Transfers
Accepted each Year:**
1,784
Middle 50% SAT range:
M: 650–750, CR:
620–720, Wr: 640–730
Middle 50% ACT range:
28–32
**Early admission program
EA/ED/None:** None

**Percentage accepted
through EA or ED:** NA
EA and ED deadline: NA
Regular Deadline: 10-Jan
Application Fee: $65
**Full time Undergraduate
enrollment:** 16,384
Total enrollment: 30,703
Percent Male: 48%
Percent Female: 52%
**Total Percent Minority or
Unreported:** 4%
Percent African-American:
5%
**Percent Asian/Pacific
Islander:** 24%
Percent Hispanic: 10%
Percent Native-American:
1%
Percent International:
7%
**Percent in-state/out of
state:** 58%/42%
Percent from Public HS:
55%
Retention Rate: 96%
Graduation Rate 4-year:
68%

Graduation Rate 6-year:
86%
**Percent Undergraduates
in On-campus housing:**
41%
**Number of official organized
extracurricular
organizations:** 642
3 Most popular majors:
Business/Marketing, Social
Sciences, Visual and
Performing Arts
Student/Faculty ratio: 9:1
Average Class Size: 10 to
19
**Percent of students going to
grad school:** Unreported
Tuition and Fees: $37,890
**In State Tuition and Fees if
different:** No difference
Cost for Room and Board:
$11,298
**Percent receiving financial
aid out of those who apply,
first year:** 67%
**Percent receiving financial
aid among all students:**
36%

To find a Trojan, you don't have to go back to Greek mythology; in fact, you can find more than 16,000 of them right here in the heart of sunny Southern California. USC students, just like the warriors for which they were named, are filled with pride and tradition. And unlike other schools that may have reputations for being "nerd schools" or "party schools," USC students say their school has the best of both worlds. As one senior said, "USC is becoming more focused on academics, which is reflected in its increasing national and international standings, but the great thing about this campus is that the social atmosphere has not taken a backseat to the greater focus on academics." From the time students step onto the beautiful campus that forms a backdrop for many a Hollywood movie, to the many years students have after graduation, USC students are and will always be Trojans.

Nuts and Bolts of the Classroom

Class sizes at USC vary, and depend on what type and level of classes you're looking for. As one junior explained, "USC boasts about having smaller class sizes, but that's not necessarily true. Just because it's a private school doesn't mean the ratios get any smaller." Average lecture halls can run up to 300 students in one room, but writing classes, which everyone has to take, are usually limited to only 12–15 students. Students say that getting into core classes isn't competitive since there are more available seats than students, but spots for interesting elective classes, such as Ballroom Dancing 101, can fill up pretty fast, especially with juniors and seniors who have priority. Both class sizes and grading usually vary between departments—popular majors on campus are Business, Biological Sciences, and Communications, and majors known for being particularly difficult are Architecture, Engineering and the sciences in general.

Grading at USC, while not super generous, is fair, students say. "Since I'm a pre-med major, my workload is immense compared to other majors. Being a science major is competitive already, but being a pre-med is even more competitive," said a student majoring in Biological Sciences. Good thing competitive core science classes are curved, then. This system saves a lot of students—students who get B's or B+'s on exams will still probably end up with an A-,or even an A, by the end of the semester. One senior added, "Most classes are curved and there also many professors who don't mind giving A's to everyone who deserves them." Smaller classes like business and language classes usually aren't curved, but the general rule of thumb is that if it's a class with a lot of people, it will be curved.

Professors, however, can be a mixed bag. While most instructors are accessible and easy to talk with during their office hours, others are less open. Professors who are here for research—since USC is a research school—are required to teach as well, so those who would rather bury themselves in work don't try to make themselves accessible to students. Luckily, Trojans have other means of finding academic support in the form of study groups, which students readily form to help each other out and create study groups. "I like that the atmosphere isn't generally a cutthroat competition. The school really wants us to do well so they make a lot of resources available to students like supplemental instruction and free tutors," a junior said.

Trojans Gone Greek

It's no coincidence that the USC has a dominant Greek scene—after all, their Greek nature is practically written in their Trojan name. A freshman noted, "Everyone knows not to make plans with a frat/sorority member on a Monday night because they have to go to Monday night dinners." Greek life is evident all throughout campus, but the core is off-campus on West 28th Street, more commonly known as The Row. With a fifth of the total student population involved with Greek life, and many more involved in service and ethnic Greek communities outside Panhellenic and Interfraternal councils, it's no surprise that much of the partying that goes on at USC happens out on The Row. However, good times are not just limited to frat parties—students often also hit up the

9-0 Bar, a local favorite, and house parties hosted in apartments. And with the City of Angels in their backyard, USC students also have the opportunity to go clubbing in the hot streets of Downtown Los Angeles.

While not everyone at USC drinks, a large majority do—one student guessed that upwards of 80 percent of the students on campus drink. While binge drinking is not·so big a problem that the University needs to address it, students recognize they have peers who regularly drink at unhealthy levels. But beyond drinking and partying, USC also offers many other opportunities to kick back and enjoy the Southern California sun. Students say having a car is nice, but not necessary since it's easy to find other friends who have cars for exploring the area. Even students who live nearby stay on campus over the weekends. It's easy to get into the heart of L.A., and there's always something fun to do. Places to explore range from Little Tokyo and Chinatown to the fashion district, and they're all within a few miles of each other. One junior enthusiastically, and simply, described USC's social life as "Great!" as she went on to explain, "I like USC because the people there are smart, but they still know how to have fun. I guess it's just the atmosphere of being in Southern California and how it's always so chill."

The social scene at USC is a dynamic one. One senior reflected on his experiences at USC and said, "There is a niche for everyone. If you are into the arts scenes, then you can find that. If you are into partying, then you can find that. There is something for everyone. It is up to the student to find the right fit."

Diversity at USC is present, but at the same time, also lacking. Students say that the typical USC student is rich—indeed, "University of Spoiled Children" is a common nickname for the school. There are frat boys and sorority girls who tend to be rich because going Greek requires a fair amount of money, but there are also many students who are on financial aid, so not necessarily everyone is loaded. "A typical USC student is a white trust fund baby, but there are also a lot of students here from a modest background," one student said. Students say there are a lot of preps, jocks, and band geeks like in high school, but that USC is less cliquish. Despite diversity in interests and geography, to name two facets, students said their peers tend to hang out within their own ethnic groups. But at the end of the day, as one junior noted, "I find that USC is really diverse and many 'groups' are just chill, down-to-earth kinds of people."

Pimp My Housing, Please?

To be frank, housing at USC is not great. Underclassmen have priority in on-campus housing, but even then, students usually move out by the time they are sophomores. This is because of USC's rather limited geographical area—the campus is right in the middle of South Central Los Angeles, so there isn't much room for expansion. "Freshmen and sophomores get priority in choosing University housing, so if you're a senior, I would say good luck in trying to find a place to live," a junior said.

Most off-campus apartments are about a block or more away from campus, and the farther away from campus you get, the more dangerous it is. While USC may get a bad reputation for being in the middle of South Central, students say the campus is safe at night, if you stay conscious about it. "They always tell us to walk in groups and not to be alone at night. The dumb students are the ones who walk home alone at 3 a.m. after a party—they're the ones who get robbed," a senior explained. Students say housing at USC needs to be improved, and the school has started what it calls a Master Plan and has already started buying property and building new housing complexes near campus.

As for meal options, one student described them as "kind of sucky." USC has two cafeterias—EVK and Parkside, the latter of which serves more international foods and is generally regarded as the better dining hall. There is the Commons area, which is kind of small, but is in the process of getting renovated. There's also Café 84 which is "alright;" one student summed up USC's dining options as "Most are mediocre." Students can also go out to the 9-0, which is a bar near campus, or stay on campus and go to Traddie's, which is short for Traditions Bar.

Hope You Like Football!

While housing and food may leave students wanting more, USC's extracurricular activity opportunities just might be the thing to fulfill a Trojan's appetite. One aspect of USC that is extremely important is students' dedication to extracurricular activities. With more than 700 student organizations, there is definitely something for everyone. One popular extracurricular is community service. "Our geographic location near Downtown Los Angeles allows us to become deeply involved in community service. I love that USC encourages community service and the strong sense of family is a strong plus," said one student who is the president of a service fraternity.

> "I felt like I was able to ease into college comfortably because the campus makes a huge effort to get people involved and people really fall in love with USC."

The most visible outside-the-classroom activity is one in which only a small fraction of the student population directly participates. But while the number of students on the field as football players and cheerleaders is quite small, practically the entire school makes it out to the stadium for football games. With pre-games, tailgates, and post-parties, football at USC is everything you've seen on national television and more. "We're practically defined by our football team. If you don't buy a spirit card, which allows you to go to football games and more, you are probably crazy for not doing so," one junior said. Even students who aren't into sports find themselves among the most hardcore of USC football fans. "There's a huge football culture on this campus. There is extreme pride and everyone from students to alumni goes all out. On game days, every single inch of the main campus is filled with people and everyone is wearing red," a senior said.

Join the Family

This dedication to USC Football reflects something larger, which is the dedication to the school as a whole. Students say they are part of "the Trojan Family" and that a strong sense of pride and tradition is instilled in them from the first day they step onto campus. "I felt like I was able to ease into college comfortably because the campus makes a huge effort to get people involved and people really fall in love with USC," a junior said. Partly because networking is so important at USC, relationships are strong within the school and outside of it. Alumni come back for career fairs and workshops looking specifically to hire fellow Trojans, and it is these lasting ties that form the core of what it means to go to USC. One student explained, "Whenever I see a fellow Trojan outside of school, even if they are a stranger, there's already a connection because of the school. Sometimes we may exchange a few words or a 'Fight On!' sign while passing by. It sounds kind of cheesy, but it's true."

Reflecting upon her time as a Trojan, one senior said, "I think that a lot of people have a misconception that USC is just a school full of rich kids, and that students basically buy their diploma. I also used to believe this before I entered, but I was surprised that most of the people I've met come from middle-class families, and most wealthy students do not flaunt their wealth." So if you're ready to challenge yourself, and have your preconceptions challenged as well, get ready to immerse yourself in the Trojan family and make friendships and connections that will last a lifetime.—*Della Fok*

FYIs

If you come to USC, you'd better bring "An open attitude to different types of people and personalities because you never know who you will end up becoming friends with here at USC."

What's the typical weekend schedule? "Thursday is the big party night because many people don't have classes on Fridays—they call it 'Thirsty Thursday.' People have small parties every night, though, and a lot of people go to Hollywood or Westwood on the weekends."

If I could change one thing about USC, "I'd change its location to an area with more shops and restaurants so there would be more things to do."

Three things every student at USC should do before graduating are "join a club, fraternity or sorority, go to at least one football game, definitely, and eat at Chano's, which is this old Mexican drive-through place that looks dirty, but it's really good Mexican food!"

Whittier College

Address: 13406 Philadelphia Street Whittier, CA 90608
Phone: 562-97-4238
E-mail address: admission@whittier.edu
Web site URL: www.whittier.edu
Year Founded: 1887
Private or Public: Private
Religious Affiliation: None
Location: Urban
Number of Applicants: 2,196
Percent Accepted: 67%
Percent Accepted who enroll: 19%
Number Entering: 282
Number of Transfers Accepted each Year: 120
Middle 50% SAT range: M: 480–602, CR: 480–600, Wr: 480–590
Middle 50% ACT range: 20–27
Early admission program EA/ED/None: EA

Percentage accepted through EA or ED: Unreported
EA and ED deadline: 1-Dec
Regular Deadline: Rolling
Application Fee: $50
Full time Undergraduate enrollment: 1,259
Total enrollment: 1,369
Percent Male: 45%
Percent Female: 55%
Total Percent Minority or Unreported: 43%
Percent African-American: 3%
Percent Asian/Pacific Islander: 8%
Percent Hispanic: 30%
Percent Native-American: 1%
Percent International: 3%
Percent in-state/out of state: 73%/27%
Percent from Public HS: Unreported
Retention Rate: 78%

Graduation Rate 4-year: 52%
Graduation Rate 6-year: 52%
Percent Undergraduates in On-campus housing: 60%
Number of official organized extracurricular organizations: 68
3 Most popular majors: Biology, Business, Psychology
Student/Faculty ratio: 13:1
Average Class Size: 10 to 19
Percent of students going to grad school: 28%
Tuition and Fees: $31,950
In State Tuition and Fees if different: No difference
Cost for Room and Board: $9,050
Percent receiving financial aid out of those who apply, first year: 92%
Percent receiving financial aid among all students: 89%

Whittier College, a small, diverse liberal arts college, is spread out over 74 acres in California, only about 18 miles southeast of the city of Los Angeles. Originally a Quaker institution, Whittier is now a secular school, but some of its original Quaker values, like emphasis on the individual and the diversity of the student body, remain an integral part of the Whittier experience.

Founding "Friends"

Whittier College began as a Quaker academy established by the Religious Society of Friends in 1887, the same year that they founded the town of Whittier itself. Although the Quaker heritage is visible in such things as the name of the weekly student newspaper, the *Quaker Campus*, there does not seem to be a large focus on the legacy of the founding Friends. One student even went so far as to say that, despite the school's reputation as a former Quaker haven, "They don't force much onto us about Quakers."

Fewer Students, More Options

With such a small student body, Whittier is able to offer smaller, more intense classes. The average class size is about 17, which fosters the development of real relationships between students and professors. As one student said, "It's nice to be able get to know your teachers." However, limiting the number of students in each classroom does create other issues. "Some of the classes are hard to get in to because of how small they are and the order of how [students] register," a junior complained.

Besides regular classes, students at Whittier can design their own major in the Whittier Scholars Program (WSP). Members of the WSP work closely with professors and other students to build their own curriculums, whether by creating their own major or fashioning a course of study around an existing one. Students can even incorporate off-campus experiences like study abroad and internships into their course of study, a large academic draw to Whittier.

Another way for students to expand their academic horizons is Whittier's one-month term in January. The courses offered for the "Jan Term" often cover more "fun" and interesting subjects, including classes that even integrate travel or other types of hands-on experiences into the session. Some of the most popular options include a class on death and dying, involving a trip to the morgue, or a trip to help clean up New Orleans. Students generally enjoy these more unconventional opportunities. "I love the Jan Term classes!" one Whittier student enthused.

Splendid Spectrum: Sports, Societies, and Student Groups

From small-town charm to the bustling activity of nearby Los Angeles, Whittier's 74-acre campus has no shortage of ways to stay busy outside of the classroom. There are tons of extracurricular activities to get involved in, from editing the *Quaker Campus*, to working on the Whittier College Radio station. And, if you can't find the club for you, never fear—the Whittier Office of Student Activities specializes in helping students create their own clubs or groups.

"I love the Jan Term classes!"

On a typical weekend, a lot of people spend time partying with societies, special fraternity-type organizations unique to Whittier. The societies host numerous social events and remain an important part of Whittier's history and traditions. Founded in the 1920s, the societies are behind most of the biggest parties on campus. If that's not your scene, never fear—students also report that there are plays, movies and concerts on campus to entertain them. And, for the more adventurous, L.A. has a whole world of restaurants, museums and shopping to amuse even the pickiest of procrastinators.

In terms of sports, Whittier has 21 Division III varsity teams on which students keep busy, the most popular of which is definitely lacrosse. Aside from the varsity teams, students can choose from a multitude of intramural sports, often played outside in the region's year-round temperate climate.

Overall, students agree that they can find whatever they want in Whittier's diverse campus. Although students may venture to downtown Los Angeles or the nearby Pacific coastline, they need not look beyond their own community for exciting opportunities among familiar faces.—*Suzanne Salgado*

FYI

If you come to Whittier, you'd better bring "pictures, posters, decorations and anything that gives you a sense of comfort from home."

What's the typical weekend schedule? "Get up at noon or so, do whatever you can on Saturday, and then Sunday is homework day."

If I could change one thing about Whittier it would be "make smaller classes easier to get into."

Three things every student at Whittier should do before graduating are "study abroad, get involved, and take advantage of the free services and fun events provided for students."

Colorado

Colorado College

Address: 14 East Cache la Poudre Street, Colorado Springs, CO, 80903
Phone: 719-389-6344
E-mail address: admission@coloradocollege.edu
Web site URL: www.coloradocollege.edu
Year Founded: 1874
Private or Public: Private
Religious Affiliation: None
Location: Urban
Number of Applicants: 4,089
Percent Accepted: 34%
Percent Accepted who enroll: 33%
Number Entering: 524
Number of Transfers Accepted each Year: 72
Middle 50% SAT range: M: 620–700, CR: 620–700, Wr: 660–730
Middle 50% ACT range: 27–30

Early admission program EA/ED/None: EA and ED
Percentage accepted through EA or ED: 27%
EA and ED deadline: 15-Nov
Regular Deadline: 15-Jan
Application Fee: $50
Full time Undergraduate enrollment: 2,053
Total enrollment: 2,075
Percent Male: 41%
Percent Female: 59%
Total Percent Minority or Unreported: 21%
Percent African-American: 2%
Percent Asian/Pacific Islander: 4%
Percent Hispanic: 7%
Percent Native-American: 1%
Percent International: 2%
Percent in-state/out of state: 27%/73%
Percent from Public HS: 58%

Retention Rate: 92%
Graduation Rate 4-year: 77%
Graduation Rate 6-year: 83%
Percent Undergraduates in On-campus housing: 76%
Number of official organized extracurricular organizations: 92
3 Most popular majors: Economics, English, Biology
Student/Faculty ratio: 10:1
Average Class Size: 2 to 9
Percent of students going to grad school: Unreported
Tuition and Fees: $33,972
In State Tuition and Fees if different: No difference
Cost for Room and Board: $8,498
Percent receiving financial aid out of those who apply, first year: 92%
Percent receiving financial aid among all students: 35%

C olorado College boasts a distinctive academic system and an amazing locale, as it is surrounded by sóme of the biggest and most beautiful mountains in North America. The college is admired not only for its solid academic foundation, but also for the wealth of outdoor opportunities available to students and for its intimate, close-knit community.

One by One
One of Colorado College's most unique and intriguing distinctions is the Block Plan, an academic system characterized by intense, focused study on one class for three and a half weeks. "The Block Plan, above anything else, is the reason I came to CC," said one student. "I love the total immersion learning." The word most commonly used to describe the system is "intense," as classes meet every day for three hours: each day of class on the Block Plan is the equivalent of a week's worth of classes on a normal semester schedule. In total, there are eight blocks per year at CC, and each block is separated by a four-day weekend. "The block breaks are a fantastic reprieve," commented one student. "You have absolutely nothing hanging over your head." Another benefit of the system is the lack of a finals week, because students have one final at the end of each block.

Students acknowledge that the Block Plan seems intimidating at first, but they say it isn't as overwhelming as it sounds because there are no other subjects, papers or homework to worry about. One outstanding advantage of the system is that it facilitates field trips, field study and classes held outside the traditional campus setting. Because the professor and the students of the course are only focusing on that one subject, "Professors have the opportunity to take students away for a week or for a block anywhere in the world." A disadvantage of the system, said one student, "is that it can be frustrating if you don't like the class you're in. Still, all you have to do is get through a couple of weeks, and then you're done. It makes the prospect of a calculus class much easier to tolerate."

At the Bidding Block

The average class size at CC is 13 students, and all classes are capped at 25. The small class size and intimacy fostered by this kind of setting encourage discussion, thereby promoting a strong student-faculty connection. Professors are extremely approachable, especially because of the fact that "this class is their life for that period of time." One student said that several of her friends have gone over to professors' houses for breakfast or dinner, and that everyone calls the professors by their first names. "Because you develop such a close relationship with them, you learn more about them as human beings instead of as lecturers in front of a big class at a larger university."

Students also develop close relationships with their classmates. Although this often leads to lasting friendships, it may sometimes lead to an unofficial phenomenon referred to as "block friends." According to one student, a "block friend" is someone whom another student gets to know really well during the block, but when the block is over and everyone is suddenly immersed in a completely new subject with completely different people, the student may never see that friend again. "The block plan, no matter how much I love it, can be a little socially staggering," he observed.

Competition between students in class is "nonexistent" because of the discussion-based setting. Because students are all going through the material together, there is a "community atmosphere" in which "You're not competing with kids for a grade; you're working with them to get the grade." Said one student, "There is definitely a certain sense of camaraderie; you're so immersed in your subject and so is the person next to you, and no one else on campus is taking that class at that time, so you're sharing a unique experience."

More than a third of the student body graduates with a degree in the natural sciences, which is the main reason why CC calls itself "a liberal arts and sciences" college. Registration for classes is a bidding process in which every student is allotted a certain number of points based on seniority. Some classes are difficult to get into, and seniors have a better chance of getting in simply because they can bid more on each class. Intro psychology is an extremely popular class, perhaps partly because each student gets a live rat at the beginning of the block (the next three weeks are focused on training that rat). Another interesting course is the biology and comparative literature class, in which students read the works of a famous butterfly expert and spend the block traveling the country and following the same path he did while tracking butterflies. Most students call the bidding system "fair," even though "it takes some strategy." All in all, people quickly get used to the Block Plan and swear that they couldn't imagine going back to the semester schedule.

Living in the Mountains

The College requires students to live on campus for the first three years, and most students choose to stay for all four. Freshmen and sophomores are usually housed in traditional dormitories, while upperclassmen have the additional option of apartment-style complexes and larger, older houses. A handful of the houses have themes that change every year, with a couple of current houses being the Mountain House (with a strong focus on the outdoors) and the Animal House (an animal appreciation group where everyone has a pet). There are also several language houses, which provide residence options for students who are studying those languages. The "mediocre" dining hall food rates a seven out of 10 for most students, but they can also use both of the different meal plan options (dining dollars and flex points) at restaurants like the charming on-campus cafe called Herb'n Farm.

The College's architecture is described as "varied," and "somewhat random," though two particularly beautiful and interesting buildings are Shove Memorial Chapel (modeled after Westminster Abbey) and the new science center, which continuously monitors the inside and outside atmospheres, self-adjusting to changes in light and temperature. The building is surrounded by different kinds of rocks that have been flown in from all over the world, making it a popular site for geology classes.

When the Weekend Rolls Around

Students at Colorado College enjoy a thriving social scene throughout the year, though the action definitely peaks on the four-day block breaks. Because almost all students live on campus, a lot of the partying occurs in dorms and residence buildings. One popular annual party is the Anything But Clothes party, where students come dressed in trash bags and cardboard boxes. Said one student, "We're not a dry campus, so people aren't flocking away to do all their partying."

The Greek system is a part of the social life, but it certainly does not dominate, and students claim that the best parties are those at houses where live bands are playing. Drinking is prevalent, as it is on most college campuses, but "It's not hard to avoid and it's not pushed or pressured on anyone." A few students observed that the use of pot is more common at CC than at a lot of other schools. One prominent group on campus, the Other Choices club, sponsors alcohol and drug-free activities that are always an enjoyable alternative to the party scene.

> "On the weekend all the hard-core people climb Pike's Peak at 10, make it to the top by sunrise, and then climb back down."

When it comes to clubs and student organizations, says one student, "We've got it all." There are four major a cappella groups, a popular improv group called TWIG, and a lot of other musical, cultural, political and random groups (such as the Carnivore Club). Intramurals are huge ("really fun and really low-key"), even for less common sports such as dodgeball and broomball. Experience is not necessary; as one student said enthusiastically, "I haven't played soccer since third grade, and this year I'm on Team Awesome!" As far as varsity sports go, the nationally ranked hockey team has the biggest following; said one student, "Every time I see the hockey players down the hall after I've just seen them on TV, I'm always a little starstruck."

One major organization is the Outdoor Recreation Committee, which hosts outdoor activities and excursions throughout the year, including the freshman orientation backpacking trip. "It's a great way to meet new people, and the upperclassmen who lead the trip give you really good insight as to what the school is like," one current freshman said. The ORC deals with "everything wilderness—the organization gets lots of funding, and you can rent out everything from skis to sleeping bags." One student summarized student extracurriculars at CC by saying, "Everyone is really active here. That's one of the things I love about it."

Also praised is the general tendency of CC students to be outgoing and incredibly friendly. "It seems like you're always getting hugs from people," commented one student. On the whole, people are pretty easygoing and casual both in dress and attitude. "We're nice people," said one student. "I walk across campus every day and I smile at nearly every person I see and just about every person smiles back at me." When asked to give a general characterization of the student body, most students said that the school had a little bit of everything and that anyone can find friends with similar interests. Another student described the students as "upper- to middle-class white hippies who are probably from one of the coasts and who are really empathetic to social and political issues." One major issue is the current lack of ethnic diversity, consistently cited as a concern of both the students and the administration.

Location, Location, Location

"You can never overlook our location," several students declared. The mountains, rivers, forests and canyons surrounding the College add a whole new aspect to college life. Students have the opportunity to take the afternoon to go fly-fishing, hiking in a canyon, white-water rafting, kayaking, skiing, snowboarding, mountain climbing, or virtually any other outdoor activity they can think of. "On the weekend all the hard-core people climb Pike's Peak at 10, make it to the top by sunrise, and then climb back down," said one student. "The area is a huge selling point for the people who come here," said another. "I've lived in Colorado all my life, so I've always taken the skiing and snowboarding culture for granted. But my peers from out of state want to ski and snowboard at every possible moment." Everyone at CC, whether or not they were born in the area, takes full advantage of the rich natural surroundings and appreciates the beautiful views from the dorm room windows. One interviewee responded to the first phone call with, "Is it OK if I call you back in like 10 minutes? There are some gorgeous clouds over the mountains right now and I just want to run down and take a few pictures."

All in all, students feel that they made the right choice in coming to Colorado College. The Block Plan is great (the block breaks are even better), the students are friendly, and the sunny skies and the beautiful mountains provide the perfect backdrop to the campus. "I love it here," concluded one student. "It truly is a fabulous place to become educated."—*Lindsay Starck*

FYI
If you come to Colorado College, you'd better bring "skis and a sleeping bag."
What's the typical weekend schedule? "A little homework, a little partying, a little adventure."
If I could change one thing about Colorado College, I'd "make the cafeteria staff more friendly."
Three things every student at Colorado College should do before graduating are "take a class off campus, go salsa dancing, and ski or snowboard."

Colorado School of Mines

Address: 1500 Illinois Street Golden, CO 80401
Phone: 303-273-3200
E-mail address: admit@mines.edu
Web site URL: www.mines.edu
Year Founded: 1874
Private or Public: Public
Religious Affiliation: None
Location: Suburban
Number of Applicants: 3,142
Percent Accepted: 61%
Percent Accepted who enroll: 29%
Number Entering: 776
Number of Transfers Accepted each Year: 128
Middle 50% SAT range: M: 600–690, CR: 540–640, Wr: Unreported
Middle 50% ACT range: 25–30
Early admission program EA/ED/None: None

Percentage accepted through EA or ED: NA
EA and ED deadline: NA
Regular Deadline: 1-Jun
Application Fee: $45
Full time Undergraduate enrollment: 3,456
Total enrollment: 4,488
Percent Male: 79%
Percent Female: 21%
Total Percent Minority or Unreported: 25%
Percent African-American: 2%
Percent Asian/Pacific Islander: 5%
Percent Hispanic: 6%
Percent Native-American: 1%
Percent International: 4%
Percent in-state/out of state: 78%/22%
Percent from Public HS: 90%
Retention Rate: 84%
Graduation Rate 4-year: 27%

Graduation Rate 6-year: 63%
Percent Undergraduates in On-campus housing: 43%
Number of official organized extracurricular organizations: 126
3 Most popular majors: Chemical Engineering, Mathematics, Mechanical Engineering
Student/Faculty ratio: 15:1
Average Class Size: 10 to 19
Percent of students going to grad school: 14%
Tuition and Fees: $25,248
In State Tuition and Fees if different: $11,238
Cost for Room and Board: $7,626
Percent receiving financial aid out of those who apply, first year: 91%
Percent receiving financial aid among all students: Unreported

Looking at the landscapes of the Rocky Mountains, the glorious foliage and the breathtaking mountainous terrain, it is very easy to overlook Golden, Colorado, an uneventful town harboring about 18,000 people. However, to about 3,300 Colorado School of Mines students, this is home. Offering 12 degree programs of which eight contain the word "engineering," Mines is strongly slanted towards the technical disciplines. Even for the most optimistic and open-minded college student, the School of Mines is "lame at first," as one senior described, but the expansive scenery and unique student body eventually become a welcoming home.

Golden Academics in Golden

According to most students, Mines does not have enough parties to really call the party scene a scene, but the parties are not what guide most students to apply to the school. Academics are clearly the main attraction at the School of Mines. The extremely rigorous curriculum challenges students with a "basically prescribed" schedule of classes for the first three years, including extensive mathematics, from calculus through differential equations, as well as physics, economics and computer programming. A typical freshman schedule includes classes (and class-related meetings) from eight to five, three times a week, and a marginally lighter load on the off-days; 15 credit hours is standard for most freshmen. Professors are generally very knowledgeable, but also have a reputation as being very demanding. Nonetheless, on the whole, the teaching staff is considered unmatched and many students cite the "opportunities for interactions with professors" as one of Mines's key advantages.

Another program mandated by the school is its EPICS program, an acronym for Engineering Practices Introductory Course Sequence. With EPICS, students are given real-world engineering problems and are asked to find innovative solutions to those problems. Additionally, in the summer following their sophomore or junior year, students participate in a Field Session program where they are introduced to skills unique to their particular area of specialization.

According to one student, the University strives to teach "the stuff you really need to be an engineer." However, students point to a lack of well-taught liberal arts classes as being the school's weakest point. With engineering as the unequivocal focus of the University, few resources are dedicated to other disciplines. Mines does have an unusually high dropout rate—around 16 percent. Of these students, most transfer to Colorado State University and other state colleges around the country. For those who remain, most are satisfied with the rigor and quality of their education. As one student put it, "it is gratifying to see how much work you actually get done by the end of each term."

Beyond the Classroom?
According to one junior, the party scene at Mines is "best thought of as a desert country . . . a quiet, lonely realm with sporadic oases of people and alcohol." Another student complained that there is "no social atmosphere and the frats are lame." Perhaps some of the trouble with social life at Colorado School of Mines lies in the fact that dorms are primarily for freshmen. After their first year, most established Miners find housing elsewhere. However, all of the traditional residence halls were recently revamped, and the school has built four new Greek houses in the past several years. A new apartment-style housing complex called Mines Parks offers something in between traditional dorm life and off-campus living. Housing is not a problem in Golden either. Students can easily find reasonably priced apartments or housing for rent within five or 10 minutes of the campus. With most people in apartments, parties are usually small groups of friends hanging out at various locations off campus, as opposed to large, campus-wide parties. One senior said that the best change for Mines would be to "open [the party scene] more to freshmen and let them get involved." Although the social scene at Mines may not be as raucous as at other schools, one student stated that, "I have class with the same people; I study with the same people; I eat dinner with the same people. CSM helps to build a real sense of community and friendship that I couldn't find anywhere else."

> "I would definitely come back. Great education, great people, great friends!"

Mines also offers a growing athletic program. Six of the past seven football seasons have been winning, and the football program was recently ranked among the top 10 Division II programs in the country. In 2007, the school completed the building of a new $25 million recreation center with facilities for club, recreational and varsity athletics. Intramural and club sports are fairly popular among students, with about 70 percent of undergrads participating.

What About the Coors Brewery?
Given the lack of gathering places on campus, the Coors Brewery, which also calls Golden, Colorado, home, serves to fill this void (literally). The brewery packs with Miners "Monday, Tuesday, Wednesday . . . every night." One student described the brewery phenomenon as the "cultural and social center of CSM." While the brewery traditionally serves free beer at the conclusion of a half-hour-long tour, with a Mines identification card, students can take "the short tour" on their way to three free servings of Colorado's best beer. Drinkers and non-drinkers should not stray from the Coor's experience, advised

one Mines junior. "It is the brewery that captures the best of CSM's social life."

For students wishing to evade the enduring call of barley and hops, the University offers a number of highly patronized alternatives. The Fellowship of Christian Athletes (or FCA) attracts many students, and athletic participation is not a prerequisite. While the FCA is a religious organization, its activities are mostly social events and community service projects. One student said that while religion (specifically Christianity) is a "big deal on campus," those who do not observe are not isolated from other students. Additionally, a large number of students associate through club sports. Although "homework is still the varsity sport of the weekends," rugby and soccer are the perennial favorites among the Miners.

Let's Party—Mines-Style

Noting the dominance of engineering in Colorado School of Mines academics, it is not surprising that the grandest production of the University is also engineering-related. In the first week of April, the school hosts "E-Days," short for—of course—Engineering Days. During this well-respected and highly anticipated event, the University presents a carnival-type fair demonstrating the newest engineering technologies. Besides a healthy dose of engineering, E-Days also boasts a spectacular pyrotechnics show. In fact, Mines is famous for its spectacular fireworks, bringing local and national bands, alumni, and students from neighboring colleges to their E-Days festival.

Beyond the Mines

When not celebrating their E-Days, Colorado School of Mines, due to its geographical location, provides numerous escapes for its students. Major cities are within a short driving distance. Denver and Boulder are within 15 minutes, while Colorado Springs is about 30 minutes away. Activities such as skiing and kayaking are frequent forms of amusement for Mines students. A senior said, "There is always something available to do, just not always time."

Clearly, Colorado School of Mines is a departure from the traditional state school education. By centering engineering as the locus of the Mines experience, the University may have narrowed its curriculum, but it has produced a praiseworthy and noteworthy academic experience. Even with a few complaints about social life, Mines students are satisfied with their college experiences. As one senior put it, "Colorado is a great place, and I like CSM." Another stated, "I would definitely come back for a second time. Great education, great people, great friends!" Those who are looking to call themselves Mines students should nevertheless heed the warning of a CSM veteran: "I would like to have known how hard it would be once I got here. The school is great but very hard."—*Anatoly Brekhman*

FYI
If you come to CSM, you'd better bring "a calculator and get ready to study hard!"
A typical weekend schedule at CSM includes "homework, going to the Coors Brewery, and doing more work."
If I could change one thing about CSM, "I'd get the freshmen more into parties."
Three things every student at CSM should do before graduating are "go to E-Days for the fireworks, get to know a professor well, and take a non-engineering class."

Colorado State University

Address: Spruce Hall,
Fort Collins, CO 80523-
8020
Phone: 970-491-6909
E-mail address:
admissions@colostate.edu
Web site URL:
www.welcome.colostate.edu
Year Founded: 1870
Private or Public: Public
Religious Affiliation: None
Location: Suburban
Number of Applicants:
12,494
Percent Accepted: 86%
**Percent Accepted who
enroll:** 42%
Number Entering: 4,392
**Number of Transfers
Accepted each Year:**
2,012
Middle 50% SAT range:
M: 500–620, Cr: 500–600,
Wr: 560–660
Middle 50% ACT range:
22–26

**Early admission program
EA/ED/None:** None
**Percentage accepted
through EA or ED:** NA
EA and ED deadline: NA
Regular Deadline: 1-Feb
Application Fee: $50
**Full time Undergraduate
enrollment:** 20,765
Total enrollment: 27,030
Percent Male: 48%
Percent Female: 52%
**Total Percent Minority or
Unreported:** 16%
Percent African-American:
2%
**Percent Asian/Pacific
Islander:** 3%
Percent Hispanic: 6%
Percent Native-American: 2%
Percent International: 1%
**Percent in-state/out of
state:** 79%/21%
Percent from Public HS:
Unreported
Retention Rate: 83%

Graduation Rate 4-year: 35%
Graduation Rate 6-year: 65%
**Percent Undergraduates in
On-campus housing:** 25%
**Number of official organized
extracurricular
organizations:** 330
3 Most popular majors:
Constructing Engineering
Technology, Kinesiology and
Exercise Science, Psychology
Student/Faculty ratio: 18:1
Average Class Size: 20 to 29
**Percent of students going to
grad school:** Unreported
Tuition and Fees: $18,858
**In State Tuition and Fees if
different:** $5,418
Cost for Room and Board:
$7,382
**Percent receiving financial
aid out of those who apply,
first year:** 71%
**Percent receiving financial
aid among all students:**
62%

Colorado State University is nestled between the edge of the Great Plains and the foothills of the Rocky Mountains in the mid-size city of Fort Collins, Colorado. Enjoying an average of 300 sunny days per year and ranked as one of the "Best Places to Live" in the western US by *Money Magazine*, Fort Collins is home to vast green spaces coupled with low stress and lower crime rates, and the students of CSU are well aware of the advantages of living in this "outdoor lovers' paradise." Besides enjoying the beauty of their surroundings, under- and upperclassmen alike appreciate their school's rigorous academics at a reasonable cost as well as the numerous opportunities to get involved in a wide array of extracurricular and athletic activities.

Decisions, Decisions

When applying to CSU, students must apply for acceptance into one of eight academic departments—Agricultural Sciences, Applied Human Sciences, Business, Engineering, Liberal Arts, Forestry and Natural Resources, Veterinary Medicine and Biomedical Sciences—and select their major before arriving on campus. However, as many as a third of the freshman class opts to take advantage of the "open option" programs that postpone the choice of a major until the beginning of sophomore year. Various individual departments offer this alternative in addition to the university-wide program that allows undecided freshmen to take courses in a variety of subject areas before committing to only one. The school also offers an honors program that provides enrichment for 190 students and features smaller honors sections in key courses within each major, priority housing in the honors dormitory, early class registration, and research opportunities with members of the faculty.

Class registration at CSU can easily be done online, but students unable to reach their computers early enough on registration day might find themselves shut out of some necessary courses and rearranging their schedules to take them the next year instead. The most frequent class size is between 20 and 29. Smaller classes naturally fill up more quickly and the competition to gain entrance can be quite fierce; larger classes are generally quite easy to get into. These larger lectures can offer frustrations of their own, however, as many of the freshman introductory classes must accommodate upwards of 200 to 300 students. While the amount of work assigned in any class can pile up, most of these introductory 100-level classes are known for being relatively easy. One of the most popular courses offered—and one that fills up very quickly on registration day—is "Psychology of Human Sexuality," which hosts a "porn day" during which the entire class watches a pornographic video for an hour in order to study and discuss its psychological implications. In order to graduate, all CSU students must take a course in English composition, although it is possible to test out of this requirement by scoring well on an AP or departmental exam. A wide variety of course options is available for fulfilling the other areas of the core curriculum, and students generally agree that it is relatively painless to do so.

At the Foot of the Mountains

Freshmen at CSU are required to live on campus, and the school does honor housing requests on a first-come, first-serve basis, so submitting dorm preferences early is a good idea. Each of the 10 residence halls has its own theme and offers related "Living Learning Communities" that provide tutoring and study groups in its focus academic area: Ingersoll, for example, is the science dorm, Newsom the honors dorm and Edwards serves the pre-veterinarians and agricultural sciences. There are also dorms with non-academic reputations: Corbett is the "Party Dorm," and most of the athletes live in The Towers. In spite of the fact that many students consider on-campus living to be enjoyable, "The food is pretty terrible and the rooms are not good," and so most move into off-campus housing after their first or second year. Huge apartment complexes such as Ram's Pointe and Ram's Village are located conveniently close to campus and cater primarily to sophomores, as upperclassmen tend to "realize that those places aren't much better than the dorms were and find a house or a better apartment." The architecture of the dorms and other buildings at CSU tends to vary in aesthetics; the older part of campus seems built in the design of the old Spanish Mission style, while other areas call to mind classical revivalist or "some kind of nasty 70s non-style," although these latter buildings have been undergoing recent renovations to improve their appearance. The Lory Student Center is a popular place to hang out for CSU students and boasts restaurants, student lounges featuring video arcades, TVs, and pool tables, a ballroom, a theater and the campus box office, and stores offering everything from textbooks and school supplies to haircuts and bicycle repairs. When this monolithic facility was renovated several years ago, *The New York Times* ranked it as one of the 10 best student centers in the country.

CSU has a firm alcohol policy and the on-campus dorms are strictly dry, but even so, alcohol often makes its way onto school property and into students' bedrooms. There are RAs on every hall to watch over their student charges, but most are not terribly severe and instead favor a policy of general oversight to stringently enforcing every rule. Binge drinking indeed is somewhat of a problem at CSU, and "at least one frat per year gets shut down for getting an underage girl sent to the hospital." With the exception of marijuana, which is somewhat popular, recreational drugs do not make much of an appearance here, and the use of harder substances is very rare.

> Fort Collins's 300 days of sunshine keep students—particularly those that love the outdoors—smiling.

Fort Collins offers a particularly vibrant bar scene, which tends to attract many CSU students. There are bars with specials every night of the week, although the most popular evenings for bar hopping tend to be Tuesdays and Thursdays, and seniors frequent these establishments more often than the underclassmen, who often prefer the party scene offered by the frats. As one student summed up, "You can see herds of freshmen walking off campus at night looking for parties, but the older classes usually just stay home or go to friends' houses."

Freshmen and upperclassmen living on campus can choose from one of six different meal plans that offer a great deal of flexibility and include the option of eating at the all-you-can-eat residence hall dining center as well as any of the restaurants housed in the Lory Student Center. Nevertheless, students are lukewarm in their enthusiasm for the food quality in the on-campus retail facilities and often end up traveling beyond the campus borders to find a satisfying meal.

Most students, particularly those from nearby towns and cities, bring their cars to campus, and those who do not have a vehicle are definitely in the minority. Although the majority do remain at CSU during the weekends, a notable minority use their cars to go home or visit nearby Denver, sixty-five miles away, for a couple of days.

Indeed, most of CSU's 20,400 undergraduates do come from within the state and are well used to Colorado's chilly winters, which in Fort Collins can reach a low of 15°F in January. Nevertheless, there are still plenty of girls who wear "mini skirts and fuzzy boots" around campus as they attempt to strike a compromise between fashion and warmth. The student body stereotypically tends to be "upper middle class and white" and sports perhaps a lower level of diversity than might be common at other universities. The Greek scene remains prevalent and drives much of the party scene, and in the weeks before rush, advertisements for the various fraternities and sororities flood the campus.

Ram-ping Up the Involvement

Football is the major player in the CSU sports arena and much of the University's sense of school spirit derives from it, although as one student admits, "The team isn't very good." Spirit organizations—the cheerleading squad, the marching band and Cam the Ram, the University's costumed mascot—support the team on game days and pull the crowd into the action. On the other hand, the varsity volleyball and lacrosse teams boast a great deal of talent but lack the attention given to football. Intramural sports are extremely popular, especially among freshmen and upperclassmen living on campus, and can become quite competitive depending on the level of ability. Everything from football to soccer to inner-tube water polo is offered, and students who want to play a sport that has not been organized are encouraged to start a new league for it. The Campus Rec center provides basketball courts, exercise rooms, an inline skating arena, a racquetball court, a pool and spa, a track and a boxing area, among many other facilities, and is popular among athletes and non-athletes alike. The only disadvantage to this altar to exercise is that it often becomes very busy and overly crowded.

Outside of athletics, CSU hosts over 300 recognized clubs, organizations and performance groups, and as with IMs, any student who finds that his or her interests are not already represented can found a new one. The student government—Associated Students of Colorado State University (or ASCSU)—is a popular extracurricular activity that makes it easy to become involved with the University through voluntary committees and associate positions as well as running for office in campus-wide election. Both the college radio station, KCSU, and the student-run TV channel Campus Television attract their share of the University audience, and the *Rocky Mountain Collegian* keeps undergraduates informed about recent news. In addition, the Curfman Gallery at the Lory Student Center offers several rotating art exhibits every year, and undergraduates can become involved in choosing and displaying the works. Volunteering off campus is also a popular pastime for CSU students, and opportunities abound to become involved with many different projects in Fort Collins and beyond. A bi-annual event called the Centertainment allows campus organizations to showcase themselves and man informational displays while interested students browse their options for extracurricular involvement.

Here Comes The Sun

Students at Colorado State University benefit from the multitude of offerings presented by their college, from the abundance of in-depth courses to the wide variety of extracurricular options, and although the food may not be gourmet or the architecture artistic, CSU undergraduates are generally quite positive about their experience. From the Lory Student Center to the themed dorms to the popular gymnasium, the amenities available on campus compare favorably with those of other universities, and Fort Collins's 300 days of sunshine keep students—particularly those who love the outdoors—smiling.—*Kristin Knox*

FYI

If you come to CSU, you'd better bring "a car—students who don't have them are definitely in the minority."

What's the typical weekend schedule? "Sleep till noon, go skiing or biking, have dinner with friends, go out."

If I could change one thing about CSU, it would be "the food options in the dining halls."

Three things every student at CSU should do before graduating are "hang out in the student center, hike to the Aggies sign above Fort Collins and go into the Old Town on Friday night."

United States Air Force Academy

Address: HQ USAF/RRS, 2304 Cadet Drive, Suite 2300 USAF Academy, CO 80840

Phone: 719-333-2520

E-mail address: rr_webmail@usafa.edu

Web site URL: www.usafa.edu

Year Founded: 1954

Private or Public: Public

Religious Affiliation: None

Location: Suburban

Number of Applicants: 9,001

Percent Accepted: 18%

Percent Accepted who enroll: 81%

Number Entering: 1,336

Number of Transfers Accepted each Year: Unreported

Middle 50% SAT range: M: 620–700, CR: 600–680, Wr: 560–660

Middle 50% ACT range: 25–29

Early admission program EA/ED/None: None

Percentage accepted through EA or ED: NA

EA and ED deadline: NA

Regular Deadline: 31-Jan

Application Fee: $0

Full time Undergraduate enrollment: 4,537

Total enrollment: 4,537

Percent Male: 81%

Percent Female: 19%

Total Percent Minority or Unreported: 23%

Percent African-American: 5%

Percent Asian/Pacific Islander: 9%

Percent Hispanic: 7%

Percent Native-American: 2.0%

Percent International: 1%

Percent in-state/out of state: 15%/85%

Percent from Public HS: 99%

Retention Rate: 93%

Graduation Rate 4-year: 70%

Graduation Rate 6-year: 72%

Percent Undergraduates in On-campus housing: 100%

Number of official organized extracurricular organizations: 77

3 Most popular majors: Aerospace, Aeronautical and Astronautical Engineering, Business, Social Studies

Student/Faculty ratio: 9:1

Average Class Size: 10 to 19

Percent of students going to grad school: 7%

Tuition and Fees: $0

In State Tuition and Fees if different: No difference

Cost for Room and Board: $0

Percent receiving financial aid out of those who apply, first year: NA

Percent receiving financial aid among all students: NA

The United States Air Force Academy demands both academic and physical excellence, a challenge that many find difficult to meet. The first challenge one meets in becoming a cadet is being admitted. Subsequently, cadets are constantly tested both in and outside of the classroom with strict rules and harsh reprimands. Although the environment is intense, the benefits of attending such a university are incalculable. Cadets are paid to attend school, become part of a closely knit squad, live in beautiful Colorado and learn how to fly.

Not an Easy Transition

When a new freshman enters the Air Force Academy compound for the very first time, the transition from high school to college takes on a new meaning. Known to the upperclassmen as "doolies," the freshmen have to adjust to many lifestyle changes. The USAFA imposes a strict daily regimen for all cadets, but freshmen experience fewer privileges and less space to live in. The beginning of a freshman's career as a cadet begins with mandatory Basic Cadet Training during the summer. This five-week long program teaches future cadets basic military skills and serves as a preliminary "weeding out" of prospects. Not everyone is able to endure such an intense lifestyle, even at the beginning.

Cadets are divided randomly into 36 squadrons of 120 each. Each squadron includes students from all four years and determines where a cadet will live. Although everyone lives in the squadrons, the living arrangements differ according to class. Freshmen live in the most crowded rooms with three roommates, while sophomores and juniors live with two, and seniors live with just one roommate. This squadron system provides smaller groups within the academy for cadets to bond.

At USAFA, hierarchy and experience are very highly valued. With each year, cadets are given more freedom and privileges. Only seniors are allowed to have a car at school, and are thus more likely to get the opportunity to party at neighboring colleges such as Colorado College and Colorado University in Colorado Springs. For freshmen, the Academy institutes strict prohibitions against underage drinking, where getting caught with alcohol can lead to expulsion. The most treasured forms of freedom are leave and phone privileges. As a first-year, cadets may only receive phone calls during the weekends and cannot leave the premises other than when on break. After the first year, cadets may leave the campus and visit local areas. Therefore, it's definitely better to be an upperclassman, but the fact of the matter is that every cadet has to go through freshman year.

The cadet dining facilities are akin to other military schools within the US. Mitchell Hall is the largest dining hall where the entire cadet wing assembles to eat family-style breakfast and lunch everyday. This type of dining means preparing and serving 12,000 meals per day. Because of this, specialized dining is very rare and many cadets view the food as "getting old very fast."

Studying Among the Best

The USAFA is ranked as the number one Baccalaureate Program in the West according to *US News and World Report*'s "America's Best Colleges 2008," making it clear that academics are taken very seriously. The average class size is small, ranging from 15 to 20 students, allowing for a more personalized form of learning. In addition to taking courses that fulfill one's major, all cadets are required to take several military courses.

Many find the academic scene highly rigorous and competitive. Once a cadet is admitted, they compete with the other students for grades as everything is graded on a curve.

Cadets usually study about 20 hours a week usually during the mandated study periods scheduled during the day when not in class. Otherwise, cadets are expected to study in their rooms or in the library during Academic Call to Quarters (ACQ). This highly regulated studying time is implemented to ensure academic success and contributes to the overall goal of efficient use of time.

Students are required to have at least 132 credit hours to graduate, but most end up having far more due to the mixture of military and major courses offered. Most cadets either major in engineering or management and each have their own reputations. One cadet said, "The engineering majors are geeks, the computer science majors don't even bother looking for dates, and the management majors don't bother doing homework because it is more of a recommendation than a requirement." The engineering major regardless of its specification is considered the hardest, where the management major is considered the easiest and most flexible major available.

EXTRAcurriculars

All cadets are required to participate in the athletic program the Air Force offers, which includes both physical education courses and competitive sports. If a cadet does not participate in a varsity sport, then he or she is expected to participate in at least one intramural sport. These sports range from Ultimate Frisbee to soccer and are very competitive.

"There truly is nothing better than to compete for the Academy."

Varsity sports are prevalent at the academy, with about one fourth of all cadets participating in them. And the teams are known to take a lot of pride in what they do. All athletes are expected to participate in their sport and fulfill all other requirements, an obligation that can prove to be difficult at times. One swimmer remarked, "Being an athlete here at the Air Force is like doubling the military requirements. It literally is like another job. However, all varsity athletes are very respected and there truly is nothing better than to compete for the Academy."

Because of the required involvement in extracurricular activities and the highly enforced regimen, cadets don't have a lot of free time. Luckily, they don't have to worry about making money, for every cadet is paid a salary monthly. A variety of scholarships is also offered to many cadets. Although they are banned from outside employment, the student salary and lack of tuition and rooming and board expenses clearly make up for it. Overall the USAFA is one of the best colleges out there for those who want to make a difference. For many cadets, being able to serve one's country and gain an education is an honor. You learn the skills you need to survive both on the battlefield and in the workplace. The highly accomplished staff, class offerings, emphasis on leadership skills, and the networking opportunities available make the Air Force an incredible experience. However, be warned that this school is not for the weak.—*Taylor Ritzel*

FYI

If you come to the Air Force Academy, you'd better bring "an ability to stick it through freshman year; it gets better from there!"

What's the typical weekend schedule? "Training classes and study hours during the weekend, however most of the time is free time."

If you could change one thing about the Air Force Academy, "I would get rid of noncommissioned officer (NCO) presence here. The AFA is training cadets to be commissioned officers, and NCOs have no part in the training of cadets."

Three things every cadet should do before graduating: "Remain standing and cheering for the football team even though it's the fourth quarter and the team is losing by over three touchdowns, use your uniform to pick up the opposite sex, deploy overseas to see what you are getting into."

University of Colorado / Boulder

Address: 552 UCB Boulder, CO 80309-0552
Phone: 303-492-6301
E-mail address: apply@colorado.edu
Web site URL: www.colorado.edu/prospective
Year Founded: 1876
Private or Public: Public
Religious Affiliation: None
Location: Suburban
Number of Applicants: 19,857
Percent Accepted: 82%
Percent Accepted who enroll: 34%
Number Entering: 5,520
Number of Transfers Accepted each Year: 1,973
Middle 50% SAT range: M: 540–650, CR: 520–630, Wr: 540–630
Middle 50% ACT range: 23–28

Early admission program EA/ED/None: None
Percentage accepted through EA or ED: NA
EA and ED deadline: NA
Regular Deadline: 15-Jan
Application Fee: $50
Full time Undergraduate enrollment: 26,155
Total enrollment: 30,945
Percent Male: 54%
Percent Female: 46%
Total Percent Minority or Unreported: 22%
Percent African-American: 2%
Percent Asian/Pacific Islander: 6%
Percent Hispanic: 6%
Percent Native-American: 1%
Percent International: 2%
Percent in-state/out of state: 69%/31%
Percent from Public HS: Unreported

Retention Rate: 83%
Graduation Rate 4-year: 41%
Graduation Rate 6-year: 65%
Percent Undergraduates in On-campus housing: 94%
Number of official organized extracurricular organizations: 300
3 Most popular majors: English, Physiology, Psychology
Student/Faculty ratio: 16:1
Average Class Size: 10 to 19
Percent of students going to grad school: 21%
Tuition and Fees: $26,756
In State Tuition and Fees if different: $7,278
Cost for Room and Board: $9,860
Percent receiving financial aid out of those who apply, first year: 42%
Percent receiving financial aid among all students: 52%

Situated in the foothills of the Rocky Mountains, the University of Colorado at Boulder presents students with unbounded opportunities to explore every aspect of college life. "CU-Boulder" simply has it all. Passionate outdoors-types can take advantage of the hundreds of miles of trails for running, biking and hiking that surround the campus. Or, daredevils can hit the slopes at over 20 ski resorts located in the vicinity. Such limitless exploration goes far beyond the outdoors, however. With over 3,400 courses in 150 fields of study, the University offers students endless ways to pursue their academic interests. The presence of six Nobel Prize winners and seven MacArthur Fellowship recipients among the faculty further reinforces CU-Boulder's high standard of academics. The unique "hippy" flavor of the town of Boulder entertains students with its laid-back but fun atmosphere. In short, CU-Boulder combines the best of many worlds, offering rigorous academic discipline in a free-spirited environment.

Open-Ended Opportunity

The first thing that students mention when referring to CU-Boulder is its freedom. With a plethora of course offerings, students may choose from thousands of courses to satisfy their intellectual desires. To help students streamline their interests, the University is divided into seven different colleges. While most take the common Arts and Sciences track, many students also enroll in the Leeds School of Business and the School of Engineering and Applied Science. The other colleges are in Architecture and Planning, Education, Journalism and Mass Communication, and Music. Students' majors vary widely, but the three most popular majors from the Fall 2008 term were psychology, integrative physiology, and English.

Without a doubt, accommodating more than 30,000 students at CU-Boulder is no small task. Although the average class size is 20–30 students, many express a frustration with the size of some classes. "I hate the big lectures!" a sophomore exclaimed. Another frequent complaint is the core curriculum requirement. The curriculum is divided between "skills acquisition" (foreign language, quantitative reasoning, writing, and critical thinking) and "content areas of study" (history, diversity, United States, literature, natural science, contemporary society, and values). Nonetheless, as at most colleges, the requirements "lessen as you progress through the years."

While finding a niche at such a large institution might seem intimidating to many incoming freshmen, CU-Boulder does provide opportunities for personalized attention. One unique aspect of the University is the presence of RAPs (Residential Academic Programs) that allow undergraduates to share experiences with others who have common interests. The sense of community engendered by the RAPs is bolstered by the fact that select relevant courses are located in the respective halls, and special events are planned just for the program. RAPs are centered on numerous concepts, including, but not limited to: Environmental Science (Baker), Diversity (Hallett), Liberal Arts (Farrand), Honors (Kittredge), American West (Sewall), and the Arts (Libby).

Beyond the RAPs, CU-Boulder offers an Honors Program for exceptionally motivated students, providing specialized curriculum and advising from faculty members. Also, the Norlin Scholars Program, a merit-based award of $3,000 per year, helps talented students achieve their goals with individual guidance.

"Everyone's really laid-back."

For those looking for diverse experiences outside of Colorado, the University offers an extensive study-abroad program in locations ranging from Perugia, Italy to Valparaiso, Chile to Cape Town, South Africa, to Ulaanbaatar, Mongolia.

Adventuresome Architecture

With over 200 "architecturally pleasing" rural-Italian-style buildings, students have plenty to gape at besides the Rocky Mountains. A common "hotspot" on campus is Norlin Quadrangle, a broad grassy area where students can go to study, meet up with friends, or simply relax and enjoy the nice weather. One student comments that Norlin Quad is "nice and open, has lots of sunshine, and is simply a nice place where you can just lie down and see the Flatirons." Slacklining—tightrope walking across climbing ropes, usually tied between two trees—is an interesting pastime commonly seen on the Quad. Other often-frequented buildings on campus include Macky Auditorium and the Norlin Library, which, with five million volumes, boasts the "largest library collection in the Rocky Mountain region."

Charles Z. Klauder designed most of the buildings on campus in a distinctive rural-North Italian fashion. The red-tiled roofs and rough walls evoke an impression of being in the mountainous regions of Northern Italy—a particularly relevant ambiance for a university placed at the base of the Rockies.

Hippie Heaven

"Everyone's really laid-back," explained one student, referring to the student body. When asked about the basic composition of the general population, most people name "Hippie" and "frat guy" as the common student types that exist at CU-Boulder. In terms of music and culture, many students list the Grateful Dead and Phish among their favorite bands. In addition, there is a recognizable presence of marijuana on campus, albeit amongst a smaller group of people.

Drinking is ubiquitous. Though the University's stated policy disallows drinking in the dorms, enforcement of the rules is characteristic of the school as a whole—laid-back. The "two-strikes" policy comes as a result of CU-Boulder's campaign as one of the first schools in the nation to systematically address student alcohol abuse. Nonetheless, drinking provides much entertainment for CU-Boulder students, especially at the fraternities and sororities that are located on "The Hill," a favorite district for students.

Recreational Respites

Located on the Eastern slope of the Rocky Mountains at an altitude of 5,400 feet, the University has the natural rocky formations as its backyard. The miles and miles of trails allow students to hike, bike, climb, or snowshoe for hours on end. During the warmer months of the year, students can opt to go whitewater rafting or kayaking on the Colorado River.

But for those who aren't willing to make the trek out to the mountains, there is plenty to do on campus. The Colorado Buffaloes

football team is a source of shared pride for nearly all CU-Boulder students. Playing in Folsom Stadium, the football team draws huge crowds during games against perennial opponents such as the Nebraska Cornhuskers. The Colorado Buffaloes also boast a strong cross-country running team, and they have produced world-class runners such as Adam Goucher and Dathan Ritzenhein.

For students who are less competitive, the intramurals program offers an array of exciting and relaxed sports to play. Among the many options, the Ultimate Frisbee team is generally regarded as a highly competitive and successful group. Other IMs include whiffleball, broomball, and inner-tube water polo.

Free Future

As successful as it has been thus far, CU-Boulder still desires to improve as an institution. In August of 2006, the stunning $31 million, 66,000 square-foot ATLAS (Alliance for Technology, Learning, and Society) Center opened, heralding a new age of advanced technological resources for student use. In September of 2006, the dedication of the new Wolf Law Building occurred. With a gigantic new law library and two high-tech courtrooms, the Law Building will be a landmark building for generations to come.

In general, CU-Boulder looks towards the future. Faculty members have won four Nobel Prizes in the last 2 decades, and have advanced the scientific knowledge of mankind in many respects. In fiscal year 2008, the school received $280 million in sponsored research awards from organizations such as the National Sciences Foundation, NASA, and the Department of Health and Human Services. With its strong, forward-looking academic program and an environment that promotes the freedom to explore, CU-Boulder provides the perfect experience for students looking to excel in new and old frontiers.—*Wookie Kim*

FYI
If you come to CU, you better bring "a tent and a beer funnel."
What's the typical weekend schedule? "Go camping, watch the football game, and drink beer."
If I could change one thing about CU, "I'd make the campus less hilly."
The three things that every student should do before graduating from CU are "hike the Flatirons, attend a frat party, and go to a CU football game."

University of Denver

Address: 2197 S. University Boulevard Denver, CO 80208
Phone: 303-871-2036
E-mail address: admission@du.edu
Web site URL: www.du.edu
Year Founded: 1864
Private or Public: Private
Religious Affiliation: None
Location: Urban
Number of Applicants: 5,072
Percent Accepted: 74%
Percent Accepted who enroll: 30%
Number Entering: 1,131
Number of Transfers Accepted each Year: 393
Middle 50% SAT range: M: 540–640, CR: 530–640, Wr: Unreported
Middle 50% ACT range: 23–28
Early admission program EA/ED/None: EA
Percentage accepted through EA or ED: 37%

EA and ED deadline: 1-Nov
Regular Deadline: 15-Jan
Application Fee: $50
Full time Undergraduate enrollment: 5,285
Total enrollment: 9,915
Percent Male: 46%
Percent Female: 54%
Total Percent Minority or Unreported: 26%
Percent African-American: 3%
Percent Asian/Pacific Islander: 5%
Percent Hispanic: 7%
Percent Native-American: 1%
Percent International: 5%
Percent in-state/out of state: 56%/44%
Percent from Public HS: Unreported
Retention Rate: 87%
Graduation Rate 4-year: 57%
Graduation Rate 6-year: 73%

Percent Undergraduates in On-campus housing: 94%
Number of official organized extracurricular organizations: 119
3 Most popular majors: Marketing, Business, Psychology
Student/Faculty ratio: 10:1
Average Class Size: 10 to 19
Percent of students going to grad school: 16%
Tuition and Fees: $33,810
In State Tuition and Fees if different: No difference
Cost for Room and Board: $9,093
Percent receiving financial aid out of those who apply, first year: 40%
Percent receiving financial aid among all students: 67%

The "oldest independent university in the Rockies" is undergoing a face-lift. Students agree that the focus of the school has shifted noticeably in the past several years. The existing emphasis on community leadership and involvement is being matched by a set of construction projects aimed at centralizing and modernizing the campus. The administration has also cracked down on the wild Greek scene. The result? A mellow, focused, and more academically oriented feel pervades the school that once was known only for its traditions of good times, great skiing and rousing school events.

Personalized Academics

To start off their time at DU, freshmen are required to take a medley of courses, including a foreign language, oral communication, math, computer science, and English. Most students are in agreement that the core curriculum lets them explore the school's strengths before choosing a major. "My favorite class to date was definitely my freshman year Spanish class, no question," one sophomore said. The student-to-faculty ratio is an impressive 10 to 1, and many commented on the personal attention received from teachers. The result is that students enjoy very small class sizes and foster "interactive" relationships with professors. TAs are a concept foreign to DU students, except in a few science courses. DU also boasts a freshman-mentoring program, which assigns all entering freshmen a faculty mentor to see them through the major decisions of the first year. After freshman year, students split their range of studies in various directions, from Arts and Literature to Creative Expression.

Popular majors include business, reflecting DU's impressive Business School; psychology and biology. Science majors are generally considered more difficult, and include killer courses in organic chemistry and cellular biology.

For all majors, DU makes an effort to foster a merit-based academic feel on campus from the very start. Freshmen can apply to be in the Pioneer Leadership Program the summer before they arrive. This highly selective program fits into their curriculum as a minor, applicable to any primary major later on. Equally selective is the Honors Program, which offers students with a 3.5 GPA or higher who apply to the program access to special lectures and seminars. The Pioneer Leadership and Honors Program students live on special, separate floors in freshman housing.

Another popular offering is the Interterm Program, which provides students with intensive programs between the formal academic quarters, both based at DU and abroad. Past Interterm opportunities, which are available in the fall, winter and spring recesses, have included An Economic History of the Caribbean taught on St. Kitts and Nevis in the West Indies, Religious and Social Justice in Vienna on location in Austria, and a course on gaming and gambling taught from the casinos of Las Vegas.

Students at DU generally like the academic term system, which divides the school year into quarters. Some complain that it is a bit fast-paced at times, leaving "no room for screwing up." The daily workload is manageable, and having more than two or three classes per day is rare.

DU students are motivated and engaged, but not over-the-top intense. One student describes academics as "Strong, but nothing I can't handle. I'm challenged, but not killing myself over work on a daily basis."

Central and Modern

"Copper is big here," commented one DU student when describing the campus. A nice blend of fresh, modern architecture and older structures makes for a very pleasant campus feel. The red brick tower of University Hall meets the low lines of Penrose Library, while pathways snake through manicured lawns and green open spaces. The wide Colorado sky and view of the Rockies add to the picturesque feel of the campus. The University prides itself on its accomplishments in enhancing the beautiful surroundings as well, with additions such as the beautiful Humanities Gardens near the center of campus. Students call the campus "very central and modern," and praise the large capital project devoted to the recently completed residence hall and science center. Recent construction projects are part of the University's efforts to move much of DU's satellite campus, Park Hill, closer to the action on the central grounds. The Ritchie Center for Sports and Wellness is another highly visible landmark, as well as a state-of-the-art athletic facility for varsity athletes and gym-rats alike.

The campus is manageably sized, so that "It never takes more than 10 or so minutes to get to class, at the extreme," one student said. Freshmen and sophomores are required to live on campus. Freshmen are housed in two dormitories, Johnson-McFarlane, or J-Mac, and Centennial Halls. Both buildings are air-conditioned and made up of suites with kitchenettes. Centennial Halls is the home of Special Interest floors, which group students by interests such as substance-free, business, math/science, all male or all female, and the Honors Program. Members of the Pioneer Leadership Program and others live in J-Mac, generally regarded as the "dorkier" of the two freshman residences. The dorms are variously described as "decent" and "kinda gross." Freshmen live with RAs on each floor, who keep tabs on alcohol, which is forbidden, and noise violations. A new residence hall, Nagel Hall, opened in 2008. Designed to keep more upperclassmen on campus, it features singles, doubles and apartments.

Students eat in cafeterias located in both of the freshman dorms, and the upperclassman dorm. After freshman year, many sophomores choose to eat in their fraternity or sorority, and there are few upperclassmen in the cafeterias at all. DU offers a "point system" allowing students extra meal points with which they can eat in local restaurants and "get a Starbucks fix."

Greek Festivities

The area around campus is "residential and cute," made up of mostly student houses. There is a small, "adequate" commercial area a few blocks from campus, and downtown Denver is only a 10-minute drive from campus. A majority of students have cars on campus, and they are permitted for freshmen. The social life at DU has many ties to the Greek system, and more than 20 percent of students are members of the nine fraternities and five sororities. As the campus continues with renovations, many of the Greek facilities will be among those revamped. Those inside the Greek system say that "It does not entirely dominate the social scene, but it is strong," and say that there are "tons of alternative, non-Greek weekend options," though some are more adamant that the Greek system "is the social scene." Students lament the increased frequency with which house parties are broken up, and say that the party scene has begun to shift towards "bar parties," where a group will rent a bar, and allow anyone over 18 (those over 21 get a wristband) to enter and enjoy dancing and drinking. Traditional fraternity events at the ever-popular SAE, Lambda Chi Alpha, and Sigma Chi fraternities include annual theme parties, such as Western, Pajama, and Principals and Schoolgirls. All formal events are Greek-based. One of the major non-Greek events is the yearly Winter Carnival, a hugely popular campuswide event in January.

Involved and Evolving

Like all universities of its size, DU has a long list of interesting extracurricular possibilities, from public service organizations to professional honors societies and dance troupes. The student newspaper, *The Clarion*, is a popular involvement, and the Alpine Club is known for organizing frequent outdoor excursions.

> **"Those who don't ski can feel a little excluded."**

The student body at DU is "not extremely diverse," and one student commented that with regards to breaking the stereotype that it's a school of rich kids, "They try but it's pretty white, fairly preppy, not a lot of punks." The 20 percent of the student body of minority background does not fail to make an impression on campus, however, forming a strong community within a community through ethnic clubs and organizations.

One student remarked that arts opportunities have not been at the forefront at DU, but that with the recent completion of the Newman Center for the Performing Arts, which includes a larger theater space, students no longer "need to be in the know to hear about the arts."

Winter Sports Rule

Skiing is a huge campus pastime and "Those who don't ski can feel a little excluded," as many students hit the slopes every weekend throughout the winter. Aside from skiing, DU offers many athletic choices to the sports-minded. Club sports are popular. They do not make any cuts and are "a lot of fun" for all involved. DU also fosters strong varsity sports teams, the most popular of which is its successful hockey team, followed by the lacrosse, soccer and swim teams. There is generally "good turnout" to games, though hockey is unquestionably king. Division I hockey games take the place of football games, as DU has no football team, and the annual game against rival Colorado College is "not to be missed."

Traditions such as the enthusiasm for the hockey team unify DU as it continues to establish itself as a rising academic institution. Students are as relaxed and ready to take advantage of its opportunities to hit the slopes and fraternity row as they are to hit the books.—*Charlotte Taft*

FYI

If you come to the University of Denver, you'd better bring "a fake ID."

What is the typical weekend schedule? "Rest up, go out, squeeze in the homework."

If I could change one thing about DU, "I'd change the rules about social activities—make them less anal about breaking up house parties."

The three things that every student should do before graduating from the University of Denver are "travel around the area because Colorado is beautiful, realize what downtown has to offer, and go to the Colorado College-DU hockey game."

Connecticut

Connecticut College

Address: 270 Mohegan Avenue New London, CT 06320
Phone: 860-439-2200
E-mail address: admission@conncoll.edu
Web site URL: www.conncoll.edu
Year Founded: 1911
Private or Public: Private
Religious Affiliation: None
Location: Suburban
Number of Applicants: 4,316
Percent Accepted: 38%
Percent Accepted who enroll: 30%
Number Entering: 492
Number of Transfers Accepted each Year: 65
Middle 50% SAT range: M: 610–700, Cr: 620–720, Wr: 670–720
Middle 50% ACT range: 25–29
Early admission program EA/ED/None: ED

Percentage accepted through EA or ED: Unreported
EA and ED deadline: 15-Nov
Regular Deadline: 1-Jan
Application Fee: $60
Full time Undergraduate enrollment: 1,996
Total enrollment: 2,026
Percent Male: 40%
Percent Female: 60%
Total Percent Minority or Unreported: 27%
Percent African-American: 4%
Percent Asian/Pacific Islander: 4%
Percent Hispanic: 5%
Percent Native-American: 1%
Percent International: 6%
Percent in-state/out of state: 27%/73%
Percent from Public HS: 55%
Retention Rate: 91%

Graduation Rate 4-year: 82%
Graduation Rate 6-year: 86%
Percent Undergraduates in On-campus housing: 99%
Number of official organized extracurricular organizations: 60
3 Most popular majors: English, Political Science, Psychology
Student/Faculty ratio: 10:1
Average Class Size: 10 to 19
Percent of students going to grad school: Unreported
Tuition and Fees: $46,675 comprehensive fee
In State Tuition and Fees if different: No difference
Cost for Room and Board: Included
Percent receiving financial aid out of those who apply, first year: 77%
Percent receiving financial aid among all students: 41%

C onnecticut College is a liberal arts institution in southeastern Connecticut, overlooking the Thames River and just minutes from Long Island Sound. With its manageable size and small student body, ConnColl has a cozy and cohesive feel. The school's honor code is an important tradition and source of pride for students, and its effects can be seen in many different aspects of college life.

Academics and Administration
With a student to teacher ratio of just 10:1, the teachers are generally very accessible, and classes are small and intimate learning environments. "One thing I really liked was the advising I received as a freshman," said one sophomore. "If you make the effort to approach them, teachers can really learn a lot about you as a student and make your transition into college that much easier." Students must fulfill general education requirements spanning seven different core areas, but few find these to be limiting. In addition, all incoming students choose from a selection of freshman seminars, giving them an opportunity to experience some of the best available courses in their first year.

The honor code allows students unique levels of comfort with their studies not found at other institutions, in particular when it comes to final exams, which are self-scheduled and not proctored.

Perhaps the most impressive college program is CELS (Career Enhancing Life Skills) through which students complete workshops to receive funding for internships. This is an incredible opportunity for students at a "small school," especially for those who would for financial reasons be less inclined to take unpaid internships in fields they enjoy. One veteran of CELS went so far as calling it "the best-run office on campus. Most who do it say it is the best thing that ever happened to them."

A point of particular interest at ConnColl is campus celebrity Leo Higdon, the College President who took office following the 2005–2006 school year. Young, energetic and student-friendly, the president can often be seen walking around campus and asking students for their input on various campus issues. Not the tallest head administrator around, he has earned such nicknames as "Big Hig" and "Higgie Smalls," according to one student who proudly claims to have a T-shirt with his face on it.

Campus

Students at ConnColl are "a pretty homogenous group of preppy white kids, most of whom are from 'right outside Boston,'" according to one interviewee. "We're not all totally preppy, though. We've got our fair share of hippies and artsy fartsy kids," said another. The student body is small enough that most faces are familiar by sophomore year, giving the campus a tight, family feeling. This unity is reinforced by campus-wide events such as "Camelympics," an inter-dorm competition organized by students that happens every fall and lasts for 48 fun-filled hours. Events range from midnight volleyball games to scavenger hunts to Scrabble.

> "My experience has been that, once you find something you like to do, the College opens up a world of opportunities."

Extracurricular activities are widely available as there are numerous clubs, organizations, volunteering opportunities, and sports teams at the varsity, club, and intramural level. Nearly all campus groups are run by students, allowing a deep level of involvement. According to one student, "My experience has been that, once you find something you like to do, the College opens up a world of opportunities."

The campus is actually comprised of several hundred acres, although "for the part you walk around on a day-to-day basis, it would take you only 10 minutes to go from the tip of south to the tip of north," said one

junior. The rest of campus is an arboretum managed by the College. Another unusual feature of the campus is that soccer and lacrosse games are played on a field situated in the middle of a cluster of dorms known as south campus, making them very convenient locations for socializing.

Some students complain about a lack of variety in the dining halls, particularly when it comes to healthy options, but the dining services work hard to take student feedback into account when preparing their menus. The meal plan is included in the comprehensive tuition, room and board fee, and is unlimited. Students can eat as much as they want and enter any dining hall on campus as many times as they want. Despite this apparent flexibility, some feel that the availability of food is too restricted due to hour constraints and the fact that only one dining hall is open on the weekends.

Housing

The campus is unofficially divided into three areas: north, central and south. South has older dorms and is loud, whereas north is newer and quieter. Central campus is less defined, but conveniently located. There is no Greek life at ConnColl, but south campus picks up the slack as far as parties are concerned. Said one admittedly biased south campus stalwart: "North has A/C and nicer rooms, but it's boring and more anti-social . . . south is way more fun."

There are no RAs at ConnColl, in keeping with the honor code and the amount of trust the administration puts in the students to behave appropriately. Instead, there is one "house fellow" in charge of each dorm, as well as SAs (student advisors) who are generally sophomores and who do not serve a disciplinary function, but rather help ease the transition into college life for freshmen.

"I know zero people who live off campus," said one sophomore. There are options for off-campus housing, but 99% of students choose to stay in the dorms, which helps draw the various years together and create a stronger feeling of campus unity. While first-year rooms are typically "nothing to write home about," the housing provided for upperclassmen is a big incentive for staying on campus. Juniors and seniors are guaranteed comfortably sized singles if they want them and many sophomores can get them as well.

New London

According to one sophomore, "It's very important to have a car or a good friend who does, although parking sucks for freshmen, and campus safety loves to ticket." The College does, however, have a free bus service that brings students from campus to downtown New London. In addition, the College sponsors monthly trips to New York City for various events, and many students take advantage of these opportunities.

The city itself receives mixed reviews from interviewed students. "Like any city, it has its bad areas; it also has beautiful areas. There are some great restaurants and also good beaches only 15 minutes away by car," said one student. Shopping opportunities are limited, but there are a Target and a Wal-Mart close by for essentials. The average student leaves campus at least once a week to eat out.

Weekend

The weekend scene at ConnColl is quite lively, especially considering the lack of a Greek scene or a true urban downtown close by. Very few students have class on Fridays, so ConnColl weekends start Thursday afternoon. Drinking is definitely the focus of most students' weekends, and there are often keg parties in the south campus dorms. Any keg on campus must be signed for by two students who have taken a one-day class called Keg 101. One sophomore resident of south campus described the

weekends as "loud. South campus is loud on Saturday because of soccer games, but the night life is just as loud."

Enforcement of drinking laws is not strict, in keeping with the honor code, and Campus Safety is generally lenient with drinking; its first responsibility is making sure students are safe, not getting them into trouble. The lack of a Greek system tends to make for a much more inclusive weekend scene at ConnColl. "I love that. I feel like everyone is equal as far as social life is concerned," one student said.

Aside from drinking, the administration makes a great effort to provide alternative activities on the weekends. FNL (Friday Nights Live) is a weekly concert on campus. In addition there are weekly Thursday Night Events, ranging from dances to comedians to movie nights to tie-dye. These events are typically more popular among freshmen, and one older student described them as "kind of lame, and definitely repetitive after a year or two." New London itself does not provide many nightlife alternatives in terms of cultural enrichment, a cause of complaint for non-drinkers.

Coming to Connecticut College, one will find a quaint, beautiful campus filled with prepsters who know how to have a good time, as well as one of the better liberal arts curricula available.—*David Allen*

FYI

If you come to Connecticut College, you'd better bring "a car, the latest copy of the J. Crew catalog and a Red Sox hat or something else related to Boston."

What is the typical weekend schedule? "Thursdays are parties, Fridays are pretty chill, and Saturdays are parties with lots of kegs in south campus."

If I could change one thing about Connecticut College, I'd "change the 'average' Conn student so it's not hard to fit in if you aren't decked out in Vineyard Vines. Oh, and also I'd get rid of the coed bathrooms. Those freak me out sometimes."

Three things every student at Connecticut College should do before graduating are "participate in Camelympics, live in south campus and ring the gong."

Fairfield University

Address: 1073 N. Benson Rd
Fairfield, CT 06824
Phone: 203-254-4100
E-mail address:
admis@mail.fairfield.edu
Web site URL:
www.fairfield.edu
Year Founded: 1942
Private or Public: Private
Religious Affiliation: Jesuit
Location: Suburban
Number of Applicants: 8,732
Percent Accepted: 59%
**Percent Accepted who
enroll:** 17%
Number Entering: 927
**Number of Transfers
Accepted each Year:** 75
Middle 50% SAT range:
M: 540–630, CR:
520–610, Wr: 540–630
Middle 50% ACT range:
23–27
**Early admission program
EA/ED/None:** EA

**Percentage accepted
through EA or ED:** 58%
EA and ED deadline: 15-Nov
Regular Deadline: 15-Jan
Application Fee: $60
**Full time Undergraduate
enrollment:** 3,469
Total enrollment: 5,128
Percent Male: 42%
Percent Female: 58%
**Total Percent Minority or
Unreported:** 15%
Percent African-American:
3%
**Percent Asian/Pacific
Islander:** 3%
Percent Hispanic: 8%
Percent Native-American:
<1%
Percent International:
Unreported
**Percent in-state/out of
state:** 23%/77%
Percent from Public HS: 55%
Retention Rate: 90%

Graduation Rate 4-year: 74%
Graduation Rate 6-year: 77%
**Percent Undergraduates in
On-campus housing:** 85%
**Number of official organized
extracurricular
organizations:** 100
3 Most popular majors:
Finance, Marketing,
Psychology
Student/Faculty ratio: 13:1
Average Class Size: 24
**Percent of students going to
grad school:** 20%
Tuition and Fees: $36,075
**In State Tuition and Fees if
different:** No difference
Cost for Room and Board:
$10,850
**Percent receiving financial
aid out of those who apply,
first year:** 70%
**Percent receiving financial
aid among all students:**
48%

F airfield University is a mid-sized Catholic university located in the picturesque town of Fairfield, CT, overlooking the Long Island Sound. Dubbed "J. Crew U," it is a place where preppy, party lovers in search of a quality education can feel at home.

A Jesuit Education

Fairfield is proud of its Jesuit tradition, evidence of which is seen in its high-quality academic programs. The University offers lucrative scholarships to top-notch incoming freshmen and high-achieving sophomores, who are invited to apply to the prestigious Honors Program. The program allows students to replace certain distribution requirements with an interdisciplinary, writing intensive program. Most students must complete core courses in five areas: natural sciences and mathematics; history and social/behavioral sciences; philosophy, religious studies, and ethics; English and visual/performing arts; and modern or classical languages. Fairfield is divided into four schools: Arts and Sciences, Business, Nurs-

ing, and the Graduate School. Students consider Biology, International Studies, Art History, Religious Studies, Sociology, Accounting and Finance, and Mechanical Engineering to all be popular and strong programs. The New Media major, similar to film studies, is gaining popularity thanks in part to the CineFest Fairfield festival that showcases the work of many students in the major.

Fairfield students love how their school's small size allows them to get individualized attention. Introductory lectures often have no more than 40 people and most seminars have less than 12. Professors are described as very knowledgeable and helpful. As one student said, they "are really concerned and devoted to the students' education." Students say the workload is the right balance—not too easy, but very manageable. "I like that we're challenged but we have a lot of time to get our work done," said one girl. The Fairfield administration and faculty are also very devoted to giving as many students as possible the opportunity to study abroad. Not only can upperclassmen elect to take the classic term or full year abroad, but all students can have an abroad experience through a variety of programs that take place during January intersession, March break, and the summer. Popular programs are in Italy, Ireland, Russia, Australia and Nicaragua.

The Beach, The Mirror, and D-I Athletics

When Fairfield students are not too busy fulfilling their core requirements or traveling abroad, they engage in their favorite activity in their favorite location. As one freshman explained, "Fairfield is a big party school; there's usually something to do every night." Fairfield has a thriving party scene despite the fact that there are no fraternities and sororities because of "The Beach," a four mile strip of land along the Long Island Sound where houses are rented by about 200 seniors. The Beach is the center of Fairfield night life, though the townhouses where many juniors live are another extremely popular location. The infamous partying that takes place at the Beach has historically caused a strain on town-gown relations. It seems that Connecticut suburbanites are not too keen on hearing hundreds of college students partying into the wee hours of the night. The Fairfield administration is now trying to exercise greater control over the partying at the Beach, causing students to bring their socializing back to the campus proper or out of town to nearby cities such as Bridgeport, New Haven and New York City, which is just a Metro-North train ride away.

> "All Fairfield students dress alike, and it really annoys a lot of people."

Students do not spend all their time drinking at the Beach. "At any party you go to, alcohol is pretty dominant, like at most colleges, but people are involved in a lot of other stuff, too," explained one student. Since Fairfield is a Catholic university, campus ministry programs with community service focuses are popular extracurricular activities. Other activities include glee club, improv groups, FUSA: the Fairfield student government, and cultural groups. Campus publications include *The Mirror*, the independent student-run newspaper, as well as a variety of literary magazines and arts publications.

Though Fairfield students aren't as into athletics as students at other Division I schools, watching the men's basketball team play at the Arena at Harbor Yard in Bridgeport is sometimes a popular activity. Fairfield usually does very well in men's and women's soccer, and women's volleyball, often getting to the NCAA tournament. Despite these facts, school spirit is not that high at Fairfield and there are more students involved in intramural sports than there are spectators at most games.

The Scoop on J. Crew U

Since Fairfield is a Catholic school in Connecticut, most students are Christians from surrounding New England states. And as the nickname would suggest, many people at Fairfield think of their fellow students as being very preppy, wealthy, and white. As one girl explained, "The typical Fairfield student is pretty laid-back, preppy, smart, and usually a partier." "All Fairfield students dress alike, and it really annoys a lot of people," complained one freshman. The University is working hard to change the stereotype of having a homogeneous population. Diversity is slowly but steadily increasing in the student body and the Center for Multicultural Relations is the home to a number of popular cultural groups and programs. Whether they fit into the idea of the typical Fairfield student or not, few students can complain about the physical appearance of their fellow students, and most say that Fairfield has a very attractive student body. And despite the fact that the administration recently got quite upset when a student group handed out condoms, hook-ups are very predominant.

To Live in a Townhouse

Students at Fairfield are guaranteed housing for all four years. Most underclassmen live in either the Quad or the Orient. The living arrangements for freshmen are often a bit cozy, to say the least. "When I first got here I found my dorm to be a lot smaller than I thought it was going to be and I'm not even in a forced triple. It's grown on me though and I like it. Some dorms are bigger than others; some are better; it just varies," summed up one freshman. Underclassmen's dreams of one day getting to live in the school-sponsored, condominium-style townhouses or the Beach allow them to put up with cramped living spaces. Housing on the Beach is not affiliated with the University, but it is one of the most popular and wished for options.

Despite their unique housing options, Fairfield students say that their food is typical college cafeteria fare. Fairfield has two dining halls, one for freshmen and one for upperclassmen. Some students complain that there is not much variety from day to day in the types of food offered, but not everyone is complaining. "I like that they have stir-fry with a lot of options so you can cook your own food. You can also eat at one restaurant and one café but you have to pay money for it; it's not on the plan," explained one girl.

Overall, Fairfield students have high praise for their school and think that potential students will love it, too. Whether you want to live on the beach, study abroad, or be educated in the Jesuit tradition, they are confident that Fairfield University would be a great place for you.—*Keneisha Sinclair*

FYI

If you come to Fairfield, you'd better bring "a car—it's essential."

What is the typical weekend schedule? "Friday and Saturday, pregame in the dorms and then go to the townhouses or the Beach. Sunday, sleep."

If I could change one thing about Fairfield, I'd "make registration be online instead of in person."

Three things every student should do before graduating from Fairfield are "go to a beach party, study abroad, and live in a townhouse."

Quinnipiac University

Address: 275 Mount Carmel Avenue Hamden, CT 06518
Phone: 203-582-8600
E-mail address: admissions@quinnipiac.edu
Web site URL: www.quinnipiac.edu
Year Founded: 1929
Private or Public: Private
Religious Affiliation: None
Location: Suburban
Number of Applicants: 14,994
Percent Accepted: 45%
Percent Accepted who enroll: 22%
Number Entering: 1,484
Number of Transfers Accepted each Year: 540
Middle 50% SAT range: M: 560–630, CR: 540–610, Wr: Unreported
Middle 50% ACT range: 23–27
Early admission program EA/ED/None: None

Percentage accepted through EA or ED: NA
EA and ED deadline: NA
Regular Deadline: Rolling
Application Fee: $45
Full time Undergraduate enrollment: 5,870
Total enrollment: 7,036
Percent Male: 40%
Percent Female: 60%
Total Percent Minority or Unreported: 12%
Percent African-American: 3%
Percent Asian/Pacific Islander: 2%
Percent Hispanic: 5%
Percent Native-American: <1%
Percent International: 1%
Percent in-state/out of state: 30%/70%
Percent from Public HS: 70%
Retention Rate: 90%
Graduation Rate 4-year: 69%

Graduation Rate 6-year: 73%
Percent Undergraduates in On-campus housing: 75%
Number of official organized extracurricular organizations: 78
3 Most popular majors: Business, General Physical Therapy, Psychology
Student/Faculty ratio: 12:1
Average Class Size: 10 to 19
Percent of students going to grad school: 37%
Tuition and Fees: $31,100
In State Tuition and Fees if different: No difference
Cost for Room and Board: $12,520
Percent receiving financial aid out of those who apply, first year: 70%
Percent receiving financial aid among all students: 68%

Quinnipiac University is a small school with huge vocational opportunities. Set in a picturesque area of New England, the University offers a rural-campus feel and family-like faculty that create an all-around homey feel. Sleeping Giant State Park looms over the campus and provides a popular hiking spot, and students can still enjoy the urban nightlife of neighboring New Haven. While the majority of students come from Connecticut and surrounding New England states, they may be pleasantly surprised by the setting. As one student said, "The combination of nature and urban convenience is a major bonus for Quinnipiac."

Campus Commuters

If you're looking for a school that complements the New England fall, this is the place. Directly across the street sits a large state park which, according to one sophomore, "looks like a patchwork quilt in the fall." An elegant pine-grove path meanders through campus providing a scenic walk to class, the library or the new gym. When asked to describe the campus, one sophomore said: "It looks like a little village. Everything is pretty close together and within walking distance. It's very picturesque too!" Another student noted, "Students literally get mad if you litter or sometimes even walk on the grass . . . It is THAT nice."

Although the campus may feel like a small village, many of the buildings are architecturally modern or even futuristic. The gym, for example, contains a suspended indoor track hanging over new tennis courts. The library also has a modern feel with a whole wall made of glass that makes it easy to enjoy the winter scenery while studying cozily in the warm library. The dorms may not be quite as elegant as the gym and library, but nonetheless students had few complaints. Freshman dorms are the smallest, but still not cramped. They are coed and accessible to all the essential campus buildings.

Freshman bathrooms are communal, but upperclassmen suites each have their own. Suites after freshman year vary in size from three to 10 students. Some students move off campus as juniors, but all seniors live off campus. As far as dining goes, students generally give high marks to their Café. One student remarked: "The Café is amazing even though people complain a lot about it. I mean, the chefs make most of the food right in front of you. It's like a mall food court; there are a bunch of different stations. I've eaten at a lot of different colleges and our Café is by far the best I've seen and eaten in."

Many students at Quinnipiac either have cars or are hankering for them. Since freshmen are not allowed to have cars on campus, some find themselves saying, "I hate waiting for shuttles and taxis when I want to get off campus; I can't wait until next year." One student emphasized, however, that cars are not a requirement: "You definitely do not need a car to have fun here. Half the time the upperclassmen take the shuttle into New Haven anyway so they don't have to drive wasted."

Partying

A lot of Quinnipiac partying takes place in nearby New Haven, but there is plenty of fun on campus, too. According to most students, it is only a minor setback that kegs are not allowed on campus. "It's not a big deal. We usually just drink in our rooms until we want to go to the bars anyway." The Greek scene is not hugely dominating at Quinnipiac, so weekend festivities revolve around the various bars surrounding campus. However, with two fraternities and three sororities and around 300 members, the frat scene certainly has a distinct presence on campus. As one sorority member said, "We're small but we're still here!"

> "The combination of nature and urban convenience is a major bonus for Quinnipiac."

One favorite hot spot off campus, especially for girls, is Toad's Place in New Haven located next to the Yale University campus. Just 10 minutes away from Quinnipiac, Toad's has dance parties every Wednesday and Saturday and often good bands on other nights. One freshman said, "Toad's is my favorite place on Saturday nights because I get to meet hot Yale boys." While upperclassmen tend to get off-campus more, this is mostly because of the accessibility of cars rather than the limitations of being underage. Consensus among underclassmen is that fake IDs are common and rarely scrutinized. But even if students don't make it off campus on the weekend there are usually options for partying on campus. For those who prefer dry events, there are also plenty of choices. As one student said, "[The] student programming board puts on tons of free campus events all weekend every weekend for kids who don't want to party or just want to have some sober fun."

Students at Quinnipiac love to talk about the tradition of May weekend. Every year in May the school spends large amounts of money for fun events like concerts. One senior said: "The entire campus turns into a drunken carnival. People run around and go crazy. It's my favorite weekend of the year."

Other social events include the school's basketball and hockey games. Both teams are quite good and the school gets excited for home games, although many students resent the lack of a football team and stadium. Other varsity sports are not as popular, but many students participate in intramural sports. "It's a great way to meet people and actually get some decent exercise," one sophomore said.

Preparing for a Job

Quinnipiac does not offer a liberal arts education, but rather provides students with training in various career paths. Among these options, Quinnipiac has gained a solid reputation in the health sciences, although these majors also seem to be the most difficult. A junior physical therapy major said, "Even though I know I'm working harder on the weekends while my friends are out partying, it's worth it knowing I can get a good job right out of college."

There are a few other majors that also receive high marks. As one student related, "The health science majors are extremely popular, and the business school and communications schools are both phenomenal. The communications school has an amazing group of teachers who are so experienced in their fields, they are on television news talk shows . . . literally every week." Students in all majors, however, note very experienced and accessible faculty members. "Teachers can be really good and even if they aren't they are usually always accessible." Classes tend to be quite small, but most students have found it relatively easy to get into the classes they want. Teachers are often flexible about letting students in even when the classes are full. Among the more interesting electives, students mention a popular art class in which students hike outdoors and make natural sculptures inspired by existing works of art. The outdoor sculptures are displayed along the campus's central pathway for all the students to admire. Outside of class time, Quinnipiac students find themselves very busy, with more than 65 student groups and clubs on campus and strong emphases on student leadership. These opportunities led one student to gush, "The student activities are amazing." By providing a rigorous pre-professional education within a small close-knit and spirited community, Quinnipiac is, in the words of one student, "a perfect fit for so many of us. I would never choose to go anywhere else."—*Quinn Fitzgerald*

FYI
If you come to Quinnipiac you'd better bring "a car and a fake ID."
What is the typical weekend schedule? "Sleeping in, homework, campus events, bars."
If I could change one thing about Quinnipiac, "it would be the lack of student enthusiasm for on-campus events."
Three things every student at Quinnipiac should do before graduating are "hike through Sleeping Giant State Park; become a leader of a team, club, or organization; and go crazy on May weekend with the rest of campus."

Trinity College

Address: 300 Summit Street
Hartford, CT 06016
Phone: 860-297-2180
E-mail address:
admissions.office@trincoll
.edu
Web site URL:
www.trincoll.edu
Year Founded: 1823
Private or Public: Private
Religious Affiliation: None
Location: Urban
Number of Applicants: 5,950
Percent Accepted: 34%
**Percent Accepted who
enroll:** 28%
Number Entering: 576
**Number of Transfers
Accepted each Year:** 24
Middle 50% SAT range:
M: 620–710, CR:
620–710, Wr: 630–720
Middle 50% ACT range:
27–31
**Early admission program
EA/ED/None:** ED

**Percentage accepted
through EA or ED:** 68%
EA and ED deadline: 15-Nov
Regular Deadline: 1-Jan
Application Fee: $60
**Full time Undergraduate
enrollment:** 2,388
Total enrollment: 2,566
Percent Male: 50%
Percent Female: 50%
**Total Percent Minority or
Unreported:** 38%
Percent African-American:
7%
**Percent Asian/Pacific
Islander:** 6%
Percent Hispanic: 6%
Percent Native-American:
<1%
Percent International: 4%
**Percent in-state/out of
state:** 17%/83%
Percent from Public HS:
47%
Retention Rate: 91%
Graduation Rate 4-year: 81%

Graduation Rate 6-year: 85%
**Percent Undergraduates in
On-campus housing:** 95%
**Number of official organized
extracurricular
organizations:** 105
3 Most popular majors:
Economics, English
Language and Literature,
Political Science and
Government
Student/Faculty ratio: 10:1
Average Class Size: 10 to 19
**Percent of students going to
grad school:** 19%
Tuition and Fees: $38,733
**In State Tuition and Fees if
different:** No difference
Cost for Room and Board:
$9,900
**Percent receiving financial
aid out of those who apply,
first year:** Unreported
**Percent receiving financial
aid among all students:**
39%

E ven though Trinity College was founded in 1823 and boasts some of the earliest examples of Gothic architecture in America, this college is not afraid of innovation. With a fresh curriculum and a large handful of renovated buildings, Trinity students enjoy constant improvements in both facilities and academics. Located in Hartford, Connecticut's capital, Trinity offers a small community feeling in an urban setting, where friendliness is a common attribute. As one sophomore said, "I was surprised in a good way, because it is so easy to fit in; you can always find a group of friends."

Small Class Conundrum

Trinity offers a wide range of classes and attracts students with a variety of interests. Though Trinity is one of the best liberal arts schools in the country, students are not deterred from pursuing science majors. Students must fulfill their distribution requirements by taking classes from five general areas: humanities, the arts, natural sciences, social sciences, and numerical and symbolic reasoning. Within each area, students are free to choose whichever classes interest them. As one sophomore declared, "I took an environmental studies course for a requirement, which I never would have chosen myself, and ended up loving it!" Students find that the requirements improve their academic experience and give just enough freedom for finding classes.

Part of Trinity's close-knit community feeling stems from the seminar classes each freshman is required to take. First-years take a seminar and live with the same group of students, fostering strong relationships and forming a comfortable environment from the very beginning of their Trinity experience. One junior commented, "these seminars are not traditional classes; they focus on unique topics and have a budget to plan activities like going to the Bushnell Theater for a show or eating out at a local restaurant." Trinity can be characterized by this focus on small classes and close student-faculty relationships.

The most popular majors on campus are history, economics and political science, which offer more classes than smaller majors such as classics or computer science. Trinity also started a new Human Rights Program and has unique classes under such disciplines as Queer Studies and Community Action. Though students are pleased with the range of courses, they comment that competition for entry into the most popular classes such as philosophy of sports or fitness classes severely limits their availability, especially to underclassmen. A current freshman moaned, "There is a lot of competition to get into classes. Most people settle for classes in their major that they need to take; only a few get to take the ones they really want."

> "Professors will even give you their cell phone number. They are willing and eager to help you with anything."

Regardless of the classes' popularity, students universally agree that the small-class environment has made for a wonderful academic experience. Students regularly eat dinner with their professors and one claimed that "Professors will even give you their cell phone number. They are willing and eager to help you with anything." Yes, the academic experience fulfills students' expectations of rigor, but students say that is just "part of what they do here; there is still plenty of time to socialize." Though some students strive to make the dean's list, others find that academics are not a dominant part of life. Professors are fair with grading, and as a savvy junior remarked, "School is just about as hard as you make it."

Community of Bantams

After freshmen year, when the students all live together in a quad, they have the ability to choose their roommates and even request themed housing. Housing for upperclassmen is integrated with a variety of buildings, including the coveted Praxis dorm. Though freshman dorms are currently being renovated, a sophomore insisted that "Dorms get bigger after freshman year with a little more to choose from, like the option of having a living room."

The RA system provides yet another way for students to form relationships with figures of authority and guidance. Though RAs are responsible for students following dorm policies and act as mediators between students and the administration, students praise the system and are happy about the bond forged between them and their RAs. "We have fantastic RAs. They are trusting and make sure you are safe, but are not an overbearing presence. They want to keep you out of trouble with authority." The college prohibits alcohol in rooms with underage students and restricts everyone from possessing hard alcohol, but students claim that the policies are not strictly enforced.

Among old Gothic architecture, a beautiful chapel, and a Victorian-style English Department building, Trinity students find new modern facilities that add even more to the college's character. Recently, students have been able to enjoy the addition of an entirely new dorm complex and a community hockey rink, while anticipating a new Trinity commons area and the renovation of some of the older buildings. When the weather is nice, students flock to the quad to socialize or play frisbee with their friends between classes and, when it's crunch time, students take advantage of quiet study spots such as Gallows Hill with comfy couches and free coffee.

The main dining hall, where most students eat on the weekdays, provides another place to meet students and socialize. There are two places available to eat other than the main dining hall, which serve a variety of sandwiches and burgers and fries.. Students pay a fee, choosing from three levels, at the beginning of the year and budget from that set amount of money. The food receives neither great praise nor terrible complaints and is occasionally surpassed by those venturing to restaurants in West Hartford or looking for a cheap meal at Trinity's, a local favorite.

Party If You Please

Trinity students agree that the social scene on campus revolves around Vernon Street, the home of the college's rowdy fraternities. A male freshman cautioned that "Some are hard to get into if you don't have girls, but you can always find a party on the weekend." The frats also host annual themed parties such as Tropical, a party ranked in *Playboy* magazine, where the students bring in sand, and Foam, where a frat house is filled with—believe it or not—foam. Some other favorite party spots include the football house or one of the cultural houses. Students usually party from Thursday through

Saturday, and drinking remains a very prominent part of the campus social life.

If these parties aren't enticing enough to relieve students' weekday stresses, they may find themselves at one of the student-run coffeehouses or attending an event hosted by "The Fred." The Fred Pfeil Community Project is a group of students who host daily events such as comedians or arts shows as an alternative to drinking. Although Trinity is a small school and most of the social scene is integrated, mostly upperclassmen can be found in The Tap, while underclassmen search for local bars that don't card. Drinking may be a part of campus culture, but "not in the absence of other options," claimed a well-rounded sophomore.

One student rejoiced that "Though there are school policies regulating alcohol consumption, everyone drinks; it happens in everyone's room." Pot is also fairly common on campus, though the harder drugs are scarce. Luckily, regardless of students' preferences of how to have fun, all rave about the general friendliness and ease of finding their own comfort zone.

Change of Heart-Ford

Students disagree about the role the surrounding city of Hartford plays in their educational and social experience at Trinity. All students either own cars or have access to a friend's for shopping trips to the Westfarms Mall or food runs down the Berlin Turnpike. One junior warned, "I would never walk around campus at night alone" and that the surrounding area can either be "really nice or really sketchy." Others comment about living in the "Trinity bubble," where it's really easy to forget the city and only use campus resources.

The administration and student-run volunteer groups strive to close the gap between the college "bubble" and the Hartford community. An involved sophomore described taking a class called Child Development, where students design a public policy project: "We had to identify a problem relating to child development in Hartford, speak to community members, formulate a solution, and present proposals to the community that were later implemented." The school also offers classes on Hartford to further familiarize the students with the city and perhaps inspire them to invest time in promoting its growth.

Squashing Opponents

Step aside, football; the 11-time national championship squash team draws the largest crowd on this campus. Though both sports enjoy support from their dedicated fans, squash remains Trinity's true claim to fame. A spirited senior said that "Around campus you can sense the Trinity pride," which carries over into other extracurricular activities as well. Everyone is involved on this campus, whether a student competes as a varsity athlete, on the intramural fields, or just cheers on a friend.

In addition to sports, Trinity students participate in a variety of clubs, from the student newspaper *The Tripod*, to student government, a wide range of volunteer groups, and even a cat alliance, which cares for cats roaming the campus. Do It Day, a campus-wide volunteer initiative, provides another outlet for students to get involved in the community by participating in activities such as painting a nursing home or planting flowers outside hospitals. There is an activity here for all interests, and as one sophomore explained, "People here are so over-involved, you hardly find anyone who only has one commitment."

Students at Trinity brag about their close relationships with amazing, compassionate professors, show their Bantam spirit through devotion to myriad activities, and save their best tropical attire to debut for weekend revelry. With so much to do, schedules are usually packed, but most students wouldn't have it any other way.—*Cara Dermody*

FYI
If you come to Trinity, you'd better bring "a pair of Uggs, a car, and a high squash IQ."
What is the typical weekend schedule? "Most spend the afternoon watching movies or playing sports, followed by pregaming for a long night at a frat or attending a concert with friends."
If I could change one thing about Trinity, "I'd bring back a dating scene."
The three things every student at Trinity should do before graduating are "Go to a squash game, volunteer in Hartford, and go to Tropical."

United States Coast Guard Academy

Address: 31 Mohegan Avenue New London, CT 06320-8103
Phone: 860-444-8503
E-mail address: admissions@uscga.edu
Web site URL: www.uscga.edu
Year Founded: 1876
Private or Public: Public
Religious Affiliation: None
Location: Suburban
Number of Applicants: 1,633
Percent Accepted: 24%
Percent Accepted who enroll: 70%
Number Entering: 274
Number of Transfers Accepted each Year: Unreported
Middle 50% SAT range: M: 600–680, CR: 570–665, Wr: Unreported
Middle 50% ACT range: 25–29
Early admission program EA/ED/None: EA

Percentage accepted through EA or ED: 29%
EA and ED deadline: 1-Nov
Regular Deadline: 1-Feb
Application Fee: $0
Full time Undergraduate enrollment: 973
Total enrollment: 973
Percent Male: 72%
Percent Female: 28%
Total Percent Minority or Unreported: 14%
Percent African-American: 3%
Percent Asian/Pacific Islander: 5%
Percent Hispanic: 5%
Percent Native-American: <1%
Percent International: 1%
Percent in-state/out of state: 6%/94%
Percent from Public HS: 81%
Retention Rate: 86%
Graduation Rate 4-year: 59%

Graduation Rate 6-year: 62%
Percent Undergraduates in On-campus housing: 100%
Number of official organized extracurricular organizations: Unreported
3 Most popular majors: Engineering, Oceanography, Political Science
Student/Faculty ratio: 9:1
Average Class Size: 10 to 19
Percent of students going to grad school: Unreported
Tuition and Fees: $0
In State Tuition and Fees if different: No difference
Cost for Room and Board: $0
Percent receiving financial aid out of those who apply, first year: NA
Percent receiving financial aid among all students: NA

The United States Coast Guard Academy provides its students with the discipline and skills useful for all tracks of life, turning its cadets into the leaders of the future. With military employment following graduation and several opportunities for development while in the Academy, cadets receive much more than a four-year education. The USCGA holds firm to its rigorous academic curriculum, strong athletics programs, and varied extracurricular offerings. Each graduate leaves the Academy with a sense of accomplishment that inevitably leads to post-graduation success.

Core Values

The United States Coast Guard Academy boasts much more than a commanding name and intimidating reputation. Founded as the Revenue Cutter School of Instruction in 1876, the USCGA offers an impressive combination of tradition, rigor, and discipline that has shaped leaders of America for over a century. In fact, the leadership skills developed during the four years at USCGA are what many cadets refer to as the best aspect of the Academy. The USCGA's set of core values is threefold, emphasizing honor, respect and devotion to duty. These values form the foundation for all programs in the Academy. The lofty reputation of the Academy often intimidates potential students, discouraging them from applying to the undergraduate program. However, prospective candidates should be encouraged "To consider the broad range of opportunities that the Academy has to offer, and acknowledge the diverse student body that enjoys the benefits of the USCGA."

The USCGA draws a student body that is about 71 percent male and 29 percent female. All cadets receive equal treatment with respect to academics, housing, and athletic training. The promise of equal opportunities at the Academy is one of the most treasured aspects of the institution, as reported by many cadets. The USCGA provides an equal playing field whether a cadet is male or female, first-class or fourth-class. You might ask: What is the difference between a first-class and a fourth-class cadet? How can delineating classes exist within a system of fair play?

All freshmen at the Academy are called fourth-class cadets, and each year students climb one rung on the ladder. Each class has special roles and duties at the Academy; this reflects the hierarchical structure of military life and prepares cadets for post-graduation military employment. Fourth-class cadets can be compared to understudies, learning the ropes of military life and closely following examples of the more experienced. Third-class cadets are assigned to advise one or two fourth-class cadets, while second-class cadets assume the responsibility of Assistant Division Officers, leading the younger cadets during training. Finally, first-class cadets have the opportunity to become Regimental Staff Officers, Company Commanders, Department Heads, and Division Officers. This specific regimentation at the Academy prepares cadets for the structured system of military duty and creates a progressive path towards increased responsibility, learning, and opportunity. At the end of four years, first-class cadets have had the experience of being followers, mentors, assistant leaders, and commanders. Each of these roles provides a wide range of opportunities for growth and enrichment unique to the mission of the Academy.

The Typical Day
With such a close parallel to military structure and core values, it is hardly surprising that discipline plays a tremendous role in the lives of cadets at the USCGA. Although cadets' names and roles change from year to year, the typical weekday schedule "falls equally upon all cadets alike." The wake-up alarm sounds at "0600" and breakfast quickly follows. Academic instruction begins promptly at 0800 and ends at 1200 for lunch. Classes then resume after lunch and end for the day at 1600. The Academy's curriculum offers a Bachelor of Science degree for all students. Classes are often competitive, though many cadets enjoy the academic challenges laid before them. The classroom setting encourages cadets to think quickly, observe objectively, and analyze deeply. Most classes do not exceed 40 students, and this fosters close relationships between students and professors, as well as interactive learning. The Academy has set core requirements, which students often complete during their first two years.

The USCGA ensures the well-roundedness of its cadets, whether they are in the classroom or on the field. Sports period runs from 1600 to 1800, and the school encourages all of its cadets to pursue athletics. The majority of students play for a varsity team, though some cadets take sports less seriously and wish there was less emphasis on it at the Academy. In addition to intramural and varsity sports, a cadet may choose from 18 other clubs and activities. These range "from glee club to aviation club to ski club to pep band." Cadets may develop a wide variety of talents and delve into many of their special interests.

> **"The friends you meet here will be the ones you keep for the rest of your life."**

Sports period doesn't end the day for cadets. Buffet dinner follows from 1700 to 1900. Then, 1900 marks the beginning of military period, and from 2000 until 2200 is study hour. Sleep becomes an option only at 2200, and all cadets must be in bed by 2400. Cadets must stay on the base during the week, and the Academy requires its students to live on the base all four years. Cadets say that living "on base" gives them a strong sense of unity with the whole student body, and this is valued very highly. Cadets report that homesickness does not often occur because of the strong bonds that cadets form while living, training, and learning together. One sophomore cadet reports that "The best thing about the Academy is the people you are surrounded by. The friends you meet here will be the ones you keep for the rest of your life."

Life Beyond the Coast
Cadets need not apply for jobs after graduation, since the Academy assures them of a career with the United States Coast Guard. Immediately following graduation, cadets receive positions as Deck Watch Officers or Engineers in Training for their first two-year tour. This embarks them on a military journey that further develops their minds, bodies, and spirits. The work ethic taught at the USCGA prepares cadets for a successful life within the military or in civilian surroundings.

Alumni of the Academy also make their mark on the outside world, often receiving honors in fields such as medicine, business and law. They attribute much of their success to the training at the USCGA and often come back to the Academy for lectures and conferences. A strong alumni network really kindles the spirit at the Academy and illustrates the fact that the Academy's core values continue to thrive in the minds of its cadets long after graduation.

The job security that the USCGA offers is one of the most attractive features of the Academy. After the first tour, cadets can apply for advanced-degree programs financed by the U.S. Coast Guard. Flight school is another appealing option for many graduates. Pay and benefits, including full medical and dental plans, continue during any tenure of employment with the Coast Guard. Cadets admit that many of them choose the USCGA because it ensures them job security when they finally embark into the world.

Graduating from the USCGA is not the end for cadets, but rather the beginning of a fruitful career of military life and much more. The USCGA asks a lot of its students but gives back just as much, if not more.—*Aleksandra Kopec*

FYI

If you come to the U.S. Coast Guard Academy, you'd better bring "a sense of humor for the many disciplining challenges you will encounter."

What is the typical weekend schedule? "Live large while freedom reigns. Leisure time increases as cadets get closer to graduation, but getting off the base is something most cadets try to do during the weekend. Maybe a little bit of studying on Sunday would ease the workload for the rest of the week, but it is important to get outside the gates and enjoy yourself."

If I could change one thing about the U.S. Coast Guard Academy, I'd "give cadets the option to get into bed before 10 p.m."

Three things every student at the U.S. Coast Guard Academy should do before graduating are "go to the Caribbean for five weeks on a 300-foot sailboat, experience swab summer—a rigorous orientation program prior to the beginning of freshman year—and become part of an athletic team."

University of Connecticut

Address: 2131 Hillside Road, Unit 3088 Storrs, CT 06268-3088
Phone: 860-486-3137
E-mail address: beahusky@uconn.edu
Web site URL: www.uconn.edu
Year Founded: 1881
Private or Public: Public
Religious Affiliation: None
Location: Rural
Number of Applicants: 21,105
Percent Accepted: 49%
Percent Accepted who enroll: 30%
Number Entering: 3,179
Number of Transfers Accepted each Year: 1,107
Middle 50% SAT range: M: 560–660, CR: 530–630, Wr: 540–640
Middle 50% ACT range: 23–28
Early admission program EA/ED/None: EA

Percentage accepted through EA or ED: 72%
EA and ED deadline: 1-Dec
Regular Deadline: 1-Feb
Application Fee: $70
Full time Undergraduate enrollment: 16,348
Total enrollment: 22,773
Percent Male: 49%
Percent Female: 51%
Total Percent Minority or Unreported: 33%
Percent African-American: 5%
Percent Asian/Pacific Islander: 7%
Percent Hispanic: 5%
Percent Native-American: <1%
Percent International: 1%
Percent in-state/out of state: 77%/23%
Percent from Public HS: 87%
Retention Rate: 93%
Graduation Rate 4-year: 56%

Graduation Rate 6-year: 75%
Percent Undergraduates in On-campus housing: 97%
Number of official organized extracurricular organizations: 303
3 Most popular majors: Business, Political Science and Government, Psychology
Student/Faculty ratio: 17:1
Average Class Size: 10 to 19
Percent of students going to grad school: 30%
Tuition and Fees: $24,050
In State Tuition and Fees if different: $9,338
Cost for Room and Board: $9,300
Percent receiving financial aid out of those who apply, first year: 50%
Percent receiving financial aid among all students: 64%

A small, unassuming town with a permanent population of around 11,000 people, Storrs, Conn., is a cartographer's speck. But a well-known university with a premier sports program has put Storrs on the map. Over the past decade, the University of Connecticut has distinguished itself academically and athletically as one of the best public universities in New England.

No Place Like Home

Three-fourths of UConn undergraduates call the Nutmeg State home. But despite the lack of geographic diversity, the student body is composed of individuals with a wide variety of backgrounds and interests: "There is a broad range of personalities that would allow any student to blend in fairly easily—from people that love to drink to people who are dedicated to studying." One consequence of a predominately New England student body is a fierce Yankee-Red Sox rivalry that often gets heated when October rolls around. Even the closest of roommates may find themselves temporarily torn apart. "Two years ago, when the Yanks were playing the Sox in the playoffs, the quad was filled," one senior remembers. "It was divided between the Sox and Yankee fans yelling at each other in the middle of the night." Playoffs time aside, students say that most people are open and friendly: "Obviously there are some exceptions, but everyone here is pretty cool." Because UConn boasts such a large student population—over 20,000 undergraduates—there is a group of people for everyone. By the same token, it can be easy to be lost in the mix: "You can stay to yourself and not meet anyone if you want and nobody will stop you. You just have to put yourself out there to make friends." Many freshmen rush fraternities and sororities; UConn, which has a detailed anti-hazing policy, oversees around 30 organizations on campus. But making friends is not contingent upon being a Greek.

Close Quarters

The real estate bubble has already burst at UConn. In recent years, the University has had to deal with serious housing shortages that have forced some students to move off campus. Unanticipated high rates of matriculation have resulted in too many students and too few rooms. Underclassmen, however, are guaranteed housing. Most freshmen live in either North or Northwest—don't be fooled by the similar names. The former is an old, rundown building known as "the jun-gle"; the latter is new and nice. Both dorms' rooms aren't particularly spacious and are usually shared by up to three people. After their first year or two, many students opt to move off campus into apartments but even those "are a hike from classes and tough to get into." In short, housing is hardly one of UConn's strong points. "Unfortunately, housing has been an on and off problem at UConn," one upperclassman said. "If you're lucky enough to have a first pick and end up in Northwest, the all-freshman housing is pretty good quality. . . . On the other hand, though, you could end up like me, in an all-girls dorm with an awful dining hall on the farthest end of campus possible. It was a much less convenient freshman experience but still a great one."

Something for Everyone

With over 100 majors and programs to choose from, undergraduates can study virtually anything. In addition to courses required for the major, students must take a certain number of General Education classes in a variety of disciplines including art, science and philosophy, affording a basic, well-rounded education. GE classes tend to be large but on average, class size ranges from 27 to 34 students. For those seeking smaller classes and a more challenging workload, UConn offers an honors program. By junior year, students interested in applying to one of the University's nine specialized schools, such as the Physical Therapy, Pharmacy or Business School, must do so: "Specialized programs like the Business School and School of Education are really prominent, apparently." Yet, the majority of students are in the College of Liberal Arts and Sciences.

> "There is a broad range of personalities that would allow any student to blend in fairly easily—from people that love to drink to people who are dedicated to studying."

The difficulty of classes depends largely on the major. Engineering courses are considered tough while human development and family studies is thought to be one of the easier majors. Some of the more acclaimed classes include David Miller's General Psychology I, which despite starting at 8 a.m. is always well-attended. "He is so good that kids want to get up and go to it," one student said. "He always starts off the class with a music video and sometimes he dresses up as former famous psychologists." Other popular courses include Children's Literature, in which students read books like *Goodnight Moon*, *Where the Wild Things Are* and *Alice in Wonderland*.

Work Hard, Play Harder

UConn has a reputation of a party school, which is well-deserved. Though the campus is billed as dry, when the weekend arrives, students don't shy from putting down the books and picking up the bottle. Underclassmen often head to the Celeron Square Apartments or make the trek to the off-campus Carriage House: "It's a fairly long path, but when you are buzzed or drunk, it goes by quickly." Those over 21—or with IDs that say they are—hit up the local bars, including Civic Pub and Huskies. Fraternities and sororities figure prominently into the party scene as well. Many have houses off campus, where they throw keggers. The Rugby House is also a weekend hotspot. Despite the occasional debauchery, students are adept at balancing school work with their social life and one senior is quick to point out that while UConn is a party school, "it's also a great place to gain a good education."

Top Dogs

UConn is perhaps best known for its sports teams. The men's and women's basketball teams have established themselves as perennial powerhouses, contending annually for national championships and making household names out of the likes of Emeka Okafor and Diana Taurasi. Come winter every year, Huskymania takes over. The campus is transformed into a frenzy as students pile into Gampel Pavilion and the nearby Hartford Civic Center to cheer on their Huskies. Tickets are not easy to come by, but the University recently instituted a lottery system to cut down on students camping out in front of the ticket booth: "People would just line up in their tents down the street. I actually saw people bring their TVs and Playstations."

Success has not been limited to the hardwood, however. The football team, which plays in the newly constructed, 40,000-seat Rentschler Field, captured the Motor City Bowl in 2004 in just its second season in Division I-A. The men's and women's soccer teams and field hockey team have all made deep runs in NCAA tournaments in the last few years. UConn also promises a wide range of intramural sports from bowling to badminton to dodge ball. The competition is intense—even to get on a team: "IMs are pretty big. The slots for teams always fill up quick, within a day or two."

UConn encourages high school seniors to come to campus and be a "Husky for a day." Students get to meet people and professors, attend classes and even eat in the dining halls. At the very least, they find out where exactly Storrs, Conn., is—and may very well find themselves returning the following fall.—*Joshua Lotstein*

FYI

If you come to UConn, you'd better bring "an open mind and a fridge to store your alcohol."

What is the typical weekend like? "Friday and Saturday, partying at Celeron, Carriage or some dorm room; Sunday, recovering and doing homework."

If I could change one thing about UConn, I'd "add more parking."

Three things every student should do before graduating from UConn are "go to a men's Basketball game, drink at Carriage or Celeron, play oozeball (volleyball in the mud) during Spring Weekend."

Wesleyan University

Address: 70 Wyllys Avenue Middletown, CT 06459
Phone: 860-685-3000
E-mail address: admission@wesleyan.edu
Web site URL: www.wesleyan.edu
Year Founded: 1831
Private or Public: Private
Religious Affiliation: None
Location: Suburban
Number of Applicants: 8,250
Percent Accepted: 27%
Percent Accepted who enroll: 32%
Number Entering: 715
Number of Transfers Accepted each Year: 110
Middle 50% SAT range: M: 660–740, CR: 640–740, Wr: 640–740
Middle 50% ACT range: 27–33
Early admission program EA/ED/None: ED

Percentage accepted through EA or ED: 43%
EA and ED deadline: 15-Nov
Regular Deadline: 1-Jan
Application Fee: $55
Full time Undergraduate enrollment: 2,796
Total enrollment: 3,222
Percent Male: 50%
Percent Female: 50%
Total Percent Minority or Unreported: 27%
Percent African-American: 7%
Percent Asian/Pacific Islander: 11%
Percent Hispanic: 8%
Percent Native-American: 1%
Percent International: 6%
Percent in-state/out of state: 8%/92%
Percent from Public HS: 57%
Retention Rate: 94%

Graduation Rate 4-year: 84%
Graduation Rate 6-year: 93%
Percent Undergraduates in On-campus housing: 99%
Number of official organized extracurricular organizations: 200
3 Most popular majors: English, Government, Psychology
Student/Faculty ratio: 9:1
Average Class Size: 19
Percent of students going to grad school: 70%
Tuition and Fees: $38,634
In State Tuition and Fees if different: No difference
Cost for Room and Board: $10,636
Percent receiving financial aid out of those who apply, first year: 79%
Percent receiving financial aid among all students: 44%

Recently named the "Most Annoying Liberal Arts College" by the gossip blog Gawker, Wesleyan University has a strong reputation for being an ultra-liberal school where political correctness is not just commendable but necessary. While this image of Wesleyan certainly rings true to many students, the University has seen a gradual shift towards a new identity. Situated in Middletown—nearly halfway between Boston and New York—Wesleyan provides a refined breeding ground for the expression of diverse perspectives for its multifaceted students.

Sincere and Studious Students

The academic atmosphere at Wesleyan can be described as being extremely genuine. Students consider learning to be an intrinsically valuable endeavor, and tend to push themselves to learn as much as they can. Although there are some people who are GPA-conscious—"You have to work hard for an A, but it's not impossible"—students "work hard because they like what they do: they're not all mindless drones." According to one sophomore, there are a good number of "ideologically driven classes with political

perspectives," especially within feminine, gender, and sexuality studies, in which "young activists are being taught by the wise, old activists." However, another student mentioned that while there is an abundance of politically motivated courses, standard "objective" classes do exist at Wesleyan. Indeed, Wesleyan's science program is one of the strongest amongst the small liberal arts colleges: it receives the largest amount of National Science Foundation grants and also recently built a $150 million science center.

The Wesleyan education focuses on developing in each student "10 essential capabilities"—including writing, speaking, interpretation, intercultural literacy, and effective citizenship. In the liberal arts tradition, students are expected to meet Gen Ed Expectations, although these are somewhat less stringent than at other comparable institutions. There are two special academic programs that Wesleyan students can enter during their sophomore year. The College of Social Studies (CSS) is a rigorous interdisciplinary program that integrates economics, political science, history, and government through colloquia, tutorials, and seminars.

CSS has a reputation as being a program "for people who want to run the world." The other alternative is the humanities-oriented College of Letters (COL)—also known as the "College of Love." Both programs involve a number of courses without grades, with written evaluations in their stead. According to one student, admitted students tend to be somewhat insular and host parties on Mondays, since they have group assignments due on Sunday nights. The CSS and COL tend to be in the student body's general consciousness, as everyone knows about the programs, and most people have probably considered applying at one time or another.

Among the academic departments, the Department of Film Studies, led by the renowned film critic Jeanine Basinger, is regarded as particularly strong. The numerous alumni have a very successful track record and have penetrated the ranks of the Hollywood elite through the achievements of the group known as the "Wesleyan mafia," which includes Michael Bay (director of *Transformers*, *Armageddon*, and *The Rock*), Joss Whedon (creator of *Buffy the Vampire Slayer*), and Laurence Mark (producer of *Jerry Maguire*). The Film Studies program attempts to integrate "history and theory with practice" and emphasizes the analysis of film over merely its production. Most of the program takes place in the state-of-the-art Center for Film Studies, which also houses a vast and unique film archive.

The academics at Wesleyan are as intimate as they are sincere. Students find that the small size of the school lends to the ease with which students can interact and eventually befriend their professors. For example, one student noted that apart from a "few arrogant professors" most of his professors had gotten to know him better, typically through relationships beyond the classroom: "Our professor took [our class] to his house and had a BBQ, where we also played croquet in his yard." The ability to get really close to a professor is a distinct benefit at a small liberal arts college such as Wesleyan. In the end, small class size and a passionate, vocal student body allow classes to "get some really great conversations going," where students pay serious attention to each other while furiously scribbling notes.

Lively Liberalism

The political climate at Wesleyan has always been—and continues to be—very liberal. One student, while speculating on the presence of conservative-leaning students on campus, remarked, "Even if there were conservative people, they're probably hiding it." Students on the right of the political spectrum seem to have trouble finding space to express themselves openly and honestly without being ostracized.

Without a doubt, Wesleyan has played a key part in many of the country's most progressive movements. According to one student, Wesleyan was a frontrunner in the civil rights movement. For example, a number of professors traveled down to Mississippi and demonstrated alongside Dr. Martin Luther King. This sort of historical precedent has affected Wesleyan's contemporary political culture. One student mentioned that the countercultural movement's lifeblood in part lies in the "sense of history that exists [at Wesleyan], a sense of Wesleyan as countercultural—even before the sixties—a sense that has extended until now."

On campus, the "social activist" groups maintain a very active presence. For example, according to one junior, the "Transgender/gay/lesbian community [and their associated clubs] host viewings of pornographic films on a regular basis." Beyond the socially aware, the assertive presence of "hipsters"—not to be confused with "hippies", although they also exist on campus—at Wesleyan elicit reactions such as "pretentious wannabes" or "elitist crowd." Without fail, a large portion of Wesleyan students draw on the lifestyle made famous by residents of Williamsburg, Brooklyn. Of all the organizations on campus, the Eclectic Society, a fraternity, provides Wesleyan's social glue: its hipster members host many of the more well-attended parties on campus.

Although it is clear that Wesleyan's student body represents a broad spectrum of ethnic, geographic, and cultural backgrounds, some students question the extent of interactions that occur between people from different comprehensive worldviews. One student cautioned that one's understanding of the diversity of the student body "depends on what kind of angle you're coming from." While he appreciated the multitude of viewpoints, he pointed out that "There are a bunch of people who don't branch out and try to meet people with fresh views." Another student mentioned that "There is a pretty clear segregation that sort of naturally happened. You wouldn't want to say that in public though—there's a lot of political correctness." Although it may look as though Wesleyan is an ideal "melting pot" of unique individuals coming together to form the Wesleyan identity, there is certainly a share of the student body that remains skeptical of the tolerance of its peers.

> "Wesleyan is a very experimental place, which is a fun thing to be as a college—it's fun to have people who aren't afraid of doing something abnormal."

In a nutshell, according to one junior, Wesleyan students can best be characterized as "socially aware and offbeat people with a variety of tastes." The student body is composed of people with a range of personalities and perspectives from all walks of life. Students place a high emphasis on the discovery of one's own identity, and the ability to express and enact such an identity with minimal restraint. The lifestyle of the inhabitants of West College ("Westco") serves as a testament to this theme. Inhabitants of the so-called "naked dorm" make their own rules on how they should live and behave in their residence. That clothing is optional should be readily apparent; in addition, meetings are planned at odd times such as 9:13 p.m. as a way to break the norm in society that events must occur on the hour or at 10- or 15-minute intervals. Westco's inhabitants—and, more broadly, Wesleyan students—are constantly pushing their creative abilities to the limit in an attempt to better expose their interests to the world around them: Wesleyan students are not afraid to confidently live their lives as they see fit.

Freedom on Foss Hill
Students find that living at Wesleyan is remarkably easy. This begins with the wide range of campus living options available to students. Freshmen usually begin their Wesleyan experience in freshman dorms, where they are paired up with other new students. As they become upperclassmen, students have the opportunity to live in normal dorms. "Program housing," where small groups of students can live in houses with unique mission statements (e.g. community service house) are available, as well as senior houses, which are semi-off-campus and wood-frame. The sprawl of the campus is very manageable and the campus living situation meets every student's needs.

Another way in which students live easier lives comes from the fact that the administration—intentionally or not—turns a blind eye toward the pervasive drug culture that exists on campus. Students tend to favor marijuana and the psychedelic effects of occasional shroom and acid trips. A number of students confirmed that a majority of the student body smokes weed. In fact, Wes Fest weekend—when accepted high school seniors come visit Wesleyan—is always scheduled to include April 20th (an important day for marijuana lovers), on which day the student body congregates en masse on Foss Hill. One student proudly asserted that Foss Hill was a "legendary place on 4/20, where literally 1,500 people with bongs meet on the Hill." Foss Hill is widely regarded as both the central location and favorite hang-out spot on campus. Students pass by it between classes and agree that "it's a place to go on the nice, sunny days for a nice game of Ultimate Frisbee."

An Experimental Experience
Upon comparing their pre-matriculation expectations to post-matriculation realities, most students seem to agree that Wesleyan does lie on the frontier of political activism. One student said the political atmosphere "surprised me, because I didn't realize just how political the school was." Above all, however, the school is about experimentation, and a number of students agree with this description. One sophomore praised the benefits of testing out new things: "Wesleyan is a very experimental place, which is a fun thing to be as a college—it's fun to have people who aren't afraid of doing something abnormal." But then again, it's okay to be "normal" too, because, at the end of the day, "If you're fine with being normal, you can still find your crowd."—*Wookie Kim*

FYI
If you come to Wesleyan, you'd better bring "weed—you'll make lots of friends."
What is the typical weekend schedule? "Wake up for brunch on Saturday, work a bit, hang out under the sun on Foss Hill, go to a performance event (like Samsara), head to Eclectic or Fountain Street. Work all of Sunday."
If I could change one thing about Wesleyan, I'd "change the repressive remnants of political correctness that actually make people self-censoring and make conversations less interesting."
Three things every student at Wesleyan should do before graduating are "do shrooms in the graveyard, go to an Eclectic party, and see Prometheus (a fire-throwing group) at the base of Foss Hill."

Yale University

Address: PO Box 208234
New Haven, CT 06520-8234
Phone: 203-432-9300
E-mail address:
undergraduate.admission
@yale.edu
Web site URL: www.yale.edu
Year Founded: 1701
Private or Public: Private
Religious Affiliation: None
Location: Urban
Number of Applicants:
22,817
Percent Accepted: 9%
**Percent Accepted who
enroll:** 68%
Number Entering: 1,320
**Number of Transfers
Accepted each Year:** 28
Middle 50% SAT range:
M: 700–790, CR:
700–800, Wr: 700–790
Middle 50% ACT range: 30–34
**Early admission program
EA/ED/None:** EA

**Percentage accepted
through EA or ED:** 18%
EA and ED deadline: 1-Nov
Regular Deadline: 1-Jan
Application Fee: $75
**Full time Undergraduate
enrollment:** 5,311
Total enrollment: 10,206
Percent Male: 50%
Percent Female: 50%
**Total Percent Minority or
Unreported:** 32%
Percent African-American:
9%
**Percent Asian/Pacific
Islander:** 14%
Percent Hispanic: 9%
Percent Native-American: 1%
Percent International: 9%
**Percent in-state/out of
state:** 6%/94%
Percent from Public HS: 55%
Retention Rate: 99%
Graduation Rate 4-year:
Unreported

Graduation Rate 6-year:
Unreported
**Percent Undergraduates in
On-campus housing:** 87%
**Number of official organized
extracurricular
organizations:** 350
3 Most popular majors:
Economics, History, Political
Science
Student/Faculty ratio: 6:1
Average Class Size: 10 to 19
**Percent of students going to
grad school:** 50%
Tuition and Fees: $35,300
**In State Tuition and Fees if
different:** No difference
Cost for Room and Board:
$10,700
**Percent receiving financial
aid out of those who apply,
first year:** 81%
**Percent receiving financial
aid among all students:**
46%

W hen Yale's newly renovated Bass Library reopened at midnight in October 2007, the event seemed more like a late-night blowout than the opening of a library. But as students raced through the underground stacks, admiring the new shelves and sampling the café's organic fare, the library extravaganza tied together the aspects of Yale life that its students cherish. With love of learning at the center of the Yale experience, students still find ways to create fun and new traditions in the unlikeliest of ways, all within the context of a university that continues to grow and reshape itself while maintaining centuries of tradition.

A Community of Scholars

Founded in 1701 by Congregationalist ministers, Yale has maintained a commitment to academic excellence ever since. But don't let the world-renowned professors intimidate you—the University is well-known for its strong focus on undergraduate education, which means that faculty members are not so pressured to publish and conduct research that they fail to throw themselves

wholeheartedly into teaching their undergraduates. One sophomore said she has found that there is a "robust dialogue between students and faculty." And while entering an academic institution filled with thousands of other motivated high-achievers may seem daunting as well, Yalies—who are known as both Bulldogs and Elis—find that their fellow students provide a supportive rather than cutthroat environment and are usually more than willing to study and brainstorm together.

As part of its liberal arts curriculum, Yale requires students to fulfill 36 credits—as opposed to the 32 mandated by the other Ivy League schools—including courses to fulfill a major and two course credits each in the humanities and arts, the sciences, the social sciences, quantitative reasoning and writing. The additional foreign language requirement may be completed with between one and three courses, depending on previous language study. While these rigorous requirements contribute to an intense academic environment, students said, rather than oppressive, they found the challenge to be more of an opportunity to thrive. One junior remarked that he felt "acceptably overwhelmed."

One reason that many students feel overwhelmed is the 2000 courses from which to choose. During the first two weeks of each semester, students take advantage of "shopping period" by attending as many classes as they wish—and sometimes as many as they can fit into a day—and deciding whether they like the professor and course material before officially enrolling. And when the time comes to enroll in courses, students report little trouble in gaining access to the ones they want, with the exception of some competitive seminars with caps of 15 to 18 participants, and even then "talking to the professor and making your case usually does the trick." Most courses have between 15 and 30 students, though some introductory lectures host more than 100. While the most popular majors are continuously history, economics, and political science, there is a lot of interest in psychology and the pre-med track, particularly biology. Professors and courses that students highly recommended included Introduction to Psychology with either Paul Bloom or Marvin Chun, History of Modern China with Jonathan Spence, Sex, Evolution, and Human Nature with Laurie Santos, and Constitutional Law with Akhil Amar.

For those looking to fulfill the distributional requirements, there are a variety of gut courses, including Biology of Gender and Sexuality (Porn in the Morn), and Computers and the Law, although some students warned that while there may be less work, these supposedly easy classes are not guaranteed A's. Humanities-oriented students who take gut classes instead of opting to hike up "Science Hill" early each morning are often ridiculed by the more scientifically inclined, and a mechanical engineering major said he and his friends do debate the relative difficulty of the sciences and the humanities. Other students said while classrooms in the different disciplines are separated geographically by the Hill, residential life and extracurriculars bring everyone together seamlessly. An English major said she enjoys that Yale's academic life "really helps stimulate interesting conversations outside the classroom. People aren't afraid to admit that they're really passionate about a subject."

The All-important Sorting Ceremony

Many of these intimate dialogues in dining halls or dorm rooms are fostered by the residential college system, which Yalies across

the board identify as one of the most distinctive, rewarding features of life as a Bulldog. Students are randomly sorted into one of the 12 colleges, which serve as a living community, social environment, intramural sports base, and source of unique pride and loyalty. That almost 90 percent of Yale students choose to live on campus for all four years is a testament to the strong bonds that are formed among those that share a college. While the 12 differ architecturally—Jonathan Edwards is Gothic, Davenport is Georgian, and Morse and Stiles are 60s-era Saarinen designs, for example—and they offer different amenities, the random assemblage of students is representative of the University at large. While Yale, with around 5,400 students, is mid-sized, the colleges help to make the school more personal. A Morse College student described the residential college system as "An amazing opportunity to escape the major college campus. It's a community within a community, with a master and dean and so many resources, like a library and buttery." Along with cheap late-night food from the buttery and the convenience of the nearby library, colleges also offer a variety of facilities, including gyms, movie theaters, performance spaces, and woodworking areas.

Old Campus houses freshmen from 10 of the 12 colleges, allowing members of the same class to get to know each other before moving into their respective colleges. Students in the larger Timothy Dwight and Silliman may live there all four years. The colleges also provide both academic and general support, from the freshman counselors who live on Old Campus to masters and deans, who live in the colleges and are enthusiastic about getting to know students. The University has almost completed the renovation of the 12 colleges, which has transformed suite arrangements, added new facilities, and beautified, all while retaining the traditional architecture and atmosphere. Each year, students in the college being renovated live in "Swing Space," a recently constructed dorm that features long hallways of suites with common rooms, kitchenettes, and private bathrooms. Students said that while Swing is less centrally located than many of the colleges, its living arrangement is a refreshing alternative from the norm, which consists of separate entryways and complex suites of between two and 10 residents, rather than the hallways common at other schools.

With the "Hogwarts-style" Commons, a dining hall in each of the 12 colleges, plus additional eateries in the University's professional and graduate schools, Yalies seem to have a lot of dining options. But some said they feel constrained by the requirement that on-campus students purchase a meal plan, even though they can exchange meals for flex dollars to be used at the convenience store or a couple of local restaurants. The benefit of eating in the dining halls, in spite of the sometimes monotonous food, is the knowledge that you will almost always have someone you can sit with, and a strong sense of community develops. The Sustainable Food Project, which brings local-grown and organic food to dining halls, may be "often healthier but not always tastier," although students said they gave the spirit of the project high marks.

Not Too Busy to Have Fun

Even as the residential colleges provide a social foundation, students raved about the many opportunities to "find your scene." Although students said there are definitely some distinct social groups—such as athletes and hipsters—a film major said he has "always felt that one can easily move throughout groups as long as you have the right disposition and outlook." Extracurricular activities are a common method of meeting new people. In terms of drinking, students estimated that about two-thirds of Yale students drink, but it is "perfectly acceptable" for someone to choose not to and still hang out with people who imbibe. Yale's policy towards alcohol consumption is fairly lenient, despite recent Connecticut laws that strengthened adherence to restrictions. A JE junior commented that "The policy of Yale has always been to give us a lot of respect in that regard, and they're not going to strongly enforce us on drinking . . . but they do take care of us when we over-drink and need help." As for drugs, the junior's perception of on-campus use was that "It's probably mostly just pot and maybe some cocaine, but I don't think too many people do really hardcore drugs."

In any case, students take advantage of campus events as well as parties, ensuring that alcohol does not by any means dominate University socializing. The myriad campus groups devoted to putting on dance, theater, comedy, and musical productions guarantee that there will always be something happening in the evenings, and periodic residential college council-sponsored dance parties and special events add to the fun. Morse and Stiles's Casino Night in November regularly draws more than 2,000 students, JE pulls out all the stops for the Spider

Ball in April, and neon-clad students dance the night away to Duran Duran at Silliman's 80's-themed Safety Dance in October. During the day, the residential colleges' "Master's Teas" are well-known for bringing interesting and prominent figures to campus for intimate talks with groups of students—recent visitors include children's folk singer Raffi, the editor of the *Harry Potter* books and the pop group Hanson, while past guests include former Supreme Court justice Sandra Day O'Connor and author Kurt Vonnegut.

The majority of Yale students are politically liberal, and those that self-identify as moderates tend towards the left as well, but there is a strong contingent of conservative students who do find a voice on campus amongst all the Yale Dems activities. When it comes to clothing, Elis know how to dress well, as befitting the New England private school stereotype, but while it's not uncommon to see guys wearing button-downs and slacks to class, sweatpants are accepted as well. Yalies are perceived as being predominantly middle-class, students said, and approximately 56 percent of the student body receives some form of financial aid. The campus is racially and ethnically diverse, and student organizations dedicated to celebrating unique cultural heritages are prominent fixtures on campus. A sizeable 10 percent of the student body hails from outside the United States, but the rest "come from New York or California, and not often in between." The openly gay community at Yale—which is often labeled the "gay Ivy"—is a testament to the high level of acceptance on campus; a gay junior remarked that "You can't really be openly prejudiced or comfortably prejudiced here because you just won't fit in." Moreover, a senior in Branford explained that labels do not have to be all-encompassing: "It's okay to be gay and not to be defined by being gay here."

Out in the Elm City

When they arrive on campus, Yalies immediately face the question of how the University integrates with the surrounding city. While New Haven still retains some of its reputation for crime and racial tension, the city is on the upswing, having undergone major efforts at revitalization over the past two decades. One area near campus that students mentioned as indicative of how the city is changing is Ninth Square, located a few blocks from campus. Formerly a district of abandoned storefronts, Ninth Square has been overhauled by a city commission. Several restaurants, including

Indian, French bistro and Malaysian cuisine, have opened in the area. Older standbys near campus include Yorkside, a multitude of Thai restaurants and "the burrito cart" for meals, while Rudy's, Hot Tomato's, and Viva's are popular nighttime stops.

But even as new businesses multiply close to campus, students still point out the University's problems integrating with the New Haven community. Occasional incidents of crime on campus, usually muggings, have students conscious of taking big-city precautions, such as not walking alone at night. One student remarked, "I think people feel safe but also realize they need to be responsible and aware." Some panhandlers are such fixtures that they have acquired quasi-affectionate monikers, such as the "Flower Lady" and the "Shakespeare Lady." The surrounding area does provide myriad opportunities for community involvement, including tutoring and canvassing for local political candidates. Furthermore, all the excitement of New York City is less than two hours away by train.

Quirky or Cultish? You Decide.

It's hard to go wrong with 277 registered undergraduate organizations. There are the campus favorites, such as political groups, publications, cultural groups, community service organizations, and a cappella groups. And then there are the quirkier niche groups, such as the Society for the Exploration of Campus Secrets, whose members sneak around campus looking for access to hidden Yale locales, and the Anti-Gravity Society, which draws the school's jugglers. The Yale College Council provides opportunity for student government involvement. Some of the organizations, including the Yale Political Union, the *Yale Daily News*, and a cappella groups, have reputations for being "cultish," but students will tell you that most undergraduates are very committed to their extracurricular activities. A good number of students have jobs as well, mostly on campus.

Except at the epic Harvard-Yale football game every November, school athletic pride doesn't surface very often. Few undergraduates regularly attend sporting events, even though the rowing and sailing teams are of international caliber, and the football team has performed well in the Ivy League recently. Furthermore, the Bulldogs' home, the Yale Bowl, holds more than 64,000 spectators, and Payne Whitney Gymnasium is the second-largest gym in the world. The Harvard-Yale game is almost better known for its tailgating, alumni reunions and pranks pulled by each school than for the football game itself.

> "People aren't afraid to admit that they're really passionate about a subject."

The Harvard-Yale rivalry certainly encompasses athletics, but it also extends into good-natured competition over which student body enjoys better quality of life, which school is ranked higher in a particular year, and other quibbles. While the jury is still out on a scientific conclusion, the emphatic Yale refrain persists: "Harvard sucks!"

And a unique Yale pride does follow students not only through their four "bright college years" in New Haven (as the school song goes), but into their later years as well, through the alumni community. While a junior affirmed, "I think there are more spectacular, friendly, and interesting people here than I thought possible," a sophomore happily pointed out that "Students didn't choose Yale to get a 4.0—they chose it because it's a genuinely intellectual place to be." Even as Yale looks to the future—for example, through globalization initiatives that connect the University intimately to China—it manages to retain an atmosphere of tradition, both in academics and fun. Any undergraduate studying grand strategy with the bells of Harkness Tower playing Britney Spears in the background can tell you that.—*Kimberly Chow*

FYI

If you come to Yale, you'd better bring "a coffeemaker and a big mug to go with it!"

What's the typical weekend schedule? "On Thursday night, go to a bar like Rudy's; try to get errands done during the day on Friday, then go out to a play, room party, organization-sponsored dance party, a cappella concert, improv show, or some combination thereof on Friday and Saturday nights; go to a late brunch and cram in as much studying as possible on Sunday, and go to bed too late."

If I could change one thing about Yale, I'd "work on the sometimes tense relationship between Yale and the city of New Haven."

Two things every college student at Yale should do before graduating are "climb Harkness Tower and go to a naked party."

Delaware

University of Delaware

Address: 116 Hullihen Hall Newark, DE 19716-6210
Phone: 302-831-8123
E-mail address: admissions@udel.edu
Web site URL: www.udel.edu
Year Founded: 1743
Private or Public: Public
Religious Affiliation: None
Location: Suburban
Number of Applicants: 21,930
Percent Accepted: 47%
Percent Accepted who enroll: 31%
Number Entering: 3,202
Number of Transfers Accepted each Year: 802
Middle 50% SAT range: M: 560–660, CR: 540–640, Wr: 540–650
Middle 50% ACT range: 23–28
Early admission program EA/ED/None: None

Percentage accepted through EA or ED: NA
EA and ED deadline: NA
Regular Deadline: 15-Jan
Application Fee: $60
Full time Undergraduate enrollment: 15,211
Total enrollment: 18,616
Percent Male: 39%
Percent Female: 61%
Total Percent Minority or Unreported: 17%
Percent African-American: 5%
Percent Asian/Pacific Islander: 4%
Percent Hispanic: 4%
Percent Native-American: <1%
Percent International: <1%
Percent in-state/out of state: 40%/60%
Percent from Public HS: 80%
Retention Rate: 90%
Graduation Rate 4-year: 67%

Graduation Rate 6-year: 77%
Percent Undergraduates in On-campus housing: 93%
Number of official organized extracurricular organizations: 200
3 Most popular majors: Biology, Education, Psychology
Student/Faculty ratio: 12:1
Average Class Size: 10 to 19
Percent of students going to grad school: 55%
Tuition and Fees: $21,126
In State Tuition and Fees if different: $8,646
Cost for Room and Board: $8,478
Percent receiving financial aid out of those who apply, first year: 42%
Percent receiving financial aid among all students: 55%

A t once known for its party scene and its academic rigor, the University of Delaware provides the proverbial balance of work and play. With abounding extracurricular options and a welcoming, involved student body, UDel students can quickly find their niche and create their own unique college experience.

Personal Attention and Flexibility at a Large School

Despite the size of the school, with 15,000 undergraduates, students said, "UDel is big, but not too large to get lost." Students say there is no need to worry about a lack of personal attention. As one freshman stated, "I was really surprised by how friendly and welcoming the upperclassmen are to us freshmen, and even the teachers are really available and eager to talk whenever." Stu-

dents agree they never have a problem getting extra help when they need it.

Another benefit of the size of the school is the range of choice and flexibility students have in their courses. As might be expected, some majors, especially the chemical engineering, biology and nursing programs, have more difficult requirements to fulfill than others do, and, as a result, course loads do vary greatly from student to student. But the consensus among students is that UDel's requirements leave them with enough flexibility in their schedules so that "As long as you pick your classes well, you'll find a load you can deal with." Students also have the core curriculum in common, though students are able to place out of some of the requirements through advanced high school courses.

UDel offers 125 majors and 75 minors—enough options to give students the ability to study exactly what they want. Many students choose to have a minor in addition to their major. The University features a prominent agriculture department, whose full-fledged farm is accessible to students of all majors. And if that is not enough, there is a special Dean's Scholar Program that allows especially motivated students to essentially design their own major and undergraduate program. There is also the Honors College at UDel, to which students may be admitted when they are accepted to the university, offering smaller class size, more student-faculty interaction and personal attention and even special dorms.

Work Hard . . .

When asked about what made UDel stand out from other schools, an undergraduate offered, "It's the classic football-frats-parties college, but has a great academic foundation as well." UDel is notorious for its intense party scene on top of its intense academic programs. With such a lively social atmosphere around them, students said, "It can be easy to let yourself start struggling if you don't keep up with the work."

"It's the classic football-frats-parties college, but has a great academic foundation as well."

A distinctive feature of UDel is its academic calendar. The Winter Session, a two-month break from mid-December to mid-February, was designed to give students the option of studying abroad for a semester during the winter. During that time, students who do not go abroad or choose to stay on campus to take additional courses are able to go home and relax for a long winter break.

. . . And Party Hard

While UDel is known for its parties and the dominance of drinking and Greek life in the social lives of students, many students agreed with one student who noted, "Yeah, it's a party school, but only if you want it to be." It is easy to find and join parties, many of which are the typical frat parties where alcohol abounds. The University is very strict, however, regarding alcohol abuse among its undergraduates on campus. Its rules include a "three-strikes-and-you're-out" policy for alcohol violations in the dorms. As a result, parties are usually taken

off-campus and away from possible crack-downs by the University.

There are also always many dry events for students who choose not to drink. The student social committee organizes a variety of events, from weekend movies and concerts to having prominent speakers on campus. One student said about UDel, "It offers all of the opportunities for you to choose exactly what you want from your college life." During the 2008 presidential election, for example, 7,000 undergraduates flocked to see vice presidential candidate and UDel alumnus Joe Biden and his wife speak at a campaign rally on campus.

Abundant Extracurricular Options

UDel students can frequently be found cheering on their school's 23 varsity sports teams, including the successful Fightin' Blue Hens football team. The UDel football team, 2003 NCAA Division I National Champions and the runners-up in 2007, has a huge following at UDel, and the games and tail-gates are a classic part of the undergraduate experience there. Thousands of students show up at every game to support the team, and games against rival Villanova draw an attendance of over 20,000 every year.

With 200 student organizations on campus, as one student remarked, "You're a fool to not get involved. There are so many options available and everyone is so welcoming." The "Hen Zone" in the Perkins Student Center is a gathering place for students of all skill levels to play a round of billiards, ping-pong, air hockey or foosball. Many UDel students are involved in sports, and there are always many activities going on around campus: a freshman aptly summarized, "Whatever you want, someone is probably doing it."

Campus Living

While many students complain about the living situation at UDel, one student remarked, "It's not a five-star hotel, but I have no complaints." Taking into consideration that there is only so much one can expect from a college dorm, another student said, the dorms are "a little on the small side, but very functional." While over 90 percent of students do stay in on-campus housing, it is fairly easy to find off-campus housing. The University also helps students to find good housing, including a Web site where students can post ads or search for local apartments.

When it comes to the food, a freshman said, "The dining halls get old fast. You learn quickly which dining halls are better. For dining halls, they're good, but get a meal plan with more points and less meals." Most students seemed to agree with going with more of UD's points when selecting a mandatory meal plan, which can be used towards purchases at any dining retail location on campus. While many students complain about the food at UDel, there is such a wide array of food on and around campus that it is difficult to not find something, though it usually is slightly more expensive than dining hall food.

Diversity?

As a state university, UDel attracts students mainly from Delaware and the states surrounding it—namely Maryland, Pennsylvania, New Jersey and New York. In terms of diversity, students expressed that UDel is a bit lacking in both geographic and ethnic diversity. "Not everyone at UDel is white, but some groups are definitely poorly represented," one student said. She added, "I would say half of my dorm is white, with more African-Americans and Hispanics than Asians or other minorities." Despite the relatively small minority population at UDel, student cultural groups like the Chinese Cultural Student Association (CCSA) often host events like the Lunar New Year Celebration that magnify the presence of minorities on campus.

In terms of campus safety, students agreed that there is really nothing to be scared of around UDel's suburban campus. Crimes are rare and "I feel very safe on campus, no matter what the time," a freshman said. Overall, students not only feel safe, but happily at home and welcome at UDel. With so much going on and seemingly endless opportunities for students to get involved on campus, students insist that it is nearly impossible to stay bored for long at UDel.—*Michelle Yu*

FYI

If you come to UDel, you'd better bring "your UDel gear for football games and maybe rain boots."

What is the typical weekend schedule? "Parties, movies, sleep. Whatever you want, someone is probably doing it."

If I could change one thing about UDel, I'd "make classes later. Everyone I know has an 8 a.m. class."

Three things every student at UDel should do before graduating are "eat at Grotto Pizza, go to the farm, and, of course, go to a football game. Also, take advantage of the great concert opportunities."

District of Columbia

American University

Address: 4400 Massachusetts Avenue NW Washington, DC 20016-8001
Phone: 202-885-6000
E-mail address: admissions@american.edu
Web site URL: www.american.edu
Year Founded: 1893
Private or Public: Private
Religious Affiliation: Methodist
Location: Urban
Number of Applicants: 15,847
Percent Accepted: 53%
Percent Accepted who enroll: 15%
Number Entering: 1,284
Number of Transfers Accepted each Year: 910
Middle 50% SAT range: M: 580–670, CR: 590–690, Wr: 580–690
Middle 50% ACT range: 25–30

Early admission program EA/ED/None: ED
Percentage accepted through EA or ED: 55%
EA and ED deadline: 15-Nov
Regular Deadline: 15-Jan
Application Fee: $45
Full time Undergraduate enrollment: 6,042
Total enrollment: 9,967
Percent Male: 37%
Percent Female: 63%
Total Percent Minority or Unreported: 37%
Percent African-American: 5%
Percent Asian/Pacific Islander: 5%
Percent Hispanic: 5%
Percent Native-American: <1%
Percent International: 6%
Percent in-state/out of state: 21%/79%
Percent from Public HS: Unreported

Retention Rate: 86%
Graduation Rate 4-year: 62%
Graduation Rate 6-year: 69%
Percent Undergraduates in On-campus housing: 75%
Number of official organized extracurricular organizations: 180
3 Most popular majors: Business, International Relations, Communications
Student/Faculty ratio: 14:1
Average Class Size: 15
Percent of students going to grad school: Unreported
Tuition and Fees: $33,283
In State Tuition and Fees if different: No difference
Cost for Room and Board: $12,418
Percent receiving financial aid out of those who apply, first year: 61%
Percent receiving financial aid among all students: 69%

When President George Washington first conceived of a "national university" in the national capital, never did he dream that it would become as prestigious as American University is today. Occupying 84 acres of Ward Circle in Northwest Washington D.C., AU provides students with an intimate yet highly academic experience. Its proximity to downtown Washington D.C. and its connections to the unlimited opportunities the city provides allows each AU student to be exposed to a vibrant and cosmopolitan environment.

Small Setting, Varied Experience

When asked about academics at AU, many students reply that classes vary in difficulty and workload. "You have to work hard in some classes, in others, barely even open a book," notes one student. All AU students are required to fulfill the General Education (GenEd) requirements, which introduce students to five innovative curricular areas: The Creative Arts, Traditions that Shape the Western World, Global and Multicultural Perspectives, Social Institutions and Behavior, and the Natural Sciences. Although some students complain that the total of 30 GenEd credit hours is "too intense," others find it a good way to discover true passions and majors and minors that they had not considered before.

The university is made up of six different schools: College of Arts and Sciences, Kogod School of Business, School of Communication, School of International Service, School of Public Affairs, and Washington College of Law. All schools except the Washington College of Law are open to undergraduate students, the most popular being the College of Arts and Sciences. The Kogod School of Business's Business Administration program is considered one of the top business schools in the country and it houses twice as many undergraduates as graduates.

Personal attention is a key concept at AU and is reflected by its limited number of lecture classes. Most classes are small, discussion-based seminars. "I love the smaller class size because it means that I truly get to know my professors and feel connected with the subject," says one student. Other students have commented that the smaller class size allows a sense of camaraderie to develop between classes, particularly between students with the same majors. "People seem to genuinely want to help each other," notes another student. "Nobody is really cut-throat."

> "People seem to genuinely want to help each other. Nobody is really cut-throat."

Students state that what often makes or breaks classes at AU are the professors. AU has a very notable faculty, including former U.S. senators, Nobel Prize winners, and a former reporter for the *Los Angeles Times*. Despite their high caliber, students laud most of their professors for being "friendly," "approachable," and "willing to go out of their way to make sure you understand something."

Are you a Northsider or a Southsider?

When asked to describe AU in one word, students often say "diverse." Culturally, AU houses students from over 130 countries and has affiliated campuses on most continents around the world. Promoting interna-tional understanding is one of AU's main objectives. A significant portion of students choose a summer internship or a semester abroad program out of the 112 that are offered during their four years at American.

Students comment that AU is also socially diverse. There are two large groups at AU: the "Northsiders" and the "Southsiders." The distinction is not only defined by the physical location on campus but also by the social activities of its denizens. As one student puts it, "Northside is quieter and studious, boring to some; Southside is more outgoing and socially oriented, way too crazy for others. AU has people on both extremes and everyone in between."

One thing common among these groups is the commitment and awareness to political and service activities. 57% of AU undergraduate students participate in significant community service and many participate in campus groups such as the Society of Professional Journalists, College Democrats, and Eco-Sense. It was also recently ranked number 7 on the Peace Corps' annual ranking of top participating colleges and universities.

Thursday, Friday, Saturday

Because many students don't have Friday classes, Thursdays mark the beginning of partying at AU. The weekend commences by "going to see a movie" and "dorm-storming" in friends' rooms. Fridays are spent studying then going out to one of the clubs or lounges in the D.C. downtown area. Students find the social and nightlife of D.C. one of the biggest advantages of AU, offsetting the fact that the campus is technically dry. However, one student notes that, "If you want to drink, you're going to find it."

Saturday nights are often spent at events hosted by fraternities and sororities off campus. AU has 11 fraternities and 13 sororities, and they seem to lead a majority of the social scene. "Greek life is huge," admits one student, "Granted, I am in a sorority, so I'm biased. But you have much better connections to getting to parties and because [AU] is so small, those connections are imperative."

AU also has many other social events that students look forward to. Musical and theatrical performances are regular events, as are nation-wide conferences and rallies held by various student groups. The school hosts big concerts on campus once or twice a year and past performers have included Ben Folds and Snow Patrol. Although not an official event hosted by the school, "Welcome Week," the week preceding the year's first classes, is also popular. "So much fun with parties thrown by organizations every night!" exclaims one student.

15 Rooms for Improvement

Residential life on AU campus is "not great, but definitely not bad" says one student. The cafeteria food is known for its great variety—able to satisfy the most outlandish cravings. Everything on campus takes meal swipe cards or Eaglebucks (money put on a school account that can be spent at cafeterias or off campus).

The dorm rooms are modern and floors are often divided into interest groups, honors groups, or majors groups. Resident Assistants (RAs) are assigned to students and most students consider them to be "pretty chill," and "just like another person living on the floor." Some RAs do enforce rules strictly but in most cases, students who are caught drinking or using drugs are sent to early morning classes—only in very rare cases are students suspended from dorms.

In order to address the qualms that students have about AU life and in order to improve AU as an undergraduate centered institution, the university in 2001 established its 15 Points Strategy. Some of the points that the university has come up with include more fundraising efforts to increase its endowment, the implementation of a highly selective interdisciplinary program called University College for freshmen and sophomores, and to increase its reach and operations abroad. Steady steps have been made for the university to reach these 15 goals and there is no doubt that student life in all aspects will see vast changes in the near future.—*Lee Komeda*

FYI

If you come to American, you'd better bring "excitement to see the monuments."

What is the typical weekend schedule? "Hit up many of the bars around the Washington, D.C., area, take advantage of special lectures at the school, and Sunday is work, work, work."

If I could change one thing about American, it would be to "allow for a more community atmosphere."

Three things every student at American should do before graduating are "go see the monuments and museums, watch the fireworks on the mall, attend a protest on campus."

Catholic University of America

Address: Cardinal Station
Washington, D.C. 20064
Phone: 202-319-5305
E-mail address:
cua-admissions@cua.edu
Web site URL: www.cua.edu
Year Founded: 1887
Private or Public: Private
Religious Affiliation: Roman
Catholic
Location: Urban
Number of Applicants: 5,180
Percent Accepted: 81.1%
**Percent Accepted who
enroll:** 22%
Number Entering: 901
**Number of Transfers
Accepted each Year:** 202
Middle 50% SAT range:
M: 500–610, CR:
510–610, Wr: Unreported
Middle 50% ACT range: 21–27
**Early admission program
EA/ED/None:** EA
**Percentage accepted
through EA or ED:**
Unreported

EA and ED deadline:
15-Nov
Regular Deadline: 15-Feb
Application Fee: $55
**Full time Undergraduate
enrollment:** 3,326
Total enrollment: 5,470
Percent Male: 46%
Percent Female: 55%
**Total Percent Minority or
Unreported:** 14%
Percent African-American:
5%
**Percent Asian/Pacific
Islander:** 3%
Percent Hispanic: 7%
Percent Native-American:
<1%
Percent International:
3%
**Percent in-state/out of
state:** 1%/99%
Percent from Public HS:
Unreported
Retention Rate: 82%
Graduation Rate 4-year:
Unreported

Graduation Rate 6-year:
Unreported
**Percent Undergraduates
in On-campus housing:**
68%
**Number of official organized
extracurricular
organizations:** 100
3 Most popular majors:
Architecture, Nursing,
Political Science
Student/Faculty ratio: 11:1
Average Class Size:
Unreported
**Percent of students going to
grad school:** Unreported
Tuition and Fees: $30,670
**In State Tuition and Fees if
different:** No difference
Cost for Room and Board:
$11,320
**Percent receiving financial
aid out of those who apply,
first year:** 91%
**Percent receiving financial
aid among all students:**
88%

D on't let the name scare you! Although CUA is a Roman Catholic institution, not everyone goes to church all the time (or at all, for that matter). Most students are "Catholics from New England, Philly and New Jersey," but people of all faiths are not only tolerated but are also encouraged to come. With D.C. as its playground, CUA is a great place to be a student: "You have no reason to be bored!" one senior said.

Not Just for Catholics

Students at CUA are required to complete a number of core courses, including "Intro to Religion," but most people don't mind it. There is a wide variety of difficulty in the course work offered at CUA, ranging from the easier political science major (after all, you are right at the heart of the American political process) to the more challenging engineering and architecture majors that students say "really set CUA apart from other universities." There is also a one-year master's program in engineering for stu-

dents who completed their undergraduate work at CUA. Students interested in social work should also take note of the opportunities CUA affords in that area—a field placement class takes you outside the classroom and puts you in a social work agency for 16 hours a week. Talk about a hands-on experience! Drama is a popular major at CUA, and the Drama School (for graduate work) is a very well-respected part of the institution. For those with a more scientific mind, the School of Nursing at CUA is an excellent school, consistently ranked in the top 10 nursing schools in the country.

Some of the best classes for undergrads are Dynamics of Christian Spirituality, World Religions, Introduction to Peace Studies, and Greek Literature in Translation. For the students not looking to work too hard there are easier classes (like Social Work 101, Anthropology, or Astronomy) but there are definitely opportunities for CUA kids to challenge themselves. Difficult courses like Fluid Dynamics make people work for their grades more than other classes. Students say that grading "depends on the professor, but it's usually fair." The workload at CUA definitely depends on the student, but many kids work and play sports while still taking a full (or more than full) course-load.

Studying at CUA is a must, and there are plenty of places to work. Some students prefer to stay in the city after work at an off-campus job, working in coffeeshops around D.C., while others enjoy the quiet rooms of Mullen, the main library. If you can't find your books there, have no fear: CUA is a member of the Washington Research Library Consortium, which also includes Howard, George Washington and American universities. "Pretty much any research material you need, you can find." Furthermore, the largest library in the United States, the Library of Congress, is only a few metro stops away from campus.

Gotta Eat Somewhere . . . Just Not on Campus!

Living arrangements at CUA make other universities look like they came from the Stone Age. Incoming freshmen can look forward to two of the greatest luxuries offered on a college campus—air-conditioning and cable. Furthermore, CUA provides a number of different housing choices for students. The University offers suite-style dorms, apartments, singles, and even trailers (yes, trailers—but only during renovation). There are also typical dorms where students share a bathroom down the hall from their rooms. All of the different styles of living "makes for a great change of pace over the four years," students say. And don't let the seemingly strict administration fool you—CUA kids know how to have a good time, even on campus.

As for food on campus, students at CUA (like at most schools) say it's not worth the money they're paying for it. One senior however, said: "There has been a huge improvement over the four years I've been here. Since our new student center opened up, the dining halls have better hours and more options." There are not always choices available to vegetarian students, and some believe the University could "cater to the more health-conscious eaters better." Students describe food prices on campus as "ridiculous," but there are always other options. Fortunately CUA is so close to downtown D.C. that you can find "any kind of food you want within 10 to 25 minutes . . . ANY kind of food."

Such proximity to a major city might make some parents nervous about their student's safety, but a modern blue-light system coupled with regularly patrolling police make students feel safe. "I've never been scared and walk alone at night without worrying," one girl said. Common sense does, however, always pay off. "I would never walk off campus in the neighborhood alone at night, though." Smart advice for just about anywhere.

It's a Party in the City

"My favorite part of CUA is the student body: they know how to party and have fun, but also how to deal with life!" Despite a reportedly "very closed-minded" administration that "cares more about the 'image' of the school than meeting students' needs," CUA is a great place to spend four years. Located right in the District of Columbia, students take full advantage of city life. There are endless numbers of museums and national monuments to visit in the city, not to mention the exciting social life an urban center provides. Although the school policy is "strict about citing underage drinkers" (there are no kegs allowed), one student pointed out that "It's a big campus." Since the school has its own Metro stop—and D.C. has an extremely well-run public transportation network—students tend to go out in the city rather than on campus. Bars dominate the social scene on party nights (generally Thursday through Saturday). Fado Irish Pub has "a great local band" on Thursdays, and Brooks and Johnny K's are popular bars for the freshmen to check out. Fortunately, drinking isn't the only thing to do around D.C. "Because we have a big Catholic identity going on, there are actually quite a number of people who don't drink at all," one student notes.

> "Because we have a big Catholic identity going on, there are actually quite a number of people who don't drink at all."

Though there isn't a significant Greek presence on campus, students "find their niche pretty easily." People at CUA love that the school is small and say that everyone is "really close," "approachable" and "friendly." One thing that incoming students should definitely know, however, is that CUA is not a place where aspiring athletes thrive. "Don't come here if you want basketball or football games to be the highlight of your weekend," says one student. CUA is a Division III school, but school pride doesn't center on athletics. There are workout facilities for health-conscious students, including a new fitness center for non-athletes. "It has great equipment, but not enough to keep up with the demand on peak-use hours," one student said.

Student life at CUA is busy—many upperclassmen get internships in the city, and student organizations are large. The Campus Ministry "has a lot to offer to one's faith life, including mass, adoration, community service, prayer groups and more," one female student said. Drama is also a popular activity for the student body. With a prestigious Drama School at the University, it's no surprise that CUA attracts aspiring actors and actresses. There are also club sports teams (including Ultimate Frisbee, soccer, and crew) and a Division I rugby team that routinely performs well. All in all there is really something for everyone at CUA. Let's not forget, of course, student-run political groups that attract students from both ends of the spectrum. What else would you expect from a school in D.C.?—*Emily Cleveland*

FYI

If you come to Catholic, you'd better bring "a passion for politics."

What is the typical weekend schedule? "Friday: go clubbing in D.C.; Saturday: spend time with friends and party at night; Sunday: go to church and study."

If I could change one thing about Catholic, I'd "make the administration better at dealing with financial issues."

Three things every student at Catholic should do before graduating are "spend a late night at Johnny K's, walk around the monuments at night, and go to a protest."

George Washington University

Address: 2121 I Street NW, Suite 201 Washington, D.C. 20052

Phone: 202-994-6040

E-mail address: gwadm@gwu.edu

Web site URL: www.gwu.edu

Year Founded: 1821

Private or Public: Private

Religious Affiliation: None

Location: Urban

Number of Applicants: 19,606

Percent Accepted: 37%

Percent Accepted who enroll: 30%

Number Entering: 2,123

Number of Transfers Accepted each Year: 980

Middle 50% SAT range: M: 600–690, CR: 600–690, Wr: 600–690

Middle 50% ACT range: 26–29

Early admission program EA/ED/None: ED

Percentage accepted through EA or ED: Unreported

EA and ED deadline: 10-Nov

Regular Deadline: 10-Jan

Application Fee: $65

Full time Undergraduate enrollment: 10,701

Total enrollment: 22,710

Percent Male: 45%

Percent Female: 55%

Total Percent Minority or Unreported: 40%

Percent African-American: 7%

Percent Asian/Pacific Islander: 10%

Percent Hispanic: 6%

Percent Native-American: <1%

Percent International: 5%

Percent in-state/out of state: 2%/98%

Percent from Public HS: 70%

Retention Rate: 90%

Graduation Rate 4-year: 72%

Graduation Rate 6-year: 77%

Percent Undergraduates in On-campus housing: 64%

Number of official organized extracurricular organizations: 220

3 Most popular majors: Social Sciences, Business, Psychology

Student/Faculty ratio: 13:1

Average Class Size: 10 to 19

Percent of students going to grad school: 20%

Tuition and Fees: $40,437

In State Tuition and Fees if different: No difference

Cost for Room and Board: $9,920

Percent receiving financial aid out of those who apply, first year: 74%

Percent receiving financial aid among all students: 37%

Going to school in the nation's capital certainly has its advantages. Just a few blocks from the White House, and a mere Metro ride from the National Archives and Capitol Hill, the GW campus is a hub of activity for its students. At GW, lazy afternoons easily turn into historical and political adventures, and even an early morning run has the unique appeal of boasting the Washington Monument and the Jefferson Memorial as backdrops. The Supreme Court is nearby, as is Embassy Row and the Smithsonian Museums. In fact, it's possible to spend four years at GW and not have enough time to explore all of the many options available. Located in the nation's political center and one of the world's most beautiful cities, George Washington University stands out for the opportunities it gives students for learning both inside and beyond the classroom. Whether you're a politics buff or not, it's certainly an exciting place to be.

One Part Academia, One Part Politics

George Washington University is comprised of six individual schools, each with its own requirements, to which aspiring freshmen apply directly: The Columbian College of Arts and Sciences, The School of Media and Public Affairs, The School of Business, The School of Public Health and Health Services, The Elliot School of International Affairs, and the School of Engineering and Applied Science. Although the six schools may seem to have a narrow focus, each student must fulfill general liberal arts requirements, and students are permitted and encouraged to take classes outside of their specific school. (Students warn, however, that it is important to be on top of your own classes and requirements, because it is surprisingly easy to "fall through the cracks" here.) In addition, GW offers a number of specialized programs including an eight-year Integrated Engineering/M.D. program, a seven-year B.A./M.D. program, and an Integrated Engineering and Law Program. The University Honors Program is a smaller, more selective college within the university that allows students a four-year, multidisciplinary, interschool undergraduate experience. Acceptance to the Honors Programs is also sweetened with a significant merit-based scholarship.

The GW faculty and classes receive solid reviews, though students are careful to warn that "It really varies based on your school, major, and professor." Most students are "happy with the accessibility of the faculty and the quality of the teaching," though students emphasize the need for their peers to make the effort to engage their professors. The workload is described as "pretty average" by most students, with some emphasizing the rigor of first-year/introductory classes. "They try to weed you out," one senior remarked. Grades are "fairly accurate," and there isn't too much "grading on a curve." Double majoring is fairly common, and not too difficult. Class sizes vary, with introductory lectures being the largest. Other classes are usually smaller, with an average of 20 to 50 students. Small discussion groups led by TAs are a popular way to master the material discussed in larger lectures.

Because of GW's central location, academics tend to go hand-in-hand with taking advantage of the opportunities available in Washington, D.C. Many students are able to intern and work during the school year, with government agencies being a popular job option. "Getting an internship or a job in government or politics may be easier during the school year," one student noted, "because fewer students are here than in the summer, when tons of undergrads want to work and live in D.C." Other advantages of GW's location include the fact that professors will frequently bring notable speakers and politicians in to speak to their classes, and field trips to museums and other attractions are often part of coursework.

A World of Social Possibilities

"Because we're in a city, people spread out a lot on weekends," said one senior. Many students head to bars or dance clubs in D.C., and while they complain about the cover charges, they generally agree that there's little to do on campus at night. "Sometimes freshmen party on campus," said one sophomore. "But as you get older, I think the bars and clubs are more of a draw. You can't really come to GW without a fake ID." That said, partying on campus can be difficult—there is officially no alcohol allowed in campus housing if you are under 21, and students caught three times with alcohol are forced to relinquish their campus housing. Any student found with an illegal substance must move off-campus at the first strike. Community Facilitators (CFs) are GW's answer to residential advisers, and while many students reported "becoming friends with" their CFs, Community Facilitators are more than willing to write up students on alcohol charges when necessary. Despite this, drinking seems to be a large part of social life at GW. Upperclassmen gravitate toward the bars in Adams Morgan, a notoriously fun part of the city, and bars closer to home, like McFadden's on New Hampshire Ave. The meal plan, called GWorld, can be used at certain local restaurants, which students reported to be a nice feature of GW dining. Students generally say that the meal plan is "good, though nothing to brag about," and are likely to dine out on the weekends, noting the restaurants on Georgetown's M Street and in Dupont Circle as particularly good options.

Drinking may be a big part of social life at GW, but fraternities and sororities are not. Greek life is an option for students that are interested, but many GWers think it unnecessary and a hindrance to enjoying all that Washington, D.C. has to offer. While students report that their peers are "pretty friendly," they also acknowledge that "The university isn't particularly helpful in helping people meet each other." Overall, being in such a great city provides a lot of opportunity, but also causes GW to lack a sense of community spirit. Most students meet their friends through their majors or extracurricular activities, even though few people feel defined by these groups. The administration attempts to foster a greater sense of community spirit by hosting events like Fall Fest and Spring Fest, and increasing the number of formal balls.

Students at GW think of themselves as "fit," and most take part in intramurals and take advantage of the beautiful Washington scenery by frequently running around the city. Many athletic teams are in the Atlantic 10 Conference as well as NCAA Division I. Students tend to show their (limited) school spirit by attending basketball games, as basketball is by far "the most popular sport on campus." Extracurricular activities are also popular, and most students get involved in at least one organization. "There are tons of options," said one student, "especially in the realm of political and cultural organizations." Students take advantage of their surroundings by joining clubs that take them to the National Gallery of Art and the Capitol, among other locales. Students tend not to feel categorized by the clubs they join, and enjoy the fact that "It always seems like you can meet someone new."

Location, Location, Location

The location of the George Washington University is its greatest draw to students, although particular departments are also very attractive. The main Foggy Bottom Campus (there is a smaller campus called Mount Vernon) is composed of four-by-four square city blocks. "It is definitely an urban, city campus," said one student, "and it is often hard to tell if someone you pass is a GW student or a government employee." While students complain about a lack of grassy space, they are always quick to realize how lucky they are to live in such a beautiful and vibrant city. Students generally feel very safe on campus, though "Of course, we're in a major city, so you have to be careful." Security measures have been increased with the threat of terrorism in recent years, and most students seem to feel that the school is doing all it can to protect their well-being.

> "It is often hard to tell if someone you pass is a GW student or a government employee."

Freshmen and sophomores are required to live on campus, and freshmen are usually split between Thurston (affectionately called "the tenements" by residents) and about four other dorms. Thurston is the largest freshman dorm on campus, and like all on-campus locations, offers apartment-style or suite living (some have kitchens, some do not). Juniors and seniors are not guaranteed on-campus housing, and may take their chances in a lottery that works on the basis of seniority. Mitchell Hall is one of the most sought after, offering attractive living conditions: all single dorms and a veranda. Many upperclassmen opt for apartments in the city (which are "SO EXPENSIVE!" warns one student) and some choose to live in the suburbs of Maryland or Virginia. For others, sorority and fraternity houses are the way to go.

The Marvin Center—the school's student union—is largely regarded as the center of campus life. The Marvin Center houses the headquarters and offices of student organizations, as well as a few fast-food and chain restaurants. Meals can be eaten in the Marvin Center or in standard dining halls, where food is described as "good but unhealthy." The center is a hub for students, a place where "Lots of kids hang out, do their work, and get meals." The center also houses a grocery store and travel agency. The Marvin Center is considered a great convenience, especially for freshmen who don't yet know their way around the city. "If you need something, chances are you can get it there."

Official school statistics show a geographically and racially diverse student population, but students tend to think the school is too dominated by the wealthy. Students complain that people at GW are ostentatious about their wealth. "People here are well-off, and they let you know it." While there are definitely stereotypes about well-dressed, BMW-driving students, others claim that it really depends on where you choose to hang

out, and with whom. "A stereotype is just that," said one articulate senior, "it underrepresents the variety of student 'types' on campus."

With a prime location in the hub of the political world, George Washington University provides an education in academics, politics, and real-life, city living. With so much to see, do, and learn, students are more than happy with their choice to come here. "I love GW," said one senior, "and I don't know many people who feel otherwise."—*Erica Ross*

FYI

If you come to GW, you'd better bring "a coffee mug for the Starbucks on every corner in D.C.!"
What is the typical weekend schedule? "Wake up late, do some work, go out all night, and wake up late again the next day!"
If I could change one thing about GW, I'd "make the administration more accessible to students."
Three things every student at GW should do before graduating are "go to the monuments at night, get a Manuche dog, and party in Georgetown."

Georgetown University

Address: 37th and O Streets, NW Washington, D.C. 20057-1270
Phone: 202-687-0100
E-mail address: guadmiss@georgetown.edu
Web site URL: www.georgetown.edu
Year Founded: 1789
Private or Public: Private
Religious Affiliation: Jesuit
Location: Urban
Number of Applicants: 16,163
Percent Accepted: 21%
Percent Accepted who enroll: 47%
Number Entering: 1,579
Number of Transfers Accepted each Year: 368
Middle 50% SAT range: M: 650–740, CR: 650–750, Wr: Unreported
Middle 50% ACT range: Unreported

Early admission program EA/ED/None: EA
Percentage accepted through EA or ED: 8%
EA and ED deadline: 1-Nov
Regular Deadline: 15-Dec
Application Fee: $65
Full time Undergraduate enrollment: 7,038
Total enrollment: 11,979
Percent Male: 45%
Percent Female: 55%
Total Percent Minority or Unreported: 30%
Percent African-American: 7%
Percent Asian/Pacific Islander: 11%
Percent Hispanic: 5%
Percent Native-American: <1%
Percent International: 8%
Percent in-state/out of state: 2%/98%
Percent from Public HS: 49%
Retention Rate: 96%

Graduation Rate 4-year: 90%
Graduation Rate 6-year: 92%
Percent Undergraduates in On-campus housing: 71%
Number of official organized extracurricular organizations: 103
3 Most popular majors: English, International Relations, Politic Science and Government
Student/Faculty ratio: 11:1
Average Class Size: 26
Percent of students going to grad school: 31%
Tuition and Fees: $37,947
In State Tuition and Fees if different: No difference
Cost for Room and Board: $12,753
Percent receiving financial aid out of those who apply, first year: 72%
Percent receiving financial aid among all students: 40%

Nestled in a distinct residential neighborhood of Washington, D.C., Georgetown University encompasses the charms of both city and suburban life. Yet, given its tremendous wealth of resources, dynamic population, and sometimes-controversial stances, the political noise generated on this campus makes for a college experience that is by no means pastoral.

Friendly Internal Rivalries

The undergraduate experience at Georgetown is markedly diverse, with four primary schools: Georgetown College, The Edmund A. Walsh School of Foreign Service, The Robert Emmett McDonough Business School, and the School of Nursing and Health Studies. Although students live, work, and play together, prospective Hoyas apply for admission to one of the four colleges, becoming affiliated with that school upon matriculation. Of the internal divisions, students said the differences only manifest themselves during mock competition, and one university tour guide described the practice as "Harry Potter-esque." In a similar vein, students admitted to the presence of some inter-school tension, but were quick to add that the tension was not strongly palpable. "We have a lot of university pride, but a lot of school pride too," said one senior.

As always, there are stereotypes about students in each of the schools. One junior explained: "There's the idea that business school kids are only there to make money; that SFS students are arrogant, conceited, naïve, and think they're the most intelligent people on campus; and that the College kids don't know what they want to do with their lives since all 900 of them come in here undeclared. The Nursing kids don't really have a reputation since there are only around 80 of them per year."

The "Georgetown Paradox"

The "Georgetown Paradox" is the understanding that "Everyone wants you for your internship, but you have no way to get to that internship," explained a sophomore. The inaccessibility of Georgetown is the primary gripe among its students. Although the University provides a bus system, many students complain about its irregularity and unreliability. "Things would be better if we had a Metro stop," said one freshman. "But I think it's because Jackie Onassis, who owned four homes in the neighborhood over the course of her lifetime, didn't want Georgetown to be accessible to just anyone." With the Georgetown stamp of approval on their resumes, most students have no problem securing competitive internships throughout the D.C. area. "Anything that I've applied for, I've gotten," said one McDonough student. "It's a matter of deciding between what you've been offered. For example, Ameriprise Financial almost exclusively recruits Georgetown students." It seems that for a Hoya the only real problem is getting there.

A Hoya Halloween

Founded alongside the country, Georgetown stands as America's oldest Catholic and Jesuit university. And with over 200 years of history, it is one with its fair share of unique traditions spanning the traditional and the innovative. Not only do Georgetown students ceremoniously steal the clock handles from Healy Clock Tower and mail them to the Vatican to be blessed by the Pope, they also dance in the Dahlgren Fountain, evoking the opening credits of the television show *Friends*.

Another Georgetown staple is the nightly 11:15 pm candlelight Catholic mass, held in the major university chapel, Dahlgren Chapel of the Sacred Heart, and most frequented on Sunday nights. On a Hoya's 21st birthday, it is practically mandated that they celebrate at "The Tombs." And around the holidays, students are known to climb up and sit in the lap of the statue of their founder (Archbishop John Carroll) and tell him what they want for Christmas.

Basketball games are another Hoya institution. As one McDonough student put it, "Attending a Georgetown basketball game will change your life." Students described the scene as a mass of gray-clad Hoyas (the school colors are gray and blue) roaring with applause each time the team scores. "Of course, some people Georgetown it up and wear a popped collar underneath," said one sophomore. The respect for Georgetown basketball extends even to the band. One New Jersey native said, "Our pep band gets more respect than any other pep band in the country." But this immense fan base lacks a football counterpart. Some students said that the football team is so bad that "People pretend we don't have a football team." With basketball characterized by a self-described "cult of followers," it is clear that Hoya pride is expressed most intensely on the court, not on the field.

The biggest campus tradition is undeniably Halloween night. The 1973 William Friedkin film, *The Exorcist*, was filmed almost entirely on Georgetown's campus. This fact adds fuel to the eerie fire driving the renowned Hoya Halloween. Students generally agreed with one senior's conclusion that "Halloween is the biggest thing on campus." That night, students dress up and proceed to the main assembly hall, where they watch the film on a jumbo screen, then go down to the intersection of M Street and Wisconsin to dance in the street. One student bragged that the Hoya holiday tradition was rated among the top towns featuring fun Halloween celebrations.

The Jesuit Influence

Students report that there are a lot of Jesuit professors, but that the Jesuit influence was only very strong around Christmas when "mangers pop up around campus." A freshman who said he was initially apprehensive of attending a Catholic-affiliated school said that his fears of "a Jesuit behind [his] back" were quickly allayed when he found their presence was not overwhelming. "The Jesuit tradition is a very welcoming and open one. There is some restriction, but they're very accommodating and open to hearing things," he said. However, other students pointed to the facts that the pro-choice group on campus is not allowed to table like other campus organizations and that, though they are permitted to flyer, anyone offended by their literature can tear them down. They also noted that none of the on-campus stores can sell condoms, though they admitted there is an unrestricted CVS just four blocks away from campus. Students further explained that Red Square is a free speech zone, where one can "pretty much say anything" without repercussions.

Not Your Average Greek

Georgetown University does not officially recognize traditional fraternities and sororities. But there are some illegitimate on-campus Greek organizations in addition to recognized professional and service organizations. "It's not your typical college Greek life; it's more of the resume-building than boozing-up kind," explained one junior. On-campus parties are not centered around Greek life, but are popular in the University townhouses, of which there are roughly 70 within a one-block radius of the front gates, populated by upperclassmen. However, recent changes to drinking policies and restrictions on parties have made on-campus fiestas almost extinct. "All it's done is push alcohol use into the surrounding areas," said one senior. Despite the enormous backlash from students and months of publications devoted to criticizing the new crackdowns, Georgetown's prime social life now exists primarily along the town's bar-lined streets.

What's in the Salad?

Georgetown students consistently commented on the University's widespread culture of looking good. "We're always ranked among the fittest campuses, and I think that's a function of the fact that when Georgetown selects its well-rounded students, a lot of them happen to be varsity athletes and come from a culture of being fit," explained one female freshman. Other students, however, were more skeptical, and sometimes sarcastic, in their justifications of the University's fit reputation. "There's a rumor that they spray carbs on the salad to get the kids to gain weight," stated one junior. "Actually, I think eating disorders are another Georgetown tradition."

> "For the most part, I feel a real sense of community here, but if you want to see a split on Georgetown's campus, come visit around November 2008."

"There is a lot of competition in terms of who can put on the biggest show of carrying the largest Louis Vuitton bag without breaking a bone," said a male Marketing major. Others elaborated on the student body's fashion choices as conclusively preppy. "We do have a large preppy contingency and that's going to happen at any higher-level school that feeds from higher-level prep schools, but Georgetown does seem to take it to an extreme," commented one freshman male. "I do feel outnumbered as a public school grad." Other students commented on the same phenomenon. "Some of the things you wonder if people do in real life, they happen here. People are playing croquet on the front lawn; kids go quail hunting," said an SFS female. Students described the overall atmosphere as reflecting "the two p's—pearls and polo's," and said that the prep level increases when people go out. One senior said, "The preppy look is definitely noticeable, but not universal."

Class, Clinton, Class . . .

Georgetown's capital location ensures proximity to a great deal of political events, an all-star faculty, various specialized courses, and famous speakers. "When people are in D.C. and want to give a speech, they come to us, we don't go to them," said a female Finance major. Students remembered instances of famous speakers coming to campus and commented on the choice between seeing Bill Clinton speak or going to class. "It was pretty funny that when Bill Clinton came to town, I remember his motorcade was blocking my path, and I actually got annoyed," recalled one senior. "The idea of choice in that situation is ridiculous, but sometimes class wins out."

It comes as no surprise that this choice would be difficult for Georgetown students who are at once notoriously studious and politically active. Hoyas are known to take it to the streets when bothered by, well, anything. Students have even mobilized to protest Wal-Mart representatives speaking on corporate responsibility. Recently, students mobilized against a series of assaults on individuals identified as homosexual, critiquing the University's position on the matter and raising the difficult issue of what a Catholic institution's position should be on such a sensitive topic. Students did, however, note that the mood at Georgetown is typically one of unity. "For the most part, I feel a real sense of community here, but if you want to see a split on Georgetown's campus, come visit around November 2008," said a junior.

Popular Georgetown majors include pre-med, finance, culture and politics, compara-tive studies and economics. The school is noted for rigorous requirements, like "Map of the Modern World." All SFS students must pass this course in order to graduate, and in order to pass this course, they must success-fully distinguish and name every country in the world, its capital, population, religion, and political system. Another requirement is "The Problem of God," fulfilled with one of 24 sections that, depending on the profes-sor, can range from getting a comparative religion approach to a psychological one to general theology. On Georgetown's general requirements, a senior said, "You're going to love them or hate them, but the fact that they're requirements means there are a lot of ways to get them done."

Georgetown students appear well-versed in working within established frameworks to accomplish their goals. They succeed at holding down impressive internships while handling full course loads, protesting for gay rights at a Catholic university, demolish-ing the competition on the basketball court and becoming scholars, while having a great deal of fun.—*Nicholle Manners*

FYI

If you come to Georgetown, you'd better bring "a pastel Polo."

What is the typical weekend schedule? "Friday: go to classes—if you have any, do work for a while in the library, go out to dinner, come back to campus to party or study, depending on the weekend; Saturday: go out to the city during the day, party at night; Sunday: spend the entire day in the library."

If I could change one thing about Georgetown, I'd "overhaul the dining hall food; it's horrendous and every prospective student should be warned."

Three things every student at Georgetown should do before graduating are "go to a basketball game, go to a performance at the Kennedy Center, and protest in Red Square."

Howard University

Address: 2400 Sixth Street, NW Washington, D.C. 20059

Phone: 202-806-2700

E-mail address: AskEM@howard.edu

Web site URL: www.howard.edu

Year Founded: 1867

Private or Public: Private

Religious Affiliation: None

Location: Urban

Number of Applicants: 7,603

Percent Accepted: 54%

Percent Accepted who enroll: 35%

Number Entering: 1,443

Number of Transfers Accepted each Year: 250

Middle 50% SAT range: M: 440–650, CR: 460–660, Wr: 410–650,

Middle 50% ACT range: 20–28

Early admission program EA/ED/None: EA

Percentage accepted through EA or ED: Unreported

EA and ED deadline: 1-Nov

Regular Deadline: 15-Feb

Application Fee: $45

Full time Undergraduate enrollment: 6,988

Total enrollment: 6,988

Percent Male: 33%

Percent Female: 67%

Total Percent Minority or Unreported: 32%

Percent African-American: 67%

Percent Asian/Pacific Islander: 1%

Percent Hispanic: 0%

Percent Native-American: <1%

Percent International: 5%

Percent in-state/out of state: 23%/77%

Percent from Public HS: 80%

Retention Rate: 84%

Graduation Rate 4-year: 43%

Graduation Rate 6-year: 63%

Percent Undergraduates in On-campus housing: 55%

Number of official organized extracurricular organizations: 150

3 Most popular majors: Biology/Biological Sciences, Journalism, Radio and Television

Student/Faculty ratio: 8:1

Average Class Size: 2 to 9

Percent of students going to grad school: 60%

Tuition and Fees: $13,215

In State Tuition and Fees if different: No difference

Cost for Room and Board: $6,976

Percent receiving financial aid out of those who apply, first year: 96%

Percent receiving financial aid among all students: 96%

From their very first footstep onto the campus, visitors to Howard University become aware of the strong sense of community that sets Howard apart from other schools across the country. Located in the nation's capital, Howard prides itself on its academic excellence as well as its reputation for turning out strong African-American students who are well-rounded and fully aware of the numerous opportunities that await them after leaving this beautiful, hilly campus situated in the heart of Washington, D.C.

Education Beyond the Classroom

In the past, in terms of majors, Howard was always synonymous with either medicine or law. Although these areas are still popular and prestigious aspects of the school, many different colleges have grown significantly in the past few years. Students choose from one of several different colleges to focus on during their time at Howard (Arts and Sciences, Communications, etc.). Another distinguishing factor of Howard is that in addition to requiring undergraduates to take a certain number of credits within their own specific concentrations, the school also places a strong emphasis on practical education, manifested in areas such as the required physical education classes.

Although there are general-education type classes that each student must take, the amount of undergraduates at Howard allows class sizes to stay relatively intimate. A senior mentioned that as she advanced into the higher-level courses within her major, most of her classes had only 15 to 20 students. Because of this, the community enjoys an excellent relationship between students and faculty members. According to another senior, "Because of the small class sizes, teachers develop strong relationships with their students. They are constantly supplying them with opportunities for internships and ways to utilize being in Washington, D.C."

It is because of these great teachers that there are certain "must-take" classes at Howard such as Literature of Love and Pan-Africanism. With readings that vary from Toni Morrison to William Shakespeare, Literature of Love is a class that encourages students to seek to understand human interaction through famous literary works. Well-known professors such as Dr. Gregory Carr and John Davis are integral parts of life at Howard and are constantly seen at functions all around campus.

On the Hilltop

With a thriving social scene, Howard has opportunities for all different types of people to get involved with student activities. HUSA, Howard University Student Association, is one of the biggest groups on campus. Other students are involved in a wide variety of extracurriculars, including everything from putting on pageants to joining step groups. *The Hilltop*, Howard's award-winning school newspaper, is very highly regarded and has won numerous accolades both nationally and at the yearly HBCU conference. In accordance with the large international student population, the African Student Association and the Caribbean Student Association are also huge forces on campus. Along with chapters of national organizations such as the NAACP and NSCS (National Society of Collegiate Scholars), Howard boasts a unique system of clubs for each of the fifty states. These clubs are known to host activities and gatherings such as the well-attended yearly party thrown by the Louisiana and Texas Clubs. There are other school-wide activities such as "ResFest" where different dormitories divide into teams and compete against other dorms in competitions such as dance contests and sporting events.

Although there are lots of different social scenes around campus, none is more dominant than Greek life. One student said that "Part of the reason the Greek scene here is so prominent is because of its legacy on campus. Greeks have a responsibility that goes beyond partying." Fraternity and sorority members hold positions of power around campus and have a very prominent place at Howard. The groups strive to be more than just social groups, emphasizing both community service and African-American unity.

Growing Up

All Howard students grow and develop in many different ways as their four years go by, and the maturity that comes with age is reflected in the various types of student housing. Freshman students are guaranteed housing and live under relatively strict rules in the dorms, many of which have to do with

student safety and the need for constant security on campus due to the high crime rate areas around campus. There are counselors and residential advisors who are there to guide freshmen along their way through the university system. According to older students, when it comes to mealtimes, the freshmen are typically seen eating in the cafeteria, which serves more or less typical college food. For most freshmen, the highlight of the "Caf" menu is Soul Food Thursdays, when the menu includes delicious items such as fried chicken and macaroni.

By the time students are upperclassmen, many are living off-campus in apartments. When talking to students, most said that after a while at school they figure out which areas are safe to go to and which areas to stay away from, in terms of safety issues. Many agreed that there could be improvements in terms of building relationships with the surrounding community and having on-campus security being more attentive while on duty. If upperclassmen are not living off-campus, they are in apartment-style dorms with kitchens, meaning that either they do not have the meal plan or they eat in the recently renovated "Punch-Out," which includes popular fast food places such as Chick-Fil-A. Most students don't have cars, probably due in part to the fact that the DC subway system, the Metro, is a very efficient way to get around the city.

> "The fact that you can meet so many people from so many different regions and backgrounds, all with the same goal in mind, is a beautiful thing."

In addition to evolving living situations and eating habits, the social scene, too, changes as students get older. The clubbing scene begins to fade and instead of heading out to clubs like H2O, F.U.R, and Love, as they did as freshman and sophomores, upperclassmen tend to socialize at bars, house parties, and more sophisticated places such as The Diner, which is a coffee-shop-like place to hang out. As the workload increases and the realization that professional life is quickly approaching, many seniors spend weekend time differently than they did their first few years at Howard.

Coming Home to Howard

Probably the most famous event all year at Howard is Homecoming. People from all over the world come to gather together and share in special activities and events that last all week long. From the moment that guests arrive on campus on Sunday, they have the option of attending chapel services, talent shows, concerts, and more. One of the most famous events is the step show that takes place at the yard, where each fraternity has its own section from which to observe the events. Although the weekend is technically centered around sports, the hype is more about the gathering of all different people in a single venue. When asked about Homecoming, one sophomore said, "The fact that you can meet so many people from so many different regions and backgrounds, all with the same goal in mind, is a beautiful thing." For those who doubt the importance of the event: Homecoming was even mentioned in a Ludacris song.

Besides the events that characterize Homecoming, alumni and other prominent members of the African-American community who return to Howard are reminded of the time they spent at the gorgeous, hilly campus lined with old, New England style buildings. At the highest point of campus is the Yard, where people study and socialize when the weather is nice. In fact, the movie *Stomp the Yard* contains references to this famous area of Howard's campus.

No matter what type of background a person comes from or what activities he or she participates in, Howard is a place where students can build on their potential and grow into future leaders. Students agree that "Even with the challenging academic life, Howard provides a unique and rewarding atmosphere for its students by allowing them to face real world problems in a lifelike setting."—*Emily St. Jean*

FYI

If you come to Howard University, you'd better bring "a portable chair to stand in lines at the admissions building."

What's the typical weekend schedule? "Go to a house party on Friday night; if it's nice out, relax outside during the day on Saturday; head to Adams Morgan or a bar on Saturday night; and then recover and relax on Sunday, take a shuttle to church in the morning and catch up on work the rest of the day."

If I could change one thing about Howard, I'd "make it so that there was a higher percentage of males on campus."

Three things every student at Howard should do before graduating are "go to Ben's Chili Bowl, get familiar with the city (especially the National Mall area), and attend a homecoming game."

Trinity Washington University

Address: 125 Michigan Avenue, NE Washington, DC 20017
Phone: 202-884-9400
E-mail address: admissions@trinitydc.edu
Web site URL: www.trinitydc.edu
Year Founded: 1897
Private or Public: Private
Religious Affiliation: Roman Catholic
Location: Urban
Number of Applicants: 441
Percent Accepted: 75%
Percent Accepted who enroll: 48%
Number Entering: 182
Number of Transfers Accepted each Year: Unreported
Middle 50% SAT range: Unreported
Middle 50% ACT range: 13–18
Early admission program EA/ED/None: EA

Percentage accepted through EA or ED: Unreported
EA and ED deadline: 1-Dec
Regular Deadline: Rolling
Application Fee: $40
Full time Undergraduate enrollment: 1,047
Total enrollment: 1,449
Percent Male: 0%
Percent Female: 100%
Total Percent Minority or Unreported: 98%
Percent African-American: 70%
Percent Asian/Pacific Islander: 1%
Percent Hispanic: 10%
Percent Native-American: <1%
Percent International: Unreported
Percent in-state/out of state: 50%/50%
Percent from Public HS: Unreported
Retention Rate: Unreported

Graduation Rate 4-year: 29%
Graduation Rate 6-year: 44%
Percent Undergraduates in On-campus housing: 22%
Number of official organized extracurricular organizations: 34
3 Most popular majors: Communications Studies/Speech Communication and Rhetoric
Student/Faculty ratio: 11:1
Average Class Size: Unreported
Percent of students going to grad school: Unreported
Tuition and Fees: $18,960
In State Tuition and Fees if different: No difference
Cost for Room and Board: $8,450
Percent receiving financial aid out of those who apply, first year: Unreported
Percent receiving financial aid among all students: Unreported

Founded by the Sisters of Notre Dame de Namur as one of the nation's first Catholic women's liberal arts colleges in 1897, Trinity has been attracting focused but fun-loving women ever since. And after becoming a university in 2004 with the addition of two professional schools, Trinity has even more resources to offer its small female population.

"At Trinity, everything is tradition. It's a very traditional school," one junior said. And indeed, the Trinity campus does abide by deep-seated social and moral standards. But with its location in the heart of Washington D.C., the campus provides plenty of opportunity to create a mix between old and new, fun and serious.

A Foundation for Leadership

With just over 1,000 undergraduates Trinity is a tight-knit community, with many specialized programs to meet the needs of its students. Trinity students complete the Foundation for Leadership Curriculum (FLC), an interdisciplinary program with a professional focus that combines courses from five areas of study: Communication Skills, Traditions and Cultural Expression, Search for Ultimate Meanings, Scientific and Mathematical Exploration, and Perspectives on Self and Society.

The most popular majors at Trinity are, understandably, politically focused, with political science as a perennial favorite, trailed by communications, business, psychology and international affairs. Trinity's political science department has graduated such political stars as California state representative and Democratic Leader of the House of Representatives Nancy Pelosi, Kansas governor Kathleen Sebelius, and several upper-level judges.

Thanks in part to its small size, and also its comfortable all-female dynamic, Trinity fosters an intimacy and camaraderie in the classroom that students cannot stop raving about. "At Trinity, you're a name, not a social security number," one student said. Another commented, "You definitely walk away with everyone pushing for you."

Students and professors are very close at Trinity, and students say it is not unusual to have a professor's home or cell phone number—or even to have class dinners at the homes of professors during the semester. "The professors at Trinity are amazing," one junior said. "They love teaching and sharing their lives and all that they have learned with their students." Another student put it more succinctly: "Trinity's professors rock!"

On the honor system since 1913, Trinity students are diligent and supportive about their work. Help abounds at Trinity, with both the Academic Support and Career Services (ASCS) offering one-on-one tutoring throughout the four-year education and also the Future Focus Program offering help specifically targeted to freshman year.

And while Trinity's academics are sufficient—with classes from Human Sexuality to Political Lives of Women to Civil Rights and Liberties on offer—the University is also part of a consortium of schools in the D.C. area, allowing students to take classes at any number of other colleges and universities, and also bringing in other students (even men!) to Trinity. Washington D.C. is also the perfect area for professional internships, and Trinity students take advantage of their connections throughout the academic year with internships at anywhere from the White House and the Department of State to the Washington Mystics and the National Zoo.

National Government and Student Government

At Trinity, extracurriculars often take a backseat to academics and internships, but they do play a part in campus life. An NCAA Division III school, Trinity is a founding member of the Atlantic Women's College conference, and competes at the varsity level in basketball, crew, field hockey, lacrosse, soccer, softball, swimming, tennis, track and field, and volleyball. Students also play a wide variety of intramural sports, but most students seem to spend their time doing individual workouts in Trinity's $20 million state-of-the-art athletic complex, the Trinity Center for Women and Girls in Sports.

Beyond athletics, Trinity extracurriculars run the gamut of usual clubs and organizations, particularly focused on the political and the journalistic. Student government is big at Trinity, as are the College Democrats and the College Republicans. Students run three publications: the literary magazine *The Record*, the yearbook *Trinilogue*, and

the newspaper *The Trinity Times*. The Latina American Caribbean Student Association (LACASA) is especially active on campus.

There are no sororities allowed on the Trinity campus, though students are free to join sororities at other schools in the D.C. Consortium. "I think one of the reasons why sororities are not recognized on our campus is that there is not really a need for them," one student explained. "Being an all women's institution necessarily connects us into a sisterhood or community that I can appreciate."

Off-Campus Life

Part of the reason why extracurriculars are not a primary focus of Trinity life is that so many students live off campus. Although the dorms themselves are considered fine, though not by any means spectacular, the University's housing crunch combined with the abundant housing in the D.C. area means that many students commute, especially after freshman year. Trinity is a dry campus, and the dorms are "very restrictive"—"It holds up to all the stereotypes of a private, Catholic women's college," one junior said—so many students also move off campus to get a bit more freedom.

The campus itself, while restrictive, is quite beautiful, sitting on 26 wooded acres. The original Main Building, completed in 1909, contains all administrative offices, most classrooms and faculty offices, the computer center, the post office, the campus bookstore, and a residence hall. In addition to the Main Building, there are two more residence halls—Cuvilly and Kerby—as well as the Science Building, the Sister Helen Sheehan Library, the Trinity Center for Women and Girls in Sports, the award-winning Notre Dame Chapel, and the Alumnae Hall, which houses the campus dining facilities.

Since most students live off campus, they don't rely heavily on the meal plan, though students say Trinity has a "wonderful catering service," which is the same company that contracts for the government and provides food for the House of Representatives and the Senate.

An Emphasis on Diversity

Trinity students' social lives also take place primarily off campus, especially because of Trinity's strict no-alcohol policy and the easy transportation into the city or to surrounding schools. Drinking and drugs are very uncommon on the Trinity campus, with most socializing taking place in D.C. itself—an easy metro ride away. Besides the strict liquor policy, the Trinity lifestyle simply does not lend itself to tons of free time for socializing. "The student organizations fight to create community on campus and have decent success," one student said. "However, Trinity women are typically extremely busy."

> "Many of the distractions that are found on large coed campuses are non-factors at Trinity. I am in college for an education and that is what I get."

The dating scene on campus is, of course, "quite non-existent." Many women, however, date men from area universities and from the D.C. area, and everyone is very enthusiastic about the all-woman atmosphere. "I would say it's comfortable," a junior said. "Many of the distractions that are found on large coed campuses are non-factors at Trinity. I am in college for an education and that is what I get."

But just because only a few men from the Consortium ever enter Trinity's campus does not mean Trinity is not diverse. The school is actually amazingly diverse—less so geographically, but with incredible racial and socioeconomic diversity. Also, because of its continuing education programs, it is not unusual for older women to be in class with the more typical twenty-somethings, lending a viewpoint that the younger students appreciate.

Constantly Evolving Traditions

As busy as they are, Trinity women always find the time to participate in Trinity traditions. "We're very into keeping up those traditions." Ultimately, these traditions are not just important to the Trinity experience, but symbolic of it: holding onto the past, but always moving forward into the future.

The many long-standing traditions at Trinity include the First Year Medal Ceremony, Sophomore Pin Ceremony, Junior Ring Ceremony, Convocation, Cap and Gown Weekend, Founders' Day, Family Weekend, and "Well Sings."

But the most important Trinity tradition, and the one that speaks most to the strong community and legacy that is a Trinity education, is the class colors. The first four graduating classes each chose a color: red, blue, green and gold. Now, at the end of the year, graduating seniors give their color to the incoming first-year class, to create a common bond between every fourth class. This is what it means to be part of a true sisterhood.—*Claire Stanford*

FYI
If you come to Trinity, you'd better bring "a well-polished résumé because you never know who you're going to meet, walking shoes, your own social life."
What's the typical weekend schedule? "Go out on Friday, protest on Saturday, sleep on Sunday."
If you could change one thing about Trinity, I'd "make the school have a bigger budget for more classes."
Three things every student at Trinity should do before graduating are "go on a midnight monument tour, go paddle-boating at the Cherry Blossom festival in the Spring, and see fireworks at the National Mall on the Fourth of July."

Florida

Florida A&M University

Address: Suite G-9, Foote-Hilyer Administration Center Tallahassee, FL 32307
Phone: 850-599-3796
E-mail address: ugrdadmissions@famu.edu
Web site URL: www.famu.edu
Year Founded: 1887
Private or Public: Public
Religious Affiliation: None
Location: Urban
Number of Applicants: 4,708
Percent Accepted: 61%
Percent Accepted who enroll: 60%
Number Entering: 1,705
Number of Transfers Accepted each Year: 605
Middle 50% SAT range: M: 440–550, CR: 440–550
Middle 50% ACT range: 19–22
Early admission program EA/ED/None: None
Percentage accepted through EA or ED: NA

EA and ED deadline: NA
Regular Deadline: 9-May
Application Fee: $20
Full time Undergraduate enrollment: 9,591
Total enrollment: 10,124
Percent Male: 43%
Percent Female: 57%
Total Percent Minority or Unreported: 97%
Percent African-American: 94%
Percent Asian/Pacific Islander: 1%
Percent Hispanic: 1%
Percent Native-American: <1%
Percent International: 1%
Percent in-state/out of state: 73%/27%
Percent from Public HS: 85%
Retention Rate: 89%
Graduation Rate 4-year: Unreported
Graduation Rate 6-year: Unreported

Percent Undergraduates in On-campus housing: 75%
Number of official organized extracurricular organizations: 10
3 Most popular majors: Business, Health Professions, Security and Protective Services
Student/Faculty ratio: 17:1
Average Class Size: 2 to 9
Percent of students going to grad school: 33%
Tuition and Fees: $15,513
In State Tuition and Fees if different: $3,572
Cost for Room and Board: $6,508
Percent receiving financial aid out of those who apply, first year: Unreported
Percent receiving financial aid among all students: Unreported

---

Tallahassee, Florida is known as a great college town. Since the city has two major universities, students who matriculate at Florida A&M (FAMU) can expect that something is always going on. In addition, as the State University System's only historically black university, FAMU has a long tradition of separating itself from the pack and retaining its individuality.

Structured Study

Undergraduates at FAMU have their pick of 94 majors within 62 fields of study in 13 different colleges. Much of the educational activity that goes on at FAMU is geared toward professional or pre-professional studies. In particular, the University's strongest programs are reputed to be in the School of Business and Industry, the College of Education, the School of Architecture, and the College of Pharmacy. The College of Engineering, which is shared with Florida State University, is also popular and well respected.

Students sometimes complain that the education they receive is a little too structured. "My academic program is way too narrowly defined," one freshman said. "There is little room for personal exploration." On the whole, however, students say the academics are "reasonable" and "manageable" if, like most FAMU students, one enters the school with a clearly defined notion of one's professional goals.

One aspect of FAMU's pedagogical goals that distinguishes the University from its State University System peers is its commitment to undergraduates. While FAMU is trying to expand its graduate program enrollment across disciplines, most of the school's energies are geared toward its undergrads. All classes are taught by professors, who as a general rule interact often and individually with their students. TAs are hired only to assist with labs and occasionally to substitute for faculty. This focus on undergraduates has always been a hallmark of the FAMU education.

Chilling at the Set

Housing headaches have long been considered a part of life at FAMU, though this may be changing for the better in the near future. Most students have traditionally lived off campus, but there are residence halls as well. The University requires all freshmen whose families live 35 or more miles away to live in the dorms. In order to create a more tight-knit community, the University has been trying to make its housing options more attractive to all students. To date, those in the dorms tend to be ambivalent about their living conditions. "[It's] fine—nothing great, nothing awful," one student said. Meal plans are required of those who do live in on-campus housing.

For those who choose their own accommodations, Tallahassee offers a wealth of housing options that cater to college students. Apartments are generally available, and local places to shop and grab a bite to eat (including two malls) are abundant. Clubs and restaurants are also popular destinations. FAMU's campus is very near downtown, which offers not only practical and social advantages but also great educational and professional-development opportunities, given Tallahassee's status as the capital of Florida. FAMU has several established internship programs with local institutions, such as the popular program that places journalism majors at the *Tallahassee Democrat*, the local daily newspaper, for a summer or more.

There is plenty to do on campus as well. One popular hangout is "the Set," which is a common area near the Student Union. It contains the post office, the bookstore, a market and a TV room. Such shared spaces give off-campus residents a great excuse to hang out with on-campus friends. "It is great to have the Set so that off-campus people like myself can still stay connected with the rest of the student body," one sophomore said.

Never a Dull Moment

Popular activities among students include the Student Government Association, fra-ternities and sororities, musical events, pre-professional societies, journalism, theater and sporting events. With so much going on, it goes without saying that FAMU students are an active, spirited group.

One of the challenges of the student government has been to keep off-campus students involved in the larger campus life. According to most accounts, they have succeeded admirably. "They do a terrific job," one student said. One popular annual event is "Be Out Day," which brings the student body out to the athletic fields for a day of food, partying and games. Another SGA-run event that "we all look forward to each year" is Homecoming.

The Greek system is another big draw for students. According to the Office of Student Union and Activities, all of the national historically black fraternities and sororities have chapters at FAMU. In addition to these more traditional college Greek houses, there are also numerous community-service organizations and honor societies.

> "I am going out into the real world with not only solid academic training, but a host of life experiences that I won't soon forget."

Music is also an important part of life at FAMU. The gospel choir is very popular, and the marching band, known as the Marching 100, has achieved an international reputation. The second largest college marching band in the world, the Marching 100 has been featured in a Bastille Day parade in Paris and played at President Clinton's second inauguration. Several predominantly black high-school bands in North Florida and other areas intentionally imitate the flamboyant, showboating style and discipline of the Marching 100.

FAMU Rattler sports are a pretty big deal in Tallahassee, even though they are often in the shadow of the larger and better-known teams of Florida State University. Students show their school spirit by decking themselves in orange and green and attending NCAA Division I sporting events, especially football, which is in Division I-AA. Intramural sports are also popular and are described as "fierce and fun."

A Close Community

With most schools in the country focusing their recruiting efforts on increasing diversity,

FAMU has bucked the trend.. The school is very proud of its status as Florida's only public historically black university, and has made the recruitment of high-achieving black students its No. 1 priority. At times, FAMU has performed as well as or better than such universities as Harvard, Yale and Stanford in recruiting National Achievement Scholars.

Students say that although they wish there were more diversity on campus, they do appreciate and enjoy the community they have. "I love this community, but . . . there is much to be desired in terms of creating a more diverse student body," one senior said. "I look outside and everyone is so much like me." Of course, the students do have diversity when it comes to their backgrounds and interests (although around 75 percent are from Florida). There is considerable political diversity, but strikingly uniform is the students' take on homosexuality. The small community of gay students isn't organized, and students say they're "not very open-minded when it comes to that."

FAMU has been a traditional top choice for many black students from Florida because of its respected pre-professional and professional academic programs, its warm environment (in more ways than one), and its commitment to undergraduate education. As one senior put it, "I am going out into the real world with not only solid academic training, but a host of life experiences that I won't soon forget."—*Jay Buchanan*

FYI
If you come to FAMU, you'd better bring "sunglasses."
What is the typical weekend schedule? "Friday, catch up on sleep; Saturday, go out and party; Sunday, do all the work from the previous week."
If I could change one thing about FAMU, "I'd improve the landscape. There are too many bushes around here."
The three things that every student at FAMU should do before graduating are "chill at the Set, volunteer in Tallahassee and attend Homecoming."

Florida Institute of Technology

Address: 150 West University Boulevard Melbourne, FL 32901-6975
Phone: 321-674-8030
E-mail address: admission@fit.edu
Web site URL: www.fit.edu
Year Founded: 1958
Private or Public: Private
Religious Affiliation: None
Location: Suburban
Number of Applicants: 3,168
Percent Accepted: 82%
Percent Accepted who enroll: 25%
Number Entering: 635
Number of Transfers Accepted each Year: 338
Middle 50% SAT range: M: 540–640, CR: 500–610
Middle 50% ACT range: 22–28
Early admission program EA/ED/None: None
Percentage accepted through EA or ED: NA

EA and ED deadline: NA
Regular Deadline: Rolling
Application Fee: $50
Full time Undergraduate enrollment: 2,594
Total enrollment: 5,118
Percent Male: 61%
Percent Female: 39%
Total Percent Minority or Unreported: 65%
Percent African-American: 8%
Percent Asian/Pacific Islander: 3%
Percent Hispanic: 6%
Percent Native-American: <1%
Percent International: 17%
Percent in-state/out of state: 55%/45%
Percent from Public HS: 56%
Retention Rate: 73%
Graduation Rate 4-year: 42%
Graduation Rate 6-year: 58%

Percent Undergraduates in On-campus housing: 37%
Number of official organized extracurricular organizations: 99
3 Most popular majors: Aerospace/Aeronautical Engineering, Aviation Management, Mechanical Engineering
Student/Faculty ratio: 13:1
Average Class Size: 10 to 19
Percent of students going to grad school: 20%
Tuition and Fees: $30,190
In State Tuition and Fees if different: No difference
Cost for Room and Board: $10,250
Percent receiving financial aid out of those who apply, first year: Unreported
Percent receiving financial aid among all students: Unreported

Nestled in a tropical, lush environment and boasting a challenging curriculum with unique research opportunities, the Florida Institute of Technology stands apart from other technical universities. Indeed, this small technical school, located five minutes from the beach, offers more than just an education: Florida Tech prepares its students for life.

Challenging Courses

Despite the appeal of relaxing on the beach, students at Florida Tech take academics seriously. Many said they find the academics to be difficult, but rewarding. As one student said, "Classes are challenging. They really put you to the test."

Students say that one of the best aspects of academics at Florida Tech is the small size of a typical class. Since many classes enroll less than 20 people, students have the chance to actively engage in classroom discussions and interact with the professor. As one sophomore said, "You're not just a number. Professors get to know your name, and you get to know a lot about them too. It's a really nice relationship, but they keep it very challenging."

On top of their classes, many students take advantage of the excellent hands-on research opportunities available at Florida Tech. From manatee preservation and beach erosion studies to working at NASA or Lockheed Martin, every student can plug into Florida Tech's extensive research program.

Along with the requirements for each major, most students have to complete core classes, which include Physics I and II, Calculus I and II, Civilization I and II, and Differential Equations and Linear Algebra. Students must also complete various communication classes, including Composition and Rhetoric, Writing about Literature, and Science and Technical Communication.

Although Florida Tech offers numerous majors through its Colleges of Engineering, Science, Aeronautics, Business, and Psychology and Liberal Arts, the two most popular majors are Aerospace Engineering and Marine Biology.

"Everything Under the Sun"

Student organizations and clubs exist for "everything under the sun," as one sophomore said. Indeed, with 100 registered student organizations on campus, "There's something here for everyone," and students have little trouble finding organizations that interest them. Popular organizations range from bowling and sport fishing to math and skydiving. Many students also get involved with community service. Florida Tech has its own organization for Habitat for Humanity as well as a program for working with local elementary school students.

Students at Florida Tech participate in 14 intercollegiate sports at the Division II level. While Florida Tech may not be known for its varsity athletics, students said that the soccer and basketball teams have recently been particularly successful. One sophomore commented that "Athletic spirit could be better, although it has improved in the last couple of years." For those not as eager to indulge in athletics at such a high level, Florida Tech also offers many opportunities to get involved with intramural sports.

Social Life

General friendliness seems to abound at Florida Tech. According to one student, "People will bend over backwards to help you." And, because Florida Tech has a small student body, "Everyone really gets a chance to get to know all the students."

On campus, "There's always something going on," as one sophomore said. The student-run Residential Hall Association and the Campus Activities Board set up popular campus events, including comedy shows, concerts and an International Fair, which allows students to explore the traditions of people from different cultures across the world.

> **"It wasn't what I was expecting . . . it was a lot better."**

Off campus, most students spend their free time hanging out on the beach. While there, people enjoy a range of water activities, including surfing, boating, kayaking or simply relaxing in the sun. Students can also drive less than an hour to get to Disney World.

Greek fraternities and sororities attract a large number of students and are a dominant presence on campus. Some students complain about a lack of on-campus parties, though they acknowledge that parties do take place off campus. Florida Tech tends to have a strict policy against alcohol, although students do not always follow it—"We still drink, of course," one sophomore commented.

Florida Tech's uneven male-female ratio affects social life on campus. Male students joke that, "If you don't find a girlfriend in the first couple of weeks in freshmen year, you won't ever find a girlfriend." However, such sentiment is not pervasive throughout the entire student body. As one male student said, "It doesn't bother me too much. I probably have more female friends on campus than male friends."

Around Campus

Students live in one of six campus residential halls and two apartment complexes. Campbell and Wood Halls offer housing primarily to freshmen, although their convenient locations draw many upperclassmen to share these residencies as well. Roberts Hall is the largest residence facility on campus and houses only freshmen. Women may choose to live in Shaw Hall, a female-only residence. Outside of the residence halls, students love the Columbia Village Suites and Southgate Apartments. The Southgate Apartments, which come with in-suite amenities and an outdoor pool, are so popular that "people wait outside and sleep in tents for a week to get in," said one student. All freshmen are required to live on campus, while about half of the remaining students choose to live off campus.

Residence halls are watched over by student RAs. One sophomore mentioned, "RAs are pretty strict compared to other schools."

Students tend to find the food at Florida Tech to be decent. As one student said, "When I come back from break, I'm excited to eat the food. But after three weeks, I'm kind of tired of it." Students often socialize at "The RAT," an eatery and pub on the lower level of Evans Hall that also features a big screen TV, game room, and computer cluster. Off campus, students enjoy eating at local restaurants such as Carrabba's Italian Grill, City Tropics Bistro and Outback Steakhouse.

Not Typically Techie

Despite its name, Florida Tech offers much more than an education in technology. From the lush botanical gardens on campus to the beautiful beaches just miles from campus, from scuba diving under the water to watching shuttle launches at Kennedy Space Center, from graphs to Greek life, Florida Tech offers the complete college experience. One student put it best, "I wasn't sure what I was getting into. It just blew me away. It wasn't what I was expecting . . . it was a lot better."—*David Flinner*

FYI
If you come to Florida Tech, you'd better bring "a calculator."
What's the typical weekend schedule? "Friday: Get out of class as early as possible and take a nap; Saturday: hang out at the beach; Sunday: Study."
If I could change one thing about Florida Tech, I'd "lower tuition."
Three things every student at Florida Tech should do before graduating are "help out with some community service projects, watch the shuttle lift off, and make many trips to the beach!"

Florida Southern College

Address: 111 Lake Hollingsworth Drive Lakeland, FL 33801-5698
Phone: 863-680-4131
E-mail address: fscadm@flsouthern.edu
Web site URL: www.flsouthern.edu
Year Founded: 1883
Private or Public: Private
Religious Affiliation: Methodist
Location: Urban
Number of Applicants: 2,559
Percent Accepted: 58%
Percent Accepted who enroll: 28%
Number Entering: 424
Number of Transfers Accepted each Year: 148
Middle 50% SAT range: M: 470–600, CR: 480–600, Wr: 460–570
Middle 50% ACT range: 20–25

Early admission program EA/ED/None: ED
Percentage accepted through EA or ED: 14%
EA and ED deadline: 1-Dec
Regular Deadline: 1-Mar
Application Fee: $30
Full time Undergraduate enrollment: 1,693
Total enrollment: 1,801
Percent Male: 40%
Percent Female: 60%
Total Percent Minority or Unreported: 20%
Percent African-American: 7%
Percent Asian/Pacific Islander: 1%
Percent Hispanic: 6%
Percent Native-American: <1%
Percent International: 4%
Percent in-state/out of state: 75%/25%
Percent from Public HS: 79%
Retention Rate: 71%

Graduation Rate 4-year: 37%
Graduation Rate 6-year: 52%
Percent Undergraduates in On-campus housing: 74%
Number of official organized extracurricular organizations: 70
3 Most popular majors: Biology, Marketing, Psychology
Student/Faculty ratio: 13:1
Average Class Size: 10 to 19
Percent of students going to grad school: 27%
Tuition and Fees: $22,145
In State Tuition and Fees If different: No difference
Cost for Room and Board: $7,850
Percent receiving financial aid out of those who apply, first year: 82%
Percent receiving financial aid among all students: 62%

Finding a pleasant atmosphere to enjoy the Florida sun is never hard at Florida Southern College. Located in the town of Lakeland, the Moccasins boast a championship-caliber women's golf team, proximity to some of the most beautiful beaches in the world, and by all accounts one of the most hospitable institutions in the South. "I would definitely choose to go here again. There are tons of great people and great professors," said one proud student.

Rockin' the Classroom

Florida Southern is known across the country for its scholastic excellence. It consistently ranks as one of the best academic colleges in the Southeast. Undoubtedly one cause for FSC's educational acumen is its small class sizes. Most classes average around 15 students, with popular lectures being the only courses where you might get lost in a crowd. One student commented that "It's a nice learning environment because classes are smaller and more intimate. The professors know you by name." Florida Southern also offers a wide variety of courses from

guts like Jogging, Waterskiing, and Physical Education, to more challenging fare such as New and Old Testament, Classical and Medieval Philosophy, and Human Genetics. Students also report that being rejected from a class you really want to take is virtually a non-issue. "If you need to get into a certain course, just talk to the professor."

Party like a Mocc-star

During the day, a plethora of leisure activities is available to your average Moccasins. They can enjoy the beautiful Florida weather on the shores of Lake Hollingsworth, hop in the car and take a 35-minute drive down the road to enjoy that same weather at Clearwater Beach, or shop at the new outdoor mall at Lakeside Village, which boasts over 100 stores. When the sun sets, however, Lakeland doesn't really offer too many party options for Florida Southern students. The scene usually starts on Thursday evenings, and begins with a trip to traditional crowd pleasers like Chili's, Bennigan's, or Applebee's. For students who don't want to go too far, the local club scene is dominated by Kau

Kau Korner, a legendary bar just off Florida Southern's campus. Students who don't mind traveling pile into their cars on the weekends to sample the sizzling nightlife of nearby Orlando and Tampa's Ybor City.

For those not into that scene, the Association for Campus Entertainment (ACE) has worked in recent years to make life in Lakeland more exciting. "The school made a concerted effort to plan weekend activities to keep students on campus," said one student. These dogged efforts have paid off. ACE has even managed to lure some comedians that have been prominently featured on networks like Comedy Central.

If you are looking for illegal drugs or a school whose drug policy is pretty lax, then Florida Southern is not the campus for you. One student reported that "the drug rules are pretty strictly enforced, especially for the freshmen." Florida Southern is also a dry campus, but the drinking restrictions are much less strict than those on drugs. Florida Southern does have Resident Assistants, who vary in temperament. "It depends on the person: some are laid-back, some not so much. Some are more involved than others." Strict RA or not, a Florida Southern senior said that "If you want to find a place to drink, you'll definitely be able to."

Oh Those Generous Greeks!

Greek life is pretty important at Florida Southern. One student estimated the Greek population to be even higher than the official statistics. Frats and sororities are quite vocal and involved on campus. Despite this, "Lakeland does not allow sorority and fraternity houses, so certain dorm rooms are considered fraternity or sorority areas," explained one sorority member. Though these dorms are set aside for Greek use, the connection is informal and no one fraternity lays claim to a whole dormitory. Also, these frats aren't all about partying and debauchery; many students report that Greeks at Florida Southern have to be well-rounded. "We're really big on philanthropy, and are also really involved in student government and other leadership roles on campus," said one fraternity member.

Doin' It Big in Lakeland

There are many students who move off campus into cheaper housing close to school after their freshman year. On the other hand, many Moccasins enjoy staying on campus for the four years they'll be there. "At this small school, if I didn't live on campus, I would really be out of the loop," said one

student. Students described their campus as "pretty diverse" with "A lot of students from Florida, but also people from up north and out west. However, there are more East Coast students."

One common complaint among FSC's pupils is the mediocre food in the dining hall. There are also concerns about the limited hours the dining hall is open. Fortunately, beneath the dining hall there is a 24-hour café to satisfy all the late-night hungers from working out, partying, or just hanging with your friends. If you prefer your meals over a good book, then you can head to the cybercafé where Moccasins stay up late nights fueled by Starbucks coffee, typing away furiously on their laptops. In addition, there is also a yogurt stand that serves smoothies for those days when the sun beats down particularly hard.

Get Up, Get Out, and Do Something

Anyone who wants to sit on their duff for their college career had better not apply to Florida Southern; students usually have their hands in a lot of pots. "We're usually pretty committed to different activities. There are lots of student athletes," explained one Moc. Florida Southern competes in Division II of the NCAA in all of its sports. The Mocs lay claim to 26 national championships. Residing in gorgeous central Florida, It comes as no surprise that FSC is home to some of the best golfers at the college level with 11 men's golf championships and four women's golf championships, including one in 2007.

> "Our location, history, and the fun stories behind the school differentiate us from other colleges."

Despite the consistent excellence of the golf team, baseball and softball are by far the most popular sports on campus. The men's baseball team has even played exhibitions with MLB's Detroit Tigers. However, in an effort to increase student participation in the school's other stellar athletics programs, a Sports Management Club has recently been founded. Also, on weekday afternoons the intramural warriors take advantage of the extensive IM fields. Moccasins are just as active off the field, too. Since Florida Southern was originally founded as a Methodist college, theology and church do play a role in the day-to-day activities of the college grounds. "Campus ministry is also a large part of the campus life," reports one student. Other students, however, don't feel pressured into taking part in the various religious activities

Everything is all-Wright

Florida Southern's most famous attribute is its bond with one of the most renowned architects of the 20th century. "We have the largest collection of Frank Lloyd Wright architecture in the world on our campus," bragged one student. One of the most popular Wright works are the underground tunnels he built for the Cold War. "Lots of kids try to get in there." There is also the recently reconstructed Waterdome, which was a part of FSC's campus as early as 1948 but has now been built to

Wright's original specifications. Consisting of a huge pool surrounded by fountains cascading together at the monument's center, the Waterdome is the crowning piece of a paean to the daring mind and bold spirit that Frank Lloyd Wright represented.

Florida Southern is also a haven for the supernatural. It seems that the residents of a particular freshman dorm have spotted a ghost. "It's [former] President Spivey's son. You'll hear a basketball bouncing, and then you have to say 'No Allen, I don't want to play,' and he'll go away." Students enjoy the color that comes with living in a place like Lakeland. "Our location, history, and the fun stories behind the school differentiate us from other colleges," said one sophomore.—*JonPaul McBride*

FYI

If you come to Florida Southern you'd better bring "a Frisbee, a car, and an open mind."
What's the typical weekend schedule? "Go see a comedy show, grab dinner at Lakeside Village, run around Lake Hollingsworth, and chill at the beach on Sunday."
If I could change one thing about Florida Southern, I would "change how different our breaks are from other schools, especially spring break."
Three things every student at Florida Southern should do before graduating are "go to Kau Kau Korner, take funny pictures with the statues, and take a religion class."

Florida State University

Address: PO Box 3062400
Tallahassee, FL 32306
Phone: 850-644-6200
E-mail address:
admissions@admin.fsu.edu
Web site URL: www.fsu.edu
Year Founded: 1851
Private or Public: Public
Religious Affiliation: None
Location: Urban
Number of Applicants:
25,485
Percent Accepted: 47%
Percent Accepted who
enroll: 42%
Number Entering: 4,992
Number of Transfers
Accepted each Year: 3,118
Middle 50% SAT range:
M: 560–650, CR: 550–640
Middle 50% ACT range: 23–28
Early admission program
EA/ED/None: None
Percentage accepted
through EA or ED: NA

EA and ED deadline: NA
Regular Deadline: 21-Jan
Application Fee: $30
Full time Undergraduate
enrollment: 31,595
Total enrollment: 39,434
Percent Male: 44%
Percent Female: 56%
Total Percent Minority or
Unreported: 28%
Percent African-American:
10%
Percent Asian/Pacific
Islander: 3%
Percent Hispanic: 12%
Percent Native-American: 1%
Percent International: 1%
Percent in-state/out of
state: 88%/12%
Percent from Public HS: 84%
Retention Rate: 89%
Graduation Rate 4-year:
Unreported
Graduation Rate 6-year:
Unreported

Percent Undergraduates in
On-campus housing:
21%
Number of official organized
extracurricular
organizations: 500
3 Most popular majors:
Criminal Justice, English,
Finance
Student/Faculty ratio: 20:1
Average Class Size:
20 to 29
Percent of students going to
grad school: 42%
Tuition and Fees: $18,243
In State Tuition and Fees if
different: $3,799
Cost for Room and Board:
$8,178
Percent receiving financial
aid out of those who apply,
first year: 50%
Percent receiving financial
aid among all students:
32%

L ocated in the heart of Tallahassee, Florida State University offers its over 41,000 students a beautiful campus, a plethora of extracurricular opportunities, and a variety of fun social venues. With excellent athletic teams and a unique sense of pride in the Seminole community, FSU is known for its students' passionate school spirit. Given its well-rounded liberal arts program and enjoyable campus environment, FSU is certainly worth considering for all those looking for a good education at a large and lively university.

Going North to Get to the South

The vast majority of FSU's students are Floridians. Yet Tallahassee's atmosphere is likely to surprise many of the state's natives. Located in the northern panhandle of Florida, Tallahassee actually seems more like the South to the Floridian freshmen than many of their hometowns. One new student proclaimed her surprise that "Everything about Tallahassee felt completely different from Florida, including the buildings, the people, and even the trees." The weather is quite different from the rest of the state. A freshman remarked that "As long as it's not August," the weather is "not bad, and high temperatures even dip into the 70s and 60s as early as October." Aside from the temperature differences, students are often pleasantly surprised that Tallahassee has less humidity and rain than the rest of Florida. As one senior said, "The weather here makes the campus feel more like Georgia or Alabama, in a really good way."

FSU's location also makes it an ideal school for both the studious scholars and collegiate socialites. As one freshman put it, "Tallahassee is a great mix between a large college town and a vibrant Southern capital." Within walking distance is the Florida Capital Building, where students can learn about politics firsthand. For those interested in the social scene, the Strip, a commercial district located right across from FSU, is a good place to enjoy free time. The Strip includes Chubby's and Potbelly's, two infamous Tallahassee hangouts that double as nightclubs, and a good number of shops and restaurants. As one freshman explained, "The unique mix of intellectually stimulating venues and upbeat social centers in this city makes Tallahassee a truly incredible college town."

A True Liberal Arts Experience

Students at Florida State University tout their well-rounded academic programs. The most popular majors include business, political science, and international studies. "Business administration seems to be the most popular major here," said one sophomore. "But, being in Tallahassee, a lot of students also choose the political science and international studies tracks." However, unlike most other state schools, Seminoles can wait until their junior year to declare a major. Many take advantage of this by trying a variety of courses. One freshman schedule included such courses as "Multicultural Film, Mythology, American Government, and German I," while another included "Chemistry I, Biology I, and General Psychology." Students at FSU find this freedom in selecting classes one of FSU's greatest academic assets.

FSU also has an excellent Honors Program with high scholastic standards and great academic rewards. Students in FSU's Honors Program receive many perks, including "really nice dorms" and "early registration for classes." In addition, FSU Honors students are allowed to live in the Honors building (Landis Hall) for more than a year, take Honors classes throughout their college years, and receive registration benefits, making this program a very desirable option.

FSU students can also choose from several other great programs. Two highly regarded alternatives include creative writing and film studies. Students brag that FSU has one of the best creative writing programs in the country. It offers a great variety of classes and, as one sophomore claimed, "FSU has world-class writing professors." Students can also take film studies as a major, if they are in The College of Motion Picture, Television, and Recording Arts. According to one junior, this is a "phenomenal program" that shows students "how to make their own cinematographic works of art, while also learning to understand other classic and contemporary works."

Though FSU's academic programs are a great fit for many students, some do see important drawbacks. Students have found that the mathematics and engineering programs are quite small, with smaller faculty and facilities. Students admit that many of their classes are lecture-based and place little emphasis on individual attention. One freshman bemoaned the "lack of availability of TAs" and also complained that professors at times were "virtually inaccessible." However, many students found that, with "persistent emailing" and "diligent planning," they were usually able to receive the help they needed. Indeed, despite these drawbacks, for a large public university FSU fosters a great learning environment with which most students are very satisfied.

A Customized, Newly Renovated Campus Life

The majority of freshman at FSU live on campus, and most have found FSU's dorms and facilities to be comfortable, easily accessible, and in great condition. Recently, 10 of FSU's 14 dormitory buildings were renovated. As a result, newly renovated dorms such as Wildwood and Degraff are by far the dorms of choice. One freshman noted that most dorms are "small but comfortable" and was also very pleased to find that most of FSU's dorms are "conveniently located near the center of campus." Special housing in Landis Hall is also available for Honors students. As one freshman Honors student noted, "Rooming with other Honors students makes the Honors program at FSU that much more enjoyable and gives you a tight-knit group of friends."

College life on campus also offers a variety of fun places for students to hang out with friends or relax. Students cite Landis Green as a major on-campus hangout. "Landis Green is a beautiful courtyard area and is a huge part of what makes FSU the school it is. We play football or Frisbee there, talk with friends, or study, and students can even sunbathe in the Florida heat while doing homework, which is very cool." Westcott Fountain also offers a place for students to cool off, and birthday swims in the Fountain are a major part of FSU tradition. Students also relax at the Suwannee Room, where they can "eat good food and have good conversation with friends." FSU's Oglesby Union Center is also a great place to find fast food: students can choose from a local Chinese food venue, a Hardee's, and a Pollo Tropical, among others. To work off those extra calories, students spend many afternoons at the Leach Center, FSU's three-story on-campus workout facility, and students are also very active in FSU's intramural sports programs.

If students at FSU wish to leave campus most find they are actually within walking distance of a vibrant social scene. Though Seminoles feel that their college is more than just a party school, they are very proud of the notorious party scene that can be found at the many nightclubs of the Strip and the fraternity and sorority houses nearby. Alcohol is "a must have" for most social events, but students are strictly forbidden to bring alcohol on campus, so most partying takes place in off-campus apartments and dance parties at Chubby's or other nightclubs on the Strip. Hook-ups are also frequent at such events. As one freshman bragged (to the concurrence of several others), "FSU takes great pride in the beauty of its women. FSU girls are by far among the prettiest you will ever see."

Most upperclassmen choose to live off campus. "That is actually for the best," said one freshman, "since FSU's dorms are already crowded, and apartments are actually cheaper." In addition, many freshmen concede that RAs here can be a problem. One freshman noted that her RA was "very unsociable and not very helpful" and that many of her friends also had problems with RAs. Also, parking at FSU, said one freshman, is "Abysmal . . . after the first two weeks I brought my car back home. It was too much of a hassle." FSU students also lament that there is not enough racial diversity on campus. However, despite these concerns, most students enjoy their on-campus living experience.

Seminole Pride and Success in Athletics and Beyond

Though FSU is known for its party scene, it is even better known for its prized football team and fan base. "Football at FSU is a religion. The Florida State Seminoles are its holy ministers, and the fans and alumni are its loyal, devout followers," one sophomore proclaimed. The FSU Seminoles boast a fan base in the hundreds of thousands both in Tallahassee and around the state. The Student Boosters sponsor massive pep rallies such as the Downtown GetDown and huge tailgating events. Tradition is also important for Seminole football games. As one sophomore explained, "Each game starts with the Seminole mascot, the Osceola, galloping onto the field with a flaming spear that is thrown into the center of the field to rile up the fans." Indeed, football at FSU is a significant source of school pride, especially during match-ups with FSU's two major rivals, the University of Florida and the University of Miami.

Though football is the major sport of choice, FSU also has a variety of excellent varsity and intramural sports. College basketball and baseball are very popular at FSU. According to one sophomore, the school has "an awesome baseball team, possibly one of the best in the country." For FSU's more casual athletes, intramural sports are an essential element of life. "FSU has an intramural league for almost every sport you can imagine," explained one freshman. "Flag football actually has over 500 participants this year." In addition, the Leach Center's athletic facilities are state-of-the-art and include two floors of workout equipment, an indoor track, and an Olympic-sized swimming pool. Yoga, spinning, and aerobic exercise classes are also offered there for free, so students of all athletic inclinations can enjoy working out.

> "Football at FSU is a religion. The Florida State Seminoles are its holy ministers, and the fans and alumni are its loyal, devout followers."

In addition to athletics, FSU has a strong set of extracurricular activities. Greek life is the predominant activity at FSU. One freshman said, "Almost everyone I know is pledging for a fraternity or sorority." Greek organizations give students leadership opportunities and can be more party-oriented or career-based depending on the chapter. FSU's Student Government Association also hosts a variety of events, including Parents' Weekend festivities and weekly movie nights. Also, students can apply to intern for the Florida State Legislature at the Capitol Building, which, as one senior noted, "is life-changing, if you have the time and the discipline to do it."

Finally, a unique and valuable gem in FSU's treasury of school pride rests in the excellent study-abroad program. One junior said that FSU "has one of the best study-abroad programs in the country." For the program in England, "It's right in the heart of London, and had so many different courses. It gave me so much cultural knowledge, was great for my political science major, and was a blast." FSU also offers programs in other locations, including Panama, Spain, France, China, Australia, Italy, and Costa Rica. Indeed, FSU's study-abroad program is something that truly distinguishes FSU from other universities.

FSU is a well-rounded academic institution that offers students unique academic opportunities and a lively atmosphere of social events. As one student said, "FSU is a place where students party hard, Seminole pride and history is celebrated, valuable lessons are learned, and life-changing opportunities are found."—*Andrew Pearlmutter*

FYI

If you come to Florida State University, you'd better bring "good walking shoes. You do a lot of walking at FSU."

What is the typical weekend schedule? "Friday nights are spent partying at a friend's apartment or clubbing at the Strip. On Saturdays, most go to the football game after tailgating and then party. Sundays are spent sleeping in and studying."

If I could change one thing about FSU, I'd "add more parking garages and bring a better variety of food to the campus."

Three things every student at FSU should do before graduating are "tour the Florida Capitol Building, study abroad with FSU's amazing study abroad program, and go to a Florida State Seminoles football game."

New College of Florida

Address: 5800 Bay Shore Road Sarasota, FL 34243-2109
Phone: 941-487-5000
E-mail address: admissions@ncf.edu
Web site URL: www.ncf.edu
Year Founded: 1964
Private or Public: Public
Religious Affiliation: None
Location: Small city
Number of Applicants: 1,221
Percent Accepted: 58%
Percent Accepted who enroll: 32%
Number Entering: 239
Number of Transfers Accepted each Year: 27
Middle 50% SAT range: M: 590–670, CR: 630–730, Wr: 600–690
Middle 50% ACT range: 27–31
Early admission program EA/ED/None: None

Percentage accepted through EA or ED: NA
EA and ED deadline: NA
Regular Deadline: 15-Feb, 15-April
Application Fee: $30
Full time Undergraduate enrollment: 785
Total enrollment: 785
Percent Male: 38%
Percent Female: 62%
Total Percent Minority or Unreported: 16%
Percent African-American: 2%
Percent Asian/Pacific Islander: 3%
Percent Hispanic: 10%
Percent Native-American: 1%
Percent International: Unreported
Percent in-state/out of state: 82%/18%
Percent from Public HS: 80%
Retention Rate: 82%

Graduation Rate 4-year: 45%
Graduation Rate 6-year: 63%
Percent Undergraduates in On-campus housing: 80%
Number of official organized extracurricular organizations: 35
3 Most popular majors: Biology, Psychology, Political Science
Student/Faculty ratio: 10:1
Average Class Size: 18
Percent of students going to grad school: 17%
Tuition and Fees: $4,127.40
In State Tuition and Fees if different: $2,376
Cost for Room and Board: $7,464
Percent receiving financial aid out of those who apply, first year: 58%
Percent receiving financial aid among all students: 39%

Imagine a college with 785 students, a laid-back atmosphere, a beach-side location, and no grades. This is no cushy finishing school; this is New College of Florida, the state's public honors college. Formerly the honors college of the University of South Florida, New College has only recently been able to stand alone in the State University System as one of Florida's, and the nation's, most unique institutions of higher learning.

Free-Form Academics

One of the most oft-cited facts about New College's academic program is its absence of formal grades. For each class, students receive from their professor a detailed evaluation of their performance that term. A common misconception is that this decreases students' motivation to do their best work. In reality, this system is a great compliment to the culture of self-motivation that is so pervasive at the school. (It's also a great boost to applications to graduate school.)

"The best education demands a joint search for learning by exciting teachers and able students," claims the college's Web site. Though this may sound idealistic, at New College these words are put into practice. "High-caliber" faculty and an eclectic, self-selected group of high-achieving students create for each other the "constructive pressure to succeed," in the words of one sophomore. In elaborating on this "constructive pressure," one art major cites not only the close relationships she has developed with the faculty in her department, but also the various student-run art shows that she and her friends have organized. Another student described the typical student-professor relationship: "You'll definitely have professors who know you well—some will probably cook your whole class dinner." Students work especially closely with their professors on their senior thesis, which is a universal graduation requirement.

In general, the academic requirements are not considered very strict. The distribution requirements are minimal at most, and many students elect to design their own major. There are, however, traditional majors available, with literature, anthropology and the sciences tending to be the most popular. Marine biology is also particularly strong, a fact enhanced by the college's proximity to the Gulf of Mexico.

An Open Atmosphere—Thanks to the "Walls"

New College has a deserved reputation as being a hotbed of activism. An overwhelming majority of its students consider themselves liberal, and radicalism—including anarchism—tends to be the rule rather than the exception. But rather than identifying themselves based on such labels, students would prefer to be seen as open-minded. Perhaps one student put it best in stating that Novo Collegians are better at "theorizing about activism" than practicing it.

> "You'll definitely have professors who know you well—some will probably cook your whole class dinner."

But there are certainly other things to do. One of students' favorite New College traditions is "the Walls." These parties are usually held multiple times a week in the school's main courtyard, the Palm Court. Students sign up to host the college-sponsored event, and the whole school is always invited. One sophomore found it hard to describe, other than that the Walls are much more "open and comfortable" than parties at other schools. "If you're not comfortable dancing," she said, "come to New College and you'll soon become a great dancer." Other popular school-wide dance parties include the Palm Court Parties (PCPs), which are more organized and happen on special occasions, such as Valentine's Day and Halloween.

Complementing this open party atmosphere is a widely accepted culture of drugs and alcohol. Marijuana and alcohol are prevalent and widely available, and it is common knowledge that the few law enforcement officials on campus are there to protect students against outsiders, not to break up social gatherings. "Cops look the other way most of the time," one student said. However, most students agree that there is little pressure on those who do not wish to participate in illicit activities.

One aspect of New College's setting that draws complaints is the town of Sarasota. Wealthy retirees are the average residents of this town, which is "a community with aspirations of being cultural and artsy." But the weather gets high marks, as do the tourist attractions: the beach and the Ringling Museum. The latter is gaining more popularity with students because of its efforts to build new student centers and libraries close to campus. And if one is desperate to get out of Sarasota for a while, there's always Tampa, which is less than an hour away by car.

There is plenty to do on campus as well. Many students are involved in such extracurriculars as *The Catalyst*, the weekly student-run newspaper; student government; and activist groups. Sports are admittedly a smaller part of life than at larger universities. New College has no varsity programs, but racquetball and soccer are popular choices for pickup games.

Beds and Bread

Dorm life receives positive reviews from most students. Lucky students are assigned to a Pei dorm or the newer Dort, or Goldstein Hall. The former are apparently the most spacious and best designed overall (originally designed as hotels by I.M. Pei), whereas the latter is more modern in all aspects and has suite-style living arrangements. The Pei dorms are reputedly the most social. "You will see your friends when you enter and leave the building, and hang out outside talking a lot," one resident said. The main drawback is that since New College is working on increasing the size of its student body, many of the rooms that were designed as doubles are suddenly becoming triples.

Campus residents are required to be on the meal plan, which is not considered a bonus. The food leaves something to be desired: "There's a reason we were ranked as the worst college food in the South," one student explained. There is one central cafeteria, but alternatives abound, including the Four Winds, a student-run cafe.

A One-of-a-Kind Experience

New College is not known to be an incredibly diverse place, as most students are white, middle-class, liberal and suburban. Other aspects of diversity, however, are present on campus. For example, the school has what one sophomore called "gender diversity." The school is very gay-friendly, and all sorts of lifestyles find acceptance at New

College. Overall, the students self-select to a large extent; while this is great for creating and sustaining a unique culture, it has the downside of perpetuating the school's homogeneity.

If you are a Florida resident, you won't find a much better education for the money than New College, as many in-state students are eligible for the state's generous scholarship programs and don't have to pay a dime to go to school. But everyone, both Florida residents and out-of-state students, shares the uniqueness of the New College experience: a noncompetitive, high-quality academic program with laid-back, intelligent students in an ideal campus setting.—*Jay Buchanan*

FYI

If you come to New College, you'd better bring "your stamina and social skills."
What is the typical weekend schedule? "Friday, relax and get ready for the party in Palm Court; Saturday, relax and play some sports; Sunday, nothing else but studying."
If I could change one thing about New College, "I'd make the student population more diverse."
Three things that every student should do before graduating are: "go to a Wall or PCP, walk around barefoot, and write a thesis."

Rollins College

Address: 1000 Holt Avenue #1502 Winter Park, FL 32789
Phone: 407-646-2161
E-mail address: admission@rollins.edu
Web site URL: www.rollins.edu
Year Founded: 1885
Private or Public: Private
Religious Affiliation: None
Location: Suburban
Number of Applicants: 3,485
Percent Accepted: 53%
Percent Accepted who enroll: 25%
Number Entering: 464
Number of Transfers Accepted each Year: 97
Middle 50% SAT range: M: 555–650, CR: 555–650, Wr: Unreported
Middle 50% ACT range: 24–29
Early admission program EA/ED/None: ED

Percentage accepted through EA or ED: 41%
EA and ED deadline: 15-Nov
Regular Deadline: 15-Feb
Application Fee: $40
Full time Undergraduate enrollment: 1,785
Total enrollment: 1,785
Percent Male: 44%
Percent Female: 56%
Total Percent Minority or Unreported: 29%
Percent African-American: 4%
Percent Asian/Pacific Islander: 4%
Percent Hispanic: 10%
Percent Native-American: <1%
Percent International: 4%
Percent in-state/out of state: 47%/53%
Percent from Public HS: 55%
Retention Rate: Unreported
Graduation Rate 4-year: 59%

Graduation Rate 6-year: 68%
Percent Undergraduates in On-campus housing: 69%
Number of official organized extracurricular organizations: 112
3 Most popular majors: Economics, Business, Psychology
Student/Faculty ratio: 10:1
Average Class Size: 10 to 19
Percent of students going to grad school: 41%
Tuition and Fees: $34,520
In State Tuition and Fees if different: No difference
Cost for Room and Board: $10,780
Percent receiving financial aid out of those who apply, first year: 70%
Percent receiving financial aid among all students: 70%

Set in idyllic Winter Park, Florida, Rollins College is "like a vacation every single day." Whether sunning by the outdoor pool, enjoying scenic Lake Virginia, or partying in nearby Orlando, Rollins students know how to have fun, and they do it in style.

Steady Studies

Academics at Rollins are "above average but not too difficult." Students who want to do well can work towards a more intense schedule, but others opt to get by in less demanding majors such as education. Science, business and foreign language majors are "competitive and demanding," required a minimum of several hours work every night, but well worth the professors they feature. "I know a lot of them wrote the text books they teach with . . . several famous politicians graduated from Rollins, too."

Rollins students have one complaint in the academic department—thick bureaucracy. It's tough to get into the classes you want, and as one freshman complained, "It's difficult to switch/drop/add classes. I spent two weeks trying to fix my schedule." But such pains are made up for with exceptionally hands-on class options. As one student raved, "Rollins offers a course that allows students to get credit by tutoring elementary kids."

High-Class Frats

For the more action-oriented, the party scene at Rollins is packed. "Everyone drinks in the dorm rooms," frat parties are frequent, and Orlando, less than ten minutes away, is packed with bars and clubs. That's a lot to handle in one weekend, especially when combined with a prevalent drug scene. "The drug scene is definitely big," one student said. "Coke is huge."

About thirty percent of the student body is part of the Greek community. One freshman said that "It isn't hard to rush and I haven't heard of any bad stories. It's expensive, but there are really fun theme parties. Golf Pro's Tennis Hoes was my favorite." ATO and Chi Psi are the "best frats," but "TKE has good parties." Kappa Delta and Kappa Kappa Gamma are the most popular sororities.

Even when they aren't going out, Rollins students dress to impress. "Many people are very preppy," a sophomore commented. "Everyone here owns a Lacoste shirt and many girls wear Lilly Pulitzer dresses and have Gucci and Louis Vuitton bags." Although diversity is lacking at Rollins, beauty is big. One girl said that "The student body is like no other. I've had several friends come and visit and they were all in shock. Everyone wears ridiculously expensive clothing, drives ridiculously nice cars and tries to outdo everyone else." And the old Spanish style campus tends to be as perfectly manicured as the undergrads themselves. The Rollins campus is "absolutely beautiful" and "covered in gorgeous foliage." And it's also a safe haven for students seeking alone time. One student said, "You can always find a place to hide down by the lake" or go running outside at night. "I love that I don't ever have to worry about anything happening."

Dumpy Dorms

For all the good-looking people and places in Winter Park, the student dorms don't quite match up. "For the price of Rollins, the dorms are disgusting. They're always filthy and covered in vomit, empty beer cans and cockroaches." "McKean is probably the worse dorm because it's always so dirty. We have a pretty big issue with cockroaches and stray cats right now. It's pretty gross." Air-conditioning is about the only perk. And interestingly enough, Florida law prohibits coed bathrooms. Considering the on-campus housing options, it is no surprise that many students opt to move off. "The apartments and houses in Winter Park are all very adorable so most people want to live close by."

> "Being on a sports team here isn't really a big deal. It's probably better to join a frat or sorority."

Luckily, the food fares a bit better. "The meal plan is great at Rollins" one undergrad said. Students get $1,700 per semester to use at dining halls and neighborhood restaurants, including Domino's pizza. There is also a deli counter and food store for kids on the run. However, "The dining hall is definitely a social scene," so students try to make time to go there and "talk with friends." When in the mood for a night on the town, Winter Park offers "amazing" restaurants, bars, and shops.

Tars Take it Slow

Extracurricular activities at Rollins "aren't huge" and "not many students work." "They're more likely to be found by the pool," one junior commented. Sports aren't very popular either, but as one student pointed out, "The baseball boys have good parties." Baseball games also attract the highest attendance, along with men's soccer (perhaps all its European recruits make it hard for even a Florida girl to resist the accents). Overall, though, "There is little team spirit," which bothers some students, especially since the Tars house a conference-leading men's basketball team.

Those students who choose to participate in extracurricular activities are well respected—particularly the members of the SGA, Rollins' Student Government Association. For theater buffs, the Annie Russell Theatre is quite the attraction. One seat is kept empty at all times for the ghost of Annie Russell, said to haunt the building. There are even students who claim to have seen and heard Annie there at night. When students aren't at a practice or in a meeting, they hit the gym. "Many people wakeboard on the lake in their free time," one student said. There is also an outdoor swimming pool and golf course nearby for athletes at heart. "Being on a sports team here isn't really a big deal. It's probably better to join a frat or sorority."—*Lauren Ezell*

FYI

If you come to Rollins, you better bring "a designer handbag, bathing suit and Lilly Pulitzer dress (for girls) and a Lacoste polo shirt, a ton of cash and a BMW (for guys)."

What is a typical weekend schedule? "Party at night, lay by the pool during the day, possibly get some homework done and do it all over again the next night."

If I could change one thing about Rollins, I'd "change the cost of tuition. It's not worth the $42,000 plus."

Three things every student at Rollins should do before graduating are: "Go to Disney World at least once, take a trip to Cocoa Beach and party at Club Paris."

Stetson University

Address: 421 N Woodland Boulevard DeLand, FL 32723
Phone: 800-688-0101
E-mail address: admissions@stetson.edu
Web site URL: www.stetson.edu
Year Founded: 1883
Private or Public: Private
Religious Affiliation: None
Location: Small city
Number of Applicants: 4,119
Percent Accepted: 54%
Percent Accepted who enroll: 28%
Number Entering: 697
Number of Transfers Accepted each Year: 100
Middle 50% SAT range: M: 500–600, CR: 500–610, Wr: 480–580
Middle 50% ACT range: 21–26
Early admission program EA/ED/None: ED

Percentage accepted through EA or ED: Unreported
EA and ED deadline: 1-Nov
Regular Deadline: 15-Mar
Application Fee: $40
Full time Undergraduate enrollment: 2,143
Total enrollment: 3,696
Percent Male: 43%
Percent Female: 57%
Total Percent Minority or Unreported: 18%
Percent African-American: 5%
Percent Asian/Pacific Islander: 3%
Percent Hispanic: 10%
Percent Native-American: <1%
Percent International: Unreported
Percent in-state/out of state: 79.7%/20.3%
Percent from Public HS: 75.10%
Retention Rate: 77%

Graduation Rate 4-year: 55%
Graduation Rate 6-year: 67%
Percent Undergraduates in On-campus housing: 72%
Number of official organized extracurricular organizations: 100
3 Most popular majors: Business, Psychology, Political Science and English, Communication Studies
Student/Faculty ratio: 12:1
Average Class Size: 18
Percent of students going to grad school: 60%
Tuition and Fees: $30,216
In State Tuition and Fees if different: No difference
Cost for Room and Board: $8,436
Percent receiving financial aid out of those who apply, first year: 22%
Percent receiving financial aid among all students: 15%

It's tough to deny the allure of packing swimsuits and tanning lotion instead of snow pants and boots in preparation for college. But Stetson University, in sunny DeLand, Florida, isn't just any laid-back, rural Florida school. It's known for solid academics—including several well-respected professional programs—and a vibrant campus atmosphere.

Academics

According to *U.S. News and World Report*, Stetson consistently ranks among the best regional schools in the Southeast. There is a lot to choose from when it come to academics: with over 60 major and minor fields available to undergraduates in the College of Arts and Sciences, the School of Business Administration and the School of Music, students can study anything from digital arts (a collaboration between the departments of Art and Computer Science and the School of Music) to chemistry to business law.

In addition to completing the requirements for a major, undergraduates in the College of Arts and Sciences must fulfill a stringent set of distributional requirements, which encompass the areas of "Foundations" (basic courses such as English, math and foreign language), "Breadth of Knowledge" (natural and social science), "Bases of Ethical Decision Making" (ethics courses), and a non-academic requirement, "Cultural Attendance," which entails attending approved cultural events every semester. Some academic requirements can be waived with AP scores, but either way, the fact remains that you will get a well-rounded education at Stetson. "All the requirements can be irritating," one junior said. "But . . . if you're an English major, at least you have the experience of having taken some science."

There are also several programs that encourage Stetson's brightest to go beyond the curricular minimum. The Honors Program, for example, gives students the opportunities to take a Junior Honors Seminar and design their own major, as well as encouraging them to study abroad. Although any entering student may apply, most accepted students have had SAT I in the 50 percent range of 1030 and 1240 and 41 percent have been in the top 10 percent of their high-school class.

As one might expect from a school with such a variety of academic disciplines and such a small student body, classes at Stetson are small, and professors are accessible. With relatively few classes within each division, majors often encompass broad areas of study. Students change their majors often, a process that is apparently neither difficult nor stigmatized. But having small class sizes—even in such traditionally impersonal disciplines as business—can make all the difference for some. "You do tend to bond with your professors, whether you like it or not," said one senior, a marketing major. "I have not been in a class with more than 50 students."

Once students have experienced the ease of getting into their desired classes and the delight of having the professor know their names from Day One, there's the actual class work to consider. More difficult subjects are rumored to be biology, chemistry and music. At one point, "Music Theory" had the highest failure rate on campus. Communications and education, according to students, are easier majors.

Dorm Life

Since freshmen, sophomores and juniors are all required to live on campus, "dorm life" at Stetson is often synonymous with "campus life." "The dorms aren't particularly nice," one sophomore said, "but they are amazing places to meet people and really learn how to live on your own." Students praised the location of the dorms—they are all within walking distance of central campus.

Other facilities are certainly not lacking. The college gymnasium and pool received high marks. The gym offers classes during the semester, and the pool is "very spacious and a good place to relax," presumably since most of the year is bathing-suit weather.

The dining halls are also decent. The main eating facility is Commons, which is apparently "fair" in terms of food and seating arrangements. Known as a social place, Commons is an area where "You can just pick up a conversation with anyone really." Stetson's flexible dining plan allows students to cash in unused meals for purchases at other eateries close by, such as the popular grill Hat Rack, Einstein Bros. Bagels, and the nearby smoothie shop.

Campus Life

Though Stetson features a variety of clubs and activities for students, the Greeks, with their six fraternities and five sororities, tend to be the biggest force on campus. They often host large parties and events in their mostly off-campus venues. Most of these events are nonexclusive.

Two other prominent groups on campus are the Council for Student Activities (CSA) and the Student Government Association (SGA). They have been responsible in the past for bringing in such big-name acts as Less Than Jake and Busta Rhymes. In addition, Stetson hosts a variety of speakers every year. "If you want to hear a speaker every week at

Stetson, you definitely can," one senior said. There are, of course, a variety of smaller organizations that cater to more specific groups; these, however, tend to be less active.

Athletics are also a big part of campus life. Although the school lacks the draw of a football team, students report that the other varsity teams' events are well-attended and popular. While the teams themselves "tend to keep together," according to a senior non-athlete, this doesn't keep the rest of the student body from going to games and cheering them on. The basketball and soccer teams receive the most attention. Intramural sports are also popular.

Outside the Bounds of Campus Grounds

The town of DeLand is not generally known as a fun place to hang out, but it has its advocates. This minority says that the town fulfills all "basic needs" with a Wal-Mart and several chain restaurants, that the historic downtown area provides a nice walk, and that "You couldn't ask for a safer place to have a school."

> "You couldn't ask for a safer place to have a school."

But those who seek a setting that includes more than McDonald's, picturesque promenades and a sense of security flock instead to Daytona or Orlando, each of which is less than an hour away. Popular destinations include malls, clubs, bars, theme parks and anything else the rural town just can't pro-vide. To this end, many students do bring cars to campus, but—as with most colleges—the limitations of on-campus parking can make owning a car more of a burden than anything. Many students use their cars to drive home to other Florida cities on a regular basis.

For those who choose to stay on campus or in DeLand, there is certainly not a dearth of things to do. The most popular parties, thrown by the Greeks, are generally held off campus, but there are large on-campus parties as well. These tend to be contained by Public Safety, Stetson's security detail. Drinking is prevalent at all of these parties, but there are alternatives. Many groups, particularly various Christian ones, host dry events on a regular basis. Drug use does occur at Stetson, but it is easy to avoid and by no means popular. According to students, alternatives to "traditional" college partying include bowling, ice skating, going to the movies, and listening to live music.

Conclusion

So why choose Stetson? For many, the appeal is that the college is "a small school close to home." Around 80 percent of the students are Floridians; it's tough for any Florida native to consider going anywhere farther north for school. But the year-round sun is not the only draw: Stetson features high-quality academics on a gorgeous campus. Although it is located in a rural town, Orlando and Daytona are close enough that students don't feel stranded. Add to that the small classes, accessible professors, school spirit and general commitment to excellence, and you've got a school that would be hard for anyone to pass up.—*Jay Buchanan*

FYI
If you come to Stetson, you'd better bring "a bathing suit, because we have a nice pool and people take trips to the beach very often."
What is the typical weekend schedule? "Friday, drive to Daytona; Saturday, spend the afternoon in Daytona and hang out with friends; Sunday, relax in DeLand."
If I could change one thing about Stetson, "I would bring a better selection of food during the weekends."
The three things that everyone should do before graduating from Stetson are "go to all the beaches, join a club or Greek organization and get involved, and enjoy it!"

University of Florida

Address: 201 Criser Hall, Box 114000 Gainesville, FL 32611-4000
Phone: 352-392-1365
E-mail address: ourwebrequests@registrar.ufl.edu
Web site URL: www.ufl.edu
Year Founded: 1853
Private or Public: Public
Religious Affiliation: None
Location: Suburban
Number of Applicants: 24,126
Percent Accepted: 42%
Percent Accepted who enroll: 63%
Number Entering: 6,390
Number of Transfers Accepted each Year: 2,150
Middle 50% SAT range: M: 580–690, CR: 560–670, Wr:** Unreported
Middle 50% ACT range: 25–29
Early admission program EA/ED/None: None

Percentage accepted through EA or ED: NA
EA and ED deadline: NA
Regular Deadline: 1-Nov
Application Fee: $30
Full time Undergraduate enrollment: 35,189
Total enrollment: 47,390
Percent Male: 47%
Percent Female: 53%
Total Percent Minority or Unreported: 36%
Percent African-American: 10%
Percent Asian/Pacific Islander: 8%
Percent Hispanic: 14%
Percent Native-American: <1%
Percent International: 1%
Percent in-state/out of state: 96%/4%
Percent from Public HS: 81%
Retention Rate: Unreported
Graduation Rate 4-year: Unreported

Graduation Rate 6-year: Unreported
Percent Undergraduates in On-campus housing: 77%
Number of official organized extracurricular organizations: 500
3 Most popular majors: Finance, Political Science and Government, Psychology
Student/Faculty ratio: 13:1
Average Class Size: 10 to 19
Percent of students going to grad school: Unreported
Tuition and Fees: $20,640
In State Tuition and Fees if different: $3,790
Cost for Room and Board: $7,150
Percent receiving financial aid out of those who apply, first year: 39%
Percent receiving financial aid among all students: 63%

G ators are known to be ruthless predators, and that remains true for the Gators at the University of Florida— UF students continue to step up their athletic, academic and overall levels of performance with every coming year. The University of Florida was the flagship school for higher education in Florida in the 1800s, and has grown to be one of the most prestigious schools not only in the state, but also in the country. And who wouldn't want to come to UF? With great weather, national champion sports teams, and an upward climbing academic reputation, students agree that there is not much you could improve about the University of Florida.

The Early Bird Gets the Worm/Dormancy in a Gator Hole

As the academic standards at UF rise, the acceptance rate keeps dropping. Many students found that applying early helped to ease anxiety about getting in, especially if UF was their first choice. An added incen-tive to apply early is that the housing application is mailed together with the main application and is handled on a first come, first serve basis. While it is not required, most freshmen live on campus and find it both very convenient and helpful in making fast friends. However, not all the dorms are created equal, and two dormitory buildings even lack air-conditioning, a necessity for most of the sultry Floridian year. There is also not enough on-campus housing for all freshmen, so space fills up fast. No one is required to live on campus at any time, and most upperclassmen move off campus after freshman year if they haven't already. Two sophomores agreed that there are perks to both, and there is "never a better time than freshman year" to live on campus. The dorm rules are relatively strict regarding overnight guests of any gender, but it all depends on the residential assistants who live on each floor. Students can even have small pets of any variety as long as their roommate approves. If you do live off campus, like the majority of students at UF, it is "pretty essential" to have a car. However, parking issues are always lurking, and it is considered a rite of passage to get a parking ticket, if not many. One student estimated that there are about three times as many cars as there are parking spots.

If a student does not end up bringing a car, he will probably know someone who did and should take full advantage. Gainesville is located in the center of North Florida, about the same distance from Orlando as from Jacksonville. Tampa and Tallahassee are also within driving distance, which is nice for when the UF-FSU game is at FSU. Another perk of Gainesville's location is its proximity to the beaches—both the Gulf Coast and the Atlantic Ocean are short drives away. One student said he usually takes a trip out of Gainesville about every other weekend, especially during the football season.

A Winning Combination
It isn't that students want to get out of Gainesville, it's that they are pulled out by tradition. Going to football games, no matter the location or the time of the year, is one of the major traditions that continues every year. Sports are huge at UF, as is the amount of school spirit; everyone claims to "bleed orange and blue." It makes sense, because while they are always top contenders, both the UF football and men's basketball teams won national championships in 2006–2007. As a result of both tradition and the championship titles, one student claimed that "Any football or basketball player is basically a god in Gainesville." Since both game tickets and Gator paraphernalia are always limited, there is a lottery system for tickets but you should bring "something orange to wear to games because everything is always sold out."

Southern Comfort
While the varsity athletes get all the glory, there are also many opportunities for less mainstream athletes to compete in either club or intramural leagues on campus. There is everything from rowing to Ultimate Frisbee to soccer in the club arena. Intramurals at UF are always expanding, and the spring of 2007 saw the first ever rock-paper-scissors intramural tournament. There really is something for everyone, including multiple gym and recreation facilities for both athletes and non-athletes.

Students also use their free time to work, to volunteer in the community, or to get involved with clubs. Students who work can choose between working a desk job on campus, or working off campus at the Gainesville Mall. The Shands Teaching Hospital provides many opportunities for interested students to volunteer and get hands-on experience in the medical world. There are also groups like GatorTRAX, which is an engineering program for students in the sixth to twelfth grades. There are almost as many groups and clubs as you can imagine, but you would be hard pressed to find a student who knew what a cappella was.

> **"Any football or basketball player is basically a god in Gainesville."**

When asked, UF students claim "There is no stereotypical Gator—we are a very diverse student body," which is a reasonable claim since the undergraduate student body is more than 35,000 strong. One senior maintained that her fellow students "range from hippies to rednecks to book worms." Although she conceded that many students come from in-state, she listed friends from "England, Saudi Arabia, South Africa, Korea, and most of the states." So while students come from all over the place, there are certain locations on campus where more visible groups can be spotted. A central spot called Plaza of the Americas is a place where "a lot of the hippie-ish people hang out."

Greeks and Gods
While the majority of students are not in fraternities and sororities at UF, Greek life plays a big role in the social scene. There are parties from Thursday night to Saturday night, and the days in between are used to go to clubs like XS on University Avenue. XS has a popular 80s theme night, but if students desire a more laid-back atmosphere, there are also many bars on the Avenue such as the Sloppy Gator. Tailgating for games is also big, and the Florida-Georgia game is touted as the "world's largest outdoor cocktail party." As at most universities, drinking is prevalent, but students say that it is not the only way students socialize at UF. Many students go bowling or see movies. One junior said that the Blockbuster "is always packed," showing that Gator students have many ways of relaxing.

Variety Is the Spice of Life
The reason students need to relax, of course, is schoolwork. UF is not the party school that some may wish it to be. There are many challenging majors, some more popular than

others, all of which have serious competition for classes. Some of the most popular majors are business, engineering, building construction and political science. The financial accounting class, a requirement for the business degree and known as the "hardest course" at UF, forces some students to change their major. One student found changing majors to be "easy," due to the fact that the University "was very accommodating." She said that her advisors, who are assigned through the student's major, are "very helpful." Some students find it easier to declare their majors even before the beginning of their freshman year so they can be sure to get in all the requirements. In addition to the specific departmental requirements, UF also has some general education requirements, which can vary depending on one's chosen major. Many students find it beneficial to transfer their AP credits from high school into college credit, and many can pass out of some requirements completely. One freshman even upgraded to sophomore standing because she had taken so many AP classes in high school.

Summer school is also an option if you have trouble fitting in all your chosen major's requirements, and the Florida legislature actually requires a minimum of six summer school credit hours. Some students find the general education requirements a good way to explore other topics. For example, one student praised the class titled Growing Fruit for Fun and Profit because even if it is not required for a major, "It's interesting and you learn something new you would have never known before. And at the end of every class they give you a bag of fruit to take home."—*Emily Matykiewicz*

FYI

If you come to the University of Flordia, you'd better bring: "some Tylenol, because there is a lot of screaming that comes along with winning 2 national titles!!! GO GATORS!!!"

If I could change one thing about the University of Florida, I'd "make it a little smaller."

What's the typical weekend schedule? "Watch the national champion basketball or football team, then head to downtown Gainesville and dance at Whiskey Room, Plasma, or Rue Bar. Maybe catch a movie on Sunday night."

Three things every UF student should do before graduating are: "experience a Saturday in the Swamp—there is nothing more exciting than cheering the Gators on with 90,000 of your closest friends—study at the new Library West, and go to Lawtey Mud Pit."

University of Miami

Address: PO Box 248025
Coral Gables, FL
33124-4616
Phone: 305-284-4323
E-mail address:
admission@miami.edu
Web site URL:
www.miami.edu
Year Founded: 1925
Private or Public: Private
Religious Affiliation: None
Location: Suburban
Number of Applicants:
19,676
Percent Accepted: 38%
**Percent Accepted who
enroll:** 27%
Number Entering: 1,980
**Number of Transfers
Accepted each Year:** 1,392
Middle 50% SAT range:
M: 600–690,
CR: 580–680, Wr: 560–650
Middle 50% ACT range:
28–31
**Early admission program
EA/ED/None:** EA and ED

**Percentage accepted
through EA or ED: EA:**
45.3% ED: NA
EA and ED deadline: 11/01
and 11/01
Regular Deadline: 15-Jan
Application Fee: $65
**Full time Undergraduate
enrollment:** 10,379
Total enrollment: 13,370
Percent Male: 48%
Percent Female: 52%
**Total Percent Minority or
Unreported:** 55%
Percent African-American:
8%
**Percent Asian/Pacific
Islander:** 5%
Percent Hispanic: 22%
Percent Native-American:
0%
Percent International: 7%
**Percent in-state/out of
state:** 50%/50%
Percent from Public HS:
Unreported
Retention Rate: 90%

Graduation Rate 4-year:
64%
Graduation Rate 6-year:
Unreported
**Percent Undergraduates in
On-campus housing:** 44%
**Number of official organized
extracurricular
organizations:** 217
3 Most popular majors:
Business/Marketing, Visual
and Performing Arts, Biology
Student/Faculty ratio: 11:1
Average Class Size: 10 to 19
**Percent of students going to
grad school:** 35%
Tuition and Fees: $34,834
**In State Tuition and Fees if
different:** No difference
Cost for Room and Board:
$10,254
**Percent receiving financial
aid out of those who apply,
first year:** 78%
**Percent receiving financial
aid among all students:**
48%

"We've got some Canes over here! Whoosh! Whoosh!" Loud cheers erupt throughout the Orange Bowl Stadium as thousands of fans gather to witness the annual University of Miami vs. Florida State University football showdown. Clad in orange and green paraphernalia, the enthusiastic spectators show vibrant support for their team. But Hurricane pride is hardly limited to the athletic field. University of Miami students have their whole school to be proud of: top academic programs, a wide array of student activities, and a beautiful campus located in sunny South Florida.

Work Hard, Play Hard

The University of Miami distinguishes itself from other schools in that it focuses heavily on both academics and athletics. What other school can lay claim to both hosting a 2004 Presidential Debate and being home to numerous championship athletic teams? In terms of academics, UM students have over 180 undergraduate programs to choose from,

offered through eight colleges: Architecture, Arts and Sciences, Business, Communication, Education, Engineering, Music, and Nursing. Freshmen accepted into the University as "undecided" majors are admitted through the College of Arts and Sciences.

The academic requirements differ depending on your college. Nevertheless, "Students have very diverse interests and are encouraged to take classes in other fields and departments," one psychology major said. The most popular majors at the College of Arts and Sciences at UM include Biology, Psychology and Political Science. Students generally agree that the "hardest majors tend to be in the science and engineering fields," such as Biology, Neuroscience, Biomedical Engineering, Physics and Genetics. Most students say that introductory courses, which generally contain between 100 and 200 students, are relatively easy. But upper-level courses, including "Organic Chemistry," "Experimental Psychology," "Ancient Greek" and "Politics of the Middle East" are known for being particularly tough. UM also offers several unique courses, including "Dance Therapy," "Horror Literature" and "Videogame Systems."

The majority of classes are taught by professors, not TAs. One junior notes, "I've had some really amazing professors here who are scarily brilliant and very approachable." Professors tend to be available and "encourage students to take advantage of their office hours."

Extending invitations to only the top 10 percent of the entering class, the University's Honors Program is considered one of the most prestigious academic tracks for incoming freshmen. Students must have a minimum SAT score of 1360 or ACT score of 31 and be ranked in the top five percent of their high school graduating class to be admitted. The Honors Program offers over 200 courses and course sections per semester, and classes are generally small seminars that foster intimate class discussion and interactive learning. In addition, the University of Miami has a highly selective Honors Program in Medicine, in which students can earn both a Bachelor of Science and a Doctor of Medicine degree in seven to eight years. Dual Degree Honor Programs in Biomedical Engineering, Marine Geology, Physical Therapy, Latin American Studies and Law are also available. Overall, the academic life is described as "pretty balanced," and "There's room for fun if you break up your time well."

Fun in the Florida Sun

University of Miami students have tons of social options on weekends, both on and off campus. There are frequent activities on campus such as concerts, movie screenings at the free campus cinema, and invited guest comedians and musicians. Frats also regularly sponsor parties where "everyone's welcome." Moreover, club-sponsored socials, such as the Hispanic Heritage Month Gala, are popular weekend options that "cater to everyone." Homecoming is another big event on campus and even includes a parade and fireworks. As one sophomore noted, "Now the school is starting to hold more events on campus on Saturdays and Sundays so that people stay more on campus." Drinking is prevalent on campus and the general feeling is that "almost everyone drinks." Nevertheless, students who do not drink say that they do not feel excluded.

Despite the active on-campus social scene, many UM students venture off to enjoy the Miami nightlife on weekends. As one student put it, "That's the beauty of being in Miami—on any given night there is something to do." Typical weekend hangouts include clubs in Coconut Grove, the Design District, South Beach and Bayside Marketplace. Usually, the minimum age for admittance into clubs is 21. On Thursdays, however, Coconut Grove has a "College Night," when students 18 and over are allowed to get into its clubs. During the day on weekends, many students catch movies or go shopping at The Shops at Sunset Place, a popular mall near campus. Of course, UM students can always be found hanging out and tanning in South Beach.

> "That's the beauty of being in Miami—on any given night there is something to do."

Although many University of Miami students have cars on campus, the school offers several transportation options to get around Miami. The Hurry 'Canes shuttle takes students to Coconut Grove and The Shops at Sunset Place, as well as areas on campus. Also, the Metrorail is a convenient way to get to Bayside Marketplace, downtown Miami and Dadeland, a huge shopping mall.

Living in Paradise

Covered with palm trees and beautiful foliage, the University of Miami is frequently praised for its beauty and described by students as "our own tropical paradise." The buildings on campus are built in modern style, and many, such as Hecht College, have been recently renovated.

The University of Miami has several central gathering areas for students. One of the most popular campus locations is the University Center (UC), which contains comfortable sofas, an arcade, a café with pool tables, a convenience store, a food court, and the offices of student organizations are located here. The Rathskeller, nicknamed "the Rat" is another popular social area, where students can play pool, watch one of the wide-screen TVs, or sit outside in the tropical warmth at swinging picnic tables. The "Rat" is also a venue for campus entertainment and frequently features live bands and dance parties. Students enjoy hanging out around the pool area to enjoy the Florida sun.

University of Miami students who choose to live on campus are assigned to one of five residential colleges—Eaton, Hecht, Mahoney,

Pearson and Stanford. The dorms are described as "relatively nice" and all are air-conditioned. As freshmen, students are randomly assigned to the dorms. Students have the option of being placed on "quiet floors," where there are stricter rules about noise. Unlike typical college dorms, a faculty master and his or her family live alongside students in each residential college. The residential colleges are also staffed by Residential Coordinators (RCs) and Residential Advisors (RAs). According to students, most RAs are "pretty strict," and "getting caught drinking or doing drugs will get people in trouble." Alcohol is only allowed in the dorm rooms of students who are 21 and over, and if they are drinking, they must keep their door closed.

The University of Miami also has a large number of commuters, some of whom belong to organizations such as the Association for Commuter Students. Upperclassmen generally decide to live off campus in apartments or houses that rent out to students in the Coral Gables neighborhood. Additionally, UM completed the University Village in 2006; the complex consists of apartments housing only upperclassmen and graduates.

Go 'Canes!

Students at the University of Miami have incredible school spirit. The University's Division One athletic teams dominate collegiate sports and have won more than 20 national championships. Sports such as football, basketball and baseball have "a huge presence on campus," and football is generally considered the most popular sport. As one student put it, "Football season gets crazy down here . . . tailgates start at least four hours before a game."

Aside from varsity sports, students are encouraged to participate in club and intramural teams. The athletic facilities for both athletes and non-athletes are "amazing." The University's multi-million dollar Wellness Center is a top-notch fitness, recreation, and wellness facility open to all students. The activities offered at the Wellness Center include intramural sports, exercise classes, and wellness programs.

University of Miami students are also passionate about extracurricular activities. Greek life is very popular, with over 1,000 un-

dergraduate members of UM's 31 sororities and fraternities. During Canefest, the organization fair at the beginning of fall semester, students are able to choose from a wide variety of clubs. Some popular organizations include Student Government, Council for Democracy, College Democrats, College Republicans, Committee on Student Organizations (COSO), and Hurricane Productions.

There are also a number of honor societies, clubs for specific majors, and community service groups. Moreover, multicultural organizations, such as La Federacion de Estudiantes Cubanos (FEC), are very prominent. Several unique activities exist on campus, such as Salsa Craze, Swing Club, and Adrian Empire, which is a Medieval/Renaissance reenactment group. And as one student remarked, "If there's something you want to do that UM doesn't have, it's pretty easy to start it up." Most students are fairly committed to their extracurricular activities. One sophomore stated, "Getting involved . . . has made it so much better because that's how you make friends and gain experience and knowledge that will help you in the future."

Cane Spirit

Despite a common stereotype that University of Miami students are "rich" and "snobby," most students claim otherwise. Students note that "The majority of people are pretty down-to-earth" and "really friendly." The University also has a great deal of diversity, with students from "all over the world and all around the U.S." A recent graduate said that the prevalent diversity on campus was a "very unique, educational and rewarding experience."

Students praise the University's commitment to both academics and athletics and attribute the University's growing prestige to President Donna Shalala, who is doing "so many things to get our school's name out there." The tropical climate, beautiful campus, and diverse and nurturing student atmosphere are all factors that draw students to the University of Miami. But what really distinguishes the school for most students is "The fact that people actually really care about their school and are proud to go to UM." Go 'Canes!—*Eileen Zelek*

FYI
If you come to the University of Miami, you'd better bring "your bathing suit, flip-flops, shorts, and sunscreen."
What is the typical weekend schedule: "For the most part it consists of lots of homework during the day and partying at night. The weekend starts on Thursday with 'College Night' in Coconut Grove and the rest of the time is usually spent tanning or clubbing in South Beach."
If I could change one thing about the University of Miami, "I'd add more parking garages and make the restaurants and dining halls on campus stay open longer."
Three things every student at the University of Miami should do before graduating are "go to a football game at the Orange Bowl, spend time at South Beach, and hang out at the Rat."

University of South Florida

Address: 4202 East Fowler Avenue Tampa, FL 33620-9951
Phone: 813-974-3350
E-mail address: admissions@admin.usf.edu
Web site URL: www.usf.edu
Year Founded: 1956
Private or Public: Public
Religious Affiliation: None
Location: Urban
Number of Applicants: 27,017
Percent Accepted: 50%
Percent Accepted who enroll: 30%
Number Entering: 3,664
Number of Transfers Accepted each Year: 7,549
Middle 50% SAT range: M: 530–630, CR: 510–610, Wr: 490–580
Middle 50% ACT range: 23–28
Early admission program EA/ED/None: None

Percentage accepted through EA or ED: NA
EA and ED deadline: NA
Regular Deadline: 15-Apr
Application Fee: $30
Full time Undergraduate enrollment: 34,897
Total enrollment: 44,395
Percent Male: 42%
Percent Female: 58%
Total Percent Minority or Unreported: 35%
Percent African-American: 12%
Percent Asian/Pacific Islander: 6%
Percent Hispanic: 14%
Percent Native-American: 1%
Percent International: 1%
Percent in-state/out of state: Unreported
Percent from Public HS: 95%
Retention Rate: 81%
Graduation Rate 4-year: Unreported

Graduation Rate 6-year: Unreported
Percent Undergraduates in On-campus housing: 13%
Number of official organized extracurricular organizations: 507
3 Most popular majors: Biomedical Sciences, Business, Psychology
Student/Faculty ratio: 4:1
Average Class Size: 20 to 29
Percent of students going to grad school: 19%
Tuition and Fees: $16,623
In State Tuition and Fees if different: $3,906
Cost for Room and Board: $8,080
Percent receiving financial aid out of those who apply, first year: 69%
Percent receiving financial aid among all students: 76%

I f you are searching for a college with a fun campus environment, a warm, sunny location, and great academic programs in business, engineering, and science, the University of South Florida is a school worth considering. In addition to enjoying USF's excellent sports teams and numerous nearby social scenes, students there take advantage of the many perks associated with being college kids in Tampa, Florida. Indeed, whether it is spending a day at the beach (only half an hour away), visiting one of the two nearby major theme parks, or enjoying exciting Di-

vision I football games, USF students always have something fun to do while they receive an excellent education.

Getting the Sunshine State Experience

Located in suburban Tampa, USF presents its students numerous benefits, creating an environment that students at other colleges only experience during spring break. Living in Florida is "a blast" according to one sophomore from out of state, who added, "Winters at USF are fantastic, since they are virtually nonexistent." The weather in Tampa is ideal during the winter and spring months, when high temperatures fall comfortably between 60 and 80 degrees, and low temperatures rarely dip below the mid-30s. Most students find the winter months to be enjoyable, and they can frequently be seen lounging about in the many green areas on campus. However, some students did complain about Florida's heat and humidity in the summer and fall months. If you play outdoor sports, be advised, "It is very, very easy to get dehydrated, especially with the high heat and humidity. The Florida heat in August, September, October, and May can be intense."

Students also find that USF is an ideal location within the city itself. One freshman noted, "Two incredible Florida theme parks, Busch Gardens and Adventure Island, are only about five minutes away from campus." In addition, USF is located "about 10–15 minutes north of downtown Tampa, which has Ybor City and Channelside as two major entertainment districts." Channelside has a variety of entertainment venues, including a movie theatre with an IMAX screen, a state-of-the-art bowling alley, and a great variety of clubs and restaurants. Ybor City not only has numerous nightclubs but also a Gameworks, a movie theatre, a line of shops, and a lot of restaurants. The beach is only a 30-minute drive away; students typically recommend Clearwater Beach as a great, year-round hangout place. The many sports teams in the area are also popular venues for students. They frequent both the Tampa Bay Buccaneers football games and the Lightning hockey games. The New York Yankees also conduct their spring training in Tampa. Furthermore, USF's football team, the Bulls, attracts massive crowds weekly, making the university a virtual Mecca for sports enthusiasts. However, one student did advise against watching one specific team. "Even though they practically give away the tickets," one junior noted, "it's just not worth seeing the Devil Rays play baseball."

USF's Academic Trifecta

USF has a strong academic program, especially in the areas of business, engineering, and pre-med. It also has all the benefits of a large university while placing emphasis on personal attention. Incoming freshmen can take a class called "The University Experience" which helps them get acclimated to college life while instructing them in the research techniques and study habits that they will need to be successful. Students report

that USF's business program is very popular on campus. "Most of the people I know are enrolled in at least some type of business-oriented class," one freshman explained, "and many of my friends have already decided to take business administration as their major."

For students not interested in a business-related major, there are lots of excellent options. USF's pre-med program is quite reputable. USF's campus includes the Moffitt Cancer Center, which is one of the top cancer research institutions in the nation and a place where many students volunteer. USF's engineering program is also noteworthy for its great faculty. One student bragged that her professor in the robotics department, Ms. Robin Murphy, missed the first day of class to deploy her robotic technology at the Crandall Canyon Mine to search for mining accident victims underground. This happens to be "just one of many examples in which USF faculty members make a difference."

While USF's academics are very strong in many aspects, students admit that it is not an ideal school for those pursuing math or humanities majors. One freshman criticized the mathematics department for having professors and teaching assistants that "do not speak English very well, are hard to understand, and not very able to help the students." The humanities department, many students complain, needs more classes and does not have enough majors from which they can choose. Despite these drawbacks, however, USF has a solid academic record overall that continues to improve each year.

Living the Good Life, On or Off Campus

A sizeable number of students at USF are commuters who live nearby. Most of these students, however, cite financial concerns for this choice. One junior noted that it was much cheaper for him to stay in an apartment nearby and that most students who opt to stay off campus do so for similar reasons. Campus living at USF is generally quite enjoyable. "I made most of my friends here by hanging out in dorms and watching movies together," noted one sophomore. "The dorms are tiny but conveniently located, and the University tries to pair you up with people you will be compatible with, so nightmare roommates are rare." Most students cite the Marshall Center as the best hangout location on campus. One freshman boasted that the Marshall Center includes "lots of pool tables, a big-screen TV, video games, a food court, and live bands that play every week." Students report that the food at USF is also quite good. In addition to a cafeteria-style meal plan, students can choose from Burger King, Subway, Einstein's Bagels, and Ben and Jerry's, among others. The library is also a great place to get together for academic and social purposes; it has a Starbucks on the first floor and is centrally located. Students also frequent the school's many courtyards and greeneries, which "have plenty of shade and are great places to study or talk to friends."

If students want to get off campus for some fun but do not have money for a night downtown or a day at Busch Gardens, the Gator Dockside is known as a good place to get together with friends. One student noted that "Gator nuggets and watching sports are a must" at this restaurant. USF students also frequent the nearby University Mall, which has a variety of shops and restaurants less than five minutes away from campus. The numerous athletic events held on campus each week, which students can get into for free, are also popular.

When on campus, students report that safety is not a major issue; in fact, "aside from the occasional bike thief," students feel safe. However, some lament that parking is an issue. While new parking lots are being constructed, "parking is terrible" at USF, and commuters complain at "having to arrive up to an hour early at times" to secure a spot close to class and that they "park really far away, which can be annoying."

A Social Scene with Something for Everyone

USF has a unique combination of athletic, Greek, and service organizations. Athletics (participating in or watching) are at the forefront of such activities. As one student noted, "Club-level and intramural sports are always fun" and are "easy to join and stay active in." By far the most popular sport at USF is football, and two major student organizations hold tailgating parties at every home game. The Student Bulls Club is probably the more universal athletic booster organization, as it is open to all students and sets up events at both home and away games for football, basketball, volleyball, soccer, and other Bulls sports. The Beef Studs is the other major athletic booster organization on campus. One freshman stated, "The Beef Studs are a one-of-a-kind, die-hard group of fans that wear body-paint at every event, always keep the crowd pumped, and travel to just about every game. I'm not even

sure if they ever remove the body paint, even during the week." There are plenty of reasons for cheering on the USF Bulls: students tout the fact that their football team is having a phenomenal season and, in October 2007, was ranked number 5 in the SEC.

> "The Beef Studs are a one-of-a-kind, die-hard group of fans that wear body-paint at every event, always keep the crowd pumped, and travel to just about every game. I'm not even sure if they ever remove the body paint, even during the week."

For those not as enthusiastic about sports, USF has a variety of other organizations. One freshman said, "Joining student government is a great way to become involved." Student government organizes school-wide social events and runs the Campus Activities Board, which oversees the funding and administration of student-run organizations on campus. The 37 fraternities and sororities represent the Greek life that plays a major but not dominant role in USF's social scene. While USF has its fair share of fun parties, students there are proud that drinking and drugs "are not a major problem." As one freshman put it, "No one really feels pressured to drink if they go to parties here."

For the more altruistic students, community service organizations and events are also thriving parts of campus life. Students work with Metropolitan Ministries, Habitat for Humanity, and other local non-profits. USF even hosts the region's Special Olympics competition every March. Indeed, as one student said, "USF has an endless number of activities that continue to grow with the interests of the student body. So even if students can't find something they are interested in, they can easily start it up and get funding from the school."

Mixing Business with Pleasure

Finally, students at USF place unique emphasis on career preparation. Alpha Kappa Psi, one of USF's coed professional business fraternities, prepares its members for successful careers in the corporate world. They frequently hold workshops, coach each other for interviews, host speakers from business-related fields, and visit the offices of major companies in the area. Furthermore, students at USF become involved in fields where they have a personal, life-long interest. One particularly driven freshman with a keen interest in hockey secured a marketing internship with the Tampa Bay Lightning, an "incredible, life-shaping experience" in which he has been able to combine "a love for hockey with a career interest in marketing and management." For him, this "has opened the door for a whole new world of opportunities." A host of similar career-oriented internships are available through the Moffitt Cancer Center and in the surrounding community. As the same freshman noted, "USF has a well-known career fair each year and is uniquely adept at helping interested students get quality internships in areas that they are really passionate about. USF really values a well-rounded education."

Overall, the University of South Florida is a strong, up-and-coming large state university that allows its students to enjoy their college experience filled with Florida-style fun, lots of school spirit, and numerous academic and career-oriented opportunities. As one student aptly and enthusiastically put it, "USF is a place where great individuals come for a great, fun experience in a great place where there are great academic programs and opportunities."—*Andrew Pearlmutter, special thanks to Steven Marsicano*

FYI

If you come to the University of South Florida, you'd better bring "something green. School spirit is big here."

What is the typical weekend schedule? "Fridays are spent hanging out with friends near campus or at someone's dorm. On Saturday, most go to a football game or some other type of athletic event, and then party or hang out that night. On Sunday, students start studying and preparing for the next week of classes."

If I could change one thing about USF, I'd "add more parking garages."

Three things every student at USF should do before graduating are "visit local landmarks such as Busch Gardens and Clearwater Beach, spend an evening at the Dockside and eat gator nuggets, and go to all the home football games. Go Bulls!"

Georgia

Agnes Scott College

Address: 141 East College Avenue Decatur, GA 30030-3797

Phone: 404-471-6285

E-mail address: admission@agnesscott.edu

Web site URL: www.agnesscott.edu

Year Founded: 1889

Private or Public: Private

Religious Affiliation: Presbyterian

Location: Urban

Number of Applicants: 1,595

Percent Accepted: 48%

Percent Accepted who enroll: 30%

Number Entering: 218

Number of Transfers Accepted each Year: 29

Middle 50% SAT range: M: 500–610, CR: 550–680, Wr: 550–660

Middle 50% ACT range: 22–29

Early admission program EA/ED/None: EA

Percentage accepted through EA or ED: Unreported

EA and ED deadline: 15-Nov

Regular Deadline: Rolling

Application Fee: $35

Full time Undergraduate enrollment: 757

Total enrollment: 885

Percent Male: 0%

Percent Female: 100%

Total Percent Minority or Unreported: 46%

Percent African-American: 21%

Percent Asian/Pacific Islander: 5%

Percent Hispanic: 4%

Percent Native-American: <1%

Percent International: 5%

Percent in-state/out of state: 54%/46%

Percent from Public HS: 80%

Retention Rate: 82%

Graduation Rate 4-year: 63%

Graduation Rate 6-year: 67%

Percent Undergraduates in On-campus housing: 87%

Number of official organized extracurricular organizations: 80

3 Most popular majors: Economics, English, Psychology

Student/Faculty ratio: 9:1

Average Class Size: 15

Percent of students going to grad school: 25%

Tuition and Fees: $3,011

In State Tuition and Fees if different: No difference

Cost for Room and Board: $9,850

Percent receiving financial aid out of those who apply, first year: 99%

Percent receiving financial aid among all students: 71%

From its origins in 1889 as a seminary for women to its recent renovations featuring a three-story rendering of Agnes Scott's DNA, Agnes Scott College has had an incredible history as a women's college famed for its liberal arts education and its warm atmosphere. Located just outside of Atlanta, the weather provides a welcoming home for students year round. But above all, strong academics with a focus on leadership and a thriving social life complete the beauty of a hip and enthusiastic women's campus.

Professors and Credits and Homework, Oh My!

Many students have said that the amount of work is "crazy," but all are quick to point out that many professors will "give extensions if you need them and will always work through things with you." Scotties do mention that their professors tend to become notorious with the Classics department taking the cake. One sophomore described how her Roman Civilization teacher came to class and conducted it in the persona of Gaius Sempronius Gracchus. "For a day or so afterwards, he signed all his e-mails to us 'GSG.'"

There are few academic requirements—approximately one per discipline, along with two PE classes and several others for a total of 128 credits across 8 semesters. These requirements can be fulfilled through a variety of unique classes; in short, there are enough options that artsy students need not fear the math requirement. One undergrad explained that she was "Immensely grateful that I was so challenged to learn and broaden my horizons."

Students agree that Agnes Scott is difficult. "There are 'marginally less difficult' majors and then there is biochemistry. Our creative writing department is fairly competitive; any of the science majors is challenging," joked one Scottie. However, the atmosphere is collaborative rather than aggressive, so "People won't sabotage you or anything."

Since there are only 910 undergraduates, the atmosphere at Agnes Scott is incredibly cozy. Class sizes range from three or four students to a maximum of 42, but with such a small student body, "They rarely fill to that point." In accordance with the liberal mindset of the school, assignments tend to be fairly innovative. One student recalled designing "a giant kids' book about a scientific experiment done with fear genes" and another professor "gave us our daily quiz one day by asking us to line up appropriately in a phalanx—spears and shields included—and we marched on Agnes Scott." And for those who want a study-abroad experience without having to undergo separation anxiety, Global Connections allows students to take "a 'trip' class and then go on a mini-study abroad trip with that class."

Working Hard, Playing like Crazy

Beyond homework and classes, Agnes Scott students keep busy. School nights tend to be set aside for homework and other extracurriculars, peppered with some trips to neighboring Georgia Tech to meet guys. Sports are very low key, with calmer fans on the sidelines. However, when asked, a student exclaimed, "Football! We have been undefeated for the last hundred years" and promised to send out shirts to anybody who asked. As at any other college campus, Frisbee is a popular pick-up game. Extracurricular groups include WAVE (the feminist group), the Anime Club, the Asian Studies Department (because the academic department does not exist), Latinas Unidas, Classics Club, Witkaze, Arabic Lunch Table, Scottie Social Dance, and many more.

The upperclassmen tend to split between the Mortar Club, which is very conservative and traditional, and the significantly more lax Pestle Club, which "just sets out to be the diametric opposite of Mortar Board." Freshmen tend to mix and mingle at larger and more organized functions, like the Red Light Green Light party, swing dance nights, movie nights and other on-campus events,

while upperclassmen tend to gravitate to Georgia Tech for the coed environment. Describing Greek life on campus, a junior joked that "Our Greek system is limited to my Theocritus class. We don't have sororities. We are a sorority."

As part of the feminist environment, people do respect personal preferences. Many students joked that first-years go in believing "Agnes will turn you gay" but in reality, people just become more supportive of the atmosphere around them. The campus is complimented for being very open and diverse. A Caucasian woman from the Midwest rattled off a list of groups with high profiles at Agnes Scott, including "Dems, Republicans, Libs, Pagans, Christians, Jews, Muslims, lesbians, transgenders, straight women, girls who look like men, girls who look very fem, black, brown, Indian, Native American, Hispanic, white and paler than white" before trailing off.

Amazing Atlanta

The campus is very calm, thanks to its scenic location just outside Atlanta. One upperclassman could not stop gushing: "It's very quaint and small and Gothic. The dining hall looks like 'The Great Hall' of Harry Potter." Just a few miles on MARTA, Atlanta's metropolitan rail system, gets you into the city, which offers incredible sports venues, nightlife, zoos, and much more.

> "We don't have sororities. We are a sorority."

The campus residences are extraordinarily varied. The freshmen are put in two dorms, Winship and Walters. Students in each consider the other their rival, although a couple of years of perspective blurs the two. Not many students live off campus, which makes the student body that much closer and intimate. And as such, there are a great number of traditions, as one student listed: "Ringing the bell in the tower when you get a job or are accepted to grad school, getting thrown in the alumnae pond if you're engaged, running around mostly naked at Black Cat, capping the spring of your junior year for Pestle Board, and, of course, the campus ghosts . . ."

Agnes Scott, more than any other women's college, offers an incredible opportunity for community as well as education. When asked if she would go back to Agnes Scott, a soon-to-graduate student said, "I'd be here in a heartbeat. I've grown up and learned both emotionally and academically. I feel like I could function in the world after being here, as a person rather than a 'woman.'" And, of course, it's just plain beautiful!—*Jeffrey Zuckerman*

FYIs

What's the typical weekend schedule? "Chill. And then panic about homework. Some people do more of the homeworking. We party or see movies or watch reruns of Project Runway. LOTS of Project Runway."

If I could change one thing about Agnes Scott, I'd "try to get just a little less homework."

Three things every student at Agnes Scott should do before graduating are "chill at Java Monkey, spend the night in the light lab, and visit the health center with a headache to see how long it takes them to give you a pregnancy test."

Emory University

Address: Emory University, Boisfeuillet Jones Ctr, Atlanta, GA 30322
Phone: 404-727-6036
E-mail address: admiss@learnlink.emory.edu
Web site URL: www.emory.edu
Year Founded: 1836
Private or Public: Private
Religious Affiliation: Methodist
Location: Urban
Number of Applicants: 12,865
Percent Accepted: 32%
Percent Accepted who enroll: 30%
Number Entering: 1,235
Number of Transfers Accepted each Year: 152
Middle 50% SAT range: M: 660–740, Cr: 640–730, Wr: 660–740
Middle 50% ACT range: 29–33
Early admission program EA/ED/None: ED

Percentage accepted through EA or ED: 31%
EA and ED deadline: 1-Nov
Regular Deadline: 15-Jan
Application Fee: $50
Full time Undergraduate enrollment: 6,546
Total enrollment: 9,300
Percent Male: 42%
Percent Female: 58%
Total Percent Minority or Unreported: 31%
Percent African-American: 9%
Percent Asian/Pacific Islander: 19%
Percent Hispanic: 3%
Percent Native-American: 1%
Percent International: 8%
Percent in-state/out of state: 29%/71%
Percent from Public HS: 64%
Retention Rate: 94%

Graduation Rate 4-year: 83%
Graduation Rate 6-year: 87%
Percent Undergraduates in On-campus housing: 66%
Number of official organized extracurricular organizations: 282
3 Most popular majors: Business, Economics, Psychology
Student/Faculty ratio: 7:1
Average Class Size: 14
Percent of students going to grad school: 65%
Tuition and Fees: $33,900
In State Tuition and Fees if different: No difference
Cost for Room and Board: $10,220
Percent receiving financial aid out of those who apply, first year: 80%
Percent receiving financial aid among all students: 53%

E very fall, former President Jimmy Carter holds an open forum with students at Emory. The Georgia native answers any question the students throw at him, formal or informal, from whether he wears boxers or briefs to his thoughts on the war in Iraq. Unique opportunities like this define the undergraduate experience at Emory, a university that fuses Southern style with challenging academics.

Academics in Atlanta

With more than 60 majors, Emory offers diverse academic opportunities for its students. The large number of pre-med students makes science departments among the most difficult and competitive. Though the programs are rigorous, one senior who plans to go to dental school said, "If you are pre-med here, you will be very well-prepared. Emory students go to some of the best med schools in the country." The emphasis on science at Emory does not mean that other areas are overlooked; the humanities and liberal arts are also intense and receive high marks from students. According to one junior, "Science majors spend more time in labs, but humanities students spend more time reading and writing papers. The workload evens out in the end, so it just comes down to what you want to spend your time doing."

The Emory College General Education requirements were recently revised for the class of 2009 and beyond. Student must take a set number of courses in each of the following six groups: Seminars and Writing; Natural and Mathematical Sciences; Social Sciences; Humanities; Historical, Cultural and International Perspectives; and Health and Physical Education. Some students dislike the requirements for the large number of classes they entail.

Emory also offers a few special programs for undergraduates through its business and nursing schools. Sophomores can apply to The Goizueta Business School, or "B-school" as it is known on campus, to receive a bachelor's in business administration. While students warn that these classes can be the most rigorous on campus, the program's national acclaim makes the challenge worthwhile for many students. There is also a program for students to receive a bachelor's in nursing through Emory's nursing school.

The average class size at Emory is between 10 and 20 students, though upper-level seminar classes can be as small as five to 10. TAs usually grade work in large introductory classes, and sometimes even teach them. However, one student pointed out that this is not always a bad thing, as TAs can be more excited about and devoted to the class than professors. In general though, professors draw rave reviews from their students for being "very accessible" and "accommodating." One sophomore appreciated the flexibility of his professors when he had to miss exam period to have surgery. Another senior remembered how one of her professors "stayed up with us until 3 a.m. at a review session the night before the midterm." Professors often have students over for dinner at their homes, and are always willing to schedule extra office hours to meet with undergraduates. One student summed up the teaching philosophy at Emory by saying: "Professors truly want to know students who truly want to learn from them. If you show that you want to learn, they'll give you everything they have to offer."

Frat Parties and Dooley's Ball

Emory's on-campus social scene centers on "Fraternity Row," the street that houses the school's 15 fraternities and 13 sororities. Frat houses (or "frat mansions," as one student called them) host parties on a regular basis, while sororities are not permitted to have parties. Statistically, about 30 percent of the student body is Greek, but some say that it can feel more like 80 percent, especially at parties. Still, many non-Greeks maintain they rarely feel left out of the social scene, and that many Greeks are friends with non-Greeks, as well. Rush takes place during second semester to allow freshmen to make friends before joining Greek organizations, and most feel that the rush process is fairly laid-back.

Frat parties usually revolve around drinking. In theory, the frats should only serve alcohol to students 21 and older, but these rules are rarely enforced. Police are strict about open-container laws, dissuading students from roaming campus with open alcoholic beverages. Because Emory is located in a residential area, party-throwers must be careful to observe local noise ordinances. One junior commented that the frat scene has "broken down over the last few years because of new regulations against alcohol, noise, and the number of people at parties." Still, frat parties continue to be popular social events on campus.

The Student Programming Council, composed of members of Emory's student body, sponsors other on-campus events throughout the year. The freshman semi-formal dance is always well-attended. The Homecoming dance is far less popular, probably because Emory has no football team. The Council also organizes band parties that bring well-known groups like Cake, The Roots, Guster, Ben Folds, and Everclear to campus each semester. Attendance at these events usually depends on the band, but according to one student, "Most people usually leave once the free food runs out." Without a doubt, the most popular school-sponsored event of the year is Dooley's Ball, a dance held in honor of Emory's mysterious unofficial mascot. Originally, Dooley was a skeleton in an 1899 biology lab that wrote anonymous articles in the school's newspaper, *The Emory Phoenix*. Nowadays, Dooley takes human form and shows up at special occasions, always accompanied by a group of bodyguards dressed in black. Dooley's identity is carefully guarded, though it's common knowledge on campus that a secret society of students maintains the tradition. Dooley's Ball is at the culmination of Dooley's Week, a celebration featuring theme days, special activities and, of course, parties. The week also includes special visits by Dooley himself, who has the authority to dismiss any class on campus with a mere squirt of his water gun. The Ball, held outdoors on the intramural fields, also features a dramatic entrance by Dooley and his entourage. One student commented that the Dooley phenomenon is "Strange and a little scary, but it's one of the things that makes Emory really unique. It's also one of the only times that you'll see any school spirit on campus."

Welcome to Atlanta

Most students cite Emory's location just outside of downtown Atlanta as one of the best attributes of the school. Emory Village, the area just outside of campus, offers an assortment of restaurants and convenience stores to serve student needs, but many students also make the 15-minute trip to downtown Atlanta to take advantage of the great shopping, eating, attractions such as Centennial Olympic Park, and the city's numerous bars and nightclubs. Off-campus nightlife forms a huge part of the social scene at Emory, and more than one student cautioned, "Having a fake ID is key to enjoying Atlanta." If you can get past the bouncers at the doors, there are bars and clubs to suit every partygoer's taste. From the upscale bars in Midtown, to the dance clubs in Buckhead, to the hippy bars in Little Five Points, Atlanta offers students a variety of alternatives to the on-campus social scene. Some clubs also sponsor well-attended Emory nights on the weekends. Being in Atlanta has more serious advantages as well. Aside from its thriving nightlife, the city is a great place for students to find jobs and internships for the summer after graduation.

With so much to do off campus, many students feel that having a car is necessary at Emory. While freshmen aren't allowed to have cars on campus, one junior suggested, "There are ways of sneaking them in." Despite the availability of public transportation and a school-sponsored shuttle service to the supermarket and a nearby mall, some students opt to use a car. However traffic has become an increasing problem that prompts some students to leave their keys at home. "The traffic can make a five-minute drive to class turn into 45 minutes. . . . With that kind of traffic, some people enjoy not having a car," remarked one student.

Preppy, Fit and Motivated

When asked to describe their peers, many Emory students agree that the majority of the student body is wealthy, upper-class, attractive and fit. Some feel that this contributes to a snobby and cliquish atmosphere, while others say that they had no problems getting to know people. One sophomore said, "Lots of people here look snobby, but once you get to know them they can be very down to earth." Many students appreciate getting to know people upon arrival at Emory through FAME, Emory's mandatory freshman advisory program, which matches groups of frosh with staff, faculty and upperclassmen. Still, they felt that the social scene gave way too quickly to separate cliques. Students are satisfied with the level of racial diversity, but feel that there is too much self-segregation among students, making it hard to get to know people from different backgrounds. Many also comment that a disproportionate number of their fellow students hail from Long Island and elsewhere in the Northeast.

Students at Emory are highly motivated and intelligent. "The majority of kids here are overachievers," one freshman said. Some feel that this creates a competitive atmosphere, particularly among the pre-med science majors. But it also means that Emory students can be involved and opinionated about their causes. "From Free Tibet to a group that advocates better wages for university workers, to experimental theater, everyone here is involved in something," says one sophomore. However another Emory student described his peers as "extremely apathetic," noting that students rarely commit to causes in large numbers.

Looking good is a priority for many Emory students, producing an attractive and image-conscious student body. One senior related that "There are too many designer purses here for my tastes, but they aren't necessarily a requirement." Students take full advantage of Emory's spacious gym facilities, which were recently renovated, and participate in many intramural and club sports. Though students are "terribly apathetic toward sports," some of Emory's Division III teams in sports like swimming, soccer, volleyball and tennis are fairly competitive. The men's and women's tennis teams have also done very well in national competition. However, many students feel Emory suffers from the lack of a football team. "It makes it difficult for students to really rally some school spirit," one junior said.

Country Club Campus

Students at Emory love their campus, which they describe as "gorgeous" and "very ritzy" with "beautiful Spanish-style architecture." Georgia's mild weather makes for beautiful landscaping, and students spend time outside year-round on Emory's spacious quads. The campus has renovated almost all of its buildings in the last 15 years. Students rave about the updates, which include the installation of computers in the gym and a gorgeous new reading room in the school's main library. Between the brand-new buildings and the well-manicured lawns, students gush that Emory's campus looks "just like a country club."

> "Where else can you get Ivy League academics south of the Mason-Dixon Line? We have better weather, and you still get a great degree."

One senior commented, "Emory has the cleanest, nicest, newest dorms of any school I've ever visited." Seven dorms house first-year students, and each has its own perks and disadvantages. Dobbs has the smallest rooms but the most central location, while Turman offers "enormous rooms" but is farther from campus. Freshmen are usually assigned to double rooms, though some singles are available. All dorms are air-conditioned and most have sinks in the rooms. There are also special theme wings or floors for students who want to live with others who share similar interests. While sophomores were allowed to move off campus in years past, they are now required to live in the dorms. Though it initially created some turmoil on campus, the administration is confi-dent that the new rule will ultimately create a strong sense of community. The most coveted dorms are on the Clairmont Campus, a short shuttle ride from Emory's central campus. Available only to upperclassmen, these apartment-style dorms are "drop-dead gorgeous." One resident lamented, "I don't want to graduate and move out of here!" Each four-person apartment includes four bedrooms, two full bathrooms, a kitchen, a washer and dryer, a living room, and a dining room. The facilities include four outdoor swimming pools (two of which are Olympic-size) as well as basketball courts, tennis courts, volleyball courts, an indoor gym and a student center called the "SAAC" with lots of study rooms and a grill-style cafeteria. These luxury dorms do come at a higher price than other campus housing, but almost everyone agrees that it is well worth it. Dining options include Dobbs University Center, which has stations for pizza, sandwiches, traditional meals, and international cuisine, as well as Cox Hall, which houses a Burger King, a Chick-Fil-A and a Starbucks. Though food options abound, one student remarked that the dining hall is "nothing to brag about."

Great Weather and a Great Degree

Students at Emory seem satisfied with their experiences. Though some bemoan the "snobby attitude" and "competitiveness" of their fellow students, almost all feel that they are getting a great education and that being in Atlanta is a huge asset. As one student observed of Emory's unique atmosphere, "Where else can you get Ivy League academics south of the Mason-Dixon Line? We have better weather, and you still get a great degree."—*Jessica Lenox*

FYI
If you come to Emory, you'd better bring a "car and a Prada handbag."
What is the typical weekend schedule? "Thursday night, dancing in Buckhead; Friday night, fraternity party or a bar in Midtown; Saturday night, off-campus party followed by late night at Maggie's; Sunday, brunch and work, work, work!"
If I could change one thing about Emory, I'd "give it a football team!"
Three things every student at Emory should do before graduating are "take a long weekend to Mardi Gras, have lunch with the dean, and lay out at the Clairmont pool instead of studying."

Georgia Institute of Technology

Address: 225 North Avenue NW Atlanta, GA 30332-0320
Phone: 404-894-4154
E-mail address: admission@gatech.edu
Web site URL: www.gatech.edu
Year Founded: 1885
Private or Public: Public
Religious Affiliation: None
Location: Urban
Number of Applicants: 9,664
Percent Accepted: 63%
Percent Accepted who enroll: 43%
Number Entering: 2,626
Number of Transfers Accepted each Year: 448
Middle 50% SAT range: M: 650–730, CR: 590–690, Wr: 580–670
Middle 50% ACT range: 27–31
Early admission program EA/ED/None: None

Percentage accepted through EA or ED: NA
EA and ED deadline: NA
Regular Deadline: 15-Jan
Application Fee: $50
Full time Undergraduate enrollment: 12,565
Total enrollment: 18,742
Percent Male: 68%
Percent Female: 32%
Total Percent Minority or Unreported: 45%
Percent African-American: 5%
Percent Asian/Pacific Islander: 18%
Percent Hispanic: 5%
Percent Native-American: <1%
Percent International: 5%
Percent in-state/out of state: 70%/30%
Percent from Public HS: Unreported
Retention Rate: 92%
Graduation Rate 4-year: 31%

Graduation Rate 6-year: 76%
Percent Undergraduates in On-campus housing: 59%
Number of official organized extracurricular organizations: 311
3 Most popular majors: Business Administration, Industrial Engineering, Mechanical Engineering
Student/Faculty ratio: 14:1
Average Class Size: 10 to 19
Percent of students going to grad school: 41%
Tuition and Fees: $25,182
In State Tuition and Fees if different: $6,040
Cost for Room and Board: $7,694
Percent receiving financial aid out of those who apply, first year: 44%
Percent receiving financial aid among all students: 32%

P art of the Public University System of Georgia, the Georgia Institute of Technology is a research-based university that, according to the school's website, is dedicated to "improving the human condition through advanced science and technology." The school is known for the rigors of its science and engineering curricula, its location in the southern metropolitan city of Atlanta, and the vast amount of school spirit among the student body.

Science and Engineering vs. Everything Else

Tech's undergraduate majors are housed under six different departments: the Colleges of Architecture, Engineering, Sciences, Computing, Management, and the Ivan Allen College of Liberal Arts. A bit of a divide exists between Tech's budding engineers, scientists, and architects—those choosing "real" majors, according to one scornful engineer—and its students pursuing a less technically oriented degree, particularly in management. The latter is known for having a less rigorous

curriculum and allowing students to retain more of their most precious commodity: free time. As one engineer asserted, "Tech is not a party school if you have an "E" next to your major." The workload for classes is "challenging" and "time-consuming," and students joke that "A normal sleep schedule isn't possible at Tech." Fortunately, tutoring is available to help students stay ahead, although the undisputed key to success for all majors is "time management."

Georgia Tech is particularly well-known for several of its more specialized engineering majors, including aerospace, biomedical, nuclear and radiological, and polymer and fiber engineering, and while these subjects are notoriously difficult to complete, they are also well respected. In the 2009 edition of the *US News and World Report* college rankings, Georgia Tech tied for fourth best undergraduate engineering program in the country. Students of all majors must satisfy the requirements of the core curriculum, which include at least one introductory calculus class, English Composition I and II, two lab-intensive sciences, and a selection of courses in the humanities, fine arts, and social sciences. These requirements receive mixed reviews from undergraduates, as some prefer to focus on their major subject while others appreciate the breadth of learning. Many of the intro-level science and math courses are known as "weed-out" classes that serve to discourage potential majors from pursuing the field. Chemistry I, Physics I, and Calculus II in particular have traditionally lower pass rates than the higher-level courses in the same subjects, a fact which makes many students question their true dedication to the subject. Success in these classes depends very much upon "your high school background and the professor," according to one student.

> **"Tech is not a party school if you have an "E" next to your major."**

Scientific research is a primary focus of Georgia Tech, and the school offers undergraduates plenty of opportunities to dive into the lab. The Undergraduate Research Opportunities Program provides students with a list of available labs for both school-year and summer research and guarantees one-on-one time with professors as well as the chance to practice techniques learned in class in a real-life setting and to make new scientific explorations and discoveries. All students are encouraged to take advantage of the many research opportunities and can work for either course credit or pay.

Another popular program—about 40% of the student body enrolls at some point in their college careers—is the co-op and internship program. Tech's Cooperative Education Program, one of the largest programs of its kind in the nation, allows interested undergrads to follow a five-year course of study in which they alternate semesters of full-time work with semesters of study as a full-time student. Local Atlanta employers in business, industry, education, and government hire these students and provide structured, educational working environments to let them gain working experience in their chosen field as well as earn money for their time. Such industry giants as Coca-Cola, General Electric, and the NASA Johnson Space Center participate as potential employers, and many of these co-ops turn into job offers after graduation, making this experience both valuable and practical.

Nerds and Greeks

Thanks to reduced in-state tuition and the popular state-administered HOPE scholarship, the majority of Tech's student body hails from nearby cities and towns in Georgia. The remaining 35%, however, represent a wide variety of states and countries, including China, India, and South Korea, and help to produce the school's diverse student body. Most freshmen matriculate as prospective engineers, but, as one student articulated, not everyone fits the "nerdy guy' with high-waters and glasses" stereotype. There are math aficionados who "tend to stay in their room" and "do talk about calculus in their free time," and happily admit to studying more than twenty hours a week, but there are also equally fun-loving students who pledge Greek and spend much of their time drinking and partying.

A common problem at technical universities tends to be an unequal gender distribution within the student body; at Georgia Tech, this disparity is dubbed "The Ratio." The Ratio, the proportion of male to female students, has hovered slightly below 3:1 for years, distorting the dating scene and inspiring the oft-repeated, tongue-in-cheek maxim of lady Techies: "The odds are good but the goods are odd." However, Tech's proximity to other North Georgia colleges, including Emory, Georgia State, Spelman, and Morehouse, allows students to mingle with other university populations and helps to offset the gender discrepancy.

The Greek scene dominates social life at Georgia Tech, and about one-fourth of the student body pledges to one of the 42 chapters on campus, usually during freshman year. Although most Tech social events are sponsored by the Greek system, non-pledgers, especially girls, are generally welcome to attend. Various fraternities and sororities sponsor activities such as parties, mixers, sports games, volunteer work, and movie screenings for members and have in the past brought such big-name bands as Sister Hazel on campus to perform.

For those not interested in Greek life, the surrounding city of Atlanta offers many possibilities for entertainment and relaxation. Those interested in more high-brow culture can enjoy an evening listening to the Atlanta Symphony Orchestra, watching a Broadway play at the Fox Theater, or perusing the displays at the High Museum of Art. In contrast, the Midtown clubs and the late-night bars in Buckhead provide an alternative party scene, most of which is easily accessible by MARTA (Metro Atlanta Rapid Transit

Authority) for those lacking a car. Many popular eateries are located within walking distance from Tech's campus, including pizza parlors Fellini's and the Mellow Mushroom as well as The Varsity, the world's largest drive-in restaurant that is famous for its hot dogs, french fries, and frosted orange drinks.

Football reigns supreme in the South, and the NCAA Division 1 Yellow Jackets often deliver an exciting time for Tech's spirit-filled spectators. The school's biggest rivalry is with the University of Georgia Bulldogs, and the huge UGA-Georgia Tech game packs tens of thousands of supporters into Tech's Bobby Dodd Stadium in a sea of bee-like yellow and black contrasting against the Bulldogs' competing red and black. Celebrated mascot Buzz works with SWARM, a student-run spirit organization, to pump up the crowd, not only for the football games, but also for the talented Tech basketball and baseball teams.

Located in the heart of Atlanta, Georgia Tech's campus has a distinct "oasis within the city" feel, as the plethora of green spaces dotting the campus help to keep the more urban senses of concrete and overcrowding at bay. However, the two major highways bordering two sides of the campus prevent students from completely escaping their urban surroundings. The campus is split into two halves—east and west—that each impart their own atmosphere to their respective residents. East Campus is older and, with its close-packed dormitory buildings and nearby Greek houses, is more conducive to socializing, while West Campus dorms are more spread apart and offer greater peace and solitude. Each side of the campus has its own dining hall and other facilities, although most upperclassmen prefer to cook at home or eat off campus.

In spite of the somewhat eccentric combination of nerds and Greeks, and science and liberal arts majors, Georgia Tech nevertheless boasts a cohesive, spirited student body with great affection for their school. No matter their major, Tech students of all stripes don the traditional Yellow Jacket stripes and support their school teams as well as dedicate themselves to their studies and classes. Tech is known for turning out some of the brightest engineering minds in the country, and its focus on first-class research helps to attract students from all over the world interested in a first-class scientific education.

FYI

If you come to Georgia Tech, you'd better bring "a ruler, a TI-89, and all the other help you can get."

What is the typical weekend schedule? "Friday and Saturday, forget about work and party at the frats; Sunday, face reality and study 'til Monday."

If I could change one thing about Georgia Tech, I'd "equalize The Ratio."

Three things every student at Georgia Tech should do before graduating are "go to the UGA-Georgia Tech football game at Bobby Dodd Stadium, try waffle fries at Chick-Fil-A, and spend a night in Buckhead or Midtown."

Morehouse College

Address: 830 Westview Drive, SW Atlanta, GA 30314
Phone: 404-215-2632
E-mail address: admissions@morehouse.edu
Web site URL: www.morehouse.edu
Year Founded: 1867
Private or Public: Private
Religious Affiliation: None
Location: Urban
Number of Applicants: 2,277
Percent Accepted: 67%
Percent Accepted who enroll: 46%
Number Entering: 700
Number of Transfers Accepted each Year: 127
Middle 50% SAT range: M: 480–590, CR: 480–580, Wr: Unreported
Middle 50% ACT range: 20–24
Early admission program EA/ED/None: EA
Percentage accepted through EA or ED: NA

EA and ED deadline: 15-Oct
Regular Deadline: 15-Feb
Application Fee: $45
Full time Undergraduate enrollment: 2,810
Total enrollment: 2,810
Percent Male: 100%
Percent Female: 0%
Total Percent Minority or Unreported: >99%
Percent African-American: 95%
Percent Asian/Pacific Islander: <1%
Percent Hispanic: 1%
Percent Native-American: <1%
Percent International: 3%
Percent in-state/out of state: 28%/ 72%
Percent from Public HS: 80%
Retention Rate: 84%
Graduation Rate 4-year: 32%

Graduation Rate 6-year: 49%
Percent Undergraduates in On-campus housing: 55%
Number of official organized extracurricular organizations: 34
3 Most popular majors: Business & Commerce, Computer & Informational Sciences
Student/Faculty ratio: 15:1
Average Class Size: 2 to 9
Percent of students going to grad school: 25%
Tuition and Fees: $20,358
In State Tuition and Fees if different: No difference
Cost for Room and Board: $8,648
Percent receiving financial aid out of those who apply, first year: 100%
Percent receiving financial aid among all students: 100%

Nothing illuminates the excellence of the Morehouse College education better than its impressive crop of graduates. Martin Luther King, Jr., Spike Lee, Samuel L. Jackson, countless distinguished professors, lead researchers, CEOs, and Rhodes scholars are examples of the "Morehouse Men" that graduate from this premier, private, historically black liberal arts college for men. Just 10 minutes from downtown Atlanta, Morehouse offers students an array of opportunities that parallels the diversity of talents and interests in its students.

Fashioning a Morehouse Man

Morehouse College, originally founded as the Augusta Institute, was established just two years after the Civil War to prepare students to be educators or enter the ministry. Under the leadership of visionaries, Morehouse became one of the leading Historically Black Colleges and Universities (HBCUs) by expanding its curriculum and acquiring the resources necessary to prepare African-American males for the challenges they face inside and outside of the classroom. More-house soon left the bottom of a church's basement for the now 61-acre campus in Atlanta.

Over 140 years later, Morehouse provides a quality liberal arts education with 26 majors from which students may choose. Although some students call the course offerings "standard and conservative," many find the variety of courses interesting, unlike those of many liberal arts colleges, and at nearly half the price. The students also report difficulties dealing with the administration, though they admit the educational opportunities far outweigh any shortcomings.

True to its mission, Morehouse's General Education requirements develop the talents necessary to graduate "empowered, informed, and responsible" men. In accordance with its goal of providing a structured learning environment, Morehouse mandates that freshmen enroll in a year-long academic and social orientation to college life. Orientation meets on a weekly basis and is on a "Pass/Fail" system that students said "would require a student to never attend" to fail.

Most students find the topics, like safe sex and personal finance, useful and interesting.

The Crown Forum is another favorite among students. Receiving its name from a famous quotation encouraging Morehouse men to grow tall enough to wear their crown, the Crown Forum helps mold students' characters and cultural competency. Students are required to attend a minimum of six events for six semesters, though many say they have attended more. Overall, students are happy with the requirements because they help them "discover unknown interests and talents" that can guide them towards their majors, and say there is flexibility in the timing of scheduling some of the less popular requirements like religion.

Nearly one-third of the students at Morehouse eventually major in Business Administration. The next most popular majors are Biology and Computer Science. Even though students find Morehouse to be a "supportive and encouraging" environment to grow academically, they acknowledged that "Business general requirement classes can be very competitive, with students contending for Fortune 500 internships." In addition, the Morehouse course load is considered intense for any student majoring in the natural sciences. However, students feel that their advisors are a "great resource," as evidenced by students' successful applications for research internships and medical school. Students reported an average of 20 students per class, which made professors accessible and "genuinely interested in their students' success."

Opportunities to Branch Out

Students searching for a greater challenge than the curriculum provides can enter the Morehouse College Honors Program (HP) during their first year, if they meet certain criteria. The HP provides students with smaller classrooms and more advanced course offerings than the regular courses, and is taught by distinguished professors. Army ROTC is also available to Morehouse students through Georgia Institute of Technology. The college also offers a plethora of internships, on-site learning opportunities, and community service projects in which roughly three-fourths of the student body participates. Through the Bonner Office of Community Service, which has partnerships with numerous organizations like the NFL YET Boys & Girls Club and Hands on Atlanta, students can easily make substantial contributions to their city. Many students also find additional service and mentoring opportunities on their own.

Morehouse's location and prestige affords its students many opportunities to learn off campus. Since they are a part of many academic consortiums, the men of Morehouse may spend a semester or academic year at universities such as Stanford and New York University, enroll in classes at colleges at Spelman, or participate in the Georgia Institute of Technology's Dual-Degree Engineering Program. These opportunities are highly recommended by students because they help Morehouse men "develop contacts, learn in unique environments, and meet women."

Life in the "A"

The single-sex education and living arrangements allow Morehouse students to "focus when it is time to focus, and party when it is time to party." "The well-known and active students" are usually leaders of popular campus organizations like student government and the NAACP. Since freshmen are required to live on campus, "class unity" quickly develops and most students become active upon their arrival. Many students meet classmates with similar interests while working on projects for science competitions or in organizations like the Morehouse Business Association.

> "Morehouse was a nurturing environment; I fell in love with the college and developed into a responsible and cognizant citizen."

After their first year, many students opt to live in the many affordable off-campus apartments near the college. Many upperclassmen have cars. "House parties and the clubs on Peachtree Street" are where students from all local colleges and universities congregate. Students report a "relatively easy time for Morehouse Men to meet other students, especially girls from other colleges in Atlanta." Greek life also attracts many Morehouse undergraduates, but problems with hazing have kept many of the "Divine Nine" National Pan-Hellenic Conference fraternities officially "off the yard."

Despite the varying interests and talents students from across the world bring to Morehouse, "a true brotherhood develops" with the men recognizing each other's talents and desiring to better not only themselves, but also their surrounding community. As one student aptly summarized his experience, "Morehouse was a nurturing environment; I fell in love with the College and developed into a responsible and cognizant citizen. In other words, I became a man of Morehouse College."—*Ayibatari Owi*

FYI
If you come to Morehouse, you'd better bring "a suit, a nice tie, and a white dress shirt."
What's the typical weekend schedule? "Most students get off work on Friday, then head to happy hour and house parties. Students study during the day on Saturday and go out to the clubs on Saturday night, sleep late, and then start the grind again on Sunday."
If I could change one thing about Morehouse I'd "change the religious foundation requirement."
Three things every student at Morehouse should do before graduating are "join extracurricular groups, mature and grow, and learn the history of the school."

Spelman College

Address: 350 Spelman Lane SW Atlanta, GA 30314
Phone: 404-270-5193
E-mail address: admiss@spelman.edu
Web site URL: www.spelman.edu
Year Founded: 1881
Private or Public: Private
Religious Affiliation: None
Location: Urban
Number of Applicants: 5,656
Percent Accepted: 35%
Percent Accepted who enroll: 30%
Number Entering: 553
Number of Transfers Accepted each Year: 101
Middle 50% SAT range: M: 490–570, CR:500–580, Wr: Unreported
Middle 50% ACT range: 21–25
Early admission program EA/ED/None: ED and EA
Percentage accepted through EA or ED: Unreported

EA and ED deadline: 1-Nov, 15-Nov
Regular Deadline: 1-Feb
Application Fee: $35
Full time Undergraduate enrollment: 2,270
Total enrollment: 2,270
Percent Male: 0%
Percent Female: 100%
Total Percent Minority or Unreported: 100%
Percent African-American: 92%
Percent Asian/Pacific Islander: 0%
Percent Hispanic: 0%
Percent Native-American: 0.00%
Percent International: <1%
Percent in-state/out of state: 31%/69%
Percent from Public HS: 84%
Retention Rate: 88%
Graduation Rate 4-year: 67%

Graduation Rate 6-year: 77%
Percent Undergraduates in On-campus housing: 43%
Number of official organized extracurricular organizations: 17
3 Most popular majors: Political Science and Government, Psychology
Student/Faculty ratio: 12:1
Average Class Size: 10 to 19
Percent of students going to grad school: Unreported
Tuition and Fees: $20,281
In State Tuition and Fees if different: No difference
Cost for Room and Board: $9,734
Percent receiving financial aid out of those who apply, first year: Unreported
Percent receiving financial aid among all students: 75%

Spelman College in Atlanta, Georgia, offers the intimacy of a women's college without the seclusion—all-male Morehouse College, which is also an historically black institution, sits directly across the street. Spelman has just over 2,200 women enrolled which, according to students, makes the experience extremely personal.

Interdisciplinary Offerings

Spelman is a liberal arts college, so students are required to take a large variety of classes before graduating. There are requirements in English, math, the humanities, women's studies/international relations, fine art, and physical education. Students say the most popular majors are Political Science and Government and Psychology but things may change with the recent introduction of a new major, African Diaspora in the World. The ADW major is interdisciplinary and focuses on the study of black people and culture throughout the world.

Class sizes are small, with an average of 20–25 students in each. The workload is also reasonable, as one student said she does about eight hours of studying a week. Spelman boasts many accomplished scholars and professors, including Pearl Cleage, a well-known author, and Dr. Christine King Ferris, the only living sibling of Dr. Martin Luther King, Jr. Both women are active professors at the College and teach classes on a regular basis. Some Spelman students expressed concern that the school's close, personal atmosphere leads professors to expect too much and to be too hard on the students, but many seniors said they were grateful for the personal attention they had received throughout the years. One student said, "They feel responsible for your success—that's why they are so hard on us. But I think it's worth it in the end."

Getting Along with the Girls
Like many women's colleges, Spelman students are constantly fighting the myth that there are no opportunities for interaction with the opposite sex. This just isn't true says one Spelman sophomore: "We do everything with Morehouse—we can cross-register for classes, their football team is essentially our football team, and most social events are jointly organized."

> "They feel responsible for your success—that's why they are so hard on us. But I think it's worth it in the end."

Students say social activities at Spelman are strongly dominated by fraternities and sororities. The city of Atlanta offers many options as well—students said their weekend activities are often centered around clubs and events located downtown. Thursdays, Fridays, and Saturdays are the most popular nights to go out, but Spelman is a dry campus, meaning no alcohol can be consumed on school grounds. Consequently, nearly all parties take place off-campus. The annual Battle of the Bands contest is one of the biggest parties of the year for Spelman students, attracting students from historically black colleges all over the country.

Atlanta offers decent public transportation, but the majority of upperclassmen still bring cars to campus. Parking is "absolutely horrible," according to one junior. Many students said MARTA, the Metropolitan Atlanta Rapid Transport Authority, is inexpensive and an excellent alternative for getting around in the city.

Spelman students come from all over the country, but in a racial sense the College is not particularly diverse. One sophomore said there are less than five non-black undergraduates enrolled at the school, though this is to be expected considering its reputation as an historically black college.

Southern Comfort
Spelman is not the kind of campus where students live in school housing all four years—most live off campus by junior year. It might have something to do with the dorms themselves. A sophomore student said the dorms "Don't have air-conditioning, they are very small, and the buildings are really old." Despite this, students feel the exterior of the dorms are aesthetically pleasing and "very pretty." Freshmen are required to live on campus, and freshman dorms are staffed by residential advisors. RAs are not generally strict, according to one freshman, but she said they are very involved in a student's freshman experience.

According to most students, dining at Spelman leaves something to be desired. There are essentially two options for meal-plan dining—Jaguar Underground Grill and Alma Upshaw Dining Hall. Both serve the typical cafeteria fare, though the Underground Grill is arranged food-court style. One junior said the décor of the dining locations is very nice, but the food is simply bad.

To earn extra cash, many Spelman students work in retail—at the mall or in local shopping centers. There are not any particularly prominent student groups on campus, but most students interviewed said most Spelman Jaguars are heavily involved in at least one activity.

Running with the Jaguars
This all-female historically black college (HBC) is all about tradition—freshmen and seniors have celebrated Founders Day for decades. During the event, held every year in April, the freshman and senior classes must wear white dresses and are joined by various alumni to celebrate Spelman's "birthday." Additionally, the Spelman campus features a grassy area known as "The

Oval" which is the location of an arch that students are not allowed to walk under until after graduation.

Students said interactions between the Atlanta community and Spelman are "nonexistent" and occasionally hostile. They said that, when help is offered by the university, the community generally rejects it and all in all Spelman and the local community do not have the "best relationship." While Spelman students say they feel safe on campus, the surrounding area has significant crime rates like any other metropolitan area. One sophomore offered this advice: "The area outside

of campus is definitely not that safe at night; you should always walk with someone else if it's late." Spelman's security force includes state-certified policemen who retain the same powers (arrest, etc.) as any member of the Atlanta Police Department.

So what is it like to go to an all-women's college? A senior student said, "Going to an all-girls school has only enhanced my college experience. I think guys and girls add a different dynamic than all one sex. With just girls, we have a more intimate setting and discussions are more productive."—*Samantha Broussard-Wilson*

FYI

If you come to Spelman, you'd better bring "a skirt."

What's the typical weekend? "Going into the city to shop, eat, and maybe going to a club at night."

If I could change one thing about Spelman, I'd "improve the administration—they are very unorganized and don't generally like students."

Three things every student should do before graduating are "cross-register at Morehouse, take MARTA into the city, and go to a sporting event."

University of Georgia

Address: Terrell Hall Athens, GA 30602
Phone: 706-542-8776
E-mail address: undergrad@admissions.uga.edu
Web site URL: www.uga.edu
Year Founded: 1785
Private or Public: Public
Religious Affiliation: None
Location: Suburban
Number of Applicants: 17,022
Percent Accepted: 54%
Percent Accepted who enroll: 51%
Number Entering: 4,696
Number of Transfers Accepted each Year: 1,524
Middle 50% SAT range: M: 570–650, CR: 560–660, Wr: 560–640
Middle 50% ACT range: 25–29
Early admission program EA/ED/None: EA

Percentage accepted through EA or ED: Unreported
EA and ED deadline: 15-Oct
Regular Deadline: 15-Jan
Application Fee: $50
Full time Undergraduate enrollment: 25,335
Total enrollment: 32,282
Percent Male: 43%
Percent Female: 57%
Total Percent Minority or Unreported: 18%
Percent African-American: 6%
Percent Asian/Pacific Islander: 6%
Percent Hispanic: 2%
Percent Native-American: <1%
Percent International: 1%
Percent in-state/out of state: 89%/%11%
Percent from Public HS: 81%
Retention Rate: Unreported

Graduation Rate 4-year: 51%
Graduation Rate 6-year: 79%
Percent Undergraduates in On-campus housing: 98%
Number of official organized extracurricular organizations: 352
3 Most popular majors: Art, Biology, Psychology
Student/Faculty ratio: 18:1
Average Class Size: 20 to 29
Percent of students going to grad school: 22%
Tuition and Fees: $22,343
In State Tuition and Fees if different: $6,031
Cost for Room and Board: $7,528
Percent receiving financial aid out of those who apply, first year: 31%
Percent receiving financial aid among all students: 49%

Located in the ideal college town of Athens, Ga., the University of Georgia is a school that takes its football seri-ously. The Bulldogs, or "Dawgs" as they are more often called, are proud of their football team and their school as a whole. And why not? UGA, with its approximately 30,000 students, is one of the top state universities in the South. Its size presents a host of extracurriculars, sports and social groups—enough to keep anyone busy for at least four years.

Inside the Hallowed Halls

Most students hail from Georgia (around 85 percent), but natives of other states and countries are not entirely missing from the classroom and social scenes. In fact, students from 127 other nations are enrolled at UGA. The overwhelming number of in-state students stems from the HOPE scholarship program, which uses state lottery funds to cover education costs. HOPE provides any student with a B average or better with free tuition and $100 toward books at any public college. Because many top Georgia students have consequently chosen to study at UGA, the University has become significantly more competitive in recent years. In-state students must now have noticeably higher GPAs and SAT scores in order to be eligible to walk around the famous Georgia "arch." In recent years, UGA has faced criticism for the low percentage of its students drawn from rural parts of Georgia—the majority of in-state students come from big cities like Atlanta.

Some students say that minorities are underrepresented for the size of the school, but efforts have been made to expand minority presence. Politically, however, UGA is fairly diverse. Even though it is "in Georgia, [and hence] still extremely Republican," liberal-minded students stand a better chance here than at many other Southern schools. Without a doubt, students appreciate the intellectual diversity that this atmosphere brings.

As the first state-chartered university in the country (founded in 1785), UGA has a broad range of architecture, both old and new, creating a beautiful campus. The large campus encompasses hundreds of buildings. The emblematic Georgia "arch" on north campus is one of the school's landmarks and symbols, but students are forbidden from walking under it until they've graduated, or else, UGA lore cautions, they won't. Sanford Stadium, known as "between the hedges," is located in the heart of the campus and is the center of attention during football season. UGA is also continually improving its campus; for example, the brand-new Coverdell Center for Biomedical and Health Sciences was recently completed

Once on campus, students have a huge variety of classes to choose from. Many take advantage of the excellent business major

or veterinary program. The sciences, as well as psychology, are very popular majors. However, those who are so inclined can also choose to major in fashion merchandising, turfgrass management or even music therapy. The abundance of majors is almost endless. Some students say there is an emphasis on the humanities—"Georgia Tech is the science school!"—but all departments have a "high level of respect for each other."

While some introductory courses are very large (as many as 300), students say that upper-level courses are much smaller and less formal. Professors "tailor the class structure to what students prefer," including discussion, group projects and case studies. Class participation is key. For overachievers, there is the prestigious honors program. Though their program is time-consuming, honors students are offered classes that are especially known for excellence and small class size, as well as for close contact with faculty.

Play Hard

The weekend at UGA begins on Thursday, and there are parties on any given night. The Greek scene is ubiquitous—the campus plays host to approximately 51 fraternities and sororities. Most of the events, however, are open to non-Greeks, as well. One student said, "Frats have a great time, but if you're not in one then you hardly know they exist." Although the administration's alcohol policies have become stricter in recent years, almost all parties provide large quantities of alcohol. If the on-campus party scene is not enough, there are a plethora of other options. Some people choose to host parties for their friends, but at the end of the night, "Many people end up in downtown Athens to round out the evening."

Athens itself is a thriving city with a buzzing bar scene. The off-campus party scene is "ridiculous," with many students choosing to concentrate their weekend activities there. With something going on every night, Athens is the ultimate college town. One student notes, though, that "It's not just a college town; it's a town with a college." That is, it has a thriving culture apart from that of UGA. In addition to great nightlife, the music scene is especially notable. Bands such as REM and the B-52s hail from Athens, and this has partly spurred huge diversity in the musical life of the city. Athens's atmosphere, that is at once "artsy and indie and fun and bohemian," is the perfect setting for a school like UGA.

Just as the city of Athens provides a wide array of distractions for students, extracurricular activities are a great way to keep busy and to meet people. The College Republicans are especially popular, as is the Greek system. Student government is another way to become involved. For students who want to give back to the community, Relay for Life and Habitat for Humanity are great options. A more unique service group is the Dance Marathon, which raises money for children's hospitals through a 24-hour dance, feast, and celebration. Religious groups, such as the Baptist Student Union and the Wesley Foundation, are many in number, as well.

The Sport is Football

Like many universities in the South, UGA keeps much of its focus on sports. But at Georgia, fans take their dose of football in over-the-top fashion. The vast majority of UGA students are active Bulldogs fans, attending games both at Sanford Stadium and in "rival territory." On game days, the excitement "encompasses the town and the area around campus." Athens swarms with student and alumni fans ready to cheer for their beloved Dawgs. Tailgating begins 24 hours prior to the kick-off, though many fans head into town as early as Tuesday or Wednesday for a Saturday game, and good tickets are often almost impossible to find by the end of the week. The all-important game against the University of Florida is an annual highlight, as well. Students are devoted to their team, and one student notes that "We bleed red and black here."

> **"We bleed red and black here."**

Other sports are also popular to watch, including basketball, swimming and gymnastics, and a variety of club and intramural sports provide ample opportunities to participate. The Ramsey Student Center for Physical Activities is one of the dominant sites on campus for recreational activities and exercise. At Ramsey, students can keep in shape using the wide variety of amenities this extensive gym provides, such as multiple swimming pools, basketball and volleyball courts, an indoor track and a weight room.

A Dawg's Pad

Being close to Ramsey and to classes is one reason for living on campus, which is an especially popular option for all freshmen. It is not mandatory that students live in dorms at UGA for any time, although most freshmen take advantage of this option. Dorms are assigned on the basis of seniority, but three high-rises (Brumby, Russell and Creswell Halls) are reserved especially for freshmen. Reed Hall is known for having a great sense of community, while Oglethorpe Hall (known as "O-House") is coveted for its prime location in the middle of campus.

Although "Every dorm is a 'party dorm' at UGA," all dorms have a resident assistant (RA). The RAs enforce general rules, but are generally friendly and encourage a sense of community within each hall. Some living quarters have special restrictions, such as all-female dorms or those with no visitation hours, but there are a wide variety of options to suit all interests.

Most students say they enjoy living in the dorms, but few students live on campus past their freshman year, so off-campus housing is commonly sought out. The campus borders a residential neighborhood, but even then some off-campus options are more than walking distance away. Almost all students on campus have a car and even freshmen are allowed to have one. According to students, however, traffic is "annoying" and UGA Parking Services is unhelpful. For those who choose to avoid the parking hassle, UGA has an extensive busing system.

Large enough to satisfy almost anyone's needs, UGA has a place for everyone. A challenging honors program and a rampant party scene exist side by side, making sure that each student can keep busy. Athens, too, provides an outlet for those who grow bored with campus-based activities. Most of all, the pride that the University of Georgia arouses in its students is inspiring: "We're the Georgia BullDawgs! Enough said, in our opinion. Students, faculty and alumni all have a sense of overwhelming pride in the University. It becomes a part of who you are."—*Andrew Beaty*

FYI
If you come to UGA, you'd better bring "a good pair of walking shoes because the campus is huge and hilly."
What's the typical weekend schedule? "Friday: hear a local band downtown; Saturday: tailgate all day until game time, and then watch the Dawgs play; Sunday: church, study, then workout at Ramsey."
If you could change one thing about UGA, I'd "make lower-level classes smaller."
Three things every student at UGA should do before graduating are "ring the victory bell behind the chapel, explore the Athens music and bar scene, and go to a Dawgs football game."

Hawaii

University of Hawaii

Address: 2600 Campus Road Honolulu, HI 96822
Phone: 800-823-9771
E-mail address: ar-info@hawaii.edu
Web site URL: www.hawaii.edu/admrec
Year Founded: 1907
Private or Public: Public
Religious Affiliation: None
Location: Urban
Number of Applicants: 6,255
Percent Accepted: 69%
Percent Accepted who enroll: 43%
Number Entering: 3,572
Number of Transfers Accepted each Year: 2,751
Middle 50% SAT range: Unreported
Middle 50% ACT range: Unreported
Early admission program EA/ED/None: None
Percentage accepted through EA or ED: NA

EA and ED deadline: NA
Regular Deadline: 2-Jan
Application Fee: $50
Full time Undergraduate enrollment: 11,283
Total enrollment: 20,051
Percent Male: 45%
Percent Female: 55%
Total Percent Minority or Unreported: 67%
Percent African-American: 1%
Percent Asian/Pacific Islander: 64%
Percent Hispanic: 2%
Percent Native-American: <1%
Percent International: Unreported
Percent in-state/out of state: 75.4%/24.6%
Percent from Public HS: 68.80%
Retention Rate: 78%
Graduation Rate 4-year: 14.70%

Graduation Rate 6-year: 54.80%
Percent Undergraduates in On-campus housing: 19.30%
Number of official organized extracurricular organizations: 150
3 Most popular majors: Biology, Art, Hospitality
Student/Faculty ratio: 13.2:1
Average Class Size: 33
Percent of students going to grad school: Unreported
Tuition and Fees: $16,608
In State Tuition and Fees if different: $5,952
Cost for Room and Board: $7,564
Percent receiving financial aid out of those who apply, first year: 41%
Percent receiving financial aid among all students: Unreported

While sun, sand and sea might first come to mind when thinking of this school's exotic location, the University of Hawaii has a whole lot more to offer than gorgeous surroundings. Its proximity to the Asia-Pacific region and unique mix of American, Asian and Pacific cultures complement the University's academic strengths and friendly environment, making this major research institution a promising place to spend four years.

East Meets West

When asked about the quality of academics, students generally agree that academics are "OK," but reported that several departments are "excellent," such as marine biology, astronomy, geology and Pacific volcanology. Ethnic studies and Pacific Asian studies were also praised for their high quality. As one student put it, "Pretty much everything is alright, but anything that specifically relates to Asia is really good." One student lauded the "eminent minds" brought in by the East-West Center, a national center that sponsors scholars from all over the world to examine economic and social issues. Others noted the presence of "renowned professors" and the strong quality of instruction, describing professors as "supportive" and the classroom environment as "progressive."

Regarding the core requirements, however, students offer differing opinions. While most like the "breadth" offered, one student regretted that the focus was primarily on Asia. Mostly, though, students found the core requirements satisfactory and do not have many complaints.

Fun in the Sun

Students rave about the range of social options at the University of Hawaii, noting that "You can pretty much do whatever you want." Most students go clubbing or to parties on Friday and Saturday nights, then recuperate by hanging out at the beach during the day. While the University of Hawaii has a Greek system, fraternities and sororities do not dominate social life. Students described the Greek scene as "not major" and said they feel little pressure to join it. Students who dislike partying can choose from a range of other options such as theater, surfing, hiking or recreational classes such as scuba diving.

Get "Lei-ed"

Occasions to dress up formally at the University of Hawaii are few and far between—guys almost never get to don their tuxedos. The dating scene, however, is alive and well, and it is common for people to go out on dates or have significant others. Random hook-ups "do happen" every once in a while, but, as one student put it, "I've been to some schools that are really promiscuous and this is not one of those." The University of Hawaii also has its fair share of attractive people, with one student raving about the "pretty girls" and their "sexy outfits." Students agreed that interracial dating is very common, but differed on the subject of gay and lesbian couples. While some described the attitude toward homosexual couples as "open and non-discriminatory," others insisted that homosexual couples generally tend to "stay low-key" because "This is not a very open climate for them."

Athletic opportunities abound at the University of Hawaii, with the most popular sports being football, volleyball, and surfing. Students are proud of their school's athletics, and there is a general "sporty atmosphere." Even students not affiliated with any of the sports clubs or teams enjoy getting outside and kicking a ball around in their spare time. It is common to see groups of students getting together to play casual sports around campus for recreation, even on weekdays.

Homogeneous and Happy

One student described the student stereotype as "people of Asian descent who were brought up in Hawaii." While there were some complaints about the student body being homogeneous, one student emphatically described the student body as "multicultural, diverse, with little segregation." Students dress very casually, with the typical day-to-day wardrobe consisting of "jeans, shorts, T-shirt." Most are happy with the school's "supportive," "friendly" and "relaxed" atmosphere and say it is easy to make friends. Extracurriculars are not a significant part of college life at the University of Hawaii, as it is a commuter school and students tend to take on part-time jobs.

Paradise Found

Students describe the campus as "spread out" and like the fact that it's "a campus unto itself." A tropical oasis, the campus consists of a lot of greenery with large lawns and lots of trees. One student enthusiastically described, "The campus is fantastic and really inspiring because it's surrounded by beautiful mountains and if you are on certain parts of campus that are on higher ground, you can look down and see the ocean." The good weather and abundant sunshine also make a good impression on students. In contrast to the beautiful natural surroundings, the buildings get low reviews. Students say the buildings "could be prettier," "could use more funding," and "need to be renovated."

Island Fare

While most students deem the dining hall food just "acceptable," one student said, "The quality is horrible." As cliques do exist, students find that there "is some pressure to always be eating with a group of friends," though it is not uncommon for people to walk into a dining hall and eat by themselves. There are complaints about the lack of great eating establishments near campus; however, "If you go a little further off campus, you can find some really good places, places that I wouldn't mind going to on a date."

> "The campus is fantastic and really inspiring because it's surrounded by beautiful mountains and . . . on certain parts of campus . . . you can look down and see the ocean."

On the whole, most students agree that the beautiful surroundings and friendly people make the University of Hawaii a great place to be. Students insist that they wouldn't trade their experiences here for anything. There is never a lack of things to do or friends to hang out with, and if classes are too stressful, there's always the beach.—*Wenshan Yeo*

FYI

If you come to the University of Hawaii, you'd better bring "a swimsuit for the beach."

What is the typical weekend schedule? "Friday, go partying; Saturday, go to the beach, more partying; Sunday, watch TV, do homework."

If I could change one thing about the University of Hawaii, I would "renovate the buildings and make them look prettier."

Three things every student at the University of Hawaii should do before graduating are "learn to surf, explore the rest of Hawaii, and learn about the culture and history of Hawaii."

Idaho

University of Idaho

Address: PO Box 444264
Moscow, ID 83844-4264
Phone: 208-885-6326
E-mail address:
admissions@uidaho.edu
Web site URL: www.uihome
.uidaho.edu/uihome
Year Founded: 1889
Private or Public: Public
Religious Affiliation: None
Location: Rural
Number of Applicants: 4,577
Percent Accepted: 77%
**Percent Accepted who
enroll:** 46%
Number Entering: 1,623
**Number of Transfers
Accepted each Year:** 966
Middle 50% SAT range:
M: 480–600, CR: 480–600,
Wr: 450–570
Middle 50% ACT range:
20–25
**Early admission program
EA/ED/None:** None

**Percentage accepted
through EA or ED:** NA
EA and ED deadline: NA
Regular Deadline: 1-Aug
Application Fee: $40
**Full time Undergraduate
enrollment:** 9,018
Total enrollment: 11,309
Percent Male: 55%
Percent Female: 45%
**Total Percent Minority or
Unreported:** 17%
Percent African-American:
1%
**Percent Asian/Pacific
Islander:** 2%
Percent Hispanic: 5%
Percent Native-American:
1%
Percent International: 2%
**Percent in-state/out of
state:** 62%/38%
Percent from Public HS: 90%
Retention Rate: Unreported
Graduation Rate 4-year: 21%

Graduation Rate 6-year: 54%
**Percent Undergraduates in
On-campus housing:**
Unreported
**Number of official organized
extracurricular
organizations:** 190
3 Most popular majors:
Education, Mechanical
Engineering, Psychology
Student/Faculty ratio: 16:1
Average Class Size: 10 to 19
**Percent of students going to
grad school:** Unreported
Tuition and Fees: $14,712
**In State Tuition and Fees if
different:** $4,632
Cost for Room and Board:
$6,762
**Percent receiving financial
aid out of those who apply,
first year:** 56%
**Percent receiving financial
aid among all students:**
75%

The University of Idaho provides a lot of things promised of a small town in land-locked America, including friendly people and a focus on agriculture. While the U of I is no mainstay of diversity, and a sometimes disconnected administration means that students do a lot of their own degree-planning legwork, students looking for an intimate campus with the social benefits of a large university will find their promised land at the University of Idaho.

Academics

Students say that the academic frontier at the University of Idaho—notable alumni of which include the first-ever female, Republican vice-presidential nominee Sarah Palin and Jack Lemley, construction manager of the Chunnel—can be really hard or really easy—it's all up to them. The University is well-known for the close relationship it has with the Idaho National Laboratory (INL), a governmental science and engineering laboratory that focuses on environmental, energy and nuclear technology. As a result, programs in engineering and the life sciences are well-funded and popular. That being said, students are quick to list engineering and chemistry classes at the University among the most difficult. Agricultural and food sciences programs are also popular choices, and feed graduates into Idaho's flourishing farming and dairy industries. U of I partners with Washington State University in nearby Pullman, Wash., in many of these departments, which contributes to the availability of equipment and talented faculty and graduate students, who often serve as TAs for large lectures. Communications is understood to be the easiest major possible. The school's Business department, while generally considered markedly less demanding than anything in the sciences, is a place where many students find common ground—"Everyone has a Business minor," notes one.

As is often the case at large universities, lecture classes required early in a student's curriculum tend to be very large and can be weed-out classes, with less-generous grading than upper-level classes. Students in every major are required to take at least one math and one science course, but most have no trouble finding an easy way around their requirements, with classes like Math 123, "Mathematics Applied to the Modern World," and Geography 100, "Physical Geography." Other favorite, unusual classes include Business 103, "Introduction to Professional Golf Management" and Psychology 330, "Human Sexuality," affectionately known as "Dirty 330."

Students note that a department's level of funding has a meaningful effect on the undergraduate experience in that department. Funding is largely a function of donation by graduates, so engineering and business-oriented disciplines are the most cash-flush on campus. One obvious way in which this disparity manifests itself is in the frequency of course offerings, even those required for the major. One French major noted such a required class that is only offered every other year, and only in the fall—it isn't uncommon that students in such situations must extend their time at the University by a semester or a year for the sake of access to that single class. That's to say nothing of what happens when students wait the semester or year, and then can't get into the class because of capped enrollment or registration bottlenecks, a circumstance for which the University administration has little sympathy.

All of which might not be so bad, if the University devoted resources to helping students plan their track to degree completion, but advising is a sore point for many students. While general advising is available for freshmen unsure about their choice of major, "As soon as you get into your department, advising goes downhill fast." The system is very decentralized, students say, with department advisors changing almost every semester and the role often filled by the newest members of the department, who may have less expertise navigating the system than the students themselves. Appointments with advisors can be hard to make, and many students remember taking classes that could have counted for more than one requirement, or which counted for no requirements at all, despite their advisors' information to the contrary.

Professors, fortunately, are another matter. Students are enthusiastic about the faculty they work with and find them accessible. Smaller departments are most intimate, and students find it possible to develop close relationships with their professors. Some even have favorite members of professors' supporting administration: "The secretary of the history department has probably saved my life multiple times."

To Greek or Not to Greek?

The course of University of Idaho students' social lives is charted early and depends a lot on their decision whether or not to go Greek. Wherever they end up, social life at U of I can be rather segmented. Greek life is prominent on campus, and frat brothers and sorority sisters tend to associate with one another, to the exclusion of students outside the circle. "I really wish there wasn't such a huge delineation between the Greek system and everything else," said one student. "I have friends in the Greek system that I really don't hang out with, and that's lame." The alternative to the Greek system for most freshmen is living in the dorms, where they make the friends they'll have for the rest of college. Even within the dorms, athletes often separate into cliques and move off campus within their first semester, and "the music kids stick together."

U of I students have a bone to pick with their reputation as a party school: "Not everyone is an alcoholic." Moscow is a small town and social life can revolve around the bar scene, but that's true even for students who aren't serious drinkers. Theirs is a nominally dry campus, and the administration makes a proactive attempt to catch offenders and educate students; punishment often centers around classes on drinking responsibly. "They're not necessarily condoning it [alcohol consumption], but they're trying to make sure people are safe." Some fraternities are expressly dry as well. Bars take the legal drinking age seriously, and fake IDs are traditionally unsuccessful, so the social world opens up a lot when students turn 21. Popular bars include John's Alley, The Plantation, The Corner Club, and Garden Lounge; Casa Lopez and The Alehouse are restaurant bars with good drink specials. One student sums up the party scene this way: "You don't have to look too hard to find a party, but it's not like the dorms are going crazy with drunk kids hanging out every door." There is a prominent coffee house subculture on the campus, with strongholds at Bucer's, The Sisters's Brew Café and The One World Café, "a bastion of liberal thinking," in one student's words.

Moscow is fairly isolated, so most students stay in the area on weekends. A car isn't a necessity in town, and can sometimes be a hassle, since parking around campus is limited and parking enforcement very stringent. A free bus system runs all over the campus and the town of Moscow, so students without cars have no trouble getting around. That said, many students keep cars, and they're necessary to get away. The nearest big-city experience is in Seattle, about a five-hour trip by car. That opportunity for escape is important to students who struggle with the small-town pace and feel of Moscow. The university system supports the town in many ways, especially the many bars, restaurants and coffee houses. Moscow hasn't forgotten it, and town-gown relations are symbiotic and pleasant. The town is small, but there is no shortage of things to do for the motivated student—the well-known Lionel Hampton School of Music supports a healthy culture of live performance, especially of jazz; the Arboretum and nearby Moscow Mountain make for nice walking and hiking; the Kenworthy Theater is a historic way to enjoy a movie; and Elizabethan enthusiasts will enjoy the Kiva Theater, which puts plays up regularly and seats in the round.

Campus Living

Two main options exist for University of Idaho freshmen making housing plans: the Greek system, which rushes at the very beginning of the fall semester, and the residence halls. Residence hall living is perfect for the student who enjoys structure, doesn't want to deal with paying bills, and enjoys a social atmosphere, since there are always people around. Some halls are explicitly restricted to first-years, most notable is the Tower, which boasts 11 stories of coed (by floor) housing. Another large residence is Wallace Hall, also coed by floor. Some housing is in the single- or double-bedroom-in-a-long-hallway tradition, and some is suite-style, but whatever the organization, the University administration is very flexible and reasonable about students interested in making changes in their housing at any time in the year, for any reason. "If things aren't working out with your roommate, or anything else, they ask you to wait it out for two weeks, and if you still want to switch, you can." Different residence halls have different personalities. Examples are a hall for students in agriculture (characterized by flannel outerwear and cowboy boots), an engineering hall, and a hall for students in the education departments. Single-sex housing is also available; Graham Hall is all-male, Houston Hall and Hayes Hall are all-female. For sophomores who choose not to move off campus or go Greek in their second opportunity to rush, there is the Living and Learning Community, a hall dedicated to second-year students. Most students on the dorm track spend one year in a residence hall before moving off-campus. Many cite RAs as a reason to escape dorm living as soon as they have friends with whom they'd like to find an apartment. While some RAs can be cool, they say, dorm living usually feels more like a police state, with strict University alcohol and furnishings policy enforcement: "Unless you get a good RA, you're going to be dealing with someone trying to catch you with an illegal candle."

Dining options on campus are dismal, which may account for the thriving restaurant business in Moscow. The largest, best-known dining halls are Bob's Café and Commons. A fair variety of foods is available, including pasta dishes, a salad bar and ever-present hamburgers, hot dogs and grilled cheese sandwiches, but the menu never changes, and as one student puts it, "You can get tired of pasta." Dining halls also keep odd hours—Commons, for example, closes at 4 p.m.—but students on a meal plan can use their VandalCard at a variety of smaller coffee-shop venues around campus, so food is always available somewhere. Favorite off-campus dining options include The Pita Pit, with varied Greek offerings, and The Breakfast Club, which does a brisk business in brunch and lunch specials.

The U of I campus is beautiful, and students appreciate it. Composed of mostly brick buildings, it's an ivy-covered haven in the woods of northern Idaho. The campus was designed by Frederick Law Olmstead, the landscape architect responsible for Central Park in New York City, and a favorite location for many is the lawn in front of the administration building. The campus is intimate, and students feel it's a factor that distinguishes their school from other, more commuter campuses in the state.

Extracurriculars

Athletics and the Greek system are major drivers in extracurricular activities at the University of Idaho. Vandal pride is strong, although students are candid about the disappointing performance of their teams. Football and men's basketball are the most popular varsity sports on campus. The former has shown especially weak performance in recent years, but game attendance remains strong and historic moments of domination over rival Boise State University are fresh in the minds of die-hard fans. An aggressive anti-BSU T-shirt campaign takes place every year leading up to the schools' annual football face-off. In addition to varsity sports, intramural activities are going on all the time, and students love the University's recently opened Student Recreation Center. Students of every level of athletic ability have access to the climbing wall—the largest of any university in the United States—massage services and "Every kind of free-weight, cardio machine or court you could ever want."

The Greek system, by design, requires a great deal of community service activity, and philanthropic pursuits are going on all the time on campus. Student government at U of I is good at organizing large events like speaking engagements or campus-wide community service trips, but students say that involvement in the voting and planning process is low. Many students have jobs for 10 to 20 hours a week, either on campus in help-desk or library services or off campus in restaurant work.

Extracurricular activities are an important way for students to experience diversity on campus, which is far from extensive, but is developing. Students characterize the campus as predominantly white and middle- to upper-middle-class, although socioeconomic perceptions are skewed downward by the proximity of Washington State University, recognized in the area as a very wealthy campus. U of I students are overwhelmingly natives of Idaho, and those not from Idaho tend to come from other Pacific-Northwestern states. Scholarships offered to multicultural students, especially those from Alaska, are improving the campus' diversity score, and the campus is adapting to broader horizons with recent introductions of multicultural fraternities and sororities. There are also a growing number of groups on campus for gay, lesbian, and transgender students.

> ## "Not everyone here is an alcoholic."

Students considering the University of Idaho should, in short, be prepared to be intrepid if they want to be challenged, and will experience four or five years of relative homogeneity in demography and opportunities for socializing. Still, students will find their classmates friendly and willing to try new things, and the community formed at the University of Idaho will likely be a lasting one.—*Elizabeth Woods*

FYI
If you come to the University of Idaho, you'd better bring "your party pants."
What is the typical weekend schedule? "Party Friday and Saturday nights, and spend all day Sunday working—and maybe, depending on the season, do something adventurous during the day on Saturday, like go for a hike or see a football game."
If I could change one thing about the University of Idaho, I would "want a Target somewhere nearby."
Three things every student should do before graduating are "go to a drag show in Pullman, WA, take advantage of the VandalCard by renting an Xbox or a laptop from the university, and sing great karaoke at the otherwise-terrible CJ's Nightclub."

Illinois

DePaul University

Address: 1 East Jackson Blvd
Chicago, IL 60604
Phone: 312-362-8300
E-mail address:
admitdpu@depaul.edu
Web site URL:
www.depaul.edu
Year Founded: 1898
Private or Public: Private
Religious Affiliation:
Roman Catholic
Location: Urban
Number of Applicants:
10,294
Percent Accepted: 70%
**Percent Accepted who
enroll:** 35%
Number Entering: 2,522
**Number of Transfers
Accepted each Year:** 2,512
Middle 50% SAT range:
M: 510–620, Cr: 510–630,
Wr: 590–670
Middle 50% ACT range:
21–26

**Early admission program
EA/ED/None:** EA and ED
**Percentage accepted
through EA or ED:** 59%
EA and ED deadline: 15-Nov
Regular Deadline: 1-Feb
Application Fee: $40
**Full time Undergraduate
enrollment:** 15,024
Total enrollment: 22,377
Percent Male: 44%
Percent Female: 56%
**Total Percent Minority or
Unreported:** 29%
Percent African-American:
8%
**Percent Asian/Pacific
Islander:** 8%
Percent Hispanic: 11%
Percent Native-American: 1%
Percent International: 1%
**Percent in-state/out of
state:** 84%/16%
Percent from Public HS: 74%
Retention Rate: 85%

Graduation Rate 4-year: 39%
Graduation Rate 6-year: 64%
**Percent Undergraduates in
On-campus housing:** 19%
**Number of official organized
extracurricular
organizations:** 170
3 Most popular majors:
Accounting,
Communications, Finance
Student/Faculty ratio: 14:1
Average Class Size: 20 to 29
**Percent of students going to
grad school:** Unreported
Tuition and Fees: $22,365
**In State Tuition and Fees if
different:** No difference
Cost for Room and Board:
$9,801
**Percent receiving financial
aid out of those who apply,
first year:** 75%
**Percent receiving financial
aid among all students:**
62%

I f you take the Brown Line to the Fuller-ton Stop on the Chicago El, you'll exit onto a bustling street in the Lincoln Park neighborhood of Chicago. But just hang a left and in a few minutes you'll be in the tree-lined heart of DePaul University. DePaul offers its students the best of both worlds: a school committed to the life and study of its under-graduates and a wealth of opportunities to be involved in the "real world" in Chicago. With 23,401 students and the whole city open to ex-ploration, few people at the University have a chance to be bored. Although it has been known as a commuter school in the past, De-Paul is rapidly attracting students from all over while maintaining its uniquely Midwest-ern warmth and sense of community both in-side the University and within Chicago through service and active learning.

Domains of Learning

DePaul takes its commitment to integrating into the surrounding urban environment very seriously. In fact, the first choice freshmen must make when they are accepted is whether to take the Discover Chicago or Explore Chicago class. In Discover, freshmen arrive at school a week early to participate in weeklong orientation programs that allow students to "totally immerse themselves in one aspect of the city's culture." These programs run the gamut from "Poverty Amidst Plenty," which gives students the opportunity to visit home-less shelters and participate in community ser-vice activities, to "Biking in Chicago," which allows students to go on bike trips that help orient them to the traffic patterns while taking in the sights. Much like Discover, but ex-panded to cover the entire first quarter,

Explore allows students to get a "more in-depth view of the inner workings of Chicago." This includes everything from a class titled Understanding Beauty in Chicago to a quarter devoted to studying the Chicago Cubs.

DePaul does not stop initiating service learning after the first quarter. The University offers many opportunities for "experiential learning," which covers study abroad, internship, and service learning areas. In fact, DePaul's Center for Community-Based Learning focuses on volunteer work and sponsors such popular classes as Peace, Social Justice, Conflict Resolution, and Psychology outreach programs that allow students to work in area clinics and get credit for it. Given the number of outside resources available, it doesn't come as much of a surprise that many students double-major and/or double-minor in applied fields such as Peace Studies and Political Science-International Relations. This interdisciplinary approach to learning permeates the atmosphere of the school, and students say that many people are very politically engaged as a result.

This sense of active engagement also extends to rest of the academic environment, as students say the "Focus of classes is more on practice than just study." For example, art history classes often come with a studio art component, just as English majors will frequently get a teaching certification in addition to their liberal arts degree. That extends in particular to the School of Commerce, which boasts "a lot of ties to accounting firms," say students, as well as a "business mindset as opposed to a pure learning mindset."

Potential Blue Demons take note: the classroom is front and center in a DePaul education, and prospective students should be prepared for a broad range of requirements that encourage active thinking and participation. The core curriculum, called the Liberal Studies Program, is comprised of a set of "learning domains," which involve completion of arts and literature, philosophical inquiry, religion, scientific inquiry, Self and the Modern World, and Understanding the Past requirements. Each of these broad-based areas allows for a great deal of freedom in choosing the classes that most interest the student, which "brings a lot more individualism into the program," say students. The Honors Program also works to tailor the broader school requirements to individual students. A member of the Honors Student Government noted that while the required classes are more specific in the honors program, "All honors classes are capped at 20,

which means that they might be a little harder to get into, but in the end, it's worth it for the close engagement with the professors." In fact, one student's "Biggest class had forty-five people in it . . . actually, there are only two or three places on campus that will even hold more than fifty people."

That closeness is also manifested in the love-it or hate-it quarter system that DePaul uses as opposed to the traditional semester. Summers are a little shorter, with school ending in late June, but students enjoy a six-week winter break. Students typically take classes three out of four quarters, as the fourth quarter is summer vacation. Students give the system mixed reviews, mentioning that "You never get bored or feel like you've wasted a semester if you end up taking a class you're not that into." A sophomore agreed, saying, "You can sample things more and experience lots of classes, and you can focus more on each one while you're taking it." And one senior hit upon a very important factor for most students, noting, "One class can't mess up your GPA because you have so many to pad any not-so-great grades."

Students also appreciate the fact that DePaul is not a research university—"Professors are very present in their fields in terms of writing and peer-reviewing, [but] the focus is clearly on teaching and coming up with new ways to present material and get students engaged."

Hit That High(Rise)

One of the hallmarks of DePaul student life is the exodus from on-campus living after freshman and sophomore year. Students are quick to say that prospectives shouldn't be turned off by this: "You stay friends with most of your friends from freshman year, and even though you don't see people congregating to go out as much, the upperclassmen are the ones who have the parties . . . so you'll see people no matter what." One junior noted that freshman year "Feels like a smaller community because you see the same people and develop a real sense of camaraderie, [but] living in an apartment becomes completely natural." Although students readily admit it is a "different lifestyle," one that includes "being independent and paying your own bills," they also say that it is "very freeing" and "exciting to live on your own with your friends." Because of the culture of living in neighborhood apartments, the campus "isn't as hoppin' on the weekends," but students insist that "Lincoln Park is a lively neighborhood, so it never feels like a dead corn town."

And never fear: there's still plenty to do, both off campus and on. When asked about the biggest party day, one junior responded, "Um, every day?" While it's clear that DePaul students are not shy about letting loose, students say that partying comes down to "less of a woo-hoo, we're in college, let's drink" atmosphere and more of a "hanging out with friends or go to a bar" environment. Students admit that many of their peers have fake IDs and that drinking is fairly prevalent on campus, but they also note that the college has a safety-first policy. DePaul provides a public safety escort from 6 p.m. to 6 a.m. every day.

For students who find that the drinking scene isn't their thing, there are plenty of events on and around campus to keep them busy. One of DePaul's most striking qualities is the diversity of its student body. As a result, there are "tons and tons of different cultural events going on all the time." Everything from the Black Student Union to a Spanish dance group to Hillel holds activities on the weekends. This is true of the diversity of the campus in general as well—as one senior said, "You definitely see people from a lot of different backgrounds."

> "A lot of people here worked really hard to be the first in their family to go to college, and it gives a very diverse perspective in class when there are people with those experiences right there—it's not just a hypothetical."

Although there are admittedly "a lot of people from Illinois and Ohio," students think there is "true diversity" at DePaul in the sense that you can "Come as you are— there is somewhere you'll fit in here." While students note that there is still separation among groups, they laud the school's particular efforts to broaden the scope of diversity by accepting students who are diverse not only in race, but also in socioeconomic status, state and country of origin, ideas, and belief systems. One junior also noted that there are "many first-generation college students at DePaul. You don't usually think about this in terms of diversity, but it really gives you perspective."

The Windy Campus

With the Chicago skyline serving as the main campus attraction, students at DePaul should never be worried about being stuck behind gates or locked into exclusively meeting people from the 18-22 set. When "the whole city is your campus," students recommend preparing for "interaction with *real people* every day." While Chicago is certainly different from many college towns, students really appreciate the cultural and community-oriented opportunities it provides. In fact, one senior noted that the "community comes into life a lot more than at other places." As an example, she pointed to the relatively large number of people from the community who come in and take classes at DePaul as well as the very large number of students who perform community service, both through DePaul and on their own initiative. On an academic level, "Things don't have to be as abstract as they are in the classroom because you can go out and experience them." This extends to the internship and work opportunities. This is particularly useful for the large number of business majors, as it gives them concentrated networking contacts from which to draw and plenty of alums who are happy to help out a fellow Blue Demon.

However, students do warn prospectives that they should prepare for a very different college experience. "It does take something away from the college experience," admitted one junior, and another student added that the whole perspective on college changes "when you're not walking across a campus to get home." Still, they note that the Student Center, the gym, the coffee shop, and study tables at the Schmidt Academic Center, known by students as SAC, tie the DePaul community together. One sophomore said, "We're definitely not separated completely, and the ways that DePaul are different are mostly really good, and add another level to the college experience."

The DePaul "Thing"

"It's not really our motto . . . and it's not really a slogan . . ." One student tried hard to describe it, but the best she could think of was "the DePaul Thing." This three-tiered saying perfectly encapsulates DePaul, students say, and it goes something like this. DePaul is: "1) Catholic—in the true root meaning of oneness, 2) Urban—in the commitment to the urban community, 3) Vincentian—in the goal of serving and loving each other." Although it may not have an overarching name, the DePaul credo, of sorts, really brings together the aspects of the school that separate it from other large, urban universities. DePaul's deep commitment to the community that surrounds it permeates every aspect of student life, and this creates a bond between students that keeps them together even in the midst of a busy city. One student captured this sense perfectly when she said: "DePaul feels real. We have all the resources and cultural opportunities of the city, but in the end, Chicago attracts down-to-earth kids from the Midwest. It's real."—*Hannah Jacobson*

FYIs

If you come to DePaul, you'd better bring "a fully loaded iPod (kids are really into music here)," "a bike lock (a bike is really useful for getting around the city)," and "warm boots!"

What is the typical weekend schedule? "Thursday, go out to the bars, meet some new people, and get great drunk food; Friday, sleep in, have a class or a club meeting, go shopping, and go to the beach if it's nice out; Saturday, do some community service, like the AIDS Walk, during the day, then at night go to a bar, go to a party, go see a show, or go to one of the tons of concert venues around Chicago; and Sunday, grab the brunch buffet at the Student Center—it's crucial for curing hangovers!"

If I could change one thing about DePaul, I'd "make it easier to get on-campus housing and streamline the bureaucracy so it would be easier to get answers from the higher-ups."

Three things every student at DePaul should do before graduating are "go on a service immersion trip to experience something outside DePaul and Chicago, get to know the city by visiting neighborhoods that are off the beaten path, and sit in the arms of the Father Egan statue!"

Illinois State University

Address: Admissions, Campus Box 2200 Normal, IL 61790-2200
Phone: 800-366-2478
E-mail address: admissions@ilstu.edu
Web site URL: www.ilstu.edu
Year Founded: 1857
Private or Public: Public
Religious Affiliation: None
Location: Suburban
Number of Applicants: 13,549
Percent Accepted: 64%
Percent Accepted who enroll: 39%
Number Entering: 5,098
Number of Transfers Accepted each Year: Unreported
Middle 50% SAT range: Unreported
Middle 50% ACT range: 22–26
Early admission program EA/ED/None: NA
Percentage accepted through EA or ED: Unreported

EA and ED deadline: NA
Regular Deadline: 15-Nov, 1-Feb
Application Fee: $40
Full time Undergraduate enrollment: 16,959
Total enrollment: 20,799
Percent Male: 43%
Percent Female: 57%
Total Percent Minority or Unreported: 11%
Percent African-American: 5%
Percent Asian/Pacific Islander: 2%
Percent Hispanic: 4%
Percent Native-American: <1%
Percent International: Unreported
Percent in-state/out of state: 99%/1%
Percent from Public HS: 88%
Retention Rate: 83%
Graduation Rate 4-year: 41%

Graduation Rate 6-year: 70%
Percent Undergraduates in On-campus housing: 30%
Number of official organized extracurricular organizations: 250
3 Most popular majors: Elementary Education, Marketing, Criminal Justice Sciences
Student/Faculty ratio: 19:1
Average Class Size: 25
Percent of students going to grad school: Unreported
Tuition and Fees: $16,444
In State Tuition and Fees if different: $9,814
Cost for Room and Board: $7,458
Percent receiving financial aid out of those who apply, first year: 60%
Percent receiving financial aid among all students: 46%

The oldest public university in Illinois, Illinois State University boasts a diverse student body of over 18,000 undergraduates. Located two hours south of Chicago in Normal, Illinois—yes, the city is really called "Normal"—the school certainly is anything but a normal state school.

Big School, Small Class

Students at Illinois State University have to complete a minimum of 120 credit hours to graduate, about one-third of which are for general education requirements. However, with over 167 fields of study and a 312-page course catalog, there are many ways for students to fulfill those hours. For example, among the University's many courses is one that allows finance majors to manage a $400,000 portfolio their senior year.

Students say that, despite the University's size, class sizes average around 30 students, with almost all classes taught by professors, and students praised the variety of professors at the school and their accessibility. As one student said, "I like how there are many different ways of teaching in one school. You'll be able to find teachers who teach to the way you learn." Grading is straightforward, most said, and tests rarely have to be curved; students who work hard generally earn As and Bs.

ISU was founded as a teaching school, and its teacher education program remains its flagship course of study, ranking among the top 10 teacher education programs in the nation. Students say ISU's strength as a teaching school has pushed the school to be stronger overall in the humanities.

Illinois State University also boasts the oldest laboratory schools in the nation. Thomas Metcalf Laboratory School and University High School, both part of ISU, teach students from nursery school through 12th grade, and education students spend much of their time at the schools. They are required to have 100 hours of work with K-12 students. However, as one senior advised, "Don't be frightened by that number [100 hours]. There are so many things that qualify for the hours; they are very easy to rack up. Personally, I already had my 100 hours by the end of my freshman year."

One of the most striking features of ISU's campus is its new College of Business building. Opened in 2005, the building has drawn more students and faculty to the program, the University claims. Perhaps even more striking than the new building, however, is the Marketing department's dress code. Students are required to wear business casual dress to their marketing classes. The policy change elicited mixed reactions from students and faculty alike. As one junior put it, "I think it's good and bad. I have a struggle every morning with what I'm going to wear . . . but it gives the class a more professional feel."

Life on a Breezeway

Although most upperclassmen live off campus, underclassmen at Illinois State University have a wide variety of residence halls from which to choose—10, to be exact. As one sophomore put it, "The dorms as a whole are a blast to live in because . . . there always seems to be something going on."

At 28 stories, Watterson Towers is the tallest residence hall in the world. It holds 10 "houses," each considered an individual residence hall. Because of Watterson's design, the central elevator only stops at each house, and students take a breezeway from the center elevator to their respective house, from where they take the stairs to their room. Student comments about Watterson, unsurprisingly, focus on the building's size—some like the close proximity to 2,000 other students, while others felt that the bustle made it harder to make friends.

Athletes generally live in Tri-Towers on the west side of campus due to its proximity to the athletic facilities, though the recently renovated rooms pull even non-athletes from the centrally located dorms. Because of that proximity to the athletic facilities, students say it has a "fun atmosphere on game days for football and basketball." Although they say that athletics haven't been too big a deal on campus, in recent years school spirit has increased largely due to the success of the men's basketball team.

The rest of the residence halls border the campus' east and west sides, and all are scheduled for renovation as part of a 15-year plan.

On-campus students are required to enroll in a meal plan, and each residential complex has a dining hall. The University recently switched from an a la carte to an all-you-care-to-eat system, which has upset some students who were used to picking up small snacks throughout the day. In general, students were very satisfied with the dining options available, which range from fast food to traditional cafeteria fare.

Students say the Resident Advisors are generally relaxed. As one freshman put it, "They are basically just there if you have any questions and to make sure you don't break the rules too much." With the exception of one floor in one residence hall for students of age, alcohol is prohibited in the dorms, and the University's stringent drinking policies mean that underage students caught with alcohol on campus may be fined. However, perhaps worse than the fine is the alcohol education class that underage students caught drinking have to take at 8:00 a.m. on a Saturday morning.

Though the school is not terribly diverse—11 percent of students identify as a minority, a statistic congruous with the demographics of the surrounding area—students say that they feel the school's atmosphere is very inclusive. Additionally, they say that the convergence of rural, suburban and urban (read: Chicago) students adds a unique mix to the student body.

The Normal Life

As one junior put it, "When the weather is nice, the quad is always packed." Whether students are doing homework, playing football, or, occasionally, reassuring their professor that it was, in fact, a good idea to move class outside, student life happens on the quad (which, for fans of foliage, also happens to be a registered arboretum). Most academic buildings are on the main quad, so it is rarely a long walk between classes, and pedestrian over- and underpasses mean that, even when traveling to buildings off the main quad, students rarely have to cross more than one street.

> "The dorms as a whole are a blast to live in because . . . there always seems to be something going on."

To the east of the University lies uptown Normal, which has a number of local restaurants, bars and stores that cater to students. Many of these businesses are open late at night. The area is currently undergoing a major facelift that is bringing a new hotel and train/bus terminal to the area. Trains make the two-hour trip between Normal and Chicago many times each day, and tickets cost about $12 each way. Further east lies Normal's twin city, Bloomington, which offers even more restaurants and shopping.

Because of University policies, most partying occurs off campus. According to one senior, "The Greek scene is pretty dominant; however, there are many other social opportunities, as well." Underclassmen tend to go to organized parties hosted by either fraternities or individual students living off campus, while upperclassmen flock to the bars in nearby uptown Normal and downtown Bloomington. One popular destination is Pub II in uptown Normal, which one junior called "THE ISU bar." Pub II is famous for its food, and finding a parking spot there any time of day is tough. Unfortunately for underclassmen, bars in the area only admit those over 21. As such, some underage students will make the 45-minute trip to the University of Illinois campus in Champaign-Urbana, where the minimum age for bars is 19.

True Midwestern Living

True to its roots in the fields of Illinois, Illinois State University simultaneously offers students Midwestern hospitality and a 21st century curriculum. Its solid academics, enthusiastic faculty, and central location make for a great environment. As one freshman said, "It has a small-town feel . . . it just has a really friendly atmosphere," as she affirmed her satisfaction with her choice to come to ISU.—*Rustin Fakheri*

FYIs
If you come to ISU, you'd better bring "notecards, because you're gonna be doing a lot of studying."
What is the typical weekend schedule? "Wake up at 11, study until about 5, eat dinner at The Rock . . . [then] go out for a couple hours to apartment parties."
If I could change one thing about ISU, "I'd make the meal plan change back to when you chose your items and your meal card was like a debit card and deducted money."
Three things every student at ISU should do before graduating are "sit in the big bowl-shaped fountain outside Stevenson Hall," "go to Pub II, THE ISU bar," and "live in a friendly dorm like Hewett or Tri Towers to make lots of friends."

Illinois Wesleyan University

Address: PO Box 2900
Bloomington, IL
61702-2900
Phone: 309-556-3031
E-mail address:
iwuadmit@iwu.edu
Web site URL: www.iwu.edu
Year Founded: 1850
Private or Public: Private
Religious Affiliation: None
Location: Urban
Number of Applicants: 2,963
Percent Accepted: 57%
Percent Accepted who
enroll: 32%
Number Entering: 538
Number of Transfers
Accepted each Year: 27
Middle 50% SAT range:
M: 590–690, CR: 540–680,
Wr: Unreported
Middle 50% ACT range: 26–30
Early admission program
EA/ED/None: None
Percentage accepted
through EA or ED: NA

EA and ED deadline: NA
Regular Deadline: Rolling
through April
Application Fee: $0
Full time Undergraduate
enrollment: 2,125
Total enrollment: 2,125
Percent Male: 42%
Percent Female: 58%
Total Percent Minority or
Unreported: 7%
Percent African-American:
5%
Percent Asian/Pacific
Islander: 4%
Percent Hispanic: 3%
Percent Native-American:
<1%
Percent International: 3%
Percent in-state/out of
state: 87%/13%
Percent from Public HS:
84%
Retention Rate: 92%
Graduation Rate 4-year:
77%

Graduation Rate 6-year:
82%
Percent Undergraduates in
On-campus housing: 77%
Number of official organized
extracurricular
organizations: 170
3 Most popular majors:
Biology/Biological Sciences,
Business/Commerce,
Psychology
Student/Faculty ratio: 13:1
Average Class Size: 10 to 19
Percent of students going to
grad school: 35%
Tuition and Fees: $32,260
In State Tuition and Fees if
different: No difference
Cost for Room and Board:
$7,350
Percent receiving financial
aid out of those who apply,
first year: 95%
Percent receiving financial
aid among all students:
91%

"Everybody here is so nice," one Illinois Wesleyan senior said, and she would probably know. With an enrollment of about 2,100 undergraduates, IWU is smaller than many public high schools, allowing students to quickly form a common identity. Studying in out-of-the-way Bloomington, students reap the rewards of the school's unique academic offerings, including the Gateway Colloquium seminars for first-years, an annual student research conference and May Term, which allows undergrads to explore non-traditional learning experiences. And if anything can be gleaned from the school's strong record of alumni giving, it is that IWU's unique programs and tight-knit community make a lasting impact on the students who step through its doors.

Challenging and Welcoming Work

Professors are very accessible to IWU students, who often develop meaningful relationships with faculty outside of class. Because the school is almost entirely under-graduates, most students are lavished with attention. Classes range from largish lectures (50–100 people) to very intimate seminars (less than 10 people), and come in varying levels of difficulty. "For the most part," said one sophomore, "the classes are as challenging as you make them."

Certain programs are developing a reputation for particular excellence, with the expectations for students in these majors rising accordingly. Biology and Business are the hot majors, and produce some of the school's top graduates. "A 3.0 in the bio program would translate to a 3.8 almost anywhere else," said one Biology major. Additionally, many science majors cite the value of being able to do research under the guidance of their professors.

The Business program boasts its own unique learning experience. "We have more discussion, more hands-on experience," one Business major said. The Business department has a successful record of placing students in summer internships in Bloomington, Chicago, or elsewhere in the country. Despite the recent prevalence of these two programs,

IWU still offers strong liberal arts programs true to its founding at 1850.

Today, most upperclassmen agree that the younger classes are smarter and more interesting every year. "I don't think I would still get in if I had to apply now," noted one senior. First-years who do make the cut benefit from the Gateway Colloquium, a series of small, discussion-oriented classes that focus on writing skills. Students also enjoy the John Wesley Powell Undergraduate Research Conference, a yearly event at which students present their research to the rest of the campus community. "You shouldn't miss it," exhorted a senior female.

Campus Culture and Living Arrangements

If there is a stereotype of IWU students, it centers on their background. "As much as the administration tries to push diversity, everyone comes from the same kind of suburb," said one transfer student. "To some extent, everybody here is a little bit of a nerd," added a physics major.

Stereotypes aside, IWU students are generally hard-working, smart, and from an upper-middle-class higher economic background. "As such," noted one student from the Chicago suburbs, "the students demand a relatively high level of living."

> "To some extent, everybody here is a little bit of a nerd."

Integral to the "high life" at IWU is gaming. Video and computer gaming are popular pastimes in the dorms, especially for the guys, with the majority of rooms linked to facilitate multi-player tournaments. "College is the ultimate gaming experience," declared one male student. Intramural sports are also an option, but casual sports, such as Frisbee on the quad, are more prevalent. One sophomore, however, disagreed, saying that the political side of university life was more interesting.

Most students applaud the on-campus housing, and though a few live off campus, all are in assigned dorms during freshman year. "I was surprised to have gotten a really cool roommate," one freshman noted. The school has a fairly successful method for putting roommates together and, according to one sophomore, it really "encourages everyone to get to know each other."

A Small Student Body Congregates

The size of the student body doesn't limit its spirit, especially on the few occasions that a large group congregates. All students agree: "Basketball is big." The team is ranked in Division III, and a home basketball game draws more than half of the student body. Other varsity teams are well-regarded, but definitely not as well-supported as basketball. In balancing the athletic experience with his academic load, one varsity swimmer emphasized the accommodation of his professors, "They are very willing to give me make-up tests." An athlete could do much worse than the facilities he will be able to use at IWU. The Shirk Center is the large athletic complex and, according to one student, "Everything is kept up very well."

The Student Senate also gathers large amounts of attention on campus, as it is the primary liaison between the school administration and the students. "The administration is genuinely receptive to student input," noted one student who worked in the admissions office.

Finally, weekend afternoons and early evenings, much of the student body congregates at the student center, which screens films, brings comedians and other live acts to campus, and acts as a simple meeting point for students before the night's activities.

Food and Drink

"The food is really good," exclaimed one excited sophomore. Still, a freshman noted that "A lot of upperclassmen claim it gets old really fast." So, if the students get tired of "Saga," the main dining hall on campus, they can go to a few on-campus alternatives or take their hunger into Bloomington. Nevertheless, "You have not had the full experience," one sophomore explained, "until you are yelled at by this crazy old lady in the dining hall."

After being chewed out by the elderly, students like to party on the weekends. The fraternities and sororities provide a large majority of the options, though there are invariably other parties on many occasions, if not on every night. Additionally, for those with ID, there are a number of bars in Bloomington that become frequent destinations.

Student opinion regarding the Greeks is mixed. Some think that the parties could be better, while others praise the generally strong social scene given the size of the student body. The truth, however, is that "If you are in the mood for a party, you'll definitely be able to find one."

Extra Opportunities

The experience at IWU would not be complete without "the monkey pit." Beneath a bridge next to the science offices, one can often see students lounging in a space that looks similar to a monkey habitat at a zoo, prompting its nickname.

But the final distinguishing element of the IWU educational experience is May Term. Students finish second semester at the end of April, but almost all continue with a three-week term immediately thereafter called May Term. During May Term, each student takes one class, which meets once a day for a few hours. While it is possible to take normal classes to satisfy major or graduation requirements, most students take advantage of various exciting opportunities.

Students take courses on campus that are offered according to a professor's hobby or special interest. Particularly popular are travel classes. During May term, students can study biology in Costa Rica or Australia, theater in New York City, international politics in the European Union, or classical music in Italy, among other options.

Yet the essence of Illinois Wesleyan remains the opportunities that await students when they leave the school. One senior said, "I feel like I will take the knowledge that I learn here into the real world."—*Peter Johnston*

FYI

If you come to IWU, you'd better bring "Mountain Dew to stay up late."

A typical weekend at Illinois Wesleyan consists of "sleeping late, partying, studying, and playing video games."

If I could change one thing about IWU, I would change "the math department."

Three things every student at IWU should do before graduating are "get yelled at by the crazy old lady at the dining hall, go to a basketball game, and play in the monkey pit."

Knox College

Address: Box K-148
Galesburg, IL 61401
Phone: 309-341-7100
E-mail address:
admission@knox.edu
Web site URL: www.knox.edu
Year Founded: 1837
Private or Public: Private
Religious Affiliation: None
Location: Suburban
Number of Applicants:
2,419
Percent Accepted: 61%
Percent Accepted who enroll: 21%
Number Entering: 307
Number of Transfers Accepted each Year: 42
Middle 50% SAT range:
M: 580–670, CR: 610–710, Wr: 580–670
Middle 50% ACT range:
26–31
Early admission program EA/ED/None: EA

Percentage accepted through EA or ED:
Unreported
EA and ED deadline: 1-Dec
Regular Deadline: 1-Feb
Application Fee: $40
Full time Undergraduate enrollment: 1,371
Total enrollment: 1,371
Percent Male: 42%
Percent Female: 58%
Total Percent Minority or Unreported: 9%
Percent African-American: 4%
Percent Asian/Pacific Islander: 6%
Percent Hispanic: 5%
Percent Native-American: <1%
Percent International: 6%
Percent in-state/out of state: 52%/48%
Percent from Public HS: 83%
Retention Rate: 91%

Graduation Rate 4-year: 64%
Graduation Rate 6-year: 74%
Percent Undergraduates in On-campus housing: 94%
Number of official organized extracurricular organizations: 102
3 Most popular majors:
Anthropology, Economics, Political Science
Student/Faculty ratio: 12:1
Average Class Size: 10 to 19
Percent of students going to grad school: 24%
Tuition and Fees: $30,180
In State Tuition and Fees if different: No difference
Cost for Room and Board: $6,726
Percent receiving financial aid out of those who apply, first year: 95%
Percent receiving financial aid among all students: 94%

Knox College welcomes students from the minute they set foot on campus. "Other schools just sort of tolerated me when I visited," one current Knox student recalled. "But Knox professors and students alike seemed to take a genuine interest in me." Students come to Knox, located in Galesburg, Illinois, from around the globe to experience the intense academics and the strong community spirit that the college has built. For many, Knox offers the best of both worlds: "Knox students know how to get it done during the week and know how to relax on the weekends."

No Tests in the Bathroom

The academic year at Knox is run on what is commonly known as a "3-3" calendar. Effectively, this breaks the year into three trimesters in which students take three classes at a time in 10-week blocks, leaving a full six weeks for winter break. While this may, on paper, appear to be an easy schedule to maintain, students at Knox know better. As one current French and Creative Writing double major asserted, "We'd die if we took any more than three classes at Knox. [Courses] are very intense and fast-paced, since we have to pack in 16 weeks of material." Furthermore, students appreciate the frequent change of classes. As one pointed out, "You never get bored of anything you take."

All freshmen are required to take a course entitled Freshman Preceptorial (according to some, also known as "How To Be A Knox Student 101"). Beyond that, there is a wide variety of directions students can take, depending on their interests. But even the introductory classes at Knox receive rave reviews. "They have a broad scope to begin with," one student explained, "but each professor I've had has created a way for the student to do a project that allows them to work on something they find interesting about the subject." In fact, the popularity of the faculty in general is undeniable. "The staff here is incredible," a current sophomore raved. "It's a great situation to be in and I am absolutely convinced that it is what makes Knox so laid-back."

When classes get really challenging, students tend to form study groups and cooperate rather than compete. "There are so many other things to worry about in college that I'm glad academic competition isn't one of them," one anthropology major said. The unique approach to academics is epitomized in the school's Honor Code. Professors do not proctor exams, so students have their choice of where to take them. In other words, according to one student, "Sometimes, we get to take our tests anywhere we want in the building except for bathrooms and stairwells."

Theme Houses and T-shirts

The unique Knox experience extends beyond the classroom. As one history major who recently spent a spring break working in New Orleans with college funding, explained, "Knox realizes that you don't just learn in the classroom . . . you need to experience the real world. And they will assist you in any way to achieve that."

In no way is this point better illustrated than through the study-abroad program that Knox offers. In addition to three college-sponsored programs in Buenos Aires, Barcelona, and Besançon, France, Knox students have a wealth of study-abroad options to choose from and are strongly encouraged to go. In fact, since a period of "experimental learning" (such as study abroad or an internship) is required for graduation, many students find the program to be an integral part of their college experience. "There are plenty of domestic study programs that are very popular here such as the D.C. semester at American University and the Arts semester at the University of Chicago," added a freshman. And to top it off, the trimester system makes it easy for students to spend a semester abroad and still be back at Knox for two full terms.

Although some students may opt to move off campus, on-campus housing varies. Dorms aside, upperclassmen have a number of different options, including the rare case of theme housing. Only three or four exist at any given time, but essentially students come together as a group to apply for a theme house, explaining both what their theme is and how it could enhance life on the Knox campus. While the types of theme houses vary every year, some current favorites include the Red House (giving its residents a taste in Communist living), and the Do-it-Yourself house.

The food, while every so often drawing predictable student complaints, is reportedly satisfying overall. One of the most popular additions to the dining hall has been stir-fry, with two chefs ready to cook whatever students put together for them. For caffeine and sugar runs on campus, students head for the Gizmo, a coffee house that is open until one in the morning.

But campus life does not end with dorms, houses, and food. In fact, it barely begins there. With more than 100 clubs and activities on campus, Knox has something to offer everyone. Best of all, the community spirit that is fostered on campus encourages many to try something new. One student, for example, came to campus with no musical background and soon found herself taking harp lessons. "Knox is so inclusive. Everyone does all that they can to help people get involved with new things and make them feel comfortable in what they choose to do," she explained.

In terms of nightlife, there is a wide variety of groups—fraternities, sororities, theme houses, and even private suites—that throw parties. And when they do, students tend to get creative. For example, the fraternity TKE hosts "Graffiti Night," during which everyone wears a white T-shirt and sports a washable marker that they are handed at the door. "There are always parties to suit any occasion," a current sophomore noted. And partying at Knox does not necessarily mean getting drunk. "There are a lot of parties that I go to where I just want to dance and not drink and there is no pressure whatsoever," one student explained. "It's definitely a personal choice here and people both acknowledge and respect that."

Pumphandle and Flunk

Among the many campus traditions at Knox, there are two that especially stand out. The first, "Pumphandle Day," occurs on the day before classes start. Everyone who is on campus that day (students, faculty, even family members!) gathers to shake everyone else's hands. As one current senior described, "People dress weird and write strange things on their name tags. It's definitely memorable." "This year we had a giant gorilla, a giant ba-

nana, a Catwoman and a Superman!" another student noted.

The second can't-miss tradition is "Flunk Day," which takes place every spring. When it arrives (the exact date is always kept a secret) the campus is woken up by fog horns in the early morning hours. Classes and meetings are canceled. In their place, a spring carnival awaits students and faculty alike. And while many students try to describe the various activities of the day, one sophomore asserted, "It's really something you just have to experience. I've never heard a description of Flunk Day that really did it justice."

> "[When students] have a paper due, they'll work on the paper for a while and THEN go to the game."

Both of these events are evidence of Knox's strong school spirit. This pride extends both to the school in general (as one student claimed, "Everyone has at least two things emblazoned with "Knox") and to sports, in particular. "Basketball and football are most popular by far," one current varsity basketball player noted, and most students agree. Even so, many keep academics as their first priority. "[When students] have a paper due, they'll work on the paper for a while and THEN go to the game."

From collaborative efforts in the classroom to dinners at professors' houses, students get to know the people around them in ways that might not be possible at other schools. Looking back, one senior noted that, "I never visited Knox before enrolling, but I felt at home from the moment I stepped on campus." Knox gives students the confidence and comfort they need to enjoy their college experience to the fullest.—*Stephanie Brockman*

FYI
If you come to Knox, you'd better bring: "sweatpants and social skills."
What is the typical weekend schedule? "Lots of work! In general, studying the whole time except for Friday and Saturday night, when there are theme and frat parties, bands, comedians, movies, performances, etc."
If I could change one thing about Knox, I'd "get a few mountains put in nearby . . . The prairie is really hard to get used to!"
Three things every student at Knox should do before graduating are: "Go sledding in the Knox Bowl (our football field), go abroad ANYWHERE, get Roger (our president) to remember your name."

Lake Forest College

Address: 555 North Sheridan Road Lake Forest, IL 60045
Phone: 847-735-5000
E-mail address: motzer@lakeforest.edu
Web site URL: www.lakeforest.edu
Year Founded: 1857
Private or Public: Private
Religious Affiliation: None
Location: Rural
Number of Applicants: 2,203
Percent Accepted: 61%
Percent Accepted who enroll: 26%
Number Entering: 356
Number of Transfers Accepted each Year: 50
Middle 50% SAT range: M: 540–660, CR: 560–660, Wr: 540–640
Middle 50% ACT range: 24–29
Early admission program EA/ED/None: EA and ED
Percentage accepted through EA or ED: Unreported

EA and ED deadline: 1-Dec
Regular Deadline: 15-Feb
Application Fee: $40
Full time Undergraduate enrollment: 1,381
Total enrollment: 1,350
Percent Male: 41%
Percent Female: 59%
Total Percent Minority or Unreported: 8%
Percent African-American: 4%
Percent Asian/Pacific Islander: 5%
Percent Hispanic: 6%
Percent Native-American: <1%
Percent International: 8%
Percent in-state/out of state: 48%/52%
Percent from Public HS: 65%
Retention Rate: 82%
Graduation Rate 4-year: 65%
Graduation Rate 6-year: 68%

Percent Undergraduates in On-campus housing: 80%
Number of official organized extracurricular organizations: 90
3 Most popular majors: Communication Studies/Speech Communication and Rhetoric, English Language and Literature, Psychology
Student/Faculty ratio: 13:1
Average Class Size: 10 to 19
Percent of students going to grad school: Unreported
Tuition and Fees: $30,600
In State Tuition and Fees if different: No difference
Cost for Room and Board: $7,326
Percent receiving financial aid out of those who apply, first year: 88%
Percent receiving financial aid among all students: 91%

Lake Forest College, often referred to as "Chicago's National Liberal Arts College," is a small school located in the quaint suburb of Lake Forest, Illinois, 30 miles north of Chicago. With a diverse, spirited, and enthusiastic student body of approximately 1,400 students representing 45 states and 65 countries, Lake Forest College promotes a liberal arts education within a cohesive student-faculty environment. As one student put it: "[Lake Forest] is a community of interesting, motivated, and most of all FUN people!"

Academics

Academic requirements at Lake Forest are not excessively rigorous. One student explained, "Graduation requires a 2.0 and certain foundational requirements that are typical of small liberal arts schools (two math or science classes, a culturally diverse class, and so on)." This flexibility allows students to explore multiple programs: "General education requirements are light, so it's easy for people to double major and minor."

One disillusioned student complained that, although "grading is relatively fair," it is somewhat inflated, and that the academics are not as challenging as some would like. However, another student pointed out that programs have become increasingly rigorous over the past few years: "The workload is getting heavier because LFC is becoming a better school. It's challenging, but doable."

The University offers a variety of popular majors such as communications, psychology, business, art history, economics and politics, as well as some more challenging majors like education, chemistry and other math- and science-oriented subjects. In general, majors in the humanities are considered much easier and more popular, while the science and math departments are more highly accredited and recognized—in particular the economics department. While there is not a large selection of course offerings in these majors, students greatly enjoy the quality of instruction and accessibility of the professors: "I love the fact that the professors who teach at LFC could teach at

Northwestern or the University of Chicago as well (lots of them used to actually), but they come here because they like teaching to undergrads in a small environment." One student went so far as to say, "I can call or e-mail professors whenever! They are very concerned with helping you do well." Specific professors mentioned were Robert Baade, Carolyn Tuttle, and Robert Lemke in the Economics Department, Les Dlabay in Business, DeJuran Richardson in the Math Department, and Spanish professor Lois Barr. Professor Marquardt's "World Politics" was also noted as a "key class."

> **"I can call or e-mail professors whenever! They are very concerned with helping you do well."**

Students who apply to Lake Forest College can also seek acceptance into the Richter Program, a competitive freshman research program. Accepted students remain on campus for the summer to pursue research with a professor.

Social Life Title

The social life on campus is dominated by sports teams, fraternities, and sororities. Lake Forest College boasts 14 varsity sports teams, in addition to various intramural and club sports. The most popular sports are hockey, football, and rugby. A large portion of the student body is involved in sports in some way. Although the facilities are often described as "inadequate," this doesn't stop the spirited and enthusiastic student body from enjoying them. A student-run organization led by the University's mascot, Boomer, supports the varsity sports teams. For a small fee, a student can join the "Athletic Council," more commonly known as the "Forest Fanatic," and take advantage of a free Fanatic T-shirt, VIP seating at home games, free food at select games, reduced bus fare to away games, e-mail notifications of upcoming events and behind-the-scenes updates and highlights.

As for Greek life, there are seven fraternities and sororities (some of which are international). One member of Delta Kappa Epsilon said, "The sororities are strong and fraternities are lacking numbers. However, I have absolutely no regrets about joining a fraternity at Lake Forest College. It has been an amazing experience for me." A member of Delta Delta Delta described the Greek scene

as "relaxed, small, personal, and authentic." Another student pointed out that, while Greeks tend to be the "most involved" at Lake Forest and often secure top positions in student government, "You don't have to be a Greek to be integrated in the school. Non-Greeks are friends with Greeks."

As the surrounding town of Lake Forest isn't exactly thriving, the overall social scene at LCF is largely campus-based. While most upperclassmen have cars, the majority stay in the area. There are a few campuswide parties, typically hosted by the fraternities, as well as semi-formals for various student organizations. The annual "Winter Ball," held in the botanical garden, the "Mr. Casanova Contest," and the "DKE Rampant Lion March Party," are particularly popular. The University has recently tightened up its alcohol policies, but the majority of the campus drinks. As for drugs, one student explained, "They are common but not socially acceptable. They are used behind closed doors (even hidden from other students)." Another stated that drugs are not common at all. As for those who are of drinking age, some venture into the city on the weekends and hit up Chicago's bars. The city of Chicago also offers many alternatives to a typical college social scene such as Navy Pier, museums like the Field Museum, an aquarium and planetarium, two major league baseball teams, a hockey team, an NFL football team and fabulous shopping on Michigan Avenue.

The University takes pride in community service activities. Although Lake Forest itself doesn't offer many opportunities, Chicago, which is only a 45-minute drive or 90-minute train ride away, provides many unique community service opportunities. The Big Brothers/Sisters program of Lake County is one such group. Located in Gurnee, a suburb about 20 minutes north of Lake Forest, this group has been around since 1904. Many Lake Forest College students volunteer for the program, which focuses primarily on mentoring throughout the Chicago community. Other activities include literary groups such as Collage, as well as political organizations including the League for Environmental Awareness, College Democrats and College Republicans. Art and performance groups exist, and the University boasts a number of additional religious, cultural, academic, and business-orientated groups.

Campus Life

Although the social scene is somewhat constrained by the general attitude and environment of the town itself, Lake Forest provides nice, on-campus living arrangements. Freshmen are assigned dorms, while upperclassmen pick through a random lottery system. There are some specialized dorms—an all-girls dorm, an international dorm, four substance-free dorms—while the remainder of the dorms are mixed. Alcohol is allowed in a select number of the dorms and only if the inhabitants of the rooms are 21. Gregory is known as the party dorm.

One girl explained, "A large majority of students live on campus because no one can afford a home in Lake Forest." The town itself is described as "very high class," "an affluent neighborhood" in a "very safe community—the safest in Illinois." One perk this exclusivity offers is the availability of high-paying babysitting jobs. However, one student noted the homogenizing effect of the school's setting: "The campus looks like a country club, the town is one of the richest in the United States, and this environment tends to influence the students; in some ways, I think, the environment 'preppifies' everyone."

There have been a few recent additions to the campus, like the brand new library and student center. As for on-campus food, one girl described it as "excellent for cafeteria food!" On-campus living includes three meals per day Monday through Friday and two meals per day on the weekend. Miramar, The Lantern, Teddy O's, The Grill and The Wooden Nickel are popular local eateries among students.

In general, this small, somewhat secluded university is able to differentiate itself from other universities through its personable professors and enthusiastic social life. One specific reason not to overlook this university, as one student put it: "It is a small liberal arts school close to a big city; it is not located in the middle of nowhere!"—*Caroline Kaufman*

FYI

If you come to Lake Forest, you'd better bring "a hat and mittens because it gets cold, an empty stomach because the cafeteria food is awesome, and a hard-working, positive attitude."

What's the typical weekend schedule? "After class on Friday, take a nap and then get ready to go out . . . South Campus is where the parties are; sleep in late on Saturday and head to the cafeteria in your PJs, watch movies, and then get ready to go out all over again! Sunday: get your work done . . . Occasionally there are All-Campus Parties that everyone attends . . . they are really fun."

If I could change one thing about Lake Forest, I'd "make the Education Major less difficult! The classes are demanding and tons of work, but it is all worth it in the end because they have a history of 100 percent job placement after graduation."

Three things every student at Lake Forest should do before graduating are "eat at the cafeteria, get involved with on-campus organizations, and study abroad—we have great programs."

Loyola University Chicago

Address: 820 North Michigan
Avenue Chicago, IL
60611-9810
Phone: 312-915-6500
E-mail address:
admission@luc.edu
Web site URL: www.luc.edu
Year Founded: 1870
Private or Public: Private
Religious Affiliation: Roman
Catholic-Jesuit
Location: Urban
Number of Applicants:
17,357
Percent Accepted: 17%
**Percent Accepted who
enroll:** 16%
Number Entering: 2,031
**Number of Transfers
Accepted each Year:** 1,830
Middle 50% SAT range:
M: 520–640, CR: 540–640,
Wr: 510–628
Middle 50% ACT range: 23–28
**Early admission program
EA/ED/None:** None

**Percentage accepted
through EA or ED:** NA
EA and ED deadline: NA
Regular Deadline:
Rolling - no closing date
Application Fee: $25
**Full time Undergraduate
enrollment:** 2,176
Total enrollment: 14,183
Percent Male: 33%
Percent Female: 67%
**Total Percent Minority or
Unreported:** 30%
Percent African-American:
3%
**Percent Asian/Pacific
Islander:** 11%
Percent Hispanic: 9%
Percent Native-American:
<1%
Percent International: 1%
**Percent in-state/out of
state:** 55% / 45%
Percent from Public HS:
66%
Retention Rate: 84%

Graduation Rate 4-year:
56%
Graduation Rate 6-year:
65%
**Percent Undergraduates in
On-campus housing:** 40%
**Number of official organized
extracurricular
organizations:** 175
3 Most popular majors:
Biology, Nursing, Psychology
Student/Faculty ratio: 14:1
Average Class Size: 10 to 19
**Percent of students going to
grad school:** Unreported
Tuition and Fees: $29,486
**In State Tuition and Fees if
different:** No difference
Cost for Room and Board:
$10,490
**Percent receiving financial
aid out of those who apply,
first year:** 84%
**Percent receiving financial
aid among all students:**
72%

Home to more than 15,500 students, spanning four main campuses, and offering a total of 72 undergraduate majors, Loyola University Chicago is the largest Jesuit university in the nation. Its location in the heart of the Windy City presents students with many opportunities for jobs, internships, entertainment, and service work, all of which help to make the city of Chicago an integral aspect of the University's mission to combine a solid academic curriculum with opportunities outside the classroom in order to provide an extremely well-rounded education.

A Solid Core
The University's goal of educating "the whole person" is demonstrated most visibly—and often most frustratingly—in the high number of credits required for the core curriculum. Each student is expected to take one writing seminar, one art course, one quantitative analysis course, and two courses each of history, literature, philosophy, science, social science, and theology. Said one student, "I haven't heard too much complaining about

the core . . . they give you a lot of options in each category." Another student disagreed: "I've thought several times that there are perhaps too many core credits. I often feel like I'm doing the same thing over and over again." One junior commented that writing is an important factor in nearly all the classes— "I've even heard of people having to write papers in math classes!" The courses are all supposed to fulfill different aspects of a well-rounded education, encouraging students to develop both academically and spiritually. Also manifest in the core curriculum is the Jesuit emphasis on social work, as many classes require service components.

When asked about common majors, students named political science, business and communications as being among the top choices. Psychology is also a popular major, and there are a large number of students in both the pre-med and the nursing programs. Most classes are small, with the average size ranging between about twenty and thirty students, with only a few classes large enough to fill an auditorium. The workload is "decent," and professors are fair and usually friendly if "you take the time to get to know them." According to one sophomore, "The workload seems relatively light when compared with some other colleges; there is usually a lot of reading to do, but I wouldn't say it's ever unbearable." Another observed, "Since the syllabi are always handed out on the first day, you should know what you're getting yourself into." In terms of specific classes, people agreed that the level of interest and difficulty of classes varied from professor to professor, but that any class related to information systems is usually hated.

In general, students feel that the academics at Loyola are strong and very diverse in their scope and focus. Said one senior, "If you ever have any questions, you can always go to your academic advisor for guidance." Most students have two advisors, one for their major and one for general education requirements, both of whom are often helpful in aspects such as career advice, opportunities for internships and events, meetings, or talks that might be of interest to their advisees. According to one student, a possible complaint about the school may be its liberal nature, and this aspect of the curriculum may often frustrate conservative students. "Still, you should know that you're going to be talking about social justice, peace, and women's studies in your classes—you *are* going to a liberal arts school, after all."

Cooler by the Lake

One of the most unique aspects of Loyola University Chicago is the division of its campus into four main parts: the Lake Shore Campus, the Water Tower Campus, Maywood Campus, and the Rome Center. The Rome Center, stationed in Italy, is a premier study-abroad location for many students from Loyola and other colleges around the country, and the Maywood Campus hosts the medical center. Undergraduate students are mostly concentrated at the Lake Shore Campus, located next to scenic Lake Michigan, and the Water Tower Campus, situated downtown on Michigan Avenue, also known as the Magnificent Mile—Chicago's most famous shopping district. Transportation between the two areas is easy and efficient due to a shuttle service that runs large coach buses for students. All students are supplied with CTA passes that allow for unlimited rides both on the buses and on the "L," the above-ground rapid transit system that runs through the city.

While many upperclassmen live off campus, freshmen and sophomores are required to live in the dorms. Previously, dorms were located only on the Lake Shore Campus, but the University recently opened new residence buildings downtown for an additional cost each semester. Said one junior, "When it comes to housing, there are a lot of options and differences in pricing to accommodate all kinds of preferences." Freshman dorms are usually single-room doubles, while sophomores reside in apartment-style housing, often with kitchens and balconies. After the first two years, most students move off campus, often to nearby Rogers Park, "because it's cheaper and you don't have all those stupid rules. Sometimes living on campus can be kind of a pain." Regulations in the dormitories, especially freshman year, are strict: in addition to the usual rules about no alcohol and no smoking, there are also rules about the opposite sex not being allowed in dorm rooms late at night, and overnight passes are always required for guests. "The rules are strict, but they're for the safety of the students. And the overnight stuff is a Catholic thing," said one sophomore. Many students did comment on the sketchy nature of the Lake Shore Campus, which is beautiful while on campus but "not a great scene" just outside. Still, campus and security police are always around to keep everyone safe, and students just need to remember to "use their common sense" as they would in any large city.

Students appreciate both the cosmopolitan nature of the downtown campus and the serene beauty at the Lake Shore. Said one freshman, "I like being so urban, but still on campus with places to lay out and sun, cafes to do work in, and wireless internet almost everywhere." Another student said, "Part of the reason I came here is because it's right on the lake, so there are a lot of great views where you can sit on a bench and face the lake or the beach to the north of campus." The campus architecture is described as "old, but nice," and the University is currently in the process of renovating older structures and adding new buildings, like Sullivan Center—the new student center. "There are so many renovations going on," said one senior. "I have no idea what the campus will look like ten years from now!"

Nightlife in the Windy City

Students say that since Greek life is not a huge part of weekend festivities, the social scene, especially for upperclassmen, is focused more on going to off-campus house parties or clubs and bars in downtown

Chicago than to frat parties. A lot of people go to Hamilton's, a bar near the Lake Shore Campus, or to house parties thrown by students who live in the neighborhood. There are a couple of streets known for their crazy parties three nights a week where students "try to replicate the idea of a state-school house party where people are doing wild things like throwing kegs out of the windows," but there are also a lot of commuters and others who avoid that scene in an effort to find weekend activities that are a little more low-key. There is a fair amount of drinking, as at many schools, and also some marijuana use. Drinking regulations in the dorms are strictly enforced, and students caught in the presence of alcohol, even if they aren't partaking, will probably be written up, fined, and perhaps even assigned community service. One junior commented, "I'd say that most people drink, but it's not a problem if you don't . . . It's no different than any other school." There are always alcohol-free campus events as well, such as films, concerts, and speakers. There are also various theatrical shows and musical entertainment in downtown Chicago.

> **"You don't feel ostracized at all if you don't share this belief system."**

Most people met their friends in the freshman dorms, as well as in classes and clubs. Overall, people are "pretty friendly" but "preppy." Students are mostly liberal, although they span a wide range of religious faiths in spite of the school's Jesuit tradition. As one senior explained, "Loyola doesn't force students to go to Mass. For those who want that aspect in their lives, they can find it here, but it isn't forced upon them." There are several different religious groups on campus, and students say that the atmosphere is very welcoming. "There's a lot of tolerance," said one sophomore. "You don't feel ostracized at all if you don't share this belief system. It's more about the Jesuit tradition of service, a tradition common in many religions, than it is about the specifics of Catholicism." Many do wish that the school were more diverse, especially in terms of ethnicity. The student and faculty population is largely Caucasian, and even though there are students from all over the country, the majority hail from the Midwest.

Favorite Pastimes

Athletics are not extremely prominent at Loyola; indeed, the University disbanded their football team in the 1940s because they wanted to place more of an emphasis on academics. While the lack of a football team (as well as the spread-out nature of the campus) may lead to less open school spirit than at many other schools, many students don't mind at all. Of course, Loyola still boasts other varsity and intramural sports, as well as other organizations such as cultural groups, religious groups, ethics clubs, and service-oriented clubs like Students Against Sweatshops and Loyola For Chicago, a group that stands for the betterment of the community and the city of Chicago. There are also political organizations, the debate team, the ethics bowl, dance teams, and theatrical societies. Said one student, "You always see flyers around for all kinds of groups, and there are lots to choose from." One complaint was that the arts are not adequately funded and that none of the literary magazines are particularly sensational. Still, it is always possible to start a new group and apply for funding from the University. In addition, many students fill their time outside of class by finding jobs downtown in shops, restaurants, or businesses related to their area of interest.

Overall, students say what differentiates their school from others is its welcoming atmosphere, its commitment to service, and the benefits of having a smaller college community within a large city. Because it is a Jesuit school, the idea behind the entire educational system is for students to be engaged in discourse, and to focus on the betterment of the whole person and the whole society instead of zeroing in on only a few particular aspects. Said one senior, "I feel that everyone here is really trying to learn, not just trying to get by, and they're always looking to literature, philosophy, and theology to find answers. A lot of people I've met and become friends with seem dedicated to seeking truth and diversity, and that's just amazing." Asked if she would choose Loyola again if she had to do everything all over again, one student replied, "It's interesting sometimes to think about where paths lead you, and I don't think you should ever regret decisions. I would come here again—I like Loyola. I like the person I have become since I've been here."—*Lindsay Starck*

FYI
If you come to Loyola, you'd better bring "a spirit of compassion."
What's the typical weekend schedule? "Get work out of the way, and go downtown!"
If I could change one thing about Loyola, "I would change the way it's so open to the city. The number of suspicious people walking around is kind of creepy."
Three things every student at Loyola should do before graduating are "take advantage of the opportunities in Chicago, have a picnic at the beach along Lake Michigan, and join an extracurricular activity."

Northwestern University

Address: PO Box 3060, 1801 Hinman Avenue, Evanston, IL 60204
Phone: 847-491-7271
E-mail address: ugadmission@northwestern.edu
Web site URL: www.northwestern.edu
Year Founded: 1851
Private or Public: Private
Religious Affiliation: None
Location: Suburban
Number of Applicants: 21,930
Percent Accepted: 27%
Percent Accepted who enroll: 33%
Number Entering: 1,981
Number of Transfers Accepted each Year: Unreported
Middle 50% SAT range: M: 680–770, CR: 670–750, Wr: 660–750
Middle 50% ACT range: 30–34

Early admission program EA/ED/None: ED
Percentage accepted through EA or ED: Unreported
EA and ED deadline: 1-Nov
Regular Deadline: 1-Jan
Application Fee: $65
Full time Undergraduate enrollment: 8,476
Total enrollment: 16,932
Percent Male: 48%
Percent Female: 52%
Total Percent Minority or Unreported: 41%
Percent African-American: 6%
Percent Asian/Pacific Islander: 17%
Percent Hispanic: 7%
Percent Native-American: 0%
Percent International: 5%
Percent in-state/out of state: 25%/75%
Percent from Public HS: 73%
Retention Rate: 97%
Graduation Rate 4-year: 86%

Graduation Rate 6-year: Unreported
Percent Undergraduates in On-campus housing: 65%
Number of official organized extracurricular organizations: 415
3 Most popular majors: Economics, Engineering, Journalism
Student/Faculty ratio: 7:1
Average Class Size: Unreported
Percent of students going to grad school: 23%
Tuition and Fees: $37,125
In State Tuition and Fees if different: No difference
Cost for Room and Board: $11,295
Percent receiving financial aid out of those who apply, first year: 77%
Percent receiving financial aid among all students: 40%

Prestigious academics, a small town located conveniently near a big city and a huge party named after an armadillo—Northwestern University has it all. Located in Evanston, Illinois, only a short train ride from Chicago, Northwestern provides a stimulating academic environment and some of the greatest opportunities for a memorable four years—cold weather notwithstanding.

Please, Not Another Exam!
Academic requirements at Northwestern are not too stressful—as one sophomore put it, there is "a good balance of what you need and what you want." Northwestern itself consists of six separate schools: Arts and Sciences, Communications, Education and Social Policy, Engineering and Applied Science, Journalism and Music. Students are required to take two classes within each school to fulfill distributional areas. However, students have many choices for the specific classes they wish to take in each area. In addition to the famous journalism and communications schools, students list economics and political science as the most popular majors on campus. The University runs on a quarter system, which consists of

three quarters during the "typical" school year, plus a summer quarter. The students describe their relationship with the quarter system as "love-hate." The coursework ends up being fast-paced and intensive, with exams every three weeks. However, the system allows Northwestern students to take a larger variety of classes, which come to an end that much quicker.

When it comes to classes themselves, there is a variety of sizes and difficulty levels to choose from. The intro classes are rather large lectures of about 300 to 500 with smaller, T.A.-led discussion sections; upper-level classes range from 20 to 50 and language classes are always capped at 20. Many students describe the coursework as very reading-intensive, but manageable. As for grades, one student summed it up by explaining that "It's hard to get an A, but it's also hard to get a C." Organic chemistry is unanimously proclaimed as the most difficult of all courses. The students find it helpful to use the University-provided online evaluation system to screen their classes; honest feedback from students who have previously taken selected courses proves to be a gold mine and an irreplaceable tool for building that perfect schedule.

In terms of forging relationships with professors, one student maintained that "If you want, it is easy to blend in." But most describe their professors as accessible, with regular office hours and willing to help out and talk. One junior even recalled a (rare) example of one economics professor who made an effort to learn the names of all of the 300 people in her lecture.

Ugg Thugs and Greeks Who Chug

The student population, as described by one student, breaks down into "one third who study all the time, one third who have too much fun and are overcommitted, and one third who manage to find some sort of a balance." Freshman year is important in terms of making friends, and the freshman dorm is overwhelmingly the primary center of social activity. After the first year, "people are not as accepting," and it becomes more difficult to meet people. Some students even complained of a clique problem. The stereotypical student as described by most is an upper-middle-class prep, complete with Uggs and North Face-clad exteriors. Students also pointed out that there is a division between the athletes and the non-athletes, and a certain degree of self-segregation occurs among ethnic groups. Diversity still abounds on campus, however, and in general, the environment is described as competitive, but definitely friendly.

The social scene for underclassmen is dominated by Greek life; about 40 percent of the student body belongs to either a sorority or a fraternity. Upperclassmen often party at off-campus apartments, and many also travel to Chicago on the weekends to go bar-hopping. In Evanston itself, the college bar scene includes Monday nights at The Keg and Thursdays at The Duce (officially the Mark II Lounge). The most highly anticipated day on campus, however, is Dillo Day (short for Armadillo Day), which takes place on the first day of reading week of the third quarter. All students gather outside for concerts and enjoy the freely flowing alcohol all day long. Yet, despite the apparent prominence of alcohol and Greek life on campus, students insisted that those who prefer not to participate in either activity could still manage to find their own ways to have fun.

North vs. South

The Northwestern campus is picturesque and beautiful. It has a mix of architecture ranging from ivy-covered old buildings to concrete boxes. As one student explained, "You can find the ugliest and the prettiest building here next to each other." As described by one sophomore, the shape of the campus is "long and skinny," polarizing the North from the South. The north side, which houses mainly athletes, Greeks and science majors, is known for its numerous parties. The south side, which houses mainly theater and communication majors, has a quieter and calmer atmosphere. All dorms are patrolled by community assistants (CAs) responsible for monitoring compliance with dorm rules. The campus is technically a dry campus. No alcohol is allowed in rooms where an underage person is present. Whether this policy is actually followed, students said, depends on the type of CA who has to make the decision.

Living options include freshman-only dorms, different size coed dorms and small and intimate residential colleges. Each class goes through its own lottery system, which generally works out so that most students actually get their first choices. Many of the dorms have stereotypes attached to them: Jones houses theater people, Elder has freshman athletes and Bobb is the party dorm. While all freshmen are required to live on campus, starting sophomore year people begin to move into off-campus apartments, and very few juniors and seniors remain in dorms. Parking is rather difficult to come by, so not many students bring cars—which is not a problem, since most people insist that everything is within walking distance.

When tired of dining hall food, which most describe rather unenthusiastically as "acceptable," Northwestern students take refuge in Evanston, universally proclaimed the "dining capital of the North Shore." Choices include a wide variety of ethnic foods, chain restaurants and cafés. There is also a newly opened crepe restaurant, and, of course, the indispensable 24-hour Burger King for those late-night cravings.

Make It Glow Purple

Varsity sports at Northwestern receive a rather lukewarm response on campus. Football games are the only sporting event that boasts consistently good attendance. However, intramural sports, the most popular of which are volleyball and Ultimate Frisbee, more than make up for the lack of varsity spirit. Athletics aside, extracurricular activities extend far and wide. Some of the many organizations on campus include the Dance Marathon, which involves planning and par-

ticipating in an all-night dance for charity, Associated Government, and the *Northwestern Daily*. The school also offers a cappella and countless culture and service-oriented groups. As for some quirkier traditions, Northwestern has a rock in a central campus location where students paint announcements. The catch? You have to guard the rock for 24 hours before you can paint it, and it can only be painted when the sun is down.

> "I was exposed to so many new things here and tried so many things I normally wouldn't!"

All of these traditions combine to help give Northwestern students a memorable and meaningful college experience. One junior said, "I was exposed to so many new things here and tried so many things I normally wouldn't." By constantly challenging its students and providing countless opportunities for something new, Northwestern breaks people out of their comfort zones and provides an environment in which students thrive and make memories to last a lifetime.—*Dorota Poplowska*

FYI

If you come to Northwestern, you'd better bring: "A warm jacket, or two, or three, or four."

What is the typical weekend schedule? "Friday go out to dinner, relax, drink, and sleep. Saturday you do it all over again, except in football season you attend a football game in the morning. Sunday intramurals happen and you do work."

If I could change one thing about Northwestern, I'd: "change how big of a role the Greek life plays."

Three things every student at Northwestern should do before graduating are: "paint the rock and guard it for 24 hours, go to Dillo Day, and spend a night on the Lakefill (a hang-out place at Lake Michigan)."

Principia College

Address: 1 Maybeck Place Elsah, IL 62028
Phone: 618-374-5181
E-mail address: enroll@prin.edu
Web site URL: www.prin.edu
Year Founded: 1898
Private or Public: Private
Religious Affiliation: Christian Science
Location: Rural
Number of Applicants: 221
Percent Accepted: 87%
Percent Accepted who enroll: 61%
Number Entering: 117
Number of Transfers Accepted each Year: Unreported
Middle 50% SAT range: M: 500–620, CR: 510–650, Wr: Unreported
Middle 50% ACT range: 21–30
Early admission program EA/ED/None: EA

Percentage accepted through EA or ED: Unreported
EA and ED deadline: 15-Nov
Regular Deadline: 1-Mar
Application Fee: $0
Full time Undergraduate enrollment: 542
Total enrollment: 542
Percent Male: 48%
Percent Female: 52%
Total Percent Minority or Unreported: 19%
Percent African-American: 1%
Percent Asian/Pacific Islander: 1%
Percent Hispanic: 1%
Percent Native-American: 0%
Percent International: 13%
Percent in-state/out of state: 12%/88%
Percent from Public HS: 61%
Retention Rate: 79%
Graduation Rate 4-year: 72%

Graduation Rate 6-year: Unreported
Percent Undergraduates in On-campus housing: 99%
Number of official organized extracurricular organizations: 29
3 Most popular majors: Business, Fine Arts, Mass Communication
Student/Faculty ratio: 8:1
Average Class Size: Unreported
Percent of students going to grad school: 27%
Tuition and Fees: $22,950
In State Tuition and Fees if different: No difference
Cost for Room and Board: $8,730
Percent receiving financial aid out of those who apply, first year: Unreported
Percent receiving financial aid among all students: Unreported

A s the only exclusively Christian Scientist college in the world, Principia College attracts followers of its faith from all over the globe. Located high above the bluffs in Elsah, Illinois over the Mississippi River, the small liberal arts school affectionately known as Prin, is a small, tight-knit community dedicated to both academic excellence and devotion to the Christian Scientist faith.

An Academic Haven

Since Principia's founding in 1898, its academic mission has evolved, placing an increased emphasis on developing students' analytical thinking, problem solving and communication skills. In order to address the specific academic needs of freshmen, Principia instituted its First-Year Experience (FYE) program in 1998. Upon arrival, each freshman enrolls in FYE, which consists of two or three courses to be taken during one's freshman year. Each program of courses has a unique theme and incorporates several classes from different departments, and the variety of programs allows freshmen to choose a theme that appeals to their personal academic interests. After FYE, students choose from 32 majors and four minors, or they may design and petition for a special major not already offered by the school.

No matter what they major in, Prin students will have a hard time skipping class or dozing off during lectures. As one junior explained, "Most of the classes are 20 students or less, and attendance is a part of the grade in most classes." The upside is that the small classroom size and campus environment makes professors very accessible. "Most of them list their home phone or cell phone numbers on the course syllabus," said one student.

Live by the Code

Outside the classroom, Principia students are held to an additional standard of integrity known as the honor code. The school's honor code is based on the principles set forth by Mary Baker Eddy, the

Discoverer and Founder of Christian Science, and by Mary Kimball Morgan, who founded Principia. While most secular liberal arts schools have some sort of general honor code loosely regulating the basics—i.e. no plagiarism and no stealing—Principia's code addresses its students' more personal and spiritual activities. It outlines specific requirements for social conduct, academic integrity and performance, financial integrity and spiritual reliance. In following the code, students agree to abstain from alcohol, tobacco, drugs and premarital sex, as well as rely exclusively on Christian Science for healing. Principia's administration finds that following these guidelines is vital in fulfilling Principia's original mission and keeping in line with the Christian Scientist faith. Enforcement of the code is taken very seriously.

Party, Prin Style
Do not be fooled by Principia's claim to be a "small" liberal arts college—its campus spans 2,500 acres. Since the nearest town is 20 minutes away, Prin has its own social committee that "provides a wide range of activities both on and off campus for the students and ways to get to them." Special events include live music courtesy of on- and off-campus bands, weekly movies screened on a large movie screen and regular parties hosted by dorms. In fact, there's so much going on at Prin that people often forget that the bustling city of St. Louis, with its restaurants, sports teams, and famous zoo, is a mere 40-minute drive from campus. Although students admit that "There is some drinking that goes on, both on campus and off," it's definitely against the code, and undergrads caught drinking can get suspended.

Feels Like Home
Nearly all students live on campus in one of 10 house-like residences, many of which were designed by the renowned architect Bernard Maybeck. In fact, Principia was designated a National Historic Landmark to honor Maybeck's exceptional architecture. All new freshmen live on campus in two dorms: Anderson House and Rackham Court. Each freshman dorm houses eight upperclassmen who serve as resident assistants (RAs). And the living ain't shabby. One Principia student even went so far as to say that ". . . Anderson House is enormous and beyond beautiful . . . we are all spoiled. I could not have asked for a better place to live my first year in college."

After freshman year, almost all students move to another house where they reside their sophomore, junior and senior years. Some students, referred to as non-traditional students, or "non-trads" (generally those students older than traditional college age), live in Hitchcock, one of three "cottages" designed by Maybeck, or in off-campus housing. Yet, most Prin students reside on campus and enjoy Maybeck's architecture and the campus's great facilities. All residences are equipped with computer labs, laundry rooms and kitchens—and there are Christian Science and academic study rooms available in each building that are open at all times. Students agreed that houses serve as smaller communities where people make friends and become involved in extracurricular activities. Each house has its own student government and board members who plan social functions, coordinate intramural athletics and lead student orientations. Aside from planning activities within the house, the board members coordinate annual campuswide activities in each residence. Rackham House kicks off the first weekend of the fall with an annual toga party, and Ferguson has a popular haunted house during Halloween. Later in winter the Sylvester House holds an 80s dance in their rec room. Members of each residence come together each year to throw some fun co-house parties, and everyone on campus gets to enjoy activities planned by all of the other houses throughout the year, which, as one junior put it, is "not a bad deal!"

> "I could not have asked for a better place to live my first year in college."

Get Involved!
The combination of Principia's small and motivated student body and the college's vast resources makes it a great place to cultivate leadership roles in extracurricular activities. In terms of sports, Principia is a Division III school and has 10 varsity sports teams for men and women, not to mention a variety of IMs. There are multiple opportunities to get involved in theater and musical groups as well, including the winter dance production and the spring play. Prin students can write for the campus newspaper, edit the yearbook, host a radio show on Principia's FM-radio station (WTPC), or even help to coordinate the annual Public Affairs Conference (PAC), which tackles questions like, "Is Democracy the Global Solution?" Getting back to basics,

the Christian Science Organization (CSO) offers undergraduates a chance to further the study of their common faith. In short, Principia offers a multitude of activities and opportunities for its students, while furthering its mission to instill in its students the values of the Christian Scientist Church.—*Suzanne Salgado*

FYI

If you come to Principia, you'd better bring "an open mind."

What's a typical weekend schedule? "Football, volleyball, or basketball game Saturday afternoon, a movie or trip into town Saturday night, church Sunday morning and homework Sunday afternoon."

If I could change one thing about Principia, I'd "change the strictness . . . Prin is fairly reasonable for why it has the rules it does, but some of them seem a bit ridiculous."

Three things everyone should do before graduating Principia are: "travel abroad, be part of a dance or theater production, and go to the City Museum with all your buds!"

Southern Illinois University / Carbondale

Address: Carbondale MC 4710 Carbondale, IL 62901-4512

Phone: 618-536-4405

E-mail address: admrec@siu.edu

Web site URL: www.siuc.edu

Year Founded: 1869

Private or Public: Public

Religious Affiliation: None

Location: Suburban

Number of Applicants: 11,785

Percent Accepted: 69%

Percent Accepted who enroll: 33%

Number Entering: 2,660

Number of Transfers Accepted each Year: 3,727

Middle 50% SAT range: M: 440–590, CR:420–570, Wr: 410–520

Middle 50% ACT range: 19–24

Early admission program EA/ED/None: None

Percentage accepted through EA or ED: NA

EA and ED deadline: NA

Regular Deadline: Rolling

Application Fee: $30

Full time Undergraduate enrollment: 14,313

Total enrollment: 15,980

Percent Male: 43%

Percent Female: 57%

Total Percent Minority or Unreported: 32%

Percent African-American: 18%

Percent Asian/Pacific Islander: 2%

Percent Hispanic: 4%

Percent Native-American: <1%

Percent International: 2%

Percent in-state/out of state: 94%/6%

Percent from Public HS: Unreported

Retention Rate: Unreported

Graduation Rate 4-year: Unreported

Graduation Rate 6-year: Unreported

Percent Undergraduates in On-campus housing: 30%

Number of official organized extracurricular organizations: 402

3 Most popular majors: Criminal Justice, Elementary Education, Trade and Industrial Teacher Education

Student/Faculty ratio: 16.5:1

Average Class Size: 10 to 19

Percent of students going to grad school: 58%

Tuition and Fees: $20,276

In State Tuition and Fees if different: $9,813

Cost for Room and Board: $7,137

Percent receiving financial aid out of those who apply, first year: 78%

Percent receiving financial aid among all students: 81%

Southern Illinois University at Carbondale, among its claims to fame, boasts one of the most unusual mascots of any American university—the Saluki, an Egyptian hunting dog. The connection between the Saluki and SIU (originally a small teacher's college founded in 1869 with a mere 143 students enrolled) remains mysterious. Nevertheless, Salukis take pride in their mascot and love their school, which has grown from humble beginnings into one of the largest and most affordable universities in the country— not to mention one of the most famous party schools in the Midwest.

Southern Illinois, Southern Hospitality

Approximately three fourths of SIU students come from Illinois, and as many students explained, there is a common misconception that all Salukis are just "southern Illinois hicks." But despite an apparent lack of geographic diversity, the student body is composed of individuals with a variety of backgrounds and interests. One student noted, "There are students here of all ages, varying from the traditional fresh-out-of-high school student to the parent of three trying to get a better job. People here come from all different backgrounds and tend to mesh together very well." The large number of students at SIU—21,000 total—makes it easy to make friends. "There are all sorts of opportunities to meet people," explained one student. "For the most part, everyone on campus is friendly. Whether you meet them in class or out at the bars, chances are you'll be friends on Facebook before the day is over."

Home Sweet Home

With such a large student body, SIU provides four main undergraduate housing areas: University Park, Brush Towers, Thompson Point, and University Hall. Each housing area has its own laundry facility and dining hall. Students are only required to live on campus during their freshman year. Salukis typically describe the on-campus housing as "pretty nice . . . besides the cinder block walls." University Park has the smallest rooms, but is located in a picturesque, wooded part of campus. Students who live in Brush Towers enjoy it particularly because of its private bathrooms and small, suite-shared kitchenettes, but some say that it can be chaotic living in a large complex of apartment-like towers. Thompson Point, said to be the "prettiest," is located on nearby Thompson Lake. University Hall is a bit farther away from the other three, but it offers the same amenities. All of the residential facilities have RAs. Students say that usually RAs are easy to talk to and helpful with problems, although some can reportedly be strict disciplinary figures. Most juniors and seniors at SIU choose to live off campus, which is where most of the famed SIU partying takes place.

There are three meal plans to choose from at SIU, and they can be used at any of the four on-campus dining halls. The meal plan is based on a points system, and any unused points at the end of the week can be used to purchase snacks and other food and drink items from the on-campus market. Unfortunately, despite the variety of options offered by the meal plan, the food at SIU is not something students brag about. Descrip-

tions of SIU food ranged from "It is disgusting" to "It sucks!" Luckily, there are many restaurants near campus. Some student favorites are Buffalo Wild Wings, Applebees, Lonestar Steakhouse and Quatros.

Work Hard . . .

At such a large research university, plenty of academic opportunities abound at SIUC. And most Salukis agree that having a variety of resources allows them lots of opportunity for hands-on work, whether on a farm for agricultural studies majors or in a broadcast station for radio and TV majors. The University has a core liberal arts curriculum that must be completed by all students before graduation. Although core classes tend to be the largest, students say that even the professors in the big lecture classes are accessible, and there are plenty of opportunities to take small classes or seminars. SIUC students' general opinion with regard to the University's professors is that they are relatively easy. As one student said, "The grading scale varies from teacher to teacher, but is generally pretty lenient." Another added, "All of my professors are really easy."

> "For the most part, everyone on campus is friendly. Whether you meet them in class or out at the bars, chances are you'll be friends on Facebook before the day is over."

In terms of majors, different ones require different workloads. In particular, science classes like engineering and aviation prove to be especially challenging. The most popular major at SIU is Criminal Justice, followed by Elementary Education and Teaching and Trade and Industrial Teacher Education. Students are asked to declare a major when they are admitted to SIU, but if they are unsure of what they want to do, they are admitted to the pre-major program with a pre-major advisor. Salukis in the pre-major program must declare a major before the end of their sophomore year.

Most students at SIU are satisfied with their overall academic experience and try to take advantage of the University's resources. "Academically we are a great school," one sophomore assured. "Departments and professors provide very hands-on learning and are willing to work with students to see that we all succeed."

. . . Play Hard

Not only is it easy to make friends at SIU, but Salukis agree that it is easy to have a good time. SIU lives up to its reputation as being a party school, but many students say that the stereotype is blown way out of proportion. One male student explained that "Underage drinking is definitely an issue here, but just as it is everywhere else." Most students agree that the drinking at SIUC seems about comparable to that of any other state school, but admit that the social scene does revolve around alcohol. People go out Wednesday through Saturday nights, but "There is a party somewhere every night if you want one." Bars on "the strip" in Carbondale are popular, and although the legal drinking age is 21, it is not hard to obtain drinks if you're underage. Furthermore, the SIU administration is relatively easygoing about alcohol monitoring. They "try to look the other way," one student explained.

Saluki Spirit

Without doubt, SIU students are definitely proud of their Division I sports teams. Among the plethora of varsity sports, football and basketball are among the most popular. Students say that club sports are competitive—especially softball—but that they're all fun to play. SIU boasts a large Rec Center where Salukis can enjoy basketball and racquetball courts, as well as an Olympic-sized swimming pool. The Rec Center also rents out sports equipment and camping supplies to students. Non-athletes will be glad to know that there are about 400 clubs and RSOs (Registered Student Organizations) on campus. Students say the most popular RSO is "definitely the sky-diving club." For some fun closer to the ground, The Student Programming Committee plans student events like dances, concerts, and movies. Greek life at SIU is relatively small, with seven sororities and 20 fraternities. Some students complain that "People here do not really understand [Greek life] because it is so small" while others say that they enjoy the minimal Greek presence on campus. Whatever their preference, Salukis can always find an organization to join during their time at SIU.

Most Salukis say they feel relatively safe on campus and very welcomed by the residents of Carbondale. Many hail Carbondale as "the perfect college town." The majority of students live on campus and do not have cars, but a lack of wheels doesn't prevent Salukis from taking advantage of a vast amount of resources and Carbondale's collegiate charm. Salukis just know how to have fun while keeping busy.—*Becky Bicks*

FYI

If you come to SIU, you'd better bring: "clothes for all seasons—the weather changes every five minutes."

What's the typical weekend schedule? "Sleeping in, drinking at night, and working on homework."

Three things every Southern student should do before graduating are "join an RSO, go to Saluki football and basketball games, and have LOTS and LOTS of fun."

One thing I'd change about SIU, I'd "improve the parking policy and build another lot or two without unfair regulations."

University of Chicago

Address: 1101 E 58th Street, Rosenwald Hall Suite 105 Chicago, IL 60637
Phone: 773-702-8650
E-mail address: questions@phoenix.uchicago.edu
Web site URL: www.uchicago.edu
Year Founded: 1890
Private or Public: Private
Religious Affiliation: None
Location: Urban
Number of Applicants: 10,362
Percent Accepted: 35%
Percent Accepted who enroll: 36%
Number Entering: 1,300
Number of Transfers Accepted each Year: 77
Middle 50% SAT range: M: 660–760, CR: 670–770, Wr: Unreported
Middle 50% ACT range: 28–33

Early admission program EA/ED/None: EA
Percentage accepted through EA or ED: 42%
EA and ED deadline: 1-Nov
Regular Deadline: 2-Jan
Application Fee: $60
Full time Undergraduate enrollment: 4,926
Total enrollment: 11,225
Percent Male: 51%
Percent Female: 49%
Total Percent Minority or Unreported: 53%
Percent African-American: 5%
Percent Asian/Pacific Islander: 13%
Percent Hispanic: 8%
Percent Native-American: <1%
Percent International: 8%
Percent in-state/out of state: 22%/78%
Percent from Public HS: 63%
Retention Rate: 98%

Graduation Rate 4-year: 86%
Graduation Rate 6-year: 91%
Percent Undergraduates in On-campus housing: 98%
Number of official organized extracurricular organizations: 400
3 Most popular majors: Biology, Economics, Political Science and Government
Student/Faculty ratio: 6:1
Average Class Size: 2 to 9
Percent of students going to grad school: Unreported
Tuition and Fees: $37,632
In State Tuition and Fees if different: No difference
Cost for Room and Board: $11,697
Percent receiving financial aid out of those who apply, first year: 48%
Percent receiving financial aid among all students: 73%

The University of Chicago is the kind of school that embraces its "nerdy" population and revels in creating enjoyable events that mirror the quirkiness of its students. Their annual scavenger hunt has been the basis of two documentaries and has prompted the arrival of CIA agents looking for the creators of a breeder reactor, all far more exciting than a game of beer pong at a frat.

Not "The Place Where Fun Comes to Die"

As the saying goes, "you can't spell UChicago without 'Chicago.'" Located in Hyde Park, the university is a short ride on the El from the city. While the area surrounding the school is not entirely student-friendly, security efforts put the population at ease, and students quickly learn how to act in a safe manner. The average student travels to the city a few times a month, providing a nice escape from the intense academic life on campus. Chicago is recognized as the improv capital of the world, and is home

to numerous jazz clubs and bars. In short, it's a cleaner version of New York, but with worse bagels.

While the city gives students great options in terms of weekend plans, most undergrads choose to remain on campus, favoring social functions and the occasional frat party. A junior tour guide stated, "I came to U of C because I wanted to go to the nerdiest school possible, while having an average social life." Some students would like to think that there is a standard "face of UChicago," but there are sharp divisions among the undergrads that make it impossible to stereotype it as a geek school. One student said, "The school doesn't have a social identity in an explicit sense; I'd be tentative in even saying that everybody is going to be smart." There are plenty of jocks and "bros" mixed in with future Noble Laureates and library junkies. As one undergrad put it, "There really are no unifying social factors."

In terms of admissions, undergrads credit high acceptance rates to self-selection among high school seniors and ill-advised guidance counselors. One student stated, "I know dozens of people from my high school who would have applied had it not been for 'that crazy application.'" In order to avoid scaring away applicants, UChicago switched to the common app from the quirky "uncommon app" to increase the number of applicants. A visit to UChicago will often provide potential applicants with a better understanding of what the school has to offer, indicating that it is not "the place where fun comes to die." Any obstacle to class diversity may be a result of the university's efforts to not reject an applicant based on "type."

Get 'er Done

UChicago is not recognized for its gorgeous students. In fact, some characterize it as the place "Where the squirrels are more attractive than the girls, and more aggressive than the guys." In UChicago students' defense, it's hard to look good and effuse machismo when classes cover a semester's worth of work in a rapid 10 weeks. Students quickly become accustomed to the massive workload, and subsequently struggle to understand how some college students "don't actually do their work." With easy access to "remarkable award-winning professors" it is no surprise that students are very academically motivated. One student remarked, "All courses have a learning for the sake of learning twist."

> **"The squirrels are more attractive than the girls, and more aggressive than the guys."**

The professors are not only accomplished (winning Pulitzer Prizes, MacArthur Fellowships, and everything in between), but accessible and uncharacteristically inviting. It is not uncommon for professors to hold wine and cheese office hours, or take time out of their home schedules to accommodate a student. Courses taught by TAs are few in number and well advertised so as not to provide any surprises. This is not to say that the TAs are not qualified teachers, as one student remarked that "some of the most interesting courses" she had taken were taught by graduate students.

UChicago's Common Core is mandatory for all students, and is meant to instill a liberal arts education within the framework of a large research institution. The core requires students to take courses on everything from the humanities and civilization studies to physical education. While this may seem like a controlling environment, students remark that if given the choice they would still opt to take core classes. Although humanities-oriented students may dread the mathematics requirement, and mathletes may fear the humanities requirement, the variety of core courses ensures that the stereotypical "black-sweatered cigarette-smoking jazz enthusiast" won't have to struggle through a semester of multivariable calculus. This is not to say that the core is easy; in fact, some students have expressed the desire to have a pass/fail "get out of jail free card" protecting GPAs from the inevitable "disastrous core class." The core provides every student with a solid foundation for upper-level classes, with the necessary "reading and analytical skills" for brilliant class discussions.

Economics and biology remain the two most popular majors amongst UChicago students. The Economics department is regarded as the "best in the nation," featuring multiple Nobel Laureates (including Gary Becker and Robert Fogel), and Steven Levitt, the brains behind *New York Times*–bestseller *Freakonomics*. There is an extensive variety of majors offered, including non-degree programs such as the popular Human Rights program. Staying true to its liberal arts foundation, the U of C steers clear of most pre-professional majors, including engineering.

Living in Chi-Town

UChicago has 10 different residence halls, ranging from brand-new orange buildings, to converted luxury hotels of the past. Two residence halls, Blackstone and Stony Island, are strictly for upperclassmen and transfers, and feature such amenities as computer rooms and solariums. Other than Blackstone and Stony Island, residence halls are not separated by year. Each Residence Hall is broken down into anywhere from one to eight "houses." There are 38 houses in total, with the average house size being 70 students. Each House has one or more Resident Heads, who work as counselors to students, while coordinating social events and forming intramural teams for sports like broomball and inner-tube water polo.

The house system puts help with math problem sets and essay editing within an arm's reach. Students will usually eat dinner, watch movies, talk politics and have small in-suite parties with fellow house members. Some are known for wacky traditions and small singles, while others are known for their prowess in intramurals marked by the assumption of the Maroon Cup. Max Palevsky, home to eight houses, is the newest residence hall and is regarded for its proximity to everything good, including "the Regenstein library, the academic quad, and recreation and music rooms." Given that Max-P is so new, it features great amenities such as air-conditioning and a meal plan with Bartlett commons, otherwise known as the best of the three campus dining halls. In fall of 2009 the University plans to unveil its new South Campus Residence Hall and Dining Commons which will add eight additional houses and be home to 811 residents. Regardless of accommodations, most students develop a great deal of house pride, and form bitter rivalries with other houses: "People in May House struggle to even talk with those in Alper." The only noted flaw with the house system is that students are not guaranteed that they will remain in their freshman house. For this reason, many students end up moving off campus with former housemates.

UChicago students meet their future housemates at O-Week (Orientation week). The U of C structures O-Week in a manner that encourages in-house mingling, as housemates are forced to eat together and talk about controversial matters regarding college students. The only events that students seem to find more enjoyable are the Polar Bear run, Shake Day and the infamous Scavenger Hunt. One sophomore remarked that his most memorable UChicago night involved "Dean of Admissions Ted O'Neil wearing his 'I admitted your mom last night' T-shirt and posting it on YouTube for [Scavenger Hunt] points."

Campus food is regarded as anywhere from "passable" to "better than my mom's cooking." The dining halls are organized in stations where students have a variety of choices charting all different types of cuisine. No matter the time, there is always a place where students can use their dining points. Students often turn to the Reynolds Club in place of a formal student union. The club is home to several eateries and shops, and serves as the headquarters for multiple organizations, including the radio station and weekly news. Even if students get tired of events and food on campus, there is a variety of great restaurants and entertainment venues in Hyde Park and downtown.

Dead Greek and Sports Life

Intercollegiate sports are not viewed as very important at UChicago, to say the least. One student remarked, "Apparently one of our teams is pretty good. I don't know which one though." An upperclassman remarked, "I don't even know where the fields are." The blatant disconnect between the athletes and the academic majority is not necessarily detrimental to the school population. The athletes still manage to find a good social scene, either by joining frats or going to bars, while other students manage to find good athletics through intramural sports. In addition to the small but sizeable number of male students who join frats, there are a slew of females who decide to join the two sororities on campus. Similar to their knowledge of sporting facilities, a lot of students have no idea where the fraternities are. One freshman noted, "I only know where the frats are because they're so close to my dorm."

More or less, UChicago provides an option for every type of person. Not everyone who attends is a turtleneck-wearing bookworm. The best description of UChicago lies not in its stereotypical nerdy student, but in its reputation as a great liberal arts college within a massive research university, a short train ride away from downtown Chicago. With a plethora of Nobel Laureates on staff, the "best economics department in the country," and the nation's best scavenger hunt, the school is worth any hardworking student's consideration.—*Zachary Fuhrer*

FYI
If you come to UChicago, you'd better bring "a laptop. Campus is incredibly wired."
What's the typical weekend schedule? "Go out Thursday night . . . don't remember anything else. Study sometime. (That's a joke.)"
If I could change one thing about UChicago I would "allow students to take one core course pass/fail."
The three things every student should do before graduating are "scare first-years about classes, play intramural broomball and hook up in the Regenstein Library."

University of Illinois / Chicago

Address: Box 5220 m/c 018
   Chicago, IL 60680-5220
Phone: 312-996-4350
E-mail address:
   uicadmit@uic.edu
Web site URL: www.uic.edu
Year Founded: 1965
Private or Public: Public
Religious Affiliation: None
Location: Urban
Number of Applicants:
   13,595
Percent Accepted: 64%
Percent Accepted who
   enroll: 38%
Number Entering: 3,272
Number of Transfers
   Accepted each Year:
   2,686
Middle 50% SAT range:
   Unreported
Middle 50% ACT range:
   21–26
Early admission program
   EA/ED/None: None

Percentage accepted
   through EA or ED: NA
EA and ED deadline: NA
Regular Deadline: 15-Jan
Application Fee: $40
Full time Undergraduate
   enrollment: 15,672
Total enrollment: 23,390
Percent Male: 48%
Percent Female: 52%
Total Percent Minority or
   Unreported: 55%
Percent African-American:
   9%
Percent Asian/Pacific
   Islander: 23%
Percent Hispanic: 16%
Percent Native-American:
   <1%
Percent International: 2%
Percent in-state/out of
   state: 98%/2%
Percent from Public HS:
   Unreported
Retention Rate: 79%

Graduation Rate 4-year: 20%
Graduation Rate 6-year: 46%
Percent Undergraduates in
   On-campus housing: 47%
Number of official organized
   extracurricular
   organizations: 348
3 Most popular majors:
   Biology, Business,
   Psychology
Student/Faculty ratio: 16:1
Average Class Size: 20 to 29
Percent of students going to
   grad school: 33%
Tuition and Fees: $24,100
In State Tuition and Fees if
   different: $11,710
Cost for Room and Board:
   $8,774
Percent receiving financial
   aid out of those who apply,
   first year: 57%
Percent receiving financial
   aid among all students:
   74%

Founded in 1965, the University of Illinois at Chicago (UIC) is one of the youngest campuses in the Illinois public university system. Located in one of America's most vibrant metropolitan areas, UIC is known for its strong ties with the city and energetic atmosphere. If you dream of going to a school in the middle of a large city filled with extracurricular distractions, you should definitely consider UIC as a potential college choice.

The Blessing of Chicago
All students live on or near the two UIC campuses (East and South) in the heart of a city known to some as one of the premier business, cultural, and entertainment centers of America. "The great thing about UIC is that you are so close to the city," explained one student. Although the school itself offers a relatively quiet learning environment, its prime location offers plenty of activities just outside the confines of its walls. Despite the fact that there are few activities organized by the University during the weekends, it is obvious that UIC students are never bored.

Since UIC has one of the lowest tuition costs amongst four-year universities, students can afford to spend more money than many other college students in the country on recreational activities.

UIC and Chicago are closely connected. UIC students frequent the countless eateries, stores, theaters, bars, and malls around the campus, while many residents of the city visit the campus to, as one student put it, "take a tour and experience the college life." On the downside, being so close to the city also means greater exposure to the city's crime, making student safety a concern.

Understated Academia
Of all the University of Illinois schools, the campus at Chicago is one of the least well known. However, this lack of reputation does not mean the school offers little in terms of academics. "Despite what other people say, people come here to study," said one senior.

One strong feature of UIC is its science departments. "Our science departments are very hard. Classes are generally very competitive," said another student. The humanities and social science classes are also known for their rigor. Most students agree that UIC has excellent faculty in a variety of fields. Classes are based on semester hours. Most classes are four hours per week, and the students need 120 semester hours to graduate; therefore, people generally take four to five classes per semester.

> **"The great thing about UIC is that you are so close to the city."**

One of the distinctive elements of UIC is that it has graduation requirements in almost all subjects offered in the school in order to help students "achieve a more rounded education." There are requirements in the humanities, the natural sciences, and the social sciences. There is also an English composition requirement and one in cultural diversity that allows students to "study the culture, social and political institutions, and value systems of social groups, regions, or nations different from those present in the dominant American culture." Students are also required to take a few of the many seminar courses offered in a variety of disciplines to supplement the large lecture courses that make up the bulk of their schedules.

The students at UIC choose their majors among the 75 different bachelor's degrees ranging from Movement Science to Social Work. The most popular majors at UIC are business management, engineering, and psychology. Students can also make their own major if they can justify having their own course of study with faculty approval and supervision.

UIC students describe the course load as challenging. According to one student, "UIC has one of the largest work loads for any class whether it be sciences, social sciences, humanities, etc. All areas are challenging and UIC encourages their students to try them all."

Living in the City
It is often very difficult for UIC students to connect with their professors because of

UIC's tendency to have mainly large lecture classes. The average class size of 29 is misleading because the classes tend to be extremely large or extremely small, and it is often very difficult to get into the tiny seminars. "The only professor I actually got to know in person led my psychology seminar. I don't think my other professors even know my name," one female student complained. Even though most professors have office hours, some students still complain about the lack of opportunities to interact with professors.

The majority of UIC students don't live in dorms; 75 percent of the students live in the greater Chicago area and commute to class every day from home or from off-campus apartments. In the recent years, however, the administration has worked to expand their campus and to decrease the number of commuters. As of the end of the South Campus expansion, 3,800 students, including over half of all freshmen, live in one of UIC's 10 residential halls. Those students who do live on campus describe their housing as being more like apartments than the typical idea of a dorm. Since many students immediately leave campus after class and Chicago is so dynamic, on-campus activities are limited. Fraternities and sororities do not have a heavy influence on the social scene. Instead, students prefer to party off campus in Chicago's bars and clubs. One student remarked, "Going to parties is a chance to mingle with the locals and students from other colleges in the area." Many reported that some bars and clubs are lenient about letting in underage students, making alcohol an important factor in UIC social life.

UIC is ranked in the top five of America's most diverse colleges. Minorities combined to make 55 percent of the college population, with 30 percent of the total population being non-native speakers of English. Also, 55 percent of the UIC population is female—a dynamic unique from other University of Illinois campuses.

Overall, students have a good opinion about their school. UIC students love their city and their fellow students, and are for the most part satisfied with the education they are receiving.—*Xiaochen Su*

FYI
If you come to UIC, you'd better bring "wind-resistant clothing."
What is the typical weekend schedule? "Go shopping and party at clubs in the city."
If I could change one thing about UIC, I'd "lower the noise level around campus."
Three things every student at UIC should do before graduating are "go to downtown Chicago, go watch a White Sox or Cubs baseball game, and take a few seminar classes."

University of Illinois / Urbana-Champaign

Address: 901 West Illinois Street Urbana, IL 61801
Phone: 217-333-0302
E-mail address: ugradadmissioins@uiuc.edu
Web site URL: www.illinois.edu
Year Founded: 1867
Private or Public: Public
Religious Affiliation: None
Location: Urban
Number of Applicants: 21,645
Percent Accepted: 71%
Percent Accepted who enroll: 45%
Number Entering: 6,948
Number of Transfers Accepted each Year: 1,148
Middle 50% SAT range: M: 630–740, CR: 540–670, Wr: Unreported
Middle 50% ACT range: 26–31
Early admission program EA/ED/None: EA

Percentage accepted through EA or ED: Unreported
EA and ED deadline: 10-Nov
Regular Deadline: 2-Jan
Application Fee: $40
Full time Undergraduate enrollment: 30,895
Total enrollment: 41,316
Percent Male: 54%
Percent Female: 46%
Total Percent Minority or Unreported: 34%
Percent African-American: 7%
Percent Asian/Pacific Islander: 13%
Percent Hispanic: 7%
Percent Native-American: <1%
Percent International: 6%
Percent in-state/out of state: 93%/7%
Percent from Public HS: 75%
Retention Rate: 93%
Graduation Rate 4-year: 62%

Graduation Rate 6-year: 80%
Percent Undergraduates in On-campus housing: 99%
Number of official organized extracurricular organizations: 1000
3 Most popular majors: Cell and Molecular Biology, Political Science and Government, Psychology
Student/Faculty ratio: 17:1
Average Class Size: 20 to 29
Percent of students going to grad school: 26%
Tuition and Fees: $26,024
In State Tuition and Fees if different: $12,240
Cost for Room and Board: $8,764
Percent receiving financial aid out of those who apply, first year: 42%
Percent receiving financial aid among all students: 65%

The University of Illinois is among the best universities in the world. It boasts 22 Nobel Laureate faculty and alumni, and 55 percent of the entering class of 2008 ranked among the top 10 percent of their respective high school classes. Home of the first Homecoming football game, the first supercomputer, the country's largest Greek scene and the nation's oldest marching band, it also has some of the best engineering, business and library science programs in the nation.

World-Class Education

Academics are taken seriously at the U of I. Students report having an average of 10 to 15 hours of work per week, more if they are majoring in science or engineering. While some of the most popular classes are taught in 600-person lectures, most classes average around 40 students. Despite the tendency towards larger class sizes, students report that professors, especially the younger ones, are accessible and eager to help students. Furthermore, the large lecture classes often offer smaller discussion sections, so students can discuss the material with a much smaller number of students and a TA.

Grades are often curved, with a preset number of students getting each grade. But students said this system works in their favor; professors reserve the right to improve the curve if the class does especially well. Students who do especially well can qualify for departmental, college or campus honors, which give students priority in registering for classes, access to additional classes, and special recognition upon graduation.

The University of Illinois's College of Engineering is its most selective college, with admission statistics comparable to those of Ivy League schools. According to students, the engineers are well aware of this fact—they "think they're better than other people," said one engineering student of his peers. The U of I's College of Business is also selective, and it does not accept transfers from other majors after freshman year.

PAR, ISR?

Students at the University of Illinois have a wide range of options to choose from for housing—as long as they choose quickly! Dorms at the U of I are assigned on a first-come, first-served basis, and buildings like the Illinois Street Residence (ISR), which is nearest the engineering campus, quickly run out of rooms. An alternative to University-owned housing for freshmen is private certified housing, which are essentially privately owned dorms on campus, complete with RAs and dining halls. Though they tend to be more expensive than traditional dormitories, they also tend to be nicer.

After freshman year, students are free to live off campus. Sophomores often stay in the dormitories if they aren't involved in Greek life, but by junior year, the majority of students live off campus in apartments. There is a wide variety of apartments available, and University buses service them, so you never have a long walk to campus. Students caution, however, that landlords are in a rush to lease their apartments, and contracts are usually signed one year in advance.

With a campus of over 30,000 students, most respondents expressed an initial fear of getting lost in the crowd, but most quickly established a group of friends within their dorm. In addition, the U of I has the largest Greek system in the nation. Although students insisted that those not involved in the system wouldn't feel left out, one sophomore said that "There is a fraternity for everyone who's interested in a Greek organization."

The majority of U of I students hail from Chicago, though there are students at the University from across Illinois, each state and over 100 countries. As such, the campus is very geographically diverse, and about 28 percent of students identify as ethnic minorities.

Krushing on the Orange

Students at the University of Illinois bleed orange. As one freshman said, "When it's game day, you can walk down the streets, and everyone knows it's game day and is wearing their orange." Athletic games often sell out, and the student section is always packed. As one freshman said, there's a lot of school pride for sports teams, "even when they suck."

Orange Krush is a 2800-member student organization that encourages that very school pride. Taking charge of much of the student ticket supply, and doing everything from requiring that students collect money for charity to attend high-demand games to effectively bribing students with prizes in exchange for their attendance at low-demand games, Orange Krush does its best to make sure the student section at each game is full.

As far as extracurricular activities go, Illinois has plenty. In fact, the U of I has over 800 registered student organizations, all of which have informational booths on the quad on the University's annual "Quad Day" at the beginning of each year, so you'll be sure to find something to fit your tastes. For example, the "October Lovers" club has autumn-themed social events and bonfires throughout the year. For nocturnal students, the "Inline Insomniacs" club goes skating at midnight once a week. Intramural sports are also popular, especially soccer and basketball, and they tend to be competitive. Despite the broad array of extracurriculars available, students say that most people really commit themselves to just one or two.

Unofficial Society

Every year, to compensate for the fact that the University is usually closed on St. Patrick's Day for spring recess, the bars in the area host Unofficial St. Patrick's Day, which students described as a "big drinking holiday." The bane of the administration's existence each year, Unofficial draws students from across the state to the University.

Over the rest of the year, students split their Thursday, Friday and Saturday nights between the bars and the frats, spending more time at the bars as the semester advances and fraternity events become more exclusive. Because students can get into bars at 19, students say social life is not significantly different for upper- and underclassmen.

> "When it's game day, you can walk down the streets, and everyone knows it's game day and is wearing their orange."

Despite the images Unofficial and the large Greek system may draw, students say binge drinking is not a huge problem, and mainly affects freshmen "getting used to it," as opposed to upperclassmen. And though the local police raid bars and ticket underage students within reach of alcohol, students report that the police rarely bust fraternities, which have houses on campus.

As one freshman said, "There's a ton of good restaurants on Green Street," and during the day, that's where students head for a bite to eat and a place to relax. The Student Union is also a popular hangout spot, with a food court, areas to sit and socialize or study, and a bowling alley. The nearby statue of the Alma Mater is also a popular gathering point, and after an athletic victory, or in 2008, after the election of President Obama, students rush toward and congregate around the statue. The library is also a popular place for studying, and it is the largest library in the nation at a public university.

30K Strong

The University of Illinois is among the nation's best public universities. With top-tier faculty, continuing research, and brilliant and involved students, the U of I can offer students with varied interests and academic aptitudes an excellent education and a great four years. As one student said, "I was kind of surprised how social it was considering it has such a good academic reputation." When asked if she was satisfied with her decision to attend Illinois, she confidently replied, "Oh yeah."—*Rustin Fakheri*

FYI
If you come to the U of I, you'd better bring "comfortable shoes because we have a huge campus."
What's the typical weekend schedule? "Get up pretty late, do all your homework, order Jimmy Johns for lunch, workout, meet friends, then go to Kans at night."
If I could change one thing about the U of I, I'd "air-condition the dorms."
Three things every student at the U of I should do before graduating are "attend a football game in the student section," "go to the top of Altgeld and watch them play the bells," and "spend a day on the quad."

Wheaton College

Address: 501 College Avenue Wheaton, IL 60187
Phone: 800-222-2419
E-mail address: admissons@wheaton.edu
Web site URL: www.wheaton.edu
Year Founded: 1860
Private or Public: Private
Religious Affiliation: Interdenominational Christian
Location: Suburban
Number of Applicants: 2,083
Percent Accepted: 62%
Percent Accepted who enroll: 45%
Number Entering: 581
Number of Transfers Accepted each Year: 102
Middle 50% SAT range: M: 610–690, CR: 600–700, Wr: 600–719
Middle 50% ACT range: 27–31
Early admission program EA/ED/None: EA

Percentage accepted through EA or ED: 48%
EA and ED deadline: 1-Nov
Regular Deadline: 10-Jan
Application Fee: $50
Full time Undergraduate enrollment: 2,365
Total enrollment: 2,915
Percent Male: 49%
Percent Female: 51%
Total Percent Minority or Unreported: 18%
Percent African-American: 9%
Percent Asian/Pacific Islander: 3%
Percent Hispanic: 3%
Percent Native-American: <1%
Percent International: 1%
Percent in-state/out of state: 22%/78%
Percent from Public HS: 61%
Retention Rate: 94%

Graduation Rate 4-year: 77%
Graduation Rate 6-year: 84%
Percent Undergraduates in On-campus housing: 95%
Number of official organized extracurricular organizations: 75
3 Most popular majors: Economics, Egnlish, Psychology
Student/Faculty ratio: 12:1
Average Class Size: 10 to 19
Percent of students going to grad school: 34%
Tuition and Fees: $22,540
In State Tuition and Fees if different: No difference
Cost for Room and Board: $7,040
Percent receiving financial aid out of those who apply, first year: 69%
Percent receiving financial aid among all students: 67%

As one of the premier Christian colleges in the United States, Wheaton College stands apart from secular institutions of higher learning with its motto, "Christo et Regno Ejus"—"For Christ and His Kingdom." Indeed, this moderate-sized liberal arts college, located in the western suburbs of Chicago, not only provides an excellent education, but also "prepares people to better the kingdom of God," as one student noted.

Wheaton College changes lives for those who seek its top-notch academics and community committed to the Christian faith.

In the Christian Classroom

As a liberal arts college, Wheaton requires all students to fulfill a general education requirement in competencies and learning courses. Competencies include foreign language, quantitative skills, oral communication, writing, applied health science and Biblical content, while learning courses include studies of faith and reason, studies in society, studies in nature, literature and the arts and the senior capstone. As part of these requirements, students must take one course in both the Old and New Testament. Yet, even with the requirements, students do not feel pressured to enroll in classes that they do not enjoy. "There are a lot of options to meet the requirements," said one sophomore.

As a Christian college, Wheaton offers a number of majors that integrate faith and learning in addition to more traditional majors. Among the majors distinctive to Wheaton are Biblical and theological studies, Christian education and various ministry-related music majors. Students report that Biblical studies and Christian education are particularly strong. In general, the high caliber of academics at Wheaton means that no single major stands out as much easier than the others. However, students say that the sciences are the hardest majors at Wheaton. Wheaton also has an excellent Conservatory of Music.

> "I've been really surprised about how true people at Wheaton stay to the whole 'For Christ' thing. It permeates the entire atmosphere."

Most students agree that the faculty enhances the challenging curriculum. "The professors are engaging and really passionate about what they teach," said one student. All professors at Wheaton are Christian, and many bring their faith to the classroom. Professors tend to open class with a devotional or thought of the day. Sometimes the devotional relates to class, but "Sometimes they just share what's in their hearts." In class and out, the professors "really love interacting with the students." Many students take advantage of special programs that allow students to travel to third-world countries to

complete service projects, such as building wells or medical clinics.

The Wheaton Covenant

Each semester, students sign an official statement of responsibility and promise to uphold certain Christian values. By signing the Wheaton Covenant, students agree to refrain from smoking, drinking alcohol, and premarital sex. Most students find that the covenant offers more benefits than restrictions. "It helps us know what we stand for," one student commented. Another student added, "I've been really surprised about how true people at Wheaton stay to the whole 'For Christ' thing. It permeates the entire atmosphere." Most students follow the covenant on the major points, but students do acknowledge that everyone does not always live up to its standards. "Obviously, no one's perfect, but in terms of the major things it's generally followed."

In addition to the covenant, Wheaton students must attend mandatory chapel services three times a week with up to nine excused absences per semester. Although Wheaton requires students to attend chapel, most people enjoy attending the services. According to one student, "At first I thought I wasn't going to like it at all, but we get pretty good speakers like government officials, famous theologians, and authors to come. Chapel is really good."

Social Creativity Required

When asked about the social life at Wheaton, one student responded, "It needs work." Some students feel that they have limited options to socialize at Wheaton, but this belief is not pervasive. According to some students, "Social life at Wheaton is what you make of it." The campus is dry and there are no fraternities or sororities. Students feel the absence of a traditional frat party lifestyle allows for a more creative social atmosphere. The college hosts events for students, such as bringing in popular Christian bands for concerts. Recent concerts have included performances by Jars of Clay and Caedmon's Call. To supplement these more contemporary concerts, students at the Conservatory of Music offer classical performances of their own, which are quite popular among the student body.

Freshmen are not allowed to have cars, but upperclassmen enjoy making quick escapes to local restaurants, bookstores, and a giant movie theater complex. One of the bonus features of Wheaton is its proximity to the city of Chicago. Students can walk from the campus to the train station and arrive in downtown Chicago in less than an hour. Students take advantage of the train to shop, catch a baseball game, or to relax on the beautiful Lake Michigan beaches.

Campus Living

Students describe Wheaton's campus as "beautiful" and an "overall really good location for a college." Safety on campus is not an issue for most students at Wheaton. As one student put it, "Wheaton's pretty much one of the safest places you can find." Around campus, students enjoy playing Frisbee outside and hanging out in the recently completed Beamer Center where they can grab a quick bite from the eatery, play pool in the game room, or enjoy a quiet respite in the study rooms or prayer chapel.

All undergraduates live on campus for the first three years. Freshmen live in either Fischer Hall or Smith-Traber Hall. Most freshmen live in Fischer, which is known as the liveliest dorm on campus. In contrast to Fischer, Smith-Traber is known as a very studious place. The Traber section of Smith-Traber houses many of the male athletes. While Wheaton has coed dorms, all floors are single sex. If you want to visit a member of the opposite sex, all dorms are open from seven to midnight on Wednesdays and Fridays, and coed lobbies located in each dorm stay open all the time for people to socialize. Students seem to like the floor rules: "There are always places you can go to hang out with people. It makes the dorms better if you need to do work." Besides the dormitories, some upperclassmen choose to live in college-owned apartments.

Wheaton tends to lack ethnic diversity, but has made efforts to increase it. What it lacks in ethnic diversity, it makes up for in Christian diversity with various denominations. Wheaton attracts believers of all denominations and a considerable amount of international students from missionary families.

Ring by Spring

Many Wheaton students find their spouses by the time they graduate. When a couple gets engaged at Wheaton, tradition dictates they climb the tower at Wheaton and ring the bell. After they ring the bell, the couple leaves a token of their visit in the tower that will stay there forever. One couple left a life-size statue of Amy Grant.

Many students feel that dating at Wheaton is a bit forced. According to one freshman, "There is this idea that if you have dinner with a girl, you're automatically going to get married." However, not all dating need be so serious. Blind dates among different floors allow students to have fun and get to know each other.

Wheaton changed its longstanding policy of prohibiting social dancing. Now, the college hosts several dances throughout the year including a swing dance, square dance, and salsa dance. A few days before each dance, the college provides lessons for students who do not know the dances. Wheaton's decision comes with much approval from the student body: "A lot of people go to the dances. They're really fun."

Getting Involved

Athletics play a major role in the extracurricular life at Wheaton. As an NCAA Division III school, Wheaton boasts 22 intercollegiate varsity sports and competes against other institutions of higher learning in Illinois and Wisconsin. While many students compete in varsity athletics, a majority of the campus participate in intramural activities. These sports run the gamut from inner-tube water polo and dodgeball to bowling and sand volleyball.

Wheaton offers a variety of other extracurricular activities. Among many options, some students participate in student government, write for *The Record* (Wheaton's student newspaper), join an improv group, or sing in a choir. Most students also get involved with community service and ministry outreach in the surrounding communities.

A Personal Choice

Wheaton College is not for everyone, but people who choose to go there have "a really strong connection to the school," as one student said. "You feel that you are connected to something bigger." Indeed, the fusion of excellent academics and devotion to faith at Wheaton College prepares its students to do big things, "For Christ and His Kingdom."—*David Flinner*

FYI

If you come to Wheaton College, you'd better bring: a Bible, time management skills, and warm clothes.

What's the typical weekend schedule? "Friday night: watch a movie; Saturday afternoon: go to the football game; Saturday night: visit Chicago; Sunday morning: attend church; Sunday night: study."

If I could change one thing about Wheaton College, I'd "give students more control over the Internet."

Three things every student at Wheaton College should do before graduating are "visit Chicago; take Intro to Christian Education with Dr. Root; play an intramural sport."

Indiana

DePauw University

Address: 101 E. Seminary Greencastle, IN 46135
Phone: 765-658-4006
E-mail address: admission@depauw.edu
Web site URL: www.depauw.edu
Year Founded: 1837
Private or Public: Private
Religious Affiliation: Methodist
Location: Surburban
Number of Applicants: 4,439
Percent Accepted: 68%
Percent Accepted who enroll: 22%
Number Entering: 664
Number of Transfers Accepted each Year: 23
Middle 50% SAT range: M: 570–660, Cr: 560–660, Wr: 620–690
Middle 50% ACT range: 25–29
Early admission program EA/ED/None: EA and ED

Percentage accepted through EA or ED: Unreported
EA and ED deadline: 1-Nov
Regular Deadline: 1-Feb
Application Fee: $40
Full time Undergraduate enrollment: 2,276
Total enrollment: 2,276
Percent Male: 44%
Percent Female: 56%
Total Percent Minority or Unreported: 16%
Percent African-American: 6%
Percent Asian/Pacific Islander: 3%
Percent Hispanic: 3%
Percent Native-American: 1%
Percent International: 2%
Percent in-state/out of state: 54%/46%
Percent from Public HS: 83%
Retention Rate: 92%
Graduation Rate 4-year: 79%

Graduation Rate 6-year: 81%
Percent Undergraduates in On-campus housing: 99%
Number of official organized extracurricular organizations: 119
3 Most popular majors: Economics, English, Communications
Student/Faculty ratio: 10:1
Average Class Size: 10 to 19
Percent of students going to grad school: 31%
Tuition and Fees: $29,300
In State Tuition and Fees if different: No difference
Cost for Room and Board: $8,100
Percent receiving financial aid out of those who apply, first year: Unreported
Percent receiving financial aid among all students: Unreported

At DePauw University, the students' sense of fun and the college's unique traditions more than compensate for the Midwestern chill. With a flourishing Greek life scene and a tight-knit population of "casual and accepting" students, this small but proud private liberal arts college offers a welcoming atmosphere. Through its distinctive combination of a strong liberal arts education and pre-professional opportunities, DePauw encourages its students to apply their intellects to the working world. As one senior put it, "De-Pauw really emphasizes putting yourself out there, getting involved, and getting everything out of the time you have in college."

Challenge, Freedom, and Excitement—All in a Day's Work

The classes and academic standards at De-Pauw "definitely require you to work," but there is plenty of freedom to choose courses, and there are several "exciting" options for learning outside of the classroom, a freshman said. Depending on the type of bachelor's degree being pursued, students need to take either 31 or 33 course credits: 31 for normal Bachelor of Arts., Bachelor of Music, and Bachelor of Musical Arts degrees, and 33 for a Bachelor of Music Education degree at DePauw's well-known music school. All students except those in the music school must take courses that fulfill three skill areas: expository writing, quantitative reasoning, and oral communication. They also have to take classes in six distributional areas: natural science and mathematics; social and behavioral sciences; literature and the arts; historical and philosophical understanding; foreign language, and self-expression through performance and participation (which can involve physical activity, the arts, or participation in a campus extracurricular activity). Students agree that these requirements hardly restrict their college experiences at all. "It's possible to get out of taking subjects you hated in high school and just take classes you're interested in," a junior said.

Meanwhile, DePauw's unusual academic calendar, which includes a month-long Winter Term in addition to the traditional fall and spring semesters, gives students the option of having adventurous, flexible learning experiences. Since Winter Term projects are graded on a "satisfactory/unsatisfactory" basis, one senior described them as "a lot of fun and not that stressful." Students can choose among dozens of short, on-campus courses ranging from EMT certification to wildlife management to campanology (the history and practice of bell ringing). They can also study at another college, do research, take an internship to build up their professional experience, or go on special study projects in different countries. One sophomore said she traveled to Morocco on a study trip just to tour the country and learn about its cultural offerings.

Yet another academic opportunity offered by DePauw is the set of five programs of distinction, which allow top students to experience "enhanced study." Students can apply to become Honor Scholars, Management Fellows, Media Fellows, Science Research Fellows or Information Technology Associates. Each program comes with its own set of benefits and hands-on experiences: while Management Fellows can enroll in special seminars and take paid semester-long internships during their junior year, Science Research Fellows are able to receive graduate-level science research opportunities.

Inside the classroom, the learning environment is both intimate and challenging. A sophomore said she had never been in a class larger than 50 people, and average class sizes hover around 15, according to students. Although the intimate, personal setting does ensure that no student slips through the cracks—"I'm afraid of sleeping in class or skipping class because my professor actually knows me," a freshman

said—students said they enjoy the personal bonds they develop with professors, who tend to be "dynamic" and liberal-leaning. In addition to high-quality teaching and mentoring, professors at DePauw will also invite students over for dinner or ask students to babysit, students said. All in all, it makes for fairly demanding academic work: classes at DePauw are challenging but not impossible.

DePauw's focus on academics is complemented by its state-of-the-art campus technology; the campus is known for being one of the most "connected" and "wireless" in the country. Professors can hold online office hours and give out exams and homework online, and the campus boasts comprehensive wireless Internet. To ensure that students can take advantage of the campus's technology, all freshmen are required to bring laptops to DePauw.

It's (Almost) All Greek to Me

Almost three-quarters of DePauw students are involved in the university's large, active Greek life scene, which dominates DePauw social life and makes for a unique party scene. With 14 fraternities and 11 sororities, including two of the oldest fraternity chapters in the country, it's "rush or be rushed," as one sophomore put it: even the minority of students who decide not to join a fraternity or sorority end up having a large circle of Greek friends and often attend parties in Greek houses. But the Greek scene is far from intimidating. Because so many students rush, "It's really easy to get into a fraternity or sorority if you want to," a senior said, adding that the Greek system is not competitive at all. Instead, it provides many traditions, great housing, and a plentiful, fun party scene. Although Greek parties do involve "a lot of drinking," students say no one is pressured to drink at DePauw.

However, some pressure still exists to join the Greek scene because so many students rush, and "independents," as students who choose not to join fraternities or sororities are called, sometimes feel ostracized. A senior said he had to work harder to meet new people and establish connections at first because he chose not to rush. Several students, both Greek and independent, criticized the Greek party scene, saying parties on campus are "hot, crowded, drunken messes that get old after sophomore year." On-campus parties are limited to the Greek houses, although organizations and the university itself often organize events such as concerts and movie screenings.

Upperclassmen often skip the Greek party scene altogether in favor of Greencastle, the surrounding town, which has several bars that are popular with both townies and college students—favorite haunts include the Duck, Topper's, and Third Degree. One bar, Moore's, even features karaoke. "You can actually hear yourself talk and you don't have to drink that much in bars, but at the frats, everyone drinks a lot," a senior said. Other than the bars, however, Greencastle has little entertainment to offer, students say; it is a small, "pretty dull" rural town. Still, students frequent Marvin's, a classic American diner that stays open later than most other Greencastle restaurants and also employs students. Marvin's special garlic cheeseburger, or "GCB," has even become part of campus culture. Nearby Indianapolis, Indiana's largest city, is a popular destination for short road trips, since many students have cars and "Indy" is only an hour away from Greencastle.

Greencastle may lack the excitement of a big city, but it is certainly safe, and features a small-town atmosphere with typical Midwestern picturesque scenery. A freshman said he felt "completely safe" at DePauw—and added that "Wherever I leave it, my stuff is completely safe too." Students regularly walk around at night and usually leave their doors unlocked. Meanwhile, students take advantage of Greencastle's "peaceful, green, and pretty" Bowman Park to just hang out and relax. The campus itself is full of greenery and attractive, classic brick buildings, such as East College, which is the oldest building at DePauw and is listed on the National Register of Historic Places.

Living on campus is required for all four years, so students live in one of eleven residence halls, with their fraternities or sororities, or in University-owned apartments. As freshmen, students all live in dorms, which usually feature coed floors and communal bathrooms as well as "small but nice and well-kept" rooms. Upperclassmen can continue to live in the dorms, move into Greek "mansions," or enter an apartment lottery for juniors and seniors. The apartments are furnished, cost about the same as living in the residential halls, and do not require their inhabitants to be on the University meal plan. Although a junior said DePauw's campus dining "isn't terrible," students agree that eating in fraternity or sorority houses or off campus in Greencastle offers better quality and more variety.

A Bell Worth Fighting For

DePauw varsity teams compete in NCAA Division III, and its women's golf, softball, and basketball teams have been especially successful in recent years. The women's basketball team has won several conference championships and one Division III national title. Still, DePauw games are not especially well-attended; students say they rarely have enough time in their busy schedules to go to games. But many students participate in intramural sports, which "are fun and keep us fit, but aren't too big of a time commitment," a sophomore said.

> "DePauw really emphasizes putting yourself out there, getting involved, and getting everything out of the time you have in college."

The one reliably popular game at DePauw is the Monon Bell Classic—simply known as "the Game"—in which the DePauw Tigers take on the rival Wabash College in football. One of the nation's oldest college football rivalries, the Game regularly attracts many current students as well as alumni, who will "pay through the nose" to get seats, according to a junior. Since the two schools are only 27 miles apart, many of the players and students on both sides are friends, relatives, or former classmates, making the Game even more heated. The teams battle for the Monon Bell trophy, a 300-pound locomotive bell that was first introduced in 1932—to keep Wabash students from stealing it when DePauw wins the trophy, the University seals the bell in a glass case.

Fun Traditions and an Easygoing Atmosphere Await

Students say DePauw's student body tends to be from the Midwest, especially Indiana, and moderate to conservative-leaning, with few minority students. However, DePauw's atmosphere is anything but dull and homogenous. Not only are the students friendly and outgoing, they also eagerly participate in a rich variety of traditions, from Boulder Run to an annual bike race in late April to a game known as "campus golf." In Boulder Run, students streak from their dorms to the Columbia Boulder, a campus landmark, while in campus golf, students dress in traditional golf attire and use golf clubs to hit tennis balls around campus courses. Although there are no actual holes, students attempt to hit their balls against specific targets while walking around student-designed unofficial golf courses.

Not only are DePauw students active in campus life, they are also generally easygoing and accepting, creating a casual, pleasant atmosphere. At DePauw, a junior said, "Everyone is definitely different, but most people still get along and manage to have a good time and get a good education at the same time."—*Vivian Yee*

FYI

If you come to DePauw, you'd better bring "a car and golf clothes for campus golf!"

What is the typical weekend schedule? "Friday is the day to hang out and go party-hopping at the frat houses or the bars; you still party on Saturday, but it's a little more laid-back. On Sunday, study, do work and hang out."

If I could change one thing about DePauw, I'd "add more minority students and more out-of-state students."

Three things every student at DePauw should do before graduating are "take a road trip to Indianapolis, eat a GCB at Marvin's, and rush a fraternity or sorority."

Earlham College

Address: 801 National Road West Richmond, IN 47374
Phone: 765-983-1600
E-mail address: admission@earlham.edu
Web site URL: www.earlham.edu
Year Founded: 1847
Private or Public: Private
Religious Affiliation: Quaker
Location: Suburban
Number of Applicants: 6,205
Percent Accepted: 69%
Percent Accepted who enroll: 27%
Number Entering: 1,156
Number of Transfers Accepted each Year: 43
Middle 50% SAT range: M: 540–660, Cr: 570–690, Wr: 560–680
Middle 50% ACT range: 24–29
Early admission program EA/ED/None: EA and ED

Percentage accepted through EA or ED: 96%
EA and ED deadline: 1-Jan
Regular Deadline: 15-Feb
Application Fee: $30
Full time Undergraduate enrollment: 1,200
Total enrollment: 1,300
Percent Male: 43%
Percent Female: 57%
Total Percent Minority or Unreported: 11%
Percent African-American: 7%
Percent Asian/Pacific Islander: 2%
Percent Hispanic: 2%
Percent Native-American: <1%
Percent International: Unreported
Percent in-state/out of state: 31%/69%
Percent from Public HS: 68%
Retention Rate: 82%

Graduation Rate 4-year: 62%
Graduation Rate 6-year: 70%
Percent Undergraduates in On-campus housing: 87%
Number of official organized extracurricular organizations: 70
3 Most popular majors: History, Psychology, Economics
Student/Faculty ratio: 12:1
Average Class Size: 14
Percent of students going to grad school: 22%
Tuition and Fees: $28,600
In State Tuition and Fees if different: No difference
Cost for Room and Board: $6,200
Percent receiving financial aid out of those who apply, first year: 90%
Percent receiving financial aid among all students: 56%

Earlham College, located in the heart of Middle America, is a Quaker school, a fact that colors every aspect of campus life. Even the sports teams are called the Quakers. Advisory committees, comprised of both students and faculty, make the decisions that govern both the current state and future direction of the college—all reached by consensus, of course. Everyone is referred to by his or her first name—the current president is affectionately referred to as "Dougie B." The school's Quaker heritage contributes to its overall emphasis on fostering individual growth. As one third year explained, "The education here is geared towards individual learning, and if you expect to be spoonfed a degree and then feel accomplished, you'll be sadly mistaken."

From India to Indiana

Through different study-abroad programs, to numerous small classes and seminars taught by professors who are actively interested in their students, Earlham offers countless academic opportunities that are there for the taking. All freshmen (or first years, as they are called at Earlham) must take two reading and writing intensive seminars. The topics of each class vary from year to year, but they often are, as one student put it, "whatever the professor is passionate about." And with class size capped at 15, there is plenty of room for professors to pass this enthusiasm on to their students. "You leave the class and everyone's still discussing the topic," recalls one second year. With subjects such as the History of Sexuality in the Nineteenth and Twentieth Centuries to Religion: For or Against the Common Good, these courses work to provide first years with an introduction to the ins and outs of Earlham academic life.

Another defining emphasis of an Earlham education is its international focus. Earlham not only attracts a large number of international students, but the college also boasts a great number of its own programs run by Earlham professors in countries around the globe. The travel opportunities offered by such programs (some remain in one city, while others take students on guided tours throughout specific areas) in conjunction with the expertise of professors, largely accounts for the popularity of studying abroad for Earlhamites.

> "[Professors] are always available to answer questions individually and personally connect with students. I don't even know what a T.A. is."

Whether they are in India or in Indiana, Earlham professors are always more than willing to work and learn with their students. "They are always available to answer questions individually and personally connect with students. I don't even know what a T.A. is," one senior asserted. Through their "enlightening discussion-based classes," professors are able to work closely with their students. "I came planning to be a journalist and pretty quickly changed to politics

mostly because of my professor . . . many professors here are inspiring and completely change the direction people go," one student said.

Hymnals and "Hash"

Outside the classroom, Earlham students can immerse themselves in a variety of extracurricular activities and sports. And if there is a part of campus life or the Earlham administration that does not satisfy students they can join a committee that addresses that particular issue. One popular committee is the Admissions and Financial Aid Advisory Committee, which recently redrafted the Earlham application. Another popular student group is the International Education Committee, which focuses on revising and expanding Earlham's international focus. As members with positions equal to the faculty that also serve on these committees, students have a great impact in creating their own college experience.

Earlham is, in the words of one student "not a jock school." But even though "Our teams suck, we are still really proud of them." Soccer, for example, never fails to draw a crowd of enthusiastic Earlhamites who sing "uproaringly funny fight songs at sports games." More often than not, students (lovingly) poke fun at their school through these cheers. In fact, the cheers themselves have been printed into a "hymnal," so that generations after generations can use them to reflect their own quirky sense of school spirit.

Although students at Earlham seem to be more than content with their choice of school, one common complaint concerns the surrounding town of Richmond. But as one student put it, "Indiana is what you make of it." Luckily, there are a number of cities within driving distance that can keep students entertained when not busy on campus.

In fact, the on-campus activities at Earlham often make students reluctant to leave, even when they have the chance. And with few other alternatives, there is a high turnout for many of the larger events sponsored by Earlham. "This makes for a good sense of campus cohesion," one senior noted. "Everyone gets to know everyone." Furthermore, the creativity of students, when it comes to finding ways to entertain themselves, is second to none. Many rave about the "quirky theme parties" that are thrown on the weekends, with some past favorites including, "Come As Your Favorite Lesbian" and "Seventh Grade."

Even though Earlham is a dry campus, one junior claimed that, "Earlham tacitly accepts and does not punish many of the known drinking gatherings that occur on a regular basis." One of the most popular of these events is an off-campus party known as "the Hash." "People gather together at two or three on a Saturday afternoon . . . they [sing] a little song while holding hands," a freshman explained. After that, students follow a long and winding flour path around campus that eventually ends at the keg provided somewhere in the 600-acre "back campus." This unconventional approach to partying is undoubtedly characteristic of the adventurous nature of the Earlham student body.

Home Away from Home

Earlham housing offers a variety of options from which students can choose. All first years live in dorms, but after that, students can choose to stay in the dorms, or move into on-campus houses (usually theme houses dedicated to a particular culture or concept). For the truly adventurous, there is an opportunity to live and work on Earlham's Miller Farm. "It has a three story treehouse with a fire pole!" one junior exclaimed.

And for those who are thinking about venturing to off-campus housing (the majority of which is owned by Earlham itself), be wary. Many students have suffered from a small sense of regret. As one student explained, "As mushy as it is to say, we have a wonderful campus community . . . I often feel that I miss out on some of that by being off campus."

Earlham's international focus, combined with the creativity of its students and its Quaker roots, enables the college to offer an unforgettable educational experience, in and out of the classroom. "In the residence halls, classes, dining halls and everywhere else on campus, I am constantly engaged," one senior said. "I am challenged in my assumptions and beliefs almost everywhere I go."—*Stephanie Brockman*

FYI

If you come to Earlham, you'd better bring a "sense of independence and willingness to find things out for yourself"

What is the typical weekend schedule? "A concert, dirt-cheap beer, a theme party, reading, and papers."

If I could change one thing about Earlham, I'd "put it closer to a big city, or have more things of interest in a closer radius."

Three things every student at Earlham should do before graduating are "go off campus for a semester, take a random class outside of your major and interest area and serve on Earlham Student Government in some way."

Indiana University / Bloomington

Address: 300 North Jordan Avenue Bloomington, IN 47405-1106
Phone: 812-855-0661
E-mail address: iuadmit@indiana.edu
Web site URL: www.indiana.edu
Year Founded: 1820
Private or Public: Public
Religious Affiliation: None
Location: Suburban
Number of Applicants: 29,059
Percent Accepted: 70%
Percent Accepted who enroll: 35%
Number Entering: 7,181
Number of Transfers Accepted each Year: 629
Middle 50% SAT range: M: 520–640, CR: 510–620, Wr: Unreported
Middle 50% ACT range: 23–28
Early admission program EA/ED/None: None

Percentage accepted through EA or ED: NA
EA and ED deadline: NA
Regular Deadline: 1-Aprl
Application Fee: $50
Full time Undergraduate enrollment: 30,394
Total enrollment: 31,626
Percent Male: 49%
Percent Female: 51%
Total Percent Minority or Unreported: 8%
Percent African-American: 4%
Percent Asian/Pacific Islander: 4%
Percent Hispanic: 2%
Percent Native-American: <1%
Percent International: 5%
Percent in-state/out of state: 67%/33%
Percent from Public HS: Unreported
Retention Rate: 89%
Graduation Rate 4-year: 50%

Graduation Rate 6-year: 71%
Percent Undergraduates in On-campus housing: 36%
Number of official organized extracurricular organizations: Unreported
3 Most popular majors: Business/Commerce, Communication, Journalism
Student/Faculty ratio: 18:1
Average Class Size: Unreported
Percent of students going to grad school: Unreported
Tuition and Fees: $12,778
In State Tuition and Fees if different: $3,196
Cost for Room and Board: $5,714
Percent receiving financial aid out of those who apply, first year: 79%
Percent receiving financial aid among all students: 71%

B loomington, Indiana, is the quintessential college town. The only unusual thing about it is that the college it surrounds has 30,000 undergrads and 38,000 total students. IU may seem like the typical big state school, but its students say that it's much more than that. It has a Midwestern warmth that brings the large campus together as a community and, despite the size, IU students are connected in school spirit and true friendliness. With unique academic programs and endless opportunities to get involved, IU is full of motivated students who want to make the most of their college experience inside the classroom and beyond.

Inside IU Academics

If reading about a big state school conjures the image of huge auditoriums seating 5,000 people and professors who probably have no idea who half the students are, fear not, say students. "My first semester was full of interactions with each of my professors on an individual basis, and I had classes ranging from 20 students to 300." The range of class sizes is normal for this university, where flexibility in the educational program is key. One junior said, "The core education differs for every major, which means I never have to take math again!" The ability to take classes that interest students on a personal level is a trademark of the Indiana education. IU encourages students to enter under the "exploratory" option, which allows them to fully experiment with a broad range of classes before settling on a major. One student said, "I think this keeps people loving school; education should be about pursuing your passions, not about a random guess as to what profession you will have at the age of forty." This focus on the individual and the awareness that each student is different sets IU apart.

With the same philosophy of exploration and a broad educational spectrum, IU offers some unique major programs that many students enjoy immensely. LAMP is the Liberal

Arts and Management Program, which allows a student to double-major in business and liberal arts. Students say that this program consistently gets rave reviews for its creative seminars and flexible approach to learning. One student explained the appeal of the program in terms of the students themselves: "The business school at IU, Kelley, is very prestigious but often students get frustrated with the thought of giving up liberal arts classes for the sake of a successful future. The clear understanding that students have more than just one interest comes through strongly with this program." Similarly, a minor in LESA, the Leadership, Ethics, and Social Action program, gives students the opportunity to explore a variety of fields while still having some direction.

> "Everyone finds something to do here. People can sit in their rooms and play Halo, but there's also a club for that."

The prestige of the Kelley School of Business, the sociology department, and the Jacob School of Music draws students to IU. But students say that what makes the academic environment truly special is the high caliber and approachability of the professors. One student said, "I think IU is unique because the professors are all well-known scholars with impressive backgrounds, yet they are down to earth and really love to teach." Although students admit that it "takes individual effort" to get to know professors in such a large environment, they also say that "IU across the board makes it easy to get one-on-one attention."

Ancient Greece

With 47 fraternities and sororities to choose from, many students at IU do decide to go through the rush process. Although officially only about 17 percent of students are involved in Greek life, students say that the campus undeniably feels the Greek presence. While one student said "You're not missing out if you're not in a frat," he also commented that frats "bring the campus together." Because on-campus housing almost exclusively contains freshmen, upperclassmen need other places to go. Students say that there is "good housing around campus," but one student also mentioned that this is

one reason to go Greek. Most people who join a fraternity or sorority end up living in the frat or sorority house, which are governed by the school even though they are not technically located on campus.

Saturday Night Fever

Fraternities and sororities clearly preside over partying, but one student asserted that "IU is too large to have a dominant social scene. There is truly a niche for everyone." Still, weekends on campus do revolve around drinking for most students. There are six bars within walking distance of central campus, and upperclassmen tend to center their partying on those. Underclassmen are "less likely to have the means to get into the bars, so they party at the frats or go to dorm and house parties." Regardless of how people decide to let loose, one student pointed out that "People hardly ever leave campus because we all want to be with the family we've formed at school." Cars are allowed, but students agree that they are more of a hassle than anything, since "IU tickets more than the entire city of Cincinnati." With downtown Bloomington only "ten steps away" from campus, students don't need to go far to find entertainment. One student summed up the weekend experience with the statement, "People here really know how to party."

On-Campus at IU

"The campus as a whole is very kind and friendly," one junior said, while a freshman agreed, "IU has such a friendly campus!" This extends to the wide range of political views that comes from a fairly equal number of liberals and conservatives on campus. Both parties are "very vocal," students say, and it "makes for great debates in political science classes!" The involvement in politics is only one way in which students can get involved. One student said, "Sports are huge here, especially the basketball team, which is ranked in the top twenty-five." The same student also said that there are many opportunities for club and intramural sports for those not quite of the varsity caliber. For those more musically inclined, the a cappella scene is prominent, with the all-male Straight No Chaser and the women's group Ladies First. Even if those particular activities don't sound particularly exciting, "Everyone finds something to do here. People can sit in their rooms and play Halo, but there's also a club for that." Another student said, "It's impossible not to get involved." IU recognizes that, just as students have more than one interest in the classroom, their extracurricular passions are varied. As such, the school makes it possible to explore many different areas, from club sports to a cappella and everything in between. "Anything you want to do, there's a way to do it."

IU in Focus

"It's fun here all the time—there's always something to do." This sense that opportunities are limitless comes through in the academics, the extracurriculars, and in the students themselves. The school creates an environment in which students are not only allowed but also positively encouraged to explore a diverse curriculum and take advantage of all the resources of a large university. IU recognizes that every student is different, and as a result the school is set up so that each person has the chance to get what he or she wants and needs out of the college experience. As one student put it, "Investigate IU! There's a lot more beneath the surface."—*Hannah Jacobson*

FYI
If you come to IU, you'd better bring "a fake ID."
What's the typical weekend schedule? "Thursday night—go out, Friday night—go out, Saturday night—go out, and Sunday do homework."
If I could change one thing about IU, I'd "make it warm all year round."
Three things every student at IU should do before graduating are "swim in Showalter Fountain, see an IU basketball game, and go to a Straight No Chaser concert!"

Purdue University

Address: 475 Stadium Mall Drive West Lafayette, IN 47907
Phone: 765-494-1776
E-mail address: admissions@purdue.edu
Web site URL: www.purdue.edu
Year Founded: 1869
Private or Public: Public
Religious Affiliation: None
Location: Suburban
Number of Applicants: 29,952
Percent Accepted: 72%
Percent Accepted who enroll: 24%
Number Entering: 7,063
Number of Transfers Accepted each Year: Unreported
Middle 50% SAT range: M: 540–660, CR: 490–610, Wr: 490–600
Middle 50% ACT range: 23–29
Early admission program EA/ED/None: None

Percentage accepted through EA or ED: NA
EA and ED deadline: NA
Regular Deadline: NA
Application Fee: $30
Full time Undergraduate enrollment: 30,468
Total enrollment: 40,090
Percent Male: 58%
Percent Female: 42%
Total Percent Minority or Unreported: 12%
Percent African-American: 3%
Percent Asian/Pacific Islander: 5%
Percent Hispanic: 3%
Percent Native-American: <1%
Percent International: 13.67%
Percent in-state/out of state: 59%/41%
Percent from Public HS: Unreported
Retention Rate: 86%
Graduation Rate 4-year: 40%

Graduation Rate 6-year: 71%
Percent Undergraduates in On-campus housing: 35%
Number of official organized extracurricular organizations: 815
3 Most popular majors: Mechanical Engineering, Management, Aero and Astro Engineering
Student/Faculty ratio: 13.8:1
Average Class Size: 20–29
Percent of students going to grad school: Unreported
Tuition and Fees: $23,224 per Semester
In State Tuition and Fees if different: $7,750 per Semester
Cost for Room and Board: $8,500 per Semester
Percent receiving financial aid out of those who apply, first year: 38%
Percent receiving financial aid among all students: 6%

Purdue University boasts about being one of the best engineering and physics schools in the nation. After all, one of Purdue's most famous alumni is astronaut Neil Armstrong. Purdue offers students a wide variety of excellent academic programs, along with a longstanding legacy of superior athletics, all in a lively and safe environment.

While Purdue University's main campus is in West Lafayette, Indiana, the University also has a number of campuses (some in conjunction with Indiana University) that are mainly commuter schools, some of which offer housing. Whether or not students choose to transfer from these schools to the West Lafayette campus, they receive diplomas with the powerful Purdue name.

Engineering, Physics and . . .

Purdue is best known for its top-ranked engineering, computer science and physics programs, but it also offers particularly well-respected opportunities in the pharmaceutical sciences, business management and veterinarian sciences. In these three subjects (on both the undergraduate and graduate level) Purdue consistently ranks among the top 20 in the nation. Despite the wide variety of excellent programs, statistics reveal that about one-fifth of all undergraduates thought about, attempted to, or did major in engineering at Purdue.

Engineering majors do not have much space for electives in their schedules, but Purdue offers incredible diversity for students pursuing other programs. The over 200 available majors attract many students seeking a wide range of options. Popular courses include glass blowing in the chemistry department, flower arranging in the horticulture department and "wine appreciation" in the food science department. The wine appreciation class is an example of the interesting and unexpected academics found at Purdue University. The recently retired professor who taught the class for 15 years has a world-renowned reputation that helped make Purdue (and the state of Indiana) the chosen host for many wineries and international wine tasting events.

At a school this size, popular and introductory classes are bound to be big. Indeed, intro-level classes range anywhere from 200 to 450 plus. But as students progress and take higher-level courses, class size decreases. While the large size of some classes may seem daunting at first, most students say that it does not significantly detract from the quality of the class, as most teachers use equipment that makes it easy for the entire class to see and hear the teacher.

As for grades, one engineer said that Purdue "does not have grade inflation, nor should you expect it to." However, liberal arts, interior design and elementary education are generally considered easier.

The Social Situation

Greek organizations on campus play a major role in the social scene. In previous years, hazing and alcohol violations by various fraternities and sororities have caused some concern. However, hazing is now practically non-existent on campus (except for the few horror stories) because of a strict no-hazing policy supported both by Purdue and by the Greek houses themselves. This change occurred recently after several fraternities had their licenses suspended for hazing activities. Of course, some mild hazing still goes on, but most students accept it as part of the rush process. In fact some students even think that the campus cracks down on hazing too much, because "hazing that just involves the rushees doing push-ups is fine." Despite the campus's strict policy on alcohol, many Greeks have continued to party and drink. Police visits, though few in number, have often ended with disputes in court.

While the freshmen and sophomores flock to the frat parties, upperclassmen tend to hang out in the local bars. The bars nearby are concentrated in one area, and the popular local bars are Where Else, the Cactus, the Wabash Yacht Club and Harry's Chocolate Shop. Harry's Chocolate Shop was once a chocolate shop and soda fountain, but was renovated into a bar. Where Else is extremely popular on Wednesday nights for its beer pong contest. During the second to last week of classes in the spring semester, the Grand Prix (a go-cart racing tournament) calls for a week of partying on campus. Luckily, Purdue's campus is generally considered extremely safe, even late at night. As one student said, "it's one of the benefits of living in the middle of nowhere."

For those seeking a tamer scene, there are plenty of alternatives to parties, including campus movie theaters with nine screens each, restaurants such as Triple XXX (Indiana's first drive-in restaurant, named after Triple XXX root beer), and local malls. Triple XXX is especially known for its biscuits, gravy and Duane Purvis All-American, a hamburger with peanut butter. Students are known to frequent Triple XXX at all times during the day—including the morning—since it's open 24 hours a day, six days a week.

While there is a great deal of interaction between students of all backgrounds, social groups are often formed along racial and ethnic lines—perhaps due to the intimidating size of the school. As one student said, "In the end, finding your group of friends is very important. While there is still a lot of interaction between all groups of people, finding your niche will help tremendously."

The Train, Purdue Pete and Rowdy

While most schools have only one mascot, Purdue boasts three, though only one is official. The train, known as the "Boilermaker Special IV," is a Victorian conception aiming to exemplify the tradition and excellence of engineering. Purdue Pete, the notable fiberglass head and hard hat, with hammer in hand, is a tradition from the '60s. Last but not least is Rowdy, Pete's younger brother, who one day hopes to be a Boilermaker.

> "While there is still a lot of interaction between all groups of people, finding your niche will help tremendously."

School spirit at Purdue is strong, especially when it comes to athletics. Purdue enjoys its status as part of the Big Ten and boasts such a strong football program that football games become an event in themselves. Tailgating, both before and after the game, allows for great parties and barbecues during the weekends, and the marching band entertains the devoted fans. The strong school spirit also carries over to both the men's and women's basketball teams. Tickets for games at Mackey Arena (for basketball) sell out quickly, and the showing at every football game is quite strong.

Football at Purdue has several longstanding traditions. One of them is the annual game against Indiana University, where the winner keeps the Old Oaken Bucket, a traveling trophy that signifies the schools' strong rivalry. The other is the "Breakfast Club" a long-standing tradition (if you are 21 and over), which is like "Halloween every Saturday." Seniors dress up in costumes, hit local bars in the morning to drink and then head to the football game to cheer for the

team in their costumes. Of course, if you can't wake up before the game (we are talking about college students), you can still go to the bars after the game to join in the tradition.

Even students who are not on varsity teams still seem to be heavily involved with sports on campus, especially in intramurals. The huge sports complex, Co-Rec as it's called, has everything you could possibly want from the expected weights, basketball, handball and squash courts, to a 50-meter indoor pool, a diving well with a 10-meter platform, and a "ridiculous" number of tennis courts.

While sports are certainly a big part of Purdue, no tuition money goes directly into the sports program. Instead, sports programs at Purdue are funded solely by individual contribution. In this sense, football and men's and women's basketball are unique programs in that they actually generate revenue.

The *Flat* Campus

Purdue's campus stretches over a wide, flat terrain about one mile long, and dormitories are all together in one location relatively far away from central campus. For those who live on campus, cars are a "necessity if you would like to do something other than study." An alternative to cars is the Lafayette-West Lafayette bus system, which is free to students, but less popular. The central campus is relatively compact, making it easy to get around by foot. Sophomores and freshmen typically choose to live in frat houses or dorms, and end up occupying almost all of the available on-campus housing. First-year students are housed in doubles in a mainly freshman dorm. While it is not recommended for freshmen to bring cars, cars become a necessity for the upperclassmen who decide to move away from central campus. Upperclassmen private apartments are mostly located closer to the bars and stadiums, and the campus apartments offered by the school are also pretty far from central campus. One student said that the apartments "are so far away that I don't see why anybody would live there." Parking is a big problem on campus—not only is it difficult to find legal parking spaces, but the police are strict about enforcing the time limits.

Purdue recently renovated many of its dining halls. The renovated dining halls are described as "pretty good," and they've even been nationally recognized, but the old ones are "less preferable" since they only serve "standard fare." The meal plan at Purdue consists of a weekly number of meal swipes and supplementary dining dollars, which can be used at on-campus mini-marts and grills. Dining dollars allow for flexibility in the plan and PDQ (Purdue Dining Quickly) allows students to use swipes on the go.

"All of the campus buildings are red brick and square," one student complained. Except for the Rawls Hall and Kannert building, which are made of limestone, all of the campus is built in classic red brick. Legend has it that John Purdue required that all of the campus buildings be made of red brick or all of his inheritance would go to his heirs. While Rawls Hall and Kannert Hall are both evidence that the legend is false, each has included red brick as part of its foundation to keep up with the tradition.

Diversity and the "Strategic Plan"

For a public university, Purdue enrolls a large percentage of international and minority students: international students comprise about 12 percent of the student body, while American minorities make up an additional 12 percent. While this figure cannot rival the percentage at top private universities, it has been increasing as a result of a new plan. Since 2001, Purdue has been implementing its "Strategic Plan," which aims to expand diversity on campus, as well as decrease the student-faculty ratio, increase interdisciplinary research opportunities, and make a stand for new innovations in technology facilities and economic development

Full of Surprises

In general, Purdue really surprises its students; it even has a nuclear reactor. While the University has its roots in agriculture and engineering, and continues to be one of the premier schools in engineering, Purdue's friendly atmosphere, variety of strong academics, lively social scene and abundant school spirit make a Boilermaker education great for engineers and non-engineers alike.—*Jesse Dong*

FYI

If you come to Purdue, you'd better bring "both a fan and winter gear—the winters are too cold, and during the hot weeks of summer, air conditioners are not allowed."

What is the typical weekend schedule? "Spend Friday and Saturday involved with sports and/or club activities. Then party on Friday and Saturday night. Sunday (and sometimes Saturday) you do all of your last-minute homework."

If I could change one thing about Purdue, I'd "add more arts and live entertainment venues and events here."

Three things every student at Purdue should do before graduating are "join the Breakfast Club, run through all the water fountains, and stand underneath the bell tower."

Rose-Hulman Insititue of Technology

Address: 5500 Wabash Avenue Terre Haute, IN 47803
Phone: 812-877-8213
E-mail address: admissions@rose-hulman.edu
Web site URL: www.rose-hulman.edu
Year Founded: 1874
Private or Public: Private
Religious Affiliation: None
Location: Rural
Number of Applicants: 3,088
Percent Accepted: 70%
Percent Accepted who enroll: 17%
Number Entering: 474
Number of Transfers Accepted each Year: 40
Middle 50% SAT range: M: 630–710, CR: 560–680, Wr: Unreported
Middle 50% ACT range: 27–31
Early admission program EA/ED/None: None

Percentage accepted through EA or ED: NA
EA and ED deadline: NA
Regular Deadline: 1-Mar
Application Fee: $40
Full time Undergraduate enrollment: 1,832
Total enrollment: 1,923
Percent Male: 80%
Percent Female: 20%
Total Percent Minority or Unreported: 11%
Percent African-American: 2%
Percent Asian/Pacific Islander: 4%
Percent Hispanic: 2%
Percent Native-American: <1%
Percent International: 2%
Percent in-state/out of state: 42%/58%
Percent from Public HS: 83%
Retention Rate: Unreported
Graduation Rate 4-year: 72%

Graduation Rate 6-year: 81%
Percent Undergraduates in On-campus housing: 60%
Number of official organized extracurricular organizations: 87
3 Most popular majors: Biomedical Engineering, Chemical Engineering, Mechanical Engineering
Student/Faculty ratio: 12:1
Average Class Size: 20 to 29
Percent of students going to grad school: 20%
Tuition and Fees: $30,243
In State Tuition and Fees if different: No difference
Cost for Room and Board: $8,343
Percent receiving financial aid out of those who apply, first year: 100%
Percent receiving financial aid among all students: 99%

R ose-Hulman Institute of Technology is a small technology/specialty school of about 1,800 students located amidst trees and rolling hills on the fringes of Terre Haute, Indiana. Rose is a utopia for those students who value a quality education over a name-brand university. It offers a more relaxed environment than its rivals, as cutthroat competition is unheard of. Because of this balance between rigor and relaxation, students are genuinely happy to be at Rose-Hulman.

Tough as Nails

Most Rose students were accustomed to getting As in high school, but things quickly change for them at Rose, where Bs are only feasible for those who work hard. Indeed, students don't exaggerate the work load when they claim "Straight As are really rare." On the other hand, if the rumors are true, no student who attends every class has ever failed a course either.

There are few easy routes to a diploma, though students agree that certain majors such as civil engineering aren't as demanding as others. The most popular majors are "anything engineering," such as mechanical engineering, electrical engineering, chemical engineering, or computer engineering. Regardless of a student's major, one sure bet is that "Most students are lucky if they get five hours of sleep a night because they are doing homework all night." Despite Rose students' work ethic, "Students here don't tend to compete with each other. We work cooperatively. Rose really stresses group projects and practical experience."

The first two years are considered the most difficult, but luckily, the work load improves after that. The sophomore curriculum is known to be brutal because it consists of classes that teach the basics for all the disciplines. Students can count on help from their professors, since they have "very good relationships." Professors often give students their home phone numbers in case they ever need help outside of office hours and professors "will help students with work for other classes as well." They are clearly "willing to put in extra hours to help students and [they] make an effort to get to know the students, and really care about us," says one student. One notorious professor, Dr. Rickert, "can solve two different math problems at the same time on the board—solving one with each hand. This is true." He also races against the computer math program, Maple, and wins sometimes. Moreover, all classes at Rose are taught by professors, though TAs are also available to help students with questions.

In spite of the work load, students are truly happy and say that the school is all they expected. One student says, "The teachers are nice, the work is challenging, and I have made a lot of new friends." Also impressive is Rose's record of nearly 100-percent job placement rate for graduating seniors and its rank in *U.S. News & World Report* as the top college in math, science, and engineering for the last nine years running, proving that the hard work is definitely worth the trouble. As one student puts it, "Rose-Hulman has given me opportunities that I could never have found anywhere else. Its supportive environment has helped me grow to become the person I am today."

When They Aren't Studying

Rose-Hulman has over 60 clubs and organizations, and students are encouraged to create a club if they can't find one that suits their needs. Apparently, "The Gun Club" has a high membership, though students are "not sure if that's to relieve stress or what." Drama, WMHD radio, student government, the student newspaper, yearbook, and other major-related clubs are also very popular, and people are dedicated to their organizations "but class work comes first."

Intramurals are also competitive; students compete in tennis, Ultimate Frisbee, indoor soccer and flag football—regardless of their skill level. Since Rose is a Division III school, it can't give athletic scholarships and this enhances the all-around feeling that classes take precedence in life at Rose. Varsity football and basketball games, however, still manage to draw fairly big crowds. Rose is also not without its own traditions. Each year during Homecoming the freshmen build a huge bonfire and guard it all week from the sophomores who try to knock it down. In past years, the bonfire has been enormous

and required air-traffic monitors, but the fire department has started enforcing stricter rules.

Beautiful, Safe Campus Living

Half of Rose's buildings have been built in the last 15 years, so it has a pretty modern feel: "The campus is cozy and pretty, with two little ponds in the center, some woods and lots of deer and squirrels." Rose has a small campus and everything is within walking distance. Those students less concerned about their appearance can roll out of bed 10 minutes before class and still make it there on time. Students are described as "geeky—few people make time to dress up, and some people wear pajamas to morning classes."

> "One of the janitors took about 45 minutes to give me a tour of the buildings, show me classrooms, and explain how to keep from getting lost."

The campus is generally considered beautiful and it is improving every day. Recent renovations include the multimillion-dollar Sports and Recreation Center, the observatory, the technology center, and new residence halls. "The school is always building something new, and our SEC [Sports and Recreation Center] is amazing and a great place to relieve stress." New apartments, affectionately called "Sammy Suites" by students, opened in 2004 and provide apartment-style living for upperclassmen.

Rose is described as "very safe since there is zero crime on campus." The campus is far enough away from the city of Terre Haute that safety isn't much of an issue. To further deter crime, emergency phones are located all over campus. Despite these efforts, most students feel comfortable enough to leave their dorm doors open all the time and say they "have never felt threatened on campus."

Dorm Life

Students have few complaints about the dorm system at Rose. Freshmen have normal dorm rooms, sophomores have suite-style ones, and juniors and seniors on campus have apartment-style dorms. The dorms are big, come with nice oak furniture, and most are air-conditioned. While freshman floors are segregated by sex, the halls are not, and upperclassmen can live on coed floors. Rooms improve each year, and dorms help foster unity among the students, especially during freshman year. "The facilities themselves are pretty good, but it's the atmosphere and staff that make them great. RAs and sophomore advisors (SAs) are really great people and help make the transition to college pretty seamless," claims one student. Each freshman has one RA and two SAs, and "You can ask anyone on campus and they see their RA as a friend more than a rule enforcer." This advising system is quite unique to Rose.

Another perk of Rose's on-campus living is that a housekeeper cleans the rooms once a week. The garbage is taken out, beds are made with fresh sheets, and the floors are vacuumed. "The housekeeping ladies are wonderfully motherly and the building janitors all take a lot of pride in their work and show good feelings toward the student body." Students say that the people who work for Rose are treated well and as a result are happy and helpful. One student describes how, during her freshman orientation, she was wandering through the academic buildings trying to find classes, and "One of the janitors took about 45 minutes to give me a tour of the buildings, show me classrooms, and explain how to keep from getting lost. He still says hi to me in the halls." Clearly, Rose has an all-together friendly atmosphere among its students, faculty, and staff.

Engineered Food

Rose-Hulman has one dining hall and food can be found on-campus until midnight. The food is described as "edible," but students warn, "Don't come here for the food." The campus has recently added a Subway, which has spurred improvement in the dining services: "Either Subway will take over campus or the cafeteria food will have to get better."

In addition to the main dining hall and Subway, "The Worx" in the basement serves burgers, chicken nuggets, French fries, and salads after dining hall hours. There are also restaurants off-campus such as Moggers, which serves sandwiches, an Italian restaurant, Mexican restaurants, and lots of steakhouses and chains. As one can see, "Terre Haute is packed with restaurants."

Nerds Have Fun Too

Terre Haute is not exactly an amusement mecca; Rose students must be adventurous in creating their own fun. On campus are nine fraternities and four sororities, and the school is small enough that Greek life dominates the social scene. Approximately half of the student body is involved. There is a frat on campus for every type of person, but "We are not the stereotypical Greeks because we are all nerds underneath." Rushing is a six-week dry process. It is a great way to meet people and is described as very non-committal. "We say that fraternities rush you because they take guys out to eat, have lots of events at their houses, and generally drop a lot of money on rush."

Since there aren't a lot of women at Rose-Hulman, guys tend to hang out with girls from Indiana State University, which is right down the road. As one student said, "Coming in I figured it would be a bunch of nerds in their rooms on weekends, but it's definitely not like that." Each fraternity has its own annual parties and students typically go out on weekends and Tuesday nights (if they don't have a lab due the next day). Each year the annual Camp Out party transforms a frat house into the wilderness, completely filled with leaves and a 25-foot-tall tree.

Diversity?

Rose-Hulman might not offer an ideal setting for those students wanting culture and diversity, since most of the student body is described as white, upper-middle-class males from the Midwest. However, while there's limited diversity, there's definitely no discrimination. "People who aren't Caucasian stick out. There is also a strong gender imbalance, but I don't think people are intolerant."

Rose has only been coed since 1995, and this attributes to the huge imbalance of male to female ratio. Rose is about 80 percent male and 20 percent female, but one girl said that instead of feeling part of the minority, "I feel appreciated for being a girl, which is a nice feeling." Along with Indiana State University, Rose men also look for girls at nearby St. Mary-of-the-Woods College to counteract the imbalance. Despite this imbalance, Rose-Hulman offers an incredible undergraduate education that is quite balanced when it comes to working hard, as students here still maintain a strong sense of fun and relaxation.—*Terren O'Reilly*

FYI

If you come to Rose-Hulman, you'd better bring "an eagerness to learn in an educational yet
relaxed environment."

What's the typical weekend schedule? "A trip to Indiana State University or St. Mary-of-the-Woods
College if you're a guy (not enough women at Rose-Hulman Institute of Technology, suck it up if
you're a girl.)"

If I could change one thing about Rose-Hulman, I would "find lots more girls or make it easier."

Three things every student at Rose-Hulman should do before graduating are "hours of homework on
a Friday night, go through rush/recruitment, and get to know everybody (at least in your major)."

St. Mary's College

Address: Le Mans Hall Notre
Dame, IN 46556
Phone: 574-284-4587
E-mail address:
admission@saintmarys.edu
Web site URL:
www.saintmarys.edu
Year Founded: 1844
Private or Public: Private
Religious Affiliation: Roman
Catholic
Location: Suburban
Number of Applicants: 1,422
Percent Accepted: 80%
**Percent Accepted who
enroll:** 40%
Number Entering: 455
**Number of Transfers
Accepted each Year:** 47
Middle 50% SAT range:
M: 520–620 CR: 520–620
Wr: 530–630
Middle 50% ACT range:
23–27
**Early admission program
EA/ED/None:** ED
**Percentage accepted
through EA or ED:** 90%

EA and ED deadline:
15-Nov
**Regular Deadline: None/
Priority Application
deadline:** 03/01
**Application Fee: Regular
fee: $30; Online:** No
application fee
**Full time Undergraduate
enrollment:** 1,601
Total enrollment: 1,628
Percent Male: None
Percent Female: 100%
**Total Percent Minority or
Unreported:** 16%
Percent African-American:
1%
**Percent Asian/Pacific
Islander:** 3%
Percent Hispanic: 7%
Percent Native-American:
<1%
Percent International: 0%
**Percent in-state/out of
state:** 28%/72%
Percent from Public HS: 43%
Retention Rate: 79%
Graduation Rate 4-year: 70%

Graduation Rate 6-year:
Unreported
**Percent Undergraduates in
On-campus housing:**
82%
**Number of official organized
extracurricular
organizations:** 70
3 Most popular majors:
Business/Commerce,
General Elementary
Education and Teaching
Nursing/Registered Nurse
Student/Faculty ratio: 10:1
Average Class Size: 10 to 19
**Percent of students going to
grad school:** 30%
Tuition and Fees: $28,212
**In State Tuition and Fees if
different:** No difference
Cost for Room and Board:
$8,938
**Percent receiving financial
aid out of those who apply,
first year:** 94%
**Percent receiving financial
aid among all students:**
91%

N estled in South Bend, Indiana, minutes from the University of Notre
Dame, is one of the nation's best-
kept secrets in women's colleges. In addition to offering top-notch academic
programs, Saint Mary's College provides a
welcoming environment for women with ambition, individuality, and faith. While "It isn't
the school for everyone," current students,
or "Belles," sing the College's praises—
when asked if she could go through the application process again, one student gushed

"I would choose Saint Mary's 20 times over."
Though many are not familiar with the small
women's College in South Bend, those seeking strong academic programs, as well as a
focus on spirituality and self-expression,
might want to give Saint Mary's a second
glance.

Getting the W

Saint Mary's strong academic programs are
a key draw for applicants. The school offers
a liberal arts education, and students are

required to take a wide range of courses in areas such as the sciences, religion and literature to satisfy their General Education requirements. Most students do not consider the requirements a hindrance, and some are even grateful for the requirements—one mathematics and economics major stressed the benefit of the liberal arts background they provide. But the same student also recommends spreading out the GEs over four years, to avoid being stuck with a semester full of classes in one discipline as an upperclassman. Those seeking a wider range of options to choose from can pursue a co-exchange program with Notre Dame, which involves taking two classes a semester at the campus across the street.

In addition to fulfilling their GEs, students must satisfy an extensive writing requirement by getting their Ws. General writing proficiency must be achieved as a first-year and again within the major as a junior and a senior—but students describe the requirement as a plus. "I feel more confident writing papers now that I have the W," one sophomore said. Writing portfolios are graded by professors from all departments and include work done in disciplines other than English. In combination with the typical course load, the writing requirement ensures that "You learn how to write and how to communicate your ideas" during your four years at Saint Mary's.

Academics at Saint Mary's are not for the weak-willed—the workload is described as "heavy" and "intimidating" but "definitely manageable." Students take around five courses, or 16–18 credits, a semester. Those seeking a laid-back academic atmosphere be warned—there is a decent amount of competition for honor societies and internship opportunities. "The college is small, all the students are women, and women can be really competitive," as one student explains. However, another described the atmosphere as encouraging rather than cut-throat: "We're all helping each other out, but we're all pushing each other at the same time." While all areas of study are demanding, some say communications majors enjoy a bit less work than others. Strong advising systems established through the Academic Affairs and First Year Studies office help students chart out their academic plans.

Benefits of the college's small size—there are only about 1,600 undergraduates on campus—include intimate class settings and tight relationships with professors. The average class size is 16 and upperclassmen re-port that they have had few classes with more than 20 students. Art students call instructors by their first names and math students share Memorial Day picnics with professors and their families. Professors typically list their home and cell phone numbers on syllabi and students have known to dial them as late as 1 a.m. with questions on the homework. This one-on-one attention also means professors are more than willing to provide career guidance, research opportunities and valuable graduate school recommendations for their students.

A Packed Social Calendar

While Saint Mary's students devote themselves tirelessly to their studies, they also find time to unwind. The Student Activities Board keeps Belles busy with a host of campus activities. Two of the biggest events are the SMC Tostal and the Twilight Tailgate; others include Jamaica Shaka (a freshman orientation mixer with Notre Dame students), pumpkin carving and Sundaes on Sundays. Dalloway's, a student-run coffee house, is a popular venue for those seeking a diversion from their studies. The organization offers karaoke, bands, dating games and other activities throughout the week.

Weekends at SMC are described as fairly low-key; students often stay in to watch movies with their friends or catch up on work. One of the benefits of SMC's proximity to the University of Notre Dame is the extra set of activities the school offers. Notre Dame's film screenings draw large crowds from Saint Mary's as do school-sponsored activities such as laser tag. While Saint Mary's permits dorm parties for those over 21, many head across the street for a more lively night life. "We go to Notre Dame if we want to go to a party," said one SMC student. A non-drinking club between the two schools, Flipside, hosts at least one activity each weekend for those who prefer to abstain. *The Observer*, a publication that serves Saint Mary's, Notre Dame, and the College of the Holy Cross, keeps students on all three campuses up to date on what's happening each weekend. As one student said, "Within this five-mile sphere, there is never a dull moment!"

The University of Notre Dame also provides a nice outlet from the same-sex environment at SMC. "You don't realize you're missing men in classes, but on the weekends, you do," confessed one student. A trolley runs back and forth between the two colleges, making intercollegiate dating a definite possibility.

Those seeking a break from the on-campus night life gravitate toward nearby bars and restaurants but one student confessed that "South Bend is sort of rundown, not the kind of place you want to hang out." Liquor locales in the surrounding area include Bookmakers, Fever, The Linebacker and Rum Runners. Trips to Chicago are also popular for those seeking respite from campus life. For those lacking a car, the school sponsors a few bus trips to the city each year.

The Facts of Life

Freshmen are placed within one of the four residence halls on campus: Le Mans, Holy Cross, Regina and McCandless. LeMans Hall, designed by a Notre Dame architecture student, is one of the more sought after dormitories. Once a building for both classrooms and dorms, it features marble in the bathrooms and chalkboards in some of the bedrooms. In general, students are pleased with the size of the rooms: "You don't feel like you're getting the shaft." Suites in McCandless even include a separate carrel for studying, because "Saint Mary's believes you should separate study from sleep."

Roommates are assigned freshman year. If the relationship becomes less than idyllic, students can seek mediation at the Counseling Center, which offers help for everything from roommate troubles to stress management to depression. Resident Advisors serve on hall floors or sections to provide guidance for underclassmen. There are also Hall Directors, who tend to be recent college graduates. While many upperclassmen opt to move off campus, "really beautiful" senior apartments opened in 2004—and that just may be enough to reel students back to campus grounds.

SMC recently revamped both the student center and the dining hall. Students cite a significant improvement in the food since the re-opening. In addition to soup, salad and cereal, students can choose from six food stations which offer pizza, hamburgers, Asian, vegetarian and home-style options. While some say the meals are "really, really good," they are also eager for more options. "I've never eaten anything that's bad, I just sometimes wish there would be more variety," said one student. Praise for the dining hall manager abounds; students who request certain goodies or recipes from home find their cravings answered within a few weeks. Some meal plans include "munch money," which can be used at the convenience store, Dalloway's, the Cyber Café, or on-campus restaurants.

Saint Mary's was founded by the Sisters of the Holy Cross in 1844, and is still sponsored by the organization today. The GE requirements include two courses in religion, but the focus on religion extends beyond the classroom. Prayer groups and intercultural groups are common. Overall, students describe their peers as open-minded when it comes to religion on campus, so students who don't practice Catholicism should not be deterred from applying. "It's not looked down upon if you don't go [to church]," explained one student. However, those who do attend services can expect to see a large number of their fellow classmates in the pews, especially on Sunday nights. "It's like a social event to go to church," said one sophomore.

> "It is just a very empowering environment to be immersed in as a female college student."

While students said they were more than pleased by most facets of the St. Mary's experience, they were unanimous in their concern for the lack of diversity on campus. In particular, they emphasized the lack of racial diversity on campus: "We need more diversity—the majority of Saint Mary's is Caucasian," said one junior. The school has made a concerted effort in recent years to address the issue, but as one student pointed out, recruitment can be difficult given the current student body makeup: "It's kind of intimidating because you have this white, conservative, Catholic student body."

Despite the lack of visual diversity on campus, a broad range of socioeconomic backgrounds is represented. A large portion of the student body receives financial aid. In addition, women come to SMC from across the country—at least 47 states are represented in a typical class.

A League of Their Own

Tight relationships exist both inside and outside the classroom at Saint Mary's. Students describe their peers as "welcoming" and "friendly," which can help ease the transition freshman year. There are no sororities on campus but that may be because they aren't needed—a running joke is that the whole school is a sorority. Annual T-shirts supporting "ΣMC" say "no rush required" and "the most exclusive sorority." Indeed students are quick to describe the sense of sisterhood that develops among women at the college.

Overall, SMC students don't seem to lament the dearth of Y chromosomes on campus. While some freshmen list the same-sex atmosphere as one of their least favorites things about Saint Mary's, upperclassmen often report just the opposite. The guy-free environment has been known to bring out the more assertive sides of some students and women can find themselves pursuing positions and activities they wouldn't have considered in a coed environment.

Saint Mary's offers students an exceptional academic experience on a campus brim-ming with a "strong sense of community and pride." As one transfer student said, "I was completely caught off guard. . . . I fell in love with the school, the professors, classes and student body immediately." Women hesitant to embrace four years without men should not be deterred from applying to Saint Mary's; the Notre Dame campus sits less than a mile away, and a same-sex learning environment does offer a host of benefits. As one SMC senior said, "all the leadership positions are held by women, our president is a woman . . . it is just a very empowering environment to be immersed in as a female college student."—*Christen Martosella*

FYI

If you come to Saint Mary's, you'd better bring "something that reminds you of your faith, your family, your friends."

What's the typical weekend schedule? "Friday: stay in for girls night and watch a movie; Saturday: work during the day, go to Notre Dame for a film screening or party at night; Sunday: go to brunch, study, go to church."

If I could change one thing about Saint Mary's I'd "increase diversity."

Three things every student should do before graduating are: "Learn how to ask questions, go through the haunted tunnels, and participate in midnight madness (a series of competitions between classes held in the athletic facility, followed by a huge all-night blow-out party)."

University of Notre Dame

Address: 220 Main Building Notre Dame, IN 46556
Phone: 574-631-7505
E-mail address: admissions@nd.edu
Web site URL: www.nd.edu
Year Founded: 1842
Private or Public: Private
Religious Affiliation: Roman Catholic
Location: Urban
Number of Applicants: 14,503
Percent Accepted: 25%
Percent Accepted who enroll: 56%
Number Entering: 1,989
Number of Transfers Accepted each Year: 191
Middle 50% SAT range: M: 630–720, CR: 640–750, Wr: 630–720
Middle 50% ACT range: 31–34
Early admission program EA/ED/None: EA

Percentage accepted through EA or ED: 48%
EA and ED deadline: 1-Nov
Regular Deadline: 31-Dec
Application Fee: $65
Full time Undergraduate enrollment: 8,371
Total enrollment: 11,134
Percent Male: 54%
Percent Female: 46%
Total Percent Minority or Unreported: 24%
Percent African-American: 4%
Percent Asian/Pacific Islander: 7%
Percent Hispanic: 9%
Percent Native-American: 1%
Percent International: 3%
Percent in-state/out of state: 8%/92%
Percent from Public HS: 50%
Retention Rate: Unreported
Graduation Rate 4-year: Unreported

Graduation Rate 6-year: Unreported
Percent Undergraduates in On-campus housing: 76%
Number of official organized extracurricular organizations: 265
3 Most popular majors: Business/Commerce, Engineering, Pre-Medicine/ Pre-Medical Studies
Student/Faculty ratio: 13:1
Average Class Size: 10 to 19
Percent of students going to grad school: 31%
Tuition and Fees: $36,847
In State Tuition and Fees if different: No difference
Cost for Room and Board: $9,828
Percent receiving financial aid out of those who apply, first year: 67%
Percent receiving financial aid among all students: 47%

At the University of Notre Dame, academics, athletics and faith blend together in a rural setting. But what truly distinguishes Notre Dame is the passion its students feel for their school. It is a passion that is evident in their spectacular displays of school pride at sporting events, in their commitment to their studies, and in their attendance at mass every week.

Academic Enlightenment

Notre Dame's rigorous curriculum motivates students with its wide variety of choices and prepares them well for the future. All freshmen enter the First Year of Studies, where they can adjust to college life while they determine which curriculum they will study for the next three years: Arts and Letters (the most popular), Engineering, Business or Science. An array of over 50 majors is available. While there is a lot of freedom within each major in fulfilling requirements, once the first-year requirements have been fulfilled, each college has their own requirements that must be fulfilled in the sophomore year before a major can be declared.

Notre Dame students enjoy small classes. With the exception of large intro classes, most have fewer than 40 students and many have less than 20. The University prides itself on its focus on undergraduates, which students commend, especially when it comes to attention from professors. Some professors hold dinners at their houses or pull crazy stunts in class to attract students' attention. One student said her finance professor would "dump a glass of water on his head because he wanted people to pay more attention." Professors are also able to eat in the dining halls for free so that classroom discussions can continue outside of class during meals. Students receive several hours of homework every night, but the university provides tutors in every subject for those who need additional help. Despite the demanding academics, most at Notre Dame are willing to embrace the challenges their education requires.

A Long-Standing Reputation

There are few people who are unaware that Notre Dame is a Catholic institution. Does that mean the entire student body is Catholic? Not necessarily. Approximately 80% of Notre Dame students are Catholic, although not all of them practice. Many students feel that religion is not overbearing on campus but it is pervasive all the same. Unsurprisingly, theology is one of the requirements for all students, although it does not have to be Catholic theology.

Each dorm has a chapel in which Mass is held every day except Saturday. Many students attend, but those who don't say there is no pressure. Some students feel that faith is a unifying factor on campus, furthering community values and lending a sense of family to the undergraduate community.

Crucifixes in classrooms and residence halls serve as a reminder of the University's Catholic affiliation. Another reminder is the single-sex dorms and the "parietals," rules for when the opposite sex can enter residence halls. To compensate for the stringency of the policy, the university does provide several 24 hour lounges where both sexes are free to socialize. Despite the unpopularity of parietals, most students agree that Notre Dame is worth the inconvenience.

Another common complaint is the lack of diversity among the student body. The minority situation was described by one student to be "Perhaps the most disheartening aspect of this campus . . . non-white and non-Catholic is a definite minority." The relative homogeneity among the student body and religious faith practiced by many result in a conservative environment in the political, sexual, and social spheres. Despite the conservative leanings of the student body, progressive proposals—such as the official recognition of the Gay-Straight Alliance—all come from the students.

Life off the Field

At Notre Dame, students know how to do more than study. Depending on their schedules, many start their weekends on Thursdays, when they go to local bars and clubs like Corby's, the Linebacker, and Fever. Attendance, however, is limited to those over 21 as all the bars scan IDs and many have been known to confiscate fake IDs. Parties also can be found on campus, but many head to off-campus venues for a livelier scene. The police have been cracking down on underage drinking recently, forcing students to change their usual social routine. On campus, the drinking policy is "beer-only." Hard alcohol is banned and punishments can be severe.

There is plenty of beer to be found, however, throughout weekends in the fall, as tailgaters gather for the football game, an amazing show of athleticism and school spirit. Almost every student buys season tickets and "the shirt," whose color changes every year, making the student section immediately recognizable. As one student put it, "There is nothing in the world like a Notre Dame football game." One Fighting Irish fan claims that words could not do it justice. On Friday nights before home games, there is a pep rally that most of the school attends, bagpipes at midnight and Saturday morning, and the entire campus is abuzz with energy and activity before students, faculty, alumni and fans alike pack into the stadium to cheer on their team. Students stand for the entire game. Enthusiasts are usually tired after a full day on Saturdays, which tends to be a more relaxed night for parties.

> "There is nothing in the world like a Notre Dame football game."

Although many social events tend to be centered on sports and involve alcohol, other options do exist. A student explained that "There is other stuff to do—hang out with friends, go to a show, go to a movie. There is an organization called Flip Side that puts on a lot of non-drinking fun activities on the weekends." In addition, every dorm has its own formal, which is often themed.

An Athletic Campus

Besides football, athletic pride and spirit is pervasive on campus. The student body is also very athletic. Most work out regularly in the excellent training facilities and almost everyone participates in dorm sports. As one student put it, "Dorm sports are HUGE. Everyone I know plays." In fact, Notre Dame is the only university with fully padded recreational football teams.

Apart from sports, students keep busy with other activities and community service. There are myriad student-run clubs and organizations on campus for all tastes and interests. The arts and theater scene puts on a student film festival every year, along with numerous plays. There is Battle of the Bands in the spring and the school has been working to bring high-profile names to campus, including Third Eye Blind and Ben Folds. Guest speakers are also common, including George W. Bush and the president of Ireland, both of whom have come to speak at graduation.

Out and About in South Bend

Living in South Bend, Indiana may not be the most exciting part of the undergraduate experience at Notre Dame, but it does offer the Morris Performing Arts center, the Coveleski Stadium, and a downtown area which is undergoing major renovation. A new strip mall is being built close to campus with student-friendly stores like J.Crew and Urban Outfitters. Restaurants including Chipotle and Buffalo Wild Wings are also new to campus.

The Notre Dame campus is closed off to traffic, making it completely self-contained. The campus landscape is beautiful, but many students complain about the weather, especially the "endless winter" when it is always "cold, or raining or snowing." Except for occasional bike thefts, campus crime is practically nonexistent. Once they are situated in a dorm, students are expected to live there for the next four years, though many move off campus in their senior year. In the absence of Greek life, the dorms tend to foster close friendships; roommates are randomly assigned to "foster community and lifelong friendships." Students take great pride in their dorms, especially since each dorm has a distinct identity, with its own mascot, hall government and reputation. The dorms are also well-equipped. Just this year, the University added cable and wireless to every room. And construction on two new dorms is about to begin in 2007 to accommodate an increasing student population. New cell phone towers were also added to improve reception.

Food options receive praise from students on campus. There are two central dining halls, North and South, and students are polled on their food preferences. Many students go to South because "It looks like Hogwarts from *Harry Potter*." Outside of the dining halls, students enjoy Burger King, Subway and Starbucks at the bustling LaFortune, the equivalent of a Student Union. Students can also head over to Recker's, a local sandwich shop on campus. Dining out is popular as well, since many students have cars on campus.

From football to religion to academics, Notre Dame is rife with rich traditions. With those traditions comes responsibility, but for most at Notre Dame, they cannot imagine it any other way.

FYI

If you come to Notre Dame, you'd better bring "boots and a North Face coat or parka."

What's the typical weekend schedule: "Thursday go to Fever; Friday go to pep rallies and campus parties or bars, depending on age; Saturdays tailgate and go to the football game and maybe to a party; Sundays recover and study."

If I could change one thing about Notre Dame, I'd "move campus closer to a city."

Three things every student at Notre Dame should do before graduating are "rush the football field, go to the Grotto/attend Mass at the Basilica and play in the intramurals."

Valparaiso University

Address: 1700 Chapel Drive Valparaiso, IN 46383

Phone: 219-464-5000

E-mail address: undergrad.admissions@valpo.edu

Web site URL: www.valpo.edu

Year Founded: 1859

Private or Public: Private

Religious Affiliation: Lutheran

Location: Suburban

Number of Applicants: Unreported

Percent Accepted: 90%

Percent Accepted who enroll: Unreported

Number Entering: 715

Number of Transfers Accepted each Year: 201

Middle 50% SAT range: M: 500–630, CR: 490–600, Wr: 480–590

Middle 50% ACT range: 22–28

Early admission program EA/ED/None: EA

Percentage accepted through EA or ED: 93%

EA and ED deadline: 1-Nov

Regular Deadline: 15-Jan

Application Fee: $30

Full time Undergraduate enrollment: 2,917

Total enrollment: 3,874

Percent Male: 48%

Percent Female: 52%

Total Percent Minority or Unreported: 4%

Percent African-American: 6%

Percent Asian/Pacific Islander: 2%

Percent Hispanic: 5%

Percent Native-American: 1%

Percent International: 2%

Percent in-state/out of state: 35%/65%

Percent from Public HS: Unreported

Retention Rate: 85%

Graduation Rate 4-year: Unreported

Graduation Rate 6-year: Unreported

Percent Undergraduates in On-campus housing: 70%

Number of official organized extracurricular organizations: Unreported

3 Most popular majors: Business/Marketing, Social Sciences, Engineering

Student/Faculty ratio: 18:1

Average Class Size: Unreported

Percent of students going to grad school: 23%

Tuition and Fees: $26,950

In State Tuition and Fees if different: No difference

Cost for Room and Board: $7,620

Percent receiving financial aid out of those who apply, first year: 83%

Percent receiving financial aid among all students: 77%

N ot far from the windy city of Chicago lies Valparaiso University, a small private Lutheran school in northwest Indiana, where students enjoy nationally recognized academic programs, an active social scene, a variety of popular extracurricular activities, and, of course, a great basketball team.

"The Human Experience"

When freshmen arrive at Valparaiso (affectionately nicknamed Valpo), they are automatically enrolled in the "Valpo Core." Also known as "The Human Experience," the core covers themes such as creation, citizenship, coming of age, vocation, love and loss through a year-long course that not only includes lectures and readings, but for-credit basketball game attendances and pasta gatherings in professors' homes. Most Valpo students value their core experiences. As one psychology major said, "At first I thought I would hate taking the required core. I thought it would be really boring since every freshman has to take it. Now that I've taken the courses, though, I really feel like core gave me a great background that I've built my entire Valpo education on top of."

Students who choose to enter "Christ College," the honors college at Valpo, substitute "Texts and Contexts: Traditions of Human Thought" for core credit; the class focuses on critical reading, writing, and discussion of great works of literature. This two-semester course includes a fall play written and performed by the students, and a spring debate before the campus community.

Aside from core, students can take classes in four other colleges at VU: Arts and Sciences, Nursing, Engineering and Business Administration. The meteorology program in the College of Arts and Sciences is a popular yet demanding major. Classes outside of the core and other general education requirements are usually small, and Valpo prides itself on the absence of TAs. Most students find their workloads manageable. As one student says, "It just depends on what you do. Like at any other college, you can make Valpo what you want it to be. If you try to do everything at once, the workload's going to seem a lot bigger."

Always Something to Do . . .

Despite the fact that Valpo is a dry campus with a zero-tolerance policy on underage drinking, students at VU find many different options when it comes to the social scene. Some students have dorm parties, while others visit the fraternity houses around campus or head up to the bars and nightclubs of Chicago. While the majority of Valpo students do drink, non-drinkers rarely feel left out. The Union Board at Valpo is extremely active, constantly arranging movies, lectures, concerts and diversity events for the entire campus.

> "Now that I've taken the courses, though, I really feel like core gave me a great background that I've built my entire Valpo education on top of."

The Greek scene at Valpo is thriving, with close to half of the students involved in the 16 fraternities and sororities. While fraternities may have houses off campus, sorority members find themselves in on-campus dorms, separated into their respective sororities by wing. The reason? As one engineering student explains, "If you have six or more girls living together in one house in Indiana, it's considered a brothel. Not that I would complain, but I think Valpo would rather avoid having all their sororities labeled as brothels. Plus, the girls probably wouldn't like it either."

Most Valpo students find it easy to meet people and make friends, especially within the student dorms, where your floor is often the source of your closest friends. Students are rarely labeled by their activities or interests, so cliques are rare at VU. Almost every student at Valpo would agree with one theology major, however, that "There is NO diversity! Everyone you meet here is white, Christian, and upper-middle-class. Practically everyone is from the Midwest, too."

From Christian Crusades to Basketball

Most students at VU are actively involved in some kind of extracurricular activity. As one student says, "Everybody has at least one thing that they do that is really theirs. Some people may do a lot of different stuff too, but everyone has got their own activity that they are really committed to." Intramural sports are very popular at Valpo, and most students are involved in community service projects; the Campus Crusade for Christ and the Voodoo Comedy Club are always fun organizations. Students interested in journalism can get involved with *The Torch*, Valpo's weekly newspaper.

While many Valpo students show their school spirit and make their way out to football games in the fall, the real source of school pride is the Valparaiso basketball team. One of the most well-attended school events of the year is Midnight Madness, when the entire school turns up to watch the first basketball practice session of the year. The players are introduced to the student body one by one and a huge pep rally led by the VU Crew is held until the players begin their first practice at midnight.

Living at Valpo

Most students at Valpo live on campus, in dorms that are single-sex by floor. Students enjoy comforts such as pullout futon beds, big windows, and sinks within their bedrooms. However, the university-regulated curfew is extremely unpopular. Members of the opposite sex must be off one another's floors after 1:00 a.m. on weekdays and after 2:00 a.m. on weekends. Drinking and smoking are prohibited in the dorms as well. RAs can be found in all dorms, but they are generally friendly and welcoming, and are seen more as companions than authority figures.

There are four main cafeterias on campus. The largest is located in the student center, where, as one student says, "You come, you eat, you leave." There are three other, smaller cafeterias, which are located in three of the dorms; their residential nature means students can often be found studying or relaxing. In addition to eating on campus, Jimmy John's and various off-campus pizza restaurants are popular dining options for students. The campus at Valparaiso is home to the second-largest university chapel in the country; its size makes it the focus of the green, gently hilly campus. Situated about an hour from Chicago and in the town of Valparaiso, Valpo creates a home for its students unlike any other. As one sociology student says, "I just love the fact that this is where I wake up every morning."

Students at VU are quickly able to find their own niches in the Valpo community and make the small Lutheran school their new home. As one Valpo student proudly boasts, "Whatever you want in a college, Valpo's got it. If you want to be in a small town community, that's Valpo. If you need the excitement of the city, Chicago's less than an hour away. If you want a lot of extracurricular activities, Valpo's got everything. If you're more concerned with the academic aspects of a college, Valpo's classes and professors are amazing. And last of all, who wouldn't want to root for our basketball team?"—*Sarah Newman*

FYI

If you come to Valparaiso, you'd better bring "a jacket, gloves, and a fan."

What's the typical weekend schedule? "Party hard on Friday night; sleep in late Saturday morning; go to the basketball game Saturday night and party with friends; go to church Sunday morning; and then study, study, study all day on Sunday."

If I could change one thing about Valparaiso, I would "make our student body more diverse."

Three things every student at Valparaiso should do before graduating are "go to El Amigos, ring the Victory Bell, and do crowd push-ups at a volleyball game."

Wabash College

Address: 301 W. Wabash Avenue Crawfordsville, IN 47933
Phone: 765-361-6225
E-mail address: admissions@wabash.edu
Web site URL: www.wabash.edu
Year Founded: 1832
Private or Public: Private
Religious Affiliation: None
Location: Suburban
Number of Applicants: 1,419
Percent Accepted: 47%
Percent Accepted who enroll: 37%
Number Entering: 250
Number of Transfers Accepted each Year: 31
Middle 50% SAT range: M: 520–630, CR 540–660, Wr: 500–610
Middle 50% ACT range: 21–27
Early admission program EA/ED/None: ED

Percentage accepted through EA or ED: Unreported
EA and ED deadline: 15-Nov
Regular Deadline: Rolling
Application Fee: $30
Full time Undergraduate enrollment: 917
Total enrollment: 1,827
Percent Male: 100%
Percent Female: 0%
Total Percent Minority or Unreported: 14%
Percent African-American: 6%
Percent Asian/Pacific Islander: 2%
Percent Hispanic: 5%
Percent Native-American: 0%
Percent International: 5%
Percent in-state/out of state: 76%/24%
Percent from Public HS: 91%
Retention Rate: 88%

Graduation Rate 4-year: 64%
Graduation Rate 6-year: 64%
Percent Undergraduates in On-campus housing: 91%
Number of official organized extracurricular organizations: 64
3 Most popular majors: English, History, Psychology
Student/Faculty ratio: 10:1
Average Class Size: 10 to 19
Percent of students going to grad school: 47%
Tuition and Fees: $25,900
In State Tuition and Fees if different: No difference
Cost for Room and Board: $7,200
Percent receiving financial aid out of those who apply, first year: 93%
Percent receiving financial aid among all students: 88%

As one of America's few remaining all-male institutions, Wabash College students benefit from the school's rich tradition of excellence, impressive endowment, small class sizes and academic rigor. From the long-held football rivalries to the major Greek presence on campus, Wabash offers a unique college experience for highly focused young men.

Small Classes, Personal Experience

Class sizes at Wabash tend to be much smaller than at competing institutions. "The largest size I have ever heard of for a class at Wabash is around 35," one student reported. When classes attract larger volumes, the school generally responds by offering several sections, rather than limiting those who can enroll. The intimate classroom environment provides students with the opportunity to foster relationships with professors, who students say "encourage individual thought and contribution in class" and are "almost uniformly excellent." After completing courses, students frequently visit and maintain lasting relationships with professors. One senior noted, "Students can build strong relations with their professors here at Wabash, and these contacts will later be valuable resources for recommendations and help in finding a career." All this personal attention seems to pay strong dividends to Wabash's graduates. In the years after graduation, approximately 80 percent of students attend graduate or professional school, and a remarkable 80-plus percent of premed students are accepted to medical school, a percentage much higher than the national average.

The academic standards at Wabash are high. Wabash requires all freshmen to participate in the Freshman Tutorial program. This set of introductory courses concentrates on everything from sculpture to nanotechnology, providing freshmen with the opportunity to critically interpret and discuss topics of interest. Many enjoy the tutorials and find them to be a great way to "get freshmen used to the college way of thinking." Another requirement, somewhat less heralded than its freshman-year counterpart, is the year-long course entitled "Cultures and Traditions," a world humanities survey offered for sophomores. Students are also required to demonstrate proficiency in writing and a foreign language. To graduate, seniors must complete "comps." These comprehensive exams, taken over the course of a week, cover every course taken in the student's given major. Some at Wabash compare this period of extensive examination to graduate school defense boards.

Life at Wabash

Wabash students generally find living without women fairly easy to get used to; however, some feel that the academic and social scenes are lacking without members of the opposite sex. One student explains the college's obligation to remain all-male: "Unfortunately (or not, depending on how you look at it), Wabash relies on alumni for our proportionally gigantic endowment, and none of the alumni want to see 'Wabash tradition' destroyed by going coed." Despite the occasional complaints about the lack of female presence, many say they feel less pressure to conform to fashion trends and are able to avoid relationship-related drama.

> "Students can build strong relations with their professors here at Wabash, who will later be valuable resources for recommendations and help in finding a career."

In terms of social life, the Greek system dominates at Wabash, with 10 nationally recognized chapters and more than half of students choosing to live in frat houses. Incoming freshmen often move into fraternities prior to the start of classes, and pledge different frats after having lived with the brothers. Alternatives to this unorthodox Greek system are, however, plentiful. Other housing options include living on campus in Martindale, College, Morris or Wolcott halls, as well as in college-owned off-campus housing.

Every fall, near the end of September, the fraternity pledges compete against one another in singing—or what has become screaming—the Wabash school song, "Old Wabash," at an event dubbed "Chapel Sing." The freshmen are judged by the Sphinx Club, an upperclassmen leadership group with fraternity-affiliated members. These seniors ultimately decide the winning house. In recent years, the students have been required to tone down this tradition as many were adversely affected by the yelling. One student described the administration's reasoning behind regulating the festivities, "[Chapel Sing] had sort of degenerated over the years into a big screaming mass of hoarse, painted, shirtless men. And we're talking bleeding-throat, can't-talk-for-a-week-screaming."

Most students complain that the social offerings of Crawfordsville, the small town of about 15,000 that's near to Wabash, aren't exactly thrilling. One student described it as a "Nowhereville along the side of I-74." Commercial outlets are few and far between, with little beyond a Wendy's, Wal-Mart, a bowling alley, and a theater. For most students, however, the limitations of Crawfordsville don't stand in the way of a good time. With regular parties and activities on campus, most deem venturing into town unnecessary. On weekends, many students also elect to travel to Indianapolis, only an hour away by car, or Lafayette, hometown of Purdue, to "sample the real college-town atmosphere." In addition, juniors and seniors have made a tradition of frequenting the Cactus Bar, a Lafayette establishment.

While students are generally "pretty satisfied—not complaining too loud" with housing and the social scene, they are less than thrilled with the food selection. As is the case at almost every college and university, the food at Wabash can be less than stellar, especially considering its high cost. Dining options at the Sparks Center have been described as "really scandalously bad." The food prepared by fraternity-hired cooks tends to be of a similarly mediocre quality, negating the perceived advantage of "living in-frat."

Athletics but No Cheerleaders

One student describes the athletic presence on campus as "pretty huge." One student reported that "Wabash has a top-notch athletics facility and is very focused on athletics, even though it is a Division III college." For over a hundred years Wabash has taken on DePauw University in one of the Midwest's longest-standing football rivalries: the Monon Bell Game. The winning team is awarded possession of the Monon Bell, a former fixture on the regular train running between Greencastle, home of DePauw, and Crawfordsville, and holds on to it until the following meeting. This trophy has historically been highly prized, with students from both schools making repeated theft attempts over the years. While Wabash places a major emphasis on football, many other athletic programs on campus are also quite popular. Wabash track and field coach Robert Johnson offered world-class athletes his expertise as an assistant coach at the 2000 Summer Olympics held in Sydney, Australia; he was the first Division III coach ever to work in that capacity. Wabash students take advantage of the great athletic resources available to them, with 40 percent of students participating in one of 10 varsity sports, and nearly 75 percent partaking in one of 23 intramural activities ranging from canoe racing to volleyball. Whether it's on the athletic field or in seminar, Wabash men are determined to get the most out of the college experience.—*Natalie Hale*

FYI
If you come to Wabash, you'd better bring "a car for all the weekend travel you'll want to do."
What's the typical weekend schedule? "Hang out with friends at frats and dorms at night, and work out or do laundry during the day."
If I could change one thing about Wabash, I would "change the town; it's boring here."
Three things every student at Wabash should do before graduating are "hang out at the Silver Dollar Bar, attend the Wabash/DePauw game, and branch out and go to a social event at a neighboring school."

Iowa

Cornell College

Address: 600 1st St. SW
Mt. Vernon, IA 52314
Phone: 319-895-4000
E-mail address:
communications@cc.edu
Web site URL:
www.cornellcollege.edu
Year Founded: 1853
Private or Public: Private
Religious Affiliation:
Methodist
Location: Suburban
Number of Applicants:
1,791
Percent Accepted: 36%
**Percent Accepted who
enroll:** 29%
Number Entering: 319
**Number of Transfers
Accepted each Year:** 39
Middle 50% SAT range:
M: 540–670, Cr: 560–670,
Wr: 620–710
Middle 50% ACT range:
24–29
**Early admission program
EA/ED/None:** EA and ED

**Percentage accepted
through EA or ED:** 25%
EA and ED deadline: 1-Nov
Regular Deadline: 1-Mar
Application Fee: $30
**Full time Undergraduate
enrollment:** 1,115
Total enrollment: 1,115
Percent Male: 47%
Percent Female: 53%
**Total Percent Minority or
Unreported:** 16%
Percent African-American:
3%
**Percent Asian/Pacific
Islander:** 1%
Percent Hispanic: 3%
Percent Native-American:
1%
Percent International: 3%
**Percent in-state/out of
state:** 30%/70%
Percent from Public HS:
85%
Retention Rate: 85%
Graduation Rate 4-year:
60%

Graduation Rate 6-year:
66%
**Percent Undergraduates in
On-campus housing:** 87%
**Number of official
organized extracurricular
organizations:** 76
3 Most popular majors:
Economics, English,
Psychology
Student/Faculty ratio:
11:1
Average Class Size: 10 to 19
**Percent of students going
to grad school:**
Unreported
Tuition and Fees: $26,100
**In State Tuition and Fees if
different:** No difference
Cost for Room and Board:
$6,970
**Percent receiving financial
aid out of those who apply,
first year:** 79%
**Percent receiving financial
aid among all students:**
68%

N o, Cornell College is not an Ivy-League university in Ithaca. Despite its small size and rural setting, however, it does attract some top talent from across the country—and it was founded 12 years earlier than that other Cornell in upstate New York. At Cornell College in Mount Vernon, Iowa, students have the opportunity to enroll in only one course at a time, join "social groups" and participate in one of the country's few college steel drum ensembles.

One-Course-At-A-Time

For students who prefer concentrating on only one subject as opposed to juggling four or five per semester, Cornell's unique One-Course-At-A-Time, or OCAAT, scheduling system is a big attraction. All courses are scheduled in blocks, with each year consisting of nine, three-and-a-half week blocks. Most courses meet for morning and afternoon sessions every day of the week, with courses requiring labs often running longer sessions than other courses. Overall students tend to give OCAAT very positive reviews. As one student described, "it allows students to focus and also to be more intense."

Additionally, students said they appreciate OCAAT for the strong student-faculty relationships it fosters as well as for the flexibility it provides. Because professors, too, have only one course at a time to focus on, they can devote all their energy and resources to the students of that particular course. Students described their professors as "awesome" and "totally dedicated" to teaching and advising. And, since so many professors live right in the small town of Mount Vernon, casual meetings outside of the classroom are very common.

Furthermore, class sizes tend to be fairly small, since all are capped at 25 students (some are even capped at 18), including introductory-level courses. The combination of small classes and block scheduling thus gives students more opportunities to attend field trips, take advantage of their own classrooms—which are not shared during the block period, and get one-on-one attention from professors.

Of course, as any student will tell you, OCAAT has its drawbacks, too—aside from the fact that taking an uninteresting course will only be that much worse when one has to go to it every day for a month. Students also acknowledged that while OCAAT works well for most classes, it can be problematic for certain areas of study. For example, it might be difficult to cram certain technical- or memorization-intensive courses, such as an introductory language course or mathematics class, into such a short period of time. But students also said Cornell is in the process of trying to adjust OCAAT slightly to better accommodate these differences. Possibilities include combining harder courses into two-block courses, or grouping some classes for interdisciplinary purposes.

Cornell also allows for a decent amount of academic flexibility. Students said they appreciated OCAAT because it allows them to take a "vacation block" if they so desire. During that time, they might decide to go on a trip, do some community service, relax, or get an early start on a summer internship. The college also makes it relatively easy for students to double-major, or to add a minor to their major. One student, who had planned on majoring in biomedical engineering before coming to Cornell, said she decided to take advantage of the school's flexibility and create her own tailor-made biophysics major. "There's a big emphasis on independence," she explained.

Not Just Another Cornfield in Iowa

Due in part to Cornell's unique academic offerings, students said the school is surprisingly not as homogenous as one would expect. "For being a small school in the middle of a cornfield in Iowa, it's really diverse," noted one junior. Although racial diversity is perhaps not as strong as in some other colleges—"it's predominantly white middle-class"—Cornell's 1,100 students do hail from all over the country, with only about 22 percent coming from Iowa. Students also said that while the campus is often described as "very liberal," voices from a broad political spectrum are heard as well. "We lean to the left, but there's room for discussion and there's a lot of it that goes on," remarked one student.

In addition to OCAAT, Cornell's diverse base of students might also be attracted to the school for its beautiful campus and lively atmosphere. "I know a lot of people who made their decision to come here solely based on the campus—we're located on a hill, one of the few in Iowa," one student joked. The architecture, too, is noteworthy. Mt. Vernon, a town of just over 4,000, boasts three National Historic Districts. "The campus is often described as a 'slice of New England hilltop in the Midwest,'" noted one student, "and I think it's kind of corny but also kind of true." Though many of the buildings on and around campus do tend to be old, they are also well-preserved and often newly renovated.

The 91 percent of students who live on campus also tend to live in older buildings, although one newly built senior dorm features a more modern suite-style setup. While the dorms may not be "as lavish as some other places," they do the trick and suit students "just fine."

Unfortunately, the quality of the food is not quite as impressive as the campus scenery and architecture. Students are required to purchase meal plans, with either 14 or 20 meals per week, and even students living off campus must still purchase a partial meal plan of seven meals a week. Although students said the quality of the food and the setup of the college's single cafeteria were "improving," they also said having a meal plan can get tiresome. "We're a 'Tier II' school when it comes to food," noted one senior. "There's even worse and I can't imagine what that would be."

Getting Involved

Cornell students also take advantage of the many extracurricular organizations available. About 90 different student organizations exist, but if there's not a group that strikes a student's fancy, he or she is easily able to start one independently. The Student Senate is in charge of doling out funds to the various organizations, which range from the Medieval Renaissance Club to the Union of Progressive Students to *The Cornellian*, the college newspaper. One of the more popular activities at Cornell is Pandemonium, a steel drums ensemble comprised of about 20 people performing a wide variety of traditional and contemporary music on four different kinds of drums.

Athletics are also very popular at Cornell, with several intramural activities offered during each block period. Though traditional sports, like basketball and volleyball, tend to be the most popular, students also participate in intramural watermelon seed-spitting contests, indoor whiffleball games, and dodgeball tournaments. While many also participate in varsity sports, students noted that there's definitely an athletic and nonathletic crowd on campus. Interest in athletics is "not campus wide," but games for football, as well as for basketball and volleyball, tend to get "pretty decent" turnouts, particularly for such a small college. Wrestling also tends to be popular, as Cornell is in one of the toughest Division III wrestling conferences in the country.

> "Because we're so small and isolated, it really pulls our campus together."

Going Social

Unlike at larger institutions, much of the social interaction at Cornell tends to take place on a smaller scale—a characteristic many students said they appreciated. "It's a small town so it's a much smaller scene, but I'm the type of person who's okay with that," explained one senior. Another noted that "because we're so small and isolated, it really pulls our campus together." The Performing Arts and Activities Council at Cornell also hosts a number of popular activities, bringing popular comedians, bands, or speakers to campus for all to enjoy on the weekends.

However, Cornell students are still able to enjoy large campus-wide parties, with "social groups" frequently hosting some of the larger off-campus gatherings. Social groups act similarly to fraternities and sororities elsewhere—but while they have Greek names, they are not nationally-affiliated and so are unique to Cornell. Some of the groups are service-based, like the Taus and Rhozes, and others are more "party-oriented," like the Delts, Owls and Phi-Os. About half of all students are members of a social group, but parties are often open to the entire university. Although events including the Delts' St. Patty's Day party and the Gamma's pig roast are popular, the social groups also host formals and semiformals every year, too.

If the pub scene is more fitting to a party-goer's interest, there are several bars within Mount Vernon, "each of which usually has a different crowd on a given weekend night." For a wider array of entertainment options, a lot of students also travel to Cedar Rapids or Iowa City (where the University of Iowa is located), both of which are a mere 20 minute car ride away. Students said that while alcohol is popular and easily accessible, there is "no more or less of a problem than at any other college."

Testing the Waters

Students suggested that potential Cornell applicants might consider spending a night or going to classes for a day or two to feel out the One-Course-At-A-Time schedule. "You either love it or hate it," remarked one student, adding that a fair number of students realize upon entering Cornell that one course at a time may not suit them as well as they thought. Regardless, incoming freshman should look forward to taking advantage of small class sizes and professor accessibility. "Professors are here because they like to teach, and the interactions we can have with them are just priceless." And, of course, they might also want to check out Cornell's social groups, scenery, and historic landmarks. One student said, "If you're looking for a good time here, you'll find it."—*Kendra Locke*

FYI

If you come to Cornell College, you'd better bring "a lot of warm clothing, because it gets pretty windy here."

What is the typical weekend schedule? "Go to social group parties, bars, or Iowa City or Cedar Rapids on Friday and Saturday nights, and relax with friends or study on Sunday."

If I could change one thing about Cornell College, I'd "put it somewhere warmer, maybe by a beach somewhere."

Three things every student should do before graduating are: "Go sledding down Pres Hill in downtown, go camping at Palisades-Kepler State Park, and take a block off and spend it however you want."

Grinnell College

Address: 1103 Park Street
Grinnell, IA 50112
Phone: 641-269-3600
E-mail address:
askgrin@grinnell.edu
Web site URL:
www.grinnell.edu/admission
Year Founded: 1846
Private or Public: Private
Religious Affiliation: None
Location: Rural
Number of Applicants:
3,217
Percent Accepted: 43%
Percent Accepted who
enroll: 34%
Number Entering: 468
Number of Transfers
Accepted each Year:
25
Middle 50% SAT range:
M: 620–710, CR: 610–740,
Wr: Unreported
Middle 50% ACT range:
28–32
Early admission program
EA/ED/None: ED

Percentage accepted
through EA or ED: 69%
EA and ED deadline:
15-Nov
Regular Deadline: 2-Jan
Application Fee: $30
Full time Undergraduate
enrollment: 1,678
Total enrollment: 1,678
Percent Male: 47%
Percent Female: 53%
Total Percent Minority or
Unreported: 19%
Percent African-American:
5%
Percent Asian/Pacific
Islander: 8%
Percent Hispanic: 6%
Percent Native-American:
<1%
Percent International:
11%
Percent in-state/out of
state: 12%/88%
Percent from Public HS:
65%
Retention Rate: 94%

Graduation Rate 4-year:
84%
Graduation Rate 6-year:
86%
Percent Undergraduates in
On-campus housing: 87%
Number of official organized
extracurricular
organizations: 300
3 Most popular majors:
Political Science,
Psychology, Economics
Student/Faculty ratio: 9:1
Average Class Size: 18
Percent of students going to
grad school: Unreported
Tuition and Fees: $35,428
In State Tuition and Fees if
different: No difference
Cost for Room and Board:
$8,272
Percent receiving financial
aid out of those who apply,
first year: 81%
Percent receiving financial
aid among all students:
Unreported

G rinnell College is a small school in a small town, but size hasn't stopped it and, in many ways, has defined its tightly knit intellectual and social community. Founded in 1846, Grinnell has since become a top choice for students thanks to its challenging academic program, quirky student body, and numerous—though often unconventional—extracurricular opportunities. Named the "Best All-Around College" in *Newsweek*'s "Hot Schools of 2004" list and ranked 14th on the *U.S. News and World Report*'s list of best liberal arts colleges for 2009, Grinnell, though located "basically in the middle of a cornfield," is a renowned institution that will provide students with an excellent education and a unique social experience.

Small Classes, Large Workload
Classes at Grinnell are small. Even popular introductory classes remain at under 30 students, which allows for close interactions with professors starting on the first day of

class in freshman year. On the downside, it also means that it is difficult to slack off or blend in.

A new system of course selection has eliminated competition for most popular classes, and students get into their top choices without a fight. "I got all my first-choice classes, even as a freshman," boasted one student.

Sociology is generally considered the easiest major on campus, and the sciences are thought to be the hardest. Weekdays "are pretty much exclusively for studying" due to a large workload with significant amounts of reading. Grinnell students, though, don't mind. Coursework is usually interesting. "We read primary documents, not textbooks about those documents. It is not about memorizing facts and regurgitating them, it is about analyzing everything yourself," said one student. "Your teachers want you to challenge them. You're not supposed to accept what is given," said another. This, in combination with small class sizes, allows students to develop close relationships with professors.

The only academic requirement at Grinnell is the first-year tutorial, in which groups of 12 students develop their writing skills on a wide range of topics, ranging from serious classes on "Russia in Revolution" to amusing courses like "The Onion, Sarah Silverman, and Flatulence: Why are Funny Things Funny?"

Grinnell also offers students the chance to create their own courses via the Mentored Advanced Project program (MAP). It allows students to work with a member of the faculty on "scholarly research or the creation of a work of art." Another option is to take ExCo, or Experimental College, which is a number of informal, often student-taught classes on a range of topics that interest students, townspeople, and staff alike.

Sound Body, Sound Mind

To study, students retreat to the Burling Library or either of the two student centers, Harris Center and Joe Rosenfeld Center. Students rave about the library's study gym, which is essentially "a playscape for studying. You can climb ladders to get to where you want to work," said one student. Traditional seating, of course, is also available. The recently renovated Harris and the brand-new JRC boast not only places to study but also an assortment of recreational facilities such as game rooms and a concert hall. Many students also choose to spend time in the lounges of their dorms.

Grinnell's new gym is popular, as are the newer dorms on East Campus, which boast air conditioning and new furniture. Students live in East, South, or North Campus. East Campus is the quietest, North Campus has many athletes, and South Campus has the most parties. Though off-campus housing is often more affordable than on-campus housing, most students choose to live on campus.

Dining at Grinnell is "pretty good," with enough selection for a student to claim that "there's definitely something for everybody." A pastry chef on staff makes "absolutely amazing" desserts. However, there are many popular dining options off campus, including AJ's Steakhouse, La Cabana, and Pizza Hut.

Not a Bunch of Dirty Hippies

Grinnell students boast about their self-governance policy, which is a variation of the honor code for everyday living to hold students accountable. In practice, this means the administration "lets you do what you want, as long as you're not dumb about it. It's pretty sensible," said one student. There are also Student Advisors, volunteers who live with undergraduates. They do not function as police or traditional residential advisors, but rather as community builders who are under no obligation to report illicit activities, such as substance abuse.

> "We joke about being a bunch of dirty hippies. Everyone showers at least once a month, whether they need it or not."

Partying includes weekly dance parties, with themes like '80s, Fetish and Cross Dress. The small campus and student body allow different cliques to socialize on the weekends and on Wednesdays, which is "a big party night, if you don't have a ton of work to get done," said one student. For nondrinkers, there is no pressure to imbibe. However, for the most part, students drink, and a large number smoke pot, which can "really overwhelm the campus social scene sometimes." The presence of marijuana on campus is what leads some students to characterize themselves self-deprecatingly as "a bunch of dirty hippies," but as one student explained, "We are aware of it, and it's not really true. We joke that people here will always shower once a month, whether they need it or not."

In their free time, students also explore the town of Grinnell, which is "the stereotypical Midwestern town with stereotypical Midwestern chain stores," commented one student. Town-gown relations are peaceful, perhaps because "there really isn't much" in Grinnell. Wal-Mart is a frequented resource, and "if you don't like Wal-Mart, you're screwed," said one student.

Work-study programs are also popular. Most participants are assigned to Dining Services, which "can be a drag," but there are other options. "I was able to find a job playing with babies in the child-care center," one freshman said.

United by Procrastination

There are "way too many different things to do" at Grinnell. No experience is needed to join extracurricular activities, which include a theater program that freshman can "actually get into." Also bountiful are community service opportunities, publications, and singing groups. A large number of famous people, bands and speakers also travel to Grinnell. "Even though it is in Iowa, Ashton and Demi were here a while back, and I could see them from my dorm window," one student said.

Sports do not draw large crowds at Grinnell. "We're good in our division, I think," said one student. Another believed that if Ultimate Frisbee were a sport, Grinnell would be ranked first in the nation "for enthusiasm at least." Some gripe about the students lacking athletic spirit, instead dedicating themselves to nontraditional sports like the Quidditch team rather than more traditional athletics.

What students love about Grinnell athletics, however, is that "the jocks here are smart." Indeed, "everyone defies stereotypes here." One student recalled how the quiet football player in her psychology class turned out to be a "huge fan of Japanese and Chinese culture and wanted to study there in the future." Another explained, "You can't make any assumptions about anyone. Every single person is enormously different." A common trait for all students is said to be "the ability to procrastinate. We're all really good at it, and it's probably one of the things that link us all together."

Most students also love the idea of going to a small school. There "is such a sense of community," and "everyone wants you to be here." Grinnell's large endowment means not only good financial aid but also good quality of life. "Everything you could possibly want is here at Grinnell," said one student. The rigorous academic experience in combination with an eclectic community of intellectuals makes life at Grinnell College truly a "one-of-a-kind experience."—*Erica Rothmam*

FYI
What is the typical weekend schedule? "Go to a free Grinnell-sponsored event during the day, watch a movie with some friends, hit a few dorm parties, and wake up the next morning to go to the library."
If I could change one thing about Grinnell, I'd "move it out of Iowa."
Three things every student at Grinnell should do before graduating are "get to know a professor well, play a game of Ultimate, and climb on the study gym."

Iowa State University

Address: 100 Alumni Hall
Ames, IA 50011-2011
Phone: 515-294-5836
E-mail address:
admissions@iastate.edu
Web site URL:
www.iastate.edu
Year Founded: 1858
Private or Public: Public
Religious Affiliation: None
Location: Suburban
Number of Applicants:
11,058
Percent Accepted: 89%
**Percent Accepted who
enroll:** 44%
Number Entering: 4,335
**Number of Transfers
Accepted each Year:**
1,527
Middle 50% SAT range:
M: 530–680, CR: 510–640,
Wr: Unreported
Middle 50% ACT range:
22–27
**Early admission program
EA/ED/None:** None

**Percentage accepted
through EA or ED:** NA
EA and ED deadline: NA
Regular Deadline: 1-Jul
Application Fee: $30
**Full time Undergraduate
enrollment:** 21,004
Total enrollment: 25,668
Percent Male: 57%
Percent Female: 43%
**Total Percent Minority or
Unreported:** 7%
Percent African-American:
3%
**Percent Asian/Pacific
Islander:** 3%
Percent Hispanic: 3%
Percent Native-American:
<1%
Percent International: 4%
**Percent in-state/out of
state:** 79%/21%
Percent from Public HS:
93%
Retention Rate: 85%
Graduation Rate 4-year:
33%

Graduation Rate 6-year: 65%
**Percent Undergraduates in
On-campus housing:** 39%
**Number of official organized
extracurricular
organizations:** 699
3 Most popular majors:
Management Science,
Marketing/Marketing
Management, Mechanical
Engineering
Student/Faculty ratio: 16:1
Average Class Size: 20 to 29
**Percent of students going to
grad school:** 17%
Tuition and Fees: $16,514
**In State Tuition and Fees
if different:** $231 per
Credit-Hour
Cost for Room and Board:
$6,715
**Percent receiving financial
aid out of those who apply,
first year:** 87%
**Percent receiving financial
aid among all students:**
79%

S
ir Lancelot and Elaine swim on placid
Lake LaVerne next to the Memorial
Union. The royal swan pair are the
pet darlings of Iowa State, second only to
the official mascot, the Cyclone. Add the
sculptures of Dutch artist Christian Petersen, Iowa State alum, to this idyllic scene
and you've got Iowa State University's
campus.

Upperclassmen say they can tell freshmen from returning students as they cross
the campus because they're dressed up and
raring to go. Upperclassmen who've been at
Iowa State for a little while are all "running
behind, still wearing their pajamas, and
haven't combed their hair." This picture of
Iowa State was pegged as "not extremely diverse." Another student put it more severely: "Since we're in the middle of Iowa, it
tends to be mostly white people . . . that's
what's in Iowa." Minority attendance is encouraged by a growing number of scholarships and cultural information sessions and
parties, but students say the school has a
difficult time retaining minority students because they're so outnumbered in the University's vast student population.

Cracking the Books

Iowa's original six colleges have multiplied to
include offerings such as business, education,
design, and liberal arts and sciences. Students
enter Iowa State in one of these colleges,
sorted according to their major. Those who
enroll as undecided are automatically placed
in the College of Liberal Arts and Sciences
(LAS), and then they "take a bunch of classes
that are designed to help you try and find
what you like to do best." One student cited
the difficulty of the engineering college as "really grueling, I think the first or second in the
nation," but offered business as a kinder, gentler alternative. "The joke here is that it's the
place engineers go to die," he said. "If they fail
out of engineering they go to business."

Some students complained about large
class sizes that make individual attention hard
to get. Class size varies depending on your college, but be reassured: students say they've
gotten individual help from professors "just by

going into their office and talking to them or asking questions." Really large classes have TA sections that break them down into more manageable groups. Students complain that TAs "usually don't know what they're doing," or "know their area, but can't teach their area." The only classes you'll find you have to tolerate, TA or not, is English. Two English credits are required for students in all colleges to graduate.

> "The joke here is that [Iowa State]'s the place engineers go to die."

One benefit on the school's large size is the vast array of academic options. The College of Liberal Arts and Sciences comprises 22 departments and over 50 majors ranging from botany, to journalism, to criminology and criminal justice. For those itching to get out of Iowa for a semester or two, LAS offers study abroad programs across the globe. Options include Belize, Florence, India and even Antarctica.

No Place Like Home
Students often start to find their niche at Iowa State by living in the dorms, and find they get a warm reception from their peers: "The doors are almost always open to everyone's rooms, and people just stop by and say hi." Resident advisors "go out of their way to make you feel part of the community." Another student added, "Up here it's pretty easy to make a small circle of friends. It's kind of hard to get lost in a crowd." The downside of the dorms is that they're none too new, though many dorm facilities are being renovated, and others are going up to replace the old buildings.

After living on campus for a year or two, most students move out of the University's old dorms. New university-owned apartments are hailed as "really really nice." There are also plenty of apartments available in surrounding Ames. While it may mean a longer walk to classes in the Iowa winter, most students choose some form of off-campus housing.

What's Doin' In Iowa
While some students complain that there's nothing to do in the Corn State, they say "it's not that bad," even though you "have to be creative." The area surrounding Iowa State University is growing to meet college students' demand for fun. Welch Avenue, the

street that separates one dorm from main campus, is lined with bars. When you're out not painting the town red, consider paintballing, go-carting, or hanging out on the University's Frisbee-golf course nearby.

Most students have cars so they can go anywhere in the city, though you won't need one on Iowa's centralized campus. The city's bus system offers another option for getting around. Wherever you are on the weekends, you can call the Moonlight Express (or, as some students have named it, "the drunk bus") to ensure a safe journey.

If you want to stay on campus for a low-key weekend, the Memorial Union has a hotel on its top floor, big halls for dances and performances, eating areas with a number of vendors, a bar, a library and a university bookstore. On the lower level you can shoot pool or even go bowling. There's no shortage of possibilities, because "there are so many people" at Iowa State who "do so many different things." Beware of Memorial Union after dark, though. An entranceway in the building that commemorates World War II and Vietnam veterans is said to be haunted by some of the wars' nurses.

Beneath the Campanile
Iowa State's oldest and most-loved tradition is campaniling. On the Friday of homecoming, students gather under the big clock tower on campus, called the Campanile. "When it strikes midnight you're supposed to kiss your significant other. That's called campaniling." Homecoming also means the height of Greek life, including a construction contest. Fraternity or sorority lawns sport such original creations as the set for Pee-wee's Playhouse or re-creations of Cy, Iowa State's yellow-headed avian mascot.

The other big event of the year is VEISHEA, an annual celebration during basketball season put together by a board of student volunteers. VEISHEA's initials represent the five original colleges at Iowa State, including veterinary medicine, engineering, industrial science, home economics, and agriculture. Events of the festival include a parade and Olympic-style competitions between teams of students. It's also a chance to reach out to the community. "They shut down a couple of the streets and they set up booths and stuff for kids and families to come," one VEISHEA fan said.

Ice, Ice, Baby
For a school whose football and basketball teams "aren't too good this year," Iowa State

offers a number of exciting intramural sports, which are recommended by students as "just too much fun" to pass up. Students pick their own teams and compete in sports such as broomball, an Iowa State tradition. "You take a ball to the ice rink where the hockey team plays," one senior explained, "and you just get a broom and you hit it to your goals." While billed as a low-contact sport, broomball can get pretty risky for those who don't slide around too well in ten-

nis shoes. For those who are less athletically or icily inclined, intramurals also offers competitions like chess and quiz bowl. Students can also compete against their professors once a year when their colleges are celebrated for a week. Business Week, for example, honors the business college, and students and teachers go up against each other in games and contests "just to get to know each other better" and have a good time.—*Stephanie Hagan*

FYI

If you come to Iowa State, you'd better bring "a beer bong."

What is the typical weekend schedule? "Friday night everybody gets dressed up, makes themselves look nice, then goes out and parties pretty much all night. Get up around noon on Saturday, sit around and watch football or study for the rest of the afternoon, and party all night. Get up at noon again on Sunday, and spend the day studying."

If I could change one thing about Iowa State, I'd "have the size of classes be smaller."

Three things every student at Iowa State should do before graduating are "go campaniling, go to VEISHEA, and party—that's just gotta happen."

University of Iowa

Address: 107 Calvin Hall Iowa City, IA 52242

Phone: 319-335-3847

E-mail address: admissions@uiowa.edu

Web site URL: www.uiowa.edu

Year Founded: 1847

Private or Public: Public

Religious Affiliation: None

Location: Urban

Number of Applicants: 14,678

Percent Accepted: 83%

Percent Accepted who enroll: 35%

Number Entering: 4,253

Number of Transfers Accepted each Year: 1,813

Middle 50% SAT range: M: 550–670, CR: 520–650, Wr: Unreported

Middle 50% ACT range: 23–27

Early admission program EA/ED/None: None

Percentage accepted through EA or ED: NA

EA and ED deadline: NA

Regular Deadline: 1-Apr

Application Fee: $40

Full time Undergraduate enrollment: 20,907

Total enrollment: 27,101

Percent Male: 48%

Percent Female: 52%

Total Percent Minority or Unreported: 15%

Percent African-American: 2%

Percent Asian/Pacific Islander: 4%

Percent Hispanic: 3%

Percent Native-American: <1%

Percent International: 2%

Percent in-state/out of state: 66%/34%

Percent from Public HS: 90%

Retention Rate: 83%

Graduation Rate 4-year: 40%

Graduation Rate 6-year: 65%

Percent Undergraduates in On-campus housing: 94%

Number of official organized extracurricular organizations: 400

3 Most popular majors: Business, Communications, Psychology

Student/Faculty ratio: 15:1

Average Class Size: 10 to 19

Percent of students going to grad school: Unreported

Tuition and Fees: $20,658

In State Tuition and Fees if different: $6,544

Cost for Room and Board: $7,079

Percent receiving financial aid out of those who apply, first year: 46%

Percent receiving financial aid among all students: 66%

Settled in the middle of vibrant Iowa City and split by a river running through campus, the University of Iowa offers a small-town community feel at a large Big Ten school. In a town where people bleed black and gold, Iowa students find their home a "gorgeous, fun, and homey location," as an enthusiastic sophomore noted. With newly renovated athletic facilities, hundreds of student organizations, and classes such as the World of the Beatles, the University of Iowa leaves little room for complaints. Students agree: the Hawkeye spirit is unmatched, the academics are challenging and the social scene will not disappoint.

Wide Variety, Extensive Requirements

With the University of Iowa's General Education Program, most students spend their first two years completing requirements in distributional areas such as rhetoric, foreign language, interpretation of literature, historical perspectives, natural sciences, quantitative or formal reasoning, social sciences and distributed general education. If reading that list leaves you exhausted, you're not alone. Iowa students agree that the requirements are excessive. Though most students apply to another college within the University, such as Iowa's business or education schools, after two years, the requirements provide a wide base with eclectic classes.

Iowa offers fun freshman seminars that liven such a requirement-centric schedule with choices like The Age of Dinosaurs, Elementary Psychology, and Stars, Galaxies, and the Universe. Students agree that physical education options such as pilates, yoga and weight training provide a welcoming break to the monotony, though they fill up quickly. After freshmen year, popular majors include communication and business; while more challenging—or "unusually hard" as one savvy junior warned—tracks include engineering, nursing, and dentistry. In addition, Iowa boasts an impressive Creative Writing department, with alumni such as Kurt Vonnegut.

With an enrollment of nearly 20,000 students, majors and departments vary in both degree of difficulty and number of required courses. Despite being a large school, students insist that professors make themselves accessible and possess a genuine interest in students' experiences. As a senior explained, "I feel we have a diverse staff and that there is really a professor out there that will touch each and every student who comes through the University." Students rave about professors eager to reach out, regardless of the lecture size. With larger lecture classes, however, comes students' control over the heaviness of their workload. Each department looks to interest students by moving them out of the classroom, and students generally appreciate the faculty's effort to instill a passion in students to pursue their interests both in school and the community.

Whether studying business management or the era marked by John Lennon and Paul McCartney's catchy lyrics, Iowa students guarantee that everyone will meet passionate professors who truly enjoy teaching. From nationally recognized writing programs to competitive nursing schools, the Iowa curriculum provides students with enough choices within requirements and chosen areas of study to form a well-rounded education.

From the Dirty Burge to the Palatial Pentacrest

Split by the scenic Iowa River, the University's campus offers a range of architecture from the east to the west side of the river. Dorms are located on either side of the river, brewing pride and a covert rivalry between those who live on either side. While one side facilitates sleeping in and the pajamas-to-class look by being closer to all the classroom buildings, the other allows a welcome break from school and the academic environment. On the west side of the river students may live in the Mayflower or Parklawn dorm, while the east side offers dorms such as Currier and the so-called "Dirty Burge." With underclassmen comprising an overwhelming majority of on-campus inhabitants, some dorms earn themselves reputations, such as the notorious "Dirty Burge," a dorm recognized in *Playboy* magazine as one of the top 10 places to get lucky. Some reputations, however, are less sexy—everyone knows Hillcrest is for athletes and Daum is for the "smart kids," as a sophomore noted.

Regardless of living on the east or west side, in the athletic or honors dorm, all students love the community feeling on-campus the housing provides to underclassmen. Specific floors, in some cases, are even designated for fields like "Women in Science and Engineering" or "Writers' Communities." Each floor also has its own RA who fosters and develops dorm communities as well as enforces dorm regulations. Though RAs must monitor their respective floors, most students enjoy their relationship with a neighboring upperclassman.

After sophomore year, the majority of students live off campus in apartments that are all within a mile of campus. Parking spots are limited around campus, but the University offers a bus from residential areas to the center of campus. Without dorms to conveniently hang out with friends, students often stop by the Iowa Memorial Union (IMU) between classes and relax in the Hawk Lounge. On warmer days, students socialize on Hubbard Park's grassy fields or enjoy the beautiful surroundings of the historic Pentacrest buildings. The five oldest buildings sit in the center of campus, most noticeably the old capitol building that can be easily recognized by its gold dome. New and renovated facilities, such as the business school's state-of-the-art Pappajohn building, join Iowa's historic Pentacrest buildings to form a mix of architecture marked by both tradition and innovation.

The meal plan elicits few complaints, offering three options for the number of meals per week and a dining hall on the east and west side of campus. The food is served buffet style, with as much food as you want for each card swipe. Overall, Iowa's campus features a strong community, a variety of architectural styles and numerous food options under the meal plan. As one junior explained about having such a close-knit campus in a city, "The residents of Iowa City have as much pride in the University as the students, making the institution and the town seemingly one."

The Greeks and Athletes
Starting with freshmen year's on-campus housing, meeting people at the University of Iowa is the least of students' worries. Students love being a Hawkeye and different social groups don't stifle the overriding pride of attending Iowa. Athletics, the Greek system, and downtown Iowa City dominate the social scene, but at Iowa, "people are friends with people from different groups. The cliques disappear at this school. Everyone is supportive of others," claimed a Hawkeye senior.

The University prohibits alcohol in dorms, but the Greek scene, consisting of 18 fraternities and 18 sororities, compensates with popular parties. Vitos, an Iowa City bar, is a popular Thursday night destination, while outgoing freshmen are found at Summit. Luckily, bars admit students who are 19 or over, leaving little divide between the underclassmen's and upperclassmen's social spheres. Though the University may have a strong reputation for drinking—as one student bragged "Iowa is definitely a huge party school"—drinking is optional and only one part of Iowa's social scene. The school's numerous student clubs and organizations plan annual events that are well attended.

Students within specific disciplines, such as engineering, enjoy close relationships with peers they lived with or recognize from class. Athletic events and celebrations, fraternity parties and local bars earn high marks from students, but by no means exclusively make up the social scene.

Midwestern Charm
Behind each student's praise of the University of Iowa and the beautiful campus lies the backbone of Iowa's Midwestern charm. Though about 52 percent of the student body is from Iowa, students agree that the University strives to admit a diverse group of students from those regions. Once students reach Iowa City, they immediately fall in love with the welcoming, vibrant community with its Midwestern charm trademark. As a nostalgic senior reminisced, "Iowa is a large school that feels small: the campus is compact, the people are friendly, and the school spirit is like no other—that I will truly miss. The residents are extremely supportive of the Hawkeyes and the students of the University."

> "Iowa is a large school that feels small: the campus is compact, the people are friendly, and the school spirit is like no other."

The Iowa River, a University of Iowa staple, also adds to the University's unique environments. As one west side native described, "I enjoy the west side because you have a separation of school and home. Walking across the river everyday gives me a chance to clear my head and get some thinking done." Few American campuses can offer such stunning scenery in the heart of their campus, and Iowa students do not take that for granted.

Harkey's Nest
Everyone loves the school's mascot Harkey the Hawkeye and students live for Iowa football. Regardless of a winning season or playing in a bowl game, every game day the Iowa City streets are a sea of black and gold. Football, basketball and Iowa's acclaimed wrestling program draw the largest crowds, but everyone on Iowa's campus is somehow involved in promoting the College and representing its student body.

Athletes enjoy perks such as the newly renovated Kinnick Stadium and their own private building for studying, but intramurals, clubs and volunteer organizations also receive campus funding with very high participation levels. Intramurals provide a great outlet to meet new people and can become very competitive. Popular intramurals include basketball, flag football, sand volleyball, rock climbing and Texas hold 'em. The University has roughly 400 student organizations and clubs such as the 24-hour Dance Marathon, the largest organization on campus that raises money for children with cancer, and the 10,000 Hour Show, where students receive a concert ticket for every 10 hours of volunteering completed.

An experienced junior said it best: "I thought Hawkeye pride was about athletics; it's about so much more than that." From day-long dance marathons, to Thursday nights at Vitos and a sold-out game at Kinnick Stadium, the University of Iowa is anything but boring. Iowa graduates leave college with a cemented love for the Midwest and unrelenting Hawkeye pride. —*Cara Dermody*

FYI

If you come to the University of Iowa, you'd better bring "a good pair of walking shoes, your Iowa apparel, and 19-year-old ID for Iowa City bars."

What is the typical weekend schedule? "Attend a football or basketball game on Saturday, drink with friends that night, and spend Sunday hanging out at the Coralville mall or finishing up some work."

If I could change one thing about the University of Iowa, I'd "flatten the hills on campus."

The three things every student at the University of Iowa should do before graduating are "participate in the dance marathon, go for a run along the Iowa River, and go to a Hawkeye football game!"

Kansas

Address: 119 Anderson Hall
Manhattan, KS 66506
Phone: 785-532-6011
E-mail address:
k-state@k-state.edu
Web site URL:
www.k-state.edu
Year Founded: 1863
Private or Public: Public
Religious Affiliation: None
Location: Rural
Number of Applicants: 6,658
Percent Accepted: 95%
Percent Accepted who
enroll: 50%
Number Entering: 3,128
Number of Transfers
Accepted each Year:
1,017
Middle 50% SAT range:
Unreported
Middle 50% ACT range:
27–31
Early admission program
EA/ED/None: None

Percentage accepted
through EA or ED: NA
EA and ED deadline: NA
Regular Deadline: Rolling
Application Fee: $30
Full time Undergraduate
enrollment: 18,545
Total enrollment: 23,081
Percent Male: 52%
Percent Female: 48%
Total Percent Minority or
Unreported: 0%
Percent African-American:
4%
Percent Asian/Pacific
Islander: 2%
Percent Hispanic: 4%
Percent Native-American:
<1%
Percent International: 7%
Percent in-state/out of
state: 86%/14%
Percent from Public HS: 81%
Retention Rate: 79%
Graduation Rate 4-year: 24%

Graduation Rate 6-year:
Unreported
Percent Undergraduates in
On-campus housing: 37%
Number of official organized
extracurricular
organizations: 594
3 Most popular majors:
Animal Sciences, Journalism,
Mechanical Engineering
Student/Faculty ratio: 10:1
Average Class Size: 10 to 19
Percent of students going to
grad school: 18%
Tuition and Fees: $15,360
In State Tuition and Fees if
different: $5,625
Cost for Room and Board:
$6,084
Percent receiving financial
aid out of those who apply,
first year: 53%
Percent receiving financial
aid among all students:
80%

A s one of the nation's first land-grant schools, Kansas State University has always been known for its top-notch agriculture programs. However, it also boasts several of the leading academic departments in the nation. Four of its nine colleges are ranked in the top ten in the United States, including the College of Agriculture, College of Human Ecology, College of Architecture and College of Veterinary Medicine. Among the state's high school seniors and community college transfers, K-state is ranked as the No. 1 choice of universities. One reason might be its outstanding Honors Program: over the past 20 years, the University has produced more Rhodes, Truman, Marshall, Goldwater and Udall scholars than any other public school in the country.

Real-World Preparation

Students have the opportunity to begin taking courses in their college of choice as early as freshman year. As the backbone of the University, the College of Arts and Sciences has the largest student enrollment, with about 7,000 undergraduates. But with more than 250 majors available and 50 minors to choose from, many students tend to mix degree programs to match their specific interests. For example, K-State has the largest Leadership Studies program in the country, with over 1,200 students earning a minor in that program.

Each department has its own general education requirements that students must meet before graduation. The requirements vary from college to college, but they can include English, math, foreign language and even public speaking courses. Though some students complain that requirements are a nuisance, others recognize that such courses help provide a "broad, well-rounded education," even though they may not be related at all to one's major.

Each student is assigned a faculty member who serves as their academic adviser at the beginning of freshman year. Students said advisors have been known to be helpful not only for providing academic assistance, but for providing "real-world" guidance as well, such as finding part-time jobs or internships in a student's field of interest. According to one student, the K-State faculty is committed to "instructing students so that we walk away with the traits needed to be successful."

Students noted that the relationship between students and professors at K-State is "pretty good," and that professors on the whole are perhaps more receptive and dedicated to the undergraduate's education than at other similarly large research universities. One sophomore remarked that the faculty has "been good as far as making undergraduates feel like they're important." He said the majority of professors are interested in interacting with their students, and receptive to speaking with anyone during designated visiting hours. While introductory classes tend to be quite large—often enrolling several hundred students at a time—upper level courses tend to be much smaller, sometimes with as few as 10 students in the more advanced ones.

K-State also provides its students with a good learning environment. All of the University's general classrooms are currently being renovated to serve state-of-the art technology, and in 2006, the campus became completely wireless. Students described their buildings as "very beautiful," with fairly uniform architecture throughout, accented by limestone and ivy.

An At-Home Atmosphere

Despite the fact that K-State boasts nearly 20,000 undergraduates, it "has the sort of atmosphere that makes everyone feel comfortable." In fact, many students enjoy studying at K-State because it has "such a friendly campus." One student noted that the administration "bends over backwards to help you out," adding that such guidance was one of the main reasons she decided to attend the University in the first place. While the majority of students are from Kansas, the quality of academic programs and the school's out-of-state affordability also make it an attractive

place for students from all over. All 50 states are represented in the student population, but most out-of-staters come from Missouri, Nebraska, Texas and Colorado.

Students agreed that most people feel very comfortable on-campus, no matter what their background is. Others, however, noted that Kansas is a conservative state and characterized the University, too, as somewhat of a "closed and conservative place." One foreign student remarked that even though the majority of people on campus and in the surrounding town are "very nice to outsiders," sometimes he got the sense that many are "just not used to dealing with people from different cultures." Still, students at K-State tend to be more moderate in their political views than one might expect, and overall the campus is "very receptive" to different opinions and backgrounds.

The Little Apple

One hundred and twenty-five miles west of Kansas City and populated by just over 50,000 residents, Manhattan, Kansas, is definitely known as a college town. Yet it is also home to Fort Riley, a large military base, so its residents are accustomed and welcoming to large amounts of people moving in and out of town.

> "[K-State] has the sort of atmosphere that makes everyone feel comfortable."

Students agreed that the University's relationship with Manhattan is a very good one—the community is involved in university activities, and students are also involved in the community. For example, the student government sends liaisons to attend all city commission meetings and some have even been elected to the city commission, so that a line of communication is maintained between the city and the student body, while the town's residents often attend many of the athletic and cultural events held on campus. Students said that residents are "generally really supportive" of the University, beyond the standard occasional complaints about things like parking, traffic congestion and noise during large events.

Some K-State students complain of a lack of activity and shopping options in Manhattan, since it's primarily a college town. However, they also noted that it is an extremely affordable place to live, and in the words of one student, "you can concentrate here pretty well." Furthermore, residents on the whole are very "nice and kind" to students who are new to the area. Some even noted that Manhattan is experiencing quite a bit of positive growth, and that several new retail and housing opportunities are being developed as well.

Housing provided by the University is separated from the city, but most students do decide to live off campus. While freshmen are not required to live on campus, it is highly encouraged and about 90 percent choose to do so. By sophomore year, students begin moving into apartment buildings, town homes or houses, and by junior year the majority of students choose to live away from campus. The University is currently in the process of completing a $100 million housing project to be completed in 2015 that will include more townhouses and apartments to complement the existing suites and residence halls.

Kicking Back in Aggieville

Despite its location in the "Little Apple," K-State campus and surrounding area provide plenty of options for students looking to have a good time. Aggieville, an approximately four-block district of bars, cafes, restaurants and nightclubs within walking distance of campus, is a popular place for crowds to gather both during the week and on the weekends. While it may not be filled with tons of "trendy, hip lounges" for students to hang out in, students said the bar scene is "great," and that there are plenty of fun places to meet up with friends.

With a fairly sizable portion of the student body deciding to join fraternities or sororities, some students considered K-State to be a "huge Greek school." As one student noted, "If you decide to go to the Greek system, your life pretty much revolves around that stuff." Though drinking is a big part of the social scene, particularly for students in the Greek system, "there's still a lot of stuff to do if you don't drink." And for students not involved in fraternity or sorority life, there's also a fairly sizable house party system.

One student described the social scene at K-State as an "at-home atmosphere that's really laid-back and accented by great nightlife." Yet for those not as interested in the bar or frat scene, there are plenty of other options as well. A union programming council coordinates activities several nights each week, while other student groups sponsor their own events. The student union, for example, puts on concerts, free movies and poker nights, among other programs.

Rooting for the Wildcats

As a member of the Big 12 Athletic Conference, K-State boasts championship football and basketball teams. Football games in the fall are an extremely popular activity with students and the Manhattan community alike, who also enjoy attending away games every once in a while. The school has big rivalries with the state's other big public school, the University of Kansas, but also competes heavily with Nebraska and Oklahoma. The Homecoming game is a fairly strong tradition at K-State, during which fraternities, sororities and other student groups create giant floats and parade around town with the marching band.

Beyond the Wildcats, students have the opportunity to participate in over 400 student clubs and organizations on campus encompassing a broad range of interests, including academics, politics and religion. Groups like the Future Financial Planners, Entrepreneurs Club and Pre-Veterinary Medicine Club also emphasize career interests. Club sports are popular as well, and include water polo, lacrosse, softball and even skydiving teams. Students said campus involvement is a strong tradition at K-State, and one added that the University does a "pretty good job of getting students interested and active in student organizations."

Students recommended that incoming freshmen get involved in some sort of student organization when they arrive on campus. Many agreed that they developed a strong sense of camaraderie working with their peers in various organizations, and that they tended also to interact socially with their groups on the weekends as well. Athletics, in particular, are a good way for students to get to know the University a little better—whether it is joining a club team, playing an intramural sport or just cheering on the Wildcats at a football game. The large number of clubs is also conducive to helping students develop leadership skills, which is something that K-State emphasizes heavily. As one student commented, "the University really empowers students to do great things if they come with an open mind and a positive attitude."—*Kendra Locke*

FYI
If you come to K-State, you'd better bring "school spirit and a love of football!"
What's the typical weekend schedule? "The bar scene is big on Thursday nights, students go out
   with friends on Fridays and Saturdays, and relax around town or study in the library on Sundays."
If I could change one thing about K-State, I'd "improve the transportation situation by adding some
   parking garages and developing a mass-transit system."
Three things every student should do before graduation are "go to an away football game, spend a
   summer in Manhattan to get to know the town a little better when there aren't so many students
   around, and check out the outdoor opportunities in the Konza Prairie Preserve, which is owned
   by the University."

University of Kansas

Address: 1502 Iowa Street
   Lawrence, KS 66045
Phone: 785-864-3911
E-mail address:
   adm@ku.edu
Web site URL: www.ku.edu
Year Founded: 1866
Private or Public: Public
Religious Affiliation: None
Location: Urban
Number of Applicants:
   10,367
Percent Accepted: 92%
**Percent Accepted who
   enroll:** 42%
Number Entering: 4,034
**Number of Transfers
   Accepted each Year:**
   1,963
Middle 50% SAT range:
   Unreported
Middle 50% ACT range:
   22–27
**Early admission program
   EA/ED/None:** None

**Percentage accepted
   through EA or ED:** NA
EA and ED deadline: NA
Regular Deadline: 1-Apr
Application Fee: $30
**Full time Undergraduate
   enrollment:** 20,298
Total enrollment: 25,619
Percent Male: 51%
Percent Female: 49%
**Total Percent Minority or
   Unreported:** 19%
Percent African-American:
   4%
**Percent Asian/Pacific
   Islander:** 4%
Percent Hispanic: 4%
Percent Native-American: 1%
Percent International: 3%
**Percent in-state/out of
   state:** 77%/23%
Percent from Public HS:
   Unreported
Retention Rate: 79%
Graduation Rate 4-year: 34%

Graduation Rate 6-year: 58%
**Percent Undergraduates in
   On-campus housing:** 22%
**Number of official organized
   extracurricular
   organizations:** 515
3 Most popular majors:
   Accounting,
   Biology/Biological sciences,
   Psychology
Student/Faculty ratio: 19:1
Average Class Size: 20 to 29
**Percent of students going to
   grad school:** 28%
Tuition and Fees: $18,909
**In State Tuition and Fees if
   different:** $7,725
Cost for Room and Board:
   $6,474
**Percent receiving financial
   aid out of those who apply,
   first year:** 48%
**Percent receiving financial
   aid among all students:**
   36%

L ocated atop Mount Oread in Lawrence, Kansas, "KU" boasts gorgeous hillside scenery and a warm, friendly student body. There is something for everyone here with the large number of students and the sheer range of activities it fosters.

Plenty of Choices
The University of Kansas offers 11 undergraduate schools. Freshmen can enter directly into the School of Engineering, the School of Architecture and Urban Design, the School of Fine Arts, or pursue a more broad-based curriculum in the College of Liberal Arts. Everyone enrolled in the College of Liberal

Arts is required to meet a core group of requirements, which includes classes in the history of Western and modern civilizations. The Western civilization classes include the study of classical thinkers like Plato and Aristotle, and the modern civilization classes focus on more recent developments and current events. While students were generally enthusiastic and deemed the course content as interesting, one student complained about the "immense amount of reading that was really demanding" and argued that "it should be pared down." Within the different programs of study, the core requirements vary greatly, and, while most students found them "helpful," one junior commented that "it would be better if the core requirements were more major-specific."

The Honors College offers a select group of students, small seminar classes known for their better student-to-faculty ratio and excellent instruction. Students not in the honors program, however, found nothing to complain about, even if they are unable to get into the smaller classes. One sophomore raved that even the largest classes at KU were "still awesome" because of the first-rate teaching staff. Students were especially enthusiastic about the broad scope of classes and agreed that, while getting into classes was not a problem, "unless you're in the honors program, it can be hard for freshmen and sophomores to get into certain science classes." The same student noted "the professors are great and really know their stuff," and that one of his favorite classes at KU was, in fact, a large lecture class. Most students found the work load sufficiently demanding without being overwhelming, though one student noted that the architectural engineering program was particularly rigorous. In particular, Dennis Dailey's class on human sexuality was described as "notoriously controversial" and always attracts large numbers of curious students.

Mt. Oread or Mt. Olympus?
The Greek scene is large and active at University of Kansas, and parties are never in short supply. Most of the Greek parties are open to the entire student body, though there are certain formal events hosted and attended only by Greeks. One student commented that "While the Greek system is fairly popular, it's not 'the thing,' so there's not much pressure to join." With the generally friendly atmosphere, students report that "it is pretty easy to make friends," saying that "you can just talk to people in classes and they will warm up to you." Students also maintain that most of their friends come from their dorms or halls. Furthermore, "there are not very many cliques" and no particular groups dominate student life. In terms of dating, students say that people tend to couple up, with one student noting that the majority of people have significant others. One single (and hopeful) student commented, "Even though there are lots of couples around, if you're single you can still find somebody to hook up with." And chances are the hookup will be a good one, according to one student who praised the "good selection" and "fair number of at-

tractive people" at the University. Students described the number of homosexual couples and interracial couples as few, but did acknowledge their presence on campus.

Cute and Preppy
Most students agreed that there was no dominant student stereotype at KU. In the words of one student, "There are 27,000 kids, and it makes me happy that there's every type of student here." However, one student noted the lack of geographic and socioeconomic diversity, stating that "there are a lot of affluent kids who come from Johnson County and drive SUVs." Another student said that the campus is "mainly Caucasian, and there's a lack of diversity that way, but [it] has improved recently." Students report a good mix of preppy and casual clothing on campus, and were happy to note that fashion at KU is "pretty much up to you—you don't have to dress up for class if you don't want to."

> **"The professors are great and really know their stuff."**

One student observed that the dressing style often develops as the day progresses, noting that "at 7 a.m. most people look like they've just rolled out of bed and are wearing jeans and pullovers, but by noon people start looking cute and preppy."

On or Off?
Students generally were satisfied and found dorms at KU ranging from "comfortable-sized" to "very nice." One student raved about the "great" facilities in the three newly renovated dorms, but described the older dorms as "basically just a 12' by 12' cubicle which two people share, unless you request a single, in which case you get the 12' by 12' cubicle to yourself." There are single-sex dorms on campus, though most of the housing is coed. However, it is important to note that at KU mainly freshmen and sophomores stay in the dorms, with most juniors and seniors opting to live off campus in apartments or houses for lease. Options for off-campus housing are plentiful with cheap rents and close proximity to campus, making it an attractive prospect for upperclassmen looking to escape the cubicles and save some money. Dining hall food is generally praised by students for its good quality; they report that there is a decent range of options, including salad bars, dessert bars and grill food. One

student said that the food was relatively reliable because "the pizzas and hamburgers are pretty decent" and agreed that "you can always find something to eat." Another student, however, complained that while food quality was satisfactory, "it can be repetitive when they keep hashing the same thing." Students were happy to report that menus are posted on the Internet, making it easy to check the day's selections before setting foot in a dining hall. Most upperclassmen eat off campus, and for those students and hungry underclassmen as well, Kansas City is a popular destination "if you want to get really good food."

Picture Perfect

Students raved about the "gorgeous" campus, with its picturesque landscaping full of "trees, flowers and hilly contours." The presence of "big red roofs, beautiful stone architecture, old buildings and bustling people" completes the idyllic scene and one student happily noted "it feels like you're in a huge park." The scenery comes at a price, though, and one student felt that the hilly landscape was a problem because it makes you develop "huge calves from walking up the hill." Because of the somewhat exhausting terrain, students generally take the bus to campus and are very happy with the efficiency of the transportation system. A female student mentioned that although "security on campus has improved recently with better lighting," she still does not feel comfortable walking alone at night and argued that improvements still were needed.

Jayhawk Rock

KU students are extremely active, as seen through the popularity of varsity sports and the prevalence of extracurricular activities. Students take great pride in their athletics. The school's basketball team is particularly strong, and basketball games are described as "always very packed—sometimes so packed that you can't get in." But while old-time favorites such as basketball and football pack the bleachers, intramural sports, community service, the law society and the medical society were also noted as being popular. Students are happy to note that the intramurals are now free, whereas in the past a small fee was charged in order to participate. At KU, new groups and activities are formed every day; as one student commented, "This semester there are at least four or five new clubs that I've personally seen start up."

Given the strong school spirit, the active social life, and vibrant extracurriculars, the University of Kansas is definitely an exciting place to be. Add to that the gorgeous campus, strong academics, and warm and friendly people and this school is guaranteed to provide an enjoyable college experience. —*Wenshan Yeo*

FYI
If you come to the University of Kansas, you'd better bring "an open mind, because you'll meet all kinds of people here."
What's the typical weekend schedule? "Party on Friday and Saturday nights; procrastinate and do homework on Sunday."
If I could change one thing about the University of Kansas, I would "make it less hilly."
Three things every student at the University of Kansas should do before graduating are "go to a basketball game, walk through the Campanile when graduating, and enjoy a leisurely walk around the gorgeous campus."

Kentucky

Centre College

Address: 600 West Walnut Street Danville, KY, 40422
Phone: 859-238-5350
E-mail address: admission@centre.edu
Web site URL: www.centre.edu
Year Founded: 1819
Private or Public: Private
Religious Affiliation: Presbyterian
Location: Rural
Number of Applicants: 2,176
Percent Accepted: 63%
Percent Accepted who enroll: 25%
Number Entering: 345
Number of Transfers Accepted each Year: 25
Middle 50% SAT range: M: 570–670, CR: 560–700, Wr: 550–680
Middle 50% ACT range: 26–30
Early admission program EA/ED/None: EA

Percentage accepted through EA or ED: 40%
EA and ED deadline: 1-Dec
Regular Deadline: 1-Feb
Application Fee: $40
Full time Undergraduate enrollment: 1,196
Total enrollment: 1,200
Percent Male: 45%
Percent Female: 55%
Total Percent Minority or Unreported: 9%
Percent African-American: 3%
Percent Asian/Pacific Islander: 2%
Percent Hispanic: 2%
Percent Native-American: 1%
Percent International: Unreported
Percent in-state/out of state: 60%/40%
Percent from Public HS: 70%
Retention Rate: 94%
Graduation Rate 4-year: 84%

Graduation Rate 6-year: Unreported
Percent Undergraduates in On-campus housing: 98%
Number of official organized extracurricular organizations: Unreported
3 Most popular majors: Social Sciences, English, Biology
Student/Faculty ratio: 11:1
Average Class Size: 18
Percent of students going to grad school: 40%
Tuition and Fees: $29,600
In State Tuition and Fees if different: No difference
Cost for Room and Board: $7,400
Percent receiving financial aid out of those who apply, first year: 60%
Percent receiving financial aid among all students: 60%

Nested in the middle of Danville, a small town of about 15,500, Centre College provides its 1,215 students with a unique education that includes going to the ballet or to see a musical for credit, a guaranteed internship and semester abroad, and over 200 years of history

Centre Commitment

Centre promises every student that he or she will graduate in four years, receive an internship, and study abroad for a semester or Centre will pay for one additional year's tuition. This promise is known as the Centre Commitment. And thanks to its small size, Centre can afford to make such promises.

All students must fulfill a General Education requirement, which includes a broad distribution of classes outside one's major, including a foreign language requirement, two health (and human performance) classes, and convocation credit. Convocations are events that "help a student become cultured." Such events range from the Nutcracker ballet, to a Martin Luther King, Jr. celebration. "Where else can I get credit for *The Nutcracker, Menopause the Musical,* and a lecture on crime in America?" boasted one student. Every year, about 40 (a minimum of 30) events are designated convocation credits, and students who attend 12 in an academic year receive one course hour of an A on their transcript. As for unusual academic classes, Stephen Rolfe Powell, a famous glass artist offers glass blowing classes that are very popular with students. Despite the enormous variety of unconventional courses, the top three most popular majors at Centre are anything but unexpected: English, history and government.

Classes generally range from 10 to 15 in size (average of 18), but the largest classes don't exceed 30 students. Competition for courses is virtually nonexistent, and for smaller classes that cap at 20, professors tend to be flexible. Although "grading is pretty hard," students agree that "it varies a lot from professor to professor." Luckily, most students receive a considerable amount of individual attention from their professors. "I routinely talk to my professors outside of class. For example, one professor and I argue about college football all the time," one student said. "Professors at Centre are wonderful. Professors are more than willing to meet up with students outside of class, and are concerned for students' academic and non-academic well-being. Where else will the college president know every student by their first name?"

At Centre, not only is fulfilling your General Education requirements a breeze, but fulfilling major requirements is so easy (not to say that the classes are), that many students can fit in a double major, as well as study abroad. Centre works on a 4-1-4 semester schedule, so that students have three weeks in the month of January, known as CentreTerm, to go abroad or take unusual classes outside of their major like the course Basketball as Religion. Popular CentreTerm classes abroad include studying volcanoes in New Zealand, primates in Barbados and history in Vietnam. About 85 percent of the student population studies abroad, and most study abroad programs are Centre college programs.

On Campus Life (Like It Or Not)
Unlike many other colleges, most of Centre's students live on campus—a whopping 93 percent. Freshmen all live together in single-sex dorms, but recently a housing squeeze allowed for one of the freshman dorms to be coed, although it is still gender-segregated by floor. Centre is embarking on building a new, larger dorm for freshmen that should be ready in 2009 that will feature suite housing, as opposed to current doubles-only system.

Except for the Independent Thought theme house, almost all dorms are single-sex. Not only is housing segregated by gender, but students at Centre also have a three week (previously six weeks) rule where students cannot be found in any of the opposite genders dorms for the first three weeks of school, and even after the three weeks, there are curfews for visitors of the opposite sex. Housing of-

fered to students varies. Centre owns dorms, as well as houses that it breaks down into apartments for rent, a popular option with upperclassmen who "want a kitchenette but still the convenience of campus housing." The upperclassmen women's dorm, Breckenridge, is supposedly haunted by dead confederate soldiers from when the dorm was used as a military hospital during the Civil War.

There are three on-campus facilities in which to eat: the Dining Commons, the Warehouse (a grill), and Jazzman's (a café). Because there is only one Dining Commons, students can generally see most of the student population at a meal. Meal plans involve different combinations of "flex dollars" and meals at the Dining Commons, as both the Warehouse and Jazzman's are à la carte. Popular places to eat off campus include Guadalajara's, Freddie's and Burke's Bakery, though most places tend to be fast food joints, national like McDonald's, or local, like the "fantastic" Mexican taco stand called La Hacienda.

Polishing Up The Greek Alphabet
Greek Row is a popular place to be. Almost all parties are thrown by the fraternities and sororities. That's not to say that they are exclusive or anything. "Everyone is welcome to any frat party, and indeed, everyone shows up, Greek or not." Some of the big annual parties include the Rave Party thrown by Phi Delta Theta, and Phi Kappa Tau's Air Guitar talent show. There a few non-Greek parties like Holiday Ball and the Beach Ball, but most parties, especially the big ones, reside in the fraternity houses. The big non-Greek event thrown every year is the Carnival, a week full of games and fun sponsored by the Student Activities Council.

Fraternities and sororities are different at Centre. More than half of the student body is in a fraternity or a sorority, but since the Greek houses can only fit about ten students, most members live on campus. Fraternities at Centre tend not to be the stereotypical party-hearty fraternities, though most frats are "jock heavy." The frats do very little hazing, but any hazing by a sorority member merits being kicked out of the sorority. "I would never have joined a sorority if I hadn't come to Centre," one student said. "It's just a different atmosphere here."

Most frat parties have a BYOB (bring your own beer) policy, since alcohol cannot be bought in Danville county at night. Students have to go on a beer run to the next county over, about a 30-minute trip by car. While alcohol and pot are prevalent on campus, there is no pressure to drink, and many choose not to. In fact, many events are required to be dry, like the Holiday Ball. Sororities also have rules against upperclassmen women giving alcohol to freshmen, which is a severe recruiting infraction.

There are many alternatives to the Greek party scene, such as the free Midnight Movies (on campus or off) that the Student Activities Committee offers, or the many musical performances that Centre brings. Pop culture artists tend not to count for Convocation credit, but national tour groups often stop in Centre to perform in the Norton Center for Arts or the theater in the newly built Crounse Hall. Participation in community service activities has increased over the past few years, and organizations like the Bonner program give students a chance to give back to the community. Other organized service activities include the likes of the Freshmen Plunge, a day of service for freshmen to get involved with the community.

The Division III soccer games are popular, as are most of the homecoming football and basketball games. "Because we are in Kentucky, and half of the people are from in state, football is a big thing." Everyone at Centre talks about the "formula for football success, "C6H0," referring to the time when Centre College beat Harvard 6-0 in 1921. That year, not only did Centre upset Harvard's then-undefeated team, but Harvard had also won the NCAA Division I championship the year before. Intramurals, on the other hand, are not quite as big of a deal, although Sutcliffe Hall, which boasts newer and bigger athletic facilities, is influencing IM participation.

Gender relations at Centre are an interesting phenomenon. As one student mused, "Sociologists have done studies on why the two different genders don't interact well here outside of parties. In the dining commons, a guy and a girl sitting with each other is a subject for gossip." That's not to say that intermingling of the different genders is not improving. The move from a six week preliminary period before coed genders can mix to a three week preliminary period, heralds change in the school policy. "Hopefully all dorms will be coed, at least by floor, with one half male and the other half female, like the freshman dorm this year," one sophomore said. Some students believe that the cause for the awkward tension between male and female undergrads is simply because most students are too busy studying to have

time to casually date, and therefore gender relations are already somewhat strained.

Centre and Danville: Too Close for Comfort?

Danville is a very quaint "Norman Rockwell" town in southern Kentucky. "While there will be a few rednecks who may stare at you, everyone is actually very friendly and helpful." The Centre bookstore is in town, but most students don't leave the "Centre bubble" for Danville, unless it's to eat.

Students complain that there isn't really too much to do in Danville and are generally pretty happy that a lot happens on campus. When students want to get away, most pile into a car and drive to Louisville or Lexington. Even though Danville is such a small town, most students need a car to get around off campus, whether it's to go to Lexington or to go on a beer run.

Danville isn't the only small thing about Louisville. "At Centre, everyone knows everyone's business, but you will also meet everyone and get to know them like your neighbor." Most people meet their close friends in class and extracurricular activities, but feel as though they know "most of the people" on campus pretty well.

Traditions, Histories, and . . . Streakers

With over 200 years of history, Centre College has built up a treasure chest of stories to share. In addition to the haunting of Breckenridge and "C6H0," Centre is truly rich in myths and legends.

"We are the Harvard of the South."

Take another interesting tradition involving former Supreme Court Chief Justice Fred Vinson, who was born in Louisa, Kentucky. A brother of Phi Delta Theta at Centre, he kept close ties with Centre after he graduated, including attending as many home games as he could. After his death in 1953, the brothers of Phi Delta decided that there was no reason that he should miss the games that he had so loved to attend. The Phi Delta brothers bring a portrait of him to almost every home sporting event, affectionately referring to the portrait as "Dead Fred." When Centre hosted the vice-presidential debates of 2000, "Dead Fred" was the first to be seated.

As for romantic tales, myth has it that if students kiss on the brass college seal at midnight in front of Old Campus, the oldest building on campus, they will end up marrying each other. With the alumni magazine reporting that two out of three Centre students end up marrying another Centre alum, it seems that there might be some truth to the myth. "My RA's boyfriend proposed to her right after kissing her on the seal [at midnight]," one student noted.

The other really popular tradition involves *The Flame*, a sculpture donated by an alumnus meaning for it to represent the lamp of knowledge on Centre's seal. For current students, "running the flame" has become a mythical tradition. To participate, students start out from a stairwell near Crounse Hall, strip down naked, run to and around the flame, and run back to where they started

from, all while avoiding being fined $100. This late night tradition can be witnessed every once in a while, especially during the rush season for fraternities, and after sports victories.

While the percentage of minorities at Centre falls less than 10 percent (4% Asian/Pacific Islander, 4% Black/Non-Hispanic and 2% Hispanic), about half of the student population is from out of state, and Centre draws for a diverse socioeconomic pool. Centre's great academics (as one student noted "We are the Harvard of the South"), its commitment to its students through both the Centre commitment and its professors, as well as its two centuries worth of history and tradition make Centre college an appealing choice for many students.—*Jesse Dong*

FYI

If you come to Centre, you'd better bring "a car and directions to Lexington and Louisville."
What is the typical weekend schedule? "Go out for Friday dinner, then go see a musical performance or play, then go to a Greek party. Saturday, sleep in, work during the afternoon, meetup with friends for dinner, go out again and probably end up at a Greek party. Sunday sleep in till brunch where you see everyone on campus, attend an athletic function, then lock yourself in the library."
If I could change one thing about Centre, I'd "improve the gender relations."
Three things every student at Centre should do before graduating are "run the flame, make a night beer run, and hang out with a professor outside of class."

University of Kentucky

Address: 100 Funkhouser Building, Lexington, KY 40506
Phone: 859-257-2000
E-mail address: admisso@uky.edu
Web site URL: www.uky.edu
Year Founded: 1865
Private or Public: Public
Religious Affiliation: None
Location: Urban
Number of Applicants: 10,024
Percent Accepted: 81%
Percent Accepted who enroll: 51%
Number Entering: 4,118
Number of Transfers Accepted each Year: Unreported
Middle 50% SAT range: M: 500–630, CR: 490–610, Wr: 470–590
Middle 50% ACT range: 21–26
Early admission program EA/ED/None: None

Percentage accepted through EA or ED: NA
EA and ED deadline: NA
Regular Deadline: 15-Feb
Application Fee: $40
Full time Undergraduate enrollment: 18,770
Total enrollment: 24,324
Percent Male: 49%
Percent Female: 51%
Total Percent Minority or Unreported: 12%
Percent African-American: 5%
Percent Asian/Pacific Islander: 2%
Percent Hispanic: 1%
Percent Native-American: 0%
Percent International: 1%
Percent in-state/out of state: 83%/17%
Percent from Public HS: Unreported
Retention Rate: 78%
Graduation Rate 4-year: 29%

Graduation Rate 6-year: 57%
Percent Undergraduates in On-campus housing: 22%
Number of official organized extracurricular organizations: 348
3 Most popular majors: Business/Marketing, Communications/Journalism, Social Sciences
Student/Faculty ratio: 17:1
Average Class Size: 20 to 29
Percent of students going to grad school: Unreported
Tuition and Fees: $15,884
In State Tuition and Fees if different: $7,736
Cost for Room and Board: $5,887
Percent receiving financial aid out of those who apply, first year: Unreported
Percent receiving financial aid among all students: Unreported

If Wildcat basketball comes to mind when you think of the University of Kentucky, you're on the right track. The thousands of students that call this campus home all come together in support of their famed team. But the excitement doesn't end there; many students at UK find themselves satisfied with the academics, busy with all the opportunities and ecstatic with school spirit.

Kentucky Academia

When students apply to UK, they apply to one of the University's 16 colleges, which include Agriculture, Engineering, Architecture, Arts and Sciences, Business and Economics, Communications, and five Medical colleges. No matter which college students attend, however, all must complete a core curriculum, called the "General Studies Program." Before graduation, students take courses in speaking, cross-cultural studies, humanities, and the social sciences. Additional math, English, and science class requirements depend on the individual college.

On the whole, students find that they "aren't that inspired" by core classes, as the classes are easy to let slide. But once students latch onto the department of their major, the academics are described as "pretty good." The science-oriented classes are cited as the most difficult, along with classes in the College of Architecture, where students can be working on projects "from 2 a.m. to 2 p.m., four days a week." Pharmacy and nursing are very popular areas of study, and the campus is "surrounded by hospitals, which makes for a lot of opportunities."

> **"Though lots come to party, those who do work find UK equally good in the humanities and the sciences."**

People choose to study many different things at UK, but most agree that "though lots come to party, those who do work find UK equally good in the humanities and the sciences." Many students receive scholarships or financial aid from the University. A good number of students also apply for the Honors Program. Once accepted into the program, students take one Honors course each semester, with the course usually focused on the humanities. All undergrads at UK have an adviser from their college and an adviser in their major, and Honors students have an additional adviser from the program.

For all students, registering for classes can be an ordeal. Though Honors students get to register first, almost everyone finds that it can be hard to get into classes. Introductory classes are often very large; one freshman commented that UK "accepts every AP credit (with a score 3 or above) to get people out of 100-level classes . . . you're lucky if you get a chair." Labs and sections for these huge classes are taught by TAs—many of whom don't speak English well.

Despite some language barriers, many students say that they are very happy with the teachers they have had. Most adopt the ritual of asking around to find out who the best professors for each class are, and are usually not disappointed. One freshman claimed: "I've been really pleased with the faculty. They have a strong background and are interested in getting the students to do their best." Many professors encourage students to come to their office hours, and this personal attention—especially noticed in the smaller-sized Agricultural College—makes UK students feel "less like a number."

Bring Out the Bourbon

Outside of academics, most Wildcats lead a very active social life. The most dominating social force is the Greek system, which provides the central scene for partying at UK. Though the fraternities and sororities are officially dry, per the school's no-alcohol policy, students often rent off-campus spaces to take their festivities outside of regulated grounds. More drinking seems to go on at UK than hard drugs; after all, "Kentucky grows tobacco and makes bourbon." Students frequent drive-thru liquor stores, and upperclassmen often go to clubs or bars.

Students say that "there're definitely the sorority-girl and fraternity-boy stereotypes" at UK. Most of the undergrads are white and middle-class, and many of the girls frequent tanning beds. A freshman noted that "there's not as much diversity as I expected," especially in reference to ethnic minorities and gays.

However, although "it can feel a little cliquey," those who aren't into the Greek scene find other ways to enjoy themselves. Sometimes "a lot of people who don't drink go home on the weekends," but often friends watch movies and go to coffeehouses, such as Starbucks, Common Grounds and Coffee Time. In addition, the University often puts on campus events such as concerts, street parties and pep rallies. The popular pep rallies are also sponsored by the student government, which puts on a Halloween party every year, as well.

On the dating front, people tend to lean towards hook-ups, but dating and steady relationships also exist. There are not many interracial or gay couples; one student said that she "doesn't see much of it" and "doesn't hear much about it."

How the Wildcats Live

The University of Kentucky is located in Lexington, where its red-brick buildings stand in green lawns full of trees. The campus is divided into three sections: North Campus, home to six dorms; Central Campus, with classroom buildings, the new library, and two dormitories; and South Campus, which has low-rise dormitory towers. Students select which dorms they want to live in on a first-come, first-serve basis. Patterson and Boyd Halls (the Honors dorms) are located on North Campus, as is Jewell Hall (the international dorm), and Blazer and Holmes Halls (all-female, all-male dorms, respectively). Also on North Campus is the Wildcat Lodge, the unofficial dorm for the basketball players, who are "treated like royalty."

On Central Campus is the "gorgeous and fairly easy to navigate" William T. Young Library. Nearby are the all-male Haggin Hall and the all-female Donovan Hall (said to be the hardest dorm to get into, because of the nice rooms). South Campus has Kirwan and Blanding Towers, along with several low-rises. The $5 million athletic complex, called the Johnson Center, is also located on South Campus. While this facility is greatly enjoyed by most, some students wish the money had been spent on "getting more teachers and more parking."

When not sleeping, partying, working out or studying, there's a good chance that students are eating. There are three dining halls around campus, one in each campus section. Blazer Hall is on North Campus, the Student Center serves meals on Central Campus, and The Commons caters to South Campus. The library also has a highly praised café called Ovid's. Though vegetarians complain about not having many options, students can charge their meal account at on-campus eateries, such as Starbucks. Also popular are fast-food restaurants like McDonald's and KFC; but for a change, there's Joe Bologna's (a small Italian restaurant) and nearby restaurants like the Macaroni Grill. Tolley-Ho, however, is the most popular off-campus restaurant. UK students have been eating and hanging out there for years, making it a real campus tradition.

We Come Together

But the biggest tradition at the University of Kentucky revolves around extracurriculars. Besides the fraternities and sororities—some of which do community outreach—students get involved in campus ministries, student boards, intramurals, the *Kentucky Kernel* (the daily newspaper), and organizations like the Green Thumb Club. As one student said, "Anything that you want to be involved in they have, or they encourage you to start yourself."

But nothing can compare to something that began a long while ago—the UK Wildcats basketball team. The men's team plays in the Rupp Arena, which now has a student section appropriately called "The Eruption Zone." Erupting is exactly what students do when they get together for a game: The "crowd is crazy" and enthusiasm skyrockets. Fireworks are set off before every home game, and afterwards the cheerleaders and band always play and sing "My Old Kentucky Home."

No matter which UK college students are in, or what their different interests are, almost everyone comes out to support their team. Students cite this common spirit that "brings so many students and groups together" as the force that really makes their university unique. With everyone cheering their Wildcats on, it makes UK, a large research university full of opportunities, "seem so much smaller."—*Elizabeth Dohrmann*

FYI

If you come to the University of Kentucky, you'd better bring "a valid ID and something blue."

What is the typical weekend schedule? "Friday: The bar of your choice with a late-night food stop at Tolly-Ho. Saturday: Football/Soccer/Basketball/Baseball game with tailgating before and hopefully a celebration afterwards. Sunday: sleep followed by cramming. Excellent Exceptions: All weekend activities in April and October revolve around tailgating and betting on horse races at the beautiful Keeneland Race Course."

If I could change one thing about UK, I'd "make the campus wet again."

Three things every UK student should do before graduating are "make an early rise and go to the Saturday morning brunch and practice runs at Keeneland in April (starts at 7:00 a.m.), sit lower level for a CATS game at Rupp Arena, and read *The Bluegrass Conspiracy* (it makes you look at all of your surroundings in a totally different light)."

Louisiana

Louisiana State University

Address: 1146 Pleasant Hall
Baton Rouge, LA 70803
Phone: 225-578-1175
E-mail address:
admissions@lsu.edu
Web site URL: www.lsu.edu
Year Founded: 1860
Private or Public: Public
Religious Affiliation: None
Location: Urban
Number of Applicants:
15,093
Percent Accepted: 73%
**Percent Accepted who
enroll:** 46%
Number Entering: 5,135
**Number of Transfers
Accepted each Year:**
1,205
Middle 50% SAT range:
M: 550–650, CR: 520–630,
Wr: 490–600
Middle 50% ACT range:
23–28
**Early admission program
EA/ED/None:** None

**Percentage accepted
through EA or ED:** Not
applicable
EA and ED deadline: Not
applicable
Regular Deadline: 15-Aprl
Application Fee: $40
**Full time Undergraduate
enrollment:** 23,396
Total enrollment: 27,824
Percent Male: 49%
Percent Female: 51%
**Total Percent Minority or
Unreported:** 21%
Percent African-American:
9%
**Percent Asian/Pacific
Islander:** 3%
Percent Hispanic: 3%
Percent Native-American:
<1%
Percent International: 1%
**Percent in-state/out of
state:** 85%/15%
Percent from Public HS: 57%
Retention Rate: 85%

Graduation Rate 4-year:
27%
Graduation Rate 6-year:
59%
**Percent Undergraduates in
On-campus housing:** 25%
**Number of official organized
extracurricular
organizations:** 300
3 Most popular majors:
Biology, Psychology
Student/Faculty ratio: 21:1
Average Class Size: 20 to 29
**Percent of students going to
grad school:** Unreported
Tuition and Fees: $13,800
**In State Tuition and Fees if
different:** $5,086
Cost for Room and Board:
$7,238
**Percent receiving financial
aid out of those who apply,
first year:** 57%
**Percent receiving financial
aid among all students:**
76%

I
t's a sunny Saturday afternoon, and the
crowd at Louisiana State's Tiger Stadium
is going wild in a sea of purple and gold.
During football season, Baton Rouge, La.,
turns into Football Town, USA. As one senior
raved, "It gets pretty rambunctious at the
games, but that's life. You plan your week
around who we play in the game. Saturday at
Tiger Stadium, it's not a date . . . it's an event!"

It Never Rains in Death Valley

The fans bleed purple and gold in Baton
Rouge. The school's unofficial color seems
to be orange, though—the color of Mike the
Tiger, LSU's beloved mascot. Fans often try
to get the tiger to roar before games for good
luck; one such student admitted, "The other
day I was walking by his cage and I heard a

huge roar. I thought to myself, 'It's going to
be a good day!' "

Tigers go crazy for the pigskin at LSU.
"Students come from out of state, specifically Texas, to attend the LSU football
games. Football's a huge deal," said one
sophomore. Everyone parks cars and trucks
around campus the Friday night before the
Saturday game. The fun begins with catered
tailgates where students and visitors alike
consume vast quantities of alcohol around
the barbecue. Out-of-state fans often arrive
in their purple-and-gold painted RVs on
Thursday night, completely filling the two
huge commuter parking lots by the stadium.
These tailgates are elaborate affairs; one
year, someone even towed along a swimming pool to the parking lot to splash

around in before the game. Tiger Stadium has been nicknamed "Death Valley," where the mantra is that it never rains. Mere drizzles, however, could never keep these fans from the stands.

Students sit in a section called the N-Zone. The demand for tickets in the Zone is so high that students often squish in, standing room only. As one girl said, "If you don't live on-campus, you'd better get there by seven in the morning on Saturday if you want any chance of getting in." To say the least, "school spirit is definitely a big deal here." Fans also come to cheer the marching band, called Golden Band from Tiger Land, as well as the popular Golden Girls dancers who lead cheers from the sidelines. The fans have many traditions; for instance, students claim they cheer "Geaux Tigers!" instead of "Go Tigers," as a nod to the area's Cajun-French culture. One junior explained, "It's a Southern thing!" Football games are more than just fun sporting events at LSU; they also serve as a bonding experience for the students. Cheering Tigers often wear T-shirts that read, "Saturday night in Tiger Stadium is the best time spent with 92,600 of your closest friends." Many students claim, "We're like a family. It's so big here so you can't say you know everyone, but we're a football school. So that's our common ground."

Life Beyond the Stadium

Of course, not all students at LSU consider football games the highlight of their college experience. As one sophomore said with a laugh, "LSU wastes all its money on sports." Luckily for others like her, there's a wide variety of activities both on campus and in the Baton Rouge area. Greek life is a huge social force at LSU. According to one senior, over 900 girls rush sororities each year. This student commented, "Greek life is a big deal here. There are always exchanges, socials, intermixing of fraternities and sororities, as well as different bar nights and themed parties where you can bring a date."

For those who don't want to join the Greek scene, there is still plenty to do. Many musical artists, such as Pat Green, give concerts on campus, and the Pete Maravich Assembly Center hosts a variety of theatrical performances and lectures. Students are also regulars at nearby movie theaters and can choose from over 625 restaurants of Baton Rouge. The bar scene is another popular social option at LSU. There are at least 30 bars and clubs, though freshmen seem particularly fond of Tigerland, a strip of six bars

where you only have to be 18 to enter, though you still must be 21 to drink. A "Drunk Bus" shuttles back and forth between Tigerland and campus every 15 minutes to pick up inebriated students and drop them off at their dorms. Other services like the campus transit also help to lower the rate of drunk driving, which until a few years ago was a big problem, since mostly everyone on campus owns a car.

Alcohol is not hard to find on campus either. Students report that the administration is generally relaxed about enforcing alcohol policies. On-campus parties where alcohol will be served do have to be approved, though. If the watchful eye of campus security catches alcohol at a party that hasn't been preapproved, the party hosts can get into a lot of trouble. Though alcohol is prevalent at LSU, many sober students "like to go out even though [they] don't drink and have no problems going to parties where alcohol is being served." Other students, however, go "wild because there's so much freedom. I wouldn't call it peer pressure, more like trying out a new lifestyle, doing things you've never done before. At home you were sheltered, but here you are responsible for yourself."

A Breeding Ground for Scholars?

While some hard-working students maintain that LSU is not as much a party school as it is reputed to be, others say that academics are not their first priority. Most undergraduates enter LSU with a major already declared. Those who aren't sure what they want to do stay in a general studies program for a year or two until they make up their minds. Switching majors can be a pain, as most credits don't transfer between programs. Dealing with registration can also be a draining and frustrating experience. One sophomore suggested that "it helps if you know your major, since getting into classes becomes a lot easier." Students agree that the science classes, particularly biology, are among LSU's toughest courses. As one freshman put it, "The biology courses weed out a lot of people." Library science is well-known as the easiest class LSU offers, and it is considered a "one-hour easy A." Class size varies greatly depending on the subject. Many English classes have only 15 to 30 students, while some popular biology and music lectures have to be held in the gym to accommodate the over 1,000 students that enroll in them. The average lecture class size hovers around 150 students, however.

LSU professors and TAs are generally responsive to student needs. They are good about returning student e-mails and setting up appointments. One senior was impressed that when he ran into one of his professors at the grocery store, she not only greeted him by name, but even had a conversation with him. LSU also offers a variety of free tutoring services. A center for freshmen is also available for academic counseling and for setting students up with the appropriate upperclassmen tutors. One student was particularly fond of the writing center, where students can get all their papers proofread. A common academic complaint, however, is that many of the foreign professors are extremely difficult to understand—so difficult, in fact, that many students drop classes because they simply cannot understand the professors. Generally the workload is decent, though the most diligent students report studying 20–30 hours weekly. Undergraduates who want to graduate within four years have to take at least 15 credit hours per semester. Often students will take lighter schedules than this, and stick around for summer school to make up the extra credits.

Beautiful Creatures in Their Natural Habitat

When one sophomore girl was asked if she thought that LSU students were on the whole an attractive bunch, she exclaimed, "My freshman year I didn't see any cute people at all, but this year I see all kinds of hot people!" A similar response came from an upperclassman, who said, "The girls are way hotter here. . . . There's a tremendous amount of gorgeous girls and a lot of guys lacking style." Needless to say, random hookups are not rare phenomena. However, the administration "strongly frowns upon shackin' up," so guys are required to sign in and out of the girls' dorms.

The students are beautiful, and "the campus is gorgeous," as well. The school invests a lot of resources to remodel buildings and to maintain the grounds. All the dorm rooms are air-conditioned, though the freshman rooms are "like closets with beds" and dorm life often involves sharing a bathroom with an entire floor of people. Many people move into off-campus apartments by sophomore year, though most agree that LSU students should try dorm life for at least one year. About 700 people live in each dorm, Herget being one of the most sought-after of the coed freshman dorms and Kirby-Smith being one of the least desirable.

While classes are never more than a mile apart, most students opt to drive to class. The abundance of cars on campus can present a problem where parking is involved. As one frustrated sophomore confided, "There are never any parking spaces! Then the ticket people get ticket-happy and we get random parking tickets." LSU offers a great bus system that transports students from their dorms and off-campus apartments right to lecture halls, though few students actually use this service.

> "We're like a family. It's so big here so you can't say you know everyone, but we're a football school. So that's our common ground."

Despite the annoyance of parking problems, LSU students love Baton Rouge and their school. They particularly enjoy the fun atmosphere and the warm and friendly people. Most students agree that "everyone's really nice" and that "LSU is not a superficial campus." However, there seems to be conflicting views regarding diversity on campus. While one senior mentioned that "LSU is not a very diverse campus right now, the majority of students being Caucasian, and the faculty being also mostly white," several others maintained that LSU is a very diverse place where there are many international students and an impressive mix of black and white students.

LSU offers a bit of something for everyone. Regardless of whether you're looking for a place to party hardy, to attend the finest football games on this side of the bayou, or to enjoy the benefits of a large university with friendly professors, LSU is definitely worth checking out. By the time you leave, you too will be bleeding purple and gold.
—*Jenny Zhang*

FYI
If you come to LSU, you'd better bring "a party cup" and "a pair of walking shoes."
What is the typical weekend schedule? "Go out until the wee hours, go to the football game, and recuperate on Sunday from the strenuous weekend."
If I could change one thing about LSU, I'd "have smaller classes."
Three things every student at LSU should do before graduating are "attend a football game, roll down Indian Mound, and go to a foam party."

Tulane University

Address: 6823 St. Charles Avenue, New Orleans, LA 70118
Phone: 504-865-5731
E-mail address: undergrad.admission@tulane.edu
Web site URL: www.tulane.edu
Year Founded: 1834
Private or Public: Private
Religious Affiliation: None
Location: Urban
Number of Applicants: 34,125
Percent Accepted: 27%
Percent Accepted who enroll: 17%
Number Entering: 1,560
Number of Transfers Accepted each Year: 425
Middle 50% SAT range: M: 620–700, CR: 630–720, Wr: 640–720
Middle 50% ACT range: 29–32
Early admission program EA/ED/None: EA

Percentage accepted through EA or ED: Unreported
EA and ED deadline: 1-Nov
Regular Deadline: 15-Jan
Application Fee: $0
Full time Undergraduate enrollment: 6,749
Total enrollment: 9,328
Percent Male: 46%
Percent Female: 54%
Total Percent Minority or Unreported: 42%
Percent African-American: 7%
Percent Asian/Pacific Islander: 4%
Percent Hispanic: 4%
Percent Native-American: 1.3%
Percent International: 3%
Percent in-state/out of state: 16%/84%
Percent from Public HS: Unreported
Retention Rate: 87%
Graduation Rate 4-year: Unreported

Graduation Rate 6-year: Unreported
Percent Undergraduates in On-campus housing: 51%
Number of official organized extracurricular organizations: 250
3 Most popular majors: Business, Health Services, Psychology
Student/Faculty ratio: Unreported
Average Class Size: 10 to 19
Percent of students going to grad school: Unreported
Tuition and Fees: $38,664
In State Tuition and Fees if different: No difference
Cost for Room and Board: $9,296
Percent receiving financial aid out of those who apply, first year: 73%
Percent receiving financial aid among all students: Unreported

G oing to jazz concerts, eating authentic Southern foods, experiencing Mardi Gras—all typical occurrences in the life of a Tulane student. Located in New Orleans, Louisiana, Tulane University is the home of the Green Waves. There are 6,449 undergraduates from all 50 states and over 35 different countries, making Tulane "one of the most diverse schools in the South," according to a current student.

Intimate Intellectualism

Students describe the academic life at Tulane as challenging and rewarding. The workload is on the heavier side and, as one Tulane junior stated, "It's a pretty big course load, but it trains you to be an adult and to learn to balance leisure and scholarship." Class sizes are relatively small, with an average of 22 students in each class, but this does not mean it is difficult to get into the courses you want to take. All students interviewed said they had never had a problem securing a spot in a class.

Business, Latin American studies, and political science are popular majors for Tulane students, with many students also choosing to identify themselves as pre-med in addition to their declared major. Tulane also offers an intensive architecture program in which students graduate in five years with a masters degree.

If you plan on pursuing Latin American or Caribbean studies, Tulane has one of the premier departments in the country. The Latin American Studies Department also gives students ample opportunity to go out into the community and experience Latin American culture. One freshman said she taught an ESL class to Spanish-speaking residents of New Orleans in conjunction with her LAS class.

Students are generally emphatic about how easy it is to speak with professors and other faculty members at Tulane. A Tulane senior said, "I can't even emphasize how easy it is to develop a relationship with our teachers. Every teacher I've had has known my name, and they are willing to go to great lengths to help you out in any way they can." There are no classes at Tulane taught exclusively by teaching assistants, which increases face-to-face interaction with the professors.

Mardi Gras Merriment

According to students, Tulane is not the place to go if you are looking for an overly competitive academic atmosphere. Students describe the environment as "not too intensive," though there is a considerable amount of work assigned. In other words, academics are important to Tulane students, but they do find time to relax and socialize.

The social scene at Tulane does not revolve around Greek life—most students say the partying goes on off campus, in the city of New Orleans. Weekends are generally eventful at Tulane, with the large majority of students staying on campus during the weekend. Students say they are never at a loss for things to do: "There are always new bars and clubs to explore," said a Tulane senior. Tuesdays and Thursdays are the most popular nights to go out, and The Boot, a local bar, is often the premier destination. The Boot's claim to fame is 50-cent-drink night on Tuesdays, with other specials throughout the week.

> "It's a pretty big course load, but it trains you to be an adult and to learn to balance leisure and scholarship."

Typically, classes do not meet on Monday and Fat Tuesday in February, so that students can enjoy Mardi Gras, a yearly festival featuring parades, food, and entertainment. The Tulane student council also sponsors a yearly Craw Fest, where local jazz bands perform on campus throughout the day. In 2007, over 14,000 lbs. of crawfish were consumed by the Tulane students who attended the event. Voodoo Fest is also held every year in New Orleans (though it is not affiliated with Tulane) and features popular rock, pop, and hip-hop acts.

Alcohol and drug policies on campus are strictly enforced, and the places and circumstances under which alcohol can be consumed on campus are very limited. Counselors closely monitor freshmen dorms to ensure that students are not violating Tulane's strict 21-and-over alcohol policy, but regardless of the grade level students interviewed

said that the majority of their classmates drink. They also said they had never felt pressured to drink and the social environment was very friendly and inviting.

Still Going Strong

Tulane students insist that the effects of Hurricane Katrina are essentially nonexistent on campus. The school's location is elevated, so even in the immediate aftermath of the hurricane damage was limited. There was flooding on the ground floor of some buildings, but all of these have been redone. The only structure currently under construction from hurricane-related damage is the library, which sustained slight water damage in the basement. In terms of Katrina's effects on the area surrounding campus, students once again said that it is limited. Damage is especially minimal in areas like uptown, where students hang out on the weekends. "The visible damage is in the residential areas where you can see abandoned houses and stuff, but Tulane students don't normally go there," said one sophomore.

Tulane is geographically diverse, with 80 percent of students coming from homes 500 miles away or further, but according to students racial diversity is not as robust. One Tulane student said the school was "mostly white" and another said that "preppy" is a popular style on campus.

Many students on campus are employed part-time in addition to their studies. Some work on campus and are involved in work-study programs. The most common campus jobs are related to housing, such as working at the front desk or being a residential assistant. Other students have retail jobs and work in the shops on Magazine Street, a popular shopping area.

There are an endless number of housing options at Tulane, including same-sex dorms, honor student dorms, and the newly opened Wall residential college, in which students live with a university fellow. Students say there are a good number of people who live on campus all four years, but there is an abundance of reasonably priced off-campus housing available. Sharp and Monroe are considered the more social freshman dorms, mostly because "they have community bathrooms, which help you make friends," said one Tulane junior.

In terms of safety, Tulane students responded that they don't feel unsafe on campus, but that New Orleans is just like any other metropolitan area and has its dangers. A junior said, "You're in a city, so you have to use common sense, but the French Quarter and Bourbon Street are generally pretty safe." The campus is also equipped with a blue light system, which allow students to call Tulane police officers at emergency stations located all over campus.

But that is not to say relations between Tulane and the surrounding community are strained. On the contrary, a freshman student was surprised by how the city and the university were interconnected. "People in New Orleans like Tulane and they are incredibly welcoming to students," she said.

Sports are not a very high priority on campus, but Tulane's baseball team is nationally ranked, and Green Wave football games take place in the famed New Orleans Superdome. Tickets to most sporting events are free to students.—*Samantha Broussard-Wilson*

FYI

If you come to Tulane, you'd better bring "rain boots."

What's the typical weekend schedule? "Take a riverboat ride down the Mississippi and finish the day off with a snack at Café du Monde."

If I could change one thing about Tulane, I'd "make the meal plan more flexible."

Three things every Tulane student should do before graduating are "experience Mardi Gras, go to the French Quarter, and eat at Giacomo's Restaurant."

Maine

Bates College, a small liberal arts school generally grouped with other Maine colleges such as Bowdoin and Colby, is located in Lewiston, Maine, a town whose claim to fame, as one student pointed out, is that "Mohammed Ali fought here." However, this middle-of-nowhere school proudly boasts such a fun-loving, tight-knit college community that students overwhelmingly proclaim that they could not imagine themselves elsewhere.

More Professors than Students?

Students at Bates know they are getting a first-class education; national surveys consistently rank Bates among the top liberal arts colleges in the nation. Though small liberal arts colleges often do not have the re-

sources to offer the wide array of subject areas and depth of study that universities can provide, students at Bates almost universally cite the small class size as something that sets Bates apart from other colleges. A large number of classes have 19 students or less, and even larger lecture classes usually don't have many more than 75 students. The Bates Web site cites the student-to-professor ratio as 10 to 1 and stresses the college's focus on small group learning in settings such as seminars and laboratories. According to one freshman, "The great thing about Bates is that the classes are pretty small. You are not merely considered a number in the classroom, but instead you become an active participant whom the professor really gets to know." Professors are also easily approachable outside the classroom and are extremely receptive to student interest; another student commented, "In my experience, professors are very happy to talk outside of class about their research, any problems you may be having in the class, concerns, or just life in general. I've also realized that professors are happy to talk to students who aren't in their classes if they show an interest in the professor's field." Though a small college, Bates offers the diversity of a liberal arts education and does have distributional requirements, including a three-science-class requirement that "for nonscience people is just too much!"

> The great thing about Bates is that the classes are pretty small. You are not merely considered a number in the classroom, but instead you become an active participant whom the professor really gets to know.

Bates is a very good school, and in terms of workload there is "a LOT of reading." According to a freshman, "the work load can be intense when midterms and finals come around, but normally it is manageable if you learn how to organize your time." Despite the workload, students observe very little competition both in and out of the classroom.

Small School, Big Parties

Bates, located in tiny Lewiston, Maine, does not boast a thriving metropolis as one of its attractions. However, students don't seem to mind; there are enough parties, events and activities on campus to keep most students from having to leave at all. According to one student, "Because there's not a lot to do in Lewiston, people stay on campus and party in the dorms and houses." Students cite dorm parties, concerts, comedy shows, dances, and off-campus parties as just some of the wide array of activities offered within the confines of Bates. The small nature of the school is conducive to creating a cohesive community, and students are generally extremely happy with their on-campus social life; as one girl commented, "Students generally don't want to leave campus because there's too much going on and they don't want to miss it. I can't imagine missing a weekend here!"

There are no fraternities or sororities at Bates; however, this is generally considered an advantage rather than a disadvantage. One freshman commented, "There is no Greek life at Bates, which I think most of the students appreciate. The social scene is much more open because of the lack of a Greek system." The students make up for this with huge annual parties, such as the '80s dance, Halloween dance, and foam dance, which are "well-attended, and everyone goes all-out and gets really into them."

In terms of drinking, the school has a relatively strict hard-liquor policy; students are subject to a three-strike rule applying to hard liquor that lasts all four years. The three strike rule requires anyone seen in a room with hard liquor to be given a strike; students with three strikes must meet with the dean. However, this rule applies only to hard liquor and drugs; the school is much more lenient in regards to wine and beer. According to students, "A lot of students do drink, but it is definitely not something you need to do to have fun here, and I know a lot of people who go out each weekend and never drink." Bates also offers a wide array of extracurricular activities, unrelated to partying, that are enjoyed by many. Athletics are popular, and students can participate on the varsity, club, or intramural level. In addition, there are four competitive a cappella groups that are extremely popular. One student exclaimed, "The Deansmen and the Manic Optimists are all male groups, the Merimanders are all women, and the Crosstones are coed. They are all amazing! They have concerts every once in a while and they are always packed!"

For those few students who have cars and want to get off campus, Lewiston is located relatively close to Freeport, a shopping hub, and Portland, which boasts great restaurants, a bustling city life, and a wide array of ski slopes. However, the center of Bates is clearly the campus itself, and students see this is as one of Bates's major attractions. Another student commented, "Every once in a while people will drive out to dinner on the weekends, or those who have cars will drive to ski resorts, but most of the time students stay on campus." As campus parties span three- or four-day weekends, starting on Thursday and continuing to Sunday, students don't want to miss out on anything that goes on!

Close quarters = Close friends

Students overwhelmingly describe the Bates population as extremely friendly, welcoming, and accepting. One student proclaimed, "If there's one reason to come to Bates, it's the people." Several students explained that, possibly due to the fact that there are two all-freshman dorms to foster a sense of family among the members of the class, their best friends have generally been people they lived with freshman year. In addition, pre-orientation programs are offered to give freshman additional chances to make friends and become comfortable in an environment away from home. Students describe the Bates campus as extremely welcoming, in part due to its small size. One student commented, "It is very easy to meet people because on the weekends you go out with friends from your floor and you end up meeting people from different dorms and classes. The students at Bates are so friendly!" Another student agreed: "It's incredibly easy to meet people because the campus is so small, and everyone's looking for new friends."

Generally, students who go to Bates are perceived as well-off, and, though the school has been making efforts to diversify the campus, it is primarily white, with a majority of students coming from the New England area. However, the environment at Bates is relatively laid-back; as one student commented, "When walking around campus, you wouldn't necessarily know that the students come from families with money—students really don't flaunt it. The 'dress-code' is very laid-back, which is great. People wear sweatpants everywhere, and that's completely accepted. While some people do get more dressed up on the weekends, it's certainly not fancy at all; I wore heels one night and felt completely out of place."

Family Away from Home

At Bates, the relatively small campus is designed to foster a sense of community among the students. Most freshmen are placed in one of three freshman dorms: Smith, Clason, and Millken. Upperclassmen often move off campus to nearby houses or, according to one student, "an area called the village, which is made up of apartment-like buildings with suites inside."

One unique thing about Bates is that there is only one dining hall, which was created in response to a request from the students to create an even more closely knit community. Commons, the dining hall, is "the hot spot on campus." The students describe the food as "surprisingly good" and describe Commons as the perfect place to hang out, chat, and people-watch. It's a lucky thing that the food in Commons is good; students explain that there are not many restaurants near campus, and other dining options are somewhat limited.

In terms of favorite hangouts, there is also Pgill (full name: Pettengill), a building open 24 hours a day and containing classrooms, lounges, professors' offices, and "really comfortable couches." Pgill is described by one freshman as "a much more relaxed study space than the library, and it's nice to have another place to go to work. It also has a wall of windows that overlooks the pond, so it's absolutely gorgeous."

Bates is known for being in the middle of nowhere, and it does not shy away from this reputation. However, its tightly knit community provides a second family for many—an aspect praised as almost everyone's favorite thing about Bates. In the midst of impressive academics and a beautiful landscape, this home away from home hosts some of the happiest students around.—*Michelle Katz*

FYI

If you come to Bates, you'd better bring "a big winter coat and slippers from LL Bean."

What's the typical weekend schedule? "Go out on Friday night, sports or homework on Saturdays and then out, work on Sundays. Weekend mornings are usually dedicated to long brunches at Commons."

If I could change one thing about Bates, "I'd create an underground tunnel for students to get to Commons and other buildings without having to freeze!"

Three things every student at Bates should do before graduating are "do the puddle jump (jump in the pond in the middle of January as part of Winter Carnival), go to Commons drunk, and spend a full night in Pgill."

Bowdoin College

Address: 5000 College Station, Brunswick, Maine 04011-8441

Phone: 207-725-3100

E-mail address: admissions@bowdoin.edu

Web site URL: www.bowdoin.edu/admissions

Year Founded: 1794

Private or Public: Private

Religious Affiliation: None

Location: Suburban

Number of Applicants: 6,033

Percent Accepted: 18.50%

Percent Accepted who enroll: 44%

Number Entering: 491

Number of Transfers Accepted each Year: 5

Middle 50% SAT range: M: 650–750, CR: 650–760, Wr: 660–750

Middle 50% ACT range: 29–33

Early admission program EA/ED/None: ED

Percentage accepted through EA or ED: 18%

EA and ED deadline: 1-Nov

Regular Deadline: 1-Jan

Application Fee: $60

Full time Undergraduate enrollment: 1,719

Total enrollment: 1,723

Percent Male: 49%

Percent Female: 51%

Total Percent Minority or Unreported: 27%

Percent African-American: 6%

Percent Asian/Pacific Islander: 11%

Percent Hispanic: 9%

Percent Native-American: 1%

Percent International: Unreported

Percent in-state/out of state: 12%/88%

Percent from Public HS: 55%

Retention Rate: 98%

Graduation Rate 4-year: 86%

Graduation Rate 6-year: 91%

Percent Undergraduates in On-campus housing: 94%

Number of official organized extracurricular organizations: 109

3 Most popular majors: Government, Economics, English

Student/Faculty ratio: 10:1

Average Class Size: 16

Percent of students going to grad school: 80%

Tuition and Fees: $38,190

In State Tuition and Fees if different: No difference

Cost for Room and Board: $10,380

Percent receiving financial aid out of those who apply, first year: 74%

Percent receiving financial aid among all students: 41%

D oes the thought of cold winters and snow banks scare you? Fear not. Bowdoin's warm community and charming campus are enough to make the ice melt! Bowdoin attracts an active student body that is ready to take advantage of all that Brunswick, Maine, has to offer, from its cute restaurants to the nearby ski slopes.

Edgy Academia

While Bowdoin does require its students to complete eight core requirements, freshmen seminars and small intensive writing workshops, one junior explained that, "although these requirements sound so stereotypically 'liberal artsy' they are also totally valid and encompass a wide range of courses the colleges offers." Bowdoin offers 42 majors and 40 minors. The faculty is also very accommodating of students wishing to create their own major. Those looking for a lighter route are advised to sign up for the government major (with an American studies concentration), which also happens to be the most popular major at Bowdoin (coincidence? I

think not). Other popular majors include economics and history. Bowdoin also boasts a fabulous science department that even has its own neuroscience program—an impressive inclusion for such a small school.

Bowdoin puts a large emphasis on student research, and pushes service learning in particular. One junior worked with a group to create their own charter school as part of a class entitled "Anarchy, Nationalism and Fundamentalism." Getting into classes is generally quite easy, and class sizes are flexible to meet demand although the average class size is kept small, about 35 in a lecture and 16 in seminar. Students are taught by professors rather than TAs, and professors are known to be friendly and welcome postclass discussions over coffee. The workload can be significant, and potential students should expect about three to four hours of homework a night. Grade inflation, as at most American colleges, is prevalent; however physics majors seem to have the toughest time of it. They have the lowest overall GPA of all the majors.

The Simple Life

While their mascot is a polar bear, and the winters can get a bit nippy, students at Bowdoin love living in Brunswick. One student described Brunswick as "wicked cute," borrowing a phrase from the local vernacular. Brunswick is filled with lots of great restaurants, ranging from Scarlet B's to the Sea Dog Brewery. For those looking for a break, Portland is not too far away (although it does require a car). Students head to Portland when in need of a really good meal or a minor-league baseball game. Freeport is a bit closer and offers great retail therapy. And of course, one of the big perks about living in Maine is that great skiing is only a two-hour drive away.

Of course, the campus isn't half bad either. Bowdoin combines charming New England red brick and ivy with modern architecture, resulting in an aesthetic that is not only easy on the eyes, but also practical and comfortable. As far as dorms go, freshmen have it best. All freshman dorms were rebuilt in the past two years and feature two doubles with a spacious common room. "My frosh room was like a palace and that was pretty universal." Freshmen are well taken care of by their RAs and proctors. Each freshman dorm is assigned a proctor who tends to be much more hands on than the RAs who live on each floor. Freshmen develop close relationships with their proctors, who are there to help them out rather than report them. "I love my first-year proctor group that lived on my floor and the floor below me and loved the relationship with our proctor, an upper-class res-life student who basically took care of us," one student said. After freshman year, the living options are a bit more limited, although housing is guaranteed for all students. Sophomores tend to live in the social houses, while juniors and seniors choose between the 16-story Cole tower, campus-owned apartments, social houses, and off-campus houses, although few opt for off-campus living arrangements. Bowdoin students are very happy with their housing options, and even more so with the food. One student raved, "Bowdoin dining is number one according to *Princeton Review* and it totally stands up to its reputation. I am a junior and still eat at least two meals a day in the dining hall."

"Home of the Original Patagucci-Prep"

One may ask, what is a Patagucci-Prep? One need go no further than this little Maine college to find the answer dressed in head to toe J. Crew, Patagonia outerwear and snow boots (although Uggs are frowned upon). The dress code is preppy-conservative, although come Halloween, all bets are off—it's time to get risqué! And the look is *au naturel*, so leave your hair pomade and curlers at home. Students agree that the campus is "pretty homogenous," with most students coming from upper-middle-class backgrounds. While it certainly has no shortage of prep school grads, Bowdoin is not the place for snobbery. Describing the general atmosphere as "like a family," Bowdoin students are proud of their tight-knit community and their "Bowdoin hello." (Note: Those too awkward to say a friendly "Bowdoin Hello" to those they pass on the sidewalk need not apply.) With a student body of just 1,710 it is easy to get to know a large portion of people—an aspect of college life here that many students love.

Life of the Party

Greek life was phased out in 2000, but that certainly hasn't put a damper on the Bowdoin social scene and for the most part, students seem glad to be rid of the Greek system. "Thank God we don't have frats or sororities . . . and I think 99 percent of students would agree with me" one student said. Instead of the Greek life, Bowdoin boasts all-inclusive social houses, which are where most of the sophomores and some of the juniors live. The administration gives the social houses money to throw parties (often themed) every weekend.

> "Thank God we don't have frats or sororities . . . and I think 99 percent of students would agree with me."

What about the freshmen? All freshmen dorms are affiliated with one of the social houses, and freshmen tend to be the main attraction at these shindigs. "No worries if you aren't 21; you just get an "X" on your hand at the door," one junior assured. "This means that if security comes, you need to put down your keg cup and look mildly sober." Upperclassmen however, tend to move away from the social houses and off campus where the place to be is the "Crackhouse." "Senior Lax Daddies reside in this classy establishment where lots of beer pong is played, there is a 'Boom Boom Room' for dance parties (black lights and '80s music included) and a keg that never seems to get kicked," one "Senior Lax Daddy" explained: The scene at the "Crackhouse" varies from year to year, but one constant that never seems to go out of style is the Pub, the local Thursday hot spot located in the student center. Students rave about the yearly Junior/Senior Ball, a senior event held in the spring (think, Prom with lots of alcohol) and the "IVIES," which includes a fun-filled weekend of drinking, cookouts, and bands. "Everyone loves Ivies, even though no one seems to ever remember it."

So what about the nonboozers out there? As is quite true on most college campuses, nonboozers are a bit more limited in their choice of weekend activities. However, the administration does make a valiant effort. "Non-drinkers are not ostracized by any means. There are not a lot of 'social' events for the non-drinking set," including a fair number of "chem-free" social houses. The weekends are also packed with opportunities to go to lectures, movies, and dance classes. The Bowdoin Film Society puts out a number of great films, some old, some new, every weekend. And the student center and the Union, which includes a gym, café, convenience store, and pub, are always booming.

All this talk about parties is definitely setting the mood! Love is in the air at Bowdoin, or for some at least. One junior reported that the love life at Bowdoin consists of people who either start dating freshman year and stay together for the four years, or a series of random hook-ups. But beware! Random hook-ups on such a small campus can get quite awkward! One student warned, "Bowdoin is politically pretty left, but suddenly becomes a bunch of gossipy moralists if people are hooking up with many different people on a semi-regular basis. And when I say many, I mean more than one person per weekend or more than a couple people a month." And while the gay scene may not be prevalent, it certainly does exist, with a number of gay-couples happily out in the open.

Bowdoin College is a little gem tucked away in Maine with a cozy, tight-knit community, a place where one can enjoy the great outdoors, a flexible class schedule, and a great social life. Bowdoin leaves students saying, "I love Bowdoin and would love to be able to do it all again."—*Victoria Wild*

FYI

If you come to Bowdoin, you better bring "a Patagonia Parka, huge boots (preferably not Uggs), and your drinking shoes."

What is the typical weekend schedule? "Watching or playing in a weekend game, going to some sort of party, and a trip to Freeport, Portland, or dinner in Brunswick."

If I could change one thing about Bowdoin I "wouldn't change a thing!"

Three things every student at Bowdoin should do before graduating are "explore downtown Brunswick, drive to the ocean, and attend as many guest lectures as possible, particularly those during Common Hour."

Colby College

Address: 4000 Mayflower Hill Waterville, ME 04901-8848	**Percentage accepted through EA or ED:** 43%	**Graduation Rate 6-year:** 88%
Phone: 207-859-4828	**EA and ED deadline:** 1-Jan	**Percent Undergraduates in On-campus housing:** 94%
E-mail address: admissions@colby.edu	**Regular Deadline:** 1-Jan	
	Application Fee: $65	**Number of official organized extracurricular organizations:** 98
Web site URL: www.colby.edu/	**Full time Undergraduate enrollment:** 1,846	
Year Founded: 1813	**Total enrollment:** 1,846	**3 Most popular majors:** Biology, Economics, Political Science
Private or Public: Private	**Percent Male:** 46%	
Religious Affiliation: None	**Percent Female:** 54%	
Location: Rural	**Total Percent Minority or Unreported:** 14%	**Student/Faculty ratio:** 10:1
Number of Applicants: 4,835	**Percent African-American:** 2%	**Average Class Size:** Unreported
Percent Accepted: 30.9%		**Percent of students going to grad school:** Unreported
Percent Accepted who enroll: 32.3%	**Percent Asian/Pacific Islander:** 8%	**Tuition and Fees:** $48,520
Number Entering: 482	**Percent Hispanic:** 3%	**In State Tuition and Fees if different:** No difference
Number of Transfers Accepted each Year: 9	**Percent Native-American:** <1%	**Cost for Room and Board:** Included
Middle 50% SAT range: M: 640–710, CR: 640–720, Wr: 630–710	**Percent International:** 5%	**Percent receiving financial aid out of those who apply, first year:** 73%
	Percent in-state/out of state: 10%/90%	
Middle 50% ACT range: 28–31	**Percent from Public HS:** Unreported	
Early admission program EA/ED/None: ED	**Retention Rate:** 96%	**Percent receiving financial aid among all students:** 43%
	Graduation Rate 4-year: 83%	

Academic, athletic, intimate and environmentally aware, Colby College offers the best of many worlds for especially talented students. Located in Waterville, Maine, this selective liberal arts college boasts everything from rigorous academics to great food, wacky traditions, and an enthusiasm for the rugged outdoors.

Academics: In the Classroom and Beyond

Chartered in 1813, Colby College is the 12th-oldest independent liberal arts college in the nation, and the depth and breadth of its current academic offerings clearly reflect such a long-standing tradition of excellence. With 53 majors and 33 minors, Colby aims to give its students an opportunity for unique intellectual exploration. Most students appreciate these offerings, but admit that "it's a lot of work."

Priding itself on giving students a truly diverse liberal arts education, Colby College has a rather hefty set of graduation requirements, in addition to those classes required

for one's particular major. Students must take a foreign language, one English composition class, one literature class, two natural sciences, one course in the social sciences, one in the arts, one in historical studies, one in quantitative reasoning, two courses that deal with diversity issues and First Year Supper Seminars. While most students do not outright dislike these requirements, some find them more burdensome than others. One senior said, "It's a lot of requirements, and people have complained about it." On the other hand, another student pointed out, "I think it's important that you at least have some diversity in your education. You're going to a liberal arts school . . . it makes sense."

Of course, as at most schools, Colby students have found ways to fulfill certain requirements they find particularly distasteful with the token "gut" classes. Students not so math and science oriented, for example, may take "Math as a Liberal Art" or "Rocks for Jocks."

One student pointed out that science majors tend to have more work. "The sciences are very challenging. They have a lot of core requirements, but the more liberal arts majors have a lot more room to take other courses." Popular majors include Government, Economics, English, History and Biology.

Perhaps what makes academic life at Colby most appealing, though, is the January Program, affectionately dubbed "Jan Plan" by the students. This plan allows students in the month of January (between semesters) to broaden their academic horizons by doing something different. This can involve taking less traditional classes on Colby's campus, such as African drumming, participating in a Colby-organized program abroad, or even coming up with a project of your own. Freshmen are generally required to stay on campus. One senior noted that she spent the month driving around the East Coast in order to write her own travel guide. "It's pretty lenient," she said. "You can get credit for a lot of stuff."

Finally, academics at Colby stand out because of the small class sizes and potential for close student-teacher relationships. Introductory classes are the biggest, but even in these classes, one student said that there are never more than 100 people. Moreover, teachers are known for looking at the class roster (which includes pictures) before class and thus being able to call students by name on the second day.

Nonetheless, some students emphasize that there is a bit of a myth that at any small school students are close with teachers. "Just because you're at a small college doesn't mean that automatically you'll have these great relations with teachers," one student cautioned. "You have to search for it." The opportunity, though, is undeniably there.

Maine Campus: Living in the Great Outdoors

As one student put it, "Colby is pretty small, and it's just absolutely beautiful. All the buildings match; you just want to have it in a little snow globe." Indeed, nestled in Maine not too far from Acadia National Park, Colby College lives up to the stereotypical quaint and rugged Maine image, with an ice-skating pond of its own and a dedication to environmental awareness and sustainability. "It's beautiful. There are trees everywhere. The grass is always very green."

As one student explained, there is definitely a "big outdoor culture." The college president recently traded in his SUV for a more environmentally friendly Prius, and "if you walk around in the winter, you'll see everyone in their Patagonia parkas."

But while students appreciate the natural beauty of the campus, they seem more disillusioned with the housing system. Students are guaranteed housing all four years, though approximately 100 people (mostly seniors) live off campus each year. Dorms are not segregated by class but rather must include a certain number of students from each class, as well as a certain number of males and females. Dorms have coed floors.

Upperclass students are assigned rooms based on a lottery system, but many complain that the current system (with the class quotas per dorm) actually discriminates against seniors who want to live together. As one student said, the system "works really well in some ways for making every dorm a diverse place age-wise, but it can really screw over juniors and seniors." One student was more blunt: "The housing is pretty sub-par. That's Colby's biggest downfall, probably."

For students who live off campus, the closest town is the city of Waterville. While Waterville is not generally considered a college town—"Waterville is not bad, it's not great"—it is only a short distance from campus. Students can bike, drive (many have cars) or even take an inexpensive taxi. The town also has a few bars and restaurants, but town-gown relations have become increasingly strained, with Waterville police becoming, according to Colby students, more eager to crack down on underage drinking and partying.

If students complain about Colby housing, though, they certainly do not complain about Colby food. Colby has three dining halls, including options for vegetarians and vegans, and "the food is great!" One student even mentioned how you can get lunch to go—not just by making a sandwich, wrapping it in napkins, and stuffing it in your backpack, but rather by picking up an actual premade bag lunch.

Preppy Partiers

With no fraternities or sororities and no major urban attractions, Colby students admit that there is a lot of heavy drinking. While the cops have been trying to crack down on underage drinking, students generally find ways to party both in the dorms and off campus. Since the dorms house students in all years, there is no strict ban on alcohol, and the HRs (head residents) are generally there more to keep students safe than to get them in trouble.

Also, Colby College itself sometimes organizes social evening activities, and a pub in the student center, Cotter Union, is popular among the students. The pub is also known to be pretty strict about carding, creating what one student described as a "more controlled environment."

> "People really like the school . . . and it's shown by how people are really involved in stuff on campus."

The social scene is also dominated, many students say, by an athletic crowd. But beyond being an athletic campus, Colby has also earned itself other reputations. One student said the "typical" Colby student "lives 20 minutes outside of Boston, went to prep school, drives a Jeep, has a house on the Cape, and wears brand-name clothing." Indeed, "it's very white. There's no getting around that."

Where Everyone Does Something

If Colby is not very ethnically diverse, it is very diverse in terms of varying student inter-

ests and passions. "Everybody here is very unique and very different and accepted," one student said. "People really like the school . . . and it's shown by how people are really involved in stuff on campus."

More specifically, Colby boasts about 100 active clubs and organizations, including everything from the skateboarding club to the Movement for Social Justice. Many students are involved in volunteer work within the surrounding communities, and many also are involved with athletics.

Colby is also known for its school spirit. The Colby-Bowdoin hockey game is particularly popular and always sells out, and, in general, sports seem to have an intense presence. Moreover, while one student admits that not everyone goes to the football games, school spirit manifests itself in other ways (even beyond athletics) as well. Every year, for example, students make boats out of nonboat materials (including everything from gardening pipes to balloons and bicycles) and then race the contraptions in a regatta across Johnson Pond.

In general, most students at Colby seem to adore their school. "The people at Colby are really great. I've loved the friends I've made."— *Jen Sabin*

FYI

If you come to Colby, you'd better bring "a warm jacket and a pair of skis."

What is the typical weekend schedule? "Thursday night: go out to a bar in Waterville; Friday night: hang out with friends, go to a smaller party; Saturday: get up at noon, sit around, work out, go to a big party off campus or to a school-organized dance."

If I could change one thing about Colby, I'd "reduce the sports culture."

Three things every student at Colby should do before graduating are "climb Mt. Katahdin, slide down the president's half-pipe, and take a walk in the arboretum."

College of the Atlantic

Address: 105 Eden Street
Bar Harbor, ME 04609
Phone: 207-288-5015
E-mail address:
inquiry@coa.edu
Web site URL: www.coa.edu
Year Founded: 1969
Private or Public: Private
Religious Affiliation: None
Location: Rural
Number of Applicants: 314
Percent Accepted: 69.1%
**Percent Accepted who
enroll:** 31.8%
Number Entering: 70
**Number of Transfers
Accepted each Year:** 18
Middle 50% SAT range:
M: 500–650, CR: 600–690,
Wr: 550–680
Middle 50% ACT range: 25–29
**Early admission program
EA/ED/None:** ED
**Percentage accepted
through EA or ED:** 44%

EA and ED deadline: 1-Dec
Regular Deadline: 15-Feb
Application Fee: $45
**Full time Undergraduate
enrollment:** 324
Total enrollment: 327
Percent Male: 36%
Percent Female: 64%
**Total Percent Minority or
Unreported:** 2%
Percent African-American:
0%
**Percent Asian/Pacific
Islander:** 1%
Percent Hispanic: 1%
Percent Native-American:
0.0%
Percent International: 14%
**Percent in-state/out of
state:** 20%/80%
Percent from Public HS:
Unreported
Retention Rate: 82%
Graduation Rate 4-year:
45%

Graduation Rate 6-year:
61%
**Percent Undergraduates
in On-campus housing:**
43%
**Number of official organized
extracurricular
organizations:** Unreported
3 Most popular majors:
Biology, Ecology, Education
Student/Faculty ratio: 11:1
Average Class Size: 12
**Percent of students going to
grad school:** 55.0%
Tuition and Fees: $31,470
**In State Tuition and Fees if
different:** No difference
Cost for Room and Board:
$8,490
**Percent receiving financial
aid out of those who apply,
first year:** 95%
**Percent receiving financial
aid among all students:**
82%

In 1969 a bunch of Harvard grads got together and decided that people would benefit by learning to understand the importance of how humans interact with their social and natural environments. The interdisciplinary approach they drew up boiled everything down to what they called Human Ecology. They chose the picturesque little seaside town of Bar Harbor, Maine, as the site for their project. Soon enough, they had created a small school of extraordinary opportunities that challenged students to rethink their roles in the world.

And the Meaning of Life Is . . .

Before graduation, every College of the Atlantic (COA) student is required to produce a thesis that answers the question "What is human ecology?" Human Ecology, the sole major at COA, introduces students to an interdisciplinary approach to defining the relationship between humans and the natural environment. Yes, it's a big topic to tackle, but when you are taking classes like "Landscapes of Power," "The Aesthetics of Violence," and "Use and Abuse of our Public Lands," somehow the answer tends to work itself out.

The degree requirements are extensive, but reveal COA's unique learning philosophy. To graduate, students must engage in community service, pursue an internship of at least one term, create a final project, and write a Human Ecology essay discussing their development as a human ecologist.

Although some struggle to find their area of focus, most say that COA "doesn't box you in with a major." Students can switch their focuses within the Human Ecology major. One senior reported that she had switched her focus from environmental law to Latin American studies to a preveterinary school track. However, with a student body of approximately 350 and faculty of approximately 35, COA is a "hard place to specialize when there are two professors who are the math department and another two who are the philosophy department," according to one third-year student. The 80 classes offered per trimester also quickly fill up to their average limit of 18. Some students find it frustrating that the small school may not offer classes within their particular interest.

In turn, COA encourages students to pursue independent studies. One student explained, "If you're motivated, good, if not, you might have a hard time here. For example, most of my work in the last year and a half has been independent, outside of class. I did an internship, then a group study, followed by a residency (the equivalent of three interconnected independent studies), and when I get back from Yucatan I'm going to do my senior project." Graduation requirements also call for students to take time off from campus to do an internship.

On average, students take three classes per trimester—"four can be a lot." The work load focuses on class presentations and "intense" papers, as opposed to exams. An 11:1 student-faculty ratio means that students get individual attention and know their professors well—everyone is on a first-name basis!

Classes also make use of research resources that include Mt. Desert Rock and Great Duck Island Lighthouse, Mt. Desert Island Biological Laboratory, Jackson Laboratory, a weather station, and a Global Monitoring System. "We may, for example, dissect whales or seals found on the coast and determine the cause of death," explains one student.

Housing: Converted Mansions, but Limited Space

COA guarantees housing, usually singles, for first-years only. The three-level horseshoe-shaped Blair-Tyson dorm houses about 40 students. Around six to eight students share a kitchen and a bathroom, which features recycled toilet paper and no stalls! Seafox, a converted mansion, is "supposedly" substance-free, but really just a more quiet dorm of 12 students with spectacular views of the ocean. RAs are pretty easygoing about marijuana and alcohol and even bring their first-years to off-campus parties to bond with upperclassmen. One RA admitted, "I'm pretty loose about it. Although if someone is having a problem, I'd certainly confront him about it."

Most upperclassmen envy the first-years who get to stay on campus. "I had a blast!" claimed a former Blair-Tyson dweller. "But there's not enough room for us, which is a bummer." Upperclassmen find apartments in town about five minutes away or in more remote locations reached by bike or car.

The Grub—A Vegan's Paradise

The environmentally conscious student body enjoys top-ranked cooking at its sole dining hall Take-a-Break, or TAB in local lingo. In 2002, PETA (People for the Ethical Treatment of Animals) ranked TAB first out of 1,200 college dining halls for its vegetarian and vegan fare and gave it the privileged title of "Veggie Valedictorian." "The worst thing about the dining hall is its dining hours: dinner between 5:30 and 6:30 is kind of ridiculous," complained one student. Also, no meals are served on the weekends, so students make use of the many on-campus kitchens.

The food is all organic and mostly from local farms, including the COA's own Beech Hill Farm where students can participate in the work-study program or volunteer. All waste is disposed of in the school's compost garden. Being on the ocean, TAB features a lot of fresh seafood. "Basically, it's not McDonald's, so don't come looking for it," affirmed one senior.

The Weekend Chill

The illegal substance of choice is reportedly marijuana, "unsurprising" for the "chill" school that enrolls many "hippied-out" students. As opposed to hard liquor, beer is the choice beverage. "My buddies and I might throw back a couple of beers, but we don't often get rip-roaring drunk," reported a third-year student. Another student warned, "There are no crazy discos or mad party places, so if that's what you're looking for you might have a hard time here. It is Maine, after all." Students claim that hard drugs are pretty rare.

Because there are no Wednesday classes (due to Student Government meetings), "there are two weekends, Tuesday nights and Friday and Saturday nights." The scene starts, according to one student, "ridiculously early! Things get started around 8:00 and end by 11:30 or 12:00." Parties are held mainly at upperclassmen residences. The Thirsty Whale, Little Anthony's, and Nakorn Thai are popular town bars. "Only really good IDs work," complained one student about the strict drinking policy.

As for the dating scene, news travels fast. One senior lamented her days as a first-year, when she "may have made one too many 'mistakes' that I couldn't escape. I saw them around nearly every day." Some students admit COA is a hard place to date because there are not a lot of new people to meet around. But the small size "makes random hookups a lot less random." COA is also very tolerant and accepting of homosexual relationships. Reportedly, "lesbians are usually more open than gay males."

Students Take Charge

The Student Government at COA is a remarkably powerful body. It has significant say in all major decisions of the school. Students even attend Trustee meetings. Classes do not meet on Wednesdays to accommodate Student Government committee meetings in which most students participate. Additionally, at 1 p.m. every Wednesday an All College Meeting to which all student organizations and committees report takes place. One student complains, however, "It's always the same people that show up and, for the most part, say the same things, so reaching common decisions has less to do with compromise and more with tiring your opponent."

The Student Activities Committee, a branch of the Student Government, brings about two or three bands per term to perform in TAB. The committee also sponsors coffeehouses, weekly Open Mike nights, the Winter Carnival and Earth Day.

For the Outdoorsman in You

COA sports teams are completely nonexistent. But students are serious about outdoor activities, rain or shine. First-years pile all the essentials—boots, bikes, backpacks, cross-country skis, you name it—into the family car when they first arrive. With Acadia National Park in COA's backyard, students can be found scaling the island's mountains (at least ten!) on weekends and have often tackled them all by graduation. Students have free passes to the local YMCA, can explore the miles of bike trails, catch a free whale-watching ride with the Allied Whale (a program for sea-mammal study and saving), or sit on the dock with their toes in the water and watch the sailboats float by.

Winter term is known as the trimester for hard work because sub-zero temperatures supposedly keep people inside. This hibernation is overstated, claimed one student. Even when Bar Harbor shuts down at the end of tourist season, COA students are still recreating outdoors with cross-country skiing, snowshoeing, Broomball and even midnight dips in the ocean. With all these activities, TV is reportedly "*not* a big pastime." At COA, something like the campus tree swing is a big attraction.

Who You'll Meet

Students at COA report that Earth Day is "the only day that we actually get off." Naturally a place like this is going to attract a certain kind of student. One student described the typical student as "someone who smells like tea-tree oil, has dreadlocks, wears Birkenstocks and is environmentally aware, politically conscious, outdoorsy, pretty athletic and earthy." Oh, and liberal. "There are maybe three Republicans here," warned one student, "I would not come here if I were a Republican." Although the school is often stereotyped, many students admit surprise at the diversity of opinion. One third-year student remarks, "I wasn't expecting anyone to challenge me." Another student determined the "dirty hippie" population to be less than a quarter of the school.

> **"I would not come here if I were a Republican."**

Students are generally from an upper-middle class socioeconomic background, and though a substantial portion of the student body hails from Maine, students come from all over the United States. For such a small school, COA boasts a significant number of international students who are attracted by the special full scholarship package as well as the uniqueness of the school. In one student's words, "COA students usually have really strong beliefs about a lot of things, and like to voice them. I guess another way to look at it is that if you took the staple "weird kids" from any high school, most of them would fit in just fine at COA."—*Baily Blair*

FYI
If you come to COA you'd better bring "a Nalgene, a backpack and long johns."
What is a typical weekend schedule? "Go for a hike, do some reading, chill with friends and lay low."
If I could change one thing about COA, I'd "move it to the tropics or a big city."
Three things every student should do before graduating are "join the Yucatan Program, go for a swim at Sand Beach on a night in January and summit all the mountains on the island."

University of Maine / Orono

Address: 5713 Chadbourne Hall Orono, ME 04469-5713
Phone: 207-581-1561
E-mail address: um-admit@maine.edu
Web site URL: www.umaine.edu
Year Founded: 1865
Private or Public: Public
Religious Affiliation: None
Location: Rural
Number of Applicants: 6,958
Percent Accepted: 77%
Percent Accepted who enroll: 34%
Number Entering: 1,839
Number of Transfers Accepted each Year: 716
Middle 50% SAT range: M: 480–600, CR: 480–580, Wr: 470–570
Middle 50% ACT range: 19–25
Early admission program EA/ED/None: EA

Percentage accepted through EA or ED: Unreported
EA and ED deadline: 15-Dec
Regular Deadline: Rolling
Application Fee: $40
Full time Undergraduate enrollment: 9,596
Total enrollment: 11,912
Percent Male: 50%
Percent Female: 50%
Total Percent Minority or Unreported: 6%
Percent African-American: 1%
Percent Asian/Pacific Islander: 1%
Percent Hispanic: 1%
Percent Native-American: 2%
Percent International: 2%
Percent in-state/out of state: 84%/16%
Percent from Public HS: Unreported
Retention Rate: 78%

Graduation Rate 4-year: 33%
Graduation Rate 6-year: 58%
Percent Undergraduates in On-campus housing: 42%
Number of official organized extracurricular organizations: 224
3 Most popular majors: Business/Commerce, Education, Engineering
Student/Faculty ratio: 16:1
Average Class Size: 10 to 19
Percent of students going to grad school: 25%
Tuition and Fees: $22,510
In State Tuition and Fees if different: $9,100·
Cost for Room and Board: $8,008
Percent receiving financial aid out of those who apply, first year: Unreported
Percent receiving financial aid among all students: Unreported

A big state school in the middle of the woods, with a cold climate to boot, might seem daunting at first. But as students at the University of Maine will tell you, there are many reasons to brave the freezing temperatures and take advantage of this vibrant community. The university that once had a live black bear as its official mascot and was known for being a legendary party school has since evolved into a respected national research university, but the students are still just as supportive of their UMaine Black Bears. From the cheering crowds at the Alfond Arena to the picnickers taking advantage of the first day of spring, it's clear that the University of Maine provides a unique opportunity for both in- and out-of-staters to make the most of the Pine Tree State.

Bear-ing All with Bananas

Founded in 1865, the UMaine campus in Orono is the largest in the University of Maine system. As a public state school, it's not surprising that 84 percent of its student body hails from Maine itself. But the 16 percent remaining call 47 states and 47 countries home, making for a campus that is surprisingly diverse for a state that one student called "one of the whitest states, if not the whitest." She continued, "The University of Maine is probably the place to go if you're looking for some ethnic and religious diversity because there is a lot of it on this campus, all things considered being in Maine." The minority students, who make up six percent of undergraduates, have the opportunity to participate in a number of ethnic and cultural organizations, including the Asian Student Association and the Black Student Union.

Most of the student population, generally either "Mainers" or New Englanders, sport a preppy style, usually American Eagle or Abercrombie, students said. Others said the campus has its fair share of rebels, both in terms of fashion and lifestyle. One girl confessed, "We're all kind of hicks." But she was quick to point out that "There are those guys who wear flannel, but they're not roaming around hunting things."

There are a few things that do unite just about all UMaine students, and one of them is supporting their Black Bears. Legend has it that the University's original mascot was a live black bear cub that lived in one of the fraternity's basements when not appearing at sporting events. Today's incarnation, Bananas the Bear, may do a better job of pumping up the crowds; the original cub was fired after attacking the University of Connecticut husky at a basketball game.

"We're all kind of hicks."

The hockey team is universally cited as the biggest draw for sports spectators. The school pep band always makes an appearance, and the roaring crowds of both UMaine students and Maine locals are a constant fixture at the Alfond Arena, usually lining up outside for tickets far in advance. The men's ice hockey team, two-time NCAA Division I national champions, in 1993 and 1999, is a great source of pride for the entire state. "People go crazy and wear jerseys and paint their faces," a junior described.

The other athletics teams, which also engage in Division I competition, may not have as much star power, but their games also attract many fans. Football is also very popular, and the basketball team's rivalry with the New Hampshire Wildcats, at 105 seasons in a row, is the longest continuous basketball rivalry between any two non-Ivy League schools.

Making a Large University Small

Black Bears can carry their determination into the classroom, too, with plenty of opportunities available at UMaine for academic excellence. The general education requirements, or "Gen Eds," are designed to produce "broadly educated persons who can appreciate the achievements of civilization, understand the tensions within it, and contribute to resolving them." Each student must take a certain number of credits in the following areas: science, human values and social context, mathematics, writing, and ethics. Every student, regardless of major, must also complete a "capstone experience," usually during the senior year, which is the culmination of his or her specific course of study. All Gen Eds must be taken for a letter grade in order to satisfy the requirement. "I'm on a one-track [course of study]," a music education major said. "The Gen Eds require me to get out of that box for a minute and open my mind to other subject areas. There's probably a little bit of groaning, but it's one of those things that gets done, often freshman year."

The most popular majors are business, education and engineering, with the latter generally cited as one of the most challenging offered at the University, as well as one of the most famous departments. The sciences in general, especially the nursing and biology programs, are well known for their rigor and progressiveness. The marine biology department is also lauded.

When students are accepted into the University of Maine, they gain entrance to specific programs based on the strength of their applications. If they do not meet the requirements for a program or are unsure of what they want to concentrate in, first-years enroll in the Exploration Program, which allows them to transition to college life and settle on an academic area, even to bolster their qualifications for a certain program. Some of the benefits of this option include an academic adviser with whom they meet on a regular basis and the opportunity to take a first-year seminar. Students looking for a more personalized education throughout their four years at the University can opt to enroll in the Honors College if they make the cut. Honors students enjoy smaller classes and close working relationships with faculty members. They also have the option of designated honors housing.

As can be expected of a large state school, students often encounter difficulties in gaining entrance to certain high-demand classes, but "teachers sometimes make exceptions." Class sizes range from around 25 in the smaller lectures to 200 to 300 in the largest survey courses, but one girl said she has a class with only three people. Classes are usually offered once a year, if not each semester, so the most common reason that students enroll for a fifth year is that they were undecided about their major, not that they could not get into core classes.

A junior cited the school's size as one of the biggest academic attractions: "I think there's something for everyone. Because we are a university, the biggest university in the state, and we have a lot of students, there's pretty much going to be a major for you."

Raising the Steins

"A lot of people have the perception that UMaine is a huge party school because at one point it was, and I don't think it necessarily is anymore," a sophomore said. Indeed, the University has recently been taking steps to curb out-of-control partying, with both reputation and students' safety in mind. "The University's known as being a party school, so it's really important to [the administration] that we crack down, and that we don't allow freshmen to be drunk all the time," a junior explained. The RAs in each dorm, where drinking is prohibited, are known for being fairly strict. The repercussions for breaking the rules include attending alcohol education meetings, and repeat offenders can be kicked out of the dorms. "Does that mean [drinking] never happens?" one student asked rhetorically. "No, but it is punishable."

Since it's fairly difficult to party in on-campus housing, much of the party scene takes place in the frats and the off-campus apartments. While one girl said she was surprised that Greek life was so present on campus, she said the presence of the frats and sororities has not been a negative part of her experience. The frats hold many of the parties, and Friday and Saturday nights are known as the big nights to go out. Pot is pretty commonplace, as it is on most college campuses, and binge drinking is not a major problem, perhaps in part because of the 2001 founding of Maine's Higher Education Alcohol Prevention Project. The initiative aimed to address the problem of binge drinking as it worsened on college campus. However, the celebrated college fight song, the Maine Stein Song, is still proudly shouted at athletic events. As undergraduates sing "Fill the steins to dear old Maine," they had better have their IDs on them.

The off-campus bar scene in Orono is not too exciting; there are a couple in town, along with a dance club that a good number of people frequent. There isn't much to do overall in Orono. Besides the legendary Pat's Pizza and a number of other coffee shops and restaurants, it is a quiet town with residents that generally have good relations with the University. In fact, many of them are affiliated with UMaine. For more bars and restaurants, as well as a grocery store, some students take the 10-minute drive to nearby Bangor, the third-largest city in the state.

Indoors and Outdoors

There's a lot to occupy students' time on campus, though. They can even get fed reasonably well. York, Hilltop, and Wells Commons offer all-you-care-to-eat dining. The latter two were recently renovated and offer a variety of standard and multi-ethnic cuisines. Students cited the Maine Marketplace in the Memorial Union as the most popular dining option, though. Here, students can use their meal plans to purchase a wide range of a la carte meals, including pizza, sandwiches, burgers, sushi, Chinese and Mexican food. They can either use one meal swipe and receive an entrée and snacks, or they can pay by the item. A number of meal plans are available, comprising both meal swipes and dining funds.

The 19 residence halls are generally considered to be acceptable, students say. Freshmen participate in the First Year Residence Experience (FYRE) and are assigned to one of the following dorms: Androscoggin, Cumberland, Gannett, Knox, Oxford, Somerset, Balentine, Penobscot, and Colvin. The latter three are designated for honors students. These are traditional undergraduate residence halls, usually with two students to a room, while upperclassmen have this option as well as the choice of living in suites. "Some of the dorms are on the older side, but I think overall they're not too awful," a sophomore concluded. As part of the FYRE, freshmen are grouped together in one part of campus and have the opportunity to make friends with many of their classmates through this close-knit community.

Theme housing includes a substance-free dorm and an "outdoorsy" dorm, the latter of which organizes trips to the mountains and the surrounding area to ski, bike, hike, and participate in all manner of recreational activities. A junior pointed out that none of the dorms, and indeed none of the buildings on the UMaine campus, are taller than four stories. She said she thinks it is because the University is built on an island in a marsh, and that buildings cannot be taller than they are because the campus will sink into the water, but she admitted that it could be just a rumor.

Many students have cars, even freshmen, and parking can be a difficult issue. The significant number of commuter students contributes to the congestion. Permits cost $50 for the year, with decals designating cars as faculty, resident or commuter, with corresponding lots. Those who trespass into other lots "are lucky if they aren't ticketed." But students point out that cars are useful for going home or just into town. While campus is considered to be "pretty safe," students interviewed did say they wish it were better lit, both because it would make them feel more secure at night and because it is difficult for drivers to see pedestrians.

The architecture on campus is mostly brick, with many trees and green spaces adding life. In the winter, snow coats everything, but it is "still aesthetically pleasing." One student said her favorite thing to do is to sit on the Mall, an open space in the middle of campus, at the beginning of spring when "the campus is buzzing and everyone is happy." With a number of constructions projects recently completed and others in progress, the UMaine campus seems to always be an exciting place. The Collins Center for the Arts was recently renovated, as was the gym.

Most UMaine students do their best to take advantage of their surroundings, often going on trips to Acadia National Park or other natural areas. But whether you're a flannel-wearing mountain man or someone who prefers to stay indoors during inclement weather, there are plenty of opportunities to do both at the University of Maine. One student said she had gotten used to the school's size, saying, "It's kind of nice having a lot more students—more things get contributed to the campus, and there are more ideas floating around." Another added, "I have plenty of time in my life to move away and see the world, but I'm glad I stayed in Maine for college."—*Kimberly Chow*

FYI

If you come to the University of Maine, you'd better bring "a pair of winter boots—it was negative 20 degrees at one point."

What's the typical weekend schedule? "On Friday, go to a hockey game, then hang out with your friends at Pat's Pizza; sleep in on Saturday, maybe go to another athletic event, then hit up the frats; Sunday, catch up on work."

If I could change one thing about the University of Maine, "I would make the weather warmer!"

Three things every student at the University of Maine should do before graduating are "go to a hockey game, sit on the Mall in the spring, and eat at Pat's Pizza."

Maryland

Goucher College

Address: 1021 Dulaney Valley Road Baltimore, MD 21204-2753
Phone: 410-337-6100
E-mail address: admissions@goucher.edu
Web site URL: www.goucher.edu
Year Founded: 1885
Private or Public: Private
Religious Affiliation: None
Location: Urban
Number of Applicants: 3,563
Percent Accepted: 66%
Percent Accepted who enroll: 17%
Number Entering: 399
Number of Transfers Accepted each Year: 118
Middle 50% SAT range: M: 510–620, CR: 540–670, Wr: 540–650
Middle 50% ACT range: Unreported
Early admission program EA/ED/None: EA

Percentage accepted through EA or ED: 43%
EA and ED deadline: 1-Dec
Regular Deadline: 1-Feb
Application Fee: $40
Full time Undergraduate enrollment: 1,472
Total enrollment: 2,362
Percent Male: 31%
Percent Female: 69%
Total Percent Minority or Unreported: 25%
Percent African-American: 6%
Percent Asian/Pacific Islander: 3%
Percent Hispanic: 4%
Percent Native-American: <1%
Percent International: 1%
Percent in-state/out of state: 23%/77%
Percent from Public HS: 67%
Retention Rate: 78%
Graduation Rate 4-year: 57%

Graduation Rate 6-year: 62%
Percent Undergraduates in On-campus housing: 80%
Number of official organized extracurricular organizations: 60
3 Most popular majors: English, Communications, Psychology
Student/Faculty ratio: 9:1
Average Class Size: 10 to 19
Percent of students going to grad school: Unreported
Tuition and Fees: $32,636
In State Tuition and Fees if different: No difference
Cost for Room and Board: $10,104
Percent receiving financial aid out of those who apply, first year: 81%
Percent receiving financial aid among all students: 59%

G oucher College, located just eight miles outside of Baltimore in the town of Towson, is a small liberal arts college that focuses on big issues. Although the school enrolls about 1,400 undergraduates, their resources for students go far beyond the 287 acres of Goucher property. With new study-abroad requirements, for which students are granted at least $1,200 to cover travel costs, interinstitutional programs with Johns Hopkins University and with Baltimore Hebrew University, and many opportunities for work and study in Baltimore and Washington D.C., Goucher's small community has become a college recognized for expanding knowledge outside of the small liberal arts college bubble.

Education Without Boundaries

With a motto like "Education without Boundaries," Goucher offers students plenty of opportunities in and out of the classroom. With thirty-one majors and six interdisciplinary areas, a five-year BA/BS program in Science and Engineering with Johns Hopkins, and numerous study-abroad programs available during the optional January term, Goucher makes it easy for students to pursue any interest they may have. Many students agree that although there are relatively few of them, their academic interests vary widely. Psychology is the most popular major on campus, and the visual and performing arts have become more popular over the years, especially with Goucher's renowned dance major. But if students still feel confined by the majors, Goucher allows them to create their own.

Goucher's general education requirements (also known as Gen Ed) include proficiency in a language, English composition, and computer technology along with a distribution of courses in the arts, natural sciences, humanities, social sciences, and mathematics. Most nonscience majors who are looking to fill their natural sciences "Gen Ed" requirement take the largest course—up to around one hundred students—at Goucher, "Introduction to Psychology," taught by the beloved Dr. Ann McKim. Dr. McKim is a "very memorable and very enthusiastic" professor who is known for keeping her students—all one hundred of them—interested and entertained.

Freshmen are also required to take two classes. One is a freshman seminar and the other is a Connections class, where freshmen meet with their upperclassmen peer mediators and talk about important issues regarding college life. However, some freshmen say the class is only effective if the peer mediator is actually dedicated to the class, which is not always the case. Overall, many freshman agree that assimilating into Goucher is easy from the beginning, and the required freshman classes can be a "great way" to meet new people and learn about a topic they would "not usually be interested in." Still, students say that freshman year can lead to some serious culture shock, as new students adjust—and even conform—to the very liberal atmosphere of the small campus.

In terms of academic difficulty, Goucher gets mixed reviews, but one senior said "that is only because some majors are more difficult than others." The English and Natural Science majors get reviews of being more difficult, while Psychology and Communications are known for being more "lenient with grading." Overall, most students agree that "you only get out of classes what you put into them" and "if you really want an A, and if you work hard enough, it is attainable." One of the reasons many students can succeed in their classes is because of the accessibility of professors. Goucher has a 10:1 student to teacher ratio and an average class size of 19, which translates into having professors "almost always able to meet when you want to schedule a meeting." Some students even said they have become friendly with professors who they've never even have "because Goucher tries to make professors and students on a more equal level; we call most teachers by their first names."

A Unique Social Experience

Even before freshman year, each class of Goucher students has the opportunity to meet people with all different interests through preorientation programs. Students agree that while the diversity—cultural, geographic, and socioeconomic—at Goucher is not very great, it improves each year. For a small liberal arts school, some students were "surprised by how many lacrosse 'bros' and athletes there are." But overall the "stereotypical" Goucher student is "very hippy-ish and free, from a middle class family on the East Coast." Overall, students are "really friendly" and "people will always be waving to you on the Van Meter Highway" (Goucher's walkway between the academic and residential quads).

"Right now, my main group of friends are the people on my floor and the people I do [activities] with," says one freshman. Seniors and freshmen both agree that the friends they have are the ones they live with and the ones with whom they participate in extracurricular activities. Usually "the athletes hang out together," but athletes agree that they "don't feel limited, even by age. Most parties have people of every age." While there is not a strong divide between students, "there are definitely different groups." One student on the women's lacrosse team said that "parties are mostly small groups of friends . . . our school is too small and parties would be broken up if they were over thirty people." With no Greek system at Goucher, parties are generally confined to students' rooms.

> "We're a very liberal school . . . it kind of comes with the territory."

While parties are small, that does not stop Goucher students from partying as hard as at any other college. Many students agree that alcohol is very common on campus, and marijuana is as well because "we're a very liberal school . . . it kind of comes with the territory." Students who are less interested in partying say that it can be "difficult to find alternatives—you have to try." While alcohol and marijuana can be found, the rules are "definitely enforced," especially by Community Assistants (CAs)—upperclassmen who oversee dorm life—who get reviews between being "really relaxed" and "pretty strict." The CAs are not just in charge of making sure parties don't get out of control, but they also deal with issues between roommates and with technical problems, and they can advise students on anything from classes to clubs.

Goucher social life at night does not consist only of small parties in dorm rooms. Students also hang out in the Gopher Hole, a coffee house on campus that's open late, often has live music on weekends, and serves food like quesadillas and "really good" smoothies. In the middle of the fall semester, students gear up for "Humans vs. Zombies," a weekend-long game that involves many pumped-up members of the student body, Nerf guns, and mild "implications of violence." Another big social event is Get into Goucher Day (GIG), when all classes are canceled on a surprise day and the campus is converted into an amusement park. Many students call it "the best day of the year." The "formal" event of the year is Gala, a night of dancing and good food. However, not every student can go to Gala, as the limited number of tickets is distributed based on seniority, starting with the seniors and "trickling down" to a few lucky freshmen.

Outside of the usual weekend events, many Gophers, as Goucher students are commonly called, are involved in volunteering, jobs, and internships. By senior year, about seventy percent of Goucher students will have had an internship. Many students find job opportunities on campus, but with Baltimore nearby and a mall in the neighborhood, many students work off campus. . The Goucher student body is also involved in helping the community, through on- and off-campus organizations. Goucher also features some "unique" clubs such as the Goucher Pirate Alliance, which is known for having bake sales where the members dress up in pirate garb. Otherwise, there are over sixty other options for students, ranging from student government to the campus radio station to student publications, such as the newspaper *The Quindecim* (*The Q*).

With seventeen NCAA Division III teams at Goucher, athletes have a big presence on campus. However, many students admit that sports at Goucher are "mostly athletes going to athletes' games." Despite the fact that sports do not get too much nonathlete spirit, students agree "we have a lot of school spirit, just not in the traditional way of going to sports games." The athletic program at Goucher is ever expanding, with brand-new fields and a new cardio center and weight room. All facilities are open for nonathletic

use, and Gophers are excited about the renovations.

Going Green at Goucher

Goucher's new initiative to "go green" has been extremely effective and gets high marks from students. Over recent years, Goucher has expanded its "green" program by building environmentally friendly buildings, selecting a "green supplier" to cater the dining halls, selling "eco-friendly" items at the bookstore, and holding many events for students to learn about sustainability. Ground broke in 2007 for the Athenaeum, Goucher's new "green building," which will hold the library, performance space, an art gallery, a computer lab, a restaurant, and many more facilities. Students are looking forward to the quadlike outdoor terrace, which will be on the roof of the building and carpeted with grass. While Goucher is calling the Athenaeum its "Crowning Jewel," students say that the campus "is [already] really beautiful" and is laid out "really well."

For students who live in dorms, there are a few buildings that students can pick based on a lottery system. Most dorms have students of all ages, but some are more "luxurious" than others.

Sophomores, juniors, and seniors can also live off campus in apartments, many of which owned by Goucher. When students want to go into Baltimore or Washington, D.C. (an hour away from campus), "about half of students have cars," but there is also a shuttle that goes between Goucher and the other universities in Baltimore, ending at the Harbor in Baltimore. "Zip cars are also an option for students who don't have cars but want to rent one."

When Goucher students get hungry, they have a lot of different options both on and around campus. Ranging from Stimson, the largest dining hall, to the Cheesecake Factory that recently opened, Goucher students have a myriad of options when it comes to eating. Students are "pretty satisfied" with the food on campus. In Heubeck Dining Hall, students have different stations to choose from, including a deli station and the sustainable Global Green Exhibition station.

Overall, Goucher students are proud of their campus and of what Goucher has to offer them. Goucher students are quick to point out the interesting facts that make their school unique. Gophers tell legends about the twenty-four mile-per-hour speed limit sign, nuclear fallout shelter, the mummy that Johns Hopkins allegedly "stole" from their school, and the beautiful trails located right off campus. Students agree that in the end, it's the school's "quirky self-expression that is inherent in most students" that makes Goucher different from any other school.—*Willi Rechler*

FYI

If you come to Goucher you better bring "plenty of warm layers for the winter," "a Nerf gun for Humans vs. Zombies," "a blanket for outside lounging," and "lots of Expo markers for your white board."

A typical weekend at Goucher is "everyone goes out Friday to the harbor or an off-campus party, then to the Gopher Hole or Game room," and Saturdays consist of "brunch in the morning, then repeat Friday night" with Sunday "a full day in the library."

If I could change one thing about Goucher I'd "make us have more school spirit."

Three things every student at Goucher should do before graduating are "Go to the Gopher Hole events, get their own radio show, and attend a Goucher party."

Johns Hopkins University

Address: 3400 North Charles Street, Mason Hall, Baltimore, MD 21218
Phone: 410-516-8171
E-mail address: apphelp@jhu.edu
Web site URL: www.jhu.edu
Year Founded: 1876
Private or Public: Private
Religious Affiliation: None
Location: Urban
Number of Applicants: 14,848
Percent Accepted: 24%
Percent Accepted who enroll: 33%
Number Entering: 1,206
Number of Transfers Accepted each Year: 26
Middle 50% SAT range: M: 660–770, CR: 630–730, Wr: 630–730
Middle 50% ACT range: 28–33
Early admission program EA/ED/None: ED

Percentage accepted through EA or ED: Unreported
EA and ED deadline: 1-Nov
Regular Deadline: 1-Jan
Application Fee: $70
Full-time Undergraduate enrollment: 4,591
Total enrollment: 6,437
Percent Male: 53%
Percent Female: 47%
Total Percent Minority or Unreported: 16%
Percent African-American: 6%
Percent Asian/Pacific Islander: 25%
Percent Hispanic: 7%
Percent Native-American: <1%
Percent International: 5%
Percent in-state/out of state: 13%/87%
Percent from Public HS: 69%
Retention Rate: 97%
Graduation Rate 4-year: 81%

Graduation Rate 6-year: 89%
Percent Undergraduates in On-campus housing: 60%
Number of official organized extracurricular organizations: 250
3 Most popular majors: Biomedical/Medical Engineering, Economics, International Relations and Affairs
Student/Faculty ratio: Unreported
Average Class Size: 10 to 19
Percent of students going to grad school: 38%
Tuition and Fees: $37,700
In State Tuition and Fees if different: No difference
Cost for Room and Board: $11,578
Percent receiving financial aid out of those who apply, first year: 47%
Percent receiving financial aid among all students: 46%

There are two things bound to bother most students at Johns Hopkins University. The first is leaving the "s" off of Johns when speaking the name of this prestigious Baltimore institution. Founded in 1876 as the nation's first research university, Johns Hopkins was named for its first benefactor whose given name was actually Johns, his mother's maiden name. The second "no-no" is the assumption that all Hopkins students are either premeds or hard-core science majors. Although celebrated for its medical school and for providing an unsurpassed premedical education, Johns Hopkins is also extremely strong in the humanities, social sciences, and engineering. Its International

Relations program is considered perhaps the finest in the nation, and its writing and art history majors are top ranked. In fact, only about 30 percent of entering freshmen at Hopkins profess an interest in medicine, a number that diminishes over time.

Homewood Bound

Although the Johns Hopkins Medical Institutions are world-renowned, the heart of the university can be found at its Homewood campus, a beautifully manicured 140-acre parklike setting adorned with red-brick Georgian Federalist-style buildings. Brick, granite, and marble walkways wend their way through lush green lawns, sculpture gardens, and beds of blue and white flowers. "The beach," an expanse of lawn that extends out from the Milton S. Eisenhower Library, is a magnet for students who want to relax, sunbathe, or socialize. All freshmen and sophomores live in or adjacent to Homewood. Freshmen live in the Alumni Memorial Residences (AMRs), or enjoy the air-conditioning in Buildings A and B. While air-conditioning in Baltimore has its advantages, many freshmen prefer the AMR setup. "I made so many friends in AMR I," one sophomore said. "It was a great place to live and a great way to meet a lot of people." Some freshmen and many sophomores live in Wolman and McCoy, which have kitchenettes and large common areas. In the past, upperclassmen have had to live off campus in apartments that abut Homewood. With the completion of Charles Commons in 2006, more students have opted to remain in university-operated facilities. Charles Commons, an extremely attractive and functional new building, houses more than 600 undergraduates as well as the 29,000-square-foot Barnes and Noble campus bookstore. Situated across Charles Street, a main thoroughfare that borders the main campus, it is a convenient and desirable residence. "Charles Commons is impressive," said one junior. "The suites are really well appointed and the opportunities for socializing in the dining facility and the common spaces really make this a fantastic place to live. It is a major addition to campus life." In addition, the University has taken over several existing apartment buildings adjacent to the new facility, performing some renovations and instituting better security.

The level of security and the degree of safety on campus in view of Baltimore's urban problems and crime rate (which is falling) are important concerns voiced by prospective students. The university has invested a great deal of time and money in assuring that there are plenty of "Hop Cops" to patrol the campus at all times, security guards at the entrances to all of the dormitories and affiliated apartments, and 24/7 walking escorts and vans available to students. "The campus is safe as long as you are aware of your surroundings," said a junior. "It's like any urban school."

Several other building projects are being pursued concurrently to both expand the campus and substantially renovate existing classroom facilities. The Decker Quadrangle venture, completed in November 2007, created a new public entrance to the campus, a new visitors and admissions center, a building to house the computational sciences departments, and a substantial underground parking facility. In addition, Gilman Hall, the heart of the Homewood, is in the process of undergoing a complete renovation, the plans of which call for the creation of a movie theater and glass-enclosed atrium.

Dining options have expanded greatly on campus and many of the dining areas and food courts have been renovated. Vegetarian and kosher foods are available at all times in certain of the venues. Freshmen are required to participate in the meal plan, while upperclassmen generally choose to prepare their own meals.

Academics: Hold the Stereotypes, Please

The student body at Johns Hopkins is ethnically diverse and a significant international population is represented on campus. The academic curriculum is rigorous, and students quickly come to realize that the "grade inflation" found at most other top colleges and universities is not characteristic of classes here. Many courses are graded on a curve. Contrary to the common stereotype that Hopkins undergraduates, particularly premeds, are intensely competitive and will work to the detriment of their fellow classmates, stealing reading materials and sabotaging lab projects, most students find their peers to be helpful and more internally motivated than externally driven by grades. "The Hopkins stereotype is ridiculous," said one senior premed. "I have never heard of a single instance of such nonsense. In fact, sophomore year my chemistry lab partner once stayed up with me all night to try to help me figure out why my data did not work out."

Perhaps to diminish the stress of grades and to promote an easier transition to the academic rigor of the Hopkins's curriculum, first-semester grades are "covered," which means they are never seen by graduate schools and are not factored into calculations of a student's GPA. First-semester grades are simply designated on the transcript as Satisfactory or Unsatisfactory. This policy has been uniformly applauded by Hopkins students, who consider covered first-semester grades to be a factor encouraging them to be more eclectic in their choice of courses and less concerned about not doing well during the period of their first exposure to the demands of academic, social, and extracurricular life at Hopkins.

Students are affiliated with one of two undergraduate divisions of Johns Hopkins, the Zanvyl Krieger School of Arts and Sciences, and the G. W. C. Whiting School of Engineering. The former is the core institution at Hopkins and enrolls approximately 63 percent of the student body, the remainder being part of the Whiting School. Most students find the professors to be extremely approachable and committed, especially in the upper-level classes, which are small. "I very quickly learned that the best person to answer a question that I might have had was the professor herself," one student said. Teachers generally do not just go through the motions at review sessions. "One evening, my biochemistry professor ran a study group until midnight and did not leave until every question was answered!" Students in Arts and Sciences choose from over 60 established undergraduate majors. Many of these programs are ranked among the best in the country. In addition, students may design an interdisciplinary major with the assistance of a faculty adviser.

> "I very quickly learned that the best person to answer a question that I might have had was the professor herself."

Distribution requirements for Arts and Science undergraduates are far from onerous and there is no core curriculum. A minimum of 30 credits out of the 120 required for the B.A. degree must be obtained in areas outside of the major. For majors in the humanities or social sciences, 12 of the 30 are required to fall within the disciplines of science or mathematics. Natural or quantitative science majors must earn at least 18–21 credits in the humanities or social sciences. In addition, Arts and Science students must take at least 4 courses that are designated writing-intensive.

Students in the G. W. C. Whiting School of Engineering pursue majors in nine distinct areas of study, including Mathematics and Statistics, Biomedical Engineering, Chemical Engineering, and Computer Science. The Department of Biomedical Engineering was ranked the best in the country by *U.S. News and World Report* and the Department of Geography and Environmental Engineering in the top five nationally. Generally between 120 and 130 credits are required for a B.S. or B.A. degree from the Whiting school.

Between semesters, Hopkins undergraduates are given a unique, voluntary opportunity to receive up to two Pass/Fail "enrichment" credits in one of four areas, including Academic Enrichment, Personal Enrichment, Experiential Learning, and Study Abroad. Academic Enrichment courses are free. Every January during Intersession, many students avail themselves of the chance to take an interesting class while enjoying part of their winter break on campus.

Taking Learning Beyond the Classroom

Research at Johns Hopkins is particularly encouraged, and there are enormous opportunities for students to become involved in projects with renowned faculty members, especially in the natural, social, and behavioral sciences. It is estimated that nearly 80 percent of Hopkins undergraduates engage in some sort of research outside of the classroom. The dedication of Johns Hopkins to research is reflected in the fact that the university ranks number one in the receipt of federal funds for research and development in science, medicine, and engineering. One female junior commented that she has "been involved in three different research projects since coming to Hopkins, both in my major (Psychology) and at the Medical School. The experience has been amazing and my advisor is always available to talk about our work."

Up to 70 percent of Hopkins students get involved in volunteer work in the community and frequently tutor inner-city elementary school students in a variety of subjects. In addition, there are 250 undergraduate clubs to attract students including a variety of publications and singing groups. "There is something for everybody's interest," said one male freshman. "I am still deciding about which of the many different school publications I want to join." The *Johns Hopkins News-Letter*, founded in 1896, is the oldest continuously published newspaper in the country and one of the most popular extracurricular venues.

Work Hard, Play Hard

No one would deny that Johns Hopkins students take their academic responsibilities very seriously. During finals period, the main library's doors are open all night, and the facility is generally full to the rafters at that time. Nevertheless, Hopkins students take their socializing seriously as well. Most students feel that the social life on campus has been steadily improving. During freshman year, the main party venue is at the fraternity houses, which are situated off campus. About 1,000 undergraduates belong to one of eleven fraternities and seven sororities. Freshman especially find frat parties an excellent way to meet classmates, albeit hot and noisy. Upperclassmen, however, generally choose "house parties" in student apartments instead of the frat scene. "Underclassmen are easy to please because they don't know any better," chuckled one male senior. "By junior year, you just don't want to chug frat Jell-O shots." Near campus, in the surrounding Charles Village, PJs and Charles Village Pub (CVP) are popular watering holes. Off campus, a short cab ride away, the Inner Harbor is a draw for stu-

dents on the weekends, especially in the area called Power Plant. In addition, many undergraduates go to Fell's Point, where there are several clubs. Excellent shopping and restaurants can be found in neighboring Towson.

Lacrosse! Lacrosse! Lacrosse!

Hopkins fields teams in all major collegiate sports, but lacrosse is unquestionably the preeminent Blue Jay sport on campus, and the source of a great deal of school spirit. In fact, Johns Hopkins lacrosse is Division I, while all other sports teams compete in Division III. Lacrosse players are actively recruited at Hopkins, and such efforts have resulted in 44 national titles for the men's team, including nine NCAA Division I titles, the most recent being awarded in 2007. Women's lacrosse too has become extremely competitive.

Hopkins has fielded top Division III teams in baseball, basketball, fencing, swimming, and water polo. For students who prefer just keeping in shape, Hopkins opened a 60,000-square-foot recreation center in 2001 that includes a climbing wall in addition to the usual cardiovascular conditioning machines.

No one would argue that Johns Hopkins is a party school. Its curriculum is intense but rewarding and the opportunities for research unsurpassed. If you are a serious student who is looking for an ethnically diverse and academically superlative school in an urban setting, and you appreciate opportunities for research, then Hopkins may just be the place for you. Loving lacrosse wouldn't hurt either!—*Jonathan Berken*

FYI
If you come to Johns Hopkins, you'd better bring "an 'I love Lacrosse' T-shirt."
What is a typical weekend schedule? "Go out Friday night, study Saturday morning, go to a lacrosse match or other sporting event in the afternoon, go to a frat or house party Saturday night, wake up late and study all day Sunday."
If I could change one thing about Johns Hopkins, I'd "get rid of bell-curve grading in classes."
Three things that every student at Johns Hopkins should do before graduating are "go to Pete's Grill, go to Fell's Point for Halloween, and cheer on the Blue Jays."

St. John's College

Address: PO Box 2800
Annapolis, MD 21404
Phone: 410-626-2522
E-mail address:
admissions@sjca.edu
Web site URL:
www.stjohnscollege.edu
Year Founded: 1696
Private or Public: Private
Religious Affiliation: None
Location: Urban
Number of Applicants:
Unreported
Percent Accepted: 81%
**Percent Accepted who
enroll:** Unreported
Number Entering: 156
**Number of Transfers
Accepted each Year:** 23
Middle 50% SAT range:
M: 590–680 CR: 640–740,
Wr: Unreported
Middle 50% ACT range:
Unreported
**Early admission program
EA/ED/None:** None
**Percentage accepted
through EA or ED:** NA

EA and ED deadline: NA
**Regular Deadline: None/
Priority Application
deadline:** March 1
Application Fee: $0
**Full time Undergraduate
enrollment:** 488
Total enrollment: 488
Percent Male: 53%
Percent Female: 47%
**Total Percent Minority or
Unreported:** 10%
Percent African-American:
1%
**Percent Asian/Pacific
Islander:** 3%
Percent Hispanic: 3%
Percent Native-American:
1%
Percent International:
Unreported
**Percent in-state/out of
state:** 18%/82%
Percent from Public HS:
Unreported
Retention Rate: Unreported
Graduation Rate 4-year:
Unreported

Graduation Rate 6-year:
Unreported
**Percent Undergraduates
in On-campus housing:**
80%
**Number of official organized
extracurricular
organizations:** Unreported
3 Most popular majors:
Unreported
Student/Faculty ratio:
Unreported
Average Class Size:
Unreported
**Percent of students going to
grad school:** 9%
Tuition and Fees: $39,
154
**In State Tuition and Fees if
different:** No difference
Cost for Room and Board:
$9,284
**Percent receiving financial
aid out of those who apply,
first year:** 78%
**Percent receiving financial
aid among all students:**
Unreported

A liberal arts education typically consists of a program of study geared toward the learning of general knowledge; it is essentially a classical form of education. St. John's College and the Great Books Program "takes serious the concept of the liberal arts, as they are literally the "freeing" arts."

Learning the Ancient Greek Alphabet

Students at the two St. John's campuses in Santa Fe, NM and Annapolis, MD have homework before their freshman year begins. In order to jump directly into the Great Books Program, all freshmen are required to memorize the Greek alphabet before arriving in their dorm rooms. Ancient Greek is one of the two languages St. John's offers, and all students take Greek for two years followed by two years of French. Learning the Greek alphabet may seem like a Herculean task, but the languages are required "not so as to be able to speak it, but more to translate great books."

The Great Books Program allows St. John's to stand apart from the hundreds of other liberal arts institutions in the country. The curriculum on both campuses is standardized with all students taking the same courses. They take music, mathematics, laboratory sciences and a classics seminar while at St. John's.

But the centerpieces of the Great Books Program are the books, so don't forget to bring a bookshelf with you freshman year. Johnnies learn geometry directly from Euclid's writings, study the classics like Virgil's Aeneid and Dante's Divine Comedy, and learn physics from Newton, though without the apples. The emphasis is not on learning from secondary sources such as textbooks; rather, "they want you to decide what you think they are saying, not what someone else believes them to be saying. It's like going back in time."

It is for these reasons that one student described the Great Books program as "freeing"—the opportunity to form one's own conclusions from venerated texts is one of the cornerstones of St. John's liberal arts education.

Nice to Meet You Mr. _____

With so much to learn and read in such a short amount of time, students rely on each other to discuss the material in seminars, led by tutors—not "professors." Tutors and students, alike, go by Mr. or Ms. and tutors can be a big part of a student's life at St. John's. Tutors are available to discuss material outside of class and often dine with their students. They are "open, accessible, and incredibly intelligent people." To win favor around the seminar table, tutors respond well to being fed—the "key is to take them out to lunch and try and win them over (even if the dining hall is pure poison)."

But in class, tutors do not so much direct as sponsor discussions of the readings for two hours two nights a week. In Arthurian-fashion, the students and their tutors sit facing each other at a seminar table. The discussion is student-led and tutors "are not there to teach you, so much as to make sure you don't get too off topic." Discussion of the literature, philosophy, and politics texts results not in a final exam or midterm but in papers throughout the year and one final paper at the end of each school year.

Though the system allows students to "formulate [their] own opinions and beliefs," the system has been criticized by some as being too subjective, due to a lack of objectively evaluated tests or exams. Because a student's grade is based on participation in seminar and his or her writing, "every class is integral to your succeeding at St. John's."

Not the Queen of Hearts' Croquet

Athletes beware—St. Johns-Annapolis offers just crew, sailing, fencing and croquet intercollegiate sports teams. But one of the most anticipated traditions at the Annapolis campus is Croquet Weekend, a sort of throwback garden party held in one of the nation's oldest cities.

Located literally around the corner from 4,400 future naval officers at the U.S. Naval Academy, St. John's has a healthy rivalry with the Midshipmen, affectionately known outside of the USNA as "middies." Croquet weekend sees the Johnnies and middies

face off in the biggest croquet match of the year for former national champion St. John's. Girls break out formal summer dresses and big hats, and "boys in nice outfits" don sport coats and loafers for the big event, while their counterparts from the USNA attend in dress whites.

"Although most don't go so much to see the game," a student said. "There are booths all around full of food, delicious oh so delicious food, as well as trinkets and alcohol."

For a school so wrapped up in tradition, another popular tradition at Annapolis is waltz parties, which a lot of midshipmen also attend. Reality, a junior group that is sponsored by the College to throw parties for the 475-strong campus, offers another form of weekend debauchery. "At Seducers and Corrupters, upperclassmen wear black and freshman wear white. 'Us' being the more experienced are supposed to welcome them by seducing and corrupting 'them.' It's really quite fun and helps everyone to get to know each other faster," a student said.

> "St. John's takes serious the concept of liberal arts, as they are literally the 'freeing' arts."

Another popular event is a Reality-sponsored weekend at the end of the year that involves a game called Spartan ball—harking back to St. John's classical outlook. "The game ends with three points, three injuries or three hours. There are no rules except the vehicles, bikes, horses, etc. are not allowed on the field, you can't wear shoes, and play only stops when the ball goes in the water or a point is scored," a participant said.

City Limits

The Annapolis campus of St. John's is nestled neatly into the historic city's waterfront, a stone's throw from the Naval Academy. But that idyllic setting has its downsides. Housing prices have risen in recent years, making housing at one of the campus dorms guaranteed only to freshman. Additionally, with food on campus drawing poor reviews, students often venture into Annapolis to grab a bite—to the detriment of their wallets. "[Annapolis] is absolutely gorgeous and has amazing food—you are just going to pay for it," a student said.

"There are three basic types of Johnnies," a student said. "There are room Johnnies who you rarely see except for the dining hall and class. There are campus Johnnies. The third type are the off-campus Johnnies who live, eat, etc., off campus." Most students at St. John's are "intellectual" and love discussing their reading and course-work away from the seminar table. "One student can be found always wearing a top hat and carrying a cane," a student said, also noting that the campus dress code varies from person to person, but that a preppy atmosphere stems from the classi-cal education at St. John's.

Though the campus is smaller than most schools, students found it to be welcoming and a way to enhance the college experi-ence. Though attempts to reinvent oneself, as is possible at large schools, are limited at St. John's because of its size, "it still feels like a pretty big school at times." —*Brittany Golob*

FYI

If you come to St. John's College you should bring "a chalkboard, a taste for classical music and a pinch of humility."

The typical weekend schedule is "basically what you make it" after Friday night seminar ends at 9:30. "Waltz parties and intramural sports are also a must-do."

If I could change one thing about St. John's College, "I'd increase the bandwith in order to watch YouTube videos," or "add more stability" to the grading system.

Three things every student at St. John's should do before graduating are "attend the Annapolis Cup at Croquet Weekend, get to know a member of the staff, and take a dip in College Creek."

St. Mary's College of Maryland

Address: 18952 East Fisher Road St. Mary's City, MD 20686-3001
Phone: 240-895-5000
E-mail address: admissions@smcm.edu
Web site URL: www.smcm.edu
Year Founded: 1840
Private or Public: Public
Religious Affiliation: None
Location: Rural
Number of Applicants: 2,723
Percent Accepted: 55%
Percent Accepted who enroll: 32%
Number Entering: 454
Number of Transfers Accepted each Year: 99
Middle 50% SAT range: M: 570–660, CR: 580–680, Wr: 570–680
Middle 50% ACT range: 24–29
Early admission program EA/ED/None: ED

Percentage accepted through EA or ED: 47%
EA and ED deadline: 1-Nov
Regular Deadline: 1-Jan
Application Fee: $40
Full time Undergraduate enrollment: 2,035
Total enrollment: 2,065
Percent Male: 43%
Percent Female: 57%
Total Percent Minority or Unreported: 24%
Percent African-American: 8%
Percent Asian/Pacific Islander: 4%
Percent Hispanic: 5%
Percent Native-American: 1%
Percent International: 2%
Percent in-state/out of state: 83%/17%
Percent from Public HS: 70%
Retention Rate: 90%
Graduation Rate 4-year: 67%

Graduation Rate 6-year: 74%
Percent Undergraduates in On-campus housing: 81%
Number of official organized extracurricular organizations: 116
3 Most popular majors: Economics, English, Psychology
Student/Faculty ratio: 12:1
Average Class Size: 10 to 19
Percent of students going to grad school: 34%
Tuition and Fees: $23,454
In State Tuition and Fees if different: $12,604
Cost for Room and Board: $9,225
Percent receiving financial aid out of those who apply, first year: 64%
Percent receiving financial aid among all students: 61%

Located in the historic St. Mary's City, St. Mary's College of Maryland (SMCM) is known as the state's Public Honors College. Founded in 1840 by the state legislature as a girl's boarding school, it has evolved to accept a more socioeco-nomically, racially, and gender-diverse stu-dent body.

Liberal Honors

As a public honors college, SMCM provides a quality education in a small liberal arts setting—the professors, as one student described, are "top class" while remaining, as another student said "warm and welcoming." When going to a school athletic game, you are just as likely to see your professor as you are your roommate. In the fall of 2008, the College implemented a new liberal arts core curriculum. In their first year, students take an "Introduction to the Liberal Arts" seminar, with a heavy focus on critical thinking, written expression, oral expression and information literacy.

Students are now required to have an "academic experience outside the classroom." To fulfill the requirement, students may study abroad, complete a course with a substantial service requirement, get an approved job or conduct independent study.

Most students enjoy the new core curriculum, expecting it to expand their academic horizons.

Classes at SMCM are kept small with the average class size at 16 students. Over 75 percent of classes have less than 20 students and rarely do even introductory courses top 35.

Some students are frustrated by a lack of academic rigor in the school, but put the blame on their peers. One student said her friends routinely mock the "honors college" designation saying that students prefer to be "chill" about their studies.

Down by the River

Students describe SMCM as being a quirky, goofy campus. The campus's location on the banks of the St. Mary's River provides students with a natural hangout spot. When the waterfront is open, students take out sailboats at no charge. And continuing the water theme, on a student's birthday they are subjected to "ponding" by their friends—being thrown into St. John's Pond at the center of campus.

Students relax and study in the multipurpose "Awesome Room" of the Muldoon River Center—the center of the campus's waterfront activities. In recent years, SMCM has hosted a cardboard boat race in addition to several more traditional clubs like crew, windsurfing, sailing, and wakeboarding.

According to students, athletics are an important part of campus life. With over 14 NCAA Division III teams and a nationally ranked sailing team, students find that if they are not playing, they are watching the games and cheering on their classmates.

Competing in the Capital Athletic Conference, SMCM often faces Gallaudet, Catholic and York Universities.

SMCM has something for everybody—over 100 clubs ranging in interest from anime to needlework. For those not participating in clubs, there are a host of recreational activities including SMCM student's favorite pastime, Frisbee Golf, in which students turn campus landmarks into holes.

SMCM takes the environmental crisis seriously. It has banned trays from its dining halls to save water and has placed bicycles around campus for student use. Additionally, each winter students organize the Polar Bear Splash, in which students—and last year one professor—dive into the frigid waters of St. Mary's River to raise awareness of climate change.

> "The quirky, hippie reputation of St. Mary's students is steadily giving way to a preppier, more clean-cut demographic."

With just under 2,000 classmates, SMCM can be as big or as small as you want it to be said students. According to students, there is a great sense of community shared by everyone from the staff and professors to the entire student body. "Everyone is just so open-minded and supportive," said one student. SMCM draws its student body from 41 countries and 40 states, though according to students, its waterfront is drawing a more homogenous crowd: "The quirky, hippie reputation of St. Mary's students is steadily giving way to a preppier, more clean-cut demographic," said one student.

Living it up in Maryland

On weekends, most students chose to stay on campus, using the school's facilities or catching a free movie at the campus theater. Others chose to travel to the closest town, Lexington Park, home to Patuxent Naval Air Station to grab a bite to eat, see a movie, or go shopping. SMCM allows all students to bring cars to campus.

Some students are upset with the lack of Greek life on campus, but a majority find they can enjoy themselves just fine without it. Nearly 80 percent of SMCM students chose to live on campus in rooms that include conventional dorms, suites, townhouses and apartments.

Housing is determined by class seniority,

leaving many underclassmen waiting until they are seniors for their pick of the college's rooming options. That said, students usually find their roommates to be their best friends with suite dinners and movie nights common across campus.

According to students, partying is fairly widespread on campus, particularly among those living in townhouses. There is a substantial group of students who use drugs on campus, and students believe the vast majority of their peers consume alcohol regularly.

Overall, SMCM students find their own niche on campus be it athletics, clubs, academics or some combination therein. As one SMCM student put it, "it's a pretty relaxed environment here." They clearly relish the opportunity to "chill" and make the most of their four years at SMCM.—*Zeke Miller*

FYI

If you come to St. Mary's, you'd better bring "your bathing suit. Especially when in the spring, its hard to find a student that's not down by the water either swimming, kayaking, sailing or just hanging out."

What's the typical weekend schedule? I usually spend my weekends catching up: catching up with friends, homework, and sleep. Because St. Mary's is in such a rural location, most of the activities happen on campus. Every weekend the school brings movies, comedians, bands and other fun activities to keep us busy and entertained. Most students live on campus, and few clear out on weekends.

If I could change one thing about St. Mary's, "it would be to increase the number of study abroad options available for students."

Three things every student at St. Mary's should do before graduating are: Have lunch/dinner with a professor, learn how to sail, and get thrown into St. John's pond on their birthday.

United States Naval Academy

Address: 117 Decatur Road Annapolis, MD 21402
Phone: 410-293-1914
E-mail address: webmail@usna.edu
Web site URL: www.usna.edu
Year Founded: 1845
Private or Public: Public
Religious Affiliation: None
Location: Urban
Number of Applicants: 10,960
Percent Accepted: 14%
Percent Accepted who enroll: 82%
Number Entering: 1,261
Number of Transfers Accepted each Year: Unreported
Middle 50% SAT range: M: 600–700, CR: 560–670, Wr: Unreported
Middle 50% ACT range: Unreported
Early admission program EA/ED/None: None

Percentage accepted through EA or ED: NA
EA and ED deadline: NA
Regular Deadline: 31-Jan
Application Fee: $0
Full time Undergraduate enrollment: 4,489
Total enrollment: 4,489
Percent Male: 80%
Percent Female: 20%
Total Percent Minority or Unreported: 25%
Percent African-American: 4%
Percent Asian/Pacific Islander: 3%
Percent Hispanic: 11%
Percent Native-American: <1%
Percent International: 1%
Percent in-state/out of state: 5%/95%
Percent from Public HS: 60%
Retention Rate: 96%
Graduation Rate 4-year: 84%

Graduation Rate 6-year: 84%
Percent Undergraduates in On-campus housing: 100%
Number of official organized extracurricular organizations: 70
3 Most popular majors: Economics, Political Science, Systems Engineering
Student/Faculty ratio: 8.5:1
Average Class Size: 10 to 19
Percent of students going to grad school: 2%
Tuition and Fees: $0
In State Tuition and Fees if different: No difference
Cost for Room and Board: $0
Percent receiving financial aid out of those who apply, first year: NA
Percent receiving financial aid among all students: NA

The United States Naval Academy is situated in Annapolis, MD. Founded in 1845 by the Secretary of the Navy, George Bancroft, the historic academy is responsible for the training of future officers of the Navy or Marine Corps. Despite its strict regiment and array of rules and hazing rites of passage that range from the silly to the unbearable, the camaraderie that develops among the midshipmen is incomparable. Students praise the institution not only for its training, but for the faculty's dedication in doing everything in their power to see their students succeed.

Fit Mind and Body

The Naval Academy stresses academia, resulting in what some students consider a "much heavier course load than that of other schools." Students are not allowed to take fewer than 15 credits a semester. As one student explained, "You don't have the option to take longer than four years. If you are on that path then you get kicked out before graduation time." Of course, the faculty's dedication to its students undoubtedly pays off in USNA's small classes, which have "between 15 and 25 students, and no graduate students" teaching. All professors have PhDs and "they're really available," one student said. Aside from its emphasis on a class hierarchy, the Naval Academy at times tends to resemble high school in other ways—"a strict high school," that is. "It's hard to do bad here because the professors are always on you." Engineering is the most popular major at USNA, perhaps due in part to the Academy's recent quota that enables "only 30 percent of the students" to be humanities majors. Balancing a heavy course load is only encumbered by fulfillment of one's military requirements. "Your final GPA is a combination of your academic grades, military grades, and physical fitness grades."

Love Hurts

"The upperclassmen run the school and they can punish you." Unfortunately, unlike high school, there's no running to the administration to escape initiation traditions or seniors with paddles, à la *Fast Times at Ridgemont High*. "The first year is basically being initiated into a superfraternity." The Academy is particularly rough with its freshmen, as that first year is key for weeding out the dedicated from the not-so-much. One student exclaimed that, "only 75 percent of the initial class size graduates." Those 25 percent might have failed following the simplest of rules, such as the one that prohibits freshmen from touching their beds from 6:30 a.m. to 10:30 p.m. Frosh regulations are severe. Plebes, first-year students, "only get to leave campus from 10 to 10 on Saturday" and, in a fraternity pledge mentality, must "run in the hallway." And newcomers ought to remember to put all DVDs away. Freshmen are prohibited from listening to music or watching movies. Of course, in addition to the strict restraints on daily activities, plebes lament that "there's a lot of bullshit knowledge you have to know" upon an upperclassmen's request, such as three current newspaper articles in advance or how many days until Thanksgiving break. Although "it's a hard system," many of the rules are relinquished in one's sophomore year. In addition to a few overnights, students agree, "the biggest thing you get as a sophomore is that you get to sleep during the day."

> **"The party scene here is in the weight room."**

The Crisco of Camaraderie

One of the Academy's most memorable traditions occurs upon completion of freshman year, when the students climb Herndon, a 21-foot structure shaped like the Washington Monument. "There's a freshman cover [hat] that's replaced with a midshipment cover," a student explained. "Before you climb it, they put grease, Crisco all around it." The inch-thick fat lining results in tedious hours during which thousands of students attempt to climb the slippery monument. Other traditions include painting the statue in the center of campus before every football game. And the easiest way Naval Academy students can guarantee a goodnight peck? It's USNA tradition that if a girl puts on a guy's cover, she owes him a kiss. "A regular girl," one student clarified, "not a Naval Academy girl."

Party in the Weight Room

"The party scene here is in the weight room." Although the Annapolis scene is "great if you're 21," since drinking is not allowed on campus and students are only allowed out during certain hours on the weekends, students find that "most people honestly do work, run, workout, and go out to eat on the weekends." Plebes are not allowed to drink, even if they are 21. Most people abide by the rigorously enforced rules, especially since "underage drinking is punished severely" and there are random weekend breathalyzers for the underage. On the other hand, seniors are allowed to buy beer at the school restaurant or drink at the officer's club, as long as they don't come back belligerent. Perhaps the slew of rules and punishments account for why intramural sports, although mandatory, provide the social aspect that is sometimes hindered by USNA's strict policies. Football is huge at the Naval Academy, with pep rallies and mandatory attendance at the games greatly promoting school spirit. While such camaraderie is prevalent throughout the school, it is stronger within each company—the 140 people or so with whom a student lives and interacts. There are 30 companies in total.

No Kissing, No Asking, No Telling

You're not allowed to show affection in any form at the Academy. There is no kissing and while PDAs are often in poor etiquette anyway, USNA makes sure to enforce Emily Post's seduction guidelines. "Girls are allowed in guys' rooms, although the door must remain open and there must be no physical contact." Students agreed that such seriousness is understandable in light of sexual harassment cases, especially the Air Force Academy scandal. "Although females are only 19 percent of the school, I feel that the administration has done an excellent job making everything equal and not tolerating any discriminative practices—no matter how mild," praised one student. Despite the female-friendly environment, one male student claimed that, "Most females here tend to have a chip on their shoulder due to the male environment." Of course, despite the rule-infused school, the Naval Academy isn't a completely hands-off boys club. "We have dances and you're allowed to bring dates to those." The dances are "a pretty big deal." One of the biggest events is the Ring Dance at the end of the year. "It's kind of like prom, that type of big, and you get your ring, and you get it in the water from the seven seas and your date is supposed to put it on you." Of course, dancing or lifting weights, "homosexuality is definitely very taboo." Students said it is "not accepted at all, but then again, nobody expects it to be in the military." Most cite the "very conservative student body" as one of the main reasons for the "don't ask, don't tell" mentality that is prevalent on campus.—*Dana Schuster*

FYI

If you come to USNA, you'd better bring a "a sense of humor and long-term perspective. The only way you will be able to survive this place is by being able to laugh it off when you get yelled at and laugh at yourself when you screw up, because both will happen . . . a lot."

What is the typical weekend schedule? "For Freshman: Start with SMT (Saturday Morning Training) around 0630. Then eat, clean, organize, do homework before liberty commences, unless there is a football game. There isn't a lot to do out in town so most either go out to eat, watch a movie, or stay back in the hall and study. Sunday: Sleep until 1:00pm or go to church services. After 1:00pm, be ready to take an exam on information you are supposed to learn about the Navy, Marine Corps, and other services. After the test, prepare for the following days classes and study!"

If I could change one thing about USNA, ". . . I wouldn't change a thing . . . The bad things and hard times, which are quite frequent, are as much a part of the experience as the good times and the opportunities are."

Three things every student should do before graduating are "sneak through the Ho Chi Min trail, join the Salsa club and mess with Master Chief Quiblin's office."

University of Maryland / College Park

Address: Mitchell Building College Park, MD 20742-5235
Phone: 301-314-8385
E-mail address: um-admit@uga.umd.edu
Web site URL: www.umd.edu
Year Founded: 1856
Private or Public: Public
Religious Affiliation: None
Location: Urban
Number of Applicants: 24,176
Percent Accepted: 47%
Percent Accepted who enroll: 37%
Number Entering: 4,204
Number of Transfers Accepted each Year: 3,672
Middle 50% SAT range: M: 600–700, CR: 570–680, Wr: Unreported
Middle 50% ACT range: Unreported
Early admission program EA/ED/None: EA

Percentage accepted through EA or ED: Unreported
EA and ED deadline: 1-Dec
Regular Deadline: 01/20
Application Fee: $55
Full time Undergraduate enrollment: 25,813
Total enrollment: 35,853
Percent Male: 52%
Percent Female: 48%
Total Percent Minority or Unreported: 43%
Percent African-American: 13%
Percent Asian/Pacific Islander: 15%
Percent Hispanic: 6%
Percent Native-American: 0%
Percent International: 2%
Percent in-state/out of state: 76%/24%
Percent from Public HS: Unreported
Retention Rate: 94%
Graduation Rate 4-year: 63%

Graduation Rate 6-year: 81%
Percent Undergraduates in On-campus housing: 41%
Number of official organized extracurricular organizations: 527
3 Most popular majors: Criminology, Economics, Political Science and Government
Student/Faculty ratio: 18:1
Average Class Size: 20 to 29
Percent of students going to grad school: Unreported
Tuition and Fees: $23,076
In State Tuition and Fees if different: $8,005
Cost for Room and Board: $9,109
Percent receiving financial aid out of those who apply, first year: 58%
Percent receiving financial aid among all students: 39%

With an undergraduate enrollment of over 25,800 , the University of Maryland, College Park, may seem at first blush intimidatingly large. Yet on this unique campus, uniting the resources and opportunities of a large research institution with the academic rigor of one of the nation's most prestigious schools and the athletic excellence and spirit of a big state university, students of every race, creed, and passion can find a niche for themselves. The diversity of the student body creates an open and welcoming environment, while the fierce pride and school spirit demonstrated by everyone on campus creates a sense of unity rivaling that of any smaller institution.

Academics: Large in Every Sense

As a large, academically prestigious research university, UMD includes an impressive array of academic departments, courses and possible majors: "They offer a wide variety of subjects, so you can take classes in whatever

you may be interested in." All undergraduates are required to fulfill the requirements of the CORE program, including nine course credits in the humanities, 10 in math and science, nine in the social sciences and history, and three in Emerging Issues, in addition to more specific English writing and math requirements. CORE also requires students to take six credits at the advanced (300–400) level in one or more fields outside their major. Students say the CORE program does a good job of "[covering] pretty much everything, from science and math to English and diversity"—and though the number of stipulated CORE classes may seem demanding to some, the sheer number of courses offered by the University creates a "large availability to fulfill requirements."

Undergrads must be enrolled in at least 12 credits per semester in order to be considered full-time students, and at least 120 are needed to graduate; further academic requirements vary depending upon your major of choice. Among the most popular majors cited by students are Business, Engineering, Journalism, Architecture, Education, Criminology, Government and Politics, Computer Science and Psychology. UMD does not permit students to minor, though multiple majors are both allowed and encouraged. The University also offers several special academic programs, including College Park Scholars, the University Honors Program, Honors Humanities and Gemstone. Benefits range from the opportunity to design and engage in independent scientific research projects together with a team of selected students (in the case of Gemstone, a four-year multidisciplinary research program) to the chance to attend special seminars and enroll in smaller classes (through the two-year University Honors Program).

At a large university like this one, the variety of classes tends to be correspondingly large—in UMD's case, including everything from introductory calculus to the perennially popular "History of Rock and Roll"—but so does their size. Students say popular introductory classes can be as large as 200 to 300 people, though "as you move higher [in course level], class sizes become smaller." Another student pointed out a further drawback in some classes, especially introductory courses with a large number of students: "Some of the more popular majors have classes with large amounts of people, so those classes tend to rely on Power Point presentations for notes, which are generally posted online. . . . I don't very much like classes where I feel like I don't need to go." To remedy some of the issues caused by large classes, many lectures with a high enrollment are split up into smaller weekly discussion sections of about 20 to 30 people, usually led by a graduate student teaching assistant. Nevertheless, students describe professors as generally "accessible and approachable" if you make the effort to interact with them, though one sophomore added that "when you're in a very large class at times it's easier to just talk with the TAs."

Overall, students say they feel both satisfied with and challenged by UMD's strong academic programs. As one student stated, "Like most universities, it's largely independent, which works for me. No one holds your hand. That can be a pro or a con, depending on your study style."

Work Hard, Play Harder

The excellence and rigor of the University's academics aside, however, College Park students are hardly all work and no play. "We are, after all, one of the Top 20 party schools!" The University boasts a thriving social scene where fraternities and sororities "are very popular, but at the same time, there are a lot of people who don't partake, and no one is ridiculed for either." Thursday, Friday and Saturday nights are a time for many students to go out and have fun with friends; some choose to stay on campus and attend sporting events or shows (the University regularly hosts concerts by artists like Ben Folds and Dashboard Confessional) or see a movie at the Hoff Theater, while others take the Metro into nearby Washington, D.C., in search of a good time. One student reported, "The most popular student hangouts are the Comcast Center for basketball games or Byrd Stadium for football games, but when those aren't options, most students go to restaurants or bars on Route 1, the main road in front of campus." Alcohol and, to some extent, drug use (particularly pot smoking) has a large presence on UMD's campus; University policy does not allow drinking in dorms, "but unless you're being really rowdy about it, it doesn't tend to be a problem." Students also add that "the good thing about a big campus is that you can find people who want to drink every night until they get sick or people that drink occasionally. Even if you don't drink at all, there are still plenty of things to do and people to hang out with."

Students have high praise for the friendliness and openness of the social scene in general: "It is easy to make friends at UMD if you are outgoing enough, and especially so if you live in the dorms." Between residence halls, extracurricular activities, jobs and classes, there are plenty of places to meet people and plenty of people to meet. Students also say that honors programs help them to make friends: one sophomore cited the Gemstone program as the place where she met many of her friends, "since most of us lived in the same dorm freshman year, and had some of the same classes."

Above all, students praise the diversity of the University's student body: "Our school is extremely diverse, and people are very tolerant and accepting." Students come from all over the globe and from all walks of life. When asked to describe the "typical" UMD student, all agreed that it was "impossible," as "there's really no stereotypical UMD student"—in fact, the one common trait students could agree on was diversity. Geographically speaking, like many state schools, UMD includes a large percentage of students from the area as well as a fairly high number of commuters—overall, according to a student, "about 95 percent of the school comes from MD, NJ, or NY (particularly Long Island), and that about 70 percent of the school comes from MD alone." Nevertheless, the campus is very ethnically, economically, and culturally diverse, ensuring that students can always find their niche.

Living it up in College Park

On a campus where finding friends often begins with your dorm, it is no surprise that many students, especially underclassmen, prefer to live on campus. In fact, as enrollment expands, the demand for on-campus housing usually exceeds the supply (with preference given to entering freshmen). The University is seeking to remedy the situation by constructing more on-campus housing, but in the mean time, many upperclassmen and transfer students must settle for apartments or other off-campus housing options.

Freshmen and students who do get lucky in the housing draw are placed in one of UMD's 36 residence halls or, in the case of some upperclassmen, in an on-campus apartment complex owned by the University. Freshmen are housed in separate dorms from upperclassmen and usually get the short end of the stick as far as amenities; students say freshman dorms are typically "fairly plain and don't have air-conditioning, and are not usually given the best of locations." On the upside, students in these dorms do tend to make more of an effort to interact with their neighbors. Students enrolled in honors programs like Gemstone and Honors Humanities live in separate dorms.

> "Everyone has school spirit and, despite it being large, it feels very close-knit."

The surrounding town of College Park, though described as "a little bit on the seedy side" and not a place to walk out alone at night, offers students a wide array of opportunities to dine, shop, or hang out. On weekends, many students frequent bars, shops, and restaurants on the aforementioned Route 1. Popular dining choices in the area include Chipotle, Mama Lucia's, DP Dough, and the Hard Times Cafe, which one student termed "the best place in the world for wings."

But students don't need to venture out into College Park to find good places to chill, eat or study. The beautiful brick architecture of UMD's campus affords plenty of places to spend time. One favorite student hangout is Stamp Student Union, which features a "very nice restaurant," Adele's, that serves as an alternative to dining hall food for students on the meal plan. The Union also boasts a pool hall, arcade and bowling alley, along with the Hoff Theater, which screens movies daily for as little as $3. Many of the University's buildings are new or recently renovated, including the Clarice Smith Performing Arts Center, the Jeong H. Kim Engineering Building and the Robert H. Smith School of Business.

"Go Terps!"

When you come to UMD, be prepared to cheer long and loud—if there's one uniting factor on this campus, it's school spirit: "Everyone has school spirit and, despite it being large, it feels very close-knit." Sports have a "HUGE presence on campus," most prominently football and basketball, and the intensity of the crowd that packs the stadium to cheer on the Terrapins (or "Terps") borders on fanaticism. So popular are Terps games that the University has instituted a lottery system for student tickets to football and basketball games, "where you earn points for each game you attend and students with more points are more likely to get tickets."

You don't have to be a star athlete to play sports at Maryland, however. UMD has a thriving intramurals program, offering sports ranging from soccer to flag football at two levels of competition, A ("competitive") and B ("just for fun, though it gets pretty competitive as well"). The Eppley Recreation Center, "well-known for its excellent facilities," provides students with excellent athletic facilities and is only one of several gyms on campus.

And the extracurricular opportunities at UMD go far beyond sports. The wide array of campus organizations offer something for everyone, and students find extracurriculars a good way to make friends at a school that can seem intimidatingly large. From service groups to ethnic organizations to a cappella to a skydiving club, chances are that no matter what your interest, there will be an organization for you. Many undergraduates also hold jobs during their time at UMD; the University offers plenty of on-campus jobs at locations like the gym, "a good opportunity for students who want to work but don't want to make a huge commitment out of it."

There is really no easy way to sum up the University of Maryland, College Park. The diversity of its student body and the sheer number of opportunities, courses and activities it offers ensure that no matter what your personality or interests, you will fit in here.

What really unites the students is a fierce pride in their university: "Everyone is so passionate about this school, and everyone has a genuine love for it."—*Amy Koenig*

FYI

If you come to UMD, College Park, you'd better bring "a red UMD shirt, for all the sporting events you're going to go to."

What is the typical weekend schedule? "Very laid-back. People sleep in, watch TV, hang out in their rooms. Lots of people go out Friday and Saturday nights. However, if it's a football game weekend, tailgating starts early, and most students are up and out hours before the game. Usually people study on Sundays or just hang out."

If I could change one thing about UMD, I'd "make the buildings closer together (it's exhausting going from class to class)."

Three things every UMD student should do before graduating are "go to a Maryland/Duke basketball game, eat a DP Dough calzone, and make sure never to step on the intersection of the lines that used to point to the campus' buildings that burned down in 1912, because if you do, you won't graduate in four years!"

Massachusetts

Amherst College

Address: PO Box 5000
Amherst, MA 01002
Phone: 413-542-2328
E-mail address:
admissions@amherst.edu
Web site URL:
www.amherst.edu
Year Founded: 1821
Private or Public: Private
Religious Affiliation: None
Location: Rural
Number of Applicants: 7,745
Percent Accepted: 15%
**Percent Accepted who
enroll:** 38%
Number Entering: 452
**Number of Transfers
Accepted each Year:** 14
Middle 50% SAT range:
M:660–760, CR: 670–770,
Wr: 670–760
Middle 50% ACT range: 31
**Early admission program
EA/ED/None:** ED
**Percentage accepted
through EA or ED:** 34%

EA and ED deadline:
15-Nov
Regular Deadline: 1-Jan
Application Fee: $60
**Full time Undergraduate
enrollment:** 1,683
Total enrollment: 1,683
Percent Male: 50%
Percent Female: 50%
**Total Percent Minority or
Unreported:** 38%
Percent African-American:
11%
**Percent Asian/Pacific
Islander:** 11%
Percent Hispanic: 11%
Percent Native-American:
<1%
Percent International: 7%
**Percent in-state/out of
state:** 10%/90%
Percent from Public HS:
58%
Retention Rate: 97%
Graduation Rate 4-year:
96%

Graduation Rate 6-year:
98%
**Percent Undergraduates
in On-campus housing:**
98%
**Number of official organized
extracurricular
organizations:** 100
3 Most popular majors:
Political Science, Psychology,
Economics
Student/Faculty ratio: 8:1
Average Class Size: 17
**Percent of students going to
grad school:** 75%
Tuition and Fees: $36,970
**In State Tuition and Fees if
different:** No difference
Cost for Room and Board:
$9,790
**Percent receiving financial
aid out of those who apply,
first year:** 80%
**Percent receiving financial
aid among all students:**
52%

The "College" in Amherst's name says it all: the anonymous and overwhelming aspects of a large university are nowhere to be found at Amherst College, where 89 percent of classes have less than 30 students and professors frequently invite their students to dinner at their homes. Yet Amherst manages to foster a supportive community without sacrificing academic rigor or the spirit of competition—and with the other four members of the Five College Consortium nearby, it's easy for Amherst students to feel like a part of a greater campus as well.

Competitive, not Cutthroat

Many students say that "one of the most fabulous things about Amherst" is the school's lack of core requirements, which affords students a significant amount of freedom when it comes to choosing classes. Freshmen are required to take a seminar in their first semester at the college, but students agree that with so many options, finding one in your area of interest is easy. "The only purpose of the seminars is to have some sort of intensive writing class when you begin college," said one sophomore. Students can enroll in seminars whose topics range from music or theater to science, philosophy, or English.

Students are required to declare a major by the end of their second year, and generally must complete eight to ten courses in that major. Students said that this continues to give Amherst scholars a real chance to explore classes that interest them. "The great thing about having so few requirements is that the students that take a certain class take it because they really want to be in that class. They aren't just there to get a requirement filled," said one sophomore. The only tricky part to registering for classes, pointed out one student, is that several courses taught by Amherst's "superstar professors"— including political science professor Austin Sarat and philosophy professor Thomas P. Smith—can be difficult to get into.

Academic enthusiasm is fundamental to the typical classroom environment at the college; with an average class size of 17, Amherst students are left with very little wiggle room when it comes to showing up to class prepared and ready to participate. "It's hard to hide," said one sophomore. Still, another student cited the school's consistently small class sizes as the best part of her academic experience thus far. The somewhat pressured environment produced by such small classes is more than offset, students say, by the close student-professor relationships that form.

One student cited the school's lack of teaching assistants as yet another perk of attending a college rather than a large university, saying, "The professors are conscious that they're there to work with the students, and you don't have to worry that they'll be preoccupied with research or focused on their graduate students." Amherst even works to foster friendships between students and their teachers, sponsoring a program known as TYPO, or Take Your Professor Out, whereby the college pays for small groups of students to take their professors out to dinner.

Despite the prevailing work ethic on campus, Amherst students insist that they are not known for being holed up in the library seven days a week. One student observed that many students, while "on the books" from Sunday to Wednesday, are equally devoted to their athletic or artistic pursuits. As another student said, "This is such a cliché, but Amherst kids really are work hard, play hard."

In keeping with their "well-rounded" reputations, Amherst students most frequently choose to be English, political science, economics, psychology, or biology majors. One sophomore who recently declared her double major of biology and theater/dance said that while the school is generally known for its offerings in the liberal arts, the professors and facilities she has encountered in her science courses have all been top-notch. "I think the science department is really an undiscovered gem at our school," she said.

While Amherst students attend a school where academic excellence is prized—"It's not the kind of place where people look down on you if you say that you think chemistry is really interesting"—one of the college's most valuable components is its atmosphere of friendly rather than malicious competition. "Everyone really supports each other," said one sophomore. "It's not a competitive or cutthroat environment at all. Everyone here works hard, and they work together."

BΘΠ? ΑΣΦ? Try TAP

While Amherst does not have any Greek life, students report that a relatively permissive alcohol policy and the close proximity of "something like 30,000 other college students" make for a lively party scene on the weekends. With an overwhelming majority of students opting to live in on-campus housing, the main part of the social life occurs in dorms on campus. Amherst also hosts a monthly TAP ("The Amherst Party") with a different theme each month—perennial favorites include Luau, Endless Summer, and "the most famous one, Madonna TAP."

Students seem to agree that drinking is a large part of Amherst's social scene, but one sophomore girl said, "The good thing is that the college isn't ignorant of that." Consequently, incoming freshmen have the ability to request substance-free housing. There are also "health and wellness dorms" for upperclassmen. Even while offering these options, Amherst remains a school with a less-than-strict approach to on-campus drinking. "I mean, if you have a keg at a party, you have to register the keg," said one sophomore. "Sometimes if a party's too loud the police will come bust it up. But they can't go into your room and search for alcohol, so it's really not hard to drink."

While it's relatively rare for most students to venture to any of the other four schools for parties, one student said that "the girls from Mount Holyoke and Smith are definitely looking for a social life outside of their schools" and added that it was more common to see them—dubbed "Mo-Hos" and "Smithies" by Amherst girls—at Amherst parties. "I don't think Amherst girls are that excited by their presence on campus," she said. "The guys . . . that might be another story." Students said that outside of this, the majority of their social interactions with students at other schools occur in town at bars. In the words of one student, "It can be nice to get off campus and meet other people.

Amherst can definitely become its own little bubble after a while."

The Amherst Bubble

One thing all Amherst students—regardless of their own personal interests—agree on is that their school is full of athletes. One varsity athlete estimated that a third of the school played a varsity sport and that almost two-thirds played either varsity or intramural sports, but she maintained that, due to the fact that athletes live in the same dorms as their less athletic counterparts, "everyone is out every weekend to support their friends and teammates. It's not a jocks vs. non-jocks situation." Another sophomore stated that, while the environment at Amherst is relatively "super-diverse as far as liberal arts colleges go," the school was also true to its classification as a place with "a lot of preppy athletes."

Jocks or no, students uniformly classify Amherst's physical campus—particularly the "insanely beautiful view from Memorial Hill that overlooks the Mount Holyoke range"—as "absolutely gorgeous." One praised "the beautiful New England feel of the entire place" and

another described Amherst as "a school that seems like a perfect philosophical place to go to college—this idyllic setting is what you imagined college would be like when you were a little girl, you know? Sitting in a coffee shop reading a book, or lying out on the grass studying in the spring." In the colder months, students often take advantage of snow by "stealing trays from our dining hall, Valentine, and going down Memorial Hill on them."

> "This idyllic setting is what you imagined college would be like when you were a little girl."

In the end, whether they are seeking out courses in specialized subjects at one of the nearby colleges, driving to Hampshire to see a dance show, playing for the Jeffs in a varsity game, or going apple-picking or hiking, Amherst students pursue their goals and passions with drive and enthusiasm. One sophomore summed up the Amherst code like this: "Generally, it's just that everything we do, we work really hard at." —*Angelica Baker*

FYI

If you come to Amherst, you'd better bring "a popped collar, some purple clothing, and money for food from town—the stuff at Valentine isn't that great."

What's the typical weekend schedule? "Wake up late, try to make it to Valentine before lunch closes, do some homework, see a sports game, and go to a great party on Saturday night."

If I could change one thing about Amherst, I'd "change its location—it's definitely not rural, but we don't trek out to Boston every afternoon either."

Three things you have to do before you graduate are: "Take a class at one of the other four colleges, swim in Puffer's Pond and climb one of the academic buildings."

Babson College

Address: 231 Forest Street
Babson Park, MA 02457
Phone: 800-488-3696
E-mail address:
ugradadmission@
babson.edu
Web site URL:
www.babson.edu
Year Founded: 1919
Private or Public: Private
Religious Affiliation: None
Location: Suburban
Number of Applicants: 3,530
Percent Accepted: 35%
**Percent Accepted who
enroll:** 34%
Number Entering: 453
**Number of Transfers
Accepted each Year:** 83
Middle 50% SAT range:
M: 590–680, CR: 560–640,
Wr: 570–650
Middle 50% ACT range:
25–29
**Early admission program
EA/ED/None:** EA and ED

**Percentage accepted
through EA or ED:**
Unreported
EA and ED deadline: 1-Nov
Regular Deadline: 15-Jan
Application Fee: $65
**Full time Undergraduate
enrollment:** 1,851
Total enrollment: 3,439
Percent Male: 60%
Percent Female: 40%
**Total Percent Minority or
Unreported:** 44%
Percent African-American:
6%
**Percent Asian/Pacific
Islander:** 14%
Percent Hispanic: 10%
Percent Native-American:
<1%
Percent International: 22%
**Percent in-state/out of
state:** 54%/46%
Percent from Public HS:
50%
Retention Rate: 93%

Graduation Rate 4-year: 84%
Graduation Rate 6-year: 87%
**Percent Undergraduates
in On-campus housing:**
86%
**Number of official organized
extracurricular
organizations:** 60
3 Most popular majors:
Accounting, Business
Operations, Finance
Student/Faculty ratio: 16:1
Average Class Size: 35
**Percent of students going to
grad school:** Unreported
Tuition and Fees: $36,096
**In State Tuition and Fees if
different:** No difference
Cost for Room and Board:
$12,020
**Percent receiving financial
aid out of those who apply,
first year:** Unreported
**Percent receiving financial
aid among all students:**
42%

Babson College, located in the Babson Park section of Wellesley, Massachusetts, is a school that strives to create the next business leaders of the world. This undergraduate program combines liberal arts and business in order to teach its students the values of a "practical business education." From the beginning of freshman year, students create their own business, immediately reinforcing the concept of experience instead of only in-class learning. Although Babson features a relatively wealthy student body, Babsonians are still ambitious to learn how to succeed in the business world.

Hands-on Preparation for the Real World

Babson students are required to start their own business—the first of many—in a freshman-year class called Foundations of Management and Entrepreneurship (FME). In this program, a team of students learns how to create and run a business, which at the end of the course is liquidated and the profits donated to charity. The course teaches students that becoming a CEO requires teamwork, plenty of effort, and true dedication.

But it is not all business at Babson. Freshmen take three additional classes that are mostly chosen for them. Two of the classes are in the liberal arts, and students say that the majority of liberal arts classes try to connect to business "every once in a while," although that does not mean that the teachers work together to distribute workloads. One sophomore said although he didn't expect professors from different departments to work together, "There have been plenty of times when I have 60 pages of reading and a test to study for on the same day. It can be overbearing at times." When students reach their junior and senior years, there is much more flexibility in their schedules.

Although Babson students are not required to pick a concentration outside of business, most do. Babson's concentrations provide ways for students to focus on the part of business that they love. Concentrations range from American studies to statistics to the literary and visual arts. The most common concentrations are Entrepreneurship and Finance. Whether a student chooses a concentration or not, everyone graduates with a BA in Business.

Babson has about 1,800 enrolled undergraduates, which translates to small classes. According to one senior, "The biggest class at Babson is FME, which has about sixty students. After that, you'll never have more than forty in a class." Most liberal arts classes are even smaller, including a few ten-person classes. The size of all classes at Babson gives students an opportunity to be in contact with some of the most influential business leaders of today. Rather than just hiring teachers who have studied business and have followed business trends, Babson also hires CEOs, CFOs, and other executives of major businesses, such as the popular professor Leonard Green, CEO of the Green Group. Although the teachers have high-powered jobs and often busy lives, Babson students give rave reviews to teacher-student relations. Professors at Babson have a reputation for helping outside of the classroom with not only class work, but in the workforce. Some teachers help students find jobs, and that provides opportunities that are "huge when you hit senior year".

Grading at Babson is notoriously difficult, but students say an "A" is attainable when enough effort is put in. One senior said that participation is a component in grading, so interaction with other students and professors "is important, and can make a little bit of a difference in your grade." Some students are convinced that there is grade "deflation" for many classes, although teachers and many students insist that it does not exist. What the real difficulty, one student said, is that "teachers have very high expectations for Babson students."

The Business Mentality

Babson's focus on business means that students are generally very driven toward their specific interests. Due to the nature of this attitude, some students say that the social environment is an even mix between collaborative and competitive. Babson fosters the idea of group work, which means that there are always people to help you. However, many point out that when they leave Babson, everyone is going into the same industry, which can create "some tension between students, because you know that you'll eventually be competing with your best friends for the same job." Many students agree that the

balance between working together and working against each other is another way that Babson mimics the business world.

> "Upperclassmen pay attention and look out for underclassmen with similar interests. Everyone wants to help freshmen because they are always looking for new people to start a business with."

The business mentality of Babson really helps the freshmen assimilate into the student body. "Upperclassmen pay attention and look out for underclassmen with similar interests. Everyone wants to help freshmen because they are always looking for new people to start a business with," one freshman remarked. The freshmen do not only get support from upperclassmen, but First Year Seminar (FYS) also provides busy freshmen with weekly information on time management along with help with classes through a peer mentor, their FYS professor, and a faculty advisor. One freshman said that it could even get "overwhelming at how many people are checking up on you."

Babson Doesn't Just Work Hard . . .

As hard as students work at Babson, a combination of three-day weekends (there are rarely classes on Fridays), monthly "Knight" dance parties in the Knight auditorium, and the on-campus Pub create an environment where students can balance work and play. Students generally agree that a vast majority of students drink. Other "hard drugs" are not too common, except many students admit to using Adderall on school nights to focus. The policy on alcohol is not completely loose, but partygoers are given several warnings by RAs before the Babson Police (affectionately called Babo) are called in to break up the party. The jobs of the RAs are to look out for the students, not get them in trouble. The new honor code states that students have an obligation to help, not to report students who get sick from alcohol.

Outside of the dorm room parties, one sophomore club athlete said "you will always find a party on campus." The pub on campus, Roger's Pub, is open to all students, and those over 21 wear wristbands so they can purchase drinks. Once the pub closes at midnight, everyone disperses from the pub to either frat parties or parties in suites where a bunch of friends—often varsity athletes—live together. With all of the events on campus, commuting to Boston is not too common among students. The students who usually travel to Boston at night are often international students who have apartments there. On campus, there are many events not based around alcohol that are widely attended by students. The Campus Activities Board plans around 50 events a year, including "Knight parties." Many campus-sponsored events attract all kinds of people, and often incorporate international culture. For example, the South Asian club throws a Bhangra dance on campus that attracts many students, especially because of the "intrigue of free food." Any time a student wants to plan a campus wide event, Babson can subsidize the party or gathering.

Who Are The Future Business Leaders of the World?

The "stereotypical" Babson student is a "white, wealthy, preppy workaholic who is very self-involved." However, diversity on campus is growing, and with every year, the numbers of international students and women increase. According to a senior girl, "The difference in numbers between men and women is not obvious at all. The only times we think about it is when people are making jokes about it." In the case of international students, who make about 20 percent of the population, the stereotype is that they are "rich" and often "royalty from some country." Most of the people who live off campus are international students, students say, and the perception is that many international students are known for having "multiple expensive cars." Overall, students agree that many Babsonians can be a "little flashy." "There are some kids who have more than one car with them." one freshman noted. But despite the stereotypes, the truth is that there are students from all socioeconomic backgrounds, and there are many students on financial aid and scholarship, with students receiving a total of about $24 million in financial aid, in addition to Babson grants, each year. Babson offers many scholarships to students that are based on all different criteria to accommodate people from all backgrounds.

When living on campus, the dorm situation "gets better with seniority," and varies depending on where you live. Few people complain about housing, as most dorms are described as being "better than those at the other colleges I've visited." Babson also gets high marks when it comes to roommate pairing. Freshmen agree that Babson "really takes your rooming form into consideration." Overall, the care that Babson puts into its social life allows students to enjoy their experience as a businessperson and a scholar.—*Willi Rechler*

FYIs
If I could change one thing about Babson, "I'd move it out of the middle of dry-town Wellesley and put the same campus in the middle of Boston!"
If you come to Babson, you'd better bring: "your Blackberry, a suit, a Northface . . . and a whole bunch of business ideas before FME starts."
Three things every student at Babson should do before graduating are: 1) "Get a 100 on an exam", 2) "Take a class with Len Green," and 3) "Stay at a Knight Party until 2 A.M."
What is the typical weekend schedule? "Weekends start on Thursday night and everyone's at pub. Friday night is a lighter night, but people go out or go to Boston, and Saturday is a big campus party night. On Sunday, everything shuts down and everyone does work."

Boston College

Address: 140 Commonwealth Avenue Chestnut Hill, MA 02467
Phone: 800-360-2522
E-mail address: NA
Web site URL: www.bc.edu
Year Founded: 1863
Private or Public: Private
Religious Affiliation: Roman Catholic
Location: Suburban
Number of Applicants: 30,845
Percent Accepted: 26%
Percent Accepted who enroll: 27%
Number Entering: 2,167
Number of Transfers Accepted each Year: 166
Middle 50% SAT range: M: 640–730, CR: 610–700, Wr: 620–710
Middle 50% ACT range: 28–32
Early admission program EA/ED/None: EA

Percentage accepted through EA or ED: 36%
EA and ED deadline: 1-Nov
Regular Deadline: 1-Jan
Application Fee: $70
Full time Undergraduate enrollment: 9,060
Total enrollment: 13,087
Percent Male: 49%
Percent Female: 51%
Total Percent Minority or Unreported: 29%
Percent African-American: 6%
Percent Asian/Pacific Islander: 9%
Percent Hispanic: 8%
Percent Native-American: <1%
Percent International: 3%
Percent in-state/out of state: 29%/71%
Percent from Public HS: 53%
Retention Rate: 96%
Graduation Rate 4-year: Unreported

Graduation Rate 6-year: Unreported
Percent Undergraduates in On-campus housing: 82%
Number of official organized extracurricular organizations: 223
3 Most popular majors: Communication, English, Finance
Student/Faculty ratio: 13:1
Average Class Size: 15
Percent of students going to grad school: 25%
Tuition and Fees: $37,950
In State Tuition and Fees if different: No difference
Cost for Room and Board: $11,610
Percent receiving financial aid out of those who apply, first year: 77%
Percent receiving financial aid among all students: 70%

The location is superb: Newton has been named one of the safest cities in America and is just a short train ride away from the exciting city of Boston. The academics are excellent; the high standards and diverse curriculum ensure quality education. To top it off, whether you prefer parties or tailgates or a cappella shows, you don't have to choose because you can attend all three in just one day. BC boasts impressive credentials on many fronts.

Attention: Get to Work!

Being a liberal arts school, BC ensures that each of its students receives a broad education encompassing many disciplines. The college is made up of four schools: the College of Arts and Sciences, Lynch School of Education, Carroll School of Management, and the Connell School of Nursing. Each school has its own set of specific requirements. However, classes in literature, modern history, philosophy, theology, the natural sciences, the social sciences, the arts, cultural diversity, and writing are common to

all. But the requirements are rarely a point of complaint since they are fairly easy to fulfill. As one junior pointed out, "While you have the required math class you dread, and a language requirement, I appreciate the core for letting me explore my options."

With options, each student can make what he or she wants out of his college experience. To make their schedules more interesting, students can take classes such as sign language, dance, or the anticonsumerist "Shop till you drop." Students recommend taking a class with Professor Seth Jacobs, who teaches history and is an expert on the Vietnam War. Class sizes vary from 12-person seminars where personal attention abounds to 200-person lectures for those who like the anonymity. Moreover, the workload, while generally manageable, can certainly be adjusted. The communications major is known for its lighter workload and higher GPAs, while the sciences are collectively acknowledged to be difficult. As one student put it, "If you want an A, you have to work for it." The professors are known to be accessible and hold regular office hours for those willing to make the effort to talk to them.

Change on the Horizon

The students are guaranteed housing for three years at BC. This means that about half of the junior class moves off campus each year. For those who do remain on campus, the choices vary by year. Dorms are assigned through a lottery. The freshmen are divided between Upper and Newton campuses, the latter being more secluded from the general population of the college while providing a close-knit sense of community. Since housing improves with seniority, the seniors get to choose from among four-to-six-person suites in apartment-style housing, featuring private bathrooms and kitchens. For the more outgoing, there is also the option of living in the senior-only mods, which are known for their spacious backyards and party-friendly atmosphere.

There are six dining halls on campus, and the food gets thumbs up from the students, although the meal plans are considered overpriced. A popular option is Lyons dining hall, affectionately named "The Rat," which features plenty of fried options. McElroy and Corcoran Commons are praised for their long hours; some days they stay open till two a.m. As an alternative, students often venture out to Cleveland Circle, where there are a large variety of restaurants ranging from sushi places to an Applebee's. Of course, there is always the option of checking out the multitude of restaurants in Boston: "Take the train in and you have the world at your fingertips," one junior points out.

There are no central hanging-out areas on campus, but the cafeterias serve as worthy substitutes. The green areas around campus also provide good spots to relax in the afternoons, and the students enjoy the beautiful flowers planted throughout. As one senior said, while the overall look of BC is very pretty, "The campus is confused." The architecture ranges from gothic to modern, and there are some in-between. Currently, BC is working on a 10-year plan to renovate the campus by updating outdated dorms and academic buildings. As one student said, "Change is on the horizon."

Party Like It's Your Job

When the weekend comes around, BC students take the opportunity to exercise their right to play hard. For seniors, the definition of a weekend is rather flexible, and the fun starts as early as Wednesday. As one student

claimed, "The school is a lot more social than I'd expected." Bars such as Mary Ann's and Roggies on Cleveland Circle (a center of shopping and social activity) are cited as local favorites for hanging out. Those of legal drinking age (read: with good fake IDs) take the opportunity to travel into the nearby Boston area, with its vibrant bar and club scene.

Most of the students, however, simply seek fun locally; while there are no frats, students take advantage of the plentiful parties at the senior mods or at the apartments of students who live off campus. The mods are also a regular tailgating site before sporting events. Another popular event on campus is the exclusive Middlemarch dance, which requires participation in a scavenger hunt to obtain tickets.

Drinking is a regular activity on campus in spite of the official dry campus rules. RAs are present in every dorm and, while most are pretty lenient, they are known to be stricter on the underclassmen. Students advise "be smart," as there are ways to get around the watchful eyes of administration.

> "The typical BC student looks like he or she 'stepped out of a J. Crew catalog with a hangover.'"

The atmosphere is generally friendly, and people meet friends through classes or dorms. Unfortunately, students often complain that the school lacks diversity in terms of ethnicity and economic background. The stereotypical BC student looks like he or she "stepped out of a J. Crew catalog with a hangover." To battle the stereotypes, groups like AHANA (African-American, Hispanic, Asian, and Native American) work on campus to increase diversity.

Super Involved

An important part of BC is its abundant school spirit. Each class has its own motto printed on the iconic gold "Superfan" T-shirt which is adorned by an eagle, the school mascot. Students proudly wear it during all sporting events. Football, basketball, and hockey have the highest attendance rates. Those who don't want the strenuous commitment of a varsity sport get involved in the popular intramural teams around campus, soccer, and basketball being the most widespread.

Outside of sports, regular extracurricular

involvement is at a high level. Among the most popular organizations are student government, College Republicans, and Democrats, and dance teams of all sorts. *The Heights* is the student-run newspaper. The Jesuit background of the college is most felt in the level of student involvement on campus. The tradition emphasizes volunteer work on campus, and the Appalachia Volunteers Program, which does work in the Appalachian region for organizations such as Habitat for Humanity, boasts a membership of over 600 students. Many students also hold jobs as part of the work-study program; the dining hall employs the most students.

"You get here and even though it might not have been your first choice, you see all the upperclassmen say they love it," one senior said. "You learn to love it as much as they do." At BC you work hard, play often, and explore plenty. A great college experience is guaranteed.—*Dorota Poplawska*

FYIs

If you come to BC, you'd better bring "money and a popped collar."
What is the typical weekend schedule? "Sleep till noon, go to a football game on Saturday, and party at night."
If I could change one thing about BC, I'd "make it more diverse."
Three things every student should do before graduating from BC are "spend the night at Bapst Library, participate in Marathon Monday [the Boston Marathon], and attend a football game at Alumni Stadium."

Boston University

Address: 121 Bay State Road Boston, MA 02215
Phone: 617-353-2300
E-mail address: admissions@bu.edu
Web site URL: www.bu.edu
Year Founded: 1839
Private or Public: Private
Religious Affiliation: None
Location: Urban
Number of Applicants: 33,390
Percent Accepted: 59%
Percent Accepted who enroll: 22%
Number Entering: 4,163
Number of Transfers Accepted each Year: 752
Middle 50% SAT range: M: 590–690, CR: 580–680, Wr: 590–670
Middle 50% ACT range: 25–30
Early admission program EA/ED/None: ED

Percentage accepted through EA or ED: 37%
EA and ED deadline: 1-Nov
Regular Deadline: 1-Jan
Application Fee: $75
Full time Undergraduate enrollment: 18,733
Total enrollment: 19,951
Percent Male: 41%
Percent Female: 59%
Total Percent Minority or Unreported: 48%
Percent African-American: 3%
Percent Asian/Pacific Islander: 12%
Percent Hispanic: 6%
Percent Native-American: <1%
Percent International: 9%
Percent in-state/out of state: 23%/77%
Percent from Public HS: 74%
Retention Rate: 91%
Graduation Rate 4-year: 75%

Graduation Rate 6-year: 80%
Percent Undergraduates in On-campus housing: 65%
Number of official organized extracurricular organizations: 400
3 Most popular majors: Business, International Relations, Psychology
Student/Faculty ratio: 14:1
Average Class Size: 15
Percent of students going to grad school: 29%
Tuition and Fees: $37,050
In State Tuition and Fees if different: No difference
Cost for Room and Board: $11,418
Percent receiving financial aid out of those who apply, first year: 80%
Percent receiving financial aid among all students: 44%

Located conveniently in the heart of Boston, Boston University presents its students with solid academics, friendly people, and a famous hockey team. And, if you're looking for off-campus adventures, the Boston T will take you anywhere you like in one of the most exciting and historic cities in the country.

What Do You Make of It?

Among BU's 18 graduate and undergraduate schools and 250 degree programs, there is plenty of room to maneuver. Still, as one sophomore commented, "it seems like everyone is either a premed or pre-law." Other popular majors include international relations, psychology, and management. The university curriculum also offers a challenging honors program for ambitious freshmen and sophomores. Like most universities, BU holds large lectures for most introductory courses with smaller discussion sections attached. Upper-level classes shrink significantly to as low as 10 or even five students. Surprisingly, competition for those classes is not really a problem, and an undergrad's chances only improve with seniority. And if lady luck is not on your side, "there are so many options, you can always find something else you will enjoy," like a class taught by Elie Wiesel, Nobel Peace Prize–winner and one of the most popular professors at BU.

Rumors about grade deflation at BU are universally acknowledged to be based on "a misconception," according to one sophomore, "no one has ever been able to prove its existence." At BU, students praise their professors for being accessible; as one student stated, the experience is "what you make of it."

No ID, No Way

Despite the strictly enforced policies against drinking, alcohol still finds its way into the lives of most BU students. Student social life is diverse in terms of locale; many undergraduates center their weekends around parties at off-campus apartments or the few off-campus frats (not funded or recognized by the university). The nearby colleges such as MIT and Harvard also offer viable party options. One student said that the Boston scene "opens up many social lives for those over 21 (or those with a really good fake ID)," and upperclassmen flock to the numerous bars and clubs in the area, such as Jillian's and The Dugout. Without an ID, students are out of luck, as Boston recently passed a law prohibiting any underage clubs, causing many undergrads to simply take their chances in the RA–monitored dorms (although some say that that is a riskier option). BU weekends typically start on Thursday for those resourceful enough to avoid the Friday classes. If you prefer your weekends dry, never fear—there are still vibrant options for a social life outside of drinking activities, many of which take place in Boston, a city that provides endless restaurants, theaters, and shopping along Newbury Street.

From Jail to Hotel

The dorms at BU vary from great apartment-style dorms to small closetlike rooms. Competition is stiff for the recently built student village apartments, as well as two other residences that were former hotels on Commonwealth Avenue. Yet getting a good dorm is a matter of luck of the draw. One student warned that some of the dorms "have been designed by an architect who used to design jails." Warren Towers, the freshman dorm, has some of the least desirable rooms; however it makes up for it by having its own vibrant and close-knit social community. Students describe the campus, which is divided into East and West, as "long and skinny." The West campus is the more lively side, since it tends to house more athletes and parties. Moreover, many students move off campus after their sophomore years. The primary complaints from all students concerned BU's old-fashioned guest policy: coed sleepovers were prohibited. And although students realize that the policy is meant to ensure safety on campus, it is commonly referred to as "outdated." Recently the student governing body at Boston University, the Student Union, worked with the administration to change the guest policy to give students more freedom as well as more responsibility.

Fortunately, food rates pretty well at BU. There are five dining halls on campus and endless restaurants, some favorites of which include T. Anthony's pizza restaurant or anything in the North End. For those on the run, there are fallback options such as the George Sherman Union and numerous small convenience stores along the campus.

BU students generally do not bring cars to campus, and as anyone who has ever driven in Boston will tell you, it is not a good idea to have a car. Besides the nightmarish parking, students agree that Boston's one-way streets will significantly impede even the most experienced of navigators. The extensive subway system known as the T, however, more than makes up for the lack of personal transportation.

East Coast Style

This ultimate East Coast university has a generally friendly atmosphere. Students say that it is easiest to meet people through dorms and extracurriculars, although sometimes smaller classes foster friendships too. Students claim that BU could be more diverse, but there are actually students from all 50 states and over 100 countries. Every race and ethnicity is represented, usually to a far greater degree than is the case at state universities.

> "There are so many options, you can always find something else you will enjoy."

Some of the most popular clubs at Boston University are student governments and the programming council. The campus is also home to many cultural clubs like the Indian Club, which is one of the biggest organizations on campus. Students report that many, if not most, of their peers have jobs. Many work on campus in dining halls through work-study programs. Others find that Boston has plentiful job opportunities, including waiting tables or working as cashiers.

Skates Are Required
Yearly balls and dances as well as weekly parties bring tradition to BU. "We also have an up-and-coming basketball program and a very popular, very involved new student spirit group nicknamed 'the Dog Pound,'" said a student representative. And, since the school does not have a football team, what spirit exists is entirely poured into the hockey team; hockey games are some of the most crowded and energetic events at BU, with the pep rallies against BU rival, Boston College, widely attended. In fact, the BU versus BC hockey game is one of the most entertaining and well-attended events on campus.

For those who have no interest in hockey, Boston provides more than enough sports teams for which to root, including the Celtics, the Red Sox, and the New England Patriots. For those hoping for an active life of their own, the university has many popular intramural teams, as well as a three-floor fitness and recreation center.

Boston University may not have the packed football stadiums of other schools, but BU students have pride in their school. And with Boston as the students' backyard playground, who could say no to that?
—*Dorota Poplawska*

FYI
If you come to BU, you'd better bring "money."
What is the typical weekend schedule? "Wake up late, gym, dinner and desserts at North End, party."
If I could change one thing about BU, I'd "improve the guest policy to something less strict."
Three things every student at BU should do before graduating are "Go to a baseball game at Fenway Park, attend a BU versus BC hockey game, and attend an Elie Wiesel lecture."

Brandeis Univeristy

Address: 415 South St., MS003 Waltham, MA 02454-9110
Phone: 781-736-3500
E-mail address: admissions@brandeis.edu
Web site URL: www.brandeis.edu
Year Founded: 1948
Private or Public: Private
Religious Affiliation: None
Location: Suburban
Number of Applicants: 7,724
Percent Accepted: 32.5%
Percent Accepted who enroll: 30%
Number Entering: 759
Number of Transfers Accepted each Year: 102
Middle 50% SAT range: M: 650–730, CR: 640–720, Wr: 540–730
Middle 50% ACT range: 29–32
Early admission program EA/ED/None: ED

Percentage accepted through EA or ED: 32%
EA and ED deadline: 15-Nov
Regular Deadline: 15-Jan
Application Fee: $55
Full time Undergraduate enrollment: 3,216
Total enrollment: 5,327
Percent Male: 44%
Percent Female: 56%
Total Percent Minority or Unreported: 19%
Percent African-American: 4%
Percent Asian/Pacific Islander: 10%
Percent Hispanic: 5%
Percent Native-American: <1%
Percent International: 8%
Percent in-state/out of state: 26%/74%
Percent from Public HS: Unreported
Retention Rate: 93%
Graduation Rate 4-year: 86%

Graduation Rate 6-year: 88%
Percent Undergraduates in On-campus housing: 77%
Number of official organized extracurricular organizations: 253
3 Most popular majors: Biology, Economic, Psychology
Student/Faculty ratio: 8:1
Average Class Size: Unreported
Percent of students going to grad school: Unreported
Tuition and Fees: $37,294
In State Tuition and Fees if different: No difference
Cost for Room and Board: $10,354
Percent receiving financial aid out of those who apply, first year: 53%
Percent receiving financial aid among all students: 48%

A sk any student at Brandeis University, and they will tell you that their school is New England's best-kept secret. Located in Waltham, Massachusetts (just a hop, skip, and jump from Boston), the University is most famous for its extraordinarily high percentage of Jewish students and for its heavily left-leaning political atmosphere. And there isn't a lot that students there could complain about. They're going to a prestigious research university that consistently shows up in top-30 lists, enjoying a campus that even boasts a castle of its own, and getting to know a wide array of students from all over the world.

Intimate Academics

Considering its prominence as a research university, academics at Brandeis are intense but rewarding. The course requirements are fairly broad, drawing on the four areas of Science, Social Science, Humanities, and Art, but there are also specific requirements in Quantitative Reasoning, Writing-Intensive courses, Oral Communication, and Non-Western and Comparative Studies. The last one is designed to "acquaint students with world views, indigenous intellectual traditions, historical narratives, and social institutions that have developed largely outside European society and its North American transplants." This intense focus on society as a whole, as well as the cultural makeup of the school itself, has made Social Sciences and Area and Ethnic Studies the two most popular majors at Brandeis; other frontrunners include Biology (a common major for premed students) and Psychology.

Incoming freshmen get to take University Seminars, which run the gamut from "Hand and Brain" to "How to Travel." These small classes taught by faculty members who would otherwise appear unapproachable are the perfect introduction for freshmen. One sophomore raved, "our professor invited us to his house at the end of the semester and he's my adviser this year ... He's actually made me think about changing my major."

All in all, the students going to Brandeis go there to learn, so they expect to work as hard as they play. Among the majors, students report that the sciences are the hardest. One premed student said "My Gen Chem class was definitely a killer weed-out and it's intense to compete against all the other premeds but . . . humanities majors don't exactly slouch either with all their papers and presentations." A math major said that, even though Brandeis students know how to have fun on weekends, "It's not uncommon for people to work until 10 on a weekend night and then go out."

Because the school is somewhat small (a little over 3,000 undergrads), almost all classes are taught by teachers, with TAs only grading papers or leading discussions. Many of the most famous professors on campus are associated with Heller School, a graduate school for social policy, and their undergraduate classes can have waitlists; one class, "War and the Possibilities of Peace" is particularly famous for its teacher, Gordie Feldman. A recent graduate called Stuart Altman's class, "American Health Care," nothing less than "one of the best classes I took at Brandeis."

Dorks in Latex?

Brandeis is a friendly campus, and a sociology major joked that it was "a school of self-proclaimed dorks." The campus has a fair number of parties every weekend, and many students use the Campus Vans to get to downtown Boston or to get off campus in general . When not visiting their friends at BU, Harvard, or MIT, many students go to Harvard Square or Newbery Street, which has many bars nearby. "As long as I've got my fake and my friends, I'm set for a Saturday night," said a sophomore. There are also concerts on campus in the fall and the spring, and many student-council-sponsored events that suffer from "good intentions, bad results." The best parties on campus are rather diverse: the South Asian Society puts on "Mela" every year, and the on-campus parties during Purim are some of the wildest. There's also "liquid latex," a night where each performer wears nothing but latex. "There are never enough people willing to perform," quipped one student who attended, "but they always sell out."

The hub of social life tends to be the dorms for underclassmen, and the Mods (a set of on-campus apartment suites) for seniors. One Mod-dweller explained that, while people in different dorms tended to become close, "the fact that Brandeis is small means that people tend to gather in the same places and it gets

to be very social" whether you live out in the Village or in the Castle. Because Brandeis does not support any type of exclusion, fraternities and sororities are not officially recognized but do provide an alternative venue for students who prefer a different milieu.

> "The fact that Brandeis is small means that people tend to gather in the same places and it gets to be very social."

Alcohol is generally not difficult to come by, and "if you're underage, it's not a problem as long as you're responsible." The campus also embraces its liberal roots in being more open to drugs than nearby colleges. Weed is most prevalent. Still, the campus is fairly easygoing and the wide array of local and international students makes it easy enough to have fun "whether you want to be a cokehead or an altarboy—nobody will feel left out."

Living on the Left

The Brandeis campus is built "on a hill, which can be pretty annoying when you have to walk up and down on it all day. You do get used to it, though." The campus does boast a wide array of buildings that attest to its 60-year history: a number of buildings had original designs by Eero Saarinen; a lake graces the area by the temple, chapel, and mosque on campus; and there is a castle that was built back when there was a veterinary school. One girl joked, "There are all sorts of towers, doors that lead nowhere, windows that don't go outside, that kind of thing. Students who live there climb around and figure it all out, everyone else gets lost just trying to find someone's room." And the Usdan dining hall is built to be riot-proof.

Riot-proof? "In the 1960s, there was a student takeover of the old student union, Ford Hall, by the black students for the civil rights movement," a women's crew club member says. "The administration had to cancel finals that semester it got so out of hand. Today, Usdan Hall has all sorts of strange halls and exits because it was built to be riot-proof." History doesn't get much more dramatic than that. Even now, the campus is very left-leaning, with protests occurring intermittently and an outspoken community at such events as Jimmy Carter's recent on-campus appearance.

In the end, every student agreed that, if they had to pick, they would definitely choose Brandeis again. One student described how "I just met the most incredible people that I just love spending my time with," and an alum said, wistfully, "I did not realize how incredibly liberal and politically active the student body is until I left. It was a really good fit for me, and I felt very comfortable." The school has successfully made itself into a diverse and accepting community with an incredible research community to make it both socially and academically an incredible value. In short, "Brandeis is better than home. No, scratch that. It's home." —*Jeffrey Zuckerman*

FYIs

If you come to Brandeis, you better bring "a fan, a big smile, and an outsized desire to right the wrongs of the world."

What is the typical weekend schedule? "Fridays we sit around and sometimes protest a controversial visitor. Saturdays we go to shul if we're orthodox and plan our parties if we're not, end up at the Mods by midnight. Sundays we wake up, eat bagels and lox, and kvetch about all the stuff that happened the night before."

If I could change one thing about Brandeis, "I'd change the buildings. But renovations are happening, so there you go."

Three things every student at Brandeis should do before graduating are "cheer on the crew and fencing teams, hang out (or live!) in the Castle, and picket against a political event."

Clark University

Address: 950 Main Street Worcester, MA 01610-1477
Phone: 508-793-7431
E-mail address: admissions@clarku.edu
Web site URL: www.clarku.edu/admissions
Year Founded: 1887
Private or Public: Private
Religious Affiliation: None
Location: Small city
Number of Applicants: 5,299
Percent Accepted: 56%
Percent Accepted who enroll: 20%
Number Entering: 650
Number of Transfers Accepted each Year: 166
Middle 50% SAT range: M: 540–650, CR: 550–660, Wr: 550–660
Middle 50% ACT range: 24–28
Early admission program EA/ED/None: ED

Percentage accepted through EA or ED: 76%
EA and ED deadline: NA
Regular Deadline: 15-Jan
Application Fee: $55
Full time Undergraduate enrollment: 2,222
Total enrollment: 3,330
Percent Male: 40%
Percent Female: 60%
Total Percent Minority or Unreported: 12%
Percent African-American: 2%
Percent Asian/Pacific Islander: 6%
Percent Hispanic: 4%
Percent Native-American: 1%
Percent International: Unreported
Percent in-state/out of state: 34%/66%
Percent from Public HS: 74%
Retention Rate: 91%

Graduation Rate 4-year: 73%
Graduation Rate 6-year: 76%
Percent Undergraduates in On-campus housing: 74%
Number of official organized extracurricular organizations: 94
3 Most popular majors: Psychology, Government, Biology/Biochemistry
Student/Faculty ratio: 10:1
Average Class Size: 21
Percent of students going to grad school: 36%
Tuition and Fees: $34,220
In State Tuition and Fees if different: No difference
Cost for Room and Board: $6,650
Percent receiving financial aid out of those who apply, first year: 74%
Percent receiving financial aid among all students: 52%

Founded in 1887, Clark University is a college with a rich history. Originally founded as an all-graduate university, it is one of three institutions that helped establish the Association of American Universities. Quietly existing in the city of Worcester, Massachusetts, Clark still retains its prestige not only as a graduate institution, but also as a place where undergraduates can grow in a learning environment. Fittingly, their motto is, "Challenge convention, Change our world."

Not Just Psych

Clark is widely known for its psychology department. As one student said, "Almost everyone here is a psych major." Clark's prominent connection with psychology dates back to its first president, G. Stanley Hall, founder of the American Psychological Association and the first person to earn a Ph.D. in psychology from Harvard. Psychoanalysis was first brought to the United States through Sigmund Freud's "Clark Lectures" at the university. Two statues commemorate Freud's visits and one student commented that "Freud is our unofficial mascot."

Although psychology is the most popular major at Clark, Government and International Relations, Biology, Business Management, and Communication and Culture fall close behind. In general, Clarkies find their classes "laid-back" and "uncompetitive." One student commented that Clark has "a lot of active and outspoken people who are passionate about what they believe in but I don't feel like people are stepping all over each other to outdo ·one another." The average class size at Clark is 15, and students tend to enjoy the intimate environment and the close relationships that fosters. It is in this intimate classroom setting where students take unique and thought-provoking classes such as "Political Science Fiction."

The Price is Right: Five for Four

Clark has 31 majors and 30 minors for students to choose from, and it is the only institution that offers Holocaust and Genocide Studies as an undergraduate minor. If those options aren't good enough for you, you can create your own major through the self-designed major program. This multi-discipline major allows students to combine over three departments to pursue research and knowledge in the field of their dreams. For more ambitious students, Clark recommends the Accelerated B.A./Master's Program, also known as the "Fifth-Year-Free" Program. Every year, 20 percent of the graduating class stays behind at Clark for a fifth year, free of charge, to pursue a Master's Degree in one of thirteen areas including management, history, chemistry, geographic information sciences, and education. Established in 1994, this program has received national attention for its admirable aim to have students "deepen their knowledge of a particular field and enhance their credentials for the job market."

Home is Where Themes, RAs, and Cheese Steaks Are

During their four years at Clark, 74 percent of students live on campus. Due to the plethora of on-campus housing options, many students have no regrets about staying there. Freshmen live in one of three first-year halls: Bullock, Wright and Sanford. Although most of these rooms are singles, doubles, or triples, some lucky denizens of Sanford Hall enjoy spacious suites with a common living space and a private bathroom.

In order to address the needs of gay, lesbian, and transgender students, Clark has adopted a gender-blind/neutral housing policy where students can opt to share a room with other students regardless of sex. For those concerned with awkward 3 a.m. bathroom encounters, Dodd Hall offers single-sex housing for women. Juniors and seniors mainly live in Maywood Street Hall where four-, five-, or six-person suites provide students with apartment-like comfort and privacy.

> "We have a lot of active and outspoken people who are passionate about what they believe in, but I don't feel like people are stepping all over each other to outdo one another."

In addition, the Theme House Program at Clark creates an opportunity for students to merge their personal and academic interests. A member of Clark's faculty is assigned to each house and, along with the Group Leader, organizes social events and educational programs to foster a sense of community on campus. Some of these Theme Houses include the Body and Soul House, the Just Yell Fire self-defense house, the Sexual Wellness and Awareness House, and Everyday is a Holiday House, a humble abode dedicated to celebrating lesser-known holidays around the world.

Unlike some schools, the presence of Residential Advisors significantly impacts the residential experience of each hall. Each year there are typically 35 RAs, of which 20 are First Year Experience RAs who specialize in the needs of freshmen. One student notes, "If you get a cool RA, you get cool activities!" RAs shape students' daily lives by throwing social functions, as well as by writing up rambunctious partiers for violating campus alcohol policies. Although RAs come in all shapes, sizes, and degrees of leniency, most agree that RAs, in general, are "chill" and "super-friendly."

Food at Clark brings a less enthusiastic response. "Boring and not really edible," commented one sophomore. After a new food distributor was brought into Clark, reactions were not favorable. "The best thing they have is probably the Philly cheese steak," said one student. No wonder vegans and vegetarians often find the food in "The Caf" unsuitable for their needs. However, there are alternatives for the ravenous Clarkie—the Bistro is an on-campus café that offers students savory sandwiches and eggs cooked every way possible. Also, the city of Worcester offers restaurants within walking distance of central campus for students looking to satiate their culinary cravings.

Out on the "Woo-town"
The city of Worcester (pronounced by locals as "WOO-stah") is 40 miles from Boston and the second largest city in Massachusetts. One student finds Woo-town "not a particularly busy city—but there are plenty of grocery stores and huge theaters where we get some great bands like Marilyn Mason and Gym Class Heroes." Although most activities off campus are hard to get to without a car, there is a Student Council Van that conveniently transports students to the mall on the weekends and the "Woo Bus" makes various parts of Worcester accessible.

Some students are concerned about the safety of Worcester, particular in Main South, the neighborhood where Clark is located. "Never walk alone," says one student. Dorm rooms are generally safe, but off-campus students should make sure to lock up properly. However, one veteran Clarkie says, "There are cop checkposts everywhere and, if you are responsible, you'll be fine. Nowhere in the world is it safe to walk around with a laptop at 3 a.m."

Hookahs and Drinking Sprees
On the weekends, some Clarkies take the train into Boston to barhop while most stay on campus for the partying. "Clark is not a dry campus," but students say it is "essential" to have an ID for the occasional "State Liquor run." Smoking culture, especially hookah smoking, is very popular at Clark. The University recently loosened their smoking policy and now students can be found puffing away on the green without being bothered.

Several times a year, campus-wide events take center stage in the social scene at Clark. One of the most beloved is "Spree Day," during the spring semester. Tradition holds that the date be kept secret, but students always seem to know when it will take place. On this most-anticipated day, classes are canceled, a carnival and concert are held on the green, livers are destroyed by 10 a.m., and hangovers nursed by 4 p.m. Though Spree Day only comes once a year, students agree that Clark is a great place to spend four wonderful years of their lives.—*Lee Komeda*

FYI
If you come to Clark, you'd better bring "a hookah."
What is the typical weekend schedule? "Friday, take the free buses during the day to go to malls and Boston. Saturday, attend a few parties and smoke a hookah. Sundays are reserved for studying."
If I could change one thing about Clark, I'd "change its size. Sometimes it's too small and gossipy."
Three things every student at Clark should do before graduating are "get involved with a student group, get to know President Bassett, and go to a foam party."

Emerson College

Address: 10 Boylston Street
Boston, MA 02116
Phone: 617-824-8600
E-mail address:
admission@emerson.edu
Web site URL:
www.emerson.edu
Year Founded: 1880
Private or Public: Private
Religious Affiliation: None
Location: Urban
Number of Applicants: 6,944
Percent Accepted: 37%
Percent Accepted who enroll: 30%
Number Entering: 774
Number of Transfers Accepted each Year: 423
Middle 50% SAT range:
M: 550–640, Cr: 580–670,
Wr: 640–700
Middle 50% ACT range:
24–29
Early admission program EA/ED/None: EA

Percentage accepted through EA or ED: 59%
EA and ED deadline: 1-Nov
Regular Deadline: 5-Jan
Application Fee: $60
Full time Undergraduate enrollment: 3,293
Total enrollment: 4,197
Percent Male: 44%
Percent Female: 56%
Total Percent Minority or Unreported: 24%
Percent African-American: 3%
Percent Asian/Pacific Islander: 4%
Percent Hispanic: 6%
Percent Native-American: 1%
Percent International: 10%
Percent in-state/out of state: 20%/80%
Percent from Public HS: 72%
Retention Rate: 88%

Graduation Rate 4-year: 72%
Graduation Rate 6-year: 72%
Percent Undergraduates in On-campus housing: 42%
Number of official organized extracurricular organizations: 60
3 Most popular majors:
Cinematograph, Writing, Arts
Student/Faculty ratio: 14:1
Average Class Size: 10 to 19
Percent of students going to grad school: 13%
Tuition and Fees: $26,880
In State Tuition and Fees if different: No difference
Cost for Room and Board: $11,376
Percent receiving financial aid out of those who apply, first year: Unreported
Percent receiving financial aid among all students: 54%

For those looking for a creative and unique learning experience in the heart of Boston, Emerson is the school for you. As one of the premier colleges dedicated to communications and the arts, Emerson makes sure to ground its specialized focus in a liberal arts context. Budding creators and performers are sure to flourish on Emerson's supportive campus.

More Than Just Arts

Emerson is far from your typical college. It uniquely combines a preprofessional art curriculum with a more traditional liberal arts experience and prides itself on striking a balance between the two. Emerson students are encouraged to cultivate their creativity and passion, while building upon a traditional foundation.

Emerson students have a variety of requirements to fulfill throughout the course of four years—some of which must be completed by the end of the freshman year. Freshmen are required to take two writing courses, which draw some complaints for being substandard. In keeping with Emer-

son's liberal arts base, students must take courses in history, non-western civilization, psychology or philosophy, and research and expository writing. The required curriculum also includes aesthetics, fine arts, and performing arts. One student commented that at times "the school definitely focuses more on its job-specific courses, and many of the liberal arts courses tend to go by the wayside as far as strong teachers go," but students generally seem to find the requirements more helpful than not. One senior reflected that, "All students appreciate the exposure to other disciplines."

Emerson students choose between two schools, the School of the Arts and the School of Communications, when declaring their major. The School of the Arts includes the performing arts, visual and media arts, and writing, while the School of Communications encompasses communication sciences, journalism, and marketing. Many students declare their major, and in effect their school, after their freshman year, but as one freshman noted, "When students are unsure of their major, they often declare it as media studies," presumably with the option of changing at a later date. Although students are technically divided by their choice of school, many students laud the benefits of having both schools under one roof. There is a great deal of involvement between the two because students are required to take classes from both, as well because of the interdisciplinary nature inherent in many of Emerson's courses. One student remarked that the existence of both schools encourages both professors and students to look at their subject in the context of other disciplines. For example, within a writing course, a professor may reference a film or television show, giving students a broader prospective.

Study abroad is a very popular option among Emerson students. Most students participate in one, if not more, of the three programs run by the University. Castle Well in the Netherlands is one popular destination that opens up all of Europe to students. The Los Angeles program sends students to California for a semester to take advantage of internship opportunities and networking in the entertainment industry. The Prague Summer Film Festival is another very popular opportunity to study abroad.

Emerson students show creativity even when picking their majors. It is extremely popular to double major, minor, or even create your own major. Some have been known to both double-major and double-minor. Students often pick unrelated subjects to study, reflecting their varied interests. Some of the more popular majors include marketing and film. Theater is known as a difficult major, as is communication disorders. Writing is another particularly rigorous major. Emerson boasts some very interesting courses, including History of Burlesque. One common complaint centers on the length of classes. Emerson classes last from between an hour and fifteen minutes to almost two hours. On the upside, classes are generally small and average at about 20 students, with the largest classes rarely topping 100 students. TAs are rare and one senior claimed, "I have never had a TA or even heard of one at Emerson." The consensus among students is that the workload is what you make it. And, on top of the normal paper writing and reading, Emerson students "come to act, produce films, write poetry, and create art."

Student Body
Emerson prides itself on representing a diverse range of opinions and people. Stu-

dents are practically required to arrive on campus with an open mind and according to one student, "I found kids I could get along with and relate to, and I think even if something isn't your style, you can still fit in." This attitude aside, there are some stereotypes for the student body, including "white, rich, gay" and crazy liberal. Many are very politically active on campus. Students laughingly joke that all incoming guys will be "gay by May," but this is offset by an extremely accepting atmosphere on campus. This does mean dating can be tough for girls on campus. Students often look to other colleges in Boston for dating opportunities. One large complaint heard among students is that Emerson is not racially or economically diverse. But the overwhelming atmosphere is one of creativity, diversity and enthusiasm.

> "I found kids I could get along with and relate to, and I think even if something isn't your style, you can still fit in."

This creativity is directly channeled into the variety of activities Emerson students take on. Many of these directly relate to majors, especially with fields such as film studies. Emerson provides the means and equipment to support creative endeavors. There are student publications, theater groups, one of the most popular college radio stations, as well as opportunities all over Boston. Emerson recently renovated the Cutler Majestic Theatre, a former opera house, as a venue for student productions, as well as visiting artists.

Not Your Average Campus
For students, "Emerson IS Boston." The school and the city are well integrated and inseparable as an experience. Weekends are jam packed because of all the bars, theaters, and events Boston offers, but that does not mean there is a lack of things to do on campus. From shows to parties, there is something to satisfy everyone. Upperclassmen often gather on campus for parties. According to one senior, "Emerson students really like to dress up for each other and spend money. It wouldn't be strange to go to a semiformal cocktail mixer." Greek life exists, but is far from a defining social force.

Emerson students are guaranteed housing for their first two years and these are not two years of suffering. Descriptions of housing have included "awesome" and "like hotels." Some students live in standard doubles off a hall in the Little Building, while Piano Row boasts newer suite-type rooms. Upperclassmen tend to move off campus into apartments. On campus, there are RAs and strict alcohol regulations in the dorms, but those over 21 are allowed to drink. Food on campus is described as "fine, but can get old." There are cafes and convenience stores in the dorm, but there are also thousands of cheap food options all around Boston. On-campus facilities also boast a library that

caters to communication majors, a new gym and soccer field, and a new performing arts theater that was featured in the Martin Scorsese film, *The Departed.*

Emerson boasts a world-class location in the heart of the theater district of Boston. Emerson's students are just as familiar with the city around them as they are with the campus. Combined with the diversity and interdisciplinary academic and art focus, Emerson is a truly unique and exciting experience for students looking to make the most of their four years at college.— *Janet Yang*

FYI

If you come to Emerson you better bring "a Mac, knowledge of art and film, and big sunglasses."
The typical weekend schedule is "dinner at a trendy restaurant in Boston, seeing an Emerson show, going to a cast party, film shoot wrap party or cocktail party."
If I could change one thing it would be "the scarcity of straight men."
Three things every student should do before graduation are "see a show in the Majestic, study abroad, and go to the EVVY awards."

College of the Holy Cross

Address: 1 College Street Worcester, MA 01610-2395
Phone: 508-793-2443
E-mail address: admissions@holycross.edu
Web site URL: www.holycross.edu
Year Founded: 1843
Private or Public: Private
Religious Affiliation: Roman Catholic
Location: Urban
Number of Applicants: 7,227
Percent Accepted: 34%
Percent Accepted who enroll: 30%
Number Entering: 738
Number of Transfers Accepted each Year: 49
Middle 50% SAT range: M: 600–680, CR: 580–720, Wr: Unreported
Middle 50% ACT range: Unreported
Early admission program EA/ED/None: ED

Percentage accepted through EA or ED: Unreported
EA and ED deadline: 15-Dec
Regular Deadline: 15-Jan
Application Fee: $60
Full time Undergraduate enrollment: 2,898
Total enrollment: 2,898
Percent Male: 43%
Percent Female: 57%
Total Percent Minority or Unreported: 39%
Percent African-American: 5%
Percent Asian/Pacific Islander: 6%
Percent Hispanic: 9%
Percent Native-American: <1%
Percent International: 2%
Percent in-state/out of state: 38%/62%
Percent from Public HS: 44%
Retention Rate: 95%
Graduation Rate 4-year: 92%

Graduation Rate 6-year: 92%
Percent Undergraduates in On-campus housing: 89%
Number of official organized extracurricular organizations: 104
3 Most popular majors: Economics, English Language and Literature, Political Science and Government
Student/Faculty ratio: 10:1
Average Class Size: 10 to 19
Percent of students going to grad school: 23%
Tuition and Fees: $38,180
In State Tuition and Fees if different: No difference
Cost for Room and Board: $10,620
Percent receiving financial aid out of those who apply, first year: 77%
Percent receiving financial aid among all students: 54%

Nestled in the city of Worcester, Massachusetts is the College of the Holy Cross, America's oldest Roman Catholic College. Initially founded in 1843 as a Jesuit school for boys, today the school prides itself in the diversity of experiences that students have, the rigor of the academic programs, and the tight-knit community formed around the city.

Optional: SATs

Holy Cross is exclusively an undergraduate institution; therefore students receive the undivided attention of faculty and administration. When asked why she chose Holy Cross over other colleges, a senior replied, "Because I knew that I would be in an environment that prioritized academics above everything." In choosing its students, Holy Cross prioritizes a candidate's interests, activities, recommendations, and high school transcript over standardized tests scores. In fact, while they are suggested, the SAT and ACT are not required for applying to Holy Cross.

A Bachelor of Arts degree is awarded to all that complete 32 semester-long courses, with requirements in arts, literature, religion, philosophy, history and cross-cultural studies. Twenty-eight majors are offered and students can also select concentrations as well. Like many liberal arts colleges, pre-professional track programs such as pre-business, pre-medicine, and pre-dental are offered as well. Holy Cross is particularly noted for its economics, chemistry, political science and English departments. Also worthy of mention is its classics department, which is one of the largest in America. Uniquely, the department integrates Greek and Latin Studies with advanced information technology and archaeology.

Academic learning outside of the classroom is also highly valued at Holy Cross, which is why they encourage students to participate in "Experiential Learning" programs. Student can take a semester or a year abroad or participate in the Semester Away Program which allows students to pursue academic interests that are not available at Holy Cross at other institutions, but many complained that the semester-long options were limited. The summer internship programs are offered to certain sophomores and juniors as an opportunity to gain professional experiences related to a student's career related goals. These internships, developed through a network of parents, alumni and friends of Holy Cross, have been extremely popular.

Holy Cross boasts a faculty to student ratio of eleven to one. However, don't expect classes to be easy because they are small. "Classes were very challenging and the professors definitely expected a lot," one recent alumna stated. But have no fear, you'll have plenty of support. "The professors always knew who you were and were great about being there for you, whether it be holding review sessions or extending office hours."

Easy Street and the "Woorats"

Residential life at Holy Cross is divided into three different areas of campus comprising 10 residence halls. As freshmen, you will be placed in one of the residence halls located at the northern end of campus known as Easy Street. While the option of moving off campus is available for second, third, and fourth year students, most Holy Cross students stay in campus housing for their entire four years. Upperclassmen mainly live in the lower part of campus, in the halls of Alumni, Carlin, Loyola and Williams. The most coveted of them all are the apartments in Williams Hall. After construction was completed in 2003, upperclassmen fought at the annual lottery for these apartments equipped with separate showers, kitchen, living room and individual bedrooms.

For food, Holy Cross students have a wide variety of options. In addition to the main dining room, there is the food court, the lunch-through-late-night Crossroads, or Cool Beans and CB2, both coffee shops. Most students have no complaints about the dining services at Holy Cross. "I really like the food at Holy Cross!" gushed one student. "They have specialty nights in the dining hall like Thanksgiving dinner and Birthday Cake night!" For those with special dietary needs, the dining services have Weight Watcher meals, heart-healthy selections, and vegetarian entrees.

While campus is generally a good place to live, Worcester (pronounced Wooster) has its ups and down. "Town-gown" relationships have gotten better in the past few years, but there is a divide between the "Woorats" and the Holy Cross Crusaders. "The locals are usually pretty nice to students as long as you don't go out of your way to offend them," said one student. Holy Cross shares Worcester with Worcester Polytechnic Institute and Clark University and is in a "consortium" with them, encouraging interaction between the students.

Bleeding Purple

Holy Cross's athletic teams are known as the Crusaders, and the official school color is the royal purple used by Emperor Constantine the Great. Holy Cross is one of the founding members of the Patriot League, which also includes American University, United State Military Academy, Bucknell University, Colgate University, Lafayette College, Lehigh University, and the United States Naval Academy. Athletic support and school spirit are very high at Holy Cross. "Holy Cross has a ton of school pride. We bleed purple! When the basketball championships were held here, everyone was painted in purple and you had to stand diagonally to fit into the gym!" gushed one track and field runner.

> "Holy Cross has a ton of school pride. We bleed purple!"

School pride is also sustained by the large number of campus-wide events and traditions held annually. Some of these events are organized by the Purple Key Society, a service honor society dedicated to increasing school spirit and community building. One of them is the 100 Days Dance, held when 100 days are left for the graduating class. This includes a dinner followed by a dance where each attendee makes a list of seniors that they try to kiss before the night is over. PKS also organizes the Purple Pride Day, when the entire school is covered in royal purple, and purple tee-shirts, cookies, balloons and stickers are given out to foster enthusiasm for the school. Another tradition is Skirt Day, which is considered the first day of spring and girls (who make up 70 percent of the student population) wear skirts for the first time in the year.

The social scene at Holy Cross is regarded with much enthusiasm as well. While there are no fraternities or sororities on campus, residence halls serve their function as smaller social communities within the campus. In particular, Wheeler Hall is known as the rowdiest hall. "It was great, everyone knew your name, and we were the only dorm [for underclassmen] not off Easy Street" says one ex-Wheeler resident. Wheeler Hall is also the birthplace of the popular campus sport, Stickball, which started in the 1940s. You can have a great time even if you aren't in Wheeler too. On Tuesdays, upperclassmen, mainly seniors, congregate at the Pub in the Hogan Campus Center. For those underage, Tuesdays mean going to the "10 spot", an open mic night for bands and performances held at Crossroads, one of the food courts. Worcester also has plenty to offer for social activities. Students often frequent the malls at Solomon Pond and the restaurants on Shrewsberry Street.

Achieving a good balance of academics, athletics, and socializing seems to be the modus operandi of these students. All three aspects of college life are met with enthusiasm and open-mindedness at Holy Cross. If this sounds like your cup of tea, "going purple" may be a good idea for next year. —*Lee Komeda*

FYI
If you come to Holy Cross, you'd better bring "purple face paint!"
What's typical weekend schedule? "Go to a sports game, study, go to the movies or a restaurant on Shrewsberry Street, hang out in friends' rooms, and study, study, study on Sunday!"
If I could change one thing about Holy Cross, it would offer "more semester-long abroad programs. It is tough to go away for a whole year."
Three things students should do before graduating: "Participate in the Appalachia service Project, go on the Silent Retreat, and enjoy Cape Week."

Hampshire College

Address: 893 West Street
 Amherst, MA 01002
Phone: 877-937-4267
E-mail address:
 admissions@hampshire.edu
Web site URL:
 www.hampshire.edu
Year Founded: 1970
Private or Public: Private
Religious Affiliation: None
Location: Suburban
Number of Applicants: 2,842
Percent Accepted: 61%
Percent Accepted who
 enroll: 27%
Number Entering: 437
Number of Transfers
 Accepted each Year: 33
Middle 50% SAT range:
 M: 540–660, CR: 610–700,
 Wr: 590–700
Middle 50% ACT range:
 26–29
Early admission program
 EA/ED/None: EA and ED

Percentage accepted
 through EA or ED: 25%
EA and ED deadline: 15-Nov
Regular Deadline: 15-Jan
Application Fee: $55
Full time Undergraduate
 enrollment: 1,428
Total enrollment: 1,428
Percent Male: 42%
Percent Female: 58%
Total Percent Minority or
 Unreported: 15%
Percent African-American:
 5%
Percent Asian/Pacific
 Islander: 4%
Percent Hispanic: 6%
Percent Native-American: 1%
Percent International:
 Unreported
Percent in-state/out of
 state: 18%/82%
Percent from Public HS: 48%
Retention Rate: 79%
Graduation Rate 4-year: 52%

Graduation Rate 6-year: 65%
Percent Undergraduates
 in On-campus housing:
 90%
Number of official organized
 extracurricular
 organizations: 94
3 Most popular majors:
 Film/Video and Photography,
 English, Fine arts
Student/Faculty ratio: 11.1:1
Average Class Size: 16
Percent of students going to
 grad school: 50%
Tuition and Fees: $37,789
In State Tuition and Fees if
 different: No difference
Cost for Room and Board:
 $10,080
Percent receiving financial
 aid out of those who apply,
 first year: 88%
Percent receiving financial
 aid among all students:
 55%

D eep in the Pioneer Valley, nestled in the quaint serenity of New England, lies a radical college devoted to inflaming the passions of its highly individualistic and motivated student body. This College was founded in the '70s by the other four colleges of the current Five College Consortium—Amherst, Smith, Mt. Holyoke, and UMass-Amherst—as an experiment in education. There are no majors at Hampshire. Every student must design his own course of study, and there is a heavy emphasis on individually driven project-based work. Hampshire College attracts a wide range of talented and self-motivated students to an energetic and liberal setting.

The Hampshire Curriculum: Div-ying up Academic Freedom

The most striking feature of Hampshire College is its "experimenting" academic program. Students must advance their way through three different divisions, called Div I, Div II, and Div III. "First-years" must start their journey in Div I, which consists of taking eight classes, and at least one in each of the five Schools of thought: Humanities Arts and Cultural Studies, Interdisciplinary Arts, Social Science, Cognitive Science and Natural Science. They must also take a tutorial class and complete some Learning Goals, which are meant to develop important academic skills. In the third "limbo semester," students complete their Div I requirements and start soliciting professors for their Div II work. Each student has a committee of two or three professors that helps him to create a unique course of study that concentrates his interests in preparation for the culminating Div III project. Once a student completes his Div III project and is reviewed by a committee of five professors, he can triumphantly ring the Div III Bell in the center of campus and declare himself "Div-Free." Because of all the committees involved in preparing one's course of study, there is a lot of paperwork. Hampshire suffers from a complex and sometimes frustrating bureaucracy. But, that is the price the students pay for an unprecedented amount of academic freedom available at no other college.

Another striking feature of Hampshire is the absence of grades. Instead, a student receives a written evaluation at the completion of a course. The students have high praises for the evaluations, which are "more telling than grades" because "they specifically relate to what [the student] can do better." Since there are no grades, the students do not feel obligated to do work that they feel isn't meaningful. That is not to say that Hampshire students are slackers. There is "a lot of outside work"—one student estimated as many as three hours of outside work for one hour of class time. Working with professors, it is not uncommon for students to rewrite a paper multiple times. Since the focus is on critical evaluation and personal improvement, many students feel it is "easy to get a good rapport [with professors] because of interaction."

There has been a movement in recent years to reform the Div I program to incorporate more individual work. This Re-Radicalization (or Re-Rad, for short) has "overwhelming" student support and is a "well-established student group." In the spring of 2004, a group of Re-Rad revolutionaries occupied the president's office in order to draw attention to their cause. This year, a Re-Rad pilot program began pairing third-semester students with Div III students for "mentored independent study."

Hampshire boasts strong programs in film, photography, and creative writing. It also created the first undergraduate interdisciplinary cognitive science program in the country. But, Hampshire is a small college and does not have the resources of a greater institution. Also, many of its classes are "narrowly focused," which hinders students who want to make a broad inquiry into a subject. Whenever a student wants a course that Hampshire does not offer, he can go to one of the other schools in the Five College Consortium. As one student succinctly said, "The Five College Consortium makes Hampshire possible." The other colleges are an invaluable academic resource, and most students take classes elsewhere, especially during Div II when they need specific courses for their concentration. The Pioneer Valley Transit Authority runs buses between all the Five College schools throughout the day and most of the night.

"Spacey" Singles and "Revolutionary" Mods

Most first-year Hampshire students live in one of two dorms—Dakin or Merrill. Ninety percent of the rooms are singles, and the students seem very happy about that. Although "most of the rooms are relatively small," the students say it is nice to have quiet space for oneself. During a housing crunch this year, some students were living in lounges, but the problem was solved as students dropped out. There is a "fair amount of socializing" in the dorms, and most people become good friends with their hallmates.

Starting into their second year, most students move into the mods, which receive high praise. A mod is essentially an on-campus apartment, in which four to 10 students share a common living space. All mods contain a kitchen, and many students go on a half-meal plan and cook meals in the mod. For this, students can buy a food share and receive inexpensive fresh vegetables year-round through the farm center and the community supported agriculture (CSA) program. There are three different mod sections—Prescott, Greenwich, and Enfield—each with its own personality and building style. The quality of the mods varies; some have been recently renovated and are dearly sought after. The housing lottery, which occurs in the spring, is "high-strung and dramatic." It takes place in a barn, where all the students mass and compete to get a good mod. Mod selections are based on seniority, so older students usually get the better housing. Most are satisfied and "the minority are horrified by the result."

There are a surprising number of options for social activity at Hampshire. There is always something happening on campus, especially in the mods. The social scene is very laid-back; one student described how most people "hang out, drink, do drugs, talk, play music or any combination of the above." Although drugs are prevalent on campus, there seems to be a consensus that there is "no pressure to do anything." The College provides lots of events for the students, such as movie nights and speakers. Local and college bands play around campus, in any space that's available. Even if something is not happening on campus, there is always the option of going to one of the other of the Five Colleges, which also have vibrant social scenes and countless activities. The "liberal, arts-friendly town" of Northampton, lined with coffee shops and bookstores, is also a popular hangout place.

Hampshire, for such a young college, already has some famous traditions. Hampshire Halloween, once called "Trip or Treat," is the biggest event of the year, a "fashion show on acid." People take their costumes very seriously, and the College plans events the whole evening. At the end of the night, the professors serve students breakfast in the dining hall. In the spring there are the Drag Ball and the Easter Keg Hunt, during which student organizations set up kegs in the woods and students bring their own cups in search of free beer. Another favorite event is the Spring Jam, a "big music festival with inflatables."

The Hampshire World: Nerds, Hipsters, Hippies, and "Earthy Types"

Hampshire admittedly suffers from a stereotype of being a haven for scruffy, pot-smoking hippies, but the students thoroughly dismiss this idea. Although there are a "fair number of hippies," that is not the only type of person on campus. Indeed, one of the greatest things about Hampshire is that there is a "niche for everyone." When students are asked to describe the typical Hampshire student, they say he is "passionate," "committed" and "not competitive." It is not uncommon for students to talk at length about their academic work. The students are very friendly, and "everybody's always discussing something, out on the quad, on the bus." Furthermore, Hampshire students have a wide range of interests and have a "greater acceptance of nontraditional things." Granted, there are a few areas in which Hampshire lacks diversity. The campus is "predominately white upper-middle class" and ideologically "very left of center." Still, the student body is quirky and interesting. For example, a number of students dressed up as pirates on Sept. 19 to celebrate International Talk Like a Pirate Day.

> "[Hampshire] did its job well; I learned how to educate myself and go after the things I want."

No matter what kind of person comes to Hampshire, he will be able to find a place. There are various groups on campus, covering all variety of interests. Hampshire Theater and its theater board, all run by students, elect student-run productions to be put on show, and host an annual play festival. Excalibur, the science fiction and fantasy fan club, one of the biggest groups on campus, hosts weekly movie screenings. Once a semester, Excalibur hosts Death Fest, a night-long role-playing-game tournament. A Circus Group was just created, where students can learn to juggle and do acrobatics. For aspiring writers, *The Hampshire Free Press* will fund periodical or book projects. Publications come and go, but the current ones are: *The Climax*, a news-paper that comes out every few weeks; *The Reader*, an annual literary arts magazine; and *The Omen*, a free-speech publication. *The Omen* is the longest-running paper at Hampshire and has been at the head of much controversy for publishing almost anything unedited. "[They're] so free speech, they won't correct your spelling." Like much of Hampshire, the writing scene suffers from "a lot of disorganization" but is "pregnant with opportunity." That is, although there are very few structures in place, if one takes the initiative, he can achieve a lot through his own effort.

SAGA and the Vegan Conspiracy

The only dining hall at Hampshire is SAGA (it's spelled in all capitals, but no one knows why). One student summed up the student opinion quite nicely when he said, "The food's fine. People complain about it because it's fun to complain about it, but it's not as bad as the complaining makes it seem." The dining hall offers a lot of options apart from the standard meal, including a salad bar, a sandwich bar, and a waffle station. It is also "very very vegetarian- and vegan-friendly." Their vegan desserts are said to be much better than the normal desserts, prompting the idea that there is a vast vegan conspiracy trying to convert the nonvegans. If SAGA is closed or a student wants something else to eat, the other places to get food on campus are the Tavern and the Bridge Café.

Hampshire was built in the '70s, and it shows. One student described the architecture of the buildings as "brutalist concrete and brick, squat and ugly." The same student described the rest of the campus as "f—ing beautiful." Although the buildings on campus are "cramped," the rest of campus is very open. The campus is crisscrossed with "woodsy paths," and many students say they enjoy taking leisurely walks around campus. The Yellow Bike program takes care of communal bikes for use by the students. When the weather is better, spontaneous drum circles overtake the campus's grassy fields. In the fall, students can pick apples all over campus. The Cultural Village is the site of the Yiddish Book Museum and the Eric Carle Children's Book Art Museum, where one can make his own children's picture book in the studio. Another popular spot is the Lemelson Design Center, where students can take lessons in blacksmithing.

Hampshire may be the most radically unique college in the nation. But it is not for everyone. It is not, as some *Saturday Night*

Live skits might suggest, a "weird slacker school." A serious caveat to anyone looking at Hampshire: It takes a certain kind of student to profit from a Hampshire education. Many come to Hampshire and find they cannot function without structure, or find the level of work too difficult. Consequently, Hampshire has a relatively high drop-out rate. But, for those who are self-motivated and have a passion for learning, a Hampshire education will do great things. One recent alum said, "[Hampshire] did its job well; I learned how to educate myself and go after the things I want." In a way, a Hampshire education is empowering, in that it frees the students from the constraints of a structured academic system. The high level of individual work and inquiry-based projects gives Hampshire the reputation of being the "graduate school for undergraduates." Hampshire prepares students well for future academic work, and graduates enjoy one of the highest grad school acceptance rates in the country.—*Ryan Galisewski*

FYI

If you come to Hampshire College, you'd better bring "a Frisbee, hippie drums and a pirate costume."

What's the typical weekend schedule? "Wake up Saturday morning, go on a crazy adventure, and then wake up realizing it's Monday."

If I could change one thing about Hampshire College, I'd "make money grow on the Hampshire tree."

Three things every student at Hampshire College should do before graduating are "occupy a building, take a class with Lynn 'don't f—ing call me Mr.' Miller, and buy a farm share."

Harvard University

Address: 86 Brattle Street Cambridge, MA 02138
Phone: 617-495-1551
E-mail address: college@fas.harvard.edu
Web site URL: www.harvard.edu
Year Founded: 1636
Private or Public: Private
Religious Affiliation: None
Location: Urban
Number of Applicants: 27,642
Percent Accepted: 7.90%
Percent Accepted who enroll: 76.20%
Number Entering: 1,658
Number of Transfers Accepted each Year: Unreported
Middle 50% SAT range: M: 700–780, CR: 690–800, Wr: 690–790
Middle 50% ACT range: 31–35
Early admission program EA/ED/None: None

Percentage accepted through EA or ED: NA
EA and ED deadline: NA
Regular Deadline: 1-Jan
Application Fee: $65
Full time Undergraduate enrollment: 6,651
Total enrollment: 20,263
Percent Male: 50%
Percent Female: 50%
Total Percent Minority or Unreported: 33%
Percent African-American: 8%
Percent Asian/Pacific Islander: 17%
Percent Hispanic: 7%
Percent Native-American: 1%
Percent International: 10%
Percent in-state/out of state: 16%/84%
Percent from Public HS: 66%
Retention Rate: 97%
Graduation Rate 4-year: 97%

Graduation Rate 6-year: 98%
Percent Undergraduates in On-campus housing: Unreported
Number of official organized extracurricular organizations: 400
3 Most popular majors: Economics, Government, Psychology
Student/Faculty ratio: Unreported
Average Class Size: <20
Percent of students going to grad school: Unreported
Tuition and Fees: $36,173
In State Tuition and Fees if different: No difference
Cost for Room and Board: $11,042
Percent receiving financial aid out of those who apply, first year: 88%
Percent receiving financial aid among all students: 60%

Harvard University. The name may call to mind a few stereotypes: arrogant, intellectual students discussing philosophy with pompous New England accents. Yet, while it maintains that time-honored reputation for academic excellence, Harvard is also an extraordinary place in which talented, creative minds can flourish and form friendships that last beyond their four years.

Beyond the Core

One of the biggest draws to Harvard is certainly its strong academic community. Harvard brings in some of the biggest professors and talented graduate students in their fields, providing students with incredible opportunities to learn. The school is famous for its Core Curriculum, which requires its students to "devote almost a quarter of their studies to courses in the following areas of the program: Foreign Cultures, Historical Study, Literature and Arts, Moral Reasoning, Quantitative Reasoning, Science, and Social Analysis." This is in addition to fulfilling a Foreign Language requirement and an Expository Writing class mandatory for freshmen. A recent revamping process in the Core program now allows students to wait till the middle of their sophomore year to declare their concentration. While the major complaints about the Core have to do with the large lectures that students must attend, overall, as one student put it, "I really liked the Core . . . at times it can feel restrictive, but it . . . 'helps you learn to study in different areas and put society in a historical perspective." Another senior agreed that, "At the time, my Core classes were kind of annoying, but looking back, it seemed to be really helpful."

In terms of concentrations, economics and government are universally recognized as the most popular, with psychology coming in a close second. However, as one student said, "in these departments, people often complain that they feel like a number, and in the smaller, quirkier departments, you can be closer to faculty." These "quirkier" departments include Folklore and Mythology and Obstructing Social Space. "Someone just sat in a box in the middle of the science center, to see how it affected people. So there's room for all kinds of projects here." Harvard's unique schedule, with a "shopping week" in the beginning of the semester and a reading week toward the end, gives students room to develop their own projects and to space out their workloads.

Regardless of concentration, professors at Harvard are always accessible. "They are always around to help," one student said. "They will even go out to lunch or dinner with you." While many lower-level lectures, especially in the science departments, are taught and graded by teaching fellows (TFs), students insist that "there are always opportunities" to find smaller classes and seminars and that class size truly depends on your concentration and course of study. When asked about grade inflation at Harvard, most students gave similar answers, saying that, "It's hard to get an A, or even a B, but it's also hard to get a D" and that "most people are just competing for that narrow band of grades in between."

Finals Clubs and the French Revolution

Outside of the classroom, Harvard students are just as talented and excited about their social lives. "I am always pretty impressed by the creativity of the student body," one junior said. "They are generally open and allow you to be yourself." One student even asserted, "The best thing about Harvard is the people. Learning from each other and having conversations allow you to learn a whole lot of new things, from new people. They're absolutely amazing." Although there is a whole host of ethnic, cultural, and geographic diversity, one student admitted that, "There are many Type A personalities here . . . sometimes, I just let other people do things like calculate tip, because eventually, it'll get done." When Harvard students channel that energy into planning their weekends, the sky's the limit. "When a bunch of smart people get into a room and start planning a party, they come up with some pretty cool stuff." In terms of partying, the options are small, but they are there. "If you want to go drink on Wednesday at 3 a.m., it might be harder. And our weekends definitely don't start on Thursdays. But, on the weekends, if you're looking for it, it's there." Another student countered that, "Getting absurdly drunk . . . is not really a part of daily life here, not even on the weekends. It's just more relaxed."

While Harvard has fraternities, they are not sponsored by the University and make up a fairly small part of the social life. Instead, there are finals clubs, which are exclusive societies that own houses and throw parties on the weekends. The clubs, most of which are all-male, are a kind of throwback to Harvard's good-old-boy reputation and are fairly controversial. As one student put it, "If people really want to party, that is an option, but some people don't like the 'old-boys-club' aspect—and, if you're a woman, it's pretty unfair." Instead, Harvard students get a bit quirkier with their parties. "One of my favorite memories is of the 'Revolution Party.' Each room represented a different revolution, from the French Revolution to the Sexual Revolution. And the last room was Dance Dance Revolution. It was great."

For those looking to leave their rooms and frat houses to have fun, Harvard Square offers a whole host of great bars and restaurants. Some popular ones include John Harvard's and the Kong, which is "the closest thing to a sketchy bar that we have." In terms of underage drinking, students report that "it is hard to drink as a frosh, but overall, the Harvard police are pretty lenient." The more adventurous can hop on the T and head to Boston itself or to the many other nearby schools. But, as one student explained, "We have a bit of a 'Crimson Bubble' here. People can plan to go to Boston on the weekends, but you have to be a bit more proactive."

Harvard Housing
Harvard is divided into a community of 12 residential houses, each of which has its own special characteristics and defining features. While all freshmen start from the same place, the dorms on Harvard Yard, they enter the housing lottery in groups (a process called "blocking") and become affiliated with a respective house starting their sophomore year. While the river houses are often thought to be the most desirable (including Eliot, Adams, and Leverett) because they are closer to the main areas of campus, the houses on the quad are not nearly as bad as their reputations would have them seem. "Some people dread being quaded, because they don't want to be cut off," one student said, "but everyone seems to enjoy living there, they have their own party and social atmosphere."

Each house has its own dining hall and facilities, its own housing council, and its own unique campus-wide parties. Some examples include the annual Eliot House party, which is invitation-only, and the Mather Lather, a giant foam party. Proctors in the freshman dorms and tutors in the upperclassmen houses "serve mostly as advisers and don't really care" about being disciplinarians. Since the housing system does make the entire school decentralized, there is no student center, but each house has its own social spaces for parties, dances, and just plain hanging out. The dining halls are all split by house as well, although one stu-

dent claims that, "Hillel [the Jewish student center] has the best food on campus. Seriously!" Overall, as one student put it, "Everyone tries to pretend that their houses are better . . . there are differences between the houses, but really it's so random, and most of the amenities are the same." And off-campus life is basically nonexistent. As one student described, "I've met two people who live off campus . . . it's difficult."

Cheering on the Crimson
When it comes to extracurriculars, Harvard has something in which everyone can be involved. There are classic Harvard mainstays, like the daily newspaper the *Crimson*, the humorous *Lampoon*, and a myriad of a cappella groups. However, there are also community service organizations, performing arts groups, and even a Chinese yo-yo club. In terms of sports, one student summed it up: "We have more varsity sports teams than any other school in the country. Whether we're any good at them is another story." Football is probably the biggest varsity draw (and the Harvard-Yale game the most popular sporting event of the year), but, as one student wryly observed, "You'll catch people reading during the football games, even if they do go." One student asserted that, "A lot of people are athletes, even though we don't have a whole 'sports pride' mentality. People will go to sports events to support their friends."

If you're not up to varsity competition, there are a whole lot of accessible and fun intramural sports to keep students occupied, the most popular of which are volleyball, Ultimate Frisbee, soccer, and basketball. Those who really get into it can join the intrahouse competition for the Straus Cup. And, if you're looking for something more than your house gym, the campus-wide sports facilities are being renovated, making it even more accessible for nonathletes.

> "You'll catch people reading during the football games, even if they do go."

Harvard offers a combination of academic stimulation, social opportunities, and a traditional New England college setting that genuinely cannot be found anywhere else. Though one senior admitted that, "It is very easy to get wrapped up in this culture of intensity, to burn out and forget about the outside world," he also countered by saying, "My stereotypes about this place were shattered when I got here. You just have to come here and experience it for yourself." If you're up to the challenge, it just may be the place for you.—*Alexandra Bicks*

FYI

If you come to Harvard, you'd better bring "your favorite book."

What's a typical weekend schedule? "Thursday nights, there are karaoke nights or trivia nights in the houses; Friday nights, stay in or go out to dinner, maybe a party; Saturday nights are bigger, more parties, concerts, plays; Sundays, brunch, homework . . . of course, no one will judge if you just want to stay in."

If I could change one thing about Harvard, I'd "change the schedule. It's really annoying to have finals after December break."

Three things every student should do before graduating are "the famous three: hook up in the library, pee on the John Harvard statue, and run Primal Scream."

Massachusetts Institute of Technology

Address: 77 Massachusetts Avenue Cambridge, MA 02139-4307
Phone: 617-253-1000
E-mail address: admissions@mit.edu
Web site URL: www.mit.edu
Year Founded: 1861
Private or Public: Private
Religious Affiliation: None
Location: Urban
Number of Applicants: 12,445
Percent Accepted: 12%
Percent Accepted who enroll: 69%
Number Entering: 1,067
Number of Transfers Accepted each Year: 17
Middle 50% SAT range: M: 720–800, CR: 660–760, Wr: 660–750
Middle 50% ACT range: 31–34
Early admission program EA/ED/None: EA

Percentage accepted through EA or ED: 30%
EA and ED deadline: 1-Nov
Regular Deadline: 1-Jan
Application Fee: $65
Full time Undergraduate enrollment: 4,172
Total enrollment: 10,220
Percent Male: 54%
Percent Female: 46%
Total Percent Minority or Unreported: 60%
Percent African-American: 9%
Percent Asian/Pacific Islander: 26%
Percent Hispanic: 12%
Percent Native-American: 1%
Percent International: 8%
Percent in-state/out of state: 10%/90%
Percent from Public HS: 70%
Retention Rate: 98%
Graduation Rate 4-year: 83%

Graduation Rate 6-year: 91%
Percent Undergraduates in On-campus housing: 90%
Number of official organized extracurricular organizations: 415
3 Most popular majors: Engineering, Computer Science, Physical Science
Student/Faculty ratio: 6:1
Average Class Size: 2 to 9
Percent of students going to grad school: 50%
Tuition and Fees: $36,390
In State Tuition and Fees if different: No difference
Cost for Room and Board: $10,860
Percent receiving financial aid out of those who apply, first year: 82%
Percent receiving financial aid among all students: 64%

Affectionately known as MIT, the Massachusetts Institute of Technology invokes stereotypical images of tech geeks holding TI-89 graphing calculators, ready to solve the world's most pressing engineering problems. In fact, it is all true. MIT undoubtedly produces some of the world's brightest minds in the field of math and science. With a reputation as the number one technical school in the nation and, quite possibly, the world, scientists at the top of their fields in math, engineering, and applied physics have emerged from the doors of the Massachusetts Institute of Technology. Therefore, one thing is certain: a world-class education awaits at MIT.

Made Like a Beaver

MIT has acquired a notorious reputation for its sometimes-ridiculous workload; thus, its students, like its mascot the beaver, will often times stay up into late hours of the night to finish problem sets. Staying up until 2 A.M. is the norm, and the number of hours for an average night of sleep hovers around five to six hours. All incoming freshman are graded on a pass/no record basis to ease transition from high school to college life. Most students find this very beneficial as there is less pressure to get A's. One freshman remarked that this system "begins to foster a sense of nonrivalry between students" right from the start.

The one drawback of the pass/no record policy is that some students may take too much advantage of the no record policy and do not put in as much effort as they could. Regardless, MIT is no easy ride. The only easy element is the physical education requirement. The core curriculum at MIT can be a bit science-rigorous at times with required courses in chemistry, physics, biology, and mathematics in addition to eight courses in the humanities and three courses in writing and communications. With MIT's reputation in the sciences, one might be inclined to overlook the humanities offerings. While less emphasized than science and engineering, the humanities departments house many distinguished prizewinning professors. In addition, MIT students also have the option of cross-registering with Harvard and taking advantage of its humanities courses.

Something else that will not be found at MIT is grade inflation. Many students do not pull off the straight A's as they were used to in high school, nor is it expected. As a current sophomore said, "You have to work really hard to get an A," a right reserved for few. Even in such intense academic rigor, competition is surprisingly subdued. "The intensity of the academics doesn't drive people apart in competition but rather brings them together in camaraderie," remarked a freshman. Long, tedious problem sets are often done cooperatively, and tight bonds develop with those with whom one spends many hours doing homework. It can be a bit overwhelming at times taking classes with a patent-holding inventor or an Intel Competition finalist. Therefore, academic insecurities do develop for some. But most classmates are more than willing to help each other.

The professors are also very approachable. In fact, most classes have fewer than 20 students so that individual attention is available. MIT also offers the innovative Experimental Study Groups (ESG) set up for incoming freshman who feel they need more individualized attention. The selection process is arbitrary with a random lottery draw that picks no more than about 50 students for the program. Students in ESG enjoy very small class sizes—often less than 10—in a more relaxed, personal atmosphere with their professors rather than the traditional lecture courses. Students go to class, eat, and often hang out with each other to form especially close bonds during their freshman year.

With all this support, it is no wonder that the most popular majors are also the most demanding, with electrical engineering and computer science taking the top prize. All other engineering disciplines and economics follow closely. Some opt to take relatively easier courses in humanities and social sciences as their concentration in addition to the core science requirements. Whichever path taken, there are many quirky classes available. Courses in video game review—where students play video games and then evaluate them—and toy-making may just be what is needed to spice up the occasionally dull MIT life, which is often problem set after problem set. For those less inclined to make toys or play video games, there are also D-Lab courses available where students fabricate simple technologies for third world nations and eventually travel there to donate the technologies as well as educating the native citizens on how to use them. Whatever the interest, each student can certainly find suitable classes at MIT.

Living in a sponge

Housing at MIT is unlike most other schools. Freshmen are allowed to choose with whom and where they live. Housing is guaranteed for all four years with the stipulation that all freshmen have to live on campus. Only approximately 10 percent of students do choose to move off campus. Others may elect to join fraternities, sororities, or cultural houses as alternatives to traditional dorms. The housing draw operates on a first-come, first-serve basis with a choice of 11 different houses. Each house has unique traditions, cultures, and architectural designs. Baker House can best be described as a wave. Bexley, Burton-Conner, and MacGregor are steeped in modern architecture with some colonial influences. Simmons Hall is, as one freshman described, a "big, metallic sponge-looking thing." With an array of options, students need to proceed with caution when making choices because not all houses are built alike. Some have better facilities and locations while others are richer in culture. A common complaint among some students is that MIT's architectural scheme is very "random and often uncoordinated."

MIT has no gothic architecture to compare to the Ivy League. Each house has a manager who takes care of most general problems. In addition, Resident Advisers (RAs) are assigned to each house to ensure the safety of students and are often available to offer advice or talk about personal issues. Most RAs are "really cool and end up being one of your good friends," said a current senior.

Most dorms are equipped with fully functional kitchens, but some houses have a higher kitchen-to-student ratio than others. A high percentage of students choose to cook for themselves due to the lack of available dining options at MIT. Out of the eleven houses, only four—Baker, McCormick, Next, and Simmons—have dining halls. An overwhelming majority of students choose to buy their own food at local cafes and restaurants, some of which are run by MIT. The dining options are not the best, but it does offer variety as each dining hall has its own "menu, culture, and characteristics," said a freshman.

Drinking . . . Out of a Fire Hose

MIT students are far from dull. Problem sets that easily intimidate the brightest of college students and a workload that has been compared to "drinking out of a fire hose," as one senior described, hardly take a toll on the social lives of MIT students. MIT's party scene is notorious around Boston with many students from other schools preferring to go there for parties. "The party scene is massive. The fraternity scene is massive," said one sophomore. Parties range anywhere from the typical dorm get-together to frat houses to the more exotic "cage" parties, which feature a cage that partygoers can dance in and on. All have been getting unanimously good rankings among the student population at both MIT and the surrounding area. The number of options and the frequency of parties mean that there is something to suit every taste. Although alcohol is a staple at these parties, people never feel pressured to drink. A senior remarked said there is a "comfortable atmosphere present at MIT parties." Some people drink, others don't. But all seem to have a good time.

The split between East Campus and West Campus is a significant characteristic of MIT. East campus has gained a reputation as a thriving counterculture. Known for their wild ways and eccentricities, these students are the ones building roller coasters and rigging stairs to play music inside their dorms as well as the annual building drops that involve objects of all sizes, shapes, and func-

tions. The most notable of these events is the annual piano drop, where a grand piano plummets from the roof of Baker House at the start of every spring semester. One of the time-honored traditions at MIT, "hacks" are harmless pranks. Some famous ones include a police cruiser on top of the Great Dome and the transformation of the Dome into R2D2 to commemorate the release of *Star Wars Episode I*. All other houses, known as West Campus, are places to find "typical" college students. Although unique in its own rights, West Campus does not draw as much interest as East Campus.

> "MIT really embraces the nerd culture."

Aside from the social and party scenes, athletics provides another venue to engage in MIT's social life. A surprising number of students partake in intramural sports. Athletics is not as emphasized at MIT as it is in other schools since most sports are in Division III. However, crew and fencing do play in Division I. Sports don't have much of a role in organizing social life at MIT because they do not have to. The social environment thrives astonishingly well on its own.

Infinite Limits

Walking through the famous Infinite Corridor of MIT, a hallway that connects the main buildings on campus, the students have infinite possibilities for success. Granted, MIT is not utopia. There will be bumps along the way. Some do feel like they are getting a science-slanted education, and students do have a love-hate relationship with MIT. At one point, they all hate the workload at MIT, but they are generally happy to be at the top school for technology, science, and engineering. Aside from the orientation toward math and science, MIT forces student to engage in their education and try new things. As one student said, "The challenge is the best part of MIT. It does push you to your limits." MIT is unique in its own right. The school is different, the students are different, and the approach to science is renowned. It is a very open and accepting place to engage in higher education since "MIT really embraces the nerd culture. There is no social posturing," as a freshman recounted. MIT is not for everyone, but for those who fit the bill, it is a great place to spend four years.—*Hai Pham*

Mount Holyoke College

Address: 50 College Street
    South Hadley, MA 01075
Phone: 413-538-2023
E-mail address:
    admission@mtholyoke.edu
Web site URL:
    www.mtholyoke.edu
Year Founded: 1837
Private or Public: Private
Religious Affiliation: None
Location: Suburban
Number of Applicants:
    3,194
Percent Accepted: 52%
Percent Accepted who
    enroll: 31%
Number Entering: 522
Number of Transfers
    Accepted each Year:
    102
Middle 50% SAT range:
    M: 590–690, CR: 640–730,
    Wr: 630–710
Middle 50% ACT range:
    26–30
Early admission program
    EA/ED/None: ED

Percentage accepted
    through EA or ED:
    Unreported
EA and ED deadline: 15-Nov
Regular Deadline: 15-Jan
Application Fee: $60; online
    application is free
Full time Undergraduate
    enrollment: 2,201
Total enrollment: 2,201
Percent Male: 0%
Percent Female: 100%
Total Percent Minority or
    Unreported: 34%
Percent African-American:
    5%
Percent Asian/Pacific
    Islander: 13%
Percent Hispanic: 6%
Percent Native-American:
    <1%
Percent International: 13%
Percent in-state/out of
    state: 20% /80%
Percent from Public HS:
    61%
Retention Rate: 94%

Graduation Rate 4-year:
    78%
Graduation Rate 6-year:
    81%
Percent Undergraduates in
    On-campus housing: 93%
Number of official organized
    extracurricular
    organizations: 150
3 Most popular majors:
    Biology, English, International
    Relations
Student/Faculty ratio: 10:1
Average Class Size: 10 to 19
Percent of students going to
    grad school: 20%
Tuition and Fees: 37,646
In State Tuition and Fees if
    different: No difference
Cost for Room and Board:
    $11,020
Percent receiving financial
    aid out of those who apply,
    first year: 85%
Percent receiving financial
    aid among all students:
    60%

Located in the quiet town of South Hadley, Massachusetts, Mount Holyoke is a small women's college with a big impact. The idyllic campus helps to foster strong bonds among the women of Mount Holyoke. As a member of the Five College Consortium, Mount Holyoke's resources are shared with those of Smith College, University of Massachusetts at Amherst, Amherst College and Hampshire College. Students are able to reap the benefits of individualized attention and support, while drawing from a wide range of academic and social opportunities.

Small, but Intense

The academic expectations at Mount Holyoke are almost universally described as "intense." Students face a variety of distributional requirements, including three courses in the humanities, two courses in math and sciences, and two courses in the social sciences. They are also required to fulfill a multicultural credit, foreign language requirement, and physical education credits. While these courses can take up a lot of time, most students seem to find them "reasonable" and flexible enough to be a positive aspect of their academic experience. Students not only need a major, but also either a minor or one of a variety of Five College certificate programs. Some of the more popular majors at Mount Holyoke include biology, English and psychology. Those not afraid of logging extra time in the library can find themselves majoring in international relations, math or one of the sciences. Students looking for an easier four years, on the other hand, tend to gravitate toward psychology or art history. While some introductory level courses can be larger in size, most classes have enrollments of less than 25, allowing for closer student-professor interaction. Professors are known for giving a sizable workload in general, with intensive assignments and reading due weekly, often to prepare for difficult exams. According to one student, "I do feel a little jealous of my friends at other schools because I feel they have more time for fun than I do." But, students agree that the quality of the professors often compensates for the sky-high expectations. Among the more well known professors are Chris Pyle, who specializes in politics, the Pulitzer Prize–winning Joseph Ellis of the History Department, and William Quillian, a well-regarded James Joyce scholar. There are also a variety of unique classes available such as "Zen and the Art of Meditation," a cryptology seminar, and horseback riding for physical education credit.

"This is definitely not a party school."

Mount Holyoke boasts some unique academic features. J-term is a period during the normal winter break when students can stay on campus to take extra, often nontraditional, courses or try out a short internship. Students are also encouraged to take advantage of the Five College Consortium. There is a free busing system among the different campuses that allows students to enroll in courses offered by other schools. This widens the course offerings available and lets students get off campus should they feel the need.

It's On (Campus) All the Way

Students rave about the beauty of Mount Holyoke's campus through all four seasons. The school's small size also contributes to its general appeal as a peaceful and friendly haven. Students agreed that South Hadley, as a town, does not contribute much to life on campus or really cater to the college. Luckily, the nearby presence of Amherst and Northampton alleviates that problem.

Over 90 percent of students live on campus, thanks to both the lack of appropriate housing in the surrounding residential areas, and the close-knit nature of the student body. Dorms vary in size and layout. The older buildings tend to have larger rooms, but dorms overall garner positive reviews. Most students live in singles by the time they are upperclassmen. There are Student Advisers on every floor and Hall Presidents for each dorm. Both groups generally make an effort to get to know the students they live with and they "usually get more worked up about noise than alcohol." There are mandatory quiet hours each night set by the halls, and these are most strictly enforced during finals. Open alcohol isn't allowed in hallways, but students generally find very few problems with this regulation.

The food on campus is highly rated by students and was even praised by one as being "great!" There are dining halls attached to each dorm, as well as one in the campus center. The school goes to great lengths to offer a variety of options for those with restricted or special diets, including vegetarian, vegan, kosher, and halal.

Sisterhood of the Traveling Party

The social life at Mount Holyoke is very much characterized by the fact that it is a women's college. Life on campus is more toned-down than at your average coed institution. As one student put it, "This is definitely not a party school." Drinking is mostly confined to weekends or special occasions. A cappella groups are a popular social outlet and sports teams are most likely to hold parties in dorms. Once a year, the school hosts Las Vegas Night, an immensely popular party that includes dancing and gambling and attracts students from other colleges. Students spend time hanging out with friends and going to movies, but they tend to gravitate off campus if they are looking for a party or members of the opposite sex. Many Mount Holyokers will leave during the weekend to visit boyfriends elsewhere. UMass and Amherst are popular destinations for fraternity parties, especially TAP, which are huge parties held at Amherst on Thursday and Saturday nights. The busing system makes the nearby colleges and bars very easily accessible.

Students participate avidly in a variety of extracurricular activities. Sports play an increasingly large role on campus, with girls participating on all levels from varsity to club. Rugby is a particularly popular and eagerly cheered sport. Other strong programs include crew, field hockey, and lacrosse. Mount Holyoke's main rival is Smith, and varsity games between the two schools are well attended. Extensive athletic facilities are also available to students, with the equestrian center often hailed as one of the shining stars. As for nonathletic activities, student government plays a large and vocal role on campus and Holyokers agreed that "the group makes sure to keep the student population well-informed of its happenings." For the musically inclined, the University boasts a selection of a cappella groups, as well as a glee club and various instrumental ensembles. No matter what one's passions are, most students find that they can discover or create a niche for whatever their particular interests may be.

Living Among Women

As a women's college, students reached a general consent that Mount Holyoke is, in many ways, not the typical college experience. According to one student, "Women's colleges certainly are not fit for everyone, but it seems that students at Mount Holyoke really considered their decision before enrolling and are ultimately very satisfied."

Although students have to work a little harder if they desire contact with the opposite sex or wish to experience the typical college party, the all-female environment more than makes up for such voids with its own unique benefits. The campus is characterized as being very friendly and students are easy to get to know, as many students interviewed found that being among all women makes for a more comfortable, accepting atmosphere on the whole, both in and out of class. The campus is also incredibly diverse on ethnic and socioeconomic levels, and although cliques do emerge, there is always a good level of interaction among the collective student body. Mount Holyokers are also "fairly open" to all sexual orientations and relationships.

Ultimately, the majority of students seem to adapt well to the all-female environment, but like at any school, at times "there are days when people are sick of Mount Holyoke," and committing to four years of being surrounded entirely by women involves particular and personal considerations for each individual. As one student expressed, "If Mount Holyoke works for you, it's a great place to be." —*Janet Yang*

FYI

If you come to Mount Holyoke you better bring "a heavy coat for those harsh New England winters."

What's the typical weekend schedule? "Sleep late, do work, go out by either taking a bus to Amherst or staying on campus and hanging out, come back late."

If I could change one thing about Mount Holyoke, "it would be to have some students lighten up and go out and have more fun."

Three things every student should do before graduating are "take a class off campus, climb Mount Holyoke on Mountain Day to get free ice cream, and eat a Chef Jeff cookie."

Northeastern University

Address: 360 Huntington Avenue Boston, MA 02115
Phone: 617-373-2200
E-mail address: admissions@neu.edu
Web site URL: www.northeastern.edu
Year Founded: 1898
Private or Public: Private
Religious Affiliation: None
Location: Urban
Number of Applicants: 35,848
Percent Accepted: 35%
Percent Accepted who enroll: 23%
Number Entering: 2,923
Number of Transfers Accepted each Year: 1,234
Middle 50% SAT range: M: 610–690, CR: 570–660, Wr: Unreported
Middle 50% ACT range: 26–30
Early admission program EA/ED/None: EA
Percentage accepted through EA or ED: Unreported

EA and ED deadline: 15-Nov
Regular Deadline: 15-Jan
Application Fee: $75, $65 online
Full time Undergraduate enrollment: 15,521
Total enrollment: 20,700
Percent Male: 50%
Percent Female: 50%
Total Percent Minority or Unreported: Unreported
Percent African-American: 5%
Percent Asian/Pacific Islander: 8%
Percent Hispanic: 5%
Percent Native-American: 1%
Percent International: Unreported
Percent in-state/out of state: 33%/67%
Percent from Public HS: Unreported
Retention Rate: 93%
Graduation Rate 4-year: Unreported

Graduation Rate 6-year: Unreported
Percent Undergraduates in On-campus housing: 47%
Number of official organized extracurricular organizations: 250
3 Most popular majors: General Business/Commerce, General Engineering, General Health Services/Allied Health
Student/Faculty ratio: 15:1
Average Class Size: 20 to 29
Percent of students going to grad school: 17%
Tuition and Fees: $33,320
In State Tuition and Fees if different: No difference
Cost for Room and Board: $11,940
Percent receiving financial aid out of those who apply, first year: Unreported
Percent receiving financial aid among all students: Unreported

I nterested in gaining the advantage of real-life work experience during your college years? If so, Northeastern and its unique co-op program might be for you. Northeastern University (NU) places a distinct emphasis on preprofessional training as well as education and offers its students a co-op internship program that places them with various companies during the academic year.

One Step Ahead: the Co-op Program

At Northeastern, students alternate between classroom study and periods of paid, professional experience. Each period is six months, which means, as one student put it, "You don't really have summers that much." It also means that the majority of students go to school for five years, rather than the typical four at other schools.

At the same time, though, students who participate in the co-op program gain a distinct advantage in the "real world." "You come out of college with a stacked resume; you know how to interview, and you know how to be professional. You just have an edge on everybody." The real-life experience also allows a student to "get a good sense of whether you're in the right field." This means, of course, that even though you don't officially select a major until sophomore year, many students applying to NU have a clear idea of what career they wish to pursue. For those who do know where they would like to end up after college, this program not only gives them a lot of resume-building experience, but it also connects them with potential employers and business opportunities. Upon graduating, many students are offered jobs at the companies they worked at in the co-op program. As one student working for an inventing company in New Hampshire declared, "I'm learning more by working than [I am] in classes."

Approximately 90 percent of NU's student body participates in the co-op program. In fact, it seems that "most kids that come to NU come for the co-op program." Students who choose to start the co-op freshman year take an orientation class and begin work sophomore year. Co-op classes are required and can focus on job-relevant skills such as interviewing or writing résumés. Students are also assigned co-op faculty coordinators who help them find opportunities that match their goals and interests. However, while these resources are available, it is up to the student to schedule and prepare for interviews, as well as perform well on the job. Even then, NU cannot guarantee that each student will have a job during the co-op term. Also, if students accept positions outside the Boston area, they are responsible for finding their own housing and transportation in the area they choose. But if a student plans to accept a local position, he or she may continue living in the NU residence hall.

> **"You come out of college with a stacked resume; you know how to interview, and you know how to be professional. You just have an edge on everybody."**

The hard work seems to be well worth it: students graduate from college and can move straight into the workforce. Another appealing incentive is the pay: students who opt to enroll in the co-op program can earn a lot of money during their six-month work periods.

The Penthouse Suite

Most students feel that the on-campus freshman housing at Northeastern is "basically like any other school"—neither exceptional nor terrible. Quality does vary, since some buildings have been renovated in recent years while others have not, but overall the freshman housing is generally described as "decent." Upperclassmen housing, on the other hand, is "so nice." "From sophomore year on, the housing is either relatively new or has been renovated within the last decade." Many residential halls, such as the West Village Halls or Davenport Commons, have units that can include two to three bedrooms, two bathrooms, a "huge" living room and a kitchen. Other amenities include cable TV, air-conditioning, and high-speed Internet. West Village E is particularly-famous; made completely of glass, it is what's known as the penthouse suite, with two glass walls that overlook a stunning view of downtown Boston. Such luxury, though, comes with a price. "It's really expensive," one student

complained, so much so that "it's actually much cheaper to live off campus"—a bold statement when weighed against the difficulty of finding affordable housing in Boston.

For those who do choose to live on campus, buildings are divided into single-sex wings, and NU offers special-interest housing, such as a "wellness" dorm (the alcohol, drug, and smoke-free Coe Hall), an honors dorm, and an international dorm. Each residential section is assigned a Resident Assistant (RA). Some students claim that their RAs have been lax about alcohol policies, provided that students respect the rules and property. One admitted, though, that this was the exception more than the rule. "I had an RA who was really relaxed about alcohol, but a lot of the RAs in other dorms were very strict and kids were always getting into trouble."

Students seem to be impressed with the campus facilities because "everything on campus is really well-maintained." This may be because the administration is "very responsive to student suggestions, and if there is a complaint, "everything gets fixed pretty quickly." Some of the facilities available to students are the Marino Recreation Center, where students, athlete and nonathlete alike, can work out, and the Matthews Arena, the oldest indoor arena in the world. This is where the hockey teams play, and games attract an enthusiastic following, outside the University as well as within. Every year, for example, the city holds the Bean Pot, a tournament in which Northeastern, Boston University, Boston College, and Harvard compete for bragging rights as the best hockey team in the city. It's held at the TD North Bank Garden arena and attracts quite a crowd. The University also maintains common areas stocked with pool tables and lounge chairs. Some of the most popular hang-out areas are the Curry Student Center and the Cyber Café in Snell Library.

Students have several options when it comes to dining. Along with its three dining halls, there are several restaurants on campus, including Taco Bell, Starbucks, Pizza Hut, Wendy's, and Qdoba. The University offers several meal-plan options, one of which includes putting money on a Husky Card, which can also be used at local, off-campus eateries. This option conveniently allows students to take advantage of NU's advantageous location in the hustle and bustle of Boston. There are several good eateries near campus, and one particular favorite is Chicken Lou's, a "little shack" at which you'll have "probably the best food you will ever eat—you would stand in line in the Massachusetts cold for that food."

So Much to Do, So Much to See

As for extracurricular activities, students at NU have a variety of choices. "The administration is very lenient with on-campus organizations," and the student government, in charge of approving clubs, distributes a hefty allocation of money to these student groups. One of the most popular clubs—and also the largest with over 600 members—is NUCALLs. Members of this organization are students fluent in other languages, and they offer peers interested in learning that language tutoring sessions for free. Intramural sports are also a popular pastime, one of the most popular sports being broom-ball. "Broom-ball is huge around campus," and students sign up for teams in the spring and fall to play a carefully organized series of games that culminate in that semester's play-offs. Other organizations are more typical, like the Student Government Association and daily newspapers, while other are more unique, like *The NU Times New Roman*, a humor newspaper. Greek life is present on campus, but it is not a driving force. Only about 8 percent of the total student body joins fraternities or sororities, and although they throw occasional parties, no one seems to be in any hurry to rush them.

Party City: Boston, the College Town

The social scene at Northeastern comes alive each weekend. Drinking is prevalent, but there is also a significant percentage of the student population that opts not to drink. And for those who do, alcohol is relatively easy to come by, as are parties. Some of the most popular events on campus are SpringFest, Midnight Madness, and International Carnevale. Partying on campus has its downside, though, because the University has strict rules about drinking. "The school is looking to get you into trouble," cautioned one student.

However, being in a city like Boston, NU's social scene is not limited to on-campus

events. It lies in the midst of several other universities—"It's a five-minute walk to Boston University, a 15-minute train ride to Boston College, and a 20-minute train ride to MIT or Harvard"—which means students at NU have several opportunities to meet students from other schools. It also gives students a wide variety of parties to choose from on weekends. "There are just so many options; I know there are always hundreds of things going on in the city." Another student said, "I can party anywhere—at a house, apartment, fraternity, or bars, clubs, concerts, and other schools."

Clubbing used to be a popular weekend activity for many NU students, but in light of new legislation, clubs are no longer 18 and up. What's more, fakes are not a good idea when partying in the city because "all the cops are out to get you." While many students enjoy spending time at bars or clubs on the weekend, these establishments tend to be extremely strict when it comes to IDs. "Every liquor store scans IDs, and several bars black light them." If a student is 21 or older, popular clubs include Avalon, Roxy, and Matrix; the most popular bar is Punter's.

The Sum Total

Overall, Northeastern students take advantage of the opportunities the school provides. The urban campus provides an endless stream of events and activities, and students actively participate in campus life, joining groups and enjoying their college years to the fullest. While enjoying the NU social scene, students simultaneously gain work experience in the co-op program, which distinguishes Northeastern from other universities. The expertise gained in real job experience gives graduating students a considerable edge post-college and is perfect for motivated, career-oriented students. All of this, combined with a respectable faculty, diverse student body, and fast-paced Boston environment, offers Northeastern students a unique and fruitful experience.—*Caroline Garner*

FYI
If you come to Northeastern, you'd better bring "skis or snowboards, to take advantage of all the ski trips the school organizes."
What's the typical weekend schedule? "Drink when and where you can, or go clubbing. Fit in a little work."
If I could change one thing about Northeastern, it would be "the proportion of students from certain regions; most are from the New England area."
Three things every student at Northeastern should do before graduating are "do the co-op program, go to a Red Sox or Patriot game, and explore what the city has to offer."

Simmons College

Address: 300 The Fenway
Boston, MA 02115
Phone: 617-521-2051
E-mail address:
ugadm@simmons.edu
Web site URL:
www.simmons.edu
Year Founded: 1899
Private or Public: Private
Religious Affiliation: None
Location: Urban
Number of Applicants: 3,222
Percent Accepted: 54%
Percent Accepted who
enroll: 22%
Number Entering: 391
Number of Transfers
Accepted each Year: 158
Middle 50% SAT range:
M: 500–590, CR:510–600,
Wr: 520–620
Middle 50% ACT range:
22–26
Early admission program
EA/ED/None: EA

Percentage accepted
through EA or ED: 57%
EA and ED deadline: 1-Dec
Regular Deadline: 1-Feb
Application Fee: $55
Full time Undergraduate
enrollment: 1,850
Total enrollment: 2,060
Percent Male: 1%
Percent Female: 99%
Total Percent Minority or
Unreported: 27%
Percent African-American:
6%
Percent Asian/Pacific
Islander: 7%
Percent Hispanic: 4%
Percent Native-American:
<1%
Percent International: 3%
Percent in-state/out of
state: 64%/36%
Percent from Public HS:
Unreported
Retention Rate: 83%

Graduation Rate 4-year:
62%
Graduation Rate 6-year: 72%
Percent Undergraduates in
On-campus housing: 55%
Number of official organized
extracurricular
organizations: 80
3 Most popular majors:
Nursing, Psychology
Student/Faculty ratio: 13:1
Average Class Size: 10 to 19
Percent of students going to
grad school: Unreported
Tuition and Fees: $27,468
In State Tuition and Fees if
different: No difference
Cost for Room and Board:
$11,138
Percent receiving financial
aid out of those who apply,
first year: 72%
Percent receiving financial
aid among all students:
70%

N estled in the bustling city of Boston rests the tranquil oasis of Simmons College. Roughly 2,000 young women attend Simmons for its liberal arts with a special focus on science. Students rave about the close-knit student body and excellent, approachable professors, which combine to form a welcoming and laid-back atmosphere.

Science Anyone?

Simmons College offers a liberal arts education with special career preparation opportunities. The nursing program feeds student internships in the city, while the physical therapy major has a six-year doctorate program. Science at Simmons is especially strong. Nursing, biology, and chemistry are considered the most difficult majors, while communications and psychology are "not as demanding, but still difficult," according to one student. Class size is small, making it easy to enroll in most classes and enabling students to take a more active role in the classroom. Students rave about their professors. One student explained, "[The professors] give you their e-mail, cell phone number, home

number, office number and office hours. They want you to come and talk to them. They are interested in helping their students."

Students must fulfill academic distributional requirements in six "modes of inquiry": Creative and Performing Arts; Language, Literature and Culture; Quantitative Analysis and Reasoning; Scientific Inquiry; Social and Historical Perspectives; and Psychological and Ethical Development. In the process, students become more well-rounded and prepared for life after college. The requirements are surprisingly unrestrictive, though, and one student commented, "I found that I was able to experiment more during my freshman year than my friends at other schools."

An Escape from Beantown

The Simmons campus receives high marks from its students. Its peaceful green quadrangle in the middle of a busy Boston neighborhood serves as a quiet haven. One student exclaimed, "Our campus is beautiful. Most people come onto campus and forget they are in a city. When you walk through the gates, it feels very much unlike a city and a lot more like home." The campus is divided into an academic portion and a residential portion separated by one city block. The residential campus consists of a picturesque quadrangle bounded by the College's residence halls and Bartol Dining Hall. Also located on the residential campus is the Holmes Sports Center, boasting an eight-lane swimming pool, suspended track, weight room, sauna, basketball court, dance studio, and squash courts. Next door is the Simmons Health Center, which offers its comprehensive services to students.

> **"[The professors] give you their e-mail, cell phone number, home number, office number and office hours. They want you to come and talk to them. They are interested in helping their students."**

Approximately a five-minutes' walk from the residential campus is the main campus. Here the College's main classrooms are located in the Main College Building (affectionately referred to as the "MCB") and the Park Science Building, where all science courses are taught. The main campus also hosts the Beatley Library and the newly constructed and unusually named One Palace Road Building. One Palace Road provides a number of student resources such as career services and counseling, as well as two graduate school departments.

Standard of Living at Simmons
The quality of dorm rooms differs at Simmons depending on renovations and specific buildings. Most freshmen live in doubles in Mesick, Morse, or Simmons Hall, but there are a few triples. There is an RA on every floor, and one student said, "They're just there to help out, and are not too strict." Students are very pleased with their living situation. Recently renovated Evans Hall and Arnold Hall are "really nice and the only ones with elevators on campus," one student reported. Praise is not as free-flowing, though, when students are asked about the food at Simmons. Bartol Dining Hall is Simmons' main dining hall and students label the food as "fair." Luckily for hungry Simmons students, the best of Boston's restaurants, with its first-class seafood and ethnic fare, lie just outside the College's gates. Other dining options available to students on campus include the Quadside Café, serving as a snack bar and grocery, The Fens, with a deli and grill, and

Java City (Simmons' Coffee Kiosk), which doles out coffee and snacks.

Livin' It Up in Beantown
One student put it best by saying, "Basically, Boston becomes your campus." For this group of young women, the possibilities of the city are boundless. Students are able to take advantage of the city's many fabulous restaurants, go shopping on Newbury Street, attend a Boston Red Sox game, and go to a concert at the Orpheum Theater. Boston offers anything and everything under the sun . . . and under the moon as well, as Simmons girls take advantage of the city's exciting nightlife.

Simmons is a dry campus, and because of alcohol and noise restrictions students often go out to Boston clubs or to frat parties at BU and MIT for a more festive atmosphere. One student comments that because of this situation, "Simmons' girls have a lot of random hookups because they really don't know when the next chance will be." These meetings often develop into something more substantial, however, and students note that many of their peers are involved in serious relationships—both heterosexual and homosexual.

From Tea to Tennis
Students describe the student body as "intelligent" and "friendly." The small class size promotes unity and school spirit. According to one student, a tradition that has been going on for a few years now is the Friday Hall Teas, where all the girls from each hall come together to "have tea or snack on goodies and just hang out and have fun."

Many Simmons students take part in sports and other extracurricular activities. The campus is described by one "as very active and involved." Simmons is home to eight Division III varsity sports, and one student described Simmons sports as "not awful"—basketball and soccer seemed to be the most popular sports among students. Other student organizations such as Simmons College Outreach, a student-run community service organization, and the Student Government Organization are just two of the many student activities and clubs in which students take part.

When John Simmons founded this college in 1899, his mission was to allow women to earn the "livelihood" they deserved and to create a new generation of well-educated women. Today his mission continues to be realized, as Simmons produces well-prepared, independent women ready to enter the world.—*Kieran Locke*

FYI
If you come to Simmons College, you'd better bring a "Boston Red Sox hat."
What's the typical weekend schedule? "Hanging out, shopping, and eating in Harvard Square or on Newbury Street and going to an occasional party at a fraternity from a neighboring college."
If I could change one thing about Simmons, I would change "the dining-hall food."
Three things every student at Simmons should do before graduating are "visit the Isabella Stuart Gardner Museum, eat Ankara Frozen Yogurt, and go on the Swan Boats in Boston Commons."

Smith College

Address: 7 College Lane Northampton, MA 01063	**EA and ED deadline:** 15-Nov	**Graduation Rate 6-year:** 88%
Phone: 413-585-2500	**Regular Deadline:** 15-Jan	**Percent Undergraduates in On-campus housing:** 90%
E-mail address: admission@smith.edu	**Application Fee:** $60	
	Full time Undergraduate enrollment: 2,588	**Number of official organized extracurricular organizations:** 134
Web site URL: www.smith.edu	**Total enrollment:** 3,101	
Year Founded: 1871	**Percent Male:** 0%	**3 Most popular majors:** Government, Psychology, Art
Private or Public: Private	**Percent Female:** 100%	
Religious Affiliation: None	**Total Percent Minority or Unreported:** 27%	**Student/Faculty ratio:** 9:1
Location: Suburban		**Average Class Size:** Unreported
Number of Applicants: 3,771	**Percent African-American:** 7%	
Percent Accepted: 48%		**Percent of students going to grad school:** Unreported
Percent Accepted who enroll: 64%	**Percent Asian/Pacific Islander:** 13%	**Tuition and Fees:** $36,058
Number Entering: 707	**Percent Hispanic:** 7%	
Number of Transfers Accepted each Year: 119	**Percent Native-American:** <1%	**In State Tuition and Fees if different:** No difference
Middle 50% SAT range: M: 570–680, CR:600–710, Wr: 590–700	**Percent International:** Unreported	**Cost for Room and Board:** $12,050
Middle 50% ACT range: 25–31	**Percent in-state/out of state:** 23%/77%	**Percent receiving financial aid out of those who apply, first year:** 87%
Early admission program EA/ED/None: ED	**Percent from Public HS:** Unreported	
Percentage accepted through EA or ED: 9%	**Retention Rate:** 90%	**Percent receiving financial aid among all students:** 53%
	Graduation Rate 4-year: 83%	

Walking around the Smith campus one night, you see students covered in duct tape and tissue paper, and some are covered in very little at all. When you ask one of the students, apparently the strange attire is a tradition for one of their famous parties known as the "Convocation Party." Convocation is just one of the interesting and bizarre traditions that make Smith such a unique liberal arts college. Students can explore more than just the typical types of courses offered by liberal arts colleges within an all-female population that most students find empowering.

The Smith Education

While students certainly have interest in entertaining traditions like Convocation and House Teas, academics are clearly the first priority for Smith women. The general expectation is that a large portion of the week is allocated to studying, as opposed to the obligatory "Sunday Afternoon Crunch" found at other schools. For most students, the work they encountered at Smith was harder than they expected, and there was more of it. And while one student felt that the academic environment was somewhat overwhelming, both because of the amount of work and the intensity of other students, another thought that since "you can choose your classes, you look forward to doing work and it's not a chore to study." Despite the intensity of the workload, most of the students felt it was an academically safe environment.

Smith students certainly do have a lot of choice when it comes to academics. There are no general education classes, and other than a writing requirement, which must be completed in freshman year, students are free to take classes in whatever field interests them. Students must have a broad curriculum, because only half of the classes taken can be in a student's major. There are no other requirements than these unless a student wishes to graduate with Latin Honors. In this case, the student must complete courses in each of the seven major fields of knowledge: Literature, Historical Studies, Social Science, Natural Science, Mathematics and Analytic Philosophy, the Arts, and Foreign Language. Most of the classes are pretty small, with the smallest under 20 and the larger classes generally under 30. There are a few larger-sized intro classes, but these are still generally kept under 50 students.

All classes at Smith are taught by professors (TAs only help grade), leading to closer relationships between students and professors than those normally found at other schools. Some of the more popular professors are Floyd Chung in the English department, Sam Intrator, and Susan Etheredge. Don't expect these classes, while interesting, to be undemanding, or even easy to get into. According to students, some of the more popular classes (such as "The American Teacher" with Intrator), are difficult to get into and do have a high level of competition within the class. Despite the difficulty of some of the classes, students tended to find the academic experience at Smith very rewarding. "There are a lot of different dimensions to learning at Smith," said one student. "You encounter many intellectuals with a lot of different perspectives."

For those not quite ready to leap into an entire course schedule full of intense classes, there are certainly easier ways to rack up credits. Students can take tai-chi, yoga, pilates, and scuba diving for credit. In addition, performance classes are a good way to get all your credits needed for a year. To complete the class, all you have to do is "show up," according to one student.

So what's the real difference between the education received at Smith at that received at another school? "Gung-ho, outspoken women," claimed one student, and she seems to be correct. While it seems as if most women at Smith would major in more typical liberal arts areas, such as English or art history, Smith women defy these stereotypes, and have just as many

majors in the sciences as in the humanities. And while English, art history, and women's studies are popular, many students are biology, premed, or engineering majors. The Picker Engineering Program is able to provide a first-class engineering program within a liberal arts education, and is the only engineering program at any women's college.

Yet another one of the reasons Smith's academic programs are so strong is because of their place in the Pioneer Valley's Five College Consortium. Smith women can take classes at Amherst, U-Mass Amherst, Mount Holyoke, and Hampshire colleges.

No Bass, but Lots of Activity

A capella is one of the major extracurriculars on campus, with groups like the Smithereens, the Smiffenpoofs, and the Vibe. Sports are also fairly popular, with soccer, basketball, crew, and rugby generally seen as some of the more popular sports. In addition, there are intramurals in which many students participate. And while some students said that people don't really attend the games, others said that attending sports events was relatively popular. "Lots of people go to the games," said one student. "There's lots of spirit, and people go to cheer on their friends."

Perhaps the largest organization at Smith is SOS, Service Organizations at Smith. There are many different organizations within this broader group, including the Smith Democrats and Republicans and the Smith College Feminists, as well as many nonpolitical organizations. According to one student, "almost everyone is involved in at least one SOS organization." In addition, some students choose to work on the Smith radio channel WOZQ, or participate in student-run religious groups or student government groups. "Everyone's involved in at least one or two things," remarked one student.

There are no sororities on campus, although students can join the ones at U-Mass or Amherst. However, sororities don't seem to be particularly popular anyway. Said one student, "they're just not really that big of a deal." Students don't seem to miss the Greek scene, according to many students. This seems most to do with the housing situation at Smith, one that is truly unique to the college.

Living and Working in Mansions

At Smith, housing is much nicer than you would find at many other colleges. Instead of living in dorms, students live in renovated mansions housing 90 to 100 people. Students live in their houses for four years, although there is certainly the ability to transfer. "It's a lot more homey, because the dorms aren't really separated," said one student.

The dorms all have different personalities, although freshman year the housing is assigned randomly. Houses on the Quad tend to be really loud and party more, while houses on Green Street tend to be more quiet and studious. The mansions all have different styles, and many once belonged to the founding families of Northampton.

Students generally live in singles or doubles freshman year and occasionally have doubles sophomore year, but all upper classmen have singles. All houses have living rooms, TV rooms, and laundry rooms. Most have dining halls located within the house, and some of the houses even have cleaning services. "The rooms are actually huge," said one student. "Every single room has amazing views, and we all have our own closets. The doubles are huge, and the singles are really big too, especially for juniors and seniors. They're probably bigger than the doubles in most other colleges."

Not only do students have the advantage of living in these mansions, but they also have the advantage of running them too. There are no faculty living in the houses, and the houses are run by two seniors, one who acts as house president and another who acts as house resident. There is an adult in charge of every five or six houses, but they're not involved in the day-to-day affairs of the students. "It just seems like at Smith there is so much trust," remarked one student. "They trust us to run the houses, and to be responsible for the most part." People usually stay on campus all four years because of the quality of the housing, although there are some co-op apartments.

Each house serves a tea Friday at four p.m. It's the responsibility of four of the freshman to set up and clean up. Students serve tea, chips, sandwiches, and a variety of different snacks, and students request the snacks for the different teas. "It's just a nice opportunity to talk to people," said one student. The food at Smith seems to be just as impressive as the housing. According to many students the food is very good. The students have a lot of choice in what they want to eat, because many of the dining halls have different themes, such as kosher, Mediterranean, and vegetarian/vegan.

Girls Know How to Have Fun
Although there is a lack of men at Smith, there is no lack of partying. Friday and Satur-

day are the biggest nights to party, and Thursday is also "pretty rowdy," according to one student. Most of the parties occur in the houses, although students can also choose to go to parties at any of the other four colleges in the Five College Consortium.

Students say that there is no pressure to drink, but if you do decide to it is harder to get alcohol if you are under 21. Alcohol can generally be found by most in smaller room parties, though. There is a no-drinking policy for students under 21, but it is not strongly enforced, as the administration generally doesn't search the rooms. Although there is certainly some drinking, other drugs are not particularly prevalent on campus.

> "Women who go to Smith are proud to be in an environment with so many other empowered and intelligent women."

The most popular on-campus parties include the Immorality Party, Halloween, and Convocation Night. For Convocation, the students of each house dress up in a particular theme. Some have had to make their costumes out of aluminum foil, or have had a theme of wearing as little as possible.

While there certainly seem to be enough on-campus activities in which to become involved, students also make regular trips into town. Northampton is only a five- or 10-minute walk from campus, and students enjoy going to town for coffee and food in cafés like Haymarket, the Woodmarket, and Thorn's. "Downtown is always nice," said one student. "It's close by, and there's a lot of stuff to do. Although there's always a lot of stuff going on every day on campus, and sometimes there were weeks where I didn't go at all."

It's a Girl Thing
Smithies talk about the friendliness of the student body, and the openness with which new students are accepted. There is a general trend of acceptance at the school, including an openness with lesbianism and sexuality that is not always seen elsewhere. As for having all women, all the time, most students say that they don't notice it after the first few weeks. "I was kind of scared about the all-women's thing, but I really forgot about it after I got to," said one student. "I only remember when people ask about it." Some students said that not having boys was not a problem, since they could meet that at

other colleges in the consortium. However, others lamented that there weren't enough boys at parties or on campus. Women who go to Smith are proud to be in an environment with so many other empowered and intelligent women. Like the motto on some of their shirts, the women seem to believe that Smith is "not a girls' school without men—it's a women's school without boys."—*Ariel Shepherd-Oppenheim*

FYI

If you come to Smith, you'd better bring "lots of CDs for house parties, rain boots, and weird things to dress up with for Convocation."

What's the typical weekend schedule? "It consists of tea on Friday, staying on campus for a concert Friday night, going to Northampton Saturday night, and studying Sunday."

If I could change one thing about Smith I'd "have more boys at parties."

Three things every student should do before graduating are "go to Immorality, take a class at another college, and jump in the pond."

Tufts University

Address: Bendetson Hall Medford, MA 02155

Phone: 617-627-3170

E-mail address: admissions. inquiry@ase.tufts.edu

Web site URL: www.tufts.edu

Year Founded: 1852

Private or Public: Private

Religious Affiliation: None

Location: Suburban

Number of Applicants: 15,619

Percent Accepted: 26%

Percent Accepted who enroll: 33%

Number Entering: 1,300

Number of Transfers Accepted each Year: 148

Middle 50% SAT range: M: 670–750, CR: 670–750, Wr: 670–760

Middle 50% ACT range: 30–33

Early admission program EA/ED/None: ED

Percentage accepted through EA or ED: Unreported

EA and ED deadline: 1-Nov

Regular Deadline: 1-Jan

Application Fee: $70

Full time Undergraduate enrollment: 5,044

Total enrollment: 8,295

Percent Male: 50%

Percent Female: 50%

Total Percent Minority or Unreported: 45%

Percent African-American: 6%

Percent Asian/Pacific Islander: 13%

Percent Hispanic: 6%

Percent Native-American: <1%

Percent International: 6%

Percent in-state/out of state: 23%/77%

Percent from Public HS: 59%

Retention Rate: 97%

Graduation Rate 4-year: 85%

Graduation Rate 6-year: 90%

Percent Undergraduates in On-campus housing: 66%

Number of official organized extracurricular organizations: 160

3 Most popular majors: Economics, English Language and Literature, International Relations

Student/Faculty ratio: 7:1

Average Class Size: 10 to 19

Percent of students going to grad school: 35%

Tuition and Fees: $38,840

In State Tuition and Fees if different: No difference

Cost for Room and Board: $10,518

Percent receiving financial aid out of those who apply, first year: Unreported

Percent receiving financial aid among all students: 41%

The geographical region between the cities of Somerville and Cambridge boasts some of the brightest and most talented young students in the world. Called the "Brainpower Triangle," its borders are delineated by the location of three of the top institutions in America—Harvard University, Massachusetts Institute of Technology, and Tufts University. Tufts , a private institution, is renowned for its internationalism,

study abroad programs, and of course, its giant elephant mascot. Tufts is located on Walnut Hill in Medford, where diligent Jumbos trek up every morning, rain or shine (or sleet, snow, hail).

An Experimental College

Tufts is divided into 10 schools, two of which are devoted to undergraduate studies: the School of Arts and Sciences and the School of Engineering. Tufts boasts a rigorous undergraduate program focusing on interdisciplinary studies. It's no surprise then, that International Relations, which combines history, politics, humanities and economics, is the most popular major. "I loved being an IR major—I got to learn everything I was interested in," one recent graduate said. The IR program is a department on its own, but it also "borrows" faculty from 16 other departments. But don't be fooled by the breadth of the major, because it's definitely not lacking in depth. While most majors only require six semesters of foreign languages, IR requires eight semesters. Many awards are given each year to graduating IR seniors—57 percent of the Class of 2008 received academic honors such as summa cum laude, which denotes having a cumulative GPA of 3.75 or higher.

IR is not the only area in which Tufts undergraduates excel. In addition to other programs that are typical of other liberal arts colleges, Tufts has a unique program called The Experimental College. "The oldest organization of its kind in the United States," the Ex College offers over 100 course that explore issues of current importance and interdisciplinary courses that are not offered in the more orthodox departments. This includes the peer-taught first-year seminar programs called Explorations and Perspectives. Seniors and juniors teach these classes and are awarded graduation credit for their leadership. Some past favorites include "Beyond BeBop: Miles and Coltrane," and "Adolescent Fiction."

This involvement of the students in teaching is indicative of the Tufts academic experience as a whole. Tufts has a student-faculty ratio of nine to one, and classes rarely exceed 100 students. Most of the classes are discussion style and Teaching Assistants are rarely needed. "During my junior year I got to know my professors really well. They're very approachable and I've gone out to a drink with one of them once!" exclaimed one senior. The caliber of professors that work at Tufts is top-notch and something that the students consider themselves lucky to have access to. Notable faculty include a former American Psychological Association president and many Nobel Prize recipients.

The Pen Is Mightier than the Jumbo

Tufts claims the honor of the first American football game between two American colleges. Although Tufts was victorious against Harvard in 1875, athletics have been somewhat lacking in recent years. Tufts is a member of the NCAA Division III in sports and is also a member of the New England Small College Athletic Conference. While the mighty Jumbos excel in particular games such as squash and sailing, athletics is not their forte. This might be attributed either to the fact that Tufts does not offer scholarships for athletes, or "because our mascot is a gigantic elephant," one student speculated. While varsity athletics may lack in school spirit, have no fear if you are a sports buff. Tufts has a 70,000 square-foot indoor sports center which includes four tennis courts, a state-of-the-art fitness center, and a six-lane indoor pool and a sauna—everything you need to stay in shape.

If you think that trekking up the hill every morning is enough exercise for you, there are plenty of other organizations to be involved in at Tufts. If you're a singer, you can join one of Tuft's six a cappella groups. "It's everywhere," said one nonsinger. "You can't escape it." Many of these groups are award-winning and go on national tours over breaks. For instance, the Beelzebubs, or Bubs, as they are commonly called, had the esteemed a cappella honor of opening for the renowned Rockapella group this winter at their concert in downtown Boston.

> **"A cappella is everywhere. You can't escape it."**

If singing's not your thing, perhaps you can find your niche in one of the numerous on-campus publications. The *Tufts Daily* is where most Jumbos get their news from, and writers for the *Daily* have gone on after Tufts to be writers for the *New York Times* and the *Boston Herald*. Those looking to do journalism on the side can opt to write for the *Tufts Observer*, a weekly magazine. "The amount of work and commitment I have for the *Observer* is great—it doesn't take over my life, but it's enough for me to take it seriously," one writer said. One of the most anticipated publications on campus is *The Zamboni*, "Tufts' only intentionally funny magazine." This 16-page tabloid is issued six times during the year, and while reviews of it are mixed among the student population ("THEY seem to think its funny"), it is your survival guide to the ins and outs of the Tufts social scene.

Fakes, Frats, and Forests

While many students may cite the school's proximity to Boston as one of the reasons why they chose to go to Tufts, in reality, most of the partying takes place on campus. Boston "sucks for underage kids" due to its strict ID-ing policy and underclassmen do not enjoy the same level of leniency with underage drinking that one may find in other big cities like New York. "Having a good fake is essential," one sophomore said. Once they are 21, Tufts kids often frequent the bars in the Medford area—the Somerville Theater is good for musical groups, and there are a few 19+ clubs that are good for a night of dancing. If you do make it to Boston for a night of fun, most of the places to go are on Lansdowne Street, where many clubs and bars are lined up for convenient "hopping around." "Avalon is the best one," said one Lansdowne Street enthusiast. "On Thursday and Friday it is 19 plus and they play really good music!"

There's plenty of partying to do on campus as well. Most of them are "keggers" thrown by frats. Tufts is very Greek-friendly, housing 11 fraternities and five sororities. While the sororities seldom throw wild, crazy parties, the frat scene is very prominent on campus as they organize large theme parties through-out the year. The Tufts administration has been "chill" about the underage drinking and partying that goes on at these frats and sees Greek life as an opportunity for Tufts students to form a community of their own and to exemplify leadership. However, students have noted that recently they have been stricter about alcohol violations than in the past.

Unfortunately, doing kegstands and going to clubs can get a little old after four years. So Tufts student take the opportunity to use the Loj, a retreat destination that is owned by Tufts and open to all of the Tufts community. Located in Woodstock, New Hampshire, the Loj offers opportunities to go skiing, hiking, apple picking, rock climbing, and swimming. To get involved in maintaining and running trips to the Loj, one can join the Tufts Mountain Club, an outdoor club dedicated to "exploring the great outdoors, physically exerting yourself," says a recent alum. So whether you have the study hard, party harder mentality of a frat brother or if you like to muse about philosophy over a fire and a glass of wine, Tufts has a little bit of something for everyone.—*Lee Komeda*

FYI

If you come to Tufts, you better bring "about 10 foldable umbrellas because chances are, you'll lose half of them and your roommate will steal the other half."

If I could change one thing about Tufts, I would change "the school color and mascot—Jumbo is just weird."

What's the typical weekend schedule? "On any given weekend you can probably find people going out to the local pubs on Thursday and Fridays. Saturday you might hit up a concert or a play and then head over to a frat house for a themed party. Sunday, if you can manage to get yourself out of bed, STUDY!"

Three things every student should do before graduating from Tufts are "take a special someone to the Library roof, have Sunday lunch at Dewick, and go to Spring Fling."

University of Massachusetts / Amherst

Address: 37 Mather Drive
Amherst, MA 01003-9291
Phone: 413-545-0222
E-mail address:
mail@admission.umass.edu
Web site URL:
www.umass.edu
Year Founded: 1863
Private or Public: Public
Religious Affiliation: None
Location: Suburban
Number of Applicants:
27,138
Percent Accepted: 66%
**Percent Accepted who
enroll:** 24%
Number Entering: 4,272
**Number of Transfers
Accepted each Year:** 1,989
Middle 50% SAT range:
M: 520–630, CR: 510–610,
Wr: Unreported
Middle 50% ACT range:
Unreported
**Early admission program
EA/ED/None:** EA

**Percentage accepted
through EA or ED:** 25%
EA and ED deadline: 1-Nov
Regular Deadline: 15-Jan
Application Fee: $40
**Full time Undergraduate
enrollment:** 20,114
Total enrollment: 25,873
Percent Male: 51%
Percent Female: 49%
**Total Percent Minority or
Unreported:** 29%
Percent African-American:
5%
**Percent Asian/Pacific
Islander:** 8%
Percent Hispanic: 4%
Percent Native-American: 0%
Percent International: 1%
**Percent in-state/out of
state:** 81%/19%
Percent from Public HS:
Unreported
Retention Rate: 86%
Graduation Rate 4-year:
51%

Graduation Rate 6-year:
68%
**Percent Undergraduates in
On-campus housing:** 63%
**Number of official organized
extracurricular
organizations:** 280
3 Most popular majors:
Biological and Physical
Sciences, English Language
and Literature, Psychology
Student/Faculty ratio: 18:1
Average Class Size: 20 to 29
**Percent of students going to
grad school:** Unreported
Tuition and Fees: $21,729
**In State Tuition and Fees if
different:** $10,232
Cost for Room and Board:
$8,114
**Percent receiving financial
aid out of those who apply,
first year:** 63%
**Percent receiving financial
aid among all students:**
53%

U Mass academics are hard," a student said, surprised. For those who remember UMass's party school reputation, they'll be amazed to find that parties now mainly happen off campus, or on a much smaller scale. Through recent renovations, new buildings, and academic reviews, UMass has recast its image as a college where athletics and academics are the main attractions.

Academic Overhaul

Amidst the formation of UMass's new public image, the University has been working to redefine itself physically, as well as academically. Recent years have seen the construction of the Center for Renaissance Studies (one of six in North America), Computer Science Building, the Child Care building and the Engineering Lab II, with a new Studio Art building on the way. Current facilities, including the WEB Dubois Library which boasts over 25 stories, are said by students to be "world class."

No matter where one's interests may lie, UMass academics will likely have an appropriate program. "I don't see any reason why you shouldn't be interested in what you're majoring here," one senior said. "We've got everything and anything to study." Majors range from Building Materials and Wood Technology to Marketing to Communication Disorders, or you could even create your own major courtesy of the Bachelor's Degree with Individual Concentration (BDIC). Not interested enough to major in it? Many majors can also be minors, or you can build a unique minor that may fulfill a more esoteric interest (UMass offer minors from Entomology to Military Leadership). While best known for its management and linguistics programs, UMass is strong in both liberal arts and the sciences, too.

If students can't find a class they wish to take at UMass, they are able to cross-enroll in classes at any of the other Five College Consortium, an intercollegiate academic program that includes Smith, Mount Holyoke,

Amherst, Hampshire College, and UMass. Whether it's merely to try out something new, or just to taste a new learning environment, many students seize this opportunity.

However, despite such leeway, all students enrolled at UMass must fulfill their general education requirements, which are aimed at increasing the width of each student's education. The writing requirement consists of a freshman college writing class and a junior year writing requirement (mandatory for every major). Six "Social World" courses must be taken, one course in each section: literature, arts, history, and social and behavioral sciences, another social and behavioral science, and another course in any section. Math and sciences require that you fulfill three natural science courses (one biological and one physical), one basic math skills and one analytical reasoning course. Finally, there must also be one interdisciplinary course. On top of that, the University requires that students take two classes on diversity, one on U.S. diversity, and another on global diversity. Surprisingly, most students stated that they "had no problem fulfilling the requirements."

Classes tend to start large in the beginning and get smaller in one's junior and senior years. "Unless you are taking a course required for a couple majors, like intro biology, you can keep your classes to under 30," an engineering major noted. One complaint was that UMass was too research-oriented. Not all classes are taught by professors. Instead, PhD students, who many undergraduates feel are less knowledgeable than professors, teach some smaller classes.

For those who are interested in more academically rigorous courses, the honors program, Commonwealth College, provides roughly 3,000 students with smaller class sizes and more challenging workloads. Commonwealth College ("ComCol") promotes strong faculty and student ties through events like "Pizza and Prof. Night" on Thursdays. ComCol also emphasizes different aspects of the college life, such as a required Dean's book seminar class, an individual "capstone experience" (a six-credit project), and community service.

Living at Amherst

Amherst, a college town in the historic Pioneer Valley of Western Massachusetts, is "a great place to go, especially to be off campus." The bus system, free to UMass students, can take you everywhere—to the four other consortium colleges, around campus, into town,

and even to the mall. Security isn't a top problem either. "I feel safe walking all alone at three in the morning," one female student said. "That's how safe it is here." Despite the lack of crime concerns, the school is still cautious, installing security cameras on the entrances, exits and the exteriors of the residential buildings, hiring a very large security detail, and having a bus that circles the large campus every 15 minutes.

There are six different residential sections of campus: North, Northeast, Central, Southwest, Orchard Hill, and Sylvan. According to the students, each has its own distinct personality. For example, Sylvan is known to be quiet, while Southwest is where most of the parties are. Orchard Hill has a lot of ComCol students, Central is very hippie, Northeast has a large Asian presence. North, opened for the first time in Fall 2006, has apartments, an attractive detail to many upperclassmen.

Special residential arrangements at Amherst include the Talent Advancement Program in which students are grouped by major, and the Residential Advancement Programs, in which students are grouped by class selection. These programs are formed to promote interaction among students with similar interests, and to facilitate easier transition into college life for freshmen. However, these special arrangements, and student selection of residential halls closest to their department buildings (for example, Northeast is closest to Engineering) often causes students to complain that "most students end up segregating themselves by major, and there is very little interaction between students of different interests."

Students eat in one of four Dining Commons (DC's) by swiping their UCARD. Students can choose their meal plans, so that they can have between 112 swipes a semester (7 swipes a week) to unlimited. Depending on one's meal plan, swipes can also be used at retail locations, like cafés around campus to buy food. Berkshire DC underwent renovation in Spring 2006 and students love the food there. "Berkshire offers a variety of delicious food," one student raved. "I hope they renovate all the other DC's too." Students can also eat at any of the nearby restaurants, like the popular Pasta E Basta and Antonio's Pizza. They also hang out in the fair trade convenience store and bagel shop People's Market, as well as a vegan/vegetarian eatery Earthfoods Café at the Student Union. But the main central hub of campus remains the Campus Center. The Campus Center offers the Blue Wall eatery and a fair trade coffee stand, and it also supplies copies of the *Daily Collegian*, UMass's daily newspaper.

There are two free athletic facilities, Boyden and Totman Gym. Those who wish to work out closer to the dorm can use the wellness facilities housed in certain residential halls. These are generally available with workout equipment, which students may use after paying a fee. Student recreational athletic facilities are separate from those used by athletes, but the campus has announced that it plans to renovate the two gyms, as well as possibly construct a new athletic facility.

Bringing down the House

While parties used to be big on campus, in recent years several fraternities have been demolished or bought out by the University. The reason for this trend can be attributed to fact that the University wants to smarten up its image. "Parties are almost always shut down by the campus police," one senior complained. "When I was a freshman, they had no problems with these parties." Neighbors complain as well about the noise level, drunken disorderly conduct, and trash left on the grounds after a party. Still, parties do occur, especially during big weekends like Orchard Hill Bowl Weekend, the Spring Concert, and after-sports victories. Most of these parties take place in Southwest and Puffton, an area where the majority of students live off-campus. After the Red Sox won the World Series, there was even a party so large that campus security had to be called in to shut down the "riot." Still, some students who are not content with the party scene on campus head to other schools for big parties, like the Halloween Party at

Smith College. Popular local bars and clubs include McMurphy's, Monkey Bar, and Sky Bar, which on Thursday nights allows students above 18 years of age.

For those who may not want to drink and party every or any night, performances and other events can almost always be found, both on and off campus. UMass has very large performance venues that are constantly showcasing various productions and concerts. UMass also offers a movie theater that shows first release films on Friday and Saturday nights.

> "I would never have expected to see so many different kinds of people at UMass."

Sports play a big role on the Division I campus. "Everyone attends the hockey games," one student said. "Where else are we going to shout at the BU students 'BC Rejects!'?" Immense school spirit is highlighted at the Mullin Center, which doubles for the arena for both hockey games and basketball games. Football games are also extremely popular and boast a significant alumni presence. Even the UMass marching band has its own share of celebrity, having won numerous national honors.

"I would never have expected to see so many different kinds of people at UMass," one student commented. "People come from all backgrounds, all ethnicities, and all over the nation and the globe with all different types of interests." And with access to four other well-respected colleges, UMass is on the way to spreading its academic wings.
—*Jesse Dong*

FYI
If you come to UMass at Amherst, you'd better bring "a better pad for your mattress."
What is the typical weekend schedule? "Attend a hockey game Friday night, go off campus on Saturday afternoon, party with friends Saturday night, and spend all of Sunday doing homework."
If I could change one thing about UMass at Amherst, I'd "renovate all the DCs."
Three things every student should do before graduating from UMass at Amherst are: "Go to Bowl Weekend, attend a hockey game and go to a frat."

Wellesley College

Address: 106 Central Street Wellesley, MA 02481-8203
Phone: 781-283-2270
E-mail address: admission@wellesley.edu
Web site URL: www.wellesley.edu
Year Founded: 1870
Private or Public: Private
Religious Affiliation: None
Location: Suburban
Number of Applicants: 4,001
Percent Accepted: 36%
Percent Accepted who enroll: 41%
Number Entering: 596
Number of Transfers Accepted each Year: 29
Middle 50% SAT range: M: 630–725, CR: 640–740, Wr: 650–740
Middle 50% ACT range: 28–32
Early admission program EA/ED/None: ED

Percentage accepted through EA or ED: 20%
EA and ED deadline: 1-Nov
Regular Deadline: 15-Jan
Application Fee: $50/free online
Full time Undergraduate enrollment: 2,190
Total enrollment: 2,344
Percent Male: 0%
Percent Female: 100%
Total Percent Minority or Unreported: 39%
Percent African-American: 6%
Percent Asian/Pacific Islander: 26%
Percent Hispanic: 7%
Percent Native-American: <1%
Percent International: 8%
Percent in-state/out of state: 12%/88%
Percent from Public HS: 64%
Retention Rate: 96%

Graduation Rate 4-year: 85%
Graduation Rate 6-year: 91%
Percent Undergraduates in On-campus housing: 97%
Number of official organized extracurricular organizations: 160
3 Most popular majors: Economics, Political Science, English
Student/Faculty ratio: 9:1
Average Class Size: 10 to 19
Percent of students going to grad school: 80%
Tuition and Fees: $36,640
In State Tuition and Fees if different: No difference
Cost for Room and Board: $11,336
Percent receiving financial aid out of those who apply, first year: 55%
Percent receiving financial aid among all students: 59%

In 1870, Henry and Pauline Durant founded Wellesley to give young women a college education as rigorous as that of their male peers. Since then, Wellesley has graduated a large number of famous alumnae, including former Secretary of State Madeleine Albright and Secretary of State Hillary Clinton. Although the college's cachet may have diminished a little after the spread of coeducation, the passion, drive, and college pride of Wellesley students is as strong as ever.

Bankers and Bluestockings

At Wellesley, schoolwork is king—or should we say, queen. Its liberal arts curriculum expects students to fulfill writing, quantitative reasoning, and foreign language requirements, and take classes in eight of nine distribution areas. In addition, they need to meet the multicultural requirement, studying one unit's worth of non-Western culture. Despite the breadth of the curriculum, students say that the variety of classes makes fulfilling requirements both easy and enjoyable. As one first-year said, "Even if you're not interested in a certain field, you can find something you enjoy." A junior who had completed her requirements sophomore year concurred: "It's really not difficult to fulfill anything."

With 30 departmental and 21 interdepartmental majors, Wellesley offers over 1,000 courses in a diverse selection of academic fields—and Wellesley women love the intellectual buffet. Students were enthusiastic about a wide variety of classes, including seminars on environmentalism, the History of Western Music, and "1968," a course devoted entirely to—you guessed it—the year 1968. One first-year student said she had met people doubling majors like "biology and political science [or] Latin American studies and music." Students agree, however, that the economics department is a big presence on campus. According to data released by the Wellesley College Office for Public Affairs, 13 percent of the Wellesley class of 2007 majored in economics and 34.6 percent went to work in business after graduation. "A lot of Econ people are trying to go into banking and finance," a junior explained. Other popular majors include political science and psychology. Although students may not declare majors in math and hard sciences in droves, one science major praised the all-female environment for cultivating interest in physics, chemistry, and math, fields that are traditionally underrepresented among women.

Students also praised the professors, who "really want students to talk to them and come to them with any problems," as one junior said. With a 9:1 student-faculty ratio, classes tend toward the intimate. This same junior named the small class sizes as her favorite thing about Wellesley's academics: "I think it makes you a lot more into your work, wanting to participate and be a part of the class." In addition, Wellesley professors tend to be both highly knowledgeable and able to transmit their knowledge to their students. Some have even written the textbooks for the classes they teach. This marriage of availability and fluency in their subject matter makes the professors one of the college's greatest assets.

> "I've met nerdy music people and nerdy politics people . . . Everyone here is nerdy about something.' "

The Wellesley workload is no joke. Academics take priority over socializing and extracurricular activities, and it shows. "During the week it's just silent, because everyone here is studying," a first-year said. Still, challenging classes don't translate into C's across the board. In 100- and 200-level classes with ten or more students, professors are required to create a curve with a B+ average. (In 300-level classes or higher, or in classes with fewer than ten students, no curve exists.) This works to students' advantage in math and science classes, while the humanities and social science departments tend to "scale down" the averages because their students usually receive higher grades. As one psychology major described, straight-A students are "either incredibly energetic and brilliant—or they study constantly, don't really socialize, and are otherwise psychotic."

Better get crazy!

Suburban Riches, Boston Fun

Wellesley is a small, affluent town outside of Boston. Students say there's not too much interaction between students and residents; and as one student put it, "I think the extent of our relationship with the town is walking into town to CVS and to the bank." Two problems keep the college from embracing its town. First, the average college student doesn't have the money for the expensive restaurants

and boutiques that the town of Wellesley offers. Second, the town is, in the words of a junior, "not a real town." Simply put, Wellesley's just not big enough to support the pizza places, concert halls, and dance clubs that would draw student interest.

But while students may consider the rich suburban-family demographics of Wellesley a drawback, the town does have some perks. Students are able to find well-paying jobs easily. Babysitting is especially popular—"The people in town are so rich, they pay really well," a junior said.

But despite living in the suburbs, students still have the city just a short ride away. Wellesley's proximity to Boston keeps students connected to urban living. The city is "very accessible" from Wellesley, and it offers good entertainment to young women about town. As one student said, "Boston always has concerts, shopping, whatever you want to do." Trips to Boston aren't exclusive to upperclasswomen. All students flock to Boston for weekend entertainment.

Wellesley Women, Cutting Loose

While an all-female student body may sound like a drag to some, Wellesley women know that single-sex education doesn't lack fun. The Wellesley Senate bus runs a route from Wellesley to the Boston-Cambridge area and back every hour. While MIT frat parties are the most popular destination, a number of colleges in the Boston area host good parties, and students choose which to attend based on the people they know at a given school. The bus goes both ways as well: "We have parties here, and guys will come from Harvard, MIT, Babson, BU, BC, Tufts . . ."

While some Wellesley students celebrate the wealth of parties in the Boston area as an opportunity to meet new people, form a larger community, and meet guys, others dislike the artificiality such party-based interactions promote. One sophomore said, "Personally, only seeing men in a frat-party atmosphere tends to reinforce negative stereotypes about them—that is, they're usually trying to hook up with girls" rather than anything more. Because of the lack of male-female interaction in a more day-to-day casual environment, "it takes a very determined individual to go out and make male friends" as opposed to just hooking up. A first-year commented that her good male friends were the boyfriends of girls on campus.

Of course, one doesn't need men to have friends, or even to date. The lesbian and bisexual community is visible and active on campus. The largest annual party at Wellesley is the Dyke Ball, which began as a prom for students who were unable to attend their high school proms due their sexual orientations. The Ball is now a campus-wide bash to which all Wellesley students can come and cut loose.

Wellesley students definitely don't need to make the trek to find close friends. Wellesley students will sometimes say that they don't need sororities "because we're all one big sorority." One first-year said she decided to matriculate at Wellesley because of how nice the students were: "Everyone is friendly. Upperclassmen will give you directions, help you with your homework." In addition, the sisterly atmosphere creates a level of freedom in intellectual and social self-expression that many students did not have in high school: "I've met nerdy music people and nerdy politics people . . . Everyone here is nerdy about something. That might be our defining feature. Even the cool kids—there's something like, 'Oh my God, I love physics!' or 'Astronomy is the coolest thing ever!'"

Diversity at Wellesley is more than intellectual. In race, socioeconomic status, political affiliation, and sexual orientation, Wellesley students represent a wide range of experiences. One student remarked, "There've been a ton of times, in a party or in a room, where I've realized I'm the only white person there." Another mentioned, "I have friends who are really rich and really poor." And while the political climate does tend toward the liberal, there is a conservative presence on campus. One first-year student said, "One of my roommates is a Ron Paul supporter, so that was interesting, what with the four pictures of Hillary Clinton on my wall."

Four Flavors at Every Meal

In a Wellesley student's first year, she is assigned a dorm. Each floor has a Resident Assistant, who is a student, and a Resident Director, an adult who usually lives in the dorm with her family. The strictness of dorm policy varies, depending on the RA and RD. After the first year, a lottery system determines what order students get to choose their rooms. Seniors get the first group of random numbers, then juniors, and then sophomores. Students said juniors and seniors are pretty much guaranteed singles. Dorms don't have official themes, but each have their own characteristics. Some dorms are considered party dorms, while another is known for being more reclusive, and still another is the "lesbian social scene" dorm. Students said the new dorms by the science center have larger rooms and quieter surroundings, but not as much character as the older buildings.

While students at many other colleges complain of monotonous meals and poorly cooked food, Wellesley women are positive about their dining halls. Wellesley students are on one of the most flexible meal plans possible—they can eat at any dining hall, at any time, as many times a day as they want. And nearly every dorm, as well as the student center, features a dining hall. Although each hall is supposed to have a theme, some are "hard to decipher." As one first-year student explained, "One of them is supposed to be comfort food, but they serve basically the same food my dorm serves, which is supposed to be eclectic cuisine." Despite the sameness, a student said, "I think that in comparison to other schools, the food is quite good, and the management does a good job of listening to student suggestions."

Apparently, one alumna thought that the dining halls lacked something, so she donated money so that every hall would have four different flavors of ice cream every day, at every meal. Do you need another reason to apply to Wellesley?—*Finola Prendergast*

FYIs

If you come to Wellesley, you'd better bring "a nice dress, because there are a lot of times where you need to wear a dress."

What's the typical weekend schedule? "If you're one of those people who's into partying, you'd probably go off campus to Harvard or MIT Friday or Saturday night, and study Sunday. Or go to Boston and shop and eat out."

If I could change one thing about Wellesley, I'd have "more on-campus social life instead of stuff in Boston."

Three things every student at Wellesley should do before graduating are "see the campus from the top of Galen-Stone Tower, skinny dip in Lake Waban, and swing next to the Chapel."

Wheaton College

Address: 26 East Main Street Norton, MA 02766

Phone: 508-286-8251

E-mail address: admission@wheatoncollege.edu

Web site URL: www.wheatoncollege.edu

Year Founded: 1834

Private or Public: Private

Religious Affiliation: None

Location: Rural

Number of Applicants: 3,833

Percent Accepted: 37%

Percent Accepted who enroll: 30%

Number Entering: 418

Number of Transfers Accepted each Year: 28

Middle 50% SAT range: M: 560–650, CR: 580–670, Wr: Unreported

Middle 50% ACT range: 25–29

Early admission program EA/ED/None: ED

Percentage accepted through EA or ED: 66%

EA and ED deadline: 1-Nov

Regular Deadline: 15-Jan

Application Fee: $55

Full time Undergraduate enrollment: 1,552

Total enrollment: 1,552

Percent Male: 40%

Percent Female: 60%

Total Percent Minority or Unreported: 11%

Percent African-American: 5%

Percent Asian/Pacific Islander: 3%

Percent Hispanic: 3%

Percent Native-American: 0%

Percent International: 3%

Percent in-state/out of state: 35%/65%

Percent from Public HS: 63%

Retention Rate: 88%

Graduation Rate 4-year: 79%

Graduation Rate 6-year: 79%

Percent Undergraduates in On-campus housing: 93%

Number of official organized extracurricular organizations: 60

3 Most popular majors: Economics, English, Psychology

Student/Faculty ratio: 10:1

Average Class Size: 10 to 19

Percent of students going to grad school: 48%

Tuition and Fees: $36,430

In State Tuition and Fees if different: No difference

Cost for Room and Board: $8,640

Percent receiving financial aid out of those who apply, first year: 70%

Percent receiving financial aid among all students: 64%

W heaton is a small liberal arts school located in the sleepy town of Norton, Massachusetts. It boasts a challenging and varied academic program where students can take classes in everything from dreams to globalization. The Wheaton community is a close-knit group where even the RAs just want to be your friend. Wheaton students have a thriving extracurricular and social scene that is greatly benefited by the campus's location between Providence and Boston, two cities just begging to be explored by car-owning and train-hopping Wheaties.

The Right Balance

Most Wheaton students are very happy with the academic environment of their campus. "The academics are just right," said one freshman. "I'm not overstressed, but I'm being challenged. And here we have the ability to do well in school and be involved in other activities, too." Popular majors include English and education. Education, along with the natural sciences, is said to be one of the hardest majors because the program involves student teaching and requires that

students double major. Wheaton is thought of as more of a humanities school, but the administration is beginning an increased focus on science. They have implemented a plan to rebuild all the science buildings on campus by 2014 and are seen as being very encouraging of students pursuing science majors.

Classes are small, usually 15 to 20 students, except in some introductory lectures. Students say that professors are very committed to getting to know them and being a part of their intellectual growth. "One of my professors gave us extra credit just for coming to her office hours so she could get to know us," said one Wheatie. There are no TAs at Wheaton, further enhancing the personalized touch. Though the professors are friendly and helpful, they are tough. Students don't think there is much grade inflation at all at Wheaton and also report relatively few curves. They stress that one must work hard to do well.

Wheaton students say their distribution requirements, called "foundation courses," are reasonable and they have an interesting array of classes in which to fill them. Foundation courses include a first-year seminar, English 101, a math course, two semesters of a foreign language, and one semester of "Beyond the West," i.e., a class that deals with a culture outside of Western society. In first-year seminars, groups of 20 freshmen become acclimated to Wheaton academic life in a laid-back atmosphere while studying topics that vary from "Surgeons and Shamans" to "The Rituals of Dinner." Wheaton also has a program called Connections, where students are able to choose a set of related courses that interest them. Examples of Connections include "Human Biology and Movement," "Modern Italy," and "Music: the Medium and the Message." Students say the Connections courses are an interesting way to fulfill requirements. Wheaties also take advantage of the fact that their college is a part of the 12-college consortium that includes, among others, Amherst, Bowdoin, Wellesley, and Dartmouth. Wheaton students can attend a college in the consortium for a semester or a year. Wheaton also offers numerous and very popular opportunities for study abroad.

A Perfect New England Family

Nearly every student has high praises for the sense of community at Wheaton. "One of the things I noticed at accepted students' day that I didn't notice at others schools was how friendly everyone was," one freshman said. Wheaton upperclassmen are especially enthusiastic about making sure new students feel welcome and are aware of the importance of not making novice Wheatie mistakes. During freshmen orientation, upperclassmen herd confused freshmen into the chapel where they begin to chant the incoming class's graduation year. After the chanting, an upperclassman runs through the chapel and squirts water on an unsuspecting frosh who automatically inherits this illustrious job. Besides being simply funny, this tradition emphasizes Wheaton's fun and family-like atmosphere. The fact that Wheaton's student body numbers fewer than 1,600 seems to be an important reason for this. "I like that it is a small school because I can get to know a lot of people well, but still see a few new faces every day," reported one girl. Additionally, "the importance of acceptance and friendship are stressed at Wheaton," says one Wheatie.

In a testament to their widespread acceptance of difference, students are quick to say that there is no "typical" Wheaton student. When pressed, they will admit that most students are middle- or upper-class and from Massachusetts, Maine, Connecticut, and surprisingly, California. "For some reason, lots of people in California know about Wheaton. I guess they like small liberal arts schools," explained one Wheatie. Another trait that bonds Wheaton students together is being physically fit. A large segment of students is involved in athletic endeavors that vary from varsity sports to the equestrian team to intramurals. There are no sororities and fraternities at Wheaton, and many say that the a cappella groups function as a more positive version of the Greek system. A cappella is very popular at Wheaton, as are a wide range of other extracurricular activities, especially community service groups. "Wheaton has a lot to offer—there's always something to join," explains one Wheatie.

Though they don't like to be typecast, Wheaton students as a whole can be summed up as both studious and typical preppy New England kids. They seem particularly fond of The North Face fleeces, colorful rain boots, and for the female students, designer purses. Wheaton students admit that their campus is not incredibly diverse, though the administration is working hard to change that. Wheaton boasts a thriving cultural center, the Marshall Center for Intercultural Learning, and is involved in a scholarship program called the Posse Program. New York City minority students receive scholarships to Wheaton in groups called posses, which helps them feel less isolated while increasing Wheaton's racial diversity.

Road Trippers

On any given weekend, a large contingent of the Wheaton student body can be found in Boston, which is 40 minutes away, or Providence, about 20. Transportation couldn't be easier since many students have cars and the school offers a shuttle that runs every 30 minutes to a nearby train station. Wheaties love hitting the restaurants, theaters and club scenes of these two New England cities. The administration encourages their students to take advantage of what their excellent location has to offer. Through the Boston and Providence Connections programs, students pay just five dollars for dinner and a concert or play on select nights. A premium outlet mall is very close to campus, giving Wheaton fashionistas yet another attractive weekend option.

Wheaton students' obvious devotion to Boston and Providence trips shouldn't be seen as a sign that there is nothing to do at Wheaton. Some students admitted that some weekends on campus are a little slow, but there are usually a wide variety of on-campus activities to choose from. The Balfour-Hood Campus Center hosts well-attended theme parties in its large lobby, called the Atrium. Wheaton often hosts concerts as well. Recently, students were surprised when a subsidized concert by a Persian pop star, which they wrote off as random and amusing, was packed with outsiders who happily shelled out $40 a ticket.

> **"I know that this might seem pretty lame, but Wheaton really would not function in the same way without the common bond and sense of belonging that the students and professors share."**

Wheaton has a campus bar, the Loft, where students can get burgers, pizza, and alcohol "if you're over 21 or have an ID that says you are." Wheaton's 11 theme houses also throw popular parties. The Lyon's Den is the campus coffee shop, and serves as a popular hangout and a more laid-back alternative to the Loft. Though many social events seem to revolve around alcohol, students report not feeling much pressure either way. The administration is fairly lax on students who do drink, and Wheaties are very accepting of students who don't.

Endless Food, and Not Just Wheaties

Most students have good things to say about Wheaton's dining system. They have unlimited access to the two dining halls, one of which stays open until midnight. Pizza and ice cream seem to be available at all times, though there are more nutritious family style options available as well. Unlimited access makes some students grow weary of the selection. "I like the food, but sometimes I get tired of it," said one girl. When this happens, students head to the nearby town of Mansfield to eat at chains like Subway.

The campus is pretty, secluded, and very Ivy League-esque with ivy-covered brick and a quaint pond that surrounds the Chase Dining Hall. The campus is not very big, which adds to the community atmosphere and also helps Wheaties easily get where they need to go. Students like their dorms when there are a proper number of people living in them. Some freshmen find themselves in forced triples on Lower Campus. Upperclassmen, on the other hand, often live on Upper Campus in newly renovated dorms that "are like hotels," said one envious freshman.

Wheaton students are overwhelmingly very pleased with their college. "I know that this might seem pretty lame, but Wheaton really would not function in the same way without the common bond and sense of belonging that the students and professors share," said one Wheatie. The combination of Wheaton's strong sense of community, challenging, but manageable academics, and prime location make it a great place to spend four years.—*Keneisha Sinclair*

FYI

If you come to Wheaton, you'd better bring "rain boots and a DVD player because there's no cable."

What is the typical weekend schedule? "Napping after last class on Friday, trips to Boston and Providence, dances at the theme houses and concerts at the Loft, playing in or going to see a game, and lots of homework on Sunday."

If I could change one thing about Wheaton, I'd "make Norton more exciting."

Three things every student at Wheaton should do before graduating are "jump in the pond, study abroad or do a college exchange, and get really involved in a Wheaton extracurricular activity."

Williams College

Address: 33 Stetson Court Williamstown, MA 01267

Phone: 413-597-2211

E-mail address: admission@williams.edu

Web site URL: www.williams.edu

Year Founded: 1793

Private or Public: Private

Religious Affiliation: None

Location: Rural

Number of Applicants: 6,478

Percent Accepted: 18%

Percent Accepted who enroll: 45%

Number Entering: 540

Number of Transfers Accepted each Year: 13

Middle 50% SAT range: M: 670–760, CR: 670–760, Wr: Unreported

Middle 50% ACT range: 29–33

Early admission program EA/ED/None: ED

Percentage accepted through EA or ED: 40%

EA and ED deadline: 10-Nov

Regular Deadline: 15-Dec

Application Fee: $60

Full time Undergraduate enrollment: 1,997

Total enrollment: 2,046

Percent Male: 50%

Percent Female: 50%

Total Percent Minority or Unreported: 29%

Percent African-American: 10%

Percent Asian/Pacific Islander: 11%

Percent Hispanic: 9%

Percent Native-American: 0%

Percent International: 7%

Percent in-state/out of state: 14%/86%

Percent from Public HS: 58%

Retention Rate: 97%

Graduation Rate 4-year: 91%

Graduation Rate 6-year: 91%

Percent Undergraduates in On-campus housing: 93%

Number of official organized extracurricular organizations: 110

3 Most popular majors: Economics, English, Art

Student/Faculty ratio: 7:1

Average Class Size: 2 to 9

Percent of students going to grad school: Unreported

Tuition and Fees: $35,438

In State Tuition and Fees if different: No difference

Cost for Room and Board: $9,470

Percent receiving financial aid out of those who apply, first year: 51%

Percent receiving financial aid among all students: 47%

On the first Friday morning in October, Williams students celebrate "Mountain Day." Bells ring to cancel class, and Ephs (named for school founder Colonel Ephraim Williams) hike up nearby Mt. Greylock to drink hot chocolate, sing songs, and enjoy the gorgeous view. Situated in the Berkshire Mountains in the northwest corner of Massachusetts, Williams boasts a "close-knit" community of approximately 2,000 students and "a really good environment to gain an education—very peaceful."

All in a Hard Day's Work

While the surroundings may be peaceful, the education at Williams is rigorous. According to one senior, "there's definitely a consensus on campus that the amount of work is greater than friends have at other institutions—even Ivy League schools." One student attributed this to "the pain of having more attention. I think that it can be really tough, just because so many of the courses are small—if there's a lot of reading for a class with four people, it's going to be pretty obvious that you didn't do it."

The flip side of such small classes is an education that is extremely personal. "You're not a number in a class of 500," said one senior. "You're a person with a personality; the professor knows who you are." Professors teach all classes and labs at Williams and often invite students over for dinner or coffee. They also encourage collaboration "ad nauseum," making for an environment that is "not at all cutthroat or competitive."

The intimate classroom environment is epitomized by the school's unique tutorial system. Starting spring semester freshman year, students can choose to take one tutorial course per semester, where two to three students meet with a professor to present and debate their weekly papers (or, in math and science tutorials, review problem sets). Despite the heavy workload, students describe tutorials as "really good, awesome—an amazing experience."

Students are also pleased with Williams' 4-1-4 schedule: four-month fall and spring semesters, with a one-month Winter Study period in between. During Winter Study, students choose from a vast array of unusual classes such as "Lego Mindstorms Robotics" and "Victorian Monsters," or submit their own proposal for a Winter Study project. Freshmen are required to stay on campus, but many upperclassmen take travel classes as varied as working at Nicaraguan eye care clinics or investigating traditional culture in Bali. Winter Study also features the Free University program, which lets students teach and take noncredit minicourses including origami, bartending, and Rubik's Cube. Because students take only one class, "there's lots of time to do other stuff—recreation, parties, skiing."

Williams requires students to take three courses in each of three divisions: Languages and the Arts, Social Studies, and Science and Mathematics. Students must also take one course relating to Peoples and Cultures, one involving Quantitative Reasoning, and two classified as Writing Intensive. In addition, students must complete four quarters of physical education, which many fulfill by playing sports at some level, while others take courses ranging from Badminton to Yoga. Generally, students "don't have a problem" fulfilling these requirements.

> "You're not a number in a class of 500. You're a person with a personality; the professor knows who you are."

Popular majors include English, psychology, economics, history, biology and art. In particular, the art history department at Williams is "world-renowned," featuring several art museums a short walk from campus and one of Williams's two graduate programs (the other is in development economics). Even nonart majors agree that art history lectures are "just unbelievable." Despite Williams's strength in the liberal arts, science majors do benefit from "a plethora of opportunities to do research as early as freshman year."

Williams students can also opt to study abroad, or they may choose Williams in New York or Williams-Mystic Program for maritime studies in Mystic, Connecticut—two programs which combine varied fieldwork with academic coursework in a new location. Williams has a lot to offer academically, and students are eager to rise to the occasion. As one high school valedictorian put it, "every single person I meet here I feel is very smart—in different ways, but all capable of having a very intelligent conversation—not just in the super-nerdy sense."

Ephs of All Breeds

"It's hard to group people at Williams," one junior said. "There's no one stereotype that fits everyone." The campus is "quite diverse" economically and geographically, and ethnic diversity is increasing. In terms of style, "Williams kids just throw on whatever they have," one student reported, while another claimed that "preppy kids are quite visible, though by no means the majority."

Despite their differences, students share one characteristic: friendliness. "The campus has a really friendly feel," marveled a freshman. "If you're walking around, there's going to be someone smiling at you and saying hello."

Ephs are involved in a wide range of activities outside the classroom. "The extracurricular involvement is unparalleled," said one student. "It continues to amaze me how people are able to juggle school with all their other activities. It really enables and encourages you to do a lot." About 50 percent (34 percent at the varsity level) of students play intercollegiate sports, and Williams is perennially ranked as the top Division III school. Intramurals are also "very big, though you don't have to be that athletic to play in them." All students can also benefit from the school's top-notch pool, field, track, squash courts, and golf course, but the weight room "is mediocre—it has what you need, but could definitely be upgraded."

Even nonathletes enjoy attending games, especially those against rival Amherst. As one student emphasized, "Physical activity is very popular at Williams—whether playing broomball with your entry freshman year or playing a sport—but you don't have to be an athlete to love Williams. The strength of other extracurriculars is enough that if sports is not your interest, you shouldn't feel that Williams isn't the place for you."

Popular activities include the student newspaper, a cappella groups, and Cap & Bells—the oldest continuously running student theater company in the nation, which enjoys the use of the theater and dance center. Also big is the Williams Outing Club, which organizes and rents equipment for hiking, kayaking, rock climbing, and winter sports. More offbeat groups include the Chocolate Lovers Association, Waffle Club, and Origami Club. Although there "isn't much political back-and-forth," students remain highly aware of current events and are "very proactive in helping out," rallying together to raise money and serve the community in times of need. Additionally, campus jobs—whether tour guiding, working in the admissions office, or working at the library—are not uncommon.

Living and Chilling on Campus

Overall, housing at Williams receives pretty high marks. Freshmen live on either Frosh Quad or the Berkshire Quad, and are divided into groups of 22 called "entries." Students in an entry live in the same building, along with two Junior Advisors (JAs) who organize events like weekly study breaks and trips to New York. JAs are generally well-liked, and exist to make sure their entries have fun and stay safe, not to police students' behavior.

"I really like the entry system," raved one freshman. "From the beginning, just to have 20 people to be able to go to dinner with or sit around your common room with put me at ease." Almost 50 percent of freshmen get singles, and upperclassmen, who pick housing in groups of up to four, "have the option of a double, but are pretty much guaranteed a single."

In the fall of 2006, Williams initiated a "cluster house" system, in which students are affiliated with a cluster of dorms in an effort to foster a sense of attachment similar to that provided by residential houses at other universities. The vast majority of students live on campus, though up to 100 seniors may live off-campus or in Williams-owned "co-op" housing.

With four dining halls to choose from, students enjoy a wide variety of food, which they describe as "really good." That's important, because "going into town involves walking across the street and walking down Spring Street—a quaint little street with a few shops, restaurants, a bar, and a bank," leaving students with few options beyond the dining halls. As one student added, "If you want a bar scene, if you want to go do cultural things in New York City, Williams is not for you. You have to acknowledge that you're choosing a school on the outskirts of rural Massachusetts, not in a big city."

The lack of nightlife in Williamstown "promotes more hanging out with your friends and socializing." Since there are no frats, students choose from parties in dorm rooms or off-campus houses, known for throwing "your typical college party with kegs, people drinking and playing beer pong." Though "alcohol is readily available at every party, it's never uncomfortable; nobody imposes or expects you to drink." All Campus Entertainment (ACE) also holds many well-attended theme parties, as well as events like homecoming, Winter Carnival, and Spring Fling. ACE even holds a weekly "Stress-Busters" event, where students can get free massages.

Cars are unnecessary for getting around, and Williams offers a shuttle on the weekends, enabling students to visit a shopping mall, supermarket, or even Wal-Mart. Getting to the airport, New York City, or Boston usually involves catching a ride with friends, but Williams also provides shuttle buses near the end of the semester or on holidays.

Students applaud the college's effort to bring the outside world to campus. "Honestly, the three years I've been here I've gone to Boston once and NYC once," a junior said. "Williams always tries to have people from outside come to campus—speakers, entertainment, that kind of stuff. There's always something to do here."—*Sameer Jain*

FYI

If you come to Williams, you'd better bring "a warm jacket and a dislike for Amherst."
What's the typical weekend schedule? "Watch or play in a sporting event, party, and then work."
If I could change one thing about Williams, I'd "cut down the preppy atmosphere a bit."
The three things every student at Williams should do before graduating are "hike up a mountain," "take a tutorial," and "either take or audit Art History 101 and 102."

Worcester Polytechnic Institute

Address: 100 Institute Road
Worcester, MA 01609
Phone: 5-8-831-5286
E-mail address:
admissions@wpi.edu
Web site URL: www.wpi.edu
Year Founded: 1865
Private or Public: Private
Religious Affiliation: None
Location: Suburban
Number of Applicants: 5,698
Percent Accepted: 66%
**Percent Accepted who
enroll:** 22%
Number Entering: 805
**Number of Transfers
Accepted each Year:** 79
Middle 50% SAT range:
M: 630–710, CR 560–670,
Wr: 560–660
Middle 50% ACT range:
25–31
**Early admission program
EA/ED/None:** EA
**Percentage accepted
through EA or ED:** 82%

EA and ED deadline: 1-Nov
Regular Deadline: 1-Feb
Application Fee: $60
**Full time Undergraduate
enrollment:** 3,016
Total enrollment: 4,157
Percent Male: 74%
Percent Female: 26%
**Total Percent Minority or
Unreported:** 12%
Percent African-American:
2%
**Percent Asian/Pacific
Islander:** 6%
Percent Hispanic: 4%
Percent Native-American:
0%
Percent International: 7%
**Percent in-state/out of
state:** 50%/50%
Percent from Public HS:
66%
Retention Rate: 94%
Graduation Rate 4-year:
63%
Graduation Rate 6-year: 64%

**Percent Undergraduates
in On-campus housing:**
59%
**Number of official organized
extracurricular
organizations:** 200
3 Most popular majors:
Computer Science, Electrical
Engineering, Mechanical
Engineering
Student/Faculty ratio:
13:1
Average Class Size: 2 to 9
**Percent of students going to
grad school:** 29%
Tuition and Fees: $34,300
**In State Tuition and Fees if
different:** No difference
Cost for Room and Board:
$10,410
**Percent receiving financial
aid out of those who apply,
first year:** 96%
**Percent receiving financial
aid among all students:**
94%

W PI is a small polytechnic institute located in Worcester, the heart of Massachusetts. This engineering haven follows a mission of educating its students on practical and theoretical levels and providing a well-rounded academic program that is sure to make future employers take notice.

Study, Study, Study!

The school operates on a system that is different from most. Instead of semesters, there are four seven-week terms, two in the fall and two in the spring. Each term students take three courses. In addition to their major requirements, every student is expected to complete nine credits or units worth of projects: a sufficiency project requiring five related courses and a project or seminar in the humanities area; a social entrepreneurship project requiring a project relating to solving a need in society via technology and science; and finally a major-qualifying project, which is a team-based project in your own major field of study. While students claim that the

projects are not difficult to finish and are enjoyable hands-on experiences, they also say that it is a good idea to get the projects not in your major out of the way early on. Electrical and computer engineering, computer science, and mechanical engineering are the most popular majors on campus. The students also mentioned Interactive Media and Games Development as one of the unique majors—one student explained, "it's basically majoring in video games." As fun as that sounds, students warn that when you come to WPI, you'd better be prepared to put in the work, no matter what you major in. The terms go by quickly and it's important to keep up with each of your classes so as not to get overwhelmed. Also be prepared to spend many hours at the lab. The Chemical Engineering major has a reputation for an overwhelming workload, and "Chemistry of Thermodynamics" and "Calculus 3" also have reputations for being difficult classes. But don't let the difficulty scare you. WPI has a student-friendly grading system with grades being A, B, C, and NR (No Record.)

This means if you get below a C, the class does not count toward your overall GPA and it's as if you never took it.

Classes are generally small with two to seven being the most frequent class size, exceptions being of course the survey courses, which can have over 50 people in a lecture. Despite their small size, the competition for a spot in a class is not a problem, and if you want to get into a class you can always turn to the professor who is likely to sign a permission sheet letting you into the class. The professors get equal praise with the classes; one senior enthused, "The unique thing [about WPI] is that the professors are extremely, extremely helpful; they will know you by your first name."

Students generally praise the academics at WPI, citing the hands-on experiences involved in projects as the best sources of learning. Classes can also be fun and hands-on, such as the Food Engineering class which teaches you all about food structure and preparation. The final project is to make something and bring it in, and students get pretty creative—some make their own chocolate from scratch or even brew their own beer. The school's focus is on technology and science, which is great for those who are sure that they want to pursue those fields. However, one student who decided that he was into humanities late in his college career complained that it was impossible for him to pursue it at WPI since the departments are small and not up to par.

Party: Calculators Optional
Students unanimously proclaim that Greek life is the hub of social life on campus. About 28 percent of males and 30 percent of females join either a fraternity or a sorority, but students commented that it can feel like much more of the student body is involved in the Greek community. While most people drink on campus there is no pressure to do so. One student explained that "there are a lot of people who are not involved in the whole party scene at all and they have their own social views," citing the game developers club and science fiction society as examples of groups that prefer to have their own gatherings. The school itself also provides entertainment options with venues such as the on-campus pub The Goat's Head and Gompei's Gutters, an on-campus bowling alley. Those few who wish to wander off campus and explore the Worcester party scene have the option of clubs and bars near Main

Street such as Irish Times and Club Red. Students warn, however, that there is very little to do in Worcester.

There is a stereotype that is associated with technical schools. As one student explained, "People tend to associate the students with the geeky look, with the thick glasses and a part on the side, but [at WPI] it's not a majority at all." But another confessed, "We're a little bit geeky," citing frequent math and science jokes that one hears on campus. Still, there are a diverse variety of students on campus, including a relatively generous community of international students that makes up a little over 8 percent of the student body. It is important to note that women are a minority at the school, making up only 29 percent of the student body. A senior girl, however, described it as not a major problem. "When you're a freshman it's a little bit awkward," she said, and while it takes some getting used to, in the end she reported, "It's not a big deal at all. We're all engineers." Another unifying characteristic is that all students are very friendly and in the freshman year the residence halls and classes offer plenty of opportunities to make good friends.

Is There Room for Me?
For the 50 percent of the student body who lives on campus the options are pretty standard. There are seven dorms in addition to an apartment complex and four smaller houses of 10 to 20 residents. Among these, East Hall is the newest dorm on campus and it's also the most coveted residence for upperclassmen. Due to space restrictions it can be pretty difficult to get into a dorm via the school's lottery system, which is based on seniority.

While the campus is considered safe, the general area outside of campus can be quite sketchy, even dangerous. This can lead to a college bubble feel on campus. At the same time, students don't mind much as they proudly proclaim that WPI is the most beautiful campus among Worcester's numerous colleges. Many like to hang out at the student center, the central hangout spot featuring pool tables, foosball tables, and a food court. When hunger strikes, Morgan Commons serves as the main dining hall. It is rated above average but has a tendency to get monotonous. Other options include a Dunkin' Donuts on campus, a convenience store, and Goat's Head, which doubles as a restaurant. For off-campus options, students recommend Highland Street, which offers many restaurants such as Sahara and Sole Proprietor and several coffee shops such as the Bean Counter.

WPI Spirit

Outside of class there is no lack of activities for the students of WPI. Among the 200 registered student organizations, there is a wide range of options including drama, a robotic team, and *The Towers*, the school newspaper that is beginning to grow in popularity. Athletics also have a great following on campus. One senior explained that there is "wicked lots of school spirit" and "almost fanatical support" for the sports teams, basketball, and football being the most popular. For the less athletically gifted there is the option of join-

ing intramural sport teams, which are not as popular but still claim a presence on campus.

> "The unique thing [about WPI] is that the professors are extremely, extremely helpful; they will know you by your first name."

With small classes, great professors, and a pretty campus, students generally report being happy with their choice of WPI. The projects focusing on hands-on work further the school's goal of preparing its students for real world jobs. One student assured, "It's an engineer's dream."—*Dorota Poplawska*

FYI
If you come to WPI, you'd better bring "a calculator."
What is the typical weekend schedule? "homework, homework and more homework, going out to party and hanging out with friend."
If I could change one thing about WPI, I'd "improve the male-to-female ratio."
Three things every student at WPI should do before graduating are "see the gold head trophy which makes rare appearances, jump through the fountain and go abroad or away for a project."

Michigan

Albion College

Address: 611 East Porter Street Albion, MI 49224
Phone: 517-629-0321
E-mail address: admissions@albion.edu
Web site URL: www.albion.edu
Year Founded: 1835
Private or Public: Private
Religious Affiliation: Methodist
Location: Suburban
Number of Applicants: 1,958
Percent Accepted: 81%
Percent Accepted who enroll: 30%
Number Entering: 484
Number of Transfers Accepted each Year: 63
Middle 50% SAT range: M: 500–650, CR: 560–630, Wr: 500–630
Middle 50% ACT range: 23–27
Early admission program EA/ED/None: EA

Percentage accepted through EA or ED: Unreported
EA and ED deadline: 1-Dec
Regular Deadline: 1-May
Application Fee: $20
Full time Undergraduate enrollment: 1,860
Total enrollment: 1,860
Percent Male: 48%
Percent Female: 52%
Total Percent Minority or Unreported: 13%
Percent African-American: 3%
Percent Asian/Pacific Islander: 2%
Percent Hispanic: 1%
Percent Native-American: <1%
Percent International: 1%
Percent in-state/out of state: 91%/9%
Percent from Public HS: 75%
Retention Rate: 86%

Graduation Rate 4-year: 63%
Graduation Rate 6-year: 71%
Percent Undergraduates in On-campus housing: 88%
Number of official organized extracurricular organizations: 110
3 Most popular majors: Biology, Economics, Psychology
Student/Faculty ratio: 14:1
Average Class Size: 15
Percent of students going to grad school: 38%
Tuition and Fees: $28,880
In State Tuition and Fees if different: No difference
Cost for Room and Board: $8,190
Percent receiving financial aid out of those who apply, first year: 85%
Percent receiving financial aid among all students: 94%

Envision approximately 1,860 students crammed into beautiful, but overpopulated, gothic buildings. Everything is surrounded by large trees. This is Albion College, set within the small city of Albion, Michigan. With its newly renovated science complex, a comprehensive First-Year Experience Program, and a recurring place on *U.S. News & World Report*'s list of the 40 "Best Value" colleges, this midwestern school provides students a strong liberal arts education with all the benefits of a small college.

No-Nonsense Academics

One student boldly remarked, "Albion is a no-nonsense school." Most students stick to standard majors such as economics, psychology, pre-med, and chemistry. The majority of the atypical classes are religious, one of the

more popular of which is called "Death and Dying." The classes are also competitive, in particular the math and science classes; to do well in physical or organic chemistry, you should expect at least 25 hours of studying a week.

In the Albion system, you need 32 credits to graduate, including major and more general liberal arts requirements. Instead of simply creating distributional requirements, each class at Albion is assigned a "mode" and a "category." "Modes"—or the approach to the subject—include Artistic Creation and Analysis, Historical and Cultural Analysis, and Textual Analysis. "Categories"—or the actual subject the class falls under—include Environmental Studies, Gender Studies, and Global Studies. In addition, all freshmen participate in the First-Year Experience, designed to ease students' academic and social transition into college. The program includes Orientation, Common Reading Experience, as well as a set of seminars on topics ranging from "Art in the Environment" to "Vietnam: Then and Now."

Albion also has a few more specific academic programs. One of the best known programs at Albion, the Carl A. Gerstacker Institute for Professional Management, is an honors business program which involves 10 semesters in four years—seven semesters of on-campus study, one summer term after sophomore year, and two internships during the fall term of junior year and the summer after junior year. Many choices for these internships are located in Europe. For students interested in political science, education, law, or community service, Albion also offers the Gerald R. Ford Institute for Public Policy and Service. Founded by the former president, the Institute allows students to pursue a major of their choice while taking classes in fields such as ethics, public policy, and government.

Fight for Your Right to Party

Historically, Albion has been known for a large party scene. But Albion officials have cracked down on the party scene in the College, doling out $500 fines to underage drinkers. There have been problems of overdrinking in the past mainly because a small group of students overdo it and, as one Albion student said, "screwed it up for the rest of us." With its isolated location, life at Albion can get monotonous, leading to occasional problems with drug use. Sometimes, though, the isolation can pay off: during the annual "Senior Week" event at the end of the year, Albion students compete in a drinking Olympics in a barn out of town—not your typical end-of-year venue.

"Albion is a no-nonsense school."

Other than the occasional novel event, one of the drawbacks of the remote campus is that many students have a difficult time finding interesting activities. But with the city of Jackson nearby and Ann Arbor less than an hour away, there are plenty of options for the many students who decide to keep cars on campus.

Fraternity parties epitomize the social scene at Albion. Since the student population is generally friendly and outgoing, the frat scene is more open than at other schools, including allowing everyone at the parties. However, the Greek life at Albion has felt the impact of the crackdown on parties, with some students and officials citing the fraternities and sororities as a major source of drinking. But other students are reluctant to call for the elimination of fraternities because many age-old traditions unique to Albion are connected to the Greek system. At least one student expressed a fear about the effect on social life in general, saying that the party scene revolves around the fraternity houses.

Living in Style

Living arrangements are standard for all four years at Albion, with most students living in the dormitories the whole time. The dorm rooms are assigned by seniority, though juniors and seniors sometimes move off campus into neighboring apartments. Freshmen are housed in either Wesley Hall or Seaton Hall; RAs live in all dormitories, and alcohol is prohibited to those who are underage. It depends, however, on how strict the RA is—some supervisors have been known to be lax about the rules.

The dorms are definitely not the only buildings that will catch your eye at Albion. The multimillion-dollar science complex, finished in 2006, is an impressive addition to the campus. Another more noticeable feature of Albion is the quad; located between all the class buildings, the quad is a great place to hang around during the warmer months. The Nature Center is also worth noting for its beautiful landscape. Thought to be the most beautiful spot on campus by many of the students, it is an "unspoiled habitat."

The dining halls are famed for their relatively good cuisine and easily managed meal plans allowing students to pick how many meals they want per week. But be warned that you will have to maintain regular eating patterns, with limited hours. Since the school is relatively small, the only times the dining halls stay open late is during finals. Also, one unique rule is that off-campus residents are not allowed in the dining halls, but with many good restaurants in the town, students have other options when they want to eat out. However when students do venture off campus, they usually try to be back before dark since the surrounding area is not particularly safe.

Extra Awesome Extracurricular

Albion College hosts extracurricular fun for everyone in many forms. Although it is a

Division III school, sports are very popular—one student estimated that "half of the campus plays a sport." Basketball and football are the most popular spectator events, but students are known for being fickle fans: at times, they rally in full force for Albion, while other times they skip homecoming games entirely to watch other local rivalries such as the University of Michigan versus Michigan State football game. Intramural sports, including soccer, basketball, volleyball, dodgeball, hockey, and tennis, are a must at this school. The IM fields are given great care and the games are known to get very competitive.

There are also some nonathletic clubs that are very popular. The most recognized are "Break the Silence" (the Gay and Lesbian Awareness Group) and the Medieval Club, which puts on mock sword fights and archery competitions.

Overall, Albion is a small school filled with friendly students. Despite the school's isolation, the campus is a beautiful and safe place where students easily become very personal with their professors and are well-prepared for life outside of college. Ultimately, Albion is a great place for students who want to have fun, but at the same time are willing to work hard.—*Benjamin Dzialo*

FYI

If you come to Albion, you'd better bring "a friendly, outgoing attitude."

What's the typical weekend schedule? "Friday: No class, or class finishes early. Workout, nap, or do nothing with your friends until you start drinking, which will last all night (or you study). Saturday: Maybe get some work done, typically don't do anything; partying at night. Sunday: Cram day. Wake up late, study all day if need be."

If I could change one thing about Albion, I'd "fix the town—people wouldn't drink so much if the town wasn't falling apart, and there was more to do."

Three things every student at Albion should do before graduating are "attend a talk by at least one of the great speakers Albion brings in, walk in the Whitehouse Nature Center in the winter, and talk with a professor outside of class."

Alma College

Address: 614 West Superior Street, Alma, MI 48801-1599

Phone: 989-463-7139

E-mail address: admissions@alma.edu

Web site URL: www.alma.edu

Year Founded: 1886

Private or Public: Private

Religious Affiliation: Presbyterian

Location: Suburban

Number of Applicants: 2,044

Percent Accepted: 73%

Percent Accepted who enroll: 26%

Number Entering: 423

Number of Transfers Accepted each Year: 59

Middle 50% SAT range: M: 520–668, CR: 498–665, Wr: 503–623

Middle 50% ACT range: 21–27

Early admission program EA/ED/None: None

Percentage accepted through EA or ED: NA

EA and ED deadline: NA

Regular Deadline: Rolling

Application Fee: $25

Full time Undergraduate enrollment: 1,384

Total enrollment: 1,384

Percent Male: 45%

Percent Female: 55%

Total Percent Minority or Unreported: 8%

Percent African-American: 2%

Percent Asian/Pacific Islander: 1%

Percent Hispanic: 2%

Percent Native-American: <1%

Percent International: 1%

Percent in-state/out of state: 96%/4%

Percent from Public HS: 91%

Retention Rate: 76%

Graduation Rate 4-year: 60%

Graduation Rate 6-year: 68%

Percent Undergraduates in On-campus housing: 88%

Number of official organized extracurricular organizations: 75

3 Most popular majors: Biology, Business, Kinesiology

Student/Faculty ratio: 13:1

Average Class Size: 15

Percent of students going to grad school: Unreported

Tuition and Fees: $249,850

In State Tuition and Fees if different: No difference

Cost for Room and Board: $8,120.00

Percent receiving financial aid out of those who apply, first year: 83%

Percent receiving financial aid among all students: 99%

The comfortable campus of Alma College can feel isolated at times, but students report that the remote location often helps them more fully assimilate into "the college experience." Characterized by its small size and convivial atmosphere, Alma provides students with the opportunity to receive a well-rounded education and prepares them to venture into the professional world.

A Liberal Arts Tradition

One Alma student describes her school's philosophy as "a little bit of everything;" in keeping with the liberal arts philosophy, there are significant general education requirements needed to complete a bachelor's degree. Students must pass composition, math, and foreign language classes, as well as distribution requirements including humanities, literature, history, social, natural and physical sciences, the arts, and more. Though one student said "it is a little hard to fit [all the requirements] in," most agree that they are necessary components of a college education.

To graduate with a bachelor's degree, students are required to take a total of 136 credits. They also must complete two spring term courses. The spring term is a month from April to May when students are able to take classes in more creative and hands-on areas. One of these courses must be an "S" course, which draws on an international, interdisciplinary perspective and often includes travel.

The most popular majors at Alma are also some of its strongest, including business administration, education, and those in the health professions. All of these prepare students very well for graduate school in medicine or law, or for professional work right out of college, and are consequently accompanied by a significant amount of homework. The curricular options for fine and performing arts are very strong, especially for a school of Alma's size. Students appreciate the training, though—as one said of the classes, "They are very challenging, but in a good way." Though work is difficult, they also report a low level of competition and believe that the on-campus atmosphere is generally conducive to doing well.

Students appreciate that the small size of their school keeps class size down and allows for a lot more interaction with their professors, who are highly attentive and devoted to teaching. One student said she appreciated "being able to go see your professor and having them know who you are." Several professors also write their own textbooks, and students agree that because of the intimate atmosphere, science demonstrations are especially "cool." One biology professor routinely "throws balls representing molecules around the room to illustrate a point." A town the size of Alma also means that professors make up a large proportion of the population. "My professor for calculus, Nyman, was the mayor of Alma," said one student, "and he cracks a lot of jokes—while still getting enough information through to my brain that it hurts after class."

Inventive Activities

Although the small size of both the college and the surrounding town leaves students without a huge number of options for the weekends, most agree that those who are inventive will find plenty to occupy them. The student body mixes and freely associates among itself. With approximately 1,300 students, in general it is "super easy to meet people—everyone is very friendly. Groups form, but they are always open to new people." Although many students join fraternities or sororities, students agree that these "don't control social life," and the parties are attended by a variety of different people. However, the frats are limited by the administration to only one alcoholic beverage party per month, and kegs are officially barred from the campus. The president is actively trying to abolish the Greek system, but one student said that "if that ever happened, I think a lot of people would leave Alma, because of the fact that there would then be NOTHING to do." Students note that in general there is a lot of hooking up, but a lack of outing destinations makes dating somewhat rare. When they do plan dates, students often go to restaurants in Mt. Pleasant, followed by bowling or ice skating.

In the rest of their free time, Alma students can see live shows at the Heritage Center, go shopping, and check out the restaurants in Mt. Pleasant (15 minutes away). Some students also choose to attend larger parties at nearby Central Michigan and Michigan State University. Students work out and play sports at the newly refurbished recreation center. And as one student noted, "Going to Wal-Mart is always an option."

Extracurricular groups and clubs also inspire devotion among the students, and many students come to be identified with the things they do outside of class. One student estimates that she spends 15 hours a week with her dance company. Musical and dramatic groups are equally rigorous, and students extol the "consistently fabulous" performances. The choirs at Alma are particularly popular, with nearly 15 percent of the student body participating in the Women's Glee Club, the College Chorale, or the Alma Choir. Community service is a common activity as well. Some students work on-campus jobs, but a few work in the surrounding community.

The Alma Scots sports teams are strong for a small school, although not usually a central part of student life. The volleyball team is especially good and recently won a state championship. Football, soccer, and golf also fare well, and games are "decently attended." Many students take full advantage of the recreation center, and both varsity and nonvarsity athletes play on the "tons" of intramural sports teams.

Living Cozily

Alma's pleasant brick campus makes its students feel "cozy." Although the buildings are not particularly unique architecturally, they are well-maintained, and the facilities are good. The campus' central location means that students often take full advantage of its proximity to neighboring cities and other schools. However, one student answers the question of whether there are enough things to do nearby the campus with a resounding "NO!"

Many students live in the dorms all four years—only upperclassmen may move off campus, and their ability to do so is regulated by a lottery system. Some dorms are coed, some are not—"however you want it to be," said one student—and though "the underclassmen dorms are kind of old, that's not to say they're not spacious." Freshmen have residential advisers, who are "pretty good about handling things." Some students opt to live in themed dorms (athletic, band, etc.) and there is a service house, as well as Greek housing.

The dining options are cited as adequate, though some students have issues with the fact that they have to apply to different meal plans and can end up being denied. However, there are opportunities throughout the day for unused meal credits to be reclaimed. Vegetarian options are plentiful, and the dining halls are clean and well supplied. Some seating arrangements are fairly established, but Alma's amiable nature means that no tensions result from this stability. As one student described, "Sororities and athletic teams usually sit in the same spot, but they'd gladly move if you were there—or sit with you."

> **"[It's] the perfect place for me. I didn't expect how much I'd not miss home."**

Alma tends to attract a vast majority of its students from Michigan, many from the suburbs of Detroit or Grand Rapids. Although many fit the bill of "the general stereotype of a middle-class white kid," this doesn't mean that everyone brings the same viewpoint. As one student said, "Though Alma isn't very culturally diverse, it is very diverse in personality." Students also believe that "there is a lot of mixing" among different social groups, and social marginalization or isolation is rare. One student noted, "[It's] super easy to meet people; everyone is very friendly."

Overall, Alma students are at school there because it offers what they want from college academics, as well as a social and congenial student body. One student said that it was "the perfect place for me. I didn't expect how much I'd not miss home." Isolated though it may be, Alma offers students the chance to live and participate fully in the collegiate environment, and to learn skills that directly enhance their futures.—*David Carpman*

FYI
If you come to Alma, you'd better bring "a car."
What is the typical weekend schedule? "Sleep until brunch at 11:30, rock climb, work, study, watch movies, play video games, party, and go to sleep around 2 a.m."
If I could change one thing about Alma, "I'd move it to a city where there are more things to do."
Three things every student at Alma should do before graduating are "go to Bar Night, go to a percussion performance, climb the rock wall."

Hope College

Address: 69 East 10th St. Holland, MI 49422
Phone: 616-395-7850
E-mail address: admissions@hope.edu
Web site URL: www.hope.edu
Year Founded: 1862
Private or Public: Private
Religious Affiliation: Reformed Church
Location: Suburban
Number of Applicants: 2,748
Percent Accepted: 83%
Percent Accepted who enroll: 35%
Number Entering: 799
Number of Transfers Accepted each Year: 57
Middle 50% SAT range: M: 540–660, CR: 530–660, Wr: Unreported
Middle 50% ACT range: 23–29
Early admission program EA/ED/None: None

Percentage accepted through EA or ED: NA
EA and ED deadline: NA
Regular Deadline: Rolling
Application Fee: $35
Full time Undergraduate enrollment: 3,226
Total enrollment: 6,391
Percent Male: 41%
Percent Female: 59%
Total Percent Minority or Unreported: 2%
Percent African-American: 2%
Percent Asian/Pacific Islander: 2%
Percent Hispanic: 3%
Percent Native-American: <1%
Percent International: 1%
Percent in-state/out of state: 70%/30%
Percent from Public HS: 88%
Retention Rate: 88%
Graduation Rate 4-year: 62%

Graduation Rate 6-year: 71%
Percent Undergraduates in On-campus housing: 78%
Number of official organized extracurricular organizations: 67
3 Most popular majors: Business/Commerce, General English and Literature, General Psychology
Student/Faculty ratio: 12:1
Average Class Size: 10 to 19
Percent of students going to grad school: 29%
Tuition and Fees: $24,780
In State Tuition and Fees if different: No difference
Cost for Room and Board: $7,650
Percent receiving financial aid out of those who apply, first year: 97%
Percent receiving financial aid among all students: 88%

S tudents at Hope College come together for many reasons. In the bleachers and on the sidelines, they all cheer on their remarkably successful athletic teams. Walking across their pine tree-lined campus, they live up to their reputation of Midwestern friendliness by saying "hi" to everyone they meet. And in chapel on Sundays, many students at this Christian Reformed college come together to celebrate their common religious values. Located near the shores of Lake Michigan in the heart of pretty downtown Holland, Hope College provides its students with solid academic programs, the personal attention only possible at a small school, and a warm social atmosphere, all structured around a core of Christian values.

Common Values

Spirituality is important to students at Hope, and religion influences nearly every aspect of campus life to some degree. Still, students maintain that nonreligious students are not pressured to participate in religious activities, which are all optional. As one junior said, "At Hope you can be as strong or as loose in your faith as you want." One of the most popular religious events on campus is the Sunday night "singing-and-celebration" service called the "Gathering." Such a great number of students pack the chapel for the Gathering that all the seats fill up, and late arrivers are left to sit in the aisles or stand in the back of the building. The Gathering is just one of the times when religion unites the student body. Groups of Hope students travel all over the world every spring break on mission trips; one junior who spent last spring break building homes for a deaf community in Jamaica described it as one of the best experiences of his life. A soccer player said his coach sometimes uses faith in his coaching style. Religion even makes its way into the classroom; according to one senior, "Some professors do incorporate [religion] in their classes." While nonreligious students are definitely in the minority at Hope, they are not excluded from campus life. A nonreligious student commented that most students come from a Christian background and are "open and not afraid to profess their opinions. However, they are usually not that overbearing."

Students say that the typical Hope student is Christian, usually conservative, and often from Michigan or the greater Midwest. One student said she liked that Hope students are "generally well-rounded and geared toward future goals." The student body is predominantly white. However, Hope, in addition to its Dutch population, also has a substantial Hispanic segment. Attempts have been made to increase the school's diversity, and a senior said she was "surprised at how many students are from out of the state and even the country." However, a sophomore expressed frustration that because so many students have similar, religiously conservative backgrounds, they tend to "generate the same old boring views and stances on subjects." Despite this, he said that there is still a substantial number of "more open-minded" people on campus.

Hitting the Books

Students at Hope universally agree that the best parts of their academic experience are the close relationships they build with the professors, who teach all their classes. One sophomore praised how "available and flexible" they are to student needs. Professors at Hope frequently go to sporting events to cheer on their students and often invite their classes to their homes at the end of the semester for dinner parties. Many students become so close with their professors that they keep in contact even after their classes are over.

Part of the reason students and teachers are able to form such close bonds centers on the small size of classes at Hope. The average class has 20 to 25 students in it. Many upper-level classes are even smaller, allowing students to get personal attention and sometimes even giving them the opportunity to get involved with their professor's research. One junior said he liked Hope's small classes because they gave him the confidence to "be more bold to ask questions" of the professor in front of the group. The small class size does cause some problems, however, since it often becomes difficult for students to get into popular classes that quickly fill up. Students in popular majors sometimes have difficulty getting into courses necessary for graduation and end up needing to either plead to the dean for class admission, or to stay on campus for a summer term in order to graduate on time.

Popular majors at Hope include biology and education, and both of these departments have excellent programs. Students majoring in education get to start doing fieldwork in local classrooms as early as their freshman year. One sophomore said that Hope "prides itself on its sciences," and the humanities majors are often less intense. Hope recently renovated its science buildings, and the premed program has a reputation for getting its students into selective medical schools. Biology is considered one of Hope's most challenging majors, as is religion. Students interested in studying religion benefit from the Western Theological Seminary—right next to Hope—and in fact, every year several students enroll in this seminary after graduation. A junior estimated that Hope students study about three hours a day; students in difficult majors put in a few more hours. Students who want a less-intense academic experience typically major in communications, although there is also substantial interest in broadcast journalism, public relations, and advertising. Academic requirements at Hope include taking several credits of religion and completing at least a 200-level foreign-language class, a class on cultural diversity and a class called "Health Dynamics," which one athlete said "is a joke. It's basically gym class, and even if you play a varsity sport, you still have to take it." Still, most students agree that the annoyance created by some of their distributional requirements and unsuccessful class registration is a small price to pay for the excellent education they receive at Hope.

Kicking Back

When they're not studying, students at Hope enjoy a wide range of social activities. Only a third to a half of the campus drinks, so while a more traditional "party scene" exists for those students who want it, nondrinkers have plenty of social options. The Student Activity Committee (SAC) sponsors $2 movie nights and brings in comedians, magicians, and bands to give performances open to the student body. The campus itself is dry, so technically no alcohol is allowed in the dorms. One junior said that while RAs can be "pretty strict" about this rule at times, people can generally get away with drinking in their dorms as long as everything stays quiet and hidden. A significant proportion of the student body is Greek, although there are few national frats or sororities on campus. Most of the Greek organizations are branches of smaller, local fraternities. They often hold theme parties, but not all of these are open to the whole student body—many are open only to other Greeks. Parties are often also held in some of the off-campus houses, especially those where members of the soccer and football teams live. Upperclassmen who want to enjoy a beer in a slightly classier atmosphere favor the New Holland Brewery, especially on Wednesday "Stein Nights," when students who bring their own beer stein can get it filled up at a discounted price.

> **"The legend goes that you'll find your soul mate at Hope."**

Walking around campus on the average Saturday night, you'll probably see a lot of good-looking people. Hope students are an attractive bunch on the whole. As one student said, "Whenever my friends come to visit from other schools, they always say how hot the girls here are." Since Hope students are over two-thirds female, this seems like pretty good odds for the guys. But Hope isn't a school for someone looking for a lot of random hookups; many students are involved in serious relationships. "The legend goes that you'll find your soul mate at Hope," said one junior in a committed relationship, and reportedly a lot of Hope students end up marrying others from their school. Students say that Hope is a friendly place. "You could go up to anyone and say hello," according to one student. Partly because of the school's small size, there aren't many cliques, and people tend to have a lot of friends of different ages.

Housing in Holland
Hope students typically live in dorms for their freshman and sophomore years. Students live in double rooms on single-sex hallways and share common bathrooms. "The dorms are overall well-kept and comfortable," said one sophomore, although all the buildings have different reputations. In addition to the coed buildings, there is one all-male dorm and three all-female dorms, including Dykstra, "where all the guys go to scope for women," according to one male student. Kollen Hall is the most social dorm; "It's the party dorm, the loudest and craziest," said one former resident. Voorhees Hall houses "a lot of artsy types," while international students tend to cluster in Scott. By junior year, most Hope students move into the "cottages." These are small houses on the perimeter of campus where groups of about six students live; they are still considered "on-campus housing" and have RAs, but they have their own kitchens and living rooms. The cottages are "a fun alternative to big-school living," according to one upperclassman. Seniors often move off campus, either to houses or to apartments in downtown Holland. In total, there are 11 residence halls, 15 apartment buildings and 63 cottages.

Hope's campus is small. "You can walk all the way around it in 15 minutes," a junior said. Most academic buildings are in the center of the campus, while the dorms and the cottages are around the perimeter. Many of the historic buildings are red brick, while some of the newer buildings, like the recently constructed science center, are more modern. One senior raved that the campus is "so cute! Hope is big on preserving the old buildings it does have, but also on adding new buildings as the college expands."

Dining hall food is "pretty good" according to most students. Freshmen often eat in Phelps Hall, which supposedly has the worst food on campus; but upperclassmen enjoy eating the much tastier food in Cook Hall, which typically serves a choice of several entrees every night, including vegetarian options. When students get bored of the dining halls, downtown Holland has a variety of unique restaurants less than a five-minute walk from campus. Windmill's is a favorite for breakfast, and students also enjoy relaxing and studying in coffee shops such as Java Joe's (which has a stage where bands perform) and Lemonjello's (pronounced le-MON-jel-lo's by those in the know).

Sports and Spirit
Students leave campus and go into Holland for more than food and coffee, however. Faith-based community service is extremely popular at the school. One junior said there are "a ton of opportunities to work in church soup kitchens or tutor kids or anything like that." Many students also spend their free time playing intramural sports ranging from inner-tube water polo to Ultimate Frisbee. When the weather is warm, students make the short trip down to the shores of beautiful Lake Michigan to hang out on the beach. Hope's Division III varsity athletic teams have had excellent records in the past few years. Both men's and women's basketball and soccer teams are extremely competitive and draw massive support from both students and members of the community who come out to watch.

The crowds are in large part due to the high level of school spirit at Hope. A combination of factors, including the small size of the student body and the shared core of Christian values, bind students closely to their school. "If I could do it all over again I would definitely, definitely choose Hope," one junior said. "It's been a place where I can get a great education while strengthening my faith. I've gotten to meet some really great people and made friendships I think are going to last for a long time."—*Katherine Kirby Smith*

FYI

If you come to Hope College, you'd better bring "a Nalgene bottle—everybody has one here."

What's a typical weekend schedule? "Friday, hang out with friends or go to a house party at night; Saturday, sleep until noon, study, go see a sporting event, then do something social or go to another party; Sunday, get up early and go to church, eat downtown at the Windmill, study, and go to the Gathering at night."

If I could change one thing about Hope College, I'd "loosen up the housing policy and make it easier to register for classes."

Three things every student at Hope College should do before they graduate are "attend Gathering, go on a mission trip for spring break and go streaking on a Chapel Run."

Kalamazoo College

Address: 1200 Academy Street Kalamazoo, MI 49006

Phone: 269-337-7166

E-mail address: admiss@kzoo.edu

Web site URL: www.kzoo.edu

Year Founded: 1833

Private or Public: Private

Religious Affiliation: None

Location: Urban

Number of Applicants: 2,092

Percent Accepted: 63%

Percent Accepted who enroll: 27%

Number Entering: 363

Number of Transfers Accepted each Year: 6

Middle 50% SAT range: M: 570–680, CR: 580–690, Wr: Unreported

Middle 50% ACT range: 26–30

Early admission program EA/ED/None: ED

Percentage accepted through EA or ED: Unreported

EA and ED deadline: 10-Nov

Regular Deadline: 1-Feb

Application Fee: $35

Full time Undergraduate enrollment: 1,340

Total enrollment: 2,748

Percent Male: 42%

Percent Female: 58%

Total Percent Minority or Unreported: 9%

Percent African-American: 4%

Percent Asian/Pacific Islander: 6%

Percent Hispanic: 4%

Percent Native-American: <1%

Percent International: 1%

Percent in-state/out of state: 69%/31%

Percent from Public HS: 85%

Retention Rate: 91%

Graduation Rate 4-year: 70%

Graduation Rate 6-year: 74%

Percent Undergraduates in On-campus housing: 77%

Number of official organized extracurricular organizations: 50

3 Most popular majors: Economics, English Language and Literature, Psychology

Student/Faculty ratio: 13:1

Average Class Size: 10 to 19

Percent of students going to grad school: Unreported

Tuition and Fees: $30,723

In State Tuition and Fees if different: No difference

Cost for Room and Board: $7,443

Percent receiving financial aid out of those who apply, first year: 98%

Percent receiving financial aid among all students: 98%

Y ou go *where*?" Students at Kalamazoo College are used to hearing this when they tell people where they go to school. First, there is the hurdle of realizing that Kalamazoo is in fact a real place, not an exotic landscape imagined by Dr. Seuss. Next, people add, "Oh, you mean you go to Western." Kalamazoo College, right in the heart of the bustling and very real city of Kalamazoo, Michigan, is not in fact connected to Western Michigan University, a large state school. K-Zoo, as students affectionately refer to it, is actually a small haven in the midst of a busy city, a community of only 1,340 scholars committed to knowing every face and every name. Despite, or perhaps because of, Kalamazoo's relative obscurity and small size, the school creates an environment where students are encouraged to try everything and stretch beyond the limits of what they think they can do.

The K-Zoo K-Plan

Catchy name aside, this academic program is renowned for its broad spectrum of classes and its emphasis on experimentation. The K-Plan encompasses, but is not limited to, classes chosen from such disparate fields as physical education, foreign language, math, world religion, and a first-quarter freshman literature seminar. Although the task of completing these requirements may seem Herculean, one freshman reassured prospective students that "the K-Plan is not strenuous to fulfill." In fact, she said, "I feel like I'm getting a broad education—I know they don't want me to limit myself." Along with the importance placed on taking a wide variety of classes, comes the out-of-the ordinary schedule. "Kalamazoo is on the quarter system. We start later, in mid-September, and we end in early June," one student explained. The fact that classes only last for 10 weeks as opposed to the typical college schedule of 15, makes the experience "really intense," said one student. However, students appreciate the fact that they can "really dive into a subject" since they take a course load of about three classes rather than the four or five one might find at a college with the standard schedule. Because of the shorter, more compressed plan, students find that they get to know their classmates and professors very well. Students reported no classes larger than around 25–30 people, which significantly contributes to the sense of having "personal relationships with professors." One student specifically commended the foreign language department on a French class of only nine people. She remarked that the small class size made it easy to "converse and not get lost in the crowd."

The foreign language department goes beyond small class sizes at Kalamazoo. It is such a large and well-established department that 80 percent of students study abroad during their time at K-Zoo. This staggering number is a nod not only to foreign languages themselves, but also to other very popular majors such as economics and international business and relations. Students say that the Center for International Programs is a widely used resource on campus and note that the staff is very helpful with

transferring financial aid. The experimentation inherent in the classes students are required to take is mirrored in the popularity of studying abroad, and students appreciate the "balance" between the familiar and the new to which they are exposed at K-Zoo.

Going to the Zoo . . .

. . . Really requires a car. The so-called "K-bubble" of the college is comforting in its very small spread, but when students want to get out into town, they say it can be difficult to find transportation. While The Rave, a theater that sells $5 movie tickets, is within walking distance, students recommend the Hot Spot Shuttle to get to the mall. The school itself is "pretty self-contained, which is kind of a drag," lamented one student. Still, students appreciate the school's attempts to reach out into the urban community with programs such as Farms to "K" and tutoring at local inner city elementary schools. The Farms to "K" program encourages everyone in the city to eat locally and practice conservation. One student said that despite the somewhat isolated campus, the students "reach out to greater Kalamazoo— K-Zoo is a very community-oriented place."

Animal House . . . or Not

It may be hard to get into the city, but the campus itself is conveniently small and compact. The hilly campus has two dorms at the top of the mound and classroom buildings and the rest of the dorms are scattered right at the bottom. Although the hillside dorms are a bit farther away, one student said, "When I say out of the way I mean about a minute out of the way. The walk across campus is five minutes tops." The two freshman dorms are very different, but students say that each has its good qualities. The largest dorm on campus houses 200 students and has movable furniture, whereas the other has two rooms connected by a bathroom. Upperclassmen have the option of living in suites in their dorms, and the housing process is one that relies on seniority for first picks. All the dorms are coed, although students note that they have single-sex halls. The fact that "most people live on campus until senior year" really contributes to a sense of community on the K-Zoo campus. One student remarked, "I was surprised by how much I mixed. There's not a big difference between classes— friends come from all years."

The lack of fraternities and sororities on campus does not mean that there are no other living options. Off-campus housing is just minutes away on foot and students call it very convenient. There are also four theme houses chosen every year. Sophomores fill out applications for a theme in a group and must agree to sponsor one event per trimester. Students are allowed to rush fraternities and sororities at Western Michigan University, but "hardly anyone does," according to one student. That's also where students go for the big parties—"it's pretty low-key on our campus."

> **"It's nice to walk around campus and see people you know. It feels like a community."**

As far as the campus itself goes, one student said, "It looks very East Coast." With its brick buildings, red brick road, and grassy quad, K-Zoo offers very much the archetypal college setting. The Capital, a big building in the middle of the quad, serves as the center for everything. While Kalamazoo is currently redoing its student center, the new glass-paned expansion of the library overlooking the campus makes up for it in spaces for students. K-Zoo students are proud of the library, redone two years ago. One student boasted, "We've increased the space by 30 percent but increased energy use by only 10 percent. We're very ecologically aware." In addition, the brand-new cafeteria boasts a wooden pizza oven. However, one student said, "I've had worse . . . but they do serve a lot of tofu."

What to Do in the Zoo

Despite the small size of the community, students assure prospective students, or "prospies" as they're known at K-Zoo, that "clubs are filled in." One student said, "I go to a school with a bunch of overachievers, and they want to do everything." As such, students describe a campus with flyers everywhere and event centerpieces on the lunch tables. "Kalamazoo is good about bringing speakers in and providing activities," and the students get "really into what they do." Although students say that the campus "is not sports-oriented whatsoever," they agree that "a lot of people are athletes." The football team may be terrible, but students proudly express their prowess in tennis: "It's what we're known for." Other activities, such as the Frelon Dance Company and the LGBT drag show, Kaleidoscope, provide a wide range of things to do on campus. One student said that "the school allows for you to try more than one thing—you can sing in five different choirs or be as overactive as you want."

The K-Zoo Experience

"People who know about Kalamazoo only have wonderful things to say about it," said one student as she admitted in the same breath that few people fall into this category. But the hidden gem with the "weird name" lives up to its reputation as a school that is challenging while being community-oriented. One student explained, "They want you to try new things and experiment. They expect you'll do great sometimes, and other times you won't do so well." That attitude of exploration and desire to grow beyond the student that arrived on campus permeates every aspect of life. One student summed up the K-Zoo experience when she said, "It's nice to walk around campus and see people you know. It feels like a community."—*Hannah Jacobson*

FYI

If you come to Kalamazoo, you'd better bring "a warm coat!"

What is the typical weekend schedule? "40-minute Fridays make all Friday classes only 40 minutes, and then we party on Friday and Saturday night, followed by everyone going to brunch on Sunday."

If I could change one thing about Kalamazoo, I'd "make it not snow so much—we get all the lake effect!"

Three things every student at Kalamazoo should do before graduating are "study abroad, do an externship, and mudslide on the hill."

Michigan State University

Address: 250 Hannah Administration Bldg East Lansing, MI 48824-0590
Phone: 517-355-8332
E-mail address: admis@msu.edu
Web site URL: www.msu.edu
Year Founded: 1855
Private or Public: Public
Religious Affiliation: None
Location: Small city
Number of Applicants: 25,500
Percent Accepted: 68%
Percent Accepted who enroll: 41%
Number Entering: 7,378
Number of Transfers Accepted each Year: 2,500
Middle 50% SAT range: M: 540–660, CR:480–620, Wr: 480–610
Middle 50% ACT range: 23–27
Early admission program EA/ED/None: None

Percentage accepted through EA or ED: NA
EA and ED deadline: NA
Regular Deadline: Rolling
Application Fee: $35 domestic; $50 international
Full time Undergraduate enrollment: 36,337
Total enrollment: 46,648
Percent Male: 46%
Percent Female: 54%
Total Percent Minority or Unreported: 16%
Percent African-American: 7%
Percent Asian/Pacific Islander: 5%
Percent Hispanic: 3%
Percent Native-American: 1%
Percent International: 8%
Percent in-state/out of state: 79%/21%
Percent from Public HS: Unreported
Retention Rate: 91%
Graduation Rate 4-year: 73%

Graduation Rate 6-year: 74%
Percent Undergraduates in On-campus housing: 43%
Number of official organized extracurricular organizations: 600
3 Most popular majors: Advertising, Finance, Education
Student/Faculty ratio: 17:1
Average Class Size: Unreported
Percent of students going to grad school: Unreported
Tuition and Fees: $25,722
In State Tuition and Fees if different: $10,264
Cost for Room and Board: $7,076
Percent receiving financial aid out of those who apply, first year: 64%
Percent receiving financial aid among all students: 45%

The best test of how long a student has been at Michigan State University is to ask him or her where in Michigan he or she goes to school. The freshest of the freshmen will just say, "East Lansing." The ones who are true MSU Spartans, though, will point to a little spot on their palms near the thumb and say, "right here!" In the Mitten State, you'll find that this is how the real Michiganders show off their home allegiance, and students at Michigan State are happy to become part of it—despite the many feet of snow they're likely to brave during the winter. And there will be lots of them around to ask: with over 36,000 undergrads and 10,000 more in the grad school, MSU has a broad population of students who are joined by an atmosphere of Midwestern friendliness, a curriculum as wide as the student body itself, and a deep love of Spartan football.

Not (Just) Another Big State School

Although it can be daunting to try to pick classes at a school that offers over 200 programs of study, students say that it is precisely that broad spectrum of educational opportunities that they appreciate about MSU. Although many choose to navigate this sea of classes in the main college, MSU offers an honors program for those who want the experience of a smaller community within the school as a whole, and three specialized residential colleges with their own unique programs of study. These residential colleges offer focused curricula ranging from the sciences in Lyman Briggs RC to politics and international relations in James Madison to liberal arts and humanities in the newest residential college, the Arts and Humanities RC. Students used many words to describe these colleges, among them "prestigious," "pompous," "reputable," "great" and "worthwhile," and they note that each college attracts students who are "really interested in the subject matter covered." All three of these colleges offer regular as well as honors programs, and require an application process. Although students say classes in the RCs are known for being "amazingly hard," they all agreed that the smaller class sizes—capped at 25—and access to the "incredible professors" make the experience well worth the extra work.

But special programs are not just for RC students. MSU offers "one of the best study abroad programs in the country—"just pick a place, and you can go there," one sophomore explained. A freshman added that the study abroad program offers opportunities "on all seven continents—yes, seven!" Students say that MSU makes it very easy to go abroad, and in fact, James Madison programs have a mandatory internship or semester abroad built in. Students really like the fact that MSU fosters an expectation of going abroad, because "at other schools, it seems like students are afraid to leave campus. Here, it's the norm." In addition, over half the students who study abroad receive some form of financial aid, which "makes a huge difference."

> "It is really easy to find small groups to hang out with and the largeness of the school enables students to have the maximum number of opportunities to pursue whatever they might be into."

This is not to say that students who stay on campus have a chance to get bored—far from it! When asked about popular majors, students came up with everything from Kinesiology to Business to Education to Veterinary Prep to the renowned Agriculture program that was part of Michigan State's original land grant. One graduating senior offered, "With such a big school, the classes offered are endless—I wish I had more time to take all the ones I've been interested in."

Spartans Gone Wild

Warriors inside the classroom, these Spartans also know how to leave the books behind and have fun. Students agree that there is "a large drinking scene" at MSU, but they are quick to say that there are plenty of ways to cut loose without breaking out the alcohol. "The Union and the Student Activities Board also have a lot of events and programs that occur on those nights for those that don't want to have the typical drunken party experience," one student pointed out. Activities ranging from bowling to free movies to student talent shows such as Spartan Idol (singing) and Last Spartan Standing (stand-up comedy) provide great weekend entertainment that does

not revolve around frats. That said, the "beer pong tournaments and special theme nights at clubs" are the more dominant social scenes at MSU, both of which make for an extremely lively campus on the weekends.

But weekends won't be the only time off, and the "Sparticipation" extravaganza at the beginning of the year will help funnel new freshmen into extracurriculars and clubs. This activities bazaar places freshmen in the middle of representatives from all the extracurricular groups, which "can be overwhelming," said one, who quickly added that it "ended up being the best way to just dive in and figure out what I wanted to do." A seasoned sophomore coming at it from the other side also noted, "You get a lot of free stuff and it is the best way to figure out what you might want to be involved in because everyone is in the same place at the same time." Popular extracurriculars include the clearly dominant frat scene, but beyond that, the "huge athletics program" provides a draw, in addition to language clubs, Student Activities Board, poetry and creative writing organizations, and even martial arts. A sophomore said, "there is a lot of pride for the sports teams, and the students are very into supporting the school through sports." This takes the form of cheering on the basketball team from the student section, called the "Izzone," gearing up for football Saturdays, or playing sports on any level from casual dorm wars to more intense club athletics. Students say that the great thing about going to such a large school is that "there is pretty much any and every extracurricular you could ever want—there is something for everyone!"

This is Sparta!

It may be a little less ancient, but the ivy-covered brick of the older buildings on the northern campus of MSU show off the school's picturesque environment. One student raved, "The Red Cedar River runs right through the center of campus and has some really awesome walking paths around it. The botanical gardens are also a must-see." While the dorms themselves are fairly standard, students say they enjoy their time living on campus. "A lot of juniors and seniors move off campus, but dorm locations do get better as you get older, so there's something to be said for that, too," one junior noted. A sophomore added that living in a dorm "has been a great way to meet people and get to know the campus."

As far as going off-campus is concerned, students say that upperclassmen are much more likely to do so if only because freshmen are not allowed to have cars on campus. Still, they say the campus is easy to get around on foot or by bus, and that East Lansing itself is "very pleasant."

Scream 4: Spartan Style

Instead of masked killers, this "scream" is an MSU tradition that takes place every finals week. One student explained that "At exactly midnight, everyone sticks their heads outside whatever room they might be studying in and screams at the top of their lungs." This de-stressing ritual serves as a good reminder that even a big school like MSU allows students to form strong bonds both to each other and to the institution. The fear of large universities is not lost on students, and one shared, "I was really worried that the campus would be too big and that I might get 'lost' with so many people. The great thing is, it is really easy to find small groups to hang out with and the largeness of the school enables students to have the maximum number of opportunities to pursue whatever they might be into." While one student noted a current lack of diversity on campus, she was quick to say that it seems that "the school is doing its best to change that." Other students mentioned the fact that "MSU draws so many different kinds of people" also helps everyone find a place to fit in despite the size. The traditions and incredible school spirit that pervade the campus of MSU give this fiery student body a lot of common ground and a huge number of opportunities to express it, both inside the classroom and out.—*Hannah Jacobson*

FYIs

If you come to MSU, "you'd better bring something green for school spirit!"

What's the typical weekend schedule? "Wake up, grab lunch/breakfast, go to work/ practice, hang out in the dorm, chill out with the floor mates (usually playing RockBand), go for early dinner, study, party, go to bed."

If I could change one thing about MSU, I'd "make the campus smaller."

Three things every student at MSU should do before graduating are, "have a picture with Sparty the Statue, paint the rock with a group of friends or an organization you are involved in, and take advantage of the study abroad program!"

Michigan Technological University

Address: 1400 Townsend Drive Houghton, MI 49931
Phone: 888-688-1885
E-mail address: mtu4u@mtu.edu
Web site URL: admissions.mtu.edu
Year Founded: 1885
Private or Public: Public
Religious Affiliation: None
Location: Suburban
Number of Applicants: 5,415
Percent Accepted: 77%
Percent Accepted who enroll: 37%
Number Entering: 1,580
Number of Transfers Accepted each Year: 524
Middle 50% SAT range: M: 590–690, CR: 530–650, Wr: 500–620
Middle 50% ACT range: 23–28
Early admission program EA/ED/None: None
Percentage accepted through EA or ED: NA

EA and ED deadline: NA
Regular Deadline: Rolling with priority consideration by Jan. 15
Application Fee: $0
Full time Undergraduate enrollment: 5,591
Total enrollment: 7, 014
Percent Male: 77%
Percent Female: 23%
Total Percent Minority or Unreported: 10%
Percent African-American: 2%
Percent Asian/Pacific Islander: 1%
Percent Hispanic: 1%
Percent Native-American: 1%
Percent International: 5%
Percent in-state/out of state: 72%/28%
Percent from Public HS: Unreported
Retention Rate: 81.90%
Graduation Rate 4-year: 24%
Graduation Rate 6-year: 64%

Percent Undergraduates in On-campus housing: 46%
Number of official organized extracurricular organizations: 180
3 Most popular majors: Engineering, Computing, natural & Physical Sciences
Student/Faculty ratio: 11:1
Average Class Size: 68% have fewer than 30 students
Percent of students going to grad school: Immediately: 14%, **Within one year:** 20%, **within 5 years:** 75%, **within 10 years:** 85%
Tuition and Fees: $22,522
In State Tuition and Fees if different: $10,762
Cost for Room and Board: $7,738
Percent receiving financial aid out of those who apply, first year: 72%
Percent receiving financial aid among all students: 58%

Originally established in 1885 to train mining engineers, Michigan Tech has evolved into a widely renowned institution with a vast array of opportunities for engineers and nonengineers alike. Located in the upper region of Michigan in the town of Houghton, this midsized college boasts a beautiful campus surrounded by snow-covered mountains, woods, and trails. But don't be fooled by the calm and quiet surroundings—Michigan Tech is one of the busiest places to spend one's college years.

Not Just For Engineers

Michigan Tech prides itself on its abundant research opportunities, especially its prized Enterprise Program. The program provides hands-on work with outfits like NASA, DaimlerChrysler, SBC Ameritech and the EPA. Teams of 20 to 30 students solve real-world engineering and manufacturing problems submitted by Michigan Tech's industry, business and corporate partners. The field of research for each group varies, including, but not limited to, aerospace, alternative fuels, robotic systems and wireless communication.

Whether you're doing engineering research or not, chances are you'll be working hard at Michigan Tech. As one student said, "Most people here are very into their schooling, so I am able to keep on track as well." The school's atmosphere is intensely preprofessional; undergraduates are often taking career goals into account as they work. One student explained, "Classes are very tough, but our job placement is very high. For pre-med majors, there is an 80 percent for med school, while the national average is 40 percent." This type of education guarantees that Michigan Tech students are prepared for the real world.

Small Town Snow Sports

Houghton, Michigan, is a very cold place, so you better bring some snow boots. The campus is covered with snow, water, woods, and trails, and the University even owns its own ski and snowboarding mountains with discounted season passes for students. The powder-covered mountains and serene hills create a calm, safe campus environment—so safe, in fact, that many people claim Houghton to be the safest town in Michigan.

> **"The people here are very laid-back . . . I like the whole 'small town' feel."**

But safe definitely doesn't mean boring. With over 150 student groups on campus, there is certainly no shortage of things to do. "[There is] almost too much to do, there are many things I want to do that I just don't have time for . . . and most people think there is nothing to do up here because we're in the middle of nowhere," one student noted. With just under 6,000 undergraduates, Michigan Tech is large enough that each activity attracts a substantial group of students. Yet, it is small enough that students can hold leadership positions without feeling too stressed out about their extracurriculars. As one student explained "The people here are very laid-back . . . I like the whole 'small town' feel."

Life in the Winter Wonderland
In terms of housing, all freshmen are required to live in one of three fully equipped residential halls, encouraging class bonding and facilitating the integration of the "frosh" into the campus scene. After that, students can choose whether or not to stay on campus for their next three years. To keep themselves entertained, Michigan Tech students take advantage of the many concerts and performances staged around campus; performers have included Mary Chapin Carpenter and Tap Dogs Rebooted. Greek life, in spite of its small numbers, has a substantial influence on the campus's social scene. Greeks coordinate several parties every semester for everyone's enjoyment. One of the biggest events of the year is the annual Winter Carnival held in February. Human dogsled races, ice bowling, snow volleyball and fireworks are all part of the extravaganza that is Winter Carnival. Groups on campus spend

weeks preparing and creating statues and snow sculptures, and teams to compete in the various races. The event is so popular that it attracts tourists from all over Michigan.

Diversity is a bit lacking at Michigan Tech: the school is about 85–90 percent Caucasian. Yet, students said that there is a growing international and minority presence, and all undergraduates have the option of participating in exchange programs or study abroad. The gender ratio is also unbalanced. Like most tech schools, the male majority leaves the lucky ladies with ample choices. "The dating scene is more competitive here . . . and the women tend to use that to their advantage," one student explained. Overall, students agreed that Michigan Tech "is very accepting" of all types and is working to improve its reputation and racial and gender diversity.

Hockey, Skiing, and . . . Broomball?
With a Division I Men's Hockey team, a dozen DII teams and many intramural teams, it is no surprise that many students choose to stay active. In fact, nearly 90 percent of students partake in intramurals. "A lot of people like to get involved with sports up here . . . it is a great way to stay in shape and meet a lot of people," one intramural athlete noted. The cold weather encourages sports unique to snow and ice. Aside from the usual skiing and ice hockey, students use the icy conditions to play a school favorite: broomball. One student explained the glories of their prized sport: "Broomball is huge up here. It is like hockey played on ice but you wear street shoes and use brooms as hockey sticks . . . you have to wear kneepads though or else you will get very bruised . . . Everybody gets really into it, everybody!" Students can be found playing broomball whenever possible—during intramural games, pickup games, and, of course, during Winter Carnival.

It is this mix of academic seriousness and fun-loving athletic spirit that continues to draw students to Michigan Tech year after year. And if you are excited by its combination of intellectual and athletic rigor, it just might be the place for you. Just don't forget your kneepads.—*Suzanne Salgado*

FYI

If you come to MTU, you'd better bring "snow shoes and a shovel."

What's the typical weekend schedule? "Days are spent at meetings or in the library, nights are for going out with friends, and Sundays especially are for homework."

If I could change one thing about MTU it would be "to have more parking—I have to get up early to get a good parking spot."

Three things every student at MTU should do before graduating are: "Go cliff jumping, explore the copper country, and learn to ski/snowboard (and if you know how to ski or snowboard, go to Mt. Bohemia)."

University of Michigan

Address: 1220 Student Activities Building Ann Arbor, MI 48109-1316

Phone: 734-764-7433

E-mail address: ugadmiss@umich.edu

Web site URL: www.umich.edu

Year Founded: 1817

Private or Public: Public

Religious Affiliation: None

Location: Urban

Number of Applicants: 27,474

Percent Accepted: 50%

Percent Accepted who enroll: 43%

Number Entering: 5,955

Number of Transfers Accepted each Year: 1,154

Middle 50% SAT range: M: 630–730, CR: 590–690, Wr: Unreported

Middle 50% ACT range: 27–31

Early admission program EA/ED/None: EA

Percentage accepted through EA or ED: Unreported

EA and ED deadline: 31-Oct

Regular Deadline: 1-Feb

Application Fee: $40

Full time Undergraduate enrollment: 26,083

Total enrollment: 38,426

Percent Male: 50%

Percent Female: 50%

Total Percent Minority or Unreported: 34%

Percent African-American: 6%

Percent Asian/Pacific Islander: 12%

Percent Hispanic: 5%

Percent Native-American: 1%

Percent International: 5%

Percent in-state/out of state: 68%/32%

Percent from Public HS: Unreported

Retention Rate: 96%

Graduation Rate 4-year: Unreported

Graduation Rate 6-year: Unreported

Percent Undergraduates in On-campus housing: 63%

Number of official organized extracurricular organizations: 1000

3 Most popular majors: Business Administration and Management, English Language and Literature, Psycholgy

Student/Faculty ratio: 15:1

Average Class Size: 10 to 19

Percent of students going to grad school: 36%

Tuition and Fees: $33,069

In State Tuition and Fees if different: $11,037

Cost for Room and Board: $8,590

Percent receiving financial aid out of those who apply, first year: 71%

Percent receiving financial aid among all students: 48%

As one of the country's most notable public institutions, the University of Michigan is wrought with history. Not only was it home to Jonas Salk's laboratory when the polio vaccine was discovered in 1955, but it was here that John F. Kennedy first proposed the Peace Corps during his presidential campaign of 1960. Yet, despite its imposing legacy and the fact that Michigan boasts the benefits of a public institution, with "millions of things to do," the University of Michigan still maintains a distinct "homey" midwestern feel.

M is for Majors . . . and Minors

With over 25,000 undergrads and over 200 academic departments in 11 undergraduate schools and colleges, the academic opportunities at Michigan are endless. In fact, many students cite this variety as their favorite aspect of the school. The choices begin with the application process—students may apply directly to one of 11 undergraduate schools. Though most first year students enroll in the College of Literature, Arts and Sciences (LSA), several other colleges are also open to freshmen, including the College of Engineering and the Art School.

Freshmen also have the option of enrolling in a number of special academic programs. The four-year honors program, for example, is offered through LSA. After being accepted into the college, select students are offered admission to the program. During their first two years, students in the honors program are offered unique advising and research programs, and can enroll in special courses not offered to the general undergraduate population. The honors program even boasts its own housing option.

Students may also opt for the Residential College (RC), a four-year interdisciplinary liberal arts program within LSA. With 900 students, and over 50 professors, RC is described as a "living-learning community." Students who choose to enroll in the program take classes and live together in the East Quadrangle Residence Hall. Another unique academic living environment is available through the Residential Programs, which are sorted through specific interests such as writing, art, women in science, and engineering. According to one freshman, "They are great ways to make this huge school feel smaller and more personal."

Regardless of major, every student in LSA must fulfill natural science, humanities, social science, and "the dreaded language requirement," among others. But most students do not consider the requirements too demanding. In fact, one freshman was told by her adviser not to worry about them, "because if I just take a full course load every semester, I'll probably fulfill my requirements anyway."

The variety of classes and departments at Michigan results in an academic environment that can invariably suit each student's individual needs. "Whether you want a class that requires five hours of studying per week, or five hours for the entire semester, you can find one," explained one student. Class size varies dramatically as well. Lower-level classes and lectures can range from 50 to 500, but most classes split into 20 to 30 student discussion sections led by Graduate Student Instructors (GSIs).

One option to keep class sizes manageable is the First Year Seminars, which are offered on a number of topics, ranging from hippies to Slavic countries, from sex to theology. Since they are led exclusively by professors, students recommend taking as many of these seminars as possible during one's first year in order to form relationships with professors early on. There is no general rule as to accessibility of the instructors. "It depends on the professor," one student remarked. "Most are very approachable, but I have come across a couple who couldn't care less about the students." Another student said that close relationships with professors are "one of those things that you kind of give up by going to a big school," but most agree that if you make an effort most professors won't turn you away. "Professors want their students to succeed," said one undergrad, "they are invested in the success of their students even if it means being flexible about their office hours, or spending a little extra time on this, and cutting back on that." Another commented that "it's easy to get to know the professors if you are interested in doing that, and it's easy to be another face in the crowd if you don't want to be noticed."

The classes at Michigan also vary in their level of competitiveness. According to one student, "my microeconomics class is a prerequisite for the business school," which inherently means it is populated by competitive students. Others note that such competition is present among architecture and pre-med students as well. But, in contrast, one student from New York City claims that she has "seen no competition whatsoever." Not only has she found that students rarely talk about their grades, but "people here in the Midwest are always willing to help one another out." This "warm and welcoming community" is for many "one of the great qualities of this school."

So does Michigan's huge academic curriculum possess any shortcomings? One undergraduate complained that Michigan has "the weakest study abroad offerings I have come across for a school of this size." Although the University claims to feature numerous specialized study abroad programs, such as the Engineering International Program, as well as study abroad scholarships, students admit they are disappointed by the offerings, especially those that don't require a foreign language.

The Animal House Way of Life

"Straight out of the movies," is how one enthusiastic freshman characterized Michigan's dominating Greek scene. With nearly 60 chapters, many students "don't know many people that aren't in frats," and for those who haven't gone Greek, the lifestyle may at times seem overwhelming and exclusive. For example, the Office of Greek Life instituted a policy that only allows those in frats and sororities to attend frat parties unless the student can somehow get his or her name on the guest-list before-hand.

But for many students, Greek life is just another way to make a huge school more manageable. One freshman noted that joining a sorority allowed her to "make a place for [herself] in such a huge community." Furthermore, because nearly 65 percent of students are Michigan natives, the out-of-state students often find fraternities and sororities an integral part of meeting new people. For girls, sorority rush is "a 10-day-long process in the fall, involving dress codes, lining up alphabetically, and a lot of fake smiling," while rush for fraternities is much more informal. Neither involves hazing, as it is strictly prohibited.

While many underclassmen join fraternities and sororities and/or attend frat parties every weekend, for those who are of age, the bar scene and house parties are common weekend activities. Some notable bars include Studio 4, Scorekeepers (aka Skeeps), Touchdowns, Necto and Rick's. The most popular nights to go out are Thursday, Friday, and Saturday, although Tuesdays are also popular bar nights.

So how do underage students manage? Although there are alcohol regulations both legally and within the Greek system, drinking ages and policies are not strictly enforced. According to one student, in terms of the Greek rules, "No one really pays attention until they've been on social probation." Similarly, an underage student is not too likely to find him or herself in trouble for drinking. "The cops are pretty strict," one freshman admitted, "but as long as you don't act like an idiot and you remain in control of yourself it isn't a problem." One sophomore agreed, stating that "for the most part, the only way to get in trouble by the police is to be obnoxious."

Not surprisingly, alcohol is extremely prevalent among the Michigan undergrad populations, and "soft drugs," such as marijuana, are fairly common among those who choose to partake. In fact, while alcohol possession by a minor will most likely result in a court appearance, marijuana possession is only a civil infraction and a violation merely results in a small fine. Though hard drugs are much harder to come by, rumor has it that cocaine use at Michigan is on the steady rise.

Regardless of their particular interests, Michigan students generally agree that finding friends is not difficult. "In such a big school, everyone is trying to find their own little niche," remarked one student, "so

everyone is really friendly and enthusiastic about meeting people." The student body at Michigan is also characterized as being extremely diverse. This does not prevent self-segregation from occurring, but one student noted that diversity has become "a huge topic of interest" since the state banned affirmative action programs in 2006.

Home Is Where Ann Arbor Is

"[As a freshman] you can live in a single or a double. You can live in apartment-style dorms or in dorm-style dorms. There are suites and there are halls. They have everything you can imagine!"

"The Hill" is composed of five dorms and is "basically the place to live if you're a freshman." Some students, as a means of ensuring that they will live in this popular area, apply to one of the residential programs that houses its students on The Hill. Dorms on The Hill include Stockwell, an all-girls dorm; Lloyd Hall (nicknamed Lloyd Island due to the numerous Long Islanders that live there); Couzens, which is rumored to have once been a mental institution; Mosher-Jordan (aka MoJo), which will reopen in the fall of 2008 after remodeling; and Markley, the "social dorm with small rooms."

"At Michigan, Bigger Is Better."

Another common freshman housing area is South Quad, which is home to both the optional honors student housing and the athletes' dorm—rumored to have the best food on campus. Students in the RC live and take classes on East Campus, while North Campus, a 15-minute bus ride away from the central campus, is home to many of the architecture, theater, and engineering students. One of North Campus's most notable dorms is Bursely, the third biggest dorm building in the country. According to one student, "Generally, the smaller the dorm, the worse its reputation is. At Michigan, bigger is better."

All freshman halls have RAs, and there is plenty of debate about their roles. "They make sure there isn't any drinking in the dorms and handle problems with roommates," one sophomore explained. "They also punish you if they find you drunk." But in the words of another student, the primary job of the RAs is to "decorate the bulletin boards and let you into your room if you get locked out."

Most students only have to deal with RAs during their freshman year, though, since the majority of Michigan sophomores move off campus. Some move into fraternity or sorority houses, while others move into co-ops where "people do chores for the house so the rent is cheap." There are also many apartment buildings and houses surrounding campus comprised mainly of students.

With 10 different dining halls on campus, "there is always something to eat." While the food might not be great, every dining hall features a salad bar, sandwich bar, pasta, and several other "staples." One student noted that "UMich food has been rated some of the best campus food in the country!" But some students disagree. As at many colleges and universities, "You can get lucky or you can eat cereal." But as one student admitted, "It's better than cooking my own food."

Other than the lack of dining hall food, it is often hard for off-campus students to tell that they are not on university property. "The off-campus neighborhoods just feel like an extension of the campus." Students often find themselves spending their free time on Main Street, which is not only full of shops and restaurants, but also Ann Arbor residents. According to one student, other than on Main Street, "I only see college kids." But she added, "There *are* 25,000 of them."

One of the favorite student hangouts on campus, especially on warmer days, is The Diag (pronounced *die*-ag), the main quad that is surrounded by classroom buildings. It is called The Diag because of the many crossing paths throughout. In the middle is a huge gold M, source of the oldest campus legend. It is rumored that if you walk over the M you will fail your first blue book exam. The curse can only be broken if someone runs naked from the Diag to the clock tower when it chimes at midnight, but since the city council banned the clock from chiming past 11 p.m., "the curse is here to stay." According to one fresh-

man, "I decided I wanted to come to Michigan when I was on The Diag."

For outdoorsy students, Nicholas Arboretum is a perfect "getaway" from campus. "It's just a million miles of nature. It's beautiful, clean, and fun to hike and walk around in."

Beer Bottles and Footballs

Although it may seem outrageous, some students actually choose University of Michigan just for the football team, and for many, it's the highlight of their college experience. "I have never been so excited to be a Michigan student as I was when I walked to my first football game," exclaimed one freshman. "The streets are filled with students all in Maize and Blue." Getting to the stadium is not a problem, as the main drag to "The Big House" is packed with fans on all sides of the stadium. "Walking down State Street is an amazing experience. You walk with 100,000 other fans to Michigan stadium to watch football."

Even if sports such as men's basketball and hockey always draw a crowd to their games, football rules at Michigan. As one student admitted, "If the football team loses, don't expect a great night out," and another added, "If you don't like beer and football, you will when you get here!"

Regardless of athletic or extracurricular interests, all students agree that one of the best aspects of the Michigan student body is its undying spirit. "You know you're at Michigan, even in the middle of winter, when everyone is bundled in their winter jackets, because Michigan hats and scarves and mittens are everywhere." And no matter where you are on campus, if you listen carefully, you will probably hear the distant chants of "It's great! To be! A Michigan Wolverine!"
—*Jessica Rubin*

FYI
If you come to Michigan, you'd better bring "Tolerance for everything that goes on here. If you don't, you won't make it past welcome week."
What's the typical weekend schedule? "Party, party, party, party . . . okay and maybe you can sleep, eat, and work a little too!"
If I could change one thing about Michigan, I'd "Move it to a warmer, sunnier place."
Three things every student at Michigan should do before graduating are "Go to a football game against Ohio State, run the naked mile, stop and listen to one of the crazy men ranting in the middle of the Diag. You may learn something."

Minnesota

Carleton College

Address: 100 South College Street Northfield, MN 55057

Phone: 507-222-4190

E-mail address: admissions@carleton.edu

Web site URL: www.carleton.edu

Year Founded: 1866

Private or Public: Private

Religious Affiliation: None

Location: Rural

Number of Applicants: 4,840

Percent Accepted: 29.8%

Percent Accepted who enroll: 35%

Number Entering: 509

Number of Transfers Accepted each Year: 22

Middle 50% SAT range: M: 660–740, CR: 650–750, Wr: 650–730

Middle 50% ACT range: 29–33

Early admission program EA/ED/None: ED

Percentage accepted through EA or ED: 36%

EA and ED deadline: 15-Nov

Regular Deadline: 15-Jan

Application Fee: $30

Full time Undergraduate enrollment: 2,005

Total enrollment: 3,991

Percent Male: 48%

Percent Female: 53%

Total Percent Minority or Unreported: 21%

Percent African-American: 5%

Percent Asian/Pacific Islander: 10%

Percent Hispanic: 6%

Percent Native-American: 0.6%

Percent International: 6%

Percent in-state/out of state: 26%/74%

Percent from Public HS: Unreported

Retention Rate: 98%

Graduation Rate 4-year: 89%

Graduation Rate 6-year: 91.0%

Percent Undergraduates in On-campus housing: 89%

Number of official organized extracurricular organizations: 132

3 Most popular majors: Biology, Economics, Political Science

Student/Faculty ratio: 9:1

Average Class Size: 18

Percent of students going to grad school: Unreported

Tuition and Fees: $38,046

In State Tuition and Fees if different: No difference

Cost for Room and Board: $9,993

Percent receiving financial aid out of those who apply, first year: 50%

Percent receiving financial aid among all students: 54%

While students searching for the ideal liberal arts college may turn their sights toward New England or the West Coast, they would be remiss if they did not consider Carleton College, a small college located in the quaint town of Northfield, Minnesota, widely hailed as one of the top liberal arts colleges in the country. Students interested in Carleton should prepare for a highly rigorous academic curriculum, not to mention one of the coldest winters found in the continental United States. But any Carleton student will cheerfully declare that he or she is happy to overlook the subzero temperatures because of the college's friendly student body, approachable professors, and beautiful campus.

A Workload Heavier than the Snowfall

Known for its academic rigor, Carleton prides itself on providing its students with a well-rounded education. While students pronounced the math and the physical science majors to be especially arduous, many agreed that there is no way to get through Carleton without doing one's fair share of work. Students praised Carleton's trimester system for allowing them to dedicate more time to fewer classes, since they are only required to take three at a time. But students also said the fast pace of classes can make each trimester seem like a blur. "If I think about what I learned in the last couple weeks, it feels like it all happened yesterday," said one freshman. Students added that the trimester system has other drawbacks, pointing to a short reading period and the early onset of midterms.

Still, midterms may seem like a small concern in comparison to the myriad distribution requirements each Carleton students must fulfill. Before graduating, each Carleton student must take two arts and literature classes, two humanities classes, three social science classes, and three math or natural science classes. Among Carleton's most distinctive requirements is the writing portfolio students must submit after their sophomore year. Said one English major: "I had a positive experience putting together my portfolio, but if you don't look at the writing portfolio as a way to reflect on yourself, then it's mostly just a hassle and waste of time. Students also have a language requirement, physical education requirement, and one final requirement known as RAD: Recognition and Affirmation of Difference. One senior said of RAD: "It was created as a requirement to improve diversity education, but it's become a little lackluster. It's kind of a useless requirement that no one really thinks about." Still, other students said they appreciated the function of the distribution requirements—including RAD—arguing that the requirements bring variety to the curriculum and provide exposure to a number of interesting topics.

But regardless of the varied opinions on campus toward Carleton's distribution requirements, students voiced unanimous approval of the school's professors and their involvement on campus. Given Carleton's small size, students work closely with their professors and form close relationships over time. "You can talk to professors about everything," one senior said. "People interact closely at Carleton. If I ever write an article for a publication, I can bank on a professor e-mailing me about it and telling me they liked it." Fortunately, small classes abound at Carleton, offering more opportunities for students to get to know their professors. Students said they found little difficulty getting into the courses they desired, noting that in the unlikely event of getting wait-listed, a student can often squeeze his or her way into the class.

But Enough about School . . .

While Carleton's coursework is tough, it is far from the only thing on students' minds. Although Minnesota's harsh winters may seem like a deterrent from social events, students said it only emboldens them to be more outgoing. "We're in the tundra, so we have to find something to do," one student said. On weekends, that "something" usually includes parties in dorms, as well as on-campus and off-campus houses. Students described Carleton's stance on alcohol to be relatively relaxed, noting that the school's main concern is that students remain safe. Beyond alcohol, students said there is very little substance use, with the exception of marijuana, which students said is used no more or less than at other colleges. Still, students said there is no pressure to use alcohol or drugs, and there are many substance-free events on campus, including dance parties occurring about every week.

Yet Carleton students know how to have fun all the time—not just during late weekend nights. Extracurricular opportunities abound on campus, from the newspaper to community service to dance groups. Among the most popular student groups is a dance group called Ebony, which has upward of 100 members. The group requires no previous training to join and has one dance each term, which is usually very well attended. Beyond dance, students find ways to stay in shape. A large majority of Carleton students participate in intramural sports. Still, trumping intramurals and varsity athletics is one sport that permeates every facet of Carleton life: Frisbee. "I've been hit by a Frisbee four times at Carleton," said one upperclassman. "Everyone plays it. It's one of the biggest things about spring." But while students are waiting for spring to arrive, they can be found playing broomball on a flooded rink in the large, open expanse called the Bald Spot.

Living by the Bald Spot

The Bald Spot marks the center of Carleton's picturesque—albeit architecturally eclectic—campus, which is flanked on all sides by Carleton's many academic, recreational, and dormitory buildings. Freshmen are assigned to various dorms with multiple upperclassmen Resident Advisors per floor. RAs at Carleton get to know their freshmen well, as one freshman noted, saying: "I was shocked that these RAs actually cared. They organize weekly study breaks and meet with us regularly." When students become upperclassmen, they have their pick of a variety of housing, including dorms or on-campus houses. Two new dorms are slated to open during the 2009–2010 school year. While about one in 10 Carleton students currently live off-campus, the college is restricting the number of upperclassmen who will be able to move off campus this coming year, as well.

Not only do students at Carleton praise the housing, but they also give positive reviews to the food, thanks to a new dining service begun this year. There are two dining halls on campus, one on the west side of campus, the other on the east side of campus. Still, students wishing to get away from dining hall food can always venture into Northfield, where a variety of cafes and eateries abound. Northfield garnered praise from students for its safe environment and quaint shops, and as one sophomore noted, "Northfield is a good college town. It's always crawling with Carleton students, and restaurants are always open late to suit your needs." But after four years spent at Carleton, Northfield can start to feel a bit confining, said one senior. "There are a million little antique stores that are way overpriced, and that's pretty much it," he said. Students needing a break from Northfield can always take a 40-minute drive up to the nearby Twin Cities, although students said almost everyone stays on campus during the weekends.

Uniquely Carleton

When asked what makes Carleton different from other colleges, students quickly point to their peers. Carleton places a high priority on diversity in its student body, and students said they are constantly impressed with the seemingly boundless knowledge and affability of their classmates. Still, students said the majority of their classmates come from upper-middle-class backgrounds, although all agreed that everyone comes to Carleton with an open mind and unique perspective. Carleton's LGBT community is small, said one gay student, but the campus is very accepting, and straight students at Carleton seek to be good allies to their queer peers.

But beyond the friendly student body and top-quality education, there are many other facets of Carleton that make it unique. Consider, for example, "Rotblatt," a campus-wide softball game played annually with as many innings as the age of the College (which has climbed above 100). Another famous facet of Carleton life is the Dacie Moses House, a residence left to the school by alumna Dacie Moses, who stipulated in her donation that the house must always have supplies inside for students to bake cookies. Yet Carleton students could not boast about surviving Minnesota without a few winter traditions. One favorite among students is to go sledding down a mammoth hill behind Evans dorm on dining hall trays.

> "I've been hit by a Frisbee four times at Carleton . . . It's one of the biggest things about spring."

While any Carleton student will name a different tradition as their favorite, many look on their time at the college with affection, noting how difficult they know it will be to leave it after graduation. From late night hangouts on the top floor of the library to lively discussions in small classes, Carleton students have myriad opportunities to learn from "the best people you'll ever meet," as one student described her classmates.—*Raymond Carlson*

FYI
If you come to Carleton, you'd better bring "long underwear and a real Frisbee."
What is the typical weekend schedule? "Friday is usually just party hopping, Saturday there's always a dance, Sunday go to brunch and start working on your paper."
If I could change one thing about Carleton, I'd "move Carleton to Minneapolis. The town is a little isolating sometimes."
Three things every student at Carleton should do before graduating are "explore the underground tunnels, even though they're off limits, participate in an intercultural retreat, and go to the Carleton football game against our major rival, St. Olaf."

Gustavus Adolphus College

Address: 800 West College Avenue St. Peter, MN 56082

Phone: 507-933-7676

E-mail address: admission@gustavus.edu

Web site URL: www.gustavus.edu

Year Founded: 1862

Private or Public: Private

Religious Affiliation: Lutheran

Location: Rural

Number of Applicants: 3,279

Percent Accepted: 71%

Percent Accepted who enroll: 29%

Number Entering: 675

Number of Transfers Accepted each Year: 79

Middle 50% SAT range: Unreported

Middle 50% ACT range: 24–29

Early admission program EA/ED/None: EA

Percentage accepted through EA or ED: 28%

EA and ED deadline: 1-Nov

Regular Deadline: 1-Apr

Application Fee: $0

Full time Undergraduate enrollment: 2,628

Total enrollment: 2,628

Percent Male: 43%

Percent Female: 57%

Total Percent Minority or Unreported: 12%

Percent African-American: 2%

Percent Asian/Pacific Islander: 5%

Percent Hispanic: 2%

Percent Native-American: <1%

Percent International: 2%

Percent in-state/out of state: 80%/20%

Percent from Public HS: 92%

Retention Rate: Unreported

Graduation Rate 4-year: Unreported

Graduation Rate 6-year: Unreported

Percent Undergraduates in On-campus housing: 77%

Number of official organized extracurricular organizations: 120

3 Most popular majors: Business, Psychology

Student/Faculty ratio: 13:1

Average Class Size: 10 to 19

Percent of students going to grad school: 34%

Tuition and Fees: $30,420

In State Tuition and Fees if different: No difference

Cost for Room and Board: $7,460

Percent receiving financial aid out of those who apply, first year: 81%

Percent receiving financial aid among all students: 66%

The Gustavus Adolphus campus, which is seated upon 350 hilltop acres, is the center of the small town of St. Peter. The College is completely self-contained, abutted by a delightful arboretum dense with trees from Minnesota and Sweden. The modern face of the "Gustie" campus owes a lot to the 1998 tornado that nearly shut down the school and after which the College "invested quite a bit in remodeling." According to students, there are "several very new buildings on campus, mixed in with older ones." These newer buildings include a new 200-resident dormitory that offers a mix of regular dorm rooms available to students of all years and apartment-style living for upperclassmen. Also recently renovated are the fitness facilities at the Lund Center, and Old Main, the oldest building on campus.

Living on the Hill

With such a high percentage of Gusties residing on campus—including all first- and second-year students—housing options are very important. Norelius Hall, known to students as "Coed," houses 400 freshmen and is located at the northern end of the campus.

The building set-up includes "sections" of 11 rooms with a common area at the center. The arrangement facilitates interactions and friendships among first-years; one junior reported that even after two years, all of her best friends lived in her "section" in Coed. The remaining freshmen, as well as the rest of the on-campus students, reside in various other mixed-years dormitories. Students of all classes may apply to live in the International Center, where both American and international students reside and participate in programs that foster cultural awareness. The Collegiate Fellow (CF) on every floor is responsible for enforcing dormitory regulations, and while "it totally depends on the CF," many will be strict only "when they have to be," such as issuing citations for underage possession of alcohol in the dorm or excessive noise in the hallways. Those with junior or senior standing may apply for permission to reside off-campus in St. Peter.

On-campus residents take meals at the highly acclaimed cafeteria, The Caf, which has "great food" and a good selection. In addition to a "grille, rotisserie, and sandwich counter," students may select from "fire-oven-baked pizza, pasta, vegetarian selections, ethnic cuisine, a salad bar, and desserts." Meals are offered on a declining balance system; students opt for one of several-sized plans and are charged for the exact amount of food they take by a swipe of their Three Crowns Card. The cafeteria is open daily from 7 a.m. until 11 p.m., although the best selection of food is available at the "usual" eating times. While students may also use meal-plan dollars at the campus center coffee bar, there are no off-campus meal options available.

Not Just a Number

Gustavus Adolphus runs on the semester system, with four-month fall and spring terms sandwiched around a January "J-term" that offers an opportunity for intensive exploration. Each course counts for one credit, and students must complete 34 credits—including three J-term courses—over their four years. Despite the "pretty extensive list of general education requirements" that forms the basis of the college's liberal arts philosophy, many students find space in their schedules to double-major; one student even reported two majors and a minor. Two semesters of foreign language study are included in the general education requirements.

> **"It's a nice feeling not to be just a number in the crowd of students. No one really falls into the masses here."**

Biology is reportedly the most popular major, with communication studies quickly gaining sway. Many students also choose to study management. Biology and physics classes are known to be difficult, and one senior called Bio 101 "the true weeding-out class for premed students." While introductory lecture courses may enroll many dozens of students, higher-level classes taken for the major often have fewer than ten people. Registration for classes is online, and students with more credits register first. While getting excluded from capped classes is sometimes a problem for underclassmen, nobody reported trouble enrolling in a class for the major.

In addition to attending some larger lecture classes, every freshman enrolls in a First Term Seminar (FTS), chosen from a wide variety of disciplines. The FTS serves both as an introduction to college writing (a much appreciated writing credit for the general edu-

cation requirements) and an opportunity to develop a relationship with a faculty member who will serve as the student's adviser until the declaration of a major.

In addition to the formal relationship with their FTS instructors and major advisers, students report the high availability of all of their professors as a great strength of the college. "I've never had a problem catching a professor," said one sophomore, who added that in addition to posting and holding regular office hours, most instructors are available by appointment or for meals. "Even the president of the college eats in The Caf!" According to another student, "when you start to get into your major, the classes get really small, and your professors will see you on campus and know your name. It's a nice feeling not to be just a number in the crowd of students. No one really falls into the masses here."

The Gustie Life

"Gusties" involve themselves in a wide variety of activities, including the *Gustavian Weekly* (the student newspaper), the student senate, College Democrats and Republicans, choir, theater, Queers and Allies, and even the "Gaming Group," which spends its early mornings fencing with foam swords while wearing capes. Because Gustavus Adolphus is a Lutheran college, "there is a huge focus on faith on campus," and there are several Christian student groups. One popular group, Proclaim, is particularly notable for its Tuesday evening contemporary worship service. The high level of participation in extracurricular organizations, religious or otherwise, makes such activities popular ways for Gusties to meet each other.

Fraternities and sororities are moderately popular, with about a quarter of the campus involved in Greek life. The two-week pledge period takes place at the beginning of sophomore year, with prerush events held at the end of the first year. Greek organizations are not allowed to have houses, but many have "unofficial houses," which are best known for their weekend parties. Even so, one sister reports that Greeks are "required to be proactive on campus and do educationals and activities for the rest of campus and for the St. Peter community."

In addition to attending parties at off-campus houses, many freshmen pass their Friday nights at "The Dive," Gustavus Adolphus's campus dance club. One sophomore describes the scene at The Dive as "drunk, sweaty freshmen dancing close together."

Having exhausted the limited social options of St. Peter, upperclassmen tend to take their cars to Mankato, about ten minutes away from campus and the home of Minnesota State-Mankato, or to the Twin Cities of St. Paul and Minneapolis, about an hour's drive. The availability of on-campus parking for less than $100 per year makes it possible for the majority of upperclassmen to bring their cars. Gusties usually take trips to Mankato "to shop, go to the bars or eat out." In addition to the traditional party nights of Friday and Saturday, many students spend Wednesday nights out because few have Thursday classes.

Gustie athletic events are another social outlet for many students, especially when the highly ranked Division III program is enjoying success on the field, court, or rink. Soccer, football, basketball, and hockey ("It's Minnesota!" one student reminds us) are all favorites. At the game, in the classroom, or on campus, there will always be people wearing Gustavus apparel. As one student notes, "If you're a Gustie, you're proud of it."

Despite the variety of activities in which Gustavus Adolphus students involve themselves, many cite the same complaint about the college: a lack of diversity. Gusties acknowledge that the recruitment of minority students is a "genuine" institutional priority but that the school has difficulty drawing students from outside of "Minnesota, Wisconsin, Iowa, and the Dakotas," as one student put it. The College has increased its recruitment of international students, but according to one student, the campus is still "more of a 'tossed salad' than a 'melting pot,'" with minority students befriending other minority students or spending time at the Diversity Center.

A Community of Scholars
Despite Gusties' brief lamentation over the things that their campus lacks, most describe the Gustavus Adolphus experience as an overwhelmingly positive one. Many look forward to the annual Nobel conference in October, when the campus hosts Nobel laureates and other renowned scholars. Previous conference topics have included "Genetics in the New Millennium," "Unveiling the Solar System: 30 Years of Exploration," and "Nature out of Balance: Unlocking the New Ecology." Other major events include the May Day Conference, held every May 1 on topics of peace, and Christmas in Christ Chapel, an annual Christmas program involving "the entire choir and dance departments."

Most of all, Gustavus Adolphus students appreciate the sense of community that the College fosters. One junior said, "I love the idea that I am able to walk around on campus and pretty much have a general sense of who people are, but still be able to meet new people. Because the campus has enough students to do that, I meet someone new practically every day!" Gusties enjoy themselves while taking advantage of the college's myriad opportunities, and many echo this simple sentiment of one senior: "I love this little campus on the hill."—*Douglas London*

FYI
If you come to Gustavus Adolphus, you'd better bring "a snowsuit, mittens, a hat, a facemask, a HUGE jacket, and a strong will to be outside in these subzero temperatures!"
What's the typical weekend schedule? "Depends on who you are. Some drink, some do homework, but it is a guaranteed good time at Gustavus!"
If I could change one thing about Gustavus Adolphus, "I would increase diversity and cultural awareness."
Three things that every student at Gustavus Adolphus should do before graduating are "go 'traying' down Old Main Hill after the first snow, spend a starry night in the Arboretum, and have a 4 a.m. breakfast at Oodles after pulling an all-nighter."

Macalester College

Address: 1600 Grand Avenue
St. Paul, MN 55105
Phone: 651-696-6357
E-mail address:
admissions@macalester.edu
Web site URL:
www.macalester.edu
Year Founded: 1874
Private or Public: Private
Religious Affiliation:
Presbyterian historic
affiliation
Location: Urban
Number of Applicants:
1,183
Percent Accepted: 41%
**Percent Accepted who
enroll:** 27%
Number Entering: 485
**Number of Transfers
Accepted each Year:**
Unreported
Middle 50% SAT range:
M: 620–710, CR: 630–730,
Wr: 620–720
Middle 50% ACT range:
28–32

**Early admission program
EA/ED/None:** ED
**Percentage accepted
through EA or ED:** 50%
EA and ED deadline: ED I:
15-Nov, ED II: 2-Jan
Regular Deadline: 15-Jan
Application Fee: $40
**Full time Undergraduate
enrollment:** 1,884
Total enrollment: 1,918
Percent Male: 44%
Percent Female: 56%
**Total Percent Minority or
Unreported:** 33%
Percent African-American:
5%
**Percent Asian/Pacific
Islander:** 10%
Percent Hispanic: 4%
Percent Native-American: 1%
Percent International: 13%
**Percent in-state/out of
state:** 18%/52%
Percent from Public HS:
68%
Retention Rate: 93%

Graduation Rate 4-year:
86%
Graduation Rate 6-year:
Unreported
**Percent Undergraduates in
On-campus housing:** 66%
**Number of official organized
extracurricular
organizations:** 80
3 Most popular majors:
Economics, Political Science,
English
Student/Faculty ratio: 11:1
Average Class Size: 18
**Percent of students going to
grad school:** Unreported
Tuition and Fees: 36,504
**In State Tuition and Fees if
different:** No difference
Cost for Room and Board:
$8,472
**Percent receiving financial
aid out of those who apply,
first year:** 87%
**Percent receiving financial
aid among all students:**
66%

Macalester is a top-notch liberal arts college. Such a description may immediately create an image of a tiny, perhaps elitist, school covered in ivy and far removed from civilization, but it could not be further from the truth. Surely, Macalester does share some features of a stereotypical liberal arts institution. It has a small enrollment of slightly less than 2,000 students and is located in a quiet residential neighborhood. Yet beyond the school's enclave is also one of the largest urban centers in the United States, the Twin Cities, which offers Macalester the unique sense of both bustling city atmosphere and serene small-town tranquility. Furthermore, despite its location in the Midwest, Macalester has a highly diverse population, with more than 10 percent of its student body coming from overseas.

A Friendly Faculty

With a highly selective admissions process that only accepts 40 percent of applicants, Macalester brings together talented students from around the world. The school ranks 25th on the *U.S. News & World Report*, and *The Princeton Review* grades its quality of life at number seven in the nation, showing that it offers a vigorous academic experience coupled with an enjoyable social environment. "The coursework is hard and competitive, as it should be," said one junior. "But I am enjoying every minute of life here."

Macalester offers more than 40 majors, and the most popular ones are Political Science, Biology, Economics, English, and Psychology. For graduation, students must complete a relatively lengthy set of requirements, designed to ensure their breadth of knowledge. These requirements are similar to those of comparable institutions and include courses on social science, natural science, humanities, writing, foreign language, and quantitative reasoning, which is an euphemism for mathematics-related classes. Unique to Macalester and true to its aspiration to become a truly global university, courses on internationalism and multiculturalism are also listed as requirements.

Another important part of the academic experience is the first-year seminar, taken by every freshman in the fall semester. These classes are small, allow close interactions between professors and students, and place a strong emphasis on writing, an essential skill for anyone who would like to succeed in college. The strong point of this program is that the students can choose from a variety of 30 different seminars, ranging from theater to cellular biology. The professor also serves as faculty advisor for students in the class.

Although the requirements sometimes help students in discovering subjects that they would not have touched otherwise, a few students are ambivalent about taking classes in which they have no interest. "I understand that we need to know different subjects, but it is really hard to find a class that interests me and fulfills the requirements at the same time," commented one student.

As a relatively small college focused solely on undergraduate education, Macalester certainly offers an engaging faculty that gives a high level of attention to the students, unlike many larger research universities, where professors are rarely seen outside of the biweekly lectures. "If you try, you can get to know some professors really well and be really good friends with them," remarked one senior.

> "St. Paul is great. It is not New York, but it is still an important city with all kinds of cultural activities and work opportunities."

The tradeoff of receiving such personal attention, however, is that the school lacks the scale and infrastructure of larger institutions. Opportunities can be limited for students seeking laboratory or in-depth research experiences. Nevertheless, the college does have state-of-the-art facilities and tries to remedy some of its disadvantages by offering summer research grants. Studying abroad at a major university can also be helpful. However, as one student said, "if you come here, understand that there are limitations to small colleges."

The Twin Cities

Macalester occupies 53 acres of a historic residential quarter. The campus is approximately a mile away from the gorgeous Mississippi River that separates St. Paul and Minneapolis. Such location allows students to take advantage of city living while enjoying the tranquility of a quiet neighborhood. "St. Paul is great," said one student. "It is not New York, but it is still an important city with all kinds of cultural activities and work opportunities."

On the downside, Minnesota doesn't exactly have San Diego weather. The winters can be very cold. In fact, it has one of the lowest average temperatures of any major metropolitan area in the United States. As one student mentioned, "the winters here are brutal, especially for those from warm places who are not used to this weather." For snow and ice aficionados, however, the Twin Cities certainly receive plenty of precipitation, both during winter—in the form of snow, hail, and sleet—and summer—in the form of thunderstorms.

The Time of Our Lives

Students are required to live on campus for the first two years. Freshmen live in one of the three residential halls specifically reserved for first-year students. Most of them are assigned to doubles, which, as noted by one freshman, "are reasonably well-kept." Lounges are also available for students to meet and socialize. Those interested in gastronomy can take advantage of the kitchens in each residential hall. The upperclassmen generally have rooms that are more spacious and apartment-like. Since Macalester is in a major city, significant portion of juniors and seniors—about half of them—prefer living off campus. The processing of finding a nice home at a low price can be burdensome, but the college does provide rental listings to help its students. In addition to these options, there are also theme houses, including five language houses, the Hebrew House, and the Veggie Co-op, available to all after one semester of study.

Despite its small size, a large number of activities can be found on campus during weekends. While some students are drawn by the attractions of the Twin Cities and drift away from the campus during weekends, the majority of students do stay within Macalester, attending different parties or simply hanging out with friends. Given the size of its student body, Macalester has neither fraternities nor sororities. Therefore, most parties happen in dorm rooms. Alcohol, as in most colleges, abounds. Those who wish to remain dry are occasionally pressured to drink, but most of them do not feel out of place by staying sober during parties. "Drinking is widespread," said one student. "But people won't look down on you if you don't drink."

The sports teams compete in Minnesota Intercollegiate Athletic Conference, which belongs to NCAA Division III. "We are a small school," said one junior. "We are not USC or Michigan State, and that shows with our football team." On the other hand, the soccer teams at Macalester are both popular and relatively successful, having achieved consecutive winning seasons. At the same time, a number of students participate in intramural and club sports. "A lot of people enjoy playing sports even though Mac is not a big sports school," said one student.

Good Old Liberals

Macalester has been long considered one of the most liberal colleges in the United States. Therefore, Republicans can feel slightly out of place if they participate in the political scene on campus. "It is rare to find a Republican on campus these days," said one student. "I don't think these people would hate someone who is an activist Republican, but I think that person would feel really uncomfortable in political discussions because he or she will be against everyone else." Never-

theless, most students agree that Macalester is generally tolerant of other people's ideas and serves as a good forum of discussions and debates.

Another unique aspect of Macalester is its large population of foreign students for a relatively small liberal arts college. The school has strongly advocated an internationalization of the campus, and the students are particularly proud of this ethnic and cultural diversity. "I think this is one of the most important parts of Mac," mentioned one student. "Seeing people from everywhere around the world is just wonderful and really help you learn more about the world."

"I think Macalester deserves more recognition and should be a highly sought-after college," said one student. Indeed, given its academic excellence, Macalester is perhaps not as well known as a few other liberal arts institutions. The location in Minnesota and the harsh winter certainly contribute to it. There are also complaints about the small size and thus the lack of different opportunities. Nonetheless, the students are generally happy and glad that they chose to attend Macalester. Ultimately, that is what is important.—*Xiaohang Liu*

FYIs

If you come to Macalester, you'd better bring "something warm to keep you warm."

What is the typical weekend schedule? "It depends. It is different every weekend. There is so much to offer in the Twin Cities during day and night. But sadly, not everyone takes advantage of it."

If I could change one thing about Macalester, I'd "move this whole place to a lower latitude."

Three things every student at Macalester should do before graduating are "visit the city during the night, live in a theme house, and start a snowball fight."

St. John's University / College of St. Benedict

Address: PO Box 7155
　Collegeville, MN 56321-7155
Phone: 320-363-2196
E-mail address:
　admissions@csbsju.edu
Web site URL: www.csbsju.edu
Year Founded: 1857
Private or Public: Private
Religious Affiliation: Roman
　Catholic
Location: Rural
Number of Applicants: 3,204
Percent Accepted: 74%
**Percent Accepted who
　enroll:** 44%
Number Entering: 1,052
**Number of Transfers
　Accepted each Year:** 51
Middle 50% SAT range:
　M: 540–660 **CR:** 500–633,
　Wr: Unreported
Middle 50% ACT range: 22–28
**Early admission program
　EA/ED/None:** EA
**Percentage accepted
　through EA or ED:**
　Unreported

EA and ED deadline: 15-Dec
Regular Deadline: None/
　**Priority Application
　deadline:** Nov 15
Application Fee: $0
**Full time Undergraduate
　enrollment:** 3964
Total enrollment: 4039
Percent Male: 48%
Percent Female: 52%
**Total Percent Minority or
　Unreported:** 10%
Percent African-American:
　1%
**Percent Asian/Pacific
　Islander:** 3%
Percent Hispanic: 1%
Percent Native-American:
　<1%
Percent International: 5%
**Percent in-state/out of
　state:** 85%/15%
Percent from Public HS: 70%
Retention Rate: 90%
Graduation Rate 4-year: 73%
Graduation Rate 6-year:
　Unreported

**Percent Undergraduates in
　On-campus housing:** 80%
**Number of official organized
　extracurricular
　organizations:** 85
3 Most popular majors:
　Biology/Biological Sciences,
　General Business
　Administration and
　Management, General
　Speech and Rhetorical
　Studies
Student/Faculty ratio: 13:1
Average Class Size: 20 to 29
**Percent of students going to
　grad school:** 14%
Tuition and Fees: $28,668
**In State Tuition and Fees if
　different:** No difference
Cost for Room and Board:
　$7,248
**Percent receiving financial
　aid out of those who apply,
　first year:** 94%
**Percent receiving financial
　aid among all students:**
　97%

T he "Bennies" and "Johnnies" of College of St. Benedict/St. John's University know they attend a unique institution. Forget for a moment the on-campus abbey and monastery, which house some of the schools' professors. CSB/SJU, one of the top Catholic liberal arts schools in the country, is actually two schools in one: College of St. Benedict, an all-women's school, and St. John's University, an all-men's school. Each boasts its own administration, athletic program, library, bookstore, and dining halls. Yet at the same time, students from both schools interact with each other on a daily basis, both in and out of the classroom. Only late at night, when everyone is (theoretically) asleep, are the two campuses single-sex.

Not only do CSB/SJU students know their campus is unique, they also know it is gorgeous. The campus is surrounded by woods and filled with trails that offer tons of opportunities for exploration and recreation. Some students, for example, enjoy the "chapel walk," a trail which leads to the Stella Maris Chapel on the SJU campus. Legend has it that if two people walk it together, they will get married.

Two of Everything

Because the institution is really two different schools, students benefit from access to facilities on both the St. Ben's and St. John's campuses. When it comes time to study, they may head to either one of two libraries. According to students, the CSB library often turns into "a social gathering" but also features a café where students can grab some caffeine to fuel late-night studying. Meanwhile, the SJU library offers a quieter atmosphere. While its basement, nicknamed "The Dungeon," is "creepy" for some students, it offers others the silence they need. One junior summed up the difference by stating that he studies "in St. John's library when I want to get things done and St. Ben's library when I don't."

Classrooms are also split between the two campuses. But the half hour between classes gives students plenty of time to commute from one side to the other by taking "The Link," a free shuttle bus service. The Link operates day and night to allow students to travel between St. John's and St. Ben's not only for academic purposes but also to visit friends and participate in extracurricular activities.

Throughout their four years on campus, CSB/SJU students have the opportunity to develop strong relationships with their professors. Even at the introductory level, students may work closely with their professors because class sizes are so small. Additionally, all first-year students participate in a symposium, a seminar capped at 18 students. The professor of the symposium class serves as the academic advisor for his or her students, and students say everyone gets to know each other extremely well. And while they do take academics seriously, students say they still maintain a deep sense of community on campus. "People get really competitive, but in a good way," one freshman observed. "It is not like they are ready to kill each other, but they really give their best to be on top."

Bennies and Johnnies have many opportunities to explore their academic options. "I switched majors more times than I can count," admitted a current double major in communications and Spanish, "and I was even able to study abroad for seven months." The sheer diversity of classes offered and opportunities extended to students is also impressive. In particular, study abroad is a very popular option for students on both campuses. One Bennie pointed out, "You ask your friends 'where are you going to study abroad,' not 'are you going to study abroad.' " CSB/SJU offers 16 different semester-long programs in several countries. In many of these programs, students participate with other Bennies and Johnnies and are taught by local professors. Academic advisers are "very helpful" in working with students to include study abroad credits in their academic schedule while still completing required classes and the requirements of their major(s).

Eating and Sleeping

Students are more than satisfied with the housing at both St. Ben's and St. John's, especially with the apartment-style residences available for juniors and seniors. Luetmer, an on-campus apartment complex for CSB seniors, offers each resident his or her own bedroom and includes a washer and dryer within every apartment. Either a community advisor (CA) in upperclassmen apartments or a resident adviser (RA) in the residence halls will act "as a program planner, conflict solver, therapist, rule enforcer, etc." Furthermore, in accordance with the Benedictine Values, students at SJU adhere to a tradition of keeping the doors to their rooms open when they are in the room. "This allows other students the opportunity to stop in, say hi and meet new people," pointed out a current sophomore.

Students give campus food mixed reviews. While one student asserted that "it's not that good and it's overpriced," another felt "the food is really good on both campuses." Regardless how they feel about the food itself, however, students do appreciate the variety of options offered. A popular eating destination is the Refectory, or "the Reef," the dining hall at St. John's.

St. John's and St. Ben's prohibit underage students from drinking on campus, a policy which is strictly enforced. However, on weekends, one freshman observed, "everybody or almost everybody is drinking." A junior added, "If people choose not to drink, they are questioned as to why they made that decision—it seems abnormal." But another student countered, "I get [pressured to drink] more at home with my friends there. I like to have a good time and am pretty crazy without the alcohol, so I seem to fit in just fine." Students over 21 can obtain permits to have parties in their rooms on campus, and St. John's University has its own on-campus pub. Otherwise, students may head to St. Joseph, the town in which College of St. Benedict is located. The small town boasts numerous "party houses" with names such as "Chubbie," "Dingleberry" and "The Chicken Shack."

But weekends at CSB/SJU are about more than just partying. There are frequent opportunities to see movies on campus, attend cultural events such as the Festival of Cultures and the Asian New Year, or even venture into nearby St. Cloud for shopping, dining, or just hanging out. Of course, students also have the option of participating in one of the many extracurricular activities at CSB/SJU. Community service is "a huge thing on campus," and additional opportunities range from writing for the school newspaper to participating in Companions on a Journey, a faith group, or campus ministry. And of course, there are the football games.

Alumni Gone Wild

Football games are some of the most important student events of the year. "People go crazy!" exclaimed one Bennie. Alumni turn out for the home games with "their spouses, kids, grandkids . . . you name it, they are there." One CSB senior bragged that "there is a lot of pride in being a 'Bennie' or a 'Johnnie.' " As a social event and as a display of school spirit, football games are "definitely a big deal," boasting the "highest attendance for football games among Division III sports." And with a 2007 NCAA Division III championship under their belts as well as consistently successful seasons, the football games' popularity is well deserved. Students also pointed to hockey and Bennie basketball as other popular sports to attend.

Of course, students have ample opportunities to participate in sports as well. A former varsity swimmer cited his athletic experience on campus as a positive one, stressing that "my coaches were really understanding that my academics come first." Student athletes, who also enjoy a large banquet and dance at the end of the year, note that sports are a great opportunity to meet others. But if the time commitment of a varsity sport is too demanding, participation in intramural sports is always an option. "There is simply no question that the best intramural sport on campus is softball," asserted one Johnnie, who added that large numbers of Bennies and Johnnies turn out every year for the sport.

Feeling Comfortable on Campus

Campus traditions are numerous. Many rave, for example, about the CSB/SJU Thanksgiving dinner. "Students are dressed formal and served as a table. Somebody from the table has to get up and carve the turkey, and then all the food is served family style," one current senior said, adding, "It's really fun." Other traditions range from a large snowball fight on the first snowfall of every year to Pinestock, an annual event in which a "big name band" comes to campus to put on a day-long music festival. "So many students look forward to April!" one Johnnie explained.

> **"Both campuses are very welcoming, and the students are very friendly."**

Time and again, Bennies and Johnnies point out the feeling of community that truly defines their college experience. "Both campuses are very welcoming, and the students are very friendly," noted one junior. Another pointed to the role of Benedictine Values, a set of 12 Christian guidelines practiced in everyday campus life. Although students may not know them by heart, they nevertheless "play a pretty big role here . . . Students are helpful and very respectful of one another." Remarked one Johnnie, "I wouldn't change my college for all the money in the world."—*Stephanie Brockman*

FYI
If you come to CSB/SJU, you'd better bring "a smile . . . fitting in means being friendly!"
What is the typical weekend schedule? "Finish classes, have some fun, do a little homework, have some fun, finish the homework you didn't do yet, go to church (time permitting)."
If I could change one thing about CSB/SJU, I'd "have more diversity on campus."
Three things that every student at CSB/SJU should do before graduating are "take the Chapel Walk, study abroad and go to the annual Thanksgiving dinner."

St. Olaf College

Address: 1520 St. Olaf Avenue Northfield, MN 55057
Phone: 507-786-3025
E-mail address: admissions@stolaf.edu
Web site URL: www.stolaf.edu
Year Founded: 1874
Private or Public: Private
Religious Affiliation: Lutheran
Location: Rural
Number of Applicants: 4,058
Percent Accepted: 59%
Percent Accepted who enroll: 35%
Number Entering: 751
Number of Transfers Accepted each Year: 48
Middle 50% SAT range: M: 600–700, CR: 600–720, Wr: Unreported
Middle 50% ACT range: 24–31
Early admission program EA/ED/None: EA and ED
Percentage accepted through EA or ED: Unreported

EA and ED deadline: ED:1-Nov, EA: 1-Dec
Regular Deadline: 15-Jan
Application Fee: $0
Full time Undergraduate enrollment: 3,073
Total enrollment: 3,073
Percent Male: 45%
Percent Female: 55%
Total Percent Minority or Unreported: 8%
Percent African-American: 1%
Percent Asian/Pacific Islander: 5%
Percent Hispanic: 2%
Percent Native-American: <1%
Percent International: 2%
Percent in-state/out of state: 55% /45%
Percent from Public HS: 84%
Retention Rate: 93%
Graduation Rate 4-year: 82%
Graduation Rate 6-year: 84%

Percent Undergraduates in On-campus housing: 80%
Number of official organized extracurricular organizations: 137
3 Most popular majors: Biology/Biological Sciences, General English Language and Literature, General Mathematics
Student/Faculty ratio: 12.8:1
Average Class Size: 10 to 19
Percent of students going to grad school: 22%
Tuition and Fees: $34,300
In State Tuition and Fees if different: No difference
Cost for Room and Board: $7,900
Percent receiving financial aid out of those who apply, first year: 82%
Percent receiving financial aid among all students: 83%

S t. Olaf College, located in the small but picturesque town of Northfield, Minnesota, is known for building a solid sense of community. With close to the entire student body living on campus and on its gourmet meal plan, the entire collegiate experience is designed to foster a tight-knit and welcoming community. This Lutheran-affiliated college has almost everything a student could want, from a rock climbing wall to a movie theater.

A Solid Liberal Arts Education

St. Olaf is at its core a liberal arts institution and it has general education requirements which every student must complete in order to graduate. These requirements include several writing courses, two religion courses, a science, a science lab, and even an ethics requirement. Students find the requirements relatively easy to fit into the 35 classes that are required to graduate, although it can be harder for some majors such as music for which the general education requirements and the major requirements do not really

overlap. There are a few classes that are considered "laid-back" that can help a student complete his core requirements. One example is a class that combines physical education with the teaching of ethics.

Perhaps due to the rigorous general education requirements, the requirements for the majors are thought to be less demanding and it is not uncommon for a student to double or even triple major. The most popular option is to have one major as well as a concentration in that major. St. Olaf has 45 graduating majors including 15 teaching certification courses, 19 concentrations and 17 pre-professional fields. The most popular majors in order are English, biology, mathematics, economics, and psychology.

St. Olaf operates on a 4-1-4 academic schedule. This means that students have two full semesters of four classes or more and an Interim Period, also called J-Term, during the month of January immediately following winter vacation. Students must register for their J-Term class the preceding spring and have a wide variety of classes to choose from. The compact schedule allows for "a truly unique class format," as one student said. These classes are entirely designed by the professor and can include a study abroad component.

At a school with a self-proclaimed "global perspective," students are encouraged to study abroad. One student said that, out of his house of 10, all 10 had studied abroad, and he estimated that nearly 90 percent of the student population will study abroad at some point during their career at St. Olaf. The J-term is different than the semester options in that it is much more affordable and it is directly under the supervision of St. Olaf professors. One class recently went to Peru to investigate the Peruvian medical experience and to learn about medicine. Another class, studying the evolution of Christianity, visited Martin Luther's hometown in Germany and the Vatican.

> "When I walk around campus and say hello to my professors, they know my name, even if I only took one class with them three years ago."

The student-faculty ratio is 13:1 and the average class size is about 22 students. Due to the small class size the students and professors really get to know each other and professors are happy to help students outside of class, take meals with students, and generally be available. One student said, "When I walk around campus and say hello to my professors, they know my name, even if I only took one class with them three years ago." Another student commented on how her professors offered to help her work on her interviewing skills when they knew she was applying for grants. The faculty goes above and beyond its academic calling to help students develop and hone their intellectual curiosity.

An Environmentalist's Haven

At St. Olaf, the environment is a part of everyday life. Surrounded by nature, the student body has an appreciation for conservation not experienced at many other schools. Students regularly talk about things the school is doing to reduce its energy usage and, despite the fact that the school recently acquired a windmill to provide a significant amount of the campus's electricity, students still feel there is more the administration could be doing.

Environmentalism and conservation are a part of the fabric of life at St. Olaf. In the month of February the entire school gets caught up in "Campus Energy Wars." As one student observed, "people get really into it in the dorms. They'll even turn off the hallway lights at night, which caused some tension because people kept on knocking into things." Another student remarked on the willingness of students to call each other out on environmental issues, exclaiming "you get reamed if you throw a can in the trash!" This spirit of environmentalism extends to the classroom. One of the most popular classes at St. Olaf is "Campus Ecology," a class with a big environmental focus that teaches student to apply environmental analyses to the St. Olaf campus and is co-taught by a senior or junior student.

Students' appreciation of the great outdoors is expressed in more leisure-oriented ways as well. The campus abounds with hiking and running trails that students take full advantage of. One student observed, "Most of the school year at St. Olaf is pretty chilly and the winter is downright frigid but you will often see people out cross-country skiing or sledding or playing a pick-up game of broomball on frozen ponds close to campus." Students even sometimes illegally camp in the nearby "natural lands," the better to appreciate the beautiful landscape that surrounds them.

A Campus of Values

St. Olaf College was founded in 1874 by a group of Norwegian-American immigrant pastors and farmers—which, incidentally, explains the prominence of St. Olaf's Norwegian-language department. The College began and continues as a Lutheran institution. There is a chapel located on campus at which many students attend the Sunday service. St. Olaf students are self-described as "homey, family- and value-oriented." While religion is not pressed upon any student and there is an active Muslim community, Protestant Christians and Lutherans in particular are the dominant religious group. There are a number of extracurricular activities that are centered on religion including Bible studies and Christian fellowships, the largest being the Fellowship of Christian Athletes. Most teams say a prayer before starting their game and it is not uncommon to see heads bowed in brief prayer before a meal in the dining hall.

However, students who are not particularly religious are not uncomfortable on campus, nor do they feel judged. One student, when asked about the presence of religion on campus, said that "it can be a little surprising," but went on to explain that people only really talk about religion in religion class as part of the core requirement. Students can find a religion class on almost all major world religions and teachers are careful to allow students to form their own opinions. Some students express their religion by abstaining from sex until marriage or not drinking. One student remarked, "Students have religious views and they follow them."

Social Life

As one student said, "you make it what you want it to be." In general students are satisfied with the social life at St. Olaf. One student describes it as "good, although it can be a little slow." In line with its Lutheran values, the campus is dry, meaning that alcohol is not allowed anywhere on campus. All students are in agreement that this does not inhibit the consumption of alcohol. One student even commented that the prohibition of alcohol leads to binge drinking behavior: "People drink stupidly because they need to pregame faster so they don't get caught." Another student, however, felt that the dry campus "was not really enforced. Usually resident life is semilenient so students drink as much or as little as other college students." This student praised the school for the number of non-alcoholic activities that it organizes in order to support its dry status. Such activities include showings of recent movies every weekend night, dances, different bands and musical groups, and dance performers. Buntrock Commons, the student center, is the home of the Pause, a completely student-run hangout that features pool tables, movies, concerts, and dances.

Due to the dry campus rule, keggers are a nonentity at St. Olaf; closed-door room parties are more the norm. About 4 percent of the student body does live off campus and these students are known for holding the bigger parties. Students also take advantage of the few bars in the town of Northfield. The Rueb'n'Stein is a campus favorite and has a big Wednesday showing. Froggy Bottom's is another popular bar with a big Thursday night following. For a more chill vibe with live music and imported beers, students go to The Contented Cow, which has more of a pub feel and is a good place for conversation. The dry campus rule also forces students to be somewhat enterprising if they want to throw a big party. Students will sometimes rent a space in the town of Northfield, usually at the Legion, and will host a party there. Such parties are announced via Facebook and generally charge $5 at the door.

Minneapolis and St. Paul are only 45 minutes from the St. Olaf campus, but trips to the twin cities are rare, according to students. Seniors are more likely to make the trek to the cities to watch a play or go to a jazz club. In order to get there students need a car, something the school allows but which few students take advantage of. One student remarked that "having a car gives you more freedom." It can be hard to get out of Northfield and sometimes students said they felt a bit isolated. Other students valued the atmosphere that the campus fosters and believe it helps to foster the sense of community that is so strong at St. Olaf.

When asked about the dating scene at St. Olaf, one student replied with some sarcasm, "I wouldn't say it's huge." Another student when asked responded with laughter and went on to explain that the gender gap at St. Olaf, which is 45 percent women and 55 percent men, seems even bigger. St. Olaf students are more likely to still be in a relationship with a high school boyfriend or girlfriend than to casually date in college. Of course, the usual casual college hook-ups do occur here although less frequently than at other schools due to the religious beliefs and values of many students. The tight-knit community feel of the campus also impedes casual dating as most students know each other and news travels fast.

St. Olaf is a beautiful college where students smile and greet each other whether they know each other or not. Students are friendly, welcoming, and open-minded despite the homogeneity of the student body. The rural setting of the campus encourages the tight-knit sense of community that pervades the campus and makes students feel they are taken care of and part of a larger St. Olaf family. St. Olaf seeks to create whole people who are intellectually curious with solid values. "You're not just getting together for class; you're in the same buildings, living together, learning together, and growing together."—*Tara Singh*

FYI
If you come to St. Olaf, you'd better bring "winter sports gear."
What is the typical weekend schedule? "Friday everyone relaxes during the day then goes to a house party or something on campus. Saturday people nap then at night they go to a sporting event or into town. Sundays are a relaxed day to do homework or watch movies."
If I could change one thing about St. Olaf, I'd "not make it a dry campus, more for safety reasons."
Three things every student at St. Olaf should do before graduating are "go to Christmas fest, climb the rock-climbing wall, and spend one night out in the natural lands."

University of Minnesota

Address: 231 Pillsbury Drive SE Minneapolis, MN 55455-0213
Phone: 612-625-2008
E-mail address: admissions@umn.edu
Web site URL: www.umn.edu
Year Founded: 1851
Private or Public: Public
Religious Affiliation: None
Location: Urban
Number of Applicants: 26,097
Percent Accepted: 57%
Percent Accepted who enroll: 36%
Number Entering: 5,266
Number of Transfers Accepted each Year: 2,981
Middle 50% SAT range: M: 580–700, CR: 540–680, Wr: 530–660
Middle 50% ACT range: 24–29
Early admission program EA/ED/None: None

Percentage accepted through EA or ED: NA
EA and ED deadline: NA
Regular Deadline: Rolling
Application Fee: $45
Full time Undergraduate enrollment: 32,294
Total enrollment: 47,240
Percent Male: 47%
Percent Female: 53%
Total Percent Minority or Unreported: 25%
Percent African-American: 5%
Percent Asian/Pacific Islander: 9%
Percent Hispanic: 2%
Percent Native-American: 1%
Percent International: 2%
Percent in-state/out of state: 73%/27%
Percent from Public HS: Unreported
Retention Rate: 88%
Graduation Rate 4-year: Unreported

Graduation Rate 6-year: Unreported
Percent Undergraduates in On-campus housing: 22%
Number of official organized extracurricular organizations: 600
3 Most popular majors: Biology/Biological Sciences, Journalism, Mechanical Engineering
Student/Faculty ratio: Unreported
Average Class Size: 10 to 19
Percent of students going to grad school: Unreported
Tuition and Fees: $14,634
In State Tuition and Fees if different: $10,634
Cost for Room and Board: $7,280
Percent receiving financial aid out of those who apply, first year: 67%
Percent receiving financial aid among all students: 51%

Nestled at the heart of a metropolis dubbed "the Twin Cities," the University of Minnesota's largest campus has twin sections as well. The Twin Cities campus acts as the center of the University of Minnesota's four-campus system, but branches of the large state university extend to Duluth, Crookston, and Morris.

"A Common Bond for All"

The University's motto says it all. The University of Minnesota, affectionately known as the "U," embraces four locations in five cities and has something to offer all its students. The Twin Cities campus boasts an enrollment of about 50,000 students, far more than the remaining three in the system.

But the flagship embraces its twin city roots and is divided into a St. Paul location, which focuses on agriculture, and the Minneapolis campus. The Minneapolis half of the U is further split into the East Campus and West Campus by the Mississippi River and connected by the iconic Washington Avenue Bridge. Adding to the U's sprawling identity, the campus has a few notable "neighborhoods"—Knoll area, Mall area, Health area, Athletic area and Gateway area. Getting around the large campus can be tricky, especially with the Mighty Mississippi in the way, so signs that make up "the Gopher Way" help students find their way.

The most notable buildings are the Weisman Art Gallery, designed by Frank Gehry, and the historic Greek row located centrally on campus on the Northrup Mall. The U offers eight residence halls and three apartment buildings and guarantees housing to all freshmen. "Living on campus is convenient," but many students commute from their homes nearby campus, making parking a challenge. Most students live in the "superblock" complex—a four-block area across from the athletics center. Freshmen can live in any of the University's seven dormitories, only two of which are explicitly designated for freshmen. Freshmen are assigned their own Community Advisors, of which there are usually two per floor in each dorm. As one student noted, much of a freshman's social life is centered around their dorm, while upperclassman life is concentrated beyond the campus.

Any students concerned about living in the heart of Minneapolis should be unduly worried; the U's president has put a significant focus on safety, and students praised the array of different resources designed to keep them safe, including security guards who walk pathways at night, security staff in all the dorms, emergency phone hubs located throughout campus, and driving services.

The campus also boasts an impressive student center called Coffman Memorial Union. Not only does the building feature a bowling alley, video games, and billiards, but it also screens movies every weekend that are free to students, faculty, and their relatives. Said one student: "Coffman is a huge component in fostering community."

Go-pher the Gopher

The U boasts a storied athletics tradition centered around the basketball, football, and ice hockey teams. The Golden Gophers participate in a long-standing rivalry game with the University of Wisconsin. "A lot of people go to games and watch them on campus," one student said. Another added, "There is a lot of school pride for sports teams." Dating back to legendary hockey coach Herb Brooks, who later coached the 1980 U.S. men's hockey team to an Olympic gold medal in the "Miracle on Ice," the U's men's ice hockey team has five national championships under its belt. Out-of-staters beware: most hockey recruits hail from Minnesota—all but two members of the current 26-man team are from the Land of 10,000 Lakes.

Athletics, though, are just one piece of the thriving campus atmosphere. Students cited Greek life, the Black Student Association, and other student organizations as prevalent on campus. "People are usually very committed to extracurricular activities," a student said. "I think they are a good way to meet people and relieve yourself from schoolwork." Still, while Greek life is popular on campus, it does not dominate social life for students at the U. The University's more than 700 student groups offer a wide array of opportunities to get involved in campus life—from the student newspaper to religious organizations. "Whatever you're into, you'll find it at the U, and probably there'll be quite a lot of people with you," one student said.

Choices, Choices, Choices

On such a large campus, academic options are hugely varied—from the agricultural programs offered in St. Paul to the College of Design. "The U of M offers very challenging courses but it also offers many fun courses such as, dance, sports and horseback riding classes," a student said. Some popular majors are political science, psychology, business and the sciences. "U of M has so many majors to choose from," a student marveled.

> "The U of M offers very challenging courses but it also offers many fun courses such as, dance, sports, and horseback riding classes."

Academic advising at the U tends to work well, one student explained, given that there is full-time staff with the specific role of advising students on their academic work. Students are advised by someone within their field of study, and while one student said getting a good adviser can be "pretty hit or miss," it helps to have a full time staff member available to help when needed.

Like any large university, class sizes reach about 100 students for introductory courses, slimming down to about 50 for specialized classes, making it relatively easy for students to get a place in a course.

The workload can get pretty heavy, with an average of two to three papers and exams per class in addition to reading. But a very descriptive course catalog helps narrow down the options. Teachers try to embrace the diversity and variety offered at the U. "I like how teachers are very open minded and teach from many perspectives," a student said. Discussions on the diverse campus are a high point for some students: "What I like most is the different people you meet and how the ranges in their experience in what is being taught is. The discussion that go on in class is really exciting."

One student mentioned the ease with which many people at the University of Min-nesota make friends: "Many people meet through classes and become friends as well. People often work and study in groups. People also hang out at the U just for fun." Ultimately, the U is a place where not only hockey-playing Minnesotans but Gophers from over 130 countries around the world can live, learn and make the most of their college years—*Brittany Golob and Raymond Carlson*

FYI

If you come to the University of Minnesota, you'd better bring "a planner."

What's the typical weekend schedule? "Friday afternoon you're either going to be out running or be at the Rec before the weekend starts, in the evening you'll most likely be at some social event in the dorms or frat row. Saturday you'll go to a sporting event or concert, Saturday night is a mirror image of Friday, and on Sunday you sleep in, maybe watch football and then get to work."

If I could change one thing about the University of Minnesota, "I'd make the class sizes smaller."

Three things every student at the University of Minnesota should do before graduating are "study abroad, participate in an extracurricular activity, and go have a burger in the Shake & 80s malt shop."

Mississippi

Millsaps College

Address: 1701 North State Streeth Jackson, MS 39210
Phone: 601-974-1050
E-mail address: admissions@millsaps.edu
Web site URL: www.millsaps.edu
Year Founded: 1890
Private or Public: Private
Religious Affiliation: Methodist
Location: Suburban
Number of Applicants: 1,266
Percent Accepted: 77%
Percent Accepted who enroll: 28%
Number Entering: 271
Number of Transfers Accepted each Year: 64
Middle 50% SAT range: M: 538–650, CR: 538–673, Wr: Unreported
Middle 50% ACT range: 23–29
Early admission program EA/ED/None: EA

Percentage accepted through EA or ED: Unreported
EA and ED deadline: 8-Jan
Regular Deadline: Oct. 1
Application Fee: $0
Full time Undergraduate enrollment: 1,013
Total enrollment: 1,118
Percent Male: 48%
Percent Female: 52%
Total Percent Minority or Unreported: 17%
Percent African-American: 9%
Percent Asian/Pacific Islander: 4%
Percent Hispanic: 2%
Percent Native-American: <1%
Percent International: 1%
Percent in-state/out of state: 43%/ 57%
Percent from Public HS: 61%
Retention Rate: 79%
Graduation Rate 4-year: 62%

Graduation Rate 6-year: 66%
Percent Undergraduates in On-campus housing: 81%
Number of official organized extracurricular organizations: 75
3 Most popular majors: Biology, Business, Psychology
Student/Faculty ratio: 11:1
Average Class Size: 2 to 9
Percent of students going to grad school: 48%
Tuition and Fees: $24,754
In State Tuition and Fees if different: No difference
Cost for Room and Board: $8,800
Percent receiving financial aid out of those who apply, first year: 71%
Percent receiving financial aid among all students: 55%

Though largely unknown outside of Mississippi, Millsaps College is highly respected throughout the area as a school that offers a well-rounded liberal arts education at a competitive price. Though Millsaps Majors may seem to have lackluster school spirit when it comes to supporting their athletic teams, most students enjoy life at Millsaps.

Work Hard

Millsaps was the first school in Mississippi to have a chapter of the academic honor society Phi Beta Kappa, and the school generally ranks high both for its academics and for its relatively low tuition. Millsaps offers 32 majors, and though the requirements vary by major, each student must complete 10 core courses, offered in topics ranging from history to science to mathematics.

A major selling point for many students is the small size of the classes at Millsaps. The average class size is 15 people, and the student/faculty ratio is 12:1. This class size fosters open discussion as well as closes relationships between professors and students. According to one student, "The classes are very engaging, very discussion-oriented." Students say that their professors "really do care about their students," and several admitted that they considered the relationships formed with their professors the most valuable part of their college experiences. "I consider some of these professors my friends." While students definitely note that the academic life is very "strenuous," most say they were fulfilled in their academic lives. "I feel like I learn so much."

Party Hard

The social life at Millsaps seems to revolve pretty much exclusively around the Greek system. There are six fraternities and six sororities governed by the Panhellenic Council and the Interfraternity Council. While students say that it is not essential to be in a fraternity or sorority—"It's not like if you aren't Greek you're going to have an awful time"—it seems pretty hard to escape the fact that the Greek scene is *the* scene at Millsaps. This is highlighted in particular by the fact that non-Greeks are referred to as "independents." Though it is perfectly acceptable to be an independent, an independent who won't set foot in a fraternity house might have a hard time finding a party, particularly during freshman and sophomore years. As students get older, however, "they tend to drift off campus more." Many upperclassmen enjoy local spots Hal & Mal's or Schimmels for drinks, music, or just hanging out with their friends. According to one student, "A lot of times you can find your professors at Fenian's."

> **"I consider some of these professors my friends"**

Drinking rules on campus seem to be pretty sensible. Though rowdy behavior in the dormitories is prohibited, students appreciated the fact that "the RAs treat us like adults." The two large campus-wide events every year are the homecoming football game in the fall and Major Madness in the spring. At Major Madness, students gather on "The Bowl"—the large, grassy area in the middle of campus—and play games, eat, drink, and listen to music. Though the musicians are rarely big-name stars—bands have included Better Than Ezra, Stroke Nine, and the North Mississippi All Stars— "It's definitely stuff you can dance to, sing to and drink to."

With the exception of the homecoming game, Millsaps students in general don't get extremely excited about sports. "It's definitely not like an SEC school, so if people come to Millsaps expecting that, then they're not going to get it." Instead, supporting athletic teams is more of a matter of supporting your friends who happen to be on those teams than a statement of school pride.

On Campus—Where It's At

Approximately 81 percent of Millsaps students live on campus. Most choose to live in the dormitories for all four years, though some upperclassmen move off campus. The housing is divided up by the North Side and the South Side. Freshman year, everyone lives on the North Side. After freshman year, students pick their rooms based on a room draw, which functions on a point system. Each student entering the room draw receives points based on his or her class year and GPA. Students then combine with their roommates and vie for the best dorms. The residence hall rooms are all double-occupancy, and the halls feature traditional double rooms, apartment-style and suite-style rooms. Though the students admit that the dormitories aren't by any means luxurious, "they do their best to make it pleasant." "My friends who are from other colleges always talk about how nice our dorms are here."

For most students, more important than the dorms themselves is the fact that the dorms provide a social outlet as well. "It's really cool when all your friends live on campus." This social atmosphere is also extended to the main cafeteria, also known as "The Caf'." The Caf' is one of two dining options on campus, the other being the Kava House, which provides quick meals to go. At The Caf', students select from a menu of salads, soups, sandwiches, and daily hot meals. Students generally seem to be quite pleased with the quality of the food, though opinions differ about the variety of food choices. While one senior said that she was "really going to miss [the food] next year," another complained that the food choices were repetitive.

The Center of the State

Students seem to have mixed feelings about being in the city of Jackson itself. In one 2008 ranking, Jackson was ranked the nation's 11th most dangerous city. For this reason, students say they must exercise caution while out on campus, but they don't feel that the crime level in Jackson is detrimental to their college experience. Students are very well aware that "Jackson isn't the safest of cities." While one student said that she generally feels "safe on campus," she was sure to note that she "wouldn't walk around alone in the dark."

One advantage of being in the city of Jackson—which has a population of just under 180,000 people—is the city's position as the capital of the state, and thus the center of state politics. Particularly for students with an interest in politics or governments, Millsaps is a good place to get a taste of the political arena. Students say it is very easy to get internships in the state or local government, and that state officials will sometimes teach classes at Millsaps as adjunct professors.

Though the city of Jackson is very much a political city, students say that campus life is "not too hardcore politically" and that the student body as a whole does not lean very heavily left or right politically. Both "the Millsaps Young Democrats and the Republicans are very well-represented and well-spoken-for." Students say that Millsaps is a place for political expression but that there are also many students who abstain from political discussion altogether.

Diversity?

Students new to Millsaps may be surprised by the lack of geographic and racial diversity. Slightly more than 50 percent of the students are from the state of Mississippi, and the 2005–2006 freshman class at Millsaps was comprised of only 17 percent minority students. While some students lamented that fact—"I'd like it to be more diverse than it is"—students across the board were impressed by the openness of students to new ideas and to different types of people. "Millsaps is very diverse if you look at the big picture, not just at race." Another noted, "What makes up for [the lack of racial diversity] is the diversity of ideas and of opinions." Though there is little racial diversity on campus, student organizations like the Black Student Association provide minority students with a sense of community.

For many students, the mere size of Millsaps contributes to this openness for different types of students. With just over a thousand undergraduates, "I feel like I've met everyone on campus one way or another," one senior said. Another student chalked up the open-minded atmosphere at Millsaps to the philosophy of education at the school. "They really teach you to be warm-hearted and open to everything and not close-minded at all."—*Susanna Moore*

FYI

If you come to Millsaps, you'd better bring "a willingness to work hard and party hard."

What is the typical weekend schedule? "Friday—go to dinner and to the fraternity houses; Saturday—watch football all day or go to the football game, eat dinner, preparty and go to the fraternity houses; Sunday—wake up late and do your homework."

If I could change one thing about Millsaps, I'd "make it farther from home."

Three things every student at Millsaps should do before graduating are "swim in the fountains, Bowl-sit, really get to know a professor."

Mississippi State University

Address: Box 6334
Mississippi State, MS
39762
Phone: 662-325-2224
E-mail address:
admit@msstate.edu
Web site URL:
www.msstate.edu
Year Founded: 1878
Private or Public: Public
Religious Affiliation: None
Location: Suburban
Number of Applicants: 7,429
Percent Accepted: 66%
**Percent Accepted who
enroll:** 51%
Number Entering: 2,478
**Number of Transfers
Accepted each Year:**
1,806
Middle 50% SAT range:
M: 538–650, CR: 490–630,
Wr: Unreported
Middle 50% ACT range:
20–27
**Early admission program
EA/ED/None:** None

**Percentage accepted
through EA or ED:** NA
EA and ED deadline: NA
Regular Deadline: Rolling
Application Fee: $35
**Full time Undergraduate
enrollment:** 13,049
Total enrollment: 16,785
Percent Male: 51%
Percent Female: 49%
**Total Percent Minority or
Unreported:** 25%
Percent African-American:
21%
**Percent Asian/Pacific
Islander:** 1%
Percent Hispanic: 1%
Percent Native-American:
1%
Percent International: 1%
**Percent in-state/out of
state:** 76% / 24%
Percent from Public HS:
Unreported
Retention Rate: 84%
Graduation Rate 4-year:
Unreported

Graduation Rate 6-year:
Unreported
**Percent Undergraduates in
On-campus housing:** 26%
**Number of official organized
extracurricular
organizations:** 326
3 Most popular majors:
Business Administration,
Elementary Education,
Physical Education Teaching
& Coaching
Student/Faculty ratio: 15:1
Average Class Size: 20 to 29
**Percent of students going to
grad school:** Unreported
Tuition and Fees: $12,503
**In State Tuition and Fees if
different:** $5,151
Cost for Room and Board:
$7,333
**Percent receiving financial
aid out of those who apply,
first year:** 76%
**Percent receiving financial
aid among all students:**
54%

The college-bound student seeking a friendly environment should take a look at Mississippi State University. MSU is an increasingly challenging university that attracts students from within the state of Mississippi and across the nation. It's a school built on unity, friendliness, and, of course, education. Tucked away from the hustle and bustle of city life in quiet Mississippi State, Mississippi, students at MSU take great pride in their school and its athletic teams.

Bulldogs and Textbooks

MSU is divided into eight different colleges of undergraduate studies, ranging from the College of Education to the liberal arts–oriented College of Arts and Sciences. MSU also offers a variety of programs in agricultural, engineering and forestry studies. At the College of Agriculture and Life Sciences, a student can major in anything from human sciences with an emphasis in interior design to food safety with an emphasis on management and production. MSU offers a wide range of pre-

professional programs ranging from premed to poultry science, but freshmen are preoccupied with a core curriculum that covers a writing course, courses in the humanities, social and physical sciences, and computer literacy. In addition, MSU has a unique and highly rated Golf and Sports Turf Management Program, as well as a Landscape Architecture program (separate from the College of Architecture). Some freshmen, especially those going into the architecture field, find that they have much more work than other students. "I have 23 hours of work a week, models to build, but that's what happens at the best architecture program in the South," said one freshman majoring in architecture. Another freshman agreed, "The architecture program is great here. But, it is a little too demanding sometimes, although I love making all the models." MSU students note that the architecture, engineering, and biology majors provide the most challenging courses on campus. A sophomore noted that "architecture and engineering, hands down" are the most time-consuming. No matter what they major in, all MSU students are required to study a foreign language. A sophomore majoring in international business explained that it is "really a double major; business and a foreign language." A psychology major said that his foreign language requirement of four credits is "not that bad; at least I get to learn French."

Athletics Are the Weekend

MSU students feel Bulldog love flowing through their veins. The school is united by the common desire for the success of their athletic teams, particularly football, baseball, and basketball. "You have to be there if there is a game going on; it's what this place is all about," said a freshman. "We usually all go to the stadium, and if the game is going well, we will all stay until the end. Lately, the wins have been difficult to come by, but it will turn around," said a hopeful MSU senior. Since most of MSU's students are from within the state, many even go home if there's no athletic event to attend that weekend.

The biggest football game of the year is the Egg Bowl, which is usually on or around Thanksgiving Day. It pits MSU against archrival Ole Miss. "The Egg Bowl is something that I always look forward to. It is so much fun, and everybody comes out and shows some school spirit," said a sophomore. No one's quite sure how the Thanksgiving-season match-up got its name, but according to one freshman, "It doesn't matter what it's called; what matters is that we beat Ole Miss, and that's all." According to legend, many years ago a cow walked onto the field during the Egg Bowl, and MSU proceeded to win the game. Ever since, MSU students proudly ring cowbells at the game for good luck. One junior said that the administration has been trying to ban the cowbells because they're considered artificial noisemakers, but "we still find a way to sneak them in. I can't wait to do it this Thanksgiving."

Greek life dominates the MSU party scene. On football weekends and other big occasions, the fraternities always "make sure that there is a party to attend." Around 25 percent of the student population is involved in the fraternity and sorority system. One sophomore observed that Greek life is a "pretty big deal here, especially if you want to party. You have to know someone in the frat if you want to drink." But a freshman who did not rush a fraternity because of his workload reassured, "I still party every weekend, and I can go to a frat if I want to. It is not frowned upon to not be a brother, or even if you don't want to

drink. It's really great." Another nondrinking junior agreed that "people are friendly to you, regardless." Most MSU students are quick to note that there is very little drug use on campus. Students who drink admit that it is easy to get around the policy, and that if you "are just careful, you aren't going to get busted," although the strictness of enforcement "totally depends on your RA (Resident Advisers)."

> **"That is the best thing about going to MSU: the people and the friendliness."**

MSU students are known for their Southern hospitality. One sophomore raved "that's part of the magic here; everybody says hello to each other." A freshman commented that it's easy to make friends at MSU and that "you find your niche faster than at any other school; it is awesome." Another freshman similarly said "that is the best thing about going to MSU, the people and the friendliness."

Southern Charm

Students love that their campus feels so "homey and cozy" and that people are "friendly wherever you go." The campus is literally the only thing in town; the borders of the school make up the borders of the city of Mississippi State, Mississippi, which borders the small town of Starkville. "It's so flat, so spread out, but everything feels so close together as time passes by," said one sophomore. Because of the campus's large size, however, many students feel that they "cannot make it here without a car." Though the school's administration has tried to introduce alternate transportation options, students often jump in their cars to get to faraway classes. "Most people just bring their cars to school, especially the people that live within driving distance. It is just something you need here," said one junior. Another reason for having a car is that most students go home for the weekend if there is "nothing going on." Cars are also helpful for the three-quarters of upperclassmen who choose to live off campus. "By the time you're a sophomore, you want to get together with your friends and move to an apartment," one junior said. There are plenty of apartment complexes in Starkville, but only a handful located within walking distance of the main part of campus.

For those students who do live in dorms, the facilities are in the process of being upgraded. The current standard freshman dorm "could be a lot worse," according to one freshman. All freshmen live in double rooms equipped with a sink and a refrigerator. Most freshman dorms are single-sex, and the coed dorms still segregate the sexes by hallway. MSU recently concluded a major dorm renovation, demolishing three of the oldest existing dorms and building three new ones: the Roy H. Ruby Residence Hall, the S. Bryce Griffis Residence Hall, and Hurst Hall. These new dorms feature private baths, wireless Internet and cable television. Upperclassmen who decide to stay on campus usually live in suites, "which are a little ratty." One junior who lives on campus says that upperclassmen live in lackluster dorms because the "school has already made a good impression on the freshmen, and most people don't usually stay on campus for the rest of their years." Upperclass suites usually have four single bedrooms and a connected bathroom.

At MSU, students feel like they are gaining more than a higher education. Not only are students learning, they feel "it is just so great here." They are quick to say that the best part about MSU is the friendliness of the student body and the faculty. One freshman said that "folks here are just good people—it is just that simple." As one senior put it, "it's just the good ol' South here, with good ol' people. I will be a Bulldog until the day I die."—*Alberto Masliah*

FYI

If you come to MSU, you'd better bring "a car. Things are all spread out."

What is the typical weekend schedule? "Wake up, study, visit friends, party, go to the game, party again."

If I could change anything about MSU, I would "make the buildings more attractive."

Three things every student should do at MSU before graduating are "go to the Egg Bowl with a cowbell, go to at least one game of every sport, get involved in an organization."

University of Mississippi

Address: 145 Martindale University, MS 38677

Phone: 662-915-7226

E-mail address: admissions@olemiss.edu

Web site URL: www.olemiss.edu

Year Founded: 1844

Private or Public: Public

Religious Affiliation: None

Location: Rural

Number of Applicants: 7,946

Percent Accepted: 83%

Percent Accepted who enroll: 37%

Number Entering: 2,437

Number of Transfers Accepted each Year: 1,543

Middle 50% SAT range: M: 460–590, CR: 460–600, Wr: Unreported

Middle 50% ACT range: 20–28

Early admission program EA/ED/None: None

Percentage accepted through EA or ED: NA

EA and ED deadline: NA

Regular Deadline: 07/20

Application Fee: $25

Full time Undergraduate enrollment: 12,682

Total enrollment: 14,459

Percent Male: 48%

Percent Female: 52%

Total Percent Minority or Unreported: 18%

Percent African-American: 13%

Percent Asian/Pacific Islander: 1%

Percent Hispanic: 1%

Percent Native-American: 0%

Percent International: 1%

Percent in-state/out of state: 66%/34%

Percent from Public HS: 70%

Retention Rate: 80%

Graduation Rate 4-year: Unreported

Graduation Rate 6-year: Unreported

Percent Undergraduates in On-campus housing: 26%

Number of official organized extracurricular organizations: 250

3 Most popular majors: Accounting, Elementary Education and Teaching, Marketing/Marketing Management

Student/Faculty ratio: 19:1

Average Class Size: 10 to 19

Percent of students going to grad school: Unreported

Tuition and Fees: $12,468

In State Tuition and Fees if different: $5,107

Cost for Room and Board: $5,914

Percent receiving financial aid out of those who apply, first year: 61%

Percent receiving financial aid among all students: 36%

The historic institution nestled in the town of Oxford, just 80 miles south of Memphis, is formally known as the University of Mississippi—but to those in the know, it's Ole Miss. First coined in 1897 as the title of the University's yearbook, Ole Miss is more than a mere nickname. It reflects the institution's deeply-rooted traditions, Southern heritage, and welcoming atmosphere. Above all, the name reflects the affection students and alumni feel for their university, with its scenic campus, close-knit feel, and growing international prestige.

An Intimate Public University

Among public universities, Ole Miss has a strong academic reputation—one that has steadily improved in recent years. With seven undergraduate schools—the College of Liberal Arts and the Schools of Accountancy, Applied Sciences, Business Administration, Education, Engineering and Pharmacy—the University has a program to offer every student, no matter where their academic interests lie. Among the various schools, the College of Liberal Arts and the School of Business Administration boast the highest undergraduate enrollments.

Over the past few years, Ole Miss has garnered a high national rank among public colleges. Students think the University's growing prestige is deserved. "Academic life at Ole Miss is great," said one student. "Most classes aren't too big, and all the professors I have come across are more than willing to help their students in any way possible."

Ole Miss's relatively small undergraduate population gives students easy access to professors and administrators. The administration has an open-door policy, encouraging students to bring concerns or suggestions straight to the top. Professors, likewise, are eager to meet with students. "Because we're not that big, the student-faculty ratio is pretty good," remarked one senior. Most students agree that class size is not overwhelming, especially compared to other public universities. Upper-level courses generally range from 20-30 students, and one upperclassman noted that many professors require participation. Introductory "core" courses, however, can hold over 150 students.

To give underclassmen the opportunity to take smaller, more specialized classes, the University offers several unique programs. Each year, the McDonnell Barksdale Honors College admits around 120 freshmen with exemplary academic records. "A lot of money has been invested in the honors college, and

it offers students great resources," said one student. The Croft Institute, Ole Miss's renowned international studies program, is even more selective, accepting only 40 students a year. But these specialized programs are not for the faint of heart. As one senior noted, "Honors College and Croft classes are more difficult than most."

For the first few months of their college careers, all Ole Miss freshmen must take an hour-a-week course called University Studies. Designed to ease the transition into college life, University Studies gives freshmen a chance to learn more about Ole Miss and to meet classmates.

Southern-style Living

Students give the University's dorms mixed reviews. "They're pretty nice," said one student. Another called them "outdated." Still another insisted that "the ladies' dorms are nicer than the men's." Whatever their opinion, freshmen are required to live on campus. All university housing is gender-segregated by building. The two main freshman dorms are Martin for women and Stockard for men. Visitation hours are relatively strict; guests must leave by 11 p.m. on weeknights and 1 a.m. on weekends, unless a dormitory's students vote in the first week of the semester to extend these hours. Men's and women's dorms are close together, and most students claim not to mind single-sex housing.

Responding to students' complaints about university housing, the administration has begun extensive renovations. Currently under construction is a massive residential college, where students can live all four years. "The residential college will have a computer lab, a gym, a cafeteria, an auditorium, and more," explained one senior. "If I could go back to my freshman year, I would definitely want to live there!"

Although many students think mandatory on-campus housing for freshmen is a good idea—as one student said, "it forces you to get to know campus and your classmates"—almost all upperclassmen live in Greek houses or off campus. Nearby apartments, while slightly less convenient than dorms, give students more freedom and flexibility. Plus, most Ole Miss students own cars, which facilitate trips to class, the grocery store, and even to Memphis (just over an hour away) to shop or go out on weekends.

Rebel Revelry

When it comes to social life, students agree: Ole Miss knows how to party. "We're not ranked the number two party school for nothing," laughed one senior.

The social scene at Ole Miss is extensive and varied. Greek life is popular on campus—35 percent of undergraduates belong to a fraternity or sorority—and rarely does a weekend go by without a fraternity party taking place. In the spring, each fraternity hosts a no-holds-barred blowout, such as SAE's "Patty Murphy" or ATO's "Gator Bash." Often these parties last an entire weekend, culminating in crawfish cookouts or barbeques with live bands. Fraternity parties are often open to non-Greeks, although students note that women have an easier time getting in than men.

While fraternity and sorority events are a big part of campus life, students agree that non-Greeks won't want for things to do on weekends. "Greek life is a great way to get to know people early on, and fraternity parties are big for freshmen," explained one student. "But as you get older, you find the social scene gears away from fraternity parties—people are over that scene."

The Oxford town square, which students described as "one of a kind," offers plenty of alternatives to the Greek party scene, particularly for the 21-plus crowd. Popular weekend hangouts include: Rooster's, a blues and barbeque joint owned by actor Morgan Freeman; Proud Larry's, a more laid-back bar with live music; and the Library, where students 18 and up can come to dance and watch sports games. Rebel Ride, a free transportation service, drives students home when the bars close at 1 a.m. Said one junior: "Oxford is a small town, but there never seems to be a shortage of things going on."

Grooving at the Grove

In the fall, no Ole Miss weekend would be complete without a Saturday afternoon trip to the Grove. Most days of the year, the 10-acre grassy knoll known as the Grove looks like a simple lawn with the occasional magnolia tree. But on game days, it transforms into what one junior calls a "huge party"—an elaborate tailgating event that is rivaled nowhere. In fact, tailgating is somewhat of a misnomer for Ole Miss's version, which doesn't involve cars, trucks, or parking lots. Rather, tailgaters at the Grove reserve open-air tents of red, white, or blue. Students and families bring grills, nice food, silverware, candles, and occasionally even chandeliers into their tents, and spend the day eating, drinking, and socializing. "Adults and students are chatting, kids are running around—

it's very family-oriented," explained one student. Ever the Southern ladies and gentlemen, many students dress up to tailgate at the Grove; girls wear sundresses and guys wear collared shirts with khakis.

School spirit abounds at Ole Miss, and football games are an integral part of the campus experience. After the Grove, students move to the stadium in their semiformal attire to cheer on the Rebels. One student notes that "tailgating used to be bigger than the football game itself," but in recent years, as the team has improved, games have become increasingly popular. In fact, many students center dates around football games, attending the game and its pre- and postparties with their date. Reflecting on the game day experience, one junior said: "There honestly isn't anything like football season at Ole Miss."

Rebelling against Racism

The shadow of slavery, segregation, and racism has long lingered over Ole Miss, much as its administration and students have attempted to distance the University from the darker aspects of its past. Founded in 1848, the University closed briefly during the Civil War after its students left to fight as "University Grays" in the Confederate army. After the war, the University remained segregated until 1962, when James Meredith became the first black student to walk the halls of Ole Miss, flanked by federal marshals. Race riots and other violence plagued the campus throughout the Civil Rights Movement.

> **"There honestly isn't anything like football season at Ole Miss."**

While most students agree that racism is a problem of the past, controversy has erupted within the past decade over the University mascot, Colonel Rebel. In 2003, Colonel Rebel—who, according to some, looks like an antebellum plantation owner—was banned from the sidelines of football games, but he remains the University's official mascot. While some students would prefer a less controversial mascot, many students, according to one senior, "just don't think about it."

The mascot controversy aside, Ole Miss has made great strides toward diversity and tolerance in the past decades. Today, 19 percent of its undergraduates are minorities, and most students feel that the University's atmosphere is inclusive. Diversity-oriented undergraduate organizations, such as the group One Mississippi, have been created to address racial issues on campus. "We've had such issues with discrimination in the past that we've really had to face these issues head on," explained one senior. Another student agreed, claiming: "We deal with this issue every day; we talk about it in every single class. We've come a really long way."

Ole Miss is an institution steeped in tradition, from its controversial mascot, to its game days at the Grove, to its beautiful and historic grounds. Throughout the past de-cades, the University has been filtering the good traditions from the bad, enhancing its academics, its facilities, and its diversity. Yet when asked what sets Ole Miss apart, most students didn't cite its academic excellence or picturesque campus. Rather, students believe that Ole Miss' close-knit, community atmosphere—rare among public universities—is what puts the University in a league of its own. As one student stated simply, "At Ole Miss, you just feel at home."—*Elizabeth Bewley*

FYI

If you come to Ole Miss, you better bring: "your tent for The Grove. If you don't, you will miss out on one of the best experiences of your life."

What is the typical weekend schedule? "Head to the bars Library or Rooster's on Thursday night, hit up a fraternity party on Friday, tailgate at the Grove and go to the football game on Saturday."

If I could change one thing about Ole Miss, I'd change: "the stereotype of Ole Miss being stuck in Civil War times and still being racist."

The three things that every student at Ole Miss should do before graduating are: "go to a football game and tailgate at the Grove, get to know Oxford, and eat catfish at Taylor Grocery just outside of town."

Missouri

Address: 203 Jesse Hall
Columbia, MO 65211
Phone: 573-882-7786
E-mail address:
MU4U@missouri.edu
Web site URL: www
.admissions.missouri.edu
Year Founded: 1839
Private or Public: Public
Religious Affiliation: None
Location: Small City
Number of Applicants:
13,102
Percent Accepted: 78%
**Percent Accepted who
enroll:** 47%
Number Entering: 5,027
**Number of Transfers
Accepted each Year:**
Unreported
Middle 50% SAT range:
M: 540–650, CR: 530–650,
Wr: Unreported
Middle 50% ACT range:
23–28
**Early admission program
EA/ED/None:** None

**Percentage accepted
through EA or ED:** NA
EA and ED deadline: NA
Regular Deadline: 1-May
Application Fee: $45
**Full time Undergraduate
enrollment:** 22,000
Total enrollment: 28,253
Percent Male: 49%
Percent Female: 51%
**Total Percent Minority
Unreported:** 12%
Percent African-American:
6%
**Percent Asian/Pacific
Islander:** 3%
Percent Hispanic: 2%
Percent Native-American:
1%
Percent International: 50%
**Percent in-state/out of
state:** 86%/14%
Percent from Public HS:
Unreported
Retention Rate: 85%
Graduation Rate 4-year:
69%

Graduation Rate 6-year:
Unreported
**Percent Undergraduates
in On-campus housing:**
37%
**Number of official organized
extracurricular
organizations:** 500
3 Most popular majors:
Business Administration,
Journalism, Psychology
Student/Faculty ratio: 18:1
Average Class Size:
Unreported
**Percent of students going to
grad school:** Unreported
Tuition and Fees: $19,514
**In State Tuition and Fees if
different:** $8,450
Cost for Room and Board:
$8,100
**Percent receiving financial
aid out of those who apply,
first year:** 64%
**Percent receiving financial
aid among all students:**
45%

W alking around the Quad, the most
striking features are the Columns,
monuments from Mizzou's earliest
days. Tradition has each year's freshmen
walk through the Columns toward Jesse
Hall to show their entrance into Mizzou.
Graduating seniors walk through the
Columns away from Jesse, signifying their
exit from college into the real world. In between are four years at the University of
Missouri at Columbia, the largest school in
the University of Missouri system and, as its
Tigers will tell you, the best. It is home to a
striking array of students. Greek life pre-
dominates on campus, with rambunctious
students holding parties regularly and there
is a wide spectrum of non-Greeks, ranging
from artsy people, Goths, anti-stereotypes,
Engineering students and many others. Just
about everybody, however, comes together
on weekends for football and basketball
games, and Mizzou pride is never as strong
as when the fans scream from the stands,
"MIZ-ZOU!!!"

Hard at Work

As Missouri's flagship state school, Mizzou
caters to a large number of students, and so
class sizes vary from 15 to 200. The largest
and most popular lecture courses, such as
Biology 1010 or Psychology 1010 can be
daunting, so smaller classes such as "History

of the 1960s" or "American Film History, 1945–Present" offer a more intimate atmosphere for students. Most students consider the workload manageable, although perennial: "I always had something to read or there'd be an online quiz or two that I had to take every day," commented a theater major.

Some students say that the most difficult courses at Mizzou are pre-med and engineering courses, including biochemistry, chemical engineering and electrical engineering, but a band member pointed out that "all majors have intensely difficult aspects to them. Business students have to struggle through Accounting 1 and 2 and macro- and microeconomics." Another student added that "a lot of majors require intensive writing courses, which are never easy, and the workload increases as you advance into your major." A few special programs help to make sense of Mizzou's large range of academic offerings—there are Freshman Interest Groups for first-year students, Sponsored Learning Communities, and academically oriented organizations on campus.

The standard distributional requirements for a Mizzou degree include college algebra and another math course, English Exposition and Argumentation, a writing-intensive course, American history or government, and a certain number of credits each from sciences, social sciences and humanities. Many courses can be fulfilled through high school coursework. One student remarked, "I often complained that it was unnecessary for me to take math and science classes . . . but now I understand why. The administration at Mizzou wanted us to be well-rounded. I'm very glad I took biology and algebra and geology, because it really opened my eyes to the world, and helped me understand current events."

Greektown or Not?

Greek life is rampant on campus, with nearly a quarter of the students participating in 48 fraternities and sororities. Opinion on this lifestyle among the remaining students is divided: a large number are very supportive of the community, from Greektown (where most of the houses are located) to the parties they provide from Wednesday through Saturday nights. The remainder complain that "if you don't belong to a Greek group, you might want to avoid living in a dorm that's located so close to Greektown, or it will drive you crazy." For them, there are many other dorms, which all tend to be fairly comfortable. Certain dorms have

become more well known for housing large populations of math and science students or artsy types; the FARC (Fine Arts Residential Community), for example, houses many music students. After freshman or sophomore year, many students will move off campus into apartments or even houses; Columbia, being a small city, offers many inexpensive housing options that are within walking distance of the rest of campus.

With so many students from so many parts of the country, Mizzou has a niche for nearly every student. The school is in the Midwest, so the stereotypical student is a "white, male, Christian Republican who belongs to a frat. Fortunately, that's usually not the case . . . the student body is very racially, ethnically, socially and politically diverse." Campus security is present, but safety is never a concern. Multiple students said they felt very safe on campus at all hours. One student living in an all-girls dorm said that "We actually are informed of any alerts through e-mail as soon as possible," which is a useful system for such a large state school.

Food is a big deal: all entering freshmen get the famous Tiger-striped ice cream, and all the dining halls have been rated as "tasty." One junior did note, though, that "you have to pay attention to dining hall hours when picking your meal plan." For late-night cravings, the most popular destination is Gumby's. Shakespeare's is also a favorite destination, claiming to have the best pizza in the Midwest.

> "Painted, tiger-ears headbands, tiger tails, and black and gold just shower the campus."

Most students are involved with multiple extracurricular groups. The ones with the largest memberships include College Democrats and College Republicans, the Asian American Student Assocation, Black Student Organization, Hillel and the Muslim Student Organization. Many students remain involved with faith-based organizations. "There are many churches, synagogues and mosques within walking distance of the campus where students can attend a service," said a business major. The biggest extracurricular is sports, though. "A LOT of students tend to wear Mizzou jerseys on days of competition," said a fan. "MU sports are pretty big in central, rural and southern Missouri. I can tell ya that, 'cause a lot of people from small towns from all over Missouri would drive up to Columbia to go to football or basketball games—it is something fun for them to do." A clarinet player for the band noted the crazy colors on game days: "Painted, tiger-ears headbands (I have one), tiger tails (have one of those too) and black and gold just shower the campus from tots to alums, students to parents." Another student said it straight out: "The one thing that sets us aside from other schools is the spirit; everyone is proud to be a Tiger. MIZ-ZOU!"

The Quad and Beyond

The campus itself stands out as one of the most beautiful areas in Columbia. One upperclassman gushed that "there is an Ivy League feel to the place. And the Quad is just amazing in the spring—people will be playing Frisbee and hanging out by the Columns even at five in the morning!" A fencer said she loves the inner architecture of Ellis, the largest of Mizzou's libraries, as well as the Art Museum. A sophomore pointed out that Mizzou has an amazing athletics center, including a "huge work-out center, many basketball courts, lazy river, saunas, pools, the list keeps going!" With so many varsity sports, the athletic center is almost a given.

When students were asked, they said that they would definitely choose to go to Mizzou again. "I had fun, I learned a lot of good stuff, I met so many cool people from all over who made me open my eyes, I made some lasting wonderful friends, and I didn't expect that I'd have such a great time here!" And the Mizzou Pride lasts the rest of your life! —*Jeffrey Zuckerman*

FYI
If you come to Mizzou, you'd better bring "a cell phone, so that you can always catch up with your pals between classes."

What is the typical weekend schedule? "Friday, go out to a party or club, hang out with your friends and go to Shakespeare's Pizza or order from Gumby's. Saturday, relax in the afternoon, take a walk in the park or go to a football game. In the evening, let loose. Sunday, study and do homework."

If I could change one thing about Mizzou, I'd "complete all the construction so our campus can be its most beautiful."

Three things that every student at Mizzou should do before graduating are "jump in the Brady Fountain, ride the Mizzou Tiger, and take a class about a subject you have no clue about."

University of Missouri / Kansas City

Address: 5100 Rockhill Road 101AC Kansas City, MO 64110
Phone: 816-235-1111
E-mail address: admit@umkc.edu
Web site URL: www.umkc.edu
Year Founded: 1929
Private or Public: Public
Religious Affiliation: None
Location: Urban
Number of Applicants: 3,458
Percent Accepted: 60%
Percent Accepted who enroll: 44%
Number Entering: 912
Number of Transfers Accepted each Year: 1,858
Middle 50% SAT range: M: 560–690, CR: 560–660, Wr: Unreported
Middle 50% ACT range: 21–28
Early admission program EA/ED/None: None

Percentage accepted through EA or ED: NA
EA and ED deadline: NA
Regular Deadline: Rolling
Application Fee: $35
Full time Undergraduate enrollment: 9,274
Total enrollment: 12,930
Percent Male: 42%
Percent Female: 59%
Total Percent Minority or Unreported: 26%
Percent African-American: 12%
Percent Asian/Pacific Islander: 6%
Percent Hispanic: 4%
Percent Native-American: 1%
Percent International: 2%
Percent in-state/out of state: 74%/26%
Percent from Public HS: Unreported
Retention Rate: 71%
Graduation Rate 4-year: 76%

Graduation Rate 6-year: 14%
Percent Undergraduates in On-campus housing: 12%
Number of official organized extracurricular organizations: 200
3 Most popular majors: Business/Commerce, Health Services/Allied Health/Health Sciences, Liberal Arts and Sciences/Liberal Studies
Student/Faculty ratio: 10:1
Average Class Size: 10 to 19
Percent of students going to grad school: Unreported
Tuition and Fees: $19,363
In State Tuition and Fees if different: $8,272
Cost for Room and Board: $8,096
Percent receiving financial aid out of those who apply, first year: 79%
Percent receiving financial aid among all students: 63%

O ver 80 percent of University of Missouri Kansas City students live off campus, but that doesn't prevent them from having a full college experience. Those UMKC students with a little bit of initiative enjoy rich academic, extracurricular and social lives throughout their years at school. With a quickly increasing enrollment and strong focus on research, the University offers a vast range of experiences on an exciting campus.

Small Classes, Big Pride

UMKC students are required to complete 120 credit hours to graduate. If they are pursuing a B.A., they must also take three semesters of the same foreign language. One popular track of study is a six-year medical program, after which graduates receive an M.D. Students may earn a bachelor's degree in over 40 concentrations in the arts, sciences, humanities, social sciences, music and nursing; UMKC's mission calls for a focus on "visual and per-

forming arts, health sciences, and urban affairs." In addition, one sophomore communications major reported an extracurricular club for almost every area of study.

Students are proud of UMKC's standing relative to its peer institutions, saying "its research is excellent and so are its teachers." While there can be "a lot of competition for classes," a first-year student reported that "most of my classes have 25 people" or fewer, and upper-level courses tend to be smaller than the required general education classes. Undergraduates commonly interact with the faculty "online through discussion boards." Though one junior mentioned eating meals with her professors "all the time," another student observed that such close interaction occurs even more often in graduate programs or the Conservatory of Music, ranked one of the top in the nation. Other unique programs include the six-year medical program, as well as the reputable Bloch School of Business and Public affairs and the School of Law.

The school boasts the only pharmacy and dental schools in the state. The University launched a major building project for Health Science 1, to provide more research space and classrooms for the health and life science departments.

Students noted the sizable population of older students and graduate students, making for a less-traditional college setting. As a result, said one undergrad, "UMKC is a great place for self-sufficient scholarly students who are interested in hitting the books."

Double Your Dorms
In the fall of 2004, UMKC opened Oak Street Hall, approximately doubling the number of students who can live on campus. Despite the high cost, the hall receives praise for the quality of housing it offers. With the leveling of Twin Oaks, the University is planning to construct a residence with town-style apartments. Nevertheless, both campus culture and economics often push students to the houses around campus, with one student noting after one year that it was "much cheaper . . . to rent a house near campus." Dorms, then, are a popular option for students arriving from outside of Kansas City only until they form a group of friends with whom they can move off campus.

One student described the University's location in the heart of Kansas City as "fantastic." Students spend much of their free time in the Country Club Plaza area of Kansas City, which offers "luxury shopping" and food options to break up the day. One freshman described this spot, along with the Westport area, as the "dominant social scene," since most students do not spend much time on campus while they aren't in class. For those on campus at meal times, the University of Missouri Kansas City offers food at its dining hall on a debit system, with students loading their cards at the beginning of the semester and spending down until the balance is zero. One student critical of the dining hall compared the food to that of her high school cafeteria. Another agreed, saying that the dining hall is "widely criticized." Students not invested in a semester-long meal plan tend not to spend much time in the dining hall because "food is expensive to purchase with cash."

Outside the Classroom and Off the Campus
Since most UMKC students live off campus, they do much of their socializing there. There are, however, many opportunities for students to get involved with university-sponsored activities as well. In addition to academically oriented groups and the Student Government Association, there are plenty of opportunities for community service in the Kansas City metro area. Ethnic organizations and academic-focused groups were noted as particularly active. Also, the University boasts seven fraternities and seven sororities. Many students, including those from outside the Kansas City area, make friends "by joining organizations," though one senior found that because so many students leave campus after class, some "organizations are begging for members."

> **"Everyone drinks, except for the really religious types."**

The campus is dry, but that is no stumbling block to the off-campus consumption of alcohol. According to a senior, "Everyone drinks, except for the really religious types." Even so, a female junior reported no pressure as the only non-drinker in her group of friends. Fridays and Saturdays are the most popular nights out, with venues ranging from small gatherings in houses to Westport, "the largest collection of bars in the Great Plains." Most students have "at least one job," at "Starbucks, in retail, work-study," and a variety of other part-time placements. Those who are employed tend to work off campus, or have an off-campus job to augment their work-study.

Typical Kangaroo?
One freshman recommended dressing up as the UMKC mascot, Kasey the Kangaroo, at least once during college. Given the make up of the student body, though, the odds are that you will find a different type of student wearing the costume at every game! "You can't really say that we have one particular stereotypical student," said one junior. "Young and old, different cultures, and different attitudes" are all represented at UMKC, even though many students are from small towns in-state. The strongest representation may be of "middle-class white" backgrounds, but students do note the diversity on campus.

To further expose students to a variety of worldviews, UMKC runs an International Academic Programs office, offering students guidance in applying for fellowships and study abroad programs. The University of

Missouri Kansas City currently has programs with schools in 21 countries in Europe and Asia, as well as ones in Mexico, Australia, and New Zealand. The office also works with students to transfer financial aid packages to study abroad programs. On campus, the school boasts an international population of around 10 percent.

UMKC competes athletically in the Mid-Continent Conference of the NCAA's Division I. The University sponsors a variety of sports, ranging from basketball and volleyball to golf, tennis, softball, and rifle, but for most of the student body, the UMKC-Valparaiso basketball game is the biggest athletic event of the year. For those not inclined to commit to Division I athletics, the Swinney Recreation Center offers fitness facilities and a swimming pool to the university community.

The University of Missouri Kansas City is a school with many opportunities for academic, extracurricular and social growth, but it requires some initiative from its somewhat scattered student body. According to those who have taken that extra step, seeking out a professor for lunch or joining a campus political organization can make for a fulfilling college experience, taking advantage of the "good education" that UMKC can provide.—*Douglas London*

FYI

If you come to UMKC, you'd better bring "a sense of humor."

The best places to hang out on the weekend are "Friday and Saturday, go to bars or go out to eat, and sleep in on Sunday."

If I could change one thing about the UMKC, "I would make parking free and plentiful."

Three things that every UMKC student should do before graduating are "go on an internship out of state or country, join a club and live in a dorm."

Washington University in St. Louis

Address: One Brookings Drive St. Louis, MO 63139-4988

Phone: 314-935-6000

E-mail address: admissions@wustl.edu

Web site URL: www.wustl.edu

Year Founded: 1853

Private or Public: Private

Religious Affiliation: None

Location: Urban

Number of Applicants: 22,428

Percent Accepted: 17%

Percent Accepted who enroll: 34%

Number Entering: 1,328

Number of Transfers Accepted each Year: 221

Middle 50% SAT range: M: 690–780, CR: 680–750, Wr: Unreported

Middle 50% ACT range: 28–34

Early admission program EA/ED/None: ED

Percentage accepted through EA or ED: Unreported

EA and ED deadline: 15-Nov

Regular Deadline: 15-Jan

Application Fee: $55

Full time Undergraduate enrollment: 6,985

Total enrollment: 12,036

Percent Male: 49%

Percent Female: 51%

Total Percent Minority or Unreported: 16%

Percent African-American: 10%

Percent Asian/Pacific Islander: 12%

Percent Hispanic: 3%

Percent Native-American: 0%

Percent International: 5%

Percent in-state/out of state: 10%/90%

Percent from Public HS: 63%

Retention Rate: 97%

Graduation Rate 4-year: Unreported

Graduation Rate 6-year: Unreported

Percent Undergraduates in On-campus housing: 73%

Number of official organized extracurricular organizations: 200

3 Most popular majors: Biology, Finance, Psychology

Student/Faculty ratio: 7:1

Average Class Size: 6

Percent of students going to grad school: 33%

Tuition and Fees: $36,200

In State Tuition and Fees if different: No difference

Cost for Room and Board: $11,636

Percent receiving financial aid out of those who apply, first year: 39%

Percent receiving financial aid among all students: 41%

Walking into the front quad through Brookings Hall, the surrounding green lawns and the collegiate twist on Gothic architecture leap out at you. They are small markers of Washington University's formidable reputation as the "truly quintessential university." Easily in the top 15 of colleges nationwide, Wash U (as it is popularly nicknamed) rivals the Ivy League and the best of small liberal-arts schools for scholarship and attention to individual students. Its location in downtown St. Louis, near the green spaces of Forest Park and the trendy stores of the Loop, is suggestive of the vivacity of its student population—vibrant, friendly and intellectually driven. The school's increasing popularity has been signified recently by unexpectedly large freshman classes, and the atmosphere is full of newfound wonder for the beauty of life in the Midwest.

Intellectualism 101: Going in Premed, Going Out with a Triple Major

The on-campus joke is that "A TON of the freshmen each year come in planning to be pre-med because the program here is so good, [which] makes the sciences notoriously rigorous and hardcore," as one senior shared. But "by the time people are required to declare a major sophomore year, the distributions across majors are much more even," so Wash U's claim to fame as a liberal arts school has always been an advantage.

The requirements are fairly clear-cut: every student must take Writing I and another writing-intensive course, a quantitative analysis class and one course each in Cultural Diversity and Social Differentiation. Additionally, two to three classes have to be taken in each of four academic areas: natural science and mathematics, social sciences, textual and historical studies, and language and the arts. Still, this set of general-education requirements is considered to be fairly flexible, and the academic areas offer many options. "Instead of having to suffer through something like chemistry, non-science people can take classes like 'Dinosaurs: Facts and Fiction.' Requirements are really flexible, which is what enables people to do things like triple major," said a female student who is triple-majoring in Political Science, Spanish, and History—hardly impossible at Washington University since requirements for a major tend to be uncomplicated, and the academic guidelines actively encourage multiple majors.

The University prides itself on its freshman programs, which range from the FOCUS program to the Text and Tradition program. There is also wide variety of freshman seminars within academic departments, which often include international travel. A sophomore who took a class on Michelangelo as a freshman raved, "We got to go to Italy after the semester was over and see some of the sculptures we'd been studying for months!" Some programs have options for a sophomore-year extension, and others lead freshman into exploring different areas of study after their freshman year.

Many introductory classes within Wash U, particularly within the sciences and psychology, enroll "over 100 [students]. Most other classes are small, between five and 20 people," said a pre-med student, who pointed out that "some very popular classes such as the Human Evolution class taught by the most eloquent speaker on campus have waitlists longer than the amount of seats in the class." An older student explained that "class size depends a lot on what you're taking. [Non-science] majors have much smaller classes. My smallest class ever was one person. Just me, alone with the professor." The professors are touted as being "super-approachable and accessible" by many students on campus, and with good reason—Washington University is primarily a liberal arts school, with scholarship as its first priority.

The workload is intense, no matter what the major. Sciences in particular are difficult due to the large number of potential pre-meds, and most people feel that "General Chemistry is the 'make it or break it' class . . . finishing it is definitely a milestone in one's academic career." The humanities tend to be easier, particularly the Classics and English, but the workload is intense, no matter what the discipline. Grade inflation is "nonexistent" and not a concern. The stereotypical Wash U student "is a really smart procrastinator, who does it because he or she is smart enough to. They know how to space out their work so they have free time. Everyone pretty much lives in the library right before finals, but generally they know how to balance their time," said a Gregg dorm resident.

Bright Colors, Tight Parties

Social life at Washington University is excellent. The events include First Friday, a campus celebration gearing up to WILD (Walk

In, Lie Down), where major bands come to perform, and Thurtene, a carnival. The fraternities, while not a dominant presence, provide entertainment for most freshmen in their first weeks of college (which is why, one member jokes, "for the first month or so all the upperclassmen avoid frat row"), and alcohol is not an issue for those who choose to seek it out. The rule, as reiterated by every student, is that they can't be "flagrant or dangerous." The University tends to stay out of alcohol-related incidents, treating them as health issues rather than disciplinary issues. Also, "one of the best things at Wash U is that there are almost as many different 'scenes' here as there are people. If you don't drink, your closest friends can become the people who also don't. If you're more into other types of activities, you can still have plenty of fun on weekends."

Many events are advertised on one of the most unusual parts of campus: the South 40 underpass. The sides of the underpass as well as underneath are regularly coated with paint, and three geometric sculptures (a square, a pyramid and a sphere), are available for similar advertising space. Groups often ask art majors to paint these areas, and they work in the evenings, making the walk around the underpass vivid and colorful. One student recalled, "The Jewish Student Union likes to paint [the sphere] to resemble a giant Matzo ball to advertise for their Passover events."

There are a wide range of activities and events at Washington University—people won't really be divided between "school-sponsored events" and "crazy in-suite parties." Frequently, people will go to lectures one evening and frat parties or bars or other suites another. The fact that the campus is very intellectual leads to some interesting twists: a chemistry major recalled one party where people played a game based on a professor's taped lectures. Sometimes the whole school will show up for more famous speakers: an Art History major said that famous people such as "Bill Nye and Paul Rusesabagina (hero of the Rwandan genocide), amongst various other political and academic names, lecture on Wednesdays" as part of the Assembly Series.

Floormate Loving

Relationships at Washington University run the gamut from casual hookups to traditional daters to engaged couples. Most people tend to end up in committed relationships by senior year, but the dating scene is still fresh as an underclassman. A female rated the general student population as "eight out of 10 for attractiveness—altogether we're a good-looking group. There's a false stereotype that girls are ugly at WUSTL; it's actually the engineering guys and they're awkward, not ugly." There are a number of gay and interracial couples, and the population is supportive of both, even though neither are a large presence on campus. STDs tend not to be an issue; an Alpha Phi Omega member said that "these smart students understand all risks they are taking and try to prevent contraction as best they can."

One upperclassman said, "One of my favorite things about Wash U is that you're always meeting new people. It's my senior year and I'm *still* making new friends every weekend." Most students have multiple groups of friends, with different activities providing new friends: classes, extracurriculars, Greek groups, even floormates. A sophomore said "the people on your freshman floor get really close and you stay really close. They're the people you're most likely to stay in contact with after college; in fact, more than half my floor moved together to the floor I'm on now." Another student said there didn't seem to be any social stereotype for Wash U students, only the academic stereotype of laid-back while intellectually intense. There's a mix of all types of students, "including some plain-and-out nerds, who are usually funnier than expected." Certainly there are wealthy students: "It's hard to say because people really don't discuss their financial situations very often, but judging by the cars in the parking lot, there's plenty of money on campus." Still, the University offers many loans and scholarships, the largest being the Compton, Mylonas, Moog, Lien, and Fossett full-tuition scholarships.

A Chancellor and a Rabbit . . .

The administration is constantly responsive to student needs; after a Facebook group called "Wash U really needs to get a fountain up in here" was created, they actually did install one—even though the campus, which includes beautiful pink granite buildings, hardly needed it. Similar responsiveness has been apparent with such issues as the decision to charge for wireless connections on campus; a succession of reactions over two weeks (in the summer, moreover) caused the administration to reevaluate their decision. The chancellor is a large presence on campus, and he is well known for inviting students to his house to go bowling or have a snack with him. Because he is a "very accomplished chemist, and he worked on creating some of the chemicals that are found in the glow stick," as a Student Admissions Committee assistant explained, hundreds of glow sticks are handed out to freshmen to carry during Convocation at the beginning of each year.

> **"As part of a class, we got to go to Italy and see Michelangelo's sculptures!"**

The campus as a whole is quite unique: it has had the honor of hosting Presidential debates consistently since 1992, and it often sets up its students with political internships. Activism is present on campus, but most students are just happy to be on the South 40, relaxing. Each student polled said that the most interesting thing about campus was The Bunny, a sculpture officially called "Thinker on the Rock." It is usually cited as the ugliest thing on campus, but also the best meeting spot. Stories abound: many students have dressed up the rabbit in clothes, although one girl stated, "Be warned: you will not get your clothes back once you donate them to the bunny."

Every student polled said that, if they had a choice, they would definitely choose Wash U again, and that they wouldn't give up all the options the school affords—study abroad, internships, classes and social events——for any other college. One sophomore said, "Academically, this is a very rigorous university. It teaches students how to think critically and to ask questions about the world. Though we put a lot of effort into our work, the reward of completion and knowledge is great." But the student triple majoring in Political Science, Spanish, and History said that what made Washington University truly unique in comparison with Ivy League school was the opportunity for individual choice: "The Wash U experience is what you make of it, and you're never limited by the preexisting system. I think that's really embodied in something that Dean McLeod, the Dean of Students, says about Wash U. As diverse as Wash U is, he says, the one thing that unites everyone on campus is that 'they want to be active participants in their own education'."
—*Jeffrey Zuckerman*

FYI
If you come to Wash U, you better bring "a laptop with wireless. You'll want the mobility."
What is a typical weekend schedule? "Thursday night: go out on the town. Friday: tie-dye shirts then watch movies on the Swamp. Saturday: homework, pre-party, club circuits. Sunday: homework, socialize in hallway circles, sleep."
If I could change one thing about Wash U, "I'd change the name so that people don't get it mixed up with other schools."
Three things every student at Wash U should do before graduating are "take Intro to Sexuality (a huge lecture class with an absolutely amazing lecturer and fantastic subject material), go bowling at the chancellor's house (at his awesome in-home private bowling alley) and attend WILD."

Montana

Surrounded by mountains and adjacent to the Clark Fork River, it's no wonder University of Montana students call themselves Grizzlies. "You can literally walk off campus into a wilderness area," raved one freshman. "It's definitely the most beautiful campus I've seen—and I was all over the West Coast looking at schools." Add to that a wide variety of academic options and the thriving small-city nightlife of Missoula, and you get a "really neat place to go to school."

Hitting the Books

UM has programs in the arts and sciences, forestry and conservation, technology, business, education, pharmacy, journalism, and fine arts, offering students a wide variety of majors, from anthropology to zoology and everything in between. Entering freshmen apply to the University of Montana at large;

students apply to a specific major before the end of junior year. The most popular majors include psychology, forestry and marketing, which is known for being relatively easy.

Regardless of major, all Grizzlies must take 120 course credits to graduate (an average course load is 15–18 credits, or 3–5 classes, per semester), at least 39 of which must be in upper-division courses. In addition, students must fulfill an English requirement, a mathematics requirement, and a foreign language or symbolic systems requirement. Also, each student must take a total of 27 credits in the following six "perspectives," with at least two credits from each: expressive arts, literary and artistic studies, historical and cultural studies, social sciences, ethical and human values, and natural sciences. To some students, the number of requirements seems like "overkill," though they are "good for someone who doesn't have a major in mind because you can figure out what you want to do." In any case, said one junior, "There's usually enough of a selection that you can find something you'll like—there's so many different choices that if you can't find something you can at least deal with, you're not trying very hard." Indeed, at least some requirements can be met with "easy and interesting" classes like "History of Rock and Roll," "Use and Abuse of Drugs," "Human Sexuality," and "Intro to Anthropology."

> **"It's definitely the most beautiful campus I've seen—and I was all over the West Coast looking at schools."**

Unfortunately, with nearly 12,000 undergrads, getting the classes you want can be "pretty hard." "Classes go really fast" in online registration, said one freshman. This leaves some students "stuck with classes at really weird times," but teachers will often sign an override slip if you talk to them in person. Students can also sign up for the Four Bear program, where they plan out a tentative four-year schedule ahead of time with an adviser and get to pick classes before everyone else.

While competition to get into classes is tough, competition within classes is almost nonexistent. "I really would not call UM cutthroat," said one junior. "While it attracts all types, people are generally pretty laid-back here." Class sizes range from 20–30 person upper-division seminars to intro lecture classes with over 400 students. Professors teach the majority of classes, though TAs (who are generally "pretty good") teach basic introductory English and math classes, in addition to leading lab sections. Even in large lecture classes, "there's a lot of access to your professor," said a junior biology major. "If you can't make it to their office hours, they'll go out of their way to meet with you," echoed a freshman. Most students are "pretty happy" with their professors, who, in addition to being "really approachable," are also "extremely knowledgeable" and "enjoy teaching."

Students seeking a more intense education can apply to the Davidson Honors College at the same time they apply to UM. Honors classes are similar in subject matter to non-honors courses, but average 22 students per class. That means "more work—because it's a smaller class, it's not as easy to sit back and tune out," but also "a lot more discussion, a

much better learning environment." Non-honors students can also take honors classes, but honors students get priority and must take at least seven honors courses, including a senior project, to graduate. UM also has a "really strong" study abroad program, which offers the opportunity to study in 38 different countries, including Australia, Canada, Chile, China, France, Morocco and Thailand.

A Grizzly's Den
Dorms at UM get mixed reviews. All are located "close to the core of campus," no more than a 10-minute walk from classes, and have laundry facilities, game rooms and lounges. However, they vary in style and quality. Jesse and Aber, the high-rise dorms, are "housing projects designed to pack in as many people as possible," while Craig and Duniway have bigger rooms, and Miller offers singles. Knowles houses honors and international students, Elrod is male-only, and Turner houses only women. Students can also choose substance-free or quiet floors if they so desire.

All students who live in the dorms must purchase a meal plan, which allows students to eat at the Food Zoo (the main cafeteria), as well as at an on-campus food court or coffee shops. The Zoo offers "pretty good variety," and the food is "good for mass production," especially with its new Farm to College program, which brings in fresh meat and vegetables from local farms.

Freshmen, who are required to live on campus, are distributed throughout the various dorms. Events like the weekly "Floor Snack" and monthly trips to a bowling alley or pizza place make it easy to meet new people. These events are organized by upperclassmen RAs, who live on each floor and range from "real well-trained" to "horrible. [They'll] write you up if you're overly loud, drinking, doing anything that's slightly weird." "Overall," said one freshman, "they're good at what they do— they keep the place running really smoothly— but they definitely stick to the rules." Even though the newest dorm, Pantzer, is reserved for upperclassmen, most students move off campus by junior year; however, many claim that "finding something that's affordable close to campus gets difficult."

Unfortunately, "parking on campus is absolutely insane—it's impossible to get a spot," and "public transportation isn't real great," so many students are forced to leave their cars in Park and Ride lots. Luckily, "it's really easy to get around" with a bike, said one Grizzly. Bike lanes are ubiquitous in Missoula, and "everything is really close—I can ride my bike to the mall, Target, and back to campus in like half an hour."

Here Come the MIP's

UM certainly lives up to its reputation as "a really big party school." Every spring, Grizzlies "dress up country style" to attend the Foresters' Ball, in which the forestry department turns the gym into a logging camp, complete with a saloon and "hitching post" where students can get "married." Other popular annual parties include Maggotfest, when rugby teams come from across the nation to compete in the spring tournament, and then have a "giant party with an absurd number of kegs and people pouring beer all over each other."

Although frats throw "their fair share of parties," Greek life is "not very big," which makes the Greek scene a "really tight-knit community" but "not a large part of the social network." Alcohol is generally "pretty easy to get," but drinking is "definitely more of an off-campus thing," since RAs zealously report underage drinking in the dorms. Even off campus, however, police "are more than eager" to cite students for "a DUI, BUI (biking under the influence) or MIP (minor in possession)."

On most weekends, students frequent house parties or head into the "very active downtown," which includes a variety of restaurants, pool halls and "a ton of bars that are always packed." Students report that "bars are pretty easy to get into if you know people that know people," even if you're not 21. Non-drinkers enjoy a variety of options as well. Popular with both students and locals is the Elks Lodge, an 18-and-up club in Missoula that invites musical performers every night. On campus, there are "Nite Kourt" events, where university organizations bring in "hypnotists, comedians, all kinds of stuff."

Grizzlies at Play

When they're not partying or studying, UM students are involved in a plethora of extracurricular activities. As one junior put it, "There's pretty much a club for anything you want." The diversity of clubs reflects a diversity of students. Although racial diversity is limited (the student body is "very, very white"), students hail from all over the country, and even as far away as Japan, Korea, Hong Kong, Australia, Germany, and Tajikistan. Organizations include the popular ASUM (student government), which organizes many events on campus, and *Kaimin*, the student newspaper, as well as unusual clubs like the "Footbag Alliance," devoted to hacky sack. As Missoula is the most liberal part of Montana (though not as liberal as some universities in other parts of the country), activism is also big. "There are a lot of causes to rally around," said a junior. "There is always something for people who want to get involved socially or politically."

But the biggest draw is the great outdoors. Students enjoy fly-fishing in the Clark Fork River right off campus, as well as hiking up to the concrete "M" on Mt. Sentinel. There are also many outdoor clubs, which organize weekend camping and backpacking trips to nearby Glacier National Park (2 1/2 hours away), Yellowstone (three hours) or Hot Springs (less than half an hour). Moreover, the Recreation Center, an on-campus facility, rents whitewater rafts, ski equipment, backpacking gear and kayaks at reduced prices.

The rec center is also "absolutely awesome" during the winter, containing an indoor track, weight machines, exercise rooms, a swimming pool and a climbing wall. Students looking for more competitive activities can play intramural sports, the most popular of which are Ultimate Frisbee, soccer, softball and basketball; and for those students who are particularly athletically-inclined, UM also offers 14 Division I varsity sports.

According to most students, there is a lot of school spirit. Students and Missoula residents regularly sell out the 23,000-seat stadium for football games, which feature skydivers jumping onto the field at halftime. Before games, "people go nuts about tailgates—they pull up in motor homes painted with the Montana colors." Whether they come for the exciting party scene, academic choices, or "gorgeous" location, students agree: "UM is a cool place to be."—*Sameer Jain*

FYI

If you come to UM, you'd better bring "Chaco sandals, a warm jacket, and a sense of adventure."

What's the typical weekend schedule? "Thursday: head out to a party. Friday: go to a pool hall or bar downtown, maybe a party. Saturday: tailgate, football game, nap in the afternoon, party at night. Sunday: homework, laundry, recovery. Or head to Glacier National Park or the Hot Springs for the whole weekend."

If I could change one thing about UM, I'd "increase racial diversity—I've seen literally four black people the three months I've been here."

Three things every student should do before graduating are "go to a football game, go to the Foresters' Ball, and hike to the M (a huge white concrete M about 1000 feet up Mt. Sentinel which people hike to all the time)."

Nebraska

Creighton University

Address: 2500 California Plaza Omaha, NE 68178
Phone: 402-280-2703
E-mail address:
admissions@creighton.edu
Web site URL:
www.creighton.edu
Year Founded: 1878
Private or Public: Private
Religious Affiliation: Roman Catholic
Location: Urban
Number of Applicants: 3,336
Percent Accepted: 89%
Percent Accepted who enroll: 32%
Number Entering: 950
Number of Transfers Accepted each Year: 165
Middle 50% SAT range:
M: 540–650, Cr: 520–630, Wr: 590–690
Middle 50% ACT range:
24–29
Early admission program EA/ED/None: NA

Percentage accepted through EA or ED:
Unreported
EA and ED deadline: NA
Regular Deadline: 15-Feb
Application Fee: $40
Full time Undergraduate enrollment: 4,104
Total enrollment: 4,647
Percent Male: 40%
Percent Female: 60%
Total Percent Minority or Unreported: 21%
Percent African-American: 3%
Percent Asian/Pacific Islander: 8%
Percent Hispanic: 3%
Percent Native-American: 1%
Percent International: 1%
Percent in-state/out of state: 37%/63%
Percent from Public HS: 55%
Retention Rate: 86%

Graduation Rate 4-year: 61%
Graduation Rate 6-year: 74%
Percent Undergraduates in On-campus housing: 62%
Number of official organized extracurricular organizations: 182
3 Most popular majors:
Business, Health, Psychology
Student/Faculty ratio: 12:1
Average Class Size: 20 to 29
Percent of students going to grad school: 70%
Tuition and Fees: $25,262
In State Tuition and Fees if different: No difference
Cost for Room and Board: $8,180
Percent receiving financial aid out of those who apply, first year: 61%

O maha may be the largest city in Nebraska, but students at Creighton University feel like they are members of a small community of familiar faces. Creighton students love the fact that their education consists of small class sizes and lots of personal attention. Students agree that "faculty involvement with students and interest in their education" sets Creighton apart from other colleges.

"The Professor Knows My Name!"

Students at Creighton all rave about the same thing: small class sizes and a personal education. With a relatively small enrollment of about 3,500 total undergraduates, even introductory classes like basic chemistry and psychology have a maximum of 50 students.

One student comments, "Most classes are small and very personable. I've had classes with anywhere from five to 25-plus students. What's great is that the professors teach all of the classes." Not only are classes more interactive, but also professors are dedicated to giving personal attention to students as individuals. The availability of professors also leads to increased research opportunities; Creighton is known as a great place for undergraduates to conduct original research.

While selecting the perfect schedule for the semester, students in the College of Arts & Sciences at Creighton need to consider the required core curriculum. Out of a total 128 required credit hours, half of those are core requirements. This demanding guideline strives to expose students to all aspects of a liberal arts education, including six classes in theology, philosophy and ethics; six in culture, ideas and civilizations; two in natural science; two in social science; and three in skills (English, math and communications). The college also has a foreign-language requirement—students must either take one year of intro-level classes in a new language, or one higher-level class for a continued language study. The core curriculum irks some students, who feel that "the core classes are stupid. They give a good overall view of every major, but for those people that already know what they want to major in, it is quite pointless." Not all students agree, however; others feel these core classes contribute to the "whole-person education."

Many Creighton students home in on pre-medical, pre-dental and pre-law studies, since Creighton has well-rounded professional graduate schools; also popular pre-professional tracks are pharmacy, occupational therapy and physical therapy. Business, biology, nursing and psychology are by far the most popular majors. The College of Business is considered to be more slack by those in the College of Arts & Sciences, but business students feel this misrepresents such difficult majors as accounting and finance. There is a lot of support for students who are interested in the health profession, and many find it exciting to be surrounded by others with the same interests. Even though many students are science-geared, Creighton offers wonderful programs in modern and classical languages and fine arts; the largest non-science major is journalism and mass communications.

While academics are not competitive in a cutthroat way, Creighton is challenging. When asked about the workload, one student responded: "Being in a school recognized for its academics, most students are overachievers. I'd say anywhere from 15 to 17 credit hours per semester is about average." Students warn prospectives against expecting gut classes in the sciences and to be prepared for many papers in other concentrations.

Comfortable Living

All freshmen and sophomores must live on-campus. Of the six dorms, three are freshman dorms and three are for sophomores. Each dorm is unique; Kiewit Hall is known as the freshman party dorm and a popular freshman hangout. Accommodations are fairly nice: Swanson, for example, consists of suites with two double bedrooms connected by a private bathroom. Each floor also has its own study room, kitchen and lounges. For juniors and seniors, who are not required to live on campus, new apartment-style housing is available—a new building was recently constructed in August 2006. Although housing is available for all four years, only about 60 percent of students live on campus.

Freshmen and sophomores must buy a meal plan, which they can use at the two main dining halls or the Student Center; the plans also include bonus dollars that can be redeemed at the four retail food stores on campus. The Student Center can satisfy all cravings for fast food, such as Blimpie's sub sandwiches, Godfather's pizza or the American Grill. With these options, some off-campus students feel that Creighton could "make the campus friendlier to those who don't have meal plans [by making] the other dining options more affordable to a college student."

Even though Creighton is situated at the heart of a large metropolitan center, students are confident in their school's security. With 24-hour foot and vehicle patrols, and transport and escort services available at all hours of the night, students consistently report feeling very safe. The city of Omaha gives ambitious and eager students the opportunity to get involved in the world outside of Creighton with a host of internships and summer opportunities. For those who enjoy the outdoors, wildlife refuges and state parks abound in the surrounding area. Students also love hanging out at the Old Market, a hotbed for "incredible restaurants and a great place for a date."

The Social Scene

Despite these attractions, many students still feel that Omaha can be "boring" and say the social scene on weekends centers around friends' rooms for house and frat parties. Greek life is pretty dominant in the social scene, as about a third of the undergrads at Creighton are in a fraternity or sorority. While this may seem like a large number, most students feel that being in a fraternity or sorority is not necessary to be in the social circuit. One student remarks: "There are also many social alternatives. Everyone will find one or many social niches."

These niches include numerous student organizations on campus. With groups ranging from the Ultimate Frisbee Organization to the Health Administration and Policy Student

Group to the Hui O Hawaii Club, students can usually find a group with their same interests. Many students are involved in community service, especially through Habitat for Humanity. Students interested in journalism can write for the *Creightonian* or work for JTV, the student-run television station. There's also a Creighton tradition of holding a candlelight mass at historic St. John's Church in the middle of campus. "Hundreds of students take a study break at 10 p.m. every Sunday night to attend a nontraditional mass celebrated almost entirely by candlelight."

> "You can always recognize and chat with a friend on the way to class. The beautiful campus is an oasis surrounded by a modern urban landscape."

Athletics at Creighton centers almost exclusively on the Division I men's basketball team. Bluejay basketball games are always well-attended, especially against Southern Illinois and Drake University. Spirited students cheer from the rowdy "Birdcage," the student section of the arena. Intramurals are huge at Creighton, with great turnouts for volleyball, baseball and soccer. This athletic spirit is complemented by a large on-campus gym featuring five basketball courts, four racquetball courts, a weight room, a swimming pool and hot tub, and an indoor track.

In reference to the makeup of the student body, many undergrads do feel that Creighton is not as diverse as other schools. However, many students notice that Creighton is "making an effort to recruit more diversity." There is a growing number of Hawaiian students on campus, and the percent of out-of-state and international students is also growing. In addition, Creighton is seeking to aesthetically improve the campus by renovating and reconstructing out-of-date buildings. Students report feeling that there is always some kind of construction going on, with new facilities popping up every year; among the university's current projects is a $50 million "Living-Learning Center," intended to integrate student services with academic support, classrooms, study areas and recreational spaces. Getting out of the dorm room, students can study beside "peaceful fountains, beautiful gardens and many neatly landscaped areas." One enthusiastic student notes, "You can always recognize and chat with a friend on the way to class. The beautiful campus is an oasis surrounded by a modern urban landscape." But still, when asked what they like best about their school, students at Creighton stress the academic acclaim and personal attention they receive in the classroom.—*Karen Chen*

FYI
If you come to Creighton, you'd better bring "a willingness to be challenged."
The typical weekend schedule is "hanging out with friends, catching up on sleep and laundry, some partying, and homework on Sunday."
If I could change one thing about Creighton, I'd "put a bar on campus."
Three things that every student at Creighton should do before graduating are "cheer on the Bluejays as part of the rowdy 'Birdcage' student section, discover yourself and others on a retreat at Creighton's rural retreat center, and take a course with Dr. Gardener in Irish literature and drama."

University of Nebraska / Lincoln

Address: 1410 Q Street
Lincoln, NE 68588-0256
Phone: 402-472-2023
E-mail address:
admissions@unl.edu
Web site URL: www.unl.edu
Year Founded: 1869
Private or Public: Public
Religious Affiliation: None
Location: Urban
Number of Applicants: 9,598
Percent Accepted: 62%
**Percent Accepted who
enroll:** 71%
Number Entering: 4,215
**Number of Transfers
Accepted each Year:**
1,246
Middle 50% SAT range:
M: 530–670, CR: 500–650,
Wr: Unreported
Middle 50% ACT range: 22–28
**Early admission program
EA/ED/None:** None
**Percentage accepted
through EA or ED:** NA

EA and ED deadline: NA
Regular Deadline: 05/01
Application Fee: $45
**Full time Undergraduate
enrollment:** 18,053
Total enrollment: 22,550
Percent Male: 54%
Percent Female: 46%
**Total Percent Minority or
Unreported:** 17%
Percent African-American:
2%
**Percent Asian/Pacific
Islander:** 3%
Percent Hispanic: 3%
Percent Native-American:
1%
Percent International: 3%
**Percent in-state/out of
state:** 83%/17%
Percent from Public HS:
Unreported
Retention Rate: 83%
Graduation Rate 4-year:
22%
Graduation Rate 6-year: 42%

**Percent Undergraduates
in On-campus housing:**
41%
**Number of official organized
extracurricular
organizations:** 335
3 Most popular majors:
Business Administration and
Management, Finance,
Psychology
Student/Faculty ratio: 19:1
Average Class Size: 20
to 29
**Percent of students going to
grad school:** Unreported
Tuition and Fees: $17,205
**In State Tuition and Fees if
different:** $6,585
Cost for Room and Board:
$6,882
**Percent receiving financial
aid out of those who apply,
first year:** 65%
**Percent receiving financial
aid among all students:**
41%

T he Big Red. Almost without fail, people across the nation know the Big Red for one thing: their football. With five National Championships under the University of Nebraska's belt, Cornhusker spirit runs deep, especially since Memorial Stadium ranks as the third-largest-populated area of Nebraska after Omaha and Lincoln on game day. To all native Nebraskans and students at the University, there is no messing around when it comes to football.

Making the Grade

Although students may not be as obsessed with academia as they are with UNL football, the University does a lot to accommodate a wide range of interests. By offering 150 majors and 10 academic colleges intended for those looking to specialize in their given field, students can find what's necessary for a thorough education. For those seeking an accelerated education, the Honors program at Nebraska offers an avenue. Requiring a cumulative 3.5 GPA to participate, those in the Honors program are provided with special housing, smaller class sizes, and close interaction opportunities with faculty and fellow high-achieving students. Students say that the most academically grueling majors include philosophy, any type of engineering, and organic chemistry. Not all classes are so demanding; UNL provides unique courses such as Introduction to Wine Tasting, Personal Defense, and Ballroom Dancing. One student emphasizes that the "liberal arts environment really encourages students to think freely and pursue individual interests, because it's all offered."

The size of most classes at the University of Nebraska echo the usual class size found at state universities, ranging from 10 to 500 students depending on the type of course with many classes averaging about 150. The general perception about the undergraduate professors is positive. "Professors are friendly and willing to work with individual students' schedules for out-of-class meetings" one sophomore noted. The TAs are a different story, however. Depending on the major, TAs can either be really helpful or hard to understand, as they may not be able to speak English very well.

Lincoln Living

During their freshman year at the University of Nebraska, students are required to live on campus. Most upperclassmen either move into on-campus apartment-style housing or move off campus entirely. Cather and Pound are two upperclassmen dorms, offering laundry facilities and computer clusters on every floor. Although many end up off campus, the majority of students seem to appreciate their freshman living experience. "You meet a lot of people that you might otherwise never get to know, some of whom become your best friends." All of the housing options offered by the University are fully air-conditioned, although those buildings not recently renovated are of noticeably lower quality.

Almost all the freshman dorms are doubles, with two beds, desks, closets, and high-speed wireless internet. RAs (Residential Advisors) are upperclassmen whose job it is to keep the freshman dorms free of alcohol and running smoothly. Those who choose to live off campus are able to take advantage of relatively low Midwestern housing prices. If a student at UNL does not reside on campus or in an apartment outside of the University's provided housing, he/she most likely lives in a fraternity or sorority. There are a total of 41 Greek houses at Nebraska-Lincoln: 14 sororities and 27 fraternities. Those involved in Greek life seem to "hold more leadership positions on campus" according to one senior. Furthermore, those brothers and sisters in Greek houses on campus have statistically higher GPAs than the overall average GPA of students at the University.

As far as food goes, the dining hall situation leaves everyone with a different taste in their mouths. Always noted as clean and not too crowded, the food's quality is recognized as anywhere from "decent but bland" to "everything one would look for in a college dining hall." However, the Training Table, a dining hall where only UNL athletes are allowed to eat, provides the best food. "They offer prime ribs, a more diversified menu, and a nutritionist is on staff in order to make sure athletes are getting the nutritional requirements they need" one junior explained.

The Union

When asked what the central hangout on campus is, students emphatically answer, "the Union!" Known to non-Cornhuskers as the Nebraska Union, the Union is unquestionably the most popular campus social center. Home to the University Bookstore, a convenience store, auditorium, copy shop, game room, food court and big-screen television lounge, the Union has it all. "If anyone ever needs to study with a group or catch up with some friends, the Union is the place to meet," declared one sophomore. Other than the Union, many Cornhuskers cite Memorial Stadium as the most prized location on campus. Renovated in 1999, the Stadium is now equipped with $40 million worth of new skyboxes.

It's All in Lincoln

If students aren't attending individual parties, team parties, or frat parties, "Haymarket is definitely the place to go" a junior explained. Located in downtown Lincoln, the Haymarket is full of restaurants and shops and is most commonly cited as the place to go for a date or to check out the bar scene on a Saturday night. Because Lincoln caters to college life and is the only real city for miles, many students will stay on campus for the better part of the year. "You really have to stay in the city because there really isn't anywhere else to go" a student said.

Aside from holding the highest grades on campus, the Greek houses are infamous for throwing some of the best parties annually. Hosting parties with themes anywhere from "Doctors and Nurses" to "Hollywood," "The frats are definitely where it's at," one student declared. Partying usually starts on Thursday nights and lasts until Saturday night. However, most Saturday nights in the fall are spent recovering from a full day at the Cornhusker tailgate rooting on the Big Red.

> **"There is a pride in being a Cornhusker that blows me away."**

Outside of academics and athletics, there are a wide range of other possibilities offered through the university and separate student organizations. Students are heavily involved in everything from community outreach volunteer programs to on-campus publications like the *Daily Nebraskan*. Cornhuskers are very satisfied overall with the extracurricular life on campus.

It's All About Football

While football most definitely pulls the biggest crowds, all athletic teams really bring a lot to Cornhusker spirit. Even when teams aren't as successful, they are still able to bring out a crowd. There are a great number of successful teams, including the men's gymnastics team, who have eight national titles under their belts, the women's indoor track and field team with three, and the women's volleyball team with two. For those athletes who aren't quite at the D-1 level, Nebraska offers a very competitive intramural sports program. Being the most popular extracurricular activity, intramural sports serve as a great way to "meet new people." For those students just looking to get a workout in, there's the Lee Sapp Recreational Center, which boasts two indoor tracks, a climbing wall, weight room, and basketball and racquetball courts. With facilities that nice, there's no excuse not to hit the gym.

For most state universities it's tricky to pinpoint one unifying factor that really seems to bring the campus together. But for Nebraska-Lincoln, it's quite obvious and goes beyond the football field. When asked what the one factor is that differentiates UNL from any other university, one sophomore noted it was "the school spirit absolutely without question. There is a pride in being a Cornhusker that blows me away." UNL is the pride of all of Nebraska and regular Nebraskans, students, and faculty aren't afraid to show it. For Nebraskans far and wide, including those who live and study on UNL's campus or are just there for the game, it really is all about football.—*Taylor Ritzel*

FYI

If you come to the U of Nebraska, you better bring "a warm winter coat. You usually have to walk a little ways to class and it can get very cold."

What's the typical weekend schedule? "Go to a frat party on Thursday and Friday nights, prime before the football game on Saturday, get pizza in Haymarket after, wake up late on Sunday and do homework in the afternoon."

If I could change one thing about the U of Nebraska, "I'd get rid of the train tracks that run through campus. You have to wait on your way to class while trains pass."

Three things every student should do at the U of Nebraska before graduating are "swim in the fountain in front of the Union, pass library class and go to a football game."

Nevada

University of Nevada / Reno

Address: Mail Stop 120 Reno, NV 89557
Phone: 775-784-4700
E-mail address: asknevada@unr.edu
Web site URL: www.unr.edu
Year Founded: 1864
Private or Public: Public
Religious Affiliation: None
Location: Urban
Number of Applicants: 4,024
Percent Accepted: 88%
Percent Accepted who enroll: 58%
Number Entering: 2,047
Number of Transfers Accepted each Year: 1,516
Middle 50% SAT range: M: 480–600, CR: 470–590, Wr: Unreported
Middle 50% ACT range: 20–25
Early admission program EA/ED/None: None
Percentage accepted through EA or ED: NA

EA and ED deadline: NA
Regular Deadline: Rolling
Application Fee: $60
Full time Undergraduate enrollment: 13,205
Total enrollment: 16,458
Percent Male: 46%
Percent Female: 54%
Total Percent Minority or Unreported: 27%
Percent African-American: 2%
Percent Asian/Pacific Islander: 7%
Percent Hispanic: 7%
Percent Native-American: 1%
Percent International: 3%
Percent in-state/out of state: 82%/18%
Percent from Public HS: Unreported
Retention Rate: 76%
Graduation Rate 4-year: 14%

Graduation Rate 6-year: 46%
Percent Undergraduates in On-campus housing: 14%
Number of official organized extracurricular organizations: Unreported
3 Most popular majors: Business/Marketing, Biology, Health Professions
Student/Faculty ratio: 15:1
Average Class Size: 20 to 29
Percent of students going to grad school: Unreported
Tuition and Fees: $15,656
In State Tuition and Fees if different: $4,561
Cost for Room and Board: $9,989
Percent receiving financial aid out of those who apply, first year: 60%
Percent receiving financial aid among all students: Unreported

Just north of downtown Reno, between the Sierra Nevada mountains and several valleys, is the University of Nevada, Reno—the state's premier public university. With its renowned specialized academic programs, a unique student population, a lively social scene, and a beautiful campus, UNR gives students the opportunity to receive a first-rate education at a great value.

Seismology, Journalism and More

At UNR, undergraduates are divided into a varied array of academic programs, including the College of Agriculture, Biotechnology, and Natural Resources; the College of Business; the College of Education; the College of Engineering; the College of Liberal Arts; the College of Science, including the well-known Mackay School of Earth Sciences and Engineering; the Division of Health Sciences (including nursing, medicine, social work and community health schools); and the Reynolds School of Journalism. Although the range of degree programs may seem daunting, students enrolled in one of the more specialized colleges will have access to focused educations and some nationally recognized faculty and research tools. "Even though you might not get a really well-rounded education, you get to really focus on what you're interested in with top-notch professors," one journalism student said. The fast-rising Reynolds School of Journalism features Pulitzer Prize–winning professors and alumni, and the Mackay School of Earth Sciences and Engineering, with the second-largest shake table—used in seismology to test earthquake conditions—in the country, is internationally recognized.

Before graduating, all students must complete the Core Curriculum, which consists of a minimum of 33 credits including a Core Humanities sequence covering the Western cultural tradition and an English or writing class, as well as different classes fulfilling mathematics, natural sciences, social sciences, fine arts, and diversity requirements depending on a student's major. To give students more chances to complete their degree requirements, UNR offers a "Wintermester" right after winter break during which students can cram entire courses into three weeks. After completing all of the other Core requirements, every student must take interdisciplinary Capstone Courses to put the final touches on their undergraduate educations. The Core Humanities courses are known to be difficult, but, as one junior noted, "They really teach important skills that are needed for the rest of college. They emphasize a lot of writing and critical reading." Overall, say students, the workload at UNR is reasonable, and students can find plenty of time to party or participate in extracurricular activities.

Not only does UNR boast renowned programs and faculty, it also offers relatively small class sizes and an honors program. Students in the honors program have access to smaller honors classes and priority registration, meaning that they are allowed to choose classes before other students, making it easier for them to take the classes they want. "Basically, all classes are open to you with early registration," a freshman said. "But the benefits kind of stop after sophomore year." Honors students explained that few majors offer upper-level honors classes, so the program "stops mattering" for juniors and seniors.

Leaving High School Behind—Or Not

Because nearly 82 percent of UNR students are from Nevada, with almost 60 percent of in-state students coming from the Reno area, some students complain that the UNR student population is "way too limited." A sophomore said most of the people she knows at UNR are people who went to her high school or nearby high schools, making the University seem like "a bigger version of my high school with the same people all over again." However, a freshman said going to college with many of his high school friends made the transition much easier,

"and besides, there are always going to be more than a few people from completely different backgrounds." Out-of-state students admit to feeling a little out of place at first, but as a freshman said, "Everyone's pretty friendly, so it's easy to meet people."

The large number of students from Nevada is no accident. UNR offers the Nevada Millennium Scholarship to all Nevada high school students who meet certain eligibility requirements, giving them considerable financial aid. It's an offer many students can't refuse: as one Millennium Scholar said, "I can go to UNR and get a great education at half the cost of going to an out-of-state college."

Another significant part of UNR's student population is the University's older students, many of whom have families and jobs in addition to their college workloads. Usually, they have chosen to pursue their college educations at the undergraduate level, without enrolling in a special program. Younger students say that although they have a hard time socializing with their older peers at first because of the age difference, the older students can add interesting perspectives to discussions in class.

Partying in the Biggest Little City in the World

UNR's 11 fraternities and eight sororities dominate the campus's social scene, with Greek house parties happening every weekend. Technically, UNR's fraternities are not allowed to serve alcohol, but students agree that it is "definitely possible" to find alcohol at parties. Drinking is common on the weekends, but as one sophomore said, "There are a lot of people at UNR, so even though I don't normally drink, it's not hard to find people who don't do it either." While many students choose to rush a fraternity or a sorority, the majority of students are not involved in Greek life and only go to the weekend parties, which are open to everyone regardless of whether they are Greek or not.

Meanwhile, although dorm parties are few and far between, students living off-campus—as well as student groups—frequently throw parties. Students 21 or over, or those who own fake IDs, can look forward to wild nights of drinking, dancing and gambling in downtown Reno. UNR's hometown isn't known as "the Biggest Little City in the World" for nothing: until the 1950s, it was the country's most popular gambling destination, and students can still find major casinos, bars and nightclubs on Virginia Street. The city is also home to numerous concerts, shows, conventions and other events, including an annual hot air balloon race. For students willing to take a short trip outside of Reno, ski resorts around Lake Tahoe are less than 50 miles away.

A Wolfpack of Activities

Outside of class and social activities, UNR students also find time to participate in over 100 campus organizations. As part of the budding journalistic tradition at UNR, the campus newspaper, the award-winning *Nevada Sagebrush*, is entirely written and produced by students with the help of some of the Pulitzer Prize–winning faculty at the journalism school. Meanwhile, many students join the Student Orientation Staff, the large student organization that helps welcome and orient new freshmen on campus, and still others compete in club sports teams or intramural sports so that they are still able to participate in athletics without making a varsity commitment. The school even has a Quidditch club, with members playing a game similar to that described in the *Harry Potter* novels. If students want to help organize social and cultural events on campus, they can join the student government or any of the residence hall councils. Various volunteering opportunities also exist, including the nearby U.S. Wolf Refuge, which takes in and provides a home for wolves and wolf-dog mixes.

Another popular campus activity is attending sports games. UNR competes in NCAA Division I's Western Athletic Conference (WAC), and has had some recent success in men's basketball. Football games against the rival University of Nevada, Las Vegas, which are known as "Battle for the Cannon" games, are especially popular. The winner of the annual contest, which attracts students, alumni, professors and Reno residents, takes home the Fremont Cannon trophy. Students are also increasingly drawn to volleyball, soccer and softball games.

UNR On and Off Campus

Unlike many other universities, UNR does not require any of its students, even incoming freshmen, to live on campus. In fact, the vast majority of UNR students—about 85 percent—live off campus. Off-campus residents usually use cars to commute to and from the school, since the public transportation system in and around Reno is "pretty inconvenient," according to one senior. If students do choose to live on campus, however, they can choose between seven differ-ent residence halls, each with its own configuration of room types and facilities: Nye Hall, Argenta Hall, Juniper Hall, Manzanita Hall, Lincoln Hall, White Pine Hall and Canada Hall. Nye Hall is the largest and oldest dorm on campus; although it has a reputation for small rooms, its traditional residence hall layout helps make it the most social of all the residence halls. Meanwhile, Juniper, White Pine and Canada halls feature apartment-style suites, with White Pine offering a fitness center and a substance-free environment. All of the halls house both men and women except for Manzanita, which only houses women, and Lincoln, which only houses men. Finally, the newest dorm, Argenta Hall, is every incoming student's dream: students describe it as having "gigantic" double rooms with private bathrooms and vaulted ceilings. UNR's Residential Advisors live with freshmen in the residence halls to give support if needed and enforce rules, especially the underage drinking policy, which states that alcohol is prohibited throughout the dorms unless all the residents are over 21. "The RAs are pretty strict and will definitely crack down if they find anything violating the policy," one freshman warned.

> **"I can go to UNR and get a great education at half the cost of going to an out-of-state college."**

On-campus residents can choose between four different meal plans, ranging from Bronze to Platinum, each with a different number and configuration of meals per week, while off-campus residents can buy meal plans allowing them to eat lunch on campus. Seven cafes, food courts and buffets dot UNR's campus, with not only traditional all-you-can-eat dining hall fare but also fast food options such as Starbucks, Sbarro and Pizza Hut. Although most of the eateries close in the evening, the campus convenience store, which sells household items as well as food, stays open until late at night.

A Great Value

Nevada's flagship state university features not only prominent and unique academic programs at a relatively low tuition, but also the attractions of Reno and a dynamic social scene. The generous Millennium Scholarship continues to draw many in-state students, but more and more out-of-state students are discovering UNR's educational benefits. Regardless of their original reasons for coming to UNR, Wolf Pack students consistently find that, as one student put it, "UNR is an amazing place, whether or not you're getting a scholarship. People who do get a scholarship just think of it as an added bonus." —*Vivian Yee*

FYI

If you come to UNR, you'd better bring "a car if you're going to live off campus—it's a must!"

What is the typical weekend schedule? "Go out and have fun on Friday nights, go to some event or sports game Saturday and hang out afterwards, catch up on work on Sunday."

If I could change one thing about UNR, I'd "bring in more out-of-state students, because it seems like everyone is from Nevada, especially the Reno area."

Three things every student at UNR should do before graduating are "try your luck at the Reno casinos, watch the Wolf Pack win the Cannon from UNLV, and get involved in an extracurricular."

New Hampshire

L ocated in the pristine wilderness of
western New Hampshire, Dartmouth
College is the smallest Ivy League college. Its roughly 4,000 students enjoy a rewarding Ivy League education filled with
academic opportunities. Dartmouth students
also enjoy the benefit of a secluded northern
New England campus, as well as an active
student community that boasts a diverse array of activities. Indeed, Dartmouth students
are very much satisfied with their college experience, exemplified by the university's
strong academic programs, exciting campus
environment and numerous extracurricular
opportunities.

Seduced by Seclusion
Located in Hanover, New Hampshire, Dartmouth boasts a beautiful natural environ-

ment that, according to one freshman, includes "hiking and biking trails amidst beautiful nature scenes, and the bliss of not having
any major cities nearby." During the fall and
spring months, this environment allows students to enjoy a variety of outdoor activities.
One of them is the Dartmouth Outing Club's
(or DOC's) freshmen trip, in which students
take a camping trip throughout northern
New England before their fall term. Taking
this trip and seeing New England's beautiful
streams, rivers, forests, hills, and valleys
gives these students a great way to bond and
explore. During the winter, according to one
sophomore, "when Dartmouth gets a thousand inches of snow and the temperature
rarely climbs above freezing, students have
frequent midnight snowball fights, take skiing trips, and even sled together on the

nearby golf course. The experience is unfathomably fun." To some students, the winter can be a bit much, however. One freshman complained, "By the time December came I had to wear three layers of clothing just to go outside." However, most find that Dartmouth's natural environment and cooler climate shapes the college experience in a positive way.

Dartmouth students enjoy the benefits of small-town life as residents of Hanover, which has a population of about 11,000. As one freshman explained, "Hanover is that quaint little town that everyone sees as part of the American Dream: it has one small street called Main Street lined with mom-and-pop stores, and everyone is really friendly." Students frequently go to Main Street to eat at small restaurants such as Mali's or shop at the Gap, the town's only major clothing store. Nevertheless, to many Dartmouth students, Hanover can at times be very dull. As one junior complained, "Hanover has almost nothing to do. It has one street with a couple of shops and restaurants and nothing else." However, most Dartmouth students generally do enjoy living in Hanover.

A New and Unique Spin on Ivy League Academics
Dartmouth's academic year is split up into quarterly terms, allowing students to take more classes and to schedule an "off" term during which they have no classes and can use their time for other pursuits, such as internships. Students also have a set of distributional requirements including, among others, a first-year seminar, a quantitative reasoning class, a literature class and three physical education classes. Though some students find this program too regimented, most appreciate it. As one freshman said, "The best part about Dartmouth's academics is that you have to try new things. For example, at a different college, I might not have been able to take a class on Slavic folklore to meet a college requirement. Having these requirements lets me get the best of all academic areas. That's what makes Dartmouth stand out."

An important component of Dartmouth academic life is the accessibility of its professors. As one sophomore said, "Professors have a strong presence, and at times even seem more like older students than faculty members." To ensure that students can have personal interactions with their professors, Dartmouth even has a "Take a Professor to Lunch" program, in which Dartmouth students schedule a lunch meeting with their professors that Dartmouth pays for. As one junior said, "This program is great because it lets me establish a personal relationship with my professors, who really seem to care." Dartmouth's uniquely amiable and accessible faculty is truly one of the best parts of its academic life. In addition, the overall scholastic program is very strong. "No matter what your major is," said one junior, "you will be able to find plenty of excellent classes and a top-notch faculty here."

> "Even during the winter months when Dartmouth gets a thousand inches of snow, students make the most of their environment. The experience is unfathomably fun."

Despite Dartmouth's great academic reputation, however, it still has a few shortcomings. Many students think that Dartmouth is not the humanities school it should be. "There aren't many history majors, language majors, or women's studies majors," said one freshman. "Also, planning to take certain classes can get complicated, since students generally need to take one term off each year to pursue internship opportunities or to relax."

Simplicity with Sophistication: Campus Life at Dartmouth
The vast majority of students at Dartmouth lives on campus, and most are quite satisfied with campus life. Due to Dartmouth's relatively small campus, most dorms are not very far from class. Such a setting allows students to bond quickly and have a positive experience. "The average dorm floor has 16 people, give or take," one freshman said. "Each floor has several bathrooms, and each building has its own kitchen and hang-out areas, so crowding is not really an issue." Undergraduate Advisors, who supervise the dorms, are also quite friendly and helpful. As one freshman put it, UGAs "are great with helping freshman and getting them acclimated to life at Dartmouth through advice and hosting dorm parties and events."

Most of the dorms have ample accommodations. By far the most coveted dorm, however, is the Wheelock building, to which the students apply separately for housing. One freshman said that his dorm "had three rooms for two people, and was huge." Wheelock students also enjoy a variety of interesting discussion groups. "Living in Wheelock feels like living in an intellectual community within an intellectual community," one student said. Though other dorms are decent, students caution prospective freshmen to be wary of the River, which is considered the worst building. One freshman complained that her room was so small that she "could only fit furniture in by squeezing it in at awkward angles," while another student complained that the kitchen at the River "is really old, and has a pipe sticking out of the wall." However, on balance, dorm life at Dartmouth is a fun experience.

Though students think that Hanover can be dull, they also believe that Dartmouth's campus life can be both entertaining and enriching. Most students cite their quad area, known as "the Green," as one of their favorite hangouts. Events at the Green include a campus-wide snowball fight and a massive student bonfire. Dinning service is also great. The 11 different eateries provide plenty of options for students. The Hopkins Center for the Performing Arts is also a student hub. The Hopkins Center hosts plays, classical and rock concerts, and movie nights. As one student put it, "The Hopkins Center is Dartmouth's house of entertainment." Overall, Dartmouth students have an enjoyable campus life and are rarely without something fun to do.

The Three Ps: Partying, Politics, and Philanthropy

Best known by many as a premier party school from the movie *Animal House*, Dartmouth has a reputation for a particularly vibrant Greek scene. As one freshman noted, "Greek life on campus is prevalent with a capital P. Socially speaking, you might almost feel restricted in your weekend options if you don't join." However, though *Animal House* does speak truth to the prevalence of Greek life on campus, most students feel it is not completely accurate. As one student noted, "Greek life here is not that intense. People party, sure, but they do so responsibly. Dartmouth also has a lot of other on-campus activities." As one sophomore put it, "Greek life is a big part of the Dartmouth social scene, but it is not coercive, and the parties are not that extreme. Even if you don't drink, Greek events can be a blast, and they really create a strong sense

of community here. Sometimes movies like *Animal House* only tell part of the truth."

Students also see community service as an integral part of Dartmouth's extracurricular offerings. The Tucker Foundation, Dartmouth's umbrella service organization, encourages student involvement with organizations such as Big Brothers Big Sisters of America, the American Cancer Society, and with projects such as AIDS Global Health Day. The Tucker Foundation also sponsors student service trips, including recovery work trips to New Orleans and service trips to Latin America. Studying abroad is also an activity in which almost all Dartmouth students participate. As one student put it, "Dartmouth has a great study abroad program with opportunities almost anywhere."

Another salient part of Dartmouth life is politics, especially during the start of every presidential election. Since Dartmouth is located in New Hampshire, which has the earliest presidential primary election in the nation, political life at Dartmouth can be quite intense. This past year, Dartmouth hosted a nationally televised debate for the Democratic Party's presidential candidates. One freshman vividly recalls the experience: "There was so much excitement on campus. Watch parties were thrown, and the auditorium was packed. I got to meet all the candidates, and the discussions with friends afterwards were incredible. One friend even told me that President Barack Obama went to one of his watch parties after the debate." In addition to presidential elections, many students find that politics affects them in other ways: students join advocacy groups, become involved in state politics, and enjoy political discussions. Overall, one of Dartmouth's best-kept secrets is its political atmosphere. Though many of its own students do not see Dartmouth as a political college, the environment is great for all those who are interested in politics.

Dartmouth is a prestigious Ivy League college that provides students with a strong academic program, an entertaining campus, and a lively social scene. As one student best put it, "Dartmouth is a place of incredible opportunity and intellectualism, where ambitious students go to challenge others, be challenged, and continue the lifelong process of enriching themselves through learning." —*Andrew Pearlmutter*

FYI
If you come to Dartmouth, you'd better bring "a warm winter coat."
What is the typical weekend schedule? "Friday nights are spent hanging out at a friend's dorm or going to a show or movie at the Hopkins Center. On Saturdays, do something athletic or do some other extracurricular activity and then go to a frat party at night. On Sundays, most students sleep in, and then study all day."
If I could change one think about Dartmouth, I'd "renovate the River dorm building and make its rooms bigger."
Three things every student at Dartmouth should do before graduating are "go on a Dartmouth Outing Club trip, participate in the annual bonfires and snowball fights on the Green and go to a frat party."

University of New Hampshire

Address: 4 Garrison Avenue Durham, NH 03824
Phone: 603-862-1360
E-mail address: admissions@unh.edu
Web site URL: www.unh.edu
Year Founded: 1866
Private or Public: Public
Religious Affiliation: None
Location: Rural
Number of Applicants: 14,382
Percent Accepted: 59%
Percent Accepted who enroll: 31%
Number Entering: 2,643
Number of Transfers Accepted each Year: 939
Middle 50% SAT range: M: 510–620, CR: 500–610, Wr: Unreported
Middle 50% ACT range: Unreported
Early admission program EA/ED/None: EA

Percentage accepted through EA or ED: Unreported
EA and ED deadline: 1-Nov
Regular Deadline: 1-Feb
Application Fee: $45
Full time Undergraduate enrollment: 12,067
Total enrollment: 15,053
Percent Male: 44%
Percent Female: 56%
Total Percent Minority or Unreported: 19%
Percent African-American: 1%
Percent Asian/Pacific Islander: 2%
Percent Hispanic: 2%
Percent Native-American: 0%
Percent International: 1%
Percent in-state/out of state: 55%/45%
Percent from Public HS: 84%
Retention Rate: 87%
Graduation Rate 4-year: 51%
Graduation Rate 6-year: 71%

Percent Undergraduates in On-campus housing: 55%
Number of official organized extracurricular organizations: 200
3 Most popular majors: Business Administration and Management, Communication, Journalism, and Related Programs, Psychology
Student/Faculty ratio: 18:1
Average Class Size: 10 to 19
Percent of students going to grad school: Unreported
Tuition and Fees: $25,236
In State Tuition and Fees if different: $11,756
Cost for Room and Board: $8,596
Percent receiving financial aid out of those who apply, first year: 72%
Percent receiving financial aid among all students: 59%

I n many ways, the University of New Hampshire serves as an exemplar of balance. Located halfway between the major cities of Boston, MA, and Portland, ME—and a stone's throw away from the White Mountains—the University's establishment in rural Durham provides its own unique environment. Additionally, the University's Congressional designation as a land-grant, sea-grant and space-grant institution demonstrates its comprehensive commitment to cutting-edge research in these fields. However, students must take the initiative to find their own equilibrium in this sea of opportunities because there are hundreds of ways to get involved in the UNH community.

Individual Initiative
Though UNH gives academic guidance through its various programs, in the end students must choose the most suitable path for themselves according to their own interests and goals. UNH comprises seven colleges, including the colleges of Engineering and Physical Sciences (CEPS), Liberal Arts

(COLA), Life Sciences and Agriculture (COLSA), and Health and Human Services (SHHS), as well as the Thompson School of Applied Science (TSAS), University of New Hampshire at Manchester (UNHM), and Whittemore School of Business and Economics (WSBE). WSBE is generally known to be a strong program and—maybe not coincidentally—its Business Administration major is by far the most popular major at UNH. Perhaps this is one reason why The Princeton Review and Forbes.com named UNH one of the nation's most entrepreneurial campuses. Other interesting majors include Justice Studies, Kinesiology and Horticultural Technology.

At the heart of a UNH education is the General Education Program, which requires students to take one course in each of eight major areas in order to learn the "fundamental skills" that allow them to make intellectual progress. While at first glance the Gen Ed requirements may look heavy, one student mentioned that it is not as harsh as it seems. Aside from First Year Writing, which every freshman must take, each of the categories includes a diverse array of courses to choose from. For example, the "Historical Perspectives" category alone has nearly 50 possible course options.

> "People take IM sports seriously. I ended up in the penalty box for one of the broomball games."

Perhaps what differentiates UNH from other comparable institutions is the number of ways in which students can take advantage of the University's unique location in pristine New England. For example, since UNH was originally incorporated as a college of agriculture and mechanical arts, and its chief benefactor was a farmer and businessman named Benjamin Thompson, the University has always emphasized agriculture. Making use of the University's resources, students majoring in Dairy Management—in addition to learning the skills necessary for the "successful management of a dairy enterprise"—can apply their classroom knowledge by tending real herds on the rural campus farms.

Furthermore, many programs take advantage of the outdoors, such as the 3,000+ acres of university-owned forestland, White Mountains National Forest, or the aquatic ecosystems of the Lakes Region of New Hampshire. In other words, the theoretical knowledge of students can be applied to real-world settings, allowing for a more balanced learning experience.

The classroom experience itself can vary in many ways. Though the intro-level courses may be dauntingly large, almost all upper-level seminars involve discussions around a circular table. In terms of workload, one student believed that the difficulty of a course was proportionate to the amount of reading: "If you don't do the reading, you can't participate in class at all." On the whole, students are encouraged to realize their potential and develop study habits that work well for them.

Friendly Folks

Sports and Greek life constitute a significant proportion of the UNH social scene. According to one student, Greek life is "a really big part of the weekend activities at UNH." This is because many students rush the dozen or so fraternities and sororities that host a number of the bigger parties on campus. "Frat parties here are the way to go," one student stated.

Like most other colleges, most students at UNH drink lots of alcohol. Though the official alcohol policies seem strict, it really depends on the enforcement by RAs on each floor of the dorms. The general policy is that one open container is permitted in a room for each person over 21 years old. However, if one's RA is easy-going, disciplinary action for alcohol abuse is unlikely. On the other hand, students mentioned that "not everyone drinks" and that many people find other activities to occupy their time when the weekend rolls around.

Meeting students at UNH is "quite easy." One student mentioned the importance of the all-freshman dorm as a way to form new friendships early on. Because "everyone is in the same boat" it was really easy to approach new people. Sports provide another avenue for making new friends. The common bond amongst students rooting for the hockey team and playing on the IM fields is "conducive to meeting new people," said one student. Regarding the character of the typical student, one student commented that "UNH students are wicked friendly."

Brilliant Brick Buildings

Most students live in dorms provided by the University for at least two years. While some eventually choose to move off campus into apartments, one student said that the upperclassmen dorms are "really nice." For those students trying to find others with similar interests, UNH offers themed housing such as the study-oriented ("Making the Grade"), substance-free ("Chem Free"), computers and technology ("Wired"), and intramural sports ("The Clubhouse") houses. As part of UNH's master campus plan, construction was completed on two residence halls in the fall of 2007, and a third opened in the fall of 2008.

The campus prides itself on the "Old Brick" look of its architecture. The primary building is Thompson Hall, built in honor of the eponymous benefactor to the University, which currently houses the administration. Because the Diamond Library is a member of the Boston Library Consortium, students have access to a large catalog of books through the interlibrary loan system. The building that is closest to the hearts of most UNH students, however, is the Memorial Union Building (also known as the "MUB"), which—with an "award-winning" and "excellent" dining hall, Holloway Commons—serves as the center of UNH's campus life. MUB is the hub; it houses an expansive food court, an entertainment center, a game room, multiple movie theaters, the Wildcat's Den (for dances and performances) and many multipurpose lecture rooms.

Hockey Is Holy

Outside of classrooms and labs, UNH offers the full spectrum of activities. The school's location in rural New England offers oudoorsy individuals an infinite number of pastimes. Because of the University's prime location, the Outing Club—"the oldest and largest club on campus"—normally offers 2–5 trips to various areas each weekend, from Nordic skiing to extreme sledding to ice climbing. Another popular on-campus activity is working for the student newspaper, *The New Hampshire*. Other prominent activities include the University's radio station, WUNH, and various a cappella groups such as the all-male Not Too Sharp. Finally, the intramural sports program is very popular and, according to one student, "very competitive." With over 28 sports and tournaments,

students have plenty to choose from. Broomball (on ice), flag football, ice hockey, indoor and outdoor soccer are among the favorite IM sports.

In a world of its own, though, is UNH hockey, which stands as the athletic face of the University. The UNH Wildcats men's and women's hockey programs are consistently title-contenders for the NCAA and Hockey East. As a result of their successes, students zealously rally around the teams during each game. One tradition that demonstrates the unifying nature of the hockey team is "White out the Whitt" ("Whitt" is short for the Whittemore Center) where, during crucial games, everyone wears white in support of UNH. Another interesting tradition is that of the brothers of the Zeta Chi fraternity, who ceremoniously toss a fish onto the ice after UNH scores its first goal of a game. The hockey games are such a central part of the school that obtaining tickets has become a feat of its own. One student described the ticket-purchasing process: "I sat in line from six in the morning. When the game came, I sat in line for another three hours just to get a good seat!" Additionally, past alums always make appearances at the hockey games to cheer their alma mater on to continued success.

Fertile Futures

In the end, the University of New Hampshire is a committed state university that constantly strives to improve itself. Its entrepreneurial spirit is supported by the Land, Sea and Space Grant programs, and it was the only public institution in New England to rank in the Top 10 for its number of Fulbright Scholars. Having produced astronauts, NHL hockey players, and acclaimed writers, UNH's production of outstanding alums is just as fruitful as the farmland around it. There are no boundaries at UNH. Students are encouraged to take their classroom knowledge and apply it directly to the outside world. Ultimately, though, it is the responsibility of student to take advantage of all that the University of New Hampshire has to offer.—*Wookie Kim*

FYI

If you come to UNH, you'd better bring "your game face, walking shoes (the campus is hilly), and a North Face jacket."

What's the typical weekend schedule? "Thursday: classes, late-night parties; Friday: classes, sports game, party; Saturday: sleep, sports game, recover, party; Sunday: study."

If I could change one thing about UNH, I'd "offer more specialized courses in specific subjects."

Three things every student at the University of New Hampshire should do before graduating are "go to the UNH/Maine hockey game, play intramural sports, study abroad."

New Jersey

College of New Jersey

Address: PO Box 7718 Ewing, NJ 08628
Phone: 609-771-1855
E-mail address: admiss@tcnj.edu
Web site URL: www.tcnj.edu
Year Founded: 1855
Private or Public: Public
Religious Affiliation: None
Location: Suburban
Number of Applicants: 9,692
Percent Accepted: 42%
Percent Accepted who enroll: 32%
Number Entering: 1,295
Number of Transfers Accepted each Year: 463
Middle 50% SAT range: M: 580–680, CR: 560–650, Wr: 560–660
Middle 50% ACT range: Unreported
Early admission program EA/ED/None: ED
Percentage accepted through EA or ED: 42%

EA and ED deadline: 15-Nov
Regular Deadline: 15-Feb
Application Fee: $60
Full time Undergraduate enrollment: 6,205
Total enrollment: 6,264
Percent Male: 40%
Percent Female: 60%
Total Percent Minority or Unreported: 34%
Percent African-American: 7%
Percent Asian/Pacific Islander: 10%
Percent Hispanic: 9%
Percent Native-American: <1%
Percent International: 0%
Percent in-state/out of state: 95%/5%
Percent from Public HS: Unreported
Retention Rate: 95%
Graduation Rate 4-year: 67%
Graduation Rate 6-year: 69%

Percent Undergraduates in On-campus housing: 48%
Number of official organized extracurricular organizations: 196
3 Most popular majors: Business Administration and Management, Elementary Education and Teaching, Psychology
Student/Faculty ratio: 13:1
Average Class Size: 20 to 29
Percent of students going to grad school: 27%
Tuition and Fees: $20,415
In State Tuition and Fees if different: $12,308
Cost for Room and Board: $9,612
Percent receiving financial aid out of those who apply, first year: 54%
Percent receiving financial aid among all students: 45%

As one of New Jersey's premier institutions of higher education, TCNJ embodies both the academic experience of a top-notch institution and the price tag of a state school. Therefore, each year, students from every corner of the United States flock to this highly regarded university to learn with each other and from each other.

An Academic Smorgasbord

Students at TCNJ are ready to work. With seven schools spanning fifty disciplines in liberal arts, it has something for everyone. The newly adopted four-credit system, along with a revamped core curriculum, challenges students to engage in rigorous academic training without wearing out. All entering freshmen participate in the "First Year Experience," a wide array of freshman-specific seminars that include anything from "Forensic Science" to "Harry Potter Literature."

The chemistry major offered at TCNJ is one of the most intensive in the nation. According to students, it is in fact more intensive than the engineering program. The chemistry major requires sixteen courses—more than the usual twelve courses per major—in a tight-knit environment where students receive direct individual attention from faculty advisors. The one drawback, as a current chemistry major noted, is that the "course schedule is pretty much fixed for all four years" due to the strenuous nature of the program.

For the medically inclined, TCNJ offers a combined seven-year B.S./M.D. program with the University of Medicine and Dentistry of New Jersey. Admission to this medical-scholar program is highly selective, but it offers a fast track to those who are set on a career in medicine.

Education is one of the most popular majors, stemming from TCNJ's original establishment as a teacher's training school. Communications, biology, accounting and nursing/exercise science are also popular. Whatever the course of study, students can expect to get very individualized care with class sizes ranging from fifteen to thirty students. Introductory courses, however, can be a little tougher with large lectures of upwards of one hundred students. Faculty advisors generally work hard to find resources for students, said one freshman. If there are still any lingering academic yearnings that have not been satisfied, the global study abroad program offers students the opportunities to experience the world.

The Lion's Den

Housing on campus can be a bit confusing for some students. TCNJ guarantees housing for all freshmen and sophomores. The proportion of freshmen who live on campus is ninety-five percent, which decreases to fifty percent for juniors and seniors. The overall on-campus housing rate is about sixty percent. Freshmen are housed in Traverse, Cromwell or Wolfe Halls, while upperclassmen are scattered in the other dorms and the many townhouses rented by TCNJ. Upperclassmen also have the options of private apartments in the city of Ewing specifically priced for college students as well as fraternity or sorority houses on and off campus.

TCNJ is in the midst of expanding its housing availability to include juniors and seniors with construction of new apartment suites, located a little farther from central campus, which are expected to open in late 2009. The rooms may be small, but many say they offer a feel of coziness. Campus living also contributes to the "tight bonds and camaraderie" among floor mates, noted one freshman. Most residences are centrally located with all buildings and facilities accessible within a ten-minute walk.

Campus safety is an important issue for TCNJ. The College has its very own campus police force that patrols at night in addition to the seventy safety posts located around campus that the students can access in case of emergency. They can also use the safety posts to ask for police escorts during the night. Resident Advisors in the dorms are also in place to ensure a safe learning environment, but they are more focused on fostering a sense of family. "You can walk into their rooms just to chat or get advice" and they will often "throw floor-wide birthday parties" to bring people together, said one junior. RAs are looked on less as authority figures and more as friends.

> **"From martial arts to campus religion to community service, there's always something to do. I'm never bored."**

Dining options at TCNJ receive mixed reviews. One trend is that students definitely need to be selective about what they do or do not eat. The food is served buffet-style in the main dining hall. There is a good selection of dishes, but they must be chosen wisely, according to a senior. Options for vegans and vegetarians are scarce. They will have the salad bar as their main staple in addition to a very limited menu of vegetarian dishes. Current students would also like to see the dining halls open a little later since the main dining hall, Eicke, closes promptly at 8 p.m, but there are also other campus-run cafes and eateries. Off-campus dining, on the other hand, might prove more satiating to the gourmet connoisseurs. The city of Ewing is very well aware of TCNJ's presence, and the students have a selection of restaurants that are moderately priced and of exceptional quality.

The Life of a Lion

Prospective students should not be fooled by the small college atmosphere of TCNJ. The party scene thrives there. Thanks to the four-credit schedule system, most students do not have classes on Wednesday, which makes Tuesday a prime time for parties. Friday, of course, is the other main party night. Options include fraternity/sorority parties, private dorms, clubs, bars, and private off-campus parties. There are also many school-sponsored events, parties, and dances, beginning with Homecoming. One complaint is that students should not expect any hot clubs or anchored social spots in the Ewing. Those dissatisfied with entertainment options choose to venture into nearby metropolitan areas such as New York or Philadelphia. Downtown Trenton is also a bus ride away with popular student hangouts, eateries, bars, and clubs. Overall, however, the off-campus social scene is a bit lacking as much of the action takes place within the TCNJ bubble.

Aside from the party scene, there are also a number of activities on campus so that it is almost impossible to be bored. "From martial arts to campus religion to community service, there's always something to do. I'm never bored," said one student. Indeed anyone can find his or her niche at TCNJ, which boasts over 180 student organizations to suit every taste. It even has a Medieval Knight Club, which is one of the more interesting favorites of students.

The Bottom Line

Many students are very happy to be a part of the TCNJ family and often show their school pride by wearing their TCNJ apparel. Sports are also major contributors to school spirit. People at TCNJ are prone to be the "athletic type," noted one freshman. People "love to exercise" and make great use of the jogging and biking trails that surround campus.

Students are generally happy with their TCNJ experience and point to the astounding hominess that they feel once arriving on campus. They are part of a community rather than a face in the crowd. This feature of TCNJ makes the freshman experience particularly enjoyable and helps their transition to college life. "No one feels alone or segregated," explained one sophomore. Although the consensus seems to point toward a general contentedness, there are also some things students would like to see improve. For one, the location of TCNJ limits nightlife off campus. Students who wish to be closer to metropolitan areas can find New York and Philadelphia to be quite a commute. However, location is the only big complaint students have about TCNJ. The mix of academics, sports, extracurricular activities, and the sense of community makes TCNJ a fulfilling place to embark on the journey of higher education.—*Hai Pham*

FYI
If you come to TCNJ, "you better bring a fan."
What is the typical weekend schedule? "Sleep in late, hang out with friends, hit up downtown Trenton, party with friends, and recuperate for the next week."
If you could change one thing about TCNJ, what would it be? "I'd like to change the location to a more urban, metropolitan area where more entertainment options are available on the weekends."
Three things every student should do before graduating are "swim in the water fountain of the science department, eat in downtown Trenton, and go to a Lion football game."

Drew University

Address: 36 Madison Avenue
  Madison, NJ 07940
Phone: 973-408-3739
E-mail address:
  cadm@drew.edu
Web site URL: www.drew.edu
Year Founded: 1868
Private or Public: Private
Religious Affiliation:
  Methodist
Location: Surburban
Number of Applicants: 4,191
Percent Accepted: 64%
Percent Accepted who
  enroll: 17%
Number Entering: 456
Number of Transfers
  Accepted each Year: 108
Middle 50% SAT range:
  M: 530–630, Cr: 530–650,
  Wr: 610–690
Middle 50% ACT range:
  24–28
Early admission program
  EA/ED/None: ED

Percentage accepted
  through EA or ED: 77%
EA and ED deadline: 1-Dec
Regular Deadline: 15-Feb
Application Fee: $50
Full time Undergraduate
  enrollment: 1,608
Total enrollment: 2,411
Percent Male: 40%
Percent Female: 60%
Total Percent Minority or
  Unreported: 34%
Percent African-American:
  5%
Percent Asian/Pacific
  Islander: 6%
Percent Hispanic: 6%
Percent Native-American:
  1%
Percent International: 1%
Percent in-state/out of
  state: 57%/43%
Percent from Public HS:
  61%
Retention Rate: 83%

Graduation Rate 4-year: 69%
Graduation Rate 6-year: 76%
Percent Undergraduates in
  On-campus housing: 87%
Number of official organized
  extracurricular
  organizations: 80
3 Most popular majors:
  Economics, Political Science,
  Psychology
Student/Faculty ratio: 11:1
Average Class Size: 10 to 19
Percent of students going to
  grad school: 33%
Tuition and Fees: $34,230
In State Tuition and Fees if
  different: No difference
Cost for Room and Board:
  $9,476
Percent receiving financial
  aid out of those who apply,
  first year: Unreported
Percent receiving financial
  aid among all students:
  51%

With just over 1,600 undergraduates, Drew is smaller than many high schools. But what the liberal arts school lacks in size, it makes up for in multiple ways, from its first-rate faculty to its beautiful campus. Belying most Garden State stereotypes, Drew is located on 200 wooded acres in northern New Jersey. New York City is also just 30 miles away, so students can experience the best of both city and country living while receiving a well-rounded education.

Friendly Faculty

Drew requires that students complete a major and a minor. But with 50 areas of study, there is no shortage of options. Students can also design their own majors and minors that focus on topics of their choosing—as long as they are approved. More popular concentrations include theater studies and English, though one student said that in general "it is pretty spread out between arts, economics, biology, political science and behavioral sciences."

Drew has several special programs, too, such as the dual-degree medical program, dual-degree programs in engineering and ap-

plied science, as well as pre-law, pre-medicine and pre-business programs.

Drew prides itself on its intimate academic setting. Classes are generally small, most with between 15 and 20 students, allowing students to interact with their classmates and professors. Students said that one of the best parts about Drew is the accessibility of the professors. Unlike at larger universities, professors teach most of the courses at Drew and make themselves available to students. "Professors are extremely easy to talk to if you need them, and they always know your name," said one student. Only first-year writing classes are taught by teaching assistants.

Drew also offers a plethora of off-campus study opportunities, giving undergraduates a chance to experience other parts of the country and the world while earning credits toward their degrees. Programs range in length and location. Students can spend a semester taking classes in London, Eritrea or New York or a summer soaking up the language and culture in Barcelona, China and Venice. Students can also take classes at nearby schools, such as Fairleigh Dickinson and St. Elizabeth's.

Cribs and Grub

Housing at Drew is guaranteed for all four years. Dorms consist of singles, doubles or suites, and students have the option of living on single-sex or coed floors. To keep an eye on things, every floor has a residential adviser. "RAs are strict in the freshman dorms," one student said. "Everywhere else is pretty relaxed as long as you are smart about things." Another student agreed, "In order to get in trouble, you really need to do something wrong."

Because on-campus housing is so habitable and housing in Madison is expensive and hard to find, most students never move off campus. The result is a close-knit community. "Though Drew is a small campus, you still see new faces everyday. Everyone is so friendly here, and it really is home to me," one junior said. Foreign language and other themed buildings—such as La Casa, a Hispanic-American dorm, and the Earth House, an especially environmentally friendly hall—are also available to upperclassmen.

Drew only has one dining hall, but students said the food is good. Plans come with 10, 14, or 19 meals a week, as well as points that may be used at the school "snack bar."

Work Hard, Play Hard

Small, quiet and quaint, Madison is not exactly the prototypical college town. Come the weekend, some students head home while others go into Manhattan, which is less than an hour's ride by train or bus. The train station is within walking distance of campus, and buses to New York are available from the main gate of the campus.

> "Drew can be a party school for some people or completely quiet and reserved for others depending on where you go and what you're looking for."

Most students, however, stick around for the weekend. Though there are no fraternities or sororities, Drew has its fair share of parties. Many take place at The Suites, a dorm for upperclassmen, where a lot of athletes usually live. For juniors, seniors and ride-bumming underclassmen—freshmen and sophomores are not allowed to have cars on campus—Morristown is just a five-minute drive away.

Drugs are not prevalent on campus, but drinking is. "Everyone I know [drinks], but you don't have to if you don't want to," said one senior, who added, "If you are caught underage drinking, which is easy to avoid, you are put on probation and possible alcohol classes." One student summed up the social scene by saying that Drew "can be a party school for some people or completely quiet and reserved for others depending on where you go and what you're looking for."

There are several special events over the course of the year, including Winter Ball, a formal dance; Festival of Lights, a holiday celebration; and 99 Nights, a party for seniors. Every year at the end of spring semester, Drew also throws the First Annual Picnic, a huge blowout where "bands play and they hold kegs for those of age."

Something for Everyone

When they are not studying or partying, students are very involved in extracurricular activities. Whether singing in an a cappella group, writing for *The Acorn* or building homes with Habitat for Humanity, Drew students take full advantage of the dozens of clubs and organizations on campus as well as one of the top-ranked theater departments in the country. Student-acted and directed productions are put on throughout the year, often attracting bigger crowds than sports events: "Going to see shows in our theatre is a big thing." Many students additionally have jobs on or around campus. As one student said, "Everyone on campus is extremely involved, and I find that every student is passionate in at least one thing."

Drew, a member of Division III, has 15 varsity teams. Most compete in the Middle Atlantic States Conference along with teams from other schools in the New Jersey and Pennsylvania area like Delaware Valley College, Wilkes University and the University of Scranton. According to one varsity lacrosse player, sports are "not overly important but a big part of the social gatherings." He added that soccer is the big sport on campus but "all sports get respect."

Drew also has clubs teams in rugby, ultimate Frisbee, volleyball and dance, which travel throughout the country to compete. For the less athletically inclined, intramural sports provide a fun and commitment-free way to get away from the books and relieve some stress. Offerings include flag football, tennis, billiards, squash, ping pong, dodge ball, racquetball, basketball, softball and wiffle ball. Students can also lift weights, run on a treadmill or take a yoga class at the state-of-the-art Simon Forum and Athletic Center.

Though most students are from the tri-state area, others come from throughout the nation and the world—27 states and 7 countries in the class of 2012, to be exact. What draws them to Drew are the small classes, the great professors, the outstanding accommodations and, yes, New Jersey.
—*Josh Lotstein*

FYI

If you come to Drew, you'd better bring "an open mind, a sled, a fan, a tool set."

What is the typical weekend schedule? "Very loud suite parties, sometimes theme parties, free movies every weekend, performances at the Space and TOE, and a cappella concerts."

If I could change one thing about Drew, I'd "make the dorms closer to the classes and the library."

Three things every student at Drew should do before graduating are "swim in Tipple Pond in the rain when it fills up, take a walk in the Arboretum and go to the Shakespeare Theatre."

Princeton University

Address: PO Box 430 Princeton, NJ 08544-0430	**Percentage accepted through EA or ED:** NA	**Graduation Rate 6-year:** Unreported
Phone: 609-258-3060	**EA and ED deadline:** NA	**Percent Undergraduates in On-campus housing:** 98%
E-mail address: uaoffice@princeton.edu	**Regular Deadline:** 1-Jan	
Web site URL: www.princeton.edu	**Application Fee:** $65	**Number of official organized extracurricular organizations:** 250
Year Founded: 1746	**Full time Undergraduate enrollment:** 4,981	
Private or Public: Private	**Total enrollment:** 6,785	**3 Most popular majors:** Economics, History, Political Science
Religious Affiliation: None	**Percent Male:** 53%	
Location: Suburban	**Percent Female:** 47%	
Number of Applicants: 21,370	**Total Percent Minority or Unreported:** 50%	**Student/Faculty ratio:** 5:1
Percent Accepted: 10%	**Percent African-American:** 8%	**Average Class Size:** Unreported
Percent Accepted who enroll: 59%	**Percent Asian/Pacific Islander:** 15%	**Percent of students going to grad school:** Unreported
Number Entering: 1,243	**Percent Hispanic:** 7%	**Tuition and Fees:** $34,290
Number of Transfers Accepted each Year: Unreported	**Percent Native-American:** 1%	**In State Tuition and Fees if different:** No difference
	Percent International: 10%	**Cost for Room and Board:** $11,405
Middle 50% SAT range: M: 700–790, CR: 690–790, Wr: 690–780	**Percent in-state/out of state:** 16%/84%	**Percent receiving financial aid out of those who apply, first year:** 85%
Middle 50% ACT range: 31–34	**Percent from Public HS:** 58%	
Early admission program EA/ED/None: None	**Retention Rate:** 98%	**Percent receiving financial aid among all students:** 54%
	Graduation Rate 4-year: 90%	

There's no doubt about it—Princeton is a hard school. It's one that's hard to get into, and maybe even harder to do well in. But to be fair most students at Princeton enjoy their experience, despite the incredible effort they put into their studies, because of the tremendous rewards that await them upon graduation. Consistently ranked first every year from 2001 to 2008 by *U.S. News* *and World Report*, it's no coincidence that Princeton offers its students an unparalleled experience in undergraduate education, something that's sure to be widely respected after graduation. Although students spend a lot of time on work, they also have a good time partaking in Princeton's many traditions, which makes their undergraduate experience particularly unique and enriching.

Work Hard and Play Hard. Really, Really Hard.

One student said, "Most people would probably agree with the following description: Princeton is a great place to be from, but not particularly great to be at." Students said that the value and prestige of receiving a Princeton diploma makes the hard work worth it, but in between the hard work, there is also a lot that can be gained through Princeton's unparalleled undergraduate experience. "The attention that we get as undergraduates from most professors is unique. Princeton focuses much more heavily on its undergraduates than its graduate students," one sophomore explained. He also added that Princeton's senior thesis, a comprehensive research project in one's major required of nearly all seniors to graduate, is something else that makes the Princeton experience especially valuable.

> "If you strike the right balance between studying and partying, it doesn't feel like school is taking over your life. I came in expecting to work with no rest whatsoever and that hasn't been the case."

But prospective students need not fear *too* much about the hard work. One freshman said, "I guess the most important thing has been to work hard and play hard. If you strike the right balance between studying and partying, it doesn't feel like school is taking over your life. I came in expecting to work with no rest whatsoever and that hasn't been the case." Students say that there is definitely a spectrum of students, ranging from those who take very easy classes and go out four to five days a week, to those who spend a large majority of their time on their studies. But students warn pre-frosh to mentally prepare themselves for the curriculum ahead of them. One sophomore said, "I definitely did not expect to be so unprepared for the difficult coursework and in general I didn't expect the workload to be so heavy." But students can find solace in the fact that they're not facing this alone. "The best thing about Princeton is the academic environment. You might be working your butt off but it's nice knowing other people are doing the same thing," one freshman said.

Deflated Spirits

While Princeton offers an unparalleled experience in an excellent undergraduate instruction, the university also has a policy of "grade deflation," which is a real and genuine concern for students on campus. Students said that Princeton began a grade deflation policy a few years ago by which approximately only 35 percent of students in a department are allowed to receive A's. Students say that the official reason is that Princeton wants to hold its students to the highest standard by fighting grade inflation and only giving A's to work that deserves the highest grades. This hasn't been happily received by the student population, and some say that it negatively affects the learning atmosphere. "The existence of a hard quota makes it seem like students not only have to do well in classes, but they have to do it better than the other 65 percent of students to get an A, so this fosters competition instead of cooperation," one student said.

In addition, students feel that institutions of similar caliber, notably Harvard and Yale, have grade inflation, which disadvantages Princeton students upon graduation as they try to apply for graduate school and professional programs, or enter the workforce. One freshman noted, "Apparently, Princeton sends out a letter explaining grade deflation to grad schools and companies, but no one knows if they actually bother reading those letters, so I, among many others, worry about that."

It's Not About the Food, It's About the Name

While Princeton does have a residential college system, there isn't intense rivalry between the colleges as is usually the case at similar schools. For the first two years, students can't transfer to be with their friends at other colleges, but by junior year students move to upperclassmen dorms and living arrangements become more flexible. There are three four-year and three two-year residential colleges, so as upperclassmen students can live in university housing on campus with college affiliation, but do not need to live in the college itself. While there are organized activities within colleges such as study breaks, trips, and intramurals, Princeton's social life entirely revolves around the eating clubs, a culture that is unique to Princeton.

In a sense, eating clubs are exactly what they sound like—places to eat. Upperclassmen have the option to either go independent or to join an eating club as their "meal plan" of sorts. There are two types of eating clubs: bicker and sign in. For bicker clubs students must go through an application process—or bickering, as Princetonians call it—and be selected by the committees of each of these clubs. These clubs are large mansions all located along Prospect Avenue, which is conveniently called the Street by Princeton students.

Ironically, the prestige of each eating club is not about the food at all, but about its name. Bicker clubs are obviously more exclusive than sign-in clubs, but some bicker clubs have such a high reputation that membership is incredibly competitive. For example, students say that Ivy consists of the wealthy, the connected, and the athletic, while Tower has mostly students from the selective Woodrow Wilson School of Public Affairs. In addition, members of certain fraternities and certain sport teams are unofficially "set" for certain eating clubs, so getting into extremely selective eating clubs is very hard, although students say that knowing "the right people" definitely helps with the process. Regarding the selectivity and prestige of the eating clubs, one student said, "The bickering process is definitely stressful and it can be very frustrating when you know there's just nothing you can do to get in because of your background. For example, Ivy costs something like $15,000 a year, so that automatically excludes the poor."

Eating Clubs or Drinking Clubs?

While eating clubs obviously serve their purpose of providing food for students, they also provide something else: drinks, drinks, drinks. Eating clubs double as party places, and although only club members can eat at the eating clubs, the clubs usually allow everyone to party, so students frequently hit up the Street on weekends. "Everyone goes to the Street, period. It's the center of Princeton's party life in the truest sense of 'party' since there aren't really any other options," one student said. He explained that free beer and music draw people to the Street on Thursday and, while most people go to dorm parties on Friday, the Street picks up again on Saturday.

Students say that the parties are usually pretty good. "There are 10 eating clubs, so you're bound to find a good one." Although it's technically illegal, it's an accepted fact that all the eating clubs serve alcohol to minors. Three eating clubs were recently closed for serving alcohol to minors, and students say that when things like that happen, eating clubs usually tighten alcohol policy, but that it usually doesn't last very long. "Princeton doesn't directly own the eating clubs so they can't really do anything about it," one student explained. Students say that administrators are in discussions about having public safety officers patrolling halls to bust parties, but before this the alcohol policy was pretty loose. Students said that they can only get in trouble for serving alcohol to minors or drinking outside, and that officers only check if students are serving alcohol to minors when parties get really loud and are reported to public safety. "Very few people get into trouble and they're usually only put on probation, but one of the few things Princeton is very anal about is that there are absolutely no drinking games."

Outside the Classroom, Inside the Bubble

Princeton is not much of a college town. Students describe it as a "rich suburb" that doesn't offer much for its college students. "Princeton feels like a tight-knit community because it's kind of isolated and everything is within walking distance. You barely ever step foot outside of campus." Students admit that this creates a "bubble culture," but one said that most people don't seem to mind, and may even really like it. "It's like a castle in the middle of nowhere, as we usually say. I like the relative isolation and peace, and having everything I need close by." However, many students still complain that the town doesn't really have things for college students to do, like bars, clubs or shopping areas.

But the lack of opportunities in the town may be good in at least one aspect—it makes Princeton students look to their own campus for activities outside the classroom. Students say that extracurricular involvement varies from person to person. Some people are heavily involved, while others might have other time commitments such as sports that prevent them from devoting lots of time to other activities. Some of the more prominent clubs include the Black Men's Awareness Group (BMAG), Student Volunteer Council (SVC), and the Asian American Student Association (AASA), while a cappella and dance groups are also very popular on campus. "Most people are committed to one thing, and I get the feeling that the majority of the students are involved in some sort of activity. There are so many things here that you're bound to find something you like, whether that's music, intra-murals, or theater stuff."

Out on the fields, Princeton boasts one of the strongest athletic programs in the Ivy League. Princeton has consistently been ranked at the top of *Time* magazine's "Strongest College Sports Teams" lists, and *Sports Illustrated* has ranked Princeton as a top 10 school for athletics. Princeton is particularly well known for its men and women's crews, which have won several NCAA and Eastern Sprints titles in recent years. In addition, Princeton's men's lacrosse team is widely recognized as a perennial powerhouse in the Division I ranks. Other successful Princeton athletic programs include women's soccer, and field hockey, which has won every field hockey conference title since 1994. Princeton athletics is a powerhouse in the Ivy League, which is a definite plus for those who are looking for a prestigious academic experience in addition to a strong athletic experience.

Keeping It Old School

While students agree that Princeton has moved away from its stereotyped image as an elitist school for stuck-up, old-money prep-school kids, the school still has strong roots and values in traditions, as the eating clubs suggest. One of Princeton's traditions is the bonfire held on Cannon Green behind Nassau Hall, which happens when Princeton beats both its rivals—Harvard and Yale—at football in the same season. "It's pretty special, since it doesn't happen that often. Everyone congregates and screams," one sophomore said. Like many other Ivy League universities, Princeton has a myth regarding exiting particular gates as an undergraduate. At the end of Princeton's graduation ceremony, the new graduates proceed out through FitzRandolph Gate as a symbol of leaving college and entering the real world. But according to tradition, anyone who leaves campus through this gate before their own graduation date will not graduate, so students use side exits instead.

Students warn that the old-school tradition of Princeton may also attract a certain type of student, namely those from "old money." While most students are generally pleasant, students warn that those who have not been thoroughly exposed to the East Coast prep school culture may be in for an initial shock. One student who came from a city public school said he was surprised by the "jock-ish" and "elitist" atmosphere at Princeton. "There are a lot more affluent and wealthy kids here—some really do flaunt it and most don't hide it. I don't have a problem with rich people, and I've certainly met people who are rich and nice, but it's just that they sometimes come across as being obnoxious in the way they act." But another student said that this attitude is not necessarily entirely related to social class, and may have a lot to do with the competitive nature of Princeton's atmosphere. "Of course, there are many rich and snobby people who dress very preppy-ish, but other people are just jerks when it comes to schoolwork, being unhelpful and arrogant. Unless you're lucky, you really have to look around for nice and helpful students."

All in all, Princeton students tend to be happy with their educational experience, even if it means that they're working incredibly hard for the four years they're at school. But between the hard work to get those coveted A's, Princeton students still find the time to pursue passions and party hard, and many keep going by keeping their eyes on the end goal: the prestige that comes with their diploma. The quality of education that Princeton students get is arguably the best on an undergraduate level, and the Princeton name will undoubtedly help students as they leave the bubble and venture off into the world. As one alumni noted, "People know that Princeton graduates will know how to solve anything if you give them enough time to figure out a way."—*Della Fok*

FYI

If you come to Princeton, you'd better bring "obnoxiously preppy clothes for lawn parties, which is when the eating clubs invite bands to come play. It starts Sunday afternoon so everyone's hungover by nine. It happens once each semester, but it's huge."

What is the typical weekend schedule? "If you're a slacker, jock, or something of that nature, you start partying on Thursday nights. If you're a nerd, you probably have 98,234 problem sets due on Friday, so you stay inside to do those. On Friday nights usually only one eating club is open, basically for the sake of the nerds, but for the rest of campus, Friday is usually pretty relaxed—the evenings are often filled with events like dance shows and concerts. Saturday is pretty dead until nighttime, which is hardcore partying, of course, and then Sunday is homework day for everyone."

If I could change one thing about Princeton, I'd "change the grading policy. Enough said."

Three things every student at Princeton should do before graduating are "go sledding with cafeteria trays at the golf course behind Forbes, one of the six residential colleges, sneak into the underground steam pipe tunnel system and make it out unscathed, and see the Triangle Show, which is this really famous theater group from Princeton that tours nationally every year."

Rutgers / The State University of New Jersey

Address: 65 Davidson Road Piscataway, NJ 08854-8097	**Percentage accepted through EA or ED:** NA	**Graduation Rate 6-year:** Unreported
Phone: 732-932-4636	**EA and ED deadline:** NA	**Percent Undergraduates in On-campus housing:** 49%
E-mail address: NA	**Regular Deadline:** NA	**Number of official organized**
Web site URL: www.rutgers.edu	**Application Fee:** $60	**extracurricular organizations:** 400
Year Founded: 1766	**Full time Undergraduate enrollment:** 3,694	**3 Most popular majors:** Biology, Engineering
Private or Public: Public	**Total enrollment:** 26,829	**Student/Faculty ratio:** 14:1
Religious Affiliation: None	**Percent Male:** 51%	**Average Class Size:** Unreported
Location: Suburban	**Percent Female:** 49%	
Number of Applicants: 28,208	**Total Percent Minority or Unreported:** 48%	**Percent of students going to grad school:** Unreported
Percent Accepted: 56%	**Percent African-American:** 9%	**Tuition and Fees:** $21,306
Percent Accepted who enroll: Unreported	**Percent Asian/Pacific Islander:** 24%	**In State Tuition and Fees if different:** $11,358
Number Entering: 5,508	**Percent Hispanic:** 8%	**Cost for Room and Board:** $9,378
Number of Transfers Accepted each Year: 2,906	**Percent Native-American:** <1%	**Percent receiving financial**
Middle 50% SAT range: M:560–670, CR:530–630, Wr: Unreported	**Percent International:** 2% **Percent in-state/out of state:** 93%/7%	**aid out of those who apply, first year:** 67%
Middle 50% ACT range: Unreported	**Percent from Public HS:** Unreported	**Percent receiving financial aid among all students:** 69%
Early admission program EA/ED/None: None	**Retention Rate:** Unreported **Graduation Rate 4-year:** Unreported	

Named most diverse national university for the 10th consecutive year in *U.S. News & World Report,* Rutgers University is a public research university that boasts a wealth of academic programs, resources, and opportunities both in and out of the classroom. With campuses in three distinct Garden State locales and roughly 50,000 students, Rutgers, the only university to reject an invitation to the Ivy League, is a serious academic institution rooted in a deep commitment to public education.

A Three-for-One Deal

Rutgers comprises three campuses, the largest and oldest of which is located in the central New Jersey cities of New Brunswick and Piscataway. The smaller southern campus at Camden and northern location at Newark flank the center, forming a university that literally spans the state. Each of the three campuses is distinct in its academic offerings, extracurricular activities and social life. One thing's for sure—the Rutgers experience is diverse.

New Brunswick students estimate that the ratio of students who live on campus versus those who live off campus is about even, while Newark students said that far more students live off campus. "Most people are dying to get off campus after their second year," revealed one New Brunswick junior resident. Because Rutgers is a public university, it is known to adhere to stringent underage drinking restrictions; students cited this fact as motivation for the move off campus. Douglass Residential College of the New Brunswick campus is an all-female housing option, though in any given year the building may include coed dorms.

All of the campuses boast a wealth of extracurricular activities and clubs, with intramural sports the most popular. Rutgers students point to the variety of options open to those looking for fun: movie theaters, the mall, restaurants and parties. The consensus among students is that their weekend parties are top-notch. "Come Friday and Saturday night, Rutgers is the place to be," bragged one sophomore. However, since many students have jobs, the weekend is not all about partying. Greek life is not very expansive, with active life primarily at its College Avenue and Livingston locations on the New Brunswick campus. The Livingston locations feature minority and ethnic fraternities and sororities.

In terms of the population's diversity, Rutgers students agree that the University hits the mark and makes continual efforts to maintain its inclusiveness. But they do criticize the disjointed nature of campus life and fault the inefficiency of the transportation system. "Even though nextbus.com reduces the wait, Route 18 construction makes traffic a constant issue," one junior said. Beyond the system of buses that attempts to connect the Rutgers experience on a practical level, the University attempts to create social spaces that foster diversity. The formation of new residential colleges (the first of which is the aforementioned Douglass) represents such an administrative attempt to foster exchange in living communities.

Rutgersfest, the annual campus-wide blowout before final exams, brings three performing artists or groups to the stage to celebrate the closing of the academic year. Even in this endeavor, students cite the diversity of acts as reflecting the diversity of those in the crowd. "Some people come to Rutgers and have an utter culture shock," said one New Yorker. However, students are quick to explain that the diversity of Rutgers is healthy and productive, and when asked about resultant tensions, dispelled the idea. "I have never encountered a problem with it," said one junior. "The people who come here with no experience with difference don't react with prejudice; they tend to be happy to get a taste of the real world."

An End to the "Rutgers Screw"

With the freshman class of 2007, the previous staples of the New Brunswick campus—Douglas, Livingston, Rutgers and University Colleges—were combined into one undergraduate liberal arts college: The School of Arts and Sciences. This advanced conglomerate offers an expanded set of over 100 majors spanning the humanities, biological sciences, mathematics and more.

The change was simply one component of the "undergraduate transformation" recently undergone by Rutgers's largest campus. And while most students have praised the effort for making their educational experience much less complicated, others have criticized it for doing the exact opposite. "It was a good idea in theory, but we weren't ready for it," remarked one junior resident advisor. She lamented that her residents "had no idea what they were doing" and that the academic advising that accompanied the new system needs work. "Academically and residence-wise, things are still in transition," she said.

Despite these administrative hassles, students generally praised the changes. A major benefit of this system is its ability to bring an end to the notorious "Rutgers Screw." Defined by students as a buzz word for the popular notion that, by the time you reach senior status, some unknown requirement or misinformation will keep you from graduating, the "Rutgers Screw" now faces extinction under the transformation's streamlined requirements and staff. Rather than being restricted by college, students can now seek advisers under the unified college to avoid the common pitfall.

Students also hailed the changes for bringing them together. Previously, each campus had its own traditions, but now Rutgers students are working to forge a single community. "Cap & Skulls," a Rutgers College secret society based on leadership and academics prowess, now extends membership invitations to the entire university. According to one exercise and sports science major, "Whatever people have to say about the transformation, it has increased campus unity."

A Warm Welcome

Freshman classes have the advantage of walking into this heightened spirit of cohesion. Upperclassmen characterized their freshman orientations as mediocre, but lauded the newest orientation efforts and the improvement of the football team as ways of bringing the class together. "This year's orientation was amazing, with all these events. We even had a throw-down where we could win prizes," a freshman New Jersey native said. One sophomore commented that the orientation "built them more into a community than [his] first year." Yet even before these changes students remembered the Rutgers freshman experience fondly. One junior exclaimed, "My freshman year at Rutgers was the most amazing experience I've ever had; I love Rutgers and I wouldn't pick another school."

Incoming classes will also be welcomed by various new, albeit uniform, academic requirements. In place of the previous "non-Western" requirement are the more expansive categories of "Diversity" and "Global Awareness." Those new to Rutgers will still have to pass "Expository Writing," a Rutgers staple known to students as "Expos," to graduate. This infamous RU requirement brought a series of groans from students across the spectrum in terms of major, interests and origin. The sole comfort students offered regarding the course was that those taking it are by no means alone. "Everyone goes through it; the beauty of it is that you have four years to knock it out," advised one senior. For those weary of getting lost in a sea of numbers, but valuing the resources of a research university, the transformation also ensures that freshman have the opportunity to engage in new first-year seminars—classes capped at 20 and taught by distinguished Rutgers faculty, aimed at engaging students in serious, speculative dialogue.

Spectacle Sports

Rutgers played Princeton University in the first ever game of intercollegiate football in 1869 (where the present-day Rutgers gymnasium now stands) and won. So it comes as no surprise that a strong tradition of university athletics continues to this day.

The Scarlet Knights have a dedicated and spirited fan base, drawing huge crowds from across the lecture hall aisle. At Rutgers, football dominates the athletic scene. Students cite the team's improvement in recent years for a surge in school spirit. "All I wear is Rutgers clothing," one senior said. Last year, the Scarlet Knights performed well enough to reach the International Bowl in Toronto, Canada, with their star player, Brian Leonard. Leonard was recently drafted into the NFL to play for the St. Louis Rams. According to students, the team has continued to improve as new stars have risen in his wake. Knights say that RU Football has become a huge campus event and school spirit has risen alongside the stats. "I have never seen so many Rutgers sweatshirts," commented one senior.

> "My freshman year at Rutgers was the most amazing experience I've ever had; I love Rutgers and I wouldn't pick another school."

Football is not the only sport that draws crowds at Rutgers. The women's basketball team is renowned for its prowess on the court and has become the media darling of college sports. The team and the school have not let the recent Don Imus controversy derail their efforts. "It really affected us when it happened, but now everything's been smoothed over," said one junior. She went on to explain how the proliferation of Facebook groups and spread of support further unified the school in the face of the media flurry. "School spirit translated into solidarity."—*Nicholle Manners*

FYI

If you come to Rutgers, you'd better bring "a Rutgers T-shirt because you'd better not be wearing another college's shirt."

What is the typical weekend schedule? "Friday, go to the dining hall, go to work, do your homework, go out; Saturday: sleep in late, go to a football game and go out; Sunday: sleep in late and do your homework."

If I could change one thing about Rutgers, I'd "change the bus system and make morning classes later."

Three things every student at Rutgers should be before graduating are "go to a football game, eat a fat sandwich at the Grease Trucks, and go to the Zimmerlie Art Museum."

Seton Hall University

Address: Seton Hall University
  South Orange, NJ 07079
Phone: 973-761-9332
E-mail address:
  thehall@shu.edu
Web site URL: www.shu.edu
Year Founded: 1856
Private or Public: Private
Religious Affiliation: Roman
  Catholic
Location: Suburban
Number of Applicants: 6,626
Percent Accepted: 79%
Percent Accepted who
  enroll: 26%
Number Entering: 1,322
Number of Transfers
  Accepted each Year: 444
Middle 50% SAT range:
  M: 480–590, CR:470–580,
  Wr: 470–580
Middle 50% ACT range:
  Unreported
Early admission program
  EA/ED/None: None

Percentage accepted
  through EA or ED: NA
EA and ED deadline: NA
Regular Deadline: Rolling
Application Fee: $55
Full time Undergraduate
  enrollment: 4,594
Total enrollment: 5,187
Percent Male: 44%
Percent Female: 56%
Total Percent Minority or
  Unreported: 50%
Percent African-American:
  11%
Percent Asian/Pacific
  Islander: 6%
Percent Hispanic: 10%
Percent Native-American:
  <1%
Percent International: 3%
Percent in-state/out of
  state: 75%/25%
Percent from Public HS: 70%
Retention Rate: 83%
Graduation Rate 4-year: 41%

Graduation Rate 6-year: 56%
Percent Undergraduates in
  On-campus housing: 46%
Number of official organized
  extracurricular
  organizations: 100
3 Most popular majors:
  Business, Health
  Professions, Social Sciences
Student/Faculty ratio: 13:1
Average Class Size: 10 to
  19
Percent of students going
  to grad school: 30%
Tuition and Fees: $27,420
In State Tuition and Fees if
  different: No difference
Cost for Room and Board:
  $11,360
Percent receiving financial
  aid out of those who apply,
  first year: 91%
Percent receiving financial
  aid among all students:
  86%

E nroll at Seton Hall University, and you will experience two dichotomous worlds: It has a strong Catholic tradition on one hand but enormous diversity on the other; it is isolated in a quiet Northern New Jersey suburb but is also less than 20 minutes from the most exciting city in the world; it is overflowing with athletic fervor but also boasts some of the country's most renowned undergraduate programs in diplomacy and business; it is considered unchallenging by some, but it actually is dominated by many career-driven students in search of double- and even triple-majors. This pattern even applies to the student body makeup, which is split almost equally between commuters from neighboring New Jersey communities and on-campus residents. Both of these highly diverse groups enjoy Seton Hall's world-renowned professors, super-charged basketball and soccer games, and thriving community service organizations and Greek life.

Heavy but Rewarding Work

Though a high acceptance rate has contributed to a perception of Seton Hall as not very selective, students say the workload is intense and requirements are heavy, but that "intelligent and supportive" teachers "who will do anything to help you" make the experience worth the stress. Undergraduates at Seton Hall apply to one of six schools: the College of Arts and Sciences, the Stillman School of Business, the College of Education and Human Services, the College of Nursing, the School of Theology, or the School of Diplomacy and International Relations. Within the largest division, the College of Arts and Sciences, many students take advantage of an innovative communications major, fostered by Seton Hall's state-of-the-art environment, offering concentrations in media, performance and graphics. Other popular majors include business, criminal justice and the social sciences. Unusual majors include sports management and diplomacy. "Girls are mostly education majors here," one student said, "and guys are usually business or diplomacy majors."

The strongest point of Seton Hall academics may be that "there are the most amazing professors here, many of whom come from Ivy League schools," as one student said. "I've learned so much from them that I don't think

I could have gotten a better education at a higher-ranked school." Jim McCartin's history class, and the History Department in general, is a favorite among students. Many of the top professors are found in the "internationally renowned" School of Diplomacy and International Relations, a school formed in 1997 in a partnership with the United Nations. The school regularly features prominent speakers including former U.N. Secretary-General Kofi Annan, former Secretary of State Henry Kissinger and the former Iranian President Mohammad Khatami.

However, many students said they were extremely burdened by core requirements, which sometimes force students into "a five-year contract with the University." Students are limited in the number of classes they can take per semester by 18 credits, but still must fulfill close to 60 credits on top of majors, second majors and minors, depending on their program. One diplomacy student said, "There's just an absurd amount of requirements. It allows you no leeway to take an additional or extra course that may be outside your major but within the realm of your field." However, another student said the core curriculum made her "very well-rounded, even though it's a pain. I know I complain a lot, but I've learned so much in my core classes."

> **"There are the most amazing professors here."**

Whether a class is a core fulfillment, introductory lecture or advanced seminar, size is small across the board. Seton Hall has very few TAs, with less than 4 percent of classes taught by them. According to one student, "It's not surprising if they close out a class after 30 people," and so it is very important to avoid "late registration." Must-take classes include "Catholic Church of the United States," which fulfills one of three required theology—not necessarily Christian-based—electives, and "Scuba Diving." When choosing these classes, advising may be hard to find, with advice coming predominantly from a "university class" that one student called "a sub par method of creating an interaction between advisors and new freshmen." But another student said she "met most of her friends in that first encounter" with her freshman advising group.

Technology is central to Seton Hall's innovative academic program. Soon after *Yahoo Internet Life* ranked Seton Hall in the top 20 of "wired" universities, it quickly became one of the most "wireless," too. Nearly all of Seton Hall's South Orange, N.J., campus is wireless, and is complete with a private cellular network. Free laptops are provided to every student upon matriculation, and technology is integrated in the classroom.

Ethnic and Location Diversity

Just as Seton Hall features state-of-the-art academics, the University also represents a cross-section of modern culture. "Everyone's different here, and that's what makes people get along," one student said. "I think that pretty much sums up Seton Hall." The student body consists of roughly 30 percent minority students. At the same time, Seton Hall is like "going to a larger high school that's not really small, but not big either . . . and a lot more fun."

The diversity of Seton Hall extends to its location, which is sandwiched between serene suburban communities and cities like Newark, which "students generally avoid" to ensure safety. Location is one of Seton Hall's major pulls, with most students, especially commuters, coming to the University from the Northeast's Tri-State Area. Though South Orange currently includes Starbucks, Cold Stone Creamery and several bars, the town is in the process of a build-up effort that may bring a movie theatre and new restaurants. According to one student, "It's not a college town—a lot of places close early, and there isn't really much to do." But for many students, Friday nights mean a 20-minute ride to New York City that provides excitement and gives the University its "edge over other smaller colleges farther from bustling cities."

An Ever-Improving Campus

Though Boland Hall is notorious for a fatal dormitory fire that broke out in 2000, Boland and every other dorm are now equipped with "like 10 sprinklers per room" and are now among the safest rooms in the country. For those who reside on campus, options also include Aquinas Hall and Xavier Hall. In spite of the small rooms, Aquinas dorms foster a sense of community, and according to one resident, "provide a great experience, because everyone gets together and is very friendly to one another." But a freshman said his Aquinas Hall dorm looks more like "the jail on Rikers Island" than his home. Xavier Hall, with suites and painted walls, is reportedly Seton Hall's best living option, which one student said, "feels like living in a hotel."

Farther from campus is the Ora Manor apartment "complex" which provides rooms smaller than those on central campus. However, a significant number of students live off campus in Greek housing since the university doesn't allow on-campus Greek life.

When students are not inside studying, they stroll Seton Hall's small campus, described by one student as a "strange hodgepodge of old and new." Contemporary Jubilee Hall, featuring marble, glass windows and a planetarium on top, is balanced by Duffy Hall, which "looks like it's straight out of the '70s." However, there have been recent upgrades to the campus, and a new 35 million dollar Science and Technology Center, which in its early stages already looks "absolutely amazing," will become one of the largest science centers in New Jersey. The Bishop Dougherty University Center is the social, nutritional, and activity hub of Seton Hall, featuring the Pirate's Cove, "a nice place to have lunch or coffee, but depressing in its magenta and turquoise color scheme," student organization meeting rooms and televisions where students gather to "watch football games."

Due to the heavy workload, students spend a great deal of time at the Walsh Library, now open 24/7. One junior described the building as "outside looking nice, but ugly inside with carpet falling off in some areas." Another student said the library does not carry enough books. "I just had to borrow a basic book from another college," she said. "It was embarrassing that we didn't carry it."

Students have mixed reactions to the campus food options. One freshman complained, "The food is an on-and-off thing; you usually end up having pizza and salad bar every night." However, take-out options are plentiful: Students order from Cluck-U Chicken, a "very good" sub sandwich shop, and the surrounding Italian-heavy neighborhood's numerous pizzeria options. The South Orange Alliance for Redevelopment promises to bring even more eateries to the community in coming years.

Service and Social Bonding
Even commuters become involved in some of the over 100 Seton Hall activities offers, which range from politically-charged to fundriven. Popular organizations include the Student Government Association; Pirate TV, the renowned campus radio station; the weekly student newspaper, *The Setonian*, which covers the extremely popular intramural sports program; a gospel choir; and the pep band. A satirical newspaper called

The Rampage, which "no one knows the editor of or who writes for it," provides weekly entertainment for students.

But the prevalent ethnic and service groups on campus distinguish Seton Hall most. These include six African-American student associations; nearly 10 other ethnic clubs for Filipino, Italian, Indian, Arabic, Asian and international students; a popular Habitat for Humanity chapter; and an award-winning chapter of the National Society of Collegiate Scholars established for top students to engage in community service. Campus events sponsored by various groups have included a concert by Third Eye Blind for the University's 150th Anniversary and the annual University Day in October for which families are invited to a festive carnival. One student recalled, "I've never seen the campus so alive before."

Sports and the SHU Experience
Although Seton Hall's once-indomitable Division I men's basketball team has waned over the past several years, enthusiasm for sports has not decreased, especially when the nationally ranked men's soccer team stole the limelight. Though Seton Hall has no football team, "basically everyone's into sports here," one junior said. "Students get really into it when we win, and very sad when we lose." At the Midnight Madness pep rally, there are games like "shootouts for thousand dollar prizes" and the chance to see the men and women basketball teams in action. But one student complained, "The culture here is dominated by sports as opposed to academia."

The social culture is also dominated by Greek life. Fraternities and sororities range from service-centered to purely social to academic. Drinking on campus is "surprisingly not prevalent," but when it does take place, it is mostly "in group settings, especially at frat parties." One student said that after a while, "Seton Hall may seem like a glorified high school, but you are comfortable because you often see people you know." But another warned, "If you don't live here, you may not get the full experience of it all." That experience—a cross between academic rigor and athletic excitement, religious bonding and exploration of differences, and South Orange serenity and New York City bustle—may be ideal, as one junior suggested, for "someone who likes diversity, a great education, not being too far from home, and absolutely awesome professors."—*Andrew M. Mangino*

FYI

If you come to Seton Hall, you'd better bring "a surge protector because they take fire safety very seriously here."

What's the typical weekend schedule? "Thursday night—come home from an internship and party; Friday night—sleep in and then take a bus to New York City or the Short Hills Mall; Saturday—see a soccer or basketball game and have a date at night; Sunday—time to study."

If I could change one thing about Seton Hall, I'd "lower the percentage of commuters, because if more people lived on campus, then it would be even more alive."

Three things every student at Seton Hall should do before graduating are "Go to Cryn's, an Irish pub in South Orange, as soon as you turn 21 as a rite of passage, explore New York City and see a Pirates basketball game."

Stevens Insititue of Technology

Address: One Castle Point on Hudson, Hoboken, NJ 07030

Phone: 201-216-5194

E-mail address: admissions@stevens.edu

Web site URL: www.stevens.edu

Year Founded: 1870

Private or Public: Private

Religious Affiliation: None

Location: Suburban

Number of Applicants: 3,058

Percent Accepted: 51%

Percent Accepted who enroll: 38%

Number Entering: 569

Number of Transfers Accepted each Year: 83

Middle 50% SAT range: M: 620–710, CR: 550–650, Wr: Unreported

Middle 50% ACT range: 24–30

Early admission program EA/ED/None: ED

Percentage accepted through EA or ED: 78%

EA and ED deadline: 15-Nov

Regular Deadline: 1-Feb

Application Fee: $55

Full time Undergraduate enrollment: 2,044

Total enrollment: 2,044

Percent Male: 72%

Percent Female: 28%

Total Percent Minority or Unreported: 39%

Percent African-American: 2%

Percent Asian/Pacific Islander: 12%

Percent Hispanic: 8%

Percent Native-American: <1%

Percent International: 6%

Percent in-state/out of state: 62% /38%

Percent from Public HS: 80%

Retention Rate: 89%

Graduation Rate 4-year: 38%

Graduation Rate 6-year: 74%

Percent Undergraduates in On-campus housing: 85%

Number of official organized extracurricular organizations: 120

3 Most popular majors: Business Administration and Management, General Computer/Information Technology Services Administration and management

Student/Faculty ratio: 8:1

Average Class Size: 20 to 29

Percent of students going to grad school: 18%

Tuition and Fees: $36,800

In State Tuition and Fees if different: No difference

Cost for Room and Board: $11,100

Percent receiving financial aid out of those who apply, first year: 82%

Percent receiving financial aid among all students: 75%

As the name of the school implies, Stevens focuses on the sciences. Though students are hard workers and want to do well, they also try to have fun and take advantage of Hoboken, New Jersey, where the school is located, and New York, which is just across the river. The juxtaposition of the small school and the two larger cities, in addition to the concentration on the sciences, makes for what students term an "atypical" college experience.

No Room for Slackers

At the start of freshman year, students choose their major and take the specific set of courses their chosen track dictates. This system means that the same group of students often has the same classes together for the entire day. "It feels a little bit like middle school," remarked a sophomore.

Students praise the fact that incoming freshmen get their own laptops for free and say that they put their computers to good use during class time. Students must take 19 to 21 credit hours a year, which is "a pretty obscene number." The large number of classes and the substantial amount of work given in each course mean that students work very hard much of the time. "You have to be self-motivated to get the work done here," said one junior. "Nobody is holding your hand. Nobody is checking up on you. It is a good thing to have that sort of academic freedom, but you have to make sure you are cut out for this kind of system."

Those looking for guidance from professors or teaching assistants (TAs) can run into trouble. "Professors can be a little hard to connect to sometimes. They are brilliant, but sometimes this doesn't translate into being able to teach." The quality of TAs varies. Some can be helpful, whereas others can be limited by their poor command of the English language.

Engineering, the most popular major, is also cited as one of the most difficult. Though "there are no easy majors here," business technology has the least amount of work, with a relatively easy core. Students can opt to lighten their academic load by spreading it over five years instead of four through the Reduced Load program. The fifth year is tuition-free.

Several other special academic programs exist at Stevens. There are seven-year doctorate, medical, and dentistry programs, as well as a co-op program in which students attend Stevens for five years but work for three semesters at a company instead of going to class. Recruiting companies in the past have included Merck and Johnson & Johnson. Co-op experiences vary. Though some students report that they worked as "personal gofers," others say they have a rewarding educational experience that can only come from "being out in the real world and seeing what it is like, without the pressure of actually having to earn your living because you are still in school."

Greeks and Athletes

Greek organizations are an important part of student life. Besides holding their own events, it often feels like "frats and sororities run everything on campus." The presence of a Greek system makes the student body segment into cliques. "It ends up that the Greeks stay with the Greeks, the athletes with the athletes, the nerds with the nerds," explained one student. However, these cliques do not stop all types of students from participating in extracurricular activities. Most people are involved with at least one group. Many students are also part of the campus work-study program.

Students tend to care little about athletics unless they are in them. Though Stevens has good lacrosse and soccer teams, the fans cheering on the sidelines at games are often exclusively composed of other athletes. Athletes seem not to mind, though, saying that the tightly knit athletic community lends a lot of support, something that is desperately needed in order to balance athletics and a demanding academic schedule.

Students who are not involved in varsity sports can use the recently renovated Charles V. Schaefer Jr. Athletic Center, which offers squash, tennis, and basketball courts as well as a gym and pool. Intramural sports are also popular.

Weekends at Stevens

There has been a recent crackdown on underage drinking on campus, which particularly affected fraternities. Any Greek organization found serving alcohol to students under 21 was forced to shut down. Much of the drinking culture was driven off campus into Hoboken and New York City. Fraternities do remain popular, sponsoring Halloween and Christmas parties, among others. The male-female ratio on campus—approximately three to one—means that girls are "rare and really have their choice of guys."

Students who look to imbibe in Hoboken are not short of places to go. Rumor says that Hoboken has more bars per square mile than any other city in the world. Being underage is sometimes a problem, but a freshman explained, "We know how to get around the age restriction." Students also frequent New York City, which offers a wealth of opportunities and nightlife right across the Hudson River.

> "People think that we spend all our time in front of our computer monitors, but we really do go out."

There are also weekend activities on campus. A lecture hall in the Buchard Building moonlights as a movie theater. Jacobus Hall has a student lounge with a climbing wall, large television, and pool table.

During the weekends, it often feels like the student population thins. Many students at Stevens are from other areas of New Jersey, and a good portion of the student body goes home on the weekends. Though many dislike the feeling of going to a "suitcase school," one freshman said that being able to go home on the weekends made his transition to college life less stressful.

The Stevens Stereotype

Campus housing is generally considered adequate. Freshmen are guaranteed housing. After the first year, upperclassmen fight for rooms in one of the five dorms. Students like that their rooms are close to their classes, especially during the winter, when the campus turns into a "wind tunnel." Despite the windiness, students like their campus, which has sweeping lawns and views of the New York City skyline.

One student explained that dining at Stevens simply, "is not good." However, the dining service is working to improve the quality of the food, and there is now more variety as well as tastier offerings. There are also many eateries in Hoboken, and, of course, there is always New York City.

Students enjoy going into both Hoboken and New York City and insist that, contrary to the "Stevens stereotype," they do go there to party. "People think that we spend all our time in front of our computer monitors, but we really do go out. Stevens in many ways is an atypical college experience, but we do do normal college things." If you have the motivation and the focus to handle the academics and the independence to handle the social scene, Stevens Institute of Technology can provide an educational and enjoyable, though "atypical," college experience.
—*Erica Rothman*

FYI
If you come to Stevens, you'd better bring "your calculator."
What is the typical weekend schedule? "Hang out on campus Friday, head into the city on Saturday, and spend all of Sunday into Monday doing schoolwork."
If I could change one thing about Stevens, I would "make it less of a suitcase school."
Three things every student at Stevens should do before graduating are "hang out at a Hoboken bar, throw a Frisbee on the lawn looking out on the city skyline, and spend lots of time complaining about all the work you have to do."

New Mexico

New Mexico State University

Address: Box 30001, MSC 3A Las Cruces, NM 88003-8001
Phone: 800-662-6688
E-mail address: admissions@nmsu.edu
Web site URL: www.nmsu.edu
Year Founded: 1888
Private or Public: Public
Religious Affiliation: None
Location: Urban
Number of Applicants: 5,960
Percent Accepted: 82%
Percent Accepted who enroll: 51%
Number Entering: 2,518
Number of Transfers Accepted each Year: 887
Middle 50% SAT range: Unreported
Middle 50% ACT range: 18–24
Early admission program EA/ED/None: None
Percentage accepted through EA or ED: NA

EA and ED deadline: NA
Regular Deadline: Rolling
Application Fee: $20
Full time Undergraduate enrollment: 13,677
Total enrollment: 17,200
Percent Male: 46%
Percent Female: 54%
Total Percent Minority or Unreported: 62%
Percent African-American: 4%
Percent Asian/Pacific Islander: 1%
Percent Hispanic: 45%
Percent Native-American: 4%
Percent International: 4%
Percent in-state/out of state: 79%/21%
Percent from Public HS: Unreported
Retention Rate: Unreported
Graduation Rate 4-year: 12%
Graduation Rate 6-year: 42%

Percent Undergraduates in On-campus housing: Unreported
Number of official organized extracurricular organizations: 263
3 Most popular majors: Business/Commerce, Curriculum and Instruction, Electronics
Student/Faculty ratio: 18:1
Average Class Size: Unreported
Percent of students going to grad school: Unreported
Tuition and Fees: $14,180
In State Tuition and Fees if different: $4,758
Cost for Room and Board: $5,766
Percent receiving financial aid out of those who apply, first year: 76%
Percent receiving financial aid among all students: 56%

L ess than an hour north of Mexico, in the middle of the desert, lies the oasis of New Mexico State University. The town of Las Cruces charms most with its Southwestern Navajo style and hospitable feel. With its strong agricultural and applied sciences programs, a spacious campus, a varied and lively social scene, and its abundance of cultural diversity, NMSU is the place for those looking for a quality education with a relaxed atmosphere.

Viewing a Wider World

New Mexico State University students enjoy a wide variety of majors incorporated in the six undergraduate colleges of Business Administration and Economics, Education, Health and Social Services, Arts and Sciences, Agriculture and Home Economics, and Engineering. While some majors, such as communication studies or family and child science, are considered easier than others, most students agree that "the workload is challenging, but rewarding at the same time."

Many students rave about the "Viewing a Wider World" program, in which students are required to take six credits in two departments other than the one in which they are majoring. In the words of one communication studies major, "You really find out a lot about other areas that you otherwise wouldn't have even thought about learning about."

All NMSU students seem to be able to agree on the accessibility and helpfulness of the faculty. One student offered, "All of the professors I've had here have been really approachable and willing to help in any way they can. Most of them are always asking students to come to their office hours, even if it's just to talk to them for a little while."

From El Paso to Mexico

NMSU students enjoy a social setting as diverse as their student body. The large university is home to an active and popular Greek system, not to mention that El Paso is less than an hour away with its restaurants, movies, theater, and other entertainment. The college often sponsors activities, such as the well-attended homecoming bonfire and a variety of cultural events. Meanwhile, the local night clubs sometimes sponsor college nights for students of all ages, and, of course, in the words of one student, "There's a lot of partying going on." Many underage students, particularly freshman, prefer to cross the border into Mexico to party, where the drinking age is 18. Greek life does exist, and although frats only attract a small percentage of the student body, they do throw parties almost every weekend.

While its students love NMSU for different reasons, an overwhelming majority agree that the school's diversity is one of its best features. As one family and child science major puts it, "Our student body is really amazingly diverse. I had expected a lot of Caucasian or Latino students, but now I've got friends from Japan, Kuwait, and Thailand." In addition to student appreciation for all the different cultures represented at NMSU, the school administration and the Union Program Council (UPC) host regular cultural events to celebrate the different customs of all the students.

The dating scene at New Mexico State University is variable as well. In the words of one student, "There are definitely random hookups. There's definitely dating. There are some homosexual couples and definitely some interracial couples. Some people find their future husband or wife here. It's such a big system that there's a lot of everything going on."

Most agree that dining out is superior to the meal plan at school, which the majority forego. In the words of one senior, "I think they've made some improvements in the food here since my freshman year, but back then, even the people who paid for their meal plans wouldn't eat that stuff." Instead, students prefer a number of on-campus restaurants that serve everything from Mexican to Chinese to pizza.

"The Horseshoe"

New Mexico State University is one of the nation's largest campuses. Much of the space comes from the school's renowned Agriculture Department, but all NMSU students can enjoy their wide, spread-out campus. Some of the favorite spots on campus include "The Horseshoe," a wide ring of buildings spread out in the shape of its name. There, students can find everything from athletic facilities and ROTC practice fields to student services and the financial aid office. One senior, however, enjoys the Horseshoe for one of its less well-known features, "I love the duck pond! It's my favorite place on-campus." What's more, the Horseshoe is just outside of the student dorms, making it a convenient place for students to visit.

> **"I'd choose to come here again without a doubt, and, in fact, I only wish I'd known about it earlier."**

Whether it is New Mexico State University's highly regarded academic programs, the great cultural diversity, the warm and sunny weather, or just the duck pond that strikes your interest, NMSU students would agree with the advice of one communication studies major, "This is a really great place to go to school. I'd choose to come here again without a doubt, and, in fact, I only wish I'd known about it earlier."—*Sarah Newman*

FYI
If you come to New Mexico State University, you'd better bring "a pair of sandals."
What is the typical weekend schedule? "Do some sort of on-campus activity, hang with friends, get some sleep and do some work."
If I could change one thing about New Mexico State University, I'd "stop raising the tuition fees."
Three things every student at New Mexico State University should do before graduating are "go to El Paso, go see the mariachis and visit the duck pond."

University of New Mexico

Address: PO Box 4895
Albuquerque,
NM 87131-00001
Phone: 505-277-2466
E-mail address:
apply@unm.edu
Web site URL: www.unm.edu
Year Founded: 1889
Private or Public: Public
Religious Affiliation: None
Location: Urban
Number of Applicants: 7,134
Percent Accepted: 74%
**Percent Accepted who
enroll:** 58%
Number Entering: 3,021
**Number of Transfers
Accepted each Year:**
Unreported
Middle 50% SAT range:
M: 470–590, CR: 470–600,
Wr: Unreported
Middle 50% ACT range:
19–25
**Early admission program
EA/ED/None:** None

**Percentage accepted
through EA or ED:** NA
EA and ED deadline: NA
Regular Deadline: 15-Jun
Application Fee: $20
**Full time Undergraduate
enrollment:** 18,743
Total enrollment: 24,814
Percent Male: 41%
Percent Female: 59%
**Total Percent Minority or
Unreported:** 49%
Percent African-American:
3%
**Percent Asian/Pacific
Islander:** 4%
Percent Hispanic: 42%
Percent Native-American: 7%
Percent International: 1%
**Percent in-state/out of
state:** 79%/21%
Percent from Public HS:
Unreported
Retention Rate: Unreported
Graduation Rate 4-year:
Unreported

Graduation Rate 6-year:
Unreported
**Percent Undergraduates in
On-campus housing:** 8%
**Number of official organized
extracurricular
organizations:** 315
3 Most popular majors:
Biology/Biological Sciences,
Business Administration and
Management, Psychology
Student/Faculty ratio: 20:1
Average Class Size: 20 to 29
**Percent of students going to
grad school:** Unreported
Tuition and Fees: $15,708
**In State Tuition and Fees if
different:** $4,834
Cost for Room and Board:
$7,336
**Percent receiving financial
aid out of those who apply,
first year:** Unreported
**Percent receiving financial
aid among all students:**
Unreported

Comprising sprawling green lawns and adobe buildings in Albuquerque, N.M., the University of New Mexico is a college that gives students the opportunity to be what they want to be. Among its 18,000 undergraduate enrollees are recent high school graduates, preprofessionals and continuing-education students returning to college. This diversity offers undergraduates a unique college experience in the heart of a Southwestern city.

Academics: Lost Among Many, but Not Lost in Life

Many students enter UNM with a good idea of their career paths. Thus, although there are a significant number of students in pursuit of their bachelor's degrees in the liberal arts, many opt to take the preprofessional route. "Everyone is pre-something," one student said, "and the premedical and prenursing tracks are huge because UNM is a great medical school." According to students, this can make the environment "very competitive," especially in the larger "weed-out" introductory science courses. Some students report

that because of the high number of students, getting into classes can sometimes be tricky, especially for undergrads who want to take graduate-level courses. Students having trouble with the material can, however, seek help from the free tutoring program offered by the library.

Despite the dominance of preprofessional programs, students also noted that the geology and photography departments are quite good. UNM also boasts a good Fine Arts school, which gives students who are undecided about their future plans a good opportunity to try out different tracks and find the one that best suits them. Classes are largely taught lecture-style at UNM and sometimes number 300-plus students, with the smaller math and English courses numbering 20 to 30. Some students complain about the large class size, but note that if a student is motivated, closer, fulfilling professor-student relationships are easy to come by. Academic facilities are outstanding, with six libraries and a number of good study and social centers, including the Student Union Building (SUB) and the Cellar. In addition, UNM is fast becoming one of the Southwest's premier research institutions, as the University just received a large amount of money for research facilities and lab upgrades.

Looking for a Party?

A portion of the UNM party scene is dominated by fraternities and sororities. According to students, the more popular fraternities are Pi Kappa Alpha and Sigma Alpha Epsilon and the most notable sororities are Kappa Kappa Gamma and Alpha Chi Omega. However, because of the dry status required of fraternities by the UNM administration, the popularity and frequency of fraternity parties has dropped off in recent years.

> "Everyone is pre-something. . . . The premedical and prenursing tracks are huge."

The widely diverse of the student body at UNM, which boasts an average age of 27, means the Greek scene does not account for all of the social life by any stretch. Older students say they prefer the "nicer" 21-and-over clubs downtown. Although UNM is officially a dry campus, most students agreed that alcohol was "easy to find," even for those underage. Several described the campus community as very "tightly knit," saying that "everyone knows everyone through someone else." Most agreed that it is relatively easy to meet new people at parties and other extracurricular gatherings.

UNM also sponsors a number of concerts and social events. Toward the beginning of the year, there is a "Welcome Back Night," where students are invited to watch a movie screened in the school's sports facility, Johnson Field. Another notable event is the "Balloon Fiesta," at which hot air balloons are launched from a nearby park built by the city a few years ago. The balloons are released every morning for a week in October, and this event attracts not only students but visitors from all over the world. UNM also attracts a number of headlining bands throughout the academic year. One event featured indie rock band The Donnas.

Off Campus and Off Hours

The city of Albuquerque offers UNM students a "fun and interesting place to live." A famous local restaurant called Frontier is a popular local hangout—"everyone is there at two in the morning on Friday nights," one sopho-

more said. Another favorite is the Student Union Building, the SUB, which reopened after renovation recently, and contains a number of restaurants and a computer center.

For students with cars, there are numerous recreational opportunities in the area. Several malls in the nearby area offer shopping, and many students leave campus on weekends to explore the greater Albuquerque area. Parking, however, is described as "very difficult," and campus parking has been alleged to overfill its lots.

Dwelling and Dining

There is a lot of variation in the quality and pricing of on-campus housing. Students apply for a particular building and are later placed according to their ranked preferences. The dorms are a social place, and a good way to make friends, especially for incoming freshmen. Many attested to the superior accommodations found in the Student Residence Centers, which consist of suites of six bedrooms connected by a common kitchen and living room area. An alternative housing option is Coronado, which has been described both as the worst of the spectrum with "a billion rooms sharing just one bathroom," and the best: "a great place to party because there are so many people in it."

The residence halls have an RA (Resident Advisors) system, which can be "a pain if your RA is strict." Despite the fact that housing is available all four years, most students choose to move off campus after freshman year. Housing is easy to find in the surrounding area, especially because "many students are from nearby." Students still advise living on campus at least one year, however, because it is a good way to meet people.

Students living on campus are automatically placed on a meal plan. Meals can be redeemed at the cafeteria, which stacks three floors of cafeteria-style options and is open continuously between 7 a.m. and 7 p.m. Several students affirmed that the cafeteria food was extremely unpopular. For those who can't stomach the cafeteria option, meal plan "point" alternatives are redeemable at the SUB, the bookstore and the on-campus Pizza Hut stand.

What Makes a Lobo

While a couple of students complained about a lack of campus cohesion and student involvement, UNM boasts several hundred undergraduate organizations that one student noted "include almost anything you could think of to do." Club and intramural sports are also "very popular," and it is "typical" to find students working out in the Johnson Center, the athletics center, late into the evening.

Varsity sports events, particularly football and basketball games, are well attended. The annual football game against New Mexico State University draws a large crowd, and festivities include a pre-game bonfire and lots of tailgating. The school's mascot, Louie Lobo, and his female counterpart, Lucy Lobo, are the inspirations for the signature cheer, in which fans howl at opponents before basketball games.

Students offer that the above lack of cohesion was due to the incredible diversity of the student body at UNM, which attracts a wide variety of students in various stages of their lives. They describe the student body as mostly middle-class, and "very culturally diverse." UNM is also remarkably ethnically diverse, and many report the feeling that white students are more of a minority on campus than ever before. There is a support network for minority students, which includes a number of student centers and the school's dedication to bilingual education. While there are student jobs aplenty, obtaining on-campus employment involves meeting a financial aid requirement; consequentially, many students hold part-time jobs in the surrounding area, which are reportedly easy to find in the commercial districts. Along with this student diversity comes an atmosphere of political freedom and protests, and though one student described the campus as "so liberal that it hurts," he maintains that liberals and conservatives alike can enjoy the activism that pervades the campus.

As one student put it, your experience at University of New Mexico is what you make of it. In a university of 24,000 overall students, it is possible to get lost in a sea of pre-professionals, but it is also possible to take advantage of unmatched diversity and resources. Students who understand this principle and are prepared to optimize their college experiences for themselves will find an outstanding value at the University of New Mexico and an extensive wealth of educational opportunities.—*Stephanie Teng*

FYI

If you come to University of New Mexico, you'd better bring "your old school notes, your skis and an attitude to work."

What is the typical weekend schedule? "Friday, frat parties, clubs or bars downtown; Saturday, sleeping in or leaving campus, finding a party or concert at night; Sunday, doing homework or going to work."

If I could change one thing about University of New Mexico, I would "improve the food."

Three things every student at University of New Mexico should do before they graduate are "try to meet a lot of new people, attend the pre-NMSU bonfire and join a student organization."

New York

T ucked away in the middle of an affluent Long Island residential district,
the Adelphi campus setting attracts
students who reside in nearby communities.
If you live on Long Island and are considering commuting to college, you'll find yourself among friends at Adelphi. Although the
student body may be comprised of a large
commuter population, the University successfully creates an intimate college experience both socially and academically. Adelphi
not only provides students with a solid base
in academics, it also offers students pre-
professional tracks so they may immediately
pursue their passions. If you are a student
looking to branch out of your home community without really leaving it, Adelphi can offer the best of both worlds. While one student
cautions "Adelphi isn't for everyone—the
commuter-school aspect sets it apart," its
tradition of strong programs and commitment to developing career opportunities
make it worth a closer look.

A Variety of Options

Students interested in Adelphi have the option of applying to the College of Arts and
Sciences, the Derner Institute of Advanced
Psychological Studies, the Honors College,
the School of Business, the School of
Education, the School of Nursing or the
School of Social Work. The schools each have
different requirements, but students in the
popular College of Arts and Sciences must
take General Education courses that, while
"fairly numerous," are "pretty easy as long as
you show up." These courses include a freshman orientation experience, an English

composition seminar, a freshman seminar, and at least six credits in each of four areas: arts, humanities and languages, natural sciences and math, and the social sciences. One student complained that of those courses there were "a handful I haven't liked." Freshmen also say the required seminar and orientation course are "a necessary annoyance."

Students cite the nursing and business programs as particularly strong. One girl raved, "My experiences working in a hospital a few times a week really prepared me for a career in nursing." However, the quality of the experience is very dependent on the teacher you get, a problem that students in various programs and majors mentioned. A communications major said that his professors' personalities had ranged from very enthusiastic about the subject to simply uninspired and "big assigners of busy work."

Many qualified students choose to enroll in the Honors Program, especially because of the generous scholarships Adelphi offers. Honors students live, attend classes and study together in this exclusive academic and living arrangement, which is "almost its own separate community." However, "you should visit the campus before you just accept the scholarship," warns one student, "because it is a pretty different college experience." For the rest of the population, one of the most common grievances is the difficulty in enrolling in classes. One student complains, "I've been trying to get into this one class for two years and haven't been able to." But once you get into courses, the atmosphere is "very tight-knit, with a close student-faculty relationship," because of the school's small size. Students even mention going into the city for performances and then to bars with their professors.

Adelphi's humanities courses are "much better and more popular" than its math and science offerings, and students "wouldn't recommend the school for pre-med." But many professors "make you think outside the box." Overall, students classified their schoolwork at Adelphi as "definitely not too hard" and found that "grading is fair and lenient."

Seeking Out the Scene

Adelphi's status as largely a commuter school situated in a wealthy Long Island suburb is one of the main obstacles to a really active social life. So many students go home on the weekends that "the campus can be pretty dead by Thursday night," and surrounding Garden City is such a sheltered community that there isn't much night life

nearby. In fact, when the campus hosted a Roots concert, it was shut down early because neighbors complained of the noise. The school hosts many other events in the University Center.

Those students who live on or near campus find a reasonable social scene at a few local bars and clubs, where Adelphi's seven fraternities and sororities often host gatherings for the student body. There are "quite a few" students in Greek organizations, and some "really make themselves known through advertising and recruiting," but because of the Garden City rule that "classifies more than six unrelated girls in a house as a brothel," the sororities don't have their own housing.

Students called Adelphi "more of a drinking school," saying that most people drink in their rooms before heading out to bars and clubs, but since the dorms are dry, "it's hard to tell how many people drink because they have to keep it pretty quiet." Overall, it's very self-controlled, and drugs "can be hard to find," although "pot is available if you want it" and "a lot of people smoke."

One student said that if you want to get socially involved at Adelphi, "you have to actively seek out the scene," whether by attending weekly comedy shows, sampling the popular theater program or heading out to New York City. The train station is on the edge of campus, just a few blocks away, and the trip takes about 45 minutes. Students really feel that the city is the redeeming factor in the otherwise quiet environment of Garden City—there are just so many opportunities for entertainment, from plays and museums to well-attended bars and clubs.

Most people meet their friends based on their living situations, whether in the dorms or off campus, but the small class sizes make it easy to meet people who share your academic interests. Students characterize the stereotypical Adelphi students as "very Long Islandish: girls get really dressed up to go to class, and boys can be very fashionable and wealthy too." However, others say that there is a lot of diversity at Adelphi, particularly because it attracts many international students. One senior explained, "There is more diversity of culture than of race, because within the largely white population, many nations are represented."

One student said that one of the most surprising aspects of Adelphi is that its student population is predominantly female. "There are a lot of hookups because guys who are hot and straight are usually taken, and you have to be quick," she admitted. The school does have an overall accepting attitude towards the gay population, which is sizable—in fact, a senior estimated that "half the males are probably gay." In the spring, the Lesbian-Gay-Bisexual-Transsexual-Queer (LGBTQ) organization puts on mock "weddings" just to show the community's support for gay couples.

People Do Live Here

Adelphi's campus is described as "truly beautiful," and students estimate that the university spends a sizable amount of money just on landscaping. The effect is a picturesque campus with spacious lawns and well-kept foliage. While many Adelphi students choose to live at home and commute to school, there is a lot of competition for housing on or near campus. Students who live in the dorms have the choice of air conditioning, which is more expensive, but students say that "it's pretty cool in Garden City, so the lack of A/C isn't a big deal." If you want housing and are new to the school, you are entered in a lottery to try to get a room in the full dorms, but if you have already been living there a semester, you have "squatter's rights" and can keep your room. One student explained, "You'll most likely get housing if you want it, but you have to be on top of the deadlines." All of the rooms are doubles and triples, and some doubles used to be triples, so "they're pretty big." The honors dorms have suites, which include a living room and two doubles.

There is an RA on each floor and a residential health director in each building, and while they do enforce the strict no-alcohol policy of the dorms, they are usually "nice and will work with you in other areas." However, "you will get in trouble and your alcohol will be confiscated if you're going to be dumb about it." New Hall is the newest dorm and is thought to be the nicest, while Earle Hall is known for housing a lot of theater majors.

Off-campus housing is apparently more difficult to find, since there are "few apartments for college students" due to the rich residential neighborhood around the campus. When they do find housing, it is usually pretty expensive as well. Students say that pricey off-campus housing is the reason why so many choose to live at home.

Downtown Garden City, a mile away, offers some shopping, including a popular mall, movies, and the nearest grocery store. A shuttle bus takes students to and from the downtown district, but "it can be unreliable or not frequent enough." It's a good idea to bring a car so you can get out of the area, but "the traffic gets pretty bad" and "one of the biggest problems on campus right now is the lack of parking available." However, the university is working to construct a new parking facility.

Students who live on campus are required to purchase a meal plan. However, many do so unwillingly. The food is reportedly "absolutely terrible," but there are other on-campus options, like at Post Hall, which houses a Sbarro, the Panther Grill and a convenience store, where students can use their meal cards like credit cards. Overall, though, there "isn't much variety and the food is of dubious quality" in the two dining halls. Students say they order takeout from local restaurants a couple times a week and sometimes go out to eat on the weekends. The nearby Chinese and Italian restaurants are "especially good," but "if you drive you can find a lot more options."

Getting Involved

One problem that many students pointed out about student involvement on campus is that it seems very low and apathetic. A senior said that she feels like "people just want to sit around and complain about how there's nothing to do instead of taking advantage of campus events." However, Adelphi does boast a number of organizations that attract loyal followings, such as the Theater Club, the NAACP, Circle K and its student newspaper, *The Delphian*. Many students also get involved in the Student Government Association, which allows them to voice their opinions about the Adelphi community and lobby for change.

> **"You won't get lost in the crowd at Adelphi."**

Adelphi is the home of a men's Division I soccer team, and all its other teams are Division II. Students say that "it's not a big athletic school, but a lot of people are interested in going to the games and supporting the Panthers." In fact, one of Adelphi's most fun annual traditions is Midnight Madness, when the men and women's basketball teams are announced at midnight at the beginning of the season, and the school's hip-hop team performs. One guy said, "It's one of the few events that almost everyone goes to and shows their school pride." For those who want to get more involved, intramural sports "always have flyers up" and can even get "intensely competitive."

Many students have jobs, whether working for the school on-campus or in the surrounding community. One popular off-campus option is working in the downtown mall. However, a particularly exciting aspect of attending Adelphi is the opportunity to participate in internships in New York City. Many students take advantage of this unique privilege and spend time learning more about their fields of interests.

While Adelphi may not be the typical college experience, it offers a variety of opportunities, from the excitement and internationalism of nearby New York City to renowned professional programs truly dedicated to preparing students for careers. While the school is ideal for many who are looking for a good school close to home, others may want to consider the additional advantages it holds. Even with the lack of an on-campus community, life at Adelphi is close-knit and friendly. As one student put it, "You won't get lost in the crowd at Adelphi."—*Kimberly Chow*

FYI

If you come to Adelphi, you'd better bring "a willingness to involve yourself in campus activities, because the school needs more participation."

What's the typical weekend schedule? "Hanging out with friends and having dinner on Friday, going to the City on Saturday, going to bars and clubs at night, or just going home for the weekend."

If I could change one thing about Adelphi, "I would increase communication between the administration and students, because sometimes I feel like I'm on my own when planning my studies."

Three things every student at Adelphi should do before graduating are "attend the Erotic Student Film Festival, participate in the Student Government Association and sneak onto the roof of the science building for the great view."

Alfred University

Address: One Saxon Drive
  Alfred, NY 14802-1205
Phone: 607-871-2115
E-mail address:
  admissions@alfred.edu
Web site URL: www.alfred.edu
Year Founded: 1836
Private or Public: Private
Religious Affiliation: None
Location: Rural
Number of Applicants: 2,355
Percent Accepted: 74%
Percent Accepted who
  enroll: 28%
Number Entering: 487
Number of Transfers
  Accepted each Year: 131
Middle 50% SAT range:
  M: 500–620, CR: 440–610,
  Wr: Unreported
Middle 50% ACT range: 22–27
Early admission program
  EA/ED/None: ED
Percentage accepted
  through EA or ED:
  Unreported

EA and ED deadline: 1-Dec
Regular Deadline: Rolling
Application Fee: $40
Full time Undergraduate
  enrollment: 2,030
Total enrollment: 2,030.
Percent Male: 47%
Percent Female: 53%
Total Percent Minority or
  Unreported: 37%
Percent African-American:
  4%
Percent Asian/Pacific
  Islander: 2%
Percent Hispanic: 3%
Percent Native-American:
  <1%
Percent International:
  3%
Percent in-state/out of
  state: 65%/35%
Percent from Public HS:
  Unreported
Retention Rate: 82%
Graduation Rate 4-year:
  49%

Graduation Rate 6-year:
  67%
Percent Undergraduates
  in On-campus housing:
  67%
Number of official organized
  extracurricular
  organizations: 90
3 Most popular majors:
  Business, Ceramics,
  Fine/Studio Arts
Student/Faculty ratio: 12:1
Average Class Size: 15
Percent of students going to
  grad school: 29%
Tuition and Fees: $24,278
In State Tuition and Fees if
  different: No difference
Cost for Room and Board:
  $10,796
Percent receiving financial
  aid out of those who apply,
  first year: 85%
Percent receiving financial
  aid among all students:
  90%

Set in a quaint and historic village in up-state New York, Alfred University is far from the frenetic pulse of Manhattan. But what the campus lacks in big-city glamour, it makes up for in small-town charm and rustic beauty. Alfred is described as a "welcoming" and "very liberal" school, with a "gorgeous campus" to boot. And don't let the University's small size fool you—with four separate schools, students can be sure to find a course of study that interests them. Home to a world-renowned ceramic engineering program, Alfred offers a plethora of academic opportunities for everyone from painters to engineers to aspiring CEOs.

An Academic Buffet

Incoming freshmen can apply to one of four schools: the College of Business, the School of Engineering, the School of Art and Design, or the College of Liberal Arts and Sciences. For those interested in entering the College of Business, Alfred offers degrees in accounting, business administration, finance and marketing. While all the schools are considered challenging, the School of Engineering is particularly work-intensive. Students also point out the internationally known School of Art and Design as offering a challenging but well-respected program. In the academic realm, Alfred is perhaps best known for its School of Ceramic Engineering. Boasting an international reputation, this "super-selective" school is the only center in the United States that offers a Ph.D. program in the field. As one student said, "Ceramics is definitely a big thing at Alfred." However, Ceramic Engineering's eminence also comes with a heavy workload—according to one student, "those people . . . never sleep."

Those seeking a more generalized course of study can enroll in the College of Liberal Arts and Sciences, which includes a First-Year Experience (FYE) Program. FYE aims to expand students' horizons by exploring issues of race, ethnicity and gender. The general education requirements also ensure that liberal arts students are exposed to a variety of topics. The requirements are divided into three "basic competencies": writing, foreign language and quantitative reasoning, as well as six "areas of knowledge": literature, philosophy or religion, the arts, historical studies, natural sciences and social sciences. Students in all schools must take a course in physical education—"I guess they want us all to be fit," one student said.

Students who want to study the arts while still enjoying the breadth of a liberal arts education can participate in BAFA, a unique program which allows fine arts scholars to gain a Bachelor of Arts degree. Unlike those seeking entrance to the School of Art and Design, BAFA applicants do not need to submit a portfolio. However, the program does require that students meet all general education requirements. Students say these differences prompt a light-hearted rivalry between Art School and BAFA students: "They just kind of rag on each other," said one student.

Alfred also has an honors program, which currently enrolls about 120 students. The program is known for offering seminars on unusual and intriguing topics. Recent course titles include "T'ai Chi," "Theory/Practice of Time Travel" and "Nip, Tuck, Perm, Pierce, and Tattoo: Adventures with Embodied Culture." In addition to enjoying classes on off-beat topics, program participants benefit from mentorship and thesis funding.

One benefit of attending a small university such as Alfred is small class size—most courses enroll fewer than 20 students, and even large lectures remain below 100. Intimate class settings are a key attribute of the Alfred academic experience: "You're not just a number," one junior said. Not surprisingly, Alfred students form close bonds with their instructors that extend outside of the classroom: "We see them all over town." As a whole, professors at this liberal university are described as "accepting," "very accessible" and "easy to talk to."

The Daily Grind

Incoming students are housed in one of the many all-freshman dorms, which are corridor-style and coed. Among these halls, the recently renovated Barresi receives high marks, while the other freshman dorms are "not so nice." Openhym, one of the largest halls, includes large lounges on each floor and a late-night study area. Resident Advisors live with the freshmen. Students say RAs vary in strictness—some write up students frequently, while others are more laid-back. Upperclassmen dorms include Kruson, Bartlett and the Brick. The Brick, used as an infirmary during World War II, houses mostly junior and seniors. As the building is a coveted residence among upperclassmen, students say one must get lucky in the housing lottery to claim a room there.

Alfred recently switched to a new dining service and now features stations for stir fry, pizza and grilled food. Students are generally pleased with the results. While the dining halls are still "working out the kinks," there are now a plethora of vegetarian options from which to choose. However one student noted that the meal plan, required for those living on campus, is "ridiculously expensive." Students who tire of the dining hall can use their "dining dollars" as a debit card at two cafes on campus. Popular off-campus spots include the Terra Cotta Coffee House; Old West; the Japanese café Nana's; and Café Za, a restaurant and bar.

Set in the foothills of the Allegheny Mountains, the University boasts a "gorgeous" and "very safe" campus. Historical brick architecture blends with the work of Alfred art students to create a "beautiful setting." One student noted that her favorite place on campus was the Bandstand, a huge gazebo beside the campus creek where students can be found playing drums on the weekends. The Powell Campus Center, which houses a radio station and most club meetings, is another popular hangout.

> **"The campus has gotten really liberal since they've gotten rid of the frats and sororities."**

While the campus may be idyllic, town-gown relations aren't always as peaceful. "Our campus is super liberal, but as soon as you go across the street, it's super conservative," one student said. Tensions can arise with the local authorities. "The police hate us!" one sophomore said. In support of this claim, a student cited the $50 "disorderly conduct" fine she received from local police for skateboarding across campus at night. That said, students feel extremely safe on campus. The school provides security phones and an escort service for those walking home at night.

Sports fanatics be warned: At Alfred, arts easily trump athletics. As one student said, "If you want to be into sports, don't go to Alfred." Despite the more artistic vibe on campus, football and lacrosse games do attract fans. Intramural sports are popular, and the newly renovated gym boasts a complete fitness center and nightly open swim. Popular extracurricular groups on campus include Pirate Theater, Spectrum (the gay, lesbian, bisexual and transgendered alliance) and the radio stations.

Seeking a Scene

When asked to describe her peers, one junior expressed her appreciation for the variety of "types" on campus. Indeed, the broad range of academic programs available at Alfred helps to ensure a diverse student body. Business students sporting "preppy collared shirts" intermingle with "artists wearing hippie clothes" and "normal liberal arts students wearing jeans and a sweater." However, another student noted the prevalence of students from upstate New York who have "face-piercings and crazy hair" and "wear thrift store clothes, or sew their own clothes out of thrift store clothes." One student also noted the well-known clique of undergrads known as "Art Stars." "They make really weird art and then say you aren't as intellectually in tune with art as they are if you don't understand it."

Given Alfred's diverse student body and unique academic programs, it's no surprise that nightlife options aren't your typical university fare. Alfred abolished Greek organizations in 2002, following the fraternity-related death of a student. While those still yearning for the traditional frat party can head to nearby Alfred State, most students remain on campus. Instead of frequenting frat row, they gravitate toward off-campus get-togethers and art house parties featuring rock bands. The Student Activities Board also brings musicians and comedians to campus on a regular basis. Popular annual events include the Winter Blues Bash, Glam Slam and Hot Dog Day, a weekend of activities held in conjunction with Alfred State to raise money for charities. The weekend is marked by performances, a parade through town, street vendors selling hand-made pottery, and the mud Olympics. During the spring event, "alcohol runs freely through the streets," and students get a welcome break from their studies.

An Eye-Opening Education

Not only has the lack of Greek activity not hindered Alfred's night life, but it also may contribute to the freethinking atmosphere that characterizes the school. "The campus has gotten really liberal since they've gotten rid of the frats and sororities," one student said. "Tolerance has definitely gone up a lot." Another cited the support among students and administration alike for Spectrum's "Gay? Fine by Me" T-shirt campaign as testament of the open-minded atmosphere that pervades campus.

For those looking to study art, ceramic engineering, business or the liberal arts, Alfred University offers stellar academic programs in a quaint, picturesque village.

The small-town surroundings and tight-knit campus make it easy for students to form fast friendships. But what students emphasize most about Alfred is its liberal, open-minded atmosphere. One previously "sheltered" student described her experience at Alfred as a "real eye-opener."—*Chrissy Levine*

FYI

If you come to Alfred, you'd better bring: "an open mind—if not, people won't even talk to you. And a really heavy coat."

What's the typical weekend schedule? "Friday: go to Nevan's theater on campus to watch a movie; Saturday: sleep in, brunch, basketball game, go dancing with your friends; Sunday: sleep in, wake up at noon, study all day."

If I could change one thing about Alfred, I'd "change the hills. It's beautiful, but it's a pain in the butt to walk everywhere."

Three things every student at Alfred should do before graduating are: "Participate in Mud Olympics, go Dumpster diving and get a radio station."

Bard College

Address: PO Box 5000 Annandale-on-Hudson, NY 12504
Phone: 845-758-7472
E-mail address: admissions@bard.edu
Web site URL: www.bard.edu
Year Founded: 1860
Private or Public: Private
Religious Affiliation: None
Location: Rural
Number of Applicants: 5,459
Percent Accepted: 25%
Percent Accepted who enroll: 38%
Number Entering: 517
Number of Transfers Accepted each Year: 79
Middle 50% SAT range: M: 650–690, CR: 680–740, Wr: Unreported
Middle 50% ACT range: Unreported
Early admission program EA/ED/None: EA

Percentage accepted through EA or ED: 65%
EA and ED deadline: 1-Nov
Regular Deadline: 15-Jan
Application Fee: $50
Full time Undergraduate enrollment: 1,873
Total enrollment: 2,148
Percent Male: 43%
Percent Female: 57%
Total Percent Minority or Unreported: 30%
Percent African-American: 2%
Percent Asian/Pacific Islander: 3%
Percent Hispanic: 3%
Percent Native-American: <1%
Percent International: 10%
Percent in-state/out of state: 24%/76%
Percent from Public HS: 64%
Retention Rate: 83%
Graduation Rate 4-year: 68%

Graduation Rate 6-year: 75%
Percent Undergraduates in On-campus housing: 75%
Number of official organized extracurricular organizations: 120
3 Most popular majors: English, Social Sciences, Visual and Performing Arts
Student/Faculty ratio: 9:1
Average Class Size: 15
Percent of students going to grad school: Unreported
Tuition and Fees: $38,374
In State Tuition and Fees if different: No difference
Cost for Room and Board: $10,866
Percent receiving financial aid out of those who apply, first year: 100%
Percent receiving financial aid among all students: 62%

Small classes, no core curriculum, and clubs like "The Surrealist Circus"—all of these are typical of Bard College. Located in upstate New York, Bard provides interested students with a very unique type of liberal arts education and the opportunity to explore all kinds of enjoyable activities during their four years—even if they involve juggling.

Academics of Choice

At Bard, students are required to design their own course of study based on what admissions materials term as a "series of active choices." This decidedly active role in shaping one's own curriculum allows students to focus in on the area they most want to explore. But this doesn't mean there are no distributional requirements. Although the requirements include, for example, a laboratory science course, such classes can thankfully be fulfilled by the likes of "Acoustics"—though one junior claimed he had to remain on a "wait list for two or three semesters before getting a chance to take it." Despite the fact that at first glance, the requirements seem to be easy, they can often be neglected by students in favor of a more major-intensive curriculum. "My advisors are brilliant professors, but maybe not as helpful as they could have been," explained one student who realized in the middle of his junior year that he was missing five distributional requirements. He also emphasized, however, that professors are "very accessible . . . and give a lot of individualized attention," even personal comments on student transcripts.

One of the features that sets Bard apart is that there are no actual "majors"; instead, students go through an intensive process known as "moderation" in which they present papers and sit before a board of professors in the department they want to study in. "You can either be accepted into your major or deferred in which case you have to re-moderate. In very few of the majors you can be rejected, such as photography or film which are the more competitive departments," explained a member of the radio group. Bard has also started a five-year business program.

That said, the most popular "majors" at Bard include film and music, which are also extremely competitive. "There is a cold-calloused filtering system . . . professors in the film department won't take you seriously until you actually declare that you're a film major," one student warned. Other difficult majors include economics and political science. Students claim that the least popular major at Bard is "probably Business Skills . . . considering the strong distaste for capitalism here."

A Change of Party Scenery

Bard was once known as one of the biggest party schools in the U.S. In recent years, however, there has been a "massive fragmentation" of the traditional party scene at Bard, forcing students to find other options for the building known as the "Old Gym," which once housed famous events such as "drag races." At present, several years after the Old Gym's closure to social events, no good candidates for a new location have been found. "There's some controversy over the newer options," one student explained.

And although many mourn the drastic change in the party scene at Bard, others say it is still "not as bad as other schools . . . we still live up to [our reputation], though it's much tamer than we used to be."

Political Un-Diversity

Bard is notorious for being one of the most liberal schools in America. "Politically, Bard is not diverse at all," one student explained. "Ethnically there's some diversity, but mostly the student body is composed of wealthy, white Americans." The students, however, are known to be extremely friendly and open-minded and, as one student put it, there is "no place where it's cooler to be gay than Bard." Putnam County, where Bard is located, is a well-known right-wing stronghold, but students claim there is no tension between the community and the more conservative college affiliates.

Tranquil, Beautiful, Isolated

Bard is located next to the Hudson River, and has some remarkable views of the Catskill Mountains. The natural surroundings, however, aren't all that Bard has to offer. Its architecture is greatly varied and noteworthy, too. The Blithewood Manor, home to the Levy Economics Institute, is frequented by students in warmer weather to hang out in the gardens. "We'll go and watch the sunset . . . the views are really beautiful." Also, the Fisher Center for the Performing Arts, designed by Frank Gehry, is extremely popular with both tourists and students.

> **"I fell in love with this place and have no desire to leave."**

As for dorms, there exists a fair amount of variety. Students can choose from a vegan co-op, the hotel-like Robbins house, or the ecologically sound Village Dorms (among many others). The Upper College Village Dorms, designed in conjunction with Bard students, are constructed from non-virgin timber sources, and are heated through a geothermal heat exchange system. About half of the dorms have singles, and most of them are coed. Students who live on campus are required to have a meal plan, which caters to vegans, vegetarians, and non-vegetarians. The food is in general pretty good, but one student warned, "The fish and pork should definitely be avoided."

Clubs and Circuses

There are approximately 60 student organizations at Bard. One of the most well-known clubs on campus is the Surrealist Circus made up of some of the "most creative and boldest people here, in a place where there are many creative and bold people." Bard also boasts several model student civic groups, such as the Bard New Orleans Project, which sent 150 student-volunteers to help repair some of the flood damage incurred by Hurricane Katrina. There is a general lack of enthusiasm for sports at Bard, but that doesn't mean that there aren't any.

Soccer is probably the most popular sport on campus, due in part to the lavish facilities donated by an heir to the Ferrari fortune. There are several varsity and club sports for those who wish to get their athleticism on.

Although the Bard College experience requires dedication and foresight on the behalf of the students, studying at Bard is incredibly rewarding. As one student put it, "On my first visit to Bard I thought it was a wondrous institution, and so far I have not been proven wrong. I fell in love with this place and have no desire to leave." —*Melissa-Victoria King*

FYI

If you come to Bard, you'd better bring "a bike."

What's a typical weekend schedule? "There is no typical anything here. There are many exceptions to week rules."

If I could change one thing about Bard, I'd "give athletes the ability to pre-register for morning classes, so they don't interfere with practice and games."

Three things every student at Bard should do before graduating Bard are "attend an American Symphony Orchestra performance or theatrical production at the Fisher Center, see the Surrealist Circus perform in the spring, and attend one of the infamous *Moderator* magazine release parties."

Barnard College

Address: 3009 Broadway New York, NY 10027

Phone: 212-854-2014

E-mail address: admissions@barnard.edu

Web site URL: www.barnard.edu

Year Founded: 1889

Private or Public: Private

Religious Affiliation: None

Location: Urban

Number of Applicants: 4,274

Percent Accepted: 28%

Percent Accepted who enroll: 47%

Number Entering: 574

Number of Transfers Accepted each Year: 135

Middle 50% SAT range: M: 610–700, CR: 640–740, Wr: 650–750

Middle 50% ACT range: 28–31

Early admission program EA/ED/None: ED

Percentage accepted through EA or ED: 48%

EA and ED deadline: 15-Nov

Regular Deadline: 1-Jan

Application Fee: $55

Full time Undergraduate enrollment: 2,302

Total enrollment: 2,359

Percent Male: 0%

Percent Female: 100%

Total Percent Minority or Unreported: 33%

Percent African-American: 5%

Percent Asian/Pacific Islander: 16%

Percent Hispanic: 9%

Percent Native-American: 1%

Percent International: Unreported

Percent in-state/out of state: 31%/69%

Percent from Public HS: 53%

Retention Rate: 95%

Graduation Rate 4-year: 82%

Graduation Rate 6-year: 89%

Percent Undergraduates in On-campus housing: 91%

Number of official organized extracurricular organizations: 100

3 Most popular majors: English, Psychology, Economics

Student/Faculty ratio: 10:1

Average Class Size: 20

Percent of students going to grad school: 22%

Tuition and Fees: $37,528

In State Tuition and Fees if different: No difference

Cost for Room and Board: $11,926

Percent receiving financial aid out of those who apply, first year: Unreported

Percent receiving financial aid among all students: 42%

Barnard is an all-women liberal arts college. This fact might turn away many female high school students searching for colleges, but a closer look at Barnard shows that it is very different from the stereotype often assigned to single-sex schools. Indeed, this top-notch university located in the middle of Manhattan offers its students not only a great education but also an exciting social life outside the classroom.

A Unique Partnership

Although it is an independent entity with its own faculty, budget, and administration, Barnard is actually an all-women undergraduate institution within Columbia University, meaning that the students have access to all the facilities, classes, and resources that characterize large research institutions. Barnard students can take classes at both their own college and Columbia. As one student noted, "The level of education at Barnard is not very different from that of Columbia because we are in the same classes." One of the interesting results of this rather special partnership is that students are selected by Barnard's own admissions office but receive Columbia degrees. But this is not to say that applying to Barnard is a much easier way of becoming a Columbia student. In fact, less than 30% of applicants were accepted by Barnard in 2008.

Following the Way of Reason

As a top-ranked liberal arts college, Barnard certainly offers a very strong academic program. True to its motto, "Following the Way of Reason," Barnard insists on providing its students with extensive training in analytical skills, both in depth and in breadth. In order to graduate, each student must have completed 122 points' worth of coursework, including two points' worth of physical education. The number of points assigned to each class varies, but it is generally around three to five.

All freshmen have to take an English class, given the importance of writing at Barnard, and a seminar offering students a chance to challenge themselves intellectually with small group discussions. In addition, all students have to fulfill the General Education Requirements in nine different subject areas, also known as the Nine Ways of Knowing, ranging from laboratory science to visual and performing arts. The student reactions to these rather extensive requirements are mixed. Some believe that "the requirements are cumbersome and unproductive." Others, however, claim that "these classes can broaden the students' horizons."

Barnard is also a highly competitive school. According to one junior, "The classes here are no joke. Most people work very hard to get good grades." At the same time, classes offered by Barnard are generally small and free of teaching assistants. One student noted, "We interact with professors, not TAs, unlike my friends at other, bigger colleges." This certainly demonstrates one of the major benefits of studying at Barnard: the combination of a small college atmosphere with the colossal resources of an Ivy League university.

Location, Location, Location

Barnard is situated in the Morningside Heights neighborhood of Manhattan. It is only two blocks away from the Hudson River and a short walk from Central Park. Its convenient location in the middle of New York City is one of the main reasons people decide to come to Barnard. In the words of one student, "I wanted to go to a liberal arts school in a big city, and Barnard fit perfectly." Despite being in the Big Apple, Barnard is actually surrounded by several other academic institutions such as the Manhattan School of Music, Jewish Theological Seminary, and most importantly Columbia University, which is right across the street.

> "The classes here are no joke. Most people work very hard to get good grades."

These surroundings not only contribute to an educational atmosphere but also offer a much more exciting social life. One student remarked, "Barnard is an all-women school, but we get to meet with guys all the time around campus and in the City." Given the cross-registration of classes, as well as an exchange program with The Juilliard School, it is not at all difficult to meet people from other colleges, both male and female, by simply staying on campus. In addition, New York City itself presents a great social environment. During the weekends, bars and clubs across the city are top choices for Barnard students, who can then meet people from practically everywhere. This lively city life, however, also has downsides. As one student pointed out, "People like to go off-campus on weekends, so the campus is depleted of people. If you like to stay on campus and do things with people from your own college, then it is sometimes difficult."

Living on Campus

First-year students must live in the Quad and can only choose between a double and a triple. This has led to many complaints from students about the lack of space. Nevertheless, one student mentioned that colleges in metropolitan areas "all have cramped dorms. We live in New York City, so people can't expect to have huge singles." Residential advisers help first-year students make the transition to college life. They are trained to help in a variety of issues and generally try to be friends and not supervisors. As one student commented, "RAs are friendly, and they can be very helpful if you take the initiative to ask them for advice."

After freshman year, students can choose to live in Barnard dorms, Columbia dorms, or one of the eight off-campus buildings. They can also find off-campus apartments themselves. Despite this opportunity of living independently in one of the busiest cities in the world, however, the cost of renting off-campus is quite prohibitive, and a great majority of Barnard students stays on-campus. In addition, Barnard and Columbia offer an educational atmosphere with quads and greens, quite different from the city high-rises, which, as admitted by many students, "can be intimidating at times."

Dining in the City

First-year students must choose Barnard's "Unlimited meals per term" meal plan, although there are three other meal plans available after freshman year. Food at Barnard can be summarized, in the opinion of one student, as "acceptable." The college offers a great variety of food options, but there are only two dining locations on campus. Many residences are equipped with kitchens, allowing students to cook their own meals. Cooking, however, can be time-consuming. According to one student, "The kitchens can be very convenient, but don't count on having the time to cook meals everyday." With countless restaurants and cafés nearby, dining out is thus a very popular, though expensive, option for the students.

Barnard Bear or Columbia Lions

Although Barnard has the Bear as its mascot, athletes can compete in varsity sports only through Columbia teams—the Lions, which do not incite much interest among Barnard students. "We really don't have that much school spirit," explained one student. "We don't know how much we should identify ourselves with Columbia." Nevertheless, the association with a prominent Ivy League school, which can be overshadowing at times, also offers many benefits that outweigh its disadvantages. Given the quality of education it provides, Barnard stands as a top choice for female students searching for first-class education in an exciting urban environment.
—*Xiaohang Liu*

FYI
If you come to Barnard, you'd better bring "clothes suitable for clubs."
What is the typical weekend schedule? "Friday tends to be comparatively quiet. Saturday is when you go to the city and have lots of fun. Sunday is for homework."
If I could change one thing about Barnard, I'd "build better dorms."
Three things every student at Barnard should do before graduating are "go to Midnight Breakfast, travel to every corner of New York City, and have fun on Barnard Spirit Day."

City University of New York Systems

New York City is unique. Known for its skyscrapers and disorderly traffic, the Big Apple is also home to over half a million students. It even has its own university system. In fact, the City University of New York, most often abbreviated as CUNY, is the largest urban public university and the third largest university system in the country, ranked after the public universities of New York State and California. It encompasses 23 schools, including 11 four-year colleges, six community colleges, and six graduate and professional schools. The number of students is also stunning. CUNY enrolls approximately 240,000 university-level students, not to mention a similar number of individuals in adult, continuing and professional education. A unique arrangement, CUNY is independent of New York State's own public university system, although it does receive funding from both the state and city governments.

Anything for Anyone
The sheer number of institutions and academic programs means a variety of options available to students. There are in fact more than 200 majors for undergraduates, thus providing the opportunity to receive training in either the traditional liberal arts or in career-oriented programs, such as Legal Assistant Studies, available at New York City College of Technology, or Television and Radio, offered by Brooklyn College. "There are all kinds of options for students, and the degrees are very practical and will help us immensely in finding jobs and doing well in them," one student said.

Given the number of options for students, CUNY has divided specialties among its schools. For example, City College is best known for its engineering program. Hunter College, on the other hand, has a large number of students enrolled in its highly acclaimed nursing school. Baruch College offers an undergraduate program within its Zicklin School, known as the largest collegiate business school in the country.

At the same time, the size of CUNY also implies a highly bureaucratic methodology of dealing with students. Surely, studying in New York City is very different from attending a small, rural college, where the school by itself represents a distinct community. The students attending any of the CUNY institutions find that they have to be independent and discover their own options rather than relying on advising from the school faculty and administrators, from whom it is sometimes difficult to obtain valuable guidance. Registering for classes can be frustrating, especially for freshmen and sophomores who are looking for relatively small classes. Nevertheless, this lack of personal attention is not unique at CUNY. In fact, students in most large universities have difficulties in navigating through the complex institutional bureaucracy. "I would like to have more individual attention. Everybody does," said one student. "But my friends in other state schools are also experiencing the same thing. And at least CUNY is now working on new programs to give us a little more personal attention."

Diverse Environment
New York City often boasts its diversity as a major strength, and the same can be said about CUNY. The location invariably means that the student body hails from all imaginable backgrounds. Indeed, more than 30 percent of undergraduates were born outside of the United States, and nearly 40 percent have a native language other than English. More than 150 countries are represented within the CUNY system. "It is a very international school. If you try, you will learn a lot about other cultures," one student explained.

Life in the Big Apple
As its name indicates, CUNY mostly serves students from New York City. Approximately 70 percent of undergraduates have attended public high schools within the City. This means that most people know about the Big Apple fairly well even before enrollment. Financially, it also makes sense for New York students to attend the school. After all, they do not have to pay the hefty charges of room and board. Many live with their families and have part-time jobs off campus.

One major drawback of CUNY is the lack of a collegiate atmosphere. Most students live off campus, and many schools do not even offer dormitories. This is because

CUNY is a commuter school. Students go to classes during the day and often have jobs at nights and during weekends. Therefore, many people take more than the traditional four years to graduate, and nearly 30 percent of undergraduates are at least 25 years old. "This is not your normal liberal arts experience," one student said. "People here are practical and have many other things going on besides school."

CUNY makes people independent. The students have to learn to take initiative and find their own opportunities. CUNY does not provide the highly protective and perhaps even insular environment of a traditional four-year college. Instead, it provides a good—and often very practical—education, and the students are on their own for other aspects of collegiate life, such as finding their own social circles and living arrangements. In the end, CUNY is for those who are looking for a good education in a diverse environment without placing too much emphasis on a traditional campus life.—*Xlaohang Liu*

City University of New York / City College

Address: 160 Convent Avenue New York, NY 10031	**Percentage accepted through EA or ED:** NA	**Graduation Rate 4-year:** 5%
Phone: 212-650-6977	**EA and ED deadline:** NA	**Graduation Rate 6-year:** 65%
E-mail address: admissions@ccny.cuny.edu	**Regular Deadline:** None/ Priority Applicaton deadline: 03/15	**Percent Undergraduates in On-campus housing:** 0%
Web site URL: www.ccny.cuny.edu	**Application Fee:** $65	**Number of official organized extracurricular organizations:** 145
Year Founded: 1847	**Full time Undergraduate enrollment:** 8,145	**3 Most popular majors:** Engineering, Liberal Arts, Psychology
Private or Public: Public	**Total enrollment:** 11,310	
Religious Affiliation: None	**Percent Male:** 47%	
Location: Urban	**Percent Female:** 53%	**Student/Faculty ratio:** 13:1
Number of Applicants: 17,816	**Total Percent Minority or Unreported:** 71%	**Average Class Size:** 20 to 29
Percent Accepted: 45%	**Percent African-American:** 21%	**Percent of students going to grad school:** Unreported
Percent Accepted who enroll: 25%	**Percent Asian/Pacific Islander:** 25%	**Tuition and Fees:** $11,129
Number Entering: 1768		**In State Tuition and Fees if different:** $4,329
Number of Transfers Accepted each Year: 1,578	**Percent Hispanic:** 34%	**Cost for Room and Board:** $1,020
Middle 50% SAT range: M: 460–590, CR: 430–550, Wr: Unreported	**Percent Native-American:** <1%	
	Percent International: 12%	**Percent receiving financial aid out of those who apply, first year:** 96%
Middle 50% ACT range: Unreported	**Percent in-state/out of state:** 98%/2%	
Early admission program EA/ED/None: None	**Percent from Public HS:** 85%	**Percent receiving financial aid among all students:** 85%
	Retention Rate: Unreported	

Located in the heart of Harlem, City College is one of the quiet academic gems of New York, producing alumni such as Colin Powell and former New York Mayor Ed Koch, and with faculty such as the co-founder of the String Theory of physics, Michio Kaku. While students at CCNY come from all sorts of backgrounds and living situations, most are from New York City itself. At CCNY, students must balance the rigorous amount of studying required to truly learn and very full personal lives.

An Immovable Foundation

Students at City College are required to maintain a 2.0 GPA or higher throughout the course of their college careers in order to graduate. At the same time, students in the Macaulay Honors College must graduate in four years, and are required to take six liberal arts courses, four of them focusing on New York City—its art, peoples, science and technology, and its future. For students in the Sophie Davis Biomedical program, which provides students with a Bachelor's degree as well as the first two years of medical school in the course of five years, every student must get a B or better in every class. Each major has its own requirements. When it comes to grading, there isn't much of a curve, but each professor makes up his or her own rubric, and so it can be kind of surprising. Stated one sophomore, "Don't come in assuming just because City's a CUNY it will be easy. I started with that notion, but my classes have changed my opinion pretty quickly."

Students all agree that the work required at CCNY is more demanding than expected, but is also quite rewarding. "For a lot of students, it's been quite some time since they were last in school, but now they are back, and are willing to work really hard to understand the material," one biology major said. In order to address the needs of a wide variety of students, the school is divided into the social sciences, the humanities, the "hard" sciences, a school of education, a school of engineering, and a school of architecture. Students major in every aspect of these programs, but everyone agrees that Engineering, the first public engineering program of its kind, and Architecture, the only public architecture program in the city, are the most popular.

As far as faculty goes, students feel that City College professors are among the most quirky and unique around. One student recalled, "I had one Earth Science professor who was also a poet. For a lecture on tornadoes, he explained it in a sort of sexual poem. I won't go into explicit detail, but I now know that tornadoes form from the friction between little tiny air molecules, that there's a building-up phase and then once all the liquid is gone . . . you know." Other students agree that the professors make the material more interesting, and insert a lot of their own personality. Furthermore, they are all very accessible to students who are willing to visit them during office hours, and are usually happy to have students assist them in research. Also, students in the Honors program and at Sophie Davis are assigned advisors who help them with everything from finding scholarships to

making sure the students are on top of their classes.

Classes run a wide range of sizes from introductory psychology lectures of about 400 people to labs with just around 15. Students feel that even though the work is very rigorous, everyone is really supportive of one another: "At Sophie, you'd expect us all to be kind of cut-throat about grades and stuff, but since we all have a seat guaranteed at med school, it's actually designed for everyone to help one another out. It's like that at the rest of the college as well."

Overall, students feel that the education they get at CCNY offers them opportunities that would otherwise not be there. "There's an openness to atypical students here, students who have kids or jobs, that I haven't heard of anywhere else," one student said. "There's a lot of support for everyone, and I think much of that comes from our diverse backgrounds and areas of study." At the same time, there is little communication between those areas of study, and students sometimes are frustrated by taking classes outside of their major.

A Commuter School Where People Know Your Name

CCNY's location at the top of a very windy hill makes it somewhat of a unique site, one that its students must trek to everyday. "The 1 Train, the A Train, the D Train, the C, the B, they all come here, but then *you* have to climb up the hill!" one student summed up. "To tell you the truth though, taking the train is a good time to do work, to catch up with friends, and to make new ones." Unfortunately, since it is a commuter school, it can be hard for the average student to meet new people, unless they share a common class or club, or are in the same program. "Most people come to campus, go to class, and then go home, unless they have a club or something," one student said.

At the same time, students tend to be very friendly, and very, very diverse: "It's a good atmosphere. A lot of people are here to get a college degree after not having the chance to for awhile, so there's camaraderie between everyone, because everyone is focused on learning and graduating." Upperclassmen tend to help out underclassmen, and there are several programs through which students can get tutoring from one another.

Students do come together for events every couple of months, such as for Relay for Life, Go Green Carnivale, a joint event between the Green Society and the Caribbean

Students Club, and the "Fifth Year Blow-out," an event at Sophie Davis where the graduating class puts on a massive talent show. Fraternities are present, and do occasionally throw parties, perform community service, and have events on-campus, although some students feel that they aren't a major scene.

Every Thursday, students have "club hours," where the organizations meet, discuss plans, and do whatever they are designed to do. Ranging from Intramural Volleyball to the Baskerville Chemical Society, clubs are designed to fulfill every student interest. "There are about a million clubs," exaggerated one student, "and if there isn't one for something you're interested in, you can start a club really easily." CCNY competes against other CUNY schools in a variety of varsity sports, but support is somewhat lacking: "Most people aren't very involved. They don't even know our mascot (it's the beaver)!" one freshman lamented.

On the weekends, students tend to do their own thing. "Most kids go home, study, and chill with their friends and family," reported one student who lives on campus. "Some of the upperclassmen go out to bars because they're legal, but underclassmen tend not to drink." Some drinking does go on in the dormitories, but the school has a zero-tolerance policy toward alcohol and drugs on campus.

Study, Eat, Breathe, Sleep—In Harlem

Most students live off campus, either at home or in apartments near the campus, in order to cut down on travel time. The school does offer housing for students a few blocks away from campus, in a building known as "The Towers", but rent is very high, with some rooms going for $1000 a month. The rooms themselves are functional and new, but many feel that the Towers are not worth the price. Also, the dorms are open to students from all over the city.

As for location, many students are big fans of the surrounding area. "There are a lot of great places to eat around here," one student said. There is some controversy amongst the students regarding safety in the area. "There's a lot of hype about, you know, 'Ohhh it's Harlem, it's not safe,'" complained a female student, "but my last lab ends at 7:50, and I feel perfectly safe." "After it gets dark, you should travel in groups," countered another. Still, there is consensus that around the campus itself, there are no major problems.

> "There's a lot of support for everyone, and I think much of that comes from our diverse backgrounds and areas of study."

Many students like to avoid the cafeteria, which tends to be expensive and doesn't offer many choices. "It's fuel, but it's not great," an engineer said. Instead, many buy food in the delis and restaurants in the neighborhood, while others bring food from home and eat it on the Quad. "The Quad is a great place in the spring and summer when the weather's nice. Otherwise, it's too cold and windy," explained a student from Brooklyn. Students also like to eat in the stairways in the North Academic Center, and to hang out in the castle-like Shepherd Hall.

At CCNY, you can find a diverse group of students coming together with one common goal and interest: learning. Students are often surprised by the challenging curriculum they deal with, but are supported by a caring and dense network of professors and friends. "When I went through the college admissions process, it wasn't until the very end that I decided to come to City," explained an Honors College student, "but it really surprised me. The tuition is lower than almost anywhere else, but what really got me was how generous the people were. There are things that you can go through, but still bounce back. City College has taught me that. I would definitely pick it again."—*Simon Warren*

FYIs
If you come to CCNY, you'd better bring "a Metrocard."
What is the typical weekend schedule? "It depends on the weekend. If you have a test coming up, it could be study eat sleep repeat, or if it's a more relaxed week, it could be go home, relax, maybe go to a party, and study on Sunday."
If I could change one thing about CCNY, I'd "make the dorms cheaper. A lot cheaper."
Three things every student at City College should do before graduating are "go to a concert at the Apollo, rub Lincoln's nose, and play pool in the Student Lounge."

City University of New York / Hunter College

Address: 695 Park Ave, Room N203 New York, NY 10065
Phone: 212-772-4490
E-mail address: admissions@hunter.cuny.edu
Web site URL: www.hunter.cuny.edu
Year Founded: 1950
Private or Public: Public
Religious Affiliation: None
Location: Urban
Number of Applicants: 24,701
Percent Accepted: 30%
Percent Accepted who enroll: 25%
Number Entering: 1,854
Number of Transfers Accepted each Year: Unrepokrted
Middle 50% SAT range: M: 500–600, CR: 480–580, Wr: Unreported
Middle 50% ACT range: Unreported
Early admission program EA/ED/None: None

Percentage accepted through EA or ED: NA
EA and ED deadline: NA
Regular Deadline: 15-Mar
Application Fee: $65
Full time Undergraduate enrollment: 15,718
Total enrollment: 21,278
Percent Male: 32%
Percent Female: 68%
Total Percent Minority or Unreported: 59%
Percent African-American: 12%
Percent Asian/Pacific Islander: 18%
Percent Hispanic: 19%
Percent Native-American: <1%
Percent International: 10%
Percent in-state/out of state: 96%/4%
Percent from Public HS: 70%
Retention Rate: 82%
Graduation Rate 4-year: 17%

Graduation Rate 6-year: 40%
Percent Undergraduates in On-campus housing: 4%
Number of official organized extracurricular organizations: 150
3 Most popular majors: Social Sciences, English, Psychology
Student/Faculty ratio: 15:1
Average Class Size: 20 to 29
Percent of students going to grad school: Unreported
Tuition and Fees: $10,800
In State Tuition and Fees if different: $4,000
Cost for Room and Board: $7,958
Percent receiving financial aid out of those who apply, first year: 55%
Percent receiving financial aid among all students: Unreported

With its well-rounded core requirements, CUNY Hunter provides students with a solid education in the middle of New York City, even if the living arrangements sometimes leave a little to be desired. Hunter draws some of the most independent students in New York City and is able to give them a good training in almost every discipline. At Hunter, students are motivated to study and maintain separate lives outside the classroom.

Well-Rounded in the Big Apple

Hunter puts a heavy emphasis on a well-rounded curriculum. All students must take classes in math, U.S. history, English, foreign language, writing, natural science, arts, social sciences, and pluralism and diversity, which deal with, for instance, non-European history and women's studies. For students at Hunter's Honors Program, they also have to take four seminars about New York City over the course of their four years in the school.

Many students are pre-med, which is known for being very challenging. Other popular majors are literature, psychology and social science. Hunter's education and nursing programs are also outstanding. For those on the pre-med track, many of the classes, such as freshman biology, are designed to "weed out" people who are not committed to becoming doctors. Still, students find that the level of difficulty allows them to appreciate the curriculum. According to one student, "Organic Chemistry tries to teach you the psychology of the carbon atom by making it personal. Don't go in expecting an easy A or B. Expect to learn."

Other classes are more varied in terms of difficulty, as well as class size. While science and honors classes fill up quickly, humanities tends to have small classes, with a maximum of 20 students. Despite the extensive general requirements, the school tries to offer very specific classes, such as "Dante's Divine Comedy," "Understanding the Sixties," and "the Psychology of Human Sexuality." These courses are very popular.

Students also greatly enjoy the classes in the Honors program. "I try to take at least one Honors class a semester," said one sophomore. "The classes are smaller, and the professors are more interested in what they are teaching and whom they are teaching." In addition to these classes, Honors students also get priority when picking classes, not to mention free laptop, free tuition, and guaranteed free housing. There is also a program called the Opportunity Fund, which provides $75,000 for study abroad, internship, projects, or other activities for each Honors student. "It's a pretty good deal. The Honors program is the only reason I'm going to Hunter," said one student.

Every student has an advisor over the course of four years who offers guidance when needed. Professors are generally reachable and helpful. While "some professors don't expect much out of students and are boring and not challenging," many are "easy to get along with and very helpful if you are serious about getting help." Students feel that advisors are excellent resources and that it is a very good idea to take the time to get their advice.

As for grading, it is varied. "In general, it is not too tough," said one student. "Depending on the class and the professor, it can be harder. Frosh bio and literature are tough, but usually classes are not too harsh, just about right."

Hunter offers its students a well-rounded education with specific classes that excite and engage students, even though the required curriculum is sometimes cumbersome. One student summed up the attitude towards the requirements: "What I like most about studying at Hunter is that as hard as it is to complete the general education requirements, you see why they exist and appreciate them. Hunter exposes you to everything. But the general education requirements are also my least favorite part. People don't like them because they are required and feel that there is no time to fulfill everything."

Close to Home

Most students at Hunter do not live on campus. Hunter is unique among the CUNYs in that it guarantees housing to all of its Honors students. Students not in the Honors program can also apply to live on campus through a very competitive online process. Every room is a single, and students get to keep the same room all four years, if they wish.

According to campus legend, Hunter's one dorm, Brookdale, was at one point an asylum for the insane. Now, instead of rooms for electroshock therapy on the first floor and a morgue in the basement, it houses a very popular game room and a swimming pool. Students love the fact that they have private rooms, and that all the rooms are identical, although half of them face a courtyard and are slightly more coveted. Living at Hunter is arranged by floor, with a RA and a CA, both undergraduates, on every floor. There are monthly floor meetings, where students can find out what is happening on their floor and settle issues. Floors can also be all-female or 24-hour quiet.

Students find that the school buildings are quite impressive. "There is a subway stop that gets off right into the school, so it is really convenient," said one student. Everyone takes public transportation to get to and from the school. In addition, the architecture makes it standout. One of four buildings that make up the school's campus, the Thomas Hunter Building, looks like a castle but has bridges on the third floor, which cross over Lexington Avenue. There are also a recently renovated swimming pool, a new chemistry laboratory, and an athletic facility for all students.

As for food, the cafeteria is not well used. It closes before dinner so that students have to go out, order food, make something, or heat up leftovers. Luckily, the options around the neighborhood are plentiful. Each floor in the dorm has a kitchen, and many students are able to go home during the weekend for home-cooked meals.

The neighborhood surrounding Hunter is mostly safe, and the school is well incorporated into the community. Since the campus is open at night, people come and go freely, but to get into the buildings, particularly Brookdale, they are required to have several ID checks.

Hunting for Friends

When it comes to social life, Hunter is unlike many others. Since most students live elsewhere in the City, many people go home or work after class and don't stay on campus. One student explained, "We're a commuter school, so there isn't much of a sense of community here. There is not an area where students can come together and relax." On the other hand, students living in Brookdale do have the opportunity to get to know their neighbors, and students can hang out between classes at an Honors lounge.

On the weekends, many students go home,

although there are house parties. Many students also go out to eat or hang out with friends. Since the school is located on Manhattan's Upper East Side, there are many excellent choices when it comes to restaurants, and some students go to bars as well. However, there is no tolerance for underage drinking. "The security guards at the dorm are very strict," explained one student. "If you come back drunk, they will call an ambulance to take you one block, and you have to pay the fee." There are harsher penalties for those caught drinking in the dorm itself. However, most students reported that binge drinking is not much of a problem at all, and that almost everything happens behind closed doors.

Most friendships are made in classes, clubs, and dorms. Those in the Honors program have an easier time of meeting new people because "you are kind of forced to, or at least you have a greater chance of meeting people. Most students come in, then go home, and don't really have a chance to sit down and get to know their classmates." Still, the consensus is that almost everyone is friendly and that the student body is one of the most diverse. "I wouldn't be surprised if every single country and nationality were represented," said one student. "You see every type of dress. You have rich people and less fortunate people. On a gradient, I would say it is completely diverse." Other students point out that people of all ages attend the school.

Hunter students also take advantage of the school's location, and get to spend time in some of New York's coolest locations. One sophomore recounted, "I once went to celebrate my friend's birthday on the Brooklyn Bridge." Every year, a big event is the Relay for Life, when Hunter and Baruch combine to form the CUNY Manhattan team. The Undergraduate Student Government also organizes events occasionally.

Big-Hearted Hawks
Hunter offers many extracurricular activities, particularly community service groups and cultural organizations. Many people have jobs or internships, and most people are highly committed to their chosen activities. Fraternities and sororities exist on Hunter's campus, but rather than being communities of people who live and drink together, Hunter's Greek life is focused almost entirely on community service. Campus publications are popular, including the newspaper, called the *Hunter Envoy*, and the literary publication, the *Olive Branch*. Groups like the Socialist Club also put out newsletters.

"What I like most about studying at Hunter is that hard as it is to complete the general education requirements, you see why they exist, and appreciate them. Hunter exposes you to everything."

When it comes to sports, the athletes themselves take their sports very seriously. However, most students feel that there is little school pride. "We may not have a football team," said one, "but I am not sure." The athletic facilities are more widely used for relaxation and fun. There are basketball courts, a gym, a pool, and a small bowling alley.

Hunter students come from everywhere. It is a fantastic place to get a solid—and for Honors students, free—education from one of the top public universities in the United States. While it is easy to feel somewhat disconnected and without a community, students do find friendships and social lives. Academically, Hunter gives students a firm background, although some students would prefer to have more freedom when it comes to choosing classes. As one student put it, "if I had to pick schools again, I think I would choose the Honors College at Hunter again. You get to be independent and don't have to rely on your parents for tuition. There are great professors and advisors who help you find internships. Overall, it is a good deal."—*Simon Warren*

FYI
If you come to Hunter, you'd better bring "sneakers."
What is the typical weekend schedule? "Go home or stay in the dorm, study or hang out. Some people volunteer or work."
If I could change one thing about Hunter, I'd "change the food plan. There is none."
Three things every student at Hunter should do before graduating are "walk from Hunter to Central Park, see the swimming pool, and get used to crowded hallways."

City University of New York / Queens College

Address: 65-30 Kissena Blvd Flushing, NY 11367	**Percentage accepted through EA or ED:** NA	**Graduation Rate 6-year:** 31%
Phone: 718-997-5600	**EA and ED deadline:** NA	**Percent Undergraduates in On-campus housing:** 0%
E-mail address: vincent.angrisani@qc.cuny.edu	**Regular Deadline:** NA	**Number of official organized extracurricular organizations:** 114
Web site URL: www.qc.cuny.edu	**Application Fee:** $65 **Full time Undergraduate enrollment:** 14,618	
Year Founded: 1937	**Total enrollment:** 18,928	**3 Most popular majors:** Accounting, Psychology, General Sociology
Private or Public: Public	**Percent Male:** 39%	
Religious Affiliation: None	**Percent Female:** 61%	
Location: Urban	**Total Percent Minority or Unreported:** 56%	**Student/Faculty ratio:** 17:1
Number of Applicants: 14,436	**Percent African-American:** 7%	**Average Class Size:** 20 to 29
Percent Accepted: 38%		
Percent Accepted who enroll: 10%	**Percent Asian/Pacific Islander:** 25%	**Percent of students going to grad school:** 17%
Number Entering: 1,642	**Percent Hispanic:** 17%	**Tuition and Fees:** $9,017
Number of Transfers Accepted each Year: 2,977	**Percent Native-American:** <1%	**In State Tuition and Fees if different:** $4,377
Middle 50% SAT range: M: 480–580, CR: 450–550, Wr: 490–550	**Percent International:** 6% **Percent in-state/out of state:** 99%/1%	**Cost for Room and Board:** $5,083
Middle 50% ACT range: Unreported	**Percent from Public HS:** Unreported	**Percent receiving financial aid out of those who apply, first year:** 55%
Early admission program EA/ED/None: None	**Retention Rate:** 84% **Graduation Rate 4-year:** 26%	**Percent receiving financial aid among all students:** 58%

S prawled over 77 acres in the residential neighborhood of Flushing, NY, just a 30-minute drive from midtown Manhattan, Queens College offers "an incredibly beautiful view of the city skyline" and a convenient location for thousands of New York City students. Less apparent, but just as spectacular, are the vast array of academic, social, and extracurricular opportunities this commuter college provides.

An Amazing Academic Assortment

Queens College offers a variety of academic options to meet the needs of a diverse group of students. The college offers over 63 majors, of which the most popular are accounting, sociology, business administration and psychology (known as a "joke major" for its relative ease). There is also "a good load of people in the sciences," which are reportedly "incredibly tough"—"much harder" than other majors.

Whatever their major, all students are re-

quired to take at least 120 credits (each class is worth three to five credits, depending on difficulty), a Freshman English Course and three additional writing intensive courses. They also must demonstrate competency in English, mathematics, physical education and a foreign language and must complete Liberal Arts and Science Area Requirements (LASAR) in seven areas. Students must also take three writing intensive units. The requirements are "somewhat inconvenient if you have a major that has lots of requirements in itself," but "it's actually not too bad to fulfill them—you just happen to end up taking them," and students averse to math and science can take "fake math and science classes" like statistics or psychology instead, while Urban Studies 101 is known as an easy way to fulfill the social science requirement. Freshmen get help planning their schedule during a mandatory advising session, and all students can consult the Advising Center on a drop-in basis, through email or by appointment.

Unfortunately, with an undergraduate

population of over 14,000 (there are also about 4,100 graduate students), many students find that registering for classes (online or in person) can be "really frustrating," especially for smaller, upper-level seminars. Students taking classes for their major get first choice, followed by seniors, juniors, sophomores and freshmen. As a result, "class registration can sometimes take a very long time, and in that time you can get closed out of classes." However, according to one senior, "if you go directly to the department or appeal to the professor, you can almost always get in."

Given its large student body, Queens College offers a surprising level of personal attention. While large introductory lectures have up to 200 students, upper level seminars, recitation sections and labs rarely exceed 20 students. Although sections and labs are often led by graduate student TA's, all seminars and lectures are taught by professors, who are, in the words of one senior, "the normal mix—some good, some not so great." Other students noted that "professors are very available and very enthusiastic, even in large lecture classes," so that "even if you're sitting in a class with 100 other people, you can get to know the professor if you want to."

While some professors are tougher than others, the workload is generally "not too much, but definitely not a walk in the park." As one sophomore put it, "You can get by taking the easiest classes, and there are definitely classes where if you're half awake you'll do fine, but you can also have an academically challenging college experience."

Students looking to take their education to a higher level can take advantage of plentiful undergraduate research opportunities or study abroad in 30 countries (popular destinations include Israel, England, Australia, the Galapagos Islands and Florence, Italy). They can also take honors track classes, which are small, rigorous classes taught by top professors.

While honors track classes are open to all students, Queens College admits only a handful exceptionally talented and motivated students per year to the Macaulay Honors College, a program where students take classes on the Queens College campus, but receive fully paid tuition, funding for internships and study abroad, an academic stipend, a free laptop and free access to museums across New York City. Honors College students must take four Honors College

seminars in addition to taking regular Queens College classes. According to one enthusiastic sophomore who had considered several Ivy League schools, these seminars offer "academically challenging, small classes" and "really amazing" professors, making for an experience comparable to that of a top small liberal-arts institution.

Queens College also features the SEEK program—which provides low-income, first-generation college students free tuition and additional guidance—as well as weekend classes, night classes, a program for adults 25 years and older and even the Center for Unlimited Enrichment, which lets senior citizens take classes at reduced cost. The college is also home to the renowned Aaron Copland School of Music, to which students apply separately.

This vast array of academic choices attracts students of all ages, races and income levels. "You have an enormous variety," raved one sophomore. "People who are 45, and people who are 18. People who are interested in politics, and people who are interested in music. The people in my medical anthropology class last semester had such varied life experiences, and the conversation took such interesting turns. It makes the education so much more enriching."

Campus Life for Commuters

Like most of the other CUNY colleges, Queens College is a commuter school. There are no dorms, and most students live at home with their parents, though a few rent apartments near campus. Students either take a public bus or drive to school, though the amount of on-campus parking, assigned by a lottery system, is "not necessarily adequate."

Because they live off campus, many students spend little time on campus outside of class. "You go to class and go home," said one sophomore. "You don't really chill there for the heck of it." Some students say this makes it difficult to get to know their classmates. Still, students report that their peers are "friendly," and for those who want to get involved on campus, plenty of opportunities are available.

Freshmen can enroll in the Freshman Year Initiative program, where students take three of their classes with the same 40 students, giving them a chance to build strong relationships. Another common way to meet people is through extracurricular clubs and organizations. The most popular clubs are cultural groups such as Hillel and Latin American Club, the weekly *Knight News* and student government; but with over 100 organizations to choose from, "if you can think of it, it's there." Most clubs have offices in the Student Union, which also has game rooms and big-screen TVs, making it a popular hangout during lunch.

On-campus dining includes a main cafeteria (which ranges from "not very appetizing" to "repetitive but pretty good"), a kosher cafeteria, a Chinese restaurant and several cafés. There are also several small restaurants right across from campus on Main St., including the popular Gino's pizzeria.

In addition to lunchtime, students have "free hours" twice a week during which no classes are held, providing a convenient time for students to hang out, hold club meetings, or "during the not-so-freezing days of summer and spring," play pickup football or Frisbee on the quad.

Although Queens is the only CUNY college to have Division II sports, there is no football team, and sports play a small role in the lives of most students. Most teams "aren't bad," but attending games is "hardly popular," though tennis and volleyball matches do draw some spectators. The on-campus gym, pool, weight room and tennis courts are free of charge to all students, but "no one really takes advantage of them" unless they are taking classes in sports or physical education. There is also a small intramural program for students who are interested.

> "It's a little bit more difficult because it's a commuter campus, but it's really what you make of it. There are definitely opportunities to have a campus life."

Because so many students live far from campus, few stick around for nighttime activities. As a result, "there is little to no drug/alcohol presence on campus. People who want to indulge in either tend to hang out off campus." There are a handful of fraternities and sororities, but since none of them have houses, they are a minor presence. However, clubs and associations will often sponsor on-campus parties, which are usually on the weekends, and "fairly well-attended." Throughout the week, students can also attend frequent lectures, concerts, and plays on campus, often held at the Kupferberg Center for the Arts.

A sophomore summed up life at Queens College with the following words: "It's a little bit more difficult because it's a commuter campus, but it's really what you make of it. There are definitely opportunities to have a campus life."—*Sameer Jain*

FYI

If you come to Queens College, you'd better bring: "passion for something—anything," "an apartment" and "a laptop."

What's the typical weekend schedule? "Go to a part-time job, internship, or use the time to study." "At night, go into the city."

If I could change one thing about Queens College, I'd change "being part of a city bureaucracy. It's really awful—getting things done means many, many forms in triplicate and many meetings and many hurdles in terms of protocol."

Three things every student at Queens College should do before graduating are "play a game of pick-up Frisbee on the main quad," "visit the on-campus museums—the art gallery in the library, all three of the galleries in Klapper Hall, the Louis Armstrong archives in Rosenthal Library and the geology exhibits," and "study abroad (huge selection, and the cost is equivalent to CUNY credit tuition)."

Clarkson University

Address: Box 5605 Potsdam, NY 13699
Phone: 315-268-6480
E-mail address: admission@clarkson.edu
Web site URL: www.clarkson.edu
Year Founded: 1896
Private or Public: Private
Religious Affiliation: None
Location: Rural
Number of Applicants: 3,204
Percent Accepted: 78.7%
Percent Accepted who enroll: 29.1%
Number Entering: 735
Number of Transfers Accepted each Year: 151
Middle 50% SAT range: M: 610–660, CR: 500–560, Wr: 480–590
Middle 50% ACT range: 24–28
Early admission program EA/ED/None: ED

Percentage accepted through EA or ED: 14%
EA and ED deadline: 1-Dec
Regular Deadline: 15-Jan
Application Fee: $50
Full time Undergraduate enrollment: 2,593
Total enrollment: 2,994
Percent Male: 73%
Percent Female: 27%
Total Percent Minority or Unreported: 9%
Percent African-American: 3%
Percent Asian/Pacific Islander: 3%
Percent Hispanic: 3%
Percent Native-American: <1%
Percent International: 4%
Percent in-state/out of state: 73%/27%
Percent from Public HS: Unreported
Retention Rate: 83%

Graduation Rate 4-year: 58%
Graduation Rate 6-year: 71%
Percent Undergraduates in On-campus housing: 82%
Number of official organized extracurricular organizations: 56
3 Most popular majors: Biology, Business, Engineering
Student/Faculty ratio: 15:1
Average Class Size: Unreported
Percent of students going to grad school: Unreported
Tuition and Fees: 32,220
In State Tuition and Fees if different: No difference
Cost for Room and Board: $11,118
Percent receiving financial aid out of those who apply, first year: 100%
Percent receiving financial aid among all students: 98%

Nestled in the small college town of Potsdam, New York, Clarkson is a thriving undergraduate university primarily dedicated to the teaching of engineering and business. With approximately 3000 undergraduate students, and with class sizes averaging only 20 students per class, Clarkson is a closely knit community where students and professors come together to solve real-world problems in a hands-on manner.

And You Thought the SATs Were Hard . . .

One thing that all students at Clarkson can attest to is the rigorous and demanding workload. As one senior put it, "Clarkson is a fast-paced school where professors have high expectations." However, few students find their workload unmanageable, with most students agreeing that what they gain from their courses is well worth the work they put in. Some of the things that students liked best about classes at Clarkson include the emphasis on interdisciplinary learning and team-based approaches to problem

solving. Although the workload might be hard at Clarkson, most students agree that their "professors are great." Not only do most professors have flexible office hours, some even make the effort to visit students or hold study sessions in student residence halls. In addition to academic interactions however, some professors also interact with students socially through intramural sports or other extracurricular activities. It seems that the only negative thing students had to say about teaching at Clarkson was the inevitable presence of TAs and professors with strong accents.

Since Clarkson is mainly an engineering and business school, most students major in those two areas, although majors in the sciences, humanities, and liberal arts are available as well. Popular majors at Clarkson include mechanical engineering, interdisciplinary engineering and management, and e-business. Regardless of what the major is, however, each student at Clarkson must complete a common set of distributional requirements. These include courses in the humanities, social sciences, natural sciences, engineering, computers, and math. Clarkson is renowned for its strong emphasis on "learning by doing" in which students are encouraged to apply the skills that they gain in classrooms to solving practical, everyday problems. For example, a program called Venture@Moore House allows a group of sophomores to design and market a new product while living together. Indeed, this is representative of the Clarkson academics atmosphere where "rather than being a competitive environment, Clarkson is more of a cooperative learning environment in which students are encouraged to work in collaborative group projects."

Living and Dining
All freshmen at Clarkson live in well-furnished doubles with "good heating." For freshmen, these rooms are located in a cluster of residence buildings (the Quad) that house approximately 60 students per floor. After freshman year, students can also choose to live in themed houses, Greek houses, or townhouses, which one junior considered "the cream of the crop." In recent years, Clark has taken an unconventional approach to student housing by allowing students to define their on-campus living experience. Through a special application process, Clarkies choose a group of friends with whom they want to live and propose a theme with related student-designed programs. Houses themes ranged from art, environmental sustainability, philosophy, and the Western frontier, to sexYOUality, cooking, knitting, and relaxation. Most students at Clarkson live on-campus for all four years and permission must be obtained to live off campus. However, off-campus housing is not too difficult to come by and is usually available within a ten-minute walk from campus. An RA (Resident Advisor) system does exist in the Clarkson dorms, although for the most part, RAs are generally viewed as fair. As one RA put it, "Just don't be stupid and you'll be fine, but if you feel the need to be stupid, at least be nice to the RA who catches you."

Food at Clarkson received mixed reviews. As one student summed it up, "the food used to be bad, but it has really improved in the past few years. For the most part they have something for everyone, and if they do not, they are more than willing to work with you on the issue." For the occasions when dining hall food simply will not do, Potsdam offers many great restaurants serving different national and international cuisines. Some of the more notable spots include The Cantina, Lobster House, and Little Italy, any of which would be "great spots for a nice date."

Filling Up Free Time
Although Clarkson is not a dry campus, partying in residence halls is forbidden, so most of the alcohol-related activities occur in either the various fraternity houses on and off-campus or the local bars. A typical freshman weekend generally includes at least one such party, and most students agree that being underage does not pose a large problem. However, one student complained that "these parties serve just beer" and that "only a few themed parties each semester serve something besides beer." Just how freely does the beer flow at these parties? When asked if drinking ever gets out of hand, one student thought that Clarkson "has a problem of not being harsh enough" about alcohol and that "problems [occur] every weekend." Another thought that most people were "very responsible" about their drinking. For students not into the party scene, Clarkson organizes movies, guest speakers, and other events for students each week.

> **"Clarkson is a fast-paced school where professors have high expectations."**

Other extracurricular activities also play a large part of life at Clarkson. Some of the more popular activities include the Outing Club, Clarkson TV, Clarkson Radio, and the Clarkson Senate. Devotion to extracurricular activities varies. While some students are "involved in way too many things," others concentrate just on a few. Overall, extracurriculars are "pretty much what you choose to make of them."

Golden (K)nights
The Greek scene at Clarkson, consisting of 10 recognized fraternities and three recognized sororities, plays a large role in the lives of many students. There is delayed rush at Clarkson, which is "great because you get to know other students well before you pledge, so you don't end up picking the wrong house." Fraternities and sororities live together in recognized Greek houses that offer their own optional meal plans. Apart from

throwing the various weekend parties mentioned above, fraternities and sororities play an important role in the Potsdam community by raising money for charities and performing countless hours of community service. It is interesting to note that Clarkson recently held the honor of having the highest fraternity and sorority average GPA in the Northeast.

But what do students do on Saturday nights, before the kegs are tapped at the frats? Why, go watch a hockey game, of course. At Clarkson "Hockey is #1." As the only Division I teams on-campus, the men and women's hockey teams are extremely important to school spirit—games against arch-rival and neighbor St. Lawrence University always sell out quickly. In order to maintain the level of their hockey team, Clarkson actively recruits players from around the country. This practice has created some resentment among students, one of whom disliked "the money wasted on athletics when many parts of the campus need fixing."

Not a varsity athlete? No problem. "If you want to play a sport but not on a school team, there are over 100 intramural teams to play on." Furthermore, Clarkson boasts a top-notch indoor recreation center that houses a long list of facilities including a gym, a pool, a weight room, and several basketball courts.

In and Around Campus

Clarkson students come from predominantly Northeast middle-class families. Ethnically, the student body is largely white, though as one student said, "a proud black community" exists on campus. Unfortunately, as one female student noted, because Clarkson is an engineering school, "the guy-to-girl ratio is so off that there are a lot of single guys out here."

The Clarkson campus is situated on 640 wooded acres and consists of 45 buildings. Although many of the buildings on-campus house state-of-the-art facilities, most students find Clarkson's buildings aesthetically "boring." What Clarkson lacks in architectural beauty, it makes up for in natural beauty, especially during the fall. However, don't forget your boots—being buried under snow for four months of each year is yet another endearing characteristic of the university.

Potsdam is a typical college town that bustles during the school year and hibernates during academic breaks. It is not unusual to hear some students complain "there is nothing to do in Potsdam." One junior countered that such people "need to get out of their rooms more, and see what [Potsdam] has to offer. [The city] may not be a metropolis but there are definitely things to do, and places to see."

When the need to get away from Potsdam arises, many options exist, most of which are within a few hours' drive from campus. These include Syracuse and Albany in New York, as well as Cornwall, Ottawa, and Montreal in Canada. Montreal, one of the renowned party cities of North America, is especially popular. Many students, however, are satisfied with the campus life at Clarkson and the small (but promising!) local community of Potsdam. Watch some hockey, play in the snow, and you'll be fine.—*Anthony Xu*

FYI
If you come to Clarkson University, you'd better bring a "warm coat and a computer."
What is the typical weekend schedule? "Saturday, sleep in, have brunch with friends, go watch the Men's Hockey game, and then party; Sunday, sleep in, do homework all afternoon, and then catch up on TV with friends."
If I could change one thing about Clarkson University, I'd "change the male-to-female ratio and the fact that it snows all year long!"
Three things every student at Clarkson should do before graduating are "cheering on your Golden Knights to victory, making 'creative' snow sculptures at night, and going clubbing in Canada."

Colgate University

Address: 13 Oak Drive
Hamilton, NY 13346
Phone: 315-228-7401
E-mail address:
admission@mail.colgate.edu
Web site URL:
www.colgate.edu
Year Founded: 1819
Private or Public: Private
Religious Affiliation: None
Location: Rural
Number of Applicants:
9,416
Percent Accepted: 23.9%
Percent Accepted who
enroll: 32.7%
Number Entering: 738
Number of Transfers
Accepted each Year: 20
Middle 50% SAT range:
M: 640–730, CR: 630–730,
Wr: Unreported
Middle 50% ACT range:
29–32
Early admission program
EA/ED/None: ED

Percentage accepted
through EA or ED:
Unreported
EA and ED deadline: 11/15
and 1/15
Regular Deadline: 15-Jan
Application Fee: $55
Full time Undergraduate
enrollment: 2,836
Total enrollment: 2,844
Percent Male: 49%
Percent Female: 51%
Total Percent Minority or
Unreported: 19%
Percent African-American: 6%
Percent Asian/Pacific
Islander: 6%
Percent Hispanic: 6%
Percent Native-American:
<1%
Percent International: 5%
Percent in-state/out of
state: 28%/72%
Percent from Public HS:
Unreported
Retention Rate: 93%

Graduation Rate 4-year:
91%
Graduation Rate 6-year:
91%
Percent Undergraduates in
On-campus housing: 92%
Number of official organized
extracurricular
organizations: 186
3 Most popular majors:
Biology, English, Psychology
Student/Faculty ratio: 10:1
Average Class Size: 18
Percent of students going to
grad school: 20.0%
Tuition and Fees: $39, 545
In State Tuition and Fees if
different: No difference
Cost for Room and Board:
$9,625
Percent receiving financial
aid out of those who apply,
first year: 81%
Percent receiving financial
aid among all students:
32%

"13 dollars, 13 prayers, and 13 articles." That was the beginning of Colgate University. In 1817, 13 men met in Hamilton, New York and founded the Baptist Education Society. Almost two centuries later, Colgate University is considered one of the country's top liberal arts universities. With a student population of about 2,750, Colgate seemingly combines the best of both worlds—the intimacy of a liberal arts college and the strong athletics program of a big university.

Nuts for Nature!

Like many of its peers in the world of liberal arts universities, Colgate is located in a small, serene location. Hamilton, a village of around 3,500 people, is nestled right in the middle of New York State, about an hour's drive from Syracuse. It is also an hour and a half away from Cornell University, Colgate's biggest rival in sports.

Quaint Hamilton Village is almost the same size of Colgate, which leads to good town-gown relationships. Even though it celebrated its bicentennial in 1995, the village, originally called "Payne's Settlement," has changed very little. Some students do feel that Colgate's location is a significant shortcoming of the university, given the fact that "there is really not much to do outside of the campus." "Everything in Hamilton revolves around Colgate," added another student, "There is really nothing for entertainment around here."

Nevertheless, students agree that the campus is beautiful. Gorgeous architecture is an important aspect of the university, especially Memorial Chapel's golden steeple, the most recognizable feature on campus. Its pristine location in upstate New York is also a prime attraction for nature lovers. "Colgate is perfect for people who enjoy the beauty of nature," one student said. Taylor Lake and Payne Creek both sit inside Colgate's campus and provide a relaxing backdrop to an otherwise hectic campus. To make use of all of its surroundings, Colgate's outdoor education program provides a fully equipped Base Camp right on campus, so students can take out rentals for snowshoeing, skiing, backpacking, and even camping. Colgate even maintains a camp in Upper Saranac Lake in the Adirondacks for the exclusive use of its faculty and students.

Despite any perceived shortcomings of the town, Colgate maintains a good relationship with Hamilton, where most of the Colgate faculty and staff live. In fact, about 85 percent of the faculty lives within 10 miles of the university. Another contributor to the goodwill between Hamilton and Colgate? As one student pointed out, "most locals go on vacation over Spring Party Weekend."

The Colgate Core

Colgate's admission process might not be as competitive as the Ivies, but it remains a highly selective school with an admissions rate below 25 percent. The average combined score on the old SAT was 1403, and more than 70 percent of its students are in the top 10 percent of their high schools. The average GPA for the class of 2012 was 3.74. "Given the admission standards," said a student, "the people here are generally smart and willing to work hard."

Colgate is a challenging school. Students need to work hard to get good grades, and several introductory classes are particularly difficult. As one student pointed out, "The intro classes are designed to cull the weak." Nevertheless, most students are happy with their classes, which are generally very small, giving students the opportunity to closely interact with their professors.

Undergrads can choose between 51 different concentrations. There is a core requirement that expects students to take four special classes by the end of their sophomore year. Two of these courses teach students about Western civilization and their contemporary challenges. The other courses are designed to give students a better understanding of a specific culture in the non-Western world and the effects of science and technology.

Colgaters have to take a minimum of 32 classes to graduate, including six classes for distributional requirements in humanities, social sciences, mathematics, and natural sciences and two physical education credits, a specialty of Colgate. Most students are fine with the requirements. According to a student, "the required Core classes are easy but usually involve a lot of reading." The gym classes, however, have mixed reviews. While some love the idea of going outdoors to learn about hiking and survival skills,

many others do not think that they should be part of the college curriculum. "I appreciate the goals of the gym classes, but I just don't think that they should still be here at the college level," said a student. "We have so many intramural sports anyway, and half of the students participate in them."

Weekends That Never End

People work hard at Colgate because of the vigorous academic standards, but they also party hard. Undergrads agree that most Colgate students have a solid sense of self-discipline that allows them to do well academically, while enjoying the nightlife.

Since a great majority of Colgate students stay on campus, there is no shortage of things to do. There are always parties going on throughout the week, not just during the weekends. Fraternity parties are probably the most prominent social scene on campus, although the sports teams are also frequent fiesta hosts. Teams often have townhouses or apartments where students go for partying and dancing. For those who grow tired of the Greek system, the Jug is the most frequented bar for Colgate students, who generally agree that everyone should go there before graduating.

> "Another contributor to the goodwill between Hamilton and Colgate? As one student pointed out, 'most locals go on vacation over Spring Party Weekend.'"

With all the partying, most students drink significant amounts of alcohol. But, as many students point out, drinking is not a particular problem on campus. Nevertheless, although there are also social opportunities for those who stay away from the parties, students agree that these are generally limited. Given the number of parties available, it becomes hard for students not to take advantage of them. Plus, since dating is "not the norm" at Colgate, parties seem to facilitate the more prominent random hook-up scene.

Dorms and Diversity

Students at Colgate are generally happy with their freshman housing, which is fortunate because 91 percent of all Colgate students live in residence halls and university-owned houses. Freshmen are required to live in residence halls, but as they move up, they are free to choose between a wide array of options, including townhouses, apartments, and suites. Another way in which Colgate differs from most colleges is that fraternities and sororities must live in university-owned houses. But most students see no problems with on-campus living. "The residences are great," said a student. "There are nice theme houses for upperclassmen."

Colgate is often seen as a relatively rich, upper-class school, and the minority population is still very small, only around 17 percent of the entire student population. Nonetheless, the school tries to attract a more diverse student body, both ethnically and financially. "Colgate is filled with rich, upper-class kids," one student admitted. "But it definitely isn't as preppy as it is made out to be. People are generally laid-back and looking for a good time."

And who wouldn't be laid-back with the serene backdrop of upstate New York and a motivated and fun-loving student body? As one student said, "Colgate is one of those schools that find the right balance between partying and studying. That's why it is so great." When the men of the Baptist Education Society met in 1819, who knew that they would make 13 such a lucky number for 2,750 undergraduates?—*Xiaohang Liu*

FYI
If you come to Colgate, you'd better bring "a worn-in hoodie."
What is the typical weekend schedule? "Friday: happy that it's Friday. Saturday: party time. Sunday: freak out at the amount of work and spend the whole day in library."
If I could change one thing about Colgate, I'd "move campus to a warmer climate."
Three things every student at Colgate should do before graduating are "go to the Jug, sled around the campus, and hit some balls at the driving range overlooking campus."

Columbia University

Address: 1130 Amsterdam Avenue New York, NY 10027
Phone: 212-854-2522
E-mail address: ugrad-ask@columbia.edu
Web site URL: www.studentaffairs.columbia.edu/admissions
Year Founded: 1754
Private or Public: Private
Religious Affiliation: None
Location: Urban
Number of Applicants: 22,584
Percent Accepted: 10%
Percent Accepted who enroll: 58%
Number Entering: 1,431
Number of Transfers Accepted each Year: 109
Middle 50% SAT range: M: 670–780, Cr 660–760, Wr: 650–760
Middle 50% ACT range: 29–34
Early admission program EA/ED/None: ED

Percentage accepted through EA or ED: 25%
EA and ED deadline: 1-Nov
Regular Deadline: 2-Jan
Application Fee: $70
Full time Undergraduate enrollment: 5,678
Total enrollment: 28,518
Percent Male: 53%
Percent Female: 47%
Total Percent Minority or Unreported: 51%
Percent African-American: 11%
Percent Asian/Pacific Islander: 23%
Percent Hispanic: 12%
Percent Native-American: 1%
Percent International: 10%
Percent in-state/out of state: 25%/75%
Percent from Public HS: 57%
Retention Rate: 98%
Graduation Rate 4-year: 85%

Graduation Rate 6-year: 94%
Percent Undergraduates in On-campus housing: 95%
Number of official organized extracurricular organizations: 450
3 Most popular majors: History, Political Science, Engineering
Student/Faculty ratio: 6:1
Average Class Size: 15
Percent of students going to grad school: Unreported
Tuition and Fees: $39,806
In State Tuition and Fees if different: No difference
Cost for Room and Board: $9,980
Percent receiving financial aid out of those who apply, first year: 79%
Percent receiving financial aid among all students: 50%

Established in lower Manhattan in 1754 as King's College by King George II of England, Columbia University has lived up to its original charge of providing an education that would "enlarge the mind, improve the understanding, and polish the whole man." First housed in a schoolhouse adjacent to Trinity Church on lower Broadway, the school moved from the East Side of Manhattan in 1857 and then to its present 36-acre site at the turn of the century. This relocation from a relatively uniform upper-class neighborhood to a far more diverse community, Morningside Heights between the Upper West Side and Harlem, is symbolic of Columbia's metamorphosis from an Anglican colonial college to a vibrant and diverse Ivy League university where free speech, student activism, and community involvement are among its most outstanding attributes.

E Pluribus Unum

Although Columbia College has always been the heart and soul of the university, it was not until the end of the 19th century that the various schools that make up the undergraduate and graduate parts of the school were incorporated under a central administration. It was at this time that the "mining school" established in 1864—that would later evolve into the Fu Foundation School of Engineering and Applied Science—and Barnard College for women came formally under the aegis of the university. At the same time, Columbia Teachers College, the Columbia University School of Law, and the Columbia University School of Medicine were officially integrated into the university system. Finally, in 1897, the newly reorganized entity moved to a new campus at 116th Street and Broadway designed by the celebrated architectural firm of McKim, Mead and White. Today, these magnificent examples of turn-of-the-century urban design, crowned by the Low Memorial Library and the huge plaza that it looks out upon, have been complemented by some rather inharmonious modern buildings, the most controversial of which is the Lerner Student Center. Completed in 1999, the design of the 225,000-square-foot edifice, with its glass walls and escalating ramps, has been nearly universally panned by critics and students alike. "It looks like a huge ant farm," complained one student. "And it is rather hard to socialize on an incline."

Cutting to the Core and Going Swimming

It is impossible to talk about Columbia's academics without immediately referring to what is known as the Core Curriculum, a series of seminar-sized required courses in literature, philosophy, history, music, art, and science that are considered to provide the essentials of a liberal education. While some latitude is afforded in the choice of science classes, courses entitled Contemporary Civilization, Literature Humanities, Art Humanities, Music Humanities, and Frontiers in Science are compulsory. While the Core Curriculum is not for everyone, most agree that it provides an excellent foundation for a liberal arts education. Literature Humanities, a year-long course in Western literature that spans Homer to Virginia Woolf, is a particularly popular class, as is Contemporary Civilization, a course that exposes students to many of the seminal texts dealing with Western philosophy.

"The Core curriculum is one of the reasons I came to Columbia," states a freshman. "The Core exposes you to so many different things you otherwise wouldn't have the chance to study. Every college student should learn from these writers and thinkers." Students find that, to some degree, the Core experience depends on the professors that you get for a particular subject. Opined one coed, "There is some luck involved in fulfilling the Core requirements, since you can't choose your profs for most courses."

In addition to the required courses in literature, philosophy, art, and music, the Core also demands the equivalent of two years of language at the college level and two courses in the Global Core, classes that deal with issues of muticulturalism, race, and gender. This requirement, in fact, is a relatively recent addition to the Core Curriculum, added by the college's Committee on the Core, in reaction to student criticism about the paucity of works by women and non-white, non-Western writers.

A rarity among colleges today, the Core Curriculum mandates that students take a minimum of two courses in physical education. "There are so many offerings," says one sophomore, "that it is always possible to find classes that suit even the most dedicated 'couch potato.'" In addition to the required gym classes, students must be able to swim seventy-five yards in the Uris Pool without resting. Although a seemingly unusual graduation prerequisite, Columbia College is not the only Ivy concerned with whether its undergraduates sink or swim. Cornell and Dartmouth also demand competence in the water.

Students must declare a "major" or a "concentration" (a less extensive version of the major that requires fewer courses) by the end of their sophomore year. Undergraduates may also "double major" or may fulfill the requirements of a major and concentration at the same time. Beyond the Core and the major or concentration, students choose from a wide variety of electives in any department in order to complete the minimum of 124 "points" necessary to graduate.

Location! Location! Location!
Columbia's location in New York, one of the world's greatest cities, is truly one of its most appealing calling cards, and it is not an overstatement to say that New York City can be viewed as an extension of the classroom. Opportunities abound to explore Manhattan's renowned museums (which are free for Columbia students) and to attend the finest theatrical and musical productions. "There are very few classes that meet on Fridays, so weekends start early," states one senior. "Many of us spend Saturday and Sunday afternoons exploring the city." In addition, the culinary diversity of New York lies at the doorstep of the University, as well as nightlife and shopping.

The Living Is Easy
The vast majority of Columbia undergraduates (99 percent of freshmen and 94 percent of upperclassmen) live on campus in university residence halls, and housing is guaranteed to all students throughout their four years. Freshmen choose to live in singles, doubles, or suites in one of five buildings located on the perimeter of South Field, the University's main quadrangle. The suite dorm is considered the most "social," while students looking for a "quieter dorm life" prefer the two mixed-suite dorms. One freshman said, "The dorms are pretty nice and having freshman housing located in one portion of the campus is really conducive to making a lot of friends right away. My floor is very close and my floor mates are my best friends. The all-freshman dorms are very social." Upperclassmen are housed by lottery. Single students share apartments or live in dormitory-style accommodations or studios, while couples generally live in studios and one-bedroom units. Families with dependent children live in "family units."

The area around Columbia University is considered very safe. "The campus is fairly small and very secure," notes a senior. "There is a security guard 24/7 at the entrance to all dorms."

Mealtime
Dining options vary from "meals" served in the John Jay dining hall Monday through Saturday, to "Columbia points" which are redeemable for à la carte selections at twelve locations on campus. While all freshmen are required to enroll in the meal plan, it is optional for upperclassmen. After the first year, students may enroll in "dining dollars" or "flex accounts," both of which have dollar balance accounts accessed through the Columbia Card, the university's ID. Kosher food can be found at the John Jay dining hall and at Barnard College for women, the Columbia affiliate located just across the street from the main campus.

Women at Columbia—the College and Barnard
Columbia College first admitted women in 1983 after merger negotiations with Barnard, an all-female college located across Broadway from Columbia, fell apart. While the University has remained closely affiliated with Barnard and students from Columbia's "sister" school can cross-register with Columbia students and freely participate in extracurricular activities, including athletics, some Columbia women do not always look at their Barnard counterparts as full equals. "Since the admissions criteria are more competitive for women at the College than they are for Barnard women, some classmates of mine consider Barnard students as being not as smart or diverse as Columbia women," said one junior. "Personally, I disagree. I have made many friends at Barnard and they are intelligent and interesting."

Outside of the Classroom
Like all outstanding colleges, the extracurricular life at Columbia is extremely diverse. There are a wide variety of publications including the *Columbia Daily Spectator*, the nation's second-oldest college newspaper, and the *Columbia Review*, the oldest student literary magazine. The *Philolexian Society* is one of the oldest collegiate literary societies in America. Columbia also fields teams in Mock Trial, Model United Nations, and debate.

There are a dozen a cappella groups and numerous musical groups, including the Columbia University Orchestra, the oldest continually performing university orchestra in the nation. Opportunities for theater performance and comedy abound, including Fruit Paunch, Columbia's improv comedy group.

Where the Lions Roar

There are 31 men's and women's sports teams representing the Lions of Columbia. Barnard students participate on the Columbia women's squads. Although the football teams have not fared well in recent years, many other sports teams have. In 2007, the Men's Track Team won the 4 x 800 Penn Relay, the first time that an Ivy League track team was victorious in this event in over three decades. Many of Columbia's athletic facilities can be found at the Baker Athletics Complex, located north of the main campus. This campus includes the football field as well as facilities for baseball, soccer, field hockey, crew, tennis, and track. "Having the football field distant from the main campus is a negative," argues one freshman. "I think that is a big reason why a lot of students do not attend the games. My friends and I would rather hang around campus or go downtown on Saturdays rather than going all the way uptown to see our team lose."

The Social Scene

With the Big Apple at their doorstep, most Columbia students avail themselves of the tremendous cultural and culinary opportunities on the weekends, although social life is usually a blend of on- and off-campus activities. "Most people go out on Thursday nights to relax, because there are only a few classes that meet on Fridays," reports one junior. "We usually sleep in on Fridays and get a head start on work and spend Saturday and Sunday afternoons exploring the city. Most people go off campus to one of the many neighborhood restaurants and bars." Students generally divide their weekend time between the Columbia neighborhood, which is full of nightlife, and downtown Manhattan. "Columbia doesn't have a big party atmosphere," notes a senior. "But students love hanging out together. On the weekends, if the weather is nice, we like relaxing in the floor lounge, hanging out on the steps of Low Library, and having lunch at one of the many on-campus dining locations."

While there are at least 20 fraternities and sororities at Columbia, only about 10 percent of undergrads participate in Greek life. "Frat life is definitely present on campus, but it is far from dominant," reports one sophomore. "You can choose to be very involved in it, or you can get through four years without ever going to a frat party."

A Tradition of Activism

Student activism has long characterized the student body. In 1968, students occupied several campus buildings in protest over the University's participation in the Institute for Defense Analyses, a weapons research agency tied to the Pentagon, and what was perceived as a lack of sensitivity toward the African-American population in neighboring Harlem. In the 1970s and 1980s, there were protests and strikes over the University's investments in companies supporting apartheid in South Africa. In 1996, student protests resulted in the addition of Ethnic Studies to the Core Curriculum. In late 2007, some students went on a hunger strike in protest over Columbia's planned large-scale expansion into Manhattanville, a neighborhood north of the main campus.

Free speech is alive and well at Columbia, regardless of the degree to which such speech goes against the grain. This was evidenced in late 2007 by the visit of Iranian President Mahmoud Ahmadinejad to the campus, a demagogic leader whose anti-American policies are well known. In fall of 2008 alone Columbia University hosted visits from Barack Obama, John McCain, and Hillary Clinton.

Columbia University is, overall, a superb academic institution that prides itself on its emphasis on the well-rounded education of its students. Its Core Curriculum is prime evidence of this, and it is essentially impossible to graduate from Columbia without having developed a broad appreciation for classical academic values. If you love learning, crave the excitement of the Big Apple, and know how to swim, Columbia may be just the school for you.—*Jonathan Berken*

FYI

If you come to Columbia, you'd better bring "a subway map."

What is a typical weekend schedule? "Sleep in on Fridays and get some work done. Explore the city Saturday and Sunday afternoons and hang out with friends on Saturday night."

If I could change one thing about Columbia, I'd "improve the advising system."

Three things that every student at Columbia should do before graduating are "get lost in the city with friends at two in the morning, eat a gigantic slice of Koronet's pizza, and hang out on the steps of Low Library."

The Cooper Union for the Advancement of Science and Art

Address: 30 Cooper Square New York, NY 10003
Phone: 212-353-4120
E-mail address: admissions@cooper.edu
Web site URL: www.cooper.edu
Year Founded: 1859
Private or Public: Private
Religious Affiliation: None
Location: Urban
Number of Applicants: 3,055
Percent Accepted: 9%
Percent Accepted who enroll: 73%
Number Entering: 206
Number of Transfers Accepted each Year: 40
Middle 50% SAT range: M: 640–780, CR: 620–710, **Wr:** Unreported
Middle 50% ACT range: 29–33
Early admission program EA/ED/None: ED
Percentage accepted through EA or ED: 16%

EA and ED deadline: 1-Dec
Regular Deadline: 1-Jan
Application Fee: $65
Full time Undergraduate enrollment: 917
Total enrollment: 969
Percent Male: 64%
Percent Female: 36%
Total Percent Minority or Unreported: 58%
Percent African-American: 5%
Percent Asian/Pacific Islander: 17%
Percent Hispanic: 7%
Percent Native-American: <1%
Percent International: 16%
Percent in-state/out of state: 60%/40%
Percent from Public HS: 65%
Retention Rate: 92%
Graduation Rate 4-year: 67%
Graduation Rate 6-year: 70%

Percent Undergraduates in On-campus housing: 20%
Number of official organized extracurricular organizations: 90
3 Most popular majors: Electrical, Electronics and Communications Engineering, Fine Arts and Art Studies, Mechanical Engineering
Student/Faculty ratio: 8.5:1
Average Class Size: 10 to 19
Percent of students going to grad school: 60%
Tuition and Fees: $35,000
In State Tuition and Fees if different: No difference
Cost for Room and Board: $13,700
Percent receiving financial aid out of those who apply, first year: 50%
Percent receiving financial aid among all students: 30%

Located in the heart of the Big Apple, The Cooper Union for the Advancement of Science and Art consists of five buildings and about 900 students residing in Manhattan's Cooper Square. Founded by philanthropist Peter Cooper in 1859, the institution is unique among its peers in that every admitted student is granted a $33,000 full tuition scholarship.

Known for its highly selective admission standards and tightly knit community, Cooper Union offers students a challenging and fun time in a diverse environment. Though only about 36 percent of students are female, and over half of the student population is from New York State, one student remarked, "Overall, Cooper is probably the most diverse school in the country. It is truly a reflection of New York City. I think at least 75 percent of the people here speak another language fluently."

A School of Polar Opposites

Cooper Union is composed of three different schools: the Irwin S. Chanin School of Architecture, the School of Art and the highly ranked School of Engineering. According to the admissions office, the average freshman class includes about 220 students—35 in architecture, 65 in art, and 120 in engineering.

Students in each of the three schools at Cooper Union have the majority of their course schedule planned for them when they enroll. In addition to the classes relevant to a student's specialty, every student must take general academic requirements within the first two years in order to fulfill his or her degree requirements. These requirements primarily include seminars in literature, history and government as well as other areas of the humanities and the social sciences. Art and architecture students must also take several natural science classes. Students do not have much flexibility in course selection until junior and senior years when they can more freely choose from a variety of electives.

Some students feel that the engineering, art and architecture students naturally divide themselves into different social circles. A chemical engineering graduate commented on the engineering school's intimidating reputation: "Cooper is very hard. I did not give it the time it deserved in order to excel. So, I graduated with a GPA which still haunts me to this day."

> "Overall, Cooper is probably the most diverse school in the country—it is truly a reflection of New York City. I think at least 75 percent of the people here speak another language fluently."

Despite the academic rigor of the engineering programs, the student added that attending Cooper Union was "the best" choice he had made in his life. "Yes, it takes work, but the more of yourself you put into something, the more you get out." Another student expressed the strength of the small community that the school fosters, exclaiming "I absolutely love it. It's a ton of work, but it's great."

A Test with No Solutions

Cooper prides itself on its selection process, especially for art and architecture school applicants. At the annual open-house and portfolio days every fall, prospective art and architecture students can meet with professors who comprise the selection committee and receive feedback on their portfolio. Talent—rather than SAT scores or GPA—is key in getting into Cooper.

The emphasis on evaluating and developing talent is part of the philosophy behind the institution's "home test." The home test is a relatively abstract assignment which enables the admissions committee to assess a student's talents and creativity in a standardized manner. There is a different "home test" for the architecture and art programs. Each one consists of a number of artistic projects to be completed within one month and returned to Cooper Union for review.

Once accepted students enroll, they can request gallery access to design an exhibition of their work. Several galleries around campus are available to exhibit the work of students and outside artists in solo and group shows. The annual student exhibition prior to commencement each year celebrates the work of art and architecture students at all levels.

Living On Your Own

Cooper Union's student residences are located across the street from the School of Engineering. Suites vary in size from three to five people with most being two-bedroom units shared by four people. Each unit contains a bedroom, bathroom, and kitchenette and each apartment building contains a study, laundry room, and common room. "The living area is usually much smaller than the bedrooms, so you will end up spending most of your time in the bedrooms," one student remarked. "However, the bedrooms are huge compared to what you would normally get in a New York City apartment for the price, and you will have, at most, one roommate."

On the top floor of the student residences are rooms affectionately known as lofts. The lofts are, in the words of one student, "very tall rooms that do not have separate sleeping areas and living areas." Artists in particular tend to like the lofts because they offer a lot of space to hang artwork, as well as providing different views of the city.

Student residence housing is only available for 178 students, and Cooper does not guarantee housing past the first year. Students who cannot secure a place in the student residence are faced with the responsibility of finding a residence in the city. While many students enjoy this challenge and freedom, others find it to be a deterring obstacle.

One plus of living off campus is that, instead of eating campus food, students eat at local restaurants or cook their own meals. "There are so many options to choose from," one student said, adding that "the food here is some of the best (food) anywhere."

Extracurricular Activities

Each school at Cooper Union has its own student council, each with its own unique constitution. The three councils also combine into the joint student council to discuss issues that affect the entire student body. Students also run a newspaper, though circulation and regular publication is difficult due in part to the fact that all upperclassmen live off campus. Cooper also sponsors a variety of cultural, ethnic and religious organizations, as well as community service clubs, art, and drama clubs and clubs that are more geared toward improving the social atmosphere on campus. While each club attracts its own aficionados, very few boast large numbers or a dedicated membership.

Campus athletics is virtually nonexistent at Cooper. There is very little commitment to intramural sports. Some students complain that the minimal athletic facilities of Cooper Union are in poor condition. Greek life also has a very limited presence on campus. Only 10 percent of male students are part of one of the two national fraternities on campus, and only 5 percent of female students are members of the local sorority.

Engineering and architecture students face particularly rigorous curriculums, so many regularly forego their social opportunities to spend time on class work. Art students often have more mobility to experience the New York City nightlife, visiting clubs and checking out the museums and Broadway shows on the weekends. Overall, all students say they love the New York atmosphere.

An Incubator for Social Progress and Creativity

Cooper Union has long been a source of many social and progressive movements. Within a year of its inception the Great Hall at Cooper Union was the site of a passionate debate between Abraham Lincoln and Stephen Douglass. Since then, the Hall has featured American Presidents Grant, Cleveland, Taft, Theodore Roosevelt, Wilson, Clinton, and Obama. Today the Great Hall remains a site for prominent performances and lectures.

The NAACP and the Red Cross were both initially organized at Cooper Union, and Susan B. Anthony located her offices there. Cooper has also been host to some of the more creative and optimistic people in the 20th century. Supreme Court Justice and ACLU founding member Felix Frankfurter attended Cooper Union and Thomas Edison enrolled in class there. Mark Twain, Samuel Gompers and Betty Friedan are also among the many influential and progressive individuals to speak at Cooper Union.

Bruce Degen, illustrator of the bestselling "Magic School Bus" children's book series, is a more recent alum of Cooper Union, and he calls Cooper Union "something that changed my life."—*Mark Schneider*

FYI

If you come to Cooper Union, you'd better bring "extra spending money for weekend activities, art supplies, and textbooks. Living in New York is expensive!"

What's the typical weekend schedule? "Eating out for dinner and studying (or painting) on Thursdays and/or Fridays, a concert, museum, movie, Broadway show, sporting event, night club or road trip on Saturdays, and hanging out and catching up on work on Sunday."

If I could change one thing about Cooper Union, "I'd expand the housing options to accommodate more students who have difficulty finding a place to live for the semester."

Three things every student at Cooper Union should do before graduating are "experience New York, get to know your professors and classmates well, and display your work in a student exhibition if you're an art student or compete in the annual egg-drop contest if you're an engineering student."

Cornell University

Address: 410 Thurston
Avenue Ithaca, NY 14850
Phone: 607-255-5241
E-mail address:
admissions@cornell.edu
Web site URL: www.cornell.edu
Year Founded: 1865
Private or Public: Private
Religious Affiliation: None
Location: Suburban
Number of Applicants:
25,617
Percent Accepted: 25%
**Percent Accepted who
enroll:** 47%
Number Entering: 3,010
**Number of Transfers
Accepted each Year:** 768
Middle 50% SAT range:
M: 660–760, Cr: 620–730,
Wr: 670–740
Middle 50% ACT range: 28–32
**Early admission program
EA/ED/None:** ED

**Percentage accepted
through EA or ED:** 37%
EA and ED deadline: 1-Nov
Regular Deadline: 1-Jan
Application Fee: $65
**Full time Undergraduate
enrollment:** 13,523
Total enrollment: 18,885
Percent Male: 51%
Percent Female: 49%
**Total Percent Minority or
Unreported:** 58%
Percent African-American: 5%
**Percent Asian/Pacific
Islander:** 16%
Percent Hispanic: 6%
Percent Native-American: 1%
Percent International: 8%
**Percent in-state/out of
state:** 38%/62%
Percent from Public HS:
Unreported
Retention Rate: 96%
Graduation Rate 4-year: 84%

Graduation Rate 6-year: 92%
**Percent Undergraduates in
On-campus housing:** 46%
**Percent affiliated with Greek
system:** 50%
**Number of official organized
extracurricular
organizations:** 823
3 Most popular majors:
Business, Engineering, Biology
Student/Faculty ratio: 9:1
Average Class Size: 20 to 29
**Percent of students going to
grad school:** 71%
Tuition and Fees: $34,600
**In State Tuition and Fees if
different:** No difference
Cost for Room and Board:
$11,190
**Percent receiving financial
aid out of those who apply,
first year:** 88%
**Percent receiving financial
aid among all students:** 40%

The youngest of the eight Ivy League institutions, Cornell University is well known both domestically and internationally as one of the premier educational establishments in the world. It boasts an immense array of resources and opportunities for its 13,500 undergraduates. In addition, its location at the southern tip of the beautiful Finger Lakes gives the prestigious university a lovely learning environment—to the delight of all who enjoy the quiet, intimate atmosphere of small college towns and the chagrin of those who prefer the lively ambiance of big cities. If you would like to study in a large, top-notch institution and do not mind a rather removed location, Cornell ought to be among your top college choices.

Enjoyment of Nature

"The beautiful campus is the reason I came to Cornell," said one student. Indeed, for all those who enjoy nature, Cornell is certainly the place to be. It is located at the southern end of Cayuga Lake in the Finger Lakes region of upstate New York. The university takes pride in its two beautiful gorges, which offer the students small areas of wildlife right in the middle of campus. Many students take the gorge trails on their way to classes to enjoy sight of the numerous waterfalls that dot the creeks. The school's location in the valley of Cayuga Lake also means that there are a lot of hills. In fact, Cornell is situated on the East Hill, which overlooks the city of Ithaca. This poses considerable inconveniences to the students. As one sophomore pointed out, "The hilly roads sometimes just make you not want to go to classes, especially during the winter."

Ithaca is a stereotypical college town, and Cornell is certainly its dominant institution. In fact, there are only about 30,000 people living in the city, a small figure considering that 20,000 students are enrolled at Cornell. Ithaca Commons is the most important downtown business hub. However, Collegetown, the southern part of the campus, also has some commercial areas and is much more accessible to students.

Despite the natural beauty, Cornell is certainly remote and hardly accessible to any major cities. "We don't even have a highway around," said one student. "You have to drive around hill after hill to get to Cornell." The location issue is certainly one of the major complaints and an important factor to consider for prospective students. "Cornell is in the middle of nowhere," remarked one student. "So if you like to leave campus for the weekend once in a while, it might not be a good idea to come here."

Private and Public

Cornell is unique among Ivy League schools for its distinct status as both a private and a public institution. The schools of Agriculture and Life Sciences, Human Ecology, and Industrial and Labor Relations are public schools. New York residents can pay about $15,000 less tuition when attending those three colleges. Other than that, "there is really no difference between the public and private parts of Cornell," said one student. "The quality of teaching is the same for all of them."

The seven colleges at Cornell include some highly specialized ones, such as Industrial and Labor Relations and Hotel Management, and broader ones, such as the College of Arts and Sciences, which is also the largest with more than 4,000 students. Also popular are the College of Agriculture and the College of Engineering, which attract most of those who are interested in science and engineering. High school students apply to one of the specific schools during the admission process, which is highly competitive for every school, as the admit rate is slightly over 20%.

The rural environment of Cornell might turn away some students, but the academics for such a large and resourceful university can be tailored to satisfy almost any kind of learner. "In terms of academics, we have something for everyone," said one student. The school offers about 80 majors, including several unusual ones such as Fiber Science and Apparel Design. Since the Finger Lakes region is also the second largest producer of wine in the United States, Cornell is well known for offering several classes in wine tasting, which are very popular.

The class size at Cornell varies widely. For freshmen, the introductory lectures are quite large, many with hundreds of students. "Some big lecture classes can have 500 people, and the personal attention that students often get at smaller schools is almost nonexistent here," said one student. Indeed, for those classes, the students almost exclusively deal with teaching assistants, not professors. For upperclassmen, the choices of classes broaden, and students can enjoy a huge selection of both large lectures and small seminars. "We have so many different opportunities," said one student. "So it is very important for the students to take advantage of them."

The coursework at Cornell is very challenging. "All incoming students should expect a lot of work," said one sophomore. The different colleges at Cornell have separate guidelines for graduation requirements, which tend to be extensive. One student said, "The required courses are sometimes good, but most of them are simply not useful." In addition, Cornell University mandates that all students take two semesters of physical education or an equivalent such as joining a sports team or even the marching band. In addition, everyone is required to pass a swim test.

Best Food

Cornell offers a variety of housing options. Most freshmen choose the traditional dorm buildings, but they also have the opportunity of living in Balch Hall, which is for first-year women only, the Townhouse Community, or one of the nine Program Houses, which are themed buildings that gather students of similar interests. Freshmen live in North Campus so that they get to know each other during their first year. The students are generally satisfied with their housing assignments, and there are generally plenty of singles available. One student pointed out, "compared to dorms in most other colleges, Cornell offers more choices, which is generally a good thing." Upperclassmen have even more options, and many of them live off-campus.

> "In terms of academics, we have something for everyone."

Cornell is known to have one of the nation's best dining services. There are 31 dining locations on campus, ranging from all-you-can-eat dining halls to à la carte cafés. In addition, there are three convenience stores to serve all those looking for snacks or daily necessities. Nevertheless, despite these excellent campus services, some upperclassmen do point out that "because of Cornell's reputation, many students' expectations of dining halls are too high when they first come here."

Fraternities

There are more than 60 fraternities and sororities at Cornell, and they boast 30% of the student population. These numbers mean that Greek life is an important part of Cornell's social scene. Freshmen especially tend to frequent the numerous frat parties during weekends. Drinking is, of course, one of the main activities there, but those who do not drink are not left out of the social scene. "If you don't drink, there are certainly a lot of activities that you are missing out on, but it's a big school. You can find many people who don't .drink and still have fun," said one student.

The life of a student at Cornell can be summarized in one word: choices. Whether it is dining, classes, housing, or weekend parties, the university offers its students a great number of options and a tremendous array of opportunities to explore. Despite its removed location and the lack of personal attention often associated with large institutions, Cornell, with the resources and reputation of a world-class university, is still a top choice for those looking for an exciting and challenging college experience.—*Xiaohang Liu*

FYI

If you come to Cornell, you'd better bring "a bicycle to ride around campus."

What is the typical weekend schedule? "Just like most universities: parties Friday and Saturday nights, and recovering from the parties the rest of the time."

If I could change one thing about Cornell, I'd "move it next to New York City."

Three things every student at Cornell should do before graduating are "travel to every part of the campus—there is always something to discover, go to every single dining hall, and go swimming in the gorge, if you dare."

Eastman School of Music

Address: 26 Gibbs Street Rochester, NY 14604
Phone: 716-274-1060
E-mail address: admissions@esm.rochester.edu
Web site URL: www.rochester.edu/eastman
Year Founded: 1921
Private or Public: Private
Religious Affiliation: None
Location: Urban
Number of Applicants: 917
Percent Accepted: 29%
Percent Accepted who enroll: 47%
Number Entering: 125
Number of Transfers Accepted each Year: 20
Middle 50% SAT range: Unreported
Middle 50% ACT range: 22–28
Early admission program EA/ED/None: None

Percentage accepted through EA or ED: NA
EA and ED deadline: NA
Regular Deadline: Rolling
Application Fee: $100
Full time Undergraduate enrollment: 500
Total enrollment: 900
Percent Male: 45%
Percent Female: 55%
Total Percent Minority or Unreported: 11%
Percent African-American: 3%
Percent Asian/Pacific Islander: 6%
Percent Hispanic: 2%
Percent Native-American: 1%
Percent International: Unreported
Percent in-state/out of state: 17%/83%
Percent from Public HS: 80%
Retention Rate: 89%

Graduation Rate 4-year: 72%
Graduation Rate 6-year: 86%
Percent Undergraduates in On-campus housing: 73%
Number of official organized extracurricular organizations: 8
3 Most popular majors: Music
Student/Faculty ratio: 4:1
Average Class Size: 5
Percent of students going to grad school: 79%
Tuition and Fees: $20,320
In State Tuition and Fees if different: No difference
Cost for Room and Board: $7,152
Percent receiving financial aid out of those who apply, first year: Unreported
Percent receiving financial aid among all students: 70%

Do you love music? Not just as a hobby, but as your life? Do you love music enough to practice until you get calluses from playing your instrument for so long? Enough to sing not just in the shower, but for hours at a time? If you do, you probably already know about this world-renowned music school. At the Eastman School of Music, serious musicians can immerse themselves in an environment where everyone thinks about, listens to, or plays music 24 hours a day.

Learning About Music

Eastman provides its students with a rigorous and thorough musical education as well as a solid humanities background. Most students are performance majors (the technical name is "applied music"). The next most popular majors are music education, composition and theory. The performance major requires three years of theory, two years of music history—covering everything from Gregorian chants to contemporary music—and, of course, weekly lessons. Performance majors must be competent piano players regardless of their chosen instrument. All performance majors must take Piano 101 and 102, or test out of this requirement. Eastman also has a humanities requirement, which can be filled with a one-semester Freshman Writing Seminar; courses in literature, history, languages, and philosophy; or a combination of these. Eastman students are serious about their humanities classes as well as their music, and classes are not easy. As one undergrad explained, "It seems like either you do really well or you completely fail." By senior year, most of Eastman's requirements are out of the way and students have more flexible schedules that allow them to audition for jobs or graduate school.

> **"It's not like a big old party school."**

Students interested in a 50:50 type course load between their liberal arts or science studies and their music concentration can pursue a B.A. or B.S. program at Eastman. Following this track, students take 40–60 percent of their courses in their music concentration of choice, compared to 80–90 percent for those pursuing a Bachelor of Music.

Because Eastman is part of the University of Rochester, students have access to the University's libraries and other facilities. Some of the humanities classes are held on the U of R campus, although as one student said, "You can make it all four years without leaving this campus." The reason many like to stay on the Eastman campus is the 15- to 20-minute bus ride to the U of R.

Students who apply to Eastman can ask to work with a particular professor, and many choose the school primarily to do just that. One student, for example, said he met his cello teacher at a summer music camp and decided to go to Eastman so he could continue to study with her. Some popular professors include clarinetist Kenneth Grant, pianist Barry Snyder and flautist Bonita Boyd. The members of the Cleveland String Quartet also teach at Eastman and attract many to their classes and concerts. Students have substantial contact with faculty members, both in lessons and in other contexts such as chamber groups.

Living and Breathing Music
Everything at Eastman revolves around music. The musical motif on campus is inescapable; the snack bar is called the Orchestra Pit and the newspaper is called *Clef Notes*. Students rave about their "access to music on hand anytime." They can go to concerts every night if they want to; Eastman's calendar is filled with student and faculty performances by soloists and groups in the Eastman Theater, concerts every other week by the Rochester Philharmonic Orchestra (Eastman students get free tickets), and limitless other performances. Eastman's Sibley Library also has an enormous music collection (the second-largest in the nation), including books, manuscripts and recordings of "just about everything," one student said. Whenever undergrads want to listen to music but just can't find a concert to go to, they can always listen to their favorite symphony or opera at the library. Students who want to participate in athletics, student government and other nonmusical extracurricular activities can journey over to the University of Rochester campus.

For those with the energy to play for more than the three to six hours they're expected to practice each day, there are plenty of opportunities to perform. Some students give several recitals a year, while others only do one in their four years at school. Many undergrads participate in chamber orchestras, quartets or other small ensembles, either for credit or for fun. Jazz bands and string quartets are in constant demand at local restaurants and bars. Traveling Broadway shows that come to Rochester sometimes need a player to fill in and look to Eastman students for help. Students also have many chances to play at church services, weddings and other special events.

Few Distractions
The Eastman campus is small, with just three buildings located in the heart of downtown Rochester: Eastman Commons, Sibley Library and a classroom building. The food at the cafeteria is "pretty normal," according to one student. "It's got a salad and pasta bar, burgers and fries, and a frozen yogurt machine." In the dorm, freshmen live in doubles, and all upperclassmen have singles. Moving off campus is a popular option for juniors and seniors, but freshmen and sophomores are required to live on campus. Many students prefer the dorm

because the surrounding neighborhood reportedly "isn't the greatest." Dorm life exposes students to an environment where everyone knows everyone else and has the same interests, so life can get a little boring. For those who need to get away, popular options include the Rochester Club, which features jazz every Friday night, and the Spaghetti Warehouse. Students also like to hang out and "go crazy" at nearby dance clubs in downtown Rochester.

Campus social life is somewhat limited. As one student explained, "It's not like a big old party school." For those who favor the Greek scene, there is one all-male fraternity, one sorority and one coed fraternity. The all-male and all-female groups each have a floor of the 14-story Eastman Commons to themselves. The all-male fraternity sponsors most of the parties, while the other Greek groups focus on community service work. Eastman

has two annual formals, one in the fall and one in the spring. Small parties in the dorm are common; one student remarked that the delivery truck from a local liquor store is frequently spotted outside the dorm. Students don't seem to mind the low-key social scene; as one sophomore pointed out, "The fewer distractions, the easier it is to concentrate on practicing—which is good, I guess."

Freshmen typically arrive at Eastman from all corners of the world with visions of their names in lights. Each dreams of being the next great viola player, soprano soloist or jazz pianist. These dreams become transformed over the next few years into more realistic aspirations. One junior explained that it doesn't matter to her whether she ends up as the soloist with a major symphony or a player in a community orchestra: "As long as I'm playing, that's cool with me."—*Susanna Chu*

FYI
If you come to Eastman, you'd better bring, "a lamp, because the dorms don't have overhead lighting."
What is the typical weekend schedule? "Practice and go to concerts."
If I could change one thing about Eastman, I would "change the weather!"
Three things every student at Eastman should do before graduating are "attend a seminar by a world-famous musician, play every instrument once and go see Niagara Falls."

Eugene Lang College

Address: 65 W 11th Street Rm. 353 New York, NY 10011
Phone: 212-229-5665
E-mail address: langadmission@newschool .edu
Web site URL: www.newschool.edu/lang
Year Founded: 1978
Private or Public: Private
Religious Affiliation: None
Location: Urban
Number of Applicants: 1,670
Percent Accepted: 63%
Percent Accepted who enroll: 30%
Number Entering: 321
Number of Transfers Accepted each Year: 239
Middle 50% SAT range: M: 490–610, CR: 555–665, Wr: 560–660
Middle 50% ACT range: 23–28
Early admission program EA/ED/None: ED

Percentage accepted through EA or ED: Unreported
EA and ED deadline: 15-Nov
Regular Deadline: 1-Feb
Application Fee: $50
Full time Undergraduate enrollment: 1,294
Total enrollment: 1,294
Percent Male: 31%
Percent Female: 69%
Total Percent Minority or Unreported: 39%
Percent African-American: 4%
Percent Asian/Pacific Islander: 5%
Percent Hispanic: 6%
Percent Native-American: <1%
Percent International: 4%
Percent in-state/out of state: 32%/68%
Percent from Public HS: Unreported
Retention Rate: 73%

Graduation Rate 4-year: 35%
Graduation Rate 6-year: 47%
Percent Undergraduates in On-campus housing: 27%
Number of official organized extracurricular organizations: 34
3 Most popular majors: Unreported
Student/Faculty ratio: 15:1
Average Class Size: 10 to 19
Percent of students going to grad school: Unreported
Tuition and Fees: $33,060
In State Tuition and Fees if different: No difference
Cost for Room and Board: $12,390
Percent receiving financial aid out of those who apply, first year: 71%
Percent receiving financial aid among all students: 51%

Students at Eugene Lang College know that theirs is not the typical college experience. They wouldn't have it any other way. "There was nowhere else I could see myself going," said one student. "I had to come to Eugene Lang." Eugene Lang College, also known as The New School for Liberal Arts, is one of eight colleges that comprise The New School, located in New York City's Greenwich Village. Founded in 1919 by a small group of intellectuals, The New School began as a forum for discussion, inviting the public to its lectures and encouraging dissent. Over the next 70 years, The New School founded seven other divisions, or colleges, including a design school and a program in jazz and contemporary music. Students apply to one of The New School's eight branches, but they reap the benefits of the close partnership of the divisions. Depending on their program of study, students are allowed to take a certain number of classes at other divisions of The New School. Students also report a great deal of "non-academic interaction" between students in different divisions, as residence halls are not divided by college, and school-sponsored events bring New School students together.

An Engaging Environment

Students agree that the school's philosophy of learning distinguishes it from other colleges. Classes at Eugene Lang are virtually all seminars, though recently a two-lecture requirement was instituted for all students. Still, at Eugene Lang, the focus is on small classes and intense discussion. Students praised the richness of the classroom environment: "Students bring so many different arenas of thought into the classes, which make the classes deep and meaningful." The curriculum at Lang is highly interdisciplinary, with such programs as Arts in Context—the study of fine or performing arts in the context of the liberal arts—and Cultural Studies and Media. Furthermore, Eugene Lang is committed to developing exceptional writers. Writing is one of the most popular concentrations at Lang (which does not have "majors"), and one student pointed out that "even if you're not in the writing program, classes at Lang are writing-intensive." All freshmen are required to take a year-long writing class, about which students had mixed opinions. One student found the first semester of the class, on essay-writing, to be unhelpful, but she raved about the class's second semester, which surveyed methods of research. In general, however, students had nothing but praise for the academic experience at Eugene Lang. The small seminars allow for a high level of engagement with the material, students claim, and Lang's interdisciplinary approach fosters an uncommon academic experience. "People think hard about what they are reading and how it applies to their lives," one student said.

To Dorm or Not to Dorm?

Lang freshmen are guaranteed housing, and most choose to live on campus. Students reflected positively on their experience in dorms, pointing out that dorm life introduced them to the Lang community and often helped establish lasting relationships. Students from different divisions of The New School live together in the dorms, and one student praised this integration as a means of "bringing different people together to share their experiences, which is what The New School is all about." Loeb Hall is particularly coveted, since University Health Services are located there. The New School's dorms include many rooms with in-suite kitchens, making on-campus living an attractive alternative to finding an apartment in the city. What's more, with the exception of two, all dorms are located close to campus, while off-campus students must pay more to live close by, or, more often, live in Brooklyn and endure the hassle of commuting to school.

Regardless, most students choose to live off campus after their freshman year. One upperclassman claimed that choosing to live on campus as an upperclassman was "a bad decision, because you're over the freshman thing—yelling in the dorms and going out a lot—but you're living with freshmen."

Because of the popularity of off-campus living, most Lang students have moderate or minimal interaction with the school's food service. Students who live on campus must purchase a meal plan, though depending on the dorm in which they live, students may be able to choose a less inclusive plan. One student maintained, "You can get better food around the city for the same price," though he did point out that the cafeterias are conveniently located.

Student Politics and Bizarre Bars

Students at Eugene Lang are involved in both the campus community and the city community. Students claim that there is "a lot of programming for people looking for a college community," including frequent, sponsored events such as conferences, lectures and readings. But students also point out that many Lang students are more interested in exploring New York City than becoming involved in the Lang community. One student admitted that Lang is "infamous for not having much community" but added that this is "a superficial judgment." Indeed, many students enjoy off-campus parties that are "packed with Lang students." In conclusion, most students enjoy the opportunity to immerse oneself in the culture of New York and "make friends all over the city" while having the chance to "make of the Lang community what you want to make of it." Students point out that the interaction between Eugene Lang and the city is essential to the college's mission to integrate the arts and ideas of the city into the learning process. For example, many classes send students out into the city to study its religious culture or art.

> "Students bring so many different arenas of thought into the classes, which make the classes deep and meaningful."

One group of students, however, is committed to building community at Lang. The Lang Student Union, which is a consensus-based rather than representative body, meets regularly and is open to all Lang students. Student Union facilitators present proposals, which a single student has the power to block. Students speak highly of the consensus system, claiming that "it's rare that a compromise can't be reached" through negotiation. One Student Union facilitator highlighted a difficulty of the consensus system, however, pointing out that at a school as diverse as Lang, it's often difficult for students to agree on what they want.

Lang students are busy off campus as well. Many students work in the city, often as event promoters or party planners. As a result, many Lang students have ins at exclusive New York clubs. Otherwise, the weekend finds Lang students at apartment parties or nearby bars and clubs such as French Roast (a combination restaurant, bar and café), Cooper 35 (a freshman hangout), and the Bulgarian Culture Club. One student described Lang haunts as "weird places, with cheap drinks, that are on the verge of being incredibly bizarre."

One thing Lang students don't experience on the weekend is the college football game. There are no varsity sports teams at Lang, and there are a few IMs coordinated through the local YMCA, but students say that they are not popular. Lang does offer less traditional physical activities, such as Capoeira, yoga, salsa dancing and meditation. One student recalled an epic dodgeball game, organized by a cultural studies professor, with particular fondness. But those looking for a traditional sports scene should look elsewhere.

To be sure, Eugene Lang is not your typical college. As students point out, taking the road less traveled is in Lang's nature: "The courses at Lang encourage you to think about things in different ways," said one student. "You piece together your own history."—*Kathleen Reeves*

FYI
If you come to Eugene Lang, you'd better bring "Said's *On Orientalism* and Foucault's *Discipline and Punish*, which are central to Eugene Lang's canon."

What's the typical weekend schedule? "The weekend starts on Thursday night. Friday is free for jobs, sleeping in or museum visits, and Friday and Saturday nights, we head to bars, coffee shops or apartment parties or visit friends at other schools around the city."

If you could change one thing about Eugene Lang, it'd be "the bureaucracy. Communication between the administration and the student body is often mediocre, and it's hard to get things changed or implement new programs."

Three things every student at Eugene Lang should do before graduating are "attend a reading by professors in the Writing Concentration, or read your own at an open mic event; read *The Weekly Observer*, an online publication, to find out about the many school-sponsored events, such as Air America tapings or a social justice conference; and attend a Student Union meeting."

Fordham University

Address: 441 East Fordham Road Bronx, NY 10458
Phone: 718-817-4000
E-mail address: enroll@fordham.edu
Web site URL: www.fordham.edu
Year Founded: 1841
Private or Public: Private
Religious Affiliation: Roman Catholic-Jesuit
Location: Urban
Number of Applicants: 18,161
Percent Accepted: 47%
Percent Accepted who enroll: 20%
Number Entering: 1,702
Number of Transfers Accepted each Year: 683
Middle 50% SAT range: M: 560–660, CR: 570–670, Wr: 560–660
Middle 50% ACT range: 25–29
Early admission program EA/ED/None: EA

Percentage accepted through EA or ED: Unreported
EA and ED deadline: 1-Nov
Regular Deadline: 15-Jan
Application Fee: $50
Full time Undergraduate enrollment: 7,994
Total enrollment: 13,181
Percent Male: 37%
Percent Female: 63%
Total Percent Minority or Unreported: 37%
Percent African-American: 6%
Percent Asian/Pacific Islander: 6%
Percent Hispanic: 12%
Percent Native-American: <1%
Percent International: 2%
Percent in-state/out of state: 54%/46%
Percent from Public HS: 47%
Retention Rate: 90%

Graduation Rate 4-year: 71%
Graduation Rate 6-year: 76%
Percent Undergraduates in On-campus housing: 56%
Number of official organized extracurricular organizations: 133
3 Most popular majors: Business, Communication, Social Sciences
Student/Faculty ratio: 12:1
Average Class Size: 10 to 19
Percent of students going to grad school: 25%
Tuition and Fees: $35,257
In State Tuition and Fees if different: No difference
Cost for Room and Board: Included
Percent receiving financial aid out of those who apply, first year: 74%
Percent receiving financial aid among all students: 63%

Combining the best of both worlds, Fordham is a small school in a big city. Featuring main campuses in Manhattan (Lincoln Center) the Bronx (Rose Hill), and most recently, Westchester, the school fosters an intimate environment while offering all the opportunities of New York City. One sophomore said, "The school is small enough that I always know at least two people who I am going out with, but it's also big enough so that I am meeting new people every day."

Up Close and Personal

The small school environment is something that Fordham students cannot praise enough. One junior gushed about how pleasant it was "to be more than just a name on the roster." The average class size is 22 and lectures hold about 40 students. The very few large lectures that the college offers hold about 100 people and are broken up into smaller discussion sections. There is also an atmosphere of intimacy with the professors, all of whom carry the reputation of being very accessible and keen to form long-term academic relationships with students.

The Fordham curriculum features an extensive list of requirements that dominate freshman and sophomore schedules. In the spirit of a true liberal arts education, the core strives to expose students to everything from math and English to theology, fine arts, and foreign languages. One junior complained that because of the core, "it's frustrating when the time comes to pick a major because you don't get into those classes until junior year." The wide variety of programs offered at Fordham does not make it easier to choose—the school's College of Business Administration, honors program, dance program, and the superb theater program are just a few of the many programs that stand out.

When it comes to academics, Fordham prides itself on rejecting grade inflation; students bemoan the grading curve as rather harsh and are used to working hard both inside and outside the classroom to earn their good grades. The introductory Accounting class is especially notorious for its level of difficulty. However, to compensate there are Music History and Life on Planet Earth which are both known to be gut courses.

Work Hard, Play in New York City

The absence of Greek life on campus escapes the notice of most Fordham students. This is no surprise, however, as the students have New York City as their playground. The freshmen are known to frequent The Jolly Tinker, also known as Tinkers, a local bar. One sophomore explained, "As an upperclassmen, you become more independent and Tinkers gets old." The students from Rose Hill campus center their social life mainly around what is known as the tri-bar area: Ziggy's, Mugzy's, and Howl at the Moon INC (or Howl for short). Meanwhile, the more centrally located students of Lincoln Center go out to various Manhattan hotspots. The technically dry campus and presence of RAs discourages dorm parties; however, it is not unusual to hear of a house party at the apartment of one of the many upperclassmen who live off campus.

One junior described the social scene as revolving around the "work hard, play hard" mentality. People are very social and go out every weekend, and since the majority of students are able to avoid Wednesday classes, Tuesday night is also a popular choice for a fun night out. Fordham is a dry campus, meaning that students cannot have alcohol unless everyone in the room is 21. Despite the restrictions, drinking is a prominent feature on campus, and drugs, while more subdued, are not uncommon. The school, however, does make an effort to provide fun events such as Homecoming, President's Ball, and Spring Weekend. The Lincoln Center campus also features endless theater and other fine arts performances, which are popular among the students.

While the school is "definitely a clique school" as one junior described it, people are generally friendly and easy to meet. Friends are made mostly through classes, but also through dorms and extracurricular activities. A typical student of Rose Hill campus is described as "well-outfitted with designer labels and likely to be from New Jersey, Connecticut, or Long Island." The more colorful and diverse Lincoln Center campus is composed of mostly international and artsy crowds. Lack of diversity is a common complaint about the university, although the various cultural groups such as the Philippine-American Club and the Hispanic club El Grito de Lares are prominent on campus and organize a variety of cultural events.

The Fordham Bubble

Despite the urban location, the picturesque campus is a bubble into which students can escape. Gothic architecture, well-kept grassy areas, and the occasional good ghost story (the campus has been featured as one of the most haunted places in the U.S.) are welcoming to students. On warm days walking past Edward's Parade which students simply refer to as "Eddie's", "the field is covered with people—students laying in the sun, playing soccer, Frisbee."

Fordham may be considered a commuter school. Most students move off campus after their sophomore year or even earlier. The scarce housing is not guaranteed for everyone, and the dorms are nothing out of the ordinary. The coveted Walsh and O'Hare apartment-style residence halls are usually reserved for upperclassmen. Housing is assigned by lottery, so students rely on accumulated "credit hours" and strokes of luck for better housing options. The administration does get a lot of credit though for its above-average efforts to honor roommate requests. Freshman housing options include Alumni Court North and South, and Hughes Hall. Queen's Court is also a popular choice for freshmen, but they must first write a letter to the nun who is the head of the house to convince her why they belong there.

The Bronx location of Rose Hill, while not ideal, is not much of a problem. The campus is unanimously hailed as very safe, complete with tall gates separating it from the neighborhood and guards who scrutinize the ID of everyone who passes through. Students are always traveling into and around the city and visiting spots such as Fordham Road, which features great alternative shopping, or Arthur Avenue, which offers excellent dining and entertainment venues. The NYC public transportation system precludes the need for a car so parking is also not a problem.

"Food, I'd give it 60 out of 100," a sophomore assessed. While the Marketplace is a pretty dining hall, it tends to disappoint in both quality and variety. The alternative options, however, offer a welcome counterbalance.

Flex dollars work at the more popular spots such as the Grill, the student deli, and Dagger John's University restaurant. One thing students cannot complain about is lack of options for dining out—restaurants are plentiful and diverse, and the Bronx version of Little Italy offers excellent choices right in Fordham's backyard.

Get Active!

Students described school pride as "up and coming." This means that currently, while there is enough support for the sports teams (basketball games sell out, so get your tickets early!), the teams don't have the most successful records. But sports on campus do have a large presence in the form of intramurals, where teams such as the Flying Jesuits Frisbee team are quite popular. The student newspaper, *The Ram*, is a weekly publication and many students also enjoy the controversial quips of *The Paper*, an alternative news source akin to *The Onion*.

Fordham students are active and committed to their extracurricular activities. Performance groups such as Mimes and Mummers and Experimental Theatre are very popular, Fashion for Philanthropy is a well-liked option and many also take advantage of the volunteer opportunities in the shelters and other social justice organizations of the Bronx. Many students also choose to take advantage of New York City, and many work in internships in various businesses around the city.

> **"Coming to New York City I expected it to be less personal but Fordham really surprised me in its friendly atmosphere."**

Opportunities are definitely not lacking at Fordham. "Coming to New York City, I expected it to be less personal, but Fordham really surprised me in its friendly atmosphere," one junior said. Whether you want a sense of close community or a big city to seek adventure, Fordham has it all.—*Dorota Poplawska*

FYI

If you come to Fordham, you'd better bring "your designer shades."

What is the typical weekend schedule? "Hit the tri-bar area on Friday, Saturday sleep in, enjoy a day in the city shopping and at night it's bars again."

If I could change one thing about Fordham, I'd "make it more diverse."

Three things every student at Fordham should do before graduating are "eat out on Arthur Ave., go streaking across Eddie's Parade, and ride the Ram statue."

Hamilton College

Address: 198 College Hill Road Clinton, NY 13323
Phone: 315-859-4421
E-mail address: admission@hamilton.edu
Web site URL: www.hamilton.edu
Year Founded: 1812
Private or Public: Private
Religious Affiliation: None
Location: Rural
Number of Applicants: 4,962
Percent Accepted: 28%
Percent Accepted who enroll: 34%
Number Entering: 472
Number of Transfers Accepted each Year: 37
Middle 50% SAT range: M: 640–720, CR: 640–740
Middle 50% ACT range: Unreported
Early admission program EA/ED/None: ED
Percentage accepted through EA or ED: 47%

EA and ED deadline: 15-Nov
Regular Deadline: 1-Jan
Application Fee: $75
Full time Undergraduate enrollment: 1,842
Total enrollment: 1,842
Percent Male: 48%
Percent Female: 52%
Total Percent Minority or Unreported: 34%
Percent African-American: 4%
Percent Asian/Pacific Islander: 8%
Percent Hispanic: 6%
Percent Native-American: 1%
Percent International: 5%
Percent in-state/out of state: 30%/70%
Percent from Public HS: 60%
Retention Rate: 96%
Graduation Rate 4-year: 85%

Graduation Rate 6-year: 90%
Percent Undergraduates in On-campus housing: 98%
Number of official organized extracurricular organizations: 80
3 Most popular majors: Economics, Mathematics, Politics and Government
Student/Faculty ratio: 10:1
Average Class Size: 10 to 19
Percent of students going to grad school: 40%
Tuition and Fees: $38,600
In State Tuition and Fees if different: No difference
Cost for Room and Board: $9,810
Percent receiving financial aid out of those who apply, first year: 78%
Percent receiving financial aid among all students: 41%

L ooking for a beautiful campus, a close community of spirited, involved and just-plain-nice people with small classes that are only taught by professors? Hamilton College, located in the picturesque village of Clinton, N.Y., might be just the school for you. Having witnessed numerous changes over recent years—including physical improvements, major changes in the curriculum, and a new president—Hamilton is an exciting and welcoming place to be.

The Curriculum: New and Improved

In the Fall of 2001, Hamilton did away with distributional requirements in an effort to encourage students to design their own curriculum. Still essential to a Hamilton education, however, is the writing requirement, which requires that students take three writing-intensive classes in any subject by the end of their sophomore year. While this may prove difficult if you don't plan your schedule well—"last semester was pretty bad because I took all writing classes, so it got a bit monotonous, always writing papers," bemoaned one freshman—Hamiltonians undoubtedly graduate with a strong foundation in writing skills. "My writing has definitely improved since I was a freshman; I thought that I had learned to write well enough in high school, but there is always room to grow in that area," a junior commented.

It's no surprise, then, that Hamilton's English department is very strong. There is also a writing center where other students are available to edit papers and hash-out ideas. Other popular majors include government, economics and psychology, while the language departments are considered weaker. Hamilton's academic offerings are strengthened across the board by the great amount of tutorial support. Such aid is not limited to the liberal arts at the writing center—if you need some help with math, you can always head over to the Q-Lit center to meet with a tutor.

Classes run small at Hamilton, ranging from around 40 in freshman classes to six in some upperclassmen courses. This can make some classes very difficult to get into, but if you make your case to the professor or if you are a major in that subject, your chances are greatly improved. Students praise the interaction with their professors, who are "very personable," and feel that small classes allow for a wealth of intellectual opportunities. "The professors are incredible and so willing to meet with and help you. Almost every professor I've had has extended office hours if needed and given us his or her home telephone number," a junior gushed. Of course, some popular departments, such as government, tend to have bigger classes, even in the upper-division major courses. In terms of Hamilton's workload, it depends on what classes you take, but one junior says that "most students are very focused throughout the year, and it gets a little more hectic during finals."

Sports, Greeks and . . . the Dog Pound?

While there is no pressure to drink, alcohol is important to the social life for many—"you're in the middle of nowhere; what else is there to do?" one student pointed out. Hamiltonians generally drink one to four nights a week, though there aren't many "four-nighters." Since the arrival of a new president, Hamilton has been enforcing its alcohol policy and underage drinking has reportedly decreased a little. "There are ways around the strictness, but it's not really worth it," said a freshman. "However, if you want something you can get it." With or without alcohol, Hamiltonians are not lacking in opportunities for fun. About 30 to 35 percent of students go Greek, so fraternities and sororities contribute greatly to the party scene by hosting most of the on-campus parties. Everyone is invited to their themed parties that are reputedly always well-themed, from '80s night to "farm party." Societies sometimes host parties off campus, but those are often invite-only because partygoers must be shuttled.

If you're not into the frats, there are other options. Non-Greek activities, like frequenting acoustic coffee-houses, are common, but as one sorority member pointed out, "It's hard to attract athletic and Greek types to stuff like that," and at Hamilton that's a large percentage of the student body. Groups like the Campus Activity Board (CAB) and the Inter-Society Council, however, try to provide a variety of gatherings that unite the student body, such as Al-Ham weekend, during which there are relay races and a carnival day.

Sports are undoubtedly a big part of the social scene—Friday nights are pretty dull, for example, because athletes don't go out in preparation for Saturday games. Even though all of Hamilton's sports are Division III and academics always come first, students love their teams. "School spirit has increased since I came here," one junior claimed. Sporting events are popular, and Hamilton has great hockey, basketball and lacrosse teams. The football team is not too fantastic, but Hamiltonians still come out to cheer, especially since the basketball fans' tradition of the "Dog Pound" has spread to other sporting events. This tradition consists of a group of exceptionally fanatical guys dressed up in costumes cheering and going crazy in a roped-off area of the field or gymnasium.

Play a Sport or Wreak Some HAVOC

Hamilton's extracurriculars are dominated by sports, and if you're on a team, that obviously takes up a lot of your free time. The less intense types play intramurals, which are very popular. Beyond the playing field, a lot of Hamiltonians are involved in HAVOC (a student-run community-service organization), yearbook, and the Hamilton Outing Club, from which you can rent just about any outdoors equipment. While extracurriculars are not as popular here as at other institutions, "after freshman year, when you don't do too much, you start wanting to get more involved," an upperclassman noted.

The Campus: Old, New, and Improving

Hamilton was once made up of two colleges: Hamilton College for men and Kirkland for women. Now it's one, but Hamilton, the north side, and Kirkland, the south side, have very distinctive architectural tones. The north side's buildings are old and "feel very New England, very prestigious," while Kirkland, built in the '60s, has "imposing" and "cold-looking" modern architecture. The two campuses are close and small enough that commuting between the two is not a problem. While there isn't a whole lot around the campus, "it's less isolated than I thought it would be when I came here," a freshman said. You need a car to get anywhere, and though freshmen cannot own cars, there is a jitney service that runs to nearby malls and to various places on campus. Clinton itself "is a beautiful town, and there are no issues with locals coming on campus—it's an open campus," one student noted. Hamilton has two main dining halls, as well as a diner and a pub that are part of the meal plan. As at any college, it's easy to get sick of the food, but there are a variety of options offered, from sushi to pizza. As a part of the college's dedication to its physical plant, Hamilton's science buildings are now undergoing major renovation: there will be a new part added, and all the labs will be brought up to date.

Hamilton's dorm options are well liked, especially since Greek houses were taken away and made into dorms for upperclassmen in 1996. "While a lot of frat members were very upset about that," a junior said, "I love it. I'm around so many different people. It's a great way to meet people by not having them segregated by societies in different houses." There is a lottery system for all students except freshmen, who live among upperclassmen. Other options are available in terms of housing; you can opt for a single-sex floor or for a substance-free dorm that is located in Root Dormitory. Off-campus housing is available to only a small number of seniors, and the administration is trying to eliminate it completely.

A Typical Hamiltonian . . .

Hamilton is not known for its ethnic diversity; most students will probably tell you that a diverse campus was not their priority when they chose their school. The student body is quite homogeneous, "it's pretty much white kids from Connecticut who wear J. Crew," and there is considerable self-segregation, from races to fraternities, the latter of which are generally divided by sports. Despite the modicum of diversity that the lack of Greek houses fosters, upperclassmen often room with members of their own society or sports team. "The administration is trying to pass a rule that will bar students in societies from living together, but that is a long way from happening," said a freshman. There is a definite conservative political presence on campus: "Hamilton's academics are liberal, but the student body is quite conservative. I thought that I would find more liberals here because of the academics," a junior noted.

According to one junior, "the dating scene is so weird." There are a lot of random hook-ups, and then couples who are all but married. Certain drugs also prevail on campus—Hamilton has a zero-tolerance policy for narcotics like cocaine, but "study drugs" like Ritalin are present. The small student population has its curses and its blessings. News travels fast in such a small institution: "Everything gets passed around so quickly and you sort of know everyone's name or face. Sometimes it can feel a bit like high school, but in a good way," a freshman said.

> "People just hang out and spend a lot of time together, and they don't really leave on the weekends. When I got here, it felt like camp."

Hamilton's close-knit community is, in fact, what students really love about it. Its small size especially allows freshmen to feel at home from the start: "All the upperclassmen are really nice and welcoming," said a freshman. "I was very attracted to the small, intimate campus," one student said. "And it sounds cliché, but everyone here is so friendly. People just hang out and spend a lot of time together, and they don't really leave on the weekends. When I got here, it felt like camp." Hamilton may be small, but Hamiltonians' love of their campus, their professors and their community is immense.—*Samantha Wilson*

FYI
If you come to Hamilton, you'd better bring "a warm jacket for the winter."
What is the typical weekend schedule? "Friday, hang out, dinner and a movie; Saturday, party, then to the bar (which is "downtown", i.e. down the hill); Sunday, homework all day.
If I could change one thing about Hamilton, I would "put it in San Diego. Everyone's so much happier when it's nice out."
Three things that every student at Hamilton should do before graduating are: "go to a Bundy party, go for a walk in the Root Glen, and dance at the diner late-night."

Hobart and William Smith Colleges

Address: 629 South Main Street Geneva, NY 14456
Phone: 315-781-3622
E-mail address: admissions@hws.edu
Web site URL: www.hws.edu
Year Founded: 1822
Private or Public: Private
Religious Affiliation: None
Location: Rural
Number of Applicants: 3,410
Percent Accepted: 65%
Percent Accepted who enroll: 25%
Number Entering: 545
Number of Transfers Accepted each Year: 27
Middle 50% SAT range:
M: 540–630, CR: 530–640,
Wr: Unreported
Middle 50% ACT range: 24–27
Early admission program EA/ED/None: ED
Percentage accepted through EA or ED: Unreported

EA and ED deadline: 15-Nov
Regular Deadline: 1-Feb
Application Fee: $45
Full time Undergraduate enrollment: 1,868
Total enrollment: 2,069
Percent Male: 46%
Percent Female: 54%
Total Percent Minority or Unreported: 4%
Percent African-American: 3%
Percent Asian/Pacific Islander: 2%
Percent Hispanic: 4%
Percent Native-American: <1%
Percent International: 2%
Percent in-state/out of state: 45%/55%
Percent from Public HS: 65%
Retention Rate: 85%
Graduation Rate 4-year: Unreported

Graduation Rate 6-year: Unreported
Percent Undergraduates in On-campus housing: 90%
Number of official organized extracurricular organizations: 77
3 Most popular majors: Economics, General English Language and Literature, General History
Student/Faculty ratio: 11:1
Average Class Size: 10 to 19
Percent of students going to grad school: 30%
Tuition and Fees: $31,850
In State Tuition and Fees if different: No difference
Cost for Room and Board: $8,386
Percent receiving financial aid out of those who apply, first year: 74%
Percent receiving financial aid among all students: 64%

Set atop a hill, adjacent to the majestic Seneca Lake, sits the campus of Hobart and William Smith Colleges. HWS is actually two schools with separate deans, admissions officers, student governments and athletic departments. Women apply to William Smith and men apply to Hobart, but all students attend the same classes and share the same beautiful campus. Due largely to its small student body of around 2,000 undergraduates, HWS is the perfect school for college applicants looking for an intimate community and a chance to build strong relationships with professors.

A Liberal Arts Education

Hobart's academics are in very much the typical liberal arts style. Following a semester schedule, students are expected to take four classes each term. It's required for students to take classes in each of the basic disciplinary areas including art and civic engagement. The art credit can be satisfied by a semester of music lessons and a credit

for civic engagement, for example, can be earned by volunteering for America Reads. Depending on the subject and professor, class sizes can vary but on average are about 20 students. With 45 majors ranging from English to Studio Art and 20 minors from Child Advocacy to Peace Studies, students are also still given the choice to design their own major. "It's a liberal arts education: strong across the board," one student affirmed. The worst academic characteristic at HWS, according to a student, is that "some of the students in the classes don't appreciate where they are. You can find peers who challenge you but sometimes they can be entirely uninspiring." Similarly uninspiring are gut classes like "Rocks for Jocks" also known as Geology 101, and "Shakespeare for Non-majors". Pat McGuire, an economics professor characterized by his sweater vests, and Craig Rimmerman, a political science and public policy professor, are both passionate and invested educators to look out for when searching for an extra class. Despite the inevitable hard professor, students consistently praise the teaching staff for their passion, accessibility and personal investment in their students.

"Because class size and the HWS community are small, you can get a lot of one-on-one time with the professors who are passionate about their subject and about teaching," a student explained. "If you stand out, you can benefit enormously from them."

With an intimate academic setting and thoroughly invested faculty, it is easy to get individual help and to form strong connections with professors, but there are always international opportunities if HWS gets too small. Taking advantage of the well-developed abroad opportunities for students, many take a break from HWS and venture off to other countries for a semester or year abroad.

Luck of the Draw

Housing, much like other college campuses, is often the luck of the draw. Freshmen are placed in a dorm before arriving on campus. Some are placed in "Dirty Durfee," though according to a student, it may not be all that dirty anymore, or in the new dorms recently constructed on the hill. As for upperclassmen, they enter a lottery with their future roommates. Choices for living range from an all-girls dorm, an all-guys dorm, coed housing, fraternities or theme housing. Students are allowed to create their own theme house by petitioning the dean and getting a group of people together. Some recent theme houses have been the Political Activism House, the Honors House, and the Outdoor Recreation House. Senior year students can live in Odell's village, a group of condominiums on the far side of campus equipped with a bathroom and kitchen. Seniors can also live off campus if they chose. "Housing is where you meet most of your friends," a student said.

Saga is the main dining hall on campus. With its 3-tiered construction, Saga has the feel of a gymnasium, and the all-you-can-eat menu can be a physical challenge for your digestive system. Saga is part of the newly renovated campus center, and students enjoy hanging out there and socializing. If Saga doesn't hit the spot, there is a café that is a la cart and a pub that serves food and beer if you are of age. Often times during the warmer months, students will take lunch out on the quad and lie out in the sun or walk up the hill to the lake.

Around the World . . . Or Not

Campus social life seems to be characterized by hanging out on the quad during warmer months, dormitory socializing, hitting up Parker's or whichever bar hasn't been shut down by the local police, and the occasional frat party (no sororities, sorry girls!). Students typically stagger into the Water Street Café or Bagels and Cakes the "morning after" for a rejuvenating breakfast. With only six fraternities, Greek life isn't a big presence on campus and there is no pressure to join. One campus party to look forward to is the spontaneous "Around the World" party, which happens a few times a year in Odell's village. Typically, a resident of one unit will decide on a whim that it's time for a night of "Around the World." Each unit chooses a different drink from some place in the world and students walk around the village trying each drink.

> "Because class size and the HWS community are small, you can get a lot of one on one time with the professors who are passionate about their subject and about teaching."

Although they have parties with diverse drinks, the attendees, for the most part, are not. The majority of the student body at HWS is white middle-class Americans, many of whom are from upstate New York or Massachusetts. The cultural clubs are strong, close-knit organizations as a result of their small numbers and provide a welcoming community within HWS for its minority students. What HWS lacks in student diversity, it makes up for in diversity of opportunities. HWS has everything from an NCAA Division I national championship-winning sailing team to a coed "drinking team with a softball problem," and students have the freedom to start their own clubs. Students are deeply dedicated to their extracurricular activities and find it easy to be "a big fish in a little pond." On Seneca Lake in beautiful Geneva, New York, with a plethora of academic and extracurricular opportunities, many students have found that they are happy where they are. One recent graduate said that HWS was the best place for him because "it gave me the opportunity to pursue any extracurricular or academic goal I wanted. The small community really offers the opportunity for leadership."—*Hayden Mulligan*

FYI
If you come to HWS, you'd better bring "a windbreaker because campus gets cold from the breeze off the lake."
What's the typical weekend schedule? "Saturdays are brunch at Saga, studying, head to Parker's, back to the frats for late night fun and Sundays are devoted to studying."
If I could change one thing about HWS, "I'd enhance the theater and fine arts departments."
Three things every student should do before graduating are "swim in Seneca Lake, go on a Finger Lakes wine tour, and eat a meal with their favorite professor."

Hofstra University

Address: 100 Hofstra University Bernon Hall Hempstead, NY 11549
Phone: 516-463-6700
E-mail address: admissions@hofstra.edu
Web site URL: www.hofstra.edu
Year Founded: 1932
Private or Public: Private
Religious Affiliation: None
Location: Urban
Number of Applicants: 18,471
Percent Accepted: 54%
Percent Accepted who enroll: 17%
Number Entering: 1,730
Number of Transfers Accepted each Year: 641
Middle 50% SAT range: M: 550–630, CR: 540–630, Wr: Unreported
Middle 50% ACT range: 23–26
Early admission program EA/ED/None: EA

Percentage accepted through EA or ED: 36%
EA and ED deadline: 15-Dec
Regular Deadline: 2/1/2009 and Rolling thereafter
Application Fee: $50
Full time Undergraduate enrollment: 8,444
Total enrollment: 11,187
Percent Male: 46%
Percent Female: 54%
Total Percent Minority or Unreported: 17%
Percent African-American: 9%
Percent Asian/Pacific Islander: 5%
Percent Hispanic: 7%
Percent Native-American: <1%
Percent International: 1%
Percent in-state/out of state: 50%/50%
Percent from Public HS: Unreported
Retention Rate: 79%
Graduation Rate 4-year: 34%

Graduation Rate 6-year: 53%
Percent Undergraduates in On-campus housing: 80%
Number of official organized extracurricular organizations: 124
3 Most popular majors: Accounting, Marketing/Marketing Management, General Psychology
Student/Faculty ratio: 14:1
Average Class Size: 10 to 19
Percent of students going to grad school: 29%
Tuition and Fees: $25,700
In State Tuition and Fees if different: No difference
Cost for Room and Board: $10,300
Percent receiving financial aid out of those who apply, first year: 90%
Percent receiving financial aid among all students: 84%

Nestled in Nassau County, New York, Hofstra University is a suburban institution in a bustling town known for being the least suburban of its kind. Hofstra offers the benefits of a large university and the intimacy of a smaller liberal arts college. It was founded as a nonsectarian coeducational university in 1935 to provide post-secondary education on Long Island. Located 25 miles from New York City, it offers the advantage of an environment that is both urban and suburban. Students have easy access to the academic, cultural, so-cial, and professional resources of the nation's largest city while studying at Hofstra.

A Little Something for Everyone

Hofstra is a comprehensive educational institution with a well-recognized academic menu. The University offers 140 undergraduate programs and 155 graduate programs spanning over ten schools and colleges. Studies covering all disciplines of arts, science, business, and humanities enable students to explore a vast array of options. As a junior noted, "There is a lot to be tried out at

Hofstra. You never feel limited to this or that at all." Students may choose to major in any number of concentrations. The Bachelor of Arts program enables greater flexibility in exploring courses in areas other than a student's intended field of concentration while the Bachelor of Science allows Hofstra students to gain breadth and depth of knowledge in a particular area. In addition, the availability of minors helps widen academic focus by including other desired disciplines of study.

Most freshmen complete a generic sequence of general studies courses during their first year and begin to focus on an area of concentration after completing 12 course-credit hours. Students also complete a University-wide distributional requirement consisting of six course credits in humanities, social sciences, and natural sciences/mathematics. Proficiency in writing as well as eight semester hours of physical education is also required. These requirements force students to "look beyond their narrow scope," according to a senior. Students usually do not have trouble fulfilling the requirements since they have the option of enrolling in classes during winter and summer sessions in addition to the regular fall and spring semesters. Hofstra also has partnerships with universities across the globe in its Off Campus Education programs. It is Hofstra's version of study abroad and enables students to study for credits across Europe, Mexico, Asia and the South Pacific.

Whatever the area of study and the mode of study, Hofstra students receive the care and attention typical of a school with low faculty-to-student ratio. In fact, Hofstra boasts an average class size of just 22 students. Even with the small classes, however, some complain about the paucity of options for science majors. Most notable is the lack of engineering programs. A current freshman said, "Although science options are available, there seems to be less emphasis and fewer options for specialization" at Hofstra. However, this may soon be rectified with the creation of a new 100,000 square foot medical school encompassing 11 acres at the Hempstead campus. Set to matriculate its first class in 2011, Hofstra University School of Medicine will be the first allopathic medical school in Nassau County, New York. Construction of the new medical school will help bring more research projects in biology, chemistry and medicine. It will also increase the number of academic programs available to the Hofstra community.

The Social Life

The academic year at Hofstra begins with Welcome Week in September when University-wide celebration and activities kick off the upcoming school year. Welcome Week usually begins with the President's Welcome Address and continues through the week with movies, a carnival, subsidized trips to New York City, and athletic socials. It finally culminates with the Hofstra Idol Talent Show. This is the week when students can enjoy all the fun of college without the workload. One freshman noted, "It was one of best weeks of the school year when everyone is making friends and getting re-acclimated to school." However, meeting new people and making friends don't end with Welcome Week. Hofstra boasts over 150 clubs and organizations. It also has 30 local and national fraternities right on campus so that everyone can find their niche and circle of friends. In fact, a Hofstra sophomore finds it "too hard to do everything you want to do because there is way too much going on."

Annual campus celebrations also provide much-needed study breaks throughout the year, such as the annual Sinterklaas Festival, the Dutch version of Christmas, complete with a tree lighting ceremony and a Dutch holiday village. Other Dutch, Italian and Irish festivals are also held throughout the year. Student-run activities, performances, concerts and socials provide even more options to get involved in Hofstra's campus life. The one drawback is that there are limited entertainment options off campus and near Hempstead. The suburban landscape of the area is more conducive to residential developments than business, so those yearning for something more exciting will have to venture into New York City. Luckily, the Long Island Railroad Station is located nearby, and a trip into Manhattan will only be around 30 minutes. Jones Beach State Park and its gorgeous boardwalk are also located about 10 miles from campus and are easily accessible by public transportation. The proliferation of these activities offsets the lack of available entertainment venues in Hempstead.

Apart from school-related activities, Hofstra offers a variety of social scenes on and off campus. The usual private dorm parties and fraternity parties can be found on most weekends. However, there are mixed reviews when it comes to rating the party scene. "People definitely need to pick and choose which ones are worth their time," according to one senior. Venturing off campus into Hempstead, students will find quaint little cafes and restaurants. Hofstra also has 18 Division I athletic teams in addition to numerous intramural sports programs. Students can choose from the usual flag football, stadium soccer, and dodgeball to the more specialized aerobics, weight training, and karate.

All the Makings of Home

Over 4,000 students choose to live on campus each year at Hofstra University in one of the 37 residence halls. Students may choose from traditional dorm settings or an apartment-style suite setup. There are also special housing options for cultural, academic, and social learning communities with at least one floor in each hall designated as "quiet floor." There is a housing option for freshmen affectionately known as "The Netherlands." It consists of 11 two-story houses that provide housing to about 55 undergraduates in each house complete with a dining facility. Others will live in similar two-story complexes or one of the numerous high-rise residence halls. The variety of housing offers every flavor for every taste. "Choosing where and how you want to live can be tricky," said a sophomore. Students also enjoy the benefits of a gorgeous campus, which includes many rare trees and outdoor sculptures in Hofstra's registered arboretum as well as the traditional buildings and high-tech facilities.

Variety also seems to be the theme when it comes to Hofstra dining. With a student meal plan, Hofstra students may choose to dine in any of the 17 dining facilities. Each establishment has its own style and options ranging from Maui Tacos to the Pizza Exchange to Nature's Organic Grille. However, large number of options doesn't imply that the options are good. "People without a doubt are very aware of what to eat and what not to eat around here," said a junior. If so desired, students can find more dinning options in the town of Hempstead and, of course, New York City.

> "There is a lot to be tried out at Hofstra. You never feel limited to this or that at all."

A home is not made with just buildings and facilities. The people are the most important assets in Hofstra's campus. Located in what is said to be one of the least suburban suburbs of New York City, Hofstra is a good reflection of the diversity of Hempstead. Students from 68 countries all study and live there. Despite the diversity, some complain that there is a preppy culture within the student body. "Some people seem a bit standoffish, like they can't relate to others not like them," said a senior. All the ingredients are there, but making them into a place to call home might prove a bit more challenging. Overall, students are content academically despite the common complaint concerning science. Socially, students may struggle to find their niche at first, but once they do, they are happy. That describes Hofstra in essence: a rewarding experience when you find your place.—*Hai Pham*

FYI

If you come to Hofstra, you'd better bring "posters, a fan, and some decorations to make your dorm feel like home."

What is the typical weekend schedule? "Stay up late talking with friends, sleep in late the next day, hang out during the day, take a trip to New York City, and maybe do some work on Sunday."

If I could change one thing about Hofstra, I'd "want there to be more off-campus social options."

Three things all Hofstra students should do before graduating are "go to Kate and Willy's, write for *The Chronicle*, and buy crafts at the annual Dutch festival."

Ithaca College

Address: 100 Job Hall Ithaca, NY 14850-7020
Phone: 607-274-3124
E-mail address: admission@ithaca.edu
Web site URL: www.ithaca.edu
Year Founded: 1892
Private or Public: Private
Religious Affiliation: None
Location: Suburban
Number of Applicants: 11,235
Percent Accepted: 74%
Percent Accepted who enroll: 22%
Number Entering: 1,797
Number of Transfers Accepted each Year: 143
Middle 50% SAT range: M: 540–630, CR: 530–630, Wr: Unreported
Middle 50% ACT range: Unreported
Early admission program EA/ED/None: None

Percentage accepted through EA or ED: NA
EA and ED deadline: NA
Regular Deadline: 1-Feb
Application Fee: $60
Full time Undergraduate enrollment: 6,260
Total enrollment: 11,999
Percent Male: 45%
Percent Female: 55%
Total Percent Minority or Unreported: 10%
Percent African-American: 3%
Percent Asian/Pacific Islander: 4%
Percent Hispanic: 4%
Percent Native-American: <1%
Percent International: 2%
Percent in-state/out of state: 46%/54%
Percent from Public HS: 75%
Retention Rate: 84%
Graduation Rate 4-year: 71%

Graduation Rate 6-year: 76%
Percent Undergraduates in On-campus housing: 70%
Number of official organized extracurricular organizations: 172
3 Most popular majors: Business/Commerce, General
Student/Faculty ratio: 12:1
Average Class Size: 10 to 19
Percent of students going to grad school: 40%
Tuition and Fees: $30,606
In State Tuition and Fees if different: No difference
Cost for Room and Board: $11,162
Percent receiving financial aid out of those who apply, first year: 90%
Percent receiving financial aid among all students: 85%

Ithaca College may have started out as a conservatory of music in downtown Ithaca, but it now offers strong academics in addition to a world-class music program. Though many students may look at Ithaca and see only Cornell, Ithaca College offers students a smaller, tightly-knit community combined with a great education.

"We're Equipped with the Biggest . . . Radio Tower"

Out of Ithaca College's six undergraduate schools—including Communications, Health Sciences, Humanities and Science, the Music School, Interdisciplinary and International Studies and the Business School—Communications, along with Health Sciences and the Music School, are the three most popular.

Most of the Roy H. Park School of Communications students (or "Parkies" as they're called) end up winning national honors from the top professional organizations and are often offered great opportunities both on campus and off campus. IC also has

two radio stations. IC's radio tower is the biggest thing on Ithaca's skyline. The Music School is considered to be the hardest school, both in terms of admittance and academic rigor. The students at this school are also the ones who "do their own thing," effectively separated from the rest of the college. As one senior music student said, "Music majors don't have a lot of free time, with recital attendances, ensemble requirements, practices, etc."

The Health Science and Human Performance School have mainly two types of majors, the Physical Therapy majors (PTs) and the Physical Education majors (PEs). Due to the physical component of the two majors, it is not surprising, said one student, that the "PTs are a bunch of jocks." The program offers several combined bachelors and masters five year programs, many of which also provide professional certification.

While there is a General Education requirement and most departments push for students to take courses outside their school, students end up really "staying within their schools." A very popular course, however, that many students across the schools end up taking is "Anatomy and Physiology," mainly because it is a requirement for many majors, and it fulfills a common science requirement.

The academics at IC "aren't necessarily hard" but they do give "a substantial amount of homework, about four-five hours' worth a night," said one student, though students at all the schools seemed to agree. Teachers are "really open and willing to talk, especially outside of class" and they're "genuinely interested in helping you in the class." IC isn't considered to be to be of the same academic caliber as its neighbor Cornell University, but that doesn't mean the teaching quality suffers. "I was surprised," one student noted, "that almost all the professors here are well-known in their fields." Due to the College's relatively small size, only intro classes are large, and most classes have only 20–30 students. "Make a good impression early," one student recommended. "IC is small enough that by the time junior and senior year comes around, you'll have a rep, and you'll want it to be a good one." Another student agreed that the smaller campus required student interaction. "Ithaca College is definitely not the place to go if you want to stay in the background."

Division III Contenders and Other Extracurriculars

The large amount of jocks from the Health Science School translates into a great athletic program and great athletic teams. Ithaca College has one of the strongest athletic programs in the NCAA's Division III. School spirit is fierce at Ithaca College, which generates not only great games, but also great attendance. The IC Bombers are well known for their football team and women's crew team, and "everyone and their mom attend the football games." The big football game of the year is the Cortaca Jug, against the SUNY Cortland Red Dragons, "which you must go to" to cheer on the team, though admittedly it's also "an excuse to get drunk." Other particularly popular sports include baseball, softball, and women's lacrosse. If you don't have the time for varsity sports, there are also club sports and recreational (intramural) sports. Students can be competitive and aggressive on the field, but they are all there "just to have fun." Despite the heavy athletic programs, the athletic facilities are still "pretty accessible."

Of course, if sports aren't your thing, there are numerous extracurricular clubs and community service opportunities. Specifically, there are a large number of performing opportunities and performances to attend. But be forewarned: "If you're not a music major, it's really hard to get lessons because they're in great demand." A lot of clubs on campus "fall in with the Ithaca atmosphere and end up being about human rights, animal rights or union rights." Everyone can get a job on campus, but finding a job off campus is a lot harder because, as one student said, "we have to compete with all those people at Cornell."

White Bread

The stereotype of the students is that they are "white bread, mainly white, upper middle class students from the Northeast" who can afford the hefty tag attached to an IC education. When asked whether there is a lot of ethnic diversity on campus, students commented "not really, unless you're in the music school." However, "the gay and lesbian population is well-sized."

> "Ithaca College is definitely not the place to go if you want to stay in the background."

The common stereotype is that IC students are either artsy, due to the strong Music School and Theatre departments, or jocks, because of the Health Science School. "Parkies are a mix—half jocks (marketing, television and radio) and half artists (visual arts and cinematography)." Most students agree that the stereotype is mainly true, but "there are enough exceptions to make life interesting."

Staying on (or off) Campus

Residential housing, one freshman said, is "nice but not that great." According to several upperclassmen, "The buildings aren't ugly, and the rooms are small but adequate." While IC offers a large variety of halls to live in (some coed, others single sex), the majority of students cite residential life as "not a strength of IC." Most students move off campus senior year, but are required to live on campus the first three years. The Towers (two large towers that are dorms) are the most prominent features of Ithaca College. Visible from almost anywhere in Ithaca, they are famous for both the fact that they sometimes have parties (one of two places to party on campus) and that on New Year's eve, the lights in the building change year numbers (i.e., from 08 to 09). The Terraces are the only dorms that offer suites, and most seniors either live in the Garden apartments, the recently built Circle apartments or move off campus to live on Prospect Street. Almost all of the halls (except the apartments) house freshmen, but the Upper and Lower quads have a larger concentration of underclassmen.

"Ithaca College really makes an effort to help freshmen transition," said one student. In addition to the three residential halls the school offers to freshmen only (with twice as many RAs), the College also hosts events, technically open to all undergraduates but specifically targeting freshmen, as an alternative to drinking. With concerts, comedians and dances, IC makes an effort to help students feel comfortable on campus. "The school really tries to limit the amount of underage drinking on campus." Drinking still occurs, just not on campus. Most parties are held off campus, specifically on Prospect Street, known as "the college town of IC." On Friday and Saturday nights, people can expect parties on Prospect Street and in the Circle apartments. However most of the partying by Ithaca College students doesn't occur there either. In fact, most partying doesn't even happen on the Ithaca College side of Ithaca. "If you want to party, go to a Cornell frat party." That's right, IC students go to Cornell frat parties, mainly because "alcohol is a lot less controlled there. And as it turns out, they aren't nerds after all."

In terms of the drug scene, IC is becoming more and more a non-smoking campus (at least in the Residence Halls), but most people at IC who smoke, smoke pot. Greek life isn't all that big on the IC campus except for a few small music fraternities and sororities. Finally, students are not thrilled with the food options on campus. "The food here isn't all that great either, unless you go to Terrace, which is pretty good." Rated between the three dining halls, Terrace is the best, Campus Center is the worst, and Towers is somewhere in-between. Terrace is described as "beautiful, because it has fountains in the dining hall, and offers a great variety of food." Meal plans are required for those who live on-campus, and they all cost the same, although different combination plans are offered with the possibility of "Bonus Bucks" that can be used for food elsewhere. "Bonus bucks make life so much simpler since I'm freed from having to eat on campus and can eat at random times."

"Ithaca Is Gorges"
Ithaca is a great, "but small," community to live in, which is "very open." "Most people take enough advantage of Ithaca" but in order to do so "you *need* a car." In fact most upperclassmen have cars, though freshmen find it harder to have a car on campus because they have to pay more for student parking. "People feel the need to get off campus sometimes, and cars are the way to do it." The other source of transportation is Ithaca's bus service TCAT, a "wonderful resource, especially if you don't want to drive during Ithaca's winters." Two of the most popular clubs among Ithaca College students are the Haunt and the Octopus downtown, known for their live (and most of the time, local) music. Popular bars are Micawbers, Moonshadow Tavern and Blue Stone, but like most bars in Ithaca, "don't expect the bars to fill up until after 11."

If partying is not your thing, the town of Ithaca offers an assortment of other things to do. The many waterfalls and state parks near Ithaca make it one of the most beautiful places to live. Right near the campus is Six Mile Creek, a "wonderful place to go skinny dipping." Another popular activity is gorge jumping (a word of caution, clear the rocks!). If it's "Ithacating—any form of precipitation with a cloudy sky"—you can always go to one of the two independent movie theaters in town, or hang around the Ithaca Commons.

A Word on the Weather
If there is one thing upon which all students agree it is this: Ithaca is cold. Yet, IC students understand that they live in Ithaca, and thus must live with Ithaca's weather. Ithaca is known for not only its freezing winters, cloudy and rainy springs and falls, but also for the erratic changes from one to another. "Only in Ithaca could you experience all the seasons in one day." It starts to snow in late October and early November, and despite the spring thaws, it's possible for it to snow in May.—*Jesse Dong*

FYI

If you come to Ithaca College, you'd better bring "good winter boots and an appreciation for sports and music."

What is the typical weekend schedule? "Party at a Cornell frat party Friday night, cheer on the IC Bombers, attend a performance, party some more at Cornell and hit up a few bars, spend all of Sunday doing homework."

If I could change one thing about Ithaca College, I'd "make it more handicapped accessible."

Three things every student should do before graduating from Ithaca College are "jump in the fountain, go to a Cornell frat party and attend the Cortaca Jug."

The Juilliard School

Address: 60 Lincoln Center Plaza New York, NY 10023-6588

Phone: 212-799-5000 ext.223

E-mail address: admissions@julliard.edu

Web site URL: www.juilliard.edu

Year Founded: 1905

Private or Public: Private

Religious Affiliation: None

Location: Urban

Number of Applicants: 2,138

Percent Accepted: 8%

Percent Accepted who enroll: 75%

Number Entering: 122

Number of Transfers Accepted each Year: Unreported

Middle 50% SAT range: Not Considered

Middle 50% ACT range: Not Considered

Early admission program EA/ED/None: None

Percentage accepted through EA or ED: NA

EA and ED deadline: NA

Regular Deadline: 15-Nov or 1-Dec, depending on major

Application Fee: $50 or $100, depending on major

Full time Undergraduate enrollment: 500

Total enrollment: 842

Percent Male: 53%

Percent Female: 47%

Total Percent Minority or Unreported: 51%

Percent African-American: 9%

Percent Asian/Pacific Islander: 17%

Percent Hispanic: 5%

Percent Native-American: <1%

Percent International: 17%

Percent in-state/out of state: 82%/18%

Percent from Public HS: Unreported

Retention Rate: 94%

Graduation Rate 4-year: 80%

Graduation Rate 6-year: 83%

Percent Undergraduates in On-campus housing: 50%

Number of official organized extracurricular organizations: Unreported

3 Most popular majors: Piano and organ, Stringed instruments, Voice and opera

Student/Faculty ratio: 3:1

Average Class Size: 2 to 9

Percent of students going to grad school: Unreported

Tuition and Fees: $28,640

In State Tuition and Fees if different: No difference

Cost for Room and Board: $11,250

Percent receiving financial aid out of those who apply, first year: 85%

Percent receiving financial aid among all students: Unreported

Centrally located in the heart of New York City, Juilliard is the serious young artist's ultimate opportunity. Not only are students immersed in the school's rigorous training programs in dance, music, and acting, but they are also constantly influenced and inspired by the cultural and artistic happenings in the hub of the creative world.

Pinnacle of Performance Arts

With an only 7.7% acceptance rate, Juilliard is one of the most competitive programs in the world for young aspiring actors, musicians, and dancers. Along with a standard application evaluation, potential Juilliard students must also undergo a rigorous audition process, in which the entire faculty of a specific department determines an applicant's admission. Unlike most universities, where SAT scores and transcripts weigh most heavily on a student's chance of admission, at Juilliard, the audition process is by far the most important piece of the application. Grades and scores are taken into account, but the student must, first and foremost, prove their musical, dance, or theatrical abilities and potential.

Although the program is a challenging one to get into, most students are happily surprised that the workload isn't too intense academically. One sophomore Juilliard student, initially intimidated by Juilliard's extremely serious artistic training was actually "pleasantly surprised to find the atmosphere much less intense and competitive than what I expected, and the classes challenging without being overwhelming." In this small, close-knit community of less than 500 undergraduates, students receive tons of individual attention. With only 90 students in both the drama and dance departments, students are under constant pressure to perform and learn at the highest, most superior level. Along with group classes focusing on their particular creative major, each student within the drama, dance, or music divisions is assigned to private, individual master classes to advance his or her talents.

Being a part of a group with such highly skilled actors, musicians, and dancers is stressful, but most of the kids at Juilliard have been training for years, and know exactly what they're getting themselves into. It seems too, for most Juilliard students, being around their classmates does not intimidate them or make them shy away from their artistic endeavors, but it actually motivates them: "some people might think that students would burn out after going through such intensive artistic training, but at Juilliard, it's just the opposite. Being surrounded by such incredible creativity in dance, music, and theater constantly re-inspires me each day."

Ping Pong and the City

Some concerns with the programs at Juilliard come from worries that students feel they won't be trained to succeed professionally outside of their artistic pursuits: "Sometimes I'm concerned that I won't be able to do anything else with my life other than music, which is natural, but a lot of times I do wish I had gone to a school that offers more pre-professional opportunities." There also are not many extra-curricular activities outside of the music, dance, and theater scene: "There aren't many organized groups—no sports teams at all (not even organized ping pong!)—though we have an art-centered service club called ArtReach that meets regularly and plans activities and projects and two Christian groups." But between master classes, performances, auditions, and academics, many students wouldn't have time for extracurriculars, and if need be, one of the most desirable places in the world, New York City, is always at their fingertips.

> **"Being surrounded by such incredible creativity in dance, music, and theater constantly re-inspires me each day."**

All freshmen and first-year students live on-campus in double bedrooms and suite-style rooms, with three bathrooms and a common living room area. There are computer labs, a gym, a cafeteria located on the lobby level, all available to students living within the dormitory. However, housing is not guaranteed for all four years of school, and many students move off-campus after their first year: "Most of my friends have moved off-campus because they're so eager to get into the New York social scene, but living on-campus my freshman year definitely helped me meet a lot of cool kids." First-time college students are always assigned to a double room, and singles become available for second year students.

Dominant social scenes are informal student groups—the dancers, the actors, people in the same year or some instrument studio, occasionally inter-disciplinary "cliques" just hanging out. There are not many academically inclined groups. One student noticed that her friends at Juilliard are "so focused on their individual art and fitting practice time into their day that many don't get excited about their academic classes, however, one notable exception is those students, mostly musicians, who take classes at Columbia College in addition to their music classes here."

Best of All Worlds

Overall, students at Juilliard seem to love their experience in such a rigorous dance, music, and theater environment, but they also seem to know what they'll be getting themselves into. Students here understand that their lifestyles will include composing and practicing music, rehearsing scenes, and choreography. At Juilliard, if students are willing to sacrifice the typical college experience and to endure this competitive environment, they have the opportunity to succeed to unprecedented heights and take in some skills of the most tenured dancers, musicians, and actors in the world. Its ideal environment located in a mecca of creativity provides inspiration and motivation for its students, and an outlet and experience unlike any other. "In one weekend I can walk over to Lincoln Center, see an opera at the Metropolitan, or see a ballet. You just can't get that anywhere else in the world."—*Catherine Reibel*

FYI

If you come to Juilliard, you'd better bring "a lot of energy to practice dance, practice piano, or rehearse for theater!"

What's the typical weekend schedule? "A lot of time is either spent working on performance pieces or actually participating in shows. If one doesn't have a show one weekend, time is spent seeing your friends' shows! Bar-hopping is always fun on less busy weekends, however they aren't a lot of large campus parties or anything."

If I could change one thing about Juilliard, I'd "make it a little bigger. I wish there were more people to meet. Sometimes it feels like a high school environment."

Three things every student at Juilliard should do before graduating are "visit a school where they can have a 'real college experience' (only to realize that frat parties suck), get to know New York City as well as possible, and embrace the fact that we have so many awesome performers and artists as resources to connect with."

Manhattanville College

Address: 2900 Purchase Street Purchase, NY 10577

Phone: 914-323-5464

E-mail address: admissions@mville.edu

Web site URL: www.manhattanville.edu

Year Founded: 1841

Private or Public: Private

Religious Affiliation: None

Location: Suburban

Number of Applicants: 3,927

Percent Accepted: 50%

Percent Accepted who enroll: 27%

Number Entering: 535

Number of Transfers Accepted each Year: Unreported

Middle 50% SAT range: M: 500–610, CR: 500–620, Wr: Unreported

Middle 50% ACT range: 20–25

Early admission program EA/ED/None: ED

Percentage accepted through EA or ED: Unreported

EA and ED deadline: 1-Dec

Regular Deadline: 1-Mar

Application Fee: $65

Full time Undergraduate enrollment: 1,845

Total enrollment: 3,022

Percent Male: 33%

Percent Female: 67%

Total Percent Minority or Unreported: 47%

Percent African-American: 7%

Percent Asian/Pacific Islander: 2%

Percent Hispanic: 15%

Percent Native-American: <1%

Percent International: 8%

Percent in-state/out of state: 64% /36%

Percent from Public HS: Unreported

Retention Rate: 74%

Graduation Rate 4-year: 51%

Graduation Rate 6-year: 57%

Percent Undergraduates in On-campus housing: 76%

Number of official organized extracurricular organizations: 48

3 Most popular majors: Business, Psychology, Visual & Performing Arts

Student/Faculty ratio: 11:1

Average Class Size: 10 to 19

Percent of students going to grad school: Unreported

Tuition and Fees: $31,620

In State Tuition and Fees if different: No difference

Cost for Room and Board: $13,040

Percent receiving financial aid out of those who apply, first year: 94%

Percent receiving financial aid among all students: 68%

With its 100-acre campus located in Purchase, New York, a small town thirty minutes from New York City, Manhattanville College offers its students the intimate academic environment of a small college while encouraging them to explore the diversity, resources, and opportunities of the nearby city. Manhattanville students receive a distinctively personal and well-rounded liberal-arts education and do not need to worry about a lack of activities to keep them busy—even if they have to travel the 30 minutes to find them.

All Planned Out: Preceptorial and Portfolio

Although Manhattanville is a small school with only 1,200 full-time undergrads, it offers over fifty majors and minors, as well as the option to design your own. As one student studying dance and business noted, "I looked at all the schools in the tri-state area. Manhattanville was the only one that said I could major in Irish Step Dancing." All students are required to have a minor in addition to a major. Some students said the choice gained in the number of majors is lost in the limitations imposed by many distributional requirements. Students must take six credits from four of five areas: mathematics and science, social sciences, humanities, languages, and fine arts. But an upperclassman offered advice, saying that these involved requirements can actually make a course load "less intimidating when your semester is not entirely consumed by classes specific to your major."

> "I looked at all the schools in the tri-state area. Manhattanville was the only one that said I could major in Irish Step Dancing."

Apart from the distributional requirements, all freshmen take the Preceptorial, a year-long seminar that functions to help students develop college-level thinking, reading, and writing skills, introduce them to important topics in various fields, and guide them in their studies at Manhattanville. Students may choose between Preceptorials covering diverse issues in current events. The instructor of a Preceptorial is also the students' freshman-year academic advisor who will be one of the many faculty members who "really care about the education of each individual student" throughout college. Manhattanville students really do gush about the degree of personal attention given to them: "I have gotten to know all of my professors personally, and I can go to them whenever I need help or mentoring."

Another distinctive feature of the Manhattanville education is the Portfolio System. Each student meets with a faculty advisor to plot his or her academic path at the beginning of freshman year. In the spring of each following year, students meet again with their advisors to assess their progress, adjust their plans, and put their best work into a portfolio. At the end of senior year, faculty members evaluate the students' portfolios before allowing them to graduate. Students find that the portfolio actually helps them greatly during their studies because it forces them to plan ahead, as well as after graduation, because they have already gathered and reflected upon their best work and are therefore prepared for graduate school or a job search.

Outside the Classroom

While Manhattanville's academic program and small size create a great sense of academic closeness, the campus, in terms of social life, is not very close-knit. This is due in part to the proximity and appeal of the city, but also because many of the students at Manhattanville are from the tri-state area and either commute daily or go home often on the weekends. As a result, the campus is not as lively as many other colleges on the weekends.

There are, however, a number of major activities throughout each year that attract most of the student body, including Fall Fest, a carnival-like music festival, and its spring counterpart, Quad Jam. Reid Hall—better known as "the Castle"—is the site of the "Castle parties," formals in the winter and spring. The Castle parties bring students together, as an upperclassmen reflected: "Most students go to the formals, and they all have different themes, which makes each one special." In addition, there are over thirty clubs and organizations ranging across broad interests, from the Latin Dance Club to the History Club to the Punk Rock Appreciation Club. Students said one of the most popular activities is writing for *The Touchstone*, the Manhattanville newspaper. The student government acts a liaison between the students and the administration, often planning activities to try to keep the campus lively on the weekends for the students who remain on campus.

But the outward migration of students on the weekends is not to say that the facilities and dorms are lacking. Students have a number of housing options, as there are four dorms, all of which are coed and said to be comfortable. Spellman, a "dry hall," is the freshman dormitory. Upperclassmen can choose from Founders, Damman, and Tenney, the latter two of which offer various suite-style living options. Students can choose between different sized suites, with the option of both singles and doubles that share a bathroom and common room. Students have a choice between meal plans that vary in number of meals taken in Benziger Dining Hall and "meal points" redeemable at local cafes and a pub. Dorms also have communal kitchens that students can use if they get tired of dining hall fare.

Manhattanville to Manhattan

Manhattanville is unique in the extent to which it encourages its students to drift from the quiet serenity of Purchase once in a while. The college sponsors trips to New York City that are often integrated into academic coursework. These trips also give students a chance to decide if they truly want to experience life in the city, in which case Manhattanville offers a Semester in New York City program. Participants who are fortunate enough to make the cut live in the city, take classes taught by Manhattanville professors, and gain working experience in internship positions at major companies located in the Big Apple.

There are also trips whose sole purpose is simply to give students a chance to explore the fun side of New York City, through events like a cruise around Manhattan, visits to the Metropolitan Museum of Art, and ice-skating in Central Park. The Office of Student Activities subsidizes some of the trips, allowing students to see shows like *The Lion King* on Broadway and the Radio City Christmas Spectacular for affordable prices. Students often also visit New York City on their own, taking in the sights and just enjoying themselves on the weekends, a possibility thanks to the Metro-North train connecting Purchase to the city.

Manhattanville is ideal for students who seek personal attention, opportunities in a nearby dynamic city, and a serene campus to return to after an exciting weekend. As one student put it, "The best thing to do is just walk around [New York City]. It's so exciting. Then I get to come back up to Manhattanville where I feel so safe."—*Michelle Yu*

FYI

If you come to Manhattanville, you'd better bring "a lot of Tupperware, Mac 'n' Cheese, and ramen noodles."

What is the typical weekend schedule? "Going out to the city, staying in the dorm drifting from room to room with friends, or going to the pub to eat and watch TV."

If I could change one thing about Manhattanville, I'd "[improve] the lack of events on campus."

Three things every student at Manhattanville should do before graduating are "go to all the Castle parties and sports events, go to the White Plains Diner at 3 a.m., and camp out on the quad."

New York University

Address: 22 Washington Square North New York, NY 10011
Phone: 212-998-4500
E-mail address: admission@nyu.edu
Web site URL: www.nyu.edu
Year Founded: 1831
Private or Public: Private
Religious Affiliation: None
Location: Urban
Number of Applicants: 37,245
Percent Accepted: 32%
Percent Accepted who enroll: 39%
Number Entering: 4,648
Number of Transfers Accepted each Year: Unreported
Middle 50% SAT range: M: 630–720, CR: 620–720, Wr: 620–720
Middle 50% ACT range: 28–31
Early admission program EA/ED/None: ED

Percentage accepted through EA or ED: 33%
EA and ED deadline: 1-Nov
Regular Deadline: 13-Jul
Application Fee: $65
Full time Undergraduate enrollment: 19,482
Total enrollment: 20,965
Percent Male: 40%
Percent Female: 60%
Total Percent Minority or Unreported: 53%
Percent African-American: 4%
Percent Asian/Pacific Islander: 19%
Percent Hispanic: 8%
Percent Native-American: 0%
Percent International: 6%
Percent in-state/out of state: 64%/36%
Percent from Public HS: 65%
Retention Rate: 92%
Graduation Rate 4-year: 77%

Graduation Rate 6-year: Unreported
Percent Undergraduates in On-campus housing: 52%
Number of official organized extracurricular organizations: Unreported
3 Most popular majors: Drama, Finance, Liberal Arts
Student/Faculty ratio: 12:1
Average Class Size: Unreported
Percent of students going to grad school: 24%
Tuition and Fees: $37,372
In State Tuition and Fees if different: No difference
Cost for Room and Board: $12,810
Percent receiving financial aid out of those who apply, first year: 80%
Percent receiving financial aid among all students: 53%

New York University was founded in 1831 by Albert Gallatin with a goal to establish "in this immense and fast-growing city . . . a system of rational and practical education fitting for all and graciously open to all." Today's NYU students agree that this goal has been met. "NYU has a variety of different schools that provide different types of education and skills," said one freshman. "It truly has something for everyone."

Fourteen Schools, Fourteen Stereotypes

The University comprises 14 different schools, colleges, and divisions that specialize in everything from the arts to business to nothing in particular. "Tisch kids work on film and production; the College kids are into liberal arts; Gallatin kids don't know what they want to do and are pretty much free to make it up as they go along," summarized one junior. The University's roughly 21,000 undergraduates are distributed amongst the schools—but not evenly. The majority of undergraduates enroll in the College of Arts and Sciences (CAS).

When asked to explain the typical NYU student, one Tisch student said the task was impossible. "I can't define a typical NYU student without splitting the stereotype into schools," he explained.

Despite the clear breakdown of these conceptions, students praised the University for fostering interaction between students, regardless of school. "We live together. We don't get separated. The lack of separation spreads into our social lives" said one sophomore. Others agreed. "There are a lot of misconceptions, but NYU is really just one school."

Size Isn't Everything

At a university this large, you might assume students are necessarily disjointed and separated. But at NYU, even without a central campus, there is something about these "Violets" that keeps everyone together.

"NYU is not too big," concluded one Stern student. "It's very possible to know a lot of people and be very involved, and by being involved, to get to know a lot more people. It's definitely what you make of it." Other students agreed, stressing that students have to be proactive to take full advantage of all that the University has to offer. "As long as you stand up and get involved it's very possible to know people high up and get your face recognized," said one senior.

Despite the size of its population, students say NYU never fails to cater to its students' diverse and eclectic appetites. "We're one of the top schools in the country for providing vegan and vegetarian options at all our dining halls, and kosher options as well," said one junior. "They observe Shabbat in one of the dining halls every week." In addition to more traditional dining hall experiences, students can eat at places like Chick Fil-A, Quiznos, Dunkin' Donuts, and Starbucks. Overall, students praised the University for providing, if not gourmet food, at least a wealth of options. "You can't complain for the most part."

The City That Never Sleeps . . . and the Students That Don't Either

To say that NYU doesn't offer your typical college experience is an understatement. With the heart of the University located in hip, bustling Greenwich Village, students have the luxury of spending four years with New York City as their workplace and playground. And since the University has seriously improved its transportation system in recent years, students at NYU freely engage in the wealth of opportunities in and around their sprawling campus.

"The social life is great, though it's not your normal college scene," explained one senior. Although NYU features some Greek life, there is not much of a formalized network of fraternal organizations on campus. Students described its members as the "few and the proud," saying that they are often indistinguishable from the general population. The University nightlife is primarily focused on the city's various offerings. "There aren't any house parties or frat parties, but you go bar and club hopping."

Some students complained that the social life is overly centered on the city itself. "You go to clubs and a lot of them are big student spots, but unless it's a 'college night,' a lot of times, I'm not even sure who my peers are," said one freshman. "It's really strange that

way. The nightlife culture almost forces you to arrive with a fake ID in hand." However, she was quick to add—"Of course, it's fun. Unlike my friends at other colleges, I'm guaranteed a party come Friday or Saturday night . . . or even Tuesday night."

Sports fans might not be as fond of the fun offered up by NYU. Without a football team, the University lacks what some might consider an intrinsic element of any college experience. Though host to spectacle-drawing varsity sports teams like volleyball, basketball, fencing, and soccer, NYU students consistently fail to flock to the stands. "Attendance at sports events is, well, there really isn't attendance at sports events," said one junior. Yet, despite lackluster athletic support, NYU students are by no means lacking in school spirit or university pride. "There's not really a sport that brings us together, but NYU kids love NYU. There's a lot of school spirit here."

But, We Work Too!

NYU maintains much of its popular academic reputation courtesy of the Leonard N. Stern School of Business and Tisch School of the Arts. But students say the University's excellence reaches far beyond the likely targets. Many cited the economics department as an undiscovered NYU jewel. "We've been the Number One Dream School for a few years now," said one sophomore. "You don't get that way by focusing only on a small group of specialized students," she continued. "Obviously, the University is offering something for us all."

> "There's not really a sport that brings us together, but NYU kids love NYU. There's a lot of school spirit here."

Other students were quick to explain deficiencies in the overall system. "I wish I had smaller classes," said one freshman. "As much as NYU tells you you're not just another number, with some professors, it just seems that way." Many courses include lectures and smaller, weekly sessions led by teaching assistants (TAs). One CAS junior succinctly declared, "TAs are pretty much a regular thing here."

Gallatin is often cited as offering more opportunities for small seminars than CAS, but as students advance in their majors, they are given preference to enter seminars in CAS, each generally including roughly 20 students. "It's a university. Lectures are part of the definition of that term. It's just part of the deal, but as you get older, you have more opportunities to take intimate classes," explained one sophomore.

Shanghai? Ghana? Don't You Wanna?

Whether or not NYU offers the most opportunities for small classes, it is certainly the ideal school for a student looking to study abroad. The University offers study abroad programs in over 25 countries—if you can bear to separate yourself from the bright city lights. Students from other college and universities are routinely offered opportunities to study abroad as part of NYU's expansive program. "Where else could you spend the semester in Shanghai or Ghana?" asked an enthusiastic junior. "It's just the best place to be for people who want to learn firsthand about other cultures."

NYU is famous (and infamous) for both its nightlife and its internships. Those looking to capitalize on a variety of resources, work on their dance moves, and master the Big Apple during their college years will find such the choice quite appealing.—*Nicholle Manners*

FYI

If you come to NYU, you'd better bring "a sense of openness because it's a very diverse school."

What's the typical weekend schedule? "Work during the day, party at night all through the weekend starting Thursday night."

If I could change on thing about NYU, I'd "improve financial aid and alumni support—excluding Stern."

Three things every student at NYU should do before graduating are "explore the city, study abroad, and meet lots of new people."

Parsons School of Design

Address: 65 Fifth Avenue New York, NY 10011
Phone: 212-229-8910
E-mail address: parsadm@newschool.edu
Web site URL: www.parsons.edu
Year Founded: 1896
Private or Public: Private
Religious Affiliation: None
Location: Urban
Number of Applicants: 2,921
Percent Accepted: 50%
Percent Accepted who enroll: 44%
Number Entering: 653
Number of Transfers Accepted each Year: Unreported
Middle 50% SAT range: M: 490–610, CR: 480–590, Wr: 490–600
Middle 50% ACT range: 22–26
Early admission program EA/ED/None: None

Percentage accepted through EA or ED: NA
EA and ED deadline: NA
Regular Deadline: 1-Mar
Application Fee: $50
Full time Undergraduate enrollment: 3,180
Total enrollment: 3,815
Percent Male: 22%
Percent Female: 78%
Total Percent Minority or Unreported: Unreported
Percent African-American: 4%
Percent Asian/Pacific Islander: 17%
Percent Hispanic: 7%
Percent Native-American: 0%
Percent International: 33%
Percent in-state/out of state: 27%/73%
Percent from Public HS: Unreported
Retention Rate: 87%
Graduation Rate 4-year: 53%

Graduation Rate 6-year: Unreported
Percent Undergraduates in On-campus housing: 23%
Number of official organized extracurricular organizations: 25
3 Most popular majors: Design, Fashion, Illustration
Student/Faculty ratio: 9:1
Average Class Size: Unreported
Percent of students going to grad school: Unreported
Tuition and Fees: $34,460
In State Tuition and Fees if different: No difference
Cost for Room and Board: $12,390
Percent receiving financial aid out of those who apply, first year: 88%
Percent receiving financial aid among all students: 44%

D o you ever dream about your name featured on white tents in Bryant Park during Fashion Week? Do you know you want to spend a life creating and designing but don't quite know how to do it? Do you watch *Project Runway* religiously? If you answered "YES!" to any of these questions, perhaps Parsons School of Design is the right place for you. Founded in 1896 as an art school, Parsons has a rich history of having the first undergraduate programs in disciplines like graphics design, interior design, and advertising. It is now part of The New School, a university network in New York City known for its avant-garde teaching style and unique philosophy. Parsons students enjoy the energy of New York, the mentorship of notable faculty, and learn the necessary skills to enter the art world after graduation.

The Foundations and Beyond

Undergraduates at Parsons can graduate in four years and obtain either a Bachelor of Fine Arts or a Bachelor of Business Administration. Those who are particularly ambitious and desire a more varied education experience can opt for the five-year joint BFA and BA program, called the BAFA program. This program is hosted in conjunction with Eugene Lang College. Students are often overwhelmed by the changes that college brings and by the stimuli that a new environment provides. Parsons tackles this problem by having every freshman take "Foundation Courses." "They're mandatory for the BFA program . . . some of the stuff seems repetitive and dull, but it just made the classes that I took my sophomore year so much more rewarding and interesting," one junior said. The program ensures that students have a necessary technical and methodological understanding of art to succeed in future classes. These classes are broad enough to be applicable to whatever majors the students choose in the end, along with being designed to enhance visual thinking.

Some of the more popular majors at Parsons are Illustration, Design and Visual Communications, and Fashion Apparel Design. The Fashion Design department at Parsons is perhaps the most renowned—its graduates include fashion designers Donna Karan and Tom Ford, plus Tim Gunn, mentor to the designers on *Project Runaway*, is the former dean of this department. Students in this major are known to be "very cutthroat" and a sense of intense competition is omnipresent in these classrooms. "People are not only very secretive about what they're designing but are constantly trying to outdo each other," one Fashion Design major said. However, she added, "But some people are genuinely helpful and will give you ideas. I guess you just have to find the right crowd."

Another program for students who are particularly driven and motivated is the Chase Scholars Program. Named for William Merritt Chase, the impressionist painter that founded the art school that eventually became Parsons, Chase Scholars have a "strong interest in design, high academic achievement and well-developed critical thinking skills but limited studio experience." Special scholarships are given to those that get into the program as well.

Jet-Setting

If you start to feel a little overwhelmed by the competition at Parsons, you may want to consider going abroad. "Many juniors take a semester or the whole year to go abroad. I was in Paris the first semester this year. It was wonderful to be studying in a different culture!" one junior raved. Paris is a popular destination for these juniors not only because "it's the only city that holds a candle to New York in terms of it being a fashion and art mecca," but because Parsons has a campus in Paris. Some areas of study in which Parsons Paris excels are Communication Design, Fashion Design, Photography and Fine Arts. Other exchange programs that are available include the Chelsea College of Art and Design in London, Sydney College of the Arts in Australia, and Bezalel Academy of Art and Design in Jerusalem, Israel.

If you can't bear to leave New York for a semester but still want to go abroad, Parsons has an excellent international summer program. These Summer Intensive Studies are open to both Parsons students and non-Parsons students, and are typically five weeks long. Classes try to mesh the subject matter with the culture and history of the host country. For instance, the Summer Intensive Studies in Paris offered "Architecture and Interiors of Paris: A Drawing Investigation and Photography in Paris."

"A Mini-Version of New York"

Even if you don't go abroad, you will be exposed to different ways of thinking, different cultures and backgrounds due to the diversity of people at Parsons. While there will be many resident New Yorkers in your classes, many students are from out of state and abroad. Parsons recognizes the importance of having a diverse learning environment and is particularly international-student-friendly. The summer before freshman year, international students attend SOPIS, Summer Orientation Program for International Students. This is an opportunity for international students to get settled in a little early but also for a chance to take English as a Foreign Language (ESL) classes and to learn about the city and how the American university system works. "Parsons is like a mini version of the city itself. There are so many people here from other places in the world—we're all learning and inspiring each other everyday," one New York native said.

The Big Apple

Not uncommon of schools in large metropolises, Parsons lacks a central campus with greens and dorms. The main campus is in Greenwich Village and the other campus is in the Garment District—fittingly, the Fashion Design is located there. Parsons has a few residence halls for its students. The Marlton House is most famous for housing Beat poets in the 1960. The most popular dorm is the Union Square Residence, where students have Union Square Park and its concerts, farmers markets and shopping right at their doorstep. Freshmen primarily live in Loeb Hall and the 13th Street Residence. Meal plans are available and there are many options in terms of eating venues that Parsons students share with students from The New School.

While the residence halls save students the hassle of finding an apartment in Manhattan, many students choose to live off campus. "Moving off was the best thing for me; I live with someone who goes to NYU and it's been awesome. I'm more independent and I've learned how to cook!" one senior said. Because so many students move off campus, the social scene at Parsons is very fragmented and school spirit is a little weak. However, most students don't seem to mind this, for "there's always something to do in New York."

> "You become a pro at finding free things to do. But otherwise you will be spending a lot of money on the weekends."

On or off campus, all students agree that New York is an expensive city to live in: "You become a pro at finding free things to do. But otherwise you will be spending a lot of money on the weekends." But New York serves as an inspiration and playground for all Parsons students. Endless galleries and museums, concerts and music, good places to eat, and the eclectic bar and clubbing scene are all taken advantage of. The fact that there are very few social opportunities on campus does not hinder these students from finding their own niche in the city. The power and the liveliness of New York City is integral to the Parsons experience—so if you think you can thrive in a bustling city life and manage the workload, Parsons may be the school for you!—*Lee Komeda*

FYI

If you come to Parsons, you'd better bring "a good winter jacket, a fake ID, and a need for creative outlet!"

What's the typical weekend schedule? "Drink and smoke at a friend's apartment and go out to hit up a few bars. Or, alternatively, I could be in the studio working non-stop."

If you could change one thing about Parsons: "A central hangout spot would be great . . . also if the two campuses were closer together."

Three things you should do before graduating: "Meet as many people and network for the future, participate in the fashion show, go to as many museums as possible."

Rensselaer Polytechnic Insititute of Technology

Address: 110 Eighth Street
Troy, NY 12180-3590
Phone: 518-276-6216
E-mail address:
admissions@rpi.edu
Web site URL: www.rpi.edu
Year Founded: 1824
Private or Public: Private
Religious Affiliation: None
Location: Suburban
Number of Applicants:
11,249
Percent Accepted: 44%
Percent Accepted who
enroll: 27%
Number Entering: 1,356
Number of Transfers
Accepted each Year: 199
Middle 50% SAT range:
M: 650–730, CR: 600–690,
Wr: 580–680
Middle 50% ACT range:
24–29
Early admission program
EA/ED/None: EA
Percentage accepted
through EA or ED: 47%

EA and ED deadline: 1-Nov
Regular Deadline: 15-Jan
Application Fee: $70
Full time Undergraduate
enrollment: 5,394
Total enrollment: 7,521
Percent Male: 73%
Percent Female: 27%
Total Percent Minority or
Unreported: 26%
Percent African-American:
4%
Percent Asian/Pacific
Islander: 11%
Percent Hispanic: 6%
Percent Native-American:
<1%
Percent International: 2%
Percent in-state/out of
state: 41%/59%
Percent from Public HS:
72%
Retention Rate: 95%
Graduation Rate 4-year:
64%
Graduation Rate 6-year:
82%

Percent Undergraduates
in On-campus housing:
53%
Number of official organized
extracurricular
organizations: 164
3 Most popular majors:
Business, Computer
Engineering, Electircal
Electronics and
Communications Engineering
Student/Faculty ratio: 14:1
Average Class Size: 10 to
19
Percent of students going to
grad school: 24%
Tuition and Fees: $36,950
In State Tuition and Fees if
different: No difference
Cost for Room and Board:
$10,730
Percent receiving financial
aid out of those who apply,
first year: 98%
Percent receiving financial
aid among all students:
94%

L ocated in upstate New York, Rensselaer Polytechnic Institute is known for churning out Noble Prize–bound engineers and NHL-bound hockey pros. Though the heavy workload and brutal winter weather can be intimidating, RPI's strong programs and cutting-edge facilities make it a mecca for engineers, architects and hockey fans alike.

A (Metric) Ton of Work

When asked why he chose RPI, one student simply said: "It sets you apart in the engineering world." RPI's stellar reputation and top-notch academic programs make it an appealing option for students interested in engineering and a host of other fields. Students can apply to one of five schools within the University: Science, Architecture, Engineering, Humanities and Social Sciences or Management and Technology. The architecture program is praised for its professors and its small size—while the University enrolls over 5,000 undergraduates, the prestigious architecture school enrolls 60–70 freshmen per year. Those who make the cut gain access to RPI's lighting research center, one of the best in the country. While RPI is predominantly known as an engineering school, the school is working to further develop its programs in other areas. The new EMPAC (Experimental Media Performing Arts Center) will mix cutting-edge technology with the arts, a reflection of the growing diversification of academic options.

Slackers beware: RPI academics are intense. As one engineering s[...] definitely a lot harder than [...] They say it's hard, but it real[...] lying." It's common knowled[...] must spend at least 30 hours [...] of class "to even have a chan[...] ting by." Most people devote[...] that, setting aside an entire [...] midnight) each week to cat[...]

At least the professors believe in curving. Though students' final grades are determined by how well they perform in comparison to their peers, competition is not cutthroat. While it does exist, some say "It's us against the teacher more than us against ourselves." Furthermore, the combination of a rigorous program and RPI's good name means that graduates are well-prepared for the working world. Students praise the career center and the University as a whole for its focus on landing students enviable jobs after graduation.

All students in the engineering program must take a set of core classes, usually during their first three or four semesters. While students say that the relevance between these core classes and their specific major can seem doubtful at first, professors aim to make the courses applicable to all programs. "You might not know what it relates to when you take it, but longer down the road you get it," said one junior.

With rigorous programs and a large student body, RPI undergrads are encouraged take a pro-active stance in their education. "If you don't put out the effort, you're a number," said one student. Extensive class preparation is required, and students must learn a number of things on their own from the textbook. Students say it "goes both ways" in terms of professor accessibility—some are always available while others are constantly traveling the world. The University is known for offering undergraduates an abundance of research opportunities.

Bricks & Bread
Campus buildings boast the best of both worlds: on the outside, the gothic structures have a "traditional, collegiate look," while on the inside they offer cutting-edge technology. The majority of campus is wireless, and every classroom is set up so that students can plug in their laptops. The University even provides incoming freshmen with a personal laptop and wireless card.

The Quad, RPI's largest residence area, sits on the main campus. It houses upperclassmen in single, double or triple rooms. There are also 10 residence halls, including five freshman dorms, surrounding the Commons Dining Hall. Upperclassmen looking ʹɔ escape traditional dorm life can live in recently-renovated apartments, which ɔmplete with a kitchen and dining ʹhile only first-year students are ʹn-campus housing, upper-class

students say they don't have any difficulty finding residences to their liking.

The dining hall receives lukewarm ratings in terms of quality—it's "hit or miss." At least "[it] doesn't cause any problems internally and tastes decent," as one content diner reported. There are six styles of food to choose from each night, so "you can always find something that you like." And for those fearing the Freshman 15—"there are lots of healthy options." Students are generally pleased with the flexible meal plans. "In theory you can go to the dining hall 15 times a day."

> "The standard issue RPI kid is probably a big computer nerd."

Most upperclassmen don't have meal plans, so they cook their own food or purchase meals at the student union. The student-run Rensselaer Union, which incorporates campus-wide technology, is a popular student hang-out. It features two floors of food courts, including a Starbucks and café. The U-shaped quad is another destination for those seeking a place to chill. But the academic rigors don't leave many stretches of time for ambitious RPI students to just lay low. "Honestly, you're going to find most people in the student union center or on their computers," said one student.

A Social Scavenger Hunt
Students agree that the low-key nightlife at RPI demands a "pro-active attitude" from those seeking a quality party. "There's stuff to do," said one student, "but it's not the University of Miami." Fraternities and sororities have a big presence on campus, with more than a quarter of the University involved, and current students encourage incoming freshmen to consider rushing. However, the RPI administration has been tightening the reins on underage drinking in recent years, making fraternities hesitant to throw full-scale parties, and leaving the nightlife-starved student body even hungrier for a full social calendar. "Our school is trying to deal with underage drinking. They feel they should be changing policies for the entire United States," said one frustrated Greek member. Outside of the Greek system, popular annual parties include the Big Red Freak-Out, to support the hockey team, and Grand Marshal week, when the elections for student representatives take

place. GM week is full of games, and students enjoy time off from classes. In general, students point to the academic intensity as the reason behind the tame party scene. "People are so busy—you don't have time to party until the weekend."

While some students complain that the surrounding town of Troy is, to put it bluntly, "pretty crappy," as well as a bit unsafe, others indicate the recent renewal effort that the city has been experiencing. Its art community in particular has made Troy more attractive. For those so inclined, students of drinking age point out worthwhile destinations like Club Lime, a rugby bar called The Ruck, and O'Learys for food. Troy and Albany also host occasional concerts. While most upperclassmen have a car on campus, few venture outside of the Troy area on a regular basis. Many students choose to hang out with friends made through activities, rather than just those from within the major.

"The Odds Are Good but the Goods Are Odd"

RPI students are known for their book smarts, but some confess that their peers' social skills could use a little fine-tuning. "The standard issue RPI kid is probably a big computer nerd," admitted one junior, echoing a common view on campus. One student painted the caricature of an RPI student as someone who "walks around in a black trench coat, doesn't speak any English, and stays in his room to play videogames or download porn." Indeed, the high-tech atmosphere can have a downside: it's not uncommon for some students to stay glued to their laptop through the weekend. "They're very computer-oriented students," explained one undergrad; "[they] make my college look bad!" However, many RPI students are witty, outgoing and have a great sense of humor; they assure that the caricature is not the norm and that "there is plenty of social interaction on campus." Overall, undergrads are described as friendly, laid-back and into outdoor activities. One junior summed up the situation by saying that there are two kinds of smarts—book smarts and wit—and every RPI student has at least one in the bag.

There are few complaints about ethnic diversity at RPI—the strong academic programs draw students from across the world. But students tend to be less enthusiastic about the gender ratio and dating prospects.

The skewed male-female ratio of 3:1 can definitely put a kink in a guy's game. As one Greek brother said: "There are 32 fraternities and five sororities—just by that fact you can kind of figure it out." Not surprisingly, long-term relationships tend to prevail over random hook-ups: "If a guy finds a girl he usually hangs on to her." Guys sometimes complain of RIBS ("ratio-induced bitch syndrome") among the minority sex, as "very pretty girls get hit on all the time, so they think they're the greatest thing in the world." Female students have their own set of troubles, though. "The guys always complain about the fact that there are no girls, but a lot of the guys are the ones who sit in the rooms and play videogames," one female explained. "Girls also have difficulty."

Puck Pros

Hockey is huge at RPI. "Going to a hockey game is like going to a professional game," explained one student. In fact some players do head straight from RPI to the NHL, including such notable alumni as Joe Juneau and Adam Oates. Men's and women's hockey are the only Division I sports at the University, but football also attracts large crowds. RPI is planning to construct the new East Campus Athletic Village, which will include a new football field, gym, 50-meter pool and tennis courts. Whether it's on the varsity, club or recreational level, many students participate in some sort of athletic activity of campus. Undergrads can often be found skateboarding, riding bikes or in the midst of a snowball fight.

Making the Most of It

While the stereotype of the RPI computer nerd seems to have some truth behind it, students have a sense of humor about it and prove that social interaction doesn't have to be limited to study sessions and videogame marathons. Facing a massive workload and large introductory classes, students are urged to shape their own paths at RPI, and to make time for fun. "You're going to go crazy if you don't take control of what you're doing," said one student. Another RPI undergrad offered this piece of advice to incoming freshmen: "Bring a willingness to do everything you can. The work is going to be really hard, but you're not going to be able to make it without friends."—*Christen Martosella*

Rochester Institute of Technology

Address: 60 Lomb Memorial Drive Rochester, NY 14623-5604
Phone: 585-475-6631
E-mail address: admissions@rit.edu
Web site URL: www.rit.edu
Year Founded: 1829
Private or Public: Private
Religious Affiliation: None
Location: Suburban
Number of Applicants: 12,725
Percent Accepted: 60%
Percent Accepted who enroll: 30%
Number Entering: 2,616
Number of Transfers Accepted each Year: 1,203
Middle 50% SAT range: M: 560–670, CR: 540–630, Wr: 520–610
Middle 50% ACT range: 24–29
Early admission program EA/ED/None: ED

Percentage accepted through EA or ED: 66%
EA and ED deadline: 1-Dec
Regular Deadline: 1-Feb
Application Fee: $50
Full time Undergraduate enrollment: 3,861
Total enrollment: 6,494
Percent Male: 67%
Percent Female: 33%
Total Percent Minority or Unreported: 32%
Percent African-American: 5%
Percent Asian/Pacific Islander: 5%
Percent Hispanic: 4%
Percent Native-American: <1%
Percent International: 11%
Percent in-state/out of state: 55%/45%
Percent from Public HS: 85%
Retention Rate: 88%
Graduation Rate 4-year: 62%

Graduation Rate 6-year: Unreported
Percent Undergraduates in On-campus housing: 68%
Number of official organized extracurricular organizations: 175
3 Most popular majors: Business, Information Technology, Photography
Student/Faculty ratio: 14:1
Average Class Size: 10 to 19
Percent of students going to grad school: 15%
Tuition and Fees: $28,035
In State Tuition and Fees if different: No difference
Cost for Room and Board: $9,381
Percent receiving financial aid out of those who apply, first year: 86%
Percent receiving financial aid among all students: 77%

Every fall, the president of the Rochester Institute of Technology (RIT) plays a softball game with students. He also bets that no one can hit a home run off his pitch. The close relationship between the faculty and students reflect the practical learning that goes on at this career-oriented university, as RIT brings technical expertise together with a liberal arts curriculum.

Real-World Academics
While many students at RIT come interested in engineering and the sciences, they often end up taking modern-day interpretative dance, pottery making or the history of the French Revolution. The foundation of the school still lies upon a liberal arts curriculum, with core classes that cover the humanities, social sciences and sciences.

But be warned, RIT academics are not for the faint of heart. The school year runs on the quarter system so there are 10-week classes followed by a final in the fall, winter and spring. Within each quarter, students typically take three to five classes. This all comes down to 40 percent more credit than other schools. Freshmen usually have relatively bad schedules since they have last pick in class registration.

With eight colleges ranging from business to the National Technical Institute for the Deaf, RIT has plenty to offer. Yet its best known feature is the co-op program. "One of the oldest in the country, the RIT co-op experience often turn into full-time jobs," a student said. Some majors require students to do a co-op, which consists of taking a certain number of academic quarters off to work at a company.

For instance, the engineering major actually takes five years to complete because of five quarters of required co-op experience. Other majors don't require a single co-op. But many students jump on co-ops because of the real-world experience and tangible rewards, like cash!

RIT also makes it easy to match you up with the type of work you would be interested in, from designing computer chips to designing fabrics for the spring fashion line. The campus career center and co-op office run year-round to match up the thousands of students with hundreds of top companies.

How to Build a Racecar
Students at RIT don't just build race cars, they swing dance! The swing dance club teaches newcomers the fine art and also competes at various dancing showoffs. For those more interested in things that may explode, many engineering majors every year have designed, built, and raced F1-like cars in competitions. If these two clubs don't whet your appetite, there are 173 others to choose from.

The photography department and art programs at RIT are very well respected. There are countless dance companies, jazz assembles and theater troupes on campus. Each year, three or four plays are produced, and many concerts are held.

The WITR is RIT's unique noncommercial and student-run radio station that reaches the greater Rochester region, a great outlet for students interested in everything from management to political commentary. *The Reporter* is RIT's undergraduate magazine, published weekly with the collaboration of writers, managers, photographers and editors. At the ESPN Sports Zone, RIT students actually tape the show *Sports Break*, which airs on ESPN 2.

Of course, if you don't find a club that exactly matches your niche, just start your own. It's very easy at RIT, and many fledgling organizations receive funding from the Student Government, which is the perfect place for the politically-oriented.

Engineers, Photographers, and Hockey Players
The first thing a student displaced from Hurricane Katrina noticed when she set foot on campus was the diversity of the student body. "Everyone's pretty well rounded," another student said. Although RIT may seem like a very technical school given its name, "there are photographers and artsy people, not just engineers," she said. However, there are more guys than girls at RIT, thus the saying around campus, "the odds are good but the goods are odd." RIT is also home to the largest population of deaf students, who are well integrated into the general student body but mostly take specially designed classes with accommodations.

> **"The odds are good but the goods are odd."**

"There are still students who play computer games in their rooms all day," one student admits. This stereotype of RIT certainly doesn't explain the facts that over half the students play in intramurals. Nonetheless, recruited athletes remain a minority on campus. All sports are Division III but hockey recently became Division I, huge news for a school that schedules homecoming around the hockey season. The lack of a football team makes hockey, as well as basketball, popular social outlets on the weekends.

Bricks, Bricks, and More Bricks
"On the outside, the campus may look bland because everything's covered in brick," one student said. But "it looks much nicer on the inside where you can enjoy the landscaping, since the buildings are roughly in a circle." The campus is medium-sized in a relatively rural area. Yet RIT is also only minutes from Rochester, a booming metropolis for weekend partiers.

"A whole new college town is being developed, with an outside amphitheater, and new stores and shops," a student eagerly revealed. Because RIT owns a lot of land, the school has been on a spending and developing spree of late, growing to keep up with their rise in popularity.

Freshmen have to live in dorms, but this gives them a chance to meet each other. The campus housing consists mainly of singles, doubles, and triples, with a few suites available. But the housing assignments are completely random. Some upperclassmen live in one of five campus apartments, while others find housing off-campus; since RIT is relatively tucked away, housing is pretty affordable. Still others go off to live in fraternities. But 68 percent of students still choose to live on campus.

Food Cornucopia

"I eat on campus every day," one student said. "The food is good." The cafeteria, situated on the freshman campus, attracts students at all times of the day. This main dining hall has a student-run pizza parlor and various fast food options.

While some tout the dining options, another student said that the food is horrible, and that students deserve better food for the relatively high cost of going to RIT. For those dissatisfied with on-campus dining options, nearby restaurants offer a welcome escape. Five to ten minutes down Jefferson Road, a major traveling route, students find plenty of places to satisfy their hunger for Mexican, Chinese, Italian, steak and good old home cooking.

On their breaks, RIT students enjoy relaxing at the coffee shops scattered around campus. The College Grind, open seven days a week, is the perfect meeting place and serves a mean espresso that will surely pick you up on those late-night study sessions. Many points along the underground halls between buildings also sell snack foods, like RITchie's, complete with the latest arcade games and big screen TV.

"Going to Wegmans at three in the morning is an awesome experience," said one upperclassman. This institutional icon is a 24-hour grocery store that's perfect for students working through the night.

Beyond the Co-op

There's always something going on along the "Quarter Mile," the busy walkway that cuts through the campus. Of course, to relax, you could go to the gym and take fencing lessons. There's also a student-run nightclub along the way. But the busiest building by far at RIT is the Union, the center of the social scene. There's a 500-seat theater that screens films, a Ben & Jerry's ice cream parlor, and various game rooms. The Union also has the unique ESPN SportsCenter desk, where you can tape your dreams of being a sports broadcaster.

Some students find having a car very useful, particularly for shopping in the surrounding areas. The Marketplace Mall is a quick drive and distraction from the busy campus. But transportation is very convenient, with free shuttles that go off-campus.

The social life on the weekends truly spans the spectrum. RIT lives by the motto, "study hard, play hard." For those into the party scene, the best places are off-campus in apartments and frats, although room parties still exist. There are 19 fraternities on campus, and 10 sororities, which undoubtedly serve as key social centers during the weekend. One student commented on the general lack of campus-wide parties, partly due to the relatively strict alcohol policy. But one weekend always alive with festivities is Brick City Homecoming, which boasts more planned events than one could ever attend and appearances by Jon Stewart and Rudy Giuliani.—*Jerry Guo*

FYI
If you come to RIT, you'd better bring "a laptop and a winter coat."
What is the typical weekend schedule? "Procrastinate, procrastinate, and procrastinate. See a drive-in movie on Thursday night, go to Friday Night at the Ritz, do a little work on Saturday, and study on Sunday."
If I could change one thing about RIT, I'd "put more hours in a day and make more students get involved in extracurricular activities."
Three things every student at RIT should do before graduating are "make a difference in the community, play Frisbee in the snow and walk the nature trails."

Sarah Lawrence College

Address: 1 Mead Way
Bronxville, NY 10708-5999
Phone: 914-395-2510
E-mail address:
slcadmit@sarahlawrence
.edu
Web site URL:
www.sarahlawrence.edu
Year Founded: 1926
Private or Public: Private
Religious Affiliation: None
Location: Urban
Number of Applicants: 2,785
Percent Accepted: 46%
**Percent Accepted who
enroll:** 27%
Number Entering: 347
**Number of Transfers
Accepted each Year:** 97
Middle 50% SAT range:
Unreported
Middle 50% ACT range:
Unreported
**Early admission program
EA/ED/None:** ED
**Percentage accepted
through EA or ED:** 24%

EA and ED deadline: 15-Nov
Regular Deadline: 1-Jan
Application Fee: $60
**Full time Undergraduate
enrollment:** 1,389
Total enrollment: 1,791
Percent Male: 27%
Percent Female: 73%
**Total Percent Minority or
Unreported:** 35%
Percent African-American:
4%
**Percent Asian/Pacific
Islander:** 5%
Percent Hispanic: 5%
Percent Native-American:
<1%
Percent International: 3%
**Percent in-state/out of
state:** 25%/75%
Percent from Public HS:
Unreported
Retention Rate: 80%
Graduation Rate 4-year:
67%
Graduation Rate 6-year:
72%

**Percent Undergraduates
in On-campus housing:**
85%
**Number of official organized
extracurricular
organizations:** 70
3 Most popular majors:
Unreported
Student/Faculty ratio:
9:1
Average Class Size:
Unreported
**Percent of students
going to grad school:**
Unreported
Tuition and Fees: $40,350
**In State Tuition and Fees
if different:** No
difference
Cost for Room and Board:
$13,716
**Percent receiving financial
aid out of those who apply,
first year:** 50%
**Percent receiving financial
aid among all students:**
53%

Located in a quiet suburb of New York City, Sarah Lawrence provides an individualized education for the atypical student, and gives students the opportunity to meet a wide variety of students. The school emphasizes a liberal arts education, while also encouraging students to apply classroom knowledge while acquiring professional experience through internships in New York City.

Where School is Tailored to You
Sarah Lawrence has few requirements, requiring only that students take one course in three out of four disciplines, which are creative and performing arts, social sciences and history, natural sciences and math, and humanities. To ensure some breadth, the school also places a limit on how many credits can be taken in each discipline, with individual caps being 50 of the total 120 needed to graduate. Typically, students take three classes a semester. The advising system provides students with a personalized educa-

tion. During freshman year, students are assigned a "don" in the field of their choice. A student's don serves as a general academic advisor as well as an aid while the student selects classes. As one sophomore said, "It is really nice having an advocate. Your don takes care of any issue you need." In addition, bi-weekly meetings with professors "ensure that you are not just another number." The consensus is that the professors have great respect for the students and do not treat them as their inferiors. "Professors are here because they want to be. They want to closely advise students." The most popular majors (known as "concentrations" at Sarah Lawrence) are writing and the humanities. Science is not as popular, but students say the science concentrations still have "a presence" on campus.

Instead of final exams, students must complete Conference Projects in many of their classes. Conference Projects range from creative group projects to research papers designed by the student under the guidance of a professor. One student commented that "conference projects, while a lot of work, teach you how to write in a way most people can't." The method of choosing classes was also described as one of Sarah Lawrence's strengths. Before a student is enrolled in a course, the student and professor interview each other to see if the class will be an appropriate match for the student. One sophomore noted, "Because it is a two-way system, I feel like I am respected by my professors and that I am not just another number in a big lecture hall." This is further reinforced by the small class size, as most courses are taught as seminars limited to 15 students. "Class size is why I chose Sarah Lawrence and what makes Sarah Lawrence Sarah Lawrence," said one senior. The workload can be challenging and "time management is key," said one student, but according to another, the environment is not competitive. "People are not cut throat because you are in competition with yourself." To supplement material learned in the classroom, many students hold internships in New York City because of its close proximity.

> **"Professors are here because they want to be. They want to closely advise students."**

Grading and advising are also unique. Sarah Lawrence gives detailed comments instead of grades. Further, grades are less a result of performance measures such as tests, but rather on effort and knowledge of the course material as perceived by the professor. One senior added that you are "graded not on your performance on a test, but on what they think you have learned. Grades/comments here are about doing the best job you can, not being in the top percentage of your class."

Overall, students like the academics at Sarah Lawrence. One senior commented that "Sarah Lawrence prepares you more broadly. SLC prepares you really well to write, understand and do work." One complaint, however, was that not all concentrations receive the same amount of resources from the College. As one senior griped, "A few departments are nonexistent, and I would like to see more equal distribution around the College."

In Between Two Cities

Located on the border of Yonkers and Bronxville in a quiet suburb of New York City, SLC does not have a very positive relationship with the locals. Those from Yonkers ignore the students, and according to students, there has been some hostility between the students and residents of Bronxville. Generally, the campus is self-contained as most students live on campus, especially freshmen and sophomores. The quality of the dorms varies, with freshman dorms described as small, and senior dorms described as "quite spacious and nice." Those who do move off campus move to Yonkers as it is less expensive than Bronxville. Freshmen are prohibited from having cars, but they are popular among Sarah Lawrence's upperclassmen.

Freshmen have a mandatory meal plan and tend to congregate at Bates Dining Hall. The meal plans are rather expensive, so upperclassmen tend to cook or get takeout. Moreover, many of the dorms have kitchens that are quite popular. During the day many students go to the on-campus pub that serves fast food, and although students acknowledge the dining halls "could use some work," many agree that they are "fine overall."

Finding Your Place at SLC

According to students, Sarah Lawrence can be socially isolating at times. The campus is often somewhat deserted during weekends because many students go to New York City. In addition, there are many types of people at SLC, and "finding your group can be difficult sometimes." It takes someone "socially outgoing to appreciate the social life." Consequently, New York is one of SLC's strengths, as it gives students the opportunity to get off campus. Shuttles as well as the train make transportation easy. "SLC attracts the type of student that will use New York for all that it has to offer."

Still, diversity can be an issue; while the campus is socially diverse, it is not ethnically. Students say the University is making efforts to change this, with days devoted to promoting education about diversity and financial issues. Financial aid remains a problem at Sarah Lawrence. One senior said that "the University is eager to use its money for financial aid. The only problem is that our endowment is not that large. They are doing great with what they have, but it is still not enough." Identity-based groups are quite popular on campus. For example, Coming Out month is popular and well received, and students say the gay population is "quite large and well accepted." The female to male ratio is higher than average, which can probably be attributed to the fact that SLC was an all women's school until 1968. In terms of finding relationships, "one must look for the dating scene, but it is there."

The drug and alcohol policy is "fairly standard." Drugs are never allowed; however, students say that marijuana and alcohol are treated less severely. If caught, a student is ticketed and then has a meeting with "student affairs." "The College has a pretty good sense of its priorities" one sophomore reported; if a student does have a problem with drugs and alcohol, the university focuses on helping the student, rather than punishing him. Still, due to the restrictions against substances, parties tend to be small and moved off campus.

Sports are not overwhelming on campus, but "are a part" of campus life. While the students interviewed could not name all of the teams, they could name many of the school's major varsity athletics. SLC has atypical school spirit. One student commented, "You won't see a bevy of sweatshirts walking around campus, but there is a sense of pride and tradition." One senior described it as a "very strong sense of tradition. The tradition is to be different from most colleges. It's a pretty wonderful place."

In general, the only complaints students had were about the occasional professor that he or she did not really enjoy, although one student commented that career services could improve their contacts and do a better job of helping students. Sarah Lawrence is a great school for those who are not looking for a restrictive environment. Sarah Lawrence is full of "self-motivated students looking for a great education in a non cookie-cutter form." SLC fosters academic growth while exposing students to many things both in and out of the classroom, and provides the opportunity for an individualized college experience unmatched by most other schools.—*Hilary Cohen*

FYI

If you come to SLC you'd better bring "an open mind and a bookshelf for all of the reading you will do."

What is the typical weekend schedule? "Thursday: Party, or leave for New York City. Friday: registered parties from a student organization. Alcohol is there but only for people of age. The rest of the weekend: schoolwork."

If you could change one thing about SLC, "it would be the size of the endowment and the amount of money available to undergraduates."

Three things you should do before you graduate are "run around naked on campus, go to a senate meeting and have at least one conference paper done on time."

Skidmore College

Address: 815 North Broadway Saratoga Springs, NY 12866-1632
Phone: 518-580-5570
E-mail address: admissions@skidmore.edu
Web site URL: www.skidmore.edu
Year Founded: 1903
Private or Public: Private
Religious Affiliation: None
Location: Suburban
Number of Applicants: 6,768
Percent Accepted: 37%
Percent Accepted who enroll: 28%
Number Entering: 682
Number of Transfers Accepted each Year: 86
Middle 50% SAT range: M: 580–670, CR: 580–680, Wr: 590–690
Middle 50% ACT range: 26–30
Early admission program EA/ED/None: ED

Percentage accepted through EA or ED: 43%
EA and ED deadline: 15-Nov
Regular Deadline: 15-Jan
Application Fee: $60
Full time Undergraduate enrollment: 2,717
Total enrollment: 2,809
Percent Male: 40%
Percent Female: 60%
Total Percent Minority or Unreported: 34%
Percent African-American: 3%
Percent Asian/Pacific Islander: 7%
Percent Hispanic: 5%
Percent Native-American: <1%
Percent International: 3%
Percent in-state/out of state: 68%/32%
Percent from Public HS: 63%
Retention Rate: 94%
Graduation Rate 4-year: 78%

Graduation Rate 6-year: 80%
Percent Undergraduates in On-campus housing: 85%
Number of official organized extracurricular organizations: 80
3 Most popular majors: Business, English, Psychology
Student/Faculty ratio: 9:1
Average Class Size: 10 to 19
Percent of students going to grad school: 19%
Tuition and Fees: $36,126
In State Tuition and Fees if different: No difference
Cost for Room and Board: $9,836
Percent receiving financial aid out of those who apply, first year: 49%
Percent receiving financial aid among all students: 50%

Students looking for a close-knit college experience are well advised to take a good look at Skidmore. Located in Saratoga Springs, New York, Skidmore offers a strong liberal arts focus, a small and supportive environment, and a great time all around. If students can handle the winter snow, Skidmore is a great place to get the whole package.

Living and Learning

Students give Skidmore's small size high marks in the classroom. The small student to teacher ratio means that students have "small classes with a lot of individual attention and the opportunity to have their voices heard." Regarding the curriculum, the much-maligned LS1 and LS2 programs for freshmen and sophomores has been replaced with the First-Year Experience. The anchors of this program are the Scribner Seminars. Freshmen are required to choose from many interesting options, including Gender Benders, Chinese Wisdom and Queens, Italian Cinema and Psych Out the Stock Market.

These well-reviewed courses are also integrated into the living experience by placing students in the same seminar within close proximity in the dorms to encourage and facilitate a learning environment that extends out of the classroom. As far as other requirements, a senior reflects that, "If taken before you declare a major, the required courses can be helpful, but if you find yourself a senior and needing to fulfill courses unrelated to your major, they're a pain."

Skidmore students find that the classes run the gamut from "classes that require a tremendous amount of work" and those that "do not require significant effort to get by." Among the majors, Business, Government, and Art are the most popular, while Economics, the sciences, and Studio Art are generally known as the majors requiring the most work. Both in and out of their majors, students can find a variety of creative and interesting courses. One of the most popular courses is MB 107, an introductory business class that draws crowds every year. Some of the more unusual courses include West

African Drumming, Dance for the Child, and a course on The Beatles.

Students have almost only positive comments on their professors and classes. Classes are described as "personal" with the normal size hovering between 15 and 20 students. "Professors for the most part are extremely qualified and genuinely enjoy their interactions with students." Professors take advantage of their proximity to students by having fun with their classes. One professor is known for occasionally bringing a banjo or guitar to class. Another advantage of the small size of the school according to students is that, "if a professor isn't good, you'll definitely hear about it from another student."

> **"You can handle everything here at your own pace and that is the benefit of being at a small school."**

Skidmore students are self-described as having a "wide range of approaches to academics." While some study around the clock, others do the least that is required. And, although certain students admit they would sometimes like to see more out of their peers, the majority seems to agree with one student's comment that, "Everyone seems to come out fine. I like it because there is no pressure to be a certain way in terms of academics. You can handle everything here at your own pace and that is the benefit of being at a small school."

Play Time
When not hitting the books, Skidmore students look to have a great time. Students are regularly out all weekend starting on Thursday night, and during the week, Tuesday nights are popular. While there is no Greek presence on campus, there are still a variety of different social groups and scenes to encompass every interest. Sports teams and former athletes, for example, dominate certain aspects of the social life. At the same time, the small size of the school encourages different groups and classes to be inclusive and socialize together. As one student expresses, "Parties that my friends throw tend to be larger because we try to incorporate all social groups." This atmosphere of camaraderie makes it easy for freshmen to meet people. Drinking plays a large role within the social scene, especially during the snowy

months that keep students indoors. While the campus has recently made an effort to become dry, certain living areas, such as the Northwood apartments, still maintain a reputation for fun. Off-campus housing, such as Stables, also serves as a focal point for weekend partying. Saratoga boasts a large bar scene that has expanded from being not only a key destination for upperclassmen, but also underclassmen. Popular destinations in downtown Saratoga include Tin 'N' Lint, a classic college bar, and Peabody's, a restaurant and club. Saratoga is described as "a great college town" and students rarely run out of things to do.

While drinking appears to be the dominant factor in Skidmore social life, one student explains, "Drinking is not essential, just easy to find if you want. The school does a fairly good job of making sure there are alternatives to drinking every weekend." These activities include movie nights, theatrical productions, and outdoor pursuits such as hiking and skiing. A few of the most popular annual events include the Junior Ring dance, a semiformal affair, Spring Fling in April, and Fun Day in May. Lake George, Saratoga Park, and Yaddo, an artist and writer's colony with botanical gardens, are also a draw for students.

Campus Life
Skidmore's administration has been putting an effort toward bringing upperclassmen back into on-campus housing. Dorms are generally rated either "not notably good or bad" or "not great," with the new apartments in Northwoods Village standing out as the best among the options. Many sophomores live in Scribner Village, which features on-campus townhouses. Starting junior year, students often move off campus, largely due to crackdowns on the social life on campus. The move to bring upperclassmen back into dorms is fairly unpopular among students, especially in light of a general feeling that overcrowding needs to be alleviated. There is a new dining hall on campus, although the food is described as "average" and "mediocre." While there are few food alternatives on campus, there are a number of restaurants within minutes of campus and many delivery options. Some popular restaurants in Saratoga include Scallions, Sperry's, and Lillian's.

The Skidmore campus benefits from its beautiful location in upstate New York surrounded by the Adirondacks and the Vermont mountains. Saratoga Springs also serves as a draw because of its appeal as a college town. On campus, notable facilities include the Tang Teaching Museum and Art Gallery, the new dining hall, and Wiecking Hall, a relatively new dorm. Scribner Library also draws positive reviews, as does the newly expanded gym.

Skidmore boasts a large number of student activities and groups on campus, enough to provide a niche for every interest. Some of the more prominent and popular groups include the Wombats, an ultimate Frisbee team, student government, and SkidTV. Outdoors activities are understandably popular in light of Skidmore's location and the great lakes and skiing and hiking opportunities in the area. Skidmore athletics do not play a huge role on campus, and many students lament the lack of school spirit. According to a former athlete, "One of the main reasons I stopped playing was due to the fact that nobody on campus cared about all the hard work we were doing to represent our school." Despite this occasional apathy, students are given a world of resources on campus to pursue whatever their interests may be.

Skidmore students agree that they are a welcoming and friendly bunch. As one senior expresses, "There are the stereotypical student groups, but they are all usually nice, friendly kids" who are easy to meet. One issue the school faces is a lack of diversity on campus as most of the students tend to be white and upper middleclass. There is also a large contingent of students from the Northeast, although there are a number of international students. The school seems to be working on its diversity issue, and students find that "there is intermixing between groups and people are accepting of kids regardless of race or orientation." Generally the campus leads toward the liberal, and even hippy, side, but there is something here for everyone.

Skidmore students may differ in their interests and activities, but they all agree that they love their school and Saratoga Springs. The cold winters are no barrier to this hard working and fun loving group.—*Janet Yang*

FYI

If you come to Skidmore you better bring "warm clothing, a lighter and a car for weekend escapes."

Three things every student should do before graduation are "go to the racetrack, go skiing on a weekend and experience a summer in Saratoga."

The typical weekend schedule is "go out to an off-campus house party, then downtown to the bars, sleep in late or go skiing, then go out some more."

If I could change one thing it would be "making the school's administration more relaxed and less likely to punish students for minor problems."

St. Lawrence University

Address: 23 Romoda Drive
Canton, NY 13617
Phone: 800-285-1856
E-mail address:
admissions@stlawu.edu
Web site URL: www.stlawu.edu
Year Founded: 1856
Private or Public: Private
Religious Affiliation: None
Location: Rural
Number of Applicants: 5,419
Percent Accepted: 34%
**Percent Accepted who
enroll:** 34%
Number Entering: 616
**Number of Transfers
Accepted each Year:** 40
Middle 50% SAT range:
M: 570–640, CR: 570–640,
Wr: 560–650
Middle 50% ACT range: 25–29
**Early admission program
EA/ED/None:** ED
**Percentage accepted
through EA or ED:**
Unreported

EA and ED deadline: 15-Nov,
15-Jan
Regular Deadline: 1-Feb
Application Fee: $60
**Full time Undergraduate
enrollment:** 2,193
Total enrollment: 2,325
Percent Male: 45%
Percent Female: 55%
**Total Percent Minority or
Unreported:** 10%
Percent African-American:
3%
**Percent Asian/Pacific
Islander:** 2%
Percent Hispanic: 3%
Percent Native-American:
<1%
Percent International:
Unreported
**Percent in-state/out of
state:** 41.5%/58.5%
Percent from Public HS:
68.90%
Retention Rate: 88%
Graduation Rate 4-year: 78%

Graduation Rate 6-year:
80%
**Percent Undergraduates in
On-campus housing:** 98%
**Number of official organized
extracurricular
organizations:** 129
3 Most popular majors:
Psychology, Economics,
English
Student/Faculty ratio:
11:1
Average Class Size: 16
**Percent of students going
to grad school:** 20%
Tuition and Fees: $37,915
**In State Tuition and Fees if
different:** No difference
Cost for Room and Board:
$9,645
**Percent receiving financial
aid out of those who apply,
first year:** 62%
**Percent receiving financial
aid among all students:**
Unreported

Tucked into a corner of the Adirondacks, in a small town in New York near the Canadian border, sits St. Lawrence University—just small enough to fit into the little town, but big enough for its students to call it home. The relatively small size of SLU allows the formation of a close-knit community, both within the student body and between the students and faculty. The rural location affords opportunities for outdoor activities and gives the campus its beautiful backdrop, the pride of many an SLU student. Even though many students complain about the huge piles of snow in the cold winter months, most agree that the warmth of the friendly people around them more than makes up for the weather.

Studying at SLU
Academics at St. Lawrence are described as difficult at times, but, as one student said, "you don't have to be doing work ALL the time." Some of the most popular departments include economics, psychology and biology. Because of the small size of SLU,

students benefit from small class sizes and they enjoy close contact with professors right from the start of their freshman year. Many professors provide students with their home phone numbers and encourage students to contact them with questions or problems. Students reported that essentially all classes enroll no more than 25 students (the average is 16), are taught exclusively by professors, and have a TA or two to give extra help to students who need it. Small class size rarely results in students being shut out of classes they want to take, though. Registration now takes place online, and involves meeting with an advisor to gain a PIN that is then used to select classes.

St. Lawrence's academic program includes a fair number of requirements. Undergraduates must take a class in each of the following areas: "Arts or Expression," humanities, math and social science. They also must fulfill a natural science requirement, which must include one course with a lab. Opinions of these requirements vary from "a hassle" to "a good way to get us to start exploring different departments." In addition, freshmen participate in the First Year Program, a semester-long course devoted to developing oral and written communication skills, taken with other students from the same dorm. While many students acknowledge the benefits of FYP, others complain about how the course often conflicts with other desired courses.

When students at St. Lawrence want to study, they often head for Owen D. Young library, the main library on campus. ODY is a fairly modern building; although its aesthetic merits are often debated, most agree that the recent renovation has made the atmosphere on the inside cheerful and stimulating. However, the lively atmosphere also frequently inspires conversation, and many students describe ODY as more of a social place than a studious one. For hard-core studying, Madill, the science library, is your best bet.

Living and Eating

Housing at SLU is mainly in dorms, although there are also off-campus options such as Greek and theme housing and athletic suites. The dorms are mostly set up in traditional singles and doubles, and are coed, but some dorms also offer the option of suites with kitchens, mostly for upperclassmen. Students cite Sykes as one of the best dorms, with Whitman as the best dorm for freshmen. On the other hand, Lee and Rebert halls are said to be the worst, although even in those less desirable dorms, rooms are reportedly spacious and nicely furnished. Almost universally, students praise their dorms, whether they live in the best or worst location, for the sense of community fostered there.

> **"You don't have to be doing work ALL the time."**

As upperclassmen, students at St. Lawrence have more housing options, although finding an apartment in Canton isn't one of them; the University requires that undergraduates reside on campus. However, many upperclassmen choose to live in Greek houses, which lie just at the edge of campus; one student living in her sorority house described her experience by saying it is "very home-like, and there is always something to do." Theme housing is another alternative to dorms available after freshman year, and such houses include a house for environmentalists, for people who enjoy

outdoor activities, and for cultural groups and international students. Seniors can also apply to live in on-campus townhouses.

SLU students tend to give their meal plan and dining options high ratings. There are three on-campus eating establishments: Dana Dining Hall (a traditional cafeteria), the Time Out Café and the Northstar Café in the New Student Center. The café has more of a relaxed atmosphere where students go to hang out and relax, and the food there is considered the best of the options on campus, particularly the chicken wrap sandwiches. There are two meal plans available to students, the 21-meal plan, which is only accepted at Dana, and a declining-balance plan which is accepted at all three on-campus locations. While students favor the declining-balance plan because of its flexibility, most agree that it is impossible not to run out of money before the end of the semester, and so that plan is better for students who are not eating all of their meals on campus.

When students get tired of the places to eat on campus, or just want to treat themselves, they look to the restaurants in the town of Canton. For quick meals, there are the standard chains: McDonald's, Burger King and Pizza Hut, and also A-1 Oriental Kitchen, which is a popular delivery choice. Other restaurants in Canton include Sergi's Pizza, which has pizza and Italian food, Jerek Subs, Josie's and Phoebe's; the Cactus Grill, a Mexican restaurant located in nearby Potsdam, is also frequented by many St. Lawrence students. During Family Weekend, students often take their parents to McCarthy's.

Life After Studying

Students at St. Lawrence spend a lot of time on extracurricular activities, and there is "always something to get involved in." One of the most active groups on campus seems to be the Outing Club, which goes on lots of trips and does other activities together. A recently founded karate club, which is student-run and student-taught, is growing rapidly, an example of the ample opportunity to start new organizations if you are interested. Many students also spend their time working for *The Hill News*, the main weekly publication of St. Lawrence.

Sports are also an option at St. Lawrence, both for fans and athletes. Varsity soccer and hockey are the most popular, with rugby and lacrosse games also drawing crowds. School spirit peaks at the time of the Clarkson-SLU hockey game, and the long-time rivalry draws huge crowds. Students say that you have to get tickets at least a week in advance if you don't want to stand up to watch the game, but that it is one of the highlights of the year that cannot be missed. Sports are not limited only to varsity athletes, though, as St. Lawrence has a wide variety of intramural teams, which allow people of all levels the opportunity to play. In addition, the athletic facilities are described as "great, and always available to everybody." All of the sports facilities have been recently renovated and according to one student athlete, "facilities at SLU are in tip-top shape." As recently as in 2007, SLU carried out a drastic multimillion-dollar expansion of its arts facilities and its Science Center. Unfortunately, the social life and weekend plans are definitely limited by the small student body and the school's rural locale. Some things that students do when they are hanging out or partying include shooting pool, going to see a movie (free on campus), going to see a band playing at Java House or going to a frat party. However, students complain that campus security and Canton police strongly frown upon student alcohol use. On top of that, on-campus and off-campus parties alike tend to get shut down soon after they begin. Thus, most students say that they spend a lot of time hanging out in bars in Canton with their friends, or taking trips on the weekend to Ottawa, the capital of Canada, or to Syracuse, both of which are within a few hours' driving distance.

Even though there may be downsides to living in a remote, rural town, students at St. Lawrence agree that the beauty of their campus and the surrounding area is worth it. The architecture of the university, a mixture of old and modern buildings, the quaintness of the town of Canton, and the beauty of the mountains and forests make St. Lawrence a scenic and pleasant place. If you are looking for a school with a fast-paced, urban environment and a restaurant and club for every night of the week, SLU may not be for you; however, if you want a school with a tight-knit community of professors and students, set in a beautiful landscape offering a place to hike or just sit and contemplate, St. Lawrence University could be the one.—*Lisa Smith*

FYI

If you come to St. Lawrence, you'd better bring "a jacket. It's really cold out."

What is the typical weekend schedule? "There are two groups on campus. For one group, the weekend starts on Thursday nights ['Thirsty Thursday'], and they go to bars. The other group is the outdoorsy group. They go to the Adirondack Mountains to go hiking, backpacking, skiing and kayaking."

If I could change one thing about St. Lawrence, I would "make it so that the clubs could be completely student-run."

Three things every student at St. Lawrence should do before graduating are "streak the Candlelight Freshman Experience," "ring the bells in the chapel," and "attend a Laurentian Singers Concert."

State University of New York System

The State University of New York System is one of the largest state university programs in the United States, consisting of 64 individual campuses and over 418,000 students. SUNY offers a variety of degrees, ranging from the one-year certificate programs at the system's 30 community colleges, which are designed to prepare students for specific employment, to the advanced doctorate degrees offered at the 13 university locations. The centers of the system lie in Binghamton, Buffalo, Stony Brook and Albany. Other campuses are scattered around New York, and are represented in Brockport, Brooklyn, Canton, Clinton, Erie, Farming-dale, New Paltz, Old Westbury, Onondaga and Syracuse. Aside from the community colleges and the University center programs, the remaining SUNY schools are divided into schools focused on cultivating different specific academic interests, including technology, veterinary medicine and forestry studies.

To simplify the process of applying to such a diversity of schools, prospective students may apply to up to eight campuses at once. In total, 49 of the 64 SUNY schools accept this common application.

Like many state university programs, the SUNY system is almost completely comprised of in-state students. Almost 90 percent of SUNY's enrollment comes from New York, and these students pay a heavily discounted price for their education. Although this makes college significantly more affordable, when combined with the increasing number of students the SUNY system admits each year, students say it also creates large lectures and low levels of attention for undergraduates.

Many SUNY students agree that the SUNY system is not one to pamper its students. In order to get involved on campus or find direction either academically or with extracurricular activities, a student must be self-motivated. According to one student, the isolated locations of most SUNY campuses make it difficult to maintain a social life and get off-campus.

Despite these challenges, the SUNY system boasts a wealth of opportunities at a very affordable price. With over 7,669 degree and certificate programs available and a niche for any student willing to make an effort to find it, SUNY provides a magnitude of resources only made possible by such a broad range of campuses and students. Following are articles about the SUNY campuses located in Albany, Buffalo, Binghamton and Stony Brook.—*Stephanie Teng*

State University of New York / Albany

Address: 1400 Washington Avenue Albany, NY 12222
Phone: 518-442-5435
E-mail address: ugadmissions@albany.edu
Web site URL: www.albany.edu
Year Founded: 1844
Private or Public: Public
Religious Affiliation: None
Location: Suburban
Number of Applicants: 20,249
Percent Accepted: 52%
Percent Accepted who enroll: 24%
Number Entering: 2,519
Number of Transfers Accepted each Year: 2,351
Middle 50% SAT range: M: 510–610, CR: 500–590, Wr: Unreported
Middle 50% ACT range: 22–26
Early admission program EA/ED/None: EA

Percentage accepted through EA or ED: Unreported
EA and ED deadline: 15-Nov
Regular Deadline: 1-Mar
Application Fee: $40
Full time Undergraduate enrollment: 11,959
Total enrollment: 12,748
Percent Male: 49%
Percent Female: 51%
Total Percent Minority or Unreported: 43%
Percent African-American: 9%
Percent Asian/Pacific Islander: 7%
Percent Hispanic: 8%
Percent Native-American: <1%
Percent International: 2%
Percent in-state/out of state: 92%/8%
Percent from Public HS: Unreported
Retention Rate: 84%
Graduation Rate 4-year: 61%

Graduation Rate 6-year: Unreported
Percent Undergraduates in On-campus housing: 57%
Number of official organized extracurricular organizations: 160
3 Most popular majors: Business/Commerce, General English Language and Literature, General Psychology
Student/Faculty ratio: 19:1
Average Class Size: 20 to 29
Percent of students going to grad school: 50%
Tuition and Fees: $12,347
In State Tuition and Fees if different: $6,087
Cost for Room and Board: $9,778
Percent receiving financial aid out of those who apply, first year: 61%
Percent receiving financial aid among all students: 60%

The State University of New York (SUNY) system is one of the best public college networks in the nation. Founded in 1844, Albany is one of the more highly regarded SUNY schools. Though it has a bit of a party school reputation, Albany offers impressive academic resources—and less impressive guidance systems—to its body of undergrads and grad students, a diverse bunch who range from nerdy bookworms to seven-days-a-week boozehounds.

A Feast of Academic Options

As one of the more prominent SUNY campuses, Albany is known for its plethora of academic resources. But as is the case in many state-run institutions, help is hard to come by. Undergraduate advisors are notoriously unhelpful. As a result, much of a student's experience at Albany depends on his or her major and ability to figure things out alone. "The thing about Albany's academics is that it can really vary from student to student as to what their experience will be," one student commented. "Some people breeze right through doing practically nothing, while other students work ridiculously hard all the time."

Albany has particularly strong programs in political science, psychology, sociology, business and physics, to name a few. Lately, the University has gained attention for its writing program after the founding of The Writers' Institute in 1983 by novelist William Kennedy. The Institute has boosted Albany's curriculum by beefing up the writing-related offerings and bringing famous authors to speak on campus. Biology is another strong department at Albany. Students interested in messing around with lab rats can check out the Mutant Mouse Regional Resource Center, a bank of specimens with "unique phenotypes" on campus. Students in the public service sector often take advantage of the internship opportunities afforded by Albany's location. Albany also offers 40 different BA/MA combination degree tracks.

Albany has a comprehensive core curriculum called the General Education Program. According to the school's Web site, the program "proposes a set of knowledge areas, perspectives, and competencies considered by the University to be central to the intellectual development of every undergraduate." Students must demonstrate proficiency in disciplinary perspectives, cultural and historical perspectives, mathematics and statistics, communication and reasoning and foreign language. Although these classes are not very difficult, some students complain that it is very hard to fulfill Gen Ed requirements. "It is almost impossible to get into Gen Ed course classes," one junior said. "[Albany] seems to be accepting more and more students, but not really opening up more classes."

A New York State of Mind

Located in upstate New York in the state capital, Albany's picturesque autumns quickly turn into brutal winters, though this is par for the course in the Northeast. Still, trekking across the frozen tundra between Albany's three campus centers is often a trying affair. While walking, students can admire the architecture of Edward Durell Stone, designer of Lincoln Center, though they may tire of this pastime when they realize that many buildings are reproduced almost identically throughout the campus.

About 93 percent of Albany's students hail from the Empire State. The freshman facebook reads like the Long Island-Westchester Yellow Pages—and with good reason. New Yorkers pay about $6,000 tuition per semester, or half what out-of-state students pay, plus roughly $9,000 for room and board.

The campus is divided into two main locations—uptown and downtown. On Uptown Campus, students live in four symmetrical quads named Indian, Dutch, Colonial and State—after New York's four historical periods. Students also live in the apartment-style Freedom and Empire Commons dorms, as well as the Alumni quad downtown. The dorms are generally described as average. Most are low-rise buildings surrounding a central tower, and consist of suites with two to three rooms with a common area.

Getting good housing can be competitive, especially when it comes to Empire, one of the nicest dorms on campus. An Empire suite consists of four singles and two bathrooms, and comes pre-furnished with couches and dressers, a full kitchen, plus a washing machine and a dryer. "It definitely beats collecting quarters and lugging your laundry to a basement," said one junior. "[Empire] is more expensive but it's worth it." Dorms such as Wellness Co-op, Bleeker Women's Leadership Project House, and Student Leadership and Healthy Lifestyle House offer themed housing for those with special interests. Recently, the University announced three new Living/Learning Communities for upperclassmen: Anime House, China House and Francophone House.

The number one complaint of Albany students is the weather, but food is a close second. The University's dining system is about as popular as MC Hammer—and Albany food didn't even experience a brief burst of popularity in the early 1990s. Students often chose to eat downtown instead of testing the mush dished out by university cooks.

Perhaps the dining situation has an impact on school spirit—Albany students are lukewarm when it comes to representing their university. According to one student, "Sports at Albany are horrible . . . there is very little school spirit and events are not well-attended. The school has tried to change that recently, but it has not been very successful yet."

> **"The freshman-sophomore party experience is nuts, but so much fun."**

Albany offers standard extracurricular fare, including intramurals, student government, performance organizations, frats and sororities. In November 2006, Albany's Earth Tones (all-male) and Serendipity (all-female) finished second and third at the collegiate a cappella Northeast Quarterfinals and are big attractions on campus. The Albany Student Press publishes a newspaper one day a week, and the Student Association governs student affairs and plans campus events.

Party Time
Though Albany no longer shows up on Top 10 Party School lists as it did throughout much of the 1990s, it is hardly a dry campus. Fraternities and sororities are not recognized by the school, but they do exist. However, it is the bar scene that dominates campus party life. "Bring enough money to drink," one student said. "That's the main source of entertainment here at Albany . . . if you wanna make it a relaxing night, you know exactly what to buy from your local provider." Famous festivities include Fountain Day, a celebration of the return of water to the campus fountain at the end of winter; Kegs and Eggs, a springtime drunkfest; and Party in the Park, a year-end party featuring live music and plenty of eats.

Despite its reputation, Albany has fairly strict rules on underage drinking: two strikes and you're kicked out of housing. But the regulations are rarely enforced. "It really depends on your RAs," one student said. "I always drank in my dorm room and never got in trouble for it . . . As long as you're not really loud it'll be fine."

Albany students report that partying is more frequent for underclassmen, and some freshmen and sophomores go out almost every night of the week. Upperclassmen don't go out as much as they start to buckle down and focus on their studies. "The freshman-sophomore party experience is nuts, but so much fun," one junior remarked. "I wouldn't trade those years for anything."

SUNY Albany is a big school with big resources, but it's not too big a drain on the pocketbook. For most, Albany is what you make of it. Students just have to make sure they don't get lost in the shuffle, and most seem to make it a productive and enjoyable time in the capital of the Empire State.—*Zack O'Malley Greenburg*

FYI
If you come to SUNY Albany, you'd better bring "an umbrella, a warm jacket, beer money, and food to keep in your room."
What is the typical weekend schedule? "Starts on Thursday, which is mainly a bar night—you won't really find parties around. Friday: hit up happy hour around four o'clock (Paulie's is the cheapest) then maybe go to some parties. Saturday morning: recover, enjoy the fine cuisine that is Chartwell's brunch omelets made to order. Saturday night: go out to the bars, unless a good friend is throwing a party. Older crowd is further downtown. Sunday: sleep in and watch movies on HBO."
If I could change one thing about SUNY Albany, I'd "change the food. It really is just bad, except the cookies . . . they're good."
Three things every student at SUNY Albany should do before graduating are "experience a warm Fountain Day, attend Kegs and Eggs and go to class drunk."

State University of New York / Binghamton

Address: PO Box 6000
  Binghamton, NY
  13902-6000
Phone: 607-777-2171
E-mail address:
  admit@binghamton.edu
Web site URL:
  www.binghamton.edu
Year Founded: 1946
Private or Public: Public
Religious Affiliation: None
Location: Suburban
Number of Applicants:
  25,242
Percent Accepted: 39%
Percent Accepted who
  enroll: 24%
Number Entering: 2,304
Number of Transfers
  Accepted each Year: 1,787
Middle 50% SAT range:
  M: 610–690, CR:
  570–660, Wr: Unreported
Middle 50% ACT range:
  25–29
Early admission program
  EA/ED/None: EA
Percentage accepted
  through EA or ED: 53%

EA and ED deadline: 15-Nov
Regular Deadline: None/
  Priority Applicaton
  deadline: 12/01
Application Fee: $40
Full time Undergraduate
  enrollment: 11,042
Total enrollment: 11,515
Percent Male: 54%
Percent Female: 46%
Total Percent Minority or
  Unreported: 44%
Percent African-American:
  7%
Percent Asian/Pacific
  Islander: 12%
Percent Hispanic: 8%
Percent Native-American:
  <1%
Percent International: 8%
Percent in-state/out of
  state: 90%/10%
Percent from Public HS:
  87%
Retention Rate: 90%
Graduation Rate 4-year:
  66%
Graduation Rate 6-year:
  Unreported

Percent Undergraduates
  in On-campus housing:
  56%
Number of official organized
  extracurricular
  organizations: 200
3 Most popular majors:
  Business Administration and
  Management, General En-
  glish Language and
  Literature, General
  Psychology
Student/Faculty ratio:
  20:1
Average Class Size: 20 to
  29
Percent of students going to
  grad school: 45%
Tuition and Fees: $12,332
In State Tuition and Fees if
  different: $6,072
Cost for Room and Board:
  $9,774
Percent receiving financial
  aid out of those who apply,
  first year: 78%
Percent receiving financial
  aid among all students:
  68%

O ne of the best, if not the best, school in the State University of New York system, Binghamton offers its diverse student body a wide variety of courses, majors, and living arrangements. The student body comes from around the country and the world, though mostly from the metro New York City area. As part of a fast-growing university, life at Binghamton is full of challenges and excitements.

Ivy of the SUNYs

At Binghamton, students can enroll and take classes in any of the five colleges: the Harpur College of Arts and Sciences, the Decker School of Nursing, the College of Community and Public Affairs, the Binghamton School of Management (SOM), and the Thomas J. Watson School of Engineering and Applied Sciences. They can also take classes in the College of Education. All students are required to fulfill general education require-

ments through Harpur. The required courses include writing, pluralism and language. After that, majors and schools have their own requirements.

The options for majors are "literally endless." At the School of Management, now one of the top fifteen public business schools in the country, Marketing, Accounting, and Finance are the top majors, but the school provides students with a solid balance of humanities and math for a future in the business world. At Harpur, English, Psychology, and Economics are very popular, while at Watson, Mechanical and Chemical Engineering are at the top. At Decker, all students major in Nursing, making up a class of around 115 students.

Another popular option is for students to create their own majors. "A lot of the majors are quite broad, but by creating your own major, you can focus it," said one senior.

The classes at Binghamton range from

large lectures to small discussion sections and seminars. For the most part, students feel that the general education requirements limit what they are able to take, but many find the classes surprisingly engaging and enjoyable. "The great thing about the critical literature class is that you spend the whole class arguing," said one sophomore.

Most students find the workload bearable, but a hundred plus pages of reading a week for one history class led one SOM student to say, "Nothing in college comes easy." At Decker, Watson, and SOM, students all have large amounts of work, but they manage to cope. As one nursing student put it, "it gets very, very tiring, but overall, it is worth it."

Students at the management school value the opportunity to address all aspects of the business world—be it from the accounting side or from the humanities side—as they are required to take classes that give them a well-rounded view. Students at Harpur enjoy the unique classes their college has to offer, such as American Sign Language, History of Pop Music, and the combined major of "Philosophy, Politics and Law."

> "Binghamton has a lot to offer. It's a growing school . . . Everyone's very active in making the school work."

When it comes to interacting with professors, most students say that, like everything else at Binghamton, the experience depends on the individual. Most professors are willing to meet with students and are approachable on all topics, but it is up to the students to reach out first.

Living it up in the Parlor City

Much of the partying that takes place in Binghamton takes place off-campus. Many students have to head into town to visit the bars or house parties in the city. Since the town relies on students for a fair amount of income, and students rely on the town for places to go, the relationship between the University and the city is relatively friendly. Students mostly go to town on the weekends, but every weeknight sees some students.

The major obstacle for students is the distance between campus and downtown Binghamton. "We're technically on the outskirts of Binghamton, so you have to take a bus or a cab to get downtown." said a student. A great number of students have cars, but parking is difficult, and freshmen are not allowed to have cars in their first year. Nonetheless, as one student pointed out, "if you don't have a car, one of your friends will." Binghamton also offers great restaurants. Places like the Lost Dog Café, Number 5, Grandes, Cyber West Café, and J-Michael's are rated highly by students. "It is really important to know these places, because it is food that you actually want to eat," said one senior. "It is a rare find, it is delicious, and it is a way to escape university life." And not only do students go downtown to visit bars and restaurants but also the fraternities. Many students feel that while the fraternities are a noticeable presence on campus, Greek life is not the entire party scene. Still, one student said, "If you're not in a sorority or a frat, you kind of miss out on a social life. I'm not affiliated with any of those clubs. I have fun, but it is not the same."

Binge drinking is not a serious problem, but the university has a zero-tolerance policy on alcohol and does everything it can to help students avoid troubles. For those who prefer to stay sober and on-campus, Binghamton offers its students an alcohol-free option called "Late-Night Binghamton," which has activities including laser tag, video game tournaments, and performances by student groups. Every year, the school organizes Spring Fling, featuring a performance by a live band, as well as carnival rides. Events like Midnight Madness, an event to kick off the men's basketball season, also garner a lot of attendees.

The student body of Binghamton reflects the multi-faceted nature of the school itself. "We're not a party school and not a very expensive school, so there's a good mix of kids from a lot of different backgrounds. It seems everyone just respects each other. I'd have to characterize them as very down to earth," said one student. Others agree that the population of Binghamton is diverse. There are a great number of international students, coming mostly from Korea, China and Turkey.

Most students are friendly, outgoing, and willing to make friends with most of their classmates. Many people are still close friends with the people they met in their first year, through either living in the same dormitories, taking the same classes, or participating in the same extracurricular activities. Everyone reports that the friendships are strong. "The people I met, I wouldn't trade them for the world," said one senior.

We Are Community

An interesting aspect of life at Binghamton is the community assignment. Prior to freshman year, students choose to live in one of the five communities that make up Binghamton. Each community has its own unique character, which comes from architecture, layout, and, of course, the students. Dickinson, the oldest community built with corridor-style dorms is known as a diverse, social dorm, while Hinman is considered a quieter, more studious community. College in the Woods has the reputation of housing a large number of "hipsters and hippies," and Newing is seen as a more Greek-oriented community. Mountainview, the newest of the communities, has air conditioning and apartment-style suites. It is home to a large number of athletes and international students. By breaking the campus into communities, students get an intimate life similar to what they would find at a smaller college while still having the resources and variety of a larger state university.

After their sophomore year, students have the choice of living off campus, either in the two upper-classmen-only housing complexes or off campus entirely. Upper-classmen feel that living off campus gives them more independence, and it's cheaper than living in student housing. Living off campus also gives students the option of making their own food. Consensus is that the food at each of the five community dining halls is decent, but, after a while, it gets tiring. Students are mixed about the pay-as-you-go plan, in which they pay for individual dishes.

In terms of aesthetics, the University has been remodeling for the past few years, and now the campus is becoming greener than ever. Two new dormitories are being built, and the natural preserve, one of Binghamton's standout assets, is becoming increasingly popular. The biggest draw for students is the size of the school. While it's a large, public university, the scale of it is rather small, with everything within ten to fifteen minutes of walking distance. Students also love that the campus, when seen from above, is in the shape of a brain. "If I'm meeting someone somewhere, it's really convenient to decide whether we should meet on the inside or the outside of the brain," said one student.

Bearcats and Other Wild Things

Even though Binghamton doesn't have a football team, there is a great deal of school pride in sports, particularly when it comes to men's basketball and soccer. The school plays Division I athletics and has a newly remodeled event center as well as two fitness centers, tennis courts, an indoor track, and space for numerous club teams. Club teams and intramurals are similarly big at Binghamton, with very competitive club teams and a wide range of intramural sports. Some students complain that the facilities are on the expensive side and hard to get to, while others feel the options available are worth the extra cost.

Students also have the opportunity to participate in extracurricular activities outside of athletics like the a cappella groups on campus or the radio station. "We have one of the last free-format radio stations in the country," said one student who currently works as a DJ. Students also get involved in the governing of their community and individual buildings, and a great number of jobs are available on campus through the school. Interested students are able to work at a wide variety of jobs, from setting up the dining halls, where the hours are considered rather inflexible, to internships at the events center. Publications like the *Pipe Dream* report on campus issues and events happening around the school.

Binghamton students are a very mixed crowd, living in a multi-faceted school. They feel that their lives and the lives of their friends are balanced between studying, work, and fun. As a senior summed up, "Binghamton has a lot to offer. It's a growing school. There's a weird stigma people have when applying to SUNYs. Binghamton breaks out of that. Everyone's very active in making the school work."—*Simon Warren*

FYI
If you come to Binghamton, you'd better bring "an umbrella, a blanket, and a willingness to work."
What is the typical weekend schedule? "Friday, go out to the bars or a party. Saturday, do your work, or whatever extracurricular you're involved in, and go out at night. Sunday, do whatever work you haven't done yet, and get ready for the week."
If I could change one thing about Binghamton I'd "make the transportation system in Binghamton run more efficiently and directly."
Three things every student at Binghamton should do before graduating are "hike to the top of the nature preserve, go to a basketball or soccer game, and eat at the Lost Dog Café."

State University of New York / Buffalo

Address: 17 Capen Hall
Buffalo, NY 14260-1660
Phone: 716-645-6900
E-mail address:
ub-admissions@buffalo.edu
Web site URL:
www.buffalo.edu
Year Founded: 1846
Private or Public: Public
Religious Affiliation: None
Location: Urban
Number of Applicants:
19,831
Percent Accepted: 48%
Percent Accepted who
enroll: 35%
Number Entering: 3,275
Number of Transfers
Accepted each Year: 3,442
Middle 50% SAT range:
M: 550–650, CR: 500–600,
Wr: Unreported
Middle 50% ACT range:
23–27
Early admission program
EA/ED/None: ED
Percentage accepted
through EA or ED: 70%

EA and ED deadline: 1-Nov
Regular Deadline: None/
Priority Application
Deadline: 11/1
Application Fee: $40
Full time Undergraduate
enrollment: 16,509
Total enrollment: 18,779
Percent Male: 53%
Percent Female: 47%
Total Percent Minority or
Unreported: 29%
Percent African-American:
6%
Percent Asian/Pacific
Islander: 10%
Percent Hispanic: 4%
Percent Native-American:
<1%
Percent International:
10%
Percent in-state/out of
state: 93%/7%
Percent from Public HS:
Unreported
Retention Rate: 85%
Graduation Rate 4-year:
28%

Graduation Rate 6-year:
36%
Percent Undergraduates
in On-campus housing:
40%
Number of official organized
extracurricular
organizations: 200
3 Most popular majors:
Business/Commerce,
General, Engineering,
General, Psychology
Student/Faculty ratio: 16:1
Average Class Size: 20 to
29
Percent of students going to
grad school: 36%
Tuition and Fees: $12,545
In State Tuition and Fees if
different: $6,285
Cost for Room and Board:
$9,552
Percent receiving financial
aid out of those who apply,
first year: 67%
Percent receiving financial
aid among all students:
75%

S UNY Buffalo, known as UB to students, is the largest of the 64 State Universities of New York. Established in 1846, UB is one of the most versatile public schools on the East Coast. Most students at UB are from the state of New York, but there are also quite a few students from all around the nation. As one of the larger public schools on the East Coast, UB students may find themselves getting lost in the crowd, but those who find their niche at the school can take full advantage of the many options available to them.

Diversity in Study

Students at UB are a diverse bunch and have academic options to match up. UB offers a great number of undergraduate majors which students can combine in double majors and minors. A junior, who has taken advantage of the many subjects available, remarked, "I am majoring in Social Science and Urban and Political Politics, and doing a minor in Sociology." In addition, there are special major programs in which individuals can devise their own programs of study. For those who are creative in designing their own majors, UB offers this option. For the ambitious, UB also offers combined-degree programs for some majors where driven students can obtain both their bachelor and master's degree in five years. "You can basically study anything you want at UB. A lot of students double-major or -minor or design their own majors," one student said.

UB encourages high achievement from its students. Every year, UB picks 250 incoming freshmen who have demonstrated academic prowess to join the University Honors College, which allows students to receive merit-based scholarships for their four years at UB. In addition, UB has the Distinguished Honors Program, which provides a free, all-expenses-paid undergraduate education.

This opportunity is given to as many as 20 lucky students a year.

While many students are pre-pharmacy, pre-business, pre-med, or pre-law at UB, architecture is surprisingly one of the most popular majors at UB. Students agree that UB is a big science and engineering school and these classes are usually harder and heavier in workload. One UB student remarked, "My workload usually depends on what classes I choose to take even if they're not science classes." To graduate, students must have completed 120 credits as well as taken all the required classes for their respective majors or minors. Freshmen also have to take a combination of core classes that usually are outside of their major. Although many students dislike these classes of 300 to 400, some freshmen find what they want to study through their core courses.

Students agree that being at a public school means that it is harder to get into classes. "People that have more credits get to register for classes first, so if you are a junior or senior you would get the classes that you need while the rest of the students who have less credits might not be able to get in," said a junior at UB. But a freshman noted, "If I really need a class for my major, I can speak to my academic counselor and have him 'force register' me into a class, which they usually will do." UB students study hard and they have the largest library system of all of the State Universities of New York, with one of the biggest collections. Libraries are usually crowded before finals and midterms.

Dorms Become Like Second Homes

Dorm life is big on campus and students and RAs alike try to make dorms and living spaces as homey as possible. A student said, "My RA is pretty cool; she's nice and comes up with events for our floor to do every month and she decorates all our halls." Students at UB participate in dorm activities sponsored by their RAs and often build great fellowships with those they live with.

One UB student who lived on campus said, "Dorms in UB are pretty okay compared to some that I've seen from other schools. The rooms are an okay size, not too small, but not too big either." For a public school, UB dorms seem to satisfy its students. Dorm life at UB is fairly typical: students learn to live with floor mates and roommates in harmony. A junior remarked, "Dorm life can get very noisy. People sometimes come back from parties at four in the morning."

UB has three different campuses. North campus is the busy, lively part of the university which is located in suburban Amherst. It has more than 100 buildings and is currently under construction for new student housing. The dorms share a public bathroom and kitchen with every floor so students tend to mingle and know those who live on the same floor. South campus is located in Buffalo. The architecture is classified as more historic, with a bell tower completing the look. South campus dorms are suite-style; students share a bathroom with their suite rather than their floor. Downtown Campus, the newest addition to the UB campus, is located in downtown Buffalo. It is known for its new buildings and state-of-the-art life sciences buildings.

Victor E. and Victoria S.

The Bulls, Victor E. and Victoria S., are UB's official mascots, and they have certainly brought a lot of victory to the school. The football, baseball, softball, volleyball, basketball, wrestling, swimming, tennis, cross country, soccer, rowing, and track and field teams are all represented in the NCAA Division I. UB athletes have their school to thank in pushing them on to victory; football is a big deal at UB and students will often go to their school's football teams to cheer for their school. A junior at UB said that of all her experiences so far at UB, "sports are a big thing at UB and football is the most popular." The UB Stadium seats 29,013 people, which adds to the exhilarating athletic experience for students and athletes alike. In addition, UB basketball players receive a lot of school pride from students; the Alumni Arena is the second-largest on-campus basketball complex in the state. UB students also participate in intramural sports with other students on campus, where they can hang out with friends and catch a game of Frisbee or just jog around campus before the heavy snows set in for the winter.

The Proof Is In the Numbers

Because UB is such a large school, there are tons of things to do and people to meet. Looking back on his years at UB, a senior said, "I ended up finding the right group of people at UB who have become my best friends . . . there are so many different people at UB that you're bound to find the right group." The diverse group of students are offered seemingly endless opportunities to get involved in clubs and activities outside the classroom, and students are very active in their extracurricular activities. One student was thankful for her work-study job at the architecture and planning library, where she can contribute to her tuition. UB offers work-study to many students on campus and quite a few students work during their undergraduate years.

> "You can basically study anything you want at UB. A lot of students double-major or -minor or design their own majors."

The biggest social events of the year at UB are Fall Fest and Spring Fest, which are held in UB's North Campus. In 2007, Spring Fest was held on Earth Day and musicians such as Jason Mraz and the band Juxtaposse per-formed for enthusiastic UB students. Other social events at UB usually happen within dorms, where suitemates or roommates may throw a party for their floor and invite friends.

Although only around 10 percent of the UB student body is involved in Greek life at UB, fraternities and sororities play a big part in the school's social scene. A student in an Asian-interest sorority at UB said, "Greek life is not as popular as it was in the past but it's still pretty big at UB. It's pretty competi-tive to rush and it definitely has a dominant presence." Although Greek organizations are competitive in looking for potentials, they also support each other when throwing so-cial or community-wide events on campus.

SUNY Buffalo offers a wide range of acad-emic and extracurricular options to its many students. Students come to accept and even enjoy the city of Buffalo and learn to find their true niche.—*Emily Chen*

FYI

If you come to UB, you better bring "snow clothes because it snows A LOT!"

What is the typical weekend schedule like? "Friday classes and parties at night, sleep in on Saturday, go off campus with some friends to the mall and eat out and spend the night watching a movie with friends, Sunday sleep in and finish up homework for the rest of the week."

If I could change one thing about UB, I'd "add more social places near the school for students to go when they just want to have fun."

Three things every student at UB should do before graduating are "take advantage of internships and international opportunities, go to the annual Welcome Back Party hosted by the Lambdas, and go to a football game."

State University of New York / Stony Brook

Address: 118 Administration Building Stony Brook, NY 11794-1901
Phone: 631-632-6868
E-mail address: enroll@stonybrook.edu
Web site URL: www.stonybrook.edu
Year Founded: 1957
Private or Public: Public
Religious Affiliation: None
Location: Suburban
Number of Applicants: 25,163
Percent Accepted: 43%
Percent Accepted who enroll: 26%
Number Entering: 4,375
Number of Transfers Accepted each Year: 3,200
Middle 50% SAT range: M: 570–660, CR: 520–610, Wr: 510–610
Middle 50% ACT range: 24–28
Early admission program EA/ED/None: EA

Percentage accepted through EA or ED: 44%
EA and ED deadline: 15-Nov
Regular Deadline: Rolling December 1 recommended
Application Fee: $40
Full time Undergraduate enrollment: 14,735
Total enrollment: 23,994
Percent Male: 51%
Percent Female: 49%
Total Percent Minority or Unreported: 38%
Percent African-American: 7%
Percent Asian/Pacific Islander: 22%
Percent Hispanic: 8%
Percent Native-American: <1%
Percent International: Unreported
Percent in-state/out of state: 87%/13%
Percent from Public HS: Unreported
Retention Rate: 89%

Graduation Rate 4-year: 44%
Graduation Rate 6-year: 59%
Percent Undergraduates in On-campus housing: 52%
Number of official organized extracurricular organizations: 286
3 Most popular majors: Biology, Psychology, Business Management
Student/Faculty ratio: 18:1
Average Class Size: Unreported
Percent of students going to grad school: 34%
Tuition and Fees: $12,070
In State Tuition and Fees if different: $5,810
Cost for Room and Board: $9,132
Percent receiving financial aid out of those who apply, first year: 72%
Percent receiving financial aid among all students: 57%

L ooking for a belly-dancing club? Sweatshop protests? A vegan club? SUNY's Stonybrook campus has enticing offerings for every kind of student. Just east up Long Island, close to Port Jefferson, the actual city of Stonybrook is two hours by train, far away from the clean, tree-covered suburban campus. While the city of Stonybrook might be "far from everything," as one student complained, its proximity to Manhattan is a major selling point for students who like to get into the city for its cultural, artistic, culinary and entertainment options.

Location, Location, Location

One undergraduate said life at Stony Brook means having "the best of both worlds," because the town is "pretty clean, you're out in the 'burbs kind of thing—but it's not that rural." The train station on campus lets students pop over to New York whenever they want. Few students stay on campus over the weekend because the city features so many things to do. The majority of students who

hail from Long Island make a mass homeward exodus weekly. Some even live at home, though others choose to live in university housing. For the first year, this means being doubled or tripled (two or three students to a bedroom), but upperclassmen get nicer room arrangements in suites of four to six with a common room and a shared bathroom. One freshman said being tripled can be really trying, but "if you tough it out for the first year it [housing] can get pretty good afterwards." Stony Brook also has a recently built apartment complex for its undergraduates, and off-campus apartments are always an option.

On DEC

All Stony Brook students have course requirements known as "DEC requirements," short for Diversified Education Curriculum. These requirements, falling in categories A through K, are "classes assigned in order to make you a more well-rounded student." They include courses in writing, literature, foreign language, math, arts, science, European, non-Western and American traditions. While one student found DEC requirements "kind of annoying" because they "make you learn a lot of stuff not really [relevant] to your major," others say DEC requirements are helpful. One senior attested, "I came into Stony Brook thinking I wanted to be a chemistry major, but then I changed my mind. As I went through my DEC classes, I found out what I wanted to do."

Big Pond, Lots of Fish

Students say class size at Stony Brook can be a problem, especially in introductory classes. Professors split large classes up into TA sections, but students say TAs can be difficult to track down and somewhat unresponsive to student needs. "It's really hard to get help, because it's a big school. You have to educate yourself. Some of the teachers are not that helpful and classes are too big." Going to professors' office hours and getting to know your department advisor helps individual students stand out among a sea of faces.

> "It's like you have lots of little worlds going on, because you have people who are into this and people who are into that."

One student said that upon first arriving at Stony Brook, she "felt like I was all by myself." To get out of the slump, Stony Brook mans its dorms with Resident Advisers (RAs), who are there to give advice and bring some college experience to the table. The RAs are "cool," and "if you have problems they'll help you out," advisees say. Part of the RAs' job, as always, is discipline, but students say, "They're not there to prevent you from having fun; they're just there to make sure everything stays in check. It's not prison-ish." Students also recommend living with other students in your area of study, so that you get to know others with similar interests. Another great way to meet people and distinguish yourself from the others around you is to be part of a club or organization. With an array of extracurricular activities ranging from belly-dancing to political protest groups, everyone is sure to find a niche. "This is a very diverse campus, so there's not one look or one way" to be, dress or act. Joining a sorority or fraternity "definitely makes you active in stuff on cam-

pus," one upperclassman said, "but it's not the only way to get involved." The unique thing about Greek life is it's something you can only get in college. If going Greek is for you, don't hold back. But don't feel pressured if that's not your style. One non-Greek said "the school is so big you can get away from" being Greek, and it's "not as rowdy as it seems on TV." Greek life is just one of many other possibilities at Stony Brook, there for the taking. Students say they appreciate that they have "people who are into this and people who are into that. It's like you have lots of little worlds going on."

That's Delivery

While one freshman said that food options at Stony Brook were great, offering variety and flexibility, upperclassmen were less enchanted. Stony Brook's campus is divided into four quads, each of which offers its own meal options, including buffet and home-style dining as well as restaurants and fast-food chains like Taco Bell and Pizza Hut. If the offerings are less than delectable, students say they "must give them props for having a lot of different options." "They have delivery too!" one student added, saying that the ever-popular college staples of Chinese and pizza were available among the delivery options. First-year students are required to have a meal plan—hardly an inconvenience when even delivery is paid for this way—but after that year students are welcome to fend for themselves. One deli in the student union offers not only meals, but also a grocery store. Every dorm on campus has a kitchen on each floor, though there are no in-suite kitchens. There is also a cooking building for students who plan on making all their own meals.

There are other ways of getting fed at Stony Brook that offer educational and cultural experiences on the side. Many groups, like the popular Caribbean Student Organization (CSO), throw parties and host workshops and lectures for their fellow students. Students come to learn about international relations and cultural differences, and for the chow. Don't look for alcohol at these gatherings and parties, though. Students say the administration is strict about keeping alcohol off campus and unavailable to those under 21.

Who Reigns in the Parade?

Homecoming week brings out the spirit of Stony Brook's Seawolves in full force. The Friday parade features floats built by student teams who represent their quads and organizations. Students make banners and enter them in competitions, and every building on campus decorates a bulletin board. As if that weren't enough, Stony Brookers also make boats every year for the Roth Regatta. So named for the quad·on which the Stony Brook pond is located, the event brings out all Stony Brook's would-be boat makers and has them race their boats on the pond. Spirit Week, an event much like Homecoming, takes place every spring. Residence halls compete in trivia and Olympic-style competitions in the gym to win glory for the Stony Brook name.

When Stony Brook students aren't competing for spirited titles, you might find them at Wang Center, a popular Asian center at the University where students can find sushi and a whole lot of information about Asian history. The Staller Center, another cultural location on campus, offers workshops and art in its theaters and galleries, or you can stop by on a Friday night to see chic in action at one of Stony Brook's fashion shows.—*Stephanie Hagan*

FYI

If you come to Stony Brook, you'd better bring "a laptop."

What is the typical weekend schedule? "Thursday's a big party night at clubs like Rumba Skies; Friday night, go to a movie on campus or take the train, go into the city, and hang out with friends; Sunday, go to the library and study."

If I could change one thing about Stony Brook, I'd "change the dorms. Some of them are really old!"

Three things every Stony Brook student should do before graduating are "realize that Manhattan is so close and actually go do something in the city, join an organization, and go to the Staller Center."

Syracuse University

Address: 900 South Crouse Avenue Syracuse, NY 13244-2130

Phone: 315-443-3611

E-mail address: orange@syr.edu

Web site URL: www.syr.edu

Year Founded: 1870

Private or Public: Private

Religious Affiliation: None

Location: Urban

Number of Applicants: 22,058

Percent Accepted: 52%

Percent Accepted who enroll: 27.40%

Number Entering: 3,473

Number of Transfers Accepted each Year: 305

Middle 50% SAT range: M: 550–650, CR: 520–620, Wr: 530–630

Middle 50% ACT range: 23–28

Early admission program EA/ED/None: ED

Percentage accepted through EA or ED: 77%

EA and ED deadline: 15-Nov

Regular Deadline: 1-Jan

Application Fee: $70

Full time Undergraduate enrollment: 12,981

Total enrollment: 19,366

Percent Male: 43%

Percent Female: 57%

Total Percent Minority or Unreported: 28%

Percent African-American: 7%

Percent Asian/Pacific Islander: 10%

Percent Hispanic: 7%

Percent Native-American: <1%

Percent International: 6%

Percent in-state/out of state: 40%/60%

Percent from Public HS: 72%

Retention Rate: 91%

Graduation Rate 4-year: 71%

Graduation Rate 6-year: 82%

Percent Undergraduates in On-campus housing: 75%

Number of official organized extracurricular organizations: 377

3 Most popular majors: Psychology, Architecture, Information Management & Technology

Student/Faculty ratio: 15:1

Average Class Size: 24

Percent of students going to grad school: 16%

Tuition and Fees: $32,180

In State Tuition and Fees if different: No difference

Cost for Room and Board: $11,656

Percent receiving financial aid out of those who apply, first year: 75%

Percent receiving financial aid among all students: 79%

At Syracuse University, rah-rah sis-boom-bah is the name of the game. There's a lot of student pride for the Orange, and there are a lot of students to provide it. Perched atop a hill overlooking the city of Syracuse in upstate New York, the University boasts over 13,000 students throughout the nine undergraduate colleges, as well as 6,000 graduate students, although "it still feels really small, and you're always going to run into people you know."

Hitting the Ground Running

While many colleges do not expect students to declare a major on their applications, Syracuse expects its students to have an idea of what they're doing and where they're going from Day One of the application process. Prospective students must apply to a particular undergraduate college: architecture, arts and sciences, education, engineering and computer science, human ecology, information studies, management, public communications, or visual and performing arts. This does not mean, however, that students must decide their academic paths during the hectic college process during the fall of their senior year of high school. Students may apply to multiple colleges, but they must select one before matriculating.

Newhouse School of Public Communications continues to hold the greatest prestige at Syracuse and is therefore the most selective in admissions, but each school has its own idiosyncrasies. While most majors require students to graduate with approximately 121 credits, engineering majors must have 30 more. Likewise, the business school requires a core group of classes that most students consider to be "sort of a pain."

The separation between the schools can also make it difficult when applying for classes outside of a given major. However, Syracuse encourages students to sample other disciplines, and students note that only certain classes, like Macroeconomics, require serious effort to get in. Several popular "gut" classes such as Human Anatomy, Religion of Sports, and Living Writers—described by one student as "the biggest joke of [her] life"—balance out more difficult courses like Biological Anthropology. For those desiring more structure, the business and communications schools give students clear direction. The College of Arts and Sciences, instead, leaves students more on their own to find an academic path.

Students are often surprised about the size of classes at Syracuse. Though the University boasts a large student body, popular lectures rarely exceed 200 students, and often remain between 50 and 75, with discussion sections of approximately 15 students. Classes also "get smaller and smaller," as well as easier to gain admittance to, each year.

Opa!

There's a reason why Syracuse Chancellor Nancy Cantor supports lowering the drinking age to 18: SU is a party school through and through. Greek life dominates the social scene at Syracuse. It is home to 27 fraternities and 20 sororities. Roughly 40 percent of undergraduates are involved in a Greek organization and most parties occur within the system. Although there are certainly students at Syracuse who do not drink, the Syracuse population as a whole "thoroughly enjoys alcohol." In fact, *The Daily Orange* runs a widely read weekly drink review called "Thirsty Thursday" outlining the weekend's recommended drink. To combat this perceived problem, the University has adopted a strict alcohol policy, particularly in underclassmen housing.

Frats aren't the only places to have fun on weekends. Marshall, or simply "M," Street just off campus is home to a string of popular bars like Maggie's and Harry's, which find themselves inundated with students throughout the weekend. The bars are strict, however, so don't expect to be allowed in without an ID.

If drinking's not your thing, there are still plenty of options to get a break from studying. The 49,250-seat Carrier Dome regularly fills up during basketball and lacrosse games for the University's nationally ranked teams. To many sports seem to be the preeminent extracurricular activity on campus, and all things considered, "it's just sick to be an athlete at 'Cuse." But this doesn't mean that you have to be a varsity athlete to participate. Intramurals are a popular option for the non-varsity athlete and a "great way to meet people."

Juicing the Orange

Apart from rushing, there are plenty of student-run organizations to stay busy outside of the classroom. *The Daily Orange*, the daily Syracuse newspaper, is a popular choice along with campus radio stations and the campus television channel, Citrus TV. For those seeking spending money for the semester, the University also makes low-key jobs very accessible to students, such as preparing food in the dining hall or sitting and swiping cards at the gym.

Freshman housing tends to be the worst experience you'll have during your time at Syracuse, but most students will admit "it's still pretty nice," and the University is currently building a new dorm for freshman named after Syracuse football legend Ernie Davis. Freshmen are randomly assigned dorms, unless there are mutual roommate requests, and live in learning communities of people with shared interests. Sophomore housing is often better, but both freshmen and sophomores are required to live on campus where alcohol is prohibited and RAs rule the land. Junior year is the time that most students move off campus and into houses and apartments around the periphery of the school, where they remain until graduation.

People and Place

Syracuse is a predominantly preppy school, with lots of "North Faces" and "popped collars." Many students hail from the suburban Northeast, but the school as a whole is far more diverse than some would think, with students from all over the world. Students also note that "everybody is really friendly," and most people are "really enthusiastic" about the university.

> **"Once you go to Syracuse, you're just obsessed."**

The city's relationship with the school is an interesting one; as one student notes, "The town would barely exist without the University." While this might create resentment in some college towns, the city of Syracuse plays an integral role in the lives of students and supports the school in a number of ways. For example, the town and University have launched a joint initiative to connect the main campus with arts and culture areas downtown by developing a "Connective Corridor" of innovative landscapes and lighting. Yet this type of relationship is not surprising but is in fact typical of the University. As one student notes, "Once you go to Syracuse, you're just obsessed."—*Michael Knowles*

FYI

If you come to Syracuse, you'd better bring "a real winter coat, in addition to your North Face."

What's the typical weekend schedule? "Go to Marshall Street bars on Friday, go to bed at five, wake up at one, do a little work, take a nap, go out again. Everyone is inside doing work on Sunday."

If I could change one thing about Syracuse, "I'd move it out of the snowbelt, because it gets really cold."

Three things every student at Syracuse should do before graduating are "rush the field at the Dome, sled down a street in a snowstorm, and take a class totally unrelated to your college."

Union College

Address: 807 Union Street Schenectady, NY 12308	**Percentage accepted through EA or ED:** 77%	**Graduation Rate 4-year:** 76%
Phone: 518-388-6112	**EA and ED deadline:** 15-Nov	**Graduation Rate 6-year:** 83%
E-mail address: admissions@union.edu	**Regular Deadline:** 15-Jan	**Percent Undergraduates in On-campus housing:** 88%
Web site URL: www.union.edu	**Application Fee:** $50	**Number of official organized extracurricular**
Year Founded: 1795	**Full time Undergraduate enrollment:** 2,240	**organizations:** 100
Private or Public: Private	**Total enrollment:** 2,240	**3 Most popular majors:**
Religious Affiliation: None	**Percent Male:** 52%	History, Political Science, Psychology
Location: Urban	**Percent Female:** 48%	**Student/Faculty ratio:** 10:1
Number of Applicants: 5,271	**Total Percent Minority or Unreported:** 19%	**Average Class Size:** 10 to 19
Percent Accepted: 39%	**Percent African-American:** 4%	**Percent of students going to grad school:** 35%
Percent Accepted who enroll: 28%	**Percent Asian/Pacific Islander:** 6%	**Tuition and Fees:** $48,552
Number Entering: 580	**Percent Hispanic:** 5%	**In State Tuition and Fees if different:** No difference
Number of Transfers Accepted each Year: 43	**Percent Native-American:** <1%	**Cost for Room and Board:** Included
Middle 50% SAT range: M: 600–680, CR: 570–660, Wr: 560–670	**Percent International:** 3%	**Percent receiving financial aid out of those who apply, first year:** 86%
Middle 50% ACT range: 26–30	**Percent in-state/out of state:** 41%/49%	**Percent receiving financial aid among all students:** 60%
Early admission program EA/ED/None: ED	**Percent from Public HS:** 70% **Retention Rate:** 93%	

The name Union College reflects the founders' belief in creating one of the country's first nondenominational colleges where there is "a sense of community devoted to unity rather than sectarianism." Located in downtown Schenectady, New York, Union College is a small liberal arts school dedicated to "broadly educating future citizens of the world." With its unique architecture, such as the 16-sided Nott Memorial built in 1813, and its long history, Union College provides its students with an experience different from any other liberal arts college.

An Education for the "life of the mind."

Union College is what one student calls an "engineering liberal arts college." Although engineering majors are required to take 40 courses over their four years as opposed to the liberal art majors' 36 courses, all students are required to fulfill their "General Education Curriculum" requirements. The General Education requirements include a distribution of courses in the humanities, social sciences, natural sciences and math.

Freshmen are required to take a Freshman Preceptorial class, which hones writing skills, sophomores are required to take a Sophomore Research Seminar and seniors must complete a thesis. The requirements may sound demanding, but many students agree that they are "rather easy to accomplish" because there are "so many options for classes." In addition to the majors and minors, Union offers several accelerated programs that provide students with the chance to earn two degrees. For example, the Leadership in Medicine eight-year program offers a combination of a bachelors, masters and doctoral degree for students in consortium with Albany Medical College. In the Law and Public Policy program, Union and Albany Law School select up to 10 incoming Union students to complete B.A. and J.D. degrees in six years.

For the students on the Union bachelors degree track, bioengineering and economics are two of the more popular majors. No matter what the major, class sizes are almost always below 25 and get smaller as the level of the class increases. "Even the lectures are small compared to most colleges," one junior said. Small class sizes also allow student-teacher relationships to be "great." One senior noted, "I never had a professor I couldn't go to for help." Some professors even take students out to dinner if the class is small enough. A first-year Union student laughed, "You know that the teachers are dedicated once your teacher asks you why you missed class the next time they see you." One of the most renowned professors on campus is Professor Stephen Berk, whose Holocaust class is extremely popular with students.

Union follows the trimester system, as opposed to the semester calendar of most other colleges. Union begins two weeks later than most schools in the fall and has a winter break of six weeks, which some students say is "too long." During that break, a student can take a three-week Mini Term abroad to one of the 10 possible country options. While most schools end in May, the end of the third trimester is in the middle of June. With the trimester system students have the advantage of taking only three to four classes per trimester. But classes that would be 15 weeks at another school are condensed to 10 weeks at Union.

A focus of the Union experience is studying abroad, which is recommended to every student, and which about 50 percent of students actually do. The Terms Abroad Programs are offered on nearly every continent. Each academic department has its own programs, which are offered for trimester periods, sometimes even for non-majors. In the Marine Studies program in the spring, students travel to conduct research from Cape Cod to Bermuda to Canada. For those who want to study abroad, conduct research or find an interesting job, Union offers many fellowships and scholarships for students of every year.

The First Greeks

Known as the "Mother of Fraternities," Union College was where the first three Greek societies were created. Greek life on campus is "pretty big," with about 50 percent of sophomores, juniors and seniors in one of the 12 fraternities and five sororities on campus. But for those not interested in joining, "you will not be ostracized," and almost all parties are open to the entire student body. In response to the social focus on Greek life, in 2004 the college created the Minerva Houses, a residential program made of seven houses to which incoming students are randomly assigned. Each house has its own council and holds its own events

ranging from lunches with professors to all-night dance parties. The houses provide another social outlet for students if Greek life is too much. But some students resent the houses for "trying to define our social lives."

Party nights at Union are usually on Wednesdays, Fridays and Saturdays because most classes meet on Mondays, Wednesdays and Fridays. Many parties, especially the frat parties, feature an abundance of alcohol, and many students agree that "binge drinking is a problem, but other drugs are not too visible on campus although they are there." But students also deal with a strongly enforced alcohol and drug policy on campus. If a student acquires five points—for being found drinking or doing drugs on campus several times—they are required to talk to the dean, and with eight points, a student is kicked out.

Students at Union have the opportunity to get to know many of their fellow students because of the small community that Union creates. Many students agree that because Union is so small, everyone is very friendly. Although the interests of students are diverse, most students are from the "northeast and white," and are from "upper-middle class families." "Most people here are pretty well-off," one student said. The "stereotypical Union kid" is often "preppy" and come winter, it "looks like a North Face factory exploded just off campus and showered everyone with fleeces and jackets."

Life in Schenectady

Union is notorious for its poor relations with the surrounding city. Most students agree that Schenectady is not the best city for a college campus, and while not too many students go into Schenectady, Union takes precautionary steps to make sure every student is safe. Almost all students live on campus, which helps foster Union's community feel. Freshmen have the choice between four different dorms, and by sophomore year, students live in suites that have two bedrooms and a common room. Upperclassmen have the option of living in their Minerva house—an option not available to freshmen—or some apartments on or off campus, as housing is guaranteed until junior year. Some of the dorms include College Park Hall, once a Ramada Inn, which includes air conditioning and individual bathrooms. Union also has theme houses where students can live, such as the Iris House, which raises LGBTQ awareness, and the Ozone House, which promotes environmental awareness.

One thing many students agree on is the beauty of Union. With the majestic Nott Memorial building at the center of the campus, other architectural features include the "modern" Olin sciences building and the "Greek-like architecture" of Old Chapel. Union makes it very clear that its architecture is unique as is its campus plan, which was the first unified college campus plan in the United States. Another distinctive part of campus is the Reamer Campus Center, which is "always bustling with activity" and there are always "at least a dozen people you know in there at a given time." The first floor of the Campus Center is the central hangout place for students, and at the Campus Center, students can get "better" food than offered in the dining halls.

Most students on campus have meal plans, including upperclassmen, because of the limited options off-campus. The West Dining Hall and the Upper Dining Hall are the main dining halls for students. Around campus, there are other options such as Starbucks, a convenience store and the sit-down Café Ozone, where students can use their student card to get lunch on Fridays. Off-campus food options are five to 10 minutes away and require a car. Getting to one of the off-campus food destinations is not a problem for the many upperclassmen who keep a car on campus. Although Schenectady does not have a good reputation among most students, some would say that during the day, Schenectady is a "quaint" and "pleasant town" to go to for a crepe, to see a movie or to go rock-climbing.

Where Hockey Rules

With student clubs abundant and ranging from politics to cultural activities to social action to sports, every Union student has the opportunity to take part in a group that they are interested in. If they can't find one, all it takes is an online form and 20 signa-tures to make a new student group. Some of the more prominent clubs are Colleges Against Cancer, which hosts the annual Relay for Life to raise cancer awareness, *Concordiensis*, the weekly school newspaper, men and women's club rugby, and Springfest, the club that organizes the annual Springfest Concert. Recent performers include Pat McGee and Rahzel.

The sport with the largest presence on campus is the Men's Hockey team, Union's only Division I sport. Hockey games are known for having a "full student section" with "screaming fans that heckle the other team." Other sports that have big turnouts include football and many games where Union is playing rival Rennselaer Polytechnic Institute. For non-athletes, the fitness center at the Alumni Gymnasium has been updated over the past five years and provides students with new equipment to stay in shape. Another option for non-varsity athletes is intramural sports, which are "very competitive" on campus. Intramurals include soccer, basketball and the ever-popular broomball.

> "It looks like a North Face factory exploded just off campus and showered everyone with fleeces and jackets."

Between its "seven traditions" that students insist everyone must take part of before graduating (such as a "naked Nott run" around the Memorial) to its unique academic opportunities, Union provides its students with a community that cannot be replicated anywhere else. One freshman noted that the campus is "very united and everyone learns everyone else's face. It's like a big high school, but better."—*Willi Rechler*

FYI

If you come to Union, you'd better bring "a HUGE winter jacket."

What is the typical weekend schedule? "Go out on Wednesday for a mostly bar night, house or frat party on Friday and Saturday" and "wake up late Sunday, have brunch at West dining hall and go back to sleep."

If I could change one thing about Union I'd "get in better touch with Schenectady. The Union bubble needs to pop."

Three things every student at Union should do before graduating are "paint the Idol, do a naked Nott run, and complete the other five traditions that you will learn when you're here!"

United States Military Academy

Address: 646 Swift Road
West Point, NY 10996-1905
Phone: 845-938-4041
E-mail address:
admissions@usma.edu
Web site URL: www.usma.edu
Year Founded: 1802
Private or Public: Public
Religious Affiliation: None
Location: Suburban
Number of Applicants:
10,778
Percent Accepted: 14%
**Percent Accepted who
enroll:** 78%
Number Entering: 1,199
**Number of Transfers
Accepted each Year:**
Unreported
Middle 50% SAT range:
M: 590–680, CR: 560–670,
Wr: Unreported
Middle 50% ACT range:
25–30
**Early admission program
EA/ED/None:** None

**Percentage accepted
through EA or ED:** NA
EA and ED deadline: NA
Regular Deadline: 28-Feb
Application Fee: $0
**Full time Undergraduate
enrollment:** 4,553
Total enrollment: 4,553
Percent Male: 86%
Percent Female: 14%
**Total Percent Minority or
Unreported:** 25%
Percent African-American:
6%
**Percent Asian/Pacific
Islander:** 7%
Percent Hispanic: 8%
Percent Native-American:
1.0%
Percent International: 1%
**Percent in-state/out of
state:** 7%/93%
Percent from Public HS: 86%
Retention Rate: 91%
Graduation Rate 4-year:
76%

Graduation Rate 6-year:
78%
**Percent Undergraduates
in On-campus housing:**
100%
**Number of official organized
extracurricular
organizations:** 105
3 Most popular majors:
Business, Economics,
Engineering
Student/Faculty ratio: 7:1
Average Class Size: 10 to 19
**Percent of students going to
grad school:** 100%
Tuition and Fees: $0
**In State Tuition and Fees if
different:** No difference
Cost for Room and Board:
$0
**Percent receiving financial
aid out of those who apply,
first year:** NA
**Percent receiving financial
aid among all students:**
NA

If your picture of college life includes sleeping in, veggin' in front of the TV while eating midnight pizza and enjoying a beer, binge drinking till you blackout at a frat party, or finding your trophy wife or husband, the United States Military Academy is not for you. West Point emphasizes leadership, service and challenge. Discipline permeates every aspect of life here for the Plebes (freshmen), the Yuks (sophomores), the Cows (juniors) and the Firsties (seniors). "Freshman Orientation" is fittingly called "The Beast" and consists of six weeks of rigorous training, including target practice and long hikes (not the scenic kind). After this intense welcome session, students prepare themselves for four years of embracing the four pillars of cadet life: Academic, Physical, Moral-Ethical and Military Development.

Hardcore Curriculum

Class size is very small, ranging from five to 20 students. As one student stated, "Class sizes are perfect, no more than 15." And despite the fact that "people are very competitive," it is "rarely at the cost of others' performance." Students have mixed responses regarding teamwork and competition. However, it is generally agreed upon that while there are those who believe in cooperation and the group spirit, some students prefer to "do it for themselves" and achieve high grades on their own.

The following core curriculum classes are required for all students: English, history, leadership, philosophy/ethics, foreign language, social sciences, law, math, chemistry, physical geography, information technology, physics, engineering/science design, military design and physical education. The first two years at the Academy are spent fulfilling these core curriculum requirements. Courses for specific majors are not taken until junior and senior year. Although one student claimed, "a Harvard 'A' is a West Point 'C'," most agree that while academics are rigorous, grading is fair. One student explained: "West Point teaches problem solving, critical thinking and effective communication. You're incredibly productive every day here."

Originally founded as an engineering school, West Point's engineering programs remain the most popular among students. Stereotypes regarding certain majors definitely exist. "People who major in Leadership just don't want to work on anything academic," and "the Nuclear Engineering major is ridiculously hard." Another student said that, "Engineering majors are geeks, Law and Management majors are slackers," while his peer claimed that, "People are always like, 'I want Foreign Language because it's easy.'" Even a Foreign Language major agreed, clarifying that, "Foreign languages, other than Chinese and Arabic, are easy."

Because Active Duty professors are on rotation and class syllabi are standardized, very few students can name "favorite" professors, though all will agree that instructors are dedicated. One female West Point student explained that, "Besides getting up every morning at 6, having two mandatory meals a day with formation, and having military training on Saturdays and the summers, what really sets West Point apart from other schools is the instructors . . . They are fully committed." Most students agreed that instructors are very accessible, often providing their home phone numbers for students to call with questions. "I appreciate the amount of time professors are willing to spend with whoever needs it."

Only Firsties Get Thirsty

Freshmen, Sophomores, Juniors, and Seniors are respectively referred to as Plebes, Yuks, Cows and Firsties. Aside from the unique names, Class/Year distinction is made very clear, especially for freshmen. "Plebes have a look on their face like a dog who just shat the carpet and got caught . . . that is to say, they look scared," explained one Cow. Plebes must walk around with their hands "at position of attention" (in a fist), do not wear rank on their uniforms, and are required to greet all upperclassmen with appropriate greetings, such as "Go Buffaloes, Sir" or "Beat Navy, Sergeant." In addition to this, perhaps the most noticeable difference between Plebes and freshmen at other schools is the strict enforcement of underage drinking violations. Freshmen can expect to be served with a brigade board, which includes 100 hours of marching around a square in the middle of campus, 60 days of room restriction, and enrollment in an alcohol course if they are found with alcohol.

The rule for alcohol is "No alcohol until you're a Cow on post." Juniors (a.k.a. Cows) who are 21 are allowed to drink at clubs on campus (a.k.a. Post) that are only open Thursday through Saturday nights. With periodic drug and alcohol tests, the substance policy is taken very seriously. Only seniors are allowed to drink Monday through Saturday nights.

"Perhaps the most coveted place on the Academy grounds is known as Firstie Club, or the First Class Club," longingly explained one Plebe. The lucky few that enter the club come to enjoy $5.50 pitchers of Yuengling and Killians beer. The club is decked out in black and white snap shots of cadets over the last 100 years in "undisciplined poses" that you won't find in the Academy's yearbooks. But don't expect to be making plans for heading anywhere after Firstie Club— with taps check, all cadets must be back in their rooms by 11:30. A mass exodus of drunken cadets leave Firstie Club and head back to the barracks. With punctuality being key, there is no time for drunken stumbling around here. Hordes of underclassmen will often stand outside of the barrack windows cheering for the seniors attempting to sprint back on time.

Checking out the 'Racks

Cadets are housed in barracks that are assigned by company. Each company has approximately 120 people, and some students claim that each company has a stereotype. "First regiment is known as 'West Point University' because it's really chill. Fourth regiment is known for doing well militarily. Third regiment is the one with the most rules and the one that is hardest on the Plebes." When asked about whether alcohol use was permitted in the barracks, one student replied, "Yeah, if you want a Brigade Board."

Barracks are immaculate on the inside. Daily room inspections require that the garbage can be empty, and that closet doors are open at a 90 degree angle, revealing evenly spaced clothes hangers. Failure to do otherwise results in incantations that "you won't survive."

In Good Company

The opening days of the Beast require people to "get pretty close pretty fast." Most students are closest with the members of their company or their sports teams. Because the entire student population is in extremely good physical shape and playing a sport is required, sports play a large role in everyday life. "Sports dominate the social scene, especially football games. If you come here, you will attend most of the home football games, if not all." Some weekends are actually designated "Football Weekend," more commonly referred to as "F weekend," where cadets have an optional Saturday breakfast and then attend a football game before being released to continue the weekend. (The other two types of weekend are: 1) A/C Weekend, which includes a mandatory breakfast and military training for 4-5 hour before being released, and 2) B weekend, which is the "free weekend" and cadets are released after class on Friday and do not have to return until an assigned time on Sunday.)

While there are significantly fewer women than men (women comprise only 14 percent of the student population), most West Point women do not feel that this is an issue. Likewise, ethnic diversity is very good, as one student praised the fact that, "students come from many countries and all walks of life."

Annual events include a Christmas/Holiday dinner where the Plebes decorate dinner tables and buy all the upperclassmen cigars. Everyone goes out to the Apron, an open area around the marching plain, and smokes it. "Even if you don't smoke, it's fun to go and stand with everyone and take part in one of the oldest traditions," explains one student. Each class also has a special event each year. The Plebes have Plebe Parent Weekend, the Yuks have Camp Illumination and Yearling Winter Weekend, the Cows have 500th night (celebrating 500 nights from graduation), and the Firsties have Ring Weekend, Branch Night and 100th Night.

Cup o' G.I. Joe, and Spirit Missions

While one student claimed that, "our life is very unpleasant," no alcohol simply means sober fun for the freshmen. While students at other colleges may find themselves having alcoholic tendencies, at West Point, "most cadets have a caffeine addiction," explained one Yuk. And where do they get their fix? Most cadets opt for Grant Hall, "an ornate, intricately decorated student union of sorts with a bunch of generals' portraits mounted on the walls and a big screen TV blaring ESPN or *The Simpsons*."

> "This is not just a school—it is a choice of lifestyle for the next nine years of life (at least) after high school."

Once one gets his or her caffeine fix, going on a spirit mission is a must for every cadet. Spirit missions are missions that occur after lights out, and include pranks on another company or cadets from the Naval and Air Force Academies. Cadets also put on a 100th Night Show, a parody of the Firstie experience in the form of a musical that is performed 100 nights from graduation. "Almost nothing is off limits. It makes fun of officers, events, cadets, etc. There are so many inside jokes, cadets always have to explain everything to their dates that they have invited."

A Choice of Lifestyle

"This is not just a school—it is a choice of lifestyle for the next nine years of life (at least) after high school," commented one senior. West Point cadets understand that much higher levels of mental agility, physical readiness and discipline are required. Living a more atypical college life is, quite simply, different. But in the end, as one cadet explained, "There's nothing I'd change about West Point. It's a military school, you know what you're getting into when you sign the dotted line."—*Christine Lin*

FYI

If you come to West Point, you'd better bring "EXCEPTIONAL PHYSICAL SHAPE. It makes everything that much easier, is one less thing to worry about while getting yelled at about everything else, and first impressions here are mainly that first day at 0520 in the morning."

What's the typical weekend schedule? "The typical weekend starts Friday night, and Saturdays will either be military training days, football games or free use. Each cadet has a number of passes to use to travel off post. When the run out, you must return to the barracks at night."

If I could change one thing about West Point, I'd "get more time off."

Three things every cadet should do before graduating are "blow post once, drink at the Firstie Club and survive."

University of Rochester

Address: 300 Wilson Boulevard Rochester, NY 14627

Phone: 888-822-2256

E-mail address: admit@admissions.rochester.edu

Web site URL: www.enrollment.rochester.edu

Year Founded: 1850

Private or Public: Private

Religious Affiliation: None

Location: Suburban

Number of Applicants: 11,633

Percent Accepted: 40%

Percent Accepted who enroll: 24%

Number Entering: 1,266

Number of Transfers Accepted each Year: Unreported

Middle 50% SAT range: M: 620–730, CR: 600–700, Wr: Unreported

Middle 50% ACT range: 27–31

Early admission program EA/ED/None: ED

Percentage accepted through EA or ED: 24%

EA and ED deadline: 1-Nov

Regular Deadline: 1-Jan

Application Fee: $60, $30 online

Full time Undergraduate enrollment: 5,058

Total enrollment: 9,160

Percent Male: 50%

Percent Female: 50%

Total Percent Minority or Unreported: 18%

Percent African-American: 4%

Percent Asian/Pacific Islander: 10%

Percent Hispanic: 4%

Percent Native-American: <1%

Percent International: Unreported

Percent in-state/out of state: 44.1%/55.9%

Percent from Public HS: 75%

Retention Rate: 96%

Graduation Rate 4-year: 70.20%

Graduation Rate 6-year: 81.30%

Percent Undergraduates in On-campus housing: 86%

Number of official organized extracurricular organizations: 250

3 Most popular majors: Biological Sciences, Engineering, Psychology

Student/Faculty ratio: 9:1

Average Class Size: 29

Percent of students going to grad school: 64%

Tuition and Fees: $37,250

In State Tuition and Fees if different: No difference

Cost for Room and Board: $10,810

Percent receiving financial aid out of those who apply, first year: 72%

Percent receiving financial aid among all students: 48%

W ith a small yet intellectually diverse student body, a focus on the freshman experience, and top-notch facilities and resources, the University of Rochester has everything that an enterprising student needs to succeed academically. Located on the outskirts of the city of Rochester in upstate New York, UR boasts a sterling academic reputation throughout the country for its strong science and engineering programs. In addition, the students at UR still know how to have fun, whether by participating in one of the many student groups or by taking full advantage of the wintry wonderland that is Rochester. The combination of these factors creates an academic and social environment that one student characterizes as "tough and challenging and frustrating, but, most of all, fun."

Interest-Driven Academics

The classes offered at UR may be harder than those at the average party school, but students find them rewarding because they can take courses that interest them. Students at UR praise the lack of a core curriculum and note that there is only one required class at the University: the freshman writing seminar. Even the required class helps illustrate the importance of choice in the UR curriculum. In fact, the seminar offerings include exciting courses like "Organized Crime in Popular Culture." Beyond the only requirement, students choose a major and study two additional areas of interest outside of the major, under the University's unique "cluster" system. For example, a student majoring in an area of the sciences will take a cluster of courses from the social sciences and the humanities. A cluster consists of three related courses, and they can be completed over the entire four years of study at UR.

Although students universally praise the freedom given by UR's lax requirements, the cluster system garners mixed reviews. One freshman noted, "The cluster system allows you to find courses that you really enjoy taking outside of your normal academic comfort zone." Another student, however, described the cluster requirements as distractions from main academic interests. "When I take the courses required for my cluster," he said, "I do not feel as if I am doing anything to move towards completing my major." A sophomore explained, "no one above freshman year takes the cluster system as a special privilege anyway. Students usually end up fulfilling their requirements without trying."

The debate raging on campus over the intricacies of the cluster system is one example among many of the intense passion that UR students share toward academic exploration. Undoubtedly, most students come to UR to study and study hard. Majoring in the sciences or engineering is popular, but Rochester is also known for its strong economics, political science and film study programs. Nonetheless, one student stated what is a generally held view on campus: "premeds are everywhere." And it is for good reason. Rochester's strong science programs are especially well equipped to prepare premedical students for the long road ahead. There are, however, plenty of students who buck the "Rochester science nerd" archetype and choose to focus on one of the many other disciplines at the University.

UR intensifies its focus on academics through a variety of special and preprofessional programs offered through the College of Arts and Sciences. Among the most notable are the REMS (Rochester Early Medical Scholars) and REBS (Rochester Early Business Scholars) programs, which offer extremely gifted students the privilege of guaranteed admission to the medical school or the business school, upon matriculation as a freshman at the university. With the Take Five program, the University offers its students an opportunity to study a completely different discipline for a fifth year, after graduation. Best of all, the Take Five program is entirely funded by the University and is tuition-free. With these and other programs, UR ensures that students will never suffer from a lack of choice and opportunity when choosing among academic offerings.

Life on the River

Even while they are immersed in Rochester's stimulating and demanding academic atmosphere, UR students find the time to enjoy themselves on Rochester's main campus, located on a bend of the Genesee River just a short drive down the highway from downtown Rochester. Most dorms are "very nice,"

with the average freshman dorm room being slightly bigger than average. RAs are generally supportive and friendly and are good sources of academic advice and counseling. One sophomore noted, "As a freshman, the University coddles you and makes Rochester seem like a magical place. The dorms are great, and we had a six-day orientation at the beginning of the year to make sure that everyone was comfortable and had found their niche before classes started." Several students described the benign oversight of freshmen as a burden when it comes to prohibited substances: "The University is probably a little too strict on drugs and alcohol." Indeed, UR is not loath to take legal action to punish repeat offenders of dormitory regulations that strictly control the use of alcohol and drugs.

These regulations and their enforcement do not, however, stifle the active social life and party scene at UR. "There are really two extremes at UR: those who go out three or more times per week, and those who never go out. But the grand majority of students lies somewhere in the middle and will drink maybe once or twice a week at most. Rochester is an intelligent party school: the morning after a big party the libraries will still be full," said a freshman. Opportunities to party on the weekends abound, from the energetic frat quad to the off-campus bars to small dorm room parties. A freshman noted, however, that one's social options are limited by the availability of transportation, given the relative isolation of the UR campus. "Cars are a really big deal at UR," said one student. "Seniors with cars can go to all the cool bars and restaurants off campus." Although anyone can technically have a car at UR, students must write to the administration for the privilege and provide evidence that they need the car to get off campus for some reason. Seniors are the most likely to obtain this privilege.

Innovation and Tradition

Even if students sometimes can't find a way to get off campus, there are still plenty of activities and fun traditions to occupy them while stuck on campus during those long upstate winter nights. "There are so many clubs, over 200 I think, that I don't even know some of them and hear about new ones all the time." said one student. An elected organization called the Student Association is responsible for disbursing funds to the myriad groups, which then hold events and organize activities. While school pride for the University's varsity teams is somewhat lacking, attendance at basketball games is usually good. Besides varsity sports, students can participate in a variety of club sports, ranging from hockey to badminton. Club and intramural sports at UR are generally not very intense and are generally regarded as study breaks rather than opportunities to display one's athletic prowess.

> "Rochester is an intelligent party school: the morning after a big party, the libraries will still be full."

As a result of its age and its active alumni association, UR holds many traditions near and dear. The Meliora weekend, celebrated every fall, is known for its "great parties and general merriment," as parents and alumni converge on the campus in a celebration of the University and its heritage. Other traditions include sledding down the campus's many hills during the long winter months and Nick Tahoe's run, an annual competition organized by fraternities that pits rushes against each other in a mad dash to an off-campus restaurant to scarf down a plate full of food and then run (or stumble) back to school. Tickets are always coveted for the annual Boar's Head dinner, in which students and faculty dress up in medieval garb and party in the ways of the 14th century.

"R U" Right for UR?

While Rochester's intense academic atmosphere is appropriate for any gifted and motivated student, more than one student commented on the lack of ethnic diversity at Rochester. "We're pretty homogenous. UR is known for being pretty white, and this is something that the University is working to address," noted a sophomore. Despite the relatively low percentage of African-Americans and Hispanics at the school, UR is a generally accepting environment, and anyone should be able to find a "group of people that you really connect with." UR students deal with the cold and the relative isolation of their campus because of the huge upside to their school: world-caliber academic programs in a small school atmosphere that often "feels even smaller and more intimate than it is."—*Patrick Hurley*

FYI
If you come to the University of Rochester, you'd better bring "a sled for Danforth Hill in the winter."
What is the typical weekend schedule? "Out to a frat on Friday night, off to a concert in the city on Saturday and then a bar on Saturday night. On Sunday everyone stays in and works."
If I could change one thing about the University of Rochester, I'd "make it more centrally located in the city and have more events off campus."
Three things every student should do before graduating are "do Nick Tahoe's run, slide down the hill in front of the dining hall, and go to a concert in downtown Rochester."

Vassar College

Address: 124 Raymond Avenue Poughkeepsie, NY 12604
Phone: 845-437-7000
E-mail address: admissons@vassar.edu
Web site URL: www.vassar.edu
Year Founded: 1861
Private or Public: Private
Religious Affiliation: None
Location: Suburban
Number of Applicants: 7,361
Percent Accepted: 25%
Percent Accepted who enroll: 35%
Number Entering: 640
Number of Transfers Accepted each Year: 29
Middle 50% SAT range: M: 650–720, CR: 670–750, Wr: 660–750
Middle 50% ACT range: 29–33
Early admission program EA/ED/None: ED

Percentage accepted through EA or ED: 38%
EA and ED deadline: 15-Nov
Regular Deadline: 1-Jan
Application Fee: $60
Full time Undergraduate enrollment: 2,389
Total enrollment: 2,389
Percent Male: 43%
Percent Female: 57%
Total Percent Minority or Unreported: Unreported
Percent African-American: 6%
Percent Asian/Pacific Islander: 11%
Percent Hispanic: 6%
Percent Native-American: <1%
Percent International: 7%
Percent in-state/out of state: 26%/74%
Percent from Public HS: 65%
Retention Rate: 96%
Graduation Rate 4-year: 87%

Graduation Rate 6-year: 0.0%
Percent Undergraduates in On-campus housing: 95%
Number of official organized extracurricular organizations: 105
3 Most popular majors: Social Sciences, Visual and Performing Arts, Foreign Language and Literature
Student/Faculty ratio: 8:1
Average Class Size: 10 to 19
Percent of students going to grad school: 20%
Tuition and Fees: $40,210
In State Tuition and Fees if different: No difference
Cost for Room and Board: $9,040
Percent receiving financial aid out of those who apply, first year: 84%
Percent receiving financial aid among all students: 57%

A small liberal arts college in upstate New York, Vassar is many a student's dream. It is home to top-notch academics and one of the most scenic campuses in the country. Even if the weather is not always pleasant, Vassar's friendly atmosphere and students' smiling faces ensure a warm welcome.

We Put the Liberal in Liberal Arts

Vassar is committed to letting their students have a variety of options that they can explore. For this reason the graduation requirements outside of one's major are minimal. Students must take a freshman writing class, a foreign language class which one can place out of with a test, and finally a quantitative analysis class which can be fulfilled with classes in a variety of fields. Moreover, Vassar offers an independent major option which allows the students to create their own major which, as one student exclaimed, can be "anything under the sun." Within the structured majors, English, political science and

psychology are the most popular majors. Even in these popular majors, however, one does not have to worry about overwhelming class sizes. The intro classes at Vassar, which are considered big, number between 25 and 35 people while most classes have only 10 people and one student even reported being one of three students in one of her classes. Students warned that "you can't hide" in these classes.

The workload in general as one student described is "very manageable and professors are very understanding." One student assured "people will work with you to accommodate your needs. It can be difficult but there is a lot of support built into the system." The professors are in general praised as very accessible. Among them the students recommended Joe Nevins, who teaches "Geography of Mass Violence," and English professor Peter Antelyes. As for other classes, organic chemistry and most intro science classes are cited as difficult while "Nutrition and Exercise" is a gut class. Among the more interesting classes, students recommended the psychology department's "Sex on the Brain" class and cited cross-departmental classes such as "Psychology of Art" and "Psychological Perspectives on the Holocaust" as worth checking out.

A School That Parties Together . . .

Vassar does not have a Greek system, but no one seems to miss it. Off campus, the town of Poughkeepsie is not considered to be very safe, and the bar scene is pretty dismal. Exceptions are Babycakes and The Dutch, which both offer cheap beer on Thursday nights. For these reasons the campus itself is center of social life. Students say that parties happen all around campus—there is a lot of camaraderie and "everyone hangs out with everyone else." The only ones that are separated are the seniors, who live separately in all-senior housing and hold their own parties there too. Students also come together at The Mug, an on-campus club/bar that features jazz night on Tuesdays, an 80s night on Wednesdays and other various themes throughout the week. In springtime the biggest event on campus is Founder's Day, which involves carnivals and other various activities on Sunset Hill. The Halloween party is another large event on campus. Most students drink on campus but there is no pressure to do so. While the campus security patrols the campus, the rules seem to be enforced rather arbitrarily and you never know if you'll get written up.

The atmosphere on campus is pretty warm as the students are described as very friendly and constantly wearing a smile. While ethnic diversity is rather limited, there is a large gay community at the college, and sexual diversity according to one student "adds another dimension" to the campus: "[Vassar] is very open about race, class and sexuality. There are always dialogues going on and [diversity] is celebrated."

How Many Gardeners Does It Take . . .

There are nine dorms on campus, and freshmen, sophomores and juniors all live integrated, thus creating "a great sense of community." This is evidenced by the fact that only about two percent of the student body chooses to live off campus. Once you get assigned to a dorm you stay there for your first three years and it is rare to transfer out. Community building begins freshman year as there are no RAs in the dorms, only Student Fellows, who are sophomores who

provide advising and guidance for the freshmen. Their role is more like that of an older sibling than a policy enforcer, and they have no power to get their advisees in trouble or written up. The communities within colleges contribute to the personalities of the dorms. Davidson is a family-oriented dorm, Lathrope is the party dorm, and Cushing is the antisocial crowd since it's out of the way from the other dorms. Strong House is the all-female dorm. In addition, each year 20 students live in the Ferry House, which is the co-op house on campus where students live, work and cook together. Seniors live in apartment complexes with four to five students to each apartment.

The campus is described as having the "classic academia feel," with brick buildings and lovely landscaping. The campus is an arboretum, so as one student described "there are lots of pretty trees and sometimes they go overboard on landscaping." She assured that "walking around on campus is definitely a pleasant experience." The Quad, which is surrounded by dorms, is the central hangout spot, and when the good weather arrives it is home to many students taking in the sunrays. Across the street from the campus there is more opportunity for outdoor activity as it is the location of the College-owned farm, cited as a great place for jogging. Otherwise students do not venture off campus much as the town-gown relations are rather strained and one student even reported having trash thrown at her when she was running on the streets of Poughkeepsie. In an effort to bridge the gap between the school and community the College decided to move the school bookstore off campus, and students are hoping that it will be the first step toward improving relations.

The main dining hall on campus is ACDC (All Campus Dining Center) and The Retreat is its smaller, to-go counterpart. The students praise the dining halls for having very good vegetarian and vegan options and generally describe the options as tasty and varied. For those wishing to venture outside of the meal plan there are nearby Thai Spice, Tokyo Express and Babycakes which are all favorites with students. For late night options students heartily recommend The Acropolis and its cheese fries.

A Traditional School

Among the 105 registered on-campus student organizations there are plenty of options. Some of the more prominent options are The Vassar Greens, an environmental club; the Barefoot Monkeys, a circus group; and also the various a cappella and drama options. The school's newspaper, *The Miscellany News*, is also pretty popular. Sports on the other hand often suffer from a lack of support. While intramurals have high participation, students complain that school spirit is rather low and not many people attend games or sporting events.

To make up for the lack of school spirit, Vassar is very rich in traditions. Primal Scream occurs each semester before finals, when all the students gather on the quad to scream in unison and let out their frustration. During this time in the spring semester, seniors also streak naked through the library. Another senior tradition is ringing the bell on top of the Main building, and throughout the designated day there are very long lines leading to the top as everyone awaits their turn to ring the bell and write their names on the wall of the room. Scantily Clad is an annual dance party involving Jell-O wrestling, but it's not the only one that involves food. In the beginning of the year as an initiation process for the freshmen, the seniors go around campus visiting freshman dorms where freshmen greet them with songs they have written for them and then proceed to enter into a food fight against the seniors.

"Vassar is very open about race, class and sexuality. There are always dialogues going on."

The community bonds at Vassar create an uncompetitive atmosphere where, according to one student, "everyone is low-key, nice and friendly, and smart but low-key." For this reason students find it easy to fall in love with the school, and when asked if they would choose it all over again, they proclaim without hesitation a definite "Yes, 100 percent."—*Dopota Poplawska*

FYI

If you come to Vassar, you'd better bring "the craziest clothes you own and a smile."

What is the typical weekend schedule? "Go out Thursday, Friday and Saturday to a play or performance after dinner and later to campus parties or the Mug; during the day relax, do laundry and read."

If I could change one thing about Vassar, I'd "improve the town-gown relations."

Three things every student at Vassar should do before graduating are "ring the bell on top of Main building, visit the Vassar farm, and try the sweet potato fries at the Retreat."

Wells College

Address: Route 90 Aurora, NY 13026
Phone: 315-364-3264
E-mail address: admissions@wells.edu
Web site URL: www.wells.edu
Year Founded: 1868
Private or Public: Private
Religious Affiliation: None
Location: Rural
Number of Applicants: 1,148
Percent Accepted: 65%
Percent Accepted who enroll: 24%
Number Entering: 174
Number of Transfers Accepted each Year: 113
Middle 50% SAT range: M: 490–590, CR: 510–640, Wr: Unrepoted
Middle 50% ACT range: 21–27
Early admission program EA/ED/None: ED

Percentage accepted through EA or ED: 80%
EA and ED deadline: 15-Dec
Regular Deadline: 1-Feb
Application Fee: $40
Full time Undergraduate enrollment: 557
Total enrollment: 557
Percent Male: 23%
Percent Female: 77%
Total Percent Minority or Unreported: 13%
Percent African-American: 6%
Percent Asian/Pacific Islander: 2%
Percent Hispanic: 4%
Percent Native-American: 1%
Percent International: 2%
Percent in-state/out of state: 69%/31%
Percent from Public HS: 88%
Retention Rate: 76%

Graduation Rate 4-year: 47%
Graduation Rate 6-year: 48%
Percent Undergraduates in On-campus housing: 86%
Number of official organized extracurricular organizations: 35
3 Most popular majors: English, History, Psychology
Student/Faculty ratio: 9:1
Average Class Size: 10 to 19
Percent of students going to grad school: 44%
Tuition and Fees: $17,580
In State Tuition and Fees if different: No difference
Cost for Room and Board: $8,420
Percent receiving financial aid out of those who apply, first year: 71%
Percent receiving financial aid among all students: 76%

P ick a tradition, any tradition. Wells has more than enough to go around. Yet despite their overwhelming popularity amongst students, one of the school's most significant traditions has recently been broken. Wells, formerly an all-girls school, admitted its first coed class in the fall of 2005. The close community spirit engendered by such a small campus, however, ensured a smooth change. "For the most part I have had no problems at all", remarked one male freshman. "I feel very at home and the people here are very nice." Indeed, at Wells, community and tradition blend to create the "relaxed and laid-back campus" students value.

One on One
Within the framework of a small student body, students have considerable access to their professors. "The one-on-one time that students at Wells get is priceless," remarked one Public Affairs major. The quality of Wells professors makes this accessibility especially appealing. "Many of my professors are literally brilliant," one freshman exclaimed. And while the grading may be tough, "you learn quite a bit."

One of the more interesting courses offered at Wells is Book Arts, in which students study the processes of book binding and book restoration, and even learn how to use a printing press. "It's really neat," one junior remarked. He also commented on the uniqueness of the college's Book Arts center. Wells also has much to offer to those interested in education. An elementary school, Peachtown, is located on campus and Wells students are greatly involved in its activities.

Science and math majors are a minority. One math major did complain about the lack of incentive to enter her field. "To give copious awards for sports or writing doesn't really encourage others to major in math," she noted. Still, she praised the department itself. "I enjoy it and find it challenging, especially the upper level courses, which is what I wanted when I came here."

'Breathtaking' Beauty
Most students are content living on campus. "The campus is absolutely breathtaking. I mean it is really, really beautiful," one freshman explained. However, the process of determining where to live on campus can be

slightly more involved. Weld "has the best kitchen and individual bathrooms" while Glenn Park, the former home of Wells' founder, boasts spiral staircases and numerous lounges. Main, the biggest residence hall, also hosts the dining hall and is effectively the center of campus. In addition, the fourth floor serves as the Healthy Lifestyles floor, which offers a living environment in which "people don't come up drunk or create havoc." While Leach "is crazy," students tend to avoid Dodge because "the style is a bit . . . retro" and it is further than the other dorms from academic buildings.

No matter where students end up, the natural beauty of Wells' campus is available for everyone to enjoy. Students have access to the nearby lake for everything from science classes to skinny dipping, and many enjoy spending time on the docks. "There are trees everywhere—I came here because of the trees," one student asserted, adding that "the town of Aurora is also incredibly picturesque".

Just as students agree on the beauty of campus, they also agree on the quality of the food. Unfortunately, the consensus is not a positive one. "The dining hall is awful," complained one junior. "It's so bad," explained a sophomore, "that I *lost* 15 pounds freshman year." Still, there are a few who have good things to say about the food served on campus, so not all is lost. One senior praised "Dean Green's macaroni and cheese at soul food/home cooking night," explaining that "the administration actually comes and serves food sometimes." Furthermore, each residence hall has its own kitchen, so students always have the option of cooking for themselves.

On and Off Campus
The close relationship between the administration and students is not limited simply to the dining hall. "Wells has a ton of committees where students go right to the administration," said one Performing Arts major. "We have committees for everything from the dining hall to student diversity that meet with the senior staff on a regular basis." Aside from such committees, students have a wide range of opportunities for involvement on campus. Since Wells is strictly an undergraduate institution, Wells women and men have the opportunity to work as TAs in different subjects. Others spend their time in activities ranging from choirs, to the Japanese Culture Club, to groups such as Q&A (Queers and Allies).

Despite the abundance of extracurricular activities on campus, Wells students usually head to nearby Cornell or Ithaca College for parties. And while drinking on campus does exist, "it is usually pretty discrete in dorms. People are fairly mellow." As one junior explained, "people come to Wells to study . . . not party." Still, many students enjoy the social activities centered at Wells. One senior pointed to Sex Collective and the Women's Resource Center as one of her favorites, crediting them with "The Erotic Ball" and "The BDP" (Big Dyke Party).

Whether or not they choose to party in Ithaca, Wells women and men tend to agree that having a car on campus is very convenient. Though Wells offers shuttle van services to a variety of locations, one sophomore points out that they "don't go to too many places and the times at which you're allowed to take the van are set by the Transportation Department." Cars offer students the freedom of movement that shuttles simply cannot provide.

Above All, Tradition
Students love the great variety of traditions on campus, citing them as a large part of what makes Wells unique. The role of traditions is deeply ingrained in campus life, and begins every year with the Senior Champagne Breakfast and Opening Convocations. "We [the entire school] all make a huge circle in front of Macmillian and . . . light candles," a current freshman described. After convocation, seniors jump into the lake wearing their lingerie.

> **"People come to Wells to study . . . not party."**

"Moving Up Day" is also a monumental event at Wells, officially marking the transition as students move from one year to the next or from student to alum. "The fire alarms are pulled around 6 or 7 a.m. and everyone gathers in front of Main building," one student recounted. "We 'circle up' and do the classes song . . . After singing the seniors race to get in line to kiss the feet of the statue of Minerva." Traditions marking the end of the school year include dancing around the sycamore tree on the last day of classes.

No matter which tradition they chose as their favorite, students are enthusiastic about the atmosphere such customs create. "I think it's special; I've never heard of these traditions anywhere else," noted one sophomore.

Wells has much to offer its undergraduates, and students find that their experiences more than exceed expectations. As one senior reflected, "the minute I stepped on campus I fell in love with it. It's exactly the place I knew I had to be and there has never been a moment . . . that I second guessed my decision." She added, "It has helped me grow as a person and challenged me in ways that I'm not sure I would have been at other schools. I love Wells and everything it has done for me."—*Stephanie Brockman*

FYI
If you come to Wells, you'd better bring "a car."
What is the typical weekend schedule? "Sleep, study, then head to Cornell."
If I could change one thing about Wells, I'd "move it closer to a city."
Three things that every student at Wells should do before graduating are "participate in all the traditions they can, skinny dip in the lake, be in a theatre or dance production."

Yeshiva University

Address: 500 West 185th Street, New York, New York 10033
Phone: 212-960-5277
E-mail address: yuadmit@yu.edu
Web site URL: www.yu.edu
Year Founded: 1886
Private or Public: Private
Religious Affiliation: Jewish
Location: Urban
Number of Applicants: Unreported
Percent Accepted: 69%
Percent Accepted who enroll: Unreported
Number Entering: 769
Number of Transfers Accepted each Year: Unreported
Middle 50% SAT range: M: 570–680, CR: 550–670, Wr: Unreported
Middle 50% ACT range: Unreported
Early admission program EA/ED/None: Rolling

Percentage accepted through EA or ED: NA
EA and ED deadline: 15-Oct, 15-Dec, 1-Feb
Regular Deadline: 1-Feb
Application Fee: $65
Full time Undergraduate enrollment: 3,076
Total enrollment: 3,076
Percent Male: Unreported
Percent Female: Unreported
Total Percent Minority or Unreported: 7%
Percent African-American: 2%
Percent Asian/Pacific Islander: 3%
Percent Hispanic: 2%
Percent Native-American: 0%
Percent International: Unreported
Percent in-state/out of state: Unreported
Percent from Public HS: Unreported
Retention Rate: 88%
Graduation Rate 4-year: Unreported

Graduation Rate 6-year: Unreported
Percent Undergraduates in On-campus housing: Unreported
Number of official organized extracurricular organizations: Unreported
3 Most popular majors: Unreported
Student/Faculty ratio: Unreported
Average Class Size: Unreported
Percent of students going to grad school: Unreported
Tuition and Fees: $31,594
In State Tuition and Fees if different: No difference
Cost for Room and Board: $9,880
Percent receiving financial aid out of those who apply, first year: Unreported
Percent receiving financial aid among all students: Unrepoted

Yeshiva University, a prominent Jewish university, offers its students the unique opportunity to spend their freshman year on the other side of the Atlantic. With 45 yeshivas and institutions located throughout Israel to choose from, YU students can earn a year's worth of credits and enter YU with sophomore standing. All credits earned are transferable from Israel to YU in New York.

Two in One Curriculum

Yeshiva University emphasizes both secular and religious studies. Undergraduates' double curriculum encompasses the Judaic areas such as Halacha (Jewish law), the Bible and the Talmud, as well as the liberal arts and sciences. YU is made up of Yeshiva College for Men and Stern College for women. The two gender-segregated campuses are located in Upper Manhattan and Midtown

Manhattan, respectively. Students may also enroll in special schools such as the Belz School of Music and the Sy Syms School of Business. In order to fulfill the Judaic studies requirement, Yeshiva College students choose from variety of classes offered at James Striar School of General Jewish Study, the Isaac Breuer College of Hebraic Studies, the Irving I. Stone Beit Midrash program and the Yeshiva Program/Mazer School of Talmudic Studies. Students generally take Judaic courses in the morning, while reserving their afternoons for secular studies. One student described the graduation requirements as "doable" and "not burdensome." Many undergrads also take advantage of the opportunity to spend their freshman year in Israel through the S. Daniel Abraham Program.

Rewarding Academics

With over 30 majors to choose from, YU also offers a plethora of joint degree program in engineering, dentistry, optometry, podiatry, Jewish studies, social work, nursing and psychology. The S. Daniel Abraham Honors Program at Stern College and the Jay and Jeanie Schottenstein Honors Program at Yeshiva College allow students with high SAT scores to enhance the rigor of their studies.

Students seem to find their classes "rewarding." One commented that "the teachers are of a sound quality" while another said that "the professors are reachable, making it not intimidating to ask a question." Some of the more popular majors are business and sociology. One sociology major said, "it is a pretty easy major" compared to the "harder majors" in the sciences. YU will also help in the job search after college. One student felt strongly that "they will hook you up with a pretty good job right after you get out." Despite the greater number of hours YU students spend in the classroom, students enjoy their dual curriculum.

Competitive Out of the Classroom

Although Yeshiva University is "sometimes lacking school spirit," the men's basketball team is the big draw of the school's varsity sports program. Recently, the Maccabees— or Macs for short—finished with a 14-11 record that included a program-record eight game winning streak. For the less athletically gifted, there is a wide range of ways to compete at YU in a non-varsity setting. YU has developed a strong, completely student-run intramural sports program that offers every-thing from bumper pool to an Iron Man competition. But do not be fooled by the intramural sports label, IMs "tend to be very competitive." Other popular ways to stay in shape are at the well-liked Furst Gymnasium and the Gottesman Swimming Pool.

The Western Capital of the Jewish World

Like many New York City schools, one of YU's greatest assets is its location. A Jewish university situated in the "Western Capital of the Jewish World," boasting the greatest Jewish population outside of Israel, provides religious students easy access to kosher dining and synagogues. Yeshiva college students love that they can get on the subway from their Upper Manhattan campus and take advantage of the Big Apple's many diversions. Stern girls find themselves in Midtown with convenient access to Times Square. Very few students have cars, so the average YU student relies on New York's public transportation system.

There are not many bars located around Yeshiva College. Thursday nights and Saturday nights are the big going out nights. One junior remarked that while "the more religious crowd tends to hang out at restaurants downtown . . . some YU kids actually experience the real NYC nightlife." This can vary from bars and restaurants to trendy clubs. The on-campus party scene is limited. There are currently no fraternities, but there is an effort being made to establish a chapter of AEPi, a national Jewish fraternity.

Basic Accommodations

The majority of those attending YU live within a three block radius of campus. Underclassmen generally live in school operated dorms while upperclassmen usually move into apartments. Some students who live in the New York-New Jersey area commute to school. There are three main dorms. The Rubin Dorm is located on top of a cafeteria and athletic center. The MUSS Dorm, considered to be the least nice of the three, is situated above the main Beit Midrash. Morge is the largest dorm and is found in the center of campus. One freshman said his dorm room "is depressing, but it gets the job done." Every floor has its own RA, who usually is "friendly and not strict." The Wilf campus, where the Yeshiva College for Men is set, spans three blocks and all the housing options lie within easy walking distance. The Stern College for Women, located at the Beren campus in Midtown Manhattan, offers independent housing in addition to three residence halls: 36th Street, Brookdale, and Schottenstein. All of these options are just a few blocks away from the Stern Campus Main Building at 34th and Lexington.

> **"There are no real traditions at YU, except for the Torah."**

Students must sign up for the school-run meal program. All the food is kosher and "it is not terrible." However, one sophomore complained, "I feel like I am paying 15 dollars for a tuna sandwich." Along with the perks of being in the NYC, including great restaurants, there are drawbacks. In the past, there have been reported muggings on or near campus. The school takes security very seriously and places 24-hour security guards on campus street corners to protect students.

The Last Word

Yeshiva University is a religious Jewish institution and as such there is little religious diversity on campus. One sophomore stressed that the typical YU student is an upper middle class, Jewish and white. But YU is filled with Jewish students from outside of the United States. The University draws students from Canada, France, Israel, and South America, among other places. Since a large portion of students spend their freshman year studying in Israel, many arrive on campus with already established friendships. The general vibe on campus is "real friendly." There is a lot of camaraderie between students of all years. Underclassmen are often in the same classes as upperclassmen, and "they tend to know each other from the same neighborhoods, high schools, or yeshivas in Israel." A religious university without much of a party scene, YU is in many ways a unique school. As one student put it, "There are no real traditions at YU, except for the Torah."—*Harry Etra*

FYI
If you come Yeshiva University, you'd better bring "a yarmulke."
What is the typical weekend schedule? "Hang out with friends on Thursday (no class on Friday), go away for Shabbat, and back to chilling on Saturday night."
If I could change one thing about Yeshiva, I'd "make it more competitive to get in."
Three things every student at Yeshiva should do before graduating are "go to a Yankees game, spend a Shabbat on campus and play in the dirty snow."

North Carolina

Address: PO Box 7156
Davidson, NC 28035-5000
Phone: 704-894-2230
E-mail address:
admission@davidson.edu
Web site URL:
www.davidson.edu
Year Founded: 1837
Private or Public: Private
Religious Affiliation:
Presbyterian
Location: Surburban
Number of Applicants: 3,940
Percent Accepted: 30%
Percent Accepted who
enroll: 39%
Number Entering: 461
Number of Transfers
Accepted each Year:
Unreported
Middle 50% SAT range:
M: 630–720, CR: 620–720,
Wr: 680–740
Middle 50% ACT range:
27–31
Early admission program
EA/ED/None: ED

Percentage accepted
through EA or ED: 41%
EA deadline: 15-Nov
Regular Deadline: 2-Jan
Application Fee: $50
Full time Undergraduate
enrollment: 1,660
Total enrollment: 1,660
Percent Male: 50%
Percent Female: 50%
Total Percent Minority or
Unreported: 24%
Percent African-American:
7%
Percent Asian/Pacific
Islander: 3%
Percent Hispanic: 5%
Percent Native-American:
1%
Percent International: 3%
Percent in-state/out of
state: 19%/81%
Percent from Public HS:
48%
Retention Rate: 95%
Graduation Rate 4-year:
89%

Graduation Rate 6-year:
91%
Percent Undergraduates
in On-campus housing:
91%
Number of official organized
extracurricular
organizations: 151
3 Most popular majors:
English, History, Economics
Student/Faculty ratio:
10:1
Average Class Size: 10 to
19
Percent of students going to
grad school: 25%
Tuition and Fees: $30,662
In State Tuition and Fees if
different: No difference
Cost for Room and Board:
$9,020
Percent receiving financial
aid out of those who apply,
first year: 64%
Percent receiving financial
aid among all students:
32%

A long with a reputation for conservatism, Davidson College boasts a reputation for excellence. Since its founding by Presbyterians in 1837, the 1,670-student residential haven has made itself known by leaving its mark on several noteworthy individuals who have passed through its grassy courtyards and majestic colonial halls. As one student noted, "Woodrow Wilson went to school here for two years then left and went to Princeton because it was too hard."

A Core that's No Bore

The crux of the Davidson education is undoubtedly its adherence to the liberal arts philosophy of expanding the mind through exposure to multiple disciplines. The core curriculum demands ten courses in six general categories: literature, fine arts, history, religion and philosophy, natural sciences/math and social sciences. If that isn't enough structure, Davidson also requires its students to take three semesters or the equivalent of a foreign language, four physical education courses, one composition credit in the first year to establish skills in college-level writing, and a cultural diversity course focusing on a non-western region. Academically claustrophobic individuals can be rest assured that Davidson's rigid core program is broadened by a unique set of in-class opportunities. One student explained, "For a composition course, 'Trial of Jesus,' my group created a newspaper meant to depict the way Jesus' execution might have been reported in the ancient Roman Empire."

Students reported that although fulfilling requirements may seem a daunting task at first, doing so is actually rather easy. Four AP credits are accepted and may be used to eliminate introductory requirements and accelerate within a discipline. What shocks incoming freshmen is the general academic rigor from which President Wilson reportedly shied away. Grade inflation is a distant myth. According to one student, "People lament that if they had gone elsewhere they would have had higher GPAs." Another student noted that, "A papers are now B or B- papers." The tougher majors are generally agreed to be those in the sciences, including Chemistry, Biology and the notorious Pre-med track, while majors such as Psychology, English and Anthropology are in most cases a bit easier to digest.

> **"People lament that if they had gone elsewhere they would have had higher GPAs."**

While there's certainly no dearth of challenges, Davidson offers an impressive set of resources in all areas of academic life. Compassionate student-professor relationship stories are commonplace—and it's no surprise in a place with a student-faculty ratio of 10 to 1. The largest classes are capped at 35 in the humanities and 32 in the sciences, but "as soon as you move into upper level courses the cap drops drastically to 20, 15, 10, eight, even five students," says one student. Classes are not difficult to get into, but if there are problems, many a solution has been reached by emailing the reputedly accommodating professors. TAs are better known as ATs and are primarily available for hour-long language sessions during which students meet in a group and speak a particular language. The CIS, or Center for Interdisciplinary Study, is the undecided, jack-of-all-trades student's academic heaven. Faculty in CIS is available to work with students who wish to construct a major Davidson does not offer. One student reported that "recent majors have ranged from neuroscience to choral conducting to international politics to medical ethics." Apparently, the sky is the limit.

Charming or Claustrophobic?

Davidson College's campus is composed of regal Georgian architecture, miles of grassy hills, a set of cross country trails that "snake through the woods next to campus," consistently temperate weather that "never seems to be overcast," the idyllic scenery of Lake Norman, and a notoriously charming wishing well. A responsible, active police force contributes to the general feeling of safety that students experience while on campus. However, the sense of intimacy that for some enhances the beauty of their "small but charming" home is a bit oppressive for others. According to one student, "Campus can get very claustrophobic after a while, [so] it is great to have your own car."

Though a convenient asset, and a means for getting to a mall (one feature that Davidson lacks), a car isn't necessary for experiencing the various charms and treats that the quaint town of Davidson has to offer. Most students report that they go off campus a few times a week, and although Davidson is only about 20 miles north of Charlotte, most tend to stick to their small-town surroundings. However, one student stated that, "if you want to go shopping, you go somewhere else." The town does have a CVS and a few small, rather expensive boutiques, but its strengths are undoubtedly its culinary highlights, which include a restaurant that is famous for its sumptuous chocolate milkshakes and Summit, an excellent coffee shop that is frequented by many Davidson Wildcats.

The majority of students live on campus and have few complaints in terms of housing and dining. All freshmen are placed in doubles according to the Myers-Briggs Personality Test, which is also applied in the arrangement of each freshman hall. Two Hall Counselors, upperclassmen in charge of enforcing rules and serving as role models and sources of advice for their corresponding freshmen, are assigned to each fresh floor. Doubles and singles are available after the first year, and most seniors live in an apartment with four or five roommates. Floors are single-sex with the exception of Belk. Freshmen start with the largest meal plan, known as "the 19," which can be reduced or eliminated as desired. The student ID can be used at multiple locations on campus and even at a few local restaurants. The dining hall, along with being aesthetically pleasing and offering a plethora of options, is not segmented by cliques and is "great for people-watching," one student noted.

Tradition Meets Innovation

The focal points of Davidson's diverse social life illustrate the clash between convention and ingenuity, habit and experiment. The Union, the group responsible for organizing campus-wide events, works to provide students with a number of stimulating pursuits, whether through lectures and talks, or more leisurely movie nights and free pottery painting sessions. The student center, which was dubbed by one student as the "hub of all campus activity," houses the campus P.O. boxes, as well as a café, and is open at all hours for casual socializing, group projects, or those notorious late-night cramming sessions.

The Union also strives to offer "social alternatives to the Patterson Court Scene." Patterson Court is the formal name for the eight international fraternities, four female eating houses and one coed eating house that compose Davidson's active Greek scene. The eating houses came about when Davidson began enrolling women. Female students rush for spots in the eating houses and about 70 percent of Davidson's female students hold membership. Forty percent of men participate in a fraternity. Though the Greek scene is rather dominant on campus, parties are open to all and generally adopt themes ranging from toga to boy band or tacky parties.

Students admit that although the school's policy is strict when it comes to alcohol, it is definitely available to those who want it. In fact, each incoming freshman is assigned an upperclassman "sibling" of the opposite sex who is officially supposed to help the student meet upperclassmen, but who unofficially is there to "mainly just buy you alcohol."

Students generally agree that random hook-ups are significantly more common than official dates, for as one student noted, the campus is almost too "excluded" for a romantic night out on the town. But despite all this arbitrary "messing around," students report that STDs are not rampant. In regards to alcohol, the administration makes efforts to involve itself through Davidson's 101 courses, which basically teach students how to act responsibly when engaging in potentially dangerous activities, such as sex and drinking. "Davidson 101 courses present sexual activity as a normal activity for college students. However, I know of many who disagree and feel targeted for not being sexually active," one student revealed.

Pearls and Polos

Davidson certainly manages to attract to its campus a "quiet, hard-working, respectful" student body, but this convention is accepted a bit more easily than the one that involves, as one student termed it, the "stereotype of the rich, snobby white kids who wear sundresses and polos to class every day." Many students emphasize the above as simply an exaggerated generalization. But according to one student, "Most people dress VERY preppy. Collared polos, khaki shorts, loafers, and pearl earrings are the standards. Most are fairly wealthy, as can be seen by their clothes, cell phones, vacations, houses, cars, and dorm rooms." Students also express dissatisfaction with the lack of international diversity and the fact that international students are housed separately. On the other hand, while, as one student noted, "most people are similar and come from similar backgrounds," another commented that, "the school is really working on diversifying the student body." Additionally, groups do not tend to self-segregate, so that the level of diversity that does exist is enhanced by a willingness to interact with various types of people.

Surely there is a general mold for the typical Davidson student's background. But this cast tends to disintegrate in the face of the manifold extracurricular opportunities that are available to every student. Sports range from the more popular football and Division I basketball to the less widely acclaimed flickerball. Students report that community service and activism groups are the most popular on campus. And there always exists the opportunity to translate a novel idea into a new club for those to whom the more conventional organizations do not appeal. According to one student on the possibility for redefinition in such a diverse extracurricular community, "I feel free to participate in what I want to here without feeling like I will get dissolved irrecoverably into a certain group or clique."—*Juliann Rowe*

FYI
If you come to Davidson, you'd better bring: "a futon, flip-flops, and plenty of suits/dresses."
What's the typical weekend schedule? "Wake up around 11 or 12, have brunch, study for a while, go out to eat, and head down to the Court/Union/or watch a movie."
If I could change one thing about Davidson, I'd "give less work and put up more swings."
Three things every student at Davidson should do before graduating are "go to Lake Campus, order food from Bonsai, and attend Thursday night worship."

Duke University

Address: 2138 Campus Drive
Durham, NC 27708-0586
Phone: 919-684-3214
E-mail address:
admissions@duke.edu
Web site URL: www.duke.edu
Year Founded: 1838
Private or Public: Private
Religious Affiliation:
Methodist
Location: Urban
Number of Applicants:
18,638
Percent Accepted: 21%
**Percent Accepted who
enroll:** 43%
Number Entering: 1,683
**Number of Transfers
Accepted each Year:** 41
Middle 50% SAT range:
M: 680–790, CR: 660–750,
Wr: 680–780
Middle 50% ACT range:
29–34
**Early admission program
EA/ED/None:** ED

**Percentage accepted
through EA or ED:** 31%
EA and ED deadline: 1-Nov
Regular Deadline: 2-Jan
Application Fee: $75
**Full time Undergraduate
enrollment:** 6,259
Total enrollment: 11,680
Percent Male: 52%
Percent Female: 48%
**Total Percent Minority or
Unreported:** 32%
Percent African-American:
11%
**Percent Asian/Pacific
Islander:** 14%
Percent Hispanic: 7%
Percent Native-American:
<1%
Percent International: 7%
**Percent in-state/out of
state:** 15%/85%
Percent from Public HS:
65%
Retention Rate: 96%
Graduation Rate 4-year: 86%

Graduation Rate 6-year:
92%
**Percent Undergraduates
in On-campus housing:**
82%
**Number of official organized
extracurricular
organizations:** 200
3 Most popular majors:
Economics, Psychology,
Public Policy
Student/Faculty ratio: 11:1
Average Class Size: 14
**Percent of students going to
grad school:** 62%
Tuition and Fees: $31,420
**In State Tuition and Fees if
different:** No difference
Cost for Room and Board:
$8,950
**Percent receiving financial
aid out of those who apply,
first year:** Unreported
**Percent receiving financial
aid among all students:**
39%

Perhaps best known among sports fans for its successful basketball team, Duke University is also recognized as one of the most prestigious establishments of higher learning in the United States. An urban school in Durham, North Carolina, Duke has a distinct Southern atmosphere as well as an intellectually stimulating environment. Given the university's athletic excellence, school spirit is, by no doubt, very strong and an important part of campus life. This unique combination of sports powerhouse and outstanding research institution offers a unique college experience, much cherished by Duke's students.

Three Schools

Duke is composed of nine schools, three of which—Trinity College of Arts and Sciences, Pratt School of Engineering, and Nicholas School of the Environment and Earth Sciences—offer degrees to undergraduate students. There are more than 40 majors available, as well as about 20 certificate programs, which are the equivalent of minors. Duke also has a distinct option at

Trinity College called Program II, which allows students to design their own interdisciplinary curriculum. According to one student, "Program II is definitely something worth exploring because it can be made to accommodate personal interests."

To graduate, students must complete 34 semester courses. Trinity College has a lengthy set of general requirements so that each student is exposed to a broad range of subjects. Everyone must take classes in what are called Five Areas of Knowledge and Six Modes of Inquiry, which range from arts and literature to science and technology. These requirements attract mixed reviews. Some students are glad they are learning a variety of topics; others are frustrated by the fact that they have to take classes they are not interested in. The Pratt School requires, in addition to classes in math, science, and engineering, one credit in writing and five credits in the humanities and social sciences.

The coursework at Duke is certainly challenging, although it always depends on the specific classes and majors. As one student pointed out, "if you choose your classes wisely, you can make it as easy or as hard as you want." In addition, the difficulty also depends on majors. The economics department is quite strict with grading, while some students find some humanities departments prone to grade inflation. This is not always the case, however, as most students agree that grading varies greatly from class to class.

Gothic and Georgian

Duke's campus is an interesting combination of Georgian architecture in the East Campus and Gothic revivalism in the West. This results in a beautiful campus as well as a great intellectual atmosphere. "The Gothic buildings here are a joy to walk by every day," said one student.

Duke owns more than 8,000 acres of land, including a 7,000 acre forest just west of the campus, a stunning botanical garden, a golf course, and a marine lab on the Atlantic coast, more than 150 miles from the main campus. "Duke has lots of resources," said one student. "You can find a lot of great facilities here that you would not find anywhere else."

> "Duke has lots of resources. You can find a lot of great facilities here that you would not find anywhere else."

Freshmen reside in the East Campus, the oldest section of the university, where are located 14 residential halls. Nine of them are conveniently built around a central quad, which also includes a science building, the Lilly Library, Baldwin Auditorium, which is one of Duke's major landmarks, and East Union, where are found two dining halls, a convenient store and other services. The other five residences for freshmen are not part of the quad but have the benefits of close proximity to Brodie Gym and air conditioning in several buildings, which is very important considering that North Carolina can be very hot during the first and last months of the school year. For upperclassmen, there are other housing options available in both the West and Central Campuses. Only seniors are allowed to live off campus, and the university has a community housing program that helps students find rentals in the Durham area.

All freshmen must enroll in a full meal plan. Upperclassmen, however, have a variety of options available. In addition, meal plans include dining points, which can be used for pizza deliveries, groceries, and restaurants. According to one student, this point system "is really flexible and allows students to explore different dining places around the area." As to the school's own dining service, most students agree that it is "good but nothing to rave about."

Weekends

Fraternities are the most important element of party scene at Duke. About 37% of the student population is associated with a Greek organization. Drinking, of course, is a dominant, though not essential, part of social life. The school is also trying to find ways to engage students in campus weekend activities, given several incidents at off-campus fraternities during recent years and complaints from Durham residents. Nevertheless, Greek life remains an indispensable part of the party nights, which are scattered throughout the week, including on some weekdays.

Although Duke has the reputation of being a "preppy" college, many students there believe that it is a misconception. "Everyone here is very friendly," said one student. "Surely there are some preppy kids just like everywhere else, but overall I think we have a great social environment."

The interactions between Durham and Duke, however, are rather limited. Durham is the fourth largest city in North Carolina and has many points of interest outside of Duke University, including bars and restaurants. Nevertheless, safety is always a concern, and most students do not venture far beyond the boundaries of the campus. "Students generally think of themselves as part of the Duke community," said one student. "There is not much feeling of being a member of the Durham community."

Blue Devils

Duke has a long history of athletic excellence. The varsity sports teams are known as Blue Devils and are part of the Atlantic Coast Conference. The men's basketball team headed by Coach Mike Krzyzewski is known as one of the most successful teams in the history of college sports. According to one student, "basketball is by far the most important sport, and everyone cares about how the team is doing." Both men's and women's lacrosse teams have also been immensely successful in the last few years, despite the recent issues surrounding the men's team that grabbed national headlines.

The best team on campus, however, is probably the women's golf team, which won three consecutive national championships from 2005 to 2007.

All the sports trophies result in the importance of athletics in the social scene at Duke and a fervent school spirit that some students describe as almost "maniacal," especially when Duke is playing against its most notable rival, University of North Carolina, Chapel Hill, which is only about 10 miles away. Out of the rivalry was created the famous tradition of Krzyzewskiville, where students live outdoors next to the Cameron Stadium in tents for weeks prior to the UNC-Duke game. "It is a great experience," said one student. "It shows how dedicated we are to school spirit."

Clearly, Duke can claim a spot among the colleges with the most ardent sports fans. In addition to this strong school spirit, however, Duke also offers top-notch facility and faculty. With its commitment to both athletics and academics, Duke stands as one of the top college choices for students around the world.—*Xiaohang Liu*

FYI
If you come to Duke, you'd better bring "a tent to camp outside Cameron."
What is the typical weekend schedule? "School work during the day, and fun time during the night."
If I could change one thing about Duke, I'd "reduce the so-called General Education Requirements."
Three things every student at Duke should do before graduating are "tent outside Cameron, go to as many basketball games as possible, and go to the Marine Lab."

Elon University

Address: 700 Campus Box Elon, NC 27244
Phone: 336-278-3566
E-mail address: admissions@elon.edu
Web site URL: www.elon.edu
Year Founded: 1889
Private or Public: Private
Religious Affiliation: United Church of Christ
Location: Small City
Number of Applicants: 9,505
Percent Accepted: 41%
Percent Accepted who enroll: 33%
Number Entering: 1,286
Number of Transfers Accepted each Year: 190
Middle 50% SAT range: M: 570–660, Cr: 560–650, Wr: 570–660
Middle 50% ACT range: 23–28
Early admission program EA/ED/None: EA and ED
Percentage accepted through EA or ED: 60%

EA and ED deadline: 1-Nov
Regular Deadline: 10-Jan
Application Fee: $50
Full time Undergraduate enrollment: 4,950
Total enrollment: 5,300
Percent Male: 40%
Percent Female: 60%
Total Percent Minority or Unreported: 13%
Percent African-American: 5%
Percent Asian/Pacific Islander: 2%
Percent Hispanic: 1%
Percent Native-American: 0%
Percent International: Unreported
Percent in-state/out of state: 30%/70%
Percent from Public HS: Unreported
Retention Rate: 90%
Graduation Rate 4-year: 74%

Graduation Rate 6-year: Unreported
Percent Undergraduates in On-campus housing: 60%
Number of official organized extracurricular organizations: 150
3 Most popular majors: Business, Communications, Education
Student/Faculty ratio: 14:1
Average Class Size: Unreported
Percent of students going to grad school: Unreported
Tuition and Fees: $22,166
In State Tuition and Fees if different: No difference
Cost for Room and Board: $7,296
Percent receiving financial aid out of those who apply, first year: 58%
Percent receiving financial aid among all students: 31%

Founded by the Christian Church now known as the United Church of Christ in 1889, and tucked away in Elon, North Carolina, in the Piedmont region of the state, Elon University's beautiful wooded campus has been recognized by the *Princeton Review* as one of the nation's finest. An hour's drive away from Raleigh, Durham, Winston-Salem and Chapel Hill, the classic Southern brick buildings intermingled with oak trees make Elon a pleasant living and learning environment. Students point to their unique academic experience, their campus-wide traditions and the vibrant student life as the selling points of this picturesque southern school.

The "Elon Experience"

Elon places extraordinary emphasis on learning outside of the walls of the classroom. Students are extremely involved in their education beyond simply attending class, an engagement that is facilitated by the "Elon Experiences" program, in which students receive a transcript that tracks their study abroad, internships, service participation, leadership roles, and experiences conducting research. Elon's admissions office proudly boasts that the university sends more students abroad than any other masters-level university in the country through the Isabella Cannon Center for Study Abroad. Students also participate in large numbers in internships and volunteer service throughout their university careers. The John R. Kernodle, Jr. Center for Service-Learning facilitates many of the programs that Elon students enroll in as part of a service-learning experience, offering courses and housing service groups. Courses are often tailored to current events or needs of the region or the country; for example, a group of Elon students recently performed service in areas affected by Hurricane Katrina. The great town-gown relations at Elon are an added bonus of the experiential learning program. Because people do a lot of work within the community as part of their experiential learning, there is a lot of interaction with the local community. One popular yearly event is the Festival of the Oak. Lots of kids from the community come to Elon's campus for a day of activities run by many Elon students.

There are approximately 4,850 undergrads at Elon and while the majority of them hail from North Carolina, Elon continues to draw students from 46 states and 45 countries. Although these numbers mark Elon as a small university, the school thinks large in terms of academics and facilities. Elon has worked hard in recent years to integrate technology in all areas of campus life. For example, the McMichael Science Center provides valuable lab space, high tech instruments, and over 70 computers to aid science students. Similarly, the Belk Library has nearly 200 computers available for public use. As the admissions office notes, "Elon's state-of-the-art facilities offer something for everyone."

Despite the large-scale technological offerings, Elon's education remains personalized to student needs: the student-to-faculty ratio is 1 to 14, and students are given many opportunities to work one-on-one with professors. Elon's year follows a "4-1-4" calendar, with a four-month fall semester, a one-month winter term, and a four-month spring semester. Many students use the one-month winter term for travel and fulfillment of the study abroad aspect of the "Elon Experiences." As one Elon senior remarked, "My winter term trip was centered around World War II and we went to France, the Netherlands, the Czech Republic, Germany, and Poland. Besides just the cultural aspects of the countries, we focused on this particular history and it was a more fulfilling experience than just traveling on my own."

> "Guys come in ties, and girls in sundresses, to tailgate and enjoy the game."

Elon provides undergraduate education in four schools: Elon College, the college of arts and science; the Love School of Business; the School of Communications; and the School of Education. In total, students can choose from among 48 major fields of study, earning Bachelors of Arts, Bachelors of Science or Bachelors of Fine Arts degrees. The most popular majors are business, communications, education, psychology and biology. A unique program at Elon is the dual-degree engineering program run in conjunction with North Carolina State University, North Carolina A & T State University, Georgia Tech, Columbia University, Virginia Tech and Washington University in St. Louis, in which students will graduate with one degree from Elon and a second from one of these affiliates.

Traditions at Elon

One of Elon's most beloved traditions takes place at 9:45 in the morning. Each Tuesday morning, students, faculty and staff gather around Fonville Fountain for refreshments and fellowship during "College Coffee." This is a great time to grab a bite to eat with a professor in a more relaxed setting, catch up with friends, or take a break before heading to class. "A lot of people go to refuel between classes," one Elon sophomore explained. "This was a great opportunity for me to meet new people as an underclassman."

Another tradition revolves around the oak tree, the symbol of Elon. The campus is still heavily populated by oaks and is located on what used to be an oak grove, and "Elon" means oak in Hebrew. Newly arrived freshmen are given an acorn in the fall, and there is a special ceremony for seniors at the time of graduation around an oak tree, symbolizing the intellectual growth of Elon students.

Sports are also a major part of creating traditions at Elon. The university boasts 16 intercollegiate varsity sports, playing in the NCAA Division I as part of the Southern Conference. You don't have to be Michael Jordan to get involved in sports, however— Elon also has 18 intramural and 21 club sports that many students take part in. "Everyone comes out for club sports or intramurals," one junior agreed. Like kids at many Southern schools, Elon students dress up for the Homecoming football game, the biggest sporting event of the year. "This was a bit of a shock for me, coming from Indiana," an Elon senior said. "Guys come in ties, and girls in sundresses, to tailgate and enjoy the game." Although the tailgates at Homecoming have an undeniable southern flavor, many students say that Elon's general atmosphere is not as Southern as other schools in North Carolina. As one senior explained, "Prevailingly, the people that go here are not from North Carolina, we have a lot of people from the Northeast, California, as far away as Maine and North Dakota. It's not like the UNC schools, which are dominated by Southern students." Another student concurred: "I feel like it's a different experience than being at UNC Greensboro or Chapel Hill."

A New Way to Look at Dining

Elon has recently introduced an innovative new meal plan system that is based on the feedback of students. All nine dining halls on campus are participating in the new plan. Students can buy 5, 9, 11, 14, 17, or 19 meals per week; unused meals carry over from week to week until the end of the semester. There are no restrictive dining times or dining zones—students can eat whenever their stomach says it's time. According to one Elon senior, the best place to grab a bite to eat on campus is Harden dining hall in the bottom floor of the Moffit dormitory, because it has the biggest variety of foods. Most students would seem to agree—it's the largest dining hall on campus.

Most students at Elon end up living off campus by the end of their college careers. Freshmen and sophomores live on campus unless they gain special approval to move off. Some juniors live on campus, and seniors who are involved in residential life, such as RAs, or athletes who are paying for housing, stay in campus housing, but the majority live in apartments or townhouses with friends. One dorm causing an exception to this rule is the newly constructed Danieley Center, a cluster of buildings boasting spacious suites and apartment-style housing. Many upperclassmen choose to live in this area. The university also owns apartment buildings such as Haggard Square and Elon Place that are technically still considered on campus housing but are a few blocks from the campus itself. As far as the dorms themselves, the best are Virginia Hall, which are single-sex by floor, and Moffit Hall, with its proximity to the dining area. Loan dorm also comes highly recommended. The Jordan Center area is considered the least desirable dorm on campus, but it is in the process of being renovated in the style of Danieley Center.

Get in the Zone

Elon students love to enjoy themselves when they're not having Elon Experiences or in the classroom. The Greek scene provides a lot of the social life of the campus, although students generally agree it's not dominant. There are 22 nationally recognized fraternities and sororities at the school, and they host a lot of social events, particularly on the weekend, but less than 20 members of the organization, usually sophomores, actually live in each of the houses that make up Greek Court. As one sorority sister put it, "You're not just in your sorority with 120 girls and that's the majority of what you do with your time. I'm still involved in my sorority but I have a ton of friends who aren't even in Greek life."

The University is also conscious about promoting the arts. Every semester get a program with all of the cultural events planned for the semester, such as musicals, plays and concerts. There is a large annual concert for Elon students, where a well-known musical group performs for the whole student body. In 2004, Maroon 5 was the big act. "Movie runs" are a popular weekend activity, particularly for those students who don't drink. The university provides discount tickets and transportation to local theaters to see the latest blockbuster hits. The Zone—a large open space in the student center—is also popular for hosting dances and big events.

Elon students generally seem to have a great time learning in a wide array of settings, enjoying Elon's gorgeous weather and making great friends. There are so many unique factors that make Elon a school that attracts people from all over the country and world. If you're looking for a balanced education, a college steeped in tradition, and an overall ideal college experience, you shouldn't look further than Elon University.
—*Elizabeth Jordan*

FYI

If you come to Elon, you'd better bring "sunglasses, because even in the winter it's still sunny."

What is the typical weekend schedule? "Wednesday and Thursday is the bar scene, Friday and Saturday party at the frats or off campus, Sunday is usually a 'party' in the library with everyone doing all their homework."

If I could change one thing about Elon, "it would be the boy girl ratio, it's pretty high in favor of the boys."

Three things every student at Elon should do before graduating are "study abroad, take advantage of the opportunities for hands-on learning and get a minor degree."

North Carolina School of the Arts

Address: 1533 South Main Street, Winston-Salem, NC 27127

Phone: 336-770-3290

E-mail address: admissions@ncarts.edu

Web site URL: www.ncarts.edu

Year Founded: 1963

Private or Public: Public

Religious Affiliation: None

Location: Urban

Number of Applicants: 679

Percent Accepted: 51%

Percent Accepted who enroll: 54%

Number Entering: 186

Number of Transfers Accepted each Year: Unreported

Middle 50% SAT range: M: 500–620, CR: 540–640, W: 600–700

Middle 50% ACT range: 20–25

Early admission program EA/ED/None: None

Percentage accepted through EA or ED: NA

EA and ED deadline: NA

Regular Deadline: 29-Jan

Application Fee: $50

Full time Undergraduate enrollment: 743

Total enrollment: 857

Percent Male: 60%

Percent Female: 40%

Total Percent Minority or Unreported: 18%

Percent African-American: 10%

Percent Asian/Pacific Islander: 2%

Percent Hispanic: 5%

Percent Native-American: <1%

Percent International: 1%

Percent in-state/out of state: 48%/52%

Percent from Public HS: Unreported

Retention Rate: 75%

Graduation Rate 4-year: 40%

Graduation Rate 6-year: 48%

Percent Undergraduates in On-campus housing: 55%

Number of official organized extracurricular organizations: Unreported

3 Most popular majors: Unreported

Student/Faculty ratio: 8:1

Average Class Size: Unreported

Percent of students going to grad school: Unreported

Tuition and Fees: $15,104

In State Tuition and Fees if different: $3,224

Cost for Room and Board: $6,831

Percent receiving financial aid out of those who apply, first year: 77%

Percent receiving financial aid among all students: 49%

With some of the most talented students around—actors, dancers, musicians, filmmakers and production designers—uniting behind their beloved mascot the "fighting pickle," the North Carolina School of the Arts (NCSA) defies categorization. This small, competitive arts conservatory is neither an ordinary college nor an ordinary arts school: quirky, intimate and friendly, NCSA attracts applicants from all over the world and commands a respect among professional artists that rivals its more well-known competitors. For students truly passionate about their arts, NCSA provides intensive training with top-notch faculty for a fraction of the price of private conservatories.

Let's Go, Pickles!

The "School of the Arts," as locals sometimes call NCSA, is comprised of five arts schools: Dance, including modern and ballet; Drama; Filmmaking; Music; and Design and Production, which trains students in set design, costuming, wigs and makeup, sound and lighting and is referred to as "D&P." Each school has its own culture and its own stereotypes— "you can usually tell what school someone is from by the way they're dressed," said a fourth-year Drama major—but the schools are united in the large quantity of work they demand. Some students chafe at the intense classes and rehearsals, which can run from 8 a.m. to midnight at peak times of year, but "the heavy workload tends to weed out those who are not up to standards."

While students from different schools may not see each other in their arts classes, General Studies classes are a different story. As NCSA's academic component, General Studies offers classes in the liberal arts and sciences, specially geared to students who care more about perfecting their plié than learning about Copernicus. That's not to say the classes are dumbed down. Students describe their academic professors as "better than you would expect for an arts school," but say it's hard to find time to do General Studies work when the arts classes are so demanding. For the most part, the faculty understands that students "are artists and don't want to major in math."

A Chance to Show Your Stuff

For a school whose goal is to teach students to create art, students say NCSA "realizes that the reason we attend is to actually do the work we are majoring in, not just to learn," and performance opportunities abound. In addition to participating in major performances, students have the option to perform chamber music, do outreach in the community and participate in the annual summer production of *The Lost Colony* on Roanoke Island, assuring that graduates of NCSA have had plenty of chances to practice their art in "exceptional" facilities.

Most students come to NCSA because of particular programs or faculty members. In general, students say the arts faculty at NCSA is "stellar" and the standards that they expect of their students are high. Each member of the faculty is an expert—ballet students are taught by former principal dancers of the New York City Ballet and music students learn from teachers that have played with the world's major orchestras. Despite their prestige in the art world, in general teachers "make themselves ridiculously accessible." In addition to the level of know-how on staff, well-known artists are often brought in for classes or concerts. But no matter how good the faculty is, "at NCSA, hands-on experience is usually considered the best teacher."

Within departments, competition can sometimes be fierce; students must be invited by the faculty to return the following year. In some departments, students speak of an unofficial cut system in which a few students are not invited back after sophomore year. This practice seems to have recently subsided—facing state budget cuts, the school "needs the money"—but some students still worry that their spot "may be in jeopardy." For the most part, though, students tend to think positively and most say that they get along very well. After all, "a little competition can be healthy."

You Want Grits with That?

Set in the laid-back, small Southern city of Winston-Salem (often known to locals as "Winston"), NCSA provides its students with a very different experience from other arts schools, which are typically located in major urban centers. While the city may not be exciting, as one student said "it has its own charm." Students say they rarely interact with the locals, but Winston-Salem residents often make up a large percentage of the audiences at student shows. The NCSA production of *The Nutcracker* is a holiday favorite in the city, selling out over a week of performances before going on tour and being shown on public television.

What, then, is there to do in Winston? Students in search of a drink often head to the

Black Bear and other bars on Burke Street, while shoppers find that Hanes Mall is "good-sized but nothing special." People looking to strut their stuff on the dance floor might not be so lucky, though: "There are no real dance clubs in Winston; you have to go to Greensboro for that," and students stress that having a car is necessary. "A car is important if you want to do *anything* off campus . . . like go out to eat, buy groceries, or go to a bar. Nothing is within walking distance and there is no ubiquitous college town shopping-eating-walking main street area," said one student.

Campus, for the most part, is "fairly safe" despite its location near some "creepy" areas. Nevertheless, "nothing really bad ever seems to happen, no matter how much people like to talk," and students say the area is improving. Straddling two neighborhoods, the campus connects the "beautiful, historic Washington Park area" with "what used to be the projects. Though they are no longer there, that neighborhood is still kind of sketchy."

Dorms like Prison Cells

All freshmen and sophomores are required to live on campus, either in the residence halls, which go by the letters A through F, or in apartment-style buildings. The residence halls get uniformly negative reviews, despite fostering a "nice feeling of camaraderie." One senior who has been an RA called the A-F buildings "gross" and mentioned the traditional rumor that they were built following the plans of a women's prison. "Though not disgusting or dirty, the rooms and halls are less than aesthetically pleasing. The walls are cinderblock and the floors are linoleum. My suggestion: get your mom/girlfriend/sister to help you decorate." Students looking to escape to the newer apartment-style buildings have to pay a bit more, but most juniors and seniors decide to live off campus. Competition is fierce for nearby houses, but students say apartments around the city are generally easy to get.

While some students complain that the dining hall food is lackluster, it has been improving since the recent renovation of the Hanes Student Commons. "I personally have seen the food go from bland to exotic," one student said. "They have a huge selection and really good vegetarian dishes." When venturing off campus for a change of taste, most students cite the nearby Acadia Grill as a popular choice, along with inexpensive Mexican restaurants.

NCSA operates a high school program on the same campus as the College, which garners mixed reactions from college students. While there is generally "no reason to interact with the high schoolers," it can be weird seeing them in the cafeteria. It's "more amusing than annoying, although on-campus life would be cooler if they weren't around," said one student.

Practice Hard, Party Harder

With the hectic schedule of classes and rehearsals which frequently spill over into the weekend, it can be difficult to find a moment to unwind. When students do get a moment, going to friends' performances is a popular choice. Generally free, the performances are "a great opportunity to see the nation's best up-and-coming artists." The Filmmaking school offers free screenings on the weekends and many students use the "well-equipped gym" to work out or play impromptu games. As for parties, most of them are off campus and students say they can get pretty wild: "there's a lot of rehearsal—we try to balance it with a lot of letting loose." Alcohol and drugs are fairly common—"it's an arts school"—but NCSA is now a dry campus, even for students over 21, so on-campus libations have to be fairly discreet.

> "An NCSA degree could get you the job. Along with your talent, of course."

The school organizes a few social events during the year, like skiing and hiking trips and Fall Fest, but most students agree that a lot of the on-campus events are "a joke." The ever popular exception is the annual Beaux Arts costume ball. Turning one of the film soundstages into a dance floor—lighting and sound are designed by D&P students and generally top-notch—the costume ball is an excuse to wear something completely outlandish or close to nothing at all. An NCSA degree serves as a lifelong Beaux Arts invitation, so the party is often a meeting place for young alumni that still live in the area.

Students describe NCSA as very accepting: "most students are progressive, open-minded and busy . . . all sorts of things that would be considered weird or even bizarre are accepted as normal." Despite a state quota requirement that about half the students must be from North Carolina, NCSA manages to attract a fairly diverse student body with students from almost every state and several foreign countries. LGBT students feel welcome as well, as the school is "sexually diverse and prides itself on being an open-minded environment."

"If your goals for college are to let loose, have fun, casually meet hundreds of people and be the stud of your favorite fraternity, you're shit out of luck," said one senior. "Though the social life is not what you'd find at a larger school, the friendships made here are formed by a love of art and are deep and real. There is a huge amount of respect among students for each other as artists . . . and a strong sense of community." With its intimate size and friendly, anything-goes culture, NCSA belies a performing arts powerhouse. With well-known alumni appearing on stages and movie screens around the world and the reputation of the school steadily growing, "an NCSA degree could get you the job. Along with your talent, of course."—*Charles Cardinaux*

FYI

If you come to NCSA, you'd better bring "something with caffeine."

What's the typical weekend schedule? "Sleep in if you can, rehearse all day, and check out the parties or a film screening at night."

If I could change one thing about NCSA, I'd "allow more unexcused absences in General Studies classes!"

Three things every student at NCSA should do before graduating are "see the work of all the various programs at least once, watch a sunrise from the library or Performance Place rooftops (officially illegal—use the trellis), and choose having fun over work from time to time."

North Carolina State University

Address: Box 7103 Raleigh, NC 27695

Phone: 919-515-2434

E-mail address: undergrade-admissions@ncsu.edu

Web site URL: www.ncsu.edu

Year Founded: 1887

Private or Public: Public

Religious Affiliation: None

Location: Urban

Number of Applicants: 17,652

Percent Accepted: 59%

Percent Accepted who enroll: 45%

Number Entering: 4,660

Number of Transfers Accepted each Year: Unreported

Middle 50% SAT range: M: 560–660, CR: 520–620, Wr: 510–610

Middle 50% ACT range: 22–27

Early admission program EA/ED/None: EA

Percentage accepted through EA or ED: Unreported

EA and ED deadline: 1-Nov

Regular Deadline: 1-Feb

Application Fee: $70

Full time Undergraduate enrollment: 24,145

Total enrollment: 24,741

Percent Male: 56%

Percent Female: 44%

Total Percent Minority or Unreported: 22%

Percent African-American: 9%

Percent Asian/Pacific Islander: 5%

Percent Hispanic: 3%

Percent Native-American: 1%

Percent International: 2%

Percent in-state/out of state: 93%/7%

Percent from Public HS: 90%

Retention Rate: 89%

Graduation Rate 4-year: 36%

Graduation Rate 6-year: Unreported

Percent Undergraduates in On-campus housing: 35%

Number of official organized extracurricular organizations: 365

3 Most popular majors: Biology, Management, Mechanical Engineering

Student/Faculty ratio: 16:1

Average Class Size: 20 to 29

Percent of students going to grad school: 31%

Tuition and Fees: $17,572

In State Tuition and Fees if different: $5,274

Cost for Room and Board: $7,982

Percent receiving financial aid out of those who apply, first year: 60%

Percent receiving financial aid among all students: 42%

If you're looking for science and technology, serious parties, and die-hard school spirit, North Carolina State University might just be the place for you. With nearly 25,000 students, NC State also offers tons of different people, perspectives and opportunities. The campus is located next to downtown Raleigh, the capital of North Carolina. Both in-state and out-of-state students consider NC State quite a deal: The University is the largest research institution in North Carolina and among the best in the nation in attracting corporate research. And students are eager to point out that, in spite of its size, the campus doesn't feel that big, and can be walked across in 15 minutes. Additionally, Raleigh offers an ample selection of museums and events, though most students stay close to campus to participate in the vibrant campus life.

'Not Just a Cow College'

Although originally an agricultural school, NC State students are quick to point out that their school is now best known as a technical school. The design, textiles and engineering programs are particularly popular. In the words of one student, "There's no question that there are a lot of engineers." This reputation has reached the point where humanities students complain that their disciplines don't get as much funding—meaning that it can be harder to get into the popular non-science classes, which are "more fun." In general, registering for classes can be really frustrating because of the sheer number of students at NC State, but "it does all get worked out in the end."

Before freshman year, students apply to the individual college within the University that contains their prospective major. For students who don't yet have a clue about what they want to do, there's the First-Year College, which requires them to take specific classes and specialized tests designed to help them settle on the right major. Students suggest, though, that if you have any idea what you want to do, it's better to go ahead and try it out since each college has faculty advisors to help you plan your academic career.

Students generally don't talk about their grades, a fact that contributes to NC State's laid-back atmosphere. Some assignments are actually optional, which also helps perpetuate this attitude among students. Optional tests are to the advantage of self-motivated students, but help disguise how much work there can be.

Introductory classes are usually very large, but students find themselves in smaller classes, as well. Although the larger classes are taught by professors, many teaching assistants—some of whom don't speak English well—are also present. Not all professors are particularly personable, but students do have the opportunity to talk to them, especially if they're willing to put forth some effort. Many of the majors, particularly the sciences, are demanding and leave little room in a student's schedule for exploration, sometimes only allowing one free course per semester outside of that major. Freshmen in particular have trouble getting into "fun classes" like Physical Education or Mythology.

Cheers, Beers and Wolfpack Pride

School pride is without a doubt a fundamental part of the NC State experience. With a history of nationally successful varsity basketball and football teams, students flock to games. As expected, tailgates for home football games are a major event, with up to 55,000 fans barbecuing, drinking and hanging out. At the games, which are "the most fun in the entire world," fans are clad in red (the school color), and notably "obnoxious, loud, fun and hilarious," particularly at games against rival UNC-Chapel Hill. It isn't all about winning, though; win or lose in the regularly sold-out stadium, NC State fans go to celebrate and party.

There aren't many school-wide, school-sponsored social events other than athletic exhibitions at NC State. As one student said, "The administration assumes we can find ways to entertain ourselves." NC State students seem more than up to the challenge, hosting their own cultural and social events "all the time." There is a movie theater on-campus, and students have the opportunity to go to a play or concert every other night if they'd like. The administration even provides free tickets to students in the Honors or Scholars program. While there is no drinking at school-sponsored events, students definitely party hard every weekend. People typically party off-campus in friends' apartments, and students report that practically everyone drinks underage. One girl commented, "I think there are people who don't drink, but I don't pay attention." NC State has its fair share of frats and sororities, but students don't feel pressured to be involved in them. One girl in a sorority noted that Greek life "can still be interesting even if you don't drink."

(A Few) Girls Gone Wild

While NC State's guy to girl ratio has been dropping, you "can still definitely notice that there are more guys." Unfortunately for wannabe Don Juans, this gives girls the advantage. However, don't let this hinder plans for romance; tons of students are dating, and there is plenty of hooking up. There is not a very active gay, lesbian, bisexual and allies association, probably because campus is not a particularly accepting place. "It would be a rough place to be gay," one student said. With almost 90 percent of students from in-state, you might expect the student body to be homogenous, but there are also students from all 50 states and 100 countries. While NC State has the demographics of a culturally diverse environment, some students complain that their school isn't very socially integrated. At the same time, one out-of-state student said he had expected more racism, but has found it to be a non-issue. While most students are physically active, making good use of the gym, one girl admitted, "You might find some beer guts" due to the hard partying.

NC State has an enormous variety of extracurricular clubs for students, ranging from political groups to club sports to community service groups. For example, the school has an enormous Habitat for Humanity chapter that meets each weekend and builds its own house every year. Religion also tends to be a "big force" at NC State: Campus Crusade for Christ is one of the largest student organizations. "But it is OK not to be religious," one student is quick to mention. Club sports are really competitive, often with serious tryouts, and if you just want to enjoy a casual game, intramural athletics is the place for you. Ultimate Frisbee and touch football are two of the more popular intramural sports. NC State also has a really popular outdoor adventures program through which students can learn how to rock-climb, hike or backpack. Not everyone at NC State cares about extracurricular activities, but those who do tend to pick one or two and get involved pretty seriously.

Sick of Brick

Campus architecture is dominated by red brick; the buildings and walkways are all brick and there is even a large open area called "The Brick Yard." One student jokingly insisted that the university receives a donation of brick every year and is obligated to use it. Just because campus looks like a brick factory doesn't mean it is ugly. On nice days,

people flock to the open areas to sunbathe and play Frisbee. On the flip side, students warn that the brick walkways flood and overflow when it rains, so invest in a good pair of galoshes. One unique building on campus is Harrellson Hall, a round concrete building. Students report having been surprised when they went to their first class because all the classrooms are shaped like pie slices, "mak[ing] the blackboards really weird."

Most freshmen live on-campus in a variety of dorms. Some dorms are freshman-only, others are single-sex; some have suites, and others halls. The administration does a pretty good job pairing up roommates, but for those who really don't get along, it's not that difficult to change housing.

One thing that students living in dorms praise is the chance to meet many new people and sleep more, because they're closer to class. The dorms are grouped into three campuses: East, West and Central. West Campus is the most popular, probably because it houses several special academic programs such as the University Scholars, and learning and living villages such as the Women in Science and Engineering (WISE) and Students Advocating for Youth (SAY). The university also offers an Honors Program which has recently moved to a new location on East Campus. One dorm, Alexander, has a program called the Global Village where every American student is paired with an international roommate.

> "I feel like I'll have a really strong background to do whatever I want when I graduate."

Most upperclassmen, however, live off-campus in apartment complexes and houses. The school provides transportation between apartments and school (known by many as "the drunk bus"). Lots of students have cars and consider them important for their social life, since public transportation in Raleigh is a "joke." Students living off campus don't usually buy meal plans but instead cook at home or eat at the many nearby restaurants and cafes. Hillsborough Street, which runs through campus, is a favorite strip of eating and watering holes.

With one dining hall on each side of campus, students can get tired of eating the same food. An on-campus food court with fast-food chains like Chick-fil-A and Taco Bell helps to break the monotony. Dining halls are not very social, but more like places to take care of business; students say they "get by" on the food there. If you want to watch sports with your meal, the Wolves' Den is the place to go—a student center where you might also go for a club meeting. The pervading campus style is very casual, including classes, and many students seem to be comfortable showing up in sweatpants and old T-shirts.

Although it has strong roots in agriculture, NC State is not just a "cow college" anymore. Among the huge student population one can find every type of person imaginable. With a lively social scene and countless activities available, students don't have trouble keeping themselves busy. On top of that, one student reported, "I feel like I'll have a really strong background to do whatever I want when I graduate."—*Alistair Anagnostou*

FYI

If you come to NC State, you'd better bring "red clothes and a Frisbee."

What is the typical weekend schedule? "Take a nap and party with friends Friday night; go to a sports event Saturday; party again Saturday night; and then catch up on work Sunday after sleeping in or going to church."

If I could change one thing about NC State, I'd "add a lot more parking."

Three things every student at NC State should do before graduating are "attend every football tailgate in a season, work for Habitat for Humanity and drink a pint in Mitch's Tavern on Hillsborough Street."

University of North Carolina / Chapel Hill

Address: Jackson Hall CB #2200 Chapel Hill, NC 27599-2200
Phone: 919-966-3621
E-mail address: unchelp@admissions.unc.edu
Web site URL: www.unc.edu
Year Founded: 1789
Private or Public: Public
Religious Affiliation: None
Location: Suburban
Number of Applicants: 20,090
Percent Accepted: 35%
Percent Accepted who enroll: 55%
Number Entering: 3,880
Number of Transfers Accepted each Year: 1,115
Middle 50% SAT range: M: 610–700, CR: 600–700, Wr: 590–690
Middle 50% ACT range: 26–31
Early admission program EA/ED/None: EA

Percentage accepted through EA or ED: Unreported
EA and ED deadline: 1-Nov
Regular Deadline: 15-Jan
Application Fee: $70
Full time Undergraduate enrollment: 17,628
Total enrollment: 25,805
Percent Male: 42%
Percent Female: 58%
Total Percent Minority or Unreported: 28%
Percent African-American: 11%
Percent Asian/Pacific Islander: 7%
Percent Hispanic: 4%
Percent Native-American: 1%
Percent International: 1%
Percent in-state/out of state: 83%/17%
Percent from Public HS: 83%
Retention Rate: Unreported
Graduation Rate 4-year: Unreported

Graduation Rate 6-year: Unreported
Percent Undergraduates in On-campus housing: 46%
Number of official organized extracurricular organizations: 557
3 Most popular majors: Biology/biological Sciences, Mass Communication/Media Studies, Psychology
Student/Faculty ratio: Unreported
Average Class Size: 10 to 19
Percent of students going to grad school: 28%
Tuition and Fees: $22,295
In State Tuition and Fees if different: $5,397
Cost for Room and Board: $7,334
Percent receiving financial aid out of those who apply, first year: 43%
Percent receiving financial aid among all students: 32%

With strong academics, great athletics and a pretty campus to boot, the University of North Carolina at Chapel Hill is a great choice for just about any student. This large southern university does everything big, including its southern hospitality. So put on your Carolina Blue shirt and come on down!

Is Bigger Better?

Starting with the class of 2010, the University introduced new graduation requirements that are quite extensive. While some students praise the system, saying that it "more fully encapsulates the purpose of a liberal arts education," others point out that changing your major is a difficult feat with all the new requirements and that you might have to stay for an additional semester to complete them unless you come in with plenty of AP credits. Survey courses are pretty much guaranteed to be 400-person classes. A good way to get a taste of a small class early on is to participate in one of the First Year Seminars. In addition to being small, which is a rare find at UNC, they are generally interesting, tackling subjects such as "US-Cuban Relations." Large sizes aside, students praised the feel of community, as most said they don't view their peers as their competition.

The school prides itself on having very strong journalism and business programs, both of which are pretty difficult to get into. With UNC's strong academic reputation also come challenging classes. Grading varies from department to department with some, such as the communications department, being more notorious for grade inflation. Students generally agree that each A requires hard work and is unlikely to be handed out easily. Students warn that the most failed course at UNC is "Calculus 231" (Calculus of One Variable I). In addition, be wary as intro classes such as intro biology, intro statistics and intro international relations are designed to weed out the people who are not serious about the major. On the other end of the spectrum, for an easy A, students recommend "Race and Ethnic Relations" and most communications classes. Like at most schools, it is still the professor that makes the class, and UNC students give high marks to their professors. The professors are generally pretty accessible and open to meeting students. One senior remarked that the professors were always "as helpful as I needed them to be." Professor Byrns in the economic dept is a favorite, drawing crowds even as early as 9:30 in the morning. Additionally UNC is home to several other famous professors, including Christopher Browning, a prominent Holocaust historian, and Professor Andrew Reynolds, who helped write the Afghani and Iraqi constitutions. The academic options are broadened via the very selective Robertson Scholars program, which allows UNC students to take classes not offered at UNC at neighboring Duke.

Party in the South [Campus]

As a state school, UNC operates under the North Carolina requirement that at least 82 percent of students must be in-state. For this reason the rare out-of-state students complain that when they initially arrived on campus, everyone else already knew at least a few people from their high school who also attended. Don't worry about being lonely in this large school, though, as freshman dorms, freshman seminars and other classes facilitate friendships. And as one student from the Northeast emphasized, the people are very friendly; in fact, he quipped, "It took me a while to get used to."

The social scene as described by one senior can be split into three categories: the Greek life, the bars and clubs on Franklin Street, and the dorm parties in the suites of South Campus. The underage underclassmen tend to gravitate toward the freshmen-dominated South Campus where the crazy parties are concentrated. Upperclassmen and those with fake IDs can usually be found on Franklin Street, an area that offers a plethora of options. Some of the more popular choices include La Rez, East End, and Top of the Hill. Frats are conspicuous during rush week when a lot of students take advantage of their parties; however, for the remaining part of the year the 16 percent of Greeks on campus are not a very big deal to the rest of the student body. While most people drink there is no pressure to join in drinking. The practical reality, according to one student, is that the University's priority is to make sure you are safe. For this reason, unless you are being obnoxious or disruptive, the RAs will leave you alone. "RAs are not secret police or anything," one senior explained. For after party options, students cite the Cosmic Cantina, a Mexican hole in the wall, as a great late-night destination.

See You in the Pit!

The campus is unofficially divided into three areas: North, South and Middle. Most of the freshman are housed on South campus, where suites and large dorms encourage socializing, although there is an integration effort going on that has the administration encouraging first years to move to other parts and mingle with the upperclassmen. While the rest of the campus is characterized by run-of-the-mill dorms, upperclassmen also have the option of living in apartment-style houses in Ram Village. Avery in Mid campus is cited as the athlete dorm. Students get assigned to dorms via a lottery system based on seniority, although there is always an option of not taking any chances and remaining in the room you currently have. The most popular option of all, however, is living off campus, and 55 percent of students do just that.

The campus draws many compliments from its students, who describe it as "scenic" and full of brick walkways. The only complaint is the never-ending and sometimes disruptive construction due to an ambitious long-term remodeling plan that the University is currently undergoing. The most popular place on campus is the Pit. A central meeting point between the student union, dining hall and a library, the Pit is home to many student organization meetings, people on their way to other destinations and "even occasionally preachers." It is said that all students pass by the Pit at least once a day.

When asked about food, the consensus, as one student summed up, is that the two dining halls on campus are "mediocre at best." However, whenever sick of the dining halls, the students can always turn to the endless stream of restaurants on Franklin Street that are bound to satisfy the choosiest of taste buds.

Duke Sucks!

If you are a basketball fan, UNC is the place to be. The Tar Heels bleed Carolina blue and the atmosphere, according to one student, can be described as "mania and fervor" and another added, "There is crazy school spirit. People here can be a little insane about sports." The basketball, baseball and football teams are successful and draw full crowds to the games. Tickets are in such high demand that the University has a lot-

tery system in place for those who wish to attend. The most anticipated game of the year is of course the one against the perennial archrival Duke. A win against Duke is lavishly celebrated by the student body on Franklin Street, where crowds gather to build fires and jump over them in joy. But sports are not confined to only varsity-level talent. The intramural program at the school is also a very popular option. To get the coveted IM champion T-shirt, students compete in a plethora of sports. "There are sports I've never even heard of," claimed one student, perhaps referring to the popular IM underwater hockey. Outside of the sports scene, other extracurriculars also abound, with the Campus Y a social advocacy umbrella group, and *The Daily Tar Heel* being some of the more popular options. There are also many a cappella groups, and proud students reported that one member participated in the 2009 American Idol competition and advanced to the final 36.

> "There is crazy school spirit. People here can be a little insane about sports."

UNC is a great deal on many fronts and a small bill for the North Carolina students. Lucky North Carolina residents take up at least 82 percent of the student population, but the coveted 18 percent left for out-of-state students is well worth the competition. The relaxed southern atmosphere makes it a pleasant environment even though students warn that it is more conservative and bigger than one might expect. Overall, however, once you get there you are bound to catch at least some of the school spirit. In no time you'll also be chanting: Go Heels!—*Dorota Poplawska*

FYI

If you come to UNC, you'd better bring "a lot of school spirit."

What is the typical weekend schedule? "go to the South Point mall on Saturday, at night go to bars and restaurants on Franklin Street and do homework on Sunday."

If I could change one thing about UNC, I'd "have more small classes."

Three things every student at UNC should do before graduating are "attend a Carolina-Duke basketball game, rush Franklin Street after beating Duke, and have fro-yo (frozen yogurt) at YoPo (Yogurt Pump.)"

Wake Forest University

Address: PO Box 7305
Reynolda Station, Winston-
Salem, NC 27109
Phone: 336-758-5201
E-mail address:
admissions@wfu.edu
Web site URL: www.wfu
.edu/admissions
Year Founded: 1834
Private or Public: Private
Religious Affiliation: None
Location: Urban
Number of Applicants: 7,177
Percent Accepted: 42%
Percent Accepted who
enroll: 37%
Number Entering: 1,124
Number of Transfers
Accepted each Year: 88
Middle 50% SAT range:
M: 610–700, CR: 630–710,
Wr: Unreported
Middle 50% ACT range:
27–31
Early admission program
EA/ED/None: ED

Percentage accepted
through EA or ED:
Unreported
EA and ED deadline: 15-Nov
Regular Deadline: 15-Jan
Application Fee: $50
Full time Undergraduate
enrollment: 4,412
Total enrollment: 5,759
Percent Male: 49%
Percent Female: 51%
Total Percent Minority or
Unreported: 14%
Percent African-American:
7%
Percent Asian/Pacific
Islander: 5%
Percent Hispanic: 2%
Percent Native-American:
<1%
Percent International: 1%
Percent in-state/out of
state: 25%/75%
Percent from Public HS:
65%
Retention Rate: 94%

Graduation Rate 4-year:
78%
Graduation Rate 6-year: 78%
Percent Undergraduates in
On-campus housing: 69%
Number of official organized
extracurricular
organizations: 168
3 Most popular majors:
Business, Political Sciene,
Psychology
Student/Faculty ratio: 10:1
Average Class Size: 10 to 19
Percent of students going to
grad school: 59%
Tuition and Fees: $36,560
In State Tuition and Fees if
different: No difference
Cost for Room and Board:
$9,867
Percent receiving financial
aid out of those who apply,
first year: 39%
Percent receiving financial
aid among all students:
34%

Nestled in Winston-Salem, N.C., is Wake Forest University, a small private university whose spirit and resources rival its larger neighbors UNC-Chapel Hill and Duke. Wake Forest's undergraduate population of about 4,400 students reaps the benefits of close contact with a celebrated roster of professors and the glory of their Division I basketball team, while enjoying a beautiful campus. Wake students, known for an abundance of school spirit, play a crucial role in maintaining Wake Forest's position as one of the top universities in the state.

"Work Forest"

Wake Forest provides its students the perks of a larger university, in a more intimate academic environment suitable for the small undergraduate body. Class size, once past introductory lectures, is typically around 20 students. This intimate class size allows Wake Forest professors to cultivate intimate relationships with students and provide more individual attention. And with professors as prestigious as Maya Angelou, who

teaches a popular poetry class, who can blame students for wanting more one-on-one time?

While professors allot a great deal of attention to their students, they also have high expectations. Wake Forest isn't known as "Work Forest" without good reason. Attendance and participation are significant factors in one's grade, so students must make a valiant effort in all of their classes. Professors are known for expecting a high level of preparedness. According to one student, some professors even "require an above average amount of work just to basically pass the course." The intimate academic setting makes it difficult to just slip by without notice, but Wake students agree the rewards are well worth the extra work.

Keeping with the "no pain, no gain" work mentality, the Calloway School of Business and Accountancy boasts a strong reputation and makes business one of Wake's most popular majors. But, it is also named one of the toughest majors, along with any of the sciences. Following in popularity are political science and communications. Many

Wake students enter the pre-med track, as well. For those students looking to avoid taking up residence in the library, communications, psychology and sociology may be the paths to take. And those looking to flee the country for a semester, year, or just the summer will be happy to hear that Wake's study abroad programs are hugely popular and are run in such locales as London, Beijing, Peru and Moscow. In fact, sometime within their four years, more than 50 percent of students take advantage of the study abroad program at the University.

Part of Wake's academic rigor stems from its extensive distribution requirements. Students are required to take one or two courses in each of five divisions: fine arts, humanities, literature, social sciences, and math and natural sciences. Freshmen are required to take a first-year seminar, a writing seminar, a foreign language and students must complete two courses in health and exercise science before graduation. While this system was implemented to ensure that students received a broad education in the liberal arts, many complain that fulfilling the requirements eats up a large portion of time and can have an impact on schedules even beyond sophomore year. Yet the general consensus is that "the requirements may be tough but they give you a good base." This sentiment reflects the overall Wake attitude toward academics—in the end, the effort students put in is well rewarded.

Kiss Me, I'm Greek!

When it's time to put aside the books, students turn to the Greek system, which dominates the social scene. One student explained that, "The Greek system IS life, and almost everyone at least tries to rush." An estimated 41 percent of the student population is involved in the Greek system, and up to 65 percent rush at some point in their four years. A major event each semester is pledge night. Freshmen rushing a sorority or fraternity are required to run around campus kissing as many people as possible, while keeping track of their make-out madness in a notebook. Although fraternities do not actually have houses, they have specific sections of dorms set aside for them and "lounges" in those areas are designated for parties open to the entire campus. Typical weekends revolve around frat parties, and students will party from one frat's lounge to the next. Wednesday, Friday and Saturday nights are the main nights for going out. During the fall, students tailgate with the intensity of a

larger state school thanks largely to their Division I status.

Students find that drinking is inevitably tied up with pledging a fraternity or sorority and Greek life in general. According to one fraternity brother, "Drinking is the primary activity of Wake Forest social life." The administration has reacted to this and has begun to come down on fraternities in particular. Many of the frats found themselves on probation for one reason or another during the past two years, which lead some of the weekend partying to move to off-campus locations. Nevertheless, for now frats continue to occupy the dominant campus social scene. And although there are regulations for drinking on campus and in dorms, residential advisors generally leave students alone unless they are disturbing others.

> "The Greek system IS life, and almost everyone at least tries to rush."

The social scene can seem very exclusive to those not involved in Greek life, but the school's budget for extracurricular activities is large. There are numerous clubs and groups satisfying almost every interest. And if you happen to find yourself without an extracurricular outlet, procuring a charter and funding for a new group is not difficult. The administration has attempted to host some social events—a recent and popular addition to the scene is Shag on the Mag, a themed dance. Unfortunately, Winston-Salem does not offer much in the way of alternatives to an on-campus scene. There are some bars, but they don't garner much traffic on weekends from Wake students. However, the city does provide a variety of restaurants popular with the undergraduate community.

Amenities, Please

Most students find residential life at Wake Forest satisfying. Dorms are characterized as "kind of old" and "small" but also "a lot of fun." Freshmen and sophomores are required to live on campus. In addition to the generic dorm, Wake also provides theme housing that creates an environment for people sharing particular extracurricular interests. For example, the Environmental House emphasizes environmentally friendly living and learning. No theme that appeals to you? Applications can be made for new theme housing. A great deal of Greek brothers move into their fraternity's section on campus, and one brother commented that he "had a blast living there." By senior year, though, many students move off campus into the numerous and inexpensive apartment complexes available. Off-campus living is facilitated by the fact that students are allowed cars all four years—and it is well advised to take advantage of that policy. Very few off-campus venues are within walking distance and there is a lack of public transportation. While complaints about public transportation are common, students give compliments of the campus facilities, including the top of the line athletic buildings. Campus technology is cutting edge, too. According to the school's Web site, "Upon enrollment students receive a ThinkPad and HP color printer/scanner/copier; computers are upgraded after two years and become the student's property upon graduation." As for the food, students say it's "not bad." There are two cafeterias on campus—the main one recently renovated in the summer of 2005. For hungry boys and girls, buffet-style options are available in the dining plan.

"Rolling the Quad"

While the student body is deemed "friendly" and "approachable," it is also somewhat homogeneous. Most people are described as "white and preppy" and generally economically well-off. Students complain that diversity is somewhat lacking on campus and there is not much intermixing among various groups. In fact, students have been characterized as what one junior referred to as "cliquey." Nonetheless, approximately 15 percent of the student body is composed of multicultural students. And on a positive note, one student noted that, "There are rarely any racial problems and people are pretty appreciative of other cultures."

One common thread running throughout all Wake Forest students is the enormous amount of school spirit that is arguably disproportionate to their school's size. This can be attributed in part to Wake's status as a Division I school. The field hockey team has won numerous national championships and the football team is always competitive and well followed, if not wildly successful. And the Demon Deacons always come out in full force for the celebrated basketball team. Wake Forest basketball is consistently ranked in the top 25 and has prominent alumni such as NBA stars Tim Duncan, Josh Howard and Chris Paul. Students make an effort to attend games, which are held just a few minutes from campus. After each major athletic team win, students come back to campus and "roll the quad." All the students grab rolls of toilet paper and throw it all over the trees and cover the entire campus in mounds of Charmin. The enthusiasm of Wake students for academics and extracurriculars plays a key role in keeping Wake Forest unique.—*Janet Yang*

FYI

If you come to Wake Forest, you'd better bring "enthusiasm—we love our school!"
The typical weekend schedule is "get out of class, meet up, and start boozing with buddies, go out, pass out, wake up and sober up a little, then start all over again. Leave all your work until Sunday morning . . . eh afternoon . . . eh probably night."
If I could change one thing about Wake Forest, I'd "make it less Greek and less preppy."
Three things every student should do before graduation are "find the underground tunnel system, participate in pledge night, go to as many basketball games as possible."

North Dakota

Address: 205 Twamley Hall
264 Centennial Drive
Street Grand Forks, ND
58202-8357
Phone: 800-225-5863
E-mail address:
enrollment_services@mail
.und.nodak.edu
Web site URL: www.und.edu
Year Founded: 1883
Private or Public: Public
Religious Affiliation: None
Location: Suburban
Number of Applicants:
4,069
Percent Accepted: 75%
Percent Accepted who
enroll: 63%
Number Entering: 1,926
Number of Transfers
Accepted each Year: 1,048
Middle 50% SAT range:
Unreported
Middle 50% ACT range:
20–25
Early admission program
EA/ED/None: None

Percentage accepted
through EA or ED: NA
EA and ED deadline: NA
Regular Deadline: Rolling
Application Fee: $35
Full time Undergraduate
enrollment: 10,085
Total enrollment: 12,070
Percent Male: 56%
Percent Female: 44%
Total Percent Minority or
Unreported: 13%
Percent African-American:
1%
Percent Asian/Pacific
Islander: 1%
Percent Hispanic: 1%
Percent Native-American: 3%
Percent International: 4%
Percent in-state/out of
state: 52%/48%
Percent from Public HS: 92%
Retention Rate: 78%
Graduation Rate 4-year:
Unreported
Graduation Rate 6-year:
Unreported

Percent Undergraduates
in On-campus housing:
31%
Number of official organized
extracurricular
organizations: 230
3 Most popular majors:
Airline/Commercial/Profes-
sional Pilot and Flight Crew,
Nursing/ Registered Nurse
RN, ASN, BSN, MSN,
Psychology
Student/Faculty ratio: 18:1
Average Class Size: 20 to 29
Percent of students going to
grad school: 24%
Tuition and Fees: $15,325
In State Tuition and Fees if
different: $6,513
Cost for Room and Board:
$5,735
Percent receiving financial
aid out of those who apply,
first year: 70%
Percent receiving financial
aid among all students:
59%

Nestled along the banks of the Red River and on the periphery of the growing city of Grand Forks lies the University of North Dakota (UND). Already acclaimed for its fantastic aeronautics and technology programs, the school is continually improving its respectable facilities and faculty, as well as expanding the opportunities it offers to its students, both in the classroom and out. The University of North Dakota recently completed the Ralph Engelstad Arena, which is known on campus as "one of the best places to watch and play hockey in the world." The school has also raised new buildings for a variety of academic departments. UND seems to be on the cusp of a dynamic and exciting future, one in which the school will continue to play an ever-larger role in its community and in the world.

Academics Take to New Heights

The University of North Dakota has 10 colleges and 193 programs of study. In the College of Arts and Sciences, which enrolls about a quarter of the University's undergraduates, students can major in a variety of liberal arts fields. Some of UND's most popular courses of study include communications, nursing and the health sciences. However, what truly separates UND from the rest of the crowd is the John D. Odegard School of Aerospace Science, touted by many as "the most technologically advanced collegiate environment for aerospace in the world." Students can major in any number of unique fields, including commercial aviation, airport management, and air traffic control. Students first go to "ground school" where they take classes in the mechanics of flying, aerodynamics, and regulations before they are paired one-on-one with flight instructors. Afterwards, the students take to the sky from the Grand Forks Airport, learning maneuvers in the air and going through takeoff and landing procedures at practice fields nearby or satellite airports as far away as Minnesota. Regardless of which school students are enrolled in, they must take courses in four core groups: communications; social sciences; arts and humanities; and mathematics, science and technology, in addition to requirements for their individual majors.

Class size never gets out of hand. According to one student, "Sometimes, I won't get into a particular section for a class, but I'm never not allowed to take the class at all because of the number of people taking it." Indeed, introductory lecture courses in the sciences may be home to around 150 to 200 students each day, but some upper-level courses and discussion classes sometimes don't make it above 10 students. Indeed, one of the assets to UND's curriculum is its favorable environment for lots of student-teacher interaction. One student explained that this was also attributable to the fact that the professors don't usually assign lots of work, preferring that their students "learn directly through discussion and contemplation." TAs offer additional help when the professor is not available, leading lab recitations and review sessions for those still struggling with yesterday's lecture.

Students who want to challenge themselves more with advanced work can apply for acceptance into the UND's Honors Program. The Program offers small, interdisciplinary classes and close faculty advising. Outside of the academic realm, the Honors Program Student Organization (HPSO) arranges trips, service projects and a special publication for participating students. Special Honors housing is also available in the wings of two residence halls.

Winter Wonderland

In the winter, the UND campus looks like the North Pole. With temperatures dipping some 20 or 30 below zero coupled with significant snowfall, it's no wonder that the weather is the one thing many UND students want to change about their campus. However student perceptions of the wintry weather differ: "For out-of-state students who are

used to a warmer climate, the winter may be a shock, but for North Dakotans and Minnesotans, it is nothing new," explained one student. According to one sophomore, the school has a few underground tunnels to provide protection from the elements and a number of "plug-ins" that students can use to prevent their cars from freezing in the parking lot. However, in the spring, the landscape of UND changes completely. After the snow has melted, the groundskeepers plant "huge amounts of flowers."

Something Old, Something New . . .

Spread out on a stretch of the flattest land imaginable, the campus of the University of North Dakota is relatively small for a state school, requiring about 15 to 20 minutes to walk from one end to the other. The older buildings (including Merrifield Hall) are in matching brick and cluster around the center of campus. Although some of the facilities are fairly old, they aren't antiquated. One junior explained "they're still very clean and comfortable, and the school has been upgrading classes with multimedia equipment." Juxtaposed with these buildings are the more modern, glass-laden Aerospace complex buildings.

Students generally agree that the school's library system gives an adequate collection of publications, including special collections with historical records of North Dakota. The school recently launched a new online library system, making its resources more accessible to the student body. Students often go to the library of their particular department for serious studying. The second floor of the recently renovated Memorial Union Student Center is another hotspot for brushing up on one's academic pursuits.

Options Galore

Freshmen are not required to live on campus, and a substantial number of undergraduates choose to live off campus. Many opt to live just west of the UND campus or in the reasonably-priced apartments that can be found downtown. Those who choose to remain in the dorms are usually given suites, with three or four people sharing one bathroom. Though only available to upperclassmen, students mention "Swanson is by far the most comfortable dorm." Swanson has a glass elevator, bathrooms in every room, and a system that allows resident students to buzz in their guests. Each dorm also houses RAs who are said to vary in terms of strictness to UND policy. Most students find them to be "welcoming and friendly," though some are inevitably "too strict."

, UND has 14 residence halls, most of which are connected to one of three dining halls. The university also opened a new apartment-style facility in the fall of 2007. Students agree that the attitude toward the school food is bipolar: either students love it or they hate it. Those opting to live in campus dorms must purchase a meal plan; for those living off campus who decide to go without one, the choices are several local coffee shops such as the Wings Airport Café, a few convenience stores and the Memorial Union Student Center, which houses a food court, ping-pong and pool tables, an arcade, and a lounge area. One of the most attractive qualities about UND, according to the students, is the feeling of safety on campus. The school provides a police force, emergency phones and an escort service for its students. The down-to-earth atmosphere of medium-size Grand Forks adds to a strong feeling of closeness and community between the students of UND and locals.

Hockey on Center Stage

UND's University Program Council works very hard to provide quality social activities to the students and sponsors performances at the Chester Fritz Auditorium by musicians such as Reba McEntire and Travis Tritt. They also sponsor what is known as the Spring Concert, which has hosted such bands as Blues Traveler and Incubus. Council members also sponsor movie nights and a coffee bar at the Memorial Student Center. In addition, there are many places for students to hang out and get a bite to eat in Grand Forks. The most popular by far is a small "hole-in-the-wall" restaurant called the Red Pepper. Serving tacos and grinders, the students rave about the quality of the food and also the college-student-friendly prices it offers. Another popular place for students to eat is the local Applebee's, which offers buy-one-get-one-free appetizers if the UND hockey team won their game that night.

Much of the social life at UND revolves around attending the school's sports games. With the completion of the Ralph Engelstad Arena, every hockey game is sold out with 11,500 screaming students, faculty and locals. Hockey attracts the biggest crowds when facing UND's chief rival, the University of Minnesota at Minneapolis. Other successful teams include men's and women's swimming, basketball, women's hockey and

football. A large portion of students also participate in intramural tennis, soccer, basketball and volleyball.

Those seeking social activity outside of the athletic scene also have options; "one doesn't have to look too hard to find a party every weekend," said one student. Students above the drinking age usually go to Whitey's, Cuckoo's Nest, Sledster's, Bonzer's, or El Roco, for a pitcher of beer. While the University is officially a dry campus, frats that decide to hold parties with alcohol can do so if they hire security guards to prevent underage drinking. Each year UND students look forward to the Springfest celebration, a party of over 5,000 students ("many of whom have a beer in their hand, or hands") that is held in University Park at the end of Spring term.

> **"At a party, it isn't unusual for two people who barely know each other through class to hit it off and spend the rest of the night hanging out."**

Students describe their peers as friendly and open. "At a party, it isn't unusual for two people who barely know each other through class to hit it off and spend the rest of the night hanging out," said one student. Though the University enrolls nearly 13,000 students, the affable student body helps create a distinct sense of community.

The Great Balancing Act

Outside of partying, UND offers 230 chartered organizations on campus. Particularly popular among students is the Wilderness Pilots Club and Sioux Crew, a group dedicated to supporting UND's athletic teams. Others write for the *Dakota Student*, a bi-weekly campus newspaper with a weekly A&E section. Students can also participate in student government or the University Program Council. Large numbers of students are also part of the school's many musical extracurriculars, including the Men and Women's Choirs, the Concert Choir, the UND Orchestra, the Drum Band, and many others. The highest student involvement reportedly occurs with clubs that are associated with particular majors, including the Engineer's Council and the Medical School Club. An annual program called the Big Event allows students to reach out to the community through a wide range of service projects.

UND places a large emphasis on the health of its students. As one student said, "Athletics is what it is all about up here." The Hyslop Sports Center attracts many students who want to unwind after a long day of classes or just keep fit. It includes an indoor track, an Olympic-sized swimming pool, dance and aerobic classes, and an extensive exercise room with modern equipment. In addition, the University recently opened the doors to a 106,000-square-foot Wellness Center. This recently constructed building is designed to provide active learning opportunities in "the multiple dimensions of wellness." Amenities include such things as a suspended running track, three wood-floor courts, a Pilates/yoga studio, a meditation lounge, a nutrition bar, a massage studio and much more.

UND is a fast-growing university, a school with potential that more than compensates for the ice-cold temperatures that it endures in the winter months. UND students come out well-prepared and eager to face whatever storminess they may encounter in the outside world. They've taken on the elements already.—*Darrick Li*

FYI
If you come to UND, you'd better bring "a snowsuit and hockey equipment."
What is the typical weekend schedule? "Party, go to the hockey game, party, recover."
If I could change one thing about UND, I'd "try to build a more diverse student body, geographically and ethnically. Oh, and build more tunnels for us in the winter."
Three things that every student at UND should do before graduating are "go to a hockey game, go fishing in the Red River and go to the Red Pepper."

Ohio

Antioch students are known for their love of a good argument. Their campus, located in Yellow Springs, Ohio, is always politically charged, and its students are always ready to push the envelope, whether they're exploring "radical research on gender" at an annual drag-themed dance party or protesting the new president's curriculum reform. But all Antioch students agree their school is all the richer for its quirks and its conflicts. One freshman summed up his school like this: "Antioch is a strange, strange place . . . but wonderful nonetheless."

Growing Pains

The college, which implemented a new academic system and saw the arrival of a new president in fall of 2005, is undergoing what one student referred to as "a major period of transition." New academic guidelines have shifted its focus slightly, with 112 credits needed to graduate and only three required terms in the co-op program. The new academic system consists of "learning communities," in which a chosen set of professors teach a set of classes focused on a certain subject or area. The idea is to unite professors in an interdisciplinary course of study and to promote a core of classes. Yet some students feel that not all professors have responded enthusiastically to the curriculum changes.

"Things are shifting," explained one senior. "A lot of professors aren't entirely pleased with the new academic system. Some of them aren't so keen on participating in it, and we're having a bit of an exodus of professors."

Despite this, many feel that Antioch's changing academic landscape renders it an even more exciting place to spend four years than it was prior to the revamping. "Antioch is changing right now, really quickly," said one senior. "The people who go to this school will have a chance to determine where it goes. If you want to be involved in the re-building of a school, the change of an entire academic structure where the community is strong, this is the place to go."

"Co-op"-erating

Antioch students agree that one of their school's most unique features is its cooperative education program, designed to give students an opportunity to travel and live independently while still in college. Experiences during co-op term have ranged from helping to run a San Francisco-based theater company to working as a case manager at a mental health residential treatment facility in Pittsburgh to teaching English as a second language at a high school in Chicago. The entire program focuses on the idea of going out into an environment that is utterly unfamiliar.

While the college maintains a list of jobs and opportunities, much of the responsibility for ensuring the program's success lies with the students themselves. The experience was described by one senior as "almost being thrown to the wolves to a certain extent. They don't really help you find housing or adjust to the area at all, although not all of the jobs require you to go out and find your own place." Part of the school's new program, however, has established "co-op communities" in Ohio, New Mexico and Washington, D.C. These areas enable students to take jobs near groups of other Antioch students and thus act as a sort of support system for each other as they settle in to their temporary homes and communities.

No grades? No problem!

Like everything else about Antioch, academics at the school are unique. In place of letter grades, students receive "narrative evaluations" in their courses. Professors are amenable to providing students with letter grades upon request, but most students say that their peers rarely use this option. This laid-back approach has its benefits and its drawbacks. Some students find that, at times, the pressure-free atmosphere goes hand in hand with a certain laziness for some of their classmates.

"The system really draws people who may not have necessarily done so well in high school, because they weren't motivated by the way a traditional high school works. But they're very bright people, and Antioch is a place with a lot of bright, critical thinkers," said one senior. "Whether they choose to use that or not . . . that's another matter."

Another student singled out Antioch's size, and in particular the extremely intimate size of the average class, as one of the highlights of attending the school. "Most classes are very small," he said. "If any class is larger than 12 students, I feel like that's too large."

Aside from the environmental studies department and the women's studies department, both popular in a student body known for its liberal, socially and environmentally conscious students, majors in the excellent communications department are the most popular. Antiochians are fond of saying that one of their communications professors, Anne Bohlen, "taught Michael Moore how to use a camera."

Costume Parties: What a Drag

Perhaps because few students have cars and because the town of Yellow Springs offers few opportunities for party-seekers, most students said that the social scene on weekends consists entirely of parties on-campus. Antioch students are generally as laid-back about their partying as they are about grades.

Students frequent the costume parties held in the student union each weekend; themes have ranged from "Cowboys and Robots" to "Mystery Prom" to "Jet-Setting Socialites A-Go-Go" to "That's Amazing . . . and Disgusting," for which past revelers have come attired in cellophane or even chocolate pudding. Another perennial favorite is "Gender F**k," an exploration ("it's become more than just a drag ball") of the more radical ideas on gender that "encourages gender-bending to the extreme" and for many students embodies the open, accepting and ever-inquiring nature of Antioch students regarding their own sexuality. "I think every Antioch student spends some time questioning, 'What gender am I? Am I really male?'" said one student. "This is also a very open community when it comes to transgender students. It's not uncommon to come back to school and see that someone has gotten a sex change."

Aside from these costume parties, however, the social scene on-campus is relatively easy-going and for the most part consists of gathering in friends' rooms or on The Stoop, a popular gathering place near the student union, to drink or smoke. Students described the presence of alcohol and some drugs on-campus, either due to administration policy or due to the make-up of the student body, as a relatively strong force in everyday life. One senior claimed that it was hard to stay away from the drug scene when living on campus, and that at least one student he knew had moved off campus to avoid that aspect of the social scene.

> **"It's not uncommon to come back to school and see that someone has gotten a sex change."**

Another student, however, said that re-gardless of the school's lenient alcohol pol-icy, no Antioch student had ever gone to the hospital in her time there and that drugs were easy to avoid. "I do drink, but I don't feel pres-sured in the slightest," said one freshman.

Passionate About Politics

In general, students feel that the stereo-typical Antioch student is defined not by how they party on the weekends—and certainly not by his or her athletic prowess. One stu-dent cited school shirts emblazoned with the slogan, "Antioch College: no football since 1929" as an example of the way the school's lack of interest in athletics "is al-most a source of pride" on-campus. Rather, Antioch students feel that they are defined by their passions—and usually, by their lib-eral politics.

One senior described the classic Antioch student as "either the idealistic hippie who spends all their time in the garden talking about auras or the black-clad, angry liberal," while another joked that "if you go to Anti-och, you have a few piercings and tattoos and have probably either colored or entirely shaved off your hair at least once in the past year." But all agreed that Antioch students are "ultra, ultra, ultra liberal" and that they love to debate, complain and protest for the causes about which they feel strongly.

"Any conservative who comes onto cam-pus is pretty quickly driven off," said one student. "People just get so emotional and energetic about their causes and issues, and that's great to see. But sometimes it can end up as these constant clashes between people and personalities, and it can get extremely uncomfortable." Despite students' concerns with political issues and social injustice,

however, one senior girl described the stu-dent body as "pretty white."

Perhaps due to the nature of Antioch's community, where "you pretty much know everyone" and everyone's ready to speak their mind and get into a debate with anyone else who does so, few students choose to move off campus at any point in their four years.

From "The Caf" to a Castle

In addition to the school's academic infra-structure, the physical campus is currently undergoing a transformation as well. Fresh-men and seniors speak of the campus's 140-year-old main building, Antioch Hall, with awe and affection. It was described by one student as "a red brick castle-like building with a copper roof" and praised for "the re-ally amazing view" from its towers by an-other. The student union, affectionately known as "the Caf," received fewer rave re-views; while one girl maintained that "it's getting a lot better" and another freshman praised "the vegan brownies," students agree that the food (and the hours of opera-tion) are less than ideal.

Aside from the cafeteria, however, the student union is spoken of as a fairly popu-lar gathering place, with one senior singling out the graffiti space in the top floor smok-ing lounge—one senior estimated that 70% of the campus smokes—as a favorite hang-out spot.

Despite the amenities on campus, how-ever, one senior recommends bringing a car as a means of occasional escape. "People can go so insane being around the same peo-ple on campus all the time," he said. "Bring a car or find a friend who has one pretty soon, so you're not always there in the whirlwind of Antioch drama."

In the end, students concur that "Antioch drama" is part of what makes their school such an unusual and one-of-a-kind place to spend four years. "It can be hard sometimes because of the nomadic nature of Antioch's educational program, but I don't think I could have gone anywhere else," said one senior. And one senior pointed to a common practice among professors as revealing of Antioch's general philosophy. "Professors are fine with you leaving to drive to Wash-ington, D.C. for a protest," he said. "They honestly are more understanding about you going to a protest than about being sick. They want you to get out there and be politi-cal, because, after all . . . that's what Anti-och's all about."—*Angelica Baker*

FYI

If you come to Antioch, you'd better bring "cigarettes, a strong sense of self, and a backpack—I've basically lived out of a hiking backpack for the past two years."

What is the typical weekend schedule? "Pick up some beer from the local beer shop on Friday, go to the party later on, wake up and go to brunch on Saturday, watch a movie or go into town and thrift shop for your outfit for that night's party . . . then play pool until two or three in the morning and dance your butt off."

If I could change one thing about Antioch, I'd "give us an endowment so we could pay our professors well. So many things that are bad here, are bad because we're such a poor school."

Three things every Antioch student should do before graduating are "get really angry at a community meeting, go hardcore at Gender F**k, and drink the yellow spring water from the Glen."

Bowling Green State University

Address: 110 McFall Center
Bowling Green, OH 43403
Phone: 419-372-2478
E-mail address:
admissions@bgsu.edu
Web site URL: www.bgsu.edu
Year Founded: 1910
Private or Public: Public
Religious Affiliation: None
Location: Rural
Number of Applicants:
11,111
Percent Accepted: 87%
Percent Accepted who
enroll: 32%
Number Entering: 3,079
Number of Transfers
Accepted each Year: 886
Middle 50% SAT range:
M: 450–550, CR: 440–600,
Wr: 435–535
Middle 50% ACT range:
19–24
Early admission program
EA/ED/None: None

Percentage accepted
through EA or ED: NA
EA and ED deadline: NA
Regular Deadline: Rolling
Application Fee: $40
Full time Undergraduate
enrollment: 14,862
Total enrollment: 17,874
Percent Male: 47%
Percent Female: 53%
Total Percent Minority or
Unreported: 21%
Percent African-American:
10%
Percent Asian/Pacific
Islander: 1%
Percent Hispanic: 3%
Percent Native-American:
<1%
Percent International: 2%
Percent in-state/out of
state: 90%/10%
Percent from Public HS:
Unreported
Retention Rate: 73%

Graduation Rate 4-year: 33%
Graduation Rate 6-year: 57%
Percent Undergraduates in
On-campus housing: 41%
Number of official organized
extracurricular
organizations: 280
3 Most popular majors:
Biology, Psychology, Speech
and Rhetoric
Student/Faculty ratio: 18:1
Average Class Size: 25
Percent of students going to
grad school: Unreported
Tuition and Fees: $16,368
In State Tuition and Fees if
different: $9,060
Cost for Room and Board:
$7,220
Percent receiving financial
aid out of those who apply,
first year: 74%
Percent receiving financial
aid among all students:
65%

If you're looking for a college town atmosphere, die-hard school spirit, and a relaxed intellectual environment, then Bowling Green State University may be the place for you. With almost 18,000 students on its main campus, BGSU is filled with tons of different people, opinions, interests, and opportunities. Students are eager to point out that in spite of the relatively small population of the town (around 29,600), Bowling Green doesn't feel that small. Located only 20 miles south of Toledo, the campus is within easy driving distance to larger cities, offering a wide variety of restaurants, events, and clubs, although most students said they usually stay close to campus to participate in the vibrant social scene.

Better than "Normal"

When classes first started in 1914, BGSU was actually called Bowling Green State Normal College, tuition was free, and the only courses offered were education classes for women. The school dropped the "Normal" from its name in 1929, and students today agree that the school is far more interesting than its founding name implies. With over 200 majors and programs offered, a competitive honors curriculum, and a very active study abroad program, BGSU has expanded to offer just about any type of academic environment for its students. And while tuition is no longer free and the campus has long been coed, students say the focus on teacher preparation and the desire to make education affordable are still at the core of BG's academic philosophy. Students agreed that education is still the most popular major, adding that "it seems like everywhere you turn, you meet another future teacher." Indeed, BGSU ranks as the 14th highest producer of teachers in the country. With such a high number in one major, it might seem that enrollment in education classes would be competitive. But students said that registering for classes in general is fairly easy. The most frustrating part is getting put on waiting lists, but "with a little determination, it all works out in the end."

No matter what major you decide to pursue, students said BGSU does a good job of offering lots of opportunities to make your education entertaining and affordable with easily accessible resources for fellowships, internships, foreign exchange programs, and scholarships or financial aid. The University can accommodate almost any of your wildest travel plans, with foreign exchange programs in over 30 different countries as well as domestic opportunities for study or work experience. The same generosity with which BG approaches study abroad also translates to their financial aid packages. Around 70 percent of students receive financial aid, and the University also offers over $20 million in scholarship money and an extensive work-study program.

Students generally don't talk about their grades or feel a lot of pressure to compete with their classmates. This laid-back atmosphere is to the advantage of self-motivated students and those in the honors program will find themselves with a demanding schedule no matter what. But others said the relaxed environment makes it almost too easy to forget about classes and only focus on the weekend.

Bleacher Creatures and Dancing Queens

Without a doubt, school pride is an important part of any student's time at BGSU. In the 1970s, a student group of die-hard BGSU Falcons fans dressed up in different Halloween costumes for every hockey game, eventually earning a spot in *Sports Illustrated* as the famous masked "Bleacher Creatures." Today, students channel this school spirit mainly during the annual football game against their arch rival, the University of Toledo Rockets, for which fans show up in unusually large numbers. "I never watch football ever, but I've never missed a BG/UT game," one student added. BG has 18 NCAA Division I varsity sports teams to cheer on, and a ton of club sports for anyone to join, including ice hockey, ultimate Frisbee and lacrosse. At games, students don their school colors, overlooking in the heat of the moment the unsightly combination of murky brown and bright orange.

In addition to sports events, there are a ton of school-sponsored activities to participate in if athletics doesn't get you going. There are nearly 325 student-run organizations on campus, and the administration makes it relatively easy to start your own group if your interests aren't already represented. BG students seem more than up for the challenge of spearheading campus events, with student-run social and cultural activities going on "pretty much all the time." Among students' favorites are homecoming, family weekend, sibs-kids weekend, and the dance marathon—student-run events that bring the large campus together and often raise funds for charities and minorities. "I've helped work on the dance marathon for two years now and it's my favorite part of the year," one student said. "It's a really unique experience that the whole student body can come together on." Students can also enjoy theatrical and musical productions at the two large performance halls in the Moore Musical Arts Center, or take a trip to the spacious Fine Arts galleries to see exhibitions from BG student artists.

Another fundamental part of the BGSU lifestyle is the Greek system. Fraternities and sororities abound on campus, with over 43 different houses for students to choose from. About 1,700 students opt for the Greek life, while others often attend the parties without choosing to rush.

Each month, BG offers its students close to 300 events and activities, ensuring that there is never a dull moment if you take advantage of the opportunities. Some students said they worried at first about the small-town setting, but the diversity of activities on campus really makes BG come alive so it can feel a lot bigger than the somewhat rural campus seems at first.

Home Sweet Home

BGSU has seven residence halls, some limited to upper- or underclassmen, and all with unique personalities and generally similar accommodations. As a rule, all underclassmen, except those who live at home, must live on campus, but students said they didn't really mind the restriction. Generally, they neither love nor hate the dorms. "The dorms are actually decent," one student said. "They can be pretty small and cramped, though, especially if you're not best buds with your roommate." Generally, the quality and size of the rooms increases as you get older. For example, Founders and Offenhauer (predominately upperclassmen dorms) have air conditioning, while the all-freshman dorm MacDonald is known for its closet-like bedrooms and sardine lifestyle.

All rooms are equipped with computer connections and cable television access. Each residential hall has its own laundry room, as well as a study area, TV lounge and computer lab for its students. All the dorms are centrally located on campus, so that you can easily get to all classes by bike or foot. Shuttle services also are available to take students to main buildings, which they said are especially useful in the winter when it gets "really freakin' cold." Although students are allowed to have cars on campus, and many do, the student parking lots are so inconvenient that "you end up walking just about as far as you would have if you hadn't driven in the first place."

> "It's nice being able to walk everywhere, and I like that I always run into somebody I know."

Even though Bowling Green is a small town, students said they are never hard-pressed for a place to eat. During the week, students often hang out at the student union, enjoying fast food or the popular Zza's pizza from the food court, a latte from the Starbucks, or a home-cooked meal at the Bowling Greenery. Commons also offers all-you-can-eat-meals, although students warned that the options can often get pretty repetitive, especially at the MacDonald's dining center.

In general, students said living at BG was comfortable and relaxing. "It's safe, friendly,

and laid-back," a student said. "It's nice being able to walk everywhere, and I like that I always run into somebody I know."

Close to 18,000 students attend BGSU, making it one of the larger public universities in the country. Only 13 percent of the students are non-residents, with about 500 international undergraduates. At about 18 percent minority, students said diversity is, of course, present on campus, but is not a major part of campus life. "I hear a lot of stuff about the preppy frat boy from BG," one student said, "but it's not really like that. That's just the stereotype we get." And with multicultural organizations, hundreds of different student groups, and so many different academic majors, students said diversity of interests is really the main point.

Campus Culture

On the weekends, BGSU's diverse student body really spreads out, with some sticking to the campus events, others partying it up with a few friends, and still others driving out of town, either for a trip home or to livelier club scenes in neighboring cities. Although Bowling Green is a dry campus, with strict enforcement in the residence halls, undergraduate students said underage drinking can thrive at BG as much as at any other college, with the aid of a fake ID, an older friend, or simply a keg at an off-campus party. "If you're underage and you want to drink, it's not hard. You can go to a frat, a bar or club, or just stay in your room and keep it down," one student said. But if drinking's not for you, many students enjoy quieter nights at the movies, the theater, or hanging out in one of the local eateries.

A large number of students do drive out of town on the weekends, either going home if they live close-by or visiting friends in Toledo or other nearby towns. Some students said commuting on the weekends can detract from the vibrant social scene BGSU tries hard to create, and that if you stick around, you'll find it can really be an exciting place to be on a Friday night.—*Maggie Reid*

FYI
If you come to BGSU, you'd better bring "a warm coat for the frigid winters."
What is the typical weekend schedule? "Friday: pre-game with your friends, go out to a frat or house party, bar hopping, some late night food. Saturday: sleep till noon, do it all again. Sunday: sleep all day and do your homework that's been piling up."
If I could change one thing about BGSU, "it would be the long months of cold, wind, and snow."
Three things every student should do before graduating from BGSU are: "make it to every UT football game, go to at least one frat party, and take advantage of the small, personal environment to really get to know your fellow classmates and your professors. You can make great lifelong connections at a place like BG."

Case Western Reserve University

Address: 10900 Euclid Avenue Cleveland, OH 44106
Phone: 216-368-4450
E-mail address: admission@case.edu
Web site URL: www.case.edu
Year Founded: 1826
Private or Public: Private
Religious Affiliation: None
Location: Urban
Number of Applicants: 7,351
Percent Accepted: 73.3%
Percent Accepted who enroll: 19%
Number Entering: 1,026
Number of Transfers Accepted each Year: 107
Middle 50% SAT range: M: 620–720, CR: 590–690, Wr: 580–680
Middle 50% ACT range: 26–32
Early admission program EA/ED/None: ED
Percentage accepted through EA or ED: 38%

EA and ED deadline: 1-Nov
Regular Deadline: 15-Jan
Application Fee: $0
Full time Undergraduate enrollment: 4,207
Total enrollment: 8,166
Percent Male: 57%
Percent Female: 43%
Total Percent Minority or Unreported: 25%
Percent African-American: 6%
Percent Asian/Pacific Islander: 17%
Percent Hispanic: 2%
Percent Native-American: <1%
Percent International: 4%
Percent in-state/out of state: 54%/46%
Percent from Public HS: Unreported
Retention Rate: 91%
Graduation Rate 4-year: 57%
Graduation Rate 6-year: 78%

Percent Undergraduates in On-campus housing: 78%
Number of official organized extracurricular organizations: 150
3 Most popular majors: Biology, Biomedical Engineering, Business Administration and Management
Student/Faculty ratio: 10:1
Average Class Size: Unreported
Percent of students going to grad school: Unreported
Tuition and Fees: $35,572
In State Tuition and Fees if different: No difference
Cost for Room and Board: $10,450
Percent receiving financial aid out of those who apply, first year: 90%
Percent receiving financial aid among all students: 84%

As the product of a merger of two established institutes of science—Case Institute of Technology and Western Reserve University—Case exemplifies the ideal of a technical university where superior academics coupled with a diverse student body provide an enlightening experience.

Academics at Case

Case is famous for its top-ranking science and engineering programs, and ranks perennially in the top 10 undergraduate biomedical engineering programs in the country. Consequently, the majority of students you'll meet at Case will be studying engineering, pre-medicine, and the "hard sciences." However, as one student commented, "Case has been working hard to increase the number of humanities majors."

Case also offers a variety of special programs aimed at students wishing to accelerate through their education, one of the most popular and selective of which is the Pre-Professional Scholars Program. Through PPSP, students are offered conditional placement in Case's graduate schools for law, social work, and dentistry. Competition for a space in the PPSP medicine program is especially intense—only around 20 to 25 students out of an applicant pool of 700 are accepted into the program annually. As a result, a coveted position in the PPSP medicine program becomes one of the most attractive aspects of Case; one pre-med student confessed, "I came to Case because I was accepted into PPSP."

Despite the heavy concentration of students in the sciences and engineering, Case is dedicated to educating their students in all areas, enabling them to become more well-rounded people with diverse interests. Case students are required to explore different areas, such as the arts, and the social sciences, as w "global and cultural diversity

The number of credits req at Case differ according While the arts and humaniti quire less credits and thus more freedom to survey othe and engineering programs require more credits. Though the requirements for science majors seem stringent, students say they leave feeling well prepared. A biomedical engineering major asserted, "The curriculum definitely takes care of every aspect of BME that's necessary, including polymers, imaging and electrics, and biomechanics."

Introductory classes are often lecture-based, with 100 to 300 students in each class. However, Case supplies "Supplemental Instructors" (SIs), who hold review sessions and are known to be "very helpful." As students progress to courses more specific to certain majors, however, typical class size decreases to a cozy 20-30, ensuring more personal attention for each student. Case also requires 16 credits in seminar classes, beginning with the freshman seminar program, SAGES (Seminar Approach to General Education and Scholarship), which is designed to encourage students to "discover . . . the endless opportunities and resources here at Case [as well as] . . . perspectives, passions, and creativity."

Social Scene

There's no question that Case students study hard, but beyond their grueling Sunday through Thursday nights, they also enjoy a vibrant and diverse social scene centered around Case's popular fraternities and sororities. Nearly a quarter of the student body is involved in the Greek scene, and as a result students report that "either you or many of your friends" are fraternity boys or sorority girls. Campus-wide Greek events are commonplace, and one of the most famous is Greek Week, when fraternities and sororities compete in numerous events. Interested students are given the opportunity to get to know their potential brotherhoods or sisterhoods through a series of events, get-togethers, and longer parties before receiving a bid to join.

Although Greek life does compose a large part of Case's social scene, students report that "the Greek community is normally very open." Although some girls complain that it is slightly more difficult to "make a ton of friends as a non-Greek," the majority of students feel that "Greeks are integrated into the campus, and are very inclusive."

While a decent percentage of students at Case come from Ohio, the student body at se still "embodies diversity in geography, city, and particularly interests." Conse-students at Case expect to meet and ds from varied backgrounds. One

student comments, "Sure, we are a nerdy school . . . but most people are socially inclined. I think that [Case] provides opportunities to meet all of the different sorts of people you'd like."

On-campus entertainment consists of performances and events run by a large variety of student groups such as IMPROVment on Friday nights and Spot Night on Wednesday nights, when local bands play. Alcohol is technically banned from campus, but one student reported it is nonetheless "easy to find," though "binge drinking and drugs are not problems on campus."

Case athletics have been increasing in popularity and rank in recent years. The Case football team ended the 2007 season with the school's first University Athletic Association Championship in football. The team was undefeated in 2008 but didn't get far in the NCAA Division III playoffs. Intramural sports, including less traditional events such as dodgeball, are "intense as heck." Three quarters of the undergraduate body participate in intramurals during their four years at Case.

> "Sure, we are a nerdy school . . . but most people are socially inclined. I think that [Case] provides opportunities to meet all of the different sorts of people you'd like."

Students can also explore the large array of off-campus entertainment. Whether you'd like to go shopping, dining, clubbing, or bowling, there are options accessible by foot or by bus. One of the most popular and unique neighborhoods near Case is Coventry, which can be reached by walking or by "Greenies," the green campus shuttle buses. Coventry is a shopping district with an eclectic mix of stores full of "books, toys, and random cool things" in addition to restaurants offering international cuisine. Sports fans can cheer on the nearby Cleveland Indians and Cavaliers, music aficionados can enjoy their favorite bands at the House of Blues, and window-shoppers can indulge themselves at Beachwood, an upscale mall accessible by bus from campus.

Of course, you can also take advantage of Case's proximity to the University Circle and enjoy masterpieces at the Cleveland Museum of Art, scientific artifacts and displays at Cleveland Museum of Natural History, shows at the Cleveland Play House, and of course the concerts of the world-renowned Cleveland Orchestra at Severance Hall, all within one mile of campus. But when you're traveling to and from locations off-campus at night, be aware that, as with most universities located in urban environments, safety is key. Although Case is currently updating emergency phones and security is "everywhere," "you should [still] definitely be smart about where you go and what you do."

Living at Case

Students are required to live on campus for the first two years of school, unless they live at home and commute. Freshmen dorms are usually doubles located in the "upper three floors of four-storied buildings" and are "fair sized, but without air conditioning." Students are allowed to choose their own rooms and dorms, pending availability, as well as their own roommates.

Many upperclassmen choose to move off campus, but a significantly larger percentage of them stay on campus due to the recent addition of the "Village at 115." Described as a "swanky hotel" by some, Village at 115 offers the luxury of an apartment with the convenience of living on campus. However, the major complaint about both upperclassmen and underclassmen housing is that "classes are too far away from the dorms."

There are two main dining halls on campus: Fribley (South) and Leutner (North). Students are free to dine at either dining hall, though Fribley is considered better. Flexible meal plans come with "Case cash," which can be used at local restaurants.

The numerous resources and opportunities Case Western Reserve University offers impact its students for a lifetime. Students describe their time at Case as "demanding but rewarding," and with its superior academics and flourishing social scene Case offers its students an ideal environment to enhance their education and social connections.—*Chaoran Chen*

FYI

If you come to Case, you'd better bring "a computer and a warm winter coat."

What is the typical weekend schedule? "Every weekend is different" and "students can generally do whatever they choose," but Friday and Saturday tend to be nights to find a party or enjoy events off campus, whereas Sunday night is reserved exclusively for studying.

If I could change one thing about Case, I'd "make everyone more positive."

Three things every student at Case should do before graduating are "go to a concert by the Cleveland Orchestra, meet Lebron James, and explore University Circle's museums."

College of Wooster

Address: 847 College Avenue Wooster, OH 44691

Phone: 800-877-9905

E-mail address: admissions@wooster.edu

Web site URL: www.wooster.edu

Year Founded: 1866

Private or Public: Private

Religious Affiliation: None

Location: Suburban

Number of Applicants: 3,445

Percent Accepted: 81%

Percent Accepted who enroll: 20%

Number Entering: 513

Number of Transfers Accepted each Year: 45

Middle 50% SAT range: M: 540–660, CR: 540–670, Wr: Unreported

Middle 50% ACT range: 23–29

Early admission program EA/ED/None: ED

Percentage accepted through EA or ED: Unreported

EA and ED deadline: 1-Dec, 15-Jan

Regular Deadline: 1-Feb

Application Fee: $40

Full time Undergraduate enrollment: 1,864

Total enrollment: 1,864

Percent Male: 47%

Percent Female: 53%

Total Percent Minority or Unreported: 10%

Percent African-American: 5%

Percent Asian/Pacific Islander: 3%

Percent Hispanic: 2%

Percent Native-American: <1%

Percent International: 5%

Percent in-state/out of state: 39%/ 61%

Percent from Public HS: Unreported

Retention Rate: 88%

Graduation Rate 4-year: 64%

Graduation Rate 6-year: 73%

Percent Undergraduates in On-campus housing: 100%

Number of official organized extracurricular organizations: 130

3 Most popular majors: Psychology, Political Science, English

Student/Faculty ratio: 12:1

Average Class Size: 17

Percent of students going to grad school: 40%

Tuition and Fees: $42,420 comprehensive fee

In State Tuition and Fees if different: No difference

Cost for Room and Board: Included

Percent receiving financial aid out of those who apply, first year: 82%

Percent receiving financial aid among all students: 17%

About an hour's drive outside of Cleveland lies the College of Wooster, named for its host, the small town of Wooster, Ohio. While its locale may be sleepy, its students are wide-awake and raring to go. The Wooster curriculum's philosophy of individual growth and self-reliance gives its approximately 1900 undergraduates a chance to experience intellectual autonomy in a safe and supportive environment. This autonomy reaches its peak in the Independent Study Program, for which each senior designs and completes a yearlong project in his or her field of study. If you are looking for challenge and freedom in equal measure, then Wooster might just be the college for you.

Life Skills in the Classroom

While Wooster places a high premium on independent exploration, its distributional requirements show that the school values tradition as well. To graduate, students must take two classes in each of three areas: Arts and Humanities, History and Social Sciences, and Mathematical and Natural Sciences. Additionally, they must fulfill—either through coursework or placement tests—requirements in writing, quantitative reasoning, foreign language, non-American or minority culture, and religion. To round off this intimidating list, Wooster requires a year-long Senior Independent Study as well as a semester-long Junior one. This course load may look burdensome, but students claim it's not as heavy as it seems: you can test out of some classes, and even if you don't, "you're able to fulfill the graduation requirements pretty easily in the first two years," said one student confidently.

Given the small class sizes and attentive professors, even required classes provide opportunity for enjoyment. As one potential science major explained, "Some of the introductory classes are about 30, which is small compared to bigger universities—and then I have a class that has ten." According to Woosterites, their small classes give them an edge over students at larger universities. One student named class sizes as his favorite part of the college's academics: "It's really nice to work with ten or eleven other kids and the professor. Everybody's input in the class is heard . . . Being in a small class forces people to do the work or do it better."

The professors contribute to the personal atmosphere, and Wooster's student-faculty ratio certainly encourages close relationships. By graduation, each student "is pretty good friends with at least two or three of the professors," claimed a junior. Students don't have to pal around with their lecturers in order to have their questions answered. The majority of professors have an open-door policy in order to better accommodate the needs of their pupils.

Of course, Wooster's academic life isn't just a good environment. It is based on intellectual rigor and the principles of the Independent Study Program. No student can blow off work and still win good grades. To get an A, "you have to study really hard for it," and tests are "harder than you would expect," according to a freshman. That isn't to say the professors are harsh or unfair: "I don't think if anyone earned an A, they would say, well I'm only giving four A's. I think they'll give you the grade you've earned. What you've done reflects the grade you get," a philosophy major opined.

The Independent Study Program, which has existed at Wooster for over 50 years, is the college's defining academic feature. While the semester-long Junior Independent Study gives students practice in a sustained, self-motivated undertaking, the Senior I.S. is an opportunity for each Woosterite to design and execute a project of his or her choosing while working one-on-one with a professor for an entire year. According to the I.S. philosophy, the program both allows students to follow their intellectual passions without restriction and prepares them for the greater autonomy and drive required in the workforce. As a junior put it, "If you're applying for a job and are even in all fields with other applicants, and you show them a 100 page independent study . . ."

Those worried about completing a liberal arts degree without having prepared for a specific profession can at least be assured they have something to show for it.

Underground Social Scene, Literally

Wooster students claim that their college remains free from cliques and other petty social divisions, "which is good, because it isn't high school anymore." While Greek life does exist at Wooster, it is not a large part of the scene. Nor are the students divided by age: seniors can hang out with freshmen without awkwardness.

Student unity is perhaps most obvious in the Underground, or UG, an on-campus, subterranean club that opens on Friday and Saturday. Dancing, food, and alcohol all make their appearances at the UG, as do a large number of students. Because of the club's popularity throughout the undergraduate body, "you get to meet a lot of different personalities," according to one appreciative student.

> **"You get to meet a lot of different personalities."**

Despite the college's small size, its students represent 46 states and 30 countries, as well as a variety of ethnic backgrounds. The political scene, however, is homogenous and overwhelmingly liberal—one student estimated that Wooster had about 20 Republicans total. The administration intends to increase college diversity in the coming years; perhaps that will include Bill O'Reilly enthusiasts as well.

Community Life, Community Service

The summer before freshman year, each student fills out an online survey to help match him or her with a roommate. The administration houses students in one of the 12 residential halls, of which each floor has a Resident Assistant. These RA's are upperclassmen who live with the freshmen: they organize weekly meetings, provide advice or counseling, and organize educational and social programs for their floors. The dorms "all come with their pluses and their negatives," but on the whole, students are lukewarm on the subject. The accommodations may be nothing to write home about, but they're certainly good enough for college students.

After freshman year, students have a choice—they can remain within the Wooster dormitories, or choose to live off-camps. For students who choose to continue dorming, they receive a draw number as part of a lottery that determines which students choose their rooms first. The numbers get better with seniority, so upperclassmen have more motivation to remain within this system. As an alternative, students can apply to live in a program house with their friends. In exchange for the use of an off-campus house, students will fulfill a community service program. Each resident must log in two hours a week in order to meet the program's requirements. Most Woosterites see this as a win-win: "We're doing something that's good for the community *and* we're all living together." Socially conscious *and* fun: who says you can't have it all?

Wooster has two main cafeterias, the Lowry Center and Kittredge Dining Halls, which boast international and vegetarian options as well as the all-American grille fare familiar to college students. On Meal Plan A, students are guaranteed 288 meals per semester, as well as 150 Flex Dollars to spend at on-campus eateries. On Plan B, they have 200 meals and 450 Flex Dollars. These Flex Dollars are meal points that can only be spent at the on-campus eateries such as Mom's Truck Stop, a diner-esque establishment and popular 3 a.m. hangout, the Old Main Café for tasty sandwiches, or the Java Hut for those who prefer caffeine to solid food.

It appears that Wooster's commitment to student freedom extends everywhere—even to breakfast.—*Finola Prendergast*

FYI
If you come to Wooster, you'd better bring "creative ideas for fun."
The typical weekend schedule "can include anything from going out to parties, dancing at the Underground, attending a sporting event, sleeping in, making Walmart trips, and procrastinating until Sunday rolls around."
If I could change one thing about Wooster, "I would have them redo the Students' Center. It's just outdated. Nobody likes to hang out there anymore because it's so old. It's from the 60's!"
Three things every student at Wooster should do before graduating are, "go to Mom's Truck Stop, go the Underground, and go to Scot Lane."

Denison University

Address: Box H, Granville, OH 43023
Phone: 740-587-6276
E-mail address: admissions@denison.edu
Web site URL: www.denison.edu
Year Founded: 1831
Private or Public: Private
Religious Affiliation: None
Location: Suburban
Number of Applicants: 5,181
Percent Accepted: 39%
Percent Accepted who enroll: 29%
Number Entering: 586
Number of Transfers Accepted each Year: 30
Middle 50% SAT range: M: 590–680, Cr: 580–690, Wr: 620–690
Middle 50% ACT range: 26–30
Early admission program EA/ED/None: ED

Percentage accepted through EA or ED: 14%
EA and ED deadline: 1-Nov
Regular Deadline: 15-Jan
Application Fee: $40
Full time Undergraduate enrollment: 2,212
Total enrollment: 2,212
Percent Male: 43%
Percent Female: 57%
Total Percent Minority or Unreported: 18%
Percent African-American: 5%
Percent Asian/Pacific Islander: 3%
Percent Hispanic: 2%
Percent Native-American: <1%
Percent International: 5%
Percent in-state/out of state: 43%/57%
Percent from Public HS: 70%
Retention Rate: 93%

Graduation Rate 4-year: 78%
Graduation Rate 6-year: 82%
Percent Undergraduates in On-campus housing: 99%
Number of official organized extracurricular organizations: 156
3 Most popular majors: Communications, Economics, English
Student/Faculty ratio: 11:1
Average Class Size: 10 to 19
Percent of students going to grad school: 27%
Tuition and Fees: $32,160
In State Tuition and Fees if different: No difference
Cost for Room and Board: $8,570
Percent receiving financial aid out of those who apply, first year: 76%
Percent receiving financial aid among all students: 43%

In the middle of Licking County, Ohio, there is a big hill with a tiny town nestled at the bottom. Granville might not be the place you would expect to find a slew of college students, but take a hike up the hill and you will come upon the warm brick buildings and expansive green areas that make up the campus of Denison University. The school may match the small size of the town at its feet, but the 2,242 undergraduates manage to create an environment where they can work—and play—with plenty of variety. While Denison is known for its traditional, preppy vibe, the genuine hominess of this "Little Utopia" is just as prevalent as a popped collar.

The Learning Curve

"A lot of my friends work pretty constantly," said one freshman, whose sentiments were echoed by other Denison students. There's no denying that the workload is heavy, and the word "slacker" does not seem to be part of the school's vocabulary. Although another student added that "teachers are tough graders and classes are challenging," in the rigorous general curriculum, ambitious students may also elect to be part of Denison's intensive honors program. But the demanding academics should not deter prospective Denisonians—the courses may be tough, but students generally praise the school's extensive academic resources.

One freshman mentioned that it can be difficult to get into the necessary introductory-level classes that are prerequisites for most of the more in-depth classes at Denison, but most students appreciate the small size of these capped classes. Students estimate that the average class ranges from about 15 to 20 people, which creates a comfortable environment for students to take risks in discussions. One student said that class is "like a dialogue between the students and the professors," which means that "students are known for their ideas—not by their ID numbers." In addition, Denison is set apart by its commitment to having only professors teach classes—TA's are around only to help grade. Students say they feel much more engaged in class because the people who really know and care about the subject are directly involved and invested in conveying material. While such a setup might be intimidating elsewhere, the small classes make interactions with the professors very easy, and students say that their teachers are both approachable and eager for students to communicate with them.

It is not only the professors who like to talk about school outside of class—the students, too, are often found debating on their way out of the classroom. One student recounted a day in the dining hall when an entire class convened spontaneously to discuss the topic of the previous day's class—not for credit, not for a grade, but because, as students note, Denisonians are passionate about what they learn. Students say most people are used to getting all As in high school, but that "it's more about actually knowing things than being able to recite details and facts."

City Upon a Hill

Denison clearly takes its role as an educator very seriously, and the campus reflects this goal. At the heart of the school are the academic buildings, which are surrounded by the residential dorms. Although the classrooms are in the middle, the real hub of campus is the Union, which students say "is always full of people." The building, with a food court and a bar for upperclassmen, provides a welcome respite from studying and a convenient meeting spot for students coming from any part of campus. Although the locations are generally divided by age, students say that almost everyone lives on campus. That, and the lack of any fraternity houses, contributes to a great deal of campus unity and a "cohesiveness that brings a lot to the school."

> "Students are known for their ideas—not by their ID numbers."

While students say that the housing is uniformly excellent, some people go a more alternative route. While still on campus, South houses many art majors, and "team" houses, such as baseball and rugby, are also popular. For more of an unconventional experience, the Homestead, which lies about a mile away from the campus, provides students with the opportunity to get just a little bit closer to nature. Students say that each dorm has its own personality, but since the housing process is done by lottery, residences hold students with many diverse interests and activities. The freshmen live on West or North quad, all in substance-free dorms. Even so, the ubiquitous college party dorm still exists in the form of Shorney, which has four coed floors and only one that is single-sex. The sophomores and juniors who live on East, meanwhile, tend to host most of the parties in conjunction with seniors in the on-campus Hayes or Sunset apartment complexes. Even better than partying, procrastination is made infinitely easier by the "amazing technology" to be found in every dorm and all across campus—students say that all the dorms and buildings are fully wireless, and one student estimated that "there are more computers on campus than people!"

The Sunset Strip

When the workweek weighs down backpacks, and minds are crammed with all the information they can handle, even the most diligent worker needs some release. "There's lots of partying, I'm not going to lie," said one student. "This is a small school in the middle of nowhere." Although most of the parties center on alcohol, students are quick to assert that people who do not drink are by no means out of luck on the weekends. One student conceded that "people definitely party with a different group if they don't drink, but it's not a big deal." Because alcohol is not allowed in the freshman dorms, most of the partying takes place in the senior Sunset Apartments. The big partying days of Wednesday, Friday, and Saturday afford plenty of time to hit the senior apartments, the sophomore and junior housing, and the club and team houses. The school is not particularly harsh with its alcohol policies, but students caution that write-ups are not unheard of, and the school cracks down hard on all illegal drugs. Still, students find the social scene to be "chill and comfortable," but stimulating because "all ages hang out together." In describing the partying at Denison, one student summed it up perfectly: "fun but not too crazy."

The Hills Are Alive

Not only with the sound of music, but also the telltale scuffling of sports, the whirring of the printing press, and every activity in between. For a very small school, Denison "really pushes that students do get involved with something, whether it's a sport, a club of some kind, or a sorority or frat." Because Granville is such a "teeny town," students find what they want right on campus. "The school provides us with lots of things to do—they know how isolated we are." Most people are very involved in activities outside of academics and are very familiar with the other students.

Denison is a Division III school, which means that, while it is "not incredibly selective as to who is capable of playing," many more people have the opportunity to participate. While students are all for playing sports, the games themselves are not particularly well attended: students caution that the football team is so bad that people almost never go to games, but lacrosse and soccer do draw some fans. Club and intramural sports also tend to be popular, especially Frisbee, rugby, soccer, and tennis.

If sports are not particularly intriguing, there are any number of activities that are "easy to get involved in." One freshman remarked, "I don't know one person who isn't involved in at least one thing outside of class." Students are part of a diverse range of extracurriculars, including environmental clubs, singing groups, and fraternities and sororities—which count one third of the student body among their brothers and sisters. Political groups are not particularly big on campus, but students mention a generally moderate to conservative vibe. One thing everyone can agree on is the popularity of the *Bullsheet*, a daily paper that is comprised entirely of student work—a better alternative to the actual school newspaper, students say. No matter what people decide to become involved in, students say it is easy to jump in immediately and be welcomed to the group.

D-Day

It may not require quite the military force of Normandy, but there is definitely an invasion of Denison's campus once a year. Each year, the school brings in a big-name musical act, which remains a surprise until announced at homecoming. Previous acts have included Third Eye Blind, Juvenile, and the Roots, and students say no one misses this event.

There is another "D" word that is not quite as much a part of the Denison tradition: diversity. "The lack of diversity surprised me," said one student, who also felt that the current homogeneity "causes problems when people of different races do come in." Students appreciate that Denison is working to make the school a more open place by sponsoring forums and dedicating itself to creating a less tense environment, but the problem is not only racial. One student candidly stated, "The tuition is quite expensive, so inevitably you are going to get a wealthier population," although others mentioned that the school gives almost everyone very generous financial aid packages.

The tradition that characterizes Denison above all is that of cohesiveness. Students may seem reserved at first, but in the end the friendliness of the student body and the accessibility of the professors create an atmosphere that allows for growth in many areas.

One student encapsulated the essence of a Denison education: "It is a good learning environment that builds you as a person rather than just a student."—*Hannah Jacobson*

FYI

If you come to Denison, you'd better bring "a lot of dress-up clothes and random things you think you'll never wear—we have tons of theme parties!"

What is the typical weekend schedule? "On Friday, take a long nap—then at six, it starts getting loud, at seven, you come out of your room to start socializing and hall bonding before pregaming and heading out to party. On Saturday, the campus is vacant until four because everyone is sleeping and/or hungover, then you do it all again until Sunday, when we do homework. And eat."

If I could change one thing about Denison, I'd "make it more diverse."

Three things every student at Denison should do before graduating are "party in the wigwam built in the woods behind the sunset parking lot, go onto the fourth floor of Talbot and look out at the amazing view of the rolling hills, and go to Brew's restaurant in Granville and Wit's for the best ice cream ever."

Kent State University

Address: Kent State University Kent, OH 44242
Phone: 330-672-3000
E-mail address: admissions@kent.edu
Web site URL: www.kent.edu
Year Founded: 1910
Private or Public: Public
Religious Affiliation: None
Location: Suburban
Number of Applicants: Unreported
Percent Accepted: 84%
Percent Accepted who enroll: 38%
Number Entering: 3,751
Number of Transfers Accepted each Year: 920
Middle 50% SAT range: M: 460–590, CR: 460–580, Wr: Unreported
Middle 50% ACT range: 19–24
Early admission program EA/ED/None: None
Percentage accepted through EA or ED: NA

EA and ED deadline: NA
Regular Deadline: 1-Aug
Application Fee: $55
Full time Undergraduate enrollment: 29,227
Total enrollment: 34,056
Percent Male: 39%
Percent Female: 61%
Total Percent Minority or Unreported: 5%
Percent African-American: 10%
Percent Asian/Pacific Islander: 2%
Percent Hispanic: 2%
Percent Native-American: 1%
Percent International: Unreported
Percent in-state/out of state: 87%/13%
Percent from Public HS: Unreported
Retention Rate: 71%
Graduation Rate 4-year: Unreported

Graduation Rate 6-year: Unreported
Percent Undergraduates in On-campus housing: 35%
Number of official organized extracurricular organizations: Unreported
3 Most popular majors: Business/Marketing, Education, Health Professions
Student/Faculty ratio: 18:1
Average Class Size: Unreported
Percent of students going to grad school: Unreported
Tuition and Fees: $15,862
In State Tuition and Fees if different: $8,430
Cost for Room and Board: $7,200
Percent receiving financial aid out of those who apply, first year: 81%
Percent receiving financial aid among all students: 63%

Kent State University, despite its place in history as a hotbed of political progressivism, is a quiet, laid-back institution. Kent offers a wide variety of academic opportunities, with a friendly atmosphere for an institution of its size. With over 18,000 un-

dergraduate students, Kent State is the second-largest university in Ohio. Although the campus is not very diverse—most of its students are in-state, Caucasian and middle-class—it offers its students various opportunities academically and socially. Kent State

University also has a network of regional campuses across Ohio, catering to commuter students.

Liberal Education at a Large University

Kent State University gives its students some freedom to choose their own schedules within the constraints of Liberal Education Requirements, or LER. Every undergraduate student must attain credit in composition, mathematics and critical reasoning, logic and foreign language, humanities and fine arts, social sciences, basic sciences and diversity. Most students seem to think that the LER is worthwhile, forcing them to explore classes they otherwise would not take.

"Human Sexuality" is a popular course, which one girl described as "one of the most fun classes I've taken in my life." Another popular class, a science class designed for non-science students, is called "Seven Ideas that Struck the Universe." Although most students seem to enjoy their classes, other students complain that the set of classes that complete the LER is too restricting.

Most introductory classes have 100 to 175 students, but the size can vary. Language classes and labs generally have less than 20 students, and class size drops once you start taking classes in the major. Professors teach all of the classes except labs, which are run by teaching assistants under the direction of a professor. Although there are no discussion sections to supplement lectures, professors have office hours set aside for helping students. The professors are for the most part approachable and helpful. Some professors even set time aside to help students on an Internet chat. These chats, as well as syllabi and class notes, are part of the Kent Web server.

Among the most popular majors at Kent, the fashion program is outstanding and is ranked as one of the top fashion programs in the nation. Some of the less popular majors are still high quality and offer excellent experiences. Many majors offer study abroad programs: The fashion and architecture programs offer studies in Venice, the journalism program in London and Paris, and the conservation program in Australia and Mexico.

Suitcasers and Party Animals

The weekend social life at Kent State is, for most of the campus, admittedly lacking. Many students describe Kent State as a "suitcase campus," where half the on-

campus students go home for the weekends. The students left on campus are left with a variety of things to do, though one must take the initiative to take advantage of the options.

Partying is a big deal for those left on campus for the weekends. Because drinking is strictly prohibited in most of the dorms, most of the partying occurs off campus at the fraternity houses. The Greek scene is influential on campus, because the frats host most of the parties. Some of the more elite national fraternities are on Frat Row, but those are mostly dry. The party fraternities are located off of East Main Street, a main strip that is a center of off-campus life. There are a lot of fast food joints on East Main, where students can often be seen "getting their 3 a.m. Taco Bell."

> Many students describe Kent State as a "suitcase campus," where half the on-campus students go home for the weekends.

For students who do not like the fraternity scene, there are a lot of other options. Upperclassmen usually hang out at their off-campus apartments. Wednesday is notorious for karaoke. On the weekends, those who are old enough go to the bars and clubs of downtown Kent. Many students spend their weekends participating in one of the multitude of extracurricular organizations. There are many different organizations on campus, some of the more popular being community service organizations, the College Democrats, the Dive (a Christian youth group started only a few years ago) and Project Sound (a group that brings local bands to campus). Other students play sports, and for those who do not go home for the weekend, joining a traveling sports team is a great alternative.

Sports are a big deal on campus. Basketball is especially popular, since the men's team enjoyed success in the NCAA tournament, reaching the Elite Eight in 2002. The football team is not as good, but still enjoys the prevalent Kent State pride. Intramural sports are also very competitive; one intramural softball team was even sponsored by a local business. The recent rage has been club dodge ball, which is played in one of the indoor facilities. The new recreation center sports two pools, indoor basketball, volleyball and track, a spa area and an indoor soccer arena.

On-Campus Housing: The "Freshman Experience" and More

Housing on campus is described as scarce. Not too long ago, a fire in one of the dorms caused students to be temporarily removed for cleanup, and the University had trouble finding space for the displaced students. Although there are some space issues, most students seemed satisfied with their experience in the dorms.

Freshmen have the option either to live in normal on-campus housing or to live in the special Freshman (or First Year) Experience dorms. Although the rooms in the Freshman Experience dorms are smaller, there are some benefits to staying in them. For one, only freshmen live in the dorms, so it makes it easy for new students to meet each other. Furthermore, they are smaller than normal dorms—at about 100 students, rather than about 750 students—which leads to a more intimate atmosphere.

Most students move off campus their junior year to apartments in the Kent area. The university requires that non-commuting students live on campus their first two years. The upperclassmen who choose to stay on campus have a pretty good choice of dorms. The standard room is a double, but some students pay more for a single, or buy out a quad with a friend for extra space. The housing has been undergoing renovation, and some "very elaborate" dorms were recently finished, which a senior called "an apartment on campus you don't have to clean." For this reason, there was an increase in upperclassmen living on campus a couple of years ago.

The security inside the dorms is fairly strict. One particularly annoyed student described the security guards as "pompous" and "self-righteous," but there is a general consensus that the policies are invasive. When an offense is committed, such as being caught drinking or partying, a strike is marked against a student. When a student accumulates enough strikes, they go to administrative courts. Although the police are not contacted, the process is still described as "irritating." Though alcohol is strictly prohibited in most dorms, there is "more [on-campus drinking] going on than people realize."

The food at Kent State gets mixed reviews from the students. One girl stated that the food is "OK, not as healthy as it could be," while another claims that "we have a very good variety." Students have a meal plan, which is based on credit that can be spent at a dining hall or at the food court. "The Hub" at the student center offers some fast food, including Quizno's, Einstein's Bagels, A&W and Ambrosia. There is even a restaurant, which offers full-service meals—a popular place to take someone out for a date. A lot of students carry a Flash Cash card, which works with the meal plan and is also accepted at most local businesses.

May 4, 1970, and Kent State Today

The incident on May 4, 1970, when four student protesters were shot and killed at Kent State, is a stunning reminder of the tension between students and the government. Today, there is a memorial to the event, and every year the campus throws a big party on the anniversary. In recent years, the partying has been curbed because of problems in the past with rowdy crowds.

The campus today is surprisingly apolitical. There is still some bad blood between the city of Kent and Kent State University, but political protests are not very common on campus. Political activism is kept at a minimum because of a "general apathy" around campus. One junior girl stated that "everyone has their own opinions, but nobody makes the effort to do anything with it." There has been some activity during recent presidential elections, but it is difficult to get the students interested in school politics. A "big protest" recently drew only 300 students.

Kent State University has a "pretty spread-out campus," with lots of open fields and sidewalks. There is a pretty forested area with a natural creek near the biology building. The architecture of the buildings varies. One can easily tell where they are by looking at the nearby buildings, as each area has a unique architecture. The art center in the center of campus is pretty and decorated with installation projects made by the students. Although a lot of students own cars, because of a parking problem most students walk around campus. The bus system has recently been revamped, and buses stop every seven minutes. Otherwise, it could take 30 minutes to walk across campus. During the "real bad-ass winter," the bus system becomes a serious boon to students, especially since the sidewalks do not always get plowed.

The campus is well-lit at night, and the students feel very safe, even when walking alone. Crime is a rare occurrence. There is an escort service available for those students who feel they need it. Overall, the campus receives high marks for atmosphere. The students are very comfortable, and all have loved their experiences there. One journalism major had misgivings when she came, but she soon changed her mind. She said, "Kent State grabbed me, pulled me in, and I never wanted to leave."—*Ryan Galisewski*

FYI

If you come to Kent State University, you'd better bring: "lots of extension cords, an umbrella and a car."

What's the typical weekend schedule? "Thursday—dance club or frat party, Friday—going to class hung-over and chilling with friends at night, Saturday—homework during the day and clubbing in Kent at night, Sunday—recovering and doing homework."

If I could change one thing about Kent State University, I'd "change the way the security is handled on on-campus living."

Three things every student at Kent State University should do before graduating are "check out the May 4 memorial and get a good understanding of what happened, experience the nightlife downtown and ride down a snowy hill on a cafeteria tray."

Kenyon College

Address: Ransom Hall Gambler, OH 43022
Phone: 740-427-5776
E-mail address: admissions@kenyon.edu
Web site URL: www.kenyon.edu
Year Founded: 1824
Private or Public: Private
Religious Affiliation: None
Location: Rural
Number of Applicants: 4,626
Percent Accepted: 29%
Percent Accepted who enroll: 34%
Number Entering: 458
Number of Transfers Accepted each Year: 10
Middle 50% SAT range: M: 630–690, CR: 630–730, Wr: 630–710
Middle 50% ACT range: 28–32
Early admission program EA/ED/None: ED

Percentage accepted through EA or ED: 41%
EA and ED deadline: 15-Nov
Regular Deadline: 15-Jan
Application Fee: $50
Full time Undergraduate enrollment: 1,663
Total enrollment: 1,663
Percent Male: 48%
Percent Female: 52%
Total Percent Minority or Unreported: 7%
Percent African-American: 4%
Percent Asian/Pacific Islander: 5%
Percent Hispanic: 3%
Percent Native-American: <1%
Percent International: 3%
Percent in-state/out of state: 20%/80%
Percent from Public HS: 47%
Retention Rate: 95%
Graduation Rate 4-year: 82%

Graduation Rate 6-year: 83%
Percent Undergraduates in On-campus housing: 98%
Number of official organized extracurricular organizations: 120
3 Most popular majors: English Language and Literature, Political Science and Government, Psychology
Student/Faculty ratio: 10:1
Average Class Size: 10 to 19
Percent of students going to grad school: 25%
Tuition and Fees: $39,080
In State Tuition and Fees if different: No difference
Cost for Room and Board: $6,590
Percent receiving financial aid out of those who apply, first year: 54%
Percent receiving financial aid among all students: 65%

Amidst the valleys and rolling hills of Gambier, Ohio, lies the rural liberal arts paradise that is Kenyon College. With only about 1,640 students, Kenyon has managed to carve out a reputation for itself as an academically challenging, artistically stimulating, and fun-loving place to spend those four formative years. And you can do it all surrounded by the pristine beauty of Kenyon's own nature preserve.

Comps but no Core

The small, intimate nature of the Kenyon community is definitely intensified when it comes to the academic community. Since the average class size is 14, students report that they definitely get a lot of one-on-one attention from their professors (and it's just professors—no TAs at Kenyon!). This can range from office hours to home visits, but professor accessibility is one of the highlights of academic life at Kenyon. In fact, one student said that, "There used to be a rule that all professors had to live on campus . . . It's not true anymore, but they're all still very close."

Rather than a standard set of core requirements, Kenyon students complete nine "units," or two semesters, of courses outside their own majors, whose requirements are often rigorous enough without the added stress. And, instead of a thesis, Kenyon seniors prepare senior "exercises," more popularly known as "comps," in which they execute some kind of culminating project that encapsulates their studies during the last four years. The comps allow for a whole range of creative freedom, but can be stressful. One senior double-major in English and Dance and Drama said that she's excited about the original play she is writing, but admitted that she "pretty much lives in the library these days."

Yet, all of these requirements do not deter determined Kenyon students from double majoring or from enjoying their classes in popular majors like English, psychology, and political science. And there are popular courses that draw in students from all sorts of specialty areas, including an anthropology seminar on drinking culture and an English course entitled, "Strange Fish and Bearded Women." Overall, while students agree that academics are "challenging, they are also definitely what you make of it—you get out what you put back in."

Frats and "Phling"

Outside of the classroom, Kenyon students are sociable and easy to get along with. As one student asserted, "Compared to other places I've been, this place is incredibly friendly." The small community makes it easy to make friends. "If you sit on the bench on Middle Path, you can see everyone at Kenyon pass by. It's impossible to walk somewhere and not see everyone you know." Yet, there is definitely a downside, as one senior admitted. "Everyone definitely knows everyone else's business here . . . we call it the fishbowl," he laughed. While the Kenyon community is made up of people from all different states and countries, the majority of the students at Kenyon are admittedly white and upper-middle-class. Yet, students are quick to say that Kenyon is an accepting and welcoming place, regardless of background.

While Kenyon is a beautiful and safe campus ("we don't even lock our doors here," one student said), it can also get to be "pretty isolated." Luckily, nearby Ohio towns and cities provide a whole host of entertainment options, including movie theaters in Columbus and bands at schools like Ohio State. Students report that while a car is helpful, it is not necessary, since there are shuttles that can take undergrads to nearby towns, and the campus itself is navigable on foot. Of course, for those who choose to stay on campus during the weekends, there is an incredible amount of things to do, from shows and concerts, to film series and frat parties. And students report that while, "you can always go to a frat party," Greek life definitely does not dominate the Kenyon social scene.

> "It's impossible to walk somewhere and not see everyone you know."

Kenyon is not a dry campus and one student claimed that, "most of the campus does drink." However, other students contended that, "you definitely don't have to drink here to have a good time." For those who prefer their weekends dry, the Kenyon After-Dark Society sponsors a whole host of activities, including first-run movie premieres and an Iron Chef Dessert contest, for people to enjoy (soberly or not). In fact, campus-wide parties and activities are an especially prominent part of Kenyon social life. One of the most popular is "Philander's Phebruary Phling," an event that takes place the first weekend in February. With a different theme every year, students get together to dance, drink, and stay warm during the onset of winter.

Life in the "Fishbowl"

All students at Kenyon must live on campus, which helps to make the housing process easier to settle than at other schools. Housing is determined by lottery, which can often be a hit-or-miss process, yet students report that they usually manage to live with friends and form even tighter bonds with roommates by the time they graduate. While one student said that, "The best way to describe our living conditions is Spartan," others insisted that the school's neo-Gothic architecture is "simple, but pretty." The different dorms at Kenyon do have their own distinct characters and features; Old Kenyon, the oldest building on campus, is supposedly haunted, while Cables is the tallest building in Knox County. There are Community Advisers (CAs) who live on both freshman and upperclassman halls, but students say that they aren't too strict.

When it comes to food, students report that the college has made a conscious effort to improve its culinary standing in the last few years. One senior stated that, "The food started out awful, but it's gotten a lot better over the last few years—there's a sushi place at the gym, and there's a lot more of a focus on vegan and vegetarian options." There's not actually a meal plan at Kenyon—students just get all-you-can-eat meals at Pierce, the school's one dining hall that has been recently renovated. For those hoping to find food elsewhere, students say that the Gambier Grille offers yummy and affordable American fare, while the Kenyon Inn is nice but a bit more expensive. And, if you're willing to drive, the Chinese and Mexican restaurants at Mt. Vernon are usually worth the trip.

Students at Kenyon can choose from a plethora of extracurricular activities to occupy their time. There are a capella and theater groups galore—in fact, many shows traditionally left a seat open during their performances for Paul Newman, one of the school's most famous alumnae. Sadly he recently died after a long-term illness and will be greatly missed. Community service is another outlet—students say that Habitat for Humanity is growing into an increasingly popular way to spend a Saturday morning. From hosting a show on Kenyon's radio station to joining the Mock Trial team, there is no shortage of opportunity to stay busy.

For the more athletically inclined, one of Kenyon's most famous Division III sports teams is the men's diving and swimming team, which has won 29 championships since 1980. The basketball and lacrosse teams are also growing in popularity, as is IM Ultimate Frisbee. In fact, the Kenyon College Ultimate Frisbee Team (KCUF) holds an event called the "Skivies Snow Bowl," in which players strip down to their underwear to play. One student admits that, "Student support for the sports teams tends to be a little lacking—we aren't a place with killer school spirit." Yet, the school's upcoming renovation of the gym and revamping of the intramural sports system leaves students optimistic about the future of Kenyon athletics.

Tradition!

Kenyon lore is rife with unique stories and enduring traditions. On the final night of freshman orientation, all freshmen stand on the steps of the theater building and sing Kenyon's four college songs as upperclassmen stand and jeer. Four years later, after their baccalaureate service, the seniors do it again, clothed in caps and gowns. It is this sense of community and continuity that binds Kenyon students together during their time together and makes the supportive and intimate atmosphere such a fun place to be, as one senior explained, "I love it here. I can safely say without feeling trite that this is truly a special place."—*Alexandra Bicks*

FYI

If you come to Kenyon, you'd better bring "a pair of boots—no one told me how cold Ohio would be and how much it would rain and snow!"

What's a typical weekend schedule? "Friday afternoon, finish up class, de-stress, dinner; Friday night, an a capella concert or a play, then a few different apt. parties (maybe the one bar on campus); Saturday, sleep in, work; Saturday night about the same (although maybe go out to eat one of those nights); Sunday, everyone does homework."

If I could change one thing about Kenyon, I'd "want there to be more diversity."

Three things everyone should do before graduating from Kenyon are: "Eat pie from Peggy Sue's (about 20 minutes away), go on Tim Shutt's ghost tour, go swimming in the nearby river down the hill."

Miami University

Address: 501 East High
Street Oxford, OH 45056
Phone: 513-529-1809
E-mail address:
admission@muohio.edu
Web site URL:
miami.muohio.edu
Year Founded: 1809
Private or Public: Public
Religious Affiliation: None
Location: Suburban
Number of Applicants:
15,009
Percent Accepted: 80%
**Percent Accepted who
enroll:** 31%
Number Entering: 3,727
**Number of Transfers
Accepted each Year:**
500+
Middle 50% SAT range:
Unreported
Middle 50% ACT range:
24–29
**Early admission program
EA/ED/None:** EA and ED

**Percentage accepted
through EA or ED:** 12%
EA and ED deadline: 1-Nov
Regular Deadline: 1-Dec,
1-Feb
Application Fee: $45
**Full time Undergraduate
enrollment:** 14,264
Total enrollment: 15,922
Percent Male: 46%
Percent Female: 54%
**Total Percent Minority or
Unreported:** 9%
Percent African-American:
3%
**Percent Asian/Pacific
Islander:** 3%
Percent Hispanic: 2%
Percent Native-American:
1%
Percent International: 1%
**Percent in-state/out of
state:** 70%/30%
Percent from Public HS:
Unreported
Retention Rate: 89%

Graduation Rate 4-year:
Unreported
Graduation Rate 6-year:
Unreported
**Percent Undergraduates in
On-campus housing:** 48%
**Number of official organized
extracurricular
organizations:** 350
3 Most popular majors:
Unreported
Student/Faculty ratio: 15:1
Average Class Size: 29
**Percent of students going to
grad school:** Unreported
Tuition and Fees: $25,207
**In State Tuition and Fees if
different:** $11,443
Cost for Room and Board:
$8,998
**Percent receiving financial
aid out of those who apply,
first year:** Unreported
**Percent receiving financial
aid among all students:**
Unreported

The deceptively named Miami University is not located in Miami, Florida. Rather, it is in Oxford, Ohio. The name came from the Miami Indians who used to live in the area. The tenth public college founded in the United States, Miami University offers "truly the quintessential college experience," said one freshman. Indeed, Miami University offers a combination of solid academics and strong party scene that is "just how I imagined college would be."

Hitting the Books

Miami University has a core curriculum of "Foundation Courses" that are usually taken during freshman and sophomore years. The requirement is met by taking 36 credit hours in English composition; the fine arts, humanities, and social sciences; cultures; natural sciences; and mathematics, formal reasoning, and technology. While introductory courses are large, the majority of classes are small. "You can really get to know your professors, though maybe less in your freshman year than as an upperclassman," said one junior.

The academic advising system is generally considered "solid." All students have a first-year advisor who lives with them in their dorm. Another advisor replaces the first one when a major is declared during sophomore year. A student's course in his or her major ends with the senior capstone, which is a project designed to combine a liberal arts education with the specialty of a major.

Because preference for class choices is given to athletes, graduate students and honor students, it can be nearly impossible for freshmen and sophomores to get into certain classes. However, "persistence pays off. If you hang around a class for long enough and talk to the teacher, you can usually find yourself a place," explained one sophomore.

Though "the schoolwork here can basically be as hard as you want to make it," students unanimously agree that the hardest majors are business and pre-med. The Oxford Scholars honors program is also challenging.

Also, Miami University ranks among the top institutions in the nation for the number of students participating in study abroad programs each year (more than 1,500). Many students opt to leave the country for a semester or a year, though the shorter summer programs are another popular option.

A Beautiful Campus

Robert Frost once said that Miami University is "the most beautiful college there is," and students take pride in their picturesque campus. "I'm a senior, and I'm still regularly in awe of how beautiful it is here," said one student. The colonial-style brick buildings divide the five sections of campus: the north, south, east, west, and central quads.

Students rave about how well their facilities are maintained. "Everything is kept very clean and pristine—my friends who visit are always surprised at how nicely our buildings are kept," said a sophomore. Dorm quality does vary, though, from the mediocre to the hotel-like. First-year residence halls are themed and offer theme-related events throughout the year. Types of hall themes include arts, foreign languages, health and wellness, honors and scholars, and leadership. After sophomore year, most students choose to move off campus and into the town of Oxford.

Dining hall food and services are well reviewed by students. Dining halls are located close to residences, and when the cafeterias close, there is a variety of late-night options available from a convenience store in the student center and other locations around campus. Popular options off-campus include the Alexander House, Kona, and Bagel and Deli.

Greek Life Dominates

Just less than half of the student body is involved with a fraternity or sorority, but students think that it often feels like many more students go Greek. "Being Greek is pretty much the only thing to do here if you want to have a social life," commented one student. "The school is located in a cornfield, and there's pretty much nothing to do but to drink," explained one freshman. "And you're going to drink with your fraternity or sorority." Indeed, the lack of any sort of off-campus scene is what drives so many students into the Greek system. Rushing is an important and stressful time on campus for the prospective Greek community.

Students enjoy the themed parties, semi-formals, and formals thrown by fraternities and sororities, but also insist that the Greek system is useful in other aspects. "Every group does support a cause and benefits the community," said one senior, who then admitted, "It's really all about the parties and socializing." Those few who insist on avoiding Greek life often live on West Campus.

> **"Every fraternity and sorority does support a cause and benefits the community . . . but it's really all about the parties and socializing."**

Aside from fraternities and sororities, there are many extracurricular activities from which to choose, ranging from career-focused groups to volunteer organizations. Intramural sports are also popular, especially broomball, a sport invented at Miami University that is played on ice without skates. Varsity sports are substantially less popular. Attendance at games is sparse, and only hockey games draw crowds.

Welcome to J. Crew U.

Students at Miami University are generally described as thin, blond, and rich. "Everyone drives huge SUVs and is very conservative," said a junior. The student body dresses mostly in clothes from J. Crew and Abercrombie, leading some to nickname Miami University "J. Crew U." The generally white, upper-middle class student body led one student to complain, "All Miami students are basically the same. It's very overbearing at times." A male student observed that much of the female population is very concerned with health, fitness, and physical appearance. However, one freshman also said that this means "everyone is very good-looking."

Miami's good academic program, beautiful campus, and lively social scene remain attractive despite the homogeneous student body and focus on physical appearance. Students say that in spite of Miami University's shortcomings, they "would definitely come to Miami if they had to do college all over again."—*Erica Rothman*

FYIs

If you come to Miami University, you'd better bring "the most recent J. Crew catalog."

What is the typical weekend schedule? "Drink on campus, drink in fraternities and sororities, and drink. Maybe you'll get some work in Sunday afternoon . . ."

If I could change one thing about Miami University, I'd "make the school more interested in its athletics."

Three things every student at Miami University should do before graduating are "play a game of broomball, spend some time abroad, and take pictures of campus to make all your friends at home jealous of how pretty your school is."

Oberlin College

Address: 101 North Professor Street Oberlin, OH 44074
Phone: 440-775-8411
E-mail address: college.admission@oberlin.edu
Web site URL: www.oberlin.edu
Year Founded: 1833
Private or Public: Private
Religious Affiliation: None
Location: Rural
Number of Applicants: 7,014
Percent Accepted: 31%
Percent Accepted who enroll: 34%
Number Entering: 745
Number of Transfers Accepted each Year: Unreported
Middle 50% SAT range: M: 610–710, CR: 640–750, Wr: 630–730
Middle 50% ACT range: 26–32
Early admission program EA/ED/None: ED

Percentage accepted through EA or ED: 60%
EA and ED deadline: 15-Nov
Regular Deadline: 15-Jan
Application Fee: $35
Full time Undergraduate enrollment: 2,839
Total enrollment: 2,865
Percent Male: 45%
Percent Female: 55%
Total Percent Minority or Unreported: 25%
Percent African-American: 6%
Percent Asian/Pacific Islander: 8%
Percent Hispanic: 5%
Percent Native-American: 1%
Percent International: 6%
Percent in-state/out of state: 10%/90%
Percent from Public HS: 60%
Retention Rate: 92%
Graduation Rate 4-year: 65%
Graduation Rate 6-year: Unreported

Percent Undergraduates in On-campus housing: 86%
Number of official organized extracurricular organizations: 125
3 Most popular majors: Visual and Performing Arts, Social Sciences, Biology
Student/Faculty ratio: 9:1
Average Class Size: Unreported
Percent of students going to grad school: Unreported
Tuition and Fees: $36,282
In State Tuition and Fees if different: No difference
Cost for Room and Board: $9,280
Percent receiving financial aid out of those who apply, first year: 88%
Percent receiving financial aid among all students: 53%

Oberlin's historical legacy as the first college to implement a number of revolutionary policies attracts an independent and diverse group of students to campus each year. The first college in the nation to admit students of color and the first to grant women a degree, Oberlin continues today to provide a freethinking atmosphere for its undergraduates.

Progressive Thinkers

Since its founding in 1833, Oberlin has always fostered liberal thinking. Just about 2,760 students attend Oberlin, with the majority enrolled in the College of Arts and Sciences and the remainder (about 500) enrolled in the highly regarded Conservatory of Music. "Obies" are required to fulfill basic distributional requirements in order to ensure a well-rounded liberal arts education. Students must take nine credit hours in each of three divisions (social and behavioral science, arts and humanities, and natural sciences and mathematics), in addition to satisfying nine hours of cultural diversity classes (i.e. foreign language classes). Demonstrated proficiency in writing and quantitative reasoning are also musts, but these skills can be proven through a wide range of classes.

Oberlin prides itself on small class sizes averaging 18 students and an easily accessible faculty. Visual performing arts, social sciences and biology are reported to be the most popular majors. For a liberal arts college of its size, Oberlin also boasts strong science programs. While students report few problems fulfilling distributions, some complained that getting into popular classes "can be really hard, especially for first years." On the whole however, students are pleased with the quality of Oberlin's academics.

> **"A great deal of latitude is granted to students in designing projects, and the final results range from historical research presentations to a newfound love of skiing."**

A number of alternative options for gaining credit are also available, and these unique opportunities are among most students' favorites. Winter Term, which takes place during the month of January, grants students an entire month to complete an independent or small group effort in one of three categories: academic study, personal growth, or field experience. A great deal of latitude is granted to students in designing projects, and the final results range from historical research presentations to a newfound love of skiing. Another of Oberlin's distinct offerings is ExCo, or Experimental College, which multiple students described as "a must-do" at Oberlin. ExCo is a completely student run department within the college that offers student taught classes in a wide variety of fields. ExCo subjects range from fishing to literature, and can be taught or taken for up to five hours of credit.

Horsecow Heaven

Oberlin is just about the furthest thing from a sports school. However, the Ultimate Frisbee team is nationally recognized and plays under quite a unique name: the Flying Horsecows. While the athletic scene may not be all that intense, music and the arts thrive at Oberlin. At the beginning of each semester, students are allowed to lease pieces of artwork by acclaimed artists such as Renoir and Warhol for a mere five dollars. As one student put it, "where else can students go to sleep with a Picasso above their heads?" Oberlin's reputation attracts a number of high quality music acts each semester, and it is possible to see a performance every night of the week.

Oberlin, Ohio (pop. 8,600) provides only a few alternatives to the on-campus social scene, and most students spend their weekends at parties in the dorms or in off-campus housing. The campus dance club, The 'Sco, is another popular hangout, as well as a major part of the music scene. Almost the entire campus can be found at the Drag Ball and Safer Sex Night, annual parties that Obies go all out for. Older students often travel the 35 miles into Cleveland to seek an alternative to the campus social scene, but most weekends there is something to be found on campus.

Hippie Haven

All kinds flock to Oberlin, but the school is well known for its "hippie environment." Shirts and shoes are seen as optional on campus, although the dining halls require both. The student body at Oberlin is truly diverse, in all senses of the term. The campus is consistently ranked as one of the most politically active in the nation, and the student body is well informed and extremely socially active.

Freshmen live on campus, generally in two person dorm rooms. The living environment is relaxed, and advisors give their charges a great deal of leniency. In addition to college-owned housing, a relatively large group of students go independent, often living in co-ops or large off-campus houses although this practice will be discontinued as of next year and all students will live in college-owned housing. Additionally, there are a number of cultural houses for those who are interested in a foreign language. The dining system isn't ideal, but the food is reported to be "pretty good, surprisingly" although some students wish that there were more options. Overall, Oberlin's students are a relatively easy-going bunch who are happy with their college and chose it for its laid-back attitude.—*Bob Casey*

FYI

If you come to Oberlin, you better bring "yourself. You as you truly are. You'll finally be in a place where you can be accepted. Not by everybody, of course, but by most of us."

What's the typical weekend schedule? "Stay up till the wee hours with friends, sleep in till the late morning/early afternoon, hip-hop dance practice Saturday evening, tumbling Sunday evening (immediately followed by fourth meal), and probably some other meetings and events in there, too. The time between all of that is full of work."

If I could change one thing about Oberlin, I'd . . . "make it easier to get into the classes you want."

Three things every student at Oberlin should do before graduating are "Take full advantage of the ExCo classes, meet lots of different people—it's an extremely diverse group with a great deal to share, and use Winter Terms to the fullest possible extent—they're a chance to learn about the things you want. It's a sweet opportunity."

Ohio State University

Address: 190 N. Oval Mall Columbus, OH 43210
Phone: 614-292-3980
E-mail address: askabuckeye@osu.edu
Web site URL: www.osu.edu
Year Founded: 1870
Private or Public: Public
Religious Affiliation: None
Location: Urban
Number of Applicants: 21,508
Percent Accepted: 59%
Percent Accepted who enroll: 49%
Number Entering: 6,168
Number of Transfers Accepted each Year: 2,198
Middle 50% SAT range: Unreported
Middle 50% ACT range: 25–29
Early admission program EA/ED/None: None
Percentage accepted through EA or ED: NA

EA and ED deadline: NA
Regular Deadline: 1-Feb
Application Fee: $40
Full time Undergraduate enrollment: 39,209
Total enrollment: 52,568
Percent Male: 51%
Percent Female: 49%
Total Percent Minority or Unreported: 15%
Percent African-American: 7%
Percent Asian/Pacific Islander: 5%
Percent Hispanic: 3%
Percent Native-American: 1%
Percent International: Unreported
Percent in-state/out of state: 89%/11%
Percent from Public HS: Unreported
Retention Rate: 92%
Graduation Rate 4-year: 46%

Graduation Rate 6-year: 71%
Percent Undergraduates in On-campus housing: 24%
Number of official organized extracurricular organizations: 800
3 Most popular majors: Biology, Political Science, Psychology
Student/Faculty ratio: 13:1
Average Class Size: Unreported
Percent of students going to grad school: Unreported
Tuition and Fees: $21,015
In State Tuition and Fees if different: $8,298
Cost for Room and Board: $7,365
Percent receiving financial aid out of those who apply, first year: 89%
Percent receiving financial aid among all students: Unreported

O hio State has its own airport. Not every university can boast that, but then and again, not every university can say that it is the largest university in the United States. Ohio State stands as the flagship establishment of the state's public system of superior education, and is widely regarded as the best public university in Ohio. In this Big Ten School, everything is supersized—from the student body to the academic choices, the football games to the extracurricular activities. As one current sophomore said, "You cannot describe Ohio State without using a superlative."

Size Does Matter!

"When I tell people I meet that I go to OSU, the first thing they say is how big it is," said one undergraduate. Located in Columbus, Ohio State University is surrounded by over a million and a half people. Ohio's government, various professional sports teams, and various unique venues all surround the school and provide tons of possibilities for students to explore their environment and act as contributing citizens.

When the school was established in 1870, the founders intended to prepare students for a career in fields related to mechanics and agriculture. School administrators have extended this traditional curriculum to include both liberal arts and technical studies. Inside the walls of the school, students intermingle, intellectualize, and enjoy the giant campus. With over 160 different majors and 20 different undergraduate schools and colleges, students are hardly limited when it comes to class choice and student interest.

"We are literally surrounded by opportunities," one junior said. "If you want to do it, it's there." Another student agreed: "OSU's big size is what makes OSU such a great school."

For such a large university, classes tend to be relatively small. Only 6 percent of classes are over 100 students, and 77 percent of classes are capped at 39 students. Undergrads say that regardless of class size, "professors are accessible and are willing to meet. Many are especially good at responding to e-mails when students have questions regarding the class material."

Living in the Buckeye State

Freshmen are required to live on campus unless they are commuting. Students reside in what OSU refers to as "towers" and "houses." The difference between the two is that towers tend to be high-rise buildings of over 20 stories, whereas houses tend to stand only three floors high. There are 31 different residence halls on campus, and many are devoted to themed housing such as the First Year Collegian Learning Community, which offers math and science tutoring in the dorms, and the Spanish Language and Culture Halls, which feature conversation tables and a close relationship with the Ohio State Department of Spanish. Most students recommend the South Campus dorms for their location and atmosphere. One student said that "the three residential areas attract very different crowds, and all three have different vibes. South Campus definitely attracts the livelier crowd."

Ohio State offers five different dining plans, ranging from the Deluxe Plan (250 "swipes" or meals per quarter) to Commuter Plus (40 swipes per quarter). As for eating locations, students may choose from places such as all-you-can-eat North Commons and Kennedy Commons, the take-out fast-food restaurant Buckeye Express, or even Viewpoint Bistro, which will cost two to three swipes in exchange for waiter service. Ohio State students also relish in the opportunity to enjoy the abundance of restaurants on High Street. As one former student said, "You can find anything your mouth desires on High Street. There are four-star restaurants and many small cafes. Food there, overall, is edible."

Greek Life and the Social Scene

Consistently ranked among the top party schools in the nation, Greek life plays a large part of the social scene at Ohio State. The biggest campus parties and events are sponsored and held by fraternities and sororities. The best place to find a good party on campus is on Indianola Street, where many of the Greek organizations are. Students tend to party-hop all night long, but the fun doesn't stop when the sun rises. During OSU football games, the streets are filled with people tailgating. Despite their killer keggers, most students agree that Greeks' contributions to the OSU community extend beyond their conspicuous penchant for partying—most notably, their involvement with community service.

> **"You cannot describe Ohio State without using a superlative."**

If the Greek scene doesn't sound appealing, there is no cause for worry. Ohio State offers more than 800 registered student organizations and the vast array of cultures, ethnicities, and religious groups make exploring new experiences at OSU an endless adventure. It's impossible to pass the Oval, which one student describes as "our huge kinda Central Park–ish thing," without seeing one student group or another promoting a cause. Ohio State students can always be seen playing football, debating, tanning, and maybe even attending an Earth Sciences class or a Tai Chi lesson smack in the middle of the Oval.

O-HI-OOOO!

"Football at OSU is almost a religion," said one junior. "Even if you don't like it coming in, you'll love it coming out." Another student said, "No one cares about hating [Michigan] the state, but definitely the school." Together, these two students are describing "The Game"—the annual Ohio State versus Michigan football game. The bitter rivalry is lived out through an intense week aptly titled "Beat Michigan Week," which is dense with partying and proud displays of the student body's hard-core school spirit, such as jumping into Mirror Lake with fellow Buckeyes while singing and chanting.

While the attachment that Ohio State students hold for their football team may be overwhelming for some, in the end, "what it comes down to is a deep love for our college and everything that endear us to it."—*Daniel Friedman and Christine Grace Lin*

FYI

If you come to OSU you better bring "a wardrobe that includes a lot of red and buckeye pride!"

What's the typical weekend schedule? "Kegs and eggs for breakfast, and football. Attend a game or watch it on TV. Either way, no exceptions."

If I could change one thing about OSU, I'd "change the police and parking rules . . . the police seem to pull people over a lot because they're bored. And parking is horrible!"

Three things every OSU student should do before graduating are: "attend an OSU football game with 100,000 ebullient people in scarlet attire, sit by Mirror Lake at night, and run across the oval naked at night."

Ohio University

Address: 120 Chubb Hall Athens, OH 45701-2979
Phone: 740-593-4100
E-mail address: admissions@ohio.edu
Web site URL: www.ohio.edu/admissions
Year Founded: 1804
Private or Public: Public
Religious Affiliation: None
Location: Rural
Number of Applicants: 14,046
Percent Accepted: 78%
Percent Accepted who enroll: 37%
Number Entering: 4,503
Number of Transfers Accepted each Year: 859
Middle 50% SAT range: M: 490–600, CR: 480–600, Wr: 470–580
Middle 50% ACT range: 21–26
Early admission program EA/ED/None: None

Percentage accepted through EA or ED: NA
EA and ED deadline: NA
Regular Deadline: 1-Feb
Application Fee: $45
Full time Undergraduate enrollment: 16,189
Total enrollment: 20,960
Percent Male: 49%
Percent Female: 51%
Total Percent Minority or Unreported: 11%
Percent African-American: 5%
Percent Asian/Pacific Islander: 1%
Percent Hispanic: 2%
Percent Native-American: 0%
Percent International: 3%
Percent in-state/out of state: 89%/11%
Percent from Public HS: 89%
Retention Rate: 80%
Graduation Rate 4-year: 48%

Graduation Rate 6-year: 71%
Percent Undergraduates in On-campus housing: 46%
Number of official organized extracurricular organizations: 360
3 Most popular majors: Recreation & Sports Sciences, Journalism, Psychology
Student/Faculty ratio: 19:1
Average Class Size: 24
Percent of students going to grad school: 25%
Tuition and Fees: $17,871
In State Tuition and Fees if different: $8,907
Cost for Room and Board: $8,946
Percent receiving financial aid out of those who apply, first year: 26%
Percent receiving financial aid among all students: 23%

According to legend, Athens, Ohio, is one of the most haunted cities in the United States. Superstition holds that Athens, home to the Ohio University Bobcats, lies at the center of a pentangle formed by five cemeteries where witches were hung in the 1700s. This geographic peculiarity supposedly causes the campus to be inhabited by a variety of spooks and spirits. Some Bobcats report that, while lying in bed while no one else is in the room, they have heard phantom typing on their computer keyboards. Others note that in one room on the fourth floor of Wilson Hall, the grains of wood on one door form a demon's face—this room has had so many reports of haunting that the University no longer assigns students to live there. Ghoulish stories, however, have certainly not scared students away from this school. Combining a well-deserved party school reputation with solid academic programs and a picturesque campus, it's no wonder that neither the ghosts nor the students want to leave OU.

Bobcats Hit the Books

OU, as one sophomore observed, is "more than just a party school; the academics are really good, too." Regardless of major, all OU students have to complete a series of requirements known as "tiers." Tier I consists of freshman English and math. Tier II involves 30 credit hours of classes in a cross-section of academic subjects. Tier III requires a junior-level English composition course. Students have mixed opinions about the tier system, some saying that they appreciate the opportunity to take classes outside of their major, while others complain that "the extra classes are a waste of tuition money."

Luckily for those who don't enjoy completing their tiers, students only have to put up with each class for two and a half months. OU operates on the quarter system, so students enroll in three ten-week terms per academic year instead of two longer semesters like at most universities. As a result, school starts in mid September, finishes in June, and provides a six-week break between the fall and winter terms that lasts from Thanksgiving until after New Years. Because of the short terms, classes meet either every day or in two-hour, twice-a-week sessions. One junior commented that a perk of the quarter system is that "we're on campus for the really nice weather in spring," while a sophomore said she liked the schedule because "if you've had a bad term, you get a fresh start in just a few weeks."

With 10 different colleges and an assortment of well-respected programs, there's something at OU to satisfy any academic interest. Boasting such standout graduates as *The Today Show*'s Matt Lauer, the Scripps College of Communication is unanimously cited as OU's best program, and one of the most selective. Other strong majors include business, engineering and pre-med, while majors in retail merchandising and in sports administration are considered somewhat less challenging. In order to begin taking upper-level classes, students must apply to the college in which they want to major. Most upper-level classes have about 20 or 30 students whereas intro classes can enroll up to 300 students. One sophomore cited this as a problem for freshmen undecided about their major, since the application process only takes place in the fall and "it can be hard to fit all your classes in four years, and lots of students end up staying for extra terms."

Students looking for an easy term can take guts like Health 101, Engineering Technology 280, art, or a "University College" class that teaches study skills and research techniques. Science classes are said to be more challenging. Chemistry 151 is known to be the hardest class at OU, and rumor has it that nearly a third of students fail the first time they take it. Despite a few particularly hard classes, OU academics are generally found to be manageable. One junior described his course load as "moderate; it's not really easy but I can get my work done." Though some grumble about TAs who speak poor English or annoying system backups during the online course-registration procedure, on the whole students are more than pleased with the quality of academics.

Good Dorms, Bad Eats

Despite occasional reports of poltergeists, most OU students are satisfied with their living arrangements. Students are required to live in the dorms for both freshman and sophomore years, in their choice of either single-sex or coed buildings. Most of the dorms have air-conditioning, and most rooms are doubles with common bathrooms on each hall. Although dorms on the West Green quad are generally considered nicer than those on the New South quad, most students like living on campus in general because "it gives you the chance to meet people you'd never think to talk to otherwise," according to one sophomore. Most students move into off-campus housing for junior and senior years. These houses are in "student ghettos" where college students rent most of the houses, and none are more than a 10-minute walk from campus. "I love living off campus; it's cheaper and more relaxed," chimed in one student.

The rooms may be popular, but the dining halls are not. The major complaint about living on campus is the dining hall food. "It's horrible," one sophomore said, "I think they put laxatives in it because it just runs right through you." A senior commented that dining hall food is "really redundant, and you can't really eat healthily at all." Others complain about the dining halls' limited hours of operation. On-campus dining does have a few perks though. The Flex 20 meal plan option allows students to get cash for the meals they don't use, and the Grab n Go café lets students use their meal plan to purchase packaged food to take back to their rooms.

Life of the Party

The best aspect of OU, according to one student, is that "everyone goes out, and every night there's something to do." While the social scene caters to partygoers, there are enough options to ensure that every Bobcat has a great time. About a third of students join a fraternity or sorority at OU, making the Greek scene a powerful social force on campus. In addition to Friday and Saturday night frat house parties that draw large crowds, Greeks sponsor some popular annual parties. One such party is Derby Days, a party held in a cornfield one Saturday during spring term where bands play and kegs flow from morning until night. With the exception of a few invite-only parties, most Greek events are open to the general student body, although one sophomore noted that "girls are pretty much always welcome at frat parties, but sometimes they're stricter about non-Greek guys." Students agree that there's no pressure to rush. One male junior observed that "it's not like you're considered un-cool if you're not in a frat," and a female student agreed that "you don't feel obligated to be in a sorority." There's no real social division between Greeks and non-Greeks, since "you have to live in the dorms for two years regardless, so you make a lot of friends both in and out of the Greek system."

> "The Halloween Party is insane; it's like nothing I ever expected!"

OU has an equally vibrant non-Greek party scene. Upperclassmen enjoy hanging out at Athens bars, of which there are more than 20, especially during the legendary themed Court Street Shuffle, when students go from bar to bar and have a drink at each one. Shuffles feature official t-shirts that students try to get signed at each bar. House parties are frequent and open to everyone. According to one sophomore, "you can basically walk into any party even if you don't know anyone and have a great time; everyone's so cool and friendly." Every year, streets populated by student houses throw huge parties like Palmer Fest, Oak Fest and High Fest, where the streets are closed off and filled with students while each house hosts a party.

Given the supernatural legends surrounding OU, it is appropriate that the biggest of these block parties is the annual Halloween festivities. Court Street, the main street in Athens, shuts down completely as more than 30,000 students descend on OU from universities all over Ohio. "Everyone dresses up and gets trashed. It's a mile-worth of kids standing shoulder to shoulder," explained one sophomore. Another student raved, "the Halloween Street Party is insane; it's like nothing I ever expected!" Clearly, drinking is an important part of the OU social life. Despite recent administrative attempts to crack down on campus drinking, including increases in the police force patrolling the streets on weekend nights, alcohol is readily accessible to those who want it. Non-drinkers need not feel excluded from OU social life however. As one sophomore said, "I didn't drink much at all my freshman year and I still went to all the parties and had a great time."

Another remarkable feature of the social scene at OU is the friendliness of the student body. "Everyone is pretty close knit here," commented one junior. A senior described the average student as "preppy, but not stuck up, really down-to-earth, friendly, good people." About 90 percent of the student body hails from Ohio, which does lead a lot of students to hang out with high school friends at first, but most upperclassmen agree that by the end of freshman year they've met most of their friends through classes or the dorms. The University is also predominantly white—whitest Ohio public university. One sophomore summed up the student body best: "students here are really chill; they're serious about school during the week so they can go out and party with their friends on the weekends."

A Red-Brick Beauty

Located in the wooded hills of Ohio, Athens was originally a manufacturing town that produced a large proportion of the country's bricks. Though most industry has since left the area, the legacy of the town's past is clearly visible on OU's campus, which many students name as their favorite feature of the school. One sophomore described the campus as "something you'd see in a movie," with large, tree-lined quads surrounded by beautiful, red-brick, colonial architecture. Students take advantage of their surroundings during the warmer fall and spring quarters by studying under a tree, sunbathing, "folfing" (Frisbee golfing), or just hanging out in the courtyards outside the dorms. Although the architecture remains old-fashioned, recent additions and renovations to science and political science buildings keep the campus updated. The Hocking River runs through the center of the hilly grounds, and the brick streets and sidewalks visually tie the campus and the city together.

The city is a "good mix between urbanism and trees," commented one junior, who added that one of the things he likes best about the small-town environment "is that Athens is basically a walking town—you can get anywhere in 15 minutes without a car." Although some students lament that Athens' small size makes them feel like they live in "the middle of nowhere," most are enthusiastic about the options available downtown. Since Athens is primarily a university town, many of the restaurants and bars cater to college students. In addition to the multitude of bars and clubs, popular late-night destinations include restaurants like the Pita Pit, Goodfellas Pizza, Burrito Buggy and a calzone restaurant called DP Dough, all of which are open until the wee hours of the morning so that students can grab a late-night meal. Policemen on horseback ensure the safety of the campus, and the mass of student housing surrounding the downtown area makes students feel at home off campus as well as on.

Athletics and Extracurriculars

After dividing their time between academics and partying, many students say they don't have much energy to devote to dozens of extracurricular interests. For those students who do wish to get involved in extracurriculars, OU offers a variety of opportunities. Many organizations relate directly to students' majors, like the business fraternity, the newspaper run by journalism students or the radio station run by telecommunications majors. Other popular organizations include the Ski Club, which takes an annual trip to Colorado during winter break and a whitewater rafting trip in West Virginia during spring break, and the student govern-

ment groups in every dorm. Many students opt to work, often in on-campus jobs in the library or dining halls. "The jobs start at minimum wage," said one sophomore dining hall employee, "but you get raises quickly and a discount on your meal plan." Intramural sports, or "IMs," are one of the most popular extracurricular options. With IM leagues in everything from flag football to Ultimate Frisbee to table tennis, students sign up in teams with friends, dorm mates, or members of their fraternity or sorority to engage in friendly competition once or twice a week.

In addition to participation in IM sports, athletically inclined OU students have the opportunity to make use of one of the finest student gyms in the country. The Ping Recreation Center, over 168,000 square feet, houses everything you could possibly want, from weights to tennis courts to a swimming pool to aerobics classes. Although the Ping Center is one of the most popular and heavily used resources on campus, attendance at varsity sporting events is much sparser. As one junior observed, "the football team sucks, so no one goes to the games." Although the basketball, baseball and club hockey teams are somewhat more popular, on the whole "there's not much school spirit in terms of athletics."

In spite of the lack of sports fans, OU students love their school and hardly mind the shoddy performance of the Bobcat athletic teams. One junior said that students enjoy being on campus so much that "no one wants to go home when classes are over in the spring!" From its wild parties to its beautiful campus, from the friendly students inhabiting it to the ghostly legends surrounding it, OU is a unique institution that inspires enthusiasm in its students. One sophomore said, "I feel at home here. It's a great atmosphere to learn in, and everyone makes you feel so comfortable. I wouldn't want to go anywhere else."—*Katherine Kirby Smith*

FYI

If you come to OU, you'd better bring "a beer bong, a fake ID, an iron stomach to handle the dining hall food and a warm coat for the frigid winter quarter."

What is the typical weekend schedule? "Friday: pre-game in the dorms, go out to a house party or frat party, hit up the bars, get some pizza at Goodfellas, go home and sleep until mid-afternoon. Saturday: do it all again. Sunday: sleep all day, try to do some work."

If I could change one thing about OU, I'd change the "strictness of the campus police."

Three things every student at OU should do before graduating are "party at Halloween, go to Derby Days, and do the Court Street Shuffle on Moms' Weekend."

Ohio Wesleyan University

Address: 61 South Sandusky
 Street Delaware, OH 43015
Phone: 740-368-3020
E-mail address:
 owuadmit@owu.edu
Web site URL: www.owu.edu
Year Founded: 1842
Private or Public: Private
Religious Affiliation:
 Methodist
Location: Suburban
Number of Applicants: 3,814
Percent Accepted: 66%
**Percent Accepted who
 enroll:** 23%
Number Entering: 576
**Number of Transfers
 Accepted each Year:**
 Unreported
Middle 50% SAT range:
 M: 540–650, CR: 530–650,
 Wr: Unreported
Middle 50% ACT range:
 24–29
**Early admission program
 EA/ED/None:** EA and ED

**Percentage accepted
 through EA or ED:**
 Unreported
EA and ED deadline: 1-Dec
Regular Deadline: 1-Mar
Application Fee: $35
**Full time Undergraduate
 enrollment:** 1,960
Total enrollment: 1,960
Percent Male: 48%
Percent Female: 52%
**Total Percent Minority or
 Unreported:** 21%
Percent African-American:
 5%
**Percent Asian/Pacific
 Islander:** 2%
Percent Hispanic: 1%
Percent Native-American:
 0%
Percent International: 9%
**Percent in-state/out of
 state:** 54%/66%
Percent from Public HS: 77%
Retention Rate: 84%
Graduation Rate 4-year: 60%

Graduation Rate 6-year:
 Unreported
**Percent Undergraduates in
 On-campus housing:** 82%
**Number of official organized
 extracurricular
 organizations:** 86
3 Most popular majors:
 Economics, Pre-med,
 Psychology
Student/Faculty ratio: 12:1
Average Class Size:
 Unreported
**Percent of students going to
 grad school:** 32%
Tuition and Fees: $33,660
**In State Tuition and Fees if
 different:** No difference
Cost for Room and Board:
 $8,270
**Percent receiving financial
 aid out of those who apply,
 first year:** 88%
**Percent receiving financial
 aid among all students:**
 60%

I f you didn't know it was there, you might drive past the tiny town of Delaware, Ohio, population 31,000, without a second glance. But at the core of this small community there is a thriving college with students passionate enough to more than compensate for their low numbers. At Ohio Wesleyan University, you will find a campus that celebrates its Midwestern friendliness, with a close-knit undergraduate community of exceptionally warm and down-to-earth students who make the town worth much more than just a passing glimpse.

A Full Spectrum of Knowledge: OWU and the Liberal Arts Education

When it comes to academics, OWU sends a clear message to its students: education requires knowledge and proficiency in a broad range of areas, which leads to the fairly expansive set of Distributional Requirements. In addition to three classes each in the humanities, social sciences, and natural sciences, students are required to take two semesters of writing-intensive classes, a for-

eign language, and diversity-geared courses as well as one fine art class and a new one-semester quantitative reasoning requirement. Although this may seem overwhelming, students say that a wide range of interesting classes can fulfill the requirements. One student remarked, "I like to be able to choose classes I like within a department." Others, however, take a different course: "Personally, I don't seek out classes that fill requirements; I just look for classes I find interesting and fulfill requirements along the way."

Nor is it a problem if a student wants a more academically challenging schedule within the OWU environment. The Ohio Wesleyan Honors Program is open to freshmen based on their high school GPA and standardized test scores, but it is also possible to join later as an upperclassman. One honors student said the program "opens up a lot of interdisciplinary courses" that she would not otherwise have been exposed to, and that while "expectations are higher in terms of quality," the quantity of work does not increase significantly. One student described the program in terms of being "faster and more in-depth," but also noted that "all the majors have difficult courses." Because of this, other students are valuable resources as unofficial advisers when choosing a schedule. Some areas are always difficult, and popular majors including Zoology, Psychology, Education, and Politics & Government all have their fair share of challenging coursework.

OWU tends to stress sciences over the humanities, although the less scientifically inclined students feel that their smaller programs give them closer relationships with professors who really care about both the material and their students. One English major said that "professors make themselves really available—they take their jobs as teachers very seriously." Professors can focus their full attention on the undergraduates, as one junior remarked: "You get to know the teachers as well as you know the other students." This extends to class work as well, since professors have a strong hand in shaping the curriculum. Because professors teach what they like, students find them engaging, dynamic, and relevant.

Dorm-Dwellers and SLUTs

OWU has all the housing fixtures one might expect in a college setting, but what sets the college apart is its unique cluster of "SLUs," or Small Living Units. The students who decide to take advantage of these themed houses are affectionately referred to as "SLUTs," or Small Living Unit Tenants. Each SLU holds events and lectures that relate to its focus, and they also offer an alternative to the frat party scene. The interests covered by the SLUs are many and varied, some of which are the Women's House, the International House, and the philosophical House of Thought. With so many areas covered, many students find a niche in SLUs. All freshmen live in the dorms along with most sophomores; it is only in the junior year that people begin to move off campus, although even juniors tend to stay. One sophomore noted that OWU is "a very residential campus."

Geography 101

When students live where they eat and study where they sleep, there will understandably be some feeling of claustrophobia. OWU combats these limitations with its unique dumbbell-shaped campus, which has academic buildings on one side with residential housing on the other, connected by a main "highway" called the JAYwalk. The walkway serves as a common meeting-place for students to see and be seen between classes, and is also flanked by the James A. Young Memorial Library. One sophomore said, "There is a consistent flow of people at certain hours of the day, and most students eat lunch on the JAYwalk." This central hangout is in the middle of an eclectic and architecturally varied campus—students all agree that the mixed architecture lends OWU a distinctly diverse feel.

The Alpha, Beta, Gammas of OWU Social Life

"Wednesday is the new Thursday," remarked one sophomore, when asked about the campus party scene. Other students concur, mentioning Friday and Saturday in addition to Wednesday as the biggest party days at OWU. As for how students get down on those nights, people mentioned a variety of locales: Delaware bars, off-campus apartment parties, SLU parties, and, most frequently, frat parties. One Delta Gamma sister estimated that 30 percent of students are somehow involved in Greek life on campus, and she said that the fraternity and sorority system has a strong presence, especially in the social life of OWU students. Although one senior mentioned that "people party with their own social groups," dance parties tend to bring people together and mix groups.

> "The professors take their jobs as teachers very seriously, and both the students and the faculty are very invested in providing an enriching experience for everyone."

As for the inevitable problems that arise from college partying, students say that the on-campus public safety officers are often willing to let alcohol charges drop if the student is polite. Students applaud the university's decision to charge students for possession rather than consumption, which allows ill students to go to the hospital for help without getting in trouble. While the off-campus police tend to be much stricter, one sophomore says that on university property, "there is an understanding that drinking occurs, and they're more worried about our safety than the fact that we drink."

Crossing the Delaware

If frat parties aren't so appealing, it might be difficult to find something to do on a weekend night. "There's not a lot to do in Delaware," admitted one sophomore, who also noted that "Columbus is a tease because it's not as close as you think it is." Delaware's small size led one senior to remark that "the town exists because the college is here." However, others point to eclectic boutiques and high-quality restaurants as characteristic of their college's hometown. Students generally feel some connection to the town and don't find relations to be particularly hostile, but all mention that there could be quite a bit of improvement. One student noted, "You could go through four years at OWU without meeting people in Delaware, but there are a lot of connections if you look for them."

After the Library Closes

OWU students are dedicated to their academic lives, but they are also committed to many activities outside the classroom. From advocacy groups such as STAND (Students Taking Action Now: Darfur) to warm and fuzzy clubs like Pet Pals, which allows students to work at animal shelters, OWU offers a large variety of extracurriculars, especially given its small size. Highlights include the WCSA, the student government, which is very active and plays a large role in decision-making on campus. Students say that it is easy to get involved with groups as early as freshman year. One sophomore noted, "Attendance can be a problem in terms of turnout, but those who are in the clubs are very dedicated."

Sports also have a large presence in the campus community. Students mention that there is a fair amount of school pride, although potentially somewhat less than at other schools. But people turn out for big games such as Homecoming and rivalry match ups, and the Division III standing attracts some athletes who want to play in more games. In addition to involvement in a varsity sport, many people decide to play at the intramural or club level. The school has recently worked on the athletic fields and the gym, so there is a clear emphasis on sports as an important part of the school environment and many athletes to reap the benefits.

According to students, the undergrads at OWU are always willing to meet new people and work in different settings. That enthusiasm permeates the entire campus, as one student pointed to the "friendly, open atmosphere" as a major reason she decided to attend OWU. At a place where "the students and the faculty are very invested in providing an enriching experience for everyone," it is important to note that a good quality to bring is the desire to know everyone on campus. One student put it perfectly: "Although there are many different small groups on campus, there is a great sense of a larger community—coming in I had a good feeling about it, and that stuck with me."—*Hannah Jacobson*

FYI

If you come to Ohio Wesleyan, you'd better bring "an umbrella—the weather in Ohio is very unpredictable!"

What is the typical weekend schedule? "Get out of class and take a nap before meeting up with people for dinner and then pregaming in a group. Go to at least one party or jump between a few on Friday night. Eat a late lunch on Saturday, go out that night, and worry about homework on Sunday. And sleep a lot—you don't have time to do that during the week!"

If I could change one thing about Ohio Wesleyan, I'd "make it more handicapped accessible."

Three things every student at Ohio Wesleyan should do before graduating are "go to an SLU party, attend a reception at Professor Olmstead's house, and go to the academic side of campus at night to see the stained glass windows in Slocum Hall!"

University of Cincinnati

Address: P.O. Box 210091
Cincinnati, OH 45221-0091
Phone: 513-556-1100
E-mail address:
admissions@uc.edu
Web site URL: www.uc.edu
Year Founded: 1819
Private or Public: Public
Religious Affiliation: None
Location: Urban
Number of Applicants:
11,876
Percent Accepted: 75%
Percent Accepted who
enroll: 40%
Number Entering: 3,528
Number of Transfers
Accepted each Year:
1,542
Middle 50% SAT range:
M: 500–630, CR: 490–610,
Wr: 470–590
Middle 50% ACT range:
21–27
Early admission program
EA/ED/None: None

Percentage accepted
through EA or ED: NA
EA and ED deadline: NA
Regular Deadline: 1-Sep
Application Fee: $40
Full time Undergraduate
enrollment: 20,501
Total enrollment: 28,332
Percent Male: 50%
Percent Female: 50%
Total Percent Minority or
Unreported: 23%
Percent African-American:
12%
Percent Asian/Pacific
Islander: 3%
Percent Hispanic: 2%
Percent Native-American:
<1%
Percent International: 1%
Percent in-state/out of
state: 90%/10%
Percent from Public HS:
Unreported
Retention Rate: 82%
Graduation Rate 4-year: 19%

Graduation Rate 6-year:
54%
Percent Undergraduates in
On-campus housing: 71%
Number of official organized
extracurricular
organizations: 250
3 Most popular majors:
Communications, Marketing,
Psychology
Student/Faculty ratio: 14:1
Average Class Size: 10 to
19
Percent of students going to
grad school: Unreported
Tuition and Fees: $23,922
In State Tuition and Fees if
different: $9,399
Cost for Room and Board:
$9,240
Percent receiving financial
aid out of those who apply,
first year: 60%
Percent receiving financial
aid among all students:
78%

Looking for "hands-on-based knowledge" that gives you that extra edge with job placement? Look no further than Cincinnati. This "not-that-spread-out" campus located in scenic downtown Cincinnati, Ohio, has everything a student could want . . . at least, it will after the construction is finished.

More Songs About Buildings

Trying to overcome its reputation as a commuter school, UC is a campus marked by rapid change and construction intended to promote campus unity and spirit. Said one engineering student, "UC stands for 'Under Construction' forever." She further explained that although the head of the University has attested that there are no plans for future projects, it was apparent that the campus would be under construction through 2010 or beyond. However, the construction is not all bad. Another student remarked "they are really trying to improve and create a nicer atmosphere for the students." To create a more central gathering place for students, a new recreational center is being built, as

well as some more on-campus dorms and buildings on Main Street. Currently, though, the best housing on campus are Turner, Jefferson and Schneider halls, which are only a few years old. These dorms have suite-style rooms, with bedrooms adjoining a shared common space connecting them all. However, most students still live off-campus in the Clifton area of Cincinnati, across the street from campus. These apartment-style accommodations are also being revamped under the name of Stratford Heights. The end of 2005 saw the completion of the Van Wormer Library renovation project, complete with a new glass dome for the oldest building on campus. The University's renovation plans are detailed and extensive and cover virtually every aspect of campus life. Additionally, the surrounding neighborhoods joined together to restructure the urbanscape during 2006, aiming to produce a university area with renewed vitality and resources.

How 'bout Dem Bearcats?

What is a Bearcat? Well, it's one hell of a basketball player. Sporting events, as any good

Ohioan could tell you, are enough to bring the community together and instill a sense of belonging and school pride. While football is the main sport at other schools in Ohio, the Bearcats actually have a strong tradition of basketball, fielding a nationally ranked team with a tradition of good play. One might wonder if it is difficult to get tickets to the games. Absolutely. One student reported camping out overnight to buy tickets to a game that was three weeks away, understanding full well that student tickets to the game would be sold out in a matter of hours. So be sure to get a spot in line early if you want to root for the rowdy Bearcats.

Day by Day

How's the weather? "Schizophrenic," one student explained. According to another student, Cincinnati "doesn't like to make up its mind what season it's supposed to be." One day in winter it may be raining, and the next there might be a wind chill of minus 15 degrees Fahrenheit. "Be prepared for anything" is one motto of the Bearcats.

While the food is reputedly "decent for dorm food," there are plenty of different stations with different types of food in the dining halls. Meals are conveniently located within the dorm buildings so hungry students don't have to brave the unpredictable weather. And if you crave something more ethnic (or just better) and don't mind heading off-campus, you're in luck. Dining options are plentiful and good in Cincinnati. Indian, Chinese, Japanese and Italian restaurants are just a hop, skip and jump away. Make sure you have a car, though, because you will need it if you want to do anything off-campus.

"Diverse people like to do diverse things, and the people at UC are diverse," noted one student. Though perhaps not as much as some schools, UC does boast some diversity. This makes for an entertaining and full social scene. There is a strong Greek presence at the school, but there is also a large contingent of GDIs (God-Damned Independents). And actually, the two groups are fairly fluid, so students don't feel too pressured to join in the frat scene if it's not for them. House parties are generally held in the nearby Clifton area.

There are also plenty of bars and clubs in downtown Cincinnati that students frequent. Aside from partying, according to one student, "there are so many clubs and activities that it's impossible not to do something." Students are very active around campus, do-

ing everything from club sports to community service, although the former is a bit more popular than the latter. Also, there are on-campus alternatives to parties, such as "Friday Night Live," at which several comics from the show "Whose Line Is It Anyway?" have been known to perform.

> "While other schools may have one thing, there are three huge things that our campus has that others don't."

If you're wondering where you can take a date, the answer's actually Kentucky. Just across the Ohio-Kentucky line is an area called Newport on the Levee. This area has a lot of non-franchise, family-owned restaurants that lend themselves to the romantic atmosphere of a date. Another popular Kentucky destination is the Cold Stone Creamery in that same area.

On campus, be sure to check out McMicken Hall's stone lions that supposedly growl when virgins walk through them, the "haunted" Cincinnati Observatory Center, and the Crosley Tower, which was reportedly created from one continuous pour of concrete.

Class? Oh, Yeah! Class!

UC students have classes too, and depending on the program they are in, most get their money's worth on their education. "While other schools may have one thing, there are three huge things that our campus has that others don't," one student said. "CCMD, AAP and the Engineering School are all awesome programs." The first stands for the College Conservatory of Music and Design, and the second for Architecture, Art and Planning. These three programs are the most competitive at UC, while the Business Program (CBA) and the Nursing Program, one student reported, are accorded less prestige among the students. The most interesting aspect of the academic program at UC, however, are the innovative co-op programs. Co-op is designed to give students real world experience in their program of study, reinforcing what they have learned in class. This experience renders students better equipped to handle their future jobs as well as gets their foot in the door with respect to potential employers. It "really helps with job placement" after school, one student said.

Fortune Telling

The University of Cincinnati does not have the school spirit of some of its other Ohio university brethren, but may get there soon. The University of Cincinnati is doing a lot to improve itself, and is on the move to provide a well-rounded college experience—while it finishes construction.—*Ashley Elsner*

FYI

If you come to the University of Cincinnati, you'd better bring a "campus map. It's confusing with all the construction going on."

What is the typical weekend schedule? "Thursday through Saturday evenings are spent out and about, and the rest of the weekend is spent putting off work to Sunday."

If I could change one thing about the University of Cincinnati I'd "have better parking and make it less expensive. Even if you have a pass, that doesn't guarantee you'll get a spot in your assigned lot."

Three things every student at the University of Cincinnati should do before graduating are "go to Skyline on Ludlow for chili, talk to people and get involved."

Wittenberg University

Address: PO Box 720
Springfield, OH 45501
Phone: 937-327-6314
E-mail address:
admission@wittenberg.edu
Web site URL:
www.wittenberg.edu
Year Founded: 1845
Private or Public: Private
Religious Affiliation:
Lutheran
Location: Rural
Number of Applicants: 2,887
Percent Accepted: 73%
**Percent Accepted who
enroll:** 26%
Number Entering: 551
**Number of Transfers
Accepted each Year:** 79
Middle 50% SAT range:
M: 500–559, CR: 490–610,
Wr: Unreported
Middle 50% ACT range: 22–27
**Early admission program
EA/ED/None:** ED

**Percentage accepted
through EA or ED:** 89%
EA and ED deadline: 15-Nov
Regular Deadline: 1-Dec
Application Fee: $40
**Full time Undergraduate
enrollment:** 1,967
Total enrollment: 1,978
Percent Male: 45%
Percent Female: 55%
**Total Percent Minority or
Unreported:** 7%
Percent African-American:
5%
**Percent Asian/Pacific
Islander:** 1%
Percent Hispanic: 1%
Percent Native-American:
0%
Percent International: 2%
**Percent in-state / out of
state:** 76%/24%
Percent from Public HS:
Unreported
Retention Rate: 80%

Graduation Rate 4-year:
56%
Graduation Rate 6-year: 57%
**Percent Undergraduates in
On-campus housing:** 82%
**Number of official organized
extracurricular
organizations:** 129
3 Most popular majors:
Biology, Business, Education
Student/Faculty ratio: 12:1
Average Class Size: 20 to 29
**Percent of students going to
grad school:** 74%
Tuition and Fees: $32,936
**In State Tuition and Fees if
different:** No difference
Cost for Room and Board:
$8,314
**Percent receiving financial
aid out of those who apply,
first year:** 99%
**Percent receiving financial
aid among all students:**
99%

Wittenberg is a breath of fresh air for those tired of visiting colleges where the campus is packed with hordes of students grubbed out in last night's pajamas and sweats heading in every direction. If you want to attend a school where the students are well dressed, always remember to accessorize with gleaming smiles, and where everybody knows your name, well then, Wittenberg is definitely the school for you.

We're talking Quality, not Quantity

When asked about why they chose Wittenberg, most students commented on the small class sizes and the atmosphere. One girl stated that, "From my visit and onward, everyone has been very friendly. Having small class sizes has been beneficial as well, because the professors are much more available when you may need one." As far as class sizes go, don't expect to be a nameless face in an auditorium lecture course. "Class sizes are wonderful! I've never been in a class with more than 30!" a student exclaimed. Class sizes generally range from 12 to 35 students, with basic introductory classes having 35. Higher-level courses are "generally in the teens, but sometimes even less."

The small size of Wittenberg presents students with a lot of personal attention. One junior stated that, "Since I have been here, I have had countless meetings with faculty discussing future career plans and paths to take. Because the school is small, focus is more on the individual."

> "Because the school is small, focus is more on the individual."

Grading at Wittenberg is done on a 10-point scale. Classes are challenging, but students love to work together, and the faculty loves to help. "The students are intelligent, the professors are incredible," a campus newspaper boasted in an article, adding that, "We have more Professors of the Year than any other school in Ohio. We have 24 Fulbright Scholars. Our faculty is incredible." Since Wittenberg professors will know students on a first-name basis, it is hard not to work hard. "There is a lot more expected out of the students . . . students definitely strive to get good grades. The library is always packed and groups of students working on projects can be found all over campus."

As far as requirements go, there are prerequisites in each of the following seven areas: Integrated Learning; Natural World; Social Institutions; Fine, Performing, and Literary Arts; Religious and Philosophical Inquiry; Western Historical Perspectives; Non-Western Cultures. Further requirements dictate that you must cover areas of writing, research, foreign language, computing, speaking and mathematics. There is also a physical activity requirement, which can be fulfilled by participation in intercollegiate athletics, or by taking various health and fitness courses. Community service is also mandatory. Sophomores must complete 30 hours of community service over the course of one term.

The most popular majors at Witt are Management and Education, but students also rave about Witt's English program. One senior pre-law English Literature major commented that, "the English department here is amazing. I get to work closely with professors; the entire English department knows me well, and is always willing to help." Be on the lookout for East Asian Studies, too, which was named as an increasingly popular major. For those students who aren't too eager to comply with a pre-arranged curriculum, there is also the option of designing your own major. Students can pick classes from a variety of disciplines to cater to their own interests and needs. Communications and Management are generally considered "the easy way out," while the sciences are considered to be the toughest courses at the university. One student commented that, "Biology is a pretty difficult major, just because so many classes are required, but it's still totally worth it." And despite not being "remotely near any large body of water," one sophomore said that, "we actually have an excellent Marine Biology program."

While students love the small school, they are also encouraged to study abroad. "The program is excellent!" exclaimed one student. Offering more than 40 options in countries all over the world—from Buddhist temples to safaris in Kenya—the school is very supportive of students going abroad for a semester, or an entire year.

Dodgeball anyone?

Despite Wittenberg's small size, there is a huge selection of clubs and organizations to join. A female student explained that, "Most everyone is involved in at least one thing. It's just so easy because Witt offers something for everyone. We have everything from Student Senate to an improv comedy group called Pocket Lint. If you're interested in something, chances are we have something for it. And if not, it's so easy to create one." Don't believe her? Wittenberg's array of sports include archery, cricket and even dodgeball!

Despite the University's efforts to branch out by implementing regional recruitment on the East Coast and in the Midwest, "Wittenberg probably isn't as diverse as it would like to be," although students all agree that the school is actively working on rectifying the problem. Currently, the minority population is lower than most other schools, but there are still many campus groups promoting diversity, including the Concerned Black Students, Jewish Culture Club, Hispanic Culture Club and Gay/Straight Alliance. The Polis House, a dorm dedicated to international awareness, promotes cultural awareness by hosting celebrations of holidays for different cultures.

The other six dorms on campus are Tower, Firesetine, Ferncliff, Myers, New Residence and Woodlawn. Dorms are assigned to freshmen based on when their applications and tuition fees are submitted. Post-freshman year, there are housing lotteries that students must attend in order to be placed in a dorm. After acquiring over 60 hours of credit, off-campus housing options are made available, though this is also done via a lottery process. Students have mixed feelings regarding whether on- or off-campus housing is better. One upperclassman stated that, "Most everyone lives on-campus, and it's so much more fun that way. People that live off-campus don't make as many friends as fast as those who live in the dorms. There are a few kids from the Springfield area who only live a few minutes away, but still choose to live on-campus anyway." (Wittenberg is located in the middle of Springfield, Ohio, which is described as being "pretty crappy on the south side, but really nice on the north side.") Most students agree that dorms are the easiest place to meet people. But while one student commented that the close proximity promoted by dorm life makes it "hard to not wanna get to know them," another student added that, "you might not always get along."

Greek-ing and Streaking

About one-third of students who live off campus at Wittenberg are in a Greek House. The six sororities and six fraternities on campus are responsible for most of the school's partying. Alcohol is allowed in dorms, but only as long as you are 21. (South Hall is the only substance-free residence hall). The school's enforcement of drugs and alcohol policies are "about middle of the road. Don't be stupid, and you won't get caught." Do not expect to see any frat boys doing keg stands here though—the school has banned beer kegs from all Wittenberg-owned housing, so fraternities do not generally provide alcohol, and parties are mostly BYOB. Despite the keg-ban, fraternities do throw parties "all the time," and "pretty good parties, actually. . . ." Aside from fraternity parties, students also enjoy hangouts such as the school's Student Union, which has yummy late-night food and a bar. The Ringside Bar is also a student favorite; kids go throughout the week to unwind with a few drinks.

A description of Wittenberg is incomplete without mention of the Hollow, a grassy valley that is perfect for sunbathing and playing Frisbee on sunny days, sledding on snowy winter days, and streaking at night, regardless of the weather. The Hollow hosts WittFest, the annual spring music festival sponsored by Union Board. Past WittFest performers have included the Nappy Roots, American Hi-Fi, Hootie and the Blowfish and 10,000 Maniacs. Springfield residents also attend the music festival, and there are carnival activities, such as inflatable obstacle courses, to provide amusement while the bands play.

Ultimately, students describe life at Wittenberg as "the perfect fit." The small-town feel of the school and the surrounding city draws people in. "The only bad thing about it being so small is that everyone knows everyone else's business. We tend to call it Wittenberg High School sometimes," explains one student. Wittenberg is a school where everybody knows your name—and then some.—*Christine Grace Lin*

FYI
If you come to Wittenberg, you'd better bring "your own case of beer or a flask."
If I could change one thing about Wittenberg, I'd "make it just a little bit bigger. An extra 500 students would spice up campus life."
What's the typical weekend schedule? "Go to the football game if it's a home game, hang out at The Hollow if it's nice out, catch up on work, and hit a few frat parties."
The three things every student should do before graduating are "study abroad, study abroad, study abroad!"

Oklahoma

Oklahoma State University

Address: 219 Student Union
Stillwater, OK 74078
Phone: 405-744-5358
E-mail address:
admit@okstate.edu
Web site URL:
osu.okstate.edu
Year Founded: 1890
Private or Public: Public
Religious Affiliation: None
Location: Suburban
Number of Applicants: 6,406
Percent Accepted: 89%
Percent Accepted who
enroll: 51%
Number Entering: 2,928
Number of Transfers
Accepted each Year:
Unreported
Middle 50% SAT range:
M: 500–620, CR: 480–600,
Wr: Unreported
Middle 50% ACT range:
22–27
Early admission program
EA/ED/None: None

Percentage accepted
through EA or ED: NA
EA and ED deadline: NA
Regular Deadline: Rolling
Application Fee: $40
Full time Undergraduate
enrollment: 18,600
Total enrollment: 22,862
Percent Male: 52%
Percent Female: 48%
Total Percent Minority or
Unreported: 22%
Percent African-American:
4%
Percent Asian/Pacific
Islander: 2%
Percent Hispanic: 3%
Percent Native-American:
10%
Percent International: 2%
Percent in-state/out of
state: 84%/16%
Percent from Public HS:
Unreported
Retention Rate: 77%
Graduation Rate 4-year: 29%

Graduation Rate 6-year:
Unreported
Percent Undergraduates in
On-campus housing: 38%
Number of official organized
extracurricular
organizations: 400
3 Most popular majors:
Accounting, Aerospace,
Agriculture
Student/Faculty ratio: 18:1
Average Class Size: 20 to
29
Percent of students going to
grad school: Unreported
Tuition and Fees: $17,241
In State Tuition and Fees if
different: $6,887
Cost for Room and Board:
$6,358
Percent receiving financial
aid out of those who apply,
first year: 73%
Percent receiving financial
aid among all students:
47%

The most challenging time of the year for most college students is undoubtedly the season when classes have finished, all graded work has been completed, and there is only one hurdle yet to be jumped: finals. And while a typical exam week unfortunately means lots of stress, lots of cramming, and not a lot of sleep, Oklahoma State University has found the perfect cure for the inevitable agony that stands between students and their vacation. Pancakes. Free, delicious, unlimited pancakes.

And while you might hesitate to judge a school based on tasty treats, students at OSU believe the free pancakes during finals week make a broader statement about how the University takes care of its students. Even with a student body exceeding 18,000, all individuals receive the attention and support they need to have a successful college career.

Orange You Going to Study Tonight?

As with any university, Oklahoma State has many different kinds of students. As one junior put it, "there are the thinking people, and the not-quite-as-smart people." Members of both categories spend a fair amount of time studying. A general rule of thumb is to spend two hours studying for every hour of class time. Upperclassmen tend to spend more time studying than freshmen, but "no matter what year you are, or what classes you're taking, you're always going to have time to have fun and chill with your friends, and still make good grades."

So what do OSU students like to study? Regardless of major, everyone is required to take two courses in each of five general areas—English, math, humanities, social studies and science. The most popular major is definitely the Business major, while the most difficult ones are Engineering and Pre-Med. OSU's Hotel and Restaurant Administration program is unique and well known across the country.

For applicants who tend to shy away from equations, Oklahoma State is also strong in the humanities. While students who choose one of these majors are definitely in the minority, they often go on to earn graduate degrees in their respective areas of study. One senior said, "You might be a business major because you couldn't really decide on anything else, but if you're a humanities major, you know that's what you want to do."

Regardless of what they choose to study, a great tutoring program is available to all OSU undergrads. For any and every subject, the school provides individual tutoring free of charge. One student who took advantage of this option found it to be rewarding: "The tutors were definitely a big help for a couple of my tougher classes."

It Takes a Village

OSU students are generally pleased with their living situations. The school's arrangements can certainly be characterized as diverse—there are on-campus apartments, lots of quads (four people with singles who share a bathroom and living room), and also more traditional housing. Compared to other large state schools, a surprising amount of upperclassmen choose to live on-campus. This is partly because of the recently completed dorm complex called The Village, which consists of six "brand-new, beautiful buildings that pretty much make you love your residential life." Each floor in The Village has a common area furnished with comfy couches and also a community kitchen—perfect for cooking up a late-night snack with some friends.

Integral to residential life at OSU are the residential advisors and Community Mentors. While one of their duties is to enforce university rules, these upperclassmen are also there to "make freshmen feel welcome, help them get involved, and generally be a friendly helper." New students will likely form a close relationship with their advisor or mentor, since there is one for every 20 or so students. And as long as you don't get caught in your dorm guzzling a beer, you can

expect that relationship to be a rewarding one.

That Rustic Feeling

Anyone who has visited the Oklahoma State campus agrees that it's pleasing to the senses. In terms of architecture, most of the buildings are old and made of bricks, with what one junior called "a little bit of a rustic feel." Another student said she was very fond of her surroundings: "Our campus is really gorgeous, especially in the spring when the flowers are blooming."

While OSU out of necessity has a fairly big campus, students have an easy time of getting from place to place by walking or biking. Conveniently located near the center of campus is Edmon Low Library, a favorite place to study or to wander stacks that contain more than 2.5 million volumes. After hitting the books, students might make a trip to the Colvin Recreation Center, which might best be described as "a glorious piece of workout heaven." The Center is very popular and includes 10 basketball courts, indoor and outdoor swimming pools, an indoor track, and racquetball and volleyball courts.

> "There's not just something for everyone, there are three things for everyone."

Another source of pride for OSU students is the Student Union building. Touted as the largest in the country, it offers a place to relax, hang out with friends, and grab some food. The Union also has the main bookstore and a clothing shop, where you'll find plenty of orange-and-black clothes for your wardrobe.

Fitting In

With about 400 undergraduate organizations, students at OSU find that they have many ways to become active. These include political, cultural, preprofessional, and recreational groups. There are also clubs for each major, and many club sports teams. One student said, "There's not just something for everyone, there are three things for everyone."

Oklahoma State also has a vibrant Greek scene. One junior estimated that perhaps one in five students are in fraternities or sororities. He said that going Greek "isn't a necessity, but it is cool if that's what you want to do. And if you don't want to do it, that's fine too." Most students agree that the Greek life is somewhat separated from other social scenes on campus—the frat parties are usually invite-only.

The Oklahoma Two-Step

Oklahoma State undergrads certainly know how to have a good time. When the weekends come around, students like to "hit up the bars on The Strip, maybe go to a party some place off campus, or go out to eat with friends." Popular campus restaurants include the West Side Café and the Service Station, both of which have fast, cheap food. Students craving a more classy setting might dine at the Rancher's Club—an upscale on-campus restaurant that attracts visitors from all over the state.

Much of social life occurs off campus. Stillwater's most well-known dance club is called the Tumbleweed. This unique joint consists of two rooms—one that plays hip/hop and modern tunes, and another that features country music favorites for a line-dancing and two-stepping crowd.

Although Oklahoma State is a dry campus, it's no secret that a majority of students like to relax after a week of classes by downing a few drinks. One popular hangout spot is Eskimo Joe's, a bar and restaurant that is considered the heart of Stillwater. Students often go there on "Thirsty Thursdays," where they can enjoy cheese fries and five-dollar unlimited beer. An OSU senior even joked that "one percent of the beer consumed in the United States is probably consumed in Stillwater."

If students want to get away for the weekend, many choose to visit Tulsa or Oklahoma City, both of which are about an hour away by car. Both cities offer opportunities to go shopping, see a movie, go to a concert, or try out a new restaurant.

It'll Be Bedlam

If there is one thing that all Oklahoma State students can agree on, it's that they love beating OU. The rivalry between these two schools, known as the Bedlam series, is a fierce one with a long history. Students clad in Cowboy orange turn out in huge numbers for the football and basketball games, because "even the people who know nothing about sports love to root against OU."

The chance to see exciting games in packed stadiums against a big rival is only one of many fun opportunities available to students at Oklahoma State. A big school that takes care of the individual, OSU is a comfortable home for its students. And don't forget about the free pancakes.—*Henry Agnew*

FYI

If you come to Oklahoma State, you'd better bring "your party hat."

What is the typical weekend schedule? "Definitely go out on Thursday, hopefully go to class on Friday then chill with friends, go to the game on Saturday, then hit the books Sunday night."

If I could change one thing about Oklahoma State, I'd "increase student involvement in campus activities."

Three things every student at Oklahoma State should do before graduating are "eat at Shortcake's diner, play Frisbee on Library Lawn, and go to a Bedlam game and root against the Sooners."

Oral Roberts University

Address: 7777 S. Lewis Avenue, Tulsa, OK 74171
Phone: 918-495-6518
E-mail address: admissions@oru.edu
Web site URL: www.oru.edu
Year Founded: 1963
Private or Public: Private
Religious Affiliation: None
Location: Urban
Number of Applicants: 1,201
Percent Accepted: 75%
Percent Accepted who enroll: 67%
Number Entering: 602
Number of Transfers Accepted each Year: Unreported
Middle 50% SAT range: M: 440–580, CR: 480–600, Wr: Unreported
Middle 50% ACT range: 20–25
Early admission program EA/ED/None: EA

Percentage accepted through EA or ED: Unreported
EA and ED deadline: 15-Nov
Regular Deadline: Rolling
Application Fee: $35
Full time Undergraduate enrollment: 2,790
Total enrollment: 3,303
Percent Male: 40%
Percent Female: 60%
Total Percent Minority or Unreported: 38%
Percent African-American: 18%
Percent Asian/Pacific Islander: 3%
Percent Hispanic: 6%
Percent Native-American: 2%
Percent International: 7%
Percent in-state/out of state: 49%/61%
Percent from Public HS: 75%
Retention Rate: 77%
Graduation Rate 4-year: 54%

Graduation Rate 6-year: Unreported
Percent Undergraduates in On-campus housing: 75%
Number of official organized extracurricular organizations: Unreported
3 Most popular majors: Marketing, Mass Communication, Theology
Student/Faculty ratio: Unreported
Average Class Size: Unreported
Percent of students going to grad school: 50%
Tuition and Fees: $18,386
In State Tuition and Fees if different: No difference
Cost for Room and Board: $7,610
Percent receiving financial aid out of those who apply, first year: 87%
Percent receiving financial aid among all students: 75%

Sixty-foot, thirty-ton bronze Praying Hands grace the main entrance to Oral Roberts University, indicating to all visitors that ORU not only offers its students academic guidance from the Ivory Tower, it also directs students to depend on a lifetime's teachings from God. Due to its religious founding, students at the University are encouraged to continually grow academically, physically *and* spiritually. They are given the unique opportunity to combine a top-notch education with a passionate religious and cultural experience. These aspects of the ORU experience require students to adhere to strict rules such as a dress code as well as to refrain from the partying that is characteristic of your "typical" college experience. Students are also required to participate in mandatory chapel services twice a week so they can continually live out the school founder's vision. Evangelist Oral Roberts claims that God instructed him to found a university based on "God's commission and the holy spirit." Roberts obeyed this mandate and in 1965 opened Oral Roberts University in Tulsa. Few universities can claim that they were built as a result of a message directly from God but Oral Roberts University is one of the few that can.

Academics

As a Christian school, Oral Roberts University emphasizes students' personal spiritual growth alongside a challenging academic education. Students at Oral Roberts say academics are noticeably "above average" and "top-notch." Students have the option to enroll in one of seven undergraduate schools: the School of Arts & Sciences, the School of Science and Engineering, the School of Theology and Missions, the School of Business, the School of Education, the School of Life-Long Education or the Anna Vaughn School of Nursing.

The seven schools vary in difficulty but all are known to be academically rigorous. According to one student, "The School of Education is very tough. There is a lot required of education majors, but it is a good thing. We have an exceptional program here and it makes the hard work worth it, because I know I am getting the best, top-of-the-line education." The School of LifeLong Education provides flexible, quality education programs to adult learners and non-traditional students. The business school is considered "exceptional" and also offers a 5-year MBA program. The School of Nursing is also "well-known and hard." Not surprisingly, the theology department within the School of Arts and Sciences is "incredible."

Especially attractive is the Honors Program, which admits 16 to 18 top applicants every year as Fellows. These students enroll in one three-credit hour Fellows Seminar each semester, in addition to one or two other Honors credit courses. Other highly qualified applicants are designated as Honors Program Scholars. Honors students are even invited to live in special dormitory wings with respected quiet hours, and a "quality academic atmosphere."

> The religious atmosphere at Oral Roberts emphasizes a non-competitive academic environment where "everybody would rather help you than compete against you." According to one student, competition is found "only in intramurals," an important part of campus life at ORU.

Faculty and staff at ORU devote themselves to building a university for God by actively participating in the lives of their students. ORU students appreciate this devotion and recognize its contribution to the successful academic environment. According to one undergraduate, "All faculty are extremely willing to go the extra mile for their students." Many students even describe faculty-student relationships as their favorite aspect of ORU academics, specifically noting the "personal help [the students] receive."

In Pursuit of Principled Social Life
ORU has been described as a place where students "get their learning and keep their burning." So life at the University goes well beyond academics. One unique feature of the ORU is an honor code which is taken very seriously and forbids the use of alcohol, tobacco and drugs, as well as lying,

cheating, cursing and premarital sex. The honor code, which is submitted with the application to the University, also requires students to attend all classes and chapel services and to participate in a physical fitness program. Unlike most universities around the country, weekend activities are not centered on drinking. This may be a result of the honor code, or it may just be a result of students' adherence to Christian values. Although drinking is not very common, it does occur, but usually off campus. According to one student, "nobody really drinks in the dorms unless they keep it on the down low." Drugs are even less prevalent than alcohol.

Instead of drinking, students who stay on campus spend their free time playing intramurals and attending dorm and sporting events. Most students do not stay on campus during the weekend. Instead, they tend to visit coffee shops, restaurants and clubs, as well as commuter students' homes away from campus. Students usually have cars so they can visit these off-campus sites, as "Tulsa does not have a good public transportation system." According to one student, "Tulsa is very boring without a car."

One student said that stereotypical ORU students may be described "as Bible beaters and Jesus-freaks but also as hard-working, honest, respected people." While the student population at ORU boasts geographic diversity, in that the school attracts students from 49 states and 50 nations, all students are connected by their faith. "For the most part everybody has a relationship with God, which makes the people pretty much all the same. But as far as culture goes, there is a good mix," said one student.

Living as "Brothers" and "Sisters"
Most students will live in dorms unless they are commuters, married or over age 25. Students generally do not mind that they are required to live on campus, because it creates a sense of "community spirit." Dorms are divided into wings, and freshmen are randomly assigned to a wing in a single-sex dorm. Each male wing is paired with a specific female wing, and "brother wings" and "sister wings" allow freshmen to meet members of the opposite sex. Brother and sister wings "plan events together, sit together in chapel, and also have designated seats" together in the cafeteria. Freshmen may request a particular dorm if they have had family in that dorm, or they may be recruited by a particular wing. The wings that "recruit, draft on,

and initiate people" are similar to fraternities, except the students live in dormitory halls, instead of separate houses elsewhere on campus. One of the oldest and most respected wings on campus is known as Young-Blood. Dorms are also known for their particular personalities. According to one student, "Claudius is the freshman, fun, social dorm. EMR is the fun, manly man's dorm. Michael and Wesley are for more of the pretty boys. Gabby is for the rich girls."

Freshmen generally find it easy to make friends in their own wings, or in their respective brother or sister wing. Additionally, freshmen do not feel excluded from upperclassmen's activities since "everybody is included in whatever is going on." But according to one senior, the upperclassmen have much less free time for socializing. Every floor has an RA and a chaplain. RAs enforce curfews, notify students of events, and maintain general order on the floor. Chaplains provide students with spiritual support.

One thing ORU students all agree on is the strangeness and originality of campus architecture. One student describes it as "space age" and another describes it as "like the Jetsons." Most find it ugly at first, but all agree that it grows on them. Currently, roofs of buildings are being improved and construction for a new student center is underway.

Students generally hang out in and around the cafeteria and at the restaurants on campus, such as the Eagle's Nest or the internet café. When the weather is nice, they spend time on the quad as well. Favorite places on campus include the Prayer Gardens, surrounding the base of the 200-foot tall Prayer Tower which serves as the visitor's center and the Kenneth H. Cooper Aerobics Center (AC), a two-story building housing athletic facilities and exercise equipment. Located in a very safe neighborhood, ORU offers an extremely safe campus environment. There are no problems between the students and the residents of the surrounding neighborhoods. As one student put it, "They love us."

There is only one cafeteria on campus, but according to a student, it has "good variety. They try hard. You have to be creative sometimes." Another student agrees it is "better than most cafeterias I have eaten in, but it still gets old and is avoided most of the time." Students are required to be on an unlimited, 17-, 14-, or 10-meal per week meal plan and each comes with a certain number of Eagle Bucks that can be used at different restaurants, as well as the coffee shop or bookstore. Even when the students tire of cafeteria food, it is not a problem since Tulsa boasts "a huge restaurant variety—anything and everything you can imagine."

Sports as a Requirement

Oral Roberts University aims to "educate the whole man: spirit, mind and body. Staying in shape and treating our bodies well is just as important as our mental state." In addition to most students' abstention from alcohol, drugs and tobacco, students are all required to participate in some sort of physical activity. One way to do this is to participate in a varsity sport. The Oral Roberts Golden Eagles compete in eight Division I sports for both men and women. Though the school is fairly young and school pride and traditions are still developing, sporting events are well-attended. Basketball is especially popular at the 10,000-seat Mabee Basketball Stadium. For students who do not want the time commitment of Division I athletics, intramurals are popular as well. Intramural sports such as basketball, soccer, volleyball, flag football, tennis, badminton and ping pong are extremely competitive.

> **"Staying in shape and treating our bodies well is just as important as our mental state."**

Outside of academics and athletics, students have many job opportunities on and off campus. Students are very committed to their extracurricular activities as well. Some students take part in mission trips, others write for the school newspaper, *The Oracle*, and some are involved in community outreach or the Leadership Academy. A unique group called the Student Association allows students to play an active role in the decision-making and programming of the university.

ORU instructs its young people in how to combine morality with worldly endeavors like business and medicine and other professional arenas featured in its academic programs. The University's facilities, high-tech amenities and space-age architecture contrast greatly with the university's embrace of an old-school mentality concerning academic life. Students all agree that devotion to God comes first; they love being in a strict academic environment where they are given the opportunity to "grow as a Christian." In the words of University Chancellor Roberts (who is son of the university's founder) ORU is a "ministry with a University not a University with a ministry." If you are seeking a spiritual, as well as an academic, collegiate experience, you may be one of the growing number of applicants considering Oral Roberts University.—*Jessica Rubin*

FYI

If you come to Oral Roberts, you'd better bring "flip-flops" and "your Bible . . . I guess."

What's the typical weekend schedule? "Friday: Coffee shops, local concerts at Cain's Ballroom, out to eat and a movie. Saturday: maybe a basketball game or a drive-in movie. Sunday: Church, lunch and a nap. Next, the campus worship service."

If I could change one thing about Oral Roberts, I'd "get rid of the curfew and allow coed dorms" and "get more people to come here!"

Three things every student at Oral Roberts should do before graduating are "swim in the fountains, run the Howard Run (streaking around Howard Auditorium) and love our President."

University of Oklahoma

Address: 1000 Asp Avenue Norman, OK 73019-4076

Phone: 405-325-2252

E-mail address: admrec@ou.edu

Web site URL: www.ou.edu

Year Founded: 1890

Private or Public: Public

Religious Affiliation: None

Location: Urban

Number of Applicants: 8,768

Percent Accepted: 89%

Percent Accepted who enroll: 49%

Number Entering: 3,843

Number of Transfers Accepted each Year: 3,500

Middle 50% SAT range: M: 540–660, CR: 510–640, Wr: Unreported

Middle 50% ACT range: 23–28

Early admission program EA/ED/None: None

Percentage accepted through EA or ED: NA

EA and ED deadline: NA

Regular Deadline: 1-Apr

Application Fee: $40

Full time Undergraduate enrollment: 20,714

Total enrollment: 27,448

Percent Male: 50%

Percent Female: 50%

Total Percent Minority or Unreported: 26%

Percent African-American: 6%

Percent Asian/Pacific Islander: 6%

Percent Hispanic: 4%

Percent Native-American: 7%

Percent International: 3%

Percent in-state/out of state: 75%/25%

Percent from Public HS: Unreported

Retention Rate: Unreported

Graduation Rate 4-year: 26%

Graduation Rate 6-year: 59%

Percent Undergraduates in On-campus housing: 28%

Number of official organized extracurricular organizations: 338

3 Most popular majors: Journalism, Management Science, Zoology/Animal Biology

Student/Faculty ratio: 18:1

Average Class Size: 10 to 19

Percent of students going to grad school: Unreported

Tuition and Fees: $17,404

In State Tuition and Fees if different: $7,423

Cost for Room and Board: $7,376

Percent receiving financial aid out of those who apply, first year: 81%

Percent receiving financial aid among all students: 49%

Nestled in America's heartland, in the small town of Norman (just south of Oklahoma City) lies the University of Oklahoma. But OU, as the university is commonly called, is much more than the visible cluster of red brick buildings and bustling students. It is truly its own world, filled with incredible school spirit and rich tradition. Just two minutes at an OU football game (especially the "Red River Rivalry," the face-off between OU and its archrival, the University of Texas) will lead any observer to realize that OU is no typical school. The "Boomer, Sooner" chant that fills the stadium will amaze visitors and excite students, alumni, and fans.

Who are the Boomers and Sooners, you ask? Well, the Boomers were pioneers who helped bring about Oklahoma's opening to settlers in the 1880s. The Sooners, on the other hand, were those unruly settlers who slipped in before President Harrison officially opened the territory. Today, the Sooners are the 20,000 plus students that make up the University of Oklahoma.

Party Like A Greek

In terms of extracurricular activities, Greek life and athletics rule the roost at OU. Fifty percent of Sooners belong to a fraternity or sorority (it's no wonder, since there are 39 of them on campus!). For Greek women, the school year starts a week early with rush in August. To accommodate this, on-campus housing permits freshman girls to move in before rush begins, so they are comfortably settled for the hectic week. Said one member, "Rush is a crazy process, but it's worth it in the end."

One aspect of Greek life that almost every participant appreciates is the exciting party scene. Theme parties, fraternity/sorority mixers, and date parties are just a few of the social events in the Greek world, and "rarely does a weekend go by without some kind of sorority/fraternity event.". The Greek system is a major part of OU's social life, but it isn't the only part. "Obviously, there is a large fraternity and sorority life but not so big that it's hard to make friends without being in one," explained one freshman. Many students find friends in other extracurricular activities—sports, theatre, political or community service organizations—and others meet people just by "going to dinner, studying, and hanging out in the dorms." For those who are part of a fraternity or sorority, parties often take place in fraternity houses, but plenty of parties are held in non-Greek houses or apartments also.

The weekend usually starts on Thursday at OU, and Sooners know how to finish off each school week in style. Thursdays are often packed with fraternity parties and house parties. Fridays can be party nights too, but as one student explains, "Fridays are usually a little more low-key." Many students choose to just "hang out and rest up" for Saturday— and if it's a football weekend, that rest is much needed. "Everyone goes to the game at least four hours early to tailgate." School spirit abounds, with face paint, OU T-shirts, and flags everywhere. "There are a lot of die-hard Sooners out there—people who literally bleed crimson." Many alumni also attend each game. "Sooner Born, Sooner Bred" seems to be a motto most OU fans live by.

However, extreme school spirit has its downsides. If the Sooners lose, prepare to mourn. One freshman described the first OU loss she witnessed: "No one talked for about three days." Some students got angry, turning over trash cans and loudly lamenting the loss, but most just "walked around like zombies." But after a win, Norman rejoices. No one throws a better victory party than a Sooner, and campus is certainly alive on these Saturday nights (and, well, most Saturday nights). Although OU has recently cracked down on underage drinking, implementing an intimidating-but-rarely-enforced Three Strike System, students don't have to look very far to find alcohol. As one student puts it, "OU is a dry campus, but I haven't seen much dryness."

> "OU may have a student body of over 20,000, but that doesn't mean hundreds of students are packed into every class."

Still, while football and partying are like oxygen to many Sooners, there are many other weekend activities to appeal to every interest. Many students spend their weekends seeing productions at the OU School of Drama, watching free new-release movies in the student union's theatre, visiting Oklahoma City, or simply relaxing. And there is certainly no lack of clubs and activities at OU. "There are millions of organizations," commented one student. "Some students seem to do everything, and others do absolutely nothing." Whether you prefer to spend your free time saving the environment, playing Guitar Hero, or partying, you can do it at OU.

A More Academic Image

OU may have a student body of over 20,000, but that doesn't mean hundreds of students are packed into every class. "I had one class of about 100 kids," states one student, "but most of my classes have about 35 students." All classes are taught by professors, and most students claim that professors are remarkably accessible, considering the number of students they teach. "You can email professors anytime, even in a class of 200. They're really good about helping students out." However, getting into first-choice classes can be challenging. "I got into most of the classes I wanted," says one freshman, "but it's hard because freshmen register last."

The work at OU can be challenging, but "once you learn how to handle it, it's definitely manageable." In recent years, the university seems to be shooting for a more "academic image." Among the current Sooner student body are nearly 600 enrolled National Merit Scholars; in fact, OU has the most National Merit Scholars in the nation enrolled per capita at a public university. The University is also among the top five in Rhodes Scholar graduates.

OU makes sure its top scholars are rewarded. Students in the Honors College (who must qualify with higher test scores and high school GPA) benefit from an early registration process, which allows them to enroll in "practically any class they want." Honors College students are the only ones who can graduate with honors, and they can enroll in small sections of about 20 students.

House Rules

On-campus housing is mandatory for all freshman students under age 20 (although there seem to be some exceptions to this rule), but many students choose to remain on campus all four years. OU's dorms are in the middle of a renovation project. Of the dorms, Couch and Walker are the most popular. "Couch is nice because it's been renovated, and all the furniture can be moved around." Couch also has the added bonus of the Couch Express, a small store and grill. Walker has a small convenience store named Etcetera, but it hasn't been renovated yet. Adams, another freshman dorm, is "not quite as nice." It has a Burger King on the ground floor, but "none of the towers connect, and the floor plan is really confusing." Freshman dorms are coed by floor, and upperclass dorms are coed by suite. RAs live on the floors with freshmen, and are "pretty helpful," although they do have to enforce the visitor rules, which state that coed visitors must leave freshman rooms by 12 a.m. on weeknights and 2 a.m. on weekends.

OU's on-campus dining facilities get mixed reviews, but most students agree that there is certainly plenty of variety available. Students can use meal points at the cafeteria, any on-campus convenience stores, and at the food court in the Student Union, which is a popular hangout. Many students move off campus after their freshman year, but plenty of students remain. "Some people think it's weird to live on campus after freshman year," explained one student, "but it's so much more convenient."

For students who live off-campus, finding parking on campus can be a real pain. "You have to get to campus pretty early just to find a parking spot." Although there is public transit around campus and Norman, most students have cars. "I don't know what I'd do without my car," one student said. "If you want to go anywhere off campus, you pretty much need to drive."

And where do students go in their cars? One favorite in Norman is the Classic 50s Drive-In, which caters to Sooners with tasty hamburgers, shakes, and other staples. There are several other popular restaurants in Norman, as well as some "cute little shops" and a mall. "Biggest surprise about OU: I looooove Norman!" exclaimed one student. "To me, it is the perfect college town." One thing that is unique about Norman is that it is "all OU, all the time." And, if the small-town scene gets too repetitive, Oklahoma City is just 15 miles down the highway.

Southern Style

At first glance, OU's student body seems pretty homogeneous. "Most of the students are white, but there are a lot of African-American and Hispanic students also." Sooners have a reputation for being an unusually attractive bunch, but they don't necessarily flaunt it. "Most people are pretty casual—you know, T-shirts, jeans, flip-flops." In other words, no one is ostracized for wearing sweats to class. Still, in true Southern fashion, most OU students try to look good and keep fit, often using the university's gym facilities or intramural sports teams to help them along the way. One stereotype most Sooners would like to banish, however, is that "we are *not* rednecks." The majority of students come from Oklahoma, the Midwest, and Texas, but students come to OU from all over the country and even outside the country. And, because of OU's theatre and arts departments and on-campus museums, Sooners have plenty of cultural outlets. "There are lots of neat, cultured people here."

But, cultured or uncultured, majority or minority, Greek or non-Greek, all OU students have one thing in common: Sooner pride. Many students make up the fourth or fifth generation in their family to attend OU. And when they make the annual 187 mile trek from Norman down to Dallas for the OU/UT game, it doesn't matter where they're from or what they look like—all that matters is the color of their T-shirt and the cheer on their lips: "Boomer Sooner!"—*Elizabeth Bewley*

FYI

If you come to The University of Oklahoma, you'd better bring "your adventurous side, your pride, and sometimes a winter jacket."

What is the typical weekend schedule? "Head to a frat party on Friday night (assuming you can get in), go to a football game Saturday morning after the tailgate, and sleep in Sunday."

If I could change one thing about The University of Oklahoma, I'd "change its proximity to outside life."

Three things every University of Oklahoma student should do before graduating are "go to the UT/Oklahoma football game, take advantage of agriculture in the area, and join a fraternity."

University of Tulsa

Address: 800 South Tucker Drive Tulsa, OK 74104-3189
Phone: 918 631-2307
E-mail address: admission@utulsa.edu
Web site URL: www.utulsa.edu
Year Founded: 1894
Private or Public: Private
Religious Affiliation: Presbyterian
Location: Suburban
Number of Applicants: 4,714
Percent Accepted: 46%
Percent Accepted who enroll: 32%
Number Entering: 692
Number of Transfers Accepted each Year: 270
Middle 50% SAT range: M: 550–700, CR: 540–700, Wr: Unreported
Middle 50% ACT range: 25–31
Early admission program EA/ED/None: None

Percentage accepted through EA or ED: NA
EA and ED deadline: NA
Regular Deadline: Rolling
Application Fee: $35
Full time Undergraduate enrollment: 3,049
Total enrollment: 3,724
Percent Male: 51%
Percent Female: 49%
Total Percent Minority or Unreported: 3%
Percent African-American: 8%
Percent Asian/Pacific Islander: 3%
Percent Hispanic: 5%
Percent Native-American: 4%
Percent International: 8%
Percent in-state/out of state: 52%/48%
Percent from Public HS: 78%
Retention Rate: 88%
Graduation Rate 4-year: 48%
Graduation Rate 6-year: 62%

Percent Undergraduates in On-campus housing: 70%
Number of official organized extracurricular organizations: 245
3 Most popular majors: Business/Marketing, Engineering, Visual and Performing Arts
Student/Faculty ratio: 10:1
Average Class Size: 10 to 19
Percent of students going to grad school: 41%
Tuition and Fees: $23,940
In State Tuition and Fees if different: No difference
Cost for Room and Board: $7,776
Percent receiving financial aid out of those who apply, first year: 49%
Percent receiving financial aid among all students: 44%

In the alphabet of life, the letter 'T' stands for many things: tortoise, telepathy, toiletries, tots. But when 't' stands for tenacity; talent, tradition and togetherness, all in one setting, that is when it also stands for TU, also known as the University of Tulsa. Now, you may be saying to yourself, TU? Did you say TU? Because then should it not be Tulsa University rather than the University of Tulsa? Perhaps yes. Perhaps no. And perhaps this grammatical flip-flop, though perplexing, perfectly demonstrates the small-size/big-time duality which TU actualizes.

Hackedemics

Across the board, TU is habitually known for its challenging academics (especially in the field of engineering). And this can be attractive to strong-minded and/or intelligent young adults (indeed one of every ten students currently enrolled at TU is a National Merit Scholar). But we all know the most attractive attribute about a college to any young adult person is how that education will help him to land an eight-figure salary, become an icon and/or hack into neighboring governments' intelligence computers. Yet, TU already knows all of that.

The University of Tulsa is "one of six pioneer institutions selected by the National Science Foundation to participate in the Federal Cyber Service Initiative (a.k.a. Cyber Corps) to train students for federal careers as computer security experts." This basically translates to "TU receiving $2.7 million to create a band of information security specialists who know how to defend the free world and defend the Internet from hackers." These students come out of the program not only with a degree in computer science and a couple years of their tuition paid for, but also "multiple federal-level computer security certificates as endorsed by the CNSS." They also get a new pick-up line: "Excuse me, I seemed to have dropped my multiple federal-level computer security certificates around here . . ."

However, if computers are not your "bag," TU also receives funding for the "Tulsa Undergraduate Research Challenge," which lets students get involved in advanced research with faculty members as early as their freshman year." It is no wonder that in 2004, four students received Goldwater scholarships (the maximum awarded annually) and that in the past year, "nine University of Tulsa students won nationally competitive scholarships." But the "level of academic strain or prowess is totally dependent on what you want and your major—communication majors have it relatively easy, whereas students with majors like nursing and engineering can easily take up residency in the library."

Classes for Claustrophobics
Come to the University of Tulsa and never feel the restless constriction of cramming into a 500-seat auditorium with a bunch of pungent, pajama-wearing cohorts for the introductory lecture of Rocks for Jocks 101. Why? Because at TU, the average class-size is 19 students, 62 percent of classes are under 20 students, and only 1 percent of classes holds 50 or more students. This allows for one-on-one instruction in an environment that "feels like home," an environment where "the teachers become easy friends and mentors, who are so approachable, accommodating, and helpful." Sounds like a little slice of heaven, eh? Except in heaven you do not have to factor in "attendance policies that can lower your grade making it so you can't skip class." In a class of 100, it is possible, but in a class of 12, hiding an absence can prove fruitless. Nonetheless, young adults (local, national, or international) continue to flock to TU in droves, thanks to the attentive faculty, the 11:1 student/teacher ratio, and the fact that "the school is small enough to not feel invis-

ible, but also big enough where you are always meeting new people."

You and Me and Greek Makes Three
This constant confluence of new friendships may be in a large part related to how actively involved the students are within campus organizations. Ninety percent of students participate in some sort of club or organization—the "big ones" being: Young Democrats, FCA, Intramurals or SA. SA is the Student Association which organizes most of the "big events" on campus, including Homecoming and Springfest—"a week of activities, free stuff and concerts (Ben Folds, Hanson, 50 Cent, Vertical Horizon, etc.), with amazing tailgating on the 'U' before the football game."

> "The school is small enough to not feel invisible, but also big enough where you are always meeting new people."

Many of the other annual events are held by Greek frats or sororities, most have "philanthropy weeks that are way fun—usually games, competitions and then parties on the weekends—all to raise money for their chosen organization." A favorite is the Lambda Chi Alpha's LUAU which is a "sand volleyball tourney where they cover a parking lot with sand and anyone can play, it's kinda a big deal." At TU, only about a fifth of the students pledge a fraternity or sorority, making Greek life "an option but not a must." If a frat holds a party or philanthropic event, anyone can attend, "so people do not feel like they have to go Greek in order to have a social life."

In fact, if you want an ample social network, intramurals might be a better bet. Eighty percent of the students partake of the intramural program, and "it is a common dream to win an intramural championship of some sort." The program is run through Collins Fitness Center, a brand-new fitness haven that came about during recent renovations (along with "amazing dorms— LaFortune is the best, the Twin dorms are the worst"). Most students describe the new fitness center as "unreal" though a few add "it is something that some huge rapper would own complete with plasma screens everywhere and every kind of workout machine you can imagine."

Running Backs, Recorders, and Robots

We know TU students love to win academic awards and that they love to play intramurals, but what happens when you combine the two? You get student-athletes who love to win and student-athletic-supporters who love to watch them win! TU basketball games have "long been known as a Tulsa tradition" and "for once, the football team is doing well!" In fact, the Golden Hurricane (or so they are known because of A. their tendency to "roar through opponents", and B. Georgia Tech was already known as the tornado) has had recent success not only in football bowl games, but also in soccer. But in the words of an insightful fan, "winning is not the best part; the best part is that the school is small enough that you know most or a lot of the athletes and this personal connection makes cheering at sporting events or watching them on TV a lot more fun because you are watching your friends."

As touching as that is, what if you do not like watching sports? Not a problem! TU has a large visual and performing arts contingency, and with the city of Tulsa boasting a professional opera company, a national ballet company, and a symphony, the two share an intimate interaction. Often "kids have gotten to fill in with the symphony" and recently the Tulsa Ballet adopted a 330-pound "fighting robot" built by TU students for a Battle Bots competition. Fortunately, "the bot had been stripped of its steel spikes and bullet-proof panels, allowing it to give a delicate ride to a full-length mirror and interact with the dancers."

Love and Leisure T-Town Style

If you are a TU student your hang-out is either the library or the "Ack-Ack." Funnily enough, at TU "the library is almost a social scene; it's fun," and ACAC is similar to a student union and the only place where you can use meal points outside of the cafeteria. Off campus, many students enjoy spending time at Utica Square, a trendy yet quaint outdoor shopping/eating/walking Mecca that is home to Santa's cottage during the winter months and Queenside's bakery year-round ("it has egg salad to die for."). They also enjoy a trip to Philbrook Museum or the Tulsa Rose Garden, "where you can have a picnic at Woodward Park and watch a movie on your laptop."

But what if you are, perhaps, more nocturnal? Where do the creatures of the night hang out? Well, a typical TU Friday night could consist of "going to a bar then ending back up at a small apartment/house party." Apparently, there used to be more house parties, but because of recent University mandates, "the parties are now being regulated and have significantly decreased in size and quantity; as a result people frequent the bar scene more." The main watering-holes are Rehab, Hardwood's or The Buccaneer (a dive-bar affectionately called The Buc). All are located across the street from campus, and "are always offering some kind of beer special or TU student discount." Then there are other, more upscale restaurant/bar districts like Brookside, Cherry Street or the Riverwalk (also a divine location to go for a jog). If you are not invited to a private apartment party, there are normally language house/frat parties, though those are known to "get kind of old after sophomore or junior year." Dorms also sometimes sponsor functions, and then "there are always City of Tulsa sponsored events like Mayfest or Oktoberfest (one fest has a lot of watercolors and live music and the other fest has a lot of potato pancakes, polka, and beer)." If those combined with Springfest are not enough fests for you, there is even a Harley Motorcycle Festival "where they close down Brookside every year and have a huge party."

But what is a party if one is alone? The dating scene at the University of Tulsa is like a good male/female relationship—discordant. Boys will tell you "it is good, there is a range of different people around and you can find your athletic or partier or smart person and dates can be as simple as going to a party together." Girls will tell you "it's not bad, there are dating prospects although not too many of quality." But one thing is sure, "it is a small school so there is a clear understanding of who is dating who."

Max Forman once said: "Education seems to be in America the only commodity of which the customer tries to get as little he can for his money." Apparently, Max Forman has never seen the University of Tulsa, especially during its current booms of a growing international student population, continuing nationally recognized academic award winners, and improving athletic victors. But the special charm of the University of Tulsa is that "as cliché as this sounds, the school feels like one big family" no matter how it orders its name.—*Jocelyn Ranne*

FYI

If you come to TU you'd better bring "a variety of clothing (for all seasons) because it could be 70 degrees one day and snowing the next, and some cash. Things are expensive on campus, and campus police only know how to do one thing—and that's give out tickets."

What's the typical weekend schedule? "Friday night can start with dinner on Brookside, then parties start around 11 p.m. (most people check out frat row). Saturday you wake up (late) do some homework, check out a sporting event, and then repeat. You do work when you can, but it is mainly partying and catching up on sleep!"

If I could change one thing about TU, "I would get more quick and good food options on campus."

Three things that every TU student should do before graduating are "camp out on the 'U' (the big U-shaped grassy area in between the dorms, library, and classroom buildings), join an organization, and climb up on the roof of the library to go stargazing."

Oregon

Address: 10015 SW Terwilliger Boulevard Portland, OR 97219
Phone: 503-768-6613
E-mail address: admissions@lclark.edu
Web site URL: www.lclark.edu
Year Founded: 1867
Private or Public: Private
Religious Affiliation: None
Location: Urban
Number of Applicants: 5,360
Percent Accepted: 56%
Percent Accepted who enroll: 17%
Number Entering: 507
Number of Transfers Accepted each Year: 68
Middle 50% SAT range: M: 590–680, Wr: 590–680, CR: 610–700
Middle 50% ACT range: 26–31
Early admission program EA/ED/None: EA
Percentage accepted through EA or ED: Unreported

EA and ED deadline: 1-Nov
Regular Deadline: 1-Feb
Application Fee: $50
Full time Undergraduate enrollment: 1,964
Total enrollment: 2,836
Percent Male: 36%
Percent Female: 64%
Total Percent Minority or Unreported: 21%
Percent African-American: 1%
Percent Asian/Pacific Islander: 6%
Percent Hispanic: 5%
Percent Native-American: <1%
Percent International: 5%
Percent in-state/out of state: 13%/87%
Percent from Public HS: 76%
Retention Rate: 83%
Graduation Rate 4-year: Unreported

Graduation Rate 6-year: Unreported
Percent Undergraduates in On-campus housing: 67%
Number of official organized extracurricular organizations: 85
3 Most popular majors: Psychology, Visual and Performing arts, English
Student/Faculty ratio: 13:1
Average Class Size: 20
Percent of students going to grad school: 10%
Tuition and Fees: $33,726
In State Tuition and Fees if different: No difference
Cost for Room and Board: $8,820
Percent receiving financial aid out of those who apply, first year: 73%
Percent receiving financial aid among all students: 86%

Lewis & Clark students love Portland. The passionate and worldly minds that attend the small classes of Lewis & Clark are also frequent visitors to downtown coffee shops and the famous Powell's Books. But it's not all about the city. Lewis & Clark's international focus, commitment to small classes and dedicated professors also draw students to this spectacular wooded estate.

Small Classes, Devoted Professors

Small classes and attentive professors are trademarks of Lewis & Clark's strong academic life. The average class size is 19 students, yet the biggest science class can hold around 70 students. While it varies among majors, most students agree that this small class size fosters discussion and "encourages students to think." Professors are "super passionate" and "want to be there and connect with students." Because of this familiar interaction, and the fact that there are no TAs, students often develop close personal relationships with their professors.

Moreover, students explain that the closely knit nature of the academic community encourages them to be committed to their schoolwork, which they describe as "challenging." Nonetheless, while students generally "do well in school," grades are not widely discussed on campus. The sole academic complaint seems to be that, being a smaller school, Lewis & Clark simply does not offer enough majors or courses from which to choose.

Perhaps to offset this disadvantage, Lewis & Clark students are encouraged to go abroad, and over 300 students each year take advantage of the school's programs in other countries. Students can choose locations all around the world, including Kenya, Germany, France, India and Australia. Most appreciate the experience of going abroad and the global perspective their comrades bring to discussions. Because of the interest in global affairs, popular majors include International Affairs and Languages.

> **"This ebb and flow of upperclassmen as some leave to study and others return from studying abroad creates a 'transient school.'"**

In terms of requirements, most students said they were "pretty standard" and not overly burdensome. All freshmen are required to take "Exploration and Discovery," a yearlong course meant as an overview of the most important works and topics of the diverse field of liberal arts. Students are split into small seminars, but each one regardless of professor is meant to cover the same material. Professors of every discipline teach the course, so students' experiences in the course vary depending on their professor. When Lewis & Clark students need to hit the books, they use the "totally awesome" Watzek Library. There are study rooms for group study, long tables, and private carrels with computer hookups that allow students to check their email from a laptop.

Hippies and Hipsters

Students at Lewis & Clark form a homogeneously progressive and liberal community. Although there is an "overwhelming number of international students," people drawn to Lewis & Clark are generally interested in a lot of the same issues. Most are liberal and interested in change, taking on issues which range from sustainability to involvement in the community. Students express a tension between a desire for a more diverse campus and the appeal of their "Lewis & Clark bubble." Indeed, in some class discussions there is "little debate," and rarely a conservative or deeply religious belief voiced. Additionally, some pessimistically feel that students may superficially judge their peers: "If you don't buy organic food you're not making the world a better place."

The social scene at Lewis & Clark is "intensely laid-back." The Greek system was abolished in the 1970s with a donor's amendment, but students don't seem to miss it. Apparently the donor would not give the school her fortune unless the school promised to prohibit Greek houses, install an all-women's dorm, and serve ice cream at every meal.

Since freshmen and sophomores are required to live on campus, many of the underclassmen social events take place on campus. As a technically dry campus, students have to find ways around the prohibition on alcohol on campus to avoid write ups by the campus police. While Lewis & Clark is not your typical "party school," students do certainly have a good time. Underclassmen manage to drink in small groups in the dorms, and bigger parties are held off campus. Binge drinking, though, is not common. Some students smoke pot, but, much like drinking, drug use is a "private hang-out thing."

Finally, Portland is a big part of the social scene at Lewis & Clark. The campus is a 10-minute drive from the city or 30 minutes on the school-run shuttle. Students often make use of the free shuttle that goes into downtown and surrounding areas every hour until 2 a.m. Once in Portland, the city has one of the most accessible public transport systems including a "great bus system." One of the major draws for many students is being able to explore the different areas of the city. Whether walking along Hawthorne Blvd. to find some new music, going to a film festival or attending "First Thursday," a program where all of the art galleries in Portland have new shows, Lewis & Clark students are drawn to the Portland scene. Coffee shops are a common place to do work or just hang out, and Powell's, the largest independent bookstore in America, is another big attraction.

"Summer Camp at a Park"

Lewis & Clark's campus is a lush, green area that used to be a rich donor's estate. As one would expect from a former estate, the buildings do not resemble typical college administrative buildings, but remind one of "Snow White cottages." On the "fairly small" campus there is a reflecting pool, a rose garden, "lots of trees, and grassy space for people to lay out on sunny days." Unfortunately, those sunny days are few and far between. The charm of a lush campus with "spectacular" views of Mt. Hood make up for the wet and misty atmosphere.

LC students live in "typical college dorms" their first two years when they are required to live on campus. Many consider this a burden and would like to have the cheaper option of living off campus. There are, however, some perks to dorm living. As a way to meet people, some of the housing facilities have themed floors, such as an "environmental activism floor" and an "international floor." Room size varies from dorm to dorm, but almost all are coed by floor.

Upperclassmen commonly move off campus either into a house with friends or an apartment. Because the area surrounding Lewis & Clark is suburban and fairly isolated, many live in Portland proper. This move off campus can create a schism between the upper- and underclassmen. Once students move off campus they "don't really see the people on campus" and sometimes become less involved in campus activities because "it's hard to get back to campus for a 7:00 meeting. You are probably only going to go if it's something really important to you." Some upperclassmen do not feel as connected to the College, but still prefer living off campus to the isolation they sometimes feel in the dorms.

The one dining hall on campus serves "reasonably good" food. Affectionately called "The Bon" after the College's catering company, Bon Appetite, it provides plenty of vegan and vegetarian options. Bon Appetite is considered one of the best food catering services in the Northwest and offers many types of food at different "stations." The meal plan is fairly flexible; students can choose the number of meals they want per week and also buy "flex points" that they can use as dollars at various a la carte places around campus.

Enjoying the Outdoors

With students living on such a verdant campus, it is no surprise that many of them enjoy outdoor activities. "College of the Outdoors" is a College-funded program that offers trips for everything from skiing to backpacking to canoeing to rock climbing. With the Oregon coast two hours away and Mt. Hood just an hour, there are plenty of spectacular sights to visit. Almost all students take advantage of these trips that can last a weekend or a day. Transportation is provided, and students can borrow any gear that they may need.

Varsity and club sports are "not big" on campus, although the ultimate Frisbee and basketball teams do have a significant following. There are "quite a few athletes" on campus and those who do not play varsity sports can compete in intramural sports. These are fairly popular activities on campus, especially volleyball, skiing, and soccer.

Beyond athletics, students can also join a variety of clubs on campus or work in the student-run co-op that serves as a popular social hang-out. The co-op is a place for students to sell their art, play music or just relax and have a cup of coffee. Social justice and activist clubs are big on campus, and other popular organizations include the women's center and the black student union.

Although students rarely display school spirit, their mascot, a Pioneer, is still a fitting symbol for Lewis & Clark students. Their attitude is reflected in one of the school's mottos, "Do not follow where the path may lead, go instead where there is no path and blaze a trail." Students enjoy the companionship of fellow well-traveled and independent students. Those committed to change and the generating of new ideas thrive at Lewis & Clark—they can get a strong liberal arts education in a small school setting.—*Rachel Jeffers*

FYI

If you come to Lewis & Clark, you'd better bring "a raincoat, tofu and a pair of Chaco sandals."

The typical weekend schedule? "Brunch in your pajamas, work in a coffee shop downtown and go to a movie or concert."

If I could change one thing about Lewis & Clark, I'd "diversify the student body in terms of background and ideology."

Three things every student at Lewis & Clark should do before graduating are "spend all day in Powell's, go to dinner with your professor and go camping on the coast."

Oregon State University

Address: 104 Kerr
Administration Building
Corvallis, OR 97331-2106
Phone: 541-737-4411
E-mail address:
osuamit@oregonstate.edu
Web site URL:
www.oregonstate.edu
Year Founded: 1858
Private or Public: Public
Religious Affiliation: None
Location: Suburban
Number of Applicants: 8,149
Percent Accepted: 86%
Percent Accepted who
enroll: 42%
Number Entering: 2,953
Number of Transfers
Accepted each Year:
Unreported
Middle 50% SAT range:
M: 490–610, CR: 460–580,
Wr: Unreported
Middle 50% ACT range:
20–26
Early admission program
EA/ED/None: EA

Percentage accepted
through EA or ED:
Unreported
EA and ED deadline:
1-Nov
Regular Deadline: 1-Sep
Application Fee: $50
Full time Undergraduate
enrollment: 16,673
Total enrollment: 19,768
Percent Male: 54%
Percent Female: 46%
Total Percent Minority or
Unreported: 30%
Percent African-American:
1%
Percent Asian/Pacific
Islander: 8%
Percent Hispanic: 4%
Percent Native-American:
1%
Percent International: 2%
Percent in-state/out of
state: 89%/11%
Percent from Public HS:
Unreported
Retention Rate: 81%

Graduation Rate 4-year:
30%
Graduation Rate 6-year:
Unreported
Percent Undergraduates in
On-campus housing: 19%
Number of official organized
extracurricular
organizations: 350
3 Most popular majors:
Business, Health, Natural
Sciences
Student/Faculty ratio: 18:1
Average Class Size: 20–29
Percent of students going to
grad school: Unreported
Tuition and Fees: $18,823
In State Tuition and Fees if
different: $6,187
Cost for Room and Board:
$8,208
Percent receiving financial
aid out of those who apply,
first year: 62%
Percent receiving financial
aid among all students:
48%

T he consensus among students at Oregon State University is that the privilege of being a Beaver is worth the constant rain in Corvallis, Oregon, a quintessential college town settled on the banks of the Willamette River in northwestern Oregon. While many students report much satisfaction with their school choice, many also struggle to define what differentiates OSU from other universities. One student echoed the thoughts of his peers when he called OSU "pretty typical for its size." Still, Oregon State offers top-notch engineering, agriculture and business programs, and those prepared to embrace a small town at the expense of cultural diversity will find a strong sense of community and a spirited atmosphere at Oregon State University.

Freshman Year, Stadium Style

Graduating from Oregon State requires a strong foundation in what the University calls the Baccalaureate Core. While some of these courses focus on basic skills such as mathematics and writing, others are designed to prepare students to participate in contemporary dialogue on topics such as "Social Processes and Institutions" and "Western Culture." Most students reflect on the "Bacc Core" with positive feelings and enjoy having common ground with all their classmates. In one senior's words, "I found it pretty enjoyable. If the Core weren't in place, most people would never take classes in, for example, 'Difference, Power and Discrimination.'" That said, another consequence of the Core is that the majority of students' classes in the first two years are part of the Core requirements, and therefore tend to be lecture classes. Students complain that these classes often have as many as 400 students and are not as challenging as they would like. Pair these required classes with those at the beginning of several large, popular majors like those in the College of Business, which also accommodate hundreds of students in large lecture halls, and the early years at OSU can feel very impersonal. Because of a limited number of choices of lower-level Core classes, registration can be a nightmare. Students who fail to plan carefully and register early are sometimes left with no option except to remain at the University a semester or a year longer than planned to get the credits they need. The problem is exacerbated for students in small or new departments. In the words of one sophomore majoring in New Media Communications, "A lot of classes are only offered once a year, so students like me have to plan their schedules very carefully." Four years can also turn into five when students retake classes in which they weren't satisfied with their grade, or change majors multiple times.

Many students choose to attend Oregon State on the strength of its engineering and forestry programs, which are well-respected and have competitive application processes and high standards for accepted students. The University is also home to an Honors College which offers an Honors Degree and smaller classes, lending students a sense of greater intimacy while still providing the broad range of classes available at a large university. OSU's College of Business, already the umbrella for a number of popular majors, recently reorganized itself in a Professional School model and a career-oriented focus, and has become increasingly popular since then. Programs in fashion design and retail management are also favorites and many students consider them to be challenging. A common thread connecting the most popular departments and courses at Oregon State is immediate applicability—students' favorite classes are the ones in which professors impart real-world experience and design a curriculum with potential for direct application to the job market.

Students say they find professors to be accessible and friendly at office hours, and reliable about responding to emails. This proves critical for students who take online classes that rely on electronic communication exclusively. Many students use former professors to plug gaps in the academic advising system, which can be hit-or-miss. Advisors are in short supply, and "don't like to meet with you very often," one junior said. "We're a large university, so it's easy to fall through the cracks," said another student. Career Services, however, is a bright spot. The office offers a sizable job fair each semester—and occasionally job fairs dedicated exclusively to the very popular engineering programs—and many companies in the Pacific Northwest recruit on campus. Career advisors can also direct students to a one-time class in which students pay eight dollars for training in dining and networking etiquette, as well as to a for-credit class on professional development where students learn the ins and outs of resume and cover letter writing and practice interviewing.

Geeked Out For Greeks

The Greek system at Oregon State University is flourishing. Greek parties are major social events on weekends and various Greek houses throw annual themed parties which students, affiliated or not, say they look forward to. OSU's campus is dry only for underage students, and even the Office of Student Conduct and Affairs acknowledges that alcohol is widely used on campus. Students agree that drinking is an ingrained feature of the social experience at the university. In one sophomore's words, "Sure, you can not drink. People will judge you, but you can make that decision." Both the Greek system and house parties are accessible to students of all ages, but the social scene opens up for undergraduates when they turn 21 and can access the bars in Corvallis, which are popular hangouts for upperclassmen. One student added that a fun activity for students who don't enjoy structured parties or the bar scene is simply "getting together with friends to have a drink and watch a basketball game."

Students at Oregon State University appreciate the outdoorsy campus atmosphere. Boating and swimming activities on the Willamette are popular in warm weather, and Corvallis boasts an impressive network of jogging and biking trails. "The ocean's about an hour away, and so are the mountains. You've kind of got it all, and not everyone can say that," one junior said enthusiastically. And of course, with so much rain, the city is perennially green, which makes for "a really pretty campus," another student said. Residents of Corvallis, meanwhile, embrace the university culture and students. "People are friendly when they find out you're a student," one junior noted, and even people not affiliated with the University call themselves Beavers and support the OSU teams.

For all their enjoyment of the area, students make no bones about the size of Corvallis and the attendant dearth of novel things to do. The nearest major retail stores and movie theaters are in Albany, about 15 miles away, which makes a car a necessity. Many students at Oregon State hail from the area and so have an easy time bringing a car to campus, and a less-easy time finding parking. A number of students maintain an even stronger tie to home and choose to live with their parents while attending OSU. These, along with the students who buy houses with friends or lease off-campus apartments, rather than reside in University dorms, make up the majority of the student body. Freshmen are "sort of expected to live in the dorms," one sophomore said; most students plug into social life on campus by way of the friends they make in these early living arrangements. After freshman year, groups of friends move off campus together, but stay close to and still spend much time on the campus, which is considered very safe at night. On-campus dining options are more than tolerable, if repetitive, and have flexible hours. Students can use money on their student IDs at a Carl's Jr. on campus, should they really need a culinary escape, and there are numerous fast food restaurants within walking distance. One senior characterized the Corvallis dining experience as "generally quick, in and out in 10 minutes or less."

Ducks and Beavers, Oh My

As one sophomore put it, "If you're a Duck or a Beaver, you're nothing else." The Ducks, of course, are the OSU rivals at the University of Oregon in Eugene. In preparation for the annual football match between the universities—known fondly as the Civil War game—the state of Oregon divides its allegiances with no looking back. With increasing successes, including a trip to the Rose Bowl, the Oregon State University football team has the whole of Corvallis behind it, and the baseball team enjoys similar successes and support. The Beaver Dam is a club for student supporters of the OSU Beavers and is one of the most popular clubs on campus, since a one-time $15 fee entitles members to priority seating at games. One student recalled that upon visiting campus, he was struck by "the huge number of people wearing the school colors, more than I'd seen anywhere else."

Student government, in the form of the Associated Students of Oregon State University, is also active and effective, with good access to University administration and much student support. Many students participate in the University's Senate, and students generally appreciate the events the ASOSU brings to campus, including stand-up comedians and a battle of the bands. Recently a group of professional snowboarders visited the campus and brought their own snow to perform demonstrations. Intramural sports are popular on campus, the most prominent being volleyball and flag football, and many students make frequent use of the athletic facilities in Dixon Recreation Center.

The OSU administration is proud of the number of cultural houses on its campus, but one member of the Hispanic Cultural Center was quick to point out that having many cultural houses does not necessarily equal diversity. He added, "I guess for someone who's never been in a diverse community before, it could be new and diverse-seeming, but if you come from another culture, it can feel like you've never seen so many white people in one spot." But few students complain of attitudes of intolerance on campus, ostensibly in part because of the explicit inclusion of coursework on diversity in the Bacc Core.

> "The ocean's about an hour away, and so are the mountains. You've kind of got it all, and not everyone can say that."

Students at Oregon State University celebrate "a real sense of togetherness," in the words of one student, even if they are unable to identify quite what it is that bonds them or sets them apart. Many students are surprised by "how small the school feels, and how you see people you know everywhere you go," even though the University is home to tens of thousands of students. In short, students who seek what is in many ways the prototypical college experience—a strong football and Greek-oriented culture at a large university—will likely have no regrets about choosing to attend Oregon State University.—*Elizabeth Woods*

FYIs

If you come to Oregon State University, you'd better bring "a rain jacket. If you bring an umbrella, the native Oregonians will think you're from California, and can't handle the rain."

What's the typical weekend schedule? "Drive to Portland for an afternoon in the city on Saturday, come back for a game Saturday night, stay up late at parties with friends, sleep in and do work on Sunday."

If I could change one thing about Oregon State University, I'd "locate it in a bigger city with more to do."

Three things every student should do at Oregon State University before graduating are "float the Willamette River, go jogging in the rain and go to the Civil War football game."

Reed College

Address: 3203 SE Woodstock Boulevard Portland, OR 97202-8199

Phone: 503-777-7511

E-mail address: admission@reed.edu

Web site URL: www.reed.edu

Year Founded: 1908

Private or Public: Private

Religious Affiliation: None

Location: Urban

Number of Applicants: 3,485

Percent Accepted: 32%

Percent Accepted who enroll: 29%

Number Entering: 330

Number of Transfers Accepted each Year: 72

Middle 50% SAT range: M: 630–710, CR: 660–760, Wr: 650–740

Middle 50% ACT range: 29–32

Early admission program EA/ED/None: ED

Percentage accepted through EA or ED: 33%

EA and ED deadline: 15-Nov

Regular Deadline: 15-Jan

Application Fee: $50

Full time Undergraduate enrollment: 1,110

Total enrollment: 1,442

Percent Male: 44%

Percent Female: 56%

Total Percent Minority or Unreported: 44%

Percent African-American: 3%

Percent Asian/Pacific Islander: 9%

Percent Hispanic: 7%

Percent Native-American: 1.18%

Percent International: 6%

Percent in-state/out of state: 14%/86%

Percent from Public HS: 59%

Retention Rate: 89%

Graduation Rate 4-year: 59%

Graduation Rate 6-year: 74%

Percent Undergraduates in On-campus housing: 64%

Number of official organized extracurricular organizations: 130

3 Most popular majors: Biology, English, Psychology

Student/Faculty ratio: 10:1

Average Class Size: 10 to 19

Percent of students going to grad school: 65%

Tuition and Fees: $37,960

In State Tuition and Fees if different: No difference

Cost for Room and Board: $9,920

Percent receiving financial aid out of those who apply, first year: 51%

Percent receiving financial aid among all students: 49%

If you dream of being either a frat brother or the girl who dates a frat brother, don't expect Reed College to be the place for you. Reed is a small school in Portland, Oregon, with a quirky student body, small class sizes, intense academic programs and a beautiful campus. If you're an open-minded intellectual who doesn't like the prep or jock factor of many other prestigious, academically challenging schools, you will feel at home at Reed.

Academic Masochism

Reedies are quick to admit that the workload at their school is a serious challenge.

One student explained that it's not uncommon to routinely spend seven hours straight working in the library. "I know that when I graduate, I'm going to have to learn how to function in the real world again, because I've been so immersed in academia," one Reedie said. However, students' academic loads are made bearable by their brilliant but approachable professors. There are no TAs at Reed since all classes are taught by professors. It's easy to get on a first name basis with them because classes are usually no bigger than 30 students. "It's great to be at a table with a few other students, sitting across from a professor who wrote the book for the course," one student noted.

Students say all majors and classes are difficult, and "there isn't anything you can slack off in." Popular majors include English, classics and religion. Psychology is considered the major for the Reedie looking for a less arduous program, but students warn that this fact means it's overwhelming instead of incredibly overwhelming. Though Reed is thought of as more of a humanities-based school, science majors are becoming increasingly popular. "The sciences are strong at Reed as well," one student said, "we even have a nuclear reactor on campus now."

Two of the school's toughest courses, a writing-intensive freshman humanities course and the senior thesis, are required, but students have few complaints about them. The mandatory freshman course is "a common experience that unifies the student body and it's a great foundation for the rest of the Reed education," said one student.

Though free-spirited, Reedies are all focused and genuinely devoted to the pursuit of intellectual growth. "You go to Reed because you want to go to grad school," one student said simply. Whether they're designing their own physics experiments or writing their senior thesis on Shakespeare, Reedies are always passionate about what they do. "It's cool to be in an environment where everyone's interesting it what they're studying," said one student. The students get to show off their laid-back side and introduce fellow students to their interests during Paideia, an event that takes place the week after winter break. During Paideia, everyone in the Reed community—except for profressors—has the opportunity to teach a class. Reedies have taught everything from bike repair to politics during this week.

Study Hard, Party Hard

"The typical Reed student basically wouldn't fit in anywhere else. They're bookish, liberal hipsters, and also friendly and fun-loving," one Reedie said. Students explain that there is no social hierarchy at their school and everyone is accepting of each other. There are no cliques of popular jocks, since Reed doesn't participate in intercollegiate sports. Reedies instead use their competitive spirit in intracollege Ultimate Frisbee and rugby games.

Students' only complaint about their fellow Reedies is the fact that there isn't enough racial diversity. "Reed is basically white and rich," one sophomore said. De-spite the racial homogeneity of the current student population, students report that Reed is working to recruit a more multicultural student body. Others compliment Reed for its financial aid efforts that attract students from a variety of socioeconomic backgrounds.

Most Reed students are heavily involved in extracurricular activities and unique student organizations. Popular groups include the Bike Co-Op and the Reed Kommunal Shit Kollectiv, which organizes parties and gives out free goodies to students in the spirit of communism. When Reedies aren't studying or involved in student organizations, they are doing their other favorite activity: partying. "I put up with five days of shit for two nights of awesome," one student noted. Most Reedies love a good party as much as they love a good lecture. "There's always something going on: parties, dances or great concerts," one enthusiastic student said. The biggest party of the year is Renaissance Fayre, a three-day party unanimously praised by Reed students that starts after the seniors turn in their theses. Alcohol and drugs are widespread at this and many other events, so much so that the other nickname for Reed students is Weedies. "There's really good pot in Oregon," one student explained. Many students said that a great deal of the smoking of this really good pot takes place at the student union. "Though there is a fair amount of alcohol and drug use, people are responsible and there's no pressure to take part if you don't want to," said one freshman.

> At Reed we say that you can have only three of the following five: good academic performance, a relationship, a good group of friends, extracurricular activities, or sleep.

For those who don't want to socialize under the influence, there is a substance-free dorm and many substance-free activities sponsored on campus. Many students said that because of Reed's pot-smoking image, the administration is now trying to keep substance use in check. However, students assure that there will continue to be many good times to be had at Reed. Because of the school's liberal Honor Principle, students can't get busted for alcohol or drug use unless they harm or embarrass another student.

"The focus of the Honor Principle is student responsibility instead of keeping us from having fun," said one student.

With their heavy workloads, many student organizations, and plentiful parties, most Reedies say that it is difficult to date seriously. "After you've been doing work all day, all you want to do is sleep. The last thing you want is to have to take someone out to dinner," explained one Reedie. Though some report having long-term relationships, most say that there are a lot of random hookups. "At Reed we say that you can have only three of the following five: good academic performance, a relationship, a good group of friends, extracurricular activities, or sleep," concluded one student.

Eating in the Reed Bubble

Most Reedies report that there is so much to do on campus, they don't often venture into Portland. "Sometimes it feels like we're in a Reed bubble and not really in Portland," one student said. There is a good selection of restaurants to visit when students do take the short bike ride to the city, but students don't seem to suffer from a lack of good food on campus either. A private food contractor, otherwise known as a catering company, provides Reedies with their meals. The food is said to be "pretty damn good" with a plethora of vegetarian and vegan options.

The only complaint Reed students do have with their dining services is the way their meal plans are set up. Each student starts off the semester with a certain amount of points, known as Commons Cash. Each food item costs a certain amount of Commons Cash, meaning students must budget the amount of money they spend at each meal. Many students find themselves very close to the end of their Commons Cash before the end of the semester is in sight. This reality forces some to leave the Reed bubble and find their nourishment in Portland, if they would rather not replenish their Commons Cash account.

Pretty Sweet Campus

Reedies have praise for their college's campus. "It's really beautiful. There are tons of trees and the buildings are all brick and pretty. Some of the dorms are sort of strange looking, but they're all fine," one student said. Even if a few of the dorms look weird, no one has any complaints about how they are set up inside. All dorms are coed and not segregated by grade. There are about 20 students per floor and one RA whose job is to offer advice and study breaks, not supervision. "Most rooms are divided doubles, which works well because everyone gets their own space," said one Reedie. Students report that the administration does a great job choosing roommates for freshmen. Old Dorm Block, which is prettier than it sounds, is one of the most popular residences. Students say that though Reed's dorms are popular, many upperclassmen live off campus. Suitable housing abounds, with plenty of apartments right across the street from campus.

Though they say that prospective students should definitely visit Reed before they make a decision, Reedies couldn't be happier with their college. As one freshman concluded, "If you're intelligent, ready to debate about anything, willing to be crazy and not afraid of weird shit, Reed is the place for you.—*Keneisha Sinclair*

FYI

If you come to Reed, you'd better bring "the mental capacity for all the work and costumes for the theme parties."

They typical weekend schedule is "work all Friday afternoon and then party, work all Saturday morning then go to a concert or play and then party, and work like crazy all Sunday."

If I could change one thing about Reed, "I'd make it more diverse."

Three things every student at Reed should do before graduating are "go to the Rhody Gardens at night, chase the Doyle Owl and write a great thesis."

University of Oregon

Address: 1217 University of Oregon Eugene, OR 97403
Phone: 800-232-3825
E-mail address: uoadmit@uoregon.edu
Web site URL: www.uoregon.edu
Year Founded: 1876
Private or Public: Public
Religious Affiliation: None
Location: Urban
Number of Applicants: 10,012
Percent Accepted: 88%
Percent Accepted who enroll: 35%
Number Entering: 3,207
Number of Transfers Accepted each Year: 2,086
Middle 50% SAT range: M: 496–611, CR: 486–606, Wr: Unreported
Middle 50% ACT range: Unreported
Early admission program EA/ED/None: EA

Percentage accepted through EA or ED: Unreported
EA and ED deadline: 1-Nov
Regular Deadline: Jan 15
Application Fee: $50
Full time Undergraduate enrollment: 16,473
Total enrollment: 20,394
Percent Male: 53%
Percent Female: 47%
Total Percent Minority or Unreported: 14%
Percent African-American: 2%
Percent Asian/Pacific Islander: 6%
Percent Hispanic: 4%
Percent Native-American: 1%
Percent International: 1%
Percent in-state/out of state: 68%/32%
Percent from Public HS: Unreported
Retention Rate: 84%
Graduation Rate 4-year: 65%

Graduation Rate 6-year: Unreported
Percent Undergraduates in On-campus housing: 22%
Number of official organized extracurricular organizations: 250
3 Most popular majors: Business Administration/Management, Journalism, Psychology
Student/Faculty ratio: 18:1
Average Class Size: Unreported
Percent of students going to grad school: Unreported
Tuition and Fees: $19,992
In State Tuition and Fees if different: $6,435
Cost for Room and Board: $8,478
Percent receiving financial aid out of those who apply, first year: 60%
Percent receiving financial aid among all students: 33%

The University of Oregon is well-regarded for its academics, its athletics and the involvement of its students. Professors engage in thrilling research while constantly cultivating young minds, which go eagerly into the world and "move mountains," as the school's slogan says. With vast resources that include a museum of natural history, a marine biology station on the coast and a sports marketing center, the University also manages to give students personal attention. Located in the town of Eugene, UO has the benefit of being in a dazzling city with small-town charm, set against the backdrop of Oregon's greenery.

Podcasts and Info Hell

The University of Oregon is comprised of seven different schools, although the Schools of Journalism and Architecture, as well as the Charles H. Lundquist College of Business, are considered particularly notable. Most freshmen begin their studies within the School of Arts and Sciences, and some choose to enter another school shortly thereafter. Those interested in a pre-professional major, such as journalism or business, must first complete the necessary prerequisites in order to be considered for acceptance into a specific school. The architecture major, a five-year program, is well-known for its difficulty and prominence, but prospective majors said they are generally excited about "the opportunities that open up after graduation."

Overall, the difficulty of classes depends on the student. Some find their classes sufficiently challenging, while others commented that "it's not a big change from high school." However, the general education requirements are diverse enough to ensure that each student is pushed out of his comfort zone at one point or another. To fulfill their requirements, students must complete 15 credits in three main categories: arts and letters, social sciences and natural sciences.

Survey class sizes are generally large, but with some effort, students say it's "easy to get ahold of" professors. To accommodate students' schedules, most hold office hours at various times during the week. And as an incentive to encourage these student-faculty relationships, if a student asks a professor to meet up in a University dining hall, the latter's meal is free. "This is a great opportunity to talk to your professors, and it's highly underused," one student reports.

For first-year students, journalism classes are very popular, particularly former broadcaster Al Stavitsky's course, "Mass Media and Society." Stavitsky creates podcasts, online audio files that include information that bridges the assigned readings and his in-class lectures. Other professors across various departments have also expressed an interest in his method, including the implementation of podcasts. On the other hand, another journalism course, the so-called "Info Hell," is notoriously intimidating and requires a 100-page research paper.

Students looking for a challenging academic opportunity might choose to apply to the Robert D. Clark Honors College, a selective program that provides its participants with an "intense" liberal arts education. It is the oldest four-year honors college in the nation, consisting of nearly 600 undergraduates. Classes are taught by some of the University's most prized professors and are capped at 25 students, allowing for plenty of personal attention. A senior thesis is required and the workload "never ever seems to end," but Honors College students agree that when all is said and done, "it's totally worth it."

Students with very specific academic interests in mind have the opportunity to choose from enrolling in over 50 Freshmen Interest Groups (FIGs). The groups vary in topic from "Introduction to Monkeys and Apes" to "Early Judaism" to "Mind and Society." Students say that participation in an FIG, which usually consists of about 25 students who take two core classes together in the fall term, is a great way to make friends right off the bat. Several of the FIGs even live together on campus.

Eating and Sleeping

Other than the specific building they will reside in, students living on and off campus have plenty of housing options to choose from. On-campus single and double rooms are both available, some with additional features such as a sink, a private bathroom or extra floor space. A single isn't guaranteed, but students who submit their housing forms earlier are more likely to get one. Spe-

cial Interest halls attract those who wish to surround themselves with other honor students, musicians, athletes or international students, to name a few. Those interested in joining a sorority or fraternity and moving into the chapter house soon into their freshman year may also sign up for a temporary housing option, to avoid breaking a residential hall contract.

Many UO dorms have their own unique characteristics. While Bean, for example, only houses freshmen, it's known for throwing the "craziest parties." However, the architect who created the dorm also designed prisons—a fact that does not seem to go unnoticed by students, one of whom referenced Bean's "small windows and poor lighting." The rooms in Carson all have sinks, and Barnhart houses a lot of athletes. Riley is the international dorm, with more than half of its students coming from overseas.

Students tend to move into cheaper apartments nearby after their first or second year, although on-campus housing is provided to all who request it. The Living-Learning Center, a large new housing complex that opened in 2006, includes classrooms in the basement and a central plaza serving as a café with outdoor seating and a setting for informal performances. The dorm rooms, primarily for first-year students, are reputed to be 50 percent larger than the current average rooms. University officials hope that the LLC will blur the distinction between residential and academic life.

Students who live on campus are required to purchase one of the University's three different meal plans. The dining program works on a weekly point system, and unused points may be rolled over. Carson and Barnhart offer all-you-can-eat buffets, while plenty of other venues around campus feature individual food items. "The food's not gourmet, but it could definitely be worse," one student said. The general consensus is that there are so many different kinds of food to choose from, it's easy enough to find something that suits the palate.

What to Do, What to Do

Greek life is relatively popular, as UO has eight Panhellenic sororities, two NPHC sororities, 12 fraternities and one fraternity colony. While sororities have a more formal and structured recruitment process that takes place in the fall, fraternities recruit year-round. Students say that initiations are "enjoyable experiences," and no complaints have been lodged in recent years. All the chapter houses are dry, as is the rest of the campus. And while many students drink, there are plenty of other activities happening around campus to keep nondrinking or non-partying students busy at any given time. Drugs aren't extremely visible, but "if you look hard enough, you can find whatever you want."

Although the school sponsors dances, students note that attendance is poor: "I went to one during freshman year, and it was just a few people standing around," one complained. Since the no-alcohol policy is strictly enforced on campus, more parties take place in the surrounding area apartments.

Downtown Eugene is a popular and inspiring location, filled with working artists, writers and musicians. While students take advantage of amenities such as a nearby theater that offers admission for only $1.50, they also warn that "everything closes after dinner." UO's rival, Oregon State University, is only half an hour away and is often a common party locale. Outdoor activities are popular with many as well, as opportunities for some great skiing or sailing are just a couple hours away by car. Many students, especially those from in state, bring vehicles to campus. Although an overnight parking permit is "a hassle to obtain," enough students have cars on campus that "it's easy to find a ride."

UO students say they are extremely happy with the security measures provided by the University. The streets are well-lit, and blue phones are liberally distributed around campus. There are several safe transportation systems, such as the Assault Prevention Shuttle (APS) and the Drunk Driving Shuttle, which provide nighttime and off-campus transport.

Go Ducks!

The majority of campus activities stem from the Erb Memorial Union (EMU), which headquarters all aspects of extracurricular organizations. While its claim to help students "discover new interests and tap hidden talents" may seem cheesy, students verify its importance on campus. Through EMU, one student discovered the Outdoor Program; another became a member of Alpha Phi Omega, the largest college service-based organization in the world; and yet another made plans to join the Peace Corps after graduation.

Opportunities to join organizations are plentiful at UO. The student newspaper, the

Oregon Daily Emerald, has a huge staff of writers. A large intramural sports league, which is grouped into three skill levels, is fairly popular as well. Joining a team for a season is highly recommended, and one student asserted that IMs are "the most fun" he's ever had. UO Debate is considered one of the best teams out of all the public universities, with two students recently placing among the top eight teams at the renowned World Universities Debating Championships. The University also hosts a plethora of music events, such as the Oregon Jazz Festival and the Oregon Bach Festival.

> **"It's easy to see why students of all backgrounds can sincerely call this campus 'home.'"**

The Ducks sports teams inspire deep loyalty among students, which is eagerly expressed at every home game. The recently renovated Autzen Stadium is almost always packed with football fans who wait in line for hours to obtain tickets. Fans are born every day, as demonstrated by a student who commented, "I brought my roommate along once and she comes to all the games now!" Along the basketball court, thousands of students who call themselves the Pit Crew line up in bright yellow t-shirts to cheer on their favorite players. They are definitely the most visible and loudest supporters, and call themselves "the greatest student basketball fan organization in the nation."

Atmosphere

As a university renowned for its politically liberal student body, it is not unusual to see large groups of students dressed in hippie garb. "If you're not used to them, it's weird at first. But eventually, you realize that the hippies are an integral part of the campus image." Although UO has made a big push to promote diversity awareness on campus—it hosts at least one diversity-building event per week—students say that it has a long way to go. One student said she wished others were "more culturally aware," recalling an incident where another student transferred because the surrounding community was considered "too white." However, students also acknowledged that most people are generally open and accepting of others' beliefs and opinions.

With such a broad spectrum of majors, political views and extracurricular options at students' fingertips, UO is a wonderful place to spend four years. Looking around, explained one student, "it's easy to see why students of all backgrounds can sincerely call this campus 'home.'"—*Catherine Jan*

FYI

If you're coming to University of Oregon, you'd better bring "an umbrella!"

What's the typical weekend schedule? "Wake up around noon, pregame, attend a sporting event, party hop at night, sleep, work, and work out."

If I could change one thing about the University of Oregon, I'd change "[the fact that] the roads have too many potholes."

Three things that every student should do before graduating are "paint your face for a football game, attend a charity event sponsored by a sorority or fraternity and join a club about something that you've never heard about."

Willamette University

Address: 900 State Street, Salem, OR 97301

Phone: 503-370-6303

E-mail address: libarts@willamette.edu

Web site URL: www.willamette.edu

Year Founded: 1842

Private or Public: Private

Religious Affiliation: Methodist

Location: Urban

Number of Applicants: 2,983

Percent Accepted: 77%

Percent Accepted who enroll: 19%

Number Entering: 435

Number of Transfers Accepted each Year: 102

Middle 50% SAT range: M: 550–660, CR: 570–690, Wr: 550–660

Middle 50% ACT range: 25–29

Early admission program EA/ED/None: EA

Percentage accepted through EA or ED: 91%

EA and ED deadline: 1-Dec

Regular Deadline: 15-Jan

Application Fee: $50

Full time Undergraduate enrollment: 1,932

Total enrollment: 2,320

Percent Male: 45%

Percent Female: 55%

Total Percent Minority or Unreported: 13%

Percent African-American: 4%

Percent Asian/Pacific Islander: 5%

Percent Hispanic: 3%

Percent Native-American: 0%

Percent International: 5%

Percent in-state/out of state: 31%/69%

Percent from Public HS: 80%

Retention Rate: 87%

Graduation Rate 4-year: 72%

Graduation Rate 6-year: 73%

Percent Undergraduates in On-campus housing: 68%

Number of official organized extracurricular organizations: 107

3 Most popular majors: Biology, Economics, Psychology

Student/Faculty ratio: 11:1

Average Class Size: 10 to 19

Percent of students going to grad school: 41%

Tuition and Fees: $28,416

In State Tuition and Fees if different: No difference

Cost for Room and Board: $7,000

Percent receiving financial aid out of those who apply, first year: 92%

Percent receiving financial aid among all students: 92%

Located in the heart of Oregon, Willamette University, the oldest college in the West, is known not only for its strong academic reputation, but also for its student body, which challenges stereotypes on a daily basis. The school's gorgeous campus with historic red-brick buildings surrounded by a bustling city is just one manifestation of the diversity of interests and opportunities found at Willamette.

Where Professors Know Your Name

As one freshman girl commented, "So far, academics at Willamette have been one pleasant surprise after another." Willamette thrives not only on its reputation for a strong academic program, but also on the emphasis it places on fostering professor-student interaction. Class sizes are generally small (the same freshman commented that her largest class contains 17 students), and this allows professors and students to get to know each other, which students cite as an important aspect of academic life at Willamette. The student-to-professor ratio is 13:1, which allows for significant, meaningful relationships to form between teachers and students. One student remarked, "I have yet to have a professor that is not demanding yet reasonable, creative yet structured, and informative yet personal. The professors make themselves easily accessible to students and genuinely do care about us." The small class size also enables increased student participation and the occasional field trip for hands-on experience.

> "I have never been taught by a faculty member whom I did not feel as though I could approach about absolutely anything."

In addition to guidance provided by professors, Willamette itself provides a structure for a course of study, as students are required to take courses in each of the following fields, or "modes of inquiry": qualitative thinking, quantitative thinking, analyzing arguments, creating in the arts, interpreting texts, thinking historically, understanding the natural world and understanding society. In addition, Willamette students must take four courses designated as "writing centered," and take a language course. This set of requirements, though extensive, ensures that students leave Willamette with an education that is broad as well as focused in a particular major or area. Popular majors include economics, political science, psychology and the domains of science and music, which are also extremely popular but challenging due to the rigors of the requirements and the quality of those departments at Willamette. Though classes are challenging, the accessibility of the faculty members makes students feel at home and comfortable enough to speak freely, both in class and out. One senior commented, "I have never been taught by a faculty member whom I did not feel as though I could approach about absolutely anything."

Seeing Through Stereotypes

As Willamette is located deep in the Northwest and many students come from surrounding areas, they could all be extremely similar; however, students overwhelmingly maintain that this is not the case. Though the majority of the student body does come from similar backgrounds, which are mostly conservative, white and middle-class, one freshman commented, "One cool thing about Willamette students is that we break a lot of stereotypes. What I mean by that is there could be a frat boy who is also a vegetarian, doesn't drink, and a Christian." Willamette students pride themselves on doing their own thing; this often doesn't fit into the stereotypical college mold, and that's OK by them.

The diversity of the student body's interests translates into a vast variety of opportunities offered at Willamette. There is a large array of organizations in which students can be involved, ranging from political groups, religious organizations, community service in Salem, and athletics. According to one female student, "The thing about this school is that there is diversity, so you are bound to find your niche." The Bearcats, a Division III team, compete in 12 different varsity sports, and a large percentage, in fact almost all, of the student body at Willamette participate in athletics in some capacity.

So Many Options, So Little Time

Like the student body, social life at Willamette is also extremely diverse—you can find entertainment at a frat party, bar, room party or just by hanging out with friends or around campus. Though Willamette students do like to party, students are quick to reassure that Willamette is "not a party school." In terms of the Greek scene, there are eight Greek organizations on campus, five of which are fraternities. The frats have parties which are open to everyone, though two of the five are dry. Though they sometimes host events such as toga or black light parties, Greek life in general does not dominate the social scene at Willamette. Students, especially upperclassmen, often visit the surrounding bars in Salem, though the city itself is not known to have a particularly vibrant nightlife, and for this reason many students travel to nearby Portland for a fun night or weekend off-campus.

Dorm and room parties are also popular weekend attractions, and some dorms, such as Doney, Terra, Lausanne and Matthews, are known to be louder, and more social than others. For quiet study, dorms such as Belknap, York, Lee, Wish and Shepard are preferable. Off-campus "keggers" are also common weekend activities, whose popularity is due in large part to the ease with which alcohol can be served. At these events students do not have to worry about campus regulations, which are strict when it comes to drinking and drug use.

However, despite these parties, tamer on-campus socializing is preferred by many students, in part because "the campus is safe at night, although Salem is not." Though the campus is well-patrolled and protected by Willamette security forces, Salem itself is not known to be a safe place to walk around at night, and students, for this reason, often prefer to stay on campus, where they know they can get home safely and securely. However, students often take trips off campus for another reason: to get back to nature. The close proximity of natural beauty to the campus, such as the nearby mountains and west coast beach, allow students who want to get off campus for a day trip or a weekend the opportunity to get back to nature and enjoy the beauty of Oregon while at the same time getting a break from the city life of Salem.

Home Away from Home
Overall, Willamette, with its setup as a small community within the larger city of Salem, has all of the characteristics necessary to provide students with a home away from home. Freshmen and sophomores are required to live on campus, which encourages them not only to form bonds when they first arrive, but to look upon Willamette as a comfortable, familiar place to come home to at the end of the day. In fall 2006, the new residential building Kaneko Commons opened for students, and promises to encourage more students to live on campus. The small size of Willamette's classes and the student body itself allows students to feel a sense of community and connection that can be much harder to achieve on larger campuses. This sense of community, highlighted by the close relationships formed and emphasized between teachers and students, is commonly agreed to be what distinguishes Willamette from the many other universities all across the nation.

It is rare to find the kind of diversity Willamette presents at such a small university; however, Willamette provides the best of both worlds. It attracts students who break every type of mold, while at the same time fostering a sense of community and common bonds between students that are vital to a fulfilling, enjoyable college experience.—*Michelle Katz*

FYI
If you come to Willamette, you'd better bring "an open mind."
What is the typical weekend schedule? "A typical weekend at Willamette is perfect for going to the mountains or the beach."
If I could change one thing about Willamette, I'd "change the hypocritical administration."
The three things that every student at Willamette should do before graduating are "get in a food fight at Goudy during 'midnight breakfast,' get thrown in Mill Stream on your birthday and start the wave at a women's volleyball game."

Pennsylvania

Allegheny College

Address: Box 5, 520 North Main Street Meadville, PA 16335

Phone: 814-332-4351

E-mail address: admissions@allegheny.edu

Web site URL: www.allegheny.edu

Year Founded: 1815

Private or Public: Private

Religious Affiliation: United Methodist

Location: Rural

Number of Applicants: 4,243

Percent Accepted: 61%

Percent Accepted who enroll: 22%

Number Entering: 591

Number of Transfers Accepted each Year: 57

Middle 50% SAT range: M: 560–650, CR: 550–660, Wr: Unreported

Middle 50% ACT range: 23–28

Early admission program EA/ED/None: ED

Percentage accepted through EA or ED: 71%

EA and ED deadline: 15-Nov

Regular Deadline: 15-Feb

Application Fee: $35

Full time Undergraduate enrollment: 2,082

Total enrollment: 2,125

Percent Male: 44%

Percent Female: 56%

Total Percent Minority or Unreported: 8%

Percent African-American: 3%

Percent Asian/Pacific Islander: 3%

Percent Hispanic: 2%

Percent Native-American: 0%

Percent International: Unreported

Percent in-state/out of state: 60%/40%

Percent from Public HS: 83%

Retention Rate: 88%

Graduation Rate 4-year: 69%

Graduation Rate 6-year: 74%

Percent Undergraduates in On-campus housing: 78%

Number of official organized extracurricular organizations: 78

3 Most popular majors: Biology, Economics, Psychology

Student/Faculty ratio: 13:1

Average Class Size: 19

Percent of students going to grad school: 54%

Tuition and Fees: $32,000

In State Tuition and Fees if different: No difference

Cost for Room and Board: $8,000

Percent receiving financial aid out of those who apply, first year: 83%

Percent receiving financial aid among all students: 69%

Founded in 1815, Allegheny is one of the oldest colleges in the United States. With a history longer than that of some of the finest and most reputed universities in the country, Allegheny College features a beautiful, pastoral campus with great learning opportunities, for which it earned a place among the top 40 schools in *Colleges that Change Lives*. If you are looking for an excellent liberal arts education and do not mind living in a quiet, small town located hours away from any major cities, consider Allegheny as a potential college choice.

Meadville? Where is That?

Meadville is a small, "post-industrial" town in western Pennsylvania. It is home to a population of only 14,000 people. The closest metropolitan area is Pittsburg, PA, which is about 90 minutes away. Cleveland, the next nearest city, requires two hours of driving. As a result, although the school offers a quiet learning environment, it certainly has "neither the number nor the quality of activities that can be found in large metropolitan areas." While the Gator Activities Programming invites entertainers to perform on campus, it is obvious that "if you've always wanted to be in a city and have flashing lights and tons of things to do on the weekends, don't bother." Nevertheless, most students agree that "Allegheny has a beautiful campus." The college covers nearly 540 acres, including a natural reserve of 283 acres, as well as 203 acres dedicated to recreation. The campus offers great facilities such as an observatory, an art gallery, and a

TV station, all for a small enrollment of about 2,125 students. With the nearby lakes and state parks, Allegheny is a great place for the enjoyment of nature and tranquility. As one student explained, "If you are looking for a small college in a rural and laid-back community, Allegheny is the place for you."

The college's relationship with Meadville, however, remains rather detached. "There tends to be clash between 'townies' and us Alleghenians," said a student. "But we are truthfully working on the relationship." While most students in the college come from middle-class families, the formerly industrial Meadville has been facing economic difficulties since the 1980s. As a result, Allegheny students are sometimes just seen as "a bunch of rich kids." At the same time, one student remarked, "The campus is rather closed off to the town of Meadville, although there are some students that go to bars and go shopping." There are about 30 restaurants in the area and several small stores. Nevertheless, with the nearest mall about 30 minutes away, "the town doesn't really have anything interesting for us to go there," one senior said.

Despite being in an isolated location, however, the students are very content with the safety of both Allegheny College and Meadville. Few dangerous incidents ever occur in the area, and the students agree that Allegheny is "a peaceful residential campus."

Majorly into Minors
A top-100 liberal arts college according to *US News & World Report*, Allegheny provides its students with a well-rounded academic program. It is a relatively selective school: more than 75 percent of its students were in the top 20 percent of their high schools. The acceptance rate is generally around 60 percent, giving Allegheny a body of capable students. "Academics are the reason that everyone comes here," said a student.

Allegheny is well known for its science departments. "We have one of the best placements into med school in the nation," one Alleghenian said. "Our science departments are very hard. We don't curve grades like other colleges." Despite the belief that humanities and social science classes are less interesting and less difficult than science classes, most students agree that Allegheny "boasts excellent faculty in all fields." The construction of a $23 million state-of-the-art communications and theater center is in the works, and will help improve the school's reputation in humanities and arts.

The classes are based on hour credits.

Most classes are four credits, and the students need 131 credit hours to graduate. People generally take four to five classes per semester. One of the distinctive elements of Allegheny is its requirement of both a major and a minor, which helps people to "achieve a more rounded education." The minor cannot be in the same academic division (humanities, natural sciences, and social sciences) as the major, meaning that the students have to take classes in very different fields, thus achieving the goal of a liberal arts education.

The school also has a vigorous set of requirements for its students. In addition to the mandatory classes in humanities, sciences, and social sciences, everyone is required to take three courses on academic planning, starting from second semester of freshman year to the end of sophomore year, to help prepare for the design of their programs of study and their activities. They also need to take three FS seminars during their freshman and sophomore years. These classes focus mostly on improving the students' ability to research and communicate ideas. There are more than 80 different seminars available to the students.

> **"'I've babysat kids for professors before. We are all equals here and students help professors and professors help students.'"**

By the end of their sophomore year, students choose their majors among the 30 offered by Allegheny. The major requires anywhere from 32 to 48 credit hours and the completion of a junior seminar and a senior project. Students can also make their own major if they can justify the point of having their own course of study. The minor requires 20 credits, 12 of which must be outside the division of the graduation major.

The course load is often agreed to be challenging among Alleghenians. According to one student, "Allegheny College has one of the largest work loads for any class whether it be sciences, social sciences, or humanities. All areas are challenging—and encouraging—which Allegheny College facilitates its students to experience."

2,125 Students, One Tight-Knit Experience
Students at Allegheny maintain close ties with their professors. "Students and professors are all very close," said an Alleghenian.

"Professors often invite students to their house for a meal." Indeed, the small classes give plenty of opportunities for the students to interact with the faculty. When asked about the relationship between the students and the faculty, one interviewee said, "I've babysat kids for professors before. We are all equals here and students help professors and professors help students."

The dorms are similar to most colleges. About 78 percent of the students live on campus. According to an Alleghenian, a typical room would be "double 17 by 15, no AC." "Only the more expensive, new dorms have AC," added another student who also pointed out that, "Bathroom and shower space is not an issue. There are plenty of those."

Greek life is an important part of Allegheny. Being part of a fraternity or sorority gives sisters and brothers access to a series of activities. Nevertheless, there are plenty of other activities on campus so that the students do not feel left out if they opt out of Greek life. Alcohol is an important part of parties, and it generally can be found by anyone.

Allegheny is trying hard to improve its diversity. Currently, less than 14 percent of Alleghenians are ethnic minorities. The administration is making it a priority to recruit more minority applicants.—*Xiaohang Liu*

FYI

If you come to Allegheny, you'd better bring "a Nalgene. We are big on those."
If I could change one thing about Allegheny, I'd "lower the cost of tuition."
Three things every student at Allegheny should do before graduating are "go to Eddie's Footlong for hotdogs, play pool in the Game Room, and take yoga classes."

Bryn Mawr College

Address: 101 North Merion Avenue Bryn Mawr, PA 19010-2859
Phone: 610-526-5152
E-mail address: admissions@brynmawr.edu
Web site URL: www.brynmawr.edu
Year Founded: 1885
Private or Public: Private
Religious Affiliation: None
Location: Suburban
Number of Applicants: 2,150
Percent Accepted: 48.7%
Percent Accepted who enroll: 35%
Number Entering: 366
Number of Transfers Accepted each Year: 25
Middle 50% SAT range: M: 580–680, CR: 620–730, Wr: 620–720
Middle 50% ACT range: 27–31
Early admission program EA/ED/None: ED

Percentage accepted through EA or ED: 19%
EA and ED deadline: 15-Nov
Regular Deadline: 15-Jan
Application Fee: $50
Full time Undergraduate enrollment: 1,287
Total enrollment: 1,745
Percent Male: 0%
Percent Female: 100%
Total Percent Minority or Unreported: 22%
Percent African-American: 6%
Percent Asian/Pacific Islander: 12%
Percent Hispanic: 4%
Percent Native-American: 10.0%
Percent International: 7%
Percent in-state/out of state: 16%/84%
Percent from Public HS: Unreported
Retention Rate: 90%
Graduation Rate 4-year: 81.0%

Graduation Rate 6-year: 85.0%
Percent Undergraduates in On-campus housing: 95%
Number of official organized extracurricular organizations: 94
3 Most popular majors: English, Mathematics, Psychology
Student/Faculty ratio: 8:1
Average Class Size: Unreported
Percent of students going to grad school: Unreported
Tuition and Fees: $36,540
In State Tuition and Fees if different: No difference
Cost for Room and Board: $11,520
Percent receiving financial aid out of those who apply, first year: 62%
Percent receiving financial aid among all students: 62%

L ocated in an ideal location just outside a major metropolis, Bryn Mawr's beautiful campus and motivated student body make it a desirable choice for many young women.

The common trait among all Mawrtyrs, as

they're called, is their overwhelming passion for their school.

Smaller is Better

Academics receive top priority at Bryn Mawr, where they are described as "challenging but so rewarding." Despite the heavy workload, most students could not be happier. The school attempts to prevent a cutthroat environment with a unique honor code forbidding the discussion of grades between students. The honor code is strictly enforced and applies to class rank as well, which is not disclosed until graduation.

The most popular majors are English, Mathematics and Psychology. All students must take a Freshman Liberal Studies Seminar, known as the College Seminar, intended to prepare freshmen for college writing, especially for classes in which papers are required such as English, History, Anthropology and Sociology. In addition to the College Seminar, students must also fulfill core requirements intended to impart a broad liberal arts foundation. These include two labs, two natural sciences, two humanities and two social sciences. One of the best classes is said to be "Identification in Cinema," a film minor/art history major course taught by perennial favorite Homay King. In addition to King, the most popular professors include Mary Louise Cookson, a mathematics professor, and Gary McDonough, director of the Growth and Structure of Cities Program. In addition to Bryn Mawr's extensive course offerings, students have the option of taking classes at nearby Haverford College, Swarthmore College and the University of Pennsylvania.

The school also allows students to design their own Independent major. One student explained, "Any gap you may find in course offerings, you can often work with professors to fill, if you are truly interested and willing to commit to it." Another student knew of friends who had majored in Feminist Studies, Theater Studies, Film, and American Cultural Studies, all as Independent majors.

Unsurprisingly, classes at Bryn Mawr are small. Intimate classes foster intimate student/professor bonds. In addition to office hours, many professors make themselves accessible to students at all hours. Outside of the academic arena, many students babysit for their professors, walk their dogs, or go to their homes for dinner on a regular basis.

Another aspect of classes at Bryn Mawr is their accessibility to all class years. With a few exceptions, classes have a mix of freshman through seniors. One student praised

this feature because it "gave me the opportunity to make friends who were older than me and acted as mentors."

Quiet but Lively

Bryn Mawr's location has a significant impact on its social scene. Students do not bewail its all-female student body because of the coed mingling afforded by the proximity of neighboring colleges Swarthmore and Haverford, with which Bryn Mawr has always enjoyed a close relationship. Haverford tends to have keg parties and dances, and the regular shuttle between the schools makes for easy access to parties.

Students at Bryn Mawr say that underage students looking to drink do not encounter many obstacles. Thursdays and Saturdays are the big party nights on campus, while Fridays are more toned down. "Thursday people party hard, and grin and bear it through their Friday classes," one student explained. When it comes to partying, as with most things at Bryn Mawr, tradition prevails. The biggest party of the year occurs at Halloween. There is usually a themed "East/West party" held in the connected Pembroke East and West dorms. Bryn Mawr and Haverford each host a drag ball; at Haverford the fall semester and at Bryn Mawr in the spring. Perry House and Radnor, both dorms, are known for throwing good parties. Radnor is sometimes unofficially used as a venue for small bands. According to one student, many of the best parties are after-parties following events like dance performances, culture shows, debate team meets, or a capella concerts.

Beyond the party scene, students hang out in local coffee shops like Cosi or Starbucks or the new coffee shop in town called Milkboy, where local musicians perform and which holds open mike nights. There is a larger Milkboy in an adjacent town two miles away. Both are affiliated with a local record production company of the same name and a current Bryn Mawr student has two albums out on their label. Another option for those interested in the arts is the renovated Bryn Mawr Film Institute, which shows art-house films and has begun cooperating with the Film Studies Department at Bryn Mawr.

For those looking to get away from campus, the local commuter rail system provides easy access to Philadelphia's Art Museum, restaurants and nightlife. The largest mall on the East Coast is 10 minutes from campus.

Most socializing takes place on campus, however, and is associated in some way with academics. One student explains that "while people are definitely social, it's nice to know you won't be the only one in the library on a Friday night." Most students hang out in their halls with friends, or in Canaday Library, which is "open, well-lit, and has sofas everywhere." The café inside, the Lusty Cup, is on the same floor as the 24-hour computing suite, making it a popular study area. A lot of socializing centers around clubs, sports and other extracurriculars because Mawrtyrs tend to be very involved.

Campus Life

At Bryn Mawr "the living is definitely good." Campus architecture is classic Gothic, with beautiful stained-glass windows and imposing stone. The newest dorm, Erdman, was designed by Louis Kahn as a modern Scottish castle. Students live in one of 13 residence halls. The absence of specially designated freshman dorms means that freshman housing can rival senior housing. Every dorm has women from all four years, and there is almost no difference in quality of rooms from freshman to senior year. Many rooms have bay windows, wood paneling, and fireplaces; some even have walk-in closets. Campus safety is not a concern. Students feel completely secure, even at night. Bryn Mawr's suburban location means that many students rarely lock their doors or their bikes, and lost wallets have been known to come back to their owners before they were noticed to be missing. Students love the dorms and campus in general, which could explain why 95 percent of the students choose to live on-campus.

The food on campus is another reason. The dining halls at Bryn Mawr receive high marks all around. They are "very vegetarian and somewhat vegan friendly." The dining halls are completely student staffed as all freshmen who desire a campus job must start in the dining halls. Outside of the dining halls, there are also many excellent restaurants in the area and in nearby Philadelphia.

Like the classes, dining halls are open to Haverford students as well, but since breakfast ends up being almost only Bryn Mawr women, you get lots of people in pajamas. In many cases, that's how they stay throughout the day. Designer brands can be spotted on campus, but for the most part dress is casual throughout the week. On the weekends students get dressed up and made up, and head out for fun. Though there may not be guys enrolled at Bryn Mawr, there are generally quite a few on campus. The women decide as a floor at the beginning of the year whether

their bathroom will be coed. Visiting men are simply expected to act responsibly.

Extracurriculars are another aspect which benefits from the small size of the school. According to one student, "If it isn't here already, you can make it happen." The small size of Bryn Mawr also allows freshmen to play an active role in their extracurricular activities. Student government is one of the largest organizations on campus, along with the *Bi-College News*, the Haverford-Bryn Mawr newspaper. There is also an active political community, with groups that span the political spectrum. Political groups are extremely active, and there are tons of dance groups (everything from Asian fusion to classical ballet) and a cappella. An active Rainbow Alliance helps to promote an open, accepting atmosphere for LGBT students.

> **"If it isn't here already, you can make it happen."**

The diversity of the student body is universally praised. Students come from all around the country and the world. Campus is described as being virtually "clique-free," and students say that there is no segregation whatsoever. "It's very, very diverse economically, socially, politically and religiously," one student said. Diversity is not only evident in the student body, but openly discussed as well. "We talk about it, a lot," a student explained. This often entails bringing up and discussing problems, as well as acknowledging any failures to address diversity issues within the community.

For all their strengths, Mawrtyrs rarely dominate the athletic field. School spirit is definitely not lacking in the least, but unfortunately that doesn't carry over to achieving many victories. There are exceptions, however. In 2007, Bryn Mawr's coed rugby team won the EPRU Division III championship and competed at nationals. Win or lose, students go out to support their teams (and Haverford's) even at away games. For the nonvarsity athletic types, there are good gym facilities, a pool, and plenty of safe places to run around campus. For almost every varsity sport there is a corresponding club team, so anyone can participate.

Tradition Reigns

Bryn Mawr's most distinguishing characteristic may be the Traditions (with a capital T). These are four events held throughout the year, aimed at welcoming the underclassmen into the community. The first Tradition is Parade Night, which welcomes the freshmen to campus with the singing of the school song. Lantern Night follows, each class holding up a lantern of a different color to identify themselves. Third is Hell Week, during which the sophomores get freshmen to do all sorts of crazy things, which the upperclassmen help them evade. Finally, in May the college president rides a horse into campus to begin the May Day celebrations, which focus on the senior class. One unspoken tradition is skinny dipping in the Cloisters, an act inspired by alumna Katharine Hepburn.

There is almost unanimous agreement among Bryn Mawr students that there is no place they would rather be: "So many of my classmates have described their attraction to Bryn Mawr as 'falling in love' or being 'magical,'" one student said. Small classes, a beautiful campus in a great location, and a diverse, passionate student body all make for a nearly ideal college experience. One student described her peers as "amazing." Another remarked that meeting alumnae is like meeting aunts or old family friends because of the shared bond that comes from the Bryn Mawr experience.—*Laura Sullivan*

FYI

If you come to Bryn Mawr, you'd better bring "passion—in studying, partying, rallying and relaxing. We are a pretty devoted-to-our-causes campus."

What's the typical weekend schedule? "Friday: relax if you have no class and go out at night. Saturday: during the day study, play a sport, volunteer, rehearse, work and then party. Sunday: spend far too long at brunch, study for an hour, eat dinner, go to SGA (our student government's open meeting), hang out with friends, stay in the library until midnight."

If I could change one thing about Bryn Mawr, I would "expand the Bryn Mawr bubble to include Philadelphia, get more students involved in off-campus communities."

Three things that every student should do before graduating are "get sunburned on May Day, join the crowd at 4 a.m. in Guild during finals, and sing good-night to the seniors during Step Sing."

Bucknell University

Address: Freas Hall
  Lewisburg, PA 17837
Phone: 570-577-1101
E-mail address:
  admissions@bucknell.edu
Web site URL:
  www.bucknell.edu
Year Founded: 1864
Private or Public: Private
Religious Affiliation: None
Location: Rural
Number of Applicants:
  8,024
Percent Accepted: 29.8%
**Percent Accepted who
  enroll:** 40%
Number Entering: 957
**Number of Transfers
  Accepted each Year:** 57
Middle 50% SAT range:
  M: 630–710, CR: 600–680,
  Wr: 610–700
Middle 50% ACT range:
  27–31
**Early admission program
  EA/ED/None:** ED

**Percentage accepted
  through EA or ED:** 39%
EA and ED deadline: 15-Nov
Regular Deadline: 15-Jan
Application Fee: $60
**Full time Undergraduate
  enrollment:** 3,583
Total enrollment: 3,719
Percent Male: 47%
Percent Female: 53%
**Total Percent Minority or
  Unreported:** 13%
Percent African-American: 3%
**Percent Asian/Pacific
  Islander:** 6%
Percent Hispanic: 4%
Percent Native-American:
  <1%
Percent International: 3%
**Percent in-state/out of
  state:** 25%/75%
Percent from Public HS:
  Unreported
Retention Rate: 95%
Graduation Rate 4-year:
  85.0%

Graduation Rate 6-year:
  88.0%
**Percent Undergraduates in
  On-campus housing:** 86%
**Number of official organized
  extracurricular
  organizations:** 150
3 Most popular majors:
  Biology, Business
  Administration, Economics
Student/Faculty ratio: 11:1
Average Class Size:
  Unreported
**Percent of students going to
  grad school:** Unreported
Tuition and Fees: $39,434
**In State Tuition and Fees if
  different:** No difference
Cost for Room and Board:
  $8,728
**Percent receiving financial
  aid out of those who apply,
  first year:** 62%
**Percent receiving financial
  aid among all students:**
  58%

Bucknell, a liberal arts school situated in rural central Pennsylvania, offers the quintessential small campus feel. Small class sizes, close relationships between teachers and students, flexible and accommodating faculty, and beautiful new facilities are all qualities that create the charming and personable feel of this community.

Accessible Academic Area

Like many small schools, Bucknell can boast an excellent student-teacher ratio that results in personal relationships between students and faculty. Students claim professors are flexible and almost always available, "You can just walk right into their office at almost any time and sit down and talk" says one student. Students' descriptions of professors have really revealed the faculty's involvement and investment in their students, "I really feel like the teachers are there to teach us, not just instruct us. It is a subtle but important difference." Only professors teach courses and teaching assistants, sometimes considered a nuisance when left in charge, are employed as a helpful supplement to lecture courses.

Perhaps one of the most impressive features of the academic curricula is the consistently small class sizes. The "large" intro level courses are sparse and usually have about 100 people. For the most part you will find yourself in more personal class settings of 20 to 30 people. As you move into the upper level courses classes are even more intimate, ranging from 13 to 20 people. Some classes are competitive to get into, especially those at the upper levels, but like one student said, "most of the time I haven't had a problem with getting into a class; the biggest problem I have had is fitting a class into my schedule when there are a lot of cool classes I want to take. The one time I had had a problem, I just spoke with the teacher and he let me in."

The workload, like at any college, "is what you make it. You can get by taking easy courses or you can challenge yourself. But to get an A you really have to work at it." The prestigious management and engineering schools draw in a lot of majors; however, economics, biology, English and psychology are common majors as well. Though Bucknell can boast a strong science and quantitative course program, its smaller majors like International Relations and Animal Behavior have strong reputations as well. Bucknell operates on a semester system and like any good liberal arts college, is invested in a well-rounded education for its students based in a core curriculum. Core requirements for freshman year are one English, one math, and one "foundational skills" class, which is designed to develop persuasive writing skills. By the end of sophomore year two lab sciences must be taken, and by graduation students must have taken four humanities, two social sciences and three writing courses. However, there is no language requirement!

Out Late Livin' the Life

With the majority of the students living on-campus and being fairly isolated, the party scene is the center of campus social life and is hard to miss every Wednesday, Friday, and Saturday. Greek life at Bucknell is big; in fact almost 50% of sophomores, juniors, and seniors are in a frat or sorority. But students are not allowed to rush until their sophomore year, so a lot of underclassman partying occurs on campus in the dorms. Though membership in a sorority or fraternity will definitely improve your party options, if that is not your thing you can still make it onto the Register list (which is the list of invites for the select campus-wide frat parties) if you have any friends in the house. Often in frats, specific sports teams will dominate the house. Perhaps this innate segregation within the student body leads to exclusive, tight-knit groups, but as one non-frat student said "the people are cliquey, but it is a big party scene and once you are out it is easy to meet people."

> "I really feel like the teachers are there to teach us, not just instruct us. It is a subtle but important difference."

About 14 percent of upperclassmen live in off-campus housing, called "downtown houses," which gives students the freedom to host their own parties on their own property. But not all this wild partying goes unchecked. It has been observed that police enforcement has been increasing over the last year or so, even in the downtown housing area. One needs to be aware that the school has in place a policy that discourages underage and out of hand drinking. It is a point system where, for example, one point will be given if an underage student is caught with an open drink, and 10 points can earn a suspension.

The school sponsors interesting non–alcohol related evening activities such as concerts and guest speakers: "Just the other day Bill Nye the Science Guy came and the auditorium was completely full, which doesn't happen that often," said one student. However, concerts and speakers are much more of a rarity than parties and are not always students' number one choice.

There isn't much of a dating scene at Bucknell. Most students would generally agree that random hook-ups are much more common and dating is not the norm. As one freshman said, "Oh yeah, hook-ups are definitely popular. I've hooked up with six people already and it's only been a month and a half!" What a statement, but overzealous freshman status is not something that should be overlooked in this case!

Wait, Who Are You?
When asked to describe the student body with a stereotype, one student said "preppy white people. You look around and all the guys are wearing red shorts, or yellow shorts, or khaki shorts with a polo and popped collar." This view that there is a homogenous student population both racially, socioeconomically, and even ideologically is consistent with student perceptions and diversity statistics. As one west-coaster put it, "there is a feeling of east coast pretension; the people are a little more self-centered than I am used to on the west coast." Though there is a fairly balanced pool of political views, that is obviously not enough to be considered truly diverse, and the school administration seems to be aware of this and has invested in long-term plans to improve the diversity of the student population.

The Bucknell Bubble
The campus is an idyllic rural setting with beautiful, mostly historic buildings in the red brick, Georgian revival architecture style with a couple modern buildings in-between. In fact, a new engineering building was added to the campus and is shared by undergrads and the small graduate population as well. Everything is easy to get to, making "it the epitome of a walking campus." For the most part all the dorms are nice places to live, maybe with the exception of some freshman housing. The freshman housing is fairly spread out, but the central freshman hall, as one can imagine, is the less desirable of the

living spaces and is assigned to you ahead of arrival. Starting sophomore year, students enter the room lottery. Bucknell has a unique system called "blockbooking rooms" which guarantees that you can live next to your friends no matter if you are in different rooms with different lottery numbers or not. It's also easy to do. Though not all dorms are a microcosm of the student body, there are two that have become the designated athlete dorms, one that is reserved for sorority living because there are no sorority houses, two dorms and one special interest house that are substance free, and one dorm that is more or less the quiet dorm, or "geeky dorm."

The meal plans and dining halls are flexible and tasty. There is an assortment of meal plans to choose from catering to different eating habits that range from the unlimited plan to the declining balance where items are charged to your account individually. There are four main dining halls each with a different taste and style and most of which are open from 7 a.m. to midnight (though not always serving hot food) which is a great convenience to late-night studiers. Most students are satisfied with their on-campus cuisine and don't go out to the "downtown" area (which is misleading because it is really just a main drag) to eat out at the restaurants or bars.

Free Time . . . What?
Students have endless opportunities to get involved in clubs, volunteering, organizations, and sports. There are over 150 clubs and organizations operating through the school and twenty-nine men's and women's varsity athletic teams. Students seem to feel that the sports teams have a large presence on campus. To facilitate such interests, the school has built impressive athletic centers including a new field house, a new basketball arena for games and there are complete weight and exercise facilities for athletes and non-athletes alike. The student body has quite a bit of team spirit and pride for their school sports, with men's basketball definitely taking the cake. Almost every game is sold out. When asked what made Bucknell unique to him, one varsity athlete answered "the mix of a Division 1 athletic program and a small school environment."—*Shaughnessy Costigan*

FYI

If you come to Bucknell you had better bring a "good self-esteem; every student on this campus is amazingly talented, and I still hold that Bucknell chooses students at least 50 percent based on looks."

A typical weekend at Bucknell consists of "procrastination, and a lot of it . . . even if you think there's nothing to do one weekend, by some miraculous turn of events, you find yourself socially booked until at least midnight on Saturday."

If you could change one thing about Bucknell, I'd "have there be a smaller Greek life."

Three things every student at Bucknell should do before graduation are "go to the Freez and the Campus Theatre, walk around downtown Lewisburg, and go wild at least once!"

Carnegie Mellon University

Address: 5000 Forbes Avenue Pittsburgh, PA 15213
Phone: 412-268-2082
E-mail address: undergraduate-admissions @andrew.cmu.edu
Web site URL: www.cmu.edu
Year Founded: 1900
Private or Public: Private
Religious Affiliation: None
Location: Urban
Number of Applicants: 13,527
Percent Accepted: 37.9%
Percent Accepted who enroll: 29%
Number Entering: 1,465
Number of Transfers Accepted each Year: 59
Middle 50% SAT range: M: 670–780, CR: 620–720, Wr: 620–710
Middle 50% ACT range: Unreported
Early admission program EA/ED/None: ED
Percentage accepted through EA or ED: 17%

EA and ED deadline: 1-Nov
Regular Deadline: 1-Jan
Application Fee: $70
Full time Undergraduate enrollment: 5,998
Total enrollment: 11,064
Percent Male: 59%
Percent Female: 41%
Total Percent Minority or Unreported: 61%
Percent African-American: 5%
Percent Asian/Pacific Islander: 22%
Percent Hispanic: 6%
Percent Native-American: 1.0%
Percent International: 15%
Percent in-state/out of state: 23%/77%
Percent from Public HS: Unreported
Retention Rate: 95%
Graduation Rate 4-year: 70%
Graduation Rate 6-year: 86%

Percent Undergraduates in On-campus housing: 64%
Number of official organized extracurricular organizations: 225
3 Most popular majors: Computer Engineering, Computer Science, Liberal Arts and Sciences
Student/Faculty ratio: Unreported
Average Class Size: Unreported
Percent of students going to grad school: Unreported
Tuition and Fees: $39,564
In State Tuition and Fees if different: No difference
Cost for Room and Board: $10,050
Percent receiving financial aid out of those who apply, first year: 75%
Percent receiving financial aid among all students: 64%

One group of students is painting a fence in the center of campus to advertise an upcoming party. Others are watching a play put on by the drama school. In the computer clusters, some students are playing Starcraft. Many engineering students are in the library working on problem sets. On a typical Saturday night at Carnegie Mellon University, students do all these things and more.

We Make Robots, but We Aren't Robots

Carnegie Mellon University is made up of six separate undergraduate colleges: the Mellon College of Science, the Carnegie Institute of Technology, the College of Fine Arts, the College of Humanities and Social Sciences, the Tepper School of Business, and the School of Computer Science. When applying to Carnegie Mellon, students are accepted into a specific school. Each school and each major has different requirements. Many consider the requirements in engineering to be the most burdensome and the requirements for majors in the College of Humanities and Social Sciences to be the easiest. Some undergraduates complain that it can be difficult to take a class outside your own college.

According to one freshman in the College of Humanities and Social Sciences, "It is close to impossible to take a class in the College of Fine Arts (art/drama/music) if you are not enrolled in that school."

Most undergraduates describe the academics as "rigorous" and "intense." The most prestigious and the most difficult majors are generally in the arts, engineering, and computer science. Classes are difficult and fast-paced, but the work often produces tangible results very quickly: "We learned how to build robots within the first three weeks of class, and then built a robot every week after that," said a student. One engineering student commented, "You get a great education because you learn how to think, not just mechanically compute. We make robots, but *we* aren't robots." On the other hand, some students refer to the School of Humanities and Social Sciences as "H & Less Stress." Students consider English, psychology, and modern languages to be the slacker majors. Carnegie Mellon offers a wide variety of majors; in fact, the school is the only college in America to offer a bagpipe major.

An engineering student raved about the quality of her professors: "I have had teachers respond to my emails within five minutes at 12:30 a.m." Some students in the College of Humanities and Social Sciences are less satisfied with the quality of the teaching: "The caliber of the professors [in arts and sciences] is nowhere near that of the other schools." Class sizes range from below 20 for seminars and electives to about 100 people for introductory classes, although the size of some popular lecture classes can be twice that.

What is a Social Life?

Because of the intense academics, some students complain about the lack of social life on campus. According to a freshman, "The social life here is what you make of it. Midnight is the time to go down to clusters, do the insane amount of work given here, or duke it out in Starcraft." One senior said the typical weekend at CMU is 70 percent work, 30 percent fun. One-dollar movies play on campus Thursday through Saturday nights. There are also weekly late-night programs sponsored by different clubs. Many students give high marks to the plays that the drama school produces. Students also go out to restaurants and bars close by in Oakland and Squirrel Hill. One student said, "Some people also take advantage of the free pool tables, ping pong, foosball and shuffleboard in the UC game room. And there is always studying."

The fraternities and sororities on campus are easy to rush and an integral part of the social scene on campus. Parties are held regularly—especially by Kappa Kappa Gamma, Phi Kappa Theta and Theta Xi. Unfortunately, parties are often little more than crappy beer and bad music, according to students, except for the occasional beach party, jungle party or foam party. "You can avoid Greek life if you just join other activities," said one student. However, freshmen usually only have the option of frat parties because they don't know enough people to go to other parties. Underage drinking is officially not allowed on campus, and those caught imbibing illegally will be punished. However, "it's pretty easy to get alcohol if you want it," said one girl. "As long as no one sees it and you're not being stupid, there haven't been many incidents involving underage drinking busts."

> "You can always find someone to hang out with who's exactly like you, or someone whose mind-set is totally different."

CMU is diverse inside as well as outside the classroom. Students hail from all 50 states and 45 different countries and are self-described as "intellectual, studious, talented, ambitious and competitive." According to one student, "You can always find someone to hang out with who's exactly like you, or someone whose mind-set is totally different." Freshman year is the best, according to a student, because "by sophomore year, a lot of people keep their doors shut." The social groups that form during freshman year often stay together over the four years. One junior said that Carnegie Mellon "is very cliquish—especially among the ethnic groups." "CMU has a varied assortment of personalities, from übergeeky (computer science majors) to the girls that you didn't like in high school (business majors)" said a senior. "Most people are really nice, although sometimes you have to be the outgoing one. . . . You definitely see a lot of clubs that I doubt exist at other schools, like the robotics club. Just the other day, they had a competition to make robots that can create root beer floats!"

Many females complain about the selection of men on campus. Even though 60 percent of the undergraduate population is male, some complain that a large percentage of the guys lack social skills. According to one female freshman, "The odds are good, but the goods are odd."

Adequate Dorms and Food

Only freshmen are required to live on campus. The quality of the dorms vary greatly from dorm to dorm. Most students feel that the housing is adequate, if a little small. Students rated RAs in the dorms as considerate, helpful and nice. Mudge, a converted mansion, is the students' favorite dorm, with suite-style, spacious rooms and a gorgeous courtyard. Some of the newer dorms, like New House, even have air conditioning, which can be nice on those still, hot days at the beginning of the school year. Donner, on the other hand, is "a dungeon, with small dingy rooms and shared bathrooms." Some students opt after the first year to live in the cheaper apartments off campus, although there aren't many nice places nearby. If you are willing to take a five-minute bus ride (which is free with tuition), many more options open up. Many students like living in the dorms because "you get to meet people, there are fun events (like pancake night, movie night, etc.) and lots of people to help with your homework!"

The food and the dining halls were given negative reviews in general, but many students say the situation is improving. Some students complain that the meal plan is too expensive. One senior female said, "Even the smallest meal plan is too much food for me." Depending on the meal plan, you get a certain number of "blocks," which can be used for all-you-can-eat cafeteria food or to buy a certain amount of food at a number of different campus eateries. The selection includes Skibo Coffeehouse, Asiana (with good BBQ chicken), and Taste of India. There is even a sushi place, a deli, and a completely vegan-friendly eatery. In addition, there is always some place to find food at 11 or 12 at night. One student said, "There aren't a lot of healthy choices, and not enough normal food, like lasagna or meatloaf kind of things. It's also pretty expensive if you just buy a meal with cash." Freshmen have to use their blocks during certain time slots and at certain places in order to avoid losing them. Upperclassmen warn future freshmen to get as small a dining plan as possible. Those in the dining hall are either "in cliques or loners," said one sophomore. Instead, people choose to eat off campus, at the numerous food trucks near campus, or to cook for themselves. For dates, students often leave campus and head over to Station Square, an area with nice restaurants.

Pittsburg

CMU is a small campus, with many patches of grass and yellow brick buildings with copper roofs that have turned green over the years. "This is a beautiful and safe campus," said one freshman. The art building is especially notable. One student said, "Every time I walk in the art building I see some new—usually odd, but amazing—work of art." "It's very pleasant here," one student said of the campus, but added a caveat: "Unless it's a really nice day, you won't see anyone hanging out outside—we're notorious for hanging out in computer clusters."

CMU is located in the suburbs of Pittsburgh, an area considered safe, although "like any big city there are some shady areas." Students give Pittsburgh high ratings, and one student happily commented, "I love the fact that I am in a city but at the same time feel that I have an actual campus." Another student said, "There are many restaurants, bars and museums within a mile of campus." The buses are free with college ID, so it is easy to get into the city. UPitt is also nearby and provides lots to do on weekends.

Filled with Traditions

One tradition at Carnegie Mellon is "painting the fence." In the center of The Cut—the green that runs across campus—is a steel fence covered with hundreds of layers of paint. Students are allowed to paint the fence between midnight and dawn. Most nights a student group will go out under the moonlight and paint the fence to advertise their event. Some students stay behind until the sun rises, guarding the fence to make sure their work does not get painted over.

The campus is also proud of the Scottish ancestry of CMU's founder, Andrew Carnegie. There is a Kiltie band and bagpipers that play at football games. Carnegie Mellon also has an annual spring carnival. Events include a Buggy race, officially called Sweepstakes, where CMU students compete in an on-land version of tobogganing around campus; Mobot, where students build robots that race though a course; and Fiesta de Primavera, an end-of-the-year celebration that includes volleyball, jousting, sumo outfits, slides, flypaper and big punching gloves.

In short, if you prefer building robots to football, and if cutting-edge technology is as important to you as a great arts program, then CMU is the place to be.—*Harrison Korn*

FYI

If you come to Carnegie Mellon, you'd better bring "your calculator."

What is the typical weekend schedule? "Read 500+ pages, write papers, do laundry, project meetings, research, eat, sleep . . ."

If I could change one thing about Carnegie Mellon, "I would make the food better."

Three things every student at Carnegie Mellon should do before graduating are "paint the fence, develop a social life, and play capture the flag in Wean."

Dickinson College

Address: P.O. Box 1773 Carlisle, PA 17013

Phone: 717-245-1231

E-mail address: admit@dickinson.edu

Web site URL: www.dickinson.edu

Year Founded: 1783

Private or Public: Private

Religious Affiliation: None

Location: Urban

Number of Applicants: 5,349

Percent Accepted: 43%

Percent Accepted who enroll: 27%

Number Entering: 621

Number of Transfers Accepted each Year: 27

Middle 50% SAT range: M: 600–680, Cr: 600–690, Wr: 650–720

Middle 50% ACT range: 26–30

Early admission program EA/ED/None: EA and ED

Percentage accepted through EA or ED: 56%

EA and ED deadline: 15-Nov

Regular Deadline: 1-Feb

Application Fee: $60

Full time Undergraduate enrollment: 2,369

Total enrollment: 2,369

Percent Male: 44%

Percent Female: 56%

Total Percent Minority or Unreported: 24%

Percent African-American: 5%

Percent Asian/Pacific Islander: 4%

Percent Hispanic: 4%

Percent Native-American: 5%

Percent International: 6%

Percent in-state/out of state: 27%/73%

Percent from Public HS: 61%

Retention Rate: 91%

Graduation Rate 4-year: 78%

Graduation Rate 6-year: 82%

Percent Undergraduates in On-campus housing: 92%

Number of official organized extracurricular organizations: 140

3 Most popular majors: Business, Political Science, Psychology

Student/Faculty ratio: 12:1

Average Class Size: 10 to 19

Percent of students going to grad school: 36%

Tuition and Fees: $35,450

In State Tuition and Fees if different: No difference

Cost for Room and Board: $8,980

Percent receiving financial aid out of those who apply, first year: 78%

Percent receiving financial aid among all students: 48%

L ocated in the tiny town of Carlisle, Pa., Dickinson is a close-knit school with prestigious international business, foreign language, and political science programs. Dickinson is perfect for the student who dreams of traveling the globe, but wants to go to a college where everyone knows his or her name and Greek life abounds. It is also a great place for preps and those who love them.

Go to Class, Go Abroad

One of the first things that Dickinson students proudly mention about their school is its small class sizes. There are virtually no classes with more than 40 students, with many Dickinsonians happily saying that their classes have even less students. Stu-

dents also praise their professors for being extremely approachable and helpful. "Our professors care a lot and are truly interested in what the students have to offer," said one freshman.

When your professors care and your classes are small, you better go to class. Dickinson assures that this happens with a strict attendance policy. Up to 20 percent of the grade for a course can be based on attendance, so those who care about their GPAs don't skip. Students say that it's relatively easy to get into classes that you want. Freshmen are encouraged to take 400-level courses with upperclassmen. Students said that you should expect to work at Dickinson, but that "it's the ideal workload. It's not too easy, but it's not too hard either."

Like most colleges, Dickinson has distribution requirements that students need to fulfill outside of their majors. They must take a writing course and a quantitative course, as well as courses in the arts and humanities, the social sciences, the laboratory sciences, U.S. diversity, Comparative Civilizations, physical education and language. Dickinsonians say that the distribution requirements are easy to complete, and just like at the local Wal-Mart, you can often get a "two for the price of one" deal where one class fulfills two requirements. However, many students admit that people put off their distribution requirements and then have to cram them all into senior year. In addition to trying to knock out a few requirements, all freshmen take a Freshman Seminar. In these seminars, students build on the research and writing skills they honed before they got to Dickinson by studying topics that appeal to them.

> **"Basically, if you're a guy, you have to join a frat or you'll be a social pariah."**

Students are equally enthusiastic about Dickinson's study abroad program. Students can go abroad for a semester or a year to a variety of Dickinson-affiliated programs around the world. Students go to countries in Europe, Africa, Asia and South and Central America simply to take classes in a setting more exciting than small-town Pennsylvania or to totally immerse themselves in a different culture. Most of the programs are not in big cities, but in small towns where students live with host families and can avoid annoying tourists. Dickinson's study abroad program is so popular that one student said, "Every winter it's like a new class of people arrives because so many juniors are coming back from study abroad." International business, foreign language and East Asian studies classes are extremely popular and renowned at Dickinson, further proving the international leanings of its students.

The Greekfest
Social life at Dickinson is dominated by Greek life. Fraternity parties are usually open to everyone and always very well attended. Students could not stress enough the importance of the frat scene. "Basically, if you're a guy, you have to join a frat or you'll be a social pariah," one student explained simply. There are four sororities on campus, including the infamous Kappas, who are known as "snobby

and exclusive," but girls do not have to join them to be a part of the social life, since guys love girls to come to their frat parties.

Just like any other school with a huge Greek life, alcohol is abundant at Dickinson. In fact, Dickinson is sometimes called "Drinkinson." The administration is not at all happy with this nickname and is very tough on alcohol. They forbid kegs on campus and will take away the house of any fraternity that has a keg for fear that they promote binge drinking. The fraternities have found clever ways around the keg restriction by having cocktail parties. Students also say that the strict rules are often unsuccessfully enforced.

Dickinson is not all about drunken debauchery. Frequent dances and concerts are hosted at The Depot and The Quarry, two on-campus hangouts. For such a small school, Dickinson attracts some big names to these events. "I was in the front row at the Death Cab for Cutie concert and there were like only 50 people there. It was amazing," one satisfied student said. These kinds of events offer a fun occasional alternative to getting drunk at the frats.

Happy Little Preppy Family
Dickinsonians are pleased with the close-knit community that makes up their school. While one student complained that she feels like she "knows the entire student body," most students like the communal feel. Dickinson must do a great job of choosing roommates for freshmen, because the friends they make in their dorms their first year are the friends they have for the next three. "Most freshmen roommates stay together," one student explained.

The fact that it's a school where everyone knows your name really has an effect on the Dickinson dating scene. "By the time they're upperclassmen, most students are in relationships here, but many freshmen are still in their high-school relationships or having random hook-ups," said one student. Some Dickinsonians utilize their study-abroad yearnings closer to home by hooking up in the East Asian Room. Dickinson students are careful not to hook up too randomly, however, because the fear of running out of attractive partners in such a tiny school is real.

Dickinson students do more than party, hook up and make phone calls to their long-distance loves. They participate in varsity, club or intramural sports with soccer, basketball and volleyball being the most popular. They are involved with student government, school publications, drama, comedy and foreign language clubs. Some students stressed that Dickinson needs to create community-service organizations to add a giving-back element to student activities.

The typical Dickinsonian, students say, is a white, upper-middle-class, private-school grad from the East Coast. "I really need to get a Polo shirt. I don't have one and everyone has them here," one student responded when asked about Dickinson's prep factor. The administration strives for diversity, but like many things at Dickinson, it ends up having an international flavor. "Our diversity is from international students. Most of the black people you'll see on campus aren't from the United States but from Africa," one freshman explained.

Pretty Campus, Ugly City

Dickinsonians have little praise for the town of Carlisle. "It's a typical mid-Pennsylvanian town: boring, kind of trashy, and there's nothing to do," complained one student. Another summed up Carlisle by simply explaining that many residents have mullets. To escape the small town stuff, students can make the 20 minute trip to Harrisburg, Pennsylvania's capital.

Though they are displeased with the town, Dickinson students don't complain too much since their campus is beautiful. "It's just what a college should look like," one student said. Dickinsonians laud their campus's limestone buildings, wide open space and lush hills. The school is not only pleasing to the eye, but also pleasing to the stomach. Its meals are time and again rated among the best of college cafeteria food. Dickinsonians have slightly less praise for their dorms, at least the inside of them. Though most are renovated and some—like Goodyear, an upperclassman dorm—are legendary, some students complain about forced triples and huge differences in the amount of students housed in different dormitories. "My dorm has 40 people and the other freshman one has 400. It's nice, because my dormmates are like my family, but sometimes I wish our dorm was bigger," one girl explained.

Dickinson seems to have it all. It offers its students the chance to be a part of a close-knit community but travel around the world, the chance to live in a small town but visit a big city, and the chance to party hard but challenge oneself academically. With all these options, Dickinsonians graduate feeling as if they made the right choice.—*Keneisha Sinclair*

FYI

If you come to Dickinson, you'd better bring "a Polo or Lacoste shirt."

The typical weekend schedule is "Friday: watch a movie, then get dressed up and pregame before going to the frats; Saturday: sleep, do work, go out to dinner, then go to the frats; Sunday: sleep and do your work."

If I could change one thing about Dickinson, "I'd make it not so focused on Greek life."

Three things every student at Dickinson should do before graduating are "hook up in the East Asian Studies room, study abroad and walk to the Wal-Mart."

Drexel University

Address: 3141 Chestnut Street Philadelphia, PA 19104
Phone: 215-895-2400
E-mail address: enroll@drexel.edu
Web site URL: www.drexel.edu
Year Founded: 1891
Private or Public: Private
Religious Affiliation: None
Location: Urban
Number of Applicants: 3,823
Percent Accepted: 72%
Percent Accepted who enroll: 45%
Number Entering: 1,238
Number of Transfers Accepted each Year: Unreported
Middle 50% SAT range: M: 560–670 Cr: 530–630
Middle 50% ACT range: 20–27
Early admission program EA/ED/None: NA

Percentage accepted through EA or ED: NA
EA and ED deadline: NA
Regular Deadline: 1-Mar
Application Fee: $50
Full time Undergraduate enrollment: 10,318
Total enrollment: 17,001
Percent Male: 57%
Percent Female: 43%
Total Percent Minority or Unreported: 26%
Percent African-American: 10%
Percent Asian/Pacific Islander: 13%
Percent Hispanic: 3%
Percent Native-American: 1%
Percent International: Unreported
Percent in-state/out of state: 52%/48%
Percent from Public HS: 70%
Retention Rate: 84%

Graduation Rate 4-year: 53%
Graduation Rate 6-year: 60%
Percent Undergraduates in On-campus housing: 35%
Number of official organized extracurricular organizations: 136
3 Most popular majors: Information Science, Mechanical Engineering, Business
Student/Faculty ratio: 15:1
Average Class Size: 14
Percent of students going to grad school: 18%
Tuition and Fees: $27,200
In State Tuition and Fees if different: No difference
Cost for Room and Board: $11,610
Percent receiving financial aid out of those who apply, first year: Unreported
Percent receiving financial aid among all students: Unreported

W ant a college experience where you can "go wireless" anywhere on campus, where you can enjoy the events, sights and tastes of the City of Brotherly Love, and where the likelihood of having to stress about finding a job after you graduate is slim to none? Check out Philadelphia's Drexel University.

A "Real-World" College Experience

Drexel's co-operative education program was recently ranked in the nation's top 10 by *U.S. News & World Report.* The Drexel Plan, required by most majors, means each student will have completed three six-month stints of full-time employment (or "co-ops") before graduation. Students browse an online database of "many large, well-established companies," choosing from over 1,500 potential employers such as GlaxoSmithKline, Children's Hospital of Pennsylvania, Lockheed Martin and Comcast Corporation. Although many co-ops are with Philadelphia-based companies, out-of-state and international op-

portunities with large companies make it so you can co-op "almost anywhere."

While some students are attracted to Drexel for its top-notch engineering programs, the fact that it offers a chance to "find out during college, rather than four years down the road, if what you're studying is what you want to do for the rest of your life" seems to truly be what sets Drexel apart from most other colleges. Almost all co-ops are salaried, and many students are offered employment upon graduation by former co-op employers.

Because most students follow the Drexel Plan, a five-year program is "pretty much standard." After attending class full-time for freshman year, these students will have a co-op each of their sophomore, pre-junior, and junior years. The regular classroom setting is standard, and most classes are structured with a lecture component and a smaller 15-20 student recitation section. One student said that while the University's engineering program (the nation's largest among private universities) is known to be tough, "most professors are well established in their fields and pride themselves" on demanding the most from their students. Although the College is known for its technology-based achievements (in addition to being a fully wireless campus since 2000, in 2002 Drexel was the first to launch a wireless Web portal service for students), the humanity department is also "pretty good, and provides a break from all of the engineering classes."

Drexel is divided into six colleges: the College of Arts and Sciences, the College of Business, the College of Media Arts and Design, the College of Engineering, the College of Information Science and Technology and the College of Nursing and Health Professions. In addition, two schools offer undergraduate B.S. degrees: the School of Biomedical Engineering, Science and Health Systems; the School of Education.

Social Scene—On Campus and Around Philly

Drexel's location in the heart of Philadelphia, while limiting the "campus feel," does make for a variety of ways to spend the weekend. As with most college campuses, drinking is almost always involved in any social activity, and is sometimes enjoyed to excess. Drugs, while readily available in a city with a population of over 1.5 million, still play a comparatively limited role in campus life.

Freshmen are required to have full meal plans and to live on campus for their first three quarters of matriculation, unless a student is married or lives at home. Residence halls Calhoun, Myers, Kelly, Towers and Van Resselaer are traditional freshman dorms, with East Hall designated as the Honors freshman hall. Another unique housing feature Drexel offers are "learning communities," where students with similar academic interests can choose to be grouped together. Business, Engineering, Future Health Professionals, Information Science and Technology and Media Arts and Design learning communities are offered.

Most upperclassmen are on limited meal plans, if any. All students seemed pleased with the options and set-up of the meal plan; Handschumacher Dining Center in the student center is the heart of the program, with a wide variety of food "stations" like the Mexican Bar and the Vegan and Vegetarian station. Other dining locations offer a la carte options and are spread throughout campus.

The majority of students opt to live off campus with a group of friends after freshman year, leading to plenty of time happily spent just hanging out, playing video games, or watching movies. Such a situation also leads to "lots of house parties, right in the city." "Even if you're under 21 you can find ways to party," remarked one minor, "whether it's at a house party or a frat party." And while the fraternity scene is present, it isn't as big as it once was. Campus events at Drexel are complemented by the proximity of St. Joe's, Temple, Villanova, and University of Pennsylvania. "Penn is a block from here, Temple's just a quick train ride away, and several others are also easily accessible by public transportation," noted one student. Given the school's male-heavy gender ratio, many students are grateful for the easy access to other schools.

> "The co-op program works to the advantage of the college student. You realize it's much easier to learn through experience, from working with so many different people."

For those of age, bars nearby like Cavanaugh's and Brownie's are popular college-student hangouts. Zocalo offers a tasty Tex-Mex dining option right near campus, and Bubble House serves up trendy, if overpriced, bubble tea and "funky" Thai fare. Overall, most students attest that there are "a lot of good little restaurants, especially ethnic places, all over the city." And of course, the corner in South Philly where Pat's and Geno's are located is "the place" to savor a bite of an "original" Philadelphia cheesesteak. Other not-to-miss activities include attending a concert by the Philadelphia Orchestra, visiting the famous Philadelphia Museum of Art, shopping on South Street or watching an Eagles, Flyers, Sixers or Phillies game. Finally, a local band scene thrives at restaurants and smaller venues, and bigger concert halls often host more mainstream attractions like O.A.R.

If you're worried your activities will be limited to watching, eating and drinking, fear not. Leading a healthy lifestyle in the city once called the "No. 1 fattest city in America" by *Men's Health Magazine* has gotten a lot easier, thanks to recent improvements that made the city more bike-friendly. And "Boathouse Row is only a five-minute walk from campus and is a great place to run or bike along the Schuylkill River, and nearby Fairmount Park has plenty of trails as well."

Student Body

Diversity on campus is improving with Drexel's rising popularity among applicants, and many students note that there are many international students. However, African-American and Latino populations account for small percentages of the total student body, and several students observed that the campus still does seem to be "a lot of people from Pennsylvania, Delaware or New Jersey."

Beyond the Classroom

Drexel's varsity teams play in a highly competitive league, and their traditionally strong basketball team provides the bulk of athletic-inspired school spirit for the Dragons. Many students lament the absence of a varsity football team, yet "intramural sports are popular, and people often sign up to play flag football, dodgeball or basketball teams with their friends." Given its location in a city that offers opportunities to pursue a wide array of interests, Drexel's on-campus extracurriculars are low key, although it still has plenty of quirky clubs such as ASE, an architectural club whose mission is to design and race concrete canoes.

Students praised campus security, reporting that numerous alarm phones and campus and city security forces made for a safe feeling near Drexel, although because of its urban location most students agreed that being aware of one's surroundings was also key.

The range of experience offered by Drexel and its surrounding city is truly dazzling. "The co-op program works to the advantage of the college student. You realize it's much easier to learn through experience, from working with so many different people. And that's what employers are looking for after you graduate."—*Katie Matlack*

FYI

If you come to Drexel, you'd better bring "a beer funnel, an appetite for cheesesteak and an appetite for learning."

What's the typical weekend schedule? "Going out on campus Thursday nights to various Thirsty Thursday events, going into the city Friday and Saturday nights, especially to Old City, and waking up late Sunday morning to do laundry and homework."

If I could change one thing about Drexel, "there would be more girls."

Three things every student at Drexel should do before graduating are "go to a giant house party and a giant frat party, run up the Art Museum steps Rocky-style and visit Boathouse Row."

Franklin and Marshall College

Address: PO Box 3003
Lancaster, MA 17604-3003
Phone: 877-678-9111
E-mail address:
admission@fandm.edu
Web site URL:
www.fandm.edu
Year Founded: 1787
Private or Public: Private
Religious Affiliation: None
Location: Suburban
Number of Applicants: 5,632
Percent Accepted: 36%
Percent Accepted who
enroll: 29%
Number Entering: 589
Number of Transfers
Accepted each Year: 42
Middle 50% SAT range:
M: 610–690, CR: 600–690,
Wr: Unreported
Middle 50% ACT range:
Unreported
Early admission program
EA/ED/None: ED
Percentage accepted
through EA or ED: 56.50%

EA and ED deadline:
15-Nov
Regular Deadline: 1-Feb
Application Fee: $50
Full time Undergraduate
enrollment: 2,164
Total enrollment: 2,164
Percent Male: 48%
Percent Female: 52%
Total Percent Minority or
Unreported: 12%
Percent African-American:
4%
Percent Asian/Pacific
Islander: 4%
Percent Hispanic: 4%
Percent Native-American:
<1%
Percent International:
8.90%
Percent in-state/out of
state: 34%/66%
Percent from Public HS:
56%
Retention Rate: 93.80%
Graduation Rate 4-year:
79%

Graduation Rate 6-year:
84%
Percent Undergraduates
in On-campus housing:
80%
Number of official organized
extracurricular
organizations: 90
3 Most popular majors:
Business, Government,
Biology
Student/Faculty ratio:
10:1
Average Class Size: 19
Percent of students going to
grad school: 25%
Tuition and Fees: $38,630
In State Tuition and Fees if
different: No difference
Cost for Room and Board:
$9,870
Percent receiving financial
aid out of those who apply,
first year: Unreported
Percent receiving financial
aid among all students:
40%

Though they call themselves Diplomats, not many Franklin & Marshall students will be heading to Washington to write legislation. Despite its liberal arts reputation and mascot, Franklin & Marshall is a school that caters to the sciences. Double majors and extracurricular leaders thrive in the close community at F&M, where high expectations are found inside and outside the classroom. Students at the College jump headlong into community service, pursue hands-on academics and research opportunities, and take advantage of unmatched faculty interactions. However, their drive doesn't force them underground—Diplomats know how to have fun like students at any other college.

Small Classes, Big Research Opportunities

Though F&M specializes in the sciences, students can experience a diverse set of classes and departments before choosing a major. "In general, it's a liberal arts curriculum," one student said. "They have a core curriculum but they really try to promote freedom in choice of study." Students must take classes from each of the three realms of study in the "Foundations" program: Mind, Self and Spirit; the Natural World; and Community, Culture and Society. This core provides the base on which upperclassmen build their majors.

Many students arrive in Lancaster expecting to major in F&M's impressive pre-med program. The pre-med track often proves to be more difficult than prospective students had imagined, as one biochemistry major pointed out: "There's a huge population of pre-med students here and that population decreases each year, pretty much exponentially." The same student, expressing a sentiment common among F&M science majors, said the only easy majors were "anything not science." Among non-science majors, the most popular concentrations include government, psychology, and business. But one English and neuroscience double major noted that "it's not unusual to see students majoring in two very different areas of study."

In either the sciences or the liberal arts, students agree that faculty interaction sets F&M apart. With a student to faculty ratio of 10:1, non-introductory classes are typically small and professors accessible. Even larger lectures often come to less than 50 students. One student doing chemistry research alongside his professor said that research opportunities at this small college "are readily available to the extent that they would be at any research university." Many students stay over the summer in nearby apartments to get involved with F&M faculty. Research, both during the year and over the summer, gives underclassmen the chance to contribute to groundbreaking work. "It's not just those in the sciences who want kids in their majors to take part in their research," one student said. "And I'm always invited over to the professors' houses for dinner afterwards to meet their families."

Lancaster Living

As one of the oldest colleges in the country, F&M is full of open spaces. In the fall and spring, Hartman Green swells with students playing Frisbee, reading, and generally enjoying themselves. Freshmen and sophomores are required to live on campus, all within a block or two of the Green. Most agree that the accommodations are comfortable but not exceptional. Hallways include both first-year and second-year students, with the latter having the option of living in doubles or suites. After sophomore year, most students move into the abundant and affordable off-campus housing across the street.

Lancaster provides F&M students with more than they usually expect when arriving on campus. Although small and relatively rural, the downtown area is full of fresh farm markets, affordable restaurants, and several clubs for students on the weekends. The restaurants become a tantalizing diversion from the typical college grub, about which one student reasoned, "I don't think college food is ever as good as home, but it won't kill you." And if you just can't resist a real home-cooked meal, many students from the East Coast use cars to escape to Philadelphia and Baltimore, which are both two hours away. "The campus doesn't become a ghost town on the weekend, but it is definitely convenient," one Philadelphian said.

The Weekend Wrap-up

Whether it's the weekend or not, students say that the campus is known to be cliquey. Fraternities and sororities are not officially recognized by the College but do exist in noticeable numbers. Nevertheless, Greek life does not dominate the social scene. "Greek life is an accessory," one student said. "By no means do you have to be in it to meet friends." Among the student body there is a clear divide between those who drink and those who do not. Those who don't drink argue that alcohol is only a small part of life at F&M: "What people say who came here 20 years ago is you have a miserable time here if you don't associate with Greek life, but what I see tells me that isn't the case." In contrast, those who do drink claim they can't imagine the school without it. Recently the administration has been increasingly strict in enforcing alcohol policies, including the prohibition of alcohol in dormitories of students under 21. In addition, local police have increased their watch over college night life—to the extent of breaking up parties and using undercover agents. Some say the police have taken it too far. "They're cracking down on us this year," said one frustrated student.

> "The first thing you notice is it's a pretty homogeneous student body. You'll probably see rich and white, for one thing."

Much like frats, athletics play an accessory role on campus. Sports teams are a popular yet limited outlet for school pride. While the Division III squash, basketball and football programs are perennially solid, few students go crazy for them. Instead, Diplomats find other ways to show their school pride. "A lot of people walk around in F&M clothing," one student said.

The Typical Diplomat

Students insist diversity improves each year, but few have any difficulty in describing the average F&M student. Almost all are academically driven. Almost all are interested in getting involved in activities outside the classroom. And almost all are upper-middle-class, white Northeasterners. "There's a distinct lack of diversity," one sophomore sighed. "The first thing you notice is it's a pretty homogeneous student body. You'll probably see rich and white, for one thing." In addition to a lack of racial and socioeconomic diversity, several students added that religious and sexual diversity is relatively rare. But religious and social minorities that do exist emerge as a vocal faction of the student body. Hillel, the center for Jewish life, hosts events geared at all students regardless of faith, in part because F&M is "still predominantly WASP." The small gay population is visibly noticeable, but not very important in the social lives of straight students.

Politically, F&M is not particularly vocal despite a fairly diverse collection of political leanings. While one sophomore suggested that there was an even split between conservatives and liberals, she added that most campus conservatives were liberal on social issues. For this reason, most students can be found in greater Lancaster volunteering. Tutoring, mentoring and volunteering with the elderly are popular options.

For most Diplomats, academics still come first. Each student comes to F&M interested in learning for learning's sake, and the drive of the typical F&M student reflects this interest. "There are a lot of competitive people here," one student conceded. "But the people who are competitive are competitive with themselves. I'd say students are definitely in it for the long haul together."—*Andrew Bartholomew*

FYI

If you come to Franklin & Marshall, you'd better bring "the drive to take advantage of all the academic opportunities."

What's the typical weekend schedule? "Thursdays and Fridays: Parties start around 11:00. Saturdays: Quiet during the day. Parties start earlier. Sunday: Homework day."

If I could change one thing about Franklin & Marshall, it'd be "the police cracking down on us."

Three things every student should do before graduating are "pee on the Ben Franklin statue while drunk," "go to the Farmers' Market downtown," and "eat dinner with your professor."

Gettysburg College

Address: 300 North Washington Street Gettysburg, PA 17325

Phone: 717-337-6100

E-mail address: admiss@gettysburg.edu

Web site URL: www.gettysburg.edu

Year Founded: 1832

Private or Public: Private

Religious Affiliation: Lutheran

Location: Suburban

Number of Applicants: 5,794

Percent Accepted: 37%

Percent Accepted who enroll: 33%

Number Entering: 714

Number of Transfers Accepted each Year: 15

Middle 50% SAT range: M: 610–670, CR: 610–690, Wr: Unreported

Middle 50% ACT range: 27–29

Early admission program EA/ED/None: ED

Percentage accepted through EA or ED: 40%

EA and ED deadline: 15-Nov, 15-Jan

Regular Deadline: 1-Feb

Application Fee: $55

Full time Undergraduate enrollment: 2,497

Total enrollment: 2,497

Percent Male: 49%

Percent Female: 51%

Total Percent Minority or Unreported: 10%

Percent African-American: 3%

Percent Asian/Pacific Islander: 1%

Percent Hispanic: 2%

Percent Native-American: 1%

Percent International: 4%

Percent in-state/out of state: 22%/78%

Percent from Public HS: 66%

Retention Rate: 92%

Graduation Rate 4-year: 80%

Graduation Rate 6-year: 84%

Percent Undergraduates in On-campus housing: 90%

Number of official organized extracurricular organizations: 140

3 Most popular majors: Management, Political Science, English

Student/Faculty ratio: 11:1

Average Class Size: 18

Percent of students going to grad school: 35%

Tuition and Fees: $37,600

In State Tuition and Fees if different: No difference

Cost for Room and Board: $9,100

Percent receiving financial aid out of those who apply, first year: 70%

Percent receiving financial aid among all students: 70%

A mention of Gettysburg College most often brings to mind the picturesque fields that served as a major battlefield during the Civil War and the location of Abraham Lincoln's famous Gettysburg Address. Come to Gettysburg though, and you will find more than just a campus steeped in history. On this site of enormous historical importance, Gettysburg students live and learn in the most thoroughly modern facilities. At this small liberal arts college, students are accomplishing more than war reenactments and historical tours. They thrive in both the intimate academic atmosphere and the extensive social scene.

Integrated Learning

Classes at Gettysburg tend to be very small, and with a student to faculty ratio of 11:1, it's no wonder classes rarely reach twenty students. Professors teach all classes, and students agree that the professors are very accessible. According to one senior, "The professors here teach what they are passionate about. They really respect us and are interested in our minds." This type of enthusiasm appears to be uniformly present through the student body. Students start out freshman year with a unique Gettysburg experience, the First Year Seminars. Freshmen pick from a variety of courses ranging from "The Makings of the Great American Musical" to "Got Porn? A Critical Approach to Pornography" and the "Critical Debates that Divided the Women's Movement." The learning experience does not stop at the end of the sixteen-person seminar, however. Residential Hall assignments for freshmen are directly linked to their freshmen seminar and college writing courses; that way informal discussion is facilitated outside the classroom setting. Students come to Gettysburg fairly aware of the requirements of the college, from the freshmen seminar to the course requirements mandating that students take courses in fields outside their major. Gettysburg students seem to agree that the requirements provide a broad liberal arts base without restricting their ability to explore. The part that draws the most complaints is the natural science requirement. But, as one student pointed out, "The science departments seem to understand and create a few courses designed for seniors to meet their graduation requirements as painlessly as possible." These include courses such as "The Chesapeake Bay" and "Natural Disasters," which fill up within minutes of the beginning of senior course registration.

Gettysburg students cite the most popular majors as political science, history, psychology and management, which is also named one of the easiest majors. Aspiring management majors should be aware though that there is talk of the major being discontinued and its nearest replacement is economics. The sciences are generally regarded as the hardest majors. Some of the more popular classes include "Philosophy of Food," "The Bible and Modern Moral Issues" and "Economics of Sports." Students here fall within a range of attitudes toward academics, ranging from the super motivated to the not motivated. Most students though "take academics pretty seriously and take an active stance in their education." According to one student, "The perfect description of Gettysburg College is that you work for a B, but you work your butt off for an A." In the words of another senior, "Gettysburg provides a great library and an amazing faculty. Anyone who claims he isn't get anything out of his academic endeavors isn't trying hard enough."

Immaculate Grounds

Students universally agree that Gettysburg provides world-class facilities. Musselman Library remains open twenty-four hours Sunday through Thursday and provides tables for group studying, as well as quiet zones with a variety of seating and lighting options and even private rooms for studying. One student professes his love for the library's availability and says, "I don't think anyone can every truly appreciate how valuable the library hours are until your computer breaks at 2 a.m. when you have a paper due or when your roommate throws a party the night before an exam." The Breidenbaugh, where most English classes are held, is cited as a particularly beautiful building on campus.

There are currently two gyms: Bream, the main gym with an indoor track and weightlifting room, and Plank, the smaller gym with a cardio and aerobics focus. There are complaints that both gyms fill up quickly because of the popularity of working out among students, but there is work being done to provide a new gym to address this issue. There are also swimming pools and numerous sports fields on campus.

The town of Gettysburg itself is somewhat sleepy and isolated and caters mostly to tourism. Students often get involved in the town via tutoring or other forms of volunteer work. Students also benefit from some of the bars and restaurants, the local movie theatre, the outlet mall nearby and the proximity to Baltimore and Washington, DC.

Trapped On-Campus

Students regard residential life as above average. According to one student, "After visiting other schools, it seems Gettysburg has some of the nicest dorms." Housing gets better as you rise through the ranks. Freshmen live in standard doubles off a hallway, but upperclassmen dorms can be described as downright luxurious. Dorms have common rooms, often with big-screen TVs. Many options are apartment style with a full kitchen, living room, and private bathroom. Seniors generally get suite-style housing with all singles in The Quarry Suites. There are also theme houses owned by the college that are often closer to campus than dorms are. Many male students opt to live in their fraternity houses. Juniors and seniors are allowed to live off campus, but over ninety percent of students choose to stay on campus. On-campus housing provides many parking options and there are even opportunities for coed living. There are Residential Advisors, but most understand the realities of college life and enforce rules reasonably. No alcohol is allowed in freshmen dorms, though.

Gettysburg food is often ranked in the top twenty nationally. One student goes as far as to call it "incredibly good for a college dining hall." One dining option, Servo, boasts a sauté line, grill and sandwich area, eggs made to order, and a vegan corner. In the College Union Building is a coffee shop, bookstore, and The Bullet Hole, another dining option that serves quick meals. Ike's serves made to order subs, soup and wraps and is open later than any of the other options. As satisfied as students are though, it is not uncommon to head off campus to eat on weekends at places such as Pizza House or nearby chain restaurants.

Popped Collars and Pearls

The Vineyard Vines and Vera Bradley sold in the school bookstore sums up the stereotype of the average Gettysburg student. Drawing its student population mostly from the Tri-State area and New England, students seem to feel that one thing Gettysburg does lack is diversity on campus, both racially and economically. Many are white and preppy and come from a privileged, private-school background that is reflected by the BMWs, Jaguars and Range Rovers littering the student parking lots. While students laud the administration for working to increase diversity on campus, there is still little intermixing between various groups. On the upside, one student remarks, "That is not to say there is an 'I'm better than you' attitude on campus and most students, regardless of income level, would feel comfortable at this school." Students are also universally described as friendly and approachable. The small, tightly-knit campus means that people are welcoming and willing to lend a hand.

> **"It's a safe bet that if you're not out at a frat sometime between Wednesday and Saturday, then you're probably not doing anything entertaining."**

Students are also involved in a variety of extracurricular activities that draw people together. Division III sports are popular, although by junior year, many nonstarters tend to drop out. Football is the most vocal and visible team because of its size, but lacrosse has also been nationally ranked for the past four years. Men and women's soccer have also been recently nationally ranked and were in the playoffs. Games often attract sports fans cheering their Bullets on. Intramurals, service organizations and various clubs also draw a large crowd.

To Be Greek or Not to Be

Gentlemen, you better step foot on campus ready to make friends with some girls! Greek life is the single largest affiliation on campus and accounts for over fifty percent of the campus population. Frat parties tend to dominate weekend activities, especially for underclassmen, and it is always advisable for guys to show up with a few extra girls in tow to ensure admittance. According to one student, "It's a safe bet that if you're not out at a frat sometime between Wednesday and Saturday, then you're probably not doing anything entertaining." On weekends, students frat-hop with ease between houses located within feet of each other. Some popular fraternities include Phi Delt, Phi Sig, and FIJI. Sororities are also popular, but because they are not allowed to live in sorority houses together, they do not play the same role that fraternities do. Gettysburg students seem to agree that many groups of friends who may have split somewhat because of their choices to go Greek or not, often reunite as upperclassmen when both Greek and independents tend to seek out non-Greek activities.

Sports teams also play a prominent role on campus. Many students enter their freshmen year affiliated with one of Gettysburg's Division III teams and that is often reflected in the social scenes. Tuesdays are a popular night to attend "Pitchers," the weekly event at a local bar involving two-dollar pitchers of beer. Some of the other social options include campus-wide activities and trips put on by the Campus Activities Board. Spring Fest is a yearly event that kicks off with a spring concert drawing students, alumni and faculty. Crab Fest is another popular event where the dining hall sets out a picnic of fresh crabs and beer set to music. Thanksgiving Dinner is eagerly anticipated during the fall semester because the dining hall orga-

nizes a family-style Thanksgiving dinner for the entire student body. Snow Ball is the annual winter dance that provides free food and drink, as well as an opportunity to dress up.

Gettysburg College is a campus rich with historical buildings, significant Civil War sites, and even rumors of hauntings. These traditions provide a background for the talented students who are drawn to both Gettysburg's history and its state of the art facilities and inspiring faculty. This beautiful school full of beautiful people boasts an intimate learning environment and social scene with something for everyone.—*Janet Yang*

FYI

If you come to Gettysburg you better bring "a bike in order to enjoy all the battlefields."

What's the typical weekend schedule? "Go to an outlet mall, go out for a nice meal with your friends off campus, drink at a frat party or somewhere else, and maybe watch a movie with friends."

If I could change one thing about Gettysburg, I'd "make it more diverse."

Three things every student at Gettysburg should do before graduating are "go on a GRAB (Gettysburg Recreational Activities Board) trip, swim in the fountain in the center of campus, and walk through the battlefields."

Haverford College

Address: 370 Lancaster Avenue Haverford, PA 19041
Phone: 610-896-1350
E-mail address: admission@haverford.edu
Web site URL: www.haverford.edu
Year Founded: 1833
Private or Public: Private
Religious Affiliation: None
Location: Suburban
Number of Applicants: 3,492
Percent Accepted: 25%
Percent Accepted who enroll: 35%
Number Entering: 315
Number of Transfers Accepted each Year: 89
Middle 50% SAT range: M: 640–740, CR: 650–750, Wr: 650–750
Middle 50% ACT range: Unreported
Early admission program EA/ED/None: ED
Percentage accepted through EA or ED: 35%

EA and ED deadline: 15-Nov
Regular Deadline: 15-Jan
Application Fee: $60
Full time Undergraduate enrollment: 1,169
Total enrollment: 1,169
Percent Male: 46%
Percent Female: 54%
Total Percent Minority or Unreported: 23%
Percent African-American: 8%
Percent Asian/Pacific Islander: 11%
Percent Hispanic: 8%
Percent Native-American: <1%
Percent International: 4%
Percent in-state/out of state: 13%/87%
Percent from Public HS: 55%
Retention Rate: 96%
Graduation Rate 4-year: 91%
Graduation Rate 6-year: 93%

Percent Undergraduates in On-campus housing: 99%
Number of official organized extracurricular organizations: 93
3 Most popular majors: Biology/Biological Sciences, General Economics, General English Language and Literature
Student/Faculty ratio: 8:1
Average Class Size: 2 to 9
Percent of students going to grad school: 18%
Tuition and Fees: $37,175
In State Tuition and Fees if different: No difference
Cost for Room and Board: $11,450
Percent receiving financial aid out of those who apply, first year: 41%
Percent receiving financial aid among all students: 42%

Founded in 1833 by members of the Religious Society of Friends, this small liberal arts college—with a student body of just under 1200—has never lost sight of its Quaker roots. A deep concern for social justice and a unique emphasis on an honor code that students say "fosters an environment of tolerance and acceptance" combine with rigorous academics, unusual traditions and a tight-knit community to give the quirky, driven students at Haverford College a truly one-of-a-kind educational experience.

On My Honor

Probably the most important single factor that shapes the Haverford experience, and one repeatedly cited by students as "what differentiates Haverford from other schools," is the Honor Code, a philosophy of integrity that is affirmed by the student body each year. The Honor Code governs all aspects of students' conduct, from academics to residential life, and all those interviewed stressed its important role in making the school "a very warm and welcoming place with an undeniable sense of community." Because it is maintained and enforced by the students (four members of each class are elected each year to serve on the Honor Council), Haverfordians have "tremendous self-governance" over the conduct of the student body: "We all have a common understanding of how we all want to be treated, and for the most part, we follow through with it." The power of the Honor Code at Haverford may seem unusual to an outsider, but students say over and over again how the Honor Code affects every facet of their lives: "The Honor Code is a huge part of the school. Sure, it may create the HaverBubble, but most of the time when it comes down to it, trust, concern, and respect really flourish here."

Tough Love (It's Academic)

Most students say they came to Haverford primarily for the rigorous academics, and it certainly lives up to its reputation. Descriptions of schoolwork range from "demanding" to "very challenging" to "incredibly heavy." As one student put it, "The workload is such that it isn't too hard to just get by, but if you want to do really well it takes a lot of hard work, much more than what you expect from a college workload." Another noted that "around midterm time, a lot of people don't sleep."

But students agree that Haverford provides an excellent academic support system; its small size and accessible faculty enable students to receive much more personal attention and guidance than they would in a large research university. Furthermore, Haverford academics are unusual in that there is almost no feeling of competition between students, resulting from a tacit don't-ask-don't-tell policy regarding grades. Said one student, "Here at Haverford, we have a sort-of rule where you don't talk about grades with people, because what we really want to avoid is one of these hyper-competitive academic scenarios."

> "The Honor Code is a huge part of the school. Sure, it may create the HaverBubble, but most of the time when it comes down to it, trust, concern, and respect really flourish here."

Like many aspects of college life, Haverford's academic requirements hearken back to its Quaker heritage. In addition to a standard set of distributional requirements—three courses each in the humanities, natural sciences and social sciences, a year of a foreign language, a freshman writing seminar and a physical education requirement—all students are also required to take a course in social justice, which "ties into our Quaker roots and an awareness of community issues." Students can satisfy these requirements with a wide range of courses. Though Haverford cannot in itself offer the broad course possibilities of a research university, it compensates by participating in a tri-college consortium with nearby Swarthmore and Bryn Mawr colleges, enabling Haverfordians to take courses at the other two institutions and receive credit through their own. Haverford's size also means that classes are much smaller and intimate: only one percent of classes have more than 50 students, and the average class size is 15. One senior reports that "even as a frosh, I was taking classes with 12 students in them. Now, as a senior, I regularly have four- to 10-person classes."

Haverford professors garner high praise from students, both for their general knowledge and for their friendliness and accessibility to students. All classes are taught by full professors, and small class sizes enable professors to pay a great deal of individual attention to each person, both in class and out of it. According to one student, "Most of my friends have babysat, house-sat, or pet-sat for a prof at some point, and it's not unusual to see professors playing with their kids or dogs around the duck pond. Because profs live on campus, they're just as much a part of the community as we are . . . They really consider us their academic colleagues, and some of my favorite friends are professors." Some particularly outstanding professors cited by students include Ashok Gangadean in the philosophy department, Bill Hohenstein, associate professor emeritus of sociology, and Bruce Partridge, the head of the astronomy department.

Furthermore, Haverford's three Academic Centers—the Center for Peace and Global Citizenship, the Hurford Humanities Center, and the Integrated Natural Sciences Center—help expand the academic experience by bringing speakers to campus and providing opportunities for research and internships.

Overall, Haverford's small size proves to be a great advantage in providing students with an exceptional undergraduate education. Students consistently praise the small class sizes and emphasis on individual student-teacher relations, which provide a support system that helps students bear the workload with aplomb. Said one student, "Haverford is a highly rigorous but incredibly nurturing academic environment. It's impossible to get lost in the shuffle here, even if you try. If you come to Haverford, you will succeed."

A Sense of Community

With Haverford's size and location—a well-to-do, wooded suburban area 20 minutes from the center of Philadelphia—it is no surprise that the vast majority of students (estimated at between 95 and 99 percent) live on campus for all four years, either in a residence hall or in college-owned apartments. Housing is assigned through a lottery system with preference given by seniority; but students say that "freshman dorms are often nicer than upperclassman dorms; they're more centrally located and are very cohesive." Some upperclassmen residences have themes or personalities; "Drinker House," home to a large number of athletes, lives up to its name by throwing regular parties.

And speaking of parties, Haverford does in fact throw them—though a student adds that "95 percent of the partying is done by 40 percent of the campus." Haverford's alcohol policy is fairly relaxed, and students say the college doesn't really stop people from partying in their rooms if they so desire. With no fraternities or sororities, Haverford's parties mostly go on in dorms or apartments, especially the so-called "party houses" like Drinker. If partying is your thing, it's only a matter of knowing where to look. One student called Haverford the "kind of place where you can either do nothing or be doing everything, depending on how much effort you put into your social life. . . . There's always something going on, but the onus is on you to figure out what's happening." Thus, students say that some people end up spending four years holed up in their rooms, while others throw themselves into extracurricular activities or parties. Socialization at Haverford, like many things in the college, is purely a matter of effort.

If you're more inclined to head off campus looking for fun, there are plenty of options in that realm as well. The local area features restaurants like Fellini's, Bertucci's and Kahurajo as well as a bar called Roaches, and though students must take a short train ride to get to the bustling city life available at urban schools, Haverford does enjoy the advantage of being completely safe by day and night. Students also like to visit nearby colleges like Bryn Mawr—incidentally, dining at Bryn Mawr is an option for students on the Haverford meal plan, head into Philly for a night on the town, or shop at the King of Prussia Mall.

In terms of diversity, ethnic and otherwise, Haverford is rather limited by its size: "It is getting much more diverse ethnically in recent years. But it is still perceived to be a school dominated by rich white kids . . . but this perception is slowly changing." In fact, 23 percent of students self-identify as minorities, and 46 states and over 40 countries are represented in the student body. Socially speaking, Bryn Mawr students are fond of saying that the stereotypical Haverfordian is "short, Jewish, and named Dan," and while that characterization is far from universally true, 'Fordians cheerfully acknowledge that "the typical Haverford student is nerdier than average [and] fairly awkward." Nevertheless, Haverfordians also tend to be friendly, tolerant and accepting, "pretty humble and down to earth. Students are chill and take life as it comes." And most agree that "making friends at Haverford is VERY easy," in large part because of the community spirit and camaraderie the small-college atmosphere fosters. "Once you meet people you know you're going to see them again at some point . . . you never go from one place to another without seeing someone you know."

School Spirit?

Perhaps not surprisingly, "rah-rah" school spirit and athletic pride aren't really Haverford's cup of tea. While over 40 percent of the student body plays varsity sports, with standouts being cross-country and track, students admit that athletics "aren't terribly large here in terms of school pride" and that "most people don't know when a game's going on." For those who are interested in sports, however, Haverford boasts a newly opened gym facility with state-of-the-art equipment.

Haverford also provides plenty of opportunities for extracurriculars, though on a rather small scale. While there are a number of organizations on campus—service groups and projects are particularly popular—they tend to attract a relatively small number of people, and students often pursue extracurricular involvement on an independent, individual basis. The partnership with Bryn Mawr does help to expand these options, however. As with partying, students report, Haverford extracurriculars are what you make of them;

some people focus exclusively on academics, while some throw themselves into outside activities. The campus also provides plenty of job opportunities for interested students, with a minimum wage of $8.50 for most positions.

On the whole, the main point students stress about life at Haverford is the unique freedom and the opportunities that they enjoy. Education, socializing and—thanks to the Honor Code—even policy enforcement are in the hands of the students, creating a sense of autonomy and responsibility unmatched at most other colleges. And nerdiness aside, Haverfordians really do know how to have fun. As one student admitted, "The only thing that surprised me about Haverford was how much fun everyone was. I expected there to be a lot of nerdy kids, and there are, but they know how to have a good conversation and a great time. I love meeting new people, and the quality and enthusiasm of those people makes the school feel much bigger than it might otherwise."—*Amy Koenig*

FYI

If you come to Haverford, you'd better bring "a dorky sense of humor, a North Face or EMS fleece, and lots of DVDs."

What is the typical weekend schedule? "Friday: have pastabilities in the DC, go to an a cappella or improv show, and make the rounds of the parties. Wake up late Saturday, hang out on campus or at King of Prussia Mall, have dinner out, and go to some parties. Sunday? Brunch at the DC, and then study all day!"

If I could change one thing about Haverford, I'd "have students relax a little more."

Three things every student at Haverford should do before graduating are "swim in the duck pond, go tunneling and sleep over in Magill (library)."

Lafayette College

Address: 118 Markle Hall
Easton, PA 18042
Phone: 610-330-5355
E-mail address:
admissions@lafayette.edu
Web site URL:
www.lafayette.edu
Year Founded: 1826
Private or Public: Private
Religious Affiliation:
Presbyterian
Location: Rural
Number of Applicants: 5,875
Percent Accepted: 37%
**Percent Accepted who
enroll:** 29%
Number Entering: 630
**Number of Transfers
Accepted each Year:** 21
Middle 50% SAT range:
M: 620–710, CR: 580–670,
Wr: 580–670
Middle 50% ACT range:
24–29
**Early admission program
EA/ED/None:** ED

**Percentage accepted
through EA or ED:** 39%
EA and ED deadline: 15-Dec
Regular Deadline: 1-Jan
Application Fee: $60
**Full time Undergraduate
enrollment:** 2,381
Total enrollment: 2,381
Percent Male: 52%
Percent Female: 48%
**Total Percent Minority or
Unreported:** 7%
Percent African-American:
5%
**Percent Asian/Pacific
Islander:** 3%
Percent Hispanic: 5%
Percent Native-American:
<1%
Percent International: 6%
**Percent in-state/out of
state:** 30%/70%
Percent from Public HS:
68%
Retention Rate: 93%
Graduation Rate 4-year: 85%

Graduation Rate 6-year:
87%
**Percent Undergraduates in
On-campus housing:** 96%
**Number of official organized
extracurricular
organizations:** 250
3 Most popular majors:
Social Science, Engineering,
Biology
Student/Faculty ratio:
11:1
Average Class Size: 10 to 19
**Percent of students going to
grad school:** 29%
Tuition and Fees: $33,634
**In State Tuition and Fees if
different:** No difference
Cost for Room and Board:
$10,377
**Percent receiving financial
aid out of those who apply,
first year:** 82%
**Percent receiving financial
aid among all students:**
56%

When summer vacation draws near, and final exams are within days, what do you do? Go to All College Day! All College Day is one of the biggest events held at Lafayette College every spring during the weekend before exams. With the quad and tailgating areas packed with students, everyone joins in the festive atmosphere. All the fraternities hold parties, while there are bands and obstacle courses set up along the quad, creating a carnival-like scene. As the school year ends, students go all out on this last weekend before getting back to the grind and preparing for exams. Strong school pride and a liberal arts mind-set define Lafayette, a small college tucked away in scenic Easton, Pennsylvania. As students become highly involved in campus activities, they generate a fervor that resonates throughout campus.

Academic Exposure

Lafayette is a liberal arts school with a strict core curriculum. From the start, Lafayette immerses its students in a series of rigorous courses that make up the "Common Course of Study." During the fall semester of freshman year, students must complete the First-Year Seminar, a writing-intensive course that covers a wide range of subjects from "Election Rhetoric" to "The Human Animal." Intensifying this focus on writing, Lafayette requires the completion of the College Writing by the second semester of sophomore year. The college also offers Values and Science/Technology seminars. These seminars focus on writing and research about issues in science. In total, students must fulfill 32 credits to graduate. The core curriculum distributes these credits among the humanities/social sciences, natural sciences, mathematics and a writing requirement that can be satisfied by the First-Year Seminar, College Writing course and Values and Science/Technology seminar, as well as at least two additional writing courses in the junior and senior years. Though this list may appear daunting, one student maintained that the core "is great because no matter what you study, you get exposed to a little bit of everything."

While many of the freshman introductory courses have about 100 students, subsequent classes are generally capped at 35 students, while seminars are capped at 15. Students commented that there is an element of competition to get into the higher-level courses as a freshman or sophomore. For those who are strictly humanities or science majors, there are courses that fulfill distributional requirements in areas outside of one's major. For example, "A Chemical Perspective" or "Baby Chem" is tailored to non-science majors looking to fulfill their natural science requirement. Of the workload, one student stated, "your professors will work you to the bone during the week, usually with small assignments, but for the most part, weekends are free with little to no work." With a strong balance between the sciences and humanities, Lafayette offers a limited range of majors that can be further expanded by specialized tracks within each. For example, a government and law major may direct his study along a political theory track. Engineering, economics and government and law rank among the most popular majors, while art and physics are on the other end of the spectrum. Mathematics and engineering are considered more difficult majors.

At Lafayette, the teacher-student relationship is an intimate one. The College focuses on developing a close setting between faculty and students. The administration pays close attention to students' feedback; at the end of each term, students fill out comprehensive evaluations. In the small classes, students are able to interact with professors on a more personal level, and professors often run into their students outside of the classroom on Lafayette's small campus. A student noted that "the teachers are always willing to sit down with you and will help you even if it isn't office hours." Despite the friendly atmosphere in the classroom, students find that it can be hard to get A's. Another complaint is that some classes only meet at 8 in the morning with no other possible times.

Bringing Students Back to Campus

Before freshman year, incoming students receive rooming cards that list the different dormitories and allow them to choose where they want to live. The College then assigns students their list of preferred housing depending on when the cards are sent in and their tuition deposit made. Freshmen are divided among all the dormitories. The freshman rooms tend to be of good size, with South College having the nicest rooms. Most dorms have been renovated rather recently, while four new dormitories were recently built.

Sophomores, juniors and seniors are entered into a housing lottery in which seniors get first pick, and girls choose before guys do. In this system, sophomores get the short end of the stick. Since they are the last group to pick and certain rooms are reserved for freshmen, they generally get the worst rooms. In choosing rooms, students have the option to form living groups composed of people with similar interests. These living groups then live on the same floor of a building. The result is a group of cultural floors, such as the French Floor and El Mundo, as well as floors dedicated to special interests groups, like the Volunteer Floor. Most of these groups are found in Keefe Hall, though Farber Hall and Ramer Hall also carry some. The residential system also features McKelvy House, a nineteenth-century stone mansion that houses 20 students of high academic distinction called McKelvy Scholars by invitation only. A common complaint among students laments the strictness of the RAs in the dorms. One student said, "Some have power trips," while another stated that dorm life becomes constricting because "you always have an RA breathing down your neck."

Upperclassmen prefer living in off-campus apartments, houses and fraternity houses. However, Lafayette recently altered its off-campus housing policy to bring students back to campus. Whereas juniors and seniors could previously live wherever they wanted, the administration has now mandated students wishing to live off campus must enter a lottery for college-owned property. Advanced application for the lottery system is currently restricted to seniors.

Lafayette features a relatively safe campus. The campus police patrol the grounds at night. However, the surrounding College Hill community can be dangerous at night, so caution is necessary. According to students, there is some tension between the community and college students as parties are generally held off campus, often resulting in noise complaints.

There are two all-you-can-eat dining facilities and one a la carte food court with different restaurants. Farinon Student Restaurant features entrees ranging from Mediterranean cuisine to Tex-Mexican food, while Marquis Student Restaurant has a wood-burning pizza oven and cook-your-own stations. The late night café, Gilbert's, offers Seattle's Best coffee and grilled foods for students from early morning to the wee hours of the night. Students say that the food is very satisfactory, and the food court is preferred over other locations. Freshmen are required to maintain the full 20-meal-per-week plan, which also comes with 100 Flex dollars that can be used at local restaurants. In subsequent years, students have the option between different meal plans.

Party Busters

If you had come to Lafayette during the 1970s, you'd have seen a campus rife with Greek life. Nowadays, there are only 12 fraternities and sororities—six of each. The College has slowly been banning these organizations from campus. However, Greek life still holds some sway on the social scene. Starting freshman year, students are allowed to rush fraternities and sororities, but are allowed to join them only after the beginning of sophomore year. The frats often hold parties for students throughout the weekend.

> "In my opinion the school needs to lighten up a little bit. After all, most Lafayette students are hard workers and should be rewarded with the right to party just as hard as they work."

The administration focuses on public safety on campus. A series of probations are handed out to those caught with drugs and drug paraphernalia, and in some cases, students may be referred to the police. With a strict alcohol and drug policy, RAs are constantly on the lookout for underage drinking, and violations can result in probation and fines. Campus police, some of whom were former police officers, enforce the school's policies, while the "liquor patrol" searches for and looks to break up raucous parties. In response to the strict rules, one student stated, "In my opinion the school needs to lighten up a little bit. After all, most Lafayette students are hard workers and should be rewarded with the right to party just as hard as they work."

Despite the policing of alcohol, students still have fun on the weekends. Starting on Wednesday, students head out to frats and parties held off campus and party on through Saturday. While underclassmen will head to off-campus parties, upperclassmen prefer to head to bars, which feature big college nights

on Thursday. Though females across the board are free to join sororities, male athletes are not allowed to pledge fraternities; so, sports teams often host their own parties. One student said about the social scene, "Everyone seems to be on the same cycle sometimes. On a good weekend it can seem like everyone is out, and the parties are amazing. Then everyone will be sick or doing work at the same time." With the newly-imposed off-campus housing restrictions, students are unsure of how the party scene will be affected. Most expect a sharp drop, but say that with time, it should readjust to normal levels.

For those not interested in the partying scene, there are many fine Italian restaurants and stores within walking distance. Campus Pizza turns into a nightclub on the weekends, while another popular hang-out is a bar called Milo's Place.

Athletic, Not Athletic, Other?

Even though Lafayette is a small school, it is a Division I school, meaning that of its small population, a large percentage are athletes. As a result, a common perception of the college is that it is very jock-oriented. While football and basketball play their games on campus, other sports have to travel off campus in order to use their facilities. As a result, the only games that most students attend are football and basketball games. The biggest game of the year is the Lafayette-Lehigh football game; with over 140 years of history, it is one of oldest college football rivalries in the country.

While the athletes have their own gym, the new $35 million Allan P. Kirby Sports Center is available to all students. The center features pools, an indoor track, billiards tables, ping pong and racquetball—just to name a few. Intramural sports are huge at Lafayette. The College features both a competitive and a noncompetitive league. Many students become highly committed to intramurals and play sports ranging from flag football to kickball to squash. Club sports also play a role in the active Lafayette student's life, with Frisbee, ice hockey and crew teams being especially popular.

But for those not satisfied by athletic activities, Lafayette's extracurricular life boasts a variety of interesting clubs and activities. Academic clubs and the Lafayette Investment Club are among the most prominent. Various other groups are involved in community service. Students are very involved in their extracurricular lives and usually find one to which they dedicate the bulk of their time. For the working student, popular jobs include the library, fitness center, career services, and—of course—being an intramural league referee.

Getting Comfy With Each Other

Most people would typify Lafayette students as preppy, rich, white kids. Still, many cultural groups are present on campus, such as the Association of Black Collegians and International Students Association. However, the lack of diversity is still very obvious. One student noted, "The international students only hang out with international students . . . There's social segregation, but not on purpose." The College is making a significant effort to recruit people of other ethnicities.

Because of Lafayette's small size, students have no difficulty meeting new people and forming close friendships. Either through joining Greek life, hanging with the party crowd or spending time with people in class, every student meets familiar faces each day on campus, and "you get close to people and hang out with them nonstop." The intimacy of Lafayette reveals no distinctions between upperclassmen and underclassmen, as everyone collectively forms a vibrant and energetic atmosphere. For many, there are no regrets about choosing a small school over a large state school, and students say that seeing the same people every day brings everyone together to form a secure network of friends that a larger school could not offer.—*Thomas Hsieh*

FYI

If you come to Lafayette, you'd better bring "a lot of backup food. You'll get sick of the food fast."

What's the typical weekend schedule? "Wake up on Saturday around noon, have lunch, do work if needed/relax and hang out, dinner, most partying generally starts at 10 or 11. Bars close at 2. Late night parties might open up then. Sunday—wake up, brunch at Farinon Dining Hall, again work if needed until it's done, or watch TV."

If I could change one thing about Lafayette, I'd "have public safety release their hold on the Greek system social scene."

Three things every student at Lafayette should do before graduating are "go to Porter's and get your own personal mug, eat the chili at Milo's Place, and buy a T-shirt that would be offensive to any student at Lehigh."

Lehigh University

Address: 27 Memorial Drive West, Bethlehem, PA 18015

Phone: 610-758-3100

E-mail address: admissions@lehigh.edu

Web site URL: www.lehigh.edu/admissions

Year Founded: 1865

Private or Public: Private

Religious Affiliation: None

Location: Suburban

Number of Applicants: 12,955

Percent Accepted: 28%

Percent Accepted who enroll: 33%

Number Entering: 1,270

Number of Transfers Accepted each Year: 65

Middle 50% SAT range: M: 640–720, CR: 590–680, Wr: Unreported

Middle 50% ACT range: 28–32

Early admission program EA/ED/None: ED

Percentage accepted through EA or ED: 40%

EA and ED deadline: 15-Nov, 1-Jan

Regular Deadline: 1-Jan

Application Fee: $70

Full time Undergraduate enrollment: 4,732

Total enrollment: 6,800

Percent Male: 57%

Percent Female: 43%

Total Percent Minority or Unreported: 27%

Percent African-American: 5%

Percent Asian/Pacific Islander: 8%

Percent Hispanic: 5%

Percent Native-American: 0%

Percent International: 5.60%

Percent in-state/out of state: 25%/75%

Percent from Public HS: 66%

Retention Rate: 94%

Graduation Rate 4-year: 72%

Graduation Rate 6-year: 83%

Percent Undergraduates in On-campus housing: 70%

Number of official organized extracurricular organizations: 150

3 Most popular majors: Finance, International Relations, Mechanical Engineering

Student/Faculty ratio: 9:1

Average Class Size: 25-30

Percent of students going to grad school: 30%

Tuition and Fees: $37,250

In State Tuition and Fees if different: No difference

Cost for Room and Board: $9,770

Percent receiving financial aid out of those who apply, first year: 42%

Percent receiving financial aid among all students: 50%

I n the little town of Bethlehem, Pennsylvania, a bright and shining star lights the way for students as they climb the central campus hillside in search of a place where they can stop to rest for the evening. The star is a large statue built on the peak of this "Christmas city," and the site of repose is a collection of Greek houses at the top of the hill. Known for its unique balance between a challenging academic curriculum and a hardcore party scene, Lehigh University offers what one student called "a dynamic learning environment customized to individual interest" and a close-knit community where students are determined to learn as much as they can while still finding plenty of time to kick back and enjoy themselves.

What Kind of Engineer Are You?

The University is composed of four different colleges: the College of Arts and Sciences, the College of Business and Economics, the College of Education (which is more focused on graduate work) and the College of Engineering and Applied Science. While Lehigh is home to students with a wide variety of academic interests, the school is particularly renowned for its engineering and its business programs. About 30 percent of the student body majors in one of the 15 types of engineering, while another 28 percent chooses to study finance, accounting, or other aspects of economics. According to one student, "When people ask you what your major is, they generally just skip right to, 'What kind of engineer are you?'" It is common for students to take on a second major or a minor, and several people commented on the interesting propensity of engineers to minor in music. One psychology major confirmed the high majority of business and engineering students, but was also quick to point out that the College of Arts and Sciences actually has the highest enrollment. About 42 percent of the student body is in arts and sciences, but because a good portion of those are only pursuing a minor in the arts, only about 20 percent have a true liberal arts major. Another student pointed out, "They're trying to tweak admissions to get more academic diversity, but right now it's heavily geared toward business and hard sciences." The newly introduced Global Citizenship program lets students give their majors an international perspective.

Most students say that they have never had trouble registering for or getting into a course, except for some of the base, extremely popular, and easy classes (there aren't many of them) such as Intro Psych or Religion 101. Lehigh prides itself on its small class sizes; apart from a few large freshman lectures, most classes have between 15 and 20 students, with language classes being even smaller. Although the University is known for its academic rigor, most students say that competition among classmates is uncommon. "People are friendly here," one sophomore said. "Classes are small enough that you can really get to know people. We study in groups a lot, especially for projects in the business school that require us to work in teams." Said another student, "You really have to be able to work as a team and help each other out." In addition to great interaction between the students, everyone has the opportunity to take advantage of an incredibly dedicated and knowledgeable faculty. "We have great student-professor relations," commented one freshman. "No matter what time I walk into a professor's office, they've never not had time to talk to me." Added another student, "I like the professor enthusiasm. You can really tell that they love what they're doing, which makes something dull more bearable. I love that they're crazy about what they're teaching."

Students call the workload "decent, as long as you go to class and keep up with the work—otherwise you have to learn everything on your own!" Grading is strict and curving is rare, so "it's very difficult to get an A." Professors do expect a lot, but students are willing to work hard in order to learn the material and get the grade.

Bottoms-Up!

The competition at Lehigh, according to one student, seems to have more to do with the social scene than it does with the classroom. "It's a competition to see who can do the best while also drinking the most," she declared. Social life is dominated by the fraternities and sororities, with about 32 percent of the student body deciding to pledge at one of the 27 Greek houses. "If you're not in a fraternity or a sorority, you're usually on an athletic team," said one varsity runner. "Or you're just weird."

Another student, when asked about Greek life, laughed and said, "It's a big part of Lehigh! It's a big deal and if that's your scene, then definitely take advantage of it; but if you don't join, you can easily find your own friends, your own group, and plenty of things to do on campus." Most parties take place Thursday through Saturday on top of the hill where all the houses are, although there are a few special occasions during the year when students party all week (usually for the annual Lehigh-Lafayette football game in the fall and Greek Week in the spring). Seniors often go with friends to bars in the surrounding area.

Drinking policies are not strongly enforced. According to one student, "The administration doesn't do much because they know we balance partying with academics. As long as we care about school as well, they're willing to let some things slide." Another noted, "The people who are most highly respected are those who are at the top of their classes but who also drink; students take pride in being able to keep studies up, but also party all the time."

> "You could hit copy and paste and 4,500 kids later you'd have Lehigh!"

Although parties are definitely enjoyable, they are not usually the best places to meet people. Most students say that they met their friends through classes or clubs, or because they lived near each other. "Classes are small and people are friendly, so it's easy to make friends," said one freshman. One major complaint about the Lehigh population is that it lacks ethnic and cultural diversity; though there are a fair number of international students, and the last three classes have been the most diverse in school history, even geographic diversity is still low. Most students hail from the East Coast. "We're a pretty homogeneous place," said one student. "You could hit copy and paste and 4,500 kids later you'd have Lehigh!" Several students described themselves and their classmates as "preppy," with many in the upper-middle class and several with "Ugg boots, messy ponytails and popped collars." Still, even though the minority population is small, everyone is inclusive and "people mix well together."

Life on the Hill

Freshmen and sophomores are required to live in dormitories on campus, while most upperclassmen move to Greek, athletic, or other residential houses in the surrounding area. Freshman dorms are randomly assigned, and several of the nicer ones are described as "palaces." There is no real separation between the campus and the town, so many "off-campus" houses are actually closer to University buildings than the dormitories are. Although underclassmen dorms are assigned randomly, they still have slight personality distinctions. Usually, the quieter dorms are at the bottom of the hill and the rowdier dorms are towards the top. In general, students enjoy living on campus in the "big, beautiful buildings," and many stay on campus as upperclassmen even though doing so is not a requirement. "I like the fact that campus is a small community where you see a lot of same people every day," said one freshman. Several people described campus architecture as "gothic, ivy-covered, with that classic college look." Another student added, "It IS built on a hill, though—that's the one drawback!" An additional disadvantage, according to some, is the drabness of the surrounding town. "I won't call it a dump," said one student, "but it isn't great." The huge difference between the economic status of the campus and the town does lead to a "bad relationship" between the students and the surrounding community, which is unfortunate but hopefully improvable through outreach programs and extracurricular community service.

When it comes to extracurricular activities, most students participate in community service programs through their Greek house or athletic team. Almost all student organizations, such as the newspaper or drama productions, are completely student-run. There are several musical organizations on campus, including the Philharmonic Orchestra, the marching band, the jazz band and a variety of smaller ensembles. Varsity sports enjoy a popular following on campus, especially the football and basketball teams. According to one student, "Football games are the place to be on the weekends and people also get crazy at basketball games, but wrestling is the most revered sport on campus. Some of the wrestlers have gone to the Olympics!" Intramurals also constitute a big part of the sporting scene on campus. "Soccer and rugby especially are pretty big and pretty competitive, but everyone can play and lots of people really get into it," said one student.

When asked what differentiates their school from others, students again remarked on the apparently equal value conferred upon both drinking and academics. "It's a little unique in its magnitude," noted one student. "People go nuts for both! You study like a maniac, and then you drink like a maniac." Most people agree that the beautiful campus, the stimulating classes and the friendly community all make them glad they chose Lehigh. Said one sophomore, "Freshman year is definitely an adjustment, as it would be anywhere. Definitely as you move up, you find more and more things you enjoy. It's a great place to spend four years!"—*Lindsay Starck*

FYI

If you come to Lehigh, you'd better bring "hiking boots, because you have to climb up that huge hill every day!"

What's the typical weekend schedule? "Thursday, drink; Friday, drink; Saturday, drink; Sunday, study."

If I could change one thing about Lehigh, I'd "do something about the homogenous student population."

Three things every student at Lehigh should do before graduating are "watch a football game on the grassy knoll, hike up to see the Bethlehem star, eat at Johnny's Bagels."

Muhlenberg College

Address: 2400 Chew Street
Allentown, PA 18104
Phone: 484-664-3200
E-mail address:
admissions@muhlenberg.
edu
Web site URL:
www.muhlenberg.edu
Year Founded: 1848
Private or Public: Private
Religious Affiliation:
Lutheran
Location: Urban
Number of Applicants: 4,703
Percent Accepted: 37%
**Percent Accepted who
enroll:** 32%
Number Entering: 551
**Number of Transfers
Accepted each Year:** 25
Middle 50% SAT range:
M: 560–660, CR: 560–660,
Wr: 560–660
Middle 50% ACT range:
24–29
**Early admission program
EA/ED/None:** ED

**Percentage accepted
through EA or ED:**
Unreported
EA and ED deadline: 1-Feb
Regular Deadline: 15-Feb
Application Fee: $50
**Full time Undergraduate
enrollment:** 2,492
Total enrollment: 2,492
Percent Male: 42%
Percent Female: 58%
**Total Percent Minority or
Unreported:** 9%
Percent African-American:
2%
**Percent Asian/Pacific
Islander:** 3%
Percent Hispanic: 4%
Percent Native-American:
<1%
Percent International: <1%
**Percent in-state/out of
state:** 23% /77%
Percent from Public HS: 70%
Retention Rate: 93%
Graduation Rate 4-year:
79%

Graduation Rate 6-year:
84%
**Percent Undergraduates
in On-campus housing:**
92%
**Number of official organized
extracurricular
organizations:** 100
3 Most popular majors:
Business/Commerce,
Drama/Theatre, Psychology
Student/Faculty ratio:
11:1
Average Class Size: 19
**Percent of students going to
grad school:** Unreported
Tuition and Fees: 35,375
**In State Tuition and Fees if
different:** No difference
Cost for Room and Board:
$8,060
**Percent receiving financial
aid out of those who apply,
first year:** 70%
**Percent receiving financial
aid among all students:**
46%

A small liberal arts college tucked away in suburban Allentown, Pennsylvania, Muhlenberg College truly offers an intimate college experience. From the quaint 80-acre campus to the modest student population, Muhlenberg is sure to make one feel like part of a small, close-knit community. However, small size doesn't mean small offerings. With over 60 majors and 100 campus organizations to choose from, Muhlenberg offers a sizable array of options for a small school. Students emerge from Muhlenberg with an excellent education, preparation for their career goals, and a stronger sense of self.

Strong Academics, Strong Students

Muhlenberg prides itself on preparing students for whatever challenge they will face, be it graduate school admissions, working towards a career, or simply being better equipped for life. Owing to the College's commitment to a liberal arts education, all

students fulfill general education requirements including two semesters of foreign language study, science, math, physical education, and the fine arts. Fear not, however, as these requirements are aimed at giving a student a well-rounded education. "No one graduates from Muhlenberg with a one-dimensional education," a senior said. "General education requirements are easily fulfilled and allow everyone to actually have a real sense of liberal arts and engage with the liberal arts in their education," a freshman remarked. Students are grounded from the very beginning in the physical sciences, social sciences and the humanities in order to expose them to academia in both breadth and depth.

The workload at Muhlenberg is also about as diverse as the number of majors the school offers. General introductory classes tend to be fairly easy while more advanced science classes can wrack any genius's brain. "It really depends on the class and the professor. Classes like fitness and wellness are jokes," a freshman said. But do not be misled. Muhlenberg is renowned for its pre-medicine program due to its highly respected science departments. They also have a praised, innovative program in neuroscience that is popular among students and gaining reputation among academic circles. Pre-med students have a pretty challenging course load that is typical of the pre-med track at any school. Most students can expect to study at least two hours per day for each class; multiplying that by the usual four-class schedule results in about eight hours of study time per day. Some majors allow for less work in the typical homework sense, but more time devoted in the art studio, theater or dance studio. Even though dance majors are not spending as much time hitting the books as pre-meds, all at Muhlenberg devote time to their education.

Devoted study doesn't mean there's no room for academic fun. Unusual classes such as "To Hell and Back" and "Bugs and Us" allow students to integrate non-traditional learning into their education with hands-on experiences in interesting subjects of study. Whatever the preference, students are sure to find something that interests them at Muhlenberg. The individualized attention that a small college affords is also an important part of the College experience. Class sizes are usually less than 20, excluding the large introductory science courses, and professors are very accessible. "Most of the professors are really nice and truly want you to succeed," a sophomore said. They can be one of the most valuable resources to students in terms of mastering course material or just building relationships.

What Muhlenberg does lack doesn't come in terms of quality but more so size. Academic departments are generally good, but some departments are undersized due to the sheer smallness of Muhlenberg's size as a liberal arts college. Some students complain that although there are many programs offered, there's just not enough of the financial pie to go around for everyone. "Some departments could use expansion," a senior opined. It is apparent that the tradeoff cost for highly individualized attention would be a smaller, less extensive program.

Ride the Mule

For a small college, Muhlenberg does have a vibrant social scene on campus. No scene dominates another here; everyone pretty much finds their place. Options are plentiful and students usually find what it is they're looking for. Weekends at the 'Berg are filled with variety—there's the frat scene, the usual dorm parties, and many non-partying alternatives. The Muhlenberg Activities Council works hard to put on events during the weekends for those for whom partying isn't their cup of tea. Movies, bowling, concerts, comedians, sports and other events are regularly held for those looking to have good, clean old-fashioned fun.

Of course alcohol is part of the party scene like at any other school, but at Muhlenberg, it doesn't dominate. Some people drink, and they find it easy to acquire alcohol. Others choose not to drink and find it equally easy to hang out with people who also choose not to drink. Just like alcohol, the Greek life at Muhlenberg is also a selective choice. Only about 20 percent of the student body is involved with Greek life. The school is large enough for people to make many new acquaintances, but small enough so that it doesn't become stifling or overpowering.

A highlight of a small college social scene is the fact that mostly everyone knows each other. People become close with most of their dormmates quite quickly due to the sheer amount of time spent interacting with each other. Classmates also quickly become good friends as many within the same major spend much academic time with each other as well. Classes, labs, performances and more begin to pile up once the semester gets rolling, so it helps to have a core group of study buddies as well as friends. If that's not enough, "everyone on campus seems to be friendly," a freshman observed. There are no social divides between majors, age or clubs. The social scene is not cliquey, but at times it can seem very homogenous. "Some people might think that Muhlenberg is a bunch of rich white kids," a senior said, but there are still plenty of opportunities for people to find their place.

Life at the 'Berg

Situated on a hilltop in the West End neighborhood of Allentown, Pennsylvania, Muhlenberg's campus offers old-school, small-town charm alongside the modernity of world-class facilities. Campus grounds are kept pristine throughout the school year. Students praise the gorgeous campus and the relative ease of walking from place to place around campus. "The best part of campus is that it is small, and it is almost impossible to be late getting to classes or appointments," a freshman remarked.

Housing at Muhlenberg can be pretty sweet as well. Even though the college and campus themselves are small, there are still lots of options for housing. Freshmen usually live on campus in one of the three designated freshman dorms with quiet dorms available for those who prefer their dorms to be a quiet study space. Then there are the party dorms for the more socially inclined. Housing is set up in a hall system where students share communal bathrooms in a hall with singles, doubles and sometimes triples that they share with roommates. Most dorms are equipped with air conditioning while Brown, the all-female dorm, is equipped with 15-foot ceilings and hardwood floors. Others might not get so lucky. But seniors have the additional option to live off campus in suite-style arrangements through the M.I.L.E program. Muhlenberg Independent Living Experience houses are owned and operated by the college. They include a kitchen, living room and multiple bedroom arrangements.

> **"The best part of campus is that it is small, and it is almost impossible to be late getting to classes or appointments."**

Dining at Muhlenberg is also very diversified. The main dining hall, affectionately known as the Garden Room, serves up traditional cuisine in a buffet-style setting. Choices are usually varied with vegetarian and vegan options consistently available. Aside from the daily hustle and bustle of the dining hall, students may also choose from Sandella's, Cyclone Salads, Freshens Smoothies, Java Joe's, and the GQ (General Quarters), the latter of which serves up late night munchies. With so much variety, students rarely get bored with the selection at Muhlenberg—but beware, choose wisely as some establishments are better than others depending on taste preferences.

If college food doesn't satiate satisfactorily, there are many restaurants around campus in Allentown. The area around Chew Street is full of businesses catering to the College community. However, town-gown relations aren't the best. Tough neighborhoods located near campus contribute to a divide between "rich" students and their counterparts who actually live in Allentown. Allentown is also just that: a town. Don't expect to find cosmopolitan entertainment options in the immediate area, but Philadelphia is only an hour away while New York City is about two hours away. Students always manage to keep themselves occupied.

Friendly Fro-Yo Fanatics

In all, Muhlenberg students claim they are some of the happiest students to be found in the Tri-State area. From the opening convocation in the chapel to the candlelight ceremony at orientation, students truly feel like an essential part of an academic community. Termed the "caring college" by its denizens, Muhlenberg is home to students known to be diverse in their interests, friends and goals. Many of them welcome newbies with open arms, often times over frozen yogurt, a campus wide obsession. As much as frozen yogurt is a part of the Muhlenberg culture, so are friendliness and acceptance. If the feel of a small, close campus doesn't feel stifling, then Muhlenberg College might be the one for some prospective students. The lack of entertainment options is mostly offset by the proliferation of activities on campus and students are generally happy in spite of the occasional feeling of living in a Muhlenberg bubble.—*Hai Pham*

FYI
Three things everyone should do before graduation are "eat fro-yo, play in the snow, see a speaker, and go to Hillel's Bagel Brunch."
What's the typical weekend schedule? "People go to parties, hang out in the dorms with their friends, participate in campus events, see a performance, go to the mall, and Sundays are mostly spent studying."
If you come to Muhlenberg you'd better bring "your work ethic, UGGs and a smile."
If I could change one thing about Muhlenberg, "I wish it weren't located in Allentown but somewhere more urban."

Penn State University

Address: 201 Shields
Building, Box 3000
University Park, PA, 16804
Phone: 814-865-5471
E-mail address:
admissions@psu.edu
Web site URL: www.psu.edu
Year Founded: 1855
Private or Public: Public
Religious Affiliation: None
Location: Urban
Number of Applicants:
48,093
Percent Accepted: 42%
Percent Accepted who
enroll: 36%
Number Entering: 7,234
Number of Transfers
Accepted each Year:
108
Middle 50% SAT range:
M: 570–670, CR: 530–630,
Wr: Unreported
Middle 50% ACT range:
27–32
Early admission program
EA/ED/None: ED

Percentage accepted
through EA or ED: 57%
EA and ED deadline: 15-Nov
Regular Deadline: 15-Jan
Application Fee: $50
Full time Undergraduate
enrollment: 37,988
Total enrollment: 44,118
Percent Male: 55%
Percent Female: 45%
Total Percent Minority or
Unreported: 13%
Percent African-American:
4%
Percent Asian/Pacific
Islander: 6%
Percent Hispanic: 4%
Percent Native-American:
0%
Percent International: 3%
Percent in-state/out of
state: 75%/25%
Percent from Public HS:
Unreported
Retention Rate: 96%
Graduation Rate 4-year:
84%

Graduation Rate 6-year:
88%
Percent Undergraduates
in On-campus housing:
82%
Number of official organized
extracurricular
organizations: 246
3 Most popular majors:
Economics, Psychology,
Biology
Student/Faculty ratio: 8:1
Average Class Size:
Unreported
Percent of students going to
grad school: Unreported
Tuition and Fees: $24,940
In State Tuition and Fees if
different: $13,706
Cost for Room and Board:
$8,270
Percent receiving financial
aid out of those who apply,
first year: 65%
Percent receiving financial
aid among all students:
48%

E ven though students tend to refer to Penn State as one entity, it is actually a composite of 26 campuses scattered throughout the state. Nevertheless, the term "Penn State" has become synonymous with the University Park campus—a vibrant academic, cultural and social center for students from all over Pennsylvania and the rest of the United States.

Options, Options, Options

Penn State was founded in 1855 when the state of Pennsylvania, responding to a request by the Pennsylvania State Agricultural Society, chartered a school focused on farming and technology—a far cry from the Greek- and Latin-based curriculum emphasized at most other colleges at the time. Throughout Penn State's rich history, the University has consistently been at the forefront of most higher education trends, such as the focus on engineering, research and even the Internet.

Penn State has general education requirements in social science and quantitative stud-ies, and such requirements generally make up one third of a student's course load. While that may seem like a lot, one junior noted that, "Most students don't mind the bulk of them, and generally they are not that hard." "My experience was that I filled most of them up without even realizing it," another student added, perhaps thanks to Penn State's incredibly diverse course catalog. One international politics major enthused, "The physical fitness requirement can be fulfilled with skiing, hip-hop dance, etc. There's even a major called Professional Golf Management." Neverthe-less, she did bemoan the lab component of the required science sequence.

Penn State students agree that academics are "as difficult as you make them out to be." Even so, many recommend that prospective students not be afraid to take more demand-ing classes, since those usually end up being the courses that have the most impact. For the academically ambitious, there is the Schreyer's Honors College, where students complete a senior-year thesis. Individual departments may also have honors programs. A student enrolled in the honors program in economics said he took "one class dedicated to writing your senior thesis, and one honors seminar in which you get to read all these things that you would never read in any other class. If I didn't do this, I'd probably be pulling my hair out in April." Said one student about the Honors Programs, "Personally, I was too lazy to apply, but through the years I have found that taking honors courses when able truly helps to avoid the B.S. work that normal classes might have. Plus you learn a lot more."

When it comes to freshman-year classes, prospective students should expect to see lecture halls of 300 to 400 students and a wide range of quality. One student highly recommended the Psychology 100 course for its professor's nutty antics. Other students stress the importance of choosing classes based on the professor, not on the course itself, since one professor rarely teaches the same introductory course in consecutive years.

Priority for course registration goes to honors students and student athletes, and then to the students with the most credits. Nevertheless, there are freshman-only sections and seminars, which one junior called "hit-or-miss." "For me, it was the hardest class of my freshman year," she explained. "For my roommate, she learned how to use the library card catalogue and that was about it."

When students come out of introductory classes, enrollment shrinks dramatically from 300 to about 25 or 30 students. Current Penn State students say that the grading might be a little bit skewed in the first year due to the different TAs, but it all evens out at the end. "Overall, grading is fair—not too harsh or lenient."

What's a Nittany, Anyways?

"When they founded Penn State, they decided to put it in the geographic center of Pennsylvania," one student said. "That means that everybody in Pennsylvania has equal access to Penn State . . . unfortunately, it also means that some would consider us in the middle of nowhere."

Despite Penn State's location, students do not lack for things to do. "Weekends are what you make of them here at PSU. You can stay in and do homework, see a movie, go out to eat, catch a concert, play pool on or off campus, or go to the bars or a friend's party. Anyone who claims that there is not enough to do in state college is, in my opinion, a toe-sucking liar."

Football is *huge* at Penn State. At this Big Ten school, the entire student population routinely turns out to support their beloved Nittany Lions. One junior echoed her classmates' sentiments when she said: "If you're on campus during game time on Saturdays, you're most likely the only person there. Not being a huge football fan myself, I was worried about this crazed reputation when I went in, but I found a lot of people use it as a chance to take a break from studying and socialize, making it more of a party than a football game."

As for weekend nights, a good majority of the student population parties—and parties hard. "After all, aren't we like, the number two party school in America?" one student mused. Students usually begin their weekends on Thursday and finish on Saturday. Frat parties are popular with freshmen, but upperclassmen gravitate toward the active, downtown bar scene or private house and apartment parties. Freshmen should be warned, however, that dorm parties rarely occur and are frequently shut down by the residential advisors. "With so much to do, it's really stupid to throw a dorm party. It's ridiculously easy to get caught," said one junior.

There are plenty of students who do not drink, and they say that they do not feel particularly ostracized for it. The HUB offers Late Night Penn State every Thursday to Saturday, and people can catch comedians, musical performers, movies, arts and crafts, game shows and more. However, that does not mean that the average Penn State student can avoid the presence of alcohol for all four years of college. "If you want a social life, you either have to drink or be around people who are drinking," said one nondrinker. "But the thing is, you'll never be pressured into doing it."

Besides football and parties, there is a notable Penn State event called THON. This is a student-run 48-hour dance-a-thon, and the proceeds go to benefit pediatric cancer. "It is the largest student-run philanthropy in the nation, and last year raised $4.21 million for the kids." It is an experience that you cannot miss. Students promise that feelings of community, camaraderie and love are never stronger than during the 48 hours of THON every February.

State College and University Park

On the topic of on-campus living, opinions vary. On the one hand, students agree that their mandatory first year of on-campus living provided them with a lot of friends and companionship. However, the common problems with living on campus, such as dirty bathrooms, mismatched roommates and loud neighbors, still apply. "Though there is a lot of camaraderie between dorm-dwellers, the experience was often times discouraging and disgusting," one student said.

The result is that many students who remain on campus after freshman year prefer to move into the suite-style dormitory. Eastview, South Halls and West Halls boast the most sought-after dorms. Most freshmen (with the exception of Schreyer's Honors students, who live in South) are placed in the East Halls. One economics major said, "My second and third years were better than my first because I lived in a suite. In fact, that's probably why I stayed in the dorm. Suites are like apartments . . . it's not like sharing a room with somebody that you don't like all that much and then having to also share a bathroom."

> **"Well, I hate to resort to clichés, but Penn State is everything and more."**

Off campus, apartments and houses are pretty easy to find, especially if distance and convenience is not the most important factor. One graduate student said, "The buses that go off campus are pretty fast and reliable, and there are two enormous 24-hour grocery stores and a Wal-Mart that are easily accessible by these buses."

Penn State is racially representative of the state of Pennsylvania, but less diverse than its peer universities. Students attest to the fact that because there are such large numbers of undergraduates on campus, "the numbers of minorities *look* big, but the percentage is actually pretty pitiful." There have been some racial incidents on campus the last few years, and students agree that what Penn State needs is more minority students.

Penn State's relationship with the town of State College can best be described as symbiotic—almost everyone who works in the town has some affiliation to Penn State. "If you go to an off-campus party and someone's from the town but not working for PSU, you look at him really strangely," one student said. There is almost no distinction between the town and campus: "If you live in South Halls, you just cross the street and you are 'downtown.' State College the town is filled with cheap restaurants and small shops, and you can get everything you need without ever setting foot inside a car or a bus."

That being said, the people of the town usually go out of their way to accommodate the needs of Penn State. When asked to describe town-gown relations, one student said, "Well, the first thing I noticed about State College is that for the kids, Halloween doesn't occur on October 31st! They go trick-or-treating two days before the actual date of Halloween. The reason for this is because the students tend to go a little crazy on Halloween, so it's not exactly safe for the kids to go door-to-door."—*Janet Xu*

FYI

If you come to Penn State, you'd better bring "a good winter jacket—waterproof, windproof and breathable!"

What is the typical weekend schedule? "The weekend starts with Thirsty Thursday. Most seniors don't have classes on Friday, but most of the underclassmen do. Friday night everybody goes out, then Saturday is just complete oblivion. Sunday is . . . 'Oh crap, I actually have to get work done.' "

If I could change one thing about Penn State, I'd "get rid of all the red tape about taking classes— I think it's ridiculous that I can only take one finance class if I wanted, and that would be Introduction to Finance."

Three things every student should do before graduating from Penn State are "go to a football game; eat at the Creamery, because it's the best ice cream you will ever find; and go to Canyon Pizza at 2 a.m. at least one Friday or Saturday night to enjoy the enormously long line of drunk people waiting for their dollar slice."

Susquehanna University

Address: 514 University Avenue Selinsgrove, PA 17870
Phone: 570-372-4260
E-mail address: suadmiss@susqu.edu
Web site URL: www.susqu.edu
Year Founded: 1858
Private or Public: Private
Religious Affiliation: Lutheran
Location: Suburban
Number of Applicants: 2,777
Percent Accepted: 73%
Percent Accepted who enroll: 31%
Number Entering: 616
Number of Transfers Accepted each Year: 69
Middle 50% SAT range: M: 520–600, CR: 500–610, Wr: 500–610
Middle 50% ACT range: 21–26
Early admission program EA/ED/None: ED

Percentage accepted through EA or ED: 83%
EA and ED deadline: 15-Nov
Regular Deadline: 1-Mar
Application Fee: $35
Full time Undergraduate enrollment: 2,137
Total enrollment: 2,137
Percent Male: 47%
Percent Female: 53%
Total Percent Minority or Unreported: 9%
Percent African-American: 2%
Percent Asian/Pacific Islander: 1%
Percent Hispanic: 3%
Percent Native-American: <1%
Percent International: 1%
Percent in-state/out of state: 49%/51%
Percent from Public HS: 85%
Retention Rate: 85%
Graduation Rate 4-year: 79%
Graduation Rate 6-year: 80%

Percent Undergraduates in On-campus housing: 74%
Number of official organized extracurricular organizations: 120
3 Most popular majors: Business Administration and Management, General, Communication Studies/Speech Communication and Rhetoric, Creative Writing
Student/Faculty ratio: 13:1
Average Class Size: 10 to 19
Percent of students going to grad school: 23%
Tuition and Fees: $31,080
In State Tuition and Fees if different: No difference
Cost for Room and Board: $8,800
Percent receiving financial aid out of those who apply, first year: 92%
Percent receiving financial aid among all students: 92%

Georgian buildings and hundreds of trees create an ostensibly quiet and arcane setting for Susquehanna University in rural Pennsylvania. However, the 306-acre campus is anything but dormant. Students buzz with enthusiasm for Susquehanna's commitment to its close-knit community, in which students partake of extensive academic and extracurricular opportunities.

Learning, Life Sciences, and Latkes

Academics at Susquehanna are all about options. Students can opt for one of six pre-professional programs or even design their own major with the help of a faculty member. Students attend one of three schools on campus, the School of Arts, Humanities and Communications; the School of Natural and Social Sciences; and the Sigmund Weis School of Business. Students enjoy the fact that the exclusively undergraduate population can enroll in classes within any of the schools. One art history major gushed that "History and Culture of Jewish Cuisine" was her favorite class, while both an early education major and a biology major chose to enroll in an honors philosophy course called "Thought and Civilization." Despite such tantalizing course options, Susquehanna does have a core of interdisciplinary requirements. Students say these core curriculum requirements are "easy to fulfill" and "comprehensive," but non-science majors dislike the requirement of one science class and one math or logic course.

Pass the Class (and the Gravy)

The core comprises approximately one-third of a student's courses and includes one class each in literature, fine arts, history, science or technology, writing, the social sciences, mathematics or logic and philosophy or religion. Despite being mandatory, students report that all these classes fully engage students. With an average class size of approximately 18 and a student-faculty ratio of 13 to 1, Susquehanna cultivates the close relationships between professors and students for which small liberal arts schools are known. Many students call their professors by their first names and are even regularly invited to dinner at their professors' homes. At the Thanksgiving dinner offered in the dining hall, faculty members become waiters and serve turkey and stuffing to students, who typically rate the meal as their favorite campus event of the year.

Northeastern Exposure

The SU student body hails mostly from the Northeast, notably from Pennsylvania, New Jersey, and New York. Attempts to increase diversity have been only somewhat successful—only eight percent of students are international or minority—but the University strongly encourages applicants of all economic, religious, and ethnic backgrounds. Indeed, Susquehanna offers need-based aid to over half of its students, has organizations affiliated with different races and religions, and boasts merit-based scholarships and an honors program to attract particularly talented applicants. A task force created by the Diversity Studies program is focusing on increasing diversity both in the curriculum and in the student body, in part through the Diversity Studies minor. Nonetheless, one African-American junior stated that he wishes "there were more diversity on campus."

> **"There's something for everyone, and if there isn't something for you, you can always start your own club or ask a professor for advice."**

Despite the relatively homogenous population, Susquehanna students have interests ranging across the board. With over 100 organizations and activities and numerous opportunities for internships and jobs in the surrounding Susquehanna Valley, it would seem that students might find so many options daunting. In fact, the opposite is true. As one sophomore explained, "There's something for everyone, and if there isn't something for you, you can always start your own club or ask a professor for advice." Over half of students participate in some form of community service, including the Habitat for Humanity program, the University's Study Buddy program in which students tutor kids at local schools, and the Ronald McDonald House for hospitalized children.

Dining at "Deg"

Students often hang out at the Degenstein Campus Center that they dub "Deg," which includes the campus bookstore, the Evert Dining Room, the Encore Café, Charlie's Coffee House, a 450-seat auditorium, and the headquarters for both the student newspaper and radio station. Although students call Evert "crowded" with "numerous options that are nevertheless usually the same day-to-day," they also say that they "run into friends all the time" there and elsewhere on campus. As on other college campuses, chicken wings, pizza, and a salad bar are staples in the dining experience.

The close-knit community can be attributed to the fact that 75 percent of students live on campus. It pays to be a veteran at SU when it comes to housing. Freshmen often find themselves in small triples, but upperclassmen have the coveted option of living in suites and townhouses in the Sassafras Complex or in Hassinger Hall, an air-conditioned dormitory that some students refer to as "Hotel Hassinger." Upperclassmen may also apply to live together in one of the volunteer project houses where students volunteering for the same cause reside. Students conducting independent research can opt to live in the Scholars' House, which includes study areas, a seminar room, a resident assistant's quarters, and a visitor's apartment that allows students to informally interact with special university guests. A few students live in the sorority or fraternity houses near campus.

Where's the Party At?

A third of students are involved in Greek life, an aspect of SU that "divides the partiers and everyone else on the weekends," said a self-proclaimed "theater guy." The two biggest party events of the year are Greek Week, which consists of mostly fraternity- and sorority-sponsored events, and Spring Weekend, a four-day outdoor festival that is run by SAC (Student Activities Committee) and features music, games, and "general craziness." Students report that, although mostly Greeks attend Greek Week, the majority of the campus turns out for Spring Weekend fun. Each year, SAC also sponsors one big annual concert; in recent years the campus has welcomed musical groups The Roots and Collective Soul.

One activity that virtually all SU students participate in is athletics. Home to 23 Varsity Division III sports teams and 14 intramural sports, "it seems like everyone does one sport or another," said a sophomore intramural volleyball player. The athletic student body is fond of the sporting facilities, the James W. Garrett Sports Complex and Lopardo Stadium. Garrett includes an impressive field house with an indoor track and courts for basketball, volleyball, and tennis, as well as a fitness center, a swimming pool, racquetball courts, and a student lounge and café.

Into the Future

The forward-looking administration at Susquehanna prides itself on offering its students resources usually found at schools twice its size. Its efforts have paid off in recent years, with the school extensively renovating its facilities and creating ambitious academic programs like the Writers Institute, the Diversity Studies program, and the Arlin M. Adams Center for Law and Society. Founded in 2001, the Law and Society Center holds an annual lecture series that sponsors renowned visitors, such as Nadine Strossen, the president of the American Civil Liberties Union, and Anthony Lewis, former *New York Times* columnist and two-time Pulitzer Prize–winning author. The Center for Career Services provides another resource on campus that proves helpful to current and past students alike. A mandatory career planning course prepares second-year students for life after college, and the results have been impressive. The program is quite successful, as 96 percent of graduates enter a job or continue their education within six months of graduation.

With the administration's commitment to providing the benefits of a large university to its students, Susquehanna is a perfect environment for college applicants who also want the comfort of a small community. Recent improvements in facilities and programs and attempts to improve diversity make Susquehanna a school to keep an eye on.—*Abigail Reider*

FYI

If you come to Susquehanna, you'd better bring "lots of sweaters."
What's the typical weekend schedule? "Sleeping, eating, going to parties, and studying on Sunday."
If I could change one thing about Susquehanna, it would be "the cold or the lack of diversity."
Three things that every student should do before graduating are "take a trip to the Poconos to go skiing, attend a fireside chat with someone famous, and get a professor you don't like to wait on you during Thanksgiving dinner."

Swarthmore College

Address: 500 College Avenue Swarthmore, PA 19081
Phone: 610-328-8300
E-mail address: admissions@swarthmore.edu
Web site URL: www.swarthmore.edu
Year Founded: 1864
Private or Public: Private
Religious Affiliation: None
Location: Suburban
Number of Applicants: 5,242
Percent Accepted: 16%
Percent Accepted who enroll: 39%
Number Entering: 365
Number of Transfers Accepted each Year: 28
Middle 50% SAT range: M: 680–760, CR: 680–780, Wr: 680–760
Middle 50% ACT range: 28–33
Early admission program EA/ED/None: ED
Percentage accepted through EA or ED: 34%

EA and ED deadline: 15-Nov
Regular Deadline: 2-Jan
Application Fee: $60
Full time Undergraduate enrollment: 1,490
Total enrollment: 1,490
Percent Male: 51%
Percent Female: 49%
Total Percent Minority or Unreported: 48%
Percent African-American: 10%
Percent Asian/Pacific Islander: 16%
Percent Hispanic: 12%
Percent Native-American: <1%
Percent International: 7%
Percent in-state/out of state: 12%/88%
Percent from Public HS: 59%
Retention Rate: 96%
Graduation Rate 4-year: 90%
Graduation Rate 6-year: 92%

Percent Undergraduates in On-campus housing: 95%
Number of official organized extracurricular organizations: 138
3 Most popular majors: Biology/Biological Sciences, General Economics, General Political Science and Government
Student/Faculty ratio: 8:1
Average Class Size: 2 to 9
Percent of students going to grad school: 21%
Tuition and Fees: $36,490
In State Tuition and Fees if different: No difference
Cost for Room and Board: $11,314
Percent receiving financial aid out of those who apply, first year: 48%
Percent receiving financial aid among all students: 50%

H undreds of acres of rolling lawns, hiking trails and—of course—a vibrant student body make up Swarthmore's intimate college campus. Founded by the Quakers in 1864, Swarthmore is an "intellectual's haven" where grades are not dwelled upon and diversity is the norm. This liberal arts college, which is now nonsectarian and has always been coeducational, has a student body of just under 1,500. The Swarthmore experience is centered on close friendships and a commitment to learning.

A senior said, "There's a wonderful, supportive community among students here." Swatties hail from all over the world, representing a wide range of backgrounds and beliefs. One student noted that her peers are praised for individuality and that, at Swarthmore, it is cool to be different. Despite its small size, Swat "celebrates the life of the mind," with a strong global outlook and an education that prepares students to become "leaders for the common good."

Straight As Don't Mean Diddly

The intimate classroom environment at Swarthmore draws many students to the school. The eight-to-one student-faculty ratio allows professors to become personally invested in their students. Many Swatties refer to their professors on a first-name basis, and one freshman said, "Professors have students over for meals in their homes and are incredibly interested to see students succeed." There are no teaching assistants at Swarthmore, meaning that professors—98 percent of whom have Ph.D.s or other terminal degrees—or guest lecturers lead every class and discussion. Seminars are capped at 12 students in order to facilitate participation and dialogue between students and faculty members.

Swarthmore has majors and programs one would not expect of a liberal arts college, like an engineering program and programs in Peace and Conflict Studies, Film and Media Studies, Interpretation Theory, Cognitive Science, and Francophone Studies. About one-third of student majors fall within the social sciences, while majors in the physical sciences are the least popular. There are internship and research opportunities in a wide variety of fields, and student-faculty collaboration is common. If a student is having trouble finding a major that perfectly suits his or her interests, designing a major is a great option that the faculty can help make possible.

A tutoring program and a writing center serve as helpful resources for students seeking extra help in academics. Additional student services include Health and Counseling Services, the Career Services Office, the Intercultural Center, the Black Cultural Center and an on-campus bookstore. A state-of-the-art science center, solar energy laboratory, observatory, and a performing arts center are further examples of Swarthmore's facilities, which rival those of much larger universities.

The college has many connections overseas and the faculty encourages students to study abroad at some point during their Swarthmore experience. Swatties have completed over 100 different programs in countries around the world. The school also has a unique honors program modeled after Oxford's tutorial system. This intensive program, centered on very small classes and dialogue, concludes with an examination conducted by outside scholars after two years of study.

> **"Because everyone is smart, people can't just be intelligent—what counts here is being passionate about something."**

For Swatties, learning does not end when class is dismissed. One student said, "Students carry their enthusiasm outside of class with them. Because everyone is smart, people can't just be intelligent—what counts here is being passionate about something." A senior added that a classroom conversation tends to spill over into lunch and can sometimes keep people talking until four o'clock in the morning.

While the students are academically driven, competition is not a factor. "No one knows anyone else's grades, or cares, even though everyone cares about doing well themselves," said one student. A freshman added, "This is the first time I've been around people smarter than me . . . and in no way have I felt intimidated by people."

The mandatory pass/fail system in the fall semester of freshman year is a "life saver" that makes the transition from high school to college life easier on young Swatties. Since a student needs only get a passing grade, this program allows students to get involved in campus life without worrying too much about grades. An academic advising program serves as an additional resource to students, although one senior warned, "The academic advising program is hit-or-miss for freshmen and sophomores . . . be pro-active about changing professors if you want to."

Both students and faculty at Swat take academics very seriously and the workload is intense. A freshman explained, "Some people complain about the fact that we don't have the same name recognition as some of the Ivies but we still have to do a ton of work."

Most Swatties have to come to terms with a GPA below 4.0. One senior explained, "No one does as well as they did in high school—but it becomes very liberating once you realize you're learning more than you ever have before." Students spend much of their time doing school work, and students can be found studying all over the campus. Popular study spots for long hours of reading and writing papers include Parrish Beach, an outdoor area with 100-year-old oak trees, various coffee bars, the McCabe or Cornell libraries, and, of course, dorm rooms.

Drunken Nights in an Arboretum

So what do Swatties do when an intense week of school work finally wraps up? One student described the weekend party scene as pub nights with all-you-can-drink beer every Thursday, and "sketchy, alcohol-soaked dance parties on Friday and Saturday nights." Students complain that the party scene gets monotonous and that costumes and fun themes are rare. Often, students have to find their own fun.

Alcohol is easy to come by, and underage drinking policies are rarely enforced. A Swarthmore senior claimed that the general rule of thumb is "act like an adult and no one will bother you." A resident assistant at Swarthmore insisted that she and the other RAs are not meant to act as the "alcohol police," as long as students don't put themselves in danger.

Swarthmore's Greek life includes only two fraternities—with just six percent of male students involved. A senior noted, "They're there for people who are interested, but social life certainly doesn't revolve around them." For those who prefer not to partake in the fraternity scene, there are plenty of party options.

Campus-wide social events are a fun option. There is the Pterodactyl Hunt, which a sophomore described as "a campus-wide role-playing game . . . a bunch of Swatties running around in a field dressed in capes and garbage bags and hitting each other with foam swords." One sophomore called the Sager Symposium the "wildest party of the year." It involves "a week of queer-themed speakers, workshops, and performances, culminating in the Sager Party (guys wear a dress, girls wear less)."

Some Swatties find that the campus starts to feel too isolated. One student explained, "It's a bubble . . . I think that's one of the biggest downsides of this school." But for a change of scenery, Swatties can easily hop on a train and end up in Philadelphia 15 minutes later. A sophomore noted, "Most people like to get away at least once a month, but hardly anyone orients their life around it."

Lifestyles of the Smart & Hippy

So where do Swatties fuel up for their long days of studying, art, and activism? The main dining hall is Sharples, which one student called "edible, but barely. People go there for the atmosphere." Other dining options include Essie Mae's (an on-campus grill) and a handful of coffee bars and sandwich shops.

Swarthmore attracts individuals seeking an intimate, rustic campus community and a rigorous academic program. This undergraduate experience educates and prepares students for leadership and for life.—*Catherine Cheney*

FYI

If you come to Swarthmore, you better bring "dirty hippy clothes you never had the nerve to wear, comfy shoes so you can walk in the woods, and Tupperware to sneak food back from the dining halls since they close so early."

What's the typical weekend schedule? "Swatties party Thursday, Friday, and Saturday, but on Sunday you don't see anyone—they're back to the books."

If I could change one think about Swarthmore, I'd "want there to be more shops in the 'Ville,' and I'd want them to be open later."

Three things every student at Swarthmore should do before graduating are "skinny dip in the creek, experience the Sager party, and date a fellow Swattie."

Temple University

Address: 1801 N.Broad Street
Philadelphia, PA, 19122
Phone: 888-340-2222
E-mail address:
tudam@temple.edu
Web site URL:
www.temple.edu
Year Founded: 1884
Private or Public: Public
Religious Affiliation: None
Location: Urban
Number of Applicants:
18,670
Percent Accepted: 61%
Percent Accepted who
enroll: 37%
Number Entering: 6,954
Number of Transfers
Accepted each Year:
3,852
Middle 50% SAT range:
M: 510–610, CR: 500–600,
Wr: 490–590
Middle 50% ACT range:
21–26
Early admission program
EA/ED/None: None

Percentage accepted
through EA or ED: NA
EA and ED deadline: NA
Regular Deadline: 1-Mar
Application Fee: $50 / $25
for online
Full time Undergraduate
enrollment: 23,027
Total enrollment: 35,822
Percent Male: 46%
Percent Female: 54%
Total Percent Minority or
Unreported: 31%
Percent African-American:
17%
Percent Asian/Pacific
Islander: 10%
Percent Hispanic: 4%
Percent Native-American:
<1%
Percent International:
1%
Percent in-state/out of
state: 79%/21%
Percent from Public HS:
81%
Retention Rate: 87%

Graduation Rate 4-year:
36%
Graduation Rate 6-year:
63%
Percent Undergraduates in
On-campus housing: 19.4
Number of official organized
extracurricular
organizations: 173
3 Most popular majors:
Elementary Education,
Psychology, Social Work
Student/Faculty ratio: 17:1
Average Class Size: 27
Percent of students going to
grad school: Unreported
Tuition and Fees: $20,468
In State Tuition and Fees if
different: $11,448
Cost for Room and Board:
$8,884
Percent receiving financial
aid out of those who apply,
first year: 72%
Percent receiving financial
aid among all students:
Unreported

W ith a diverse student body, a dynamic city and a multitude of liberal arts and preprofessional programs, Philadelphia's Temple University offers its undergraduates an incredible four-year experience. In fact, Temple Owls report that "an education from Temple is far more than class time and books—it's about culture . . . independence and growth."

Build Your Core
Meant to help students acquire skills in areas ranging from math and science to arts and culture, Temple's required "Core Program" demands a lot of class time. One frazzled freshman became overwhelmed as he listed some requirements: "An individual and society course, a race course, a science, a math, language requirements, international studies, etc." But for the most part students appreciate the rigorous liberal arts workout of the Core. As one student said, "It's good to have to take a class outside your major. I learned things I never would

have otherwise." Besides, none of the core requirements are anywhere near as difficult as Temple's upper-level science courses. "We are infamous for our difficult science classes," lamented one science major. "It's a hard life. Being a bio major—it becomes your life if you even want to stand a chance." But Owls love a challenge because bio is one of the most popular majors, along with psychology, public health, education, and business. Music, tourism, and hospitality are not quite as popular. After the demands of the Core, Owls can choose from over 120 undergraduate majors. Average class size is 27, and students reported that "most professors are easily accessible." In terms of grading, one student said that "some professors are more liked than others" but that "the grading is usually fair." Students can also study abroad at Temple's international campuses, which include Tokyo, Rome and London, or partake in an honors program that offers smaller classes to its students and is taught by the most prestigious professors. Overall, students agreed that "no one's going to hold your hand here, but the professors are accessible, and the facilities are everything you could ask for."

Living on the Edge

Housing options at Temple include coed dorms, special housing for disabled students, and Living/Learning Center apartments for single students. "We are only provided housing the first two years, unless you are an athlete or an RA," one student explained. The luck of the draw is the only thing that separates the "nice, new suite dorms that have air conditioning and kitchenettes" and "the older community-living dorms that are tiny." Owls don't complain though. One even swore by the tiny dorms, saying that "they are so much fun. They offer more of the dorm experience than the newer ones." RAs are usually cool, but students admit that some can be "pretty strict."

> "No one's going to hold your hand here, but the professors are accessible and the facilities are everything you could ask for."

Despite the dorm fun, most students live in apartments next to campus. When asked about quality of life in the apartments, one student said, "They are nice, but also offer that college experience because you are surrounded by Temple students." Some popular apartment complexes include University Village, the Edge, and YONO apartments.

As Scene on Campus

While there "are a good amount of commuters," students at Temple say that most undergrads don't own cars. "We are right smack in the middle of Philadelphia; there isn't much room for parking, and public transportation and shuttles are easily accessible." Together, Temple and Philadelphia offer a virtual playground of activity. On campus, there are tons of sports facilities, including the Independence Blue Cross Student Recreation Center, which is a 59,000-square-foot building full of fitness equipment frequently populated by athletes. Other popular hangouts include the campus bell tower and The Wall, which is "a collection of small food shops." Regarding the city, one female student said, "Philadelphia offers fabulous history, art, dining, and shopping. What's not to love?" Owls are happy with their campus design, as one

student explained: "The SAC (Student Activities Center) is beautiful and new, and many of our older buildings like Mitten Hall and Conwell have classic beauty."

The University's jewel is definitely the new Teaching, Education, Collaboration, and Help Center, referred to as the TECH center. Offering over 600 computer workstations, 80 loaner laptops, and wireless Internet access throughout the 75,000-square-foot structure, it's no wonder students "spend all Sunday at the TECH center doing work." Of course the 24-hour Starbucks, lounge furniture, and cable channels only add to the atmosphere.

All that studying requires brain food, and Owls have their pick from the SAC, the dining halls in Johnson and Hedwick, and various on-campus restaurants and fast food places. A typical student food plan combines meal dollars for dining halls and "diamond dollars" for restaurants. One dining hall is buffet-style, and the other is restaurant/deli-style. Students generally reported that "both are good." One expert eater added, "The food trucks rock, and be careful of the beef from the Taco Bell in SAC."

Greek Life

Even though only one percent of the male and female populations go Greek, sororities and fraternities rule Temple's nightlife. One student said, "Greek life is huge, especially minority Greeks such as the African-American and Latino/Latina fraternities and sororities." The university offers 24 recognized Greek organizations, but students wouldn't mind some more. As one student explained, "It's annoying because there's always a line to get into the frat parties." If the frats are too crowded, Owls hit up the city scene with its laundry list of bars, such as "the Draught Horse, Maxi's, Pyramids and—of course—Old City Clubs and Lounges." Although Temple University recently prohibited alcohol on campus, students aren't worried. "That only applies to the dorms on campus now . . . there are so many students in apartments and their parties aren't technically on campus." Alcohol is a mainstay of the party scene, but generally "people don't call others losers if they don't drink and drugs have never been an issue."

"Diversity University"

Temple University Owls are definitely a diverse and active group. Indeed, the Princeton Review ranked Temple University as the nation's second most diverse campus. One student explained, "I'm learning languages because it seems like I'm the only one speaking English!" Owls describe their campus as a friendly melting pot. "People are very nice; it's easy to meet people anywhere and everywhere. We are a big campus, and there are crowds of people everywhere you look during the semester."

Temple University offers an incredible amount of extracurricular activities. One student said, "The list is never-ending! We have so many student organizations and clubs!" Sports are big on campus, and Owls are dedicated fans. "Even though our foot-ball team has had a losing streak, their fans are so loyal." Basketball, soccer, fencing and softball also draw crowds. For those who like to be in on the action, intramurals are "competitive and popular."

Temple is known for its vibrant student body, thriving city backdrop and state-of-the-art academic facilities. Most importantly, its students are happy where they are. As one asserted, "I have to keep an open mind and to make the most of opportunities."—*Eliza Crawford*

FYI

If you come to Temple, you'd better bring "an open mind and a smile on your face or you'd miss out on the amazing experience Temple offers!"

What's a typical weekend schedule? "Party, Party, Party, and then recover by spending your Sunday at the TECH center doing work."

If I could change one thing about Temple, I'd "offer students more individual attention; the university can be very disorganized sometimes."

Three things every Temple student should do before graduating are "check out the free galleries offered the first Friday of every month, go to a concert at the Liacouras Center, and take a million and one pictures because you never want to forget your years here!"

University of Pennsylvania

Address: 1 College Hall Philadelphia, PA 19104
Phone: 215-898-7507
E-mail address: info@admissions.ugao.upenn.edu
Web site URL: www.upenn.edu
Year Founded: 1740
Private or Public: Private
Religious Affiliation: None
Location: Urban
Number of Applicants: 22,645
Percent Accepted: 16%
Percent Accepted who enroll: 66%
Number Entering: 2,385
Number of Transfers Accepted each Year: 296
Middle 50% SAT range: M: 680–770, CR: 650–750, Wr: 660–750
Middle 50% ACT range: 29–33
Early admission program EA/ED/None: ED

Percentage accepted through EA or ED: Unreported
EA and ED deadline: 1-Nov
Regular Deadline: 1-Jan
Application Fee: $75
Full time Undergraduate enrollment: 9,687
Total enrollment: 16,545
Percent Male: 51%
Percent Female: 49%
Total Percent Minority or Unreported: 55%
Percent African-American: 8%
Percent Asian/Pacific Islander: 17%
Percent Hispanic: 6%
Percent Native-American: 0%
Percent International: 10%
Percent in-state/out of state: 19%/81%
Percent from Public HS: 54%
Retention Rate: 98%

Graduation Rate 4-year: 88%
Graduation Rate 6-year: 94%
Percent Undergraduates in On-campus housing: 64%
Number of official organized extracurricular organizations: 350
3 Most popular majors: Business Administration and Management, Finance, Nursing/Registered Nurse RN, ASN, BSN, MSN
Student/Faculty ratio: 6:1
Average Class Size: 10 to 19
Percent of students going to grad school: 18%
Tuition and Fees: $37,526
In State Tuition and Fees if different: No difference
Cost for Room and Board: $10,622
Percent receiving financial aid out of those who apply, first year: 76%
Percent receiving financial aid among all students: 40%

Bearing the imprint of Benjamin Franklin, arguably America's most celebrated philosopher, the University of Pennsylvania was imbued with a spirit of liberal thinking and scholarship even before it enrolled its first students. Conceived in 1740 and opened in 1751, Penn has lived up to its goal of providing a practical education devoted to liberal arts, business, and public service. Generally acknowledged as the nation's first true university, it is credited with having developed the first modern liberal arts curriculum. Today, Penn's architecturally varied and attractive 269-acre campus located in West Philadelphia is home to an undergraduate student body that has grown to over 10,000 students, many of whom are international in origin. Despite its growth, the college has remained true to its original mission since its inception.

Four Schools in One

The academic interests of Penn's undergraduates run the gamut, and despite differences in career plans, all students are completely integrated into the fabric of the college. Nevertheless, successful applicants to Penn enter one of the four schools that together create the undergraduate institution. The largest of the schools is the College of Arts and Sciences, to which over six in 10 students belong, followed by the highly competitive Wharton School of Business, which enrolls about 18 percent of Penn students. Wharton is the only undergraduate business school in the Ivy League and has an unparalleled international reputation. The School of Engineering and Applied Science enrolls just slightly fewer students than does the Wharton undergraduate program, and the relatively small but excellent School of Nursing includes approximately 500 undergrads. Thus, Benjamin Franklin's original goal that Penn teach "everything that is practical, and everything that is ornamental" is certainly well-addressed by the broad range of opportunities available to undergraduates here.

The College of Arts and Sciences allows the most freedom of choice of the four schools at Penn. In this undergraduate school at Penn, students are generally required to take between 12 to 14 courses in their major and around 20 outside of their area of concentration. Included in the latter are courses that fulfill distribution requirements. Beginning in 2006 and starting with the Class of 2010, the college has reduced the number of distributional courses necessary to graduate, with the intention of increasing curricular flexibility. Students must now take one course in each of the following areas: Society, History and Tradition, Arts and Letters, Physical World, Living World, Humanities and Social Sciences, Natural Science and Math. Within the framework of these disciplines, undergraduates in the College of Arts and Sciences must also fulfill requirements in quantitative reasoning, foreign language and writing. Noted one sophomore, "Mine was the first class with the new curriculum. My junior and senior friends say that the reduction in distribution requirements makes it much easier to complete your major and still take some great courses that are outside the beaten path." Students preregister for courses, but can change their schedules during a "shopping period." However, noted a junior, "for courses with restricted enrollment, such as seminars, it can be difficult getting in if you have not pre-registered, unless someone drops out of the class. Teachers generally try to be accommodating, but they can't always be."

The Wharton School of Business at Penn is world-renowned and the list of its graduates who went on to distinguish themselves in the business world is staggering. It is arguably the best undergraduate business school in the country and, as such, the most competitive of the four schools at Penn in terms of admissions. In contrast to the curriculum of the College of Arts and Sciences, the course of study in this school is much more predetermined. Thirty-seven courses are required to graduate, only two of which must be taken outside of Wharton. There is theoretically a wide variety of possible "concentrations" available within the context of the Bachelor's of Science in Economics degree that is awarded to all students, but the vast majority concentrates in the area of finance.

Penn's School of Engineering and Applied Sciences, or SEAS, like Wharton, has a fairly fixed curriculum. The course of study is traditional, and most students take classes in math, science, engineering, and little else. "I am very happy with my courses," said one senior. "If I wanted to take Old English poetry, I wouldn't be in SEAS."

The School of Nursing prepares its students for a variety of fields related to nursing and the health sciences. A total of 28 classes in nursing and medicine are required, but there is ample room to take other courses in the College of Arts and Sciences. Students concentrate in one of two programs in the school: Family and Community Health and Foundational Sciences and Health Systems.

There are many opportunities for

interdisciplinary study at Penn, and the school encourages this type of exploration. Students may pursue dual degrees within, for example, the School of Arts and Sciences, or may enroll in one of the joint degree programs at the school. For example, the Huntsman Program in International Studies and Business awards two simultaneous degrees, a Bachelor of Arts in International Studies from the School of Arts and Sciences and a Bachelor of Science in Economics from the Wharton School. The Lauder Institute of Management and International Studies awards an MBA from Wharton and a MA in International Studies from the School of Arts and Sciences.

Academics are rigorous at Penn, and most students put in a good amount of study time. Students are well aware that exams and course grades are curved, especially in the sciences and math, so there is a fair amount of competition among students. In addition, many undergraduates are premed and prelaw. "That alone leads to competition," said a senior, "but I don't think that Penn students are any more cutthroat than pre-professional students at other schools."

Campus in the City
Penn touts the opportunities of its situation in the city of Philadelphia, a bustling metropolis with a long and interesting history. Undergraduates choose to live in a variety of different types of housing, both on and off campus. Only about 60 percent of undergrads live on campus. Many upperclassmen prefer living off campus in fraternities and sororities or apartments that are generally less expensive than the University housing options.

For those living on campus, there are 11 College Houses, each with its own architectural style, ranging from 24-story high-rise apartment buildings to historic buildings with hardwood floors. Most freshmen live in dorms that surround the Quad. Each facility is home to about 400 students. Dining facilities are in close proximity. Residents of the high-rises have bathrooms and kitchenettes in their suites. In addition to these options are "theme houses" which allow students with similar cultural backgrounds and interests and students with similar academic interests to live together. In addition, fraternities and sororities have been active on campus since the mid-1800s and represent another significant housing option.

Food for Thought
First-year undergraduates are required to enroll in one of four meal plans, all of which include "Dining Dollar$" that can be redeemed at all Penn dining locations, including Starbucks and several on-campus cafés and retail institutions nearby. Upperclassmen who choose to live and eat on campus can choose from among 10 different plans. Dining Dollar$ can be easily added to their accounts. Kosher food is found at Falk Dining Commons and is under Orthodox supervision. In addition, a variety of foods can be purchased at a new "convenience area" in the same facility. The nutritional composition of all meals can be found at kiosks located in each of the dining facilities. Most students do not complain about the food options. "There is always something to fit your dietary needs and preferences," said a sophomore. "And there is an increasing interest in foods that have been grown and prepared with attention to ecological considerations."

An Extracurricular Smorgasbord
Penn boasts a wide array of extracurricular opportunities, including participation on numerous intercollegiate athletic teams. There are 17 men's sports teams and 16 women's teams. In addition, students may participate on intramural teams in 12 sports and on a variety of club sports. Beyond organized sports, huge numbers of students go to the gym on almost a daily basis. The facilities are open Monday through Thursday from 6 a.m. to 1 a.m., so there is little excuse for being a "couch potato." The gyms are also open on the weekends with less extensive hours.

Many students are involved with the numerous publications on campus as well as student government organizations such as the Undergraduate Assembly, the debate team, and the Model UN. In addition, opportunities to sing, dance, and act abound. There are numerous a cappella groups on campus. "Penn is a real extracurricular smorgasbord," said one senior. "I have done a lot of acting and a lot of writing out of class."

Living in and Giving to West Philadelphia
West Philadelphia provides an active and multiethnic neighborhood for Penn students, as well as tremendous opportunities for community service. But many students voice concerns about their safety on campus, especially its immediate environs. They often point to the great "town-gown" discrepancy between the wealth of the University and the majority of its students when compared to the socioeconomic status of the residents of the surrounding neighborhood. Students call

this disparity the "Penn Bubble." "I have been here for three years," stated one student, "and I still feel uncomfortable walking around West Philly at night. I don't like going out alone. But many great universities are located in areas where the underprivileged live. You have to be careful, but there are so many opportunities to get involved. On balance, the neighborhood is really a plus." The University has actively focused on security on campus in recent years.

> "Many great universities are located in areas where the underprivileged live. You have to be careful, but there are so many opportunities to get involved."

Penn students actively participate in a wide variety of community service projects. Civic House is the main hub for those interested in such endeavors, providing a liaison between the University and the community. Civic House maintains a community agency database that allows students to locate volunteer organizations that serve the greater West Philadelphia neighborhood.

I'll Drink to That
Like students at the other Ivies, Penn students tend to study hard and play hard. The fraternities and sororities are where a great deal of socializing takes place, especially for the lowerclassmen. Alcohol plays an important role at most weekend parties and it flows more freely in the frats. Most students agree that a significant amount of booze is consumed at Penn. They also note that although there are definite dictates against the availability of alcohol in these venues, the enforcement of such policies is lax. "The RAs and GAs don't allow things to be completely freewheeling," noted one junior, "but they let things go as long as no one gets really out of hand."

As is the case at many other universities, the social scene generally shifts to private parties in students' apartments during the upperclass years. Many Penn students live off campus as juniors and seniors and are less inclined to spend their weekends at the frat parties.

Beyond the Parties
Philadelphia affords virtually unlimited opportunities for social activities beyond the party scene. Every Thursday, Penn's school newspaper, *The Daily Pennsylvanian*, catalogues the numerous concerts, theatrical performances, and dances that will be taking place that weekend. Most students avail themselves of the city and frequent restaurants, bars, and clubs there. "There are so many things to do in Philly," said a senior. "Sometimes it's nice to get off campus and do some exploring. I am certainly going to miss being in this city after I graduate."

Here's a Toast to Dear Old Penn!
School spirit is alive and well at Penn, and their strong athletic teams reinforce the identification of Penn students with their school. Men's basketball is unquestionably the most popular intercollegiate sport on campus, and Penn's teams have been exceptional in recent years. Games against Princeton, the University's archrival on the court, are packed, and Penn football games have become increasingly popular as well, as a function of the fielding of more competitive teams in recent years.

Penn students traditionally throw toast on the football field after singing a song entitled "Drink a Highball," ever since the drinking age was raised from 18 and most undergraduates could no longer consume the intended cocktail.

. . . As a "Button"
In the center of the Penn campus, there is a huge white button, split asymmetrically, measuring 16 feet in diameter and weighing over 5,000 pounds. Designed by Claes Oldenburg and cast in reinforced aluminum, it faces Benjamin Franklin in front of Penn's Van Pelt Library. According to legend, Benjamin Franklin once popped off a button from his pants after gorging on a huge meal, with the projectile then splitting in two. While the artist himself once remarked that the split in the button divides it into four parts, representing William Penn's original division of Philadelphia into four squares, some argue that it represents the four undergraduate schools at Penn. Others ascribe a variety of other traditions and functions to this sculpture, including as a place to engage in some more risqué public behavior. The Button can, more broadly, be seen as representing a starting point for discussion, inquiry and debate. Students at Penn have never been accused of not thinking.

When polled, the vast majority of students at this exciting Ivy League university, whose national standing in a variety of published surveys has steadily increased in the last decade, love being students there. The diversity of the student body, the quality of the faculty, the opportunities for extracurricular involvement in a large array of activities, the strong sense of school spirit and a commitment to the betterment of the surrounding community are but a few of the elements that have made Penn a truly great place to live and study. If you are willing to work hard and find intellectual challenge up your alley, then you may well find that Benjamin Franklin had the right idea when he popped a few buttons while throwing his weight behind the University of Pennsylvania.—*Jonathan Berken*

FYI
If you come to Penn, you'd better bring "the ability to throw toast like a discus."
What is a typical weekend schedule? "Party like a rock star all weekend long."
If I could change one thing about Penn, I'd "make West Philly safer."
Three things that every student at Penn should do before graduating are "go see Mask and Wig, read Ben Franklin's autobiography and have sex under the Button."

University of Pittsburgh

Address: 4227 Fifth Avenue, First Floor Alumni Hall Pittsburgh, PA 15260
Phone: 412-624-7488
E-mail address: oafa@pitt.edu
Web site URL: www.pitt.edu
Year Founded: 1787
Private or Public: Public
Religious Affiliation: None
Location: Urban
Number of Applicants: 19,056
Percent Accepted: 56%
Percent Accepted who enroll: 32%
Number Entering: 3,419
Number of Transfers Accepted each Year: 1,157
Middle 50% SAT range: M: 580–670, CR: 570–670, Wr: Unreported
Middle 50% ACT range: 24–30
Early admission program EA/ED/None: None

Percentage accepted through EA or ED: None
EA and ED deadline: None
Regular Deadline: Rolling
Application Fee: $45
Full time Undergraduate enrollment: 17,427
Total enrollment: 25,715
Percent Male: 49%
Percent Female: 51%
Total Percent Minority or Unreported: 19%
Percent African-American: 8%
Percent Asian/Pacific Islander: 5%
Percent Hispanic: 1%
Percent Native-American: 0%
Percent International: 1%
Percent in-state/out of state: 83%/17%
Percent from Public HS: Unreported
Retention Rate: 90%
Graduation Rate 4-year: 56%

Graduation Rate 6-year: 75%
Percent Undergraduates in On-campus housing: 45%
Number of official organized extracurricular organizations: 450
3 Most popular majors: Marketing/Marketing Management, Psychology, Speech and Rhetorical Studies
Student/Faculty ratio: 16:1
Average Class Size: 10 to 19
Percent of students going to grad school: 38%
Tuition and Fees: $23,290
In State Tuition and Fees if different: $13,642
Cost for Room and Board: $8,600
Percent receiving financial aid out of those who apply, first year: 68%
Percent receiving financial aid among all students: 52%

In the early 1780s, Hugh Henry Brackenridge, newly elected to the Pennsylvania State Assembly, sought funds from the state to build a new academy at the edge of the western frontier. And in a little log cabin in 1787, the Pittsburgh Academy was founded. Today, University of Pittsburgh stands as one of the oldest, most prestigious public universities in America. Located in the Oakland suburb of Pittsburgh, just a block away from the picturesque Schenley Park, the affectionately named "Pitt" has grown into a 132-acre mammoth of a university, boasting over 17,400 full-time undergraduates.

ABC, Pitt, and Me
A little over half the undergraduates at Pitt enroll in the School of Arts & Sciences,

while the rest are dispersed throughout the colleges of Engineering, Nursing, Business Administration, Health & Rehabilitation Services, Information Services, Social Work, Education, and General Studies. In order to graduate from the School of Arts & Sciences, students must fulfill requirements in their major, general education, and skills. Skills requirements were created to ensure that all Pitt graduates have competency in writing, algebra, and quantitative and formal reasoning. Students are placed into or exempt from skills classes based on exams taken during high school or upon arrival at Pitt. The other, specialized colleges require that students fulfill a certain number of credits within the college and the rest through the School of Arts & Sciences.

Students at Pitt agree that their classes are generally pretty large—lectures often contain a couple hundred students, especially during the freshmen and sophomore years. However, these larger classes often have recitation once a week so that students can receive the individual attention that can be lost in a large university. Sometimes, though, all it takes is a little initiative. "I find that the professors are really accessible," said one engineering student. "They usually all have office hours where you can just walk in and talk to them. Sometimes students get intimidated by them, but most of the professors honestly really enjoy being there and getting to know you better."

Pitt's size alone can make anybody—especially a freshman—a little overwhelmed academically, but students say the pressure dies down after a while. The trick lies in Pitt's many different schools and majors, which help break up a large student body into smaller, academic environments. "Sooner or later, you start to connect with your department, and then it's like you're going to a small school," one recent graduate asserted. Indeed, there are over 90 registered, academic-related organizations on campus, furthering the connections made in the departments.

Panther Central

Of course, Pitt wouldn't be Pitt without athletics. Football is arguably the biggest sport on campus. In its history, the Panthers have won nine NCAA national football championships. Football games are often heralded by huge tailgates, pep rallies, and victory celebrations. In 2004, the University hired Dave Wannstedt, former NFL head coach and Pitt alumnus, as the new Panthers coach, hoping to bring back the football hey-days of the 1970s and 1980s.

In the past few years, basketball has also grown into a major sport at Pitt. The men's basketball team won the Big East Tournament in 2003, and has perennially been one of the most successful basketball teams on the East Coast. In fact, basketball tickets have become so coveted that they are now "impossible to get." To foster fledgling sports, Pitt recently instituted a program of ticket distribution. Attendance at some of the lesser-known sport games, such as certain women's sports, generates a certain number of points. Those points can then be used towards applying for tickets for a men's basketball game. The higher the number of points, the higher the priority. "That policy really helps ensure a rowdy ground at every home game, no matter what sport. Our student stands are never empty, and that really helps generate some serious school spirit," said one student.

There is no doubt that Pitt students also take the athletics of their new home city very seriously. "After the Steelers won the Superbowl, there were riots right on campus!" The successful athletics teams also contribute to a huge sense of school pride. Every time the football team wins a victory, the lights on top of the Cathedral of Learning shine blue and gold—an apt symbol of the close relationship of athletics and academics in this University.

All Night Long

Pitt students have their own underground, student-run Web site, which functions as a giant online announcement board for campus parties. To date, over 8,000 users have registered, and a quick glance around the website turns up ads for frat parties, house parties, and even party reviews. This is hardly unusual for a college where the majority of students head out three nights a week, and some party every single day.

"House parties are by far the most popular, probably because it's really hard to get into bars underage," said one student. Another attested, "I went to this one party where they were playing beer pong on the front lawn. The cops were driving by and didn't even care!" Inside Pitt buildings, however, alcohol policy is much more stringent. One Pitt graduate explained, "Since we live in an urban environment, we do have a security guard who checks your Panther card before you go into your dorm, so if they can smell the alcohol on your breath or see you falling over, they *will* report you."

Even though Pitt is a relatively large state school, the Greek life is pretty subdued. The percentage of both male and female students in fraternities and sororities hovers around eight percent each. Most students' social lives do not revolve around Greek letters. "Most sororities and fraternities have on-campus houses . . . Their parties are geared towards underclassmen and the people that live there or are part of the group," said one student.

> **"The great thing about Pitt is that one minute you can be on campus, in the hustle and bustle of Pittsburgh, and then you walk over a bridge, and all of a sudden you almost forget that you're in a city."**

Students at Pitt take full advantage of the fact that they are living in a vibrant city teeming with culture. "There are always concerts and other musical events going on, and there are a ton of bars in Oakland," said one undergrad. "CMU [Carnegie Mellon University] is nearby, so a lot of CMU students come down to our frat parties and sometimes we go up to CMU. You really never get bored of the scene."

Besides weekly house parties and barhopping, Pitt also sponsors many big events. Not surprisingly, Homecoming Weekend is "*huge*." The Bigelow Bash is also spectacular. One weekend in late March or early April, Pitt closes down Bigelow Boulevard for a day of live music, games and perhaps even some exotic animals and sumo wrestling.

Living at Pitt

Even though full-time undergraduate students are not required to live on campus, they are guaranteed on-campus housing for the first three years. Pitt owns many residential halls and apartment buildings on campus, and is currently in the midst of building more. The largest housing complex, Litchfield Towers, was finished in 1966 and encompasses three towers, each 22 stories high. The Towers are coed and house about 1,800 students—many of them freshmen. Each room is equipped with furniture, a telephone, cable TV, and Internet access. Resident directors and assistants live in these halls to address any questions or concerns that may arise. The majority of Pitt's eateries

are located in the lower level of the Towers, given its convenient and accessible location on campus. "Every student has to live in the Towers at some point," one student asserted. "You meet absolutely everyone there."

The University housing system also features all-female dorms Holland and Amos, with Amos hosting nine sororities. Because of its proximity to Petersen Events Center and the major athletic facilities, Sutherland Hall primarily consists of athletes. Pitt also features Special Living Communities that cater to students who share a common academic or social interest. Some examples include Alcohol-Free, Engineering Living-Learning Community, and the International Living Community.

Upperclassmen have the choice of apartment-style housing, which offers more self-reliance and independence than the traditional residential halls. They often include kitchens complete with stoves, refrigerators, garbage disposals, and dishwashers. Despite this option, however, many juniors tend to move off campus because of high housing costs. Dorms at Pitt usually run around $2,200 per semester, in addition to a required meal plan. Moving off campus usually means cheaper rents, more freedom, and more control over food.

The Pitt meal plans work a little differently than those of most colleges, striking a very good balance between the two traditional types. With every meal plan purchased, a student gets a certain amount of Meal Blocks and Dining Dollars. Meal Blocks can be best used in the Marketplace or for buying entrees. They are worth $5.40 per block. Dining Dollars can be swiped anywhere, for the exact amount of the purchase, and they are often used for smaller purchases. The Marketplace, an all-you-can-eat dining hall open for all three meals, is located in the lower level of the Litchfield Towers. The William Pitt Union's Schenley Café includes Pizza Hut Express, Freshens Smoothie Company, and Sub Connection. There are also a host of coffee carts and snack shops for those on the go. All in all, students don't complain much. "The food on campus is good—very good. It does get a little monotonous at times, but I think that's the same everywhere you go."

Log Cabins, Operas, and Observatories

Perhaps the best-known piece of architecture at Pitt is the Cathedral of Learning. Soaring over 42 stories and 535 feet tall, the

Cathedral is the second-tallest education-oriented building in the world. Its construction halted in the middle of the Great Depression, and the lore goes that it was only finished with the help of over 97,000 area school children who each chipped in a dime to buy a brick. The Cathedral of Learning is also famous for its two floors of Nationality Rooms. The project started when John Gabbert Bowman, the tenth chancellor of Pitt, invited different national groups in Allegheny County to decorate a classroom in the Cathedral to reflect their own heritage. Today, the 26 Nationality Rooms boast palatial furniture from China, sixth-century mosaics from Israel, and an iroko wood entry door that portrays nine ancient and medieval African kings. "If you come to Pitt, even for a visit," said one student, "you have to see Cathedral Lawn and the Nationality Rooms."

The general feeling of the Pitt campus is urban. "No matter what time of the day it is, there's always going to be people walking around, doing things," one student proclaimed. "We do live in Pittsburgh, after all." But those fond of the country do not need to worry. Just a bridge west of campus lays Schenley Park, the third-largest public park on the East Coast. This 400-acre park features hills, woods, walking trails, a botanical conservatory, a swimming pool, tennis courts, a golf course, a nature center and an ice skating rink—all within walking distance of Pitt. "The great thing about Pitt is that one minute you can be on campus, in the hustle and bustle of Pittsburgh, and then you walk over a bridge, and all of a sudden you almost forget that you're in a city."

The city of Pittsburgh also cannot be forgotten. In recent years, Pitt's administration has made great efforts to open up the ample opportunities of Pittsburgh to the undergraduates of the University. Called PITT ARTS, the program annually gives away thousands of free tickets to operas, ballets, theaters, film, and museums. Pitt students automatically receive free admission at the Andy Warhol Museum, the Phipps Conservatory and Botanical Gardens at Schenley Park, the Carnegie Museum of Art and Natural History, and the Mattress Factory museum. PITT ARTS now gives more than 30,000 students each year the chance to experience the vibrant city that they live in. Joked one student, "See? We can be alcoholics *and* cultured!"

The original log cabin where Hugh Henry Brackenridge first built his Academy still stands today, wedged between the Cathedral of Learning and the Heinz Chapel. "It is the perfect spot," admitted one student. "You can hardly believe you are still in a city." Perhaps that is the perfect portrait of the University of Pittsburgh—the crossroads of innovation and history, athletics and globalization, culture and education.—*Janet Xu*

FYI

If you come to Pitt, you'd better bring "an umbrella and waterproof shoes (it rains a lot and it will be muddy 50 percent of the time)."

What's the typical weekend schedule? "Frat parties and house parties starting Thursday night, and maybe some bars if you're over 21, and maybe go into Pittsburgh on Saturday to catch a play."

If I could change one thing about Pitt, I'd "change the advising system for freshmen. They just don't give us enough info!"

Three things every student at Pitt should do before graduating are "look at the Nationality Rooms and then go to the top of the Cathedral, go to all the museums around campus that we get into for free, and go to a Panthers football game."

Ursinus College

Address: Box 1000
Collegeville, PA 19426-1000
Phone: 610-409-3200
E-mail address:
admissions@ursinus.edu
Web site URL:
www.ursinus.edu
Year Founded: 1869
Private or Public: Private
Religious Affiliation: None
Location: Suburban
Number of Applicants: 6,192
Percent Accepted: 55%
Percent Accepted who
enroll: 55%
Number Entering: 3,387
Number of Transfers
Accepted each Year: 11
Middle 50% SAT range:
M: 570–670, CR: 570–680,
Wr: 560–660
Middle 50% ACT range: 25–29
Early admission program
EA/ED/None: EA and ED
Percentage accepted
through EA or ED:
62%/62%

EA and ED deadline: 1-Dec,
1-Jan
Regular Deadline: 15-Feb
Application Fee: $50/free
online
Full time Undergraduate
enrollment: 1,680
Total enrollment: 1,680
Percent Male: 46%
Percent Female: 54%
Total Percent Minority or
Unreported: 28%
Percent African-American:
6%
Percent Asian/Pacific
Islander: 4%
Percent Hispanic: 3%
Percent Native-American:
0%
Percent International: 1%
Percent in-state/out of
state: 58%/42%
Percent from Public HS:
61%
Retention Rate: 88%
Graduation Rate 4-year:
71%

Graduation Rate 6-year:
74.0%
Percent Undergraduates
in On-campus housing:
95%
Number of official organized
extracurricular
organizations: 88
3 Most popular majors:
Biology, Economic,
Psychology
Student/Faculty ratio:
12:1
Average Class Size: 2 to 9
Percent of students going to
grad school: 34%
Tuition and Fees: $36,910
In State Tuition and Fees if
different: No difference
Cost for Room and Board:
$8,800
Percent receiving financial
aid out of those who apply,
first year: Unreported
Percent receiving financial
aid among all students:
91%

From day one, students at Ursinus College are placed on an even playing field. All freshmen enter the same rooming lottery, all freshmen are issued Dell laptops, and all freshmen take part in the CIE program. But to say that life in Collegetown, Pennsylvania, is ordinary or simple is utterly false. With a lively student body and traditions dating back to the eighteenth century, this small college provides students with the opportunity to work closely with an esteemed faculty and the tools to grow into mature adults who actively explore and question the world around them.

Cooperation and Collaboration

Known for the close relationships between faculty and students, this small college includes a wide range of majors in both the sciences and the humanities. Although Ursinus is known as a popular choice of premed students, the most popular majors for undergraduates are psychology and economics. But UC has majors for everyone—even

dancers—with the addition of dance as a major in recent years.

Part of this collaboration between faculty and students is developed starting from their first days during freshman year, when all Ursinus students participate in the CIE Program—The Common Intellectual Experience. This liberal studies seminar epitomizes the value that the staff at Ursinus puts on the development of the conversation ability and well-roundedness of its students. Freshmen are required to take the class for both semesters. Groups of sixteen freshmen address major life questions such as: "what does it mean to be human?", "how should humans live their lives?", and "what is the universe and what should our place be within it?" The course was designed so that each freshman student would be reading the same material at the same time, facilitating discussion amongst the entire entering class. By looking at works of art, classical writing and political theory, professors are leaders but at the same time members of the discussion group. The

CIE instructors are from a wide range of disciplines, and this means that there is no expert on the subject, instead, everyone takes part in the learning and growth.

Collegeville, PA: Location, Location, Location

Students at Ursinus are not lacking in things to do. With the city of Philadelphia only 30 miles away and free shuttle buses to the city, UC students are not too far away from the Liberty Bell, the Rocky Steps, concerts and urban life. But even with this at their fingertips, many students say they rarely leave their dorms in the quaint town of Collegeville. With 97% of students living on campus, location of dormitories is a big deal. Students living on campus enter the lottery system to determine their living situation. Older students get preference and the prizes tend to be the restored Victorian-Era homes that are located right on campus. But no fear, even for freshmen, the living quarters are definitely not like your stereotypical cinderblock high rise, and most freshmen seem to enjoy the dorm atmosphere.

Thanks to its renowned collection of American arts, the Berman Museum brings a great number of art lovers to Collegeville and Ursinus. Besides the beautiful brick walkways and historic buildings, the campus at UC is enhanced by the famous sculptures from the museum. These statues are all over campus and some of them are extremely realistic. One freshman said that everyone "freaks out" when they see the well-known statue of the old lady who is so lifelike it's "creepy." It is pretty common to see tourists and students taking pictures with the old lady.

Mixin' it Up

According to students, there is hardly any difference socially between upperclassmen and "the new kids." Even juniors and seniors involved in frats do not act superior and this is partially due to all the efforts by the administration at Ursinus to raise school unity and keep all the grades mixed. Therefore, for students of many different ages, a typical night out at Ursinus consists of starting out in the Reimert, which is a residence hall made up of large suites that house some local fraternities and sororities. Although there are only a few nationally recognized Greek organizations on campus, some of the favorite social events of the year for many Ursinus students are the "Dated." Joint-hosted by a fraternity and a sorority, these events are always memorable

occasions. Students sign up ahead of time, and they are taken on buses off campus where there are big parties at places like firehouses with dancing, music, etc. Students like the Reimert because it is always open and there are always people ready to have a good time. But if you are not at Reimert, then you'll probably start your night off at one of the houses on Main Street, which tend to be known for their great parties as well.

With all these parties going on, it makes sense to wonder about the drug policy at Ursinus. Students describe the administration as relatively lenient for everyone except those living in freshman dorms, where rules tend to be stricter. As long as you keep the alcohol within the confines of the buildings, trouble tends to stay away—but things become a little trickier when going outside with alcohol. If caught, a common punishment was said to be community service. But even with the party scene at Ursinus, students appreciate the fact that there is not a big drug scene at the school and that students are not typically pressured into doing things which they do not feel comfortable about.

Activities Galore

Some of the most prominent clubs on campus are *The Grizzly* (the student paper), the Campus Activity Board, Student Government and the Residence Hall Association. According to students, the CAB always has stuff going on in the lounge underneath Wismer Cafeteria such as prerelease movies and casino games. Recently, the Student Council successfully kicked off "Late Night Lower Wismer," where there is popcorn, videogames such as Rockband, a Wii system, a pool table and karaoke. The Wismer Center is considered a major social center on campus that houses dining facilities, social lounges, a snack bar and game room. But even with big clubs such as the CAB and *The Grizzly*, it doesn't mean there aren't any obscure or unique organizations in Collegeville. There is a scuba club and a meditation group that meets once a week to "de-stress."

Athletics is also a big part of extracurricular activities at Ursinus, and about 50% of students compete on varsity sports teams. The Bears are part of the Centennial Conference, founded in 1992 for small mid-Atlantic academic institutions, and compete at the NCAA Division III level against schools such as Dickinson, Bryn Mawr, and Johns Hopkins. In fact, in 2006, the Ursinus field hockey team was the Div. III National Champions.

Even though the majority of students participate in either varsity or intramural athletics at school, most still say that sports are not the major focus on campus. But even so, UC students are fortunate to have great facilities. With a marvelous fitness center that boasts new machines and an indoor track, students have little reason not to be active.

History and Tradition

According to lore, the tree under which author J. D. Salinger wrote his book *Catcher in the Rye* while he was a student at Ursinus still stands today near the end zone of the football field. A plaque is now placed outside the room where he lived during his time in Collegeville as a student. Ursinus is a place where tradition and history matter. According to campus tour guides, Ursinus was even at one point in the *Guinness Book of World Records* for having the most marriages among students. From the moment undergraduates go through the typical icebreaker games during their first day as freshmen, a sense of unity is apparent, and this lasts through the years. By the time Ursinus students are seniors and ready to graduate, the majority is even comfortable enough with each other to slide down one of the fountains on campus completely naked. Every year

there is also an event called Air Band, which is a lip-synch and dance competition for charity. Ursinus's tradition of equality even extends to the technological realm. Since 2000, Ursinus's laptop initiative has provided every student and faculty member with a laptop. Some of the goals of the project were to improve communications between students and faculty, to bolster the sense of community around campus and to provide equal computer access for all students.

> "The campus and the people at Ursinus are personable and it is almost impossible to get lost in the shuffle."

It is this sense of togetherness that brings students to Ursinus. Instead of just being a number, students make real connections that last. There is an appreciation for the small, picturesque campus and the welcoming community where everyone is equally appreciated: students, faculty and staff. According to one sophomore, "The campus and the people at Ursinus are personable and it is almost impossible to get lost in the shuffle."—*Emily St. Jean*

FYI

If you come to Ursinus College, you'd better bring "plenty of snacks because the cafeterias and other eating areas have terrible hours."

What's the typical weekend schedule? "Wake up around 11 or 12, go to brunch until one, study or watch football during the afternoon, dinner, and then out for the rest of the night."

If I could change one thing about Ursinus, I'd change "the school name, because it gets really old hearing people mispronounce the name or make dumb jokes about it."

Three things every student at Ursinus should do before graduating are "slide down a fountain naked before graduation, take a picture with one of the statues on campus (preferably the old lady), and go to a 'Dated.'"

Villanova University

Address: 800 Lancaster Avenue Villanova, PA 19085-1672
Phone: 610-519-4000
E-mail address: gotovu@villanova.edu
Web site URL: www.villanova.edu
Year Founded: 1842
Private or Public: Private
Religious Affiliation: Roman Catholic
Location: Suburban
Number of Applicants: 15,102
Percent Accepted: 39%
Percent Accepted who enroll: 27%
Number Entering: 1,729
Number of Transfers Accepted each Year: 125
Middle 50% SAT range: M: 620–710, CR: 580–680, Wr: Unreported
Middle 50% ACT range: 28–31
Early admission program EA/ED/None: EA

Percentage accepted through EA or ED: Unreported
EA and ED deadline: 1-Nov
Regular Deadline: 7-Jan
Application Fee: $75
Full time Undergraduate enrollment: 6,390
Total enrollment: 10,152
Percent Male: 49%
Percent Female: 51%
Total Percent Minority or Unreported: 18%
Percent African-American: 4%
Percent Asian/Pacific Islander: 7%
Percent Hispanic: 7%
Percent Native-American: 1%
Percent International: Unreported
Percent in-state/out of state: 25%/75%
Percent from Public HS: 55%
Retention Rate: 95%
Graduation Rate 4-year: 82%

Graduation Rate 6-year: 88%
Percent Undergraduates in On-campus housing: 70%
Number of official organized extracurricular organizations: 250
3 Most popular majors: Nursing, Finance, Communication
Student/Faculty ratio: 11:1
Average Class Size: 22
Percent of students going to grad school: 23%
Tuition and Fees: $36,950
In State Tuition and Fees if different: No difference
Cost for Room and Board: $10,000
Percent receiving financial aid out of those who apply, first year: 80%
Percent receiving financial aid among all students: 45%

At Villanova, students take full advantage of everything their school has to offer. Students immerse themselves in their studies, a vast array of community service, its ideal suburban Philadelphia location and—of course—the school's wildly successful basketball team. While football's not much of a big deal, Villanova students "go crazy over basketball." "Hoops Mania" isn't just the season opener where the basketball team is introduced; it's a Villanova fever that has been contagious since the school was founded. Villanova's basketball team made it to the Elite 8 in 2006, and students say, "they're really good—that's why we are basketball crazy." In fact, during halftime at one of the games, it is possible to win a cruise or a brand new Mustang just for shooting a couple hoops.

Players, Greeks, and Saints

Basketball is just one of Villanova's many traditions. A Catholic university located only about 15 minutes away from Philadelphia, it is nestled right in the center of the Main Line—a well-known upscale area of suburban Philadelphia. While Villanova's campus is gorgeous, the University also boasts an exciting night life and a Greek system devoted to perpetual partying. However, whether or not you choose to go Greek, an active social life is a must. One student confessed, "As important as our grades are to us, [partying] is a really important aspect of our school." That said, about 20 percent of the student body belongs to one of 19 fraternities or sororities. They make their presence known during "Greek Week" when Greeks wear their letters and have contests and games around campus. Greek life is prevalent on campus, but since fraternities and sororities do not have houses, they do not consume the social life on campus and students say that anyone can survive without belonging to a fraternity or a sorority. But fraternities and sororities are not all about drinking and dancing the night away; they also avidly promote philanthropy. Each fraternity and sorority is affiliated with a different community service organization and organizes two events per year to raise money for their chosen charities. The service-based Greek life yields events like the Special Olympics on Villanova's campus, as well as a number of projects in Philadelphia city schools, shelters and soup kitchens. "Habitat for Humanity is huge on our campus," one senior said, recommending that everyone go on mission trips during fall or spring break to build houses. "I know for some of my friends who go to big universities, it's not the cool thing to get involved in community service," she explained. "But here, it's the cool thing to do."

The Holy Grounds

For entertainment on college grounds, students go to Connelly Center, where free movies are shown on weekends. The school also hosts "Late Night Villanova" where students stay up all night doing various activities and all proceeds go to charity. Many also venture into Philadelphia. Railways line either side of campus and make it possible for freshmen and sophomores, who are not allowed to have cars, to explore the city. Weekend shuttles also run into the heart of Philadelphia and to the nearest mall. On the first Friday of every month and every Sunday, art galleries and museums are free for the public, and students often take advantage of this deal and swarm into the city. One sophomore recommended the popular South Street: "Shopping is fun because there are lots of random boutiques, but it's even fun just to sit and watch the people go by and see the random happenings." Another student agreed: "The people there are very different from what you see on campus; it's a breath of fresh air." South Philly, as it's known by locals, is "the place" to get an authentic Philly cheesesteak at the corner where Pat's and Geno's are located. Downtown Philadelphia also boasts several clubs, including "Shampoo" and "Envy," which host college nights for students and a bar called Brownie's. "When you turn 21," one senior said, "it's the rite of passage—you go to Brownie's."

Villanova hosts a handful of annual, campus-wide events. The St. Thomas of Villanova Day Parade is held in the fall when students return from summer vacation. St. Thomas Villanova Day includes a feast and some speeches to recognize the founder of the University, St. Thomas of Villanova. A similar carnival, NovaFest, is hosted at the end of the year. "NovaFest is a huge weekend party that we look forward to all year. We never really get good bands, but it's crazy and everyone drinks all weekend long." However, do not expect to obtain easy access to alcohol at these parties or at any other social gatherings; Villanova has a strict alcohol policy that is enforced by Resident Advisors. No alcohol is allowed for underage students, and students over 21 are only allowed to keep a certain amount of alcohol in their dorm rooms. Students say the RAs are "pretty strict on it. They make themselves very friendly, and very approachable, but we know that they're the arm of the law." However, students contend that while the University is strict on alcohol possession, "there are many ways to get around it." As for food and sustenance, Villanova offers a number of dining options in addition to regular dining hall meal plans. Meal plan points pay for items at the convenience store, the Italian kitchen, and the grill. Coffee shops like "The Holy Grounds" can be found all over campus, in libraries and in classroom buildings. The Bartley Exchange "has great sandwiches and meals . . . everyone agrees it is the best place to eat on campus." There's also a traveling coffee cart that tries to capture customers from the nearby Starbucks.

Holy Wisdom

Applicants apply to one of Villanova's four colleges: Arts and Sciences, Commerce and Finance, Engineering or Nursing. Students have the option of changing their college program once they are enrolled and are not required to declare a major until the end of sophomore year. Students in the college of Arts and Sciences must fulfill a number of distributional requirements. "They try to make you as well-rounded as possible," one senior said, listing the requirements in science, math, theology, history, foreign language, English, and ethics. "Our school is very much broken up by the college you're in," one senior said. "Academic-wise, you're very segregated." The freshman core, however—a survey of Western Literature and history from the ancient medieval period through the Renaissance and the Enlightenment to the present—is required of all freshmen and is "a big mixing pot." These core Humanities classes also have a very religious base. As an Augustinian university, "we read the Bible as one of our books in them and also Augustine's *Confessions*."

Goin' to the Chapel

One amorously-minded sophomore noted the beauty of Villanova's on-campus church. "It's the most gorgeous chapel," she said, noting that couples are married there every weekend. The wait list to get married there is "so long there are at least two marriages a day on the weekends. Freshman year you're supposed to put your name on the list." While no one actually signs up to be married that far in advance, you might be able to arrange a marriage in a different way; couples who kiss under the arch in Coor Hall as freshmen are said to be destined for wedding bells in the chapel.

> As important as our grades are to us, partying is a really important aspect of our school.

When it comes to other chapel-going, students say the Catholic tradition of the school is more like background noise than an omnipresent affiliation. "I was expecting it to be a whole bunch of Catholics," one freshman said, "But only some go to Mass." He soon discovered that Villanova was "more religiously diverse" than he had expected. The majority of students on campus are in fact Catholic, but as one sophomore noted, "they are not necessarily stringent Catholics; it is present, but I wouldn't say it pervades social life." The 8 p.m. and 10 p.m. masses are very popular times for students. Feel free to walk into Coor Hall or the chapel as you please, but watch your step at St. Mary's on West Campus. Not only do students tell great ghost stories about this and other buildings, they also warn that if you step on the seal in the floor there, you won't graduate in four years.

Posterchild for Preppy

"Basically everybody at this campus is out of an Abercrombie & Fitch catalog," one sophomore confessed. "But there are still some people who throw everybody on campus for a loop." Students describe the typical Villanova student as "upper-middle-class white—just your basic kid who grew up in the suburbs and whose parents are together . . . and they have brothers or sisters who go here or who've graduated from here; there's a lot of legacy at Villanova." While one sophomore conceded that many students come from a privileged background and "drive BMWs," "there are a lot of people who don't go with that crowd and who don't really care about that stuff." The homogeneity of the student population is a widespread complaint, although one sophomore optimistically reported, "The incoming class was far more diverse than ours," and "a lot more cultural clubs have popped up on campus recently."

Overall, students say the size and atmosphere of Villanova help make everyone feel at home. One sophomore remarked, "Villanova's big on community, and I think that's one of the things that really attracted me: leaving home I'd kind of have a new family as soon as I got here." Another student appreciated that Villanova is "not so big that you get lost in the masses, but not so small that everybody knows everything about everyone else; it makes for a comfortable feel." Remember, though, whether headed toward class, the chapel, or Philadelphia—watch out for those seals.—*Laura Sullivan*

FYI

If you come to Villanova, you'd better bring "readiness to work hard and party hard, a Louis Vuitton bag and a fake ID."

What is the typical weekend schedule? "Friday nights party, Saturday sleep in, do some work during the day or watch football, Saturday night more parties, Sunday go to meetings and study with everyone in the Bartley Exchange."

If I could change one thing about Villanova "I'd make the student body more diverse."

Three things every student at Villanova should do before graduating are "go to the basketball games, watch the chariot races and go on a community service trip."

Rhode Island

Brown University

Address: 45 Prospect Street
  Providence, RI 02912
Phone: 401-863-2378
E-mail address:
  admission_undergraduate@
  brown.edu
Web site URL:
  www.brown.edu
Year Founded: 1764
Private or Public: Private
Religious Affiliation: None
Location: Urban
Number of Applicants:
  20,633
Percent Accepted: 13.7%
**Percent Accepted who
  enroll:** 55%
Number Entering: 1,550
**Number of Transfers
  Accepted each Year:** 117
Middle 50% SAT range:
  M: 670–780, CR: 650–760,
  Wr: 660–770
Middle 50% ACT range:
  28–33
**Early admission program
  EA/ED/None:** ED

**Percentage accepted
  through EA or ED:** 36%
EA and ED deadline: 1-Nov
Regular Deadline: 1-Jan
Application Fee: $70
**Full time Undergraduate
  enrollment:** 6,095
Total enrollment: 7,909
Percent Male: 48%
Percent Female: 52%
**Total Percent Minority or
  Unreported:** 32%
Percent African-American:
  7%
**Percent Asian/Pacific
  Islander:** 16%
Percent Hispanic: 9%
Percent Native-American:
  <1%
Percent International: 8%
**Percent in-state/out of
  state:** 5%/95%
Percent from Public HS:
  Unreported
Retention Rate: 97%
Graduation Rate 4-year:
  83.0%

Graduation Rate 6-year:
  92.0%
**Percent Undergraduates in
  On-campus housing:** 79%
**Number of official organized
  extracurricular
  organizations:** 400
3 Most popular majors:
  Biology, Economic,
  International Relations and
  Affairs
Student/Faculty ratio: 8:1
Average Class Size:
  Unreported
**Percent of students going to
  grad school:** Unreported
Tuition and Fees: $37,718
**In State Tuition and Fees if
  different:** No difference
Cost for Room and Board:
  $10,022
**Percent receiving financial
  aid out of those who apply,
  first year:** 44%
**Percent receiving financial
  aid among all students:**
  44%

Students considering Brown should not let its centuries-old Ivy League traditions fool them; Brown's history of progressive teachings has been a hallmark of its undergraduate experience since the school's founding in 1764. Today, you'll find that Brown has carried this tradition of intellectual and extracurricular curiosity into the twenty-first century, cementing its place as a true haven for fine academics and passionate interests in an environment that celebrates free thought.

So Chill and Satisfied

The absence of any general requirements at Brown is part of its overall atmosphere of freedom and experimentation. The "New Curriculum" allows Brown students to shape their own programs of study, which they said offers a number of advantages. One senior explained that "when you don't have requirements, it works for both people who don't know what they want to do and people who know exactly what they want to do; it helps you structure your education for whatever fits you best." He added that, "you get a school full of people doing what they love." Brown also offers its famous Satisfactory/No Credit option, where students can opt to take as many classes as they like on a pass/fail evaluation basis instead of for a letter grade. While most students only choose to do this a few times a year, it lets them experiment in a subject outside their normal area of interest without having to worry about their numerical performance. One student said that it "goes in line with Brown's whole philosophy of giving you freedom to explore new fields without feeling that it all has to be related to your future success and your résumé."

Although many students choose to major in International Relations or Biology, they can specialize in more unusual majors or "concentrations" as well. Brown reportedly has the only Egyptology concentration in the Western Hemisphere, and the Neuroscience department is well-known for its professors and cutting-edge research. Professor Emeritus Barrett Hazeltine's popular business management classes attract many students, and Biology professor Ken Miller was recently a leading witness in the Supreme Court case debating the teaching of evolution in schools. Adventurous students interested in the arts may cross-register at the nearby—and equally famed—Rhode Island School of Design.

Students agreed that while introductory courses can have up to a few hundred people in them, upper-level classes shrink in size considerably. Freshmen also have the option to sign up for First Year Seminars capped at 20 students, which offer an opportunity for first-years to get to know each other and a professor in a lively, intimate discussion setting. Professors are described as being very accessible if students need them to be. In addition to being required to host weekly office hours, many Brown professors get to know their students' names, even in large lecture courses. As one student put it, "If you're willing to take a little initiative, you can build really strong relationships."

The pervasive laid-back attitude regarding academics is another strong characteristic of Brown. One senior confided that, "while it's really competitive to get into Brown, it's really not competitive when you get here." Although "the vast majority of people here are still working really hard," students say that it is rare for people to lose their cool about GPAs or class curves—in public, at least. This relaxed philosophy allows people to collaborate on work and generally to "stay away from bragging about how hardworking or stressed you are." Another senior explained that "it's hard to compete because everyone's passionate about their own interests and has their own achievements along different dimensions."

Conservative Commentators Need Not Apply

Every year at Brown, the Queer Alliance hosts "Sex Power God," a wild party at which students are encouraged to wear as little clothing as possible. In 2005, SPG got some surprise attention when it was featured on the TV show "The O'Reilly Factor" as an example of Ivy League–sanctioned debauchery. Although Bill O'Reilly may not approve, students said that one of their favorite aspects of Brown is its liberalism and free-spirited atmosphere. Although they caution against giving in entirely to the conception of Brown students as "pot-smoking, flannel-wearing hippies," in general, students concurred that there's some truth to the image. The campus is "overwhelmingly liberal," although conservatives do have a voice, and students said that "everyone here is interested in making the world a better place."

In terms of encouraging diversity, students said that the admissions office is doing a good job geographically, but social divisions based on income and ethnicity are sometimes apparent. Students agreed that the mostly generous financial aid policy has improved in the past few years and has made attending an elite private school a reality for many low-income students.

Although the actual number of students in fraternities and sororities at Brown may be relatively small, their weekend parties are still very popular, especially among underclassmen. Everyone also finds themselves at parties in the dorms, usually earlier in the night, before they head out to some of the local bars and clubs in the downtown area or on nearby Thayer Street. The club Fish Co. is reportedly the place to be on Wednesday nights. Upperclassmen often attend parties at off-campus houses. Brown's policies on alcohol and drug use are described as "extremely loose," and campus police and Residential Counselors in the dorms "are really there just to make sure that you're being safe and not causing trouble." One girl said that she would often come back to her dorm hall at night and smell pot, but she said that "it's not at all something that people will pressure you to do, although it's definitely there if you want it."

Brown students find it easy to take the bus or train to Boston or New York on the weekends, but many find that just staying on College Hill in Providence is satisfactory. Brown's NCAA Division I teams usually have games, although few students reportedly attend them.

Life on College Hill

Upon setting foot on campus, visitors to Brown immediately notice the striking colonial-style brick buildings and the wide, inviting Main Green. The campus is described as "very New England," complete with ivy and impeccable grounds. However, today's Brown students have adapted their school's austere backdrop to the twenty-first century. On sunny days, students crowd the lawns with lemonade stands, soccer games, back massage stations, and the occasional hookah.

Most freshmen live in Keeney Quadrangle, which houses about 600 students and is known as the "freshman zoo." The rest live in dorms that range from a few blocks to a 10-minute walk away. While Keeney is agreed to be the most social dorm, people said that the other dorms foster long-term relationships as well. Everyone is assigned a roommate in a double, and the traditional long hallways are coed. The bathrooms are supposed to be single-sex, but some students reported having members of the opposite sex invade when their lines were too long. Freshmen are organized into units of 40 to 60 and are assigned undergraduate RCs. Students said they made the majority of their friends in their first-year units, since "it's a large enough group of people that you get a good variety of interests and personalities." After freshman year, students enter the Housing Lottery to draw for several different arrangements, ranging from triples to suites.

The two main all-you-can-eat dining halls, the "V-Dub" and the "Ratty," got mixed reviews, with most students agreeing that the fare quickly grows monotonous, even though the "V-dub" does have a vegetarian line. The meal plan was recently expanded to allow diners more freedom to use their plans at after-hours eateries on campus, including the Ivy Room and Joe's. Nearby Thayer Street is an ever-popular option for a wide variety of food, from the famous falafels at East Side Pocket to Antonio's Pizza. If you want to venture off the Hill into the downtown area, the Dominican food gets good reviews for its affordability and exotic allure, while Café Paragon is "a good place to go for a good meal with your parents."

While one junior said she did not know why Brown students would need to leave College Hill to entertain themselves, the recently-renovated and revitalized downtown Providence is an enticing reason. The city has spruced itself up in the past several years, and its museums, events on the river, and "humongous" mall are attractive study breaks for students.

Campaigns and Cracked Pots

At Brown, students know how to balance ambitious activities with downtime. A sophomore said he thought that "everyone here is involved in at least two or three extracurricular activities, usually very different from each other, and in a very driven way." Politics are a common interest, with the Brown College Democrats widely cited as the most popular organization. One sophomore even said that "a popular joke is that the Brown Green Party is bigger than the campus Republicans." No matter which party you pick, students say that the small size of Rhode Island is conducive in allowing them to get involved in local and statewide politics. "I have a lot of friends who feel like they're making changes in social policy and education reform—they really have an impact on who gets elected." The Queer Alliance draws many members, as do cultural heritage groups and a number of social activism organizations like the Brown Darfur Action Network and Amnesty International. A capella and dance groups also have a strong presence.

Recent years have seen an increase in the involvement of students in community service organizations in downtown Providence, challenging the belief that all Brown students avoid leaving College Hill. Some students also have jobs down the hill, although "Brown provides a lot of opportunities for employment, especially through Dining Services."

> "It's very Brown to think 'I'm free and naked and helping people by giving them donuts.'"

Brown students revel in a number of zany traditions that pervade the college's freeform atmosphere. Every finals period, a group of students organizes in secret and shows up on campus at a random time to run through the buildings, from the libraries to the dorms, in what is termed the "Naked Donut Run." "It's very Brown to think 'I'm free and naked and helping people by giving them donuts,'" one student remarked. A legend surrounding a mysterious figure from Brown's past has also become tradition. On

Friday the 13th, students pay homage to the mythical professor Josiah Carberry, who supposedly studied "psychoceramics," or cracked pots.

"I don't think we conform to non-conformity, but people are not afraid to express themselves," one student said. Indeed, Brown does leave its undergraduates many opportunities for freedom of expression, whether it is by letting students choose their own classes, run a medley of organizations or spearhead campaigns. While it may be famous for its unstructured atmosphere, Brown students find that their self-motivation and passionate interests help them to shape unique college experiences.—*Kimberly Chow*

FYI

If you come to Brown, you'd better bring "liberal political beliefs and a scarf."

What's the typical weekend schedule? "Friday night go to a room party; Saturday sleep in then do community service in Providence; Saturday night go to a frat or a party thrown by an organization, then do work all Sunday."

If I could change one thing about Brown, "I would want people to venture off College Hill into downtown Providence more."

Three things that every student at Brown should do before graduating: "March against the University, like to protest the bookstore going corporate, take a completely ridiculous class that has nothing to do with your major, and try to get to the tops of as many buildings as you can."

Rhode Island School of Design

Address: 2 College Street Providence, RI 02903
Phone: 401-454-6300
E-mail address: admissions@risd.edu
Web site URL: www.risd.edu
Year Founded: 1877
Private or Public: Private
Religious Affiliation: None
Location: Urban
Number of Applicants: 2,511
Percent Accepted: 34%
Percent Accepted who enroll: 47%
Number Entering: 398
Number of Transfers Accepted each Year: 151
Middle 50% SAT range: M:550–670, CR:530–660, Wr:** Unreported
Middle 50% ACT range: Unreported
Early admission program EA/ED/None: EA
Percentage accepted through EA or ED: Unreported

EA and ED deadline: 15-Dec
Regular Deadline: 15-Feb
Application Fee: $50
Full time Undergraduate enrollment: 1,882
Total enrollment: 1,882
Percent Male: 35%
Percent Female: 65%
Total Percent Minority or Unreported: 49%
Percent African-American: 2%
Percent Asian/Pacific Islander: 14%
Percent Hispanic: 5%
Percent Native-American: <1%
Percent International: 12%
Percent in-state/out of state: Unreported
Percent from Public HS: 60%
Retention Rate: Unreported
Graduation Rate 4-year: Unreported
Graduation Rate 6-year: Unreported

Percent Undergraduates in On-campus housing: 33%
Number of official organized extracurricular organizations: 35
3 Most popular majors: Graphic Design, Illustration, Industrial Design
Student/Faculty ratio: 11:1
Average Class Size: Unreported
Percent of students going to grad school: Unreported
Tuition and Fees: $27,510
In State Tuition and Fees if different: No difference
Cost for Room and Board: $7,709
Percent receiving financial aid out of those who apply, first year: Unreported
Percent receiving financial aid among all students: Unreported

The Rhode Island School of Design does not offer your "typical" college experience—there are not many sports teams, social life is secondary to schoolwork, and your English teacher might not care if you don't finish your reading assignment because she knows you spent eight hours doing studio work the day before. RISD (pronounced "RIZ-dee") is a serious school for serious art students. Students at RISD, a small campus in Providence, Rhode Island, that is adjacent to Brown University, can major in apparel design, art education, graphic design, industrial design, illustration, textiles, sculpture, glass, or animation, and there are many other options where those came from.

The campus is home to about 2,300 students total, with approximately 1,900 undergraduates. Students say the relatively low number of students allows for very intimate classes, in which the average size is 13 students.

All RISD freshmen are required to take Foundation Studies, a fundamentals program which consists of three classes: Drawing, Two-Dimensional Design, and Three-Dimensional Design. The program is meant to immerse students in the basics of art and visual design, and to help them explore their options in terms of majors. Freshmen are also given second priority (after seniors) in class selection so that they can experiment with classes before making a final decision on their area of concentration.

RISD is organized on a trimester schedule, which has positives and negatives according to students. Students are only given two weeks off for winter break, but they are also able to take more classes in one year. The second semester, which takes place right after winter break, is also unofficially designated as "relaxation time." According to one RISD junior, no one takes more than two classes during this period in January and February. "Most people only take one class during second semester because the first and third semesters are hardcore," she said.

Liberal arts courses are also required of every student, but they are definitely not the concentration of a RISD education. According to a RISD sophomore, History of Art and Visual Culture is the most popular liberal arts department and some students even choose to major in this field rather than in a visual art. Students say the most popular visual art department is illustration because it offers students a great deal of freedom in their studies and concentration. "It's a very open and free department—you can really take it anywhere you want and there aren't a lot of technical restrictions," one RISD junior said. The consensus among RISD students is that the hardest major is architecture, which some students playfully refer to as "archi-torture."

Getting into the class you want can be a nightmare at RISD, mostly because the class sizes are so small. There is also a precise hierarchy of preference in which seniors get first choice during enrollment, freshmen second choice, juniors third and sophomores are left to fend for themselves at the bottom. As mentioned earlier, freshmen are given second priority so they can explore different classes before they pick their major. "As a sophomore, it was incredibly difficult to get the classes I wanted. I guess it's fair in the long run, but it's still pretty frustrating," a current junior said.

According to interviewed students, the workload at RISD is rigorous to say the least. "There's not a lot of time to sleep because you're spending all night cutting paper, making books, and putting together your portfolio," said one RISD senior. Students also emphasize the necessity of attending class and say you are required to get a note from the nurse if you miss class due to illness, "just like high school." RISD students also have the option of taking classes at Brown, so if a RISD student wants to take a math class, there is nothing stopping her. Beginning in the 2008–2009 academic year, Brown and RISD began to collaborate to offer students a dual degree—the completion of a five-year program will allow students to receive a BA from Brown and BFA from RISD. Participating students must live on both campuses for two years each and must complete both degrees.

> **"There's not a lot of time to sleep because you're spending all night cutting paper, making books, and putting together your portfolio."**

Social life has been a point of contention among RISD students, mostly because the school's social scene is somewhat limited. According to one junior, the amount of work assigned to RISD students makes partying difficult, though some students do go to parties at Brown or to bars. All in all, social life is very much contained within the campus and mostly consists of private parties. "This is not a party school; it's a very serious school. If you're someone who wants to go somewhere with lots of parties and things, RISD probably isn't the school for you," one RISD freshman said. But that is not to say students don't make meaningful relationships or have close friends. A junior said everyone has a very good relationship with almost everyone else simply because the school is so small.

RISD freshmen and sophomores are required to live on campus, and many juniors and seniors choose to do so anyway. Freshmen are housed in the Quad, conveniently located right next to the main dining hall, the Met. Construction was recently completed on 15 Westminster, a new dorm building that also happens to be the location of the main library. Students say the new building is "great," "beautiful," and "centrally located," just a quick walk from the graphic design and illustration building. Housing is done by lottery after freshman year.

Despite the statistic that 69 percent of RISD students are female and 31 percent are male, most students said RISD was very diverse, and that you are able to "meet all sorts of people." There is large population of international students, especially from Korea.

Student Alliance, the student governing body, is the primary student group on the RISD campus. It meets weekly to discuss student issues, which most recently have included concerns regarding social life at RISD. The Alliance is working to get administrative approval for a student center on campus to increase "hang out" space for students. Other student clubs include a cappella groups and cultural clubs. RISD has two varsity sports, basketball and hockey, both of which compete on the Brown campus. "Sports are not that big of a deal on campus," said one sophomore. "But we still support our teams."

Students describe the food at RISD as "decent" and "pretty good," but they do acknowledge that some dining halls have more options than others. A junior student said the best place to grab a quick bite to eat is the Portfolio Café, located right next to the library in Westminster 15.

The bottom line for students at RISD is their artistic education, and most are more than satisfied with the training they have received at the university. "RISD is the perfect school for me because I'm doing what I love," said one senior. "Make sure you really love this kind of work before you decide to come to RISD."—*Samantha Broussard-Wilson*

FYI
If you come to RISD, you'd better bring "your sketchbook."
What is the typical weekend schedule? "Work, work, and maybe a little extra work before bed."
If I could change one thing about RISD, I'd "give the students more time to sleep."
Three things every student at RISD should do before graduating are "go to a hockey game, explore the coffee shops in Providence, and go on any of the excursions offered, like Newport, New York City, or skiing."

Salve Regina University

Address: 100 Ochre Point Avenue Newport, RI 02840-4192
Phone: 401-341-2908
E-mail address: sruadmis@salve.edu
Web site URL: www.salve.edu
Year Founded: 1947
Private or Public: Private
Religious Affiliation: Roman Catholic
Location: Suburban
Number of Applicants: 5,937
Percent Accepted: 59%
Percent Accepted who enroll: 16%
Number Entering: 560
Number of Transfers Accepted each Year: 121
Middle 50% SAT range:
M: 510–590 ,CR:510–580,
Wr: Unreported
Middle 50% ACT range: 22–26
Early admission program EA/ED/None: EA

Percentage accepted through EA or ED: 26%
EA and ED deadline: 1-Nov
Regular Deadline: NA
Application Fee: $50
Full time Undergraduate enrollment: 2,127
Total enrollment: 2,700
Percent Male: 31%
Percent Female: 69%
Total Percent Minority or Unreported: 23%
Percent African-American: 1%
Percent Asian/Pacific Islander: 1%
Percent Hispanic: 3%
Percent Native-American: <1%
Percent International: 1%
Percent in-state/out of state: 16%/84%
Percent from Public HS: 62%
Retention Rate: 73%
Graduation Rate 4-year: 63%

Graduation Rate 6-year: 67%
Percent Undergraduates in On-campus housing: 58%
Number of official organized extracurricular organizations: 42
3 Most popular majors: Criminal Justice, Education, Nursing
Student/Faculty ratio: 14:1
Average Class Size: 10 to 19
Percent of students going to grad school: 20%
Tuition and Fees: $31,500
In State Tuition and Fees if different: No difference
Cost for Room and Board: $10,700
Percent receiving financial aid out of those who apply, first year: 68%
Percent receiving financial aid among all students: 71%

Salve Regina College was founded under the tutelage of the Sisters of Mercy, and was originally intended to be a liberal arts college in the Catholic tradition. It changed its name to Salve Regina University in 1991, but it still remains a serious liberal arts college with a considerable Catholic bent. Originally started as a nursing program, today's Salve Regina boasts both a popular and competitive nursing component and a wealth of additional programs of study. Students receive a well-rounded, liberal arts education, centered on an intensive core.

Liberal Arts with a Side of Catholicism

Salve Regina's most striking academic feature is the Core Curriculum, which every student must complete in order to graduate. The core is extremely intensive, covering a wide range of subjects and disciplines. The Core Curriculum consists of the Common Core, five courses which every single student takes; and the Core Complement, for which there is a choice between classes that fulfill the require-

ments. The Common Core includes Philosophy and Religious Studies courses, aimed at helping students understand the widespread influence of Judeo-Christian thought in the world, with a focus on Catholicism. One student described the curriculum as "definitely liberal arts by nature, but with a very religious overtone." Some students do not take kindly to having religion "stuffed down their throats," but others accept it as part of the school's mission. There is also an introductory course taken during freshman year entitled "Portal: Seeking Wisdom," which serves to introduce students to the liberal arts. The core received mixed reactions from the students. One claimed that it was too restricting and the long list of requirements prevented her from going abroad for a semester. Another found the experience enlightening and instructive, albeit at times overwhelming. Although many of the core classes deal with very similar subjects, each new subject is somehow refreshing, as one will "get something different out of it looking at it from a different angle than before."

Without a doubt, Salve's greatest academic strength is its commitment to student-professor interaction. One student earnestly said, "I absolutely adore my professors at Salve." When class sizes are so small and such a focus is placed on discussion and student participation, it's no surprise that students and instructors share a strong bond. Most classes have fewer than 20 students, and only the most popular introductory classes have classes larger than 30 students. Such great emphasis on exploration leads to some very lively discussions; students are "always engaged in class." Even in the larger classes, "there's really good discussions that come up" and the professors are still accessible.

> "Our classes are held in mansions . . . can you say that about another school?"

Salve students have many choices for their majors. Most liberal arts disciplines are covered, but the most popular majors are reportedly Nursing and Administration of Justice. The nursing program is one of the most difficult tracks at Salve. It has strict requirements; getting a C—in any nursing course—is considered "failing" and results in expulsion from the major. The popularity of the nursing program may explain one of Salve's most interesting facets. The nursing department has "very few male students" and, seeing as it's one of the largest majors, the university as a whole has a high female-to-male ratio.

Salve Girls and Some Salve Guys

One student noted that, "Walking around it's pretty obvious that you run into more girls than guys," but she didn't feel that it was "very noticeable." Unlike many student bodies, Salve's seems very comfortable with itself. The school is markedly homogeneous. Naturally, the majority of students are affiliated with the Catholic Church in some way. Although there may be plenty of Catholics, one student warned that "the chapel is small and only a small percentage of students attends mass on Sundays." Furthermore, many of the students are described as white, preppy, and wealthy. One girl noted that, "Many people dress up for classes and carry around their Louis Vuitton and Coach bags." Only one student expressed an odious dislike of the stereotypical Salve kid, bemoaning

their New England preppiness, although still admiring the school's quality of teaching. A word for the wise: although it may be difficult to fit into such a crowd, the students are for the most part pretty amiable and social. The typical student also "parties a lot and is very concerned with working out at the gym."

Salve students like to party. The campus is strictly dry, so most students have to go off campus, to the apartments of upperclassmen, in order to drink on the weekends. Despite being a dry campus, there are a lot of alcohol and drugs; there is a prevalence among the more well-to-do of some "rich man's drugs." It remains difficult and somewhat of a hassle for students to party, especially those that are underage. Many students go to nearby Newport on the weekends to go clubbing and to escape the strict campus rules. For those that do not want to stray far from campus or drink, the University hosts many dry events for the student body. Every spring the campus holds a concert. On top of that, a comedian performs every week, and every once in a while, bands or singers come to the weekly performance.

Newport: Bars, Beaches, and Villas

Salve Regina has "a beautiful campus." Located in the historic city of Newport, Rhode Island, the campus is well-known for the mansions it has acquired for university use; the school was originally founded when the gorgeous Ochre Court was donated to the Sisters of Mercy. Ochre Court is a Newport mansion, built to be the luxurious residence of a wealthy banker in the Gilded Age of the late nineteenth century. It remains today as the heart of Salve Regina's campus, just as it has always been. When Salve was just a nursing school, it housed the faculty, the students and the classrooms. It is now the location of the admissions office and a small chapel. Today, much of the campus shares the same historic grandeur of the Gilded Age. Classes are held in mansions; some of the main academic buildings, Wakehurst and McCauley, were also donated to the school by wealthy Newport families. The campus lies over the water and is described as "amazingly beautiful" by the students.

Downtown Newport is rather touristy, and the location boasts various places to shop and eat. Some favorite student eateries include the Brick Alley Pub, Sardella's, Puerini and the Red Parrot. Newport has a lot of unique stores and bars popular among Salve students on the weekends. The most popular beach for students is First Beach, which can be reached from campus on the Cliff Walk. The Cliff Walk stretches over three miles, and goes alongside a precipice overlooking the Atlantic Ocean. It is yet another one of the interesting vistas to be found at this uniquely Catholic liberal arts university founded in the historic city of Newport.—*Ryan Galisewski*

FYI

If you come to Salve Regina, you'd better bring "common sense, money (it would be a shame to put all those awesome stores downtown to waste), and a diverse sense of style."

What is the typical weekend schedule? "Go clubbing in Providence Friday night. Work during the day on Saturday and then go to a friend's party in Newport. Sunday either go to mass or sleep in and then do work the rest of the day."

If I could change one thing about Salve Regina University, I would "make it a little bit more diverse. It gets boring having to see people who look exactly the same walking around campus."

Three things every Salve Regina University student should do before graduating are "go for a drink at all of the bars on Thames Street and/or Broadway, visit the Breaker's Mansion before Christmas and go for a drive on Ocean Drive—it's the most beautiful road in the world!"

University of Rhode Island

Address: 14 Upper College Road Kingston, RI 02881-1322
Phone: 401-874-7000
E-mail address: admission@uri.edu
Web site URL: www.uri.edu
Year Founded: 1892
Private or Public: Public
Religious Affiliation: None
Location: Rural
Number of Applicants: 14,272
Percent Accepted: 79%
Percent Accepted who enroll: 28%
Number Entering: 3,155
Number of Transfers Accepted each Year: 1,068
Middle 50% SAT range: M: 500–590, CR: 480–570, Wr: Unreported
Middle 50% ACT range: Unreported
Early admission program EA/ED/None: EA

Percentage accepted through EA or ED: 64%
EA and ED deadline: 15-Dec
Regular Deadline: 1-Feb
Application Fee: $50
Full time Undergraduate enrollment: 12,516
Total enrollment: 15,080
Percent Male: 42%
Percent Female: 58%
Total Percent Minority or Unreported: 16%
Percent African-American: 4%
Percent Asian/Pacific Islander: 2%
Percent Hispanic: 5%
Percent Native-American: 1%
Percent International: <1%
Percent in-state/out of state: 61%/39%
Percent from Public HS: Unreported
Retention Rate: 81%
Graduation Rate 4-year: 38%

Graduation Rate 6-year: 57%
Percent Undergraduates in On-campus housing: 45%
Number of official organized extracurricular organizations: 100
3 Most popular majors: Business/Marketing, Communications/Journalism, Education
Student/Faculty ratio: 19:1
Average Class Size: 20 to 29
Percent of students going to grad school: Unreported
Tuition and Fees: $21,294
In State Tuition and Fees if different: $6,440
Cost for Room and Board: $8,828
Percent receiving financial aid out of those who apply, first year: 63%
Percent receiving financial aid among all students: 52%

While the URI administration tries hard to shed the school's "Animal House" reputation of old, collegiates at this public university still enjoy a fun-filled four years. Students are drawn to URI's strong academic departments, such as business and management, and to its low in-state tuition. Of course, its reputation as a party school "doesn't hurt, either."

The "School" Part of a Party School

While URI students certainly have their fun, academic requirements are a central part of each student's life. The University of Rhode Island requires students to complete a number of courses in order to graduate, including classes in the natural sciences, fine arts, mathematics, languages and social sciences.

While this subject load may seem daunting, current URIers say that prospective students have nothing to fear. "Really, as long as you go to class, you'll be fine," said one male junior. "Teachers here tend to understand that this is college . . . they let some stuff slide."

It's also pretty easy to skip class and get notes from a friend—especially since introductory classes here can be so large that a professor would never notice your absence. Some courses at URI enroll as many as 500 students. This can be a good thing—you can get into any class "as long as you have taken the prerequisites." Plus, according to students, the average class only has 40 to 50 students. Certain majors are also required to take specific classes. Students rave about the German and business departments, and URI has long been known for its marine biology programs. The most popular major seems to be communications, which is also ranked by students as one of the school's easiest. The human development/family studies major is also considered to be among the less demanding, while engineering is considered particularly difficult. The pharmacy major is also considered one of the hardest, as students must maintain a higher-than-average GPA to be allowed to continue in the program. Classes can be "as competitive as you want." It may be true that many students "don't care," but there is definitely some competition among those who are "top in their programs."

URI faces a common problem of many large universities—TAs must teach many of the recitations that accompany the professor's lectures. Despite this, students say that professors are "approachable, if you make the effort." Grading tends to be "pretty reasonable," although grade inflation and scaling of grades varies by course and department. According to several undergraduates, the same course taught in sections by different professors will have "totally different material, grading, and workload."

For the more academically inclined graduate of the Rhode Island public school system, the University offers an impressive and prestigious honors program. The class sizes are generally smaller and the courses more rigorous. Students can apply directly after high school or at any point during their college years. Like most other universities, URI extends to its students the possibility of study abroad, which, for some weary of Rhode Island, is a great chance to "escape and have a blast." URI also offers a "Centennial Scholarship" for motivated and quali-fied students, which provides the lucky chosen few with a full ride.

In terms of upgrades, the University of Rhode Island is in the process of building a new $60 million center for biotechnology and life studies on the Kingston Campus. A new business building has also popped up recently, and new dorms and dining halls are in the works.

Home Sweet Home

URI's campus is a random smattering of gothic, colonial and modern architecture. The Quad, at the center of campus, is picturesque and a great place to "hang out or do work." While the Quad is home to a large number of academic buildings, the Greek houses are farther away on the outskirts of the sprawling campus. Campus dorms, the student center and the library are all nearby.

The dorms at Rhode Island get mixed reviews. While the dorms tend not to have specific identities—there is really no particular "party dorm" or "frat dorm" (though there is a discrepancy between more social and less social ones)—they vary greatly by condition and age. "Some dorms are really beautiful," said a senior, "but I was very disappointed freshman year to learn that mine was not one of them." All dorms are coed by floor. There is a substance-free dorm, although the alcohol policy is "strictly enforced" in all on-campus housing. The policy states that students under 21 may not have any alcohol in their rooms, while those of legal drinking age may possess "only a small amount, like a six-pack." According to students, the RAs "vary, but are basically there to make sure things don't get out of control," although one student was convinced his RA was put in place "to ruin my life." Penalties are high for breaking the alcohol policy, helping to explain why most students not only prefer to party off campus, but also often opt for off-campus housing after freshman or sophomore year. Sorority and fraternity houses, as well as apartments and private houses near campus, are popular with upperclassmen. Since on-campus housing is not guaranteed after freshman year, and students complain that "there is a serious housing shortage at URI," off-campus living is a popular option. Of course, that also means that many students have cars to get around. Fortunately, the relationship with locals is described as "very good," and students generally feel very safe around campus and beyond it.

URI students can chow down at one of the school's three main dining rooms or the oft-praised Ram's Den. Several meal plans are available to URI students, who praised the flexibility, if not the fare. "The dining hall food is okay," said one sophomore, "it just takes some getting used to." At the Ram's Den students use food points purchased at the beginning of the semester to buy the delectable goodies offered at "the best place on campus." The other dining halls vary, with some serving fast food while others offer more complete entrees. Several students complained about the selection of local restaurants, noting that "Kingston is not the place for five-star dining."

Kingston is a rather uneventful place, leading most students to feel that "drinking and partying is really the only thing to do here." While one student pointed out that "of course nothing important ever happens at URI—this is Rhode Island!" the administration tries to keep things lively with academic lectures and on-campus social events. When students need a night of hard drinking and wild fun, they turn to the Greek scene and to the bars and clubs of Providence to let off some steam.

Getting Soaked on a Dry Campus

After URI was named "America's Top Party School," the administration made the alcohol policy much tougher and started to be stricter with fraternity parties. Despite this, most students claim URI campus is "officially dry, but really, very wet." As with most large state universities, Greek life is the dominant form of social activity on campus, despite the fact that only about 10 percent of students are involved in the 20 fraternities and sororities. This is the case because parties, which must be registered with the university police, are generally open to the URI public. Despite the tendency of Greek life to dominate, students reported relatively little tension between Greeks and non-Greeks. While most students agreed that, "almost everyone here drinks," they also concurred that "not drinking doesn't necessarily mean you have no social life." Overall, students agreed that "everyone at URI is very friendly, and it's easy to meet people no matter what you're into."

Extracurricular activities are a major part of students' lives at URI, although the student body generally laments the lack of

school spirit. Basketball and football games are popular draws, especially when URI heads out against rival Providence College. Other notable sports teams are volleyball, baseball, soccer and sailing. Club sports are very popular, although for some, "it can be hard getting people to show up."

The student senate and the student-run newspaper, *The Good 5 Cent Cigar*, are also big campus extracurriculars. The Student Entertainment Committee is responsible for making sure that URI undergrads have plenty of fun, social options. A variety of other activities, including the Experimental Art Society and the Surf Club keep students' minds busy and their bodies outdoors. Yes, that's right, the Surf Club—the beach right near URI is "definitely one of the best parts of going to school here."

In addition to clubs and sports, a great number of students have part-time jobs. "It's pretty easy to get a work-study job at the event center, academic halls, or dining halls," remarked one senior.

Diversity is celebrated on the URI campus, with recent efforts by student groups, as well as the administration, to ensure that students of all backgrounds are tolerant of one another. As one student explained, "It would be hard to define a certain, stereotypical URI student. Basically everyone here has their own style." Students also spoke of the surprising geographic diversity, despite the fact that URI is a state school.

> "It's much more fun than I ever imagined Rhode Island could be."

Overall, URI collegiates seem content. While some undergrads wished there was slightly more emphasis on academics than on partying, most agreed that motivated students can combine a good learning experience with a lot of fun. Many echoed one senior's statement that, "I wouldn't change my decision to come here for anything in the world." In the words of one sophomore: "It's much more fun than I ever imagined Rhode Island could be."—*Erica Ross*

FYI

If you come to URI, you'd better bring "your smile, because everyone else here will have theirs."

What is the typical weekend schedule? "Start drinking on Wednesday. Continue through Monday morning."

If I could change one thing about URI "I'd build a parking garage."

Three things every student should do before graduating from URI are "swim at Narragansett beach, learn to surf, and spend an afternoon on the Quad with friends."

South Carolina

Address: 105 Sikes Hall
Clemson, SC 29634-5124
Phone: 864-656-2287
E-mail address:
cuadmissions@clemson.edu
Web site URL:
www.clemson.edu
Year Founded: 1889
Private or Public: Public
Religious Affiliation: None
Location: Rural
Number of Applicants:
Unreported
Percent Accepted: 54.0%
Percent Accepted who
enroll: Unreported
Number Entering: 2,813
Number of Transfers
Accepted each Year: 816
Middle 50% SAT range:
M: 587–680, CR: 550–640,
Wr: Unreported
Middle 50% ACT range:
25–30
Early admission program
EA/ED/None: None

Percentage accepted
through EA or ED: NA
EA and ED deadline: NA
Regular Deadline: 1-May
Application Fee: $50
Full time Undergraduate
enrollment: 14,713
Total enrollment: 18,317
Percent Male: 54%
Percent Female: 46%
Total Percent Minority or
Unreported: 10%
Percent African-American:
7%
Percent Asian/Pacific
Islander: 2%
Percent Hispanic: 1%
Percent Native-American:
<1%
Percent International: 1%
Percent in-state/out of
state: 71%/29%
Percent from Public HS:
Unreported
Retention Rate: 92%
Graduation Rate 4-year: 49%

Graduation Rate 6-year:
77%
Percent Undergraduates in
On-campus housing: 42%
Number of official organized
extracurricular
organizations: 292
3 Most popular majors:
Biology, Business,
Engineering
Student/Faculty ratio:
14:1
Average Class Size: 31
Percent of students going to
grad school: Unreported
Tuition and Fees: $24,130
In State Tuition and Fees if
different: $11,108
Cost for Room and Board:
$6,556
Percent receiving financial
aid out of those who apply,
first year: 87%
Percent receiving financial
aid among all students:
71%

Six out of seven days of the week, Clemson, S.C., is the typical Southern town. With a population of 12,000, which is significantly lower than the number of students at Clemson University, the town's small, quaint, charming, and filled with "white upper-class Republicans." But on Saturdays, you're transported to a whole new color palette, as "the whole town just turns orange." At Clemson, football games are the main events, and students very rarely miss a home game. "Everyone falls in love with football, tailgating is a way of life, and you are late if you're not partying by noon for an 8 p.m. game." Fans, visitors, and alumni travel miles to see the orange and purple Tigers play in a gigantic stadium capable of seating 80,301 roaring fans.

A Smorgasbord of Majors

Students at Clemson report that there seems to be a major for everyone, even those individuals whose "major" interests do not include academics. "'Party Right Through May'—that's what all the slackers and athletes major in," one student said. "I'm not really sure what they do." Believe it or not, "Party Right Through May" does have an official title, and those fun-loving students holding "Parks, Recreation, and Tourism Management" degrees are especially attractive to the U.S. Army recruiters seeking trip schedulers for soldiers.

At the opposite end of the spectrum, many students are drawn to Clemson for its excellent engineering program. Current undergraduates eagerly await the completion of an automotive engineering graduate center paid for by a $10 million endowment by BMW for automotive research and development. An excited freshman said: "BMW only has one American plant and it's here and that's sweet. Clemson is going to be one of the best places to study automotive engineering." However, prospective engineering students and car enthusiasts should be warned that the program is not easy. Students report that engineering's high number of requirements significantly cut down course options for underclassmen.

Clemson students apply to one of five different colleges: Agriculture, Forestry, and Life Sciences; Arts, Architecture and Humanities; Business and Behavioral Science; Engineering and Science; or Health, Education and Human Development. Each semester, students must take 12 to 17 hours worth of classes a week. However, not all classes last the full duration of the semester. The ever-popular "Camping and Backpacking" course in the leisure skills department, for example, consists of two 75-minute classes for five weeks.

Clemson is a big public school, but students consider the class sizes to be about average. While some courses, such as the general chemistry lecture, can number up to 150 students, the average class size is 29. In terms of grading policies, grade inflation won't be found at Clemson, and, as one student simply put, "There is no rounding up here." The University recently completed a controversial two-year trial period of a plus/minus grading system in 2004 and is currently considering whether or not to implement such a system.

Sweet Home South Carolina?

Not quite. According to its students, Clemson apparently isn't so Southern in its hospitality. The rooms and the food earn subpar ratings and while there are new dorms, students complain that most on-campus facilities are "pretty run down and old." For this reason, it is not mandatory for freshmen to live on campus, but surprisingly "the 'horseshoe' is the place to be freshman year—on warm days the grassy area behind the highrises, 'Lever Beach,' is covered with bikini-clad girls tanning and guys tossing the football around; at night there's tons of people hanging around outside—normally waiting for shuttles to the big frat parties going on that night." Those who do choose to stay and live in freshman dorms, including one not-so-affectionately called Shoeboxes, give the experience high acclaim. As one student

put it, "You might rag on the rooms while you live there, but the social scene and good times make it a place you never stop missing and reminiscing about long after you have to move out."

Looking to foster intellectual and social relationships, Clemson tends to group students in dorms based on interests. Marveled one student: "My entire hall is engineering students. It makes it easier in terms of studying." Another emphasized, "It's better to be closer to the people in your field because you can get input and feedback from them more easily and vice versa." A few particularly sought out housing options are the Stadium Suites and the Lightsey Apartments, but such options are also significantly more expensive. Stadium Suites is a four-story building right by the stadium, making it an ideal location for football fans, though one student lamented, "there's one tree in the way that prevents you from seeing the game from your suite."

The food options at Clemson are far from gourmet. They consist mostly of retail food courts and there are two dining halls—one for east campus and one for west campus. While some students say the food quality has improved in recent years, others complain that "the food gets old. They're the same thing everyday." A popular student center called the Hendrix Center was erected in the year 2000. Along with other standard food court items, at Hendrix, students can purchase Clemson ice cream and Clemson's other, slightly more eclectic, specialty: blue cheese. Such delicacies are due in large part to Clemson's Department of Food Science and Human Nutrition, and students appreciate its contributions in the center. "The Hendrix Center is the central spot. [Clemson] kind of centralized everything that was once a bit scattered. You used to have to walk really far to get good food."

Zoom Zoom

While the BMW engineering center awaits completion, most students (freshmen included) satisfy their thirst for automotives by keeping their cars on campus. One student warned, "You absolutely need a car." Many students find Clemson isolated and a bit too "in the middle of nowhere." Anderson is the closest "decent-sized" town and Greenville is in the vicinity as well, but both are beyond walking distance. Other students defended the campus and one insisted that "it's beautiful. A lot of the colleges are in the city, but here, you have a real campus feel because you know everyone on campus is pretty much a student." Many bored students go off campus and into the town on weekends to party and go to bars. Since most of the Clemson population is from South Carolina, many also visit home on weekends but only if there's an away game. Stated one student, "If there's not a football game, it's pretty dead. . . . We become a suitcase college. Everyone packs up and goes."

> "If there's not a football game, it's pretty dead. . . . We become a suitcase college. Everyone packs up and goes."

Where Is My Car?

So what's the catch to Clemson's well-known reputation as being a party school? According to students, the boast-worthy reputation only holds for the 25 percent of students in fraternities and sororities. One dejected student lamented, "I don't know how welcome I'd be. They're not too inviting." Another said, "If you're not a friend, for the most part, you can't get in [to the fraternities and sororities]." With only four bars and one on-campus pub around, one frat brother said, "I'm glad I pledged." So what's a fun-seeking non-Greek Clemson student to do? Turn to the strong athletic community, of course. Students note that some of the "big sports teams" step up and are known to throw their own parties and dances.

Alcohol is prevalent on campus, but if anyone gets caught, the University cracks down seriously for a period of time. "They know you're going to drink, but they want you to keep it inside. You can definitely get away with drinking." The University apparently prefers to being kept in the dark about its students' drinking habits. According to one student, "Signs around campus say 60 percent of students have 0–4 drinks a week, but I seriously don't believe that."

Southern Belles and Gentlemen

While the alcohol may flow freely, students report no need for beer goggles at Clemson. One male student raved that "the girls are hot. There are slightly more guys than girls, but there are a lot of good-looking girls. It's not like Georgia Tech." Are such claims too good to be true, or at least too good to last? Some Clemson students are upset at the University's recent attempts to make the admission process more difficult. One upset individual complained that "They're making entrances too hard. They're trying to get into the top 20 list because they're 27 right now on some list . . . so they're making everything ridiculous and we're just getting more and more engineering dorks."

Dorks included, the Clemson student body as a whole can be characterized as typically Southern and some say even a bit closed-minded. Students report very little diversity in terms of color and perspective. One student expressed that "the only black people here are pretty much athletes. Honestly, if I were black, I wouldn't want to go here." A minority student confirmed his sentiments: "The education is everything I expected. Clemson doesn't have the total package of college I was expecting, but I got the main thing I came here to get. I'd do the college thing over if I could." Yet another student stated that, in the dining halls, "It's a little bit self-segregated. Nothing new from high school." Students went as far to say that one campus building, the Strom Thurmond Institute, proves disconcerting to the numerous students who pass it on their way to classes everyday and one student wondered, "I'm wondering what sort of message that sends to students."

While students report that Clemson may not provide the varying and stimulating perspectives a more diverse college might provide, they also stress its strengths and the high quality of its education. "It would be almost impossible for someone to find a school with more pride than Clemson." It's definitely the place to be.—*Robert James*

FYI

If you come to Clemson, you'd better bring "orange."

What is the typical weekend schedule? "Party or stay in with movies or go out to eat Thurs and Fri. On football weekends, Saturday is entirely football—tailgates before and after the game, and usually a party afterwards, whether we win or lose. Sunday is the recovery and study day."

If I could change one thing about Clemson, I'd "make it snow in the wintertime, because it only gets cold enough to snow every so often."

Three things every student at Clemson should do before leaving are "go swimming off of the dam, play our Frisbee golf course, and get involved with one of our student organizations."

Furman University

Address: 3300 Poinsett Highway Greenville, SC 29613

Phone: 864-294-2034

E-mail address: admissions@furman.edu

Web site URL: www.furman.edu

Year Founded: 1826

Private or Public: Private

Religious Affiliation: None

Location: Urban

Number of Applicants: 4,414

Percent Accepted: 57%

Percent Accepted who enroll: 30%

Number Entering: 754

Number of Transfers Accepted each Year: 45

Middle 50% SAT range: M: 590–690, CR: 590–690, Wr: 580–680

Middle 50% ACT range: 26–30

Early admission program EA/ED/None: ED

Percentage accepted through EA or ED: 56%

EA and ED deadline: 15-Nov

Regular Deadline: 15-Jan

Application Fee: $50

Full time Undergraduate enrollment: 2,801

Total enrollment: 2,970

Percent Male: 43%

Percent Female: 57%

Total Percent Minority or Unreported: 20%

Percent African-American: 7%

Percent Asian/Pacific Islander: 3%

Percent Hispanic: 2%

Percent Native-American: <1%

Percent International: 2%

Percent in-state/out of state: 30%/70%

Percent from Public HS: 63%

Retention Rate: 92%

Graduation Rate 4-year: 80%

Graduation Rate 6-year: 84%

Percent Undergraduates in On-campus housing: 91%

Number of official organized extracurricular organizations: 143

3 Most popular majors: Communications, History, Political Science and Government

Student/Faculty ratio: 11:1

Average Class Size: 10 to 19

Percent of students going to grad school: 40%

Tuition and Fees: $34,568

In State Tuition and Fees if different: No difference

Cost for Room and Board: $8,966

Percent receiving financial aid out of those who apply, first year: 69%

Percent receiving financial aid among all students: 42%

Upon entering the gates of Furman University, many students forget that they're at college as they stand before what looks like the grounds of a country club. Located 15 minutes away from downtown Greenville, South Carolina, Furman offers its students a strong liberal arts education in a traditional Southern setting. Furman boasts an extraordinarily beautiful and welcoming campus, featuring numerous fountains, a giant lake, a golf course, a spectacular rose garden, and even a black swan (a gift from an alumnus). One student described the appeal of Furman's campus as "so perfect, it's almost unreal."

Spending Time with "James"

While the country club allure and what one student described as the "Fantasy of Furman" are striking, the way students and faculty treat academics is far from a walk in the park. "Academically, students at Furman have a high regard for themselves," a sophomore noted. "There are a lot of people who take their school work very seriously." With the amount of General Education requirements they have, it's no wonder that Furman students have the option to hit the books at all hours of the night, as the library study lounges are open 24/7. However, one student noted that, "While there's a pretty big laundry list of GC's you have to have, they're not extremely difficult courses." One of these requirements is dubbed "Ultimate Questions," an interesting name for a course in religion and ethics that reflects Furman's former religious affiliation. Freshmen are also required to take two seminar-style classes as an introduction to Furman, covering topics such as "Contemporary Issues in Film," "How Science Shapes our Views," and "What is and isn't Language." This is a newly instituted program, and current freshmen expressed mixed feelings about these seminars, saying that they are "either a hit or a miss." At Furman, there's also another unique set of requirements, called Cultural Life Programs or "CLP's" where students must attend 32 events, performances, and speakers.

Furman students have a tendency to

double major, and one sophomore observed, "What really sets Furman apart, students say, is its excellent faculty. "For some reason, middle of nowhere South Carolina has just brewed incredible teachers," marveled one student. There is also widespread agreement that "the class size really differentiates Furman from other schools." The average class size is 18, and the largest lectures contain a mere 35 people. Teachers strongly urge students to attend their office hours and expect to establish a relationship with them. As one student put it, "Everyone cares so much about their education, it's contagious."

It's No New York . . .

Students from farther north than Maryland be warned—you may be in for a culture shock. Despite sharing the liberal arts model of schools in the Northeast, Furman University is culturally very Southern. The majority of its students hail from the southern states of South Carolina, Tennessee and Georgia, and the sound of "Yes ma'am's" and "Yes sir's," is as central to Furman as the lake located in the middle of its campus. Sundresses, pearls, boat shoes and bow ties dominate tailgates, and smiling and waving to people who you may have met only once is the norm. "You definitely won't see people wearing hipster, New York-ish stuff," laughed one student. However, some students urge against this stereotype, saying that there is definitely an "outdoorsy," "borderline hippie" sub-culture if you look for it, and the predominantly southern demographic "doesn't mean that everyone will fit into that southern lady, southern gentleman mold."

Even taking this subculture into account, there seems to be an agreement that "the main student, to be perfectly honest, would be a conservative, preppy, kind of straight laced person," as one student described. Furman students also tend to be fairly wealthy, as evidenced by the numerous high-end cars on campus and their weekly forays to restaurants in Greenville.

Students also commented on the homogeneity of Furman, which is widely acknowledged as an issue, if not a pressing one. "Race-wise, it's definitely predominantly white and it's not very integrated," said one student. "In general, you tend to see the same kind of person. It's one of the more negative things about Furman."

That Southern Tradition

At Furman, it's not uncommon to see a student squealing and laughing as he or she is unceremoniously dumped into a lake. While someone on a tour of the school might be alarmed, most onlookers at Furman don't cringe at this spectacle; they know that it's an affectionate way for a student's brother hall to offer its birthday wishes. Each dormitory is divided into halls, and each hall has a "brother" or "sister" hall with which it participates in social activities. It's light-hearted traditions like these that make Furman so much fun for its undergraduates. Freshmen begin their life at Furman with the famed "my tie" dance at "O week," knowing that as seniors they will mark the end of their four years with an epic session of "fountain hopping." Some traditions, however, are slightly more serious. For example, if a student kisses someone under the bell tower, word is that they'll probably be getting hitched to that person in the near future. One freshman explained, "A lot of people talk about marriage. It's very much a 'find your one' kind of thing."

> **"For some reason, middle of nowhere South Carolina has just brewed incredible teachers."**

During "O week," freshmen are introduced to what will initially dictate their social life (at least until spring, when rush takes over): their hall. Over the course of a week, they make cheers, compete with other halls, create silly dances, and get to know their peers in a setting that is "exactly like summer camp." Each hall has a theme like the "Harlem Globetrotters," "Where's Waldo," and "Lilly Pulitzer." Halls plan outings and participate in activities together throughout the school year, providing an immediate and nurturing community. While Greek life is a huge feature at Furman, one sorority girl noted, "The difference is you still maintain close friendships with your hall." However, "Hall is not a make or break kind of situation. If you don't like your hall, stick it out, because spring semester is a ton more fun than fall," she added.

Lakeside Divides

Furman's Southern flavor is mixed with the aftertaste of the school's former Baptist affiliations. The result: a schism on campus between drinkers (typically Greek) and their more religious peers. "Some people who go to church and who are a little more religious do separate themselves. They have their cliques," admitted one student. "It can be hard to find people who both drink and go to church. It's either one or the other," added another student. However, one sophomore stated that if you do party at Furman, you're most likely the "good Southern Christian boy who parties on Saturday night and gets cleaned up to go to church on Sunday morning."

While Furman claims to be a dry campus, it's been revealed to be a "damp campus" in reality. Drinkers generally party off campus at frats or at their favorite bars in Greenville. While alcohol policies certainly aren't lenient, and there can be some "crazy RA's," for the most part, students can get away with their debauchery if they're smart about it.

For those who don't frequent the drinking frats, there is always something to do on campus. Furman Undergraduate Student Activities Board (FUSAB) is constantly putting on events and concerts, bringing in speakers (including all of the presidential candidates for the 2008 election), and sponsoring screenings of movies such as *Pineapple Express*. However, most students are content with their weekly routine of dinner in Greenville and a movie night in the dorm with friends.

Purple . . . and GREEN

While you may see students clad in purple at a football game, it's probably by accident. Students reported a lack of school spirit at athletic events, and after the Saturday morning football tailgate, most students call it quits after the first quarter. "We're kind of apathetic when it comes to sports," said a former cheerleader.

Fortunately, there are plenty of other arenas that Furman students get passionate about. There are myriad student groups on campus, ranging from those addressing social justice issues to the ever-popular Christian organizations, like the Fellowship of Christian Athletes. The Outdoor Club is incredibly well funded, as is Furman's Student Activities Board, which has worked with budgets of over $250,000. Students also take advantage of the campus itself in their spare time. "Because campus is so beautiful, you can run around the lake or into the woods. You can't do that in big city schools," acknowledged one appreciative student.

Recently, Furman has made a concerted effort to address sustainability. It hosts Cliffs Cottage, *Southern Living*'s first showcase of a sustainable home, right on campus. The public is encouraged to explore the home, and Furman's Office of Sustainability and Environmental Education is soon to be relocated there. Students and faculty alike are the driving force behind the University's exciting green initiatives, and there are plenty of opportunities to get involved.

The Progressive South

Furman is the type of place where students can finish a complex lab report while sitting in rocking chairs on a porch and chatting with friends. It offers a Southern lifestyle with progressive approaches to the areas like technology and environment, designating it as a "new age type of university." With its friendly students and nurturing (though somewhat homogenous and conservative) environment, Furman is a wonderful place to be. When asked, more than one student said, "Oh yeah, I'd choose Furman all over again."—*Raphaella Friedman*

FYIs

If you come you'd better bring "Pearls and a sundress, and be able to tie a bow tie."

What's the typical weekend schedule? "Finish classes on Friday, might study for a few hours, go out to dinner with friends downtown. You might stay out a little later at a frat on Friday, or go back and watch a movie with some friends. Saturday, put on your pearls, go to the tailgate, go to the football game, maybe study for a few hours, do something low key at night like walking along the waterfall downtown, come back, go to sleep early because you have church in the morning, after church study all day."

If I could change on thing about Furman, I'd "make it more diverse in all senses of the word. Geographically, racially, socially, politically."

University of South Carolina

Address: Admissions Office
Columbia, SC 29208
Phone: 803-777-7000
E-mail address: admissions
ugrad@sc.edu
Web site URL: www.sc.edu
Year Founded: 1801
Private or Public: Public
Religious Affiliation: None
Location: Urban
Number of Applicants:
Unreported
Percent Accepted: 59%
**Percent Accepted who
enroll:** Unreported
Number Entering: 3,719
**Number of Transfers
Accepted each Year:** 2,055
Middle 50% SAT range:
M: 550–650, CR: 540–640,
Wr: Unreported
Middle 50% ACT range: 23–28
**Early admission program
EA/ED/None:** EA
**Percentage accepted
through EA or ED:**
Unreported

EA and ED deadline: 1-Oct
Regular Deadline: 1-Dec
Application Fee: $50
**Full time Undergraduate
enrollment:** 18,827
Total enrollment: 25,823
Percent Male: 43%
Percent Female: 57%
**Total Percent Minority or
Unreported:** 4%
Percent African-American:
8%
**Percent Asian/Pacific
Islander:** 3%
Percent Hispanic: 2%
Percent Native-American:
<1%
Percent International: 1%
**Percent in-state/out of
state:** 62%/38%
Percent from Public HS:
Unreported
Retention Rate: 87%
Graduation Rate 4-year:
Unreported
Graduation Rate 6-year:
Unreported

**Percent Undergraduates
in On-campus housing:**
40%
**Number of official organized
extracurricular
organizations:** Unreported
3 Most popular majors:
Business/Marketing,
Social Sciences,
Communications/Journalism
Student/Faculty ratio:
16:1
Average Class Size: Less
than 30
**Percent of students going
to grad school:** Unreported
Tuition and Fees: $22,908
**In State Tuition and Fees if
different:** $8,838
Cost for Room and Board:
$6,652
**Percent receiving financial
aid out of those who apply,
first year:** 56%
**Percent receiving financial
aid among all students:**
41%

I n spite of initial reservations, "within a week I was obsessed," one senior said of her initial experience at South Carolina University. This passion seems to extend to most of USC students, who sing their school's praises and show their collegiate pride at the drop of a hat or the blow of a whistle. Displays of devotion are especially evident at the popular, and often over the top, football games. But South Carolina University offers so much more than just grand sporting events. The academic programs, extensive extracurricular choices and an exhausting party scene all contribute to forming a memorable experience that most students, when given the choice, would wish to live all over again.

University 101

Despite South Carolina's large student body, there are few complaints about becoming just a number. The class sizes at the University vary widely from 20 to 300, with intro classes generally on the high end of the spectrum. However, large lectures come equipped with smaller discussion sections to ensure that each student gets personal attention. "I have never taken a class that had more than 50 students," one Honors College student said. Other students praised the numerous options for more intimate academic settings, often citing the professor for "making" the class. One senior raved that "[the professors] have been nothing but awesome," and students have generally described the professorship as being friendly, easily accessible, and diligent to learn the names of all of their students. Among the faculty sit several famous names such as Don Fowler, the former chairman of the Democratic National Committee.

With 14 schools to choose from, the University offers something for everyone. The major unanimously proclaimed as the most popular and also the most difficult is the number one, nationally-ranked International Business program. The major accepts only 50 people each year and attracts students from all over the country, as well as many from overseas. South Carolina also offers unique majors such as Sports and Entertainment Management or Hotel and Restaurant Tourism Management. And for the top qualified students of each year, the University features an Honors Program and Capstone Scholars. For freshmen, an atypical class that is offered and sometimes required is University 101, a class that focuses solely on helping students adjust and make the best of university life. Aside from the required English, social science, and history courses (all of which students can place out of), there is a unique assortment of ways students can expand their knowledge, whether by learning how to shag—the dance, that is—or by taking a wine-tasting class or studying Super Bowl commercials (it's actually a class) to vary their schedules. Overall, the workload itself is deemed manageable. Some students complain about the large amounts of reading they receive, but as one sophomore explained, "People are not missing out on social life."

Where the Beer Is Green and the Beach Is Near

South Carolina offers many great ways to have a good time. Although many students contend that no particular social scene dominates, the Greek parties are the most common ones listed. For the 21+ crowd (or those with really good IDs) there are the Five Points downtown bars. People usually start going out on Thursday night, especially with Thursday being "college night" in the downtown area.

Even though only about 16 percent of students belong to a sorority or a fraternity, students generally agree that Greek life is "really noticeable." During the first week of school, one of the most prominent things on campus is the excess of flyers inviting people to rush. And students estimate that a majority of the population does rush, especially girls. "During my freshman year half the kids on my floor rushed," one senior remembered. The Greeks, in addition to hosting regular weekend parties, also organize many exclusive theme parties and are the driving force behind Homecoming week festivities.

Nevertheless, as a senior pointed out, "you can have fun even if you're not Greek." Big annual celebrations include St. Patrick's Day at Five Points, when everything is blocked off from the city and the beer is green. Halloween weekend is "always fun." Many alternative entertainment options are provided by the student-run Carolina Productions. The group organizes main events on campus such

as concerts, the Wacky Wednesday Booth that plans something new and fun for each Wednesday at the Student Center, and has even been responsible for bringing Bob Saget to campus. For a more low-key night, there are the dorm parties, which are especially popular for underclassmen. But be forewarned. Despite the abundance of partying on campus, the drinking rules are strict—SLED or undercover officers patrol the area and are quick to enforce the rules. All freshman dorms are labeled dry and all rooms in the upperclassmen dorms in which persons under 21 reside are dry, as well. However, as one freshman observed, "You can drink in the dorm—if you can get away with it." The ability to "get away with it" mainly depends on your RA and on how belligerent you become. One junior pointed out that although "we are not a dry campus," people are understanding of those who do not drink. As an alternative to partying, many students take weekend trips to the plentiful beaches of Charleston.

Our Stereotypes Are Diverse

Many come to South Carolina with the expectation of a crowd of typical southern girls and frat-guy types. But more often than not, students are pleasantly surprised by the diversity on campus. Although one junior described the day-to-day look as having "a beachy atmosphere—there are shorts and sandals everywhere," there is a greater stylistic range. But it doesn't mean there aren't stereotypes. As one sophomore put it, "You can definitely pick out the Greeks by their clothes, and you can definitely pick out 'emos' by their clothes." Nevertheless, there is a fair amount of geographic and ethnic diversity. Students hail from all 50 states and there is a well-represented international community at South Carolina. Some students acknowledge, however, that the campus often has segregation lines among groups—whites and blacks have their own separate frats and parties. "Walking around campus you [would] think it is segregated," said one student. Students, however, assure that there is no tension on campus, and that the relations among races are by no means "uncivil." Students are making strides to creating a more unified collegiate atmosphere, which even in its current state is still generally described as very friendly.

Horseshoes and Pizza Huts

Due to numerous dorm renovation projects, one senior explained that "housing right now is in limbo." Still, all freshmen are required to live on campus, spread out between the freshman-only dorms, many of which are single-sex with strict visitation rules for prospective guests of the opposite sex. All freshman dorms feature suite-style rooms (two double bedrooms, a common room and a bathroom). Due to dorm renovations, the upperclassmen are not guaranteed housing. However, this lack of guarantee is not a major problem; many, if not most, upperclassmen prefer off-campus housing—especially at the nearby university-exclusive apartment complexes. For those who choose to stay on campus, there are several coed options, including Roost, which mainly houses athletes, and The Green Dorm, a completely environmentally friendly habitat. The University also offers several themed communities such as the French community, the Spanish community (where they speak only the language of affiliation), the International community, and the Music community. Currently, the University is building a multimillion-dollar Research community. The Greeks, especially in their sophomore year, often opt to reside in the multimillion-dollar houses that populate the Greek Village. All students are able to bring cars, and it seems like all do. Parking, or lack thereof, is the most common complaint heard from the students. "To get to class on time, you have to get there 30 minutes before to find a spot to park," one student warned.

> **"Everyone here is obsessed with football, even those who are not athletic."**

South Carolina University students vote the campus food as "Most likely to make you gain the Freshman 15." There are five dining halls, including the Russell House, which serves both as the student union and the grand marketplace or main dining hall. Dining options include everything from a salad bar to an overabundance of fast food chains like Burger King, Chic-Fil-A, Taco Bell, and Pizza Hut, where students can use their meal plans. Luckily, the city houses many privately owned restaurants that, all in all, "give the city more character."

The campus itself is pretty with a smattering of modern industrial buildings, many newly renovated buildings, and—of course—the horseshoe with "an old, traditional, southern feel to it." The horseshoe—you guessed it—is shaped like a horseshoe and serves as the main, grassy hangout area for students looking to picnic or play Frisbee. Most importantly, the campus is regarded as safe. "Considering the size of this university, they have done a good job of protecting us," one student praised. Call boxes which are located throughout campus (you can't turn around without seeing at least one) serve as emergency call services. A shuttle service also operates on campus.

The Loyal Gamecocks

Many students at South Carolina "rely on organizations to find [their] niche" a senior observed. Some of the more prominent groups include Student Government, the Triple A's (Association of African-Americans), and Carolina Productions. For the politically aspirant, there are the College Republicans and Young Dems; for the journalistically inclined, there is the *Daily Gamecock*; and for the socially focused, there are 14 sororities and 19 frats from which to choose.

If all else fails, the uniting theme of the University seems to be sports. Club and intramural sports serve as competitive, but very fun, alternatives to varsity. But perhaps the most popular ways for being involved in the athletic life is actually just attending the varsity games. South Carolina's talented teams are fun to watch and support. The baseball and basketball games are both very well attended, but football remains king. People fight for tickets, which sell out almost immediately. "Everyone here is obsessed with football, even those who are not athletic," one sophomore declared. The annual game against archrival Clemson is among the most exciting and is preceded by the Tiger Burn—a pep rally and ceremonial burning of a papier-mâché Clemson Tiger. The proud Gamecocks attend the games dressed in their best—pearls, cocktail dresses, blazers, and bow tie. The tailgates begin at noon and last for about five or more hours until the game begins. The Gamecocks are known for their loyalty; they cheer loudly until the last minute, win or lose.

It is easy to get swept up in the enthusiasm of the football crowd of the always-filled-to-the-brim William-Brice Stadium. Such an exhilarating feeling is a good reflection of the mentality of South Carolina University's students. Any initial reservations incoming students might have are quickly replaced by feelings of school pride and affection. Because whether it be the campus, the vast array of extracurriculars or the friendly people, it is good to be a Gamecock.—*Dorota Poplawska*

FYI

If you come to South Carolina, you'd better bring "Rainbows (sandals that everyone wears) and dressy clothes for those football games."

What is the typical weekend schedule? "Thursday attend college night at Five Points and party on Friday. Saturdays are dominated by tailgates and football games that take up all day. Catch up on work Sunday after sleeping in or going to church."

If I could change one thing about South Carolina, I'd "add more parking spaces."

Three things every student at South Carolina should do before graduating are "go to Five Points, stay till the end of a football game, and get to know a professor on a more personal basis."

Wofford College

Address: 429 North Church Street Spartanburg, SC 29303
Phone: 864-597-4182
E-mail address: boggsdw@wofford.edu
Web site URL: www.wofford.edu
Year Founded: 1854
Private or Public: Private
Religious Affiliation: United Methodist
Location: Suburban
Number of Applicants: 2,278
Percent Accepted: 59%
Percent Accepted who enroll: 31%
Number Entering: 415
Number of Transfers Accepted each Year: 17
Middle 50% SAT range: M: 570–680, CR: 560–660, Wr: 560–660
Middle 50% ACT range: 22–27

Early admission program EA/ED/None: ED
Percentage accepted through EA or ED: 64%
EA and ED deadline: 15-Nov
Regular Deadline: 1-Feb
Application Fee: $50
Full time Undergraduate enrollment: 1,389
Total enrollment: 1,389
Percent Male: 52%
Percent Female: 48%
Total Percent Minority or Unreported: 13%
Percent African-American: 6%
Percent Asian/Pacific Islandler: 3%
Percent Hispanic: 2%
Percent Native-American: 0%
Percent International: 3%
Percent in-state/out of state: 60 %/40%
Percent from Public HS: 61%
Retention Rate: 91%

Graduation Rate 4-year: 79%
Graduation Rate 6-year: 83%
Percent Undergraduates in On-campus housing: 96%
Number of official organized extracurricular organizations: 105
3 Most popular majors: Biology, Finance, Government
Student/Faculty ratio: 11:1
Average Class Size: 20
Percent of students going to grad school: 49%
Tuition and Fees: $29,465
In State Tuition and Fees if different: No difference
Cost for Room and Board: $8,190
Percent receiving financial aid out of those who apply, first year: 52%
Percent receiving financial aid among all students: 52%

Wofford College offers a tight-knit community and strong teacher-student relationships for a student body that is smaller than that of most high schools. With approximately 1,300 students, Wofford reserves its solid, liberal arts education for a select group of students. Its location in the traditional South impacts student culture; it's no surprise to students that "many of the ladies went to debutante balls." But Wofford stands out primarily for its Division 1 Athletics. With such a small student body, "one in six guys plays football." Pearls, sports, and prep don't diminish the fact that Wofford is widely respected for its premedi-

cine program and "many students go into politics" after graduation. There's no doubt that Wofford grads impact the lives of South Carolinians since "three of the South Carolina State Supreme Court justices graduated from Wofford."

Is There a Doctor in the Classroom?

Opened in 1854 and still affiliated with the Methodist Church, Wofford has remained small by choice. The administration reportedly has no plans to expand enrollment, but instead plans to concentrate on providing a select group of students with a strong education in the humanities, arts and sciences. Students say that "the small class sizes are really nice." One student warned, however, that due to Wofford's size, "there is not a wide variety of classes." Professors are especially accessible and maintain an "open door policy," according to students. "I didn't expect the professors to be so understanding, but they are like high school teachers in that sense. They want to help you out." Undergraduates are required to take courses in the humanities, English, fine arts, foreign language, science, history, philosophy, math, physical education and religion. These general education requirements are meant to ensure that, by the end of their first two years, students will have taken some classes they normally would not have considered. Students are also required to complete four interim projects. The month of January is designated as Interim, a time between the two regular semesters when students can research, travel, take an internship, or work on an independent project. Interim projects on campus can include courses such as *The Passion of the Christ* as Film, Sacred Art, Theology, and Cultural Maelstrom" or "Web Design For People Who Do Other Things For a Living." Off-campus travel programs in January 2009 included "Cornbread and Sushi on the Road" and "Intense in Tents: African Culture & Ecology in Namibia." Internship projects and service learning can even take you to Capitol Hill for a month. The Interim permits and encourages teachers and students to explore the new and untried. Even more exciting, most interim projects are graded Pass/Fail.

Among the most popular majors at Wofford are biology, business economics, political science, history and English. "Business Economics is seen as a fairly easy program," one student said, "and sociology is picked on for having the easiest major." But "in general everyone respects each other because every major requires a lot of time and effort." The science department is reported to be particularly strong. One student said that, as a physics major, "people tend to hold me in somewhat (unwarranted) high regard because there are so few of us. I have a class this semester where I am the only student in the class." But there is no doubt that the sciences and particularly the biology major are "top-notch" at Wofford and many students go on to medical school.

Tech Savvy

Wofford's efforts to provide cutting-edge technical services to its students are highlighted in a January 2006 article on "Coolest Campus Tech" on the *Forbes* Web site (www.forbes.com). The article focuses on the Wofford program called FYI (First Year Interface), which allows freshmen to meet and greet via a MySpace-style Web site. After sharing profiles, photos, bedtimes and partying habits on the site, Wofford lets students who hit it off become roommates. Students may also contact members of the Student Life staff with questions about what to expect when preparing to come to Wofford. The student profiles are searchable for similar interests, geographic areas and other information. Wofford also has begun posting podcasts to its Web site (www.wofford.edu) for downloading and listening to audio recordings of campus programs and events. Wofford not only uses technology to help its students acclimate to campus. In 2002, Wofford began The Novel Experience—a program that asks incoming students to read an assigned novel over the summer and to write essays prior to arrival in Spartanburg. In early September, a town-gown exercise takes place when student groups and professors are assigned to eat at local restaurants through a lottery, discussing the novel over dinner. About a week later, the author comes to campus for a special address. "Talking with the author and the professors was definitely a highlight," one student said. "Because it happens in the first week of school, you go with your humanities class and you get to know them really well. It helped to make it more comfortable." Rising freshmen also have the option to attend a program called The Summit. This program takes place before the start of school, and new students spend a few days at a summer camp and go whitewater rafting. "It's where you first meet most of the people you come to hang out with."

Dorm Life: A Necessary Experience

An online lottery system sorts all dorm assignments and seniority is prioritized. Halls are coed in four of the dorms; two other dorms have two all-girl halls and all-guy halls per floor. The two freshman dorms accommodate men and women separately. Marsh Hall—the freshman dorm for men—is known as "particularly miserable, crazy, and disgusting all at the same time. But all in all, a necessary experience." Greene Hall is the freshmen girls' dorm and "where freshman guys spend most of their time." All students living in dorms have the convenient advantage of a five- or 10-minute walk to classroom buildings. "If I wake up late at 9:20 I can still get to a 9:30 class." On the way, students enjoy the shade of many oak trees or stop to lounge on the benches near the central campus field. There are plans in the works to provide a type of campus "village" to students, comprised of apartment-like facilities in renovated houses Wofford has purchased. Campus is "much safer" than the surrounding areas in Spartanburg. According to students, "it's kind of a rough town in places" and "people tend to stay within the 'Wofford bubble.'"

Frat Row, Football, and More

"Greek life at Wofford is huge" and more than 50 percent of the student body is Greek. The fraternity row (location on campus for fraternity houses and called "the row" by students) is the dominant social scene on campus. It's a popular site for a shaving cream fight and "you can't miss out on slip-and-slide at the row." "The frat row is a typical site of first-time meetings between folks." One of the most talked-about days of the year is Guys' Bid Day, when freshman boys find out which fraternity they're pledging. A popular celebration follows. Spring Weekend has many activities and is a time when "you should party extremely hard." In addition to the popular varsity athletic teams, like men's and women's basketball, "we have an ultimate Frisbee team and a fly fishing organization—which is funded by the school for their equipment and trips." One student called it "a sweet gig."

Wofford and Spartanburg are not interchangeable. With the exception of a few bars and the "gracious discounts" many local businesses offer to students, there is not much interaction. "I don't think that the two are intertwined unless there is an athletic event," one student said. Another student pointed out that "the town's heyday was gone years ago because it was once a big textile city." Wofford is located in "an underprivileged area, so we interact with the community in a variety of ways through service learning and volunteer work," a student said. Wofford reportedly hosts two events during the school year for children in the area to attend. One student said that "Wofford does a great job interacting with the surrounding community." Student groups on campus include Campus Ambassadors, students who volunteer their time to give tours to prospective students, and the Fellowship of Christian Athletes (FCA), which involves many students and "is held in high regard." The Outdoors Club is another option for bikers, hikers and climbers. "Most students are passionate about the clubs they are involved in" and "each group has their fanatics."

Southern Ladies and Gents

There's no getting around it. Most students say that "Wofford is typically viewed as a white, conservative school." Students who attend Wofford are "particularly preppy and from 'old money' families or parents with white-collar careers." One student said, "It seems like everyone's dad is either a doctor or an attorney." While some students admitted there is geographic diversity and students definitely come to Wofford from a variety of states in the Southeast—"there seems like there are as many out-of-state students as there are in-state"—ethnic diversity is not strong. "It's not diverse. Only about 10 percent of the school is made up of minority students." The "frat look" is very popular with "Sperry's, khakis, and sunglasses with Croakies making a dominant appearance all over campus" and "pastel colors are worn by both guys and girls." According to another student, "The attitude is a positive and confident one. Students are proud to be at Wofford." While the Wofford student is stereotypically characterized as rich and preppy, "there are many people who do not fit this stereotype at all. In general, everyone here is friendly and you can always expect a hello when walking down the sidewalks on campus." The same mentality translates to the classroom where "there's always a comfortable setting. You just raise your hand if you have a question and the teacher will answer you."

"Students Are Proud to Be at Wofford."

Any school that takes as much pride in its history as Wofford does is bound to have unique traditions. Old Main was the foundational building of the University and features a misspelled plaque that reads "benificent" rather than "beneficent." For Wofford students, rubbing the mislaid "i" brings them luck on exams. If you're a student who desires personal attention at a small liberal arts college and hopes for the benefits of an incredible network of alumni—"who are always there to offer jobs to the next graduates"—Wofford's luck is just waiting to rub off on you.—*Bess Hinson*

FYI

If you come to Wofford, you'd better bring "sunglasses with Croakies, polo shirts, pearls, and a flask."

What's the typical weekend schedule? "A sports game or workout during the day. Next, dinner or a movie with friends and then to fraternity row all night."

If you could change one thing about Wofford, it'd be "more diversity—a larger variety of students who are also more open-minded."

Three things every student at Wofford should do before graduating are "swim in the fountain after jumping in the mud on Guys' Bid Day, ring the bell in the Old Main building, and date someone."

South Dakota

University of South Dakota

Address: 414 East Clark Street Vermillion, SD 57069

Phone: 605-677-5434

E-mail address: admissions@usd.edu

Web site URL: www.usd.edu

Year Founded: 1862

Private or Public: Public

Religious Affiliation: None

Location: Rural

Number of Applicants: 3,499

Percent Accepted: 80%

Percent Accepted who enroll: 37%

Number Entering: 1,031

Number of Transfers Accepted each Year: 1,252

Middle 50% SAT range: M: 480–610, CR: 470–660, Wr: Unreported

Middle 50% ACT range: 20–25

Early admission program EA/ED/None: None

Percentage accepted through EA or ED: NA

EA and ED deadline: NA

Regular Deadline: Rolling

Application Fee: $20

Full time Undergraduate enrollment: 6,844

Total enrollment: 8,721

Percent Male: 38%

Percent Female: 62%

Total Percent Minority or Unreported: 15%

Percent African-American: 2%

Percent Asian/Pacific Islander: 1%

Percent Hispanic: 2%

Percent Native-American: 2%

Percent International: <1%

Percent in-state/out of state: 70%/30%

Percent from Public HS: 94%

Retention Rate: 72%

Graduation Rate, 4-year: 20%

Graduation Rate 6-year: 44%

Percent Undergraduates in On-campus housing: 31%

Number of official organized extracurricular organizations: 130

3 Most popular majors: Business/Marketing, Education, Health Professions

Student/Faculty ratio: 14:1

Average Class Size: 20 to 29

Percent of students going to grad school: 50%

Tuition and Fees: $7,148

In State Tuition and Fees if different: $5,828

Cost for Room and Board: $5,442

Percent receiving financial aid out of those who apply, first year: 64%

Percent receiving financial aid among all students: 53%

The University of South Dakota simply refuses to allow its students to have the normal college experience. Residential assistants routinely inspect dorms for alcohol and fine guilty students $100 in addition to enforcing probation. Vermillion, the town in which USD is located, lacks the clubs and pubs college students live for in other states. And football games, held outdoors at most colleges nationwide, are held indoors in the Dakota Dome, where students report it generally "gets kind of warm." It may all sound a tad bit stifling, but a closer look at USD shows that in fact quite the opposite is true.

Live, Local and Late-Breaking Majors . . .

USD is comprised of four different colleges: the College of Arts and Sciences, the School of Business, the School of Education, and the College of Fine Arts. The conveniently located School of Law and the School of Medicine also provide guidance and resources for students interested on a prelaw or premed track. Most USD students enter the College of Arts and Sciences and focus on a variety of majors within the wide-reaching and traditionally defined liberal arts realm. While there are many interesting majors to choose from, some concentrations, such as communications and business, rise to the top and attract the most students. And with distinguished alumni in media such as Tom Brokaw and Pat O'Brien, is it any wonder that most USD students flock to the strong mass communications department? While such large majors at USD dominate the spotlight, prospective students should also be aware of the comparatively smaller yet well-received concentrations that USD has to offer. Students sing the praises of the criminal justice department and describe the classes as "particularly interesting." Although USD is a state school, students are quick to point out that it's not overwhelming. With a student to faculty ratio of 15:1, USD rivals many state schools unable to boast such close interaction between students and staff.

USD students are generally described as "laid-back" and "not stressed," which may be attributed to the lack of pluses and minuses in the grading system as well as the open opportunity to take classes satisfactory/unsatisfactory (known in other college systems as "pass/fail"). One student even suggested that on a given weekday, most students, depending on major, are "all out getting drunk." However, another student disagreed with this assessment, stating that classes can be "pretty tough" and that studying is "what a lot of people do during the week, mainly." Regardless of whether USD students are holding a pen or a bottle on most weekday nights, students warn about exercising caution in choosing classes, as confused students might find that advising at USD is unable to meet their needs. As one student noted, "Even if you go down to talk to the advisors, they don't really help you all that much. You've got to do your own work and talk to older students."

More Tests?
Requirements at USD are atypical of the larger state university. Students are required to take a standardized test, the Collegiate Assessment of Academic Proficiency, before graduating, in addition to fulfilling a certain number of credit hours. These requirements, depending on college, focus on the study of mathematics, natural sciences, social sciences, and humanities and fine arts. Students are also required to take Introduction to Computers but can test out of it by taking an Information Technology Literacy Exam. All students are also required to take a test in Information Literacy. Non-compliance with taking these standardized tests, or failing them, results in an inability to graduate. With

all these tests, you'd expect USD students to be nervous wrecks, constantly walking around with their noses in books or perhaps lined up at the nearest coffee shop. Quite the opposite is true, in fact, students report that few of their peers are even aware of them. "I'm not aware of any such tests," said one student. And anyway, USD students are in good company, as there are also exam requirements for students at the five other state schools in South Dakota.

The Return of the Native . . . or Not
Since USD offers so many areas of studies, students find that they have the opportunity to meet a lot of different types of people. According to one student, "The personality of the student body is split because of all the different colleges. There's a really good mix." However, another student noted, "In a state with so much Native American history and culture, you'd expect to see more Native Americans on campus, but there aren't. There are a lot in the state and the area, but not here." The mostly white student body tends to dress "preppy in winter coats." It is, after all, South Dakota, where parkas are hot and the weather is not. Students report that while "the beginning of the school year and a bit of the end of year has nice weather," the rest of the year can be quite rough. However, most students at USD are native to South Dakota and have already acclimated themselves to cold climates. With the non-South Dakotans on campus hailing from Minnesota, Nebraska and Iowa, one can't expect too much complaining. The homogenous student body doesn't seem to bother many on campus. Overall, students state that USD is "big enough so that you get to know people and you can run into some people and have classes with them, but still get to meet new people."

And the Crowd Goes Wild
The Coyotes sure do know how to howl. Or maybe it's just the way the acoustics work inside the Dakota Dome. USD football players feel the love because in the Dome "it gets loud really fast and that makes us more excited to play," said one football player. The dome is just a short walk for students on campus. Other sports, including softball, track and field, swimming, volleyball, and basketball, also hold events inside the Dome. For the winter basketball season, the basketball court is placed in the middle of the Dome, bleachers are placed all around it, and

the result is the largest basketball arena in NCAA Division II. While this might sound appealing, one student actually said, "It kind of sucks for basketball though, because you never get enough people in the big Dome for it to get pretty loud." But while the acoustics of the large space might sometimes hamper the cheers, overall, school spirit on campus is widespread. One student noted that "you always see people wearing red stuff and stuff always supporting USD."

> **"[The Dome] gets loud really fast, and that makes us more excited to play."**

During homecoming week, the school sponsors a week-long festival officially called Dakota Days but fondly dubbed D-Days by the students. Involving the whole college, D-Days is "pretty crazy and the weekend is even crazier." On the weekdays, there are concerts by various artists and events such as Jell-O wrestling and mechanical-bull riding. On the Saturday, there is a parade and plenty of tailgating sponsored by booster clubs and local city businesses.

Runaway Students

After freshman and sophomore year, most students move off campus or into their fraternities or sororities. Why? Although residential assistants inform students about forthcoming alcohol searches and though "[residential assistants] don't want to get you in trouble," many students seek the freedom acquired from living off campus in houses. Students call their off-campus housing "a place of their own," and report that such residences are generally "fairly new, pretty big, and shared between six and eight people." These houses are also the epicenter of college life, with most non-fraternity and -sorority parties taking place at them. The dorms are in the process of slowly being renovated. Most rooms are doubles in a hallway where 40–60 people share five or six showers. The dorms, according to one gloomy student, "are the smallest in the state." Thus, fraternities and sororities prove a promising solution to many unhappy, cramped dorm-dwellers and also provide social opportunities.

Dancing Greeks, Halloween Treats

Students see fraternities and sororities as places there "to make finding friends a lot easier" and even "get into parties that only girls are usually let into." Students at USD keep busy. Many students are active in the Greek scene, which is active within the local community. During "Strollers," the Greek groups get together for "not quite a dance-off, but you stay up for 24 hours straight and you try to raise money and see who can dance the longest." During Halloween, students are requested to stay in their dorms for a period of time so little kids from around town can trick or treat.

Speaking of frat parties, USD policy is stringent on drinking—on-campus drinking, that is. One student said, "There are campus police walking around and if you get caught on campus, the penalty's usually pretty stiff, so not that many people drink on campus." Elaborated another: "The cops are not nice. They're out to get us. They should let us have fun. They'll stop us if we're even wearing backpacks to a party." Yet another student explained that generally "people go out in the field, build a fire. Drink." Other students stressed that alternatives to the drinking/fire-building/mad cop scene include going "to parties, concerts, and shows. We're not too far from Sioux Falls." Many students who live close to home also go home for the weekends, which is not surprising given that most USD students voice the opinion that "Vermillion is boring."

A Bit of the Old and a Bit of the New

USD is a campus in transition, and with many building projects and renovations in the works, its face is constantly changing. Lazy students will be happy to note that academic buildings at USD are within close proximity to each other, and the building facilities are "all pretty nice." With the exception of a few dorms, the campus buildings are relatively recent, and the fine arts building is "almost brand new." The medical school is currently under renovation, and a new Coyote Student Center opened in February 2009. Students report that the campus overall is "pretty safe" and the "biggest crime is probably having parties and getting busted for underage drinking." Dining halls are also conveniently located around campus and even were reported to be "better than expected" by one student. Students have the option of eating at Lakota Marketplace in the student center, Commons Dining Hall, and Charlie's Grille. Most students avoid Commons and eat at Lakota or Charlie's, where selection is said to be much better.

University of South Dakota is different from any other college. At USD, it is necessary to learn to balance an on-campus life of academics and community involvement with your off-campus life of cultural events and socializing in order to experience all that USD has to offer. Despite the apprehensions voiced about the size and isolation of Vermillion, strict RAs, and tests, students report that USD is still "better than expected."—*Anna Yu*

FYI
If you come to USD, you'd better bring "a ridiculously insulated winter coat."
What's the typical weekend schedule? "Study, sleep, and party."
If I could change one thing about USD I would have "nicer cops and more parking."
Three things that every student at USD should do before graduating are "attend Dakota Days, visit a frat, and visit upperclassmen houses."

Tennessee

Rhodes College

Address: 2000 North Parkway
  Memphis, TN 38112
Phone: 901-843-3700
E-mail address:
  adminfo@rhodes.edu
Web site URL:
  www.rhodes.edu
Year Founded: 1848
Private or Public: Private
Religious Affiliation:
  Presbyterian
Location: Urban
Number of Applicants: 3,747
Percent Accepted: 50%
**Percent Accepted who
  enroll:** 26%
Number Entering: 477
**Number of Transfers
  Accepted each Year:** 28
Middle 50% SAT range:
  M: 580–670, CR: 580–680,
  Wr: Unreported
Middle 50% ACT range: 26–30
**Early admission program
  EA/ED/None:** ED

**Percentage accepted
  through EA or ED:** 14%
EA and ED deadline: 1-Nov
Regular Deadline: NA
Application Fee: $45
**Full time Undergraduate
  enrollment:** 1,647
Total enrollment: 1,664
Percent Male: 43%
Percent Female: 57%
**Total Percent Minority or
  Unreported:** 22%
Percent African-American:
  7%
**Percent Asian/Pacific
  Islander:** 5%
Percent Hispanic: 2%
Percent Native-American:
  <1%
Percent International: 2%
**Percent in-state/out of
  state:** 26%/74%
Percent from Public HS: 50
Retention Rate: 85%
Graduation Rate 4-year: 69%

Graduation Rate 6-year: 72%
**Percent Undergraduates
  in On-campus housing:**
  76%
**Number of official organized
  extracurricular
  organizations:** 90
3 Most popular majors:
  Biology, English, Business
Student/Faculty ratio: 10:1
Average Class Size: 10 to
  19
**Percent of students going to
  grad school:** 36%
Tuition and Fees: $32,136
**In State Tuition and Fees if
  different:** No difference
Cost for Room and Board:
  $7,842
**Percent receiving financial
  aid out of those who apply,
  first year:** 80%
**Percent receiving financial
  aid among all students:**
  80%

In the midst of the bustle of Memphis, Tennessee lies the small liberal arts paradise of Rhodes College. Students from across the country flock to Rhodes to learn from talented professors, live in Gothic-style dorms, and play Frisbee on a tree-lined campus. The small, close-knit community provides a place where "Rhodents," as students are affectionately known, can thrive and grow for their four-year-experience.

Not Just a Number

Academics at Rhodes are definitely challenging, yet students agree that the course load is manageable thanks in part to the small class size and individual attention each student receives. In order to graduate, Rhodents must fulfill requirements in seven different areas, ranging from English and social sciences to fine arts and physical education. Popular ma-

jors include biology, English, and business administration, which one student said "has the beginner-level courses with some of the largest numbers of students of any class, around 30."

No matter what you major in, you'll be working pretty hard. "I undoubtedly do more homework here than I did in high school," one student admitted. "Most classes are reading-intensive, and professors demand that students come to class prepared." Many professors even have strict attendance policies, which students cite as a downside to the small size of most classes. Yet, overall, students say that the class size is a perk rather than a pitfall, since "small classes allow for complete engagement and a better relationship with the professor." Indeed, Rhodes professors are incredibly accessible. "All of my professors know me by name. I'm not a number." One senior even said, "It is not unusual to go to dinner at a professor's home or enjoy coffee at our Starbucks on campus. I love the student-teacher ratio here."

The "Rhodes Bubble"

When not hitting the books, Rhodes students are incredibly sociable and friendly. "Everyone I've met at Rhodes has been so nice," one first-semester freshman enthused. "I know so many people already!" The small number of students, coupled with an intimate learning atmosphere, makes for a tight-knit community in which people make fast friends. Historically, that community has always been a bit homogeneous. Students of color make up only 17 percent of the College. Yet students maintain that Rhodents are "all really open and interested in meeting new people" and support the college's commitment to building up the diversity of its population.

> "If you want a school with killer school spirit, don't come to Rhodes. I don't think I even made it to our homecoming football game."

Regardless of background, sports and extracurriculars provide a plethora of opportunities for Rhodents to get to know one another. Although Rhodes has a whole host of Division III varsity sports teams, they don't often get enough student support. "If you want a school with killer school spirit, don't come to Rhodes," one student warned. "I don't think I even made it to our homecoming football game." Nevertheless, students insist that the school is making a concerted effort to boost attendance and school spirit, and many say that intramural and club teams are becoming more popular, especially football and basketball. Anyone just looking for a workout can take advantage of the newly renovated Mallory-Hyde Gym and its facilities, or simply join the multitudes tossing Frisbees on Rhodes' manicured lawns.

Off the field, community service seems to be a typical Rhodent's pastime of choice. Students say that one of the most popular ways to become involved in service is through the Kinney Volunteer Program, which organizes and arranges volunteer service activities on campus and throughout the city of Memphis. From volunteering at soup kitchens to working with children at Memphis' famed St. Jude Children's Research Hospital, Kinney provides Rhodes students with a way to truly en-

gage with the Memphis community and break out of what one student called "the Rhodes bubble."

The Land of the Delta Blues

The social scene at Rhodes is dominated by the Greek system—over half of the student body is involved in fraternities and sororities. But students are quick to stress that the Greek parties are open to the entire student body, and that, as one senior explained, "you do not have to go Greek to have a social life." One freshman female admitted, though, that "joining a sorority has really helped me to meet people on campus . . . but of course, there are other ways." Despite the fact that Rhodes "is pretty strict about alcohol," drinking is prevalent on campus. "As long as you're careful about where you drink, you won't get in trouble," a junior said. Campus security is committed to protecting students. "Even if I walk across campus at late hours, I'm completely confident that I'll be safe." For those looking to party off campus and away from the frat houses, downtown Memphis has a whole host of bars and clubs Rhodes students love to frequent, like the Flying Saucer and Silky's. The University even provides buses that shuttle students downtown to cut down on the risk of drunk driving on campus.

If you prefer your weekends dry, never fear—Rhodents maintain that "there is always an alternative to drinking." Memphis provides Rhodes students with many of these alternatives. One Memphis native enthused, "I was worried that [my experience] would be different than that of students from out of state . . . [but] midtown and downtown Memphis are full of exciting and new places and things that I'd never seen or experienced." Cars are a must for getting around the city, but, as one student explained, "A lot of people have cars, so someone can usually give you a ride . . . everyone I've met is really generous about giving rides." Music buffs can frequent the blues clubs on Beale Street, as well as the Rock and Soul Museum and, a bit further away, Graceland itself. Rhodes students often receive discount tickets to basketball games at the new FedEx Forum Stadium, and to local movie theaters, too. From eating soul food at Isaac Hayes' restaurant to seeing the pandas at the Memphis Zoo, there is never a shortage of ways for Rhodes students to entertain themselves in the city around them.

Rat Snack Attack

Housing at Rhodes is, like many other aspects of campus life, intimate and

community-based. Freshmen and sophomores are required to live on campus, but
there is no difference in quality between any of
the beautiful, Gothic-style dorms. "When my
friends [at other schools] saw my dorm, they
got really jealous!" one freshman laughed. Juniors and seniors are able to live off campus,
but many choose not to. In fact, three-fourths
of Rhodes students choose to stay on campus
with the community they have built. In terms
of food, Rhodents all feast at one on-campus
dining hall known as the "Rat." When describing the Rat, one student said, "You can always
get something you like, but sometimes you
can get sick of the same stuff." The Lynx Lair
provides a fast-food-style alternative—some
students say it's better than the Rat, which is

mostly renowned for its omelets. For more
tantalizing off-campus fare, the nearby
Cooper-Young neighborhood boasts restaurants like the Young Avenue Deli and Café Ole
that draw in students.

Whether playing Frisbee on the quad,
studying in the newly renovated library, or
wolfing down omelets at the Rat, Rhodes
students are experts at carving out communities of their own and taking advantage of
the resources around them. A nurturing liberal arts school in the middle of a big city,
Rhodes offers its students the best of both
worlds. "It's really nice to get off campus
and leave the 'Rhodes bubble,' but it's also
really nice to come back. It feels like
home."—*Alexandra Bicks*

FYI
If you come to Rhodes, you'd better bring "a raincoat and umbrella, it rains a lot here!"
What's a typical weekend schedule? "When it's warm, people will be playing Frisbee on Friday
   afternoons. At night, there are some people downtown, some people hanging out in the dorms or
   fraternity houses, and some people off campus. Usually on Saturday or Sunday afternoons,
   people are relaxing or doing homework."
If I could change one thing about Rhodes, I'd "require students to live on campus all four years."
Three things everyone should do before graduating Rhodes are "ride the Lynx statue, enjoy
   Friday's Fried Chicken at the Rat, and attend at least one concert on campus."

University of Tennessee / Knoxville

Address: 320 Student Services Building, Circle Park Drive, Knoxville, TN 37996-0230
Phone: 865-974-1000
E-mail address: admissions@utk.edu
Web site URL: www.utk.edu
Year Founded: 1794
Private or Public: Public
Religious Affiliation: None
Location: Urban
Number of Applicants: 12,824
Percent Accepted: 71%
Percent Accepted who enroll: 47%
Number Entering: 4,331
Number of Transfers Accepted each Year: 1,909
Middle 50% SAT range: M: 540–640, CR: 530–630, Wr: Unreported
Middle 50% ACT range: 23-28

Early admission program EA/ED/None: None
Percentage accepted through EA or ED: NA
EA and ED deadline: NA
Regular Deadline: 1-Dec
Application Fee: $30
Full time Undergraduate enrollment: 21,369
Total enrollment: 27,632
Percent Male: 49%
Percent Female: 51%
Total Percent Minority or Unreported: 1%
Percent African-American: 9%
Percent Asian/Pacific Islander: 3%
Percent Hispanic: 2%
Percent Native-American: <1%
Percent International: 1%
Percent in-state/out of state: 86%/14%
Percent from Public HS: Unreported
Retention Rate: 84%

Graduation Rate 4-year: 29%
Graduation Rate 6-year: Unreported
Percent Undergraduates in On-campus housing: 33%
Number of official organized extracurricular organizations: 450
3 Most popular majors: Business/Marketing, Psychology, Social Sciences
Student/Faculty ratio: 16:1
Average Class Size: 20 to 29
Percent of students going to grad school: 20%
Tuition and Fees: $18,908
In State Tuition and Fees if different: $6,250
Cost for Room and Board: $6,676
Percent receiving financial aid out of those who apply, first year: 49%
Percent receiving financial aid among all students: 46%

UT has it all—country, campus, and cityscape, with sky-high school spirit to match. Whether the Tennessee Volunteers are camping in the Rockies, singing about it in Neyland Stadium, or bar hopping in Knoxville, they know how to have a good time. They also know when to buckle down and study. Says one particularly dedicated junior, "My major concern with my classes is finishing on time with all A's by monitoring my work schedule with my study schedule."

Work Is What You Make It

Students at the University of Tennessee reiterate the fact that "it is the student that makes or breaks the academics." A given semester's load is "definitely manageable," and determined by the student's major, as well as his or her class attendance and effort. Some of the harder majors include nursing, engineering, and architecture, while psychology and exercise science are less demanding. The General Education track demands 36 hours before graduation and basic core subjects like English, biology, and math—overall, "a bit excessive," in the words of one sophomore.

The University requires a minimum GPA of 2.0. Failure to meet that minimum results in academic probation and, eventually, expulsion. One junior noted, however, that "the academic requirements at the University of Tennessee are very easy to abide by." Her classmate added that consistent class attendance yields a B average in most 100- and 200-level courses. (Many of the professors actually give five-point pop quizzes in lecture.) In higher-level courses, there is more work involved, and attendance itself is graded.

Big on School, Not on Student-Professor QT

According to students, one of the difficulties at a large university like UT is that "getting into classes is difficult, and it's very frustrating" when you get shut out. A sophomore reported stories of students having difficulty with graduating on time because they could not get into the courses required to do so. However, her friend added that "the system is improving." Lecture class size can be from 250 to 600 students, whereas discussions cap at 7 to 25. Though there are professor-student relationships in those smaller seminars, one sophomore finds them lacking in lecture. "I am having to get used to the fact that I am just a number in most of my classes," he said. To boot, many of the TAs employed to ease that feeling do not speak adequate English and make comprehension very difficult.

For its "mediocre" classification, the academic program at UT has many redeeming and unique qualities. For one, the University is making an effort to replace professors who can't manage the language barrier. Dr. Kris Koehne, who teaches human sexuality and child-family studies, is praised for teaching the "most interesting and hysterical class offered at the University of Tennessee." There are also some special programs for those with early ambitions. The Education program in particular is unique, as are the Volunteer Community and Design Community programs. Other students raved about outdoor projects in the nearby mountainside, and one junior spoke of how much she valued an assignment in which she tried to prove the existence of God: "It was probably the hardest paper I have written in my entire life, but it taught me a lot about the human psyche and its perception of the outside world."

Living the Life

Social life at UT revolves around the Greek system. Freshmen spend their weekend evenings at dorm, house, and frat parties where they are usually charged for a cup, but not for admission. Upperclassmen frequent "the Strip"—home of the Knoxville bar scene—but it is difficult to get in without being of age or having an expert fake ID. "UT is a 'dry' campus," explained one junior. "There is no alcohol allowed on campus, but there is always a lot available. The police department would say that there is a huge problem, but the students would say it's not." As a result, "cops are everywhere" and underage drinking has become an issue in the last few years, especially in light of recent citations and pedestrian accidents with drunk drivers. Drugs have a presence, too, but are generally kept "behind closed doors."

Outlets for nondrinkers include numerous organized activities throughout the week, including lectures, film screenings, and concerts. The Ewing Gallery and McClung Museum hold regular art exhibitions. Social and service-oriented organizations host formal events for their members throughout the year. For 10 years running, the University has hosted a dance marathon to benefit the local children's hospital. The Student Center, which is home to the bookstore, computer store, three cafeterias, and a quick mart, is "one of the most popular places on campus during the day." Since the center also houses lecture halls and study areas, it is constantly in use.

Actual dating is rare at UT, but random hook-ups are commonplace. One student concluded that "girls are better looking as a whole," while her classmate commented that "it is an attractive campus simply because it is in the South, but it definitely could not compete with UNC, UGA, Ole Miss or SMU in the 'hot people' factor." According to one student who quoted the University Clinic, 80 percent of the school is sexually active, and the STD rate is 50 percent (one out of two). One freshman noted that she has "yet to see a homosexual couple or interracial couple" on campus. A sophomore described the UT student population as middle-class "southern prep and granola hippie people." However, another student asserted that there are students from all walks of life, all income brackets, and many races and sexual orientations. Self-segregation is predominantly in the form of ethnic fraternities.

As mentioned earlier, Greek life dominates most students' social debuts at UT. One frosh swore that she "cannot imagine going out not in a sorority. It has helped me meet so many new people and given me stuff to do such as pledge mixers and fraternity parties." The most popular sororities are AOPi, Tri-Delta, Chi Omega, Alpha Delta Pi, Kappa Kappa Gamma, Kappa Delta, and Phi Mu. Getting into one of them is not easy: "Rush is very draining and exhausting, and sororities have grade cuts, so good grades are important," said one sorority-struck freshman. Fraternities like Pike, Sigma Chi, and Kappa Sigma throw parties on the weekends and most special events, like when Pike had Pat Green perform at their house. SAE has recently been kicked off campus but still holds festivities and theme parties in line with its contemporaries. Some of the most highly anticipated parties include SAE's boxing tournament, Pike's Fall Fiesta, Volapalooza, Super Hero's Day Off, Peace Love Chi O, Casino Date party, Country Clubbers mixers, Halloween parties, and more themes than you can shake a stick at—"Wild Wild West," "Secs and Execs," Luau, "Lifestyles of the Rich and Famous," and—of course—"80s." Most of the cliques on campus are formed through the Greek system, though students also meet close friends through class and dorm assignments freshman year.

Ditch the Dorms
Freshman dorms are "small and old." They have air-conditioning, but students have no control over the temperature, and "visiting hours" determine when friends can come over and only friends of the same sex are allowed to sleep over. All of the dorms have Residential Advisors, but they are only strict in the girls' dorms. "No limit" Clement, on the other hand, is known for its laid-back RAs. South Carrick, Humes, North Carrick, and Reese are the best freshman dorms because they surround a courtyard called the "Presidential" where the students can meet and socialize. Sophronia Strong, said to be the worst dorm, has small rooms and no air-conditioning. It's also rumored to be haunted. "Sophie" gets upset when she hears residents arguing on her birthday, one student explained. Hess, commonly known as "the zoo," is considered the craziest dorm on campus.

> **"As long is there is a lot of school spirit, which Tennessee has, it really does not matter to me if it is not the prettiest campus."**

After freshman year, Greek and racial factors distribute students throughout the dorms. However, there are many off-campus options including sorority houses, apartments, and private houses that are within walking distance of campus. Rent is $350–$450 a month on average, and the most popular off-campus housing is in "The Fort," where there is usually a waiting list.

A Concrete Jungle
UT's campus is no architectural marvel, but it has the feel of a college atmosphere. One student maintained that "as long as there is a lot of school spirit, which Tennessee has, it really does not matter to me if it is not the prettiest campus." The campus also provides easy access to Knoxville, so students have the option of remaining in the campus bubble or venturing out into real life. In fact, as most have cars, University of Tennessee students frequently leave campus to rock climb, camp out, water-ski, or go rafting in nearby outdoor areas. Added one sophomore, "There are also lovely places like Gatlinburg and Dollywood just a few miles down I-40 which can be really fun if you are in the mood for a cheesy weekend!"

Within the bubble, UT boasts great student facilities. "Exercising is very social and popular," and the gym, "T-Rec," features state-of-the-art exercise and recreation equipment including "tons of machines, weights, weight equipment, an indoor track, four basketball courts, three racquetball courts, an outside intramural field [four, actually], and an indoor and outdoor swimming pool." Not to mention the Smoothie King inside. Students rave about the library and surrounding movie theaters and parks available to them on the weekends. Neyland Stadium, of course, is the prize of UT. It seats over 100,000 football lovers, including just about every student on any given Saturday. "The Hill" is the home of most science and math facilities and is currently under construction. One junior praised the work being done: "The University is finally making much-needed changes to the physical structure of the buildings on campus."

All-Star Eats

Tennessee dining hall food is "great but fattening." All-Star plans are the best, as well as any plan (there are five) with "bonus bucks" that can be used outside of the dining halls. "The dining halls are very clean and the food is exquisite. Sometimes there are even theme parties! They cater to all appetites and are typically open at convenient hours but close around 8 p.m." Although UT dining has happy customers, the dining hall is not a social environment. When asked if she might go to the dining hall alone and find someone to sit with, one sophomore answered, "No way. Most people don't go to a dining hall without friends." And most people don't stay there longer than necessary. "There are lots of other places to go to hang out" or eat off campus. On a date you might go to the Tennessee Grill or the Riverside Tavern. "Sawyers and Vic and Bill's Deli are great little holes in the wall that you'll only know about or go to if you live around the area."

Venerable Volunteers

At a school as big as UT, "most everyone is in an organization of some sort; otherwise you would not meet very many people." Greek life and intramurals dominate student interest, but the Baptist Collegiate Ministries, Vol Nation (the pep club), and the Student Government Association are well-respected, too. One thing is for sure—community service has a high profile at UT. "We are the Volunteers for a reason," said an emphatic sophomore. For the more eccentric minds, there are also "funny organizations" like the fly fishing club that demand less time—two hours a week on average. Further, about half of the student body works a job on the side.

In accordance with their track records, football and women's basketball are the most popular spectator sports on campus. "The football players are dumb and cocky, but most everyone goes to the football games decked out in orange," said a student. Athletics are a source of pride at UT. Students participate in the Vol Walk, a procession before every game; sing "Rocky Top" at the top of their lungs during play; and tailgate religiously. There is even a large population of students who follow their football team as far as Florida for away games. Tennessee boasts celebrity status for a few coaches and former players. Peyton Manning, currently the quarterback for the Colts, retired his jersey on October 29, 2004, and Pat Summitt is the most winning coach in history. When it comes down to it, UT is defined by its "colors and school spirit."—*Lauren Ezell*

FYI

If you come to University of Tennessee, you better bring a "closet full of orange clothes."

What is a typical weekend schedule? "Sleep . . . drink . . . FOOTBALL . . . drink . . . sleep . . . drink . . . sleep. . . . study on Sunday night."

If I could change one thing about University of Tennessee, "I'd power-wash all the concrete buildings."

Three things every student at University of Tennessee should do before graduating are "paint the Rock, do a pub crawl, camp in the Smokies."

University of the South (Sewanee)

Address: 735 University Avenue Sewanee, TN 37383-1000
Phone: 931-598-1000
E-mail address: admiss@sewanee.edu
Web site URL: www.sewanee.edu
Year Founded: 1857
Private or Public: Private
Religious Affiliation: Episcopal
Location: Rural
Number of Applicants: Unreported
Percent Accepted: 64%
Percent Accepted who enroll: Unreported
Number Entering: 402
Number of Transfers Accepted each Year: Unreported
Middle 50% SAT range: M: 580–680, CR: 568–680, Wr: Unreported
Middle 50% ACT range: 25–30
Early admission program EA/ED/None: ED

Percentage accepted through EA or ED: 50%
EA and ED deadline: 15-Nov
Regular Deadline: 1-Feb
Application Fee: $45
Full time Undergraduate enrollment: 1,475
Total enrollment: 1,491
Percent Male: 41%
Percent Female: 59%
Total Percent Minority or Unreported: 1%
Percent African-American: 4%
Percent Asian/Pacific Islander: 3%
Percent Hispanic: 2%
Percent Native-American: 1%
Percent International: 1%
Percent in-state/out of state: 27%/73%
Percent from Public HS: Unreported
Retention Rate: 88%
Graduation Rate 4-year: Unreported

Graduation Rate 6-year: Unreported
Percent Undergraduates in On-campus housing: 93%
Number of official organized extracurricular organizations: Unreported
3 Most popular majors: Social Sciences, English, Visual and Performing Arts
Student/Faculty ratio: Unreported
Average Class Size: Unreported
Percent of students going to grad school: Unreported
Tuition and Fees: $32,760
In State Tuition and Fees if different: No difference
Cost for Room and Board: $9,360
Percent receiving financial aid out of those who apply, first year: 68%
Percent receiving financial aid among all students: 41%

In the midst of the beautiful rolling hills of East Tennessee lies the small liberal arts paradise of the University of the South at Sewanee. Sewanee, as it is more commonly known, offers a supportive learning environment coupled with a friendly and laid-back social scene. The small and intimate community allows Sewanee kids to spend four years learning from, and partying with, some of the most talented college students in the country.

Class Without TAs

One of Sewanee's biggest draws is its nurturing and accessible academic community. As one student describes it, "Students are able to get valuable personal instruction from the professors in a very interactive environment where studies are based on discussion, not lecture." The school requires its students to fulfill a set of core requirements, including English, math, history and foreign languages. Some of the more popular majors include forestry and geology, even though they are "extremely challenging." English and history are also favorites, with physics and chemistry universally less popular.

Since Sewanee has no TAs, every single class is taught by professors, a move that elicits only praise from students despite the fact that "grading is fairly strict." Discussions are, as one student puts it, "fun and stimulating" due to the small class size, truly encouraging Sewanee kids to get the most out of their classroom experiences. Professors are described as "friendly and accessible" and "willing to meet with students at any time." One junior even goes so far as to say that "perhaps Sewanee's greatest academic strength is the relationship between students and professors . . . It is very difficult to find a bad teacher here."

Life in the "Bubble"

Outside of the classroom, Sewanee kids are incredibly sociable. As one junior said, "Sewanee people are some of the friendliest people on the planet . . . if there is any true stereotype, it's that all Sewanee students are usually able to get along with everyone." One male student even asserts that "some say we are all Southern hicks . . . but truth be told, I would rather be a Southern gentleman here [than anywhere else]." The stereotype that the population is made up of "privileged white students in a bubble" does admittedly "apply to many people," yet students are quick to defend their school's take on diversity. While the school may be "predominantly white," students insist that "we have a multicultural institute, and we try to promote racial awareness and cultural appreciation," recognizing the University's commitment to strengthening the diversity of the "close, but somewhat isolated, community."

> **"Perhaps Sewanee's greatest academic strength is the relationship between students and professors."**

Regardless of background, sports and extracurricular activities provide a plethora of opportunities for people to get to know their peers. While Sewanee does have a large football team, one junior claims that "sports like basketball and football are not a huge draw for students," while soccer and especially rugby seem to be gaining popularity as the teams score more victories on the field. Intramural sports are also prominent at Sewanee, with women's field hockey and men's basketball described as the most "intense" in which students can participate. If you're just looking to stay in shape, the Fowler Center is a "fairly pleasant" gym with accessible facilities such as a pool, track, and weight room. For non-athletes, Sewanee offers roughly 110 clubs, including community service organizations, publications, and theater groups, giving students a variety of different social outlets.

The Sewanee residential community is made up of a variety of dorms and houses, each of which has its own unique character. Freshmen don't have separate housing, but are instead integrated into upperclassmen dorms from the very beginning, with the only difference being that singles are reserved for juniors and seniors. Most students live on campus, since Sewanee seniors are the only group permitted to apply for off-campus housing. Well-known dorms include Cannon Hall, the universally recognized "party dorm," and Humphreys, which "looks like a hotel, inside and out." There are also special language houses, in which students commit to speaking only the particular language of the house, as well as a few single-sex dorms. Student proctors live in the dorms and fulfill the role of RAs, while Assistant Proctors (or APs) "work with freshmen to help them adjust to college life and enforce dorm rules."

Architecturally, students state that "most of the buildings at Sewanee are rather distinctive . . . think Oxford." The gorgeous All Saints' Cathedral, complete with stained glass windows, serves as a prominent campus landmark, while the towers of McClurg Dining Hall have earned it the nickname "Phallus Palace." Inside McClurg, Sewanee's only dining facility, students on a meal plan enjoy the "great number of choices" that the school has to offer. If the campus food starts to get old, Mi Casa Mexican restaurant and Shen Chinese buffet offer quick and easy alternatives.

It's All Greek To Me

The party scene at Sewanee is notorious for being one of the craziest in the country. One student admits, "Sewanee students work hard all week, and yes, we drink hard on the weekends . . . If you're against alcohol, you probably shouldn't go here." The prevalence of alcohol on campus is abetted by the Greek system, which essentially dominates the available social options. However, Sewanee kids are quick to assert that "the fraternity system promotes friendship in the community." The huge number of frats provides interested pledges with a variety of different alternatives, and they all have an open door policy, meaning that "anyone is allowed to party at any house on any given night."

However, some students warn that "lately the drinking policy has been getting stricter" and that officials have been cracking down on the amount of alcohol the fraternities and sororities are allowed to serve. To get around these regulations, people can also head off-campus for parties in senior residences, where the drinks continue to flow all night long. The University even has its own Tiger Bay Pub, a restaurant that serves beer until 10 p.m. and breakfast for the rest of the night, a sure sign of just how much alcohol serves as a hallmark of the school's social experience.

Despite Sewanee's self-proclaimed status as a wet campus, there are definitely weekend activities that don't necessarily involve alcohol. The Sewanee Union Theater offers sneak previews of upcoming films, while the nearby Lake Cheston club has occasional concerts and shows. Sewanee's proximity to the woods also allows students to enjoy outdoor activities like hiking and camping. The campus is incredibly safe, and town-gown relations are friendly, as many students comment that "[The town of Sewanee] generally tolerates the students, and the beer and liquor stores are especially appreciative of them." In terms of venturing off campus to explore the surrounding areas, Sewanee kids agree that "most people have cars." Indeed cars are necessary for everything from making Wal-Mart runs in nearby Cowen or Monteagle to making the treks to Nashville or Chattanooga. Popular off-campus clubs include Tubby's in Monteagle, while the coffee house Stirling's and Shenanigans bar and grill draw rave reviews from students. The Four Seasons even offers home cooking, but it is closed during the winter because it serves fresh food directly from nearby farms, a reminder of the advantages of Sewanee's rural location.

A Place Where Angels Dwell

Sewanee lore is rife with unique stories and enduring traditions. Students still "dress for class," meaning that they wear nicer clothes out of a sense of propriety and respect for the professors. Tour guides tell of nearby Civil War bombs and battles, while stories of ghosts and haunted buildings continue to circulate. Legend even has it that angels dwell at the gates of Sewanee, and many students admit to tapping the roof of their car when entering or exiting campus to "summon a 'Sewanee angel'" to protect them. Truly a charmed place, Sewanee offers prospective students a chance for a supportive and rewarding college experience. As one junior states, "Sewanee is just the greatest. Period."—*Alexandra Bicks*

FYI

If you come to Sewanee, you'd better bring "hiking boots, dress attire for class, a smile, and sense of adventure."

What's a typical weekend schedule? "Friday night, party hard; Saturday morning, sleep; Saturday afternoon, go see some sports events; Saturday night, party hard; Sunday, go to church to make up for Friday and Saturday night, and then study!"

If I could change one thing about Sewanee, I'd "make it closer to a real city—it can get kind of isolated out here."

Three things everyone should do before graduating are "hike the perimeter trail, take interesting classes, and watch a sunset at Morgan's Steep."

Vanderbilt University

Address: 2305 West End Avenue Nashville, TN 37203

Phone: 615-322-2561

E-mail address: admissions@vanderbilt.edu

Web site URL: www.vanderbilt.edu

Year Founded: 1873

Private or Public: Private

Religious Affiliation: None

Location: Urban

Number of Applicants: Unreported

Percent Accepted: 33%

Percent Accepted who enroll: Unreported

Number Entering: 1,673

Number of Transfers Accepted each Year: 193

Middle 50% SAT range: M: 680–760, CR: 650–740, Wr: 650–730

Middle 50% ACT range: 30–33

Early admission program EA/ED/None: ED

Percentage accepted through EA or ED: Unreported

EA and ED deadline: 1-Nov

Regular Deadline: 3-Jan

Application Fee: $50

Full time Undergraduate enrollment: 6,637

Total enrollment: 10,587

Percent Male: 44%

Percent Female: 56%

Total Percent Minority or Unreported: 13%

Percent African-American: 10%

Percent Asian/Pacific Islander: 7%

Percent Hispanic: 6%

Percent Native-American: 1%

Percent International: 4%

Percent in-state/out of state: 16%/84%

Percent from Public HS: Unreported

Retention Rate: 96%

Graduation Rate 4-year: Unreported

Graduation Rate 6-year: Unreported

Percent Undergraduates in On-campus housing: 89%

Number of official organized extracurricular organizations: 329

3 Most popular majors: Social Sciences, Engineering, Foreign Languages and Literature

Student/Faculty ratio: 9:1

Average Class Size: Unreported

Percent of students going to grad school: Unreported

Tuition and Fees: $37,005

In State Tuition and Fees if different: No difference

Cost for Room and Board: $12,028

Percent receiving financial aid out of those who apply, first year: 86%

Percent receiving financial aid among all students: 46%

Smack-dab in the middle of Music City, USA, Vanderbilt University's idyllic brick buildings and grassy lawns are just blocks away from the good food and quirky culture of Nashville, Tennessee. Competitive both academically and socially, Vandy is a place for those who like to work hard, play hard, and eat great burgers.

Atypical "A's"

On Vanderbilt academics, one freshman concluded: "I am confident that the academics of Vanderbilt are perfectly balanced to allow its students to enjoy the college life, while still being rigorous enough to create respect in the job world and promote learning while on campus." But grade-grubbers be warned: Vanderbilt supports grade *de*flation, an oft-forgotten phenomenon of a pre–SAT tutor America. As one junior elaborated, "B's are easy to get; A's are hard."

Students might have an easier time pushing 4.0's at the Peabody School of Education.

The Human and Organizational Development major is one of the easiest on campus. Engineers, premed students, and economics majors have a tougher time. Some students argued, though, that "each major is challenging . . . but not impossible." According to many students, "curriculum is an integral part of Vanderbilt."

Even in the more difficult majors, most Vanderbilt professors have an open-door policy and boast small class sizes. Upperclassmen say 30 students is the average campus wide, though large lectures border on 50. Freshmen seeking name-brand profs should enroll in Brian Griffith's Intro to Human Development, John Lachs' Intro to Philosophy, or Stephen Buckles' introductory economics courses.

Music City Madness

Vanderbilt has "top 20 academics according to *US News* and a top 20 party scene according to *Playboy*." And Hugh Hefner certainly knows his parties—the entertainment options at Vanderbilt do not disappoint. Among fraternity parties, downtown Music City, movies on Peabody lawn, and on-campus concerts and lectures, Vandy students are never bored. "Being underage is only a problem if you want to go to bars downtown and you don't have a fake ID. Most take anything halfway legit," one junior said. Upperclassmen who are interested, however, can enjoy the Nashville nightlife courtesy of student-friendly cabs that frequent Vanderbilt's campus on the weekends. Underclassmen attend frat parties more often, and enjoy "cool live bands, literally every weekend."

> **"Vanderbilt has top 20 academics according to *US News* and a top 20 party scene according to *Playboy*."**

There are many non-drinkers on campus, but they are well accepted and included in regular goings-on. As one freshman explained, "I know several of my closest friends and I don't drink, but we can still go to the frats and have fun." There is also a Christian fraternity that hosts dry parties. During the daytime, Vanderbilt has hosted many famous lecturers in years past including Maya Angelou and Tennessee native Al Gore. Further, the "Chancellor's Lecture Series" is mandatory for freshman and open to the public, while the "Sarratt Student Center is a popular hang-out place." Students agreed that the highlight of Vanderbilt social life comes in April with the Rites of Spring. Just before finals, the school hires bands and performers for "a two-day orgy of music" on Alumni Lawn. Past performers include Ludakris, Maroon 5, and Robert Earl Keen.

On-campus dating is, for the most part, limited to formals, but there is a "small scene." It is mostly overwhelmed by "lots of random hook-ups." What does set Vanderbilt apart, according to one student, is that the "student body is unusually attractive," especially the women, he added.

The Vandy Vibe

The Vanderbilt stereotype is what you might expect at a southern school. One freshman listed the following perceived stereotypes: "Vanderbilt is an all-wealthy white school. Girls are blonde, preppy, fake, and dependent. Guys are party animals and southern gentlemen. Everyone is from the South, and everyone dresses to impress." In reality, however,

"there are more middle-class students than most people think. About half of the student body receives financial aid." Many students express satisfaction with the student body profile, but a considerable number wish there were more diversity.

Some of the homogeneity around the Vandy campus is attributed to the "huge Greek system." One sophomore wrote that second semester rush is "stressful but fun!" Chi Omega, Delta Delta Delta, Kappa Alpha Theta, Kappa Kappa Gamma, and Kappa Delta are the coveted sororities, while guys elbow to get into Sigma Chi, Sigma Alpha Epsilon, Kappa Alpha, and Pi Kappa Epsilon. The Greek system seems to be a significant forum for making friends at Vandy, and on the homogeneity that it creates, the same student argued that "smart and interesting people are definitely here . . . lots of students who actually care about political and social issues as well as what they look like!"

The Lowdown on Living

All Vanderbilt freshmen live on campus in one of three dorms. Kissam is the least well kept. Composed of single bedrooms, it is viewed as a "bookworm" area. Branscomb, neighbor to Greek row, boasts the best party scene. And Vandy-Barnard is the most popular dorm for freshmen. Most upperclassmen stay on campus, hopefully in Scales or Vaughn, the best upperclass dorms, while others live in fraternity or sorority houses or in other off-campus accommodations. There is an international house called McTyeire "where you have to speak a foreign language and eat dinner there four nights a week" and there is also a philosophy house.

On-campus dining plans are "decent . . . not great but not horrible." Rand, the main dining center, is a nice place to sit and chat with friends for hours on end. When students need a change of pace, however, they can use their meal points at surrounding restaurants: P.F. Chang's, Ken's Sushi, Pancake Pantry, and Bread & Company are all popular. Amerigo's is the hot spot for dates, and Rotier's is the home of the world's best cheeseburger. Vanderbilt also features a significant number of options for those with certain eating requirements, such as the kosher and vegetarian establishments on campus.

Commodores in the Community

Vandy students are avid sports fans. Though the basketball and baseball teams are the most successful, more students frequent weekly football games in the fall—often with a date and a dress. There is even a "Vanderbilt Fanatics" club that organizes the cheering effort. One nice tradition, according to students, "is for the students to stand and sing the alma mater after each game, win or lose."

For nonvarsity athletes, there are a number of sporting options. One freshman said, "The club and intramural programs are popular and well run." Additionally, there are great facilities for recreational exercise such as swimming, weight lifting, tennis, and basketball. On nice days, many students can be seen running "the loop," a three-mile course around campus.

In terms of nonathletic extracurriculars, Vanderbilt students are very community service oriented. Alternative Spring and Winter Break, which "take several hundred students to another state or country," and Habitat for Humanity are very well respected. Student who aren't involved in community service or the Commodore yearbook (another popular pastime), might take jobs on campus, although most students with jobs are part of the work-study program. Sororities and fraternities are the most time-consuming extracurriculars but Vandy students insist that "academics come first."—*Lauren Ezell*

FYI

If you come to Vanderbilt you better bring "a sundress for football games."
What is a typical weekend schedule? "Study hard, play hard."
If I could change one thing about Vanderbilt, I'd "add more diversity to the student body."
Three things every student at Vanderbilt should do before graduating are "take a drunk picture with Chancellor Gee, take an ASB trip, and get painted up for a football game."

Texas

Address: One Bear Place #97056 Waco, TX 76798-7056
Phone: 254-710-3435
E-mail address: admissions@baylor.edu
Web site URL: www.baylor.edu
Year Founded: 1845
Private or Public: Private
Religious Affiliation: Baptist
Location: Urban
Number of Applicants: 25,501
Percent Accepted: 51%
Percent Accepted who enroll: 24%
Number Entering: 3,062
Number of Transfers Accepted each Year: 404
Middle 50% SAT range: M: 560–660, CR: 540–650, Wr: 530–630
Middle 50% ACT range: 23–28
Early admission program EA/ED/None: None

Percentage accepted through EA or ED: NA
EA and ED deadline: NA
Regular Deadline: 1-Feb
Application Fee: $50
Full time Undergraduate enrollment: 11,878
Total enrollment: 14,541
Percent Male: 43%
Percent Female: 57%
Total Percent Minority or Unreported: 29%
Percent African-American: 8%
Percent Asian/Pacific Islander: 8%
Percent Hispanic: 11%
Percent Native-American: 1%
Percent International: Unreported
Percent in-state/out of state: 81%/19%
Percent from Public HS: Unreported
Retention Rate: 84%

Graduation Rate 4-year: 49%
Graduation Rate 6-year: 72%
Percent Undergraduates in On-campus housing: 39%
Number of official organized extracurricular organizations: 237
3 Most popular majors: Biology, Psychology, Nursing
Student/Faculty ratio: 15:1
Average Class Size: 28
Percent of students going to grad school: Unreported
Tuition and Fees: $26,084
In State Tuition and Fees if different: No difference
Cost for Room and Board: $7,895
Percent receiving financial aid out of those who apply, first year: 78%
Percent receiving financial aid among all students: 54%

The history of Baylor University began before Texas even entered the Union as a state. In fact, its official establishment in 1845 was chartered by the then-Republic of Texas. Over one and a half centuries later, Baylor has become not only a well-respected academic institution, but also the largest Baptist-affiliated university in the world, with a total of over 14,000 students. Furthermore, due to its dedication to research activities across all disciplines, Baylor has also emerged as a highly regarded global university, attracting students and faculty from around the world.

No-nonsense Academics

The quality of education offered by Baylor is widely recognized as one of the best in the country. *U.S. News & World Report* recently ranked Baylor as the 76th best national university. In 2007, *Relevant* magazine listed the university as the best Christian college in the country. This means competitive students and challenging academics. "Surely, finding easy classes is not that hard, and sometimes it depends on what you want to achieve in college," said one senior. "But overall, the classes are hard and make you work quite a bit."

Baylor students are also keen on boasting about the range and number of academic opportunities. After all, the University provides 145 different areas of study, not to mention the fact that it also offers 50 study-abroad programs, a rarity even among the largest academic institutions in the United States. Given Baylor's status as a leading research university, undergraduate students who seek to enrich themselves even further can easily gain exposure to the numerous in-depth research projects on campus.

In addition, the undergraduate education at Baylor goes far beyond the traditional liberal arts subjects. The University is divided into 11 different schools, and eight of them—ranging from the customary Arts and Sciences to the Hankamer School of Business to the School of Social Work—have degree-granting programs for undergraduates. Several certification programs are also available for those who seek to link their education directly to future employment, like students who are planning for a career in teaching. "The School of Education is great here at Baylor," affirmed one student. "It gives a lot of opportunities to students to have field experiences and do some actual teaching in classrooms. It prepares us well for our careers."

As its Baptist affiliation would suggest, Baylor maintains considerable emphasis on Christianity in the education of students. The core curriculum that everyone must fulfill before graduation reflects this religious commitment by requiring students to attend Chapel regularly during at least two semesters. Furthermore, everyone must take two specific religion classes: Introduction to Christian Scripture and Introduction to Christian Heritage. "I particularly enjoyed my religion classes. I now know so much more about what it means to be a Christian," one student explained.

The rest of the curriculum varies significantly, given the large differences between majors. However, as in most universities of similar academic vigor, students are required to take classes in a variety of fields, such as English, foreign language, and mathematics. These skills are deemed highly valuable regardless of major. "The required classes can be a pain, but I feel I learned a lot of new things from them," said one student.

Life in Waco

Located on the south side of Waco, Texas, Baylor is generally considered an urban school, but its surroundings are certainly more reminiscent of the suburbs, with low-rise apartments and small houses. Although Waco does employ a large number of commuters, it is certainly not a major metropolitan area and has been suffering from urban decay for several decades. Nevertheless, efforts are now underway, with the help of Baylor, to revive the city. On the other hand,

students do not necessarily feel it is necessary to be part of Waco, and prefer staying on campus. "We have a very big university," one student said. "So I don't feel the need to go to the city, which doesn't have much anyway."

Life on Campus

Freshmen are required to live on campus, unless they live with their parents in McLennan County or have extenuating circumstances such as being married or having dependents. In applying for housing, students can ask for a specific roommate and indicate residential hall preferences. Although there is no guarantee that these requests will be honored, students certainly have a certain degree of control over their living arrangements. "The rooms are reasonable," one student said. "I have been to dorms of my friends in other colleges, and, compared to them, I think Baylor's housing is not bad." Nevertheless, upperclassmen tend to move off campus to the many surrounding apartments. This means that less than half of the students are currently living in university facilities; however, Baylor has recently indicated that it recognizes the importance of campus living to education and aims to achieve 50 percent of students living on campus by 2012.

As a Baptist university, the way students behave certainly reflects Christian values. Alcohol, for example, is strictly monitored on campus. Therefore, many parties happen off of University property. Baylor has more than 40 fraternities and sororities, making them an important part of the social scene. For those uninterested in Greek life or alcohol, many other options are also available, especially the different artistic and sporting performances where many people gather and socialize. Furthermore, unlike at most universities in the country, another major and well-attended weekend activity is church. "Of course people go to church on Sundays," one student said. "At the end of the day, this is a Christian university, and going to church is essential for many people here."

Baylor Bears

Baylor, like many other large Texan universities, is a major force in collegiate athletics. The Bears, named after the school mascot, participate in the Big 12 Conference, a highly competitive and prestigious conference of NCAA Division I. Although the football team has not been very successful due to the quality of its adversaries, the games still attract large crowds and are famous for the Baylor Line, a large number of freshmen wearing yellow shirts cheering for the team and intimidating the opponents.

The more successful programs include the baseball team, which regularly provides quality players to Major League Baseball; the women's basketball team; and the track and field team, which is known to have produced one of the most celebrated sprinters in recent memory, world-record holder Michael Johnson. The most outstanding team award, however, probably goes to the tennis team, which has been winning consecutive titles since 2005. "Our teams are very good, so it is only natural that sports are big at Baylor," one student concluded. "The teams and the crowd help us to have a strong school spirit," added another.

Diversity in a Baptist Institution

One of the major factors that may turn away many prospective applicants is the image of a heavily religious university that focuses on proclaiming Christian values. Undoubtedly, Baylor does have a strong emphasis on religion. In fact, its mission statement unambiguously affirms that the goal of the institution is to combine Christianity with academic excellence. "My religion is important to me," one student explained. "That is why I chose to come here." The requirement of Chapel attendance clearly shows that the school is deeply committed to teaching students about not only religion, but also faith.

On the other hand, Baylor's student body does have substantial diversity, at least for a school of such strong religious affiliation. Minority students account for roughly 30

percent of the total enrollment, a considerable number for most universities. At the same time, more than 70 countries are represented on campus, and the school enrolls about 200 international students. Furthermore, despite the preaching of Christian values, there are a small number of non-Christians. "I know people who are atheists here," said one student. "As long as you can stand having plenty of pious people around you, I don't think you will find it really hard to get by." One drawback, however, is that the University is predominantly Texan in nature. In fact, four out of five students come from the Lone Star State. "You will learn a lot about Texas during your time at Baylor," affirmed one student.

> "You will learn a lot about Texas during your time at Baylor."

Baylor is unique. With its combination of qualities and weaknesses, students choose to attend this school for a particularly large variety of reasons. Sometimes it is because Baylor is academically industrious. Sometimes it is because of Baylor's religious traditions. Sometimes it is the school spirit. Regardless of their reasons, most students are happy about their choice. Surely the strong emphasis on Christian values and the location in Waco may turn away some potential suitors. At the end of the day, however, Baylor remains a top destination for students from around the world.—*Xiaohang Liu*

FYI
If you come to Baylor, you'd better bring "work ethic."
What is the typical weekend schedule? "Parties, but you have to make sure that you will get up in the morning on Sunday for church."
If I could change one thing about Baylor, I'd "make more upperclassmen live on campus."
Three things every student at Baylor should do before graduating are "visit Dallas, study abroad, and go to as many sports games as you can."

Rice University

Address: MS 17 PO Box 1892 Houston, TX 77251-1892	**EA and ED deadline: ED:** 1-Nov, EA 1-Dec	**Graduation Rate 6-year:** 92%
Phone: 713-348-7423	**Regular Deadline:** 10-Jan	**Percent Undergraduates in On-campus housing:** 68%
E-mail address: admi@rice.edu	**Application Fee:** $50	
Web site URL: www.rice.edu	**Full time Undergraduate enrollment:** 3,154	**Number of official organized extracurricular organizations:** 215
Year Founded: 1912	**Total enrollment:** 5,456	
Private or Public: Private	**Percent Male:** 52%	**3 Most popular majors:** Biology, Economics, Psychology
Religious Affiliation: None	**Percent Female:** 48%	
Location: Urban	**Total Percent Minority or Unreported:** 47%	**Student/Faculty ratio:** 5:1
Number of Applicants: 8,776		
Percent Accepted: 23%	**Percent African-American:** 6%	**Average Class Size:** 10 to 19
Percent Accepted who enroll: 34%	**Percent Asian/Pacific Islander:** 18%	**Percent of students going to grad school:** 41%
Number Entering: 714		
Number of Transfers Accepted each Year: 106	**Percent Hispanic:** 12%	**Tuition and Fees:** $25,606
	Percent Native-American: <1%	**In State Tuition and Fees if different:** No difference
Middle 50% SAT range: M: 680–780, CR: 650–740, Wr: 640–740	**Percent International:** 4%	**Cost for Room and Board:** $10,250
	Percent in-state/out of state: 53%/47%	
Middle 50% ACT range: 30–34	**Percent from Public HS:** Unreported	**Percent receiving financial aid out of those who apply, first year:** 65%
Early admission program EA/ED/None: ED and EA	**Retention Rate:** 97%	
	Graduation Rate 4-year: 79%	**Percent receiving financial aid among all students:** 64%
Percentage accepted through EA or ED: 32%		

With its cleanly manicured lawns, lush green vegetation, and park-like atmosphere, one would hardly guess that Rice University is located just a few miles from downtown Houston, Texas. As one of the nation's top universities, it offers students an unmatched education in addition to a beautiful learning environment.

"We Study a Lot"

In describing Rice, one student said, "You will work so hard here. The students I know could not work more if they wanted to." Even those who choose to take the easier route must fulfill Rice's academic requirements, which can vary in intensity depending on the major and the number of AP credits an individual has coming in. There are three areas of distributional requirements—the humanities, the social sciences, and the natural sciences. Students point out that the requirements have their "ups and downs," but one student said it is beneficial, since "taking classes outside of your major really helps to open your mind." Many students take a lot of science courses

regardless, but there are complaints about the "perfectionist premeds." It is common for students to continue their research at Rice over the summer. One of Rice's most well-known programs is the Rice-Baylor program, which guarantees acceptance to Baylor College of Medicine, the largest medical center in the country, located "right across the street." However, the program only accepts approximately 10 undergrads per year. Unfortunately, many premed students do not have the luxury of going abroad—a hefty sacrifice, considering that about half the University's students do so for at least a semester.

In terms of getting into classes, freshmen often have the most difficulty procuring a spot for the more coveted lectures. The upside for freshmen is that general education classes such as introductory humanities tend to be capped, so they range from 20 to 30 people. Other introductory courses, including biology, chemistry, physics, and constitutionalism, are generally quite large, "which for Rice isn't that big—maybe 100 students." One Rice freshman bragged that "my smallest class is an amazing Introduction to Theater class, which only has about 10 students." Upper-level courses are extremely small at Rice; typically less than 20 to 30 people. One upperclassman said, "I had four classes with fewer than 10 students last year."

While most Rice students are committed to their studies, few deny that some majors are harder than others. Mathematics, physics, and computer science top the list of most demanding majors. However, "every discipline at Rice has very serious students, and those are the ones that study the most—it doesn't depend on the major." "You will spend your four years at this school either working or feeling like you should be working." This deep commitment to academics and intensive studying does have its payoff, however. "There's a deeper level of satisfaction here than at most other schools because we know that 'excellence' should be hard to achieve (and that things can only get easier.)"

The workload is more bearable when students have the opportunity to take classes from famous professors like Dennis Huston, a humanities teacher famous for lectures in which "he spits out obscenities left and right." People actually camp out in front of the registrar's office to ensure a spot in Huston's public speaking class. Bombs and Rockets, a class about the "Politics of American National Security," is another hot ticket: And these classes don't disappoint, with enjoyable assignments to hold students' interest. One premed student was assigned the task of creating artificial blood for one of his science courses.

Grade inflation doesn't seem to be a prominent concern at Rice, where students joke about its prevalence at Ivy League schools. Some classes, such as chemistry, do have what are called "redemption points." In this system, if a student's score on a portion of the final exam is better than that on a test from the beginning of the year, the earlier test score replaces final questions pertaining to the earlier test, resulting in the higher grade.

For all their positive attributes, academics at Rice do have some drawbacks. One student noted that some "professors and classes are not as liberal-artsy or teaching-focused as advertised. You get a lot of indifferent professors and big lecture classes, especially in the math and science departments." For more difficult classes, recitation sessions taught by the TAs are offered. Students seem to have mixed feelings about TAs, some complaining that they only muddle the information and

that it can be "really hard to understand" those with foreign accents. This is not always the case, however, and one student praised the grad students at Rice, calling one of her TAs "better than the professor." Whatever the case may be, "between the office hours of the TAs and professors, you can always get help if you need it."

Studying Aside

Rice isn't all brains and no beer (despite its Greek-free status). "Even though Rice students are hardworking, you can find a lot of students that like to party a lot." Although most parties serve up alcohol, there are "always other things to do," one student emphatically pointed out, and nondrinkers are not at all ostracized. "I can't imagine a more accepting social scene." The residential colleges throw a lot of the parties. Well-known bashes include the Annual Night of Decadence, "which is basically a nude party;" Disorientation (at the end of orientation week); and the Tower Party. Late-night games of powderpuff football or just "chilling" with card games or a movie are options for those students who just want to veg out. The dating scene (or lack thereof) at Rice is often blamed on the common stereotype that "most of us guys tend to be shy," one male Rice student explained. And the males' shyness only works to their disadvantage, since "there's a good amount of cute girls on campus." The verdict is still out, however, because other Rice students feel that "you're either in a very serious relationship or you're not dating anyone at all."

Instant Family

The social life at Rice is supplemented by the University's "amazing" residential college system. About 400 people (100 from each grade) live in each of nine colleges, providing an instant family atmosphere ingrained in freshmen from the start of "a great orientation week." Freshmen from each college are divided into groups of eight to 10 students during "O-Week." "You're really tight with them from the start and you do all your activities with your group," a student explained. The colleges "make a very concerted effort to put people from very different backgrounds and with very different interests in each group," one student said. And yes, the residential colleges definitely do have different personalities, students said, which "are all brainwashed into us during our orientation week." Most students are positive about the system and their experience. One student noted that the system is like "the best parts of a fraternity and a dorm all put together." And don't worry about meeting people outside of your residential college. Classes, parties, or common friends are all ways to extend your social circle, although it does "take a little bit more effort."

Each college has its own master and staff of associates. The master is a tenured professor at the University and handles academic and personal matters, in addition to organizing social events. He or she lives and eats with the students in the residential college. The associates are faculty members, most of whom live outside of Rice, except for the two associates who reside in each college. They provide academic advice and help direct students' career choices.

Dorms vary from college to college, but most students would agree that none are terrible. Rooms range from singles to quads, most of which are located on coed floors and share single-sex bathrooms. There are more singles in the newer colleges, but there's no reason to fear being lonely—usually four singles comprise a suite, with its own common room and bathroom. And don't worry about playing your music too loudly: the RA system is fairly lenient and the RAs "tend to be really cool here and enjoy hanging out with us."

> "The education you receive outside the classroom at Rice is what makes me feel like I could have never been happy anywhere else."

Each college has its own dining hall, and though the quality varies, overall the food at Rice is "good by college standards." Even seniors opt to eat in the dining halls because "one of the great things about the college system is that students from all classes interact on a daily basis (primarily at lunch)." On Saturday nights, the cafeterias are closed for all students—a mixed blessing because "it forces one to go off campus." And there are more than enough places to choose from, with a great range in price and quality." When the clock strikes two in the morning, Taco Cabana, "a better, cheaper version of Taco Bell," is the place to be for post-party munchies. House of Pies is another Rice novelty.

A World Away

What's green, flat, and pretty all around? Why, the campus of Rice University, of course. It features beautiful landscaping and sprawling quads that students said "people are actually encouraged to walk on," although some prefer to utilize the plush grass for napping. The main local attraction is Rice Village, an outdoor mall with a mix of franchises and independent retailers that is "packed with restaurants." But who wants to walk when you can hitch a ride with any of the estimated 40 percent of Rice students who have cars on campus? Beyond campus, Houston has so much to offer, including the Theater District, Chinatown and the Galleria, a "really famous, really large mall," but one student did lament the insular nature of the school. The hedges that surround the "spacious campus sometimes make Rice students forget that there's the city of Houston and even an entire world outside Rice." When they do get outside, favorite Rice bar hangouts in Houston include Bar Houston, Brian O'Neil's, Brock's Bar, and Two Rows. Little Woodrow's is another popular bar in the Village (along with Brian O'Neil's). Luckily for students not blessed with the luxury of wheels, a rail system makes getting places a bit easier. Last year, Rice's President implemented "Passport to Houston," so now all undergraduates can ride the light rail for free, "which makes going to bars, baseball games, and restaurants downtown, as well as the museum district and apartment complexes, very easy."

Outside the Classroom

"The education you receive outside the classroom at Rice is what makes me feel like I could have never been happy anywhere else," one student said. "People game, take salsa lessons, play ultimate Frisbee," and do anything to "enrich themselves," another said of the extracurricular scene at Rice. Although some organizations are more "official" than others, "as long as you have a group of people with a common shared idea, it can be made into an official club." The Cabinet, Parliament, and Diet among others are the names of residential college student governments, and these are a popular activity, even more than their counterpart, the official University student government. Future journalists can take a stab at writing for Rice's widely read newspaper, *The Thresher*. High participation rates show more than just an interest to beef up résumés. "Everybody does their own thing," and they are appreciated for it. One student went so far as to say that "Rice people will change your life."

Although Rice's athletics are not the pinnacle of the University, the school's baseball team won the College World Series in 2003, made the NCAA tournament in 2006, and advanced to the NCAA Super Regionals. Rice students don't just cheer for the champs, though. A surprising number of people attend the football games "even though we're quite pathetic," one student said. College sports are another popular option—teams from various residential colleges compete against one another for the President's Cup.

Although there are separate workout facilities for varsity athletes, the general public facility "pales in comparison to Duke's," as one student put it. "You're probably going to have to wait for cardio equipment anytime in the afternoon or evening, and most mornings as well. But the Board of Trustees has stated that a new Rec Center is a priority."—*Laura Sullivan*

FYI

If you come to Rice you'd better bring "water balloons for O-Week, Beer Bike, and general mayhem."

What is the typical weekend schedule? "A lot of studying and a lot of procrastinating with your friends either partying, going out in Houston, or hanging out at your college."

If I could change one thing about Rice, I'd "help the premeds relax."

Three things every student at Rice should do before graduating are "support their powderpuff team, explore Houston without a car, and advise during O-Week (it's more fun for the advisers than for the freshmen, shhh!)."

Southern Methodist University

Address: PO Box 750181 Dallas, TX 75275-0181
Phone: 214-768-3417
E-mail address: ugadmission@smu.edu
Web site URL: www.smu.edu
Year Founded: 1911
Private or Public: Private
Religious Affiliation: Methodist
Location: Urban
Number of Applicants: 8,270
Percent Accepted: 50%
Percent Accepted who enroll: 34%
Number Entering: 1,397
Number of Transfers Accepted each Year: 558
Middle 50% SAT range: M: 590–680, CR: 560–660, Wr: 560–660
Middle 50% ACT range: 25–30
Early admission program EA/ED/None: EA
Percentage accepted through EA or ED: Unreported

EA and ED deadline: 1-Nov
Regular Deadline: 15-Mar
Application Fee: $60
Full time Undergraduate enrollment: 6,240
Total enrollment: 10,000
Percent Male: 47%
Percent Female: 53%
Total Percent Minority or Unreported: 26%
Percent African-American: 5%
Percent Asian/Pacific Islander: 6%
Percent Hispanic: 8%
Percent Native-American: <1%
Percent International: 6%
Percent in-state/out of state: 55%/45%
Percent from Public HS: 61%
Retention Rate: 89%
Graduation Rate 4-year: 58%
Graduation Rate 6-year: 73%

Percent Undergraduates in On-campus housing: 31%
Number of official organized extracurricular organizations: 180
3 Most popular majors: Business, Public Relations, Social Science
Student/Faculty ratio: 12:1
Average Class Size: 10 to 19
Percent of students going to grad school: Unreported
Tuition and Fees: $31,200
In State Tuition and Fees if different: No difference
Cost for Room and Board: $12,445
Percent receiving financial aid out of those who apply, first year: 82%
Percent receiving financial aid among all students: 65%

Many Southern Methodist University students are frustrated with the stereotypes associated with common perceptions of their beloved school, complaining that "everyone assumes because we go to SMU we must be rich and Southern." But never fear. "SMU is really working to change its image from 'Southern Millionaires'

University' to an academically charged, more demanding and well-respected and recognized university," asserted one proud Mustang. And while there are elements of that academic millionaires' club that still linger on campus (one sophomore insisted that every girl should know to bring "a Lily Pulitzer dress and pearls" to school), this is not by any means all that SMU has to offer. "SMU has top-notch academics, opportunities, professors, location, and students," one senior explained.

Life on a Movie Set

SMU offers nationally recognized programs in fields ranging from business to dance. Although the offerings are rigorous, requirements are flexible enough to allow students to double major, to pick up minors, or to participate in one of the many study-abroad programs that SMU offers. But between the wide variety of academic programs and extensive extracurricular involvements, students must quickly learn to balance their time. One Mustang observed, "There is always something to do, but the library is also always packed!"

"First-years" (never call them "freshmen"!) are required to live on campus. There are a number of different housing options, including an Honors dorm. "I enjoy on-campus living because I don't have to drive much unless I'm going out to eat or shopping," a sophomore RA said. "It's nice being close to all of my classes." Another Mustang chimed in that he "loved living in the dorms! It can get a little loud in the freshman dorms at times, but it is essential to the freshman experience." After first year, the housing choices expand immensely. Sophomore males may decide to move into their fraternity houses (girls have to wait until their junior year to live in the sorority houses), but there are also on-campus as well as off-campus apartments ("It's not cheap, but it's very doable"), and of course, various on-campus residence halls and houses.

The on-campus eating options, centered around the offerings of Umphrey Lee Center, are enough to keep most Mustangs happy. Its pasta bar has a loyal following amongst students, as do the omelets at Mac's Place. In general, on-campus dining offers enough variety that at least one item will please every student's palate. And, for at least one first-year, there's more than enough to keep her happy. "It's all pretty delicious," she said.

But even if the beauty of SMU is not in its dining halls, then the breathtaking campus landscape more than makes up for it. "The whole thing is amazing!" one senior raved. Another added, "It's like a movie campus!" Indeed, the school takes full advantage of the sunny Dallas weather. "The groundskeepers change all the flowers in the flower beds once a month so they're always in season and beautiful." All of this is encased in what one Mustang described as the "Highland Park Bubble." Highland Park, one of the wealthiest neighborhoods in Dallas, surrounds the campus. And while this may make things expensive for students, it also provides them with "small-town shops and little diners." Furthermore, it provides an outstanding level of safety on campus. "I literally walked from one end of the campus to the other at midnight and felt extremely safe," one sophomore said. Indeed, thanks to the fact that the campus lies within the jurisdiction of four different police forces (Highland Park, neighboring University Park, SMU Campus Police, and the Dallas Police), students are well protected at all times.

TVs and Tailgating

On the surface, there is a large element of homogeneity within the student body. "SMU is really conservative. It's kind of like a scaled-down version of UGA or Ole Miss," one sophomore noted. However, there is a subtle streak of diversity that quickly becomes apparent upon closer investigation. For example, the campus boasts far more religious diversity than a school with the word "Methodist" in its name would be expected to have, with 31 religious groups, including Hillel, the Hindu Club, the Baha'i Club, and the Muslim Student Association operating under the office of the campus chaplain. As one junior explained, "I would say the majority of campus often feels predominantly Christian. However, when you really start to meet people and talk to them, you will find out just how diverse we all really are."

There are a number of ways to get involved in athletics on campus, from intramural sports to the varsity level. And although the school is successful in a number of different sports, football is an undeniable favorite at SMU. Some students complained that this favoritism can be to the detriment of other sports. "Our men's soccer team is ranked number one in our conference, and many people do not have any interest."

Still, there's something to be said for the enthusiasm amongst students when it comes to supporting their football team. Aside from the requisite body-painting and jersey-wearing, Mustangs list tailgating amongst their favorite

SMU traditions. Sure, this may sound like a relatively common pastime for a college campus, but don't be fooled. As one first year explained, "It's 'SMU tailgating.' People have big-screen TVs, satellite dishes, leather couches, and other ridiculous tailgating items." Indeed, tailgating draws crowds of Mustangs, alumni, and other fans to the "Boulevard," the road that runs north to south through the center of campus. Groups such as fraternities, sororities, and even different colleges rent out the red and blue tents that line the Boulevard to wait for the game to begin, aided by the large, digital countdown clocks that are scattered throughout the crowd. "Seeing friends, the free food, and the whole aspect of body-painting with fraternity brothers right before the game makes the whole experience a great one."

> **"It's 'SMU tailgating.' People have big-screen TVs, satellite dishes, leather couches, and other ridiculous tailgating items."**

Going Greek

Despite the fact that only about one third of Mustangs are members of a fraternity or sorority, it is also true that Greek life has a disproportionately strong presence on campus. "At SMU Greek life is huge," one sorority sister asserted. "The school, particularly the admissions office, tries to play it down. But in reality, as proven by statistics, it is the students that are in sororities and fraternities that have the highest average GPA and are the most involved in other programs on campus."

But the Greek system's visibility does not end there. The rush process virtually takes over the entire campus during the week before the start of spring semester in January. Rushees return early to SMU in order to participate in a full week of rush activities, described across the board as "intense." Sorority rushees, for example, have to dress for a different theme each day, whether it be business casual or formal. At the end of the rush process, all accepted sorority rushees participate in a "Pig Run," which requires the girls, dressed identically in white tops and jeans, to run from the center of campus to Sorority Row, all the while cheered on by the new fraternity pledges. And the enthusiasm extends well past rush. "In the spring everything kind of revolves around Greek life because everyone is so excited about it," a sophomore said.

The process is taken extremely seriously, to the point that potential pledges are not even allowed to interact with Greek members in the fall semester, for fear that groups will attempt to unfairly lure hapless first years into their sororities or fraternities. A small percentage of students, however, may take the process a little too seriously. "There's people who talk about girls transferring because they didn't get the house they wanted," one Mustang remarked, but later admitted to not knowing "how true that is."

The prominence of fraternities and sororities on campus often calls into question the issue of drinking on campus. In fact, aside from tailgates (at which those 21 and older wear bands indicating that they can drink), SMU is a dry campus. Campus police are strict in enforcing the rules. Students do have the option of going both to fraternity parties and to the bars surrounding campus, and many actively take advantage of these opportunities. But at the same time, there are more than enough opportunities for those who choose to stay on campus and not to drink. "SMU does a great job of providing many things to do, such as sneak peek previews for upcoming movies." At times, Southern Methodist University may live up to its reputation as "where rich white kids go to become Greek, party, and find their spouses." But that is far from all the school has to offer. From academics to tradition, SMU provides its students with the opportunity to have a world-class education within the "movie campus" that SMU calls home.—*Stephanie Brockman*

FYI

If you come to SMU, you'd better bring "a sundress for tailgating if you're a girl, and a polo shirt if you're a boy."

What is the typical weekend schedule? "Sleep almost all day on Saturday, wake up in time to tailgate, go pregame and then tailgate, and then go to sleep. Sundays, sleep in, shop, and do some studying."

If I could change one thing about SMU, I'd "dispel the negative stereotypes and rumors about SMU. I think many strong and focused students buy into the rumors and therefore believe SMU would not be a good fit for them."

Three things every student at SMU should do before graduating are "go to Plucker's (a local restaurant with GREAT wings) late night, take Crime and Delinquency with Richard Hawkins, and explore, and probably get lost in, downtown Dallas."

Texas A&M University

Address: P.O. Box 30014
College Station, TX
77843-3014
Phone: 979-845-3741
E-mail address:
admissions@tamu.edu
Web site URL: www.tamu.edu
Year Founded: 1876
Private or Public: Public
Religious Affiliation: None
Location: Rural
Number of Applicants:
20,887
Percent Accepted: 70%
**Percent Accepted who
enroll:** 55%
Number Entering: 8,093
**Number of Transfers
Accepted each Year:**
2,295
Middle 50% SAT range:
M: 560–670, CR: 520–630,
Wr: 500–610
Middle 50% ACT range: 23–29
**Early admission program
EA/ED/None:** None

**Percentage accepted
through EA or ED:** NA
EA and ED deadline: NA
Regular Deadline: 15-Jan
Application Fee: $60
**Full time Undergraduate
enrollment:** 35,271
Total enrollment: 38,430
Percent Male: 50%
Percent Female: 50%
**Total Percent Minority or
Unreported:** 27%
Percent African-American:
4%
**Percent Asian/Pacific
Islander:** 5%
Percent Hispanic: 16%
Percent Native-American:
1.0%
Percent International: 2%
**Percent in-state/out of
state:** 97%/3%
Percent from Public HS:
Unreported
Retention Rate: 92%
Graduation Rate 4-year: 41%

Graduation Rate 6-year:
77%
**Percent Undergraduates in
On-campus housing:** 24%
**Number of official organized
extracurricular
organizations:** 725
3 Most popular majors:
Business/Marketing,
Agriculture, Engineering
Student/Faculty ratio:
19:1
Average Class Size: 20 to 29
**Percent of students going to
grad school:** Unreported
Tuition and Fees: $22,184
**In State Tuition and Fees if
different:** $7,844
Cost for Room and Board:
$8,000
**Percent receiving financial
aid out of those who apply,
first year:** 68%
**Percent receiving financial
aid among all students:**
61%

Aggie pride and tradition are two of the defining characteristics of Texas A&M, located in College Station, Texas. At A&M, football reigns, making for "awesome school pride" and "one of the proudest, borderline cocky schools in Texas." From the folly of ring-dunking and pond-hopping to the somber Aggie Muster and Silver Taps, as one senior said, "There are so many events here that bring people together as Aggies."

Finding an Academic Niche

Although introductory-level classes at Texas A&M can be as large as 300 to 400 people, according to one senior, "Once you get more specific, class size shrinks"—often to about 20-30 students. For a more intimate academic experience from the start, A&M offers honors programs that include smaller classes taught by distinguished professors. But despite the fact that A&M has more than 36,000 students, professors are generally accessible, especially when students make an effort to talk to them after class. "I've never had any problems being able to talk to professors," one junior said.

Getting into popular classes—generally those that are fun or easy—can be a challenge, especially for freshmen, who get last pick in the registration process. One student tried to register for "History of Rock & Roll" three times before nabbing a spot in the popular lecture. But student workers and honors students get to register early, and all students are generally able to get into classes required for their majors. "Any class that you need to get, you can get into," a senior said.

Across Texas A&M's 10 different colleges, the sciences feature most prominently. "A lot of people want to be doctors," one junior said. Engineering, biomedical science, and business are among the most popular majors. But the liberal arts are by no means insignificant, nor are the social sciences; one student said the political science major is becoming more popular, especially with the influence of the George (H.W.) Bush Presidential Library and Museum on campus.

Majors in math and science are generally considered harder than liberal arts programs; architecture majors are said to "never leave the building," and engineering majors "usually have no lives." But "they enjoy what they're doing," one junior said. On the flip side, students consider communications, education, and recreational parks and tourism among A&M's easiest majors. Still, "You get out of it what you put into it," the student said. And no matter one's major, as another junior put it, at A&M, "You're gonna earn that degree; you're not gonna coast."

The school's agricultural roots (A&M once stood for "agricultural and mechanical") still loom large with strong veterinary and agriculture programs. The agriculture department offers courses including agribusiness, agricultural journalism, agricultural leadership ("Nobody really knows what it is," one sophomore said), and poultry science—not to be confused with political science, another student joked.

Overall, students cite the variety of Texas A&M's programs of study as a favorite aspect of academics at their school. Whether spending hours in biomedical engineering labs or taking niche classes like "Feminism in Hip Hop" and "History of 18th-Century Dress," Aggies have a vast array of academic options from which they can choose.

Campus and Beyond

A&M's campus architecture is "a hodge-podge" of styles, as one junior put it, and construction is "nonstop." The biggest current project is the planned renovation of the Memorial Student Center—a popular campus hangout that is set to close for three years beginning in 2009, much to the dismay of many students.

Most campus housing at Texas A&M is located on either the Northside—which students say is known to be a more tight-knit, sometimes rowdier community—or the Southside—where student residents live in newer dorms, including the popular Commons, a complex of four connected dorm buildings. While most Aggies choose to live in the dorms for their first year, after that, "everyone lives off campus," one sophomore said, explaining that sophomores, juniors and seniors often opt to live in nearby apartments or in fraternity or sorority houses. Campus is considered "very safe," and College Station, at least the area near campus, is generally also secure.

With the move off campus, many Aggies opt out of A&M's meal plans, which one junior said are convenient for freshmen but have "really limited choices." Still, the most popular dining hall on campus, Sbisa, offers a variety of ethnic foods and is generally

considered "really good." There are also smaller eateries throughout campus, as well as numerous popular College Station restaurants, many of which accept "Aggie Bucks."

Students describe College Station as a small town with housing and restaurants aplenty. And town-gown relations are generally amicable; "The town wouldn't exist without the University," one junior pointed out. "Most of the joints in town have some sort of maroon or A&M logo" in their storefronts, another junior said.

Sports, Soldiers, and Social Life

Even in off years, athletics dominate A&M's social scene, with Kyle Stadium's more than 80,000 seats filled to capacity on football Saturdays. "They pretty much rule the school," one junior said of Aggie sports. On the Friday nights preceding home football games, students flock to the stadium for Midnight Yell—a massive pep rally where Yell Leaders direct students in practicing traditional Aggie yells. On football Saturdays, students in attendance cheer on the team with "wildcats"—distinct noises and corresponding motions made by each class. Students stand for the whole game to honor the story of the "Twelfth Man," a 1920s football attendee who came down from the crowd and suited up for one game, standing at the ready if he should be needed by the injury-ridden team, which eventually managed to pull out a win.

Outside athletics, one unique part of campus life at Texas A&M is the Corps of Cadets—a vital remnant of the school's founding as a military college. The Corps is a body of about 2,000 male and female Aggies who sign up for military training along with their A&M education. Corps members are not obligated to serve in the military after graduation unless they choose to sign up for the ROTC. Students not preparing for military service often participate to carry on family tradition or to be a part of Texas A&M's all-Corps marching band. Corps members are seen in uniform in class, but the Corps dorms are "almost like a different world from the campus," one senior said. Corps members "like to hang out with other people so they don't go crazy," but "they definitely tell you from day one that your best friends are in the Corps," the student said.

As for Greek life at A&M, "It's not a super big emphasis," according to one junior. Whereas sororities are quite popular, fraternities have less of a presence—the result of an age-old tension between fraternities and the Corps. "If you want to get hazed, join the Corps instead of the frats," a senior said.

On the weekends, the main social scene is at North Gate—a strip of restaurants, two-step dance halls, and bars near campus. Most students have cars to go off campus, as strict alcohol policies in the dorms often deter on-campus parties. Enforcement of alcohol rules is up to the discretion of individual RAs, but, according to one junior, throwing parties on campus is "pointless"; students know that if they get caught they will "get in big trouble." Though largely off campus, drinking at A&M is as prominent as at most other colleges, students said, but drugs have a minimal presence.

Aggie Pride

With over 800 student organizations, extracurricular activities at A&M are "a huge deal," comprising the so-called "other education" that Aggies seek outside the classroom. "Everyone is involved in at least one thing," one junior said. Among the most prominent activities are student government, including freshman leadership organizations (FLOs); student publications like the school's newspaper, *The Battalion*; intramural sports; student employment; and Fish Camp—a freshman orientation program.

Even with such variety of interests among the student body, diversity is one front where students said the school could improve. "Diversity is one of the big problems here—there's not much of it," one senior said, noting that Texas A&M is often stereotyped as a school of white, Christian conservatives. But the administration is "making a conscious effort," one junior said, to push for a more diverse population, especially as part of the Vision 2020 program—a plan launched in 1997 to establish Texas A&M as one of the nation's top public universities by the year 2020.

Still, unifying traditions abound at A&M. On Ring Day, which takes place each semester, students who have completed 95 hours of class time invite family and friends to watch them receive their class rings. "Aggies are obsessed with our Aggie rings," one senior said. When their parents have left, students take part in the traditional "ring dunk,"

each dropping their new ring into a pitcher of beer and chugging the beer until only the ring remains. Another favorite tradition is pond-hopping, during which students jump into the various fountains on campus.

But some traditions are more somber. At the annual Aggie Muster, roll calls of Aggie soldiers who have died in battle that year are read aloud at ceremonies throughout the world, the largest one taking place on A&M's campus. And when any current students die during military service, they are remembered that month during a solemn observance called Silver Taps. Bonfire is another major tradition at A&M. Until 12 students were killed when the fire collapsed during construction in 1999, the event was held on campus each year to energize Aggies for the annual football game against rival the University of Texas at Austin. Since Texas A&M officials cancelled Bonfire, students have continued to lead it independently off campus.

Traditions such as these unite Aggies in a spirit of camaraderie echoed by the famous "Howdy"—the Aggie custom in which students greet everyone they pass on the street with the warm salutation. From the moment students arrive at A&M to the time they graduate, such friendliness is constantly encouraged: "Aggies are nice, Aggies are friendly, Aggies stay happy," one senior said. Although the rise of the iPod culture is making the Howdy a "dying tradition," according to one junior, still "it's a very friendly population."

> **"Aggies are nice, Aggies are friendly, Aggies stay happy."**

Even among so-called "two-percenters," the few A&M students who do not attend football games and are less involved with school traditions, the power of the "Aggie family" is strong. Whether in the classroom, in the dance halls or on the football field, "it's ridiculous how much culture A&M has," a senior said. As Aggies say, "From the outside looking in, you can't understand it; from the inside looking out, you can't explain it."—*Margy Slattery*

FYI

If you come to Texas A&M, you'd better bring "anything maroon-colored" and "good walking shoes—the place is gigantic."

What is the typical weekend schedule? Thursday night, students pack College Station's dance halls; Friday night is dominated by parties and, during football season, Midnight Yell; Saturday is spent tailgating and then cheering on the football team at the game, followed by bar-hopping at North Gate ("to celebrate or mourn" the game's result); Sunday, many students go to church and then "buckle down and study for the week."

If I could change one thing about Texas A&M, I'd make the student body "more open-minded and more diverse."

Three things every student should do before graduation are "dunk your ring," "go pond-hopping," and "witness A&M beating the hell out of UT [the University of Texas at Austin] at some sport."

Texas Christian University

Address: 2800 S. University Drive Fort Worth, TX 76129

Phone: 817-257-7490

E-mail address: admissions@tcu.edu

Web site URL: www.tcu.edu

Year Founded: 1873

Private or Public: Private

Religious Affiliation: Christian Church, Disciples of Christ

Location: Urban

Number of Applicants: 12,212

Percent Accepted: 50%

Percent Accepted who enroll: 27%

Number Entering: 2,039

Number of Transfers Accepted each Year: 826

Middle 50% SAT range: M: 540–640, CR: 520–630, Wr: 530–640

Middle 50% ACT range: 23–28

Early admission program EA/ED/None: ED

Percentage accepted through EA or ED: Unreported

EA and ED deadline: 1-Nov

Regular Deadline: 15-Feb

Application Fee: $40

Full time Undergraduate enrollment: 7,143

Total enrollment: 8,696

Percent Male: 41%

Percent Female: 59%

Total Percent Minority or Unreported: 17%

Percent African-American: 5%

Percent Asian/Pacific Islander: 3%

Percent Hispanic: 7%

Percent Native-American: <1%

Percent International: Unreported

Percent in-state/out of state: 73%/27%

Percent from Public HS: 72%

Retention Rate: 86%

Graduation Rate 4-year: 54%

Graduation Rate 6-year: 69%

Percent Undergraduates in On-campus housing: 46%

Number of official organized extracurricular organizations: 205

3 Most popular majors: Business Administration, Nursing, Advertising/Public Relations

Student/Faculty ratio: 14:1

Average Class Size: 27

Percent of students going to grad school: 21.90%

Tuition and Fees: $28,250

In State Tuition and Fees if different: No difference

Cost for Room and Board: $10,000

Percent receiving financial aid out of those who apply, first year: 86%

Percent receiving financial aid among all students: 68%

Texas Christian University lies in the heart of Dallas/Fort Worth, and it embodies the heart of Texas. From the football stands to the classroom, TCU students carry a "go get 'em" attitude and a horned frog football cheer. As one sophomore so eloquently put it, "I will bleed purple until the day I die."

The Perfect Fit

Texas Christian University offers its students a well-rounded liberal arts education that "gives you a broad experience but [doesn't] force you to delve too deeply into subjects you're not interested in," according to one sophomore. His classmate elaborated: "I revel in the academic life here." That life requires an "essential" core curriculum which consists of credits in the humanities, social sciences, natural sciences, fine arts, mathematics, writing, and oral communication. There is also a Heritage, Mission, Vision, and Values requirement with emphases on religion, culture, and history. In addition, students at TCU must complete their majors' requirements. One sophomore explained that "people in 'technical' majors like nursing or engineering have it much tougher than the liberal arts majors." Students name biology, physics, mathematics, chemistry, accounting/finance, engineering, and nursing as the difficult majors, and advertising/public relations, communications, interior design, and nutrition as the less demanding ones.

The Neeley School of Business houses the most competitive majors, while hard-core studiers are found racing along the pre-med track. TCU also offers a highly praised Honors Program, which awards early class registration to students invited to the program upon acceptance to TCU, as well as those who prove themselves capable by first semester grades. In order to stay in the Honors Program, students must fulfill additional class requirements. Many pursue the Chancellor's Leadership Program and specialized programs in the business school in place of the generalized honors curriculum. Texas Christian University strives to maintain small classes of 30 to 40 students. Therefore, class registration for popular majors like communications can be difficult when many students compete for the same courses. (Athletes and honors students have the privilege of registering early). According to TCU students, the process, though potentially frustrating, results in "perfect" class sizes and a manageable workload. One sophomore stated "I feel like academics at TCU are challenging but not burdensome for the most part; students are still able to have a social life and keep a good GPA."

Although lacking worldwide fame, the professors at Texas Christian University are praised by their students. One student caringly described his favorite teachers: "Dr. Patrick Nuss is an amazing teacher in the business school. I particularly enjoy Dr. Blake Hestir of the Philosophy Department (the existentialist, he has a delightfully sinister sense of humor) and Dr. Timothy Parrish of the English Department (the classic ponytail, glasses, preoccupied, brilliant, bad-at-spelling English professor)." Other students reiterated the fact that they cherish their close relationships with professors and cited rare, yet positive, experiences with teaching assistants. "The only grievance I have with classes," one sophomore said, "is that sometimes there are not enough of them." However, the same student went on to explain the University's extraordinary focus on accommodating student concerns. For example, the Schieffer School of Journalism recently added several classes in response to student demand.

Living It Up

TCU party life is divided in two ways: underclassmen and upperclassmen, and Greeks and non-Greeks. Underclassmen go to frat parties, house parties, and mixers on the weekends, while upperclassmen prefer bars. However, obtaining alcohol is not much of a problem for anyone at TCU, even for those who are underage.

Since the University is a Christian school, there are many non-drinkers and more alternative social venues for them to enjoy. A number of concert venues are near campus, and the TCU theater has scheduled performances on most weekends. Further, the Bass Performing Arts Hall provides musical performances, and the Programming Council, part of the student government, plans movies and concerts for students. There is a student center on campus with a ballroom.

Most campus-wide events at TCU are hosted by independent or Greek organizations. Approximately 37 percent of men join fraternities, and 39 percent of women join sororities. The rush process consumes a large amount of student energy. Though fraternity rush is relatively laid-back at TCU, sorority rush is incredibly stressful, noted one sophomore. However, another added that "cool" frats and sororities just depend on your preference of people. "Everyone has different ideas about which ones are the best," so there is no real hierarchy in the Texas Christian Greek society. The parties are usually fun and girls are rarely charged for admission or drinks. Most often, it's the fraternity members who fund alcohol purchases and theme parties, the best of which come at Halloween, Christmas, and the end of the year—barring any police presence: "Fort Worth has the largest police force in Texas." The TCU administration is also tough on drinking. Kegs are allowed on campus only for tailgates, and Greek organizations are held liable for any out-of-control events. However, the University has recently installed a "medical amnesty" policy that protects students with alcohol-induced sickness from punishment in order to insure their safe treatment.

A Deficit in Dating and Diversity

The dating life at TCU is minimal. "A lot of people joke that at TCU, you either have a boyfriend or you hook up, but there is little 'dating,'" one sophomore said. This phenomenon may make sense considering that the college is smack in the middle of a state famous for its attractive populace. Who wants to settle down when there's so much to go around? One male student elaborated: "The girls are hot. The guys aren't too shabby from what I hear either. Overall the campus is generally pretty gorgeous. It's easy to forget that there are unattractive people in the world." Aside from all of the ogling on campus, sex keeps a pretty low profile at TCU. There have recently been articles in campus publications about the lurking threat of STDs, but none of the interviewed students cited a significant presence.

In particular, homosexual and interracial couples are few and far between. "There are very few gays," one student noted. Further, the school has a very small minority population. And although most students seem pleased with the student population, they do wish it were more diverse. The overwhelming homogeneity has made minority students somewhat exclusive. "The African-American crowd typically associates solely with each other," one senior said. "Many students assume that if a TCU student is black, he or she is an athlete, which is certainly not the case." The TCU stereotype is "white, rich and Greek." One student passionately described the "typical student" as a "sorority girl wearing her silly big sunglasses and carrying her Prada bag while she talks on her cell phone. She's probably driving her Mercedes, too." Since TCU was rated one of the fittest campuses in the country by *Men's Fitness* magazine, and the Rec Center is one of the hottest daytime spots on campus, chances are that girl is probably worked hard enough to deserve those designer jeans.

Living On, Eating Off
The average freshman dorm at TCU provides "the basic necessities and nothing more." Space is tight, and visiting, alcohol and drug restrictions are even tighter, but students still find the overall dorm experience to be "fine." All dorms come with air-conditioning, heat, and RAs. Most students agreed that the best dorms are Moncrief Hall and Foster Hall, which also happen to be coed. The worst dorm is reportedly Milton Daniel: "It has broken water fountains and smells like puke and carrots on a fairly regular basis." Interestingly, binge drinkers and wild parties are mysteriously attracted to Milton's conditions.

TCU has a separate endowment dedicated to landscaping, so you can be sure that the physical campus is beautiful—and safe. "I absolutely feel safe at TCU," affirmed one student. The police are easily accessible, and TCU has an all-male organization called "Froggie-Five-O" that gives rides to girls when they have to walk at night. Despite the friendly security services, most upperclassmen move off campus to enjoy apartment or house setups and lower prices. Added one sophomore, "Underclassmen are allowed to live off campus, but it is strongly discouraged."

> "The campus is generally pretty gorgeous. It's easy to forget that there are unattractive people in the world."

Most students, even residents, eat a fair number of meals off campus, because of the dining halls' expensive prices and inconvenient timing (although the University is planning to improve the cafeterias in the near future). "The only thing that stays open past 2:30 in the afternoon is the Main, which is really fattening and heavy food. Edens, Deco Deli, and Sub Connection are all better options if you don't mind eating really early." The Main's main draw is its social appeal. Most campus cliques (fraternities, athletes) are represented there during the day, so groups of friends might appear just to socialize.

As for off-campus eateries, "the most famous restaurant in Fort Worth is undoubtedly Joe T. Garcia's. It's been around forever!" Italian Inn is also a great, but undiscovered date restaurant where the waiters serve and entertain. And although there is a local Starbucks, the Panther City Coffee Co. is heralded as the best spot for an espresso shot.

Texas Is for Football
Football is the most popular spectator sport at Texas Christian University. The Horned Frogs recently won the Poinsettia Bowl and draw much school spirit from students and alumni alike. In fact, TCU's traditional spectator chant, "Riff Ram Bah Zoo," is one of the oldest cheers in college history.

Unique to TCU are the Purple Hearts, a student organization that helps lure high school football players to the University. "We recruit senior football players for the TCU team through visits to the stadium and the athletic complex at home games," a student explained. For more recreational athletes, IM sports are prevalent at TCU, and the Campus Recreation Center offers state-of-the-art athletic equipment. "Every cardio machine has its own flat-screen TV, and there are really nice weights and stuff. There are also aerobic classes and yoga every day, an indoor and outdoor swimming pool, and indoor and outdoor track."

According to one sophomore, "TCU students are very involved, and spend quite a bit of their time on other activities." About half of the student body works a part-time job, and most are identified by their extracurricular activities. Social organizations, performance groups, intramurals, academic organizations, and service organizations are the most popular. The most heralded organization is Frog Camp, an orientation trip for freshmen for which upperclassmen are leaders. Also highly touted are the Student Government Association, Order of Omega Greek honors society, sports appreciation organizations, and the "eleven40seven" journal of written and visual arts.

Texas Tradition
One thing is clear: TCU is a university bathed in tradition. Along with legendary cheers, students are indoctrinated by a wealth of myth when they accept admission to the school. One student cited the following examples: "When the purple light is on in Frog Fountain, the Chancellor is on campus. If you kiss the nose of the iron Horned Frog statue, you will have good luck. The bodies of Addison and Randolph Clark (TCU's founders) are actually cremated inside their bronze statues. It is tradition to raise your right hand and make the horned frog sign with your fingers when the chapel bell rings the alma mater." Another noted that President Lyndon B. Johnson himself broke the ground for the Sid Richardson Science Building when it was built in the seventies.

TCU is a place that people fall in love with, from its glorious oaks to its cheesy mascot: "People take a lot of pride from being Frogs—we're the only Horned Frogs in the nation!"—*Lauren Ezell*

FYI
If you come to TCU, you better bring "a lot of Polos."
What is a typical weekend schedule? "Study by day, party by night."
If I could change one thing about TCU, I'd "make it more diverse."
Three things every student at TCU should do before graduating are "Study abroad, jump in Frog Fountain, and go to Joe T's and Ol' South."

Texas Tech University

Address: Box 45005 Lubbock, TX 79409-5005	**EA and ED deadline:** NA	**Percent Undergraduates in On-campus housing:** 26%
Phone: 806-742-1480	**Regular Deadline:** 1-May	
E-mail address: admissions@ttu.edu	**Application Fee:** $50	**Number of official organized extracurricular organizations:** 399
Web site URL: www.ttu.edu	**Full time Undergraduate enrollment:** 21,062	
Year Founded: 1923	**Total enrollment:** 23,021	**3 Most popular majors:**
Private or Public: Public	**Percent Male:** 54%	Business/Marketing, Family and Consumer Sciences, Engineering
Religious Affiliation: None	**Percent Female:** 46%	
Location: Urban	**Total Percent Minority or Unreported:** 24%	
Number of Applicants: 13,976	**Percent African-American:** 5%	**Student/Faculty ratio:** 18:1
Percent Accepted: 77%		**Average Class Size:** 20 to 29
Percent Accepted who enroll: 41%	**Percent Asian/Pacific Islander:** 4%	**Percent of students going to grad school:** Unreported
Number Entering: 4,439	**Percent Hispanic:** 13%	**Tuition and Fees:** $15,213
Number of Transfers Accepted each Year: 2,818	**Percent Native-American:** 1.0%	**In State Tuition and Fees if different:** $6,783
Middle 50% SAT range: M: 500–610, CR: 480–580, Wr: 460–560	**Percent International:** 1%	**Cost for Room and Board:** $7,310
	Percent in-state/out of state: 96%/4%	**Percent receiving financial aid out of those who apply, first year:** 46%
Middle 50% ACT range: 21–26	**Percent from Public HS:** Unreported	
Early admission program EA/ED/None: None	**Retention Rate:** 83%	**Percent receiving financial aid among all students:** 44%
Percentage accepted through EA or ED: NA	**Graduation Rate 4-year:** 27%	
	Graduation Rate 6-year: 54%	

At a school with over 22,000 undergraduates, it's hard to define the "typical student." But students at Texas Tech are united by their commitment to the University and to the community at large. "This is one of the most exciting times to be a part of Texas Tech," explained one student, who sees a renaissance beginning for the school. "We're an emerging research university now," he said, citing several recently-hired faculty members and the acquisition of a new Vice President of Research for the University. "We want to become a top one."

Such ambition is characteristic of Tech students and is exemplified by the school's Student Government Association. Officers spend up to 40 hours per week at the SGA office, working to promote student needs and to develop and execute initiatives of their own. The SGA created programs such as Take a Kid to the Game, which allows local underprivileged kids to watch the Red Raiders play football and spend the day with a Tech student. The SGA has also worked with the University's career center to attract the attention of prominent Texas-based companies. "We want to do a better job of getting Tech's image out there," said a member of the SGA.

Academics on the Upswing

Students say they are generally happy with the courses offered at Tech, but deciding which classes to take can be a bit of a headache. Students criticized the advising program, claiming that counselors "aren't always helpful." One student, who complicated her degree plan by changing her major, said "it's hard for students who don't know what they want to do right away." While one student remarked that his interactions with advisors "left something to be desired," others reported that advisors can actually be helpful.

> **"This is one of the most exciting times to be a part of Texas Tech"**

Small classes tend to give students the most positive academic experiences at Texas Tech. Introductory classes, particularly in popular departments like business, biology, architecture, and English, may have 400 or more students. One student called his experiences in these classes "disappointing," pointing out that he never got to actually meet his professors. Upper-level classes, however, which contain between 30 and 70 students, are "more fulfilling."

Regardless of class size, professors are "very accessible," offering regular, frequent office hours. Students also praised Tech's academic atmosphere. "It doesn't seem like a high-stress, competitive setting," said one student. "The professors and students are really friendly and open."

One student highlighted Tech's recent academic improvement and potential for future growth. He said that while he is "not happy with where we are right now," the school has made a lot of progress in the past five years, as a greater number of small classes are offered and the quality of professors improves.

At Large in Lubbock

Most students at Texas Tech, especially non-freshmen, live off campus. However, a new on-campus option of two- to three-bedroom apartment-style housing is popular among upperclassmen, one student said. Students said high-quality off-campus housing is relatively easy to find. In addition to the three apartment complexes across the street from campus (one of which is newer and more expensive than the other two), students also live in a residential neighborhood south of campus known as "Tech Terrace." Other popular apartment complexes may be found farther away from campus, but travel to and from these locations usually requires a bus trip.

The University requires that freshmen live on campus, and most students claimed that the experience of living in a dorm was valuable. One student noted that even though she moved off campus by sophomore year, she was "grateful" for her on-campus experience because it was "a great way to meet people." Students also have the option of living on specially assigned Intensive Study or Substance-Free floors (although technically, alcohol and other drugs are prohibited in all dorms).

Student attitudes are generally positive, but not extremely enthusiastic, about the town of Lubbock. One student said that she wished she were in a bigger city—"though I love Lubbock," she added. Students say that the town is safe, and there is a separate on-campus police force. One student explained, "You either love Lubbock or you hate it, because there's not a whole lot to do except get involved with things on campus and in the town."

Gregarious Greeks

Getting involved is what Tech students do best. Whether it's involvement in a community outreach program, writing for Tech's newspaper, *The Daily Toreador*, or membership in a service sorority or fraternity, there is no shortage of extracurricular pursuits at Texas Tech.

While Tech's 411 student organizations cater to a variety of interests, Greek organizations are especially popular. "Greek life is really big, whether you're in it or not," said one student. Fraternities and sororities throw most of the parties at Tech, although because so many students live off campus, non-Greek house parties are common as well. Greek students pointed out that by joining a fraternity or sorority, you are not only part of the single organization, but also a member of the greater Greek community at Tech. "It's nice to know that you can go to any local bar on a Thursday night and see all your friends," said one sorority member. Students at Tech are also attracted to Greek life for its service component, and some choose to join service sororities, which place an even greater emphasis on philanthropy. A student who joined both a Greek sorority and a non-Greek service sorority pointed out that while she enjoys Greek life, she has made closer friends through the service sorority because of its smaller size and more personal atmosphere.

The Center for Campus Life, which is the central office for all registered organizations on campus, is located in the Student Union Building. Since its recent renovation, the Student Union, which houses a bookstore, meeting rooms, TVs, and a computing assistance center, has been especially popular among students. Furthermore, students are enthusiastic about the Student Union's food court, which includes a Chick-fil-A and a Starbucks.

The Center for Campus Life also provides a host of entertainment programs and events that range from concerts, interactive games, and movies to more academic-oriented programs like workshops and lecturers. TAB, the Tech Activities Board, also organizes events such as open mike nights, bowling, and foreign film screenings for those looking for an alternative to the Greek life. When football season is in play, countless students participate in RaiderGate, co-hosted by the student government, which is Texas Tech's version of tailgating, complete with live music and barbeque.

A "Dry" Town

Though Lubbock is a "dry" town and liquor stores are prohibited, bars are exempted from this law. In fact, Lubbock has a colorful bar scene—Bleacher's Sports Café, The Library, Rocky's, and Timmy's are student favorites. In order to purchase alcohol, students drive to an area called the Strip (apparently modeled after Las Vegas) outside of town. "It would be easier to go down to the convenience store and pick something up," one student griped.

While one student said that "a lot of partying goes on" at Tech, another pointed out that there is a "growing minority" that doesn't drink. In any case, students agreed that non-drinkers do not feel uncomfortable at Tech.

Red Raiders in a Red State

Students agree that the political climate at Tech and in Lubbock is "very conservative." One student put it this way: "If you don't love George Bush, you're in the minority." However, an officer of the University Democrats pointed out that liberal students are more common than you might expect, adding that liberalism is "an underground thing."

The student body at Tech is not very diverse, although students claim that the school is taking steps to increase racial diversity. While there is a Gay Straight Alliance at Tech, students agree that the gay community is not very visible. Of the 37 religiously-affiliated student organizations at Tech, 30 are Christian groups. One student pointed out that Bible studies are common and well-attended at Tech. Another student agreed that Christian groups are plentiful on campus but added that non-Christians "don't feel out of place."

Tech Takes the Field

Texas Tech is known for its high-caliber sports teams and enthusiastic fans. Cheering on the Red Raiders at football and basketball games is a central part of the Tech experience. Coach Bobby Knight, who retired in February of 2008, helped vault the basketball team into the spotlight, and women's basketball is drawing higher attendance than it ever has before—higher, sometimes, than the men's team. Football, though, is the main attraction, according to students. The pregame festivities alone are impressive, with fraternities, sororities, alumni groups, and even local rodeos sponsoring tailgates. On the Thursday before a game day, students decorate a statue of Will Rogers and his horse, Soapsuds, with red crepe paper. Even without the streamers, this Tech landmark is full of Tech pride. The horse's behind points straight in the direction of Tech's biggest rival, Texas A&M.

Non-varsity athletes at Tech are not just devoted fans; they are devoted players. Tech students are passionate about intramural sports, and since the expansion of the Student Recreation Center, IMs are more popular than ever. Student organizations, Greek organizations, and dorms field IM teams, and, as one student explained, "everybody plays; everybody wants to be the best." The Rec Center offers classes, workshops, and even massage therapy.

In the classroom, on the football field, or in the community, Red Raiders are proud to be part of the growth and improvement that characterizes Texas Tech. With a wide array of academic offerings, facilities that are constantly improving, and a rich extracurricular scene, Texas Tech is gaining popularity with Texans and non-Texans alike.—*Kathleen Reeves*

FYI

If you come to Texas Tech, you better bring "a day planner, because so many activities are offered on campus, and rain boots, because of the ineffective drainage system."

What's the typical weekend schedule? "Wednesday: Hit up a bar called South Beach; Thursday: Go to the Depot District of town; Friday: Hear a country band play at Wild West; Saturday: Football game day! Afterwards, head to a house party or the bars. Sunday: Wake up, spend all day at the library."

If I could change one thing about Tech, I'd "change the restrictive parking system."

Three things every student at Tech should do before graduating are "attend a football game, get involved in an on-campus organization, and go to Carol of Lights, an annual, nationally recognized holiday lighting ceremony."

Trinity University

Address: One Trinity Place
San Antonio, TX
78212-7200
Phone: 210-999-7207
E-mail address:
admissions@trinity.edu
Web site URL: www.trinity.edu
Year Founded: 1869
Private or Public: Private
Religious Affiliation: None
Location: Urban
Number of Applicants: 3,754
Percent Accepted: 58%
Percent Accepted who enroll: 30%
Number Entering: 655
Number of Transfers Accepted each Year: 37
Middle 50% SAT range:
M: 610–690, CR: 600–690,
Wr: Unreported
Middle 50% ACT range: 27–31
Early admission program EA/ED/None: EA and ED
Percentage accepted through EA or ED:
Unreported

EA and ED deadline: 1-Nov
Regular Deadline: 1-Feb
Application Fee: $40
Full time Undergraduate enrollment: 2,489
Total enrollment: 2,703
Percent Male: 47%
Percent Female: 53%
Total Percent Minority or Unreported: 40%
Percent African-American: 4%
Percent Asian/Pacific Islander: 7%
Percent Hispanic: 11%
Percent Native-American: 1%
Percent International: 6%
Percent in-state/out of state: 73%/27%
Percent from Public HS: 72%
Retention Rate: 90%
Graduation Rate 4-year: 69%
Graduation Rate 6-year: 79%

Percent Undergraduates in On-campus housing: 71%
Number of official organized extracurricular organizations: 130
3 Most popular majors:
Business Administration/Management, English, Communications and Media Studies
Student/Faculty ratio: 9.5:1
Average Class Size: 10 to 19
Percent of students going to grad school: 34%
Tuition and Fees: $27,699
In State Tuition and Fees if different: No difference
Cost for Room and Board: $8,822
Percent receiving financial aid out of those who apply, first year: 67%
Percent receiving financial aid among all students: 83%

Trinity University sits on the top of a hill, overlooking the beautiful San Antonio skyline. The attractive campus is ideally situated in a private setting in the midst of a growing, modern Texas city just minutes from the popular downtown tourist area, as well as the San Antonio airport. Year-round mild Texas weather, coupled with an equally "warm" campus community, allows students to party heartily while still partaking in a comparatively rigorous liberal arts education. Although the University is historically Presbyterian-affiliated, the religious feel of the campus is not as strong as the "family feel" that makes Trinity so unique.

High Educational Standards

Trinity University gives its students a strong liberal arts and science education and prepares them for "a lifetime of success in any endeavor." According to one student, "Although Trinity is considered to be a liberal arts school, the science department is very strong and continues to grow. The humanities aspect of Trinity is also thriving, and new interdisciplinary majors are being added every year." The school claims that compared to other universities, Trinity students receive a truly practical education. The academic program contains three components. The first component is the Common Curriculum, which provides a foundation in the arts and sciences. The Common Curriculum consists of a First Year Seminar Program and a Writing Workshop; proficiency in foreign language, computer, and mathematics skills; fitness education; a senior experience; and a core liberal arts foundation consisting of "Five Fundamental Understandings." The second component of academic requirements is the major, which allows students to study a specific field in depth. Trinity offers its students 37 majors and 49 interdisciplinary minors. Thirdly, students must take elective courses in order to round out their curriculum and explore new areas.

Students generally agree that the "academic requirements are fairly stringent," but they also vary by department. According to one student, "Everyone is held to a high standard and the requirements are set forth to push even the brightest of students." Workload and class size all vary by department as well. Some students spend as much as 40 hours a week doing work, while many can get away with doing much less. Normal classes range in size from 25 to 80, but upper-level courses in some departments have fewer than 10 students. One student observes that "the majority of the departments are well known on Trinity's campus, especially since it is such a small school." Because Trinity is small, it also allows for low faculty-to-student ratios. "Every student has the opportunity to get to know their professors very well if they

wish. Many people take advantage of this and have developed extremely close relations with certain [professors]."

One unique aspect of Trinity's academic environment is the Academic Honor Code. Initiated by students in 2004, the Honor Code is signed by all freshmen at new student orientation and requires that students sign every assignment, affirming that they have been honest in their academic endeavors.

Students at Trinity do not find much competition among their peers academically. According to one student, "The students at Trinity put more stress on their own academics rather than competing with others. There are some who do put stress on competition, but they are in the minority." Another student notes, "Everyone does their own thing academically, but there is a sense of competition in sports." For students who wish to go beyond the typical academic rigor, there are many honors societies at Trinity. These include Alpha Lambda Delta (a first year academic distinction), Golden Key National Honor Society, Phi Beta Kappa (general distinction; liberal arts and sciences), Alpha Epsilon Delta (pre-med honors society), and an honors society for just about every academic department.

Sports and Frats Rule

On the weekends most students generally find themselves splitting time between fraternity parties and sporting events, as these tend to be the most popular social scenes on campus. According to one freshman, "Frats usually control the party scene on weekends." But a senior argues, "There is a large percentage of the student body involved in Greek life, but it doesn't dominate." In fact, the Greek scene incorporates about 25 percent of the student body and consists of six sororities and six fraternities. An interesting fact about the Greek life at Trinity is that all of the sororities and fraternities are local; they are not affiliated with any national Greek organizations, and as a result students do not have to pay high dues like at most other universities. The school does not allow Greek on-campus houses, but there are some "informal" off-campus houses.

Trinity University has 18 varsity sports teams, and they are some of the most competitive sports teams in the NCAA Division III and the Southern Collegiate Athletic Conference. Trinity has won an incredible number of SCAC President's Cup Trophies, awarded to the conference's best overall sports program. According to one student, "Sports rule

Trinity!" Students can often be found attending as many sporting events as they can on the weekends before going to the frat parties or local bars.

Many students at Trinity have cars, and there is "a good deal of parking on campus." Even so, since students are required to live on campus for three years, most of the weekend activity remains on campus. Only seniors live off campus, so according to one student, "they *do* have a different social life, since most of their friends also live off campus and parties are off campus." Other students can use their cars on the weekends by going to local bars, one of the most popular being Bombay's Bicycle Club. San Antonio also provides many other opportunities for evening activity; students often go to Cowboys Dance Hall to see concerts or to the popular commercial River Walk, along the banks of the San Antonio River.

> **"Sports rule Trinity!"**

Alcohol at Trinity is very common, but probably just as common as at most universities—in the words of one student, "No more, no less." Drug use seems to the students to be just as widespread as at other schools as well. Students are aware that "there is a very strict drug and alcohol policy on campus and campus security responds very quickly to complaints." Even students who are 21 or older are only allowed to have beer in their rooms—no hard liquor.

Typical Trinity students have been described by their peers as "preppy" and "rich," but surprisingly, there "are not very many snobs." There is not much diversity at Trinity, but the diversity that is present is "well-represented." The students at Trinity are all very friendly, and freshmen find it easy to meet others like themselves. According to one student, "Many people freshman year leave their doors propped open, and hanging out in other people's rooms is very common."

Community Living
Living on campus is "integral to the educational experience" at Trinity, and for this reason Trinity has imposed a Three-Year Residency Requirement on its students. Students are also guaranteed housing on campus senior year if they want it. As a result, about 70 percent of the student body lives on campus. First year students all live together in one area of campus, in one of seven dorms. This creates a freshman community. All residence halls are set up as suites, so two rooms share a bathroom and there are two students in each room. On-campus housing is considered "pretty decent," and this is not surprising given that students are required to live there for three years. About every 18 freshmen are assigned an upper-class Resident Mentor who guides them through New Student Orientation and "keeps the peace, mostly." Trinity also offers its freshmen First Year Special Interest Housing, including options for Quiet Living and Substance-Free Living. After freshman year, students can request where they would like to live and may also request a roommate. Dorm personalities "change a little each year depending on who lives there," but often the upperclassmen dorms Thomas and Lightner are said to be party dorms. The dorms maintain their own traditions such as the annual baby powder–covered Calvert Halloween "ghosts."

There are two places to eat on campus: Mabee Dining Hall and The Commons, a food court. The food on campus is, according to one student, "better than I thought it would be." The Commons is open until midnight, so students can buy late-night, fast-food snacks. There are also many good restaurants in nearby downtown San Antonio, if students get tired of the on-campus offerings.

Outside of the Classroom: Sports and More
At Trinity, athletics are much more than just a weekend diversion. In addition to the 18 competitive varsity teams, 65 percent of students at Trinity participate in club or intramural sports. Student-run club sports are very diverse, and include sports such as men's and women's lacrosse, equestrian sports, water polo, and even trap and skeet shooting. Intramural sports give all students an opportunity to join in the athletic competitions, as there are teams for "almost anything you could think of."

Students also participate in many other activities outside of the classroom. About half of the students at Trinity participate in community service through the Trinity University Voluntary Action Center. There are also many religious groups on campus, as well as political action groups and student publications such as the daily newspaper *The Trinitonian*. Some students also work during the school year, and there are plenty of job opportunities for those students. Some of the most popular part-time work includes positions at local high schools or at Trinity's admissions office, or work as a lifeguard. Again, accessibility to downtown San Antonio and its famed River-walk bars and restaurants is another perk of living in the middle of this modern city and popular tourist destination.

The sense of community resulting from Trinity's secluded campus, where most students live on campus, makes Trinity University a welcoming place. If that isn't enough,

rigorous academics and stellar sports and social opportunities will likely satisfy almost anyone. Warm Texas weather and the University's nice facilities and private but accessible location in a modern city with great restaurants, bars, and professional sports nearby contribute to creating a very satisfied student body.—*Jessica Rubin*

FYI

If you come to Trinity, you'd better bring "lots of flip-flops."

What's the typical weekend schedule? "It's all about sports at Trinity. . . . You'd better be at the football, soccer, basketball, volleyball, and baseball games!"

If I could change one thing about Trinity, I'd "change the temperature of the classrooms . . . they are so chilly."

Three things every student at Trinity should do before graduating are: "Go abroad if you can, take advantage of the variety of student organizations on campus, and get to know a professor."

University of Dallas

Address: 1845 East Northgate Drive Irving, TX 75062
Phone: 972-721-5266
E-mail address: ugadmis@udallas.edu
Web site URL: www.udallas.edu
Year Founded: 1956
Private or Public: Private
Religious Affiliation: Roman Catholic
Location: Urban
Number of Applicants: 1,060
Percent Accepted: 91%
Percent Accepted who enroll: 35%
Number Entering: 342
Number of Transfers Accepted each Year: 81
Middle 50% SAT range: M: 550–650, CR: 560–680, Wr: 530–670
Middle 50% ACT range: 24–29

Early admission program EA/ED/None: EA
Percentage accepted through EA or ED: 35%
EA and ED deadline: 1-Dec
Regular Deadline: 1-Aug
Application Fee: $40
Full time Undergraduate enrollment: 1,299
Total enrollment: 2,977
Percent Male: 49%
Percent Female: 51%
Total Percent Minority or Unreported: 32%
Percent African-American: 1%
Percent Asian/Pacific Islander: 5%
Percent Hispanic: 16%
Percent Native-American: <1%
Percent International: 2%
Percent in-state/out of state: 50%/50%
Percent from Public HS: 45%

Retention Rate: 80%
Graduation Rate 4-year: 46%
Graduation Rate 6-year: 56%
Percent Undergraduates in On-campus housing: 92%
Number of official organized extracurricular organizations: 35
3 Most popular majors: Biology, Business, English
Student/Faculty ratio: 13:1
Average Class Size: 20 to 29
Percent of students going to grad school: 25%
Tuition and Fees: $24,770
In State Tuition and Fees if different: No difference
Cost for Room and Board: $7,885
Percent receiving financial aid out of those who apply, first year: 65%
Percent receiving financial aid among all students: 81%

Amidst the wide variety of colleges and universities in the greater Dallas area, the University of Dallas stands out for its combination of academic rigor and traditional Catholic sensibilities. With a strong emphasis on the Western canon, a comprehensive core curriculum, and a wildly popular study-abroad program in Rome, UD offers

its students a structured, traditional education that will serve them well both in and out of the classroom.

Nerdy to the Core

UD has a reputation for being, as one student puts it, a "nerdy" school because of its comprehensive set of requirements known as the core curriculum. The UD core is mostly made up of primary sources that allow students to engage directly with the texts that shaped the foundations of Western thought. Of the credits needed to graduate, 15 are the same for everyone, made up of classes in English, history, theology, philosophy, economics, and politics. In addition, there are science lab, math, and language requirements that complete the core. English is one of the most popular majors at UD, despite the large amounts of reading, writing, and memorization it requires. Psychology is also a favorite, even though majors have to complete a thesis over 100 pages long to graduate. Language and math majors are universally less popular.

No matter what you're majoring in, classes at UD seem to be challenging all around. As one student explains, "UD is hard, a lot harder than the other schools my friends go to . . . you can't find an easy class to shrug off." Though the University is generous with academic and athletic scholarships, they are difficult to maintain: "The academic demands for retaining any scholarships . . . are rigorous, so many students aren't able to slack off even if they don't care." Adding to the academic intensity, there is a very strict attendance policy at UD—missing four classes automatically means that you are dropped from the course. Luckily, students have the support of the faculty to guide them through the rough waters of UD academics; most students are happy with their professors, saying that they are "very accessible—they *want* you to contact them when you need them." Some popular ones include English professor Father Robert Maguire and economics teacher William Doyle, who help UD kids achieve their "number one goal" of truly learning and internalizing the material that they grapple with.

TGIT: Thank God It's Thursday

Of course, there is much more to life at UD besides its standout academic program. While sports admittedly "aren't the focus of UD," students enjoy participating in and cheering on the teams that they have, including the men's rugby and basketball teams, whose games draw a huge following. Support for women's teams is a little "less vigorous," but both genders play baseball, soccer, and lacrosse. In fact, the UD lacrosse team is currently the only collegiate varsity lacrosse team in Texas. The newly renovated athletic center also provides lots of resources for students to stay in shape, including trainers and state-of-the-art equipment. Overall, as one student puts it, sports are "compatible" with the typical UD student way of life, even if they don't dominate it.

While there are over 35 extracurricular activities and clubs in which UD kids can participate, the consensus is that "club life isn't too popular in general, [since] a lot of students are busy studying." However, the student government and activities committee is large and attracts more and more people to its ranks in hopes of increasing the popularity of its events. Since there are no sororities or fraternities, on-campus social life at UD seems to revolve around parties in upperclassmen apartments either on campus or across the street in a group known as "Old Mill." Though some students say that "Student Apartment kids tend to stick to themselves," the parties they throw attract partygoers from all over the UD community. As one girl explains, "Younger and older students intermingle, making it easy for there to always be a party to go to if you have the right connections."

UD is a wet school, meaning that drinking is tolerated and prevalent throughout campus. While the drinking scene "never really gets out of control," one student admits that "technically, drinking policy is according to the law of the state of Texas, and if you get caught underage, you do get in trouble." Drinkers "tend to stick together" and congregate either at various parties or at a campus bar and grill called the Rathskeller that is actually on the student meal plan. For those who prefer their weekends dry, the student government sponsors a weekly event known as TGIT ("Thank God It's Thursday"), during which students party and dance to live music without the addition of alcohol.

Living in "the Convent"

Socially, UD provides a safe, friendly environment in which students can get to know each other. Despite the small size of the school (only about 1,200 total), most students claim that its nurturing environment is a help rather than a hindrance. "It's super easy to meet people your first semester, mostly because the school is so small . . . you immediately find your group of friends and settle in for the haul," said one junior. Diversity is a bit lacking at UD, since "most kids are white, hail from a Catholic (or at least Christian) household, and hold the same basic beliefs in common." However, some students claim that "there is a fair amount of diversity in religions and races," emphasizing that the University recognizes the importance of diversifying the student body and is making a conscious effort to do so. Either way, there is no lack of community at UD. As one junior raves, "That's one thing I love about this school . . . absolutely one hundred percent of [students] are genuine. Students are true to what they believe, kind and caring, and the farthest from a fake crowd you will ever find."

> "Students are true to what they believe, kind and caring, and the farthest from a fake crowd you will ever find."

The Dallas residential community is made up of a variety of houses, each of which has its own unique character. Freshmen and sophomores must live on campus in specific dorms, only one of which is coed. The prevalence of same-sex living "though it may seem like a bother, is actually pretty fun . . . dorm spirit is [awesome]." Of the eight dorms, the all-male Gregory and all-girl Jerome are known as the "party dorms," and Catherine, by contrast, is sometimes called "the Convent." All of them, however, have at least two RAs who are "strict" and "are pretty serious about their roles." While some upperclassmen continue to live on campus after sophomore year, most move to the Old Mill apartments across the street or into those in the Student Apartment complex, which are "a lot nicer . . . there's usually a waitlist to get in." The architecture on campus is "not very pretty to look at, but it serves its purpose"— some of UD's architectural standouts include the Braniff Memorial Tower, which is a "landmark for the University" and the newer Art Village, in which a whole group of buildings is "put on stilts, so . . . they pretty much [look like] they're in the trees."

All UD students who live on campus must be on a meal plan, and freshmen can choose between 14- or 19-meal-per-week plans. After freshman year, you can choose between plans of 19, 14, or 10 meals, and the declining balance can be used at the Rathskeller, which is located below the campus's only dining hall in the Haggar University Center. Most upperclassmen tend to get either the lowest amount of meals or no plan at all, since food-wise, "some days are better than others." Others are less diplomatic, saying, "Let's just put it this way—one of the most popular groups on Facebook is 'I starve myself to go to UD.' No one goes here for the dining services." Despite the lack of gourmet options, the dining hall and student center remains one of the central hangout locations on campus.

Dallas to Rome

Since there's "not much to do on campus," many UD students spend their weekends enjoying the restaurants and club scene in the surrounding Texas areas. The town of Irving itself is "a little scruffy" and not quite as nice as the school itself, yet town-gown relations are so calm as to be almost nonexistent, as one student describes: "Some people that live 15 minutes from the University have never even heard of it." To really get a taste of college town life, students recommend heading into the bigger city of Dallas itself for the best bar, shopping, and restaurant scenes. They agree, however, that "[since] most places are a few miles away . . . if you want to hang out outside of campus, you need a car." Whether you want to party in downtown clubs, shop in the popular West End or Las Colinas districts, or just grab dinner and a movie with friends, Dallas offers a plethora of opportunities for fun and relaxation off campus.

Perhaps the most well-known component of life at UD and the one that draws in the most students is its Rome program. Most sophomores spend at least one semester studying at UD's campus at Due Santi, just 20 minutes away from Rome itself. For many UD students, Rome is the highlight of their college career, as they take classes in subjects like ancient architecture and travel throughout Italy and Greece on weekends to see the very monuments they study. The Rome program, with its synthesis of Western tradition and Catholic values, and its application of the concepts learned in the classroom to real life, is the epitome of what makes the University of Dallas "a real, true, Catholic, strenuous liberal arts education that will influence all aspects of students' lives."—*Alexandra Bicks*

FYI

If you come to Dallas, you'd better bring: "a formal gown, cowboy hat and boots."

What's a typical weekend schedule? "Sleep it off from the night before, go to an occasional extra credit lecture on campus, do homework for a couple hours, hit Old Mill or the Student Apartments to do it again."

If I could change one thing about Dallas, I'd: "Make it a little bigger, and pretty up some of that architecture."

Three things everyone should do before graduating are: "[participate in] all the activities you can, go to Rome, and attend mass at the Cistercian Abbey of Our Lady of Dallas."

University of Houston

Address: 122 E. Cullen Building Houston, TX 77204-2023
Phone: 713-743-1010
E-mail address: admissions@uh.edu
Web site URL: www.uh.edu
Year Founded: 1927
Private or Public: Public
Religious Affiliation: None
Location: Urban
Number of Applicants: 9,935
Percent Accepted: 75%
Percent Accepted who enroll: 43%
Number Entering: 3,218
Number of Transfers Accepted each Year: 4,119
Middle 50% SAT range: M: 490–610, CR: 460–580, Wr: Unreported
Middle 50% ACT range: 19–24
Early admission program EA/ED/None: None

Percentage accepted through EA or ED: NA
EA and ED deadline: NA
Regular Deadline: 1-Apr
Application Fee: $50
Full time Undergraduate enrollment: 27,400
Total enrollment: 32,631
Percent Male: 49%
Percent Female: 51%
Total Percent Minority or Unreported: 66%
Percent African-American: 14%
Percent Asian/Pacific Islander: 20%
Percent Hispanic: 21%
Percent Native-American: <1%
Percent International: 4%
Percent in-state/out of state: 98%/2%
Percent from Public HS: Unreported
Retention Rate: 77%

Graduation Rate 4-year: 11%
Graduation Rate 6-year: 11%
Percent Undergraduates in On-campus housing: 25%
Number of official organized extracurricular organizations: 300
3 Most popular majors: Engineering, Psychology
Student/Faculty ratio: 20:1
Average Class Size: 20 to 29
Percent of students going to grad school: Unreported
Tuition and Fees: $16,597
In State Tuition and Fees if different: $8,167
Cost for Room and Board: $6,935
Percent receiving financial aid out of those who apply, first year: 56%
Percent receiving financial aid among all students: 85%

Students who choose the University of Houston prepare for the professional world in a number of unique academic colleges, while enjoying the opportunity of living at home yet remaining involved on campus through intramural sports and numerous clubs. UH remains nearly unmatched among state universities in diversity of student background. Students travel from afar seeking Houston's requirement of a broad field of study, either with a liberal arts education offered by the Honors College or pursuing a mandated minor or double-major.

Renowned Academic Colleges

Opportunity for specialization abounds in the University's 12 academic colleges. In addition to the College of Liberal Arts and Social Sciences, numerous specialized colleges receive wide acclaim. The Conrad N. Hilton College of Hotel and Restaurant Management is "intense like the rest of the school," demanding much of its students in courses that include tours of restaurant and hotel facilities, economic theory, language and etiquette devel-

opment, and food and beverage courses. Practicum courses put students in real-life employment situations to learn career skills. The C. T. Bauer College of Business, a home to "great minds," ranks third among public Texas universities. The Colleges of Optometry and Pharmacy garner respect across the state as well. The Gerald D. Hines College of Architecture boasts amazing professors who are also known to solicit their students' help on projects and assist their students in finding internships.

The most selective of the colleges is the Honors College, a highly-ranked liberal arts program that enrolls 300 students to study literature and philosophy in a discussion environment. These students take a heavier-than-average course load, possibly 15–16 credit hours instead of a typical student's 12–13 credit schedule. Each semester, Honors students must enroll in at least one course specific to the Honors College. They also must complete a Senior Honors Thesis to finish the program. The Honors College is located "in one of the better parts of campus," with classes held in the University's newly renovated main library. Additional perks include priority registration, a private lounge and study space, and more structured advising. Advising within the Honors College does not require that you "hunt down an advisor," as meetings are preplanned for all Honors students.

For students who desire a less intense experience than the Honors College, the Scholars' Community, a supplementary course for which all students can apply, caters to the part of the student body that wants to be considered "more academic." The Scholars' Community is reportedly "not as intense" as the Honors College, and these students also enjoy priority registration and may take advantage of free tutoring sessions and special advising.

The University of Houston requires that all students take a core curriculum of 42 credit hours. This core curriculum does not limit students' freedom to explore possible majors, as students can and do change their major any number of times before junior year, when they must decide. Another distinctive aspect of the UH curriculum is that students within the College of Liberal Arts and Social Sciences must complete a minor or second major in addition to their first. Such a requirement ensures that all students study a diversity of topics.

Remarkable Courses

UH Colleges feature talented professors. "I've never had a professor I didn't like," reports one student. Even in comparison to the Honors College, professors are "just as good," but classes are larger. For example, one introductory chemistry course taught by the enthralling professor Dr. Simon Bott is one of the most interesting but one of the largest courses, with an enrollment of approximately 600 students. Another popular course entitled "Principles of Drug Action" attracts a large number of students who ultimately find a seat in the class before graduating: "It seems like 80 percent go through it." "Beverage Appreciation," offered by the School of Hotel and Restaurant Management, is a popular wine-tasting course for juniors and seniors over 21 aspiring to become hospitality professionals. "Human Situation," an element of the Honors College curriculum, stands out from other courses as a "totally different" approach to reading works of literature and philosophy.

Students notice a constant flow of professors in and out of the University, which can enhance variety and opportunity, but can also make building relationships difficult. "I am having trouble finding professors who are still around to write letters of recommendation," laments one graduate school applicant. Although professors are easily reachable during office hours and by e-mail, "you would really have to work at a relationship" to get to know a member of the faculty.

Uncommon Diversity

The University of Houston has also been identified to its students as "one of the most diverse campuses in the nation." Indeed, few public universities can claim such a high number of international students and such a heterogeneous racial breakdown as the University of Houston. International students commonly hail from countries in Africa and Asia, among others. Students say the University's generous financial aid policies contribute to a diverse student body.

The Commuter Lifestyle

Many students cite a close proximity to home and feasibility of living at home as major reasons for coming to the University of Houston. Alternatively, students who choose to live on campus avoid the stress of a morning commute: "Having to drive is a disadvantage because of traffic." In the past, parking space has been limited, but is expected to improve with the completion of a new parking garage.

In general, students feel that the student body is distributed fairly evenly between commuting students and students who choose to live on campus. Commuting students do not feel separated from their on-campus peers: "I practically live there. I stay so late that some of my classmates don't even know that I commute."

Constant Campus Improvement

The UH campus is set three-quarters of a mile away from a major freeway: "It's a great location because the campus is not totally downtown, so there is less traffic." One disadvantage of an urban campus, however, is that the UH campus adjoins economically troubled areas: "The area around it is not one of the nicest." Although students generally avoid the immediate vicinity, downtown Houston is always accessible. Still, the campus itself is peaceful and refreshing, featuring fountains and architecturally impressive structures. Also, construction seems to be constantly underway. Recent completions include renovations to the main library and a new Science and Engineering Center.

Living Options for Non-Commuters

Dormitories are the most common choice for housing at UH. "The Quads," which include the preferable Honors dorms, are regarded as the nicest dorm rooms. The basement of one building has a game room and kitchen equipment. Some regard Moody Towers as less appealing than the Quads. One student compares the dorms by the music they play in the cafeterias: nice classical music is standard for the Quads, while a visitor may hear "ghetto hip-hop" in the Towers. Each dorm features a lounge, computer lab with Internet access, small convenience stores, and cafeterias for student use. Apartment-style living is also available in either university-owned or third-party buildings.

Dining options at UH are varied and commended. "UC Satellite," a newer dining area located underground, is "the best secret on campus." In addition to a deli with great sandwiches and a popular sushi bar, it features more commercialized restaurants like Smoothie King; Starbucks; Pizza Hut; Taco Bell; and Kim Son, serving Asian food. In addition, the Hilton Hotel on campus contains an upscale restaurant and a student-run café that operates during the night. Two dorm cafeterias serve "typical dorm food."

The Attractive Force of Activities

Clubs give many students a reason to stay on campus after class. Students remark that "there is a club for everything." Phi Theta Kappa, an honors society, is active and popular for résumé-building. Student Governing Board plans parties and fundraisers. Model UN, although not affiliated with UH, operates on the UH campus. Religious organizations have high membership. For example, the large Lakewood Church holds Sunday service and bible studies in a part of the campus recently bought out by the church. Interest groups and political organizations represent all sides. A unique Student Alumni Organization plans dinners and events to network undergraduates with alums. Guest speakers can also be arranged by department.

Recreational sports connect the student body outside of class. The Rec Center features rock climbing, a competition swimming pool, a hockey area, and racquetball courts, among other activities. Students often take recreational sports classes and play intramural sports, in which they sometimes go on to compete regionally. Flag football is known as one of the largest intramural programs. Respected varsity sports include competitive cheerleading and diving, which has generated Olympians.

School Spirit Sometimes Lacking

Although the effervescent competitive cheerleading squad is highly ranked, their spirit does not always pour out into the rest of the student body: "Most people didn't even know what was going on during Spirit Week." One reason could be that many students leave campus: "It's a commuter school, so many students don't participate." Some students report that there is "hardly any school pride," but pride seems to be more "a matter of who you hang out with." In response to these complaints, the Cougar Club and the Bleacher Creatures, two pep squads, set out during games to amplify audience enthusiasm.

> **"Most people didn't even know what was going on during Spirit Week."**

One popular social event on campus is the Frontier Fiesta that occurs around the time of Homecoming. It involves tailgating, games, fire shows, and food. Most of the social life on campus revolves around the fraternities and sororities near the apartment buildings, which can be expected to host parties most weekend nights.

Downtown Action

One benefit of the University's location is that it allows access to the downtown, Richmond, and trendy Montrose, all of which are popular destinations for students seeking diversion. A shopping center near Rice University attracts UH students after school. Amy's Ice Cream and the 59 Diner also deserve a visit from every student. A collection of small, family-collection museums and the theaters of the Theater District in downtown Houston offer student discounts.

In Need of a New Reputation

UH is sometimes overlooked by Houston residents who are "in a hurry to get away from their parents." Because the University of Houston is located near the homes of many prospective students, they misjudge its value: "It's underestimated because it's in town." And so UH surprises many prospective students. To obtain an accurate perception of the University of Houston, one must investigate its numerous strong academic colleges and its diverse and involved student body.—*Eric Klein*

FYI

If you come to the University of Houston, you'd better bring "workout clothes for the Rec Center and Intramural Sports."

What's the typical weekend schedule? "Either go to a restaurant or club in downtown Houston, or get a home-cooked meal if you commute."

If I could change one thing about the University of Houston, I'd "increase the level of school spirit."

Three things every student at the University of Houston should do before graduating are "Go to the Frontier Fiesta, see a play in the theater district, and take 'Principles of Drug Action.'"

University of Texas/Austin

Address: 2400 Inner Campus Drive Austin, TX 78713-8058
Phone: 512-471-3434
E-mail address: NA
Web site URL: www.utexas.edu
Year Founded: 1883
Private or Public: Public
Religious Affiliation: None
Location: Suburban
Number of Applicants: 27,237
Percent Accepted: 51%
Percent Accepted who enroll: 54%
Number Entering: 7,419
Number of Transfers Accepted each Year: 2,859
Middle 50% SAT range: M: 570–690, CR: 540–660, Wr: 540–670
Middle 50% ACT range: 23–29
Early admission program EA/ED/None: None

Percentage accepted through EA or ED: NA
EA and ED deadline: NA
Regular Deadline: 15-Jan
Application Fee: $60
Full time Undergraduate enrollment: 37,459
Total enrollment: 48,401
Percent Male: 47%
Percent Female: 53%
Total Percent Minority or Unreported: <1%
Percent African-American: 6%
Percent Asian/Pacific Islander: 20%
Percent Hispanic: 20%
Percent Native-American: <1%
Percent International: 3%
Percent in-state/out of state: 94%/6%
Percent from Public HS: Unreported
Retention Rate: 92%
Graduation Rate 4-year: 48%

Graduation Rate 6-year: 76%
Percent Undergraduates in On-campus housing: 20%
Number of official organized extracurricular organizations: 900
3 Most popular majors: Social Sciences, Communication/Journalism, Business/Marketing
Student/Faculty ratio: 18:1
Average Class Size: 10 to 19
Percent of students going to grad school: Unreported
Tuition and Fees: $26,672
In State Tuition and Fees if different: $8,090
Cost for Room and Board: $9,246
Percent receiving financial aid out of those who apply, first year: 82%
Percent receiving financial aid among all students: 57%

Life at the University of Texas has something for everyone. With more than 48,000 students, this flagship state school is a world unto itself. Not only is there an enormous range of quality course offerings, but students can enjoy a vibrant social life as well. In addition to the wealth of resources offered by the University, students can take advantage of the exciting scene in surrounding Austin. And, of course, there's nothing like a football game to get the weekend going. Life at UT is full of possibilities—according to one student, "If you make an effort to talk to people at the gym, on campus, at gatherings, you could have 48,000 friends." This vast array of opportunities offers students a wide range of experiences and options that is harder to find at smaller universities.

Charging into Classes

UT's size affords a wide variety of course offerings. While many introductory classes have Teaching Assistants, upper-level courses can have as few as 15 students. If you're in a popular major, signing up for courses can be difficult. UT anticipates that this can be a challenge to incoming freshmen, and provides an orientation program to ease the transition to life at UT and help students navigate the class registration process.

All students must fulfill certain graduation requirements, including a foreign language requirement, writing proficiency, and a course on Texas government, politics, or history. As at most universities, classes at UT can range from "awesome to absolutely awful." The education major is generally regarded as one of the easiest; students in the math and science departments tend to have the most rigorous academic programs. Some students double major to take advantage of the breadth of course offerings found at UT. A small and select group of students enroll in the Plan II Honors Program, a multidisciplinary liberal arts major offering small classes taught by some of the University's best professors. Students applying for this competitive program must fill out a secondary application in addition to their general application to UT. Plan II students live in separate dorms in the Honors Quad for their four years as undergraduates. As a result, students in Plan II tend not to meet as many students outside their small program.

Several undergrads agree that one class everyone should take before graduation is Interpersonal Communications taught by Dr. John Daly. "The class is a blast," explained one student.

Longhorn Life
Though many freshmen live on campus, UT's large size necessitates that some students move off campus. Many high school seniors send in a housing application and deposit even before they are accepted to the school. Indeed, housing is limited, and competition for on-campus housing can be fierce. Jester, the largest dormitory—and often cited as the "worst" dorm—is a high-rise building housing almost 3,000 students. Jester has parts, East and West, and even has its own zip code! All dorms, however big or small, have air-conditioning, and students can elect to live in coed or single-sex dorms.

Most upperclassmen live off campus and seem to enjoy the opportunity to get to know the city of Austin a bit better. Off-campus housing options range from reasonable to costly; those students living particularly far away make use of a UT-operated shuttle service.

Although most Longhorns live off campus, there are extensive dining hall and eating options on campus. On-campus students usually purchase meal plans, allowing them to eat at any on-campus dining hall. Students tire of the options as the "choices are the same throughout the year," and many complain about the quality of the food.

Awesome Austin
Nestled in the heart of Austin, UT thrives on its location in the midst of a vibrant and exciting city. While some students complain that the campus "feels scrunched" and "lacks the big quads you see at Northern universities," there are "tons of activities" happening off campus. Many Longhorns enjoy Sixth Street for its nightclubs, bars, and trendy restaurants. "A slice of pizza from one of the street-side places on Sixth Street will even cure a hangover," one UT senior said. Known as "The Live Music Capital of the World," Austin also affords endless opportunities for listening to music. With a range of high-tech firms in the city and the State Capitol building a few blocks from campus, students are constantly in the midst of activity. "One thing that differentiates UT from other schools is Austin," one student noted. Indeed, after graduation, many students elect to remain in Austin, claiming that "you won't find a more exciting city to go to school in on the face of the planet."

> "You won't find a more exciting city to go to school in."

For those Longhorns who crave outdoor activities, Austin's weather is nearly ideal. Many students enjoy going to lakes and swimming areas like Barton Springs, Lake Travis, Lake Austin, and Canyon Lake. Although the summer begins to heat up toward the end of the school year, winter temperatures rarely drop below freezing, so students can take advantage of the outdoors for much of the school year. Students feel safe on campus and regularly venture off campus for "camping, running, fishing, hiking, and mountain biking."

Longhorn Pride
"Texas is football, no ifs, ands, or buts." Athletics are huge at UT—and why not? The football team consistently ranks in the top 15, and the school invests heavily in its athletic facilities. "The gym is gorgeous, albeit busy,"

one student said. "There are more than enough machines and weights to keep you busy and sweating."

Athletics is not the only thing that unite students. The large Greek system also provides ample opportunities for socializing. Though many students "go Greek," those who don't can still attend the parties. Frat parties occur frequently, however, and some students feel that too much of the campus social life centers on such Greek-hosted social events. The Greek community also has political sway on campus; however, UT also has several activist groups and a large number of students who are driven to start their own if they feel passionate about a certain cause.

Some students work paying jobs either on or off campus, but many spend time in ex-tracurricular activities. Students participate in service, volunteer, and faith organizations of all sorts. And since Austin is the state capital, students interested in politics can easily seek internships in government offices.

Being a UT student means having a lot of energy and pride—UT students are nothing if not spirited. With so many different opportunities at their fingertips, students can have an educational experience characterized by both breadth and depth. While the school's size may seem overwhelming at first, students agree that freshmen should jump right in and get involved: "The community is a welcoming one." According to one student, "If I had to choose again, I'd definitely take UT over any other school."—*Lucinda Stamm*

FYI
If you come to UT Austin, you'd better bring "a cowboy hat."
What is the typical weekend schedule? "Thursday, Friday and Saturday nights students tend to go out. During football season, Saturday is 'game day,' and most students start the day drinking with the masses of people at the game. By Sunday, students are back to work."
If I could change one thing about UT Austin, I'd "make the social life less dependent on the Greek system."
Three things every student at UT Austin should do before graduating are "swim in the campus fountains, take John Daly's Interpersonal Communications class, and take advantage of the music scene in Austin—they don't call it the 'Live Music Capital of the World' for nothing."

Utah

Address: A-153 ASB
Provo, UT 84602
Phone: 801-422-2507
E-mail address:
admissions@byu.edu
Web site URL: www.byu.edu
Year Founded: 1875
Private or Public: Private
Religious Affiliation: Church
of Jesus Christ of Latter-Day
Saints
Location: Small city
Number of Applicants:
10,182
Percent Accepted: 68%
Percent Accepted who
enroll: 77%
Number Entering: 7,000
Number of Transfers
Accepted each Year: 1,500
Middle 50% SAT range:
M: 570–680, CR: 550–670,
Wr: Unreported
Middle 50% ACT range: 25–30
Early admission program
EA/ED/None: None
Percentage accepted
through EA or ED: NA
EA and ED deadline: NA

Regular Deadline: 1-Feb
Application Fee: $30
Full time Undergraduate
enrollment: 30,000
Total enrollment: 32,992
Percent Male: NA
Percent Female: NA
Total Percent Minority or
Unreported: 11%
Percent African-American:
<1%
Percent Asian/Pacific
Islander: 3%
Percent Hispanic: 3%
Percent Native-American:
<1%
Percent International: 3%
Percent in-state/out of
state: 33%/67%
Percent from Public HS:
Unreported
Retention Rate: Unreported
Graduation Rate 4-year:
21%
Graduation Rate 6-year:
54%
Percent Undergraduates
in On-campus housing:
11%

Number of official organized
extracurricular
organizations: 390
3 Most popular majors:
Business, Education, Social
Sciences
Student/Faculty ratio: 23:1
Average Class Size:
Unreported
Percent of students going to
grad school: Unreported
Tuition and Fees: Member of
The Church of Jesus Christ
of Latter-day Saints:
$2,040 per semester,
Non-member of The
Church of Jesus Christ of
Latter-day Saints: $4,080
per semester
In State Tuition and Fees if
different: No difference
Cost for Room and Board:
$6,460
Percent receiving financial
aid out of those who apply,
first year: 54%
Percent receiving financial
aid among all students:
20%

S et on 560 pristine acres in Provo, Utah, Brigham Young University offers a strong academic education in a beautiful environment. With its religious affiliation with the Church of Jesus Christ of Latter-day Saints, BYU is certainly not your typical college. One of the most significant differences that you might notice is the policy against drinking—and the students' willing adherence to it.

Integrated Secular and Spiritual Education

BYU is known for strong academics, and the reputation is well-deserved. Students say there is a pretty heavy workload, but that

they always find time to have fun. A student, reflecting on his and his friends' academic schedules, said "it's not extreme unless you make it that way." Students are also very satisfied with the range of classes offered for every interest at every level. They say that some of the strongest and most popular majors are in business and marketing, education, and social sciences.

The most distinctive aspect of BYU lies in the university's religious affiliation with the Church of Jesus Christ of Latter-day Saints. Academically, the philosophy of BYU is that truth comes from God, so secular learning and spiritual learning are parts of a whole. Often, students defer enrollment, taking a gap year to do missionary work in a foreign country. Other students attend BYU for their freshman year, and then take a year or two off to complete a mission. The missions also act as immersion programs, allowing students to experience a new and foreign culture. Forty-five percent of students go on mission trips, adding to the international cultural awareness of the campus.

As part of its undergraduate degree requirements, BYU has a University Core consisting of 18 requirements that are divided into five categories: Doctrinal Foundations; The Individual and Society; Skills; Arts, Letters, and Sciences; and Electives. The Doctrinal Foundations requirements include studying the Book of Mormon, the New Testament, and Doctrine and Covenants. These contribute to the 14 credits of required religion coursework throughout a student's time at BYU. Every Tuesday, BYU holds Devotionals and forums where students can go to listen to and meet prominent figures in the Church, world leaders, and scholars. Professors in other subjects at the University are encouraged to make connections between their material and religion as well.

Housing and Food

Also, because the Church owns the university, operating costs, tuition, and fees are greatly subsidized, and many students receive full merit-based scholarships. As a result, students laugh about how "food is more expensive than tuition." Meal options for BYU students vary greatly. There are a large variety of places on campus where meal cards can be used, from Cannon Commons, the cafeteria, to the fancy Skyroom Restaurant on the top floor of the student center or the Jamba Juice on campus. Students can also use points from their meal plans to buy groceries from the Creamery.

Students have the options of apartment-style living with in-suite kitchens as well as a foreign language immersion dorm. The housing policies at BYU reflect the University's emphasis on chastity. The dorms at BYU are separated by gender with restrictions on people of the opposite sex being in housing buildings after 1:30 a.m. on Fridays and after midnight on all other days. These policies are actually a part of the Honor Code, which dictates specific visiting hours for each individual dorm and even off-campus housing for single students.

Fun without Alcohol

One significant characteristic that distinguishes BYU from other universities is the spirit and atmosphere of the students' social life. BYU has an honor code that students and faculty alike take very seriously. Among the provisions of the Honor Code are the typical "be honest" and "respect others," but there is also a rule that men must be clean-shaven at all times. The one policy that is most prominently evident—and often shocking to students at other universities—is abstinence from alcohol and caffeine, as dictated by Mormon beliefs.

For many schools, students' social activities will often involve drinking, and it can even be hard to imagine a university where alcohol is not present. But at BYU, students embrace the policy, arguing instead that "it's great for social life." One student said, "People are more creative about things to do because there needs to be more to a party than just an open cooler."

> "People are more creative about things to do because there needs to be more to a party than just an open cooler."

Instead, students have fun at events like dances run by the student government, often multiple times a week, that have themes like swing, 80s, and country. Students say there are always people hanging out in the dorms and around campus. At later hours at night though, students migrate to outside the dorms because of the gender restrictions on housing buildings. In terms of interaction between the sexes, students say that one of the biggest myths about BYU—namely that students go to BYU to get married—is not that far off the mark. One student noted that students do marry earlier than at other colleges.

Sports and Leisure

BYU's symbol is a giant white "Y" on the mountain above the school. Yes, the mountain is above the school. Apart from skiing and snowboarding, students are extremely active in sports. BYU's intramural sports program is very popular, and creative adjustments are made to promote participation. One student remarked, "My favorite weird one is inner-tube water polo. The idea is to make the game more accessible to people who aren't amazing swimmers."

Apart from intramural sports, BYU competes in the NCAA's Division I-A Mountain West Conference. The University's varsity sports are competitive, with its football and men's basketball teams ranked fairly high. Other sports in which BYU's Cougars are a major force are volleyball, rugby, and soccer.

People of Provo

Perhaps it is the beauty and peacefulness of Provo that causes it, but the people at BYU are very friendly. One freshman explained, "When you walk past someone here that you don't know, they always say hi instead of awkwardly looking away like anywhere else. It's weird for a few days, but after that, it's wonderful." Additionally, BYU's huge expanse of a campus creates a very serene and isolated environment for students. Many students said that BYU is such a safe place and the students are so respectful toward one another that they don't worry about nodding off to sleep on the grass with their laptops next to them: "The crime report section of the paper is a big joke."

As might be expected by the school's religious affiliation, the vast majority of students are Mormon. At the same time, the Mormon population is largely distributed throughout the world, with the majority living outside of the United States. As a result, even though BYU's student body is religiously homogenous, cultural diversity is not completely lacking. BYU also has a focus in international studies, offering courses in over sixty languages. One third of the student body is enrolled in foreign language courses, a proportion that is four times the national average, and BYU's Russian program is one of the largest in the nation.

BYU provides its students with an academic and social environment that is really unlike that of any other university. While restrictions abound, from the dress code to an emphasis on chastity, students love their beautiful school and the unique experience it gives them.—*Michelle Yu*

FYIs

If you come to BYU, you'd better bring "a snowboard or skis, and a razor if you're a guy."
What is the typical weekend schedule? "At least one dance and a well-organized group date, normally something silly and free/cheap."
If I could change one thing about BYU, I'd "loosen the dress code and un-restrict dorm visiting hours."
Three things every student at BYU should do before graduating are "hike the Y, take a dance class, and attend all of the devotionals and forums."

University of Utah

Address: 201 South 1460 East, Salt Lake City, UT 84112
Phone: 801-581-7281
E-mail address: admissions@sa.utah.edu
Web site URL: www.utah.edu
Year Founded: 1850
Private or Public: Public
Religious Affiliation: None
Location: Urban
Number of Applicants: 7,234
Percent Accepted: 81%
Percent Accepted who enroll: 51%
Number Entering: 4,057
Number of Transfers Accepted each Year: 2,721
Middle 50% SAT range: Unreported
Middle 50% ACT range: Unreported
Early admission program EA/ED/None: None

Percentage accepted through EA or ED: NA
EA and ED deadline: NA
Regular Deadline: 1-Apr
Application Fee: $35
Full time Undergraduate enrollment: 14,504
Total enrollment: 28,211
Percent Male: 55%
Percent Female: 45%
Total Percent Minority or Unreported: 13%
Percent African-American: 1%
Percent Asian/Pacific Islander: 6%
Percent Hispanic: 5%
Percent Native-American: 1%
Percent International: 3%
Percent in-state/out of state: 83%/17%
Percent from Public HS: Unreported
Retention Rate: 83%
Graduation Rate 4-year: 20%

Graduation Rate 6-year: 51%
Percent Undergraduates in On-campus housing: 8%
Number of official organized extracurricular organizations: 154
3 Most popular majors: Economics, Mass Communications, Psychology
Student/Faculty ratio: 13:1
Average Class Size: 30
Percent of students going to grad school: Unreported
Tuition and Fees: $16,600
In State Tuition and Fees if different: $5,285
Cost for Room and Board: $5,972
Percent receiving financial aid out of those who apply, first year: 68%
Percent receiving financial aid among all students: 30%

At the feet of the Wasatch Mountains and in the heart of Salt Lake City, the University of Utah, in many ways, offers the best of the west. Motivated students will find it offers all the intellectual challenge they are looking for, and it is an unusual example of a large university where student input matters a great deal. Those seeking a friendly, small-town feel in the setting of a large university and who are willing to forego cultural diversity will find a happy home at the University of Utah.

Hidden Opportunities for Challenge

Students of all levels of seniority agree that it can be easy to coast at the University of Utah ("the U," to those in the know), since there is a strong flow of student-to-student information about which are the easiest classes and most lenient professors. Several of the largest majors also require many large lecture classes—which tend to be the easiest—and relatively few small seminar-style classes. Those same large lecture classes are the road to general education credits for many students, few of whom struggle to fulfill the distributional requirements. Many students take advantage of this opportunity to get outside their discipline for a painless foray into Survey of Jazz or Introduction to Music, for example.

All the same, students hoping to be challenged will not be disappointed if they are willing to do their own legwork. The University divides its academic disciplines into colleges, including an Honors College, which offers Honors Degree and Honors Certificate options to accepted applicants. The University has expanded the honors program in the last several years, and students who take part sing the praises of more engaged professors, more classroom discussion, and assignments that are, in one student's words, "more open-ended, rather than 'Answer 10 questions from the book.'" The U is also very willing to accept credit for advanced high school classes and even "life experience." One senior remarked with candor, "I knew it was going to be an okay education that would qualify me for graduate school, but the opportunities available surprised me, and I've been very impressed."

There can be no doubt that the University of Utah is a research institution where science is king. The University's engineering and pre-medical programs are regarded as the most challenging, and the students in them as the "smartest" at the University. Many students at the U come expressly to take advantage of the science faculty and facilities, and engineering, biology, and chemistry are popular majors. Changing majors and double majoring are very common at the U, so many students have experience in both the sciences and the humanities—located on opposite sides of the very large campus—and have an easy time finding common academic ground. But students do feel a stark disparity in department funding, with the sciences garnering the majority of state grants to the school. The Utah Science Technology and Research (USTAR) program is a special initiative that directs state funding to scientific research initiatives that program directors hope will result in company and job creation in the state of Utah. And the University continues to draw national attention for its cardiology division and such faculty as geneticist Mario Capecchi, who won the 2007 Nobel Prize in Physiology or Medicine and is a source of pride for students in all disciplines.

> "I knew it was going to be an okay education that would qualify me for graduate school, but the opportunities available surprised me, and I've been very impressed."

The U is well connected to Salt Lake City, where the majority of University of Utah alumni remain after graduation. Many students benefit from the Career Services office, which has access to a strong network of internship and job opportunities in the city. Academic advising is markedly less popular. Students complain of advisors recommending classes that are too easy or unnecessary for their major. Some intrepid students supplement their advising needs: "When the advisors aren't helpful, I turn to former professors. Every time I've wanted to meet with a professor, they've made time for me," explained one student. Faculty at the U is broadly regarded as friendly, accessible, and generally interested in the success and satisfaction of their students. Bad professors are weeded out of the undergraduate teaching body through student advisory committees' input or through dwindling class sizes that speak for themselves.

Alternatives to Mom and Dad's House

The phrase "commuter campus" is deeply entrenched in University of Utah students' vocabulary. An overwhelming majority of students live off campus, and because much of the student body is from the Salt Lake City area, many live with their parents. Similarly, many students come into the U with the same group of friends they had in high school, and socialize primarily with that group. Those who choose not to live with their parents often find off-campus housing—which is generally cheap in the area around campus—with their network of high school friends. Meanwhile, on-campus housing presents opportunities for students who want to look outside their high school crowd. The University, the International Olympic Committee, and Salt Lake City joined to rebuild University housing when the city hosted the 2002 Winter Olympics and used residence halls for athletes' housing. Dorms are now spacious, and located in one of the prettiest parts of campus. "The residence buildings are red brick, and it's really nice when you can be in your dorm room, and then walk five or 10 minutes and be on the trails where you can walk or hike," said one junior.

Freshmen living on campus are required to buy a meal plan, but upperclassmen's housing often includes kitchens. Few students at the U have complaints about the quality of the food, but many find its repetition disappointing. As the U undertakes extensive property development—including renovations of many class buildings and the Marriott Library and construction of a new Student Life Building to replace The Field House as the home of student recreation—the administration is increasingly focusing on taking the University in a greener, more renewable direction. On-campus and off-campus students alike enjoy the social benefits of two fraternity and sorority systems at the University of Utah. The first is the traditional Greek system common to many large universities. "Greek row" is as close to the University proper as it could be while remaining nominally off campus, and therefore exempt from the University's well-enforced dry campus policy. Parties on Greek row are a weekend activity that draws even off-campus students. The other system of fraternities and sororities is an outgrowth of the large number of practicing members of the Church of Jesus Christ of Latter-Day Saints at the U, who make up about half the student body. "The LDS Institute, across the street from campus, is a big hangout," said one student. "They have their own activities and their own version of the Greek system."

Students often occupy themselves outside class at The Gateway, an open-air promenade in downtown Salt Lake City with restaurants and a movie theater, and on nearby ski slopes such as Alta, Snowbird, and Park City, the last of which hosted numerous Winter Olympics events and boasts, in one student's opinion, "the best snow in the world." The U of U OneLove Ski and Snowboard Club and the Utah Freeskier Society are two of the largest student groups on campus. While students do need transportation to the slopes, a car is not a real necessity for taking part in most activities around Salt Lake City. The city is home to a well-developed bus system and light rail, both of which run in and around the campus and are free to University of Utah students. But because so many students come from the area and live off campus, many have cars, so parking near the U is competitive.

Social goings-on at the U are accessible to students of all years and ages. Because the University is home to a large "nontraditional" student population, including older-than-average and married students, many undergraduates find that, in the words of one senior, "They have no idea what year people are," so all comers are welcome at social events.

"I Am a Utah Man, Sir, and Will Be Till I Die; Ki!Yi!"

Recent sports seasons have been good to the University of Utah Utes, which is good news for students at the U, and for residents of much of the Salt Lake City valley, which divides its fervent allegiance between the University of Utah and nearby rival Brigham Young University. Utah fans sign up in droves to be part of The Mighty Utah Student Section (The MUSS, taken from a line in the school song), which has a waiting list. Membership entitles students to prime seating at Utah games, and one member describes it as "the best rush you could ever have. Since we are a dry campus, where else are you going to get 5,000 students together at a game to cheer and have a good time?"

The MUSS has done much to address worries about lackluster student involvement at the U. Club officers can be hindered, when organizing events, by the volume of students who live off campus, many of whom also work 20-40 hours per week, and so do not endeavor to participate in the hundreds of student groups on campus. Those students who are involved on campus have undertaken efforts to raise student awareness of the extracurricular opportunities at the U. One such effort is the U Book, a brainchild of the

Student Alumni Board. The U Book contains information about various student groups, 50 U of U traditions, including athletic events like Homecoming and the Utah-BYU football game, places to visit on campus and around Salt Lake City, and annual student events like the Hunger Banquet.

Still, the size and influence of the Associated Students at the University of Utah—the school's student government—are especially noteworthy given the challenges of engaging a geographically spread out student body with diverse interests. A relatively large number of students take part and most of the remaining student body is well-informed about current issues up for debate. ASUU efforts also produce results. A recent example is the Graduation Guarantee, under which the University guarantees that by fulfilling a series of advising requirements, all incoming freshmen and transfer students will graduate in four years, or the University will pay for or waive the remaining requirements for graduation. The University approved and began implementing the Guarantee shortly after the ASUU passed the student initiative.

The University of Utah adheres to and helps define the libertarian spirit that prevails in much of Utah. Students define the course and rigor of their own education, and many find that what they learn is immediately applicable in the work force; they work together to govern themselves as much as possible, and many remain in the Salt Lake City area and continue to engage with the U as donors, board members, and die-hard Ute fans. In the words of a nostalgic second-semester senior, "I didn't expect to feel this way, but I want to come back, and I want to support my school."—*Elizabeth Woods*

FYIs

If you come to the University of Utah, you'd better bring "your skis and good walking shoes to get around campus."

What is the typical weekend schedule? "Go to a concert or other student performance Friday night, sleep in Saturday and have a leisurely brunch with friends, head to the MUSS tailgate and then the football game, and spend the rest of the night at after parties."

If I could change one thing about the University of Utah, I'd "have more people live on campus, to create more of a community."

Three things every student should do before graduating are "join the MUSS, spend time in the Wasatch Mountains, and finish the U Book."

Vermont

Bennington College

Address: One College Drive
Bennington, VT 05201
Phone: 800-833-6845
E-mail address:
admissions@bennington.edu
Web site URL:
www.bennington.edu
Year Founded: 1932
Private or Public: Private
Religious Affiliation: None
Location: Rural
Number of Applicants: 1,057
Percent Accepted: 62%
**Percent Accepted who
enroll:** 29%
Number Entering: 190
**Number of Transfers
Accepted each Year:** 56
Middle 50% SAT range:
M: 560–660, CR: 620–720,
Wr: 646–768
Middle 50% ACT range:
24–28
**Early admission program
EA/ED/None:** ED

**Percentage accepted
through EA or ED:** 60%
EA and ED deadline: 15-Nov
Regular Deadline: 3-Jan
Application Fee: $60
**Full time Undergraduate
enrollment:** 618
Total enrollment: 759
Percent Male: 34%
Percent Female: 66%
**Total Percent Minority or
Unreported:** 17%
Percent African-American:
2%
**Percent Asian/Pacific
Islander:** 2%
Percent Hispanic: 3%
Percent Native-American:
<1%
Percent International: 4%
**Percent in-state/out of
state:** 4%/96%
Percent from Public HS:
59%
Retention Rate: 89%

Graduation Rate 4-year: 45%
Graduation Rate 6-year: 59%
**Percent Undergraduates in
On-campus housing:** 98%
**Number of official organized
extracurricular
organizations:** 21
3 Most popular majors:
Drama, English, Visual and
Performing Arts
Student/Faculty ratio: 9:1
Average Class Size: 15
**Percent of students going to
grad school:** Unreported
Tuition and Fees: $38,270
**In State Tuition and Fees if
different:** No difference
Cost for Room and Board:
$10,680
**Percent receiving financial
aid out of those who apply,
first year:** 87%
**Percent receiving financial
aid among all students:**
77%

L ocated in the Green Mountains of Southwestern Vermont, Bennington College boasts 300 wooded acres, five acres of tilled farmland, 15 acres of wetland, 80 species of trees and 121 species of birds. How's that for diversity?

Small and remote, Bennington attracts an equally intellectually diverse range of students, who come for the individualized academics and the intimate campus—not to mention the theme parties.

Flex Your Academic Muscle

Bennington's academic system is unique. There are no majors at Bennington; instead, students develop a "focus" or a "concentration" themselves with large input from a faculty adviser. Focuses can range from the more traditional, such as mathematics, to the absolutely untraditional, such as storytelling. With the help of a faculty adviser, students plan their course load to best suit their focus, a method called the Plan Process.

Some students relish this academic freedom, saying that it forces you to really "think about your education" and engage in your academic career. For example, one student, who is focusing on "painting and education," said he planned his course load to involve a lot of sciences so he could learn things like the chemistry used to make paint pigment. A junior with a focus in literature said, "The best students are the ones who do take advantage of the flexibility." Indeed, students agreed that the best academic careers are the ones that are cross-disciplinary, to use all of Bennington's resources.

But while many students laud this different take on academics, others say it encourages floundering, and in fact sometimes attracts "terrifically unmotivated" students. "No one is forced to get specific, so everyone is doing everything," one junior said. "Freedom is good for some people, but for most it is just too much." Along with no majors, grades are also optional at Bennington, with narrative evaluations available as an alternative option. Those with grad school plans typically opt for grades, but many other students opt out, helping to contribute to the somewhat misguided perception of Bennington as a "slacker school."

The most popular concentrations at Bennington are the visual arts, dance, writing, and language programs. In fact, much of modern dance was developed at Bennington, whose program was founded by pioneer Martha Graham. The current faculty boasts many literature standouts, and a recent project brought a group of South African leaders to campus to lead classes in the social sciences.

Because of the "planning" system's built-in one-on-one time with faculty members, and because of the small size of the school, students are very close to professors. "I call most professors by their first name," said the student concentrating in painting and education. Other students say they frequently have lunch with their professors, and know their families. But again, this closeness seems to be a double-edged sword; some students complained that professors are almost "too nice," and as a result there is a kind of pressure to befriend all your professors to get ahead. "Something that goes hand in hand with extremely personal relationships is that there is favoritism."

One of the biggest draws to Bennington is the Field Work Term (FWT), a seven-week winter term during which students take internships at various institutions across the country and the world. An annual requirement for graduation, the FWT provides the opportunity to work at places such as the San Francisco Museum of Modern Art, the Pittsburgh Zoo, and Houghton Mifflin Publishing Company. Many students enjoy the FWT as an opportunity not only to apply what they've learned to the real world, but also to take a break from life at Bennington's small and remote campus.

Do-It-Yourself Extracurriculars

Although it is a small campus, Bennington offers any extracurricular group you might want—if you're willing to create it. Because it is such a small school, most clubs come and go, with students forming new ones every year. Long-term groups include the school newspaper; the literary magazine *Silo*; the campus radio station, WHIP; and the perennially popular Outing Club, which sponsors skiing, horseback riding, rock climbing, and hiking trips in the neighboring Green Mountains. There are also community service groups, including the Student Action Network (SAN) and the Community Outreach Leadership Team (COLT). One current club, sure to be a keeper, is Sugar Bush, in which students make maple syrup from nearby trees.

If you're looking for sports at Bennington, though, you're out of luck. As one junior bluntly puts it, "Why would anyone interested in sports come to Bennington?" There are no varsity sports team, and the only club team is coed soccer, which has been known to play nearby high schools. And forget about intramurals. (Students have recently started a dodgeball team, though.) Instead, Bennington students focus their energy on the great outdoors, the free fitness classes, and the "great" rec center—complete with climbing wall and sauna.

The Birthplace of the Theme Party

What Bennington may lack in athletics, it surely makes up for in theme parties. "Bennington is pretty much the birthplace of the theme party," one arts concentrator said. Another seconded, "You'll pretty much never go to a party at Bennington that isn't a theme party." Popular parties in the past have included pirates versus ninjas, Pigstock (a pig roast with live music), the "office party," and the huge roller-disco party Rollerama. Every year, the college puts on SunFest, a music festival on the central lawn featuring 10 to 15 bands during the day. The recent addition of MoonFest the night before is also popular.

Although theme parties are truly the dominant social scene, there are a few other outlets for those not wanting to get dressed up. The campus brings in two to three live bands each week, most of which are small, indie-rock groups, most famously the White Stripes. There is also the occasional unthemed house party, though those are few and far between.

Drinking and drugs are both prevalent at Bennington, though not out of control. "Drugs are in your face if you look for them, they are not in your face if you do not," one male junior said. "They don't dominate the social scene. Parties are still fun if you aren't into that stuff—no one is going to force them on you, or think you're not cool if you're not into them."

From Colonial to Co-op

Bennington's version of student housing is as unique as its take on academics. Bennington offers five types of housing: a drug-free house on campus, an organic co-op off campus, colonial houses, 1970s modern houses, and 2001 contemporary houses. Each house accommodates 25 to 30 students and is managed by two students selected by their peers. These students run Sunday evening "coffee houses" to discuss community issues or just to chat. Students across the board describe Bennington housing as "amazing." Not only are the houses beautiful, but the system guarantees that you'll end up living with your friends—and guarantees a single for junior and senior years.

Students are less unequivocally enthusiastic about the meal plan. Though the food is good by college standards, with plenty of vegetarian and meat options, all students must be on the same three-meal-a-day meal plan for all four years. So even though most houses come equipped with a kitchen, students rarely eat anywhere but the dining hall.

In fact, for the most part, students rarely venture far off the Bennington campus. Many students have cars, and thanks to a "ride board," rides are easy to find, but most choose to stay on what they consider a "really self-sufficient campus." That campus, while intellectually and increasingly socioeconomically diverse, is noticeably lacking in ethnic or cultural diversity. "It is sad," one student said.

"This is one thing Bennington is—and needs to be—working on." The campus also has an overwhelming majority of women, running to around 70 percent of the undergraduate population. Female students say that this ratio is not as much of a problem as you might think, however, especially since they can meet people much more easily during the Field Work Term. "Ultimately people still have boyfriends, people still meet people."

If students are really itching to meet more people, they can go to nearby Hampshire or Williams Colleges. Most, however, stay in the area of North Bennington—the "ridiculously New England" town where Bennington College is actually located—or Bennington, a larger city. One especially nice aspect of such a remote lifestyle is that students never have to worry about their safety: "Vermont feels like the safest place in the world. I never worry."

> "I feel like the main thing you learn at Bennington is how to educate yourself."

Overall, a Bennington education is what you choose to make of it. It is unique, to be sure, but it is that unusual character that allows many students to flourish. For those expecting an easy ride, however, Bennington is not the place, nor is it the place for those who need much hand-holding: "I feel like the main thing you learn at Bennington is how to educate yourself."

And how to throw a damn good theme party.—*Claire Stanford*

FYI
If you come to Bennington, you'd better bring "roller skates, costumes, and false eyelashes."
What's the typical weekend schedule? "Some sort of 'thirsty Thursday' celebration, class Friday, Friday night find out who is having a party in their room. Galavant around after, maybe see what band is playing. Saturday night, dress up in whatever you can find that remotely fits the theme of whatever party is going on, and get drunk. Sunday, recover."
If you could change one thing about Bennington I'd "only admit students who would be terribly excited."
Three things every student should do before graduating are "go in the catacombs, take a private tutorial, and run naked across the Commons lawn."

Marlboro College

Address: P.O. Box A, 2582 South Road, Marlboro, VT 05344-0300
Phone: 802-258-9236
E-mail address: admissions@marlboro.edu
Web site URL: www.marlboro.edu
Year Founded: 1946
Private or Public: Private
Religious Affiliation: None
Location: Rural
Number of Applicants: 459
Percent Accepted: 68%
Percent Accepted who enroll: 30%
Number Entering: 93
Number of Transfers Accepted each Year: 55
Middle 50% SAT range: M: 510–650, CR: 590–690, Wr: 640–720
Middle 50% ACT range: 24–32
Early admission program EA/ED/None: EA and ED

Percentage accepted through EA or ED: Unreported
EA and ED deadline: ED: Dec. 1; **EA:** Feb. 1
Regular Deadline: 15-Feb
Application Fee: $50
Full time Undergraduate enrollment: 330
Total enrollment: 330
Percent Male: 43%
Percent Female: 57%
Total Percent Minority or Unreported: 13%
Percent African-American: <1%
Percent Asian/Pacific Islander: 6%
Percent Hispanic: 4%
Percent Native-American: 1%
Percent International: 1%
Percent in-state/out of state: 10%/90%
Percent from Public HS: 70%
Retention Rate: 73%

Graduation Rate 4-year: Unreported
Graduation Rate 6-year: Unreported
Percent Undergraduates in On-campus housing: 80%
Number of official organized extracurricular organizations: 22
3 Most popular majors: English, Social Sciences, Visual & Performing Arts
Student/Faculty ratio: 8:1
Average Class Size: 2 to 9
Percent of students going to grad school: Unreported
Tuition and Fees: $32,180
In State Tuition and Fees if different: No difference
Cost for Room and Board: $9,040
Percent receiving financial aid out of those who apply, first year: Unreported
Percent receiving financial aid among all students: Unreported

Located in rustic Vermont, a 20-minute drive from the nearest town, Marlboro College offers its students an academic sanctuary in the midst of the New England mountains and greenery. With a small student body and a focus on the outdoors and schoolwork, Marlboro provides an intimate environment perfect for those looking for a unique and self-driven collegiate experience.

An Intense Learning Environment

Marlboro, with its lack of athletics and scarcity of extracurricular activities, is primarily a learning-driven college. Students unanimously concur that most non-class time is spent on schoolwork. "It's a really rigorous setting," one junior said. "People just do work all the time. It really affects the social scene." Another junior agreed, "Work *is* our extracurricular activity."

The academic program is lauded as extremely strong all around. Classes are small, with most classes consisting of about 10 students: "Eighteen students in a class is huge." If students are interested in a topic not offered, one-on-one tutorials can be arranged with professors in fields such as Arabic or fiction writing. There are no required classes except for a writing seminar that must be completed during freshman year.

Because of the small classes and intellectual environment, it is easy for students to form strong bonds with the faculty members leading their classes. "It's up to the students to enhance the faculty-student bond," one junior explained. Another student said professors often eat in the dining hall and are for the most part extremely "affable and approachable." But another student pointed out the one downfall of small classes: students who don't do the reading generally stand out. "You can't hide," said one senior. "Professors will call you if you don't show up for class."

Classes are divided into five basic categories: humanities, social sciences, natural sciences, world studies, and arts. In general, the humanities and literature departments are seen as the strongest, though there is also a notable "film culture," and political science is a very popular concentration. The math and science departments are "growing," though most students concede that those programs are slightly weaker. Recent additions to campus include the Serkin Arts Center and a new World Studies building.

Students choose a self-designed Plan of Concentration (known as the "Plan") to complete their studies at Marlboro. The plan can take many different forms: anything from a 120-page paper to an architectural model to writing a musical. Junior year is spent designing the plan, and the project is executed during senior year. "Everything culminates in the Plan," one junior said.

> **"Work *is* our extracurricular activity."**

Though most find the academic experience "intense" and "wonderful," for others it can be a little overbearing. "It can definitely be too much for some people," a junior said. In general, though, students say they appreciate the unique structure because it creates a noncompetitive atmosphere, with the focus more on the "academic process." Some people transfer out, one sophomore said, because of the heavy workload, as they look for a college experience where the learning is "less individually driven."

An Intimate Community

The extremely small student body—there are only 311 students enrolled—makes for a unique collegiate social life. There are rarely huge on-campus parties, and there are no frats or sororities to host gatherings. "Most of our parties are pretty mellow," one junior said. "People will dance; there will be a band playing; people will drink and smoke."

For some students, though, living in such isolation can be restricting. "It kind of feels like we're living in a bubble," a senior said. Brattleboro, the nearest town, does offer "cool coffee houses and a co-op, which everyone loves because we're all hippies." Students also get off campus to participate in numerous outdoor activities in the surrounding Vermont mountains and lakes.

Despite the lack of prominent social activities, one junior said it was easy to find ways to have fun. "You just have to make things happen," she said. "There's not the consistent night life that you might find at a large university, but there's usually a few big parties every year and things to do."

Students at Marlboro tend to be of a certain mold. Most students hail from the mid-Atlantic states and New England. A senior summed up the typical Marlboro student: "We tend to be white, of a similar socioeconomic category, and—in general—people who didn't fit in during high school." The small community also means that everyone knows everyone's business. "You can't really avoid the gossip," one freshman said.

Dorms, "Cottages," and a Barn-Turned-Building

The dorms that house Marlboro students reflect the intimate feel of the campus. The dorms are "really small," one senior said—each of the nine on-campus residence halls houses roughly 12 to 30 students, with roughly 80 percent of students living on campus. In general, the rooms are large, though some of the rooms are arranged in an unusual fashion—some freshmen complained about having to live in triples.

While housing is guaranteed for freshmen, it is not guaranteed for the next three years. Typically, 50 or so students (usually sophomores) are forced to live off campus each year. The off-campus dormitories—only a quarter-mile away from central campus—offer an appealing option due to their intimate feel (students described them as "little cottages"). Other students choose to live in Brattleboro in an apartment. One senior who lives in Brattleboro said she enjoys the change of pace after living on the close-knit Marlboro campus for three years: "There's a huge art and music scene."

There are residential advisers in every dorm, though they do not often take on the disciplinarian role. "No one is policing you," a sophomore said. Instead, RAs serve as resources for students and are able to offer advice and answers.

In general, the campus itself is "pretty rustic." A junior said, "The landscape is definitely really nice with all the white buildings, though the architecture could use some work." The on-campus dorms—each built in a slightly different era—are marked by a variety of architecture styles. The main classroom building is a converted barn, and the campus center—marked by its huge wooden rafters—was designed by a student for his "Plan."

Food Complaints, Pride, and Broomball

One thing that all Marlboro students seem to agree on is the unappealing food on campus. There is one dining hall on campus and one basic meal plan for all students. A "big issue on campus" according to one junior, the food is a constant source of consternation for students. "There is just no selection whatsoever," one junior said. Though some students said the food was passable and not as bad as it was made out to be, many students have taken to creating their own food options. Many students said the lack of vegetarian and vegan options forced even the most devout vegetarians to start eating meat again; vegetarians currently have the option of filling out forms to request chicken or fish.

In general, as one junior put it, "extracurriculars don't really exist" at Marlboro. Unlike at other schools, where there are certain clubs that exist from year to year, students at Marlboro start up new clubs each year based on interests, which may fizzle and change at any given point in the year. "You can make happen pretty much whatever you want here," one senior said.

"Pride"—the campus shorthand for the Gay-Straight Alliance—is considered the most prominent on-campus organization. Music ensembles tend to attract a fair number of students as well. Many students also join committees to help plan events and deal with other Marlboro-related issues.

While there are no official sports teams, the club soccer team is a source of school pride, as the student body often comes out to support the soccer squad. Frisbee and fencing are other popular sports. The Outdoor Program also plans many trips and excursions every year. Every winter, the whole school participates in a "broomball" tournament—a kind of makeshift hockey game—on the frozen pond on campus, at which school spirit and enthusiasm is often at its highest.

Marlboro College certainly stands out from the endless list of colleges because of its small size and intense academic atmosphere. Though some students said it becomes suffocating and small at times, most students appreciate the closeness of the campus and the bonds they are able to form with faculty. As one student put it, "A typical Marlboro student is one who is interested in his or her education and wants to play a role in it."—*Josh Duboff*

FYI
If you come to Marlboro, you'd better bring "a winter coat, motivation, and a stick of deodorant."
What is the typical weekend schedule? "Eat brunch, read a few books, go to the pond/sledding, eat dinner, read more, party, dance, listen to music, have some good conversations, go to bed."
If I could change one thing about Marlboro, I'd "give the school a lot more money."
The three things every student should do before graduating from Marlboro are "play broomball, skinny-dip in South Pond, get to know each other well."

Middlebury College

Address: The Emma Willard House, Middlebury, VT 05753-6002
Phone: 802-443-3000
E-mail address: admissions@middlebury.edu
Web site URL: www.middlebury.edu
Year Founded: 1800
Private or Public: Private
Religious Affiliation: None
Location: Suburban
Number of Applicants: 7,823
Percent Accepted: 17%
Percent Accepted who enroll: 44%
Number Entering: 576
Number of Transfers Accepted each Year: Unreported – 14 enrolled
Middle 50% SAT range: M: 640–740, CR: 630–740, Wr: 640–740
Middle 50% ACT range: 29–33
Early admission program EA/ED/None: ED

Percentage accepted through EA or ED: 27%
EA and ED deadline: 1-Nov
Regular Deadline: 1-Jan
Application Fee: $65
Full time Undergraduate enrollment: 2,422
Total enrollment: 2,422
Percent Male: 50%
Percent Female: 50%
Total Percent Minority or Unreported: 41%
Percent African-American: 5%
Percent Asian/Pacific Islander: 10%
Percent Hispanic: 7%
Percent Native-American: 1%
Percent International: 12%
Percent in-state/out of state: 5%/95%
Percent from Public HS: 52%
Retention Rate: 95%
Graduation Rate 4-year: 88%

Graduation Rate 6-year: 92%
Percent Undergraduates in On-campus housing: 97%
Number of official organized extracurricular organizations: 100
3 Most popular majors: Economics, English, Psychology
Student/Faculty ratio: 9:1
Average Class Size: 10 to 19
Percent of students going to grad school: Unreported
Tuition and Fees: $49,210
In State Tuition and Fees if different: No difference
Cost for Room and Board: Included
Percent receiving financial aid out of those who apply, first year: 48%
Percent receiving financial aid among all students: 79%

O ften described as the "picture-perfect New England campus," Middlebury College is truly the ideal environment for students who are active and outdoorsy, who appreciate a rigorous academic curriculum, and who want to enjoy delicious dining hall meals. Nestled within the famous green mountains in the cold, snowy, beautiful state of Vermont, Middlebury offers students a cozy environment where they can keep busy indoors with solid course schedules and a wide array of extracurricular activities, as well as amusing themselves outdoors in the natural beauty of their surroundings by skiing, hiking, or merely sitting back and enjoying the view of a sunrise over the mountains.

Parlez-vous Français?

Middlebury requires that all students fulfill seven out of eight distribution groups, which cover literature, language, deductive reasoning, science, art, history, social analysis, foreign language, and philosophy/religion. In addition, everyone must fulfill four cultural distributions: Asian/Latin American, North American, European, and a comparative course, as well as taking two college writing classes and one freshman seminar. The majority of students say that the requirements are easy to fulfill; according to one junior, "I finished all mine freshman year." The top three majors are economics, English, and psychology ("it's pretty nice to do pre-med here"), though other popular and interesting majors include biology, environmental studies, and international politics. "We have a lot of people who double-major," said one sophomore. "Basically, we all try to do as much as we can." Middlebury is world-renowned for its language program, and a large number of students study abroad for a semester or a summer program. The summer language program on campus is so intensive that it is possible to receive an M.A. in a language over the summer. The school year is actually split into three parts, with a fall semester, a spring semester, and a one-month interim period known as "J-term" when students take only one class (either getting an intensive course like organic chemistry out of the way as quickly as possible, or taking it easy with a light and fun class). As far as specific classes go, language classes are always highly recommended and organic chemistry is usually abhorred, but there are many unique courses such as an anatomy class that is also a dance class and an English/environmental studies class where students read Thoreau and Emerson and travel to a farm where they learn to birth sheep.

Class size depends on subject; the largest introductory science classes have 75–85 people, but most classes have 10–19. One student reported, "I've had classes as small as four people!" All classes are taught by professors who "are always willing to sit down and talk to you about anything." One student said, "I feel like our professors are teachers first and foremost—we are their priority, and it shows." Although registering for classes can be a frustrating process, students who don't get into the classes they want are often able to go talk to the professors, who are nearly always willing to make room for them. "Basically, if a student shows any interest whatsoever, a professor will bend over backwards trying to help them get into a course or better understand the material." The workload—though manageable—can be daunting, and sometimes students say that they feel overwhelmed. "Still," said one senior, "we work hard, we play hard. You learn a lot if you keep up, but if you fall behind you may never catch up again."

One particularly unique aspect of Middlebury is that in addition to the regular matriculating class in September, there is another group of about 100 students—"the Febs"—who start in February. They also graduate a semester later, and are therefore able to ski down one of the hills for their graduation tradition.

Something in Common[s]

Residential life at Middlebury is broken into five "commons," a system somewhat like the four houses in the *Harry Potter* books. Freshmen are assigned to a commons based on their choice of freshman seminars, and the professor of the seminar becomes their advisor. Each commons has a certain number of residential buildings on campus, a dining hall, a game collection, different events, and various speakers. Changing commons is simple to do and often just means a change in housing; the main benefit to staying in a commons are

the housing points students receive when deciding where to live in an upcoming semester. Inter-commons rivalries are common, especially in intramural sports. These smaller communities within the larger community of Middlebury are designed to make life easier for incoming freshmen and foster a greater sense of belonging; while some students see this as an admirable objective, others complain about the housing discrepancy between commons (although the college is currently undergoing major renovations in order to create a more balanced living situation) and the fact that they feel "punished" by the points system if they choose to live with friends instead of staying in their original commons.

Dorm quality increases with seniority, from basic singles and suites freshman year to apartment-style rooms senior year with a common room, kitchenette, and in-suite bathroom. The majority of students live on campus all four years—"We have great rooms, they get cleaned for us, and the dining hall food is amazing. Why would we want to leave?" One junior admitted, "Sometimes we call this Club Midd, because we're really spoiled here. We're not ready for the real world." Dining hall food is, indeed, very delicious. Much of the food offered is locally produced, and the basic meal plan allows for unlimited trips to the dining hall and unlimited food while you're there. "The people who work there are really nice, too," one sophomore said. "When one girl said that she missed the salmon from her area of Alaska, they flew it in." The staff takes students' suggestions seriously (you can always fill out dining hall cards); many students have even given their own family recipes to the cooks, who have then proceeded to make those dishes. One freshman said, "We often end up at dinner for over an hour, and we keep getting snacks over the course of the evening. Plus, we always have Ben & Jerry's Ice Cream!"

When it comes to eating off-campus, students say that the greater Vermont area also "takes food very seriously, and it shows." One person cited a restaurant called Flatbread as having amazing pizzas, though the downside of living in rural Vermont is that there are no places that deliver pizza or Chinese late at night (and also no Starbucks!). One sophomore said, "Food here is less expensive than in a big city and we go out occasionally, but when my parents come they always want to eat in the dining hall because it's so delicious!"

Work Hard, Play Hard

Students say that after a long week of study-ing, they are more than ready to party when the weekend rolls around. Drinking is preva-lent on campus: "You always see everyone out at the same parties . . . dancing, drinking, and merrymaking." Instead of frats, Middle-bury has social houses, coed groups of stu-dents (often affiliated with a commons) who throw parties. There are three bars that up-perclassmen often frequent on Wednesday or Thursday nights, and since Middlebury is a small town, they will most likely run into other students at the same places. On cam-pus, people socialize with friends in dorms or attend one of the many themed dance parties thrown by teams or clubs, such as eighties dances, contra dances, and the popular neon dance party thrown by the ski team. Non-alcoholic social activities include concerts by student bands, free movies on Friday nights, late-night snacks at the Grille (the union), and events organized by the Middlebury Campus Activity Board. One student said, "On week-ends people go out and party like crazy, then get up the next morning at 7 or 8 a.m. to go running!" Another reported, "It's a varied but close-knit social scene. I've never been to a party where I didn't know someone." Annual parties include the Winter Carnival, when students go to cheer on the ski teams at home during the day and then dress up for a formal ball at night, and two other formals in fall and spring. Students also spend much of their free time at varsity hockey games, which draw fans from all over campus as well as the surrounding community.

> "Once we even ran into a professor's pond! It's dark, you're naked, it's fun!"

Middlebury boasts a wide variety of ex-tracurricular groups, with everything from literary and art magazines to political orga-nizations to Lovers of the Garden State ("I don't know what they do, but apparently they really like New Jersey"). There is a bird-watching club, a sign language club, re-ligious and cultural groups, community ser-vice organizations, theatre, "too many a cappella groups for our size, in my opinion," dance groups, band and orchestra, the Mid-dlebury Outdoors Club, and Sunday Night Group—a group that started out as an envi-ronmental activism group directed at cli-mate change, but which has now "turned into a social justice group for anyone who wants to change the world." The list could go on and on. Particularly adventurous stu-dents enjoy the Polar Bear Club, where they drive to nearby lakes at night and run naked into the freezing water. According to one member, "Once we even ran into a profes-sor's pond! It's dark, you're naked, it's fun!" Intramural sports, especially broomball, are also popular. "We were in the *Wall Street Journal* for our Quidditch team," one stu-dent said. "The players wear capes and run around with brooms between their legs." This comment prompted another student to remark, "Everyone here is kind of quirky. Not weird or anything, just very social, very interesting, very open."

"Midd Kids" are definitely lauded as being friendly, outgoing, and outdoorsy individuals. "I met most of my friends in the dorm fresh-man year," said one senior. "But you can really sit down with anyone at mealtimes and you'll be welcomed." When asked to describe the typical student, people listed adjectives such as "athletic, health-conscious, well-rounded, upper middle class, white, sometimes preppy, and good at something—whether it be play-ing an instrument or being a star athlete." Said one junior, "My little brother would tell you that I've turned into such a hippie since being here; I get food from an organic garden, talk about climate change all the time, and am al-ways outside." The student body is extremely international, with students from all over the world, even "exciting places such as Burma, Kazakhstan, and Bhutan!" One senior com-mented, "The diversity in some areas is cer-tainly lacking . . . and granted, it's hard to bring inner-city kids here, because who would want to come to Vermont?"

A Close-Knit Community

Although most students stay mainly on cam-pus, people say it is good to know someone with a car because it is necessary to use one for skiing or grocery shopping. Everyone agrees that the campus is extremely safe at night. Said one student, "I mean, who could possibly attack you? . . . Cows, maybe?" Said another, "I never lock my door, and people always leave their stuff in the library unattended." Middlebury prides itself on its Honor Code, which is manifested in ways such as self-scheduled exams and the fact that the professor is never in the room when students take an exam. "There is a sense of community that everyone respects," one se-nior said. "You would never talk or cheat because it would be a violation of your respect for your professor and your peers. It's taken really seriously here."

The sense of community at Middlebury is indeed, for many students, one of the most distinctive aspects of the college. For others, the best part of the college is "the people— everyone is so passionate about what they do and about what everyone else is doing. You go to your friends' events, they come to yours, you sit down and have crazy conversations all the time . . . there's just a lot of passion here!" Another student cautioned, "Sometimes Mid-

dlebury can turn into kind of a bubble that distances you from the outside world. As you long as you make an effort to stay in tune, you'll be okay." And as one junior summed up, "We all got into Middlebury because we were stellar in our high schools. Then you get to Midd where everyone is like that, you can face rejection for the first time, get grades you've never seen before, and it can be frustrating . . . but also invigorating, because you're surrounded by all these people who are going to change the world."—*Lindsay Starck*

FYI

If you come to Middlebury, you'd better bring "a warm jacket."

What's the typical weekend schedule? "Sleep, brunch (order omelettes!), do work, sleep again, eat dinner, pre-game, go out."

If I could change one thing about Middlebury, I'd "make it less of a bubble from the outside world."

Three things every student at Middlebury should do before graduating are "streak the campus, study a language, watch a sunrise while sitting on a roof."

University of Vermont

Address: 194 South Prospect Street, Burlington, VT 05405-0160
Phone: 802-656-3370
E-mail address: admissions@uvm.edu
Web site URL: www.uvm.edu
Year Founded: 1791
Private or Public: Public
Religious Affiliation: None
Location: Suburban
Number of Applicants: Unreported
Percent Accepted: 70%
Percent Accepted who enroll: Unreported
Number Entering: 2,450
Number of Transfers Accepted each Year: 741
Middle 50% SAT range: M: 550–650, CR: 540–640, Wr: 540–640
Middle 50% ACT range: 23–28
Early admission program EA/ED/None: EA
Percentage accepted through EA or ED: 70%

EA and ED deadline: 1-Nov
Regular Deadline: 15-Jan
Application Fee: $45
Full time Undergraduate enrollment: 10,504
Total enrollment: 11,824
Percent Male: 45%
Percent Female: 55%
Total Percent Minority or Unreported: 1%
Percent African-American: 1%
Percent Asian/Pacific Islander: 2%
Percent Hispanic: 2%
Percent Native-American: <1%
Percent International: <1%
Percent in-state/out of state: 26%/74%
Percent from Public HS: Unreported
Retention Rate: 86%
Graduation Rate 4-year: 54%
Graduation Rate 6-year: 69%

Percent Undergraduates in On-campus housing: 54%
Number of official organized extracurricular organizations: Unreported
3 Most popular majors: Social Sciences, Business/Marketing, Education
Student/Faculty ratio: Unreported
Average Class Size: Unreported
Percent of students going to grad school: Unreported
Tuition and Fees: $29,682
In State Tuition and Fees if different: $12,844
Cost for Room and Board: $8,534
Percent receiving financial aid out of those who apply, first year: 76%
Percent receiving financial aid among all students: 55%

Why is University of Vermont abbreviated UVM? It actually comes from its Latin name, *Universitas Viridis Montis*, which means "University of the Green Mountains." Founded in 1791, the same year Vermont became a state, the University of Vermont lives up to its Latin name, boasting both natural beauty and an environmental focus. With construction of modern suite-based residence halls, a new honors college, and the recent switch to dry dorms, UVM is shedding some of its party image in hopes of emphasizing its appealing academics and location.

ABCs the UVM Way

Undergraduate academics at UVM are broken down into seven different colleges. The most popular majors at UVM are business administration, English, and psychology. While each major belongs to a specific college, every student is required to fulfill one three-credit Race and Racism in the U.S. and one Human and Societal Diversity requirement, as well as complete various education requirements in the other colleges, including two semesters of physical education. Luckily breaking a sweat isn't hard to do in Vermont. UVM owns a few natural areas like Mount Mansfield, which it uses for teaching, recreation, and physical education classes.

Because of its close proximity to Canada (a one-hour drive to the border), UVM offers a Canadian Studies major. From anthropology to art history, English to business administration, UVM gives students a unique opportunity to learn about the U.S.A.'s neighbor to the north. It even offers the class Due North, which culminates in a weeklong field trip to Canada to watch a hockey game and visit the Parliament.

UVM offers an array of unique classes like the History of Rock and Roll; The Role of Drugs in Society; Films and Novels of Stephen King; Tolkien's Hobbits; and Pirates, Tacks, and Seadogs. The two classes known for being easy are Introduction to English and Personal Health. But be forewarned: With all the varying courses UVM offers, most students wake up at 6 a.m. on registration day to get into the section they want. However, if students really want to get into a particular class or section, they can petition the professor for an override. Following the prevalent Vermont attitude, professors are required to let in students if the class is required for their major, but they let in almost all students who petition regardless of reason.

Classes tend to be on the rather large side in the beginning of freshman year and get smaller as students progress through their undergraduate careers. Introduction to Psychology has about 200 students, while most introductory classes range from 60 to 100. Upperclassman classes hover around 40 to 60 students, although most seniors will take two or three seminars, which are capped at 20. The main exception is with languages. All foreign language classes are kept small, at around 20 people. All classes are taught by professors, though sections and labs are taught by TAs. "I have had great experiences with TAs," one student said. "I have never had trouble communicating or finding times to meet outside of class with mine." Some professors, like Brookes Cowan, who teaches Introduction to Sociology, are known for being laid-back. Professor Cowan lives in the student off-campus area and interacts very comfortably with her students. "Teachers are very professional, but they're not stuffy, they're very down to earth and very understanding. They understand if something is late due to a family function."

For those seeking an academically rigorous course load, the new Honors Program offers about 400 students such an opportunity. Honors Program students still belong to one of the seven academic colleges, but one class every semester is an honors program seminar of no more than 20 people. All freshmen in the program must take the Making Ethical Choices, Personal, Public, and Professional seminar, but after their first year, they are allowed to choose their seminars. Along with the cohesion of living together in a Residency under a Dean in the new University Heights Complex, the Honors Program offers students special co-curricular and extracurricular opportunities, like field trips to Boston and Montreal, as well as small perks like early registration, extended library borrowing privileges, and discounted tickets to performing arts events.

New Campus Living

UVM just recently finished building new residential halls on Athletic Campus. These residential halls are all LEED certified, which is the highest environmentally sustainable construction certification a building can receive. All freshmen and sophomores are required to live on campus, and then are free to move off as juniors and seniors. Even so, housing is now guaranteed for all four years.

Campus dorms cluster in three places—North Campus, Athletic Campus, and Redstone Campus—although there are a few dorms buildings on Central Campus, as well. North Campus is where most of the "shoebox" dorms are. Redstone campus is the southeast campus, named after the Redstone Residential buildings. Athletic Campus, the east campus, is noted for its close proximity to the Patrick Gymnasium and is home to the recently constructed new University Heights residential halls and the Living and Learning Buildings. Living and Learning (L&L) are theme dorms, either by suite or by floor. Some examples of themes range from the outdoor floor to the live music floor to the community service floor.

Although UVM is trying to make its dorms a new home away from home for students, most students view them as "a place where you live, not your home." Still, most students agree that they have made some of their most lasting friendships through the dorms.

Meal plans at UVM come in many variations, with different amounts of points and blocks. Points are essentially dollars that you can use at à la carte cafés on campus, while blocks are swipes you use at one of the two all-you-can-eat dining halls that serve standard fare. While the points cafés are really well liked, points can also be used to order pizza from Domino's and Pizza Hut any time of the day and late night, though most off-campus places take Cat Scratch, the UVM student debit account, instead. If students get tired of eating on campus, popular restaurants and cafés in Burlington include Three Tomatoes, Mountaintop Brew, American Flatbread, and Red Onion Sandwich. Fitting in with the hippy image of UVM, most eateries are organic with many vegetarian options, but "are absolutely delicious and cheap!"

Residential Advisors (RAs) may be as young as sophomores and as old as graduate students, and how strict your RA may be depends on who your RA is. However, one student reported that "all RAs still adequately enforce the rules." UVM is not exactly a dry campus (the soon-to-be-finished Davis Student Center will have a pub), but all residence halls are alcohol-free: "With respect to that rule, RAs make almost no exception." Response to the dry dorm rule has been mixed, because most students drink off campus at house parties and bars. However, "strict enforcement of rules by the administration and the police has diminished our reputation as a party school," one student said. There has been some countereffect such that students have been turning to drugs in dorms as opposed to alcohol. While the person who

phones in a drunken friend receives amnesty, anyone found drunk and underage will receive medical attention but will also have to attend counseling, perform community service, and pay a fine after recovery.

Skis, Views and Booze

Burlington is a small, quaint city that feels like a town. With a population of about 40,000, and home to four colleges, Burlington is a true college town. "Almost all stores are mom and pop stores, and with UVM on the hill, and Burlington downtown by the shore of Lake Champlain, it's the most beautiful place to live." The center of downtown Burlington is Church Street, a cobblestone-paved, pedestrian-only eight square blocks, at the end of which sits a majestic old church.

> "We all consciously chose this school. We didn't come here because we thought it was the best thing to do, it was what we were supposed to do next, or because we couldn't go somewhere else."

Off-campus living in junior/senior years "is sort of an informal agreement . . . it is ten times cheaper and a different scene." While there are a few frats and sororities at UVM, even some that are community service-based, different social groups tend to mingle and mix off campus at house parties or at bars. The five to six blocks between campus and downtown are where almost all upperclassmen live, and with all of it leading downhill to downtown and Lake Champlain, there is no bad view. Looking across Lake Champlain, students can see the Adirondack Mountains in New York State. Popular sports bars and pubs are RJ's, What Ale's You, and Nectar's. Auggies on Tuesday nights serves, Hurricanes for four dollars, massive alcohol drinks that make Auggies the most popular place for college students to beat the midweek blues. The main dance club is Rasputin's, but newly opened club Plan B is gaining popularity, though mainly for an older crowd. Burlington's live music scene is always an option, as well as its many performing arts events for those seeking a different night out.

Of course, if arts are not your definition of a night out, UVM is part of Division I athletics and "everyone attends the [men's] hockey games," one student said. All sporting event tickets are free to students, but since there are no season tickets available, students must wait in line for tickets to each game. Also highly attended are men's and women's basketball games. UVM has not had a football team since 1974, "presumably to fund our other sports instead." Rather, rugby football remains a popular club sport. But for less competitive players, the big intramural sport is broomball. Over 100 teams sign up for broomball every year, and students rave that "it's so much fun!"

Other popular extracurriculars include Outdoor Club, Skiing and Snowboarding Club, and Volunteers in Action, the umbrella organization for most community service and social justice organizations that sponsors the Alternative Spring Break Trip every year, where groups of ten students go on ten different trips, nine domestic and one abroad, to do community service. The Outdoor Club sponsors really cheap weekend trips every year that are publicized to all students via e-mails. And thanks to the proximity of the many great skiing locations and the discount provided by the club, the Skiing and Snowboarding Club is always a popular activity to join.

A Different Diversity

"What we lack in racial and ethnic diversity, we make up for in a different type of diversity," a senior said. Vermont is the second-whitest state, so racial diversity at UVM is not surprisingly lacking. However students come from all different sorts of socioeconomic classes. Even though the University of Vermont is a public university, the majority of its students—74 percent, as a matter of fact—come from out of state. This is in part due to Vermont's small population, but it is also due to UVM's initial status as a private university, which was only changed in 1865. The result is that both UVM's in-state and out-of-state tuitions fall somewhere between private and public universities.

UVM students still have a liberal and environmental bent, living up to some degree to its "tree hugger" stereotype. "Everyone buys local dairy and veggies," one student explained, while another student added that "there are recycling bins everywhere, and if you don't recycle, anyone on the street would stop to correct you." That's just the Vermont attitude toward life and nature. "That's what makes UVM special," one student said. "We all consciously choose this school. We didn't come here because we thought it was the best thing to do, it was what we were supposed to do next, or because we couldn't go somewhere else. It was because this was the University of *Vermont*."—*Jesse Dong*

FYI
If you come to UVM, you'd better bring "environmental conscience."
What is the typical weekend schedule? "Attend a hockey game Friday night, go hiking or skiing Saturday afternoon, party with friends off campus Saturday night, and spend all of Sunday doing homework."
If I could change one thing about UVM, I'd "make the residences more of a home."
Three things ever student should do before graduating from UVM are: "go to the top of Mt. Mansfield, take part of the naked bike ride, and participate in the polar bear jump."

Virginia

College of William and Mary

Address: PO Box 8795
Williamsburg, VA
23187-8795
Phone: 757-221-4223
E-mail address:
admission@wm.edu
Web site URL: www.wm.edu
Year Founded: 1693
Private or Public: Public
Religious Affiliation: None
Location: Suburban
Number of Applicants:
11,636
Percent Accepted: 34%
Percent Accepted who
enroll: 35%
Number Entering: 1,386
Number of Transfers
Accepted each Year: 356
Middle 50% SAT range:
M: 620–710, CR: 630–730,
Wr: 610–720
Middle 50% ACT range:
27–32
Early admission program
EA/ED/None: ED

Percentage accepted
through EA or ED: 50%
EA and ED deadline: 1-Nov
Regular Deadline: 1-Jan
Application Fee: $60
Full time Undergraduate
enrollment: 5,850
Total enrollment: 7,300
Percent Male: 45%
Percent Female: 55%
Total Percent Minority or
Unreported: 23%
Percent African-American:
7%
Percent Asian/Pacific
Islander: 8%
Percent Hispanic: 8%
Percent Native-American: 1%
Percent International: 2%
Percent in-state/out of
state: 59%/41%
Percent from Public HS:
Unreported
Retention Rate: 94%
Graduation Rate 4-year:
90%

Graduation Rate 6-year:
Unreported
Percent Undergraduates in
On-campus housing: 67%
Number of official organized
extracurricular
organizations: 378
3 Most popular majors:
Business Administration,
Psychology, Government
Student/Faculty ratio: 11:1
Average Class Size:
Unreported
Percent of students going to
grad school: Unreported
Tuition and Fees: $29,116
In State Tuition and Fees if
different: $10,246
Cost for Room and Board:
$8,030
Percent receiving financial
aid out of those who apply,
first year: 82%
Percent receiving financial
aid among all students:
58%

The College of William and Mary, founded in 1693, is the second-oldest university in the United States. As its tour guides are quick to tell you, it was the college that Thomas Jefferson attended, the college where George Washington was chancellor, and the college that gave birth to the Phi Beta Kappa society in 1776. Yet William and Mary isn't all about tri-corner hats and resting on past laurels, despite its location in touristy Colonial Williamsburg. What distinguishes William and Mary nowadays, aside from having Sandra Day O'Connor as its chancellor, is its reputation for academic excellence. *U.S. News & World Report* ranked it first among public universities for undergraduate teaching. Results like that have many students here proudly embracing their label of being a "public Ivy." But William and Mary isn't all about staying locked in the library. The school has a beautiful campus, a successful football team, and serious cash flow from recent donations, donations that are funding a number of renovations and new buildings all around campus.

A Public Ivy

Most students agree that academics take precedence. According to one student, "At William and Mary, it's cool to be smart. People here are a different kind of intelligent." Students must complete 120 credits to graduate, and the average course counts for three or four credits. In addition, students must also fulfill the GERs, or General Education Requirements, which include one course in mathematics and quantitative reasoning; two courses in the natural sciences; two courses in the social sciences; three courses in world cultures and history; one course in literature or art history; two credits in creative or performing arts; and one course in philosophical, religious, or social thought. Classes at W&M vary in size but all generally fall into one of three categories. The largest are introductory lectures with 100 to 250 people, and the smallest are seminars capped at 15, with classes of 25 to 35 people in between. All freshmen are required to take a freshman seminar; these are generally praised. Students register by class year in a relatively painless process.

William and Mary also rewards its incoming overachievers (generally the top seven percent of each class) with its James Monroe Scholar Program. In addition to having one of the best dorms on campus (Monroe Hall) reserved exclusively for freshman Monroe Scholars, they get first pick in freshman seminars, have a chance to apply for a $1,000 grant for the summer after freshman year, and are guaranteed $3,000 for an independent project the summer after their sophomore or junior years. Of him to whom much is given, however, much is expected. In an already intense academic environment, the Monroes feel the pressure even more than most.

Among the 35 concentrations offered at William and Mary, there is the usual mix of easy and difficult majors. Some of the usual suspects like geology, psychology, and anthropology are popular with the less academically motivated crowd, while biology, chemistry, physics, and computer science are some of the hardest, and most well taught, majors. For those interested in economics, W&M offers a business major affiliated with its business school. For all their stellar reputation, one student believes W&M's academics are actually underrated. "I don't think people are quite aware of how good they are," he explained. Perhaps part of what makes the academics so good is that, for the most part, classes are taught by full professors. In four years, one senior could recall having been taught by a TA only once. Students also give the professors rave reviews, calling them approachable, interested, and "brilliant."

Partying at a Deli?

Students bring the same passion to social activities as they do to their classes. "The same people who hide out in Swem all week and study, party on the weekends (and during the week)." So what do William and Mary students do when they're not in the newly renovated library? Options abound. Student organizations, which number over 350, are popular, and most people belong to at least one or two clubs: "In all honesty I can say that W&M is where the kids who were involved in high school come to be even more involved in college." There are numerous performing arts and a cappella groups; several publications like the *DoG Street Journal* (referencing Duke of Gloucester Street, the main drag for students and locals) and the *Flat Hat*, W&M's weekly student newspaper; a number of Christian groups; and a whole host of others, from the chess club to the Russian club. Many students' social lives revolve around their organizations, as many clubs sponsor a number of parties and formals. Athletics, of course, play a big part in school life, as was especially the case a few years ago, when the Tribe football team made it all the way to the NCAA I-AA semifinals. Stands were more crowded than they had been in years, and Tribe Pride promises to stay inflated for years to come.

Greek organizations play a large role in the campus social scene as well. According to the W&M administration, 25 percent of undergrads are involved in Greek life, but according to one frat brother, the majority of those students belong to exclusive social service frats, evidence of W&M's passion for volunteerism. "Students praise volunteerism and community service as cool things to do." The school boasts the largest chapter in the country of Alpha Phi Omega and the largest collegiate service fraternity, and the governor recently visited campus to commend W&M for its commitment to service.

The percentage of people who live in traditional party-oriented frat houses is much smaller, and continues to shrink as frats lose their charters or housing by violating alcohol or other policies. The school has attempted to crack down on underage drinking in recent years, but students still manage to circumvent the system. Although the school requires that fraternity parties serving alcohol receive advance approval from the administration, "people can and do drink at the frats." Pregaming in dorm rooms is also popular among underclassmen.

For upperclassmen, off-campus parties, held by clubs, sports teams, or even Greek members living off campus, are popular. Because of regulations, there are no bars near W&M, but several so-called "delis" in the area reportedly serve the same purpose. In recent years, the delis have started to card more strictly, but for the persistent, alcohol is still available. Since "the most popular of the delis tends to rotate throughout the year," the reputations tend to depend on who and when you ask. The "nicest" of these delis is the Green Leafe, which has Mug Night every Sunday, when you can bring in a mug and they'll fill it with beer for a small price. College Delly, now under new ownership, is also popular and, last spring, Paul's was "the place to go." Aside from the delis, however, students report that there really isn't much off-campus nightlife, though there's always plenty to do on campus. In addition to the party scene, more toned-down events include forums with a host of visiting speakers: "In my years at the College I've seen Ralph Nader and Jon Stewart (he's an alum of ours), and even Kofi Annan and Supreme Court Justice Antonin Scalia."

Multinational Neighbors

In terms of housing, many students stay on campus all four years; as one student said, "I think people stay living on campus because it's very convenient and we have a really tight community." The dorms, which, with a few exceptions, are all coed, are generally pretty nice. Yates, Monroe, and Barret may be a little better than average, and Jamestown North and South are so far away that people dread getting placed there, but the halls are actually in decent shape. The housing system revolves around a lottery that most agree "ends up being pretty fair." Freshman housing is generally pretty good, and friends made in freshman halls often end up being friends for all four years. For those into foreign languages, W&M offers the opportunity to live in houses geared toward a specific language, whether it be Russian, Spanish, or French. Each house has a tutor from one of the countries where the language is spoken and hosts various cultural events. The language houses provide a warm, tight-knit community.

Dining services at William and Mary were significantly better before a budget crisis a few years ago led to cutbacks in quality. The university is, however, trying to remedy this: the main dining hall, "the Caf," recently received a facelift, with improvements including "amazing" food and an Internet café. Students can still find other good-quality offerings around, such as the daily-made sushi, which one student describes as "not sketchy. It's really good." When the options feel limited, though, students can take a walk around town and find plenty of ways to

spice up their dining. Local restaurants like The Fat Canary, Aromas, Trellis, and the Cheese Shop receive good ratings, though the ones in the tourist part of colonial Williamsburg are pretty pricey. There are also two convenience stores open 24-7 in Williamsburg, including the WaWa, without which "students would go crazy."

What really sets William and Mary apart from most colleges, in the opinion of several students, is the sheer beauty of its campus. When these students talk about how spectacular their campus looks, they don't just mean the sites that every William and Mary tour guide points out: the colonial architecture of Old Campus, the famous Sunken Gardens, or even the Crim Dell pond with its storied bridge. (Supposedly, any couple who kisses on the bridge has to get married unless one of them throws the other one off.) These students mean places that are far less touristy, like the amphitheater at Lake Matoaka, which a couple of students said was the most beautiful place they had ever been in their lives.

> "At William and Mary, it's cool to be smart. People here are a different kind of intelligent."

The students at William and Mary are aware of its history and traditions. As one student said, "We all know that the Wren Building is the oldest academic building in the country still in use, almost all of us can recite the great history of our college, and almost all of us know the chorus to the alma mater. Our big tradition events such as the Yule Log and Convocation Ceremonies are incredibly crowded and bring us together."

One of the most interesting traditions at W&M is the Triathlon: swimming the Crim Dell pond, streaking the length of the Sunken Gardens, and jumping the Governor's Mansion wall to complete the garden maze inside, all in the same night. True triathletes complete the entire thing nude. It is not uncommon to see people streaking the Sunken Gardens on a typical weekend in the wee hours of the morning "Some students are so gung-ho as to complete the triathlon not once but many times!"

So in the end, what does William and Mary have to offer? It has a beautiful campus, and thanks to a number of donations it is also poised to complete a number of major renovations. People here are generally pretty studious folks, with a grasp on tradition. If you're looking for a gorgeous place to live and an Ivy League–level education for a public school price, the College of William and Mary is the place for you.—*Laura Sullivan*

FYI

If you come to William and Mary, you'd better bring "a camera."

What's the typical weekend schedule? "Friday: UCAB event/party at a frat; Sat.: sleep in, study some, football game, or other athletic event, dance party; Sun.: study day/stay in."

If I could change one thing about William and Mary, it would be "the food; on-campus food leaves much to be desired, but that's why God created WaWa."

Three things that every student at William and Mary should do before graduation are "camp out and sleep under the stars in the Sunken Gardens (beware of streakers, Matoaka Ampitheater may be a safer bet), take a class in the Wren Building, and complete the triathlon."

George Mason University

Address: 4400 Univ. Drive Fairfax, VA 22030

Phone: 703-993-2400

E-mail address: admissions@gmu.edu

Web site URL: www.gmu.edu

Year Founded: 1972

Private or Public: Public

Religious Affiliation: None

Location: Urban

Number of Applicants: 12,943

Percent Accepted: 63%

Percent Accepted who enroll: 31%

Number Entering: 2,497

Number of Transfers Accepted each Year: 3,710

Middle 50% SAT range: M: 520–610, CR: 500–600, Wr: Unreported

Middle 50% ACT range: 22–26

Early admission program EA/ED/None: EA

Percentage accepted through EA or ED: 18%

EA and ED deadline: 1-Nov

Regular Deadline: 15-Jan

Application Fee: $70

Full time Undergraduate enrollment: 18,589

Total enrollment: 29,803

Percent Male: 47%

Percent Female: 53%

Total Percent Minority or Unreported: 57%

Percent African-American: 7%

Percent Asian/Pacific Islander: 16%

Percent Hispanic: 6%

Percent Native-American: <1%

Percent International: 4%

Percent in-state/out of state: 90%/10%

Percent from Public HS: 85%

Retention Rate: 84%

Graduation Rate 4-year: 41%

Graduation Rate 6-year: 59%

Percent Undergraduates in On-campus housing: 25%

Number of official organized extracurricular organizations: 250

3 Most popular majors: Accounting, Political Science, Speech and Rhetorical Studies

Student/Faculty ratio: 15:1

Average Class Size: 20 to 29

Percent of students going to grad school: Unreported

Tuition and Fees: $22,476

In State Tuition and Fees if different: $7,512

Cost for Room and Board: $7,360

Percent receiving financial aid out of those who apply, first year: 59%

Percent receiving financial aid among all students: 34%

F ounded as an independent university in 1972 after originating as a branch of the University of Virginia, George Mason University is a rising star among American colleges. Its location less than an hour from the nation's capital affords students ample opportunities for work and play, and its three main campuses offer a wide array of curricular and extracurricular options. With a student body recently termed the most diverse in the nation by the Princeton Review, and a faculty that brings practical experience as well as academic prestige to the table, GMU is perfectly suited to almost any type of student—and despite its relative youth, it's by no means short on college spirit.

Beyond the Books

George Mason students average around 15 credit hours, or about five courses, per semester, a workload that students find rigorous but manageable. Academic requirements vary depending on area of study, but every student must complete a set of general course requirements. Students add, however, that "it doesn't take as long to complete the general education requirements as it sounds like it does."

Of GMU's 100+ degree programs, those that are most popular with students include several offered by the School of Management, as well as biology, government and international politics, and psychology. Besides the main Fairfax campus, George Mason also offers classes and facilities in Arlington County, Prince William County (where the Freedom Aquatic and Fitness Center, "the largest fitness and aquatic center on the East Coast," is located), and Loudoun County, a location that just opened in 2005. The number and variety of programs available mean that GMU students have a plethora of options. Students do warn, however, that "GMU doesn't really allow students to double-major," though it is easy for those with diverse interests to pursue one or more minors. The University also caters to students transferring in from another institution; a significant percentage of incoming students hold associate's degrees from the neighboring Northern Virginia Community College.

GMU's faculty includes top names in their fields, such as Economics professors and Nobel laureates Vernon Smith and James Buchanan. Professors at Mason are generally deemed "very approachable," and students praise the fact that "many of the professors have real-world experience that they are able to bring in to their lectures, which is very helpful." Class sizes average around 20–29, and larger lecture courses are broken up into discussion sections taught by graduate teaching assistants. Many professors also communicate with their students using WebCT, an online program that allows students to upload assignments, check grades, and discuss material on a class Web page. Students can also use the Internet to track their degree requirements using the PatriotWeb database, a convenience that means they "don't have to see an advisor constantly if they have questions."

A Capital Place to Be

The University's location close to Washington, D.C. and the large number of commuter students make George Mason's social scene truly unique. Proximity to the nation's capital gives Mason students a wide variety of options for term-time work and weekend fun, and students tend to be very involved outside campus. According to one junior, "Many students intern with political campaigns or work for government agencies or large corporations." Most GMU students either live in the surrounding area and commute to classes (many take advantage of the local Cue Bus system, which is free for students, and the Washington Metro subway system), or "live on campus during the week, but leave and stay with family or friends off campus for the weekend." Of about 18,500 undergraduate students, only 25 percent live on campus. As a result, students say that "most people socialize off campus" by taking advantage of the various opportunities for entertainment afforded by the University's surroundings, including local bars or clubs.

This doesn't mean, however, that the campus itself lacks a thriving social scene. GMU has 22 fraternities and 13 sororities, which are "either adored by their members or scorned and scoffed at by non-members" and often host parties open to all students, though the frats do not have separate housing on campus. The University also sponsors "Every Freakin' Friday," an event hosted, as per the name, every Friday that features "movies, food, comedians, live entertainment, and much more" (including, recently, Adam Pascal of *Rent* fame). A campus film committee also sponsors movies on weekend nights, "anything *from United 93* to *Thank You For Smoking* to *The Devil Wears Prada!*" Partying in dorms and nearby student apartments is also popular, which sometimes leads to trouble with the administration. Despite enforcement policies that have recently become increasingly strict, students report that drinking is prevalent on campus. Overall, most students are happy with the social aspect of the University. One sophomore reported, "It is very easy to make friends at GMU."

Mason Madness

Because of the high percentage of commuters, students often meet most of their friends in classes and clubs, and student organizations function both as a way to get involved on campus and as a means of finding friends with similar interests in a large and extremely diverse student body. George Mason has a wide variety of "exceptionally organized and dedicated" extracurricular organizations, ranging from community service organizations and cultural interest clubs to art, theater, and dance groups. GMU's weekly newspaper, *The Broadside*, is one of the top student publications in the nation and has a strong following on campus. The University also boasts a "very popular" radio station and literary magazine. On the whole, students are very committed to their extracurriculars: "People are always going to meetings, starting up organizations, or planning activities."

Mason athletics, both varsity and intramural, also have a strong presence on campus. The campus offers a wide array of new and newly renovated athletic facilities, including the Aquatic and Fitness Center, which was recently renovated. Much of the University's athletic pride is centered around the basketball team, whose Final Four performance in 2006 in the NCAA has brought it, and George Mason with it, into prominence. One student said, "The nation fell in love with us, and we were the Cinderella story of the year." Rather than having its homecoming in football season as is standard practice for many colleges, GMU's is centered around basketball and occurs in the spring semester along with the annual celebration of Mason Day. "Mason Madness" (formerly "Midnight Madness"), which kicks off the basketball season as students gather to watch the team's first practice of the season, is a well-attended event. Still, students tend to assert that "sports aren't that huge on campus," and that there is "more pride in the school itself, the reputation of the school," than in athletics themselves.

Living It Up, Off Campus or On

Because George Mason is a relatively "young" university, most of its buildings are either new or newly renovated, and it boasts a picturesque variety of modern architecture. A man-made lake near central campus provides a pleasant setting for students to walk and chat; the nearby, "beautifully sculpted" Center for the Arts and Patriot Center host a variety of events on behalf of both the University and outside organizations. Students also frequent the George W. Johnson Center (or JC), dubbed the "hangout for everyone," which houses the University bookstore, a food court, a movie theater, dance studios, study areas, and "overflow from our already massive library."

Those who do live on campus reside in one of GMU's dorm complexes, though most students consider on-campus housing a "rip-off" and choose instead to commute from home or to rent apartments nearby. Freshmen live in President's Park, which has a very strict no-alcohol policy. The best rooms ("very nice, write-home-about quality") are in Potomac Heights, available only to upperclassmen. George Mason also has a number of dining options, with several dining halls, on-campus restaurants (including the JC's food court), and a cornucopia of local restaurants in the surrounding Old Town Fairfax.

> "I'd say that students are focused academically and are very career-oriented, without being cutthroat or being overly uptight."

More than any physical feature or facility, the characteristic that most sets George Mason apart in the eyes of its students is its diversity—one student termed the University "insanely diverse." Over 130 nationalities are represented on campus, and student interests run the gamut from politics to physics to dance. Mason students do have something in common, however: "I'd say that typical GMU students are focused academically and are very career-oriented, without being cutthroat or being overly uptight. The casual, friendly attitude is a constant." With dynamic professors, state-of-the-art facilities, and convenient location, George Mason University is the perfect place for those who want to change the world and enjoy themselves while they're at it.—*Amy Koenig*

FYI
If you come to George Mason, you'd better bring "a Metro card. You'll probably need to use it more than once, especially if you work."
What's the typical weekend schedule? "Friday night: bar hopping in D.C. or Old Town Fairfax. Saturday: study. Sunday: parties in D.C. or at fraternities."
If I could change one thing about GMU, I'd change "the Orientation Program. Over the summer, they ran three large orientations during finals week. The orientation itself isn't a problem, but they should schedule more effectively."
Three things every Mason student should do before graduating are "go to Mason Day, take advantage of your resources, and go to the *The Price Is Right* taping in LA wearing your school colors."

Hampden-Sydney College

Address: P.O. Box 667
Hampden-Sydney, VA 23943
Phone: 800-755-0733
E-mail address:
admissions@hsc.edu
Web site URL: www.hsc.edu
Year Founded: 1775
Private or Public: Private
Religious Affiliation:
Presbyterian
Location: Rural
Number of Applicants: 1,553
Percent Accepted: 63.60%
**Percent Accepted who
enroll:** 31.80%
Number Entering: 333
**Number of Transfers
Accepted each Year:** 18
Middle 50% SAT range:
M: 515–610, CR: 500–610,
Wr: 480–590
Middle 50% ACT range: 20–26
**Early admission program
EA/ED/None:** EA and ED
**Percentage accepted
through EA or ED:**
Unreported

EA and ED deadline:
15-Nov
Regular Deadline: 1-Mar
Application Fee: $30
**Full time Undergraduate
enrollment:** 1,120
Total enrollment: 1,120
Percent Male: 100%
Percent Female: 0%
**Total Percent Minority or
Unreported:** 13%
Percent African-American:
4%
**Percent Asian/Pacific
Islander:** 1%
Percent Hispanic: 1%
Percent Native-American:
<1%
Percent International:
1.90%
**Percent in-state/out of
state:** 68.1%/31.9%
Percent from Public HS:
57.80%
Retention Rate: 78.70%
Graduation Rate 4-year:
61%

Graduation Rate 6-year:
66%
**Percent Undergraduates in
On-campus housing:** 94%
**Number of official organized
extracurricular
organizations:** 50
3 Most popular majors:
Economics, History,
Government and Foreign
Affairs
Student/Faculty ratio:
10.5:1
Average Class Size: 14.8
**Percent of students going to
grad school:** 20%
Tuition and Fees: $28,250
**In State Tuition and Fees if
different:** No difference
Cost for Room and Board:
$9,228
**Percent receiving financial
aid out of those who apply,
first year:** 98%
**Percent receiving financial
aid among all students:**
54%

Since its 1775 founding, the mission of Hampden-Sydney College (HSC) has been to form "good men and good citizens in an atmosphere of sound learning." This small all-male school maintains its tradition of excellence by holding students to the highest standards of character, curriculum, and climate. Tucked away in a small Virginian pocket of tranquility, HSC exudes a picturesque, old-school charm. Its effective and extensive honor system creates a sense of both citizenship and brotherhood.

The Core Curriculum, Liberal Arts at Its Finest

Hampden-Sydney has a broad core curriculum that ensures that each student has taken "at least two courses in every discipline" before graduation. Because these requirements are so extensive, it is common to find seniors still trying to fulfill them. For this same reason, many people double major. The curriculum within the majors is very broad, and each student must have a complete understanding of a subject. Popular majors include econom-

ics, political science, and history, although in the past few years, religion has become increasingly popular. While science may not be quite as popular, students rave about the "must-take class" of "Caveman Chemistry," a hands-on lab class in which students start off by making fire as the cavemen did, working their way though human history, and making plastic as their final project.

But when it comes to academics, Hampden-Sydney College is not all fun and games. Students must complete the Rhetoric Program, which consists of enrolling in challenging English classes, writing ten papers every semester, testing grammar proficiency, and taking an overall final exam. The Rhetoric Program is tough in the sense that "if you don't pass it, you don't graduate," but as a result, "everyone who graduates here can be proficient in writing, and write something that is worth reading." Furthermore, teachers are personally attentive and usually generous with extensions, "It's almost impossible to graduate with a 4.0 here because being perfect in your class is viewed as unattainable," one senior said. There is reportedly no grade inflation, and a C is often considered average.

We Eat Here, We Sleep Here, We . . . Fish Here?

A 1,100-member all-male college, Hampden-Sydney allows for "an atmosphere where you leave your door open and get to know all of the guys in the hall." Before they arrive, freshmen can chose to live in one of three dorms. Most choose Cushing because of its large rooms and the sense of community fostered by its 16-person corridors. Juniors and seniors have more options, and can even apply to live in college-owned off-campus housing. About 50 students per year do so, "but it's more convenient to live on-campus." The college allows about 35 upperclassmen to live outside college-owned housing. Because the nearest town, Farmville, is a 10-mile drive away, hardly anyone chooses to live in apartments not affiliated with the College. The housing draws are done first by seniority and then by GPA.

The architecture is "old Federal; red brick with white trim." And behind the commons area, at the foot of a hill, is a pond where students like to fish. Concerts, cookouts, pig roasts, and barbeque buffets are also hosted in that area. As far as the dining hall is concerned, food is said to be good, especially in comparison to that at other colleges. However, many students complain about "getting sick of the same good food by the end of the semester."

Intramural Life

The dominant extracurricular is most definitely intramural sports, with a 45 percent participation rate. Intramurals run all year round, and essentials such as soccer, softball, flag football, and basketball are all offered.

With about 25 percent of the school participating, varsity athletics also receive much support, particularly the football team, whose homecoming game kicks off a week of partying with students from the competing school. The football team is also the only sports team large enough to be "a group unto themselves."

In light of the fact that forming clubs at Hampden-Sydney involves little more than "filling out a form," the football players have even formed the Tiger Athletic Club, an organization bearing a likeness to its own frat, "especially due to the fact that they own a house." Other popular activities involve the Outsiders Club (which sponsors outdoor trips such as whitewater rafting), student

government, the Young Republicans, and the debate society.

In Style and at Leisure

Although Hampden-Sydney is changing rapidly, it is still typecast as attracting "upper-middle-class white guys who drive SUV's." If dress is any indicator of anything, HSC boys are "not afraid to wear pink or Rainbow sandals, year-round." Popped collars, khakis and shaggy hair are also common sights. Students report that if you wear plaid, people will compliment your "cool pants." Dressing up during the day may not be the norm, but it definitely doesn't stand out.

As far as nightlife is concerned, an attendance policy prevents most students who have Friday classes from going out on Thursday nights. However, on Friday and Saturday nights, students will congregate in the off-campus houses or throw room parties. The alcohol policy is fairly lax. RAs do not go out to search and storm rooms, and most students feel comfortable with the degree of independence accorded them. Over 25 percent of students are members of frats. Fraternity Circle, the location of the frat houses, is the dominant (if not the only) social scene. But fraternity parties are not exclusive to the point where frats throw parties only for themselves; they often host parties specifically for the entire student body. During Greek Week, fraternities open their houses to all students and host popular bands; past acts have included Vanilla Ice and Galactic.

> "The honor system sets us apart. It is really strong and plays a large role on campus."

Contrary to popular belief, meeting girls is really not an issue at Hampden-Sydney College. Girls from other colleges, including the neighboring all-girls college Hollins, visit for the weekend just as boys from HSC visit the girls' schools. Also, the fraternities have frequent mixers with sororities from the University of Richmond and the University of Virginia. The College Activities Committee also hosts events, and effort to increase the female presence at social events is definitely noticeable. When asked about girls, one student replied, "It enhances our situation being that we are all male. We certainly do form friendships with girls, but during the week when you have work to do, it's nice to hang out with the guys."

Southern Culture of Honor

Although some may be turned off by the "rolling hills and grazing cattle" that surround the school, others like the security of being able to leave their car doors unlocked and not having to swipe to access buildings. For the men of Hampden-Sydney, this sense of trust is a foundation for brotherhood. One student noted, "The honor system sets us apart. It is really strong and plays a large role on campus." Often, professors give tests and leave the room or give take-home tests with the instructions not to use books and to return in two hours. This honor code is strictly enforced: The minimum punishment for lying, cheating, stealing (or tolerating those who do) ranges anywhere from one semester's suspension to expulsion. The Student Court maintains the code and is responsible for assigning any student accused of an infraction to an undergraduate lawyer while also determining the punishment. Albeit strict, "[the honor code's] effects benefit the entire community." According to one senior, the sense of trust and brotherhood "is really strong and plays a huge role on campus. On the whole, you can do what you want, but you have to grow up quick if you want to make it."—*Christine Kim*

FYI

If you come to Hampden-Sydney, you'd better bring "Seersuckers and loafers."

What's the typical weekend schedule? "Get out of classes, drink with the guys, and wait for the ladies to arrive from SBC, Hollins, and other schools. Go to the frats, dance and get obliterated. Wake up Saturday—during football season, throw on the coat, go to the Founders lot and get completely drunk for free—wear off the hangover, start drinking again. Sunday: wake up, say goodbye to the weekend catch, watch football, do homework."

If I could change one thing about Hampden-Sydney, "We'd have girls. Just kidding. It would be slightly smaller. We're on the verge of becoming too big to be doing what we've been doing since we were founded, such as upholding our honor code."

Three things every student at Hampden-Sydney should do before graduating are "a bell run, take 'Caveman Chemistry,' and play rugby."

Hollins University

Address: PO Box 9707 Roanoke, VA 24020-1707

Phone: 800-456-9595

E-mail address: huadm@hollins.edu

Web site URL: www.hollins.edu

Year Founded: 1842

Private or Public: Private

Religious Affiliation: None

Location: Urban

Number of Applicants: 651

Percent Accepted: 84%

Percent Accepted who enroll: 35%

Number Entering: 193

Number of Transfers Accepted each Year: 50

Middle 50% SAT range: M: 490–620, CR: 500–670, Wr: 490–620

Middle 50% ACT range: 21–28

Early admission program EA/ED/None: ED

Percentage accepted through EA or ED: Unreported

EA and ED deadline: 1-Dec

Regular Deadline: 1-Feb

Application Fee: $35

Full time Undergraduate enrollment: 799

Total enrollment: 1,049

Percent Male: 0%

Percent Female: 100%

Total Percent Minority or Unreported: 9%

Percent African-American: 8%

Percent Asian/Pacific Islander: 2%

Percent Hispanic: 3%

Percent Native-American: <1%

Percent International: 2%

Percent in-state/out of state: 52%/48%

Percent from Public HS: 77%

Retention Rate: 73%

Graduation Rate 4-year: 57.%

Graduation Rate 6-year: 59%

Percent Undergraduates in On-campus housing: 80%

Number of official organized extracurricular organizations: 46

3 Most popular majors: Communication and Media Studies, English Language and Literature, General Psychology

Student/Faculty ratio: 10:1

Average Class Size: 10 to 19

Percent of students going to grad school: 22%

Tuition and Fees: $25,110

In State Tuition and Fees if different: No difference

Cost for Room and Board: $9,140

Percent receiving financial aid out of those who apply, first year: 97%

Percent receiving financial aid among all students: 93%

Respect for tradition and a love for tight-knit community are just some of the values held close to the hearts of students at Hollins University. Academics being no exception, the talented women at Hollins effectively utilize the honored ways of the past to explore and live bright futures as graduates of this distinguished institution.

Scales and Perspectives

A four-year women's university, Hollins divides coursework into four different categories including humanities, social sciences, fine arts, and natural sciences. Rather than taking particular required courses, students must take eight credits from each of these divisions. Though some popular majors at Hollins include economics, history, and psychology, English is by far the largest major. In fact, many students were drawn to Hollins by the reputation of its well-rated, well-funded creative writing program. A unique major is the interdisciplinary major, a program in which students work with two faculty members to compile a major from two or more disciplines suited to students' interests. Challenging classes at Hollins include upper-level political science classes, but all senior seminar 400-level classes, according to one senior, "have as much work as should be expected." While most students are humanities majors, the natural science facilities are still fairly up-to-date, and a new visual arts center sparkles on campus. Hollins also offers a dance program that is always popular with students, who must complete two zero-credit physical education courses before graduation. Second-semester freshmen also apply to enroll in the three-year Batten Leadership Institute, a noncurricular program designed for students to "go above and beyond" to focus on their leadership skills.

Germany in January?

Hollins divides its year into three parts—two semesters plus a four-week January short term. During short term, the University offers intense seminars, internships for upperclassmen, and study-abroad opportunities in Greece, Spain, and Germany. Competition at Hollins is not cutthroat, but many students report a sporting competitiveness in classes. Students at Hollins feel this sense of competition enhances the spirit of sisterhood at the college. As one student noted, "You want to strive to be the best in your class or a particular class, but it's a natural, healthy competitiveness." The "Hollins family" also extends to the faculty. Many professors live on nearby "faculty row," and it is not uncommon for classes to be moved there, sometimes just in time for dinner. It's no wonder that, with a low student-faculty ratio of ten to one and with 79 percent of classes under 20 students, by their fourth year, many students come to appreciate the special relationships forged with their faculty.

Good Living, Bad Food

Freshman dorms are unusually nice and new, often making the transition from home go much more smoothly. Each single or double is air-conditioned, and each hallway of 15 girls shares a bathroom, kitchen, social room, and study room. Upperclassmen reside in apartments and themed houses such as the Spanish house, French house, or fine arts house. Although these residences lack air-conditioning, most rooms are spacious singles, and one senior living in the Spanish house even boasted of her two closets and hardwood floor.

> "We have all kinds of girls here, from extreme liberal girls to true Southern belles who wear pearls, khakis, and Oxfords."

The food situation at Hollins, however, does not receive such positive reviews. The dining hall has dinner hours (4:30–6:30 p.m.) that most find unusually early, and does not provide as much variation as many would hope for. However, Hollins is very sensitive to the needs voiced by various committees on religious and vegetarian sensitivity, and strives to ensure that an array of specific diets are accommodated. For those who need a quick fix (and we're talking of the fried variety), students can also eat at The Rat, a student center specializing in fast foods.

One- to Two-Beer Kind of School

Many freshmen spend Friday to Sunday at nearby Virginia schools to visit friends and boyfriends. And although Hollins is "a little bit on the outskirts of Roanoke," groups of girls sometimes frequent downtown clubs and bars. Students maintain that they "have all kinds of girls here, from extreme liberal girls to true Southern belles who wear pearls, khakis, and Oxfords." Students note that Hollins is too small to be cliquish, and as students grow older, greater numbers of on-campus parties occur that are hosted in upperclassman apartments. Hollins girls have been known to occasionally get the party started on Thursday, but Friday and Saturday nights usually prove to be the most exciting. Some find it problematic that Hollins "shares its brother school," Hampden-Sydney College, with the four other women's colleges in the area. All boys aside, Hollins' own student body contains a good mix of partiers and "staunch sober girls" who choose not to drink. However, in general, Hollins students "play by the rules" and don't consider their campus to be a wild party school where students are "allowed to have open glasses anywhere, walking down the hallways . . . drinking themselves silly every weekend." As one student summed it up, "It's a one- to two-beer kind of school."

Let's Get Physical

Hollins' activity board is particularly strong, and "from concerts, to cultural events, to poker nights, there is always something to do no matter what your interests are." Many women are active in student government and community service. HOP, Hollins Outdoor Program, offers mountain climbing, whitewater rafting, and other outdoor excursions. Its being a Division III school, the sports teams at Hollins are not big enough to be too exclusive, socially or athletically. While no club sports are offered, Hollins gives interested students a chance to walk on to teams otherwise populated by mostly recruited athletes. For those disinterested in organized sports, Hollins has a gym equipped with a rock-climbing wall—donated by a Hollins alum, the first woman to climb Mount Everest—a sauna, a pool, and a fencing studio that is also used for aerobics.

Sisterhood

Although sororities are prohibited by Hollins, the sense of sisterhood is campus-wide, and many campus activities still revolve around tradition. On Tinker Day, the day of the first autumn frost, students wake up to the sound of seniors banging on pots and pans as they run down underclassman hallways. Students head to breakfast in the dining halls "in the craziest outfits imaginable," and afterward ditch classes for the day to trek up nearby Tinker Mountain for a picnic buffet at the summit, where the day is spent performing songs and skits. Another popular tradition is Ring Night, when juniors are officially inducted as seniors. This three-day celebration culminates with juniors receiving gift baskets full of senior "necessities" such as pots and pans (for Tinker Day) and four bottles of champagne from their secret senior sisters. Why four bottles of champagne at this "one-to two-beer school?" Another tradition, of course. One of the champagne bottles is used for the women's first-step tradition. Only seniors are allowed to walk on the front quad grass, and, on first-step day, seniors take their first steps on the beautiful front quad while popping the cork of their first bottle of champagne.

With so many fun yet meaningful traditions and a strong sense of community and support, it is no wonder that students grow to love Hollins for both its strengths and its weaknesses. As one student noted, "This school wasn't necessarily my top choice, but looking back on it, Hollins really was my perfect school."—*Christine J. Kim*

FYI

If you come to Hollins, you'd better bring "something unusual to wear for Tinker Day."

What's the typical weekend schedule? "Most classes will end around noon on Fridays. About a third of the students will jump in their cars and head for JMU, VMI, or Virginia Tech. However, there's usually a party going on somewhere either Friday or Saturday, and these tend to follow all-day events like Arts Fest and the Hollins Theater shows. Sundays tend to be laid-back and quiet, with limited hours in the dining hall."

If I could change one thing about Hollins, "I'd alter the policies of the career development center to be more conducive to finding jobs rather than identifying possible career choices."

Three things every student at Hollins should do before leaving are "climb Tinker Mountain, see a Hollins dance performance, and participate in Ring Night."

James Madison University

Address: Sonner Hall, MSC 0101, Harrisonburg, VA 22807
Phone: 540-568-5681
E-mail address: admissions@jmu.edu
Web site URL: www.jmu.edu
Year Founded: 1908
Private or Public: Public
Religious Affiliation: None
Location: Suburban
Number of Applicants: 19,245
Percent Accepted: 65%
Percent Accepted who enroll: 32%
Number Entering: 3,956
Number of Transfers Accepted each Year: 659
Middle 50% SAT range: M: 540–630, CR: 520–620, Wr: 520–620,
Middle 50% ACT range: 22–26
Early admission program EA/ED/None: EA

Percentage accepted through EA or ED: 46%
EA and ED deadline: 1-Nov
Regular Deadline: 15-Jan
Application Fee: $40
Full time Undergraduate enrollment: 16,916
Total enrollment: 18,454
Percent Male: 40%
Percent Female: 60%
Total Percent Minority or Unreported: 14%
Percent African-American: 4%
Percent Asian/Pacific Islander: 5%
Percent Hispanic: 2%
Percent Native-American: <1%
Percent International: 1%
Percent in-state/out of state: 71%/29%
Percent from Public HS: Unreported
Retention Rate: 91%
Graduation Rate 4-year: 66%

Graduation Rate 6-year: 81%
Percent Undergraduates in On-campus housing: 36%
Number of official organized extracurricular organizations: 328
3 Most popular majors: Finance, Health and Physical Education, Psychology
Student/Faculty ratio: 16:1
Average Class Size: 20 to 29
Percent of students going to grad school: 35%
Tuition and Fees: $9,229
In State Tuition and Fees if different: $3,482
Cost for Room and Board: $3,586
Percent receiving financial aid out of those who apply, first year: 54%
Percent receiving financial aid among all students: 52%

I n the midst of the stunning Shenandoah Valley lies a purple and gold gem, uncovered and raised from its modest beginnings as a Virginia teachers' school to become one of the leading schools in America. From the moment freshmen step onto James Madison University's campus, they are swept into the friendly bustle that defines the student body.

Academia Is Nuts (in a Good Way)

James Madison University offers a wide range of course offerings and lauded academic programs. Majors range from popular categories such as business and political science to the less popular (but nonetheless adored) social services program. Freshmen tend to attend larger lecture classes, while upperclassmen enjoy about a 16:1 student-professor ratio. Almost all classes, large or small, are taught by full professors who hold consistent office hours and make themselves extremely accessible. In fact, there are "a ton of professors whom you can run into out on the town in bars and restaurants and they're almost always happy to chat."

Although some students complain about the general education requirements, there is no shortage of enthusiasm about particular departments. A senior describes the College of Integrated Science and Technology as "groundbreaking," a division with an entire portion of campus dedicated to it and a curriculum that incorporates biology, chemistry, physics, computer science, and technology. Students also love the School of Media Arts and Design (SMAD); one student remarked that "everyone should take at least one class in SMAD with Rusty Greene." JMU features a fantastic education program, in which education majors can earn their masters in JMU's five-year program. Some Dukes will admit that "people have a lot of trouble with Elementary Statistics," Macroeconomics, and College of Business 300 (COB 300, which includes four separate classes taken at once), but add that even these are recommendable and very worthwhile. Almost all Dukes agree that, no matter what you take, there is still plenty of time to immerse yourself in extracurriculars.

Outside the Classroom

As one student aptly stated, "You'd be hard-pressed to find someone here who's not involved in some sort of student activity." The student body offers over 300 active student-run groups. Not necessarily the most popular but one of the most famed among these is IN8, JMU's secret society. Every year, it gives out eight letters to students and faculty who have significantly impacted their society to let them know that their work does not go unnoticed. In addition, in 2003, they donated a human sundial, a spot in the middle of campus where a person stands on a particular month's mark and casts a shadow on plaques six or seven feet away that designate the time.

When it comes to nightlife, fraternities and sororities provide a nice opportunity to make friends and get involved in the "party scene." Greek life only involves about 12 percent of students, but the ones who go Greek love it. Men rush only one fraternity, while women rush all eight sororities and slowly narrow down their options. Other people get involved with groups such as religious organizations, student government, the yearbook committee, activist groups, a cappella groups, or the sailing club, to name a few.

> "[Dukes are] active and productive, and excited about what they're doing."

All sports at JMU are NCAA Division I. Football, which plays in the Colonial Athletic Association, and basketball provide nearly the strongest crowd draws, second only to the nationally acclaimed marching band. Although most Dukes do not attend all the games, everyone attends homecoming. The school annually provides a famous speaker to address a student body decked out in JMU's purple and gold, which proceeds to "tailgate all day and party all night." In general, students become involved in several activities over their four years and often still find time to work in local restaurants or as tutors, dining hall attendants, or teaching and information assistants. A stimulating environment succeeds in keeping Dukes, as one phrased it, "active and productive, and excited about what they're doing."

Relaxing Down Under

JMU is incredibly friendly; its social graces tend to alleviate what might otherwise be a stressful academic lifestyle. Additionally, the campus accommodates students' busy schedules exceedingly well. JMU provides plenty of student facilities, including one of the most popular lounges on campus, Taylor Down Under. Students can go to places like this and find access to computers, the Internet, billiards, board games, study areas, and comfortable futons ("Great for napping!"). The university also sends a constant flow of music over Taylor Down Under's PA system, interrupted only for common evening events such as "open mic nights," poetry readings, bands, comedy acts, and other entertainment. Other popularly frequented hangouts include the quad in the spring, where someone is always lying out doing homework or playing frisbee, or even the on-campus dining halls, some of which stay open until 10 p.m. on weeknights.

Well-Catered

Students who linger in the dining halls find everything from all-you-can-eat buffet style meals to food courts and more specialized sandwich bars and salad bars. The school "keeps experimenting with the menu" and actively responding to student complaints to keep its students satisfied. Recently the dining halls relieved the threat of student uproar over the removal of a certain beloved chicken wrap. For a different taste, Chick-fil-A and an Einstein Bros. Bagels are located on campus, where students can use "dining dollars" that come with the standard 12-meal weekly plan. Of course, typical chain restaurants are scattered around Harrisonburg, especially after the recent addition of a new shopping center. Local favorites, however, include Mr. J's Bagels, known for its "AMAZING bagel sandwiches"; El Charro, a Mexican restaurant; and Luigi's, an Italian pizzeria. When they leave the table, students will be happy to find that no eatery is too far from home.

In the Hall of the Mountain King: The Suite Life

All freshmen and many sophomores live on campus in centrally located buildings, making "rolling out of bed three minutes before class starts incredibly possible (and done frequently)," according to one upperclassman veteran. In general, these residential halls vary from hall to suite style and offer warm, beautiful, and historical dorms. Many Dukes claim that "Old Campus," a group of dorms constructed between 1908 and 1948 with blue stone, stands out as the nicest housing in the area, especially since all of its buildings have been renovated during the past decade. For those not lucky enough (or not inclined) to live there, the "Village" is available, offering advantages of its own. Its nine residential halls are standard cinder block structures, including both standard freshman housing and interest-related accommodations. Students can live in leadership communities, biology-themed communities, substance-free communities, international halls (where international students are paired with American roommates), and more. All dorms have remained coed since the last all-girls dorm opened its doors to men. The system seems to produce fast friends: One senior praised, "I still live with five girls from my freshman hall, and I've had the same (randomly assigned) roommate since freshman year."

On-campus housing is also available for upperclassmen, but most elect to enter the myriad of apartment and townhouse complexes that have sprouted around the school in response to the quickly growing student population. This growth has created what one apartment dweller termed a "mini satellite campus off campus," consisting of various buildings. The student body has approximately doubled to 15,000 in the past 20 years, necessitating extra housing. Although parking spaces are generally scarce and the commute to class from the apartments is slightly longer than from on-campus housing, residents love where they live. Each of these complexes "has its own reputation and theme," providing off-campus essentials for their inhabitants.

Bust out the Party Hat

"Everyone from freshmen to super-seniors (5th years) show up at the apartment parties for mingling, dancing, flip cup, beer pong, and just some basic chatting over beer" when the weekend rolls around. Some Dukes start their nightlife on Wednesday or Thursday night, either in local bars or apartments. Mainstreet Bar and Grille, in particular, keeps some people dancing until 2 a.m. on Wednesday nights. Since no alcohol (JMU makes this very clear) is allowed in freshman dorms and no one underage can drink on campus, most partiers migrate to the apartments by Friday.

Not everyone drinks, but those who do usually have the option to party hard: "At some universities, a cover is required by the owners of the house to pay for the alcohol, but at JMU, it's pretty much open and free to all, which is so nice to know that you're welcome everywhere." JMU students seem responsible about their habits, a trait best shown by the student-run "SafeRides" program that offers free taxi service to those who have been drinking.

Moreover, the school's "three strikes" program forces them to proceed with relative caution, especially with respect to local police or higher-up administrators. Residential assistants purportedly "are always there for you, and do what they need to do to keep us all safe but let us enjoy ourselves, too." Some of the less strict ones "have even been known to play beer pong with us," says a freshman, though this is rare. Dukes who would rather not party or drink can hit the student lounges, which stay open late, or go to a movie at the campus movie theater for only $2.50. Wherever students are, campus police, vigilant "campus cadets," and a "blue light system" (a series of blue lights all over campus, each within view from the last, that can be used to summon help or safety escorts) keep them safe all night.

The Bottom Line

As a recent student body president remarked in an interview, "I've never met a single person who left because they didn't like it here. The only ones who leave are the ones who think that maybe they wanted something different academically." As the school develops, however, this latter concern is becoming less and less prevalent. JMU provides a terrific liberal arts education and continues its history of producing successful alumni today, while fostering an inclusive and high-spirited atmosphere that complements its beautiful area. Most Dukes echo the testimony of one upperclassman: "If I had to choose all over again, I'd stick with JMU. Wouldn't change anything."—*Hugh Sullivan*

FYI

If you come to JMU, you'd better bring "a friendly attitude."

What's the typical weekend schedule? "Go to bars on Wednesday and Thursdays, apartment parties on Friday. Saturday, work out during the day; go to a frat party at night. Sunday, sleep in and study!"

If I could change one thing about JMU, I would "move it closer to a major city. JMU does a good job of bringing stuff down, and Charlottesville isn't too far away, but I would prefer to have the D.C. nightlife available."

Three things that every student at JMU should do before graduating are "swim in Newman Lake (not as pleasant as it may sound), ring the bells in the bell tower, and find the hidden underground tunnels that were originally built so that women could avoid the cold weather between classes but have since been shut down. (The bell tower is rumored to be haunted on foggy nights by the ghost of the girl whose death in the tunnels caused the tunnels' closing.)"

Randolph College

Address: 2500 Rivermont Avenue, Lynchburg, VA 24503

Phone: 434-947-8100

E-mail address: admissions@randolphcollege.edu

Web site URL: www.randolphcollege.edu

Year Founded: 1891

Private or Public: Private

Religious Affiliation: Methodist

Location: City

Number of Applicants: 1,585

Percent Accepted: 83%

Percent Accepted who enroll: 11%

Number Entering: 144

Number of Transfers Accepted each Year: 53

Middle 50% SAT range: M: 490–600, CR: 500–630, Wr: Unreported

Middle 50% ACT range: 23–27

Early admission program EA/ED/None: EA

Percentage accepted through EA or ED: 73%

EA and ED deadline: 1-Dec

Regular Deadline: 1-Aprl

Application Fee: $35; online application is free

Full time Undergraduate enrollment: 649

Total enrollment: 656

Percent Male: 18%

Percent Female: 82%

Total Percent Minority or Unreported: 36%

Percent African-American: 9%

Percent Asian/Pacific Islander: 3%

Percent Hispanic: 7%

Percent Native-American: 1%

Percent International: 11%

Percent in-state/out of state: 48%/52%

Percent from Public HS: 78%

Retention Rate: 70%

Graduation Rate 4-year: 66%

Graduation Rate 6-year: 66%

Percent Undergraduates in On-campus housing: 88%

Number of official organized extracurricular organizations: 40

3 Most popular majors: Biology, Political Science, Psychology

Student/Faculty ratio: 7:1

Average Class Size: 2 to 9

Percent of students going to grad school: 31%

Tuition and Fees: $27,890

In State Tuition and Fees if different: No difference

Cost for Room and Board: $9,310

Percent receiving financial aid out of those who apply, first year: 83%

Percent receiving financial aid among all students: 96%

Randolph College, formerly Randolph-Macon Women's College, is beginning a new chapter of its 115-year history. In fall of 2007, this small liberal arts college admitted its first coeducational class. The school also began, in 2007, to fulfill its plans to release a new, enhanced curriculum. Yet with all these dramatic changes, the school insists that "the essential elements of the Randolph-Macon experience will remain constant."

A Close-Knit Community

Randolph College is described as a "gorgeous" college, set against the backdrop of the Virginia hills, and it is distinctive for its classic redbrick buildings and a matching redbrick wall that surrounds the entire campus. The student body is made up of only about 715 students, and all of them are required to live on campus for their full four years. "I like that everyone lives here," said one student. "We have such a wonderful sense of community, and it only takes five minutes to get from one part of campus to another." Most people have "no real complaints" about the living situation, as the rooms are larger than those at many other colleges and each of the dorm buildings has a unique attribute such as air conditioning, elevators, larger rooms, a better location, or extended quiet hours. Freshman dorms are assigned based on student preference forms, and upperclassmen draw for rooms in spring. Most of the dormitories are divided proportionally among the classes (except for the senior dorm and the mostly freshmen dorm) in order to facilitate and encourage interaction among upperclassmen and underclassmen. One senior commented, "My first year, I had so many upperclassmen coming into my room, welcoming me, letting me borrow books, telling me about professors, giving me tips, asking me about my clubs . . . people just take you under their wing!"

Another student commented, "It's really easy to meet people here because it's such a small school. There is only one dining hall and everyone has the same set meal plan, so "sometimes people will stay at dinner for hours, just talking. Of course there are a couple of cliques, but there will be groups in any community and no one is exclusive."

Students say they met their friends through athletics, clubs, classes, or freshman orientation groups. "There are a ton of mixers," said one student. "You'd have to live in a hole not to have any friends at Macon. And that's not possible to do here, either!" The college is very geographically diverse and boasts a large international student population, but ethnic diversity could use some improvement. "We could use more diversity, but I'm glad that we're at least as diverse as we are now," said one student. "It brings a lot to the classroom to have so many different vantage points."

From Homework to Happy Hour

The academics at Randolph are rigorous, to say the least. Students have a variety of requirements to fulfill, spanning such subjects as religion, philosophy, English, physical education, and a lab science. "Because of the liberal arts requirements, I get exposed to a lot of classes that may not be my strengths," commented one student. "But if you come in with an open mind and you push yourself to do well, they're really great." The most popular majors are psychology, politics, biology, and English, and if a student can't find a major

that suits her among the list of more than 25 possibilities, she always has the opportunity to design her own major. Most students agree, "All the majors are difficult—[Randolph] definitely doesn't give anything out for free." Registration is based on seniority and usually people are satisfied with the system, but the popularity of certain majors (particularly biology), the limited selection of classes, and the small class size can sometimes make it difficult to get into certain courses. Class size varies from four or five students to 30, although the average is 12. Workload, too, varies and depends on the class, the professor, and the preparation of the students. While one described it as "pretty heavy compared to other colleges," another observed, "It's not too different from high school AP classes. It can be overwhelming at first, but it's definitely manageable." Said one student, "Standards are fairly high, but there's no animosity within the classroom. People just want to do their own personal best."

According to many students, grading can be stringent. "We have a saying here: 'Anywhere else it would have been an A,'" said one. "I don't know if that's true, or if that's just us complaining about it." Still, student-faculty relations are "amazing. There's a lot of interaction with professors, especially on independent research projects." Another said, "A lot of professors have students babysitting, house-sitting, pet-sitting, whatever!" Most professors have an open-door policy, where students can come by and talk or ask questions even if it's not during office hours. "Professors want students to do well," noted one junior. The faculty is also highly involved in student extracurricular life, participating in award shows or other activities and often attending a Macon Community Happy Hour. Overall, students appreciate their professors and their academic opportunities, believing that the rigor of the curriculum is "worth it, because we're working hard for our education and becoming stronger in the process."

We Like to Party?

The extracurricular activity at Randolph is centered around a wide variety of student clubs and organizations. "We're very involved in our clubs," said one student. "We're always out to save the world in one form or another." Several of the larger groups include Amnesty International, the Environmental Club, the Black Students Alliance, various religious organizations, language clubs, and the Macon Activities Council, which brings in speakers and musicians and organizes events such as horseback riding or whitewater rafting. There are also multiple drama productions, musical ensembles, and a whole host of other clubs. "We have upwards of 100 clubs for a student body of only 1,150 people, if that gives you any idea of how important clubs are to us," one student said.

> "You'd have to live in a hole not to have any friends at Macon. And that's not possible to do here, either!"

Varsity athletics, however, has a slowly growing following, thanks to the college's recent infusion of males. In fact, nearly half of the male students are varsity athletes. "The people involved are really dedicated and the faculty is supportive, but I don't know how much attention the student body pays to the WildCats," said one student athlete. Intramural sports are not big; most students get their exercise by working out on their own, lifting weights or going running. A large majority of students have jobs on campus, especially since many of them participate in the work-study program.

As far as the weekend social scene is concerned, Randolph is not a party school. "We go off campus to party," one student said. "I'd say that on the weekends, almost half the campus goes home or goes to another college to party, while the other half stays behind to do work or club stuff." Another student said that weekend socializing can consist of a variety of activities such as drinking in people's rooms, going to a movie or out to dinner, going to see guest speakers or musicians, or going out to a club. "One club across the street has Wednesday college night, but generally, there's not a whole lot to do in Lynchburg," commented one sophomore. "Occasionally an organization on campus will host a bigger party, but for the most part people stick to smaller groups in rooms." One famous annual celebration is the "Never-Ending Weekend," with Friday night being the Tacky Party (the name is self-explanatory) and Saturday night being Fall Formal. Weekend activities in the surrounding town are limited, since Lynchburg "is not really a college town, so you have to drive to get to a movie theatre and most good restaurants." When asked to comment on the town's relationship with the college, one student responded, "We're definitely a separate community, but the town respects Randolph students and they have no real reason to complain about us because we're not a party school."

Daisy Chains and Pumpkin Parades

One particularly distinctive tradition at Randolph is the inter-class rivalry. Students identify themselves as "evens" or "odds," depending on the year of their graduation, and they enthusiastically participate in a vast collection of activities—such as water balloon fights and painting each other's banners—associated with the even-odd rivalry. "Sister classes" (freshmen/juniors and sophomores/seniors) have a strong connection, and they show their support for one another during Ring Week, when freshmen give small gifts to the juniors and create a scavenger hunt for them to find their class rings, and the Pumpkin Parade, where each senior receives a pumpkin carved by a sophomore. Right before graduation, sophomores make a huge daisy chain and pass it to the seniors. The class rivalry is even physically built into the school: a special staircase in the main lobby has one side for evens and one side for odds, and if a student goes up or down the wrong side, rumor has it that she won't graduate on time.

Randolph is certainly not for everyone. But for those who are willing to brave the tough academics and enjoy a somewhat quieter social scene, the college offers a vibrant community of dedicated, intelligent students who are working to better themselves and their society. One senior's final comment was, "It's a wonderful place. I've been exceedingly happy with what I've experienced there in the past four years."—*Lindsay Starck*

FYI
If you come to RC, you'd better bring "a whole lot of class spirit for the even-odd rivalry!"
What's the typical weekend schedule? "Relax, maybe party a bit or take a trip off-campus, then hit the books on Sunday."
If I could change one thing about RC, I'd "have more faculty available so that it's easier to get into popular or required classes."
Three things every student at RC should do before graduation are "join a club or several of them, ring the bell in Main Hall, and participate in the traditional Dell Run (running naked across the Greek-style ampitheater)."

S w e e t   B r i a r   C o l l e g e

Address: P. O. Box B
  Sweet Briar, VA 24595
Phone: 434-381-6142
E-mail address:
  admissions@sbc.edu
Web site URL: www.sbc.edu
Year Founded: 1901
Private or Public: Private
Religious Affiliation: None
Location: Rural
Number of Applicants:
  619
Percent Accepted: 81%
Percent Accepted who
  enroll: 40%
Number Entering: 202
Number of Transfers
  Accepted each Year: 21
Middle 50% SAT range:
  M: 480–590, **CR:** 510–620,
  Wr: Unreported
Middle 50% ACT range:
  21–26
Early admission program
  EA/ED/None: ED
Percentage accepted
  through EA or ED: 91%

EA and ED deadline: 1-Dec
Regular Deadline: 1-Feb
Application Fee: $40
Full time Undergraduate
  enrollment: 675
Total enrollment: 675
Percent Male: 0%
Percent Female: 100%
Total Percent Minority or
  Unreported: 10%
Percent African-American:
  1%
Percent Asian/Pacific
  Islander: 1%
Percent Hispanic: 3%
Percent Native-American:
  1%
Percent International: 1%
Percent in-state/out of
  state: 57%/43%
Percent from Public HS:
  72%
Retention Rate: 75%
Graduation Rate 4-year:
  68%
Graduation Rate 6-year:
  70%

Percent Undergraduates in
  On-campus housing: 90%
Number of official organized
  extracurricular
  organizations: 53
3 Most popular majors:
  Biology/Biological Sciences,
  General Business/
  Commerce, General Political
  Science and Government
Student/Faculty ratio:
  Unreported
Average Class Size:
  Unreported
Percent of students going to
  grad school: 24%
Tuition and Fees: $26,995
In State Tuition and Fees if
  different: No difference
Cost for Room and Board:
  $10,160
Percent receiving financial
  aid out of those who apply,
  first year: 90%
Percent receiving financial
  aid among all students:
  93%

Though small and rural, Sweet Briar College's quaint, historical campus seems to house the best of everything—except for men, of course. According to a locally printed bumper sticker, at Sweet Briar College, "women are leaders and men are *guests*." That's an overstatement considering the male visitation privileges and security clearance they have to gain just to get on campus. They don't call Sweet Briar the "pink bubble" for nothing!

Workin' It

Don't think that all that pink means these girls aren't working hard. Academics are taken very seriously at Sweet Briar College. Writes one junior, "There is a lot of reading and paper writing, etc . . . and it can be really hard but we're all at Sweet Briar to gain an education and so we do what it takes." The girls are required to meet general education requirements including fulfilling certain knowledge areas and skill areas, but course options allow for students to do so according to their own interests. For example, one junior took a course on the "History of Crime and Punishment in the West" to fulfill the Quantitative Reasoning requirement.

Sweet Briar girls agree that there are no "hard" or "easy" majors offered there. "Sweet Briar academics aren't for the faint of heart, no matter which major or minor you choose. We are a very small school . . . but it does ensure that none of our 40-something programs are weak." That may mean no coasting, but it also means that Sweet Briar students have full reign over their course options. Honors classes are available to all who are interested, and Sweet Briar offers certificate programs in Arts Management, Equine Studies, and Leadership. Furthermore, the average class size is 12 students. That kills all hopes of unnoticed absences on especially early- or late—mornings, but students have no trouble working their way into capped courses. All they have to do is ask nicely.

The workload can be heavy at Sweet Briar, but "girls learn to balance things quickly. Study parties are a popular and fun way to get work done, but have a little fun at the same time." Professors are also very accessible for outside help, and no classes are taught by TAs, so girls enjoy lots of one-on-one time with their instructors. Moreover, they are able to complete special projects researching the local history in nearby Amherst and Lynchburg. Twenty-one of Sweet Briar's 30 campus buildings are part of the "Sweet Briar College National Historic District" on the National Register of Historic Places.

Out on the Town

Social life at Sweet Briar is different than at other schools because girls go off campus to party. "The campus is pretty evenly split between the girls who like to go to other area school and girls who like to stay around SBC on the weekends." Shopping, dining out, and movie-going are popular. Though drinking is not unheard of, the Sweet Briar honor code disallows underage drinking, ensuring that non-drinkers are satisfied by a myriad of alternatives. The Campus Events Organization plans concerts and events on the weekends, including two annual formal events, the "Fall Formal" and the "Junior Banquet." The CEO also organizes lectures and exhibitions on a weekly basis. Recent guests have included Salman Rushdie, DanceBrazil, and the Roanoke Opera. Not bad for a small college town.

There's no Greek system at Sweet Briar College, but, as one T-shirt reads, "SBC: We're one big sorority." Tap Clubs are similar institutions, all but one of which are exclusive. Bum Chums and Ants 'N' Asses are the most popular, and many sponsor boathouse parties. However, on-campus cliques "change and morph frequently," so meeting new people is not a problem. In fact, most faces are familiar anyway on such a small campus.

According to a traditional jingle, "Diamonds are pretty and so are pearls, but nothing compares to Sweet Briar girls." It's not surprising, then, that boys come from nearby Hampden-Sydney to take Sweet Briar girls on dinner and movie dates in Lynchburg. Only about half of the student body is sexually active, however, so the jury's out on after-dinner activities. Says one junior, "a large percentage of the school is sexually active, but as educated women, I'm sure many, if not all of them make sure to use protection so STDs are not a perceived problem".

The Sweet Briar student body is "diverse in terms of personality types and backgrounds" but not much else. One girl writes that "Sweet Briar students are stereotyped as preppy girls who wear pearls, pink and green, and Vera Bradley bags." Most girls dress more casually than expected, however, and would prefer that the campus as a whole were more diverse.

Dorms and Dining

Unless they're married or over 22, Sweet Briar students are required to live on campus or at home. Freshmen are divided into floors and halls based on their chosen "male visitation option," but upperclasswomen are automatically allowed visitors at all hours, unless enough students request otherwise. Meta Glass and Grammer Halls are for first-year students and are monitored by upperclasswomen called FYAs or First-Year Assistants, and even the upperclass dorms have Community Assistants (CAs). Dew is the worst dorm, and Manson has the best kitchen, but according to one student, "All of the dorms on campus are pretty nice . . . they all have nice big rooms and are really good compared to other college dorms I have seen." They had better be if there's no way out of them.

> ### "It's like a four-year slumber party with great classes interspersed!"

Along with a four-year residential plan comes a 21-meal fixed dining plan. Sweet Briar girls can eat in the dining hall or have wraps made at a station on the way to class. They can also purchase food from the "Bistro" or the "Café" at their expense, but the dining hall overlooks the mountain, so it's absolutely worth the time. "One could easily spend hours sitting in our dining hall and chatting, and I have on several occasions," says one student. Many student groups also hold meetings in the dining area. Girls who need a change of pace dine out at The Briar Patch in Amherst, or grab coffee at The Drowsy Poet.

Loving the Locals

Sweet Briar students can't say enough about their campus—almost as beautiful as the students. Writes one student, "[Sweet Briar] is the one college that I visited where I felt the pictures in the brochures didn't do it justice." The original campus buildings were built by Ralph Adams Cram, who also designed many of Princeton's buildings, and the recent ones emulate his style so that the architecture blends with the natural surroundings. "The campus feels very peaceful and is just a really pleasant place to be." At least there's something for these ladies to feast their eyes on.

The "Dell" is the grassy courtyard in the center of campus—a popular perch for students in search of a little sun. Other students, assured by the vigilance of the Campus Police, like to take walks around the "Dairy Loop." Those who want a break from nature can explore the shopping districts in Amherst and Lynchburg, both of which have healthy relationships with the College. Local elementary school students enjoy campus and gallery tours and science and art days given by Sweet Briar students. The girls also host a school supply drive and teach dance classes in town.

Down Time . . . Or Not

Sweet Briar girls don't take academics lightly, and the same goes for extracurriculars. One junior writes that "Sweet Briar students in general are extremely active in extracurricular activities, almost to the point of insanity." So when they're not in class, girls engage with respected groups like the student government, student newspaper, and intramurals. Tap Clubs are also popular, but more fun than structured. Girls who need a good football fix have to travel to nearby Hampden-Sydney or VMI to catch a boy in uniform. The Sweet Briar Equestrian Team, however, is well-supported and fitted with a recruiting office. Less competitive souls get their workouts in the recreational gym, swimming pool, or tennis court.

When they're not excelling in the classroom or on the IM fields, the Sweet Briar Vixens are participating in one of the college's many traditions—or hiding from them. Daisy, the daughter of the College's founder, is rumored to haunt the place. More wholesome rituals include "The Ring Game," which roots out those lucky girls who are engaged—yes, to be married—and the "Big/Little Sister" program, which partners juniors and freshmen, not to mention Scream Night, Lantern Bearing, Step Singing, and Founders' Day. Wherever they choose to expend their energies, the girls of Sweet Briar College are wed to their alma mater. Quirky traditions and an idyllic campus are their favorite parts. One student comments, "It's like a four-year slumber party with great classes interspersed!" Pillow fights, anyone?—*Lauren Ezell*

FYI
If you come to Sweet Briar, you better bring "a car."
What is a typical weekend schedule? "Whatever you want!"
If I could change one thing about Sweet Briar, I'd "make the student body more diverse."
Three things every student at Sweet Briar should do before graduating are "go sledding on a dining hall tray, walk the Dairy Loop, and admire just how beautiful the campus is."

University of Richmond

Address: 28 Westhampton Way, Richmond, VA 23173
Phone: 804-289-8640
E-mail address: admissions@richmond.edu
Web site URL: www.richmond.edu
Year Founded: 1830
Private or Public: Private
Religious Affiliation: None
Location: Suburban
Number of Applicants: 7,970
Percent Accepted: 32%
Percent Accepted who enroll: 29%
Number Entering: 787
Number of Transfers Accepted each Year: 108
Middle 50% SAT range: M: 590–680, CR: 580–680, Wr: 590–690
Middle 50% ACT range: 26–30
Early admission program EA/ED/None: ED
Percentage accepted through EA or ED: 28%

EA and ED deadline: 15-Nov, 15-Jan
Regular Deadline: 15-Jan
Application Fee: $50
Full time Undergraduate enrollment: 2,735
Total enrollment: 3,445
Percent Male: 49%
Percent Female: 51%
Total Percent Minority or Unreported: 13%
Percent African-American: 6%
Percent Asian/Pacific Islander: 4%
Percent Hispanic: 3%
Percent Native-American: 1%
Percent International: Unreported
Percent in-state/out of state: 17%/83%
Percent from Public HS: 61%
Retention Rate: 91%
Graduation Rate 4-year: 82%

Graduation Rate 6-year: 87%
Percent Undergraduates in On-campus housing: 91%
Number of official organized extracurricular organizations: 275
3 Most popular majors: Business Administration, Accounting, International Studies
Student/Faculty ratio: 9:1
Average Class Size: 16
Percent of students going to grad school: 40%
Tuition and Fees: $38,850
In State Tuition and Fees if different: No difference
Cost for Room and Board: $8,200
Percent receiving financial aid out of those who apply, first year: 75%
Percent receiving financial aid among all students: 42%

When you head off to the University of Richmond, you'd better be prepared for a four-year marathon. The serene campus is bustling with activity, ambitious students, and unique educational opportunities. Students throw themselves into every aspect of the Richmond experience and reap the benefits. A recently revamped science center, gym, and dining hall, plus a new residence hall, are just a few of the new perks at the already impressive school. Students come ready to work hard, play hard, and make the most of all that Richmond offers.

The Richmond Difference

The Robins School of Business at Richmond was recently ranked number 20 by *Business-Week* for undergraduate business programs. Most students agree that business is one of the most popular majors for students to pursue at UR. Meanwhile, the Jepson School of Leadership Studies is one of a kind. If they don't choose business, students often select this interdisciplinary major in leadership studies, which is unique to UR. "Anything in the science field is known to be killer," one junior said. "Most people on campus are political science, business, or leadership majors." There is also praise for international business, which easily complements a language major. Students at Richmond must fulfill General Education requirements, the "gened's," that range from science and math to literature and history. The Core Course, a combination of philosophy and literature that "not many people love" is one of the most notoriously hard requirements that everyone must suffer through, explained one student. Students also take Wellness classes, which address various health and lifestyle issues.

Richmond students agree that the workload is challenging. "You'd be hard-pressed to find an easy class at Richmond," one junior said. Students spend a significant amount of time in the library, which has almost become another location to socialize. "People are always in the library; you can find everyone there," one student described. Recent renovations to the main library make it an even more attractive destination. Richmond has an undergraduate student-faculty ratio of 9:1 and most students find it very easy to seek out help from professors. Small class size also aids in roundtable discussions and the free exchange of ideas in an intimate environment.

Students find it very easy to become involved on campus from Greek life to student government and an array of clubs and organizations. Richmond students approach their extracurriculars with the same intensity as their classes and often find it easy to become overcommitted. "I was surprised by how easy it is to become involved here," one junior noted. At Richmond, involvement creates a close-knit community to which everyone can contribute.

From the Lodges, to D-Hall

To balance out all that work, Richmond students never find their weekends dull. "Greek life pretty much rules here," one junior girl said. The lodges—fraternity houses—are known for their great throw-downs on Saturdays. Friday nights usually consist of going to the senior apartments and partying there. Drinking is prevalent but most agree that everyone is able to find his or her own comfortable social scene.

In between parties, friends cherish their moments in the dining hall, affectionately known as "D-Hall," to debrief the past nights' events. All students living on campus must have a meal plan and the food is generally satisfactory. Some complain of a lack of variety while others rave about new additions of brick oven pizza and a Mongolian grill. For those seeking more diverse options, venturing into the city of Richmond offers many local restaurants and two nearby shopping malls. Some students keep cars on campus, which is important for escaping the "Richmond Bubble," although the University also provides a free shuttle service and city bus passes. One student complained of the contained campus, citing that "most students are too timid to get off campus and do their own thing."

If you're looking for a sports-oriented college, Richmond is not the place. "Nobody really cares about sports here," one sophomore declared. Basketball is perhaps the most popular team to follow, but attendance at most sporting events is low. Football also tends to bring students out, and tailgating is a social event in itself. "Everyone gets dressed up as preppy as possible and drinks in the parking lot at the sta-

dium," a senior described. After mingling in a mixture of pearls and popped collars, many students head back to the dorms without making it to the game. Still, the football team has recently made its mark and garnered special attention by winning the 2008 NCAA Division I National Championship—the school's first such championship in any sport.

The Richmond Bubble

It may be a very contained world, but Richmond students are happy and quite comfortable in their bubble. "It's definitely sheltered away from the 'real world'" a student explained, "but it's a safe, friendly, and caring environment with every opportunity you would ask for." Students praise the beautiful campus and enjoy warm afternoons swimming or laying out by the James River. The Richmond community is friendly and fluid, making it easy to constantly meet new people. The student body lacks some diversity and despite University efforts to attract a more international crowd, everyone agrees that the majority of students appear to be preppy, middle-class northerners.

> "It's definitely sheltered away from the 'real world,' but it's a safe, friendly, and caring environment with every opportunity you would ask for."

There is a prevalent sense of integrity within the student body due to a strong honor code that everyone signs freshman year. Freshman men and women take part in respective honor code signing ceremonies—Investiture for men and Proclamation for women. The women wear white dresses and the men dress up as well, making each event a formal and special occasion. Crime is low and while most people agree you should not leave your laptop lying around, they feel very safe. For girls worried about walking home late at night or just looking to escape the cold, there is a campus shuttle service, but sorry boys: this one is strictly for the ladies so you'll be traveling on foot after your nights out.

The View Across the Lake

White no one is required to live on campus at any point, freshmen, sophomores and juniors who live on campus must live in residence halls or themed houses until they are seniors, when they have the option of moving to an on-campus apartment. Over 90 percent of students choose to remain on campus for all four years. "Nobody likes moving off campus because it's hard to stay in the social scene," one junior said. Housing is decent but some students lament having to live in doubles until they are juniors, as well as being confined to single-sex dorms—though coed options exist for upperclassmen in living and learning communities. The University has converted some doubles into suite-style dorm rooms that can accommodate a greater number of students. Richmond was historically divided by the lake in the middle of campus into two separate colleges, Richmond College for boys and Westhampton College for the girls. Rumor has it that whomever you kiss on the gazebo in the middle of the lake will be the person you marry. Nowadays each sex lives on both sides of the lake, but dorms remain single-sex. All freshman girls live in Lora Robins Court or Moore Hall, and freshman boys are assigned to Dennis, Marsh, and Wood Halls. Students easily form solidarity within their class years, but the separation of sexes is said to have some negative effects. "Intermixing seems more forced and based around sexual attraction," one student complained. "If you see a guy in Lora Robins you know he is there to see a girl."

The students relish several Richmond traditions that date back many years. Breaking out the traditional white dress again, the junior girls take part in "Ring Dance." This black-tie event takes place at the old Jefferson Hotel, with each girl accompanied by her father and a date. A much less formal but equally important event is Festivus, a campus-wide outdoor event. Festivus takes place every March and is the "best day of the year" according to several students. The day commences early with a slew of students decked out in sundresses and ties, drinking mimosas. The party moves to the apartments and then continues at the lodges for this all-day affair.

Overall, students are thrilled with their choice to attend Richmond, which is evident in the high level of enthusiasm and involvement in the school community. People are happy to take advantage of every aspect of their four years. One sophomore raved, "The people here are genuinely nice and excited about life! We really do all work hard and play hard." If you're ready to take it all in, be prepared to hit the ground running. —*Jennifer Hansen*

FYI

If you come to Richmond you'd better bring . . . "a polo shirt in every color, collar popped."

What is the typical weekend schedule? "Either apartment parties or, even better, fraternity lodge parties! Go shopping in Carytown, and every Saturday and Sunday afternoon, everyone piles into D-Hall for brunch."

If I could change one thing about Richmond I'd . . . "make more apartment-style or coed housing. Living in a dorm till you're a junior just sucks!"

Three things every Richmond student should do before graduating are "go all out at Festivus, spend a few lazy afternoons by the James River, either attend Ring Dance (if you're a junior girl) or go with a junior girl to Ring Dance."

University of Virginia

Address: PO Box 400160
Charlottesville, VA
22904-4160
Phone: 434-982-3200
E-mail address:
undergradadmission@
virginia.edu
Web site URL: www.virginia.edu
Year Founded: 1819
Private or Public: Public
Religious Affiliation: None
Location: Urban
Number of Applicants:
17,798
Percent Accepted: 35%
Percent Accepted who
enroll: 52%
Number Entering: 3,246
Number of Transfers
Accepted each Year: 850
Middle 50% SAT range:
M: 620–730, CR: 600–710,
Wr: 600–710
Middle 50% ACT range:
Unreported
Early admission program
EA/ED/None: None

Percentage accepted
through EA or ED: NA
EA and ED deadline: NA
Regular Deadline: 2-Jan
Application Fee: $60
Full time Undergraduate
enrollment: 15,078
Total enrollment: 22,533
Percent Male: 43%
Percent Female: 57%
Total Percent Minority or
Unreported: 6%
Percent African-American:
5%
Percent Asian/Pacific
Islander: 12%
Percent Hispanic: 11%
Percent Native-American:
<1%
Percent International: 5%
Percent in-state/out of
state: 72%/28%
Percent from Public HS:
75%
Retention Rate: 97%
Graduation Rate 4-year:
84%

Graduation Rate 6-year:
91%
Percent Undergraduates in
On-campus housing: 43%
Number of official organized
extracurricular
organizations: 604
3 Most popular majors:
Social Sciences,
Engineering,
Business/Marketing
Student/Faculty ratio: 15:1
Average Class Size: 10
to 19
Percent of students going
to grad school: Unreported
Tuition and Fees: $29,798
In State Tuition and Fees if
different: $9,505
Cost for Room and Board:
$7,820
Percent receiving financial
aid out of those who apply,
first year: 45%
Percent receiving financial
aid among all students:
25%

N estled between the cosmopolitan, mid-sized city of Charlottesville, and the scenic beauty of the Blue Ridge, The University of Virginia (UVa) offers a combination of tradition and pride. UVa was founded by Thomas Jefferson, and both Edgar Allan Poe and Woodrow Wilson attended the University. Further tradition dictates the fact that UVa has no "freshmen" and "sophomores;" instead, there are first-years and second-years and so on. This convention started because Thomas Jefferson, the school's founder, believed learning is continuous, and therefore "freshmen" are simply in their first year of a lifelong education. Other idiosyncrasies include the "Wahoos'" reference to their campus as "Grounds," or simply calling UVa "the University." Learning the lingo as a first-year at the University is key to fitting in on Grounds.

A Lifelong Education and Free Lunches

The University breaks down undergraduates into seven schools: the Architecture School,

the Engineering School, the McIntire School of Commerce, the Nursing School, the Batten School of Leadership and Public Policy, the Curry School of Education, and the College of Arts and Sciences. Each school has its own academic requirements determined by major. The academic requirements in the College are "basic:" 12 credits of math and science, six of humanities, three of history, six of social science, and three in non-Western perspectives. There are also additional foreign language and writing proficiency requirements. The Jeffersonian vision of academia is the cornerstone of the University, and requires students to "follow truth wherever it may lead," and it always leads to multiple disciplines.

Most students do not find the requirements burdensome "since they are really flexible, and you can space out anything that you detest so that you aren't stuck with a ton of courses that you hate in any given semester." Class sizes vary greatly "depending on which classes you take." The University offers a range of classes, from large lectures of 500 students down to a two-student seminar.

Some classes are difficult to get into, such as Media Studies and Public Speaking, and during the beginning of class sign-ups "it is frustrating because it seems like everything is full and nobody can get the classes they want, but by the end of the drop period a lot of slots open up, so students just have to be patient and vigilant." UVa has "gut" classes like any other school, and Physics 105 (How Things Work), Mental Health, lower-level astronomy classes, and physical education classes are considered to be a few examples.

Once students get into their courses, they say, professors "are very accessible." Most students are very happy with their professors; a UVa third-year pointed out that "the professors here want you to learn, so they try and be available as much as possible." Students say "grading is usually tough but fair;" however, the Jeffersonian ideal definitely resonates with students. As one third-year summed up, "I love it here . . . [It is] challenging, but you always learn something."

> "Mr. Jefferson wanted students and professors to interact regularly and freely because that was how education was truly found."

In keeping with the University's tradition and history, Professors are either addressed as "Mr." or "Mrs." or "Professor," but never "Dr." because "Mr. Jefferson did not want that sort of division between students and faculty." Instead, as one student said, "Mr. Jefferson wanted students and professors to interact regularly and freely because that was how education was truly found." In response to this tenet, the College of Arts and Sciences Council has a "take your professor to lunch" program, in which the council will pay for your lunch with your professor as a way to increase interactions between students and the faculty outside of the classroom. One student even said, "I have been on a rowing machine at the Aquatic Fitness Center rowing next to my Organic Chemistry professor."

Students say the coursework at UVa is intense yet manageable. "There is still time for play, but the work comes first and during the week it takes a decent part of my schedule." While "tradition" and "history" resonate deeply with the Wahoos, the word "honor" has even more significance on Grounds. The Honor System attempts to provide students with substantial benefits dependent on self-governance, such as unproctored exams in their rooms or in a pavilion garden. Self-governance is a huge tradition at UVa; "not only do we have a completely student-run Honor Committee and University Judiciary Committee, but the Student Council has a great deal of influence, distributing over $300,000 annually to student groups." However, the Honor System has become a "contentious issue here at UVa, especially the single sanction, which means automatic expulsion for anyone convicted by the Committee." Moreover, "a lot of professors give proctored exams and don't allow the freedom and trust promised in the prospectus. The University has done a good job of perpetuating the myths and there are examples of the benefits of the honor code, but they are the exception rather than the rule."

Life as a Wahoo

UVa students are known as "Wahoos" (or "Cavaliers"), and Charlottesville is nicknamed "Hooville," an epithet said to originate from the legend of the wahoo fish, which can drink its weight in water. UVa students live up to these nicknames because "alcohol is everywhere on campus." However, "a student can go out and have a good time with or without alcohol." Between hanging out in the vibrant town of Charlottesville and going to a cappella concerts, intramurals, rock concerts, and smaller parties, students boast that "there is something for everyone here." One first-year said, "I think that UVa is diverse when it comes to social scenes."

The University's policies on alcohol tend to be pretty strict, but "as long as you don't do anything stupid, you're fine." Students mostly go out on the weekends, "restricted to Thursday [through] Saturday or Sunday nights, but there are definitely places to go every night of the week." The fraternities lined up on Rugby Road tend to run the social scene "until students are of age to go to bars and purchase alcohol." Being underage is a problem at bars, but not at fraternities. Bid Day, Halloween, and Springfest are reportedly the biggest parties on campus. Third- and fourth-year students frequent house and apartment parties, bars, and other colleges, and they often travel into Washington, D.C.

Dating among Wahoos is said to be "very common," and students agree "there are enough attractive people." Attractive or not, students love to dress up, and there are many occasions on Grounds. Besides the formal events for fraternities and sororities, another tradition at UVa is to get dressed up for football games. There has recently been a split among the student body with regards to wearing formal clothing to football games. Many students "now opt for donning orange-dominated school colors in an effort to create what's known as the 'Sea of Orange.'" Dress as you please, because UVa offers tons of other activities on the weekends besides football games.

There are always "local bands playing all over the place." The UVa movie theater showcases $3 movies every weekend: one old movie and one new movie. Big Hollywood names, including Anthony Hopkins and Sigourney Weaver, come to the annual Virginia Film Festival in Charlottesville. The Dalai Lama and Ralph Nader were among high-profile campus speakers in the last few years. Campus-wide organized activities provide "good movies and amazing lectures."

Polos and Popped Collars?

While opinions on the student body differ from "very diverse" to "too homogeneous (predominantly white)," the stereotypical UVa student is: "white, preppy, and well-groomed; wears khakis and polo shirts, or skirts with nice tank tops; probably upper middle class." An aspect that most students agree on is that "there is a lot of self-segregation," which is "a big issue here." One student said: "There's definitely a lot of tension over the issue. I do think there has been minor progress over the years, however." Race relations aside, the University has the highest black student graduation rate, approximately 87 percent, of any public university in America.

One Wahoo said, "There is a reputation of pretentiousness and preppiness that seems to follow UVa everywhere, but I think that the school is very diverse and accepting; I know people who wear polo shirts each day, and I know people that wear T-shirts and jeans."

The Grounds

First-years live on campus and are divided between the New Dorms and the Old Dorms. Although rooms in the Old Dorms tend to be "small," they are also "more social." First-years in the New Dorms "get really big rooms with a suite area for every five rooms, and some rooms have air-conditioning." There is an RA for every 20 first-years, and they vary in strictness. Some are strict, some couldn't care less. "Most are strict when they need to be," one student said.

Lots of students move off Grounds after their first year and either relocate to fraternity and sorority houses or the two residential colleges on Grounds. The residential colleges, Brown and Hereford, "have personality, but other than that, the housing areas are pretty standard." There are also houses for students with common interests, including French, Spanish, and Russian Houses. Living off-grounds is "very popular"; however, rents and proximity to the grounds can vary greatly. Students warn that off-grounds housing "is a ridiculous problem here in Charlottesville" because "most first-years are forced into signing a lease in October or early November with roommates they barely know yet."

While the dining halls tend to be "fairly clean," some students complain about dinner ending too early. The dining hall food reportedly is "not terrible, but not good either, and the wait is often bad." The University just built a new "Observatory Hill Dining Hall," which serves mostly first-years, "and it sounds like the food will be better there as well." Students have "plus dollars" that come with their meal plans, and this allows students to eat at different stores and bakeries and the Pav, Crossroads, and the Castle, which are food courts that house chain restaurants like Pizza Hut and Chick-Fil-A. There is a large food selection for vegetarians, and "the restaurants in Charlottesville are great, basically one from each cost category that are about five minutes away."

The Good Ole Song

People at UVa are "very devoted" to their extracurricular activities, and although "almost everyone belongs to some society or another, many belong to more than one." Some of the most well-respected organizations include the Madison House (community service), the Jefferson Society (debate), *The Cavalier Daily*, and the University Guides. The Madison House "is the epicenter of volunteerism at the University." They run programs in tutoring, medical aid, pet care, elderly companionship, and more. Some students also hold real jobs on the side, and the University also offers a lot of jobs for work-study students.

True to tradition and history, secret societies are "a large part of students' life here." These philanthropic societies are "very secretive about their workings in the community." While the IMP's are secret in their actions, everyone knows who they are. The Z's are secret until graduation, and the 7's are unknown until they die. "When individuals in the 7 Society pass, the chapel bell rings seven times at 7:07 p.m., then plays an eerie song on the seventh chord."

Although football is the most popular sport at UVa by far, soccer and basketball are also big. "There is so much school pride—especially with football." Both students and alumni go to football games, and "if you walk around campus on game days, all you see is beer everywhere and everyone is dressed up," one student said. In sticking with tradition, Wahoos can be seen putting "their arms around each other and sway[ing] while singing 'The Good Ol' Song' after the team scores." Another tradition is the "fourth-year fifth," which is "a challenge of fourth-year students drinking a fifth of bourbon at the last football game of the season." Although the administration is working to curtail this last tradition, the Cavalier fans possess and express a great amount of team spirit. Students boast that their Aquatics and Fitness Center has great facilities for swimming, weight-lifting and the like. "The Aquatics [and] Fitness Center is a top-of-the-line student and faculty resource." The new John Paul Jones Arena hosts all basketball games as well as community events, such as major concerts and even circuses, in the hopes of continuing to draw members of the Charlottesville community into the life of the University. Aside from varsity sports, many students play intramurals; and there are always pick-up games around the grounds.

History and Beauty Unite

The grounds are "beautiful . . . hilly, open, historical architecture yet with a modern vibe." "Classic buildings" and "lots of trees and grassy areas" contribute to the attractiveness of the campus. The University is centered around the Lawn, which neighbors the Rotunda, hosts a statue of Homer and Frisbee games on sunny afternoons, and serves as a popular hangout on Sundays. "I love the Lawn. There are trees on the sides where you can sit and read or study," said one student. If you prefer studying indoors, UVa's main library, Alderman Library, is the backup to the Library of Congress. "Our libraries are pretty amazing."

UVa is a "really friendly place" where people are "generally enthusiastic and happy, and they don't stress out like at other schools." The "great thing about UVa is for a public university, you get an Ivy League education for about half price and the campus is great. . . . Plus, it's also a huge party school if you dig that sort of thing. There is something for everyone."—*Terren O'Reilly*

FYI

If you come to UVa, you'd better bring "a tie and polo shirts for guys and a sundress for girls."

What's the typical weekend schedule? "Everyone goes out Thursday through Saturday, and goes to fraternity parties or bars, depending on the weekend. Everyone tailgates all day on Saturday during football season."

If I could change one thing about UVa, it would be "the disproportion of in-state students (about 70 percent) to out-of-state students (30 percent)."

Three things every student at UVa student should do before graduating are "streak the lawn, learn the 'Good Ol' Song' and sing it at a football game, and enjoy the beauty of the lawn, gardens, and architecture because you will not find them at other schools."

Virginia Polytechnic Institute & State University

Address: 201 Burruss Hall
Blacksburg, VA 24061
Phone: 540-231-6267
E-mail address:
vtadmiss@vt.edu
Web site URL: www.vt.edu
Year Founded: 1872
Private or Public: Public
Religious Affiliation: None
Location: Rural
Number of Applicants: 19,429
Percent Accepted: 67%
Percent Accepted who
enroll: 39%
Number Entering: 5,119
Number of Transfers
Accepted each Year: 1,434
Middle 50% SAT range:
M: 530–630, CR: 570–670,
Wr: 530–630
Middle 50% ACT range:
Unreported
Early admission program
EA/ED/None: ED

Percentage accepted
through EA or ED: 50%
EA and ED deadline: 1-Nov
Regular Deadline: 15-Jan
Application Fee: $50
Full time Undergraduate
enrollment: 23,041
Total enrollment: 29,537
Percent Male: 58%
Percent Female: 42%
Total Percent Minority or
Unreported: 14%
Percent African-American:
4%
Percent Asian/Pacific
Islander: 7%
Percent Hispanic: 3%
Percent Native-American: 0%
Percent International: 2%
Percent in-state/out of
state: 25%/75%
Percent from Public HS: 95%
Retention Rate: 93%
Graduation Rate 4-year: 50%

Graduation Rate 6-year: 53%
Percent Undergraduates in
On-campus housing: 39%
Number of official organized
extracurricular
organizations: 600
3 Most popular majors:
Biology, Engineering, Nursing
Student/Faculty ratio:
16:1
Average Class Size: 24
Percent of students going to
grad school: 24%
Tuition and Fees: $20,825
In State Tuition and Fees if
different: $8,198
Cost for Room and Board:
$5,476
Percent receiving financial
aid out of those who apply,
first year: 36%
Percent receiving financial
aid among all students:
34%

O n a fine day each winter, masses of cadets and members of the all-male dorm Pritchard Hall can be observed on the Drill Field at Virginia Polytechnic Institute, using their respective strategies to bombard the other side with snowballs. More students begin to gather around the field to watch the groups duke it out. On one side, the disorderly males of Pritchard defend their territory, while on the other, the cadets gather in military formations and use their learned military tactics to gain the upper hand. This epic snowball fight occurs every winter, only at Virginia Polytechnic Institute.

Virginia Tech, better known as "VT," is known mostly for its technical background, but it provides for humanities as well. With its mascot, the Hokie Bird or Hokie (a large purple turkey), the University sets itself apart in the little town of Blacksburg, Va.

School Is for the Hokies

Freshmen who are sure of what they want to major in can enroll in one of Virginia Polytechnic's seven undergraduate colleges: Agriculture and Life Sciences, Architecture and Urban Studies, Pamplin College of Business, Engineering, Liberal Arts and Human Sciences, Natural Resources, and Science. Students who are undecided are placed in the University Studies program and have until the end of sophomore year to apply to a college. Students find it rather easy to switch from college to college, with only a few days' wait for the paperwork to be processed. However, with rigorous academic requirements, students are given very little time to explore other fields outside their major. Virginia Tech requires students to fulfill 36 to 44 semester hours distributed among the seven core areas: Writing and Discourse; Ideas, Cultural Traditions, and Values; Society and Human Behavior; Scientific Reasoning and Discovery; Quantitative and Symbolic Reasoning; Creativity and Aesthetic Reasoning; and Critical Issues in a Global Context. Of all the majors, engineering and architecture are the hardest, with the most work and competition. One mechanical engineering major said that "the professors load you with work, while other majors don't." Communications, engineering, business, and biology are the most popular majors, while some of the more unusual majors include wood science and forestry, as well as horticulture.

Virginia Tech also has a University Honors Program, which is made up of the top academic students. Incoming freshmen with excellent high school GPAs and high SAT scores are allowed to apply for the program. Honors students have better access to faculty, intensive academic advising, priority in class registration, and honors-only courses. In addition, students in the program are given more opportunities for independent study and research. Upon acceptance, the program requires students to maintain a 3.5 GPA in order to keep their standing.

Introductory classes tend to have 200 to 300 people in each class, while the major-specific classes are much smaller with around 30 people. Because of the large classes and number of students, some students feel that the student-teacher relationship is not a good one. This tends to be especially true for the engineering and chemistry departments. One student said that "many professors just teach, and if you don't get it, they send you to a graduate student or teaching assistant." In addition, because there are so many students within these majors, many of the labs and sections are led by graduate students who often do not have a strong grasp of the subject and have poor English. However, many non–engineering majors feel the opposite way about their professors. An environment science major said: "You get to know all your professors really well. I had really good professors in geography and almost got into that because of them."

Keeping House

Students are required to live on campus for at least one year. The majority of on-campus students are freshmen, while some sophomores stay on campus. Most of the residences are coed with a few single-sex dorms. Pritchard, an all-male dorm, is the largest male dorm on the East Coast. Students say that female dorms are typically a lot better than the male dorms. One male student said, "Guys' dorms are dirtier, and you have to deal with fire alarms every night. Plus, the bathrooms are gross." In addition, there are some complaints about RAs who can be really strict and dampen dorm life. Virginia Tech prohibits alcohol in the dorms and has visitation restrictions. Despite the downsides of dorm life, students enjoy the ability to walk to wherever they want to go and the close proximity of the dining halls and gym. People enjoy hanging out on the quad outside of Pritchard, where, when the weather is nice, students can play a game of volleyball. Some of the dorms are GPA-oriented, while others are not. The athletes' dorm is near the gym and connected to the dining center, West End Market. The oldest dorms are for the ROTC cadets and are separated from the rest of campus.

After their first year, most students move off campus to townhouses and apartments in search of more private and cheaper living conditions. While many students bring their own cars, Virginia Tech provides a bus line that transports off-campus students to and from campus. Students note that while security on campus is not an issue, the off-campus community can get a little more out of control. Often after big sporting events, crowds can get rowdy. The administration provides a Safe Ride program that will pick up students if they prefer not to walk somewhere, and emergency phone stations are available throughout the area.

The dining hall food receives great reviews from the students. The most preferred site is West End Market, where students can get fresh Maine lobster and London broil. The many other dining centers, such as D2 and Shultz Dining Center, have all-you-care-to-eat buffets. Virginia Tech also offers many food courts with restaurants such as Sbarro, Au Bon Pain, and Chick-fil-A. In addition, there is an on-campus grocery store. Students can select from among many different meal plan options involving Flex dollars, which can be used to purchase food and for doing laundry. Even with the various dining plans, students have to watch how much they spend, as they can easily run out of Flex dollars before semester's end; they warn that "you have to read the fine print." Besides eating on campus, there are many bars and restaurant in nearby Christiansburg, where the mall and other retail stores are located, and the University provides transportation to and from the town.

Where's the Party at?

While not in the classroom, students are busy partying it up. Around 20 percent of the students at Virginia Tech are involved in Greek life. Many of the frats hold open parties and tend to dominate the social scene. The students who join frats find it to be a memorable experience and form a close network of friends that can aid in securing jobs and recommendations. Even though the frats are fun, students have to be able to balance the time commitments to the fraternity and to academics, and many drop out of the pledging process because of this.

Virginia Tech has a zero-tolerance policy

for drugs and is also strict regarding alcohol. Alcohol is not allowed in the dorms, and students are given judicial restrictions (JR) if they are caught with it. Three JRs result in suspension for one semester. While campus police do look out for violations of the alcohol policy, one student noted that "as long as you don't act stupid, you'll be OK."

> **"As long as you don't act stupid, you'll be OK."**

The parties tend to be held off campus, where all the frats and apartments are. Students head out starting Thursday and party until Saturday. Generally, underclassmen have no difficulty finding things to do and can usually be found at the different parties held at the apartment complexes. While underclassmen spend their time at off-campus parties, upperclassmen tend to enjoy their time downtown where the bars and clubs are. Those not interested in spending their weekends inebriated head off into the nearby Appalachian mountains, where they go hiking and camping and enjoy the beautiful scenery.

Passing the Time in Blacksburg

In Blacksburg, Va., people's minds are on one thing only during the fall: college football. With a perennially top-ranked team, a large amount of school pride is invested in Virginia Tech athletics. A student remarked, "Everyone, on their AIM profiles, has stuff from football and fight songs, too." Football is the most notable team on campus, with players who are frequently in the media and have hopes of following in the paths of many all-star alumni. Many games are broadcast nationally and are always packed, giving Virginia Tech a reputation for being one of the toughest places to play. Fans congregate around campus, and all that can be seen around Blacksburg is Virginia Tech paraphernalia. Tailgating is big, and all the alumni come down to party and barbecue.

The varsity athletes live in separate dorms and have their own gym. However, students say that the athletes "basically have their own fraternities and get in a lot of fights." For those not involved in intercollegiate athletics, there are also other venues to get out the competitive urges. The club lacrosse team is highly competitive because there is no varsity team. In addition, intramural sports are very competitive, and the frats and sororities get involved. There are different sports to participate in such as flag football, basketball, dodgeball, and inner-tube water polo. There are also many student gyms, some of which are located in dorms such as Pritchard. The main gyms for students feature basketball courts, lifting machines, and swimming pools.

While athletics can take up a significant amount of time, other clubs are also prominent on campus. The business clubs are very popular, and the Student-managed Endowment for Educational Development (SEED) group is notoriously difficult to get into. SEED manages over a million dollars from a portion of the Virginia Tech Foundation's endowment and uses it to invest in stocks, and usually, the group is able to turn a profit. Around 40 to 100 students apply for membership, but only 10 to 20 are accepted after an application and interview process. There are also many societies for each major that provide forums for the students of that major to meet their classmates and get to know each other better. Because the students in each major have similar interests, the societies help to form close friendships. In addition, social events are planned to help take students' minds off of academics. Plus, advisers help them with getting job offers, and events are planned to help students get to know the major better. One engineering major said, "I got to know many of my friends through engineering classes." A large percentage of the students are also involved with ROTC and Virginia Tech's Corps of Cadets program, which offers a structured military lifestyle for those looking for leadership development.

When a mass shooting on campus in April 2007 put the campus under an intense media spotlight, the educational community and many others around the world joined with Hokies in solidarity. Following the attacks, the school established the Hokie Spirit Memorial Fund in honor of the victims. While classes were canceled for the week and students were given the option of taking off the rest of the semester, Virginia Tech makes a continued effort remember the victims while putting the tragedy behind it and is well on its way to normalcy.

Red-blooded Hokies?

The students at Virginia Tech are typified as "hard-core football fans and very conservative." While the majority of students are from Virginia, there is a good blend of students from North and South. One student said of Virginia Tech's diversity: "It's mostly white, but there are many people from different countries and backgrounds. I see a lot of different people every day." Students find it easy to relate to their easygoing classmates and are able to meet new people often. Forums such as frats, societies, and clubs help to further cement the friendships between all sorts of people. Because Virginia Tech draws its students mostly from neighboring states, some students know each other from home and therefore are able to network through friends' friends. Though the campus is big, the students all share the same interests and draw from each other's energy to create a friendly and homelike atmosphere for each other.—*Thomas Hsieh*

FYI

If you come to VT, you'd better bring "a map, because it is very big and you can easily get lost, and also to explore the beautiful mountains around the city."

What is the typical weekend schedule? "Typically stay out late Friday; sleep in Saturday, do some fun stuff during the afternoon, party at night; sleep in Sunday and do homework the rest of the day."

If I could change one thing about VT, I'd "change the dorm situation because Pritchard is an all-male dorm and is pretty bad."

Three things every student at VT should do before graduating are "go to a football game, go hiking and fishing in the Appalachian Mountains, and travel around Virginia because there are a lot of different schools nearby."

Washington & Lee University

Address: 204 West Washington Street Lexington, VA 24450-2116
Phone: 540-458-8710
E-mail address: admissions@wlu.edu
Web site URL: www.wlu.edu
Year Founded: 1749
Private or Public: Private
Religious Affiliation: None
Location: Rural
Number of Applicants: 6,388
Percent Accepted: 27%
Percent Accepted who enroll: 42%
Number Entering: 456
Number of Transfers Accepted each Year: 17
Middle 50% SAT range: M: 650–730, CR 650–740, Wr: Unreported
Middle 50% ACT range: 28–32
Early admission program EA/ED/None: ED

Percentage accepted through EA or ED: 38%
EA and ED deadline: 15-Nov
Regular Deadline: 15-Jan
Application Fee: $50
Full time Undergraduate enrollment: 1,752
Total enrollment: 2,155
Percent Male: 50%
Percent Female: 50%
Total Percent Minority or Unreported: 10%
Percent African-American: 3%
Percent Asian/Pacific Islander: 4%
Percent Hispanic: 2%
Percent Native-American: 1%
Percent International: Unreported
Percent in-state/out of state: 15%/85%
Percent from Public HS: 94%
Retention Rate: 94%
Graduation Rate 4-year: Unreported

Graduation Rate 6-year: Unreported
Percent Undergraduates in On-campus housing: 61%
Number of official organized extracurricular organizations: Unreported
3 Most popular majors: Social Science, Art, History
Student/Faculty ratio: Unreported
Average Class Size: Unreported
Percent of students going to grad school: Unreported
Tuition and Fees: $37,412
In State Tuition and Fees if different: No difference
Cost for Room and Board: $9,400
Percent receiving financial aid out of those who apply, first year: 73%
Percent receiving financial aid among all students: 35%

Just by knowing the name of Washington and Lee University, located in Lexington, Virginia, you already know a great deal about the school. Named for the two famous American generals—George Washington and Robert E. Lee—the University boasts a rich historical tradition, an emphasis on honor and traditional American values, and a predominantly southern outlook. At Washington and Lee, you will find an extremely happy, though not particularly diverse, group of southern ladies and gentlemen.

A Liberal Arts Education That Covers All Bases

At Washington and Lee, a strong academic background is a main focus, and there is a large set of General Education Requirements to ensure that students receive the full benefits of attending a liberal arts institution. In addition to required classes in areas as widely varied as mathematics, social sciences, and foreign language, Washington and Lee students must fulfill a Physical Education requirement, though students praise the "really interesting" classes that fulfill this requirement. One student commented, "I took figure skating, skiing, and fitness—which pretty much just got me credit for going to the gym! They also have bowling, horseback riding, basketball, and many other [sports]." In general, the requirements are extensive, though they do have the benefit of allowing students to sample classes in several different fields as opposed to staying within their majors.

Popular majors at Washington and Lee include History, Business Administration, and Economics. English, Biology, and Neuroscience are generally considered to be harder majors, though all of the departments are considered comparable in terms of quality. Washington and Lee also houses the Williams School of Commerce (also known as C-School), one of the few fully accredited undergraduate business schools in the nation.

Washington and Lee is a relatively small school, and as a result classes are usually not very big, thus fostering much closer professor-student relations. According to one male sophomore, "the student-faculty relations are generally very good. We have a speaking tradition that helps foster this. You can walk into a professor's office at any time for help or just to talk." Another student described the benefits of the small class size, saying, "The student-faculty ratio is very low due to the extremely small size of the school. Also, the small classes mean that the professors really know who you are, and they take attendance in almost every class. Lexington is a very small town, and most of the professors live here. I had two that hosted cocktail parties for their classes at their homes." Despite the accessibility of the professors, grading is generally considered difficult, though fair. According to one student, "the workload is always doable." However, another commented that "grading is hard. It is a very competitive school and they let you know first trimester freshman year that your GPA will go down."

In terms of schedule, Washington and Lee is divided into a trimester system, with a third "spring term" that lasts six weeks and during which students are required to take only two classes. Students enjoy this last term; one girl noted that "although you finish later in the year, during the last trimester you only take two classes, so it's kind of a nice break from the rigorous five you take at most schools."

On My Honor
Another unique characteristic of Washington and Lee is its honor system, described by one male student as a "student-governed, zero-tolerance system." The honor code is an extremely strict code that prohibits students primarily from three actions: lying, cheating, and stealing. The code is taken extremely seriously, and a code violation can result in expulsion from the university.

> "Because of how seriously students take the honor code, professors are never present for tests and exams."

Many students appreciate the increased level of trust they receive from professors as a result of the code; one student described the test-taking situation at Washington and Lee, saying, "because of how seriously students take the honor code, professors are never present for tests and exams. Many tests are self-administered anywhere (library, dorms, outside), and professors trust that the students will bring the exams back at the proper time. During exam weeks students may choose when and where to take their finals. Professors only write one copy of the exam, as they know students will not discuss the test." Another student described the seriousness of the honor code: "Every time you take a test or hand in a paper you have to sign it with the honor code. If you get caught cheating or plagiarizing, you're kicked out of the university, no questions asked." However, for most students, the benefits outweigh the risks, as the honor code allows them a far greater degree of freedom than most of their peers at other universities.

An American Tradition of Beauty
The option of taking tests anywhere on campus is especially nice because Washington and Lee is widely known for its beautiful grounds. According to one current student, "the architecture of the campus is beautiful. The Colonnade is a National Historic Landmark." Washington and Lee's Web site confirms this statement: "Constructed between 1820 and 1842, Washington and Lee's Colonnade is a National Historic Landmark district and has been described by the National Park Service as forming 'one of the most dignified college campuses in the nation.' It is

not only the heart of campus but also a symbol of Washington and Lee."

The school's historical traditions are described as "too many to name," though one sophomore explained, "many buildings are thought to be haunted due to the age of the school."

Due to the beauty of the campus, freshmen enjoy their required first year on campus. Many juniors and seniors elect to move off campus, as the surrounding areas are just as beautiful as the campus itself. One student commented, "Most juniors and seniors live off campus in apartments in town or houses out in the beautiful countryside." The town, Lexington, is "so small that on- and off-campus living are not that different."

This beautiful campus is rich in history, and prides itself on reflecting the American tradition of higher learning. However, one potential disadvantage to the campus environment, students claim, is the student body's lack of diversity. One sophomore described the student body as relatively homogeneous, saying that "it would be characterized as conservative and upper middle class. Most students come from the south." Another student went further into the problems of diversity when describing her freshman year experience: "[There is] almost none. Confederate flags are printed on some of the school shirts at the bookstore, and students hang the flags in their dorm rooms. It is very hard for some people to understand and accept diversity. My freshman suitemate was from Africa, and her direct roommate was from Virginia and had a hard time adjusting to sharing a room with someone of a different race."

Go Greek or Bust

At Washington and Lee, social life is almost exclusively focused on fraternities and sororities; one student conjectured that "almost 80 percent of kids are involved in Greek life" (the actual number is close, at 75 percent). Greek life is the focus of most students to the exclusion of most else, as athletics are not all that popular, though lacrosse and soccer garner the most atten-

tion. Greek life starts from the moment students set foot on campus, which fosters not only an almost immediate sense of community, but also an opportunity to become friends with upperclassmen that is unique to Washington and Lee. One student said, "Since freshmen are rushed the moment they step on campus, upperclassmen and underclassmen are mixed very well. Age and year doesn't really play a role in who your friends are." An upperclassman echoed this sentiment: "You will pretty much have the same social life from freshman to senior year because you will be in the same sorority or fraternity."

Social life is Greek or very little else; one student explained that "I never go to a bar. I always go to a fraternity house or an off-campus frat house." However, just because the social life is Greek-dominated doesn't mean there isn't always something to do. According to one proud student, "Washington and Lee is the second biggest party school in the country. There is somewhere to go almost every night." A sophomore noted that "the big nights are Wednesday, Friday and Saturday." Students generally attend either fraternity parties, which often feature bands, or house parties located out in the countryside. Drugs and alcohol are often fixtures of these parties. Students describe drug and alcohol use as relatively common, though there is little use within the dorms themselves. More special parties include cocktail parties, semi-formals, and "fancy dress balls, due to the Greek social scene and southern values of the school."

Washington and Lee is the perfect place for future sorority girls and fraternity boys who want to immerse themselves in an environment rich in history and tradition, while at the same time enjoying the benefits of a school that offers both an extensive education and seven-day-a-week parties. One student summed it up perfectly: "I expected a southern and conservative school, and that's what I got. If I had to choose again, I would absolutely pick Washington and Lee over anywhere else!"—*Michelle Katz*

FYI

If you come to Washington and Lee, you'd better bring "a collared shirt."

What is the typical weekend schedule? "Get out of class and start hanging out and go out to the country that night. Sleep in Saturday and watch college football and go out again Saturday night. Most students start their work Sunday evening."

If I could change one thing about Washington and Lee, I'd "make the administration realize that diversity isn't necessarily based on color."

Three things every student at Washington and Lee should do before graduating are "go tubing in the river, go for a drive out to Goshen, and sneak around the school's underground tunnels without getting caught!"

Washington

The Evergreen State College

Address: 2700 Evergreen Parkway NW, Olympia, WA 98505

Phone: 360-867-6170

E-mail address: admissions@evergreen.edu

Web site URL: www.evergreen.edu

Year Founded: 1967

Private or Public: Public

Religious Affiliation: None

Location: Urban

Number of Applicants: 1,989

Percent Accepted: 94%

Percent Accepted who enroll: 35%

Number Entering: 659

Number of Transfers Accepted each Year: 1,318

Middle 50% SAT range: M: 470–600, CR: 530–660, Wr: Unreported

Middle 50% ACT range: Unreported

Early admission program EA/ED/None: None

Percentage accepted through EA or ED: NA

EA and ED deadline: NA

Regular Deadline: 1-Mar

Application Fee: $50

Full time Undergraduate enrollment: 4,364

Total enrollment: 4,696

Percent Male: 54%

Percent Female: 46%

Total Percent Minority or Unreported: 32%

Percent African-American: 4%

Percent Asian/Pacific Islander: 5%

Percent Hispanic: 5%

Percent Native-American: 3%

Percent International: 1%

Percent in-state/out of state: 72%/28%

Percent from Public HS: Unreported

Retention Rate: 70%

Graduation Rate 4-year: 51%

Graduation Rate 6-year: 57%

Percent Undergraduates in On-campus housing: 22%

Number of official organized extracurricular organizations: 61

3 Most popular majors: Social Sciences, Humanities, Visual Performing Arts

Student/Faculty ratio: 22:1

Average Class Size: 20 to 29

Percent of students going to grad school: 21%

Tuition and Fees: $16,189

In State Tuition and Fees if different: $5,329

Cost for Room and Board: $8,052

Percent receiving financial aid out of those who apply, first year: 67%

Percent receiving financial aid among all students: 54%

A state school with a lush, thousand-acre campus just outside Olympia, Washington, Evergreen was founded in the 1960s and has been popularly known ever since as "that hippie school up north." As one student put it, "the stereotype is built up that there are a lot of hippies and we all eat granola and live in the woods." However, students insist that this is nothing more than a myth and that Greeners, as they are called, are much more than granola-eaters. One junior said, "[The stereotype is] that people here just smoke pot and talk about Buddhism, but I'm pretty positive I haven't had one conversation about Buddhism." While there is indeed a "liberal undertone" at the school, students emphasize that one can still find a rich diversity of ideas in the classroom. As one sophomore recounted, "In my seminar, I'm reading George W. Bush's favorite book (next to the Bible), and half of the class agrees with it and half of the class disagrees. You don't just have a bunch of liberal kids patting each other on the back." One senior added, "One thing we do have in common is that we're all pretty open-minded on campus. A lot of people recycle, and you could say, 'Oh, you're a hippie,' but we're just normal people."

Although students maintain that Evergreen's population is as diverse as any other school's, Evergreen State College has not completely abandoned the liberal ideas (or types of people) from the era in which it was founded. In fact, one could say that Evergreen State continues to thrive on vestiges of the 1960s, giving it a unique educational style that grants students a sense of independence and interdisciplinary integration rarely found in the modern college.

Academic Liberation

Students at the Evergreen State College eagerly talk about the remarkable degree of freedom that their school allows them in their academic pursuits. "[The freedom] can be a beautiful thing for certain people," praised one student. "For students who have a drive to learn, and who don't need someone to be constantly on their back [about] turning something in, I really think Evergreen is a great place."

> "[The stereotype is] that people here just smoke pot and talk about Buddhism, but I'm pretty positive I haven't had one conversation about Buddhism."

Evergreen State's academic repertoire encourages students to be masters of their own scholastic destiny through four special features: academic programs, independent study contracts, internships, and study abroad. The bulk of Evergreen State's curriculum is in the form of academic programs, in which students register for a coordinated three-quarter set of classes centered on a unifying theme rather than signing up for several classes individually that, in all likelihood, would not be as integrated. One student focusing (Evergreen has no majors—only foci) on environmental studies noted that the program Ocean Life and Environmental Policy, which he pursued in his first year at Evergreen State, has been his main academic inspiration. "That class was basically an introduction to marine biology and ecology, but we also did environmental policy and linked it to ocean life." In order to accommodate such cross-disciplinary studies as well as to satisfy the 25:1 student-faculty ratio that every class must uphold, programs are taught by more than one professor, with each professor specializing in the respective academic areas covered by the course.

This connection across the disciplines—such as biology, ecology, and politics—is the distinguishing feature of Evergreen State's academic programs. Such integration allows Evergreen State to be lax when it comes to formal distribution requirements, without sacrificing an emphasis on basic skills. One student commented, "Whenever you put together a program at Evergreen, you're going to get the writing skills, the math skills, and you would have to search really hard *not* to get those things."

Evergreen State students also can choose contracts, in which select students can set up independent study programs in cooperation with a faculty member. "You specify the books you're going to read, where you're going to be, and how often you're going to contact your faculty member," one student said. "You could say, 'Hey, I want to do a contract about rainforest ecology.'" Students maintain that contracts are not an opportunity to avoid class, but instead, as the name suggests, they require a substantial amount of commitment of which not all students are deemed capable. "To get a contract they choose you. [Faculty] will talk to your old professors and ask, 'How good would they be?'"

Similarly, select students are allowed to take leave from Evergreen and study abroad or do internships for credit. "You'll say what you're going to do and what you're going to be learning, and the faculty will make sure that you're doing work and not just sweeping floors," one senior said. Such internships can lead to even bigger opportunities. "My friend worked on the movie *S.W.A.T.* and was offered a job," the senior said.

"No Grading," Not "No Work"

Perhaps the most striking feature of the Evergreen State education is the lack of numerical grading. Instead, at the end of each quarter professors write what is known as a narrative evaluation, which is essentially like the recommendation letters given to students at other colleges, but with painstaking detail of a student's improvement over the course of a quarter. Students value the flexibility that the narrative evaluation system offers as opposed to numerical grading. "Everything that you do extra in class reflects [in your evaluations] because your teacher can write about it, so you're not limited to an A." Another student praised the amount of detail that can go into an evaluation; he said that with Evergreen State evaluations, employers were probably more likely to get a "better impression of me and my work ethic and to judge me as a student better as opposed to with an A, B, or a C."

Yet with such a novel approach to academics, one might wonder whether there's the temptation just to slack off at Evergreen, or a necessity to be self-motivated and driven to take charge of one's own work. Evergreen students insist that the case is mostly the latter. "I would say that people are very hardworking and [Evergreen's academic programs] force you to be very self-motivated," said one sophomore. Another student added, "There are not many students who just go to school. There's not really anyone who doesn't go to class. Everyone who is here wants to be here, and everyone who is here wants to learn. And if they don't, they leave."

In fact, one senior noted that Evergreen State is far from a slacker's dream. "I spent 40 to 50 hours a week doing homework my first year. It's pretty common, and my friends don't look at me funny when I say, 'I have to go do work now,' because they have to, too. I wouldn't say there's too much work, but there is a lot of work." Another student added: "School is hard here! But it's the attitudes of the people around you that help you relax and not feel overwhelmed." Students concurred that the work is manageable, especially because the academic program system allows professors to "coordinate so that they can assign a steady amount of homework." A senior noted that at one point during a program, "[Everyone] handed in their homework late, and the professors apologized and said that they had assigned too much work." The student concluded that this cooperation between the students and professors does help. "You can really get in the groove of a schedule that works for you," he said.

The Green and the Concrete
Evergreen State has a wide selection of rooming options. One student cited two examples, "They've got apartment-style living with four to six bedrooms with a furnished living area; they also have modular housing which is further down with their own parking lots. It's more secluded." Evergreen State offers several specialized dorms, such as "A" Dorm, a freshmen-only building, and according to one sophomore, a sustainable living housing option is in the works, in which environment-conscious students can live according to the "concept of living without depleting your resources." Added another student, "Sustainable living rocks!"

Yet perhaps an inevitable consequence of having so many different housing options is wide variation in housing quality. While one student said, "The dorms are so much bigger than anyone else's dorms I've ever seen," another said, "I lived in housing my first year and I hated it. It's cramped and pretty rowdy."

Moreover, despite the multiplicity of housing options, students living on campus are in the minority. "I wish that there were more students living on campus," complained one sophomore. "There's 4,300 students, and only 1,000 kids live on campus. Some of them commute from their hometowns [in Washington]. A lot of people live in houses or apartments off campus." She conceded, however, "It doesn't affect student life that much, but in terms of walking over to your friends' dorms to say hi, you can't really do that." In spite of this difficulty, however, the majority of the party scene takes place in the dorms. According to one freshman, "Awesome dorm parties are easy to have. You can register your parties and the cops won't come and bust it, unless it's really late and really loud."

Students generally agree that the dining hall food has improved by leaps and bounds in recent years. Once catered by the Marriott hotel chain, Evergreen State now offers a dining option prepared by Aramark. "They make crêpes right in front of you," one senior raved. Evergreen State also prides itself on its organic farm, much of whose produce goes to the dining halls. "Seventy percent of the food is organic, and they're working their way up to making it 100 percent," one sophomore said. Evergreen State also offers a convenience store called The Corner, which is conveniently located near the dorms of Lower Campus and offers "fruits and breads, vegetables, juice, and the basic necessities—chips and candy."

Evergreen State also offers a good range of extracurriculars, including six intercollegiate sports and many clubs. Students explained that there are "lots and lots of student clubs, so many that you don't have time for them all!" One senior spoke of his involvement with the Student CD Project, which puts out a yearly collection of songs from Evergreen student bands. Students also have good things to say about Olympia and its vibrant nightlife and rich music scene, concentrated along streets such as the famous 4th Avenue Strip. Many people enjoy a one-day festival known as Super Saturday as well as events such as a Punk Rock Prom, sponsored by an animal-rights organization.

Greeners do admit that Evergreen State does not fit the mold of other colleges, yet they insist that that isn't a bad thing. As one senior said, "It's a shame that some students may be scared off by the hippie stereotypes that abound about Evergreen State." He concluded, "I really feel sorry for people who don't know how great Evergreen State is and who would do really well here."—*Christopher Lapinig*

FYI

If you come to The Evergreen State College, you'd better bring "an umbrella. It's basically temperate rainforest and it rains half of the year."

What is the typical weekend schedule? "Do work, go to the gym with my friends, go to basketball or soccer or volleyball games depending on what season it is, go up to Seattle or Olympia for concerts, eat out a lot, and do homework, of course."

If I could change one thing about The Evergreen State College, I'd "ask for more jobs off campus. It's really hard to find a job in Olympia, and I think most people at Evergreen work, but it's much easier to work off campus."

Three things that every student at The Evergreen State College should do before graduating are "go to the organic farm, rappel from the Clocktower, and go for a swim in the Sound on campus."

University of Puget Sound

Address: 1500 North Warner Street, Tacoma, WA 98416-1062
Phone: 800-396-7191
E-mail address: admission@ups.edu
Web site URL: www.ups.edu
Year Founded: 1888
Private or Public: Private
Religious Affiliation: None
Location: Suburban
Number of Applicants: 5,580
Percent Accepted: 65%
Percent Accepted who enroll: 19%
Number Entering: 748
Number of Transfers Accepted each Year: 173
Middle 50% SAT range: M: 570–670, CR: 570–680, Wr: 560–660
Middle 50% ACT range: 25–29
Early admission program EA/ED/None: ED

Percentage accepted through EA or ED: Unreported
EA and ED deadline: 15-Nov, 2-Jan
Regular Deadline: 15-Jan
Application Fee: $50
Full time Undergraduate enrollment: 2,536
Total enrollment: 2,858
Percent Male: 42%
Percent Female: 58%
Total Percent Minority or Unreported: 17%
Percent African-American: 3%
Percent Asian/Pacific Islander: 9%
Percent Hispanic: 4%
Percent Native-American: 1%
Percent International: Unreported
Percent in-state/out of state: 30%/70%
Percent from Public HS: 75%
Retention Rate: 85%

Graduation Rate 4-year: 70%
Graduation Rate 6-year: 76%
Percent Undergraduates in On-campus housing: 59%
Number of official organized extracurricular organizations: Unreported
3 Most popular majors: Business, Psychology, English/International Political Economy
Student/Faculty ratio: 11:1
Average Class Size: 18.3
Percent of students going to grad school: 55%
Tuition and Fees: $33,975
In State Tuition and Fees if different: No difference
Cost for Room and Board: $8,760
Percent receiving financial aid out of those who apply, first year: 83%
Percent receiving financial aid among all students: 60%

Located near the cities of Tacoma and Seattle and the natural landmarks of Mount Rainier and the Puget Sound, University of Puget Sound gives its students a unique experience that is both urban and rural. With a variety of social and academic areas to explore, Puget Sound offers all the opportunities of a larger university while structuring its academics and extracurriculars around what is most important: a personal experience for each and every student.

A Unique Introduction

Students' holistic experiences at University of Puget Sound begin as soon as they step foot on campus. Puget Sound's unique three-part orientation is called Prelude, Passages and Perspectives. It introduces students to the environmental, academic, and community-oriented aspects of the university. Students are first given a taste, or "Prelude," of Puget Sound academics with a sample of a typical day of classes. Then, during Passages, students are sent on a camping trip in Hood

Canal, three hours away from campus. Through three days of hiking through the wilderness, watching the sunrise from the top of a mountain, and gathering around huge bonfires, students learn to appreciate the natural beauty surrounding Puget Sound and develop bonds with their fellow students. One student recounted, "There is a special kind of bonding that takes place when you spend three days backpacking in the wilderness without a shower." The third segment, Perspectives: Urban Plunge, demonstrates Puget Sound's involvement with the Tacoma community. In Perspectives, students engage in service projects ranging from cleaning the Puget Sound to working with mentally disabled people. These three components let students experience three important parts of a Puget Sound education: environment, academics and community.

Small College Treatment, Large College Selection

As a liberal arts college, University of Puget Sound encourages its students to explore numerous academic fields outside of their own majors. In order to fulfill the core requirements, which consist of eight different courses in different academic areas, students must take at least one core course every semester over their four years at Puget Sound. However, the university's unique core class system makes it simple to find classes that fulfill the core requirements and that interest students from every major by offering these classes in almost every department. For instance, one potential English major student claimed, "I can fulfill my math core requirement with a class in the philosophy department."

Although the ways through which students can fulfill their core requirements are numerous, some students may find it difficult to get the exact classes that they want. Course scheduling for freshmen is a laborious process because some popular classes fill up quickly or are offered in only a couple of time slots. As a result, some students may find it difficult to "take the classes [they] need to take while fitting them into a feasible schedule."

Once students get into their desired classes, however, they are likely to find a unique and personal experience. The majority of courses at Puget Sound consist of classes with fewer than 25 students, and each student should expect to pay attention in every class. Because of the small class sizes, one student noted, "people attend class and pay attention to the discussion because,

when there is no back row, sleeping is not an option." Similarly, students expect to receive personal attention from their professors. As one student reported, when she began to pay less attention in class, her professor e-mailed her, writing, "I noticed that your in-class participation has dropped off a little, and I wanted to say that I value your opinion very much and encourage you to talk." Eager to ensure that each of their students performs well, professors are available for assistance outside of class, by office hours, or by e-mail appointments. In addition, professors encourage students to meet with them on other subjects. For example, one student said, "I spent one afternoon going over a German test and the meeting ended talking about places in Washington to go spelunking."

Although teachers want their students to do well, good grades are by no means easily achieved at Puget Sound. One student says, "In one of my classes the professor told us that A's were reserved for perfect work only." However, getting good grades is not impossible. Students agree that professors grade fairly. One student said, "I have never felt cheated out of the grade I deserved, nor have I felt I've gotten good grades when I least deserved them."

Daring You to Try Something New

Extracurriculars at Puget Sound are numerous and diverse, from political clubs such as Young Democrats and Young Republicans to entertainment groups such as the Circus Club. Puget Sound is not a sports school—in the words of one student, "You won't find 10,000 students at the football games"—but on the whole its athletic teams are competitive. Among the most competitive of the Division III teams are the swim team–the women's team is ranked number one in the region–the women's soccer team, and the crew team. For those who would rather participate than observe, Puget Sound intramurals are extensive and popular as well.

The variety in Puget Sound's extracurriculars dares the University's students to try something new. One of the most popular extracurricular groups at Puget Sound is the Repertory Dance Group (RDG). A no-cut campus dance troupe that performs one show every semester, RDG is composed of expert and novice dancers and choreographers of every style. The most unique extracurricular activities at Puget Sound, however, take advantage of its proximity to natural reserves. One of the most popular activities is Puget

Sound Outdoors, which organizes "reasonably priced outdoors trips like weekend backpacking trips, ski trips, rock climbing trips, etc." Puget Sound even has its own student-run equipment rental shop, the Expeditionary (affectionately called the Expy), which equips students for outdoor excursions from camping to cross-country skiing.

At Puget Sound, not only are students encouraged to try a variety of extracurriculars, but they are also given motivation to pursue them. The unique system of credits at Puget Sound awards 0.25 credits for certain co-curricular activities. For instance, students majoring in Communication Studies may earn activity credits for participating in competitive forensic programs like the National Parliamentary Debate Association (NPDA) debate.

Of Castles and Cafés

University of Puget Sound is located in a suburban neighborhood. Puget Sound has taken advantage of the University surroundings and purchased houses surrounding the campus for student living. Consequently, many juniors and seniors live in these on-campus houses instead of dorms. However, off-campus housing in the neighborhood surrounding Puget Sound is also abundant.

On-campus housing is available in the form of themed houses and residence dorms, many of which have distinct personalities. For instance, Todd/Phibs is the unofficial "party dorm." Puget Sound's official themed dorms are not, as one student described it, the "look, all the potheads live together" unofficial kind. For example, Harrington features the official Healthy Options floor, and Schiff Hall houses the Outdoors dorm. Themed on-campus houses like the Comic House and House of Ramen line the famous "Theme Row."

Campus food at Puget Sound, like typical cafeteria food, can get tiring. However, students consistently boast of its variety. With sandwich lines and theme nights, there is usually something worth trying. Other on-campus restaurants, such as the Oppenheimer Café ("the OC"), Diversions Café, and the Cellar, which serves late-night pizza and ice cream, give students several dining and snacking options no matter what time of day or night they want to eat. Puget Sound also has one of the most vegetarian-friendly dining systems in the country and has been rated by PETA as one of the top 10 universities for most vegetarian options. For those who still want to dine off campus, there are numerous choices. Silk Thai offers delicious Thai cuisine. Farelli's and Garlic Jim's pizza are popular, and cafés like the Mandolin and Rosewood Cafés serve delicious sandwiches and other simple fare. Puget Sound's proximity to Tacoma gives students ample opportunity to explore the city's best restaurants.

> "I spent one afternoon going over a German test and the meeting ended with us talking about places in Washington to go spelunking."

Student opinion on campus security varies depending on who is asked. While some contend that they have "never felt unsafe on campus" and emphasize that there have been "no crimes and no thefts," others say that they feel uncomfortable walking alone at night, as they would in any other area. However, students consistently report that Puget Sound has drilled into them that security is always available to escort students both on and off campus.

Puget Sound 101: How to Change the World

Appropriate to its proximity to nature and its devotion to the outdoors, Puget Sound is a university that makes sustainability one of its priorities. For example, the university participates in numerous sustainable programs around campus, such as the vermicomposting program, which is run by Students for a Sustainable Campus in conjunction with Dining Services and turns the University's food waste into fertile soil by using red worms. Puget Sound's eco-friendly beliefs also manifest in its mascot. While the Puget Sound athletic teams are called the "Loggers," the university's official mascot has changed from a logger to a grizzly bear, "Grizz." As one student reports, "Grizz is our mascot, because at such an eco-friendly school, we felt a logger was too unsustainable . . . we take our sustainability very seriously." In addition to sustainability, Puget Sound students have been passionate about many other domestic and international issues, such as the 2008 presidential election and the genocide in Darfur. As part of the "number one liberal college feeder into the Peace Corps," Puget Sound students are, as one student describes, "the ones who will change the world."

For the student who is passionate about resolving current issues, University of Puget Sound offers a personalized education and numerous opportunities to explore in academics, extracurriculars and life experience. As one student put it, Puget Sound is "for dedicated, intelligent, outdoorsy, active, passionate, open-minded people. [It] will give you a unique education [and] teach you to think in a forward, global way."—*Chaoran Chen*

FYI

If you come to UPS, you'd better bring "your hiking boots and rain slicker."
What's the typical weekend schedule? "Friday night, prepare for a hiking trip or find a party;
  Saturday night, watch a movie or hang out with friends; Sunday, wake up late and do homework."
If I could change one thing about UPS, I'd "find a way to encourage ethnic diversity on campus."
Three things every student at UPS should do before graduating are "spend a weekend in the
  mountains, devise a plan to steal the Hatchet, and participate in the Repertory Dance Group."

University of Washington

Address: Box 355852
  Seattle, WA 98195
Phone: 206-543-2100
E-mail address: NA
Web site URL:
  www.washington.edu
Year Founded: 1861
Private or Public: Public
Religious Affiliation: None
Location: Suburban
Number of Applicants:
  17,777
Percent Accepted: 65%
**Percent Accepted who
  enroll:** 46%
Number Entering: 5,278
**Number of Transfers
  Accepted each Year:** 1,807
Middle 50% SAT range:
  M: 570–680, CR: 530–650,
  Wr: 530–640
Middle 50% ACT range:
  23–29
**Early admission program
  EA/ED/None:** None

**Percentage accepted
  through EA or ED:** NA
EA and ED deadline: NA
Regular Deadline: 15-Jan
Application Fee: $50
**Full time Undergraduate
  enrollment:** 28,570
Total enrollment: 38,415
Percent Male: 46%
Percent Female: 56%
**Total Percent Minority or
  Unreported:** 3%
Percent African-American:
  3%
**Percent Asian/Pacific
  Islander:** 31%
Percent Hispanic: 6%
Percent Native-American:
  1%
Percent International: 3%
**Percent in-state/out of
  state:** 84%/16%
Percent from Public HS:
  Unreported
Retention Rate: 92%

Graduation Rate 4-year: 48%
Graduation Rate 6-year: 74%
**Percent Undergraduates in
  On-campus housing:** 20%
**Number of official organized
  extracurricular
  organizations:** 550
3 Most popular majors:
  Social Sciences, Biology,
  Business/Marketing
Student/Faculty ratio: 12:1
Average Class Size: 20 to 29
**Percent of students going to
  grad school:** Unreported
Tuition and Fees: $23,219
**In State Tuition and Fees if
  different:** $6,802
Cost for Room and Board:
  $8,640
**Percent receiving financial
  aid out of those who apply,
  first year:** Unreported
**Percent receiving financial
  aid among all students:**
  Unreported

N estled in the shadows of the Cascade and Olympic Mountain Ranges, the University of Washington embraces its Seattle location by combining the distinction of a prominent research institution with a "relaxed, west-coast atmosphere."

Living in Husky Territory

Despite the rumors, Seattle is far from being the rain capital of the nation. In fact, Seattle's annual precipitation is actually less than that of Miami, Boston, New York, Philadelphia, and Washington D.C! That being said, the city's rainy reputation stems from the dreary winter months, when for several weeks the region is enveloped in cloudy skies and light drizzle.

UW is a large university, enrolling more than 40,000 undergraduate and graduate students on three campuses. The main location is in Seattle, Washington, with smaller campuses in Bothell and Tacoma. All three facilities serve an incredibly diverse student body, offering combinations of day and evening classes for either full-time or part-time students. Raved one junior, "The [Seattle] campus is absolutely gorgeous. We have over 700 acres of trees, grass, and amazing Gothic architecture. The people are amazing and it honestly doesn't rain that much!"

"UW is a very self-directed university," another student noted. "You need to know what you want in order to get it. Because it's so big, no one does it for you." With over 25,000 undergraduates on the Seattle campus alone, many incoming freshmen worry that they will become a nameless face in the crowd. However, current students repeatedly declared that friends are easy to find, and with "over 500 student groups, there's always something going on!"

> "The campus is absolutely gorgeous, the people are amazing, and it honestly doesn't rain that much!

Most students begin to associate with a certain social circle early in their college experience. Social life at the UW, despite its diversity, is described as fairly segregated between the Greeks, the dorm kids, and the commuters. While the Greeks are sometimes described as "the rich white kids who wear Uggs and North Face jackets," the dominant campus fashion is decidedly practical: "fleeces, jeans, comfy stuff to stay dry and warm." One student cited the social groups as the main difference between underclassmen and upperclassmen; the older students tend to already have their social circles established, while the incoming freshman are much more open to hanging out with whomever.

Dorm Life and Coffee Breaks
Most UW students live on campus for their freshman year. Hansee (all singles) and McCarty halls are the two most popular. There are also theme dorms based on a student's interests, each occupying one or two floors inside the larger buildings. "I lived in the Honors House for two years, which was all the honors students. There's also a substance-free dorm and an outdoor focus dorm," one student said. Even though the dorms are always full, UW is also "a huge commuter school."

When it comes to dining, Huskies claim that "we have the best campus food service in the country!" The meal plan is fairly simple, as students place a certain amount of money in their dining accounts to spend like cash. Even though there are dining halls all over campus, Huskies may also choose to take advantage of the "cheap, amazing ethnic food places" in the U-District. As is to be expected in the birthplace of Starbucks, "The coffee shops are

good, and there are tons of cute little secret ones all over, so go search for them!"

Upperclassmen often move off-campus into the surrounding neighborhoods. The Greek system occupies the north neighborhood, with 29 frats and 16 sororities owning off-campus houses. The area ten or so blocks north, Ravenna, is "nice, a little quieter." Despite the slightly higher rent, the U-District is a vibrant, diverse neighborhood, filled with cheap eateries, popular hangouts, and cool stores.

With over 85 percent of the undergraduate student body hailing from Washington State, the campus can often feel empty on Saturdays when students go home for the weekends. Most do not have cars, as parking is expensive. The bus system is easy, efficient, and free for students because part of their tuition goes toward a bus pass that allows for free rides on all Seattle public transportation. With the Sea-Tac airport, the ferry docks, and the Amtrak train station only a bus ride away, most UW students find they can travel fairly conveniently.

Sleepless in Seattle
In keeping with the diverse student body, there are many options for nighttime activities, though students listed a few particularly notable events. The residence halls throw a weeklong extravaganza called "Winterfest," complete with casino nights, dances, and bonfires. The annual "Pow Wow" and "Spring Cruise," in addition to the Greeks' annual Homecoming and "Anchor Splash" parties, also received high praise. On normal weekends, upperclassmen party more at bars or houses, while freshmen tend to flock to the larger frat parties.

UW's student body incorporates the complete spectrum of attitudes toward student drinking: some students go out every night of the week, while other students never touch alcohol. Students claim that, depending on one's social circle, there is not a lot of pressure to drink. Because the residence halls actually have a pretty strict alcohol and drug policy—including probation and mandatory alcohol counseling following certain offenses—most of the drinking takes place off campus. These regulations, however, are met with mixed reviews. According to one student, "if you get caught smoking pot by the campus police, you get in less trouble than you do for jaywalking."

Husky Fitness and Pride
Since Seattle has been named "the fittest city in the U.S" (according to rankings released

by *Men's Fitness* in 2005), it comes as no surprise that the University of Washington is also recognized as one of the top athletic programs in the country. It is not unusual for the 10 men's and 11 women's varsity teams to earn national honors. If you are more inclined to cheer from the stands, Huskies hold the gold standard for the student cheering sections: "There is a lot of pride invested in being a Husky!" exclaimed a junior. All sports, except basketball and football, are free for students. During the fall, volleyball and football dominate the scene, as the "campus literally shuts down on football Saturday." During the annual Apple Cup, thousands of UW Huskies flock to the football stadium to cheer their school to victory over archrival Washington State. During the winter, die-hard basketball fans camp outside the gym for days before games even if they already have tickets—just to show their support! This student section is one of the best in the country; affectionately called the "Dawg Pack," this group of devoted fans even has its own locker in the men's locker room.

For the non-varsity athletes, there is a state-of-the-art gym called the "IMA." It has an elevated running track; a 5,000-square-foot weight room; over 300 machines; four basketball courts; racquetball, squash and tennis courts; a pool; saunas; and an indoor climbing wall. Free for all students, the gym also offers a diverse array of fitness classes, over 30 club sports, and the Dawg Bites Sports Café. Intramural sports are also a popular activity, ranging from very competitive to purely recreational: Examples include inner-tube basketball, ultimate frisbee, rowing, and bowling.

There are over 550 student clubs on campus, ranging from living groups to multicultural societies to political associations to "just plain weird" groups. Students listed a medley of different organizations, including the Filipino American Student Association, the Amateur Porn Club, the Peanut Butter and Jelly Club, and Habitat for Humanity. A sophomore claims that the "funniest group" is an organization of extreme liberals called the LaRouche, who aggressively hand out pamphlets as students walk to class. "Do not take this group seriously," the sophomore laughs. "Many people joke about them." Extremist or not, students dedicate a lot of time to their organizations, and social groups are often defined by extracurricular activities.

Many students also manage to balance their studies and a job—either on campus as RAs or tutors, or in the local "U-District"

neighborhood as waiters or store clerks. Since Huskies love their coffee, 22 espresso stands on campus supply students with part-time jobs, hang-out places, and delicious, cheap coffee.

In the Classroom

With over 1,800 undergraduate courses offered every quarter, incoming freshmen might feel slightly overwhelmed. Freshmen may choose to join the FIG (Freshman Interest Group) program, where small groups of freshmen with similar academic interests share the same courses during their first quarter. The Honors Program is highly regarded, though a junior stressed that the program's diverse and interesting classes can be hard to get into.

Don't be surprised if many classes your freshman year, are on the higher end of the student-to-faculty ratio. Said one sophomore, "My first quarter, all my classes had over 700 people in them, which was really daunting." Although the workload of a specific course almost directly corresponds with the difficulty of a class, a sophomore noted an important exception in the introductory classes. "The introductory grading can be very hard," she said, "as the main purpose of many of the intro classes is to 'weed out' those students who cannot handle the workload." However, once a student becomes more involved in a department, the focus is more on the material and the learning process. "I didn't expect the professors to be as open to students as they were," one student explained. "They really made an effort to get to know us, so it wasn't at all impersonal."

The academics at the UW are extremely varied, as the requirements for graduation differ from college to college. The most competitive programs include the business school, the architecture school, and the college of engineering. The science majors are also widely cited as being difficult, due to the UW's top-tier medical school and the large number of students who enroll for UW's stellar scientific research facilities. Many other majors do not have any prerequisites for admission or a competitive admissions process. Several students testified to the discrepancy between the science and the humanities programs: "I have friends who take communications and history classes and they can easily get 3.6's or 3.7," said a sophomore, "while science majors often have GPAs an entire point lower." Students recommended Comparative History of Ideas, International Studies, and Near Eastern Languages and Civilization as being unique and intriguing majors.

Among UW's 3,600-plus faculty are six Nobel Laureates, a National Book Award Winner, and 43 members of the National Academy of Sciences, not to mention many other widely renowned scholars and scientists. Freshman seminars offer incoming students the opportunity to establish a relationship with these faculty members while exploring their fields of study. But don't get too excited, a sophomore warns, as "in all honesty, the school is so big it is really hard to identify famous professors. There are celebrity profs, you just have to be part of the department to realize it." The competition for popular classes varies depending on the department, but as one student noted, "if you're a good enough student and stubborn enough, you can get into anything."

Even given the rare circumstance that a student does not find a niche on campus, Seattle and the surrounding area provide countless opportunities for adventure and entertainment. The school's proximity to both the Cascade Mountains and the Puget Sound leads to many diverting weekend trips. Seattle itself is a fascinating city, home to Starbucks, Microsoft, Amazon.com, REI, and Nintendo. Clearly, the University of Washington and the surrounding area can cater to the interests of all 40,000 undergraduate and graduate students, whether athletes, baristas, scholars, or ski bums. One student's comment in particular emphasized the enthusiasm characteristic of all Huskies: "I love the UW. It's a fantastic education, I get exposed to a huge amount of cutting-edge research, and there are so many opportunities I don't know where to start!"

FYI

If you come to UW, you'd better bring "a raincoat."

What's the typical weekend schedule? "Friday: hit up a party or lay low with friends; Saturday: shop, cheer on the Huskies at the football game, go out; Sunday: sleep till noon, get up and study, study, study!"

If I could change one thing about UW, I'd "make the registration process during freshman and sophomore year easier to get the classes you need."

Three things every student at UW should do before graduating are "jump off the bridge that goes to nowhere, eat at Burger Hut at 2 a.m., and take the bus to class even though it's only a 10-minute walk."

Washington State University

Address: Lighty 370, Pullman, WA 99164-1067
Phone: 888-468-6978
E-mail address: admiss2@wsu.edu
Web site URL: www.wsu.edu
Year Founded: 1890
Private or Public: Public
Religious Affiliation: None
Location: Rural
Number of Applicants: 9,314
Percent Accepted: 77%
Percent Accepted who enroll: 40%
Number Entering: 2,699
Number of Transfers Accepted each Year: 4.039
Middle 50% SAT range: M: 500–610, CR: 480–590, Wr: Unreported
Middle 50% ACT range: Unreported
Early admission program EA/ED/None: None

Percentage accepted through EA or ED: NA
EA and ED deadline: NA
Regular Deadline: Rolling
Application Fee: $50
Full time Undergraduate enrollment: 19,554
Total enrollment: 23,612
Percent Male: 48%
Percent Female: 52%
Total Percent Minority or Unreported: 14%
Percent African-American: 3%
Percent Asian/Pacific Islander: 6%
Percent Hispanic: 4%
Percent Native-American: 1%
Percent International: 3%
Percent in-state/out of state: 89%/11%
Percent from Public HS: 99%
Retention Rate: 82%
Graduation Rate 4-year: 34%

Graduation Rate 6-year: 34%
Percent Undergraduates in On-campus housing: 33%
Number of official organized extracurricular organizations: 200
3 Most popular majors: Communication, Education, Engineering
Student/Faculty ratio: 15:1
Average Class Size: 10 to 19
Percent of students going to grad school: 62%
Tuition and Fees: $16,087
In State Tuition and Fees if different: $6,447
Cost for Room and Board: $7,326
Percent receiving financial aid out of those who apply, first year: 73%
Percent receiving financial aid among all students: 75%

Pullman is a small and sleepy town, unless you happen to arrive when the WSU Cougars play the University of Washington Huskies in the Apple Cup. Students suddenly stream out into the streets, and Pullman overflows with crimson, gray, and cougar. Washington State University has long had a reputation for being the largest party school in the state. However, that party scene has been subsiding in recent years, and in turn, WSU has also amped up its science programs to provide quality academics. Some claim that these changes are helping WSU shed its reputation and that the school is now becoming a well-respected university with numerous resources and the latest research facilities.

Do you Wazzu?

The president of the school in 2002 restricted the printing of the slang term for the university, "Wazzu," on all endorsed clothing to discourage the reputation of its being a party school. While it seems few would argue that this move changed the school's atmosphere, all agreed that the school's academics certainly weren't as easy as the school's party-hard reputation in the state made them seem. The school has a top-notch veterinary program, and students agree that popular majors, like communications, business, and science, all have high-quality classes.

Remarked one student, "My overall experience with classes has proven that WSU has a rigorous academic structure. If you are thinking of becoming a veterinarian or working in agriculture, WSU is a definite prospect." Others argued that, while there are some hard classes, students who know which courses to take can find a lighter workload. But if you are willing to work, some of the best and most challenging classes are in the sciences. Most consider WSU a science school, and one junior said that he had yet to take a humanities class. However, there are some General Education Requirements, such as a world histories course, a course in English composition, and some math and science courses. Like most of the other classes geared toward freshmen, the lectures are usually larger in number, with the average size of a general education class at 58 students. According to one student, some of the more popular classes can have a few hundred students, although English classes are generally capped at 26. There are teaching assistants to help out, though, and students said they were usually helpful.

If students need extra help, there are certainly ample resources. The professors have available office hours, and the college has a students' center on campus known as the "CUE," where TAs wait inside to help students with any paper or problem set they may be having trouble with. For many science and math lectures, there are also tutorial "classes," which are not mandatory but are helpful to attend. In these classes, a teaching assistant will help further explain concepts and review material. One student noted, "After freshman year, you kind of get it. They're there to help you, and it helps a lot to go."

> **"WSU's motto is 'World class, face to face.' So far the statement has proven to be accurate."**

Students say they can generally get into the classes they want to, although it is sometimes hard as a freshman, because preference is given to upperclassmen. If a student makes it past the large introductory classes, he or she can generally get into whatever upper-level class he or she wants, and those classes are usually much smaller. Students usually do not have to take specific required classes after freshman year besides those in their major, and they are freer to take classes they want to take to fulfill their General Education Requirements and credit hours. They can choose from a wide variety of classes not often offered at smaller colleges, or any college at all, such as billiards, scuba diving, hip hop, and, for any would-be gymnasts, beginning tumbling. One student remarked, "I love the broad class base." For students looking for vigorous academics, WSU also has much more intense courses. Freshmen can choose to enroll in the Honors College of WSU; they live in an "Honors Dorm" and may begin working on a thesis project in their junior year.

Majors are often career-based, and most students choose their classes and direction with careers in mind. The concepts of liberal arts and traditional education are much less popular than classes dealing with hard facts or specific skills. When asked about which was the worst major at WSU, a sophomore responded, "Philosophy is the worst. It might be taught well, but who have you heard of making millions with this kind of degree?" Overall, students are impressed by the quality of academics. One student said "WSU's motto is 'World class, face to face.' So far the statement has proven to be accurate."

Palouse-a-Palooza

"You can't go home every weekend, and you're definitely more on your own because Pullman is so isolated," one student noted. However, while the area known as the "Palouse," generally offers little but farmland, students certainly find enough to do in the small town of Pullman. While upperclassmen frequent bars such as Valhalla and the Coug, underclassmen are more likely to be found at popular coffee shops such as the Daily Grind and the Bookie. Many students are likely to hang out at the Rec Center, a giant gymnasium where students can play basketball, lift weights or head to the Jacuzzi. The Compton Union Building (the CUB) is a recently renovated student center with a ballroom, movie theaters, meeting rooms, cafés, and other resources and spaces.

Partying in the Palouse

Fraternities certainly throw a lot of the parties on campus, although students have mixed feelings about the entities themselves. One student claimed that Greek life is not a big deal, while another said that "[frats are] very important. There are a lot of negative stereotypes about fraternity boys and sorority girls. Although there are some people who fit the criteria, the majority of those living on Greek Row are smart, goal-oriented individuals."

Most students don't feel at all pressured to drink. Those who want to will certainly have to go off campus. WSU has a strict alcohol policy on campus, and rooms are monitored by RAs who patrol the dorms at 9 p.m. and midnight on weekdays and even at 3 a.m. on weekends. Drugs are less prevalent, and one student remarked that some students do harder drugs, but that they form a small minority.

The first time a student is caught with alcohol, there is a $50 fine and a mandatory alcohol awareness class. The second time students are caught, the fine is larger, their parents are notified, and they have to meet one-on-one with a counselor to determine if they have a problem. After the third strike, a student is technically supposed to be sent home, but one sophomore claimed to know people on their fifth and sixth strikes. The same student said that the policy is "mostly to scare freshmen," and that

students didn't have to worry about the policy off campus.

All freshmen are required to live in approved University housing their first year, which includes fraternities and sororities. About 30 percent of students decide to live on campus after freshman year. The ones who move off campus either get apartments or houses with their friends or move into a fraternity or sorority. Most students say they do not really like the freshman dorms, although they do say there is fun to be had there. Stephenson is usually the party dorm ("party" being a loose word as the dorms are dry), while Scott-Coman is quieter. Many of the buildings on campus are redbrick buildings, which most students find very pretty. The campus is currently growing with renovations and new buildings. Several new science buildings have opened over the past few years, and the new Palouse Ridge Golf Club is already world-renowned.

Cougar Pride

School spirit is rampant at WSU, and everyone is a die-hard Cougar fan. According to one student, Pullman and the campus are literally transformed on game day, with many more people out than are normally in town. The most exciting game of the year is the Apple Cup, in which the Cougars face off against their rivals, the University of Washington Huskies. "A football weekend is unlike any other," one student said. "It's ridiculous with UW." Everyone sports Cougar T-shirts and sweatshirts, and Cougar license plates are also very popular.

However, for those students who aren't quite up to varsity level, Washington State still has a lot to offer. Intramural sports are the most popular extracurricular, and almost every sport is offered. One student said that people are "very passionate" about intramurals. The Outdoor Recreation Center also has quite a bit to offer in the way of outdoor activities, and students can take river-rafting trips, go rock climbing, or even take one of the outdoor trips to Alaska. Pullman students are generally active, as a lot of the preferred activity involves the outdoors or hanging out at one of the recreation centers; at least, until it starts to snow.

Pullman prides itself in its friendly environment, and people are generally treated very well. As one student noted, "It's a pretty welcoming student body. If you randomly said hello to 20 people, you would easily get 18 hellos back."—*Molly Shepherd-Oppenheim*

FYI

If you come to WSU, you'd better bring, "Cougar gear, Cougar gear, Cougar gear."

What's the typical weekend schedule? "Friday: go to classes, work out, go to a party. Saturday: go to a football game, go to another party. Sunday: try to catch up on homework."

If I could change one thing about WSU, I'd "place it in a more vibrant location."

Three things every student at WSU should do before graduating are, "Go see the grizzly bears, go on one of the outdoor rec trips, and go to the Haunted Palouse, a Halloween haunted house and corn maze."

Whitman College

Address: 345 Boyer Avenue
Walla Walla, WA 99362
Phone: 509-527-5176
E-mail address:
admission@whitman.edu
Web site URL:
www.whitman.edu
Year Founded: 1883
Private or Public: Private
Religious Affiliation: None
Location: Rural
Number of Applicants: 3,096
Percent Accepted: 46%
Percent Accepted who enroll: 28%
Number Entering: 401
Number of Transfers Accepted each Year: 50
Middle 50% SAT range:
M: 610–700, CR: 630–730,
Wr: 620–710
Middle 50% ACT range: 28–32
Early admission program EA/ED/None: ED
Percentage accepted through EA or ED: 75%

EA and ED deadline:
15-Nov
Regular Deadline: 15-Jan
Application Fee: $50
Full time Undergraduate enrollment: 1,458
Total enrollment: 1,458
Percent Male: 45%
Percent Female: 55%
Total Percent Minority or Unreported: 19%
Percent African-American: 2%
Percent Asian/Pacific Islander: 10%
Percent Hispanic: 6%
Percent Native-American: 1%
Percent International: 3%
Percent in-state/out of state: 40%/60%
Percent from Public HS: 75%
Retention Rate: 93%
Graduation Rate 4-year: 84%

Graduation Rate 6-year: 85%
Percent Undergraduates in On-campus housing: 62%
Number of official organized extracurricular organizations: 60
3 Most popular majors:
Biology, History, Political Science
Student/Faculty ratio: 9:1
Average Class Size: 10 to 19
Percent of students going to grad school: Unreported
Tuition and Fees: $34,880
In State Tuition and Fees if different: No difference
Cost for Room and Board: $8,820
Percent receiving financial aid out of those who apply, first year: 70%
Percent receiving financial aid among all students: 74%

If you love nature, the outdoors, and learning, then Whitman College in Walla Walla, Washington is the place for you. With a generally laid-back attitude and overall liberal mindset, Whitman students can take advantage of the abundance of activities offered on campus, as well as enjoy the outdoors in the beautiful Pacific Northwest.

Welcoming "Whitties"

Students say that one of the greatest perks of a Whitman experience is going to school in Walla Walla. Whitman students (called "Whitties") say that Walla Walla is the perfect college town—small and friendly with lots to do. One student remarked, "The cam-

pus and surrounding areas are so safe . . . I can leave my purse and belongings in a public place and know that when I return they'll be sitting right where I left them." Another described the campus and Walla Walla as "incredibly safe. You wouldn't believe it. I can trust anyone on this campus."

At Whitman, it's not uncommon to say hi to or strike up a conversation with a stranger on the street. Freshmen at Whitman even said that the welcome they received on their first day at college was almost overwhelming. "Since it is a school of maybe 1,400 students, you end up meeting a lot of people pretty easily," one junior explained. "As far as friendliness goes, Whitman students are some of the friendliest people I have ever met." But the student population of Whitman is "not diverse." "There is not much diversity," and Whitties are "mostly white," with a very "small population of international students," one Whittie noted. Despite the lack of diversity, Whitties maintain that they are extremely accepting of any student. One Whittie summed up the student body by saying, "I was surprised by the kindness and acceptance I found here that I have never found anywhere else."

Love the Core

Many undergrads agree that one of the most important qualities of Whitman students is a "genuine interest in learning." Academics have always been central to life at Whitman, and many students say that the only thing Whitties love as much as the outdoors is learning.

At the center of a Whitman education is the core curriculum. Students describe the Core program as one to "ensure some kind of exposure to all areas of the liberal arts." In addition to taking two semesters of Core classes ("Antiquity" and "Modernity") freshman year, Whitties are also required to fulfill a plethora of distributional requirements, including two social science classes, two humanities, two fine arts, two sciences, two alternative voices classes, and a quantitative analysis course before graduating.

While premed and the sciences are popular majors, they are also known to be the most difficult. Of course, it is possible to be "challenged by any program you pursue," although reportedly there is a fair amount of grade inflation. And students maintain that it is hard to do poorly at Whitman because so many academic resources are available outside of class.

> "I can leave my purse and belongings in a public place and know that when I return they'll be sitting right where I left them."

Whitties rave about their professors, describing them as "highly regarded" and "very accessible." "I love the profs here . . . they are highly accessible people, and very friendly and helpful," one junior said.

What About the Weekends?

Whitties report a great social scene on campus. Students say that unofficial on-campus parties, fraternity and sorority parties, and dances and events hosted by official Whitman clubs are the dominant activities for Friday and Saturday nights. One third of the student population is involved in Greek life. Sorority members live in the all-female Prentiss Hall. Frat parties are popular social events, but students report that they are "exclusive" or hard to get in to.

Students say that, "like any other college," alcohol is very present on campus. The school's alcohol policy "is very laid-back." Most students drink "in a private space that is somewhat contained (i.e., in one's room with the door closed). If an RA catches you drinking in public, they pour out your drink, and that is all," one Whittie warned. However, many students stress that there are "plenty of activities on campus if you don't drink." And students seem to agree that there are almost no drugs present on campus.

Whittie Winners

Whitties describe their campus as "beautiful." The campus is centered around Ankeny Field, which is pretty much "your typical college quad." Freshmen and sophomores live on campus and are required to have an on-campus meal plan. The biggest dorms on campus are Anderson and Jewitt Halls. There are also several smaller residence halls for juniors and seniors. In addition to the traditional dorm housing, Whitman also has many different theme houses, ranging from a volunteer house to a writing house, which, as one student described, "allow upperclassmen to live within a community of people with similar interests."

The meal plan at Whitman allows students to eat at two dining halls and the student center, Reid Campus Center. Students assert that Reid Center has better food than the halls, but the halls have "exceptional salad bars."

In terms of sports, jocks should take heart—Whitman has no football team or cheerleaders. However, students are quick to say that "tennis, cross country, and skiing are very popular." There is also a biking team that is growing in popularity. Whitman's new tennis facility and indoor pool are proclaimed by most to be "high quality."

Because of the lack of varsity sports, Whitman students take intramural sports very seriously. Some of the most popular are bowling, flag football, ultimate Frisbee, basketball, and soccer. And despite a high level of competition, Whitties say that IMs are "fun!"

Whitman draws much of its appeal from its

beautiful Pacific Northwest surroundings. While Whitties hold a great appreciation for nature, they are quick to refute common stereotypes that Whitman students care more about their hiking boots than their grades or extracurriculars. In truth, while the typical Whitman student is outdoorsy and free-spirited, he or she is also friendly, accepting, hard-working, and high-achieving. One student summed up his experience at Whitman by saying, "Being a 'Whittie' is an amazing experience, and if this school is the right place for you as a person, it's the best place in the world."—*Becky Bicks*

FYI

If you come to Whitman, you'd better bring: "Hiking boots, a Frisbee, a spirit of adventure, and an open mind."

If I could change anything at Whitman, I'd "push the food service provider (Bon Appetit) to improve overall quality."

What's a typical weekend schedule? "Party on campus Saturday and sleep in and study on Sunday, or go on a camping trip Friday night and come back Sunday."

Three things everyone should do before graduating from Whitman are: "Run the Beer Mile, complete the Frisbee golf course, go on as many camping trips as possible."

West Virginia

Marshall University

Address: One John Marshall Drive, Huntington, WV 25655
Phone: 304-696-3160
E-mail address: admissions@marshall.edu
Web site URL: www.marshall.edu
Year Founded: 1837
Private or Public: Public
Religious Affiliation: None
Location: Suburban
Number of Applicants: 2,409
Percent Accepted: 83%
Percent Accepted who enroll: 83%
Number Entering: 1,661
Number of Transfers Accepted each Year: 762
Middle 50% SAT range: M: 440–560, CR: 450–560, Wr: 440–550
Middle 50% ACT range: 19–25
Early admission program EA/ED/None: None

Percentage accepted through EA or ED: NA
EA and ED deadline: NA
Regular Deadline: Rolling
Application Fee: $30
Full time Undergraduate enrollment: 8,904
Total enrollment: 13,562
Percent Male: 45%
Percent Female: 55%
Total Percent Minority or Unreported: 11%
Percent African-American: 6%
Percent Asian/Pacific Islander: 1%
Percent Hispanic: 2%
Percent Native-American: 1%
Percent International: 1%
Percent in-state/out of state: 74% / 26%
Percent from Public HS: Unreported
Retention Rate: 71%
Graduation Rate 4-year: Unreported

Graduation Rate 6-year: Unreported
Percent Undergraduates in On-campus housing: Unreported
Number of official organized extracurricular organizations: 100
3 Most popular majors: Business, Education, Liberal Arts
Student/Faculty ratio: 19:1
Average Class Size: 20 to 29
Percent of students going to grad school: 27%
Tuition and Fees: $11,702
In State Tuition and Fees if different: $4,598
Cost for Room and Board: $7,210
Percent receiving financial aid out of those who apply, first year: 68%
Percent receiving financial aid among all students: 44%

For the many West Virginia residents on campus, Marshall University can seem like a larger version of high school: a familiar environment surrounded by classmates they have known since kindergarten. While this can promote a lack of diversity on campus, Marshall is able to boast accessible professors, brand-new facilities, and a tight-knit community available to students who live both on and off campus.

One Class at a Time

All students must satisfy the requirements of the Marshall Plan, which is composed of a course or two in math, science, computer literacy, writing, multicultural studies, international studies, and a senior capstone experience involving both oral and written presentations. Although the Plan is considered more annoying than demanding, many students would like to see changes to these general education requirements or at least a decrease in the time they must devote to them. Furthermore, several students, particularly those who commute, complained of not having enough time for electives. And at the same time, many of the "coolest" electives are only offered through the Marshall Community and Technical College. "I don't want to sacrifice the authenticity of regular Marshall courses for the coolness of the technical school ones," said one senior.

Although the Marshall Plan consumes large portions of students' academic hours, one psychology major said he loves the freedom within his major. "You don't really have to take a lot of hours in your major," he said. Many students concentrate in business or nursing, but other departments also receive praise from students. "Take as many history classes as you can. Those are the best professors," one student said, while another described his first-year experience in the music department as "amazing." Science majors are generally regarded as more difficult, and those students not in the science departments do bemoan a lack of opportunities in humanities and social sciences. The University seems to propel this perspective, having recently unveiled the Robert C. Byrd Biotechnology Center in 2006.

Nevertheless, students agree that the workload at Marshall is not strenuous. "I would definitely apply myself more if I were in a more intense academic environment," one senior said. Students said that many professors implement curves, and one freshman laughed when she was asked about the difficulty of the course load. "My favorite thing about Marshall is how easy my classes are," she said. "But Drinko library is always packed."

However easy the classes are, Marshall University does attract talented students with not only the promise of intimate student-teacher interaction but also financial incentives. The University offers myriad scholarships, particularly for in-state students, based on ACT scores and cumulative GPA. There is also the prestigious Yeager Scholarship, which provides tuition, room and board, a semester abroad for foreign language study, a summer program at Oxford University in the United Kingdom, and convenient benefits like early registration for classes.

Living the Dream

Many West Virginia residents view Marshall and its rival, West Virginia University, as the only college options. The West Virginia state government encourages this idea with a scholarship called the PROMISE. The result is a student population that is overwhelmingly homogenous and can often make out-of-state students feel like outsiders. Most in-state students continue associating with their friends from high school, so it can be difficult for out-of-state students to acclimate. However, students say that the social scene at Marshall depends greatly on the living situations.

Marshall requires students to live in dorms for the first two years on campus. However, the two-year rule only applies to those living outside of a 50-mile radius, so commuters have very different opinions of Marshall and its social scene. Students who live in the dorms rate Marshall as much more diverse, and they praise the quality of freshman dorms. When asked if rooms get better with seniority, one freshman said, "No, not at all." This is because Marshall recently constructed new buildings designed just for freshmen, and the additions are expected to attract more students to on-campus living.

> "The most political that the campus gets is during elections for Mr. and Miss Marshall."

There exists a thriving off-campus life as well. Many students live in designated off-campus apartments and enjoy more freedom than those who opt for dormitory living, probably because of the strict dry policy enforced by on-campus housing authorities.

Eat, Drink, and Be Merry

One student who had lived in the small city her entire life commented that "Huntington is the place to be if you want to go to church, go out to eat, or get totally drunk." Being located in what the Centers for Disease Control and Prevention recently named the unhealthiest city in America does have advantages. The City of Huntington recently constructed a complex called Pullman Square that caters to college students looking for both daytime and nighttime fun. Pullman Square offers restaurants, a movie theater, an independent bookstore, a comedy club, shops, and plenty of parking for all the commuters.

Students also frequent Huntington's numerous bars and nightclubs. One student spoke passionately about "quarter-pitcher night" at The Eager Beaver, while others never miss an opportunity to go club-hopping on Friday and Saturday nights. In addition, Marshall has a large Greek scene that provides weekend parties for the entire community.

Students praise the amount of extracurricular options available to Marshall students. One freshman noticed that students are "very committed" to their extracurricular activities, particularly those that are entirely student-run. There are plenty of activities and resources available for religious students in particular, but those looking for political activism should search elsewhere. "The most political that the campus gets is during elections for Mr. and Miss Marshall," said one senior. The student newspaper, *The Parthenon*, is extremely popular on campus, and most students are kept up-to-date by reading it.

Sports also have a dominant presence on campus. Excitement abounds during football season, and students are dedicated to their football team, the "Thundering Herd," known to provide quality players to the NFL. The Marshall basketball program also gets significant attention, particularly during the Marshall-WVU game, which brings large audience of both current students and alumni. "There is a ton of school pride," said one sophomore. "Go Herd!" he added.

'We Are Marshall'

Nothing better illustrates the closeness of the Marshall campus than the sentimentality associated with the plane crash that killed almost the entire football team, coaching staff, and some fans in November of 1970. Often called the "worst sports-related disaster in United States history," the tragedy continues to affect students, staff, and area residents. The Memorial Fountain that commemorates the catastrophe is not only considered one of the "prettiest" parts of campus, but also the most meaningful.

The overall atmosphere at Marshall University can be summed up by the school's motto, "We Are Marshall." This sentiment is a testimony to the enormous pride that students, faculty and alumni feel about their school. The recent renovations and additions demonstrate that Marshall is expanding, and many students see their school changing from being known a commuter school to becoming a leading university in the near future.—*Lauren Oyler*

FYIs
If you come to Marshall, you'd better bring "a ton of green clothes."
What is the typical weekend schedule? "On Wednesdays, it's quarter-pitcher night at Eager Beaver. Thursdays and Fridays are frat parties or clubbing. Saturday is football or basketball games. Then on Sunday, go to church and start studying."
If I could change one thing about Marshall, I'd "decrease the number of requirements of the Marshall Plan."
Three things every student at Marshall should do before graduating are "eat the peach pie at Harless, take advantage of the Marshall Artist Series, and see *We Are Marshall* to understand the school's history."

West Virginia University

Address: PO Box 6009
Morgantown, WV
26506-6009
Phone: 304-293-2121
E-mail address:
go2wvu@mail.wvu.edu
Web site URL: www.wvu.edu
Year Founded: 1867
Private or Public: Public
Religious Affiliation: None
Location: Rural
Number of Applicants:
15,094
Percent Accepted: 88%
Percent Accepted who enroll: 39%
Number Entering: 5,099
Number of Transfers Accepted each Year: 1,495
Middle 50% SAT range:
M: 480–580, CR: 470–560,
Wr: Unreported
Middle 50% ACT range: 20–28
Early admission program EA/ED/None: None

Percentage accepted through EA or ED: NA
EA and ED deadline: NA
Regular Deadline: Rolling
Application Fee: $25
Full time Undergraduate enrollment: 21,145
Total enrollment: 26,740
Percent Male: 55%
Percent Female: 45%
Total Percent Minority or Unreported: 7%
Percent African-American: 3%
Percent Asian/Pacific Islander: 2%
Percent Hispanic: 2%
Percent Native-American: 0%
Percent International: 2%
Percent in-state/out of state: 54%/46%
Percent from Public HS: Unreported
Retention Rate: 84%
Graduation Rate 4-year: Unreported

Graduation Rate 6-year: Uneported
Percent Undergraduates in - On-campus housing: 25%
Number of official organized extracurricular organizations: 300
3 Most popular majors:
Business, Engineering,
Health Professions
Student/Faculty ratio: 23:1
Average Class Size: 2 to 9
Percent of students going to grad school: Unreported
Tuition and Fees: $15,770
In State Tuition and Fees if different: No difference
Cost for Room and Board: $7,434
Percent receiving financial aid out of those who apply, first year: 69%
Percent receiving financial aid among all students: 86%

West Virginia University is better known for its football and basketball teams than academics, but this nationally ranked party school certainly offers much more than just a good time outside of classes.

All Play and No Work?

Despite its reputation as a party school, students at WVU actually do study. Popular majors include business, communications and journalism, and engineering, but many students take advantage of WVU's more esoteric programs, such as Exercise Physiology or Textiles, Apparel and Merchandising. By the time students are juniors, they apply to a specific college within the University, such as the Perley Isaac Reed School of Journalism, the College of Human Resources and Education, or the Eberly College of Arts and Sciences. WVU also offers over 60 minors, including disciplines like Native American Studies, Conservation Ecology, and Pest Management, a great variety.

In addition to the range of majors and minors offered, WVU students love the large number of class choices. The only drawback is the size of classes. "All of my classes this semester are too big," said one sophomore majoring in chemistry. "I'm talking 250 or so students." Although the classes do become progressively smaller with seniority, many students feel that they have trouble choosing a major because "lecture hall classes are impossible to pay attention in."

Because the school is so large, many students receive relatively little advising. All students must complete the requirements of the General Education Curriculum, which ultimately takes up about one third of each student's course schedule. Although students are assigned to an academic advisor, one freshman said she didn't even know she had to complete the GEC and "expected much more help with scheduling" from the advisors.

The Honors College at WVU provides a more intimate learning environment for students who have demonstrated academic prowess throughout high school. The Honors Program allows students to graduate with honors as well as take small classes that are unheard of for students not in the program. These courses, which are capped at 20 students, are offered in departments ranging from microbiology to theater. They make it possible for honors students to engage in discussions and debate with their professors and peers. Students in the Honors Program say that they don't know what they would do without the additional benefits of the program, which include better housing, priority course registration, and more easily available study abroad opportunities. In return, students must complete at least 24 credit hours of Honors courses and maintain a high GPA.

On the other hand, the Honors program at WVU reportedly lacks academic diversity. Students claim that the number of science majors in the Honors College is significantly disproportional to the number of science majors in the overall undergraduate population. "The only time I hear anyone talking about humanities is when they are trying to fill GECs," said one sophomore in the Honors College. This disparity contributes to the overarching belief around campus that social sciences and humanities are easy. "Whenever I'm at a party and tell people that I'm a biology major, people cringe," said one junior. "They usually follow up with something like 'Oh, that's so hard. I could never do that.'"

Country Roads

Located in the Mountain State, WVU's campus boasts great opportunities for hiking, which may be required to get to classes. West Virginia has two campuses, the Evansdale campus and the Downtown campus. To connect them, the University constructed a monorail system, called the PRT (Personal Rapid Transit). While riding the PRT remains a uniquely Mountaineer experience, students' overall impressions of the PRT are negative. "The PRT is like a rollercoaster for little children," one WVU junior said.

Running from 6:30 a.m. to 10:15 p.m. on weekdays, 9:30 a.m. to 5:00 p.m. on Saturdays, and closed on Sundays, the PRT schedule is not designed for convenience. It is also known to break down frequently, leaving students without cars stuck on their respective campuses. Even students who do have cars have trouble getting around because parking is "severely limited."

Instead of solving the parking or the PRT problem, many students would prefer that the University somehow unify the two campuses, which are separated by about one and a half miles. While the Downtown campus is known as the heart and soul of WVU, the Evansdale campus has many necessary resources as well, including many athletic facilities, making transportation between the two unavoidable. One freshman complained that the dual campus structure of WVU makes it "impossible to see anyone."

The West Virginia hills are also considered

inconvenient by some students. There is even a Facebook group called "I Got 99 Problems and 82 of them are the Steps by the Life Science Building," dedicated to commiserating about the hilly terrain at WVU. However, the hills are also beloved by students. Active students utilize the area's natural resources by hiking, walking, or jogging on trails located next to the Monongahela River. They can also make frequent visits to Coopers Rock State Forest, make use of the nearby ski resorts, and enjoy whitewater rafting.

Take Me Home

Ironically, the dorms at WVU are unwaveringly dry, even for students over the age of 21. The school's policy on alcohol in the dorms is strict: All students found drinking in the dorms will be written up and fined. Students looking to drink need not search far, however, for an off-campus house party or a bar. Because Greek life is not particularly important on campus, students say that the social scene at WVU truly revolves around Morgantown's bounty of bars and clubs, frequented by students every night of the week. On the other hand, the easy access can be problematic when finals approach. The dilemma of juggling the bustling social scene and academics contributes to WVU's relatively low freshman retention rate, and one sophomore estimated that "probably 95 percent" of the student body drinks.

For those not looking to imbibe, WVU has WVUp All Night, a weekly event that takes place in the Mountainlair, the student union on the Downtown campus. Each Thursday, Friday, and Saturday night beginning at 7 p.m., the Mountainlair is transformed into Up All Night, where students can get free food, watch movies, go bowling, and enjoy myriad other activities. Although many students view Up All Night as a way to sober up after a long night of drinking, it is still lauded as one of the country's best weekend alternatives to the "college party scene."

The school also sponsors another entertainment event called FallFest. Every year the University welcomes students back to campus with a huge outdoor concert featuring several headlining bands. This event is so impressive that it even attracts students from rival Marshall University, whose students are often willing to make the two-and-a-half-hour drive from southern West Virginia to enjoy big-name acts at WVU.

> "'WVU is like being a kid trying to do a jigsaw puzzle at a carnival.'"

Sports are also an essential part of student life at WVU. With sports teams that consistently rank among the top 25 in the nation, loyal Mountaineer fans look forward to game days with passion. On Saturday mornings in the fall, fans in gold and blue shirts flock to the Pit for unforgettable tailgates before moving on to Milan Puskar Stadium, where they cheer on the Mountaineers in what is usually a spectacular game. School spirit is also palpable during the basketball season, when Mountaineer fans religiously follow NCAA rankings to see if their team prevails.

Students are envious of the "sweet" athletic facilities reserved for varsity athletes, but the Student Rec Center is more than adequate for non-athletes. Boasting everything from standard exercise equipments to a 50-foot climbing wall, badminton courts, and an elevated track, the Student Rec Center is home to WVU's intramurals, which are fairly popular among students.

To the Place I Belong

"My economics professor really said it best," commented one junior majoring in accounting. "He said 'WVU is like being a kid trying to do a jigsaw puzzle at a carnival.' You can get the education at WVU that you could get anywhere, but there is so much going on around you that it's really a test to see if you can concentrate, which is something I think is unique. It probably prepares you for the real world better than a lot of places in that sense." The majority of students are proud of their school and their Mountaineers. Students are known to sing along to John Denver's "Country Roads," which is usually done at sporting events. This is because, to them, WVU really is "home."—*Lauren Oyler*

FYIs

If you come to West Virginia, you'd better bring "an appreciation for beer."

What is the typical weekend schedule? "Go out to bars or an off-campus party on Thursdays and Fridays, wake up early for a tailgate on Saturday, cheer on the Mountaineers, and have a victory celebration on Saturday night."

If I could change one thing about West Virginia, I'd "bring the two campuses together."

Three things every student at West Virginia should do before graduating are "walk down High Street to see all the crazy parties, go to a football game at Milan Puskar Stadium, and see Coopers Rock."

Wisconsin

Beloit College

Address: 700 College Street
Beloit, WI 53511
Phone: 608-363-2500
E-mail address:
admiss@beloit.edu
Web site URL: www.beloit
.edu/admissions
Year Founded: 1846
Private or Public: Private
Religious Affiliation: None
Location: Urban
Number of Applicants:
2,248
Percent Accepted: 63%
**Percent Accepted who
enroll:** 24%
Number Entering: 362
**Number of Transfers
Accepted each Year:** 25
Middle 50% SAT range:
M: 560–690, CR: 570–700,
Wr: Unreported
Middle 50% ACT range:
25–30
**Early admission program
EA/ED/None:** EA

**Percentage accepted
through EA or ED:**
Unreported
EA and ED deadline: 1-Dec
Regular Deadline: 15-Jan
Application Fee: $35
**Full time Undergraduate
enrollment:** 1,297
Total enrollment: 1,388
Percent Male: 44%
Percent Female: 56%
**Total Percent Minority or
Unreported:** 13%
Percent African-American:
4%
**Percent Asian/Pacific
Islander:** 3%
Percent Hispanic: 4%
Percent Native-American:
<1%
Percent International:
Unreported
**Percent in-state/out of
state:** 22%/78%
Percent from Public HS: 78%
Retention Rate: 89%

Graduation Rate 4-year: 72%
Graduation Rate 6-year: 78%
**Percent Undergraduates in
On-campus housing:** 95%
**Number of official organized
extracurricular
organizations:** 95
3 Most popular majors:
Creative Writing, Sociology,
Anthropology/Political
Science
Student/Faculty ratio: 11:1
Average Class Size: 15
**Percent of students going to
grad school:** 40%
Tuition and Fees: $31,540
**In State Tuition and Fees if
different:** No difference
Cost for Room and Board:
$6,696
**Percent receiving financial
aid out of those who apply,
first year:** 80%
**Percent receiving financial
aid among all students:**
62%

Founded in 1846 in territorial Wisconsin with just $7,000 and a desire to bring education to the Midwest, Beloit College has now become an internationally recognized college famed for its liberal arts education and its distinctive atmosphere. A few students may whine about the cold winters of Wisconsin, but the environment at Beloit is very welcoming. Strong academics with a focus on global relations and a thriving social life complete the beauty of a hip and enthusiastic campus.

Interdisciplinary Innovation

Although some students call the workload "challenging," most agree that it is quite rewarding, thoughtful, and interdisciplinary. Beloiters also rave that their professors are accessible and helpful. One freshman said that her professor offered her class an opportunity to work and learn in Africa with the professor over the summer.

A First-Year Initiatives program brings all Beloit's freshmen together through interdisciplinary seminars and orientation programs. This is complemented by a Sophomore-Year Initiatives program that works with sophomores to overcome the dreaded "sophomore slump" and helps them to become more aware of their aims and goals in college. Beyond that, there are few academic requirements—two courses in natural sciences or math, two in social sciences, and two in humanities. Additionally, each student must complete three writing-focused classes and one interdisciplinary class. These requirements can be fulfilled through a variety of unique classes;

the course catalogue has such offerings as Egyptian, History of Physics, Dinosaurs and Their Lost World, and even Film Music. "The requirements are good in that they offer structure, but they are quite flexible and can be tailored to your individual interests," one undergrad explained.

To help students through difficult classes, Beloit offers a number of resources. The Learning Support Services Center often tutors students either individually or in groups, and the Writing Center, where tutors "work with students on a collaborative basis" is open until 10 p.m. on school nights. Students agree that the workload is just as intense as that at any first-rate university, regardless of the department. Classics is said to be a somewhat easy major, but one junior pointed out that the sciences tend to be more challenging "because of time and difficulty. There is certainly less wiggle room in [science majors] to take classes you are interested in" outside the major. Beloit's specialties, international relations and anthropology, are fairly difficult, but are both popular and renowned majors. Anthropology, in particular, received rave reviews. One student gushed that "Indiana Jones was based on one of our archeology graduates named Roy Chapman [Andrews]. He donated all his artifacts to the school upon his death!" Luckily, living professors tend to be just as amazing. The reigning celebrity is Tom McBride of the English department, who is the creator of the annual "mindset lists" and is described as "very Texan" with a "loud teaching style." There is also an archaeology professor, Dan Shea, who "frequently takes students along on his digs in Chile," and Pablo Toral, a specialist on development and Latin America, a favorite of students.

The atmosphere at Beloit is intimate, considering that the college only has 1,300 undergraduates. Classes are usually smaller than 20 students and always under 30. Even the introductory survey classes are personal, although one philosophy major whined that they were "lacking in depth . . . but also unavoidable." Assignments, according to students, tend to go beyond the standard papers. One student recalled "performing the entire *Paradise Lost* in front of an audience for an English class," while another said, "In my African studies class we had to do oral presentations because African culture is more oral than ours."

Frisbee and Freak-Dancing

Beyond homework and classes, Beloit students keep busy. For those not writing for the *Round Table*, the school paper, school nights are devoted to homework and other extracurriculars. Sports are very low-key. When asked, a student said, "Sports? We have sports? Oh, yeah, intramurals. I've heard rumors of varsity sports but never witnessed them. Kind of like ghost stories." When it's warm enough, Frisbee is surprisingly common on the grounds. Extracurricular groups include Young Democrats, Young Republicans, the Gay-Straight Alliance, Black Students United, Voces Latinas, and even fencing.

Thursday through Saturday nights, "everyone parties together on campus, which is awesome and friendly, but can always be awkward the next morning, since you know everyone," one female undergrad said. Freshmen tend to mix and mingle at larger and more formal functions, while upperclassmen parties are usually more private, "but they are still very much out in public with the rest of us mortals." The Greek scene, with only eight percent of men and six percent of women involved, is small but key to the party circuit. One fraternity member commented that "Greek life affects the community, but does not run it like on other schools. That's why I joined." All the parties have different themes, from a "Talking Heads" party to the soccer team's 70s-style "Playaz Ball" party, but students uniformly have a good time together. Beloit also organizes a Folk and Blues weekend every fall that brings a number of bands to campus for two nights.

As part of the hippie environment, people do respect what alcohol can do to the body. Most people who do drink end up at Aldrich residential hall. One girl who lives there said that "when I didn't drink, I didn't feel out of the loop, but sometimes I feel that drinkers can be really inconsiderate about others, especially when it's a Wednesday night." Students said that IDs are rarely checked, and private parties are very common and very open. There is a zero tolerance policy on drugs. However, since there is a large proportion of hippies on campus, "there is certainly a lot of pot here, but you have to look harder to find stronger drugs." Coed dorms make hooking up and sex fairly common. "Students at Beloit can't be described as polyamorous," said one student. "They are just plain amorous." Of course, "there are also a fair amount of committed couples of all preferences."

Wild, Wonderful Wisconsin

The campus is very idyllic, thanks to its scenic location in the woods of Wisconsin.

Beloit's greatest claim to landscape fame is its Native American burial mounds, which no other college in the States has. One of the burial mounds is shaped like a turtle, from which was derived Beloit's unofficial turtle mascot. "We're freaking Beloit College," one student exclaimed. "Everything begins and ends here! We also have a rich history of hippiedom." The campus incorporates Georgian and colonial architecture, and the woods add natural beauty. The city of Beloit is fairly unexciting, but just seven dollars buys a bus ticket to Madison, which is 45 minutes away.

> **"Everything begins and ends here! We also have a rich history of hippiedom."**

The campus residences are extraordinarily varied. One college radio announcer gave a quick rundown of the major dorms: "Peet is the stoner dorm. Aldrich is where the drunks go. 810 [College Street] is where soccer players usually live. Avoid the '64 halls—they were built to be riotproof and thus are ugly as sin. The worst dorm would be 609 Emerson, a freshman dorm with cinderblock walls and dingy lighting."

The students, however, make up for the buildings. Of course, the student body can still easily fall into stereotypes: "You know those white kids with dreadlocks who are actually from the 'burbs of Chicago? A lot of those go here. A fair amount of indie kids/art students. But all the rest are pretty normal." There is some self-segregation, but the large number of international students really balances out the student body. A student government leader said, "I feel comfortable sitting with anybody" in the cafeterias.

From the campus to the classes to the night scene, there is a focus more on connections and understanding than just textbook learning at Beloit. It is "this emphasis on experiential learning and international perspectives," one freshman explained, "that makes Beloit truly excellent." Oh, yeah, and it's fun, too!—*Jeffrey Zuckerman*

FYI

If you come to Beloit, you better bring "lots of costumes because people here LOVE theme parties."

What's the typical weekend schedule? "Friday night: party. Saturday: Sleep it off, do a little bit of homework. Party at night. Sunday: Do a lot of homework."

If I could change one thing about Beloit, I'd "get more diversity. Tons more. As in people who are not white and from Chicago."

Three things every student at Beloit should do before graduating are "Study abroad, have tea at a professor's house, and dance their ass off at as many campus parties as possible."

Lawrence University

Address: P.O. Box 599
Appleton, WI 54912-0599
Phone: 800-227-0982
E-mail address:
excel@lawrence.edu
Web site URL:
www.lawrence.edu
Year Founded: 1847
Private or Public: Private
Religious Affiliation: None
Location: Suburban
Number of Applicants:
2,618
Percent Accepted: 59%
Percent Accepted who
enroll: 25%
Number Entering: 414
Number of Transfers
Accepted each Year: 68
Middle 50% SAT range:
M: 610–720, CR: 590–720,
Wr: 610–690
Middle 50% ACT range:
27–31
Early admission program
EA/ED/None: EA and ED

Percentage accepted
through EA or ED: 39%
EA and ED deadline: 15-Nov
for EA, 1-Dec for ED
Regular Deadline: 15-Jan
Application Fee: $40
Full time Undergraduate
enrollment: 1,503
Total enrollment: 1,503
Percent Male: 46%
Percent Female: 54%
Total Percent Minority or
Unreported: Unreported
Percent African-American:
4%
Percent Asian/Pacific
Islander: 2%
Percent Hispanic: 1%
Percent Native-American:
<1%
Percent International:
Unreported
Percent in-state/out of
state: 27%/73%
Percent from Public HS:
Unreported

Retention Rate: 90%
Graduation Rate 4-year: 63%
Graduation Rate 6-year:
79%
Percent Undergraduates in
On-campus housing: 97%
Number of official organized
extracurricular
organizations: 130
3 Most popular majors:
Biology, History, English
Student/Faculty ratio: 9:1
Average Class Size: 15
Percent of students going to
grad school: 22%
Tuition and Fees: $33,264
In State Tuition and Fees if
different: No difference
Cost for Room and Board:
$6,957
Percent receiving financial
aid out of those who apply,
first year: 66%
Percent receiving financial
aid among all students:
Unreported

L awrence University's 84 acres in Wisconsin barely contain the vibrancy and excitement of the 1,500 students that bring the school to life. Lawrence is renowned for its music conservatory, and a sizeable percentage of students choose to follow its five-year double-degree program for a Bachelor of Music and Bachelor of Arts. At the same time, the close, intimate atmosphere of its liberal arts curriculum provides the opportunity for budding English and Biology majors alike to shine. And as if that wasn't enough, Lawrence students regularly go on retreats to Björklunden (pronounced "Bee-york-lun-den"), an estate on the shore of Lake Michigan, for seminars and weekend trips and to enjoy nature at its most beautiful. "I had my choice of so many schools," one sophomore said, "and I picked Lawrence because it had everything I could ask for."

So a Connie and a Bio major are in a Frosh Studies class . . .

The hallmark of any Lawrentian's education is the Freshman Studies program, which every professor teaches and all students take in their first year at school: "It's unique to Lawrence, because all the freshmen read the same works, which cross different disciplines . . . so the curriculum covers works mostly from literature but also from science and math, history, and of course music." One student mentioned looking at Martin Luther King Jr.'s "I Have a Dream" speech alongside John Coltrane's song "Alabama" and realizing with her classmates that the two texts shared the same rhythms and cadences: "It was just fascinating to uncover things like that, that you would never notice outside of the classroom!"

The distributional requirements are a writing-intensive and speaking-intensive class, a quantitative class, classes with elements of diversity, a lab science class, a humanities class, a social science class, a fine arts class, a semester of a foreign language (or its equivalent), and a year of Freshman Studies. An English major noticed that "especially with the 'diversity' classes, the distributional requirements encourage people to have a broad view of the foundations of our world. Dead white males have been powerful forces, yes, but there's so much more than that." Classes are on the small side, and one student said she was surprised when her roommate was in a chemistry lecture class with 60 students, "and I had just never heard of anything that big at Lawrence. Classes are usually closer to 15 or 20, but they get smaller as you take more advanced courses."

Lawrence's music conservatory adds a unique twist to the school, and a significant number of students take classes at the Con, as it is called. One student considering a degree in music spent her free hours in a new way: "My workload is a different kind because I'll practice for several hours every day rather than reading books and writing papers or working in a lab." Still, she added, the amount of work is not unreasonable: "I've heard about people pulling all-nighters, but usually it's their fault because they've been putting off something too long."

With such small classes, professors focus on students and strive to make the work interesting. "In Music Theory we each wrote our own four-part chorales and then had people in that class perform them on their respective instruments . . . Viola was a really popular instrument," said a viola player from that class. Geology classes have also gone out into Wisconsin's geologic deposits, and students have dug up rather sizeable artifacts.

Life in between Brewed Awakenings and Björklunden!

When Lawrentians are not hard at work (and most of them do have some time to relax on weeknights), they take the time to enjoy themselves. On weekend afternoons, people usually go to a coffee shop in Appleton "and pretend to work while socializing and enjoying the day." Most students are split between the smaller, cozier Brewed Awakenings and the slightly more posh Copper Rock with its high ceilings, exposed brick walls, and cool art. "On weekend nights, there's usually one or two main parties that have been advertised, usually at the theme house or frat house," so the campus tends to split into the "party" groups and the "relaxed" groups. When asked about parties, one underclassman said, "The Coop's Nearly Naked parties are really neat—the point is to be creative and dress in anything other than clothing. We've even had dresses made out of juice boxes."

True to Lawrence's focus on music, the all-around coolest frat on campus is Sinfonia, a music fraternity that is almost all brass and percussion, with a lot of jazz musicians. "They provide the music for all their parties, and I just think that's really cool," said a staff writer for the school paper.

"If I had to nail down a stereotypical Lawrence student," said the writer, "it would be a music nerd. Nice, yes, but nerdy. There are definitely jocks on campus, though, and both groups have their female counterparts." On a 1-to-10 scale, Lawrence students rate an eight for all-around attractiveness. Downer Commons, where most students tend to eat, has three rooms that segment the student body in an interesting way: "A lot of the huge jocks sit in the A room, probably because it's closer to the food. The 'cool and alternative' people, including the outdoorsy people, sit in B, because it gets the best sunlight. And people who want peace and quiet sit upstairs in C, but everybody talks to them because the soft-serve ice cream machine is upstairs!" Lucinda's Dining Hall, the smaller dining facility, is a dining hall with an amazing view of the Wisconsin landscape that Lawrence borders. A vending machine is being added to the Con, and "now Connies won't ever go outside the Con again," joked a musician.

> "I had my choice of so many schools and I picked Lawrence because it had everything I could ask for."

Almost all students live on campus, with a very small handful of super seniors, or fifth-year students in the double-degree program, living in apartments. A major part of dorm life is theme housing, "a hot-button issue every spring. The validity of the Swing (Dancing) House and SoundBoard House are the topics of much debate, in comparison to the CompSci House, the GLOW (Gay, Lesbian, or Whatever) House and the oft-discussed but never realized French House." While most floors are single-sex, "coed floors are creeping slowly onto campus." The Lawrence campus is small enough that news often spreads over Saturday and Sunday brunch at Downer.

On some weekends, for a change of pace, students can go to Björklunden to explore the beautiful 425-acre estate that the University owns along Lake Michigan on the Door County peninsula. There is a lodge, and often student concerts are performed there.

Different student groups go each weekend, and some students manage to go two or three times per term. Many students would tell you that a memorable part of a weekend at Björklunden is the food. It's a weekend of nonstop eating, and the food is a nice break from cafeteria food. A notable treat is Chef Steve's famous bread pudding.

One Lawrence student said that, even in the cold of winter, "Lawrence is a bit like Lake Wobegon (which makes sense since we're pretty close to Minnesota), because all the women are strong, all the men are good looking, so all us students are above average." With such a tight-knit community, an intimate liberal arts curriculum, nightlife as cozy as the town of Appleton, and the wild beauty of Wisconsin all around, how could any student *not* pick Lawrence?— *Jeffrey Zuckerman*

FYI

If you come to Lawrence University, you'd better bring "an active love of music."

What is a typical weekend schedule? "Friday: dinner at the Coop, concert, dance party. Saturday: yoga, Farmer's Market, study until your friend's recital, dance party. Sunday: brunch, studying, and maybe another recital, SoundBoard at the coffeehouse in the evening."

If I could change one thing about Lawrence University, "I'd spend more time at Björklunden."

Three things every student at Lawrence University should do before graduating are "visit the cupola on top of Main Hall, answer phones all night during the Great Midwest Trivia Contest, and spend all Saturday attending student recitals."

Marquette University

Address: P.O. Box 1881 Milwaukee, WI 53201-1881
Phone: 414-288-7302
E-mail address: admissions@marquette.edu
Web site URL: www.marquette.edu
Year Founded: 1881
Private or Public: Private
Religious Affiliation: Roman Catholic–Jesuit
Location: Suburban
Number of Applicants: 13,375
Percent Accepted: 67%
Percent Accepted who enroll: 20%
Number Entering: 1,811
Number of Transfers Accepted each Year: 351
Middle 50% SAT range: M: 550–660, CR: 540–630, Wr: 530–640
Middle 50% ACT range: 24–29

Early admission program EA/ED/None: None
Percentage accepted through EA or ED: NA
EA and ED deadline: NA
Regular Deadline: 1-Dec
Application Fee: $30
Full time Undergraduate enrollment: 7,742
Total enrollment: 10,472
Percent Male: 46%
Percent Female: 54%
Total Percent Minority or Unreported: 17%
Percent African-American: 5%
Percent Asian/Pacific Islander: 4%
Percent Hispanic: 5%
Percent Native-American: 1%
Percent International: 2%
Percent in-state/out of state: 43% / 57%
Percent from Public HS: 54%
Retention Rate: 89%
Graduation Rate 4-year: 57%

Graduation Rate 6-year: 74%
Percent Undergraduates in On-campus housing: 51%
Number of official organized extracurricular organizations: 230
3 Most popular majors: Communication, Business, Biomedical Sciences/Journalism
Student/Faculty ratio: 15:1
Average Class Size: 10 to 19
Percent of students going to grad school: 33%
Tuition and Fees: $28,128
In State Tuition and Fees if different: No difference
Cost for Room and Board: $9,280
Percent receiving financial aid out of those who apply, first year: 75%
Percent receiving financial aid among all students: 58%

Welcome to Milwaukee, the famous Brew City of Middle America. Cold weather, cold beer, and cheese are the staples of this lovely city, dotted with parks for hiking and picnicking and situated on the edge of sparkling Lake Michigan. Despite the icy weather and long winter, students of Marquette University are quite happy with their location and have plenty of school spirit to prove it. College unity transcends even the sports arena at this medium-sized urban university, as its Catholic affiliation pervades the student body, which takes pride in its religious traditions.

A Couple of Requirements

Marquette has much to offer in terms of academic variety across several schools, including colleges of Arts and Sciences, Communication, Nursing, Business Administration, Engineering, Health Sciences, and Education. Students enjoy the many options and varied resources, but they sometimes feel overwhelmed with the amount of requirements: 36 credits in areas including Rhetoric, Literature, Math, Diverse Cultures, and Science. The university strives to maintain the Jesuit tradition of strong theological education, with six credit hours required in that field. One student lightheartedly commented, "I am not a huge fan of all theology, but, God dammit, we go to a Jesuit university," while another said it was hard to cram everything into her schedule in addition to her major requirements.

As for majors, the ones attracting the most students are communication, business, and biomedical sciences (the latter being one of the hardest), along with journalism. Marquette has other strengths as well, such as its unique programs in dental hygiene and physical therapy and its study-abroad incentives. It is also associated with the Milwaukee Institute of Art and Design, a major perk for those interested in art.

Class size varies from major to major, but in general, courses range from large 200-person intro lectures to 12- to 30-student courses by junior and senior year as students further specialize. Even courses taken by first-year and second-year students are often small enough to foster a healthy, interactive relationship between the students and the professors. According to a current junior, "Every time I run into my old professors, even if I took their course my freshman year, they not only remember me but ask how I am doing. The professors are usually genuinely interested in your well-being as a student and a person."

There are virtually no complaints about the course load, as most students can afford to start partying on Thursday straight through Saturday, but spending up to 30 hours a week on schoolwork is not uncommon at Marquette. In addition, it is very common for students to double-major. Many seem happy not only with the education they are receiving, but also with the personal growth afforded by close contact with professors and great study-abroad opportunities. A junior political science and criminology major raved about her favorite professor: "She was very informal and had her office hours outside. She would always offer to go to the bars and things like that with us. She was great!" A couple of classes that were praised were Dynamic Media and Politics and Juvenile Delinquency, which took students to juvenile court for a field trip.

Getting Better at Diversity

Besides doing schoolwork, Marquette students fill their time up with a diverse array of extracurricular activities. There are many clubs on campus that reflect a variety of interest groups, from the medieval reenactment club to community service groups. According to one student, service is "huge" at Marquette, and a large percentage of the student body comes out for Hunger Clean-Up, a day of cleaning up around Milwaukee. Basketball is definitely the biggest sport on campus, and people holding tickets are referred to as "fanatics" for their enthusiastic school spirit. Games were described as "energetic, loud, lots of singing, lots of pride! Just plain fun!" by one student, who also mentioned that Notre Dame and Madison were big rival teams.

> **"Most students are Christian so they share some sort of unity in that."**

Although the extracurriculars on campus may be diverse, the student body is slightly less so. Many students are from the Wisconsin and Illinois area, especially from Chicago, and are Caucasian and conservative. One student summed it up as "no diversity at all." But another said that the school isn't just a sea of "homogenous Midwestern white Republican Christians—some of the students are, but plenty aren't." The Marquette administration is striving to diversify the school's homogenous population while still maintaining its Jesuit traditions. Many students enjoy the comfort of a uniform student body, and some frequently attend very traditional events like the Mass of the Holy Spirit at the Joan of Arc Chapel located at the center of campus. Students take pride in this beautiful service and enjoy the Catholic affiliation of their school. Says one, "Most students are Christian so they share some sort of unity in that." Still, another pointed out that "Marquette isn't such a tight community because all the people are the same, but rather because they are committed to similar ideals and goals."

The Scoop on Brew City Living

Party all the way, dude. Yes, as you would expect at this Catholic school, the weekend starts on Thursday and no one follows the "strict" alcohol policy. In the Brew City, bars and clubs are never lacking, although a timeless favorite among the student body is the Water Street Bar. Chilling with friends on campus often involves drinking; keggers are common and often revolve around the hype of the basketball games. There is also a moderately sized Greek system on campus that provides social outlets through a variety of theme parties. A notable annual party is the ABC: "anything but clothing." Such partying often leads to random hookups, but most agree that this is an underclassman trend. There is more to the social life than drinking, however, since Milwaukee offers a wide variety of cultural events, concerts, art exhibits, and shows. Because many students are from the area and get internships in the area during the summer, local summer festivals provide great entertainment. They pervade the city, and Milwaukee residents make merry with music, parades, drinking on the streets, and dancing. Irish Fest week is always popular among college students.

No [Insert Opposite Sex Here] Allowed!

Although students reportedly do not abide by the no-alcohol rules, they do abide by the rules in the dorms. When living with RAs and priests, there is no escaping the patrols. Although several dorms on campus are coed, members of the opposite sex are not allowed to visit after 1 a.m. on weeknights or 2 a.m. on weekends.

Frosh dorms are small and cramped, and some students described them as "rundown" and "sorta ghetto," definitely "not the cleanest." But the architecture of the eight residence halls on campus, along with that of some other buildings, is quite remarkable. It has a modern touch that has received mixed reviews. McCormick, which maintains a reputation for crazy revelry at all times, is a round building with pie-slice-shaped rooms. Tower and East are quieter and have typically shaped, larger rooms.

The upperclassman dorms get better, although a large number of students move off campus to nearby university-owned apartments after the first two years. Part of the draw of these more spacious quarters is the lack of living restrictions and RAs, not to mention the convenient nearby coffee shops and laundromats.

Although many Marquette students move off the main campus, no one feels isolated. Everything on campus and in the vicinity is "clumped together." This is convenient because all the main classroom buildings, the library, the St. Joan of Arc Chapel, and even the main dorms are easily accessible—no trudging long distances in the icy weather! Marquette also receives much praise from its student body for its fantastic gym and athletic facilities.

Although the gym and the library got rave reviews, the food provided by the dining halls did not: "Perhaps the worst part of the university," as one student referred to it. Not only is the food not tasty, but it's also unhealthy, which means students often subsist on pizza, chicken nuggets, and burgers. However, if you're into Papa John's Pizza or Jimmy John's sandwiches, this could be the place for you. A car on campus is useful for grocery shopping if you decline to be on the meal plan, and it can also be convenient for shopping, road trips to Chicago (only an hour and a half away), or simply exploring Milwaukee. Marquette is the sort of school that does not become a ghost town on weekends. It's fun and alive and has a lot of pride, school spirit, and a strong alumni connection. Satisfied with the education and college experience they receive, most say they would do it all over again if they could.
—*Carolina Galvao*

FYI

If you come to Marquette, you'd better bring "a good fake ID."

What is the typical weekend schedule? "Basketball games, bars, beer, enjoying the city of Milwaukee, and sleep."

If I could change one thing about Marquette, I would change "the food."

Three things every student at Marquette should do before graduating are "attend a game, attend at least one mass of the Holy Spirit, and study abroad."

University of Wisconsin / Madison

Address: 716 Langdon Street
Madison, WI 53706-1481
Phone: 608-262-3961
E-mail address: onwisconsin
@admissions.wisc.edu
Web site URL:
www.admissions.wisc.edu
Year Founded: 1848
Private or Public: Public
Religious Affiliation: None
Location: Urban
Number of Applicants: 25,478
Percent Accepted: 53%
Percent Accepted who
enroll: 43%
Number Entering: 7,067
Number of Transfers
Accepted each Year: 1,777
Middle 50% SAT range:
M: 620–730, CR: 540–670,
Wr: 570–670
Middle 50% ACT range:
26–30
Early admission program
EA/ED/None: None

Percentage accepted
through EA or ED: NA
EA and ED deadline: NA
Regular Deadline: 15-Nov,
1-Feb
Application Fee: $44
Full time Undergraduate
enrollment: 27,680
Total enrollment: 42,041
Percent Male: 47%
Percent Female: 53%
Total Percent Minority or
Unreported: 13%
Percent African-American:
3%
Percent Asian/Pacific
Islander: 6%
Percent Hispanic: 3%
Percent Native-American: 1%
Percent International: 6%
Percent in-state/out of
state: 66%/34%
Percent from Public HS:
Unreported
Retention Rate: 93%

Graduation Rate 4-year: 49%
Graduation Rate 6-year: 80%
Percent Undergraduates in
On-campus housing: 24%
Number of official organized
extracurricular
organizations: 700
3 Most popular majors:
Political Science, Biology,
Psychology
Student/Faculty ratio: 13:1
Average Class Size: 29
Percent of students going to
grad school: Unreported
Tuition and Fees: $21,820
In State Tuition and Fees if
different: $7,570
Cost for Room and Board:
$7,770
Percent receiving financial
aid out of those who apply,
first year: 54%
Percent receiving financial
aid among all students:
32%

C onsistently rated among the top 10 public universities in the nation, the University of Wisconsin/Madison is a thriving, bustling campus happily situated between two beautiful lakeshores in the heart of the city. The University is well-known and widely respected for its challenging academics, its strong athletic teams, its groundbreaking research in a variety of fields, and—most importantly—its large and terrifically vibrant study body.

Work Hard . . .
Because Madison is such a large university, it has the resources and the faculty available to offer its students more than 4,300 courses in over 100 majors. About half of the undergraduate student body enrolls in the College of Letters and Science, but other options for study include business, agriculture, engineering, and education in the University's other schools and colleges. Popular majors are psychology and economics (Madison has one of the best undergraduate business schools in the nation), while the majors offered in engineering are ruefully described

as "ridiculous" in terms of their level of difficulty. Certain majors are sometimes referred to as "underwater basket-weaving majors" in reference to their being undemanding and not particularly useful, although most students generally do respect courses of study different from their own. As for unusual majors, the University boasts an amazing African language department with an extremely popular class on the African storyteller. The course is taught by Harold Scheub, one of the world's foremost experts in the field. Generally speaking, the variety of departments and majors available for study is so remarkable that one recent graduate commented, "Even during my senior year, I kept meeting people whose majors I had never heard of!"

Class sizes vary from large introductory lectures to smaller classes as students become more specialized in their studies. Large classes almost always meet in smaller discussion groups, and most students say that even in big lectures they feel encouraged to ask questions without worrying about a professor being "insulted by the interruption."

In addition, professors are available to talk to anyone who makes an effort to get to know them during office hours or through e-mail. Registration for classes can be frustrating; the system is based on seniority by number of credits, so it is often difficult for underclassmen to get into the classes they want. The workload is "manageable if you have a good work ethic," with "plenty of opportunities to excel," including the Honors Program, the Medical Scholars Program, study abroad, research, or any number of double majors, minors and certificates. The motto at Madison has long been "Work hard, play hard," and most students can attest to the fact that "work hard" is no joke. As one junior noted, "People can overlook academics when they look at the school because they see us on TV during a Badger game when we're all pepped up and when we're not representing the academic rigor that goes on here." In truth, however, classes can be very challenging, which means that when the weekend rolls around, students are always ready to close their books and focus instead on maintaining their reputation as one of the top party schools in the nation.

. . . Party Hard . . .

A typical Madison weekend runs from Thursday to Saturday and includes everything from frat parties and room parties during the evenings to barbecues and tailgating on a game day. Of course, as at any school, the amount of partying that goes on really varies from person to person. Drinking is definitely a big part of the social scene—especially at the very popular parties along Frat Row—though there are always other social activities for those who would rather stay sober. Memorial Union, a popular student hangout located on the edge of Lake Mendota, has recently initiated "Fashionably Late," a series of gaming nights, movies, concerts, and shows "which are definitely an option if you don't feel like drinking." When asked if drinking was considered a problem on campus, most students felt that things usually settled down after freshman year when people began to solidify their groups of friends and stopped feeling like they had to go out every single weekend. Perhaps the craziest party night of the year is Halloween, when "out-of-towners flood into the city" and a crowd of 40,000 people celebrates all along State Street. Another famous Madison party is the Mifflin Street Block Party, a huge outdoor gathering right before the end of spring semester that boasts live bands and great barbecues.

A vast majority of students say they met their friends not at parties, but in class or through social organizations. Madison has hundreds of clubs and associations, including two great a cappella groups, a wide variety of intramural sports (including favorites such as badminton, dodgeball, and flag football in addition to the more commonly popular sports like Frisbee), and "clubs for everything." One well-known group is the Hoofers club, which offers a wide array of outdoor activities such as mountaineering, "outing" (hiking), riding, skiing and snowboarding, scuba, and sailing. There are also a lot of political action groups and religious groups. Joining a club is a great idea, students say, because "once you find your place on campus, it stops feeling so big."

> **"The amount of school spirit at this university is incredible."**

The student body, however, is not quite as diverse as the extracurriculars. While the school does attract a large group of international students, the majority of students hail from Wisconsin or the surrounding area. As one student put it, "We're just a nice bunch of Midwestern kids." The University is currently working on attracting more minority students and therefore improving cultural and racial diversity. Diversity does exist in terms of interests and backgrounds, said one student, because "there are just so many people who all come here with different beliefs and different life experiences."

. . . Play Hard

According to one student, "Madison is truly a college sports town." The campus "goes nuts" over football, hockey, basketball, and volleyball, switching off based on the season. "The amount of school spirit at this university is incredible," one person said. According to one student fan, "We have the most formidable student section in the country, and we've definitely turned the tide in a lot of close games." A member of the old-school style marching band explained that game day rehearsals start at 7:00 a.m. and end at 9:00 a.m., at which point the band members often run to the dorms and loudly play school songs outside students' windows. "Usually it's pretty hard to sleep in on game day, no matter where you are," he said. During the week, Madison students display their school spirit by wearing school sweatshirts, hats, T-shirts, and anything else Badger-related.

Even apart from the sports teams, students here have a lot of pride in their school and are always more than willing to show it off.

Life on the Lakes

The campus is situated on an isthmus between Lake Mendota and Lake Monona, a unique location that provides beautiful scenery as well as the resources for sailing, fishing, rowing, and a number of other outdoor activities. The University is also connected to the Capitol via State Street, which runs from the Capitol on one end to the library mall on the campus side, and offers visitors and students a wide variety of shops, restaurants, and theaters. State Street has everything from fine Italian restaurants such as Tutto Pasta to the quicker and more economical Noodles Inc., a multitude of other vegetarian and ethnic restaurants, a great cookie store, an impressive array of bars, vintage and off-beat clothing stores, and more commonly recognized stores like the Gap and Urban Outfitters. A walk through some of the shops on State Street can often be reminiscent of the University's "hippie days" of the '70s, when Madison was a hotspot for war protestors. Today the University retains its reputation as the stomping grounds for many liberal groups, and students say that there is always "some kind of protest happening on any given day on State Street." One student explained that a unique aspect of Madison is the variety of different environments in a small area. "You can walk through the whole campus in about 15 minutes, but within those 15 minutes you will cover everything from State Street and the downtown area, to the Capitol, to the lakeshore where you'll feel like you're in the North Woods, to the agriculture part of campus that looks like typical dairy-farm Wisconsin, and then back to the middle of campus and the academic world."

Dorm living is divided into three basic areas: the Southeast dorms, known as the party area; the Lakeshore dorms, a quieter, calmer area right on Lake Mendota; and the private dorms, which are "slightly more expensive but have a lower people-per-bathroom ratio." Students are assigned to dorms based on a "preference system" where they rate their housing choices. Each dorm area "has its own little community" with eating places, workout centers, and a particular atmosphere. A lot of students move into nearby apartments or Greek houses after a year or two in the dorms. The area around campus is relatively safe, and while students point out that you need to be as careful at night as you should be anywhere, many feel perfectly comfortable walking to or from parties either alone or in a group.

Dining hall food is said to be "adequate" and "always hot and ready." One student observed, "The food is good for the first couple of weeks, then they start serving the same stuff over and over again!" The meal plan works through a prepaid card, which students can use to buy convenience-store-style grocery items as well as to swipe in a standard cafeteria setting. The University is famous for its "wonderful" Babcock ice cream, made fresh right on campus in conjunction with the Food Science major in the College of Agricultural and Life Sciences. According to one student, "You can even visit the cows that they're milking!" Architecture on campus is described as a "random mix" of old and modern, and the University is currently undergoing several renovation projects.

On Wisconsin!

All things considered, most students at the University of Wisconsin-Madison are satisfied with their college choice. Its huge size provides students with a wealth of opportunities both inside the classroom and out, but everyone is still able to find his or her own smaller community of classmates and friends. One student commented, "At first I wasn't happy about going to a big state school because I thought I'd just be a number. But if you approach it as a challenge and as a place where there are opportunities for development and ways to distinguish yourself, the possibilities are limitless." And in a perfect example of the famous school spirit, when asked if she would choose Madison if she could do everything over again, one recent graduate replied, "Absolutely! Go Badgers!"—*Lindsay Starck*

FYI

If you come to the University of Wisconsin/Madison, you'd better bring "something red—school spirit here is huge."

What's the typical weekend schedule? "Friday night: party; Saturday: sleep in, then party, especially if there's a game; Sunday: study."

If I could change one thing about the University of Wisconsin/Madison, I'd "introduce a better bus system."

Three things every student at the University of Wisconsin/Madison should do before graduating are "go sledding down Bascom Hill, go to a Badger game and stay for the fifth quarter, and enjoy a cool evening at the Terrace on Lake Mendota—it's beautiful!"

Wyoming

University of Wyoming

Address: 1000 E. University Avenue, Laramie, WY 82071
Phone: 307-766-1121
E-mail address: why-wyo@uwyo.edu
Web site URL: www.uwyo.edu
Year Founded: 1886
Private or Public: Public
Religious Affiliation: None
Location: Suburban
Number of Applicants: 3,371
Percent Accepted: 96%
Percent Accepted who enroll: 51%
Number Entering: 1,633
Number of Transfers Accepted each Year: 1,474
Middle 50% SAT range: M: 500–640, CR: 470–610, Wr: Unreported
Middle 50% ACT range: 21–26
Early admission program EA/ED/None: None
Percentage accepted through EA or ED: NA

EA and ED deadline: NA
Regular Deadline: 10-Aug
Application Fee: $40
Full time Undergraduate enrollment: 9,492
Total enrollment: 12,433
Percent Male: 49%
Percent Female: 51%
Total Percent Minority or Unreported: 9%
Percent African-American: 1%
Percent Asian/Pacific Islander: 2%
Percent Hispanic: 3%
Percent Native-American: 1%
Percent International: 1%
Percent in-state/out of state: 43%/57%
Percent from Public HS: Unreported
Retention Rate: 74%
Graduation Rate 4-year: Unreported

Graduation Rate 6-year: Unreported
Percent Undergraduates in On-campus housing: 21%
Number of official organized extracurricular organizations: 198
3 Most popular majors: Business/Marketing, Education, Engineering
Student/Faculty ratio: 15:1
Average Class Size: 20 to 29
Percent of students going to grad school: Unreported
Tuition and Fees: $11,031
In State Tuition and Fees if different: $3,621
Cost for Room and Board: $7,707
Percent receiving financial aid out of those who apply, first year: 56%
Percent receiving financial aid among all students: 45%

Not many universities can claim a location at 7,200 feet. Amidst mountain ranges and grassy plains, the height only adds to the remote, yet urban setting of the University of Wyoming, one that most students come to love. With the University of Wyoming being the only big college in the state, the University continually draws fans to cheer for the brown and gold.

The State University

With just over 8,000 undergraduates claiming their loyalty to UW, many students feel that the size is perfect. One sophomore commented that the student body population is "the perfect size, enabling individual attention and creating an atmosphere for better learning, but also big enough to see unfamiliar faces." Like any university, the class sizes vary with specialization. While introductory courses can range anywhere from 200 to 500 students, the higher-level courses cater to crowds of 30 students or less.

At U of Wyoming, one will find most students looking to major in Business Administration or Education, but don't be fooled, Wyoming offers a variety of fun areas of study. "In order to fulfill the physical education requirement, I've known people who have taken Ballroom Dancing, Ballet, and even Tai Chi," one senior said. The University of Wyoming offers strong honors programs and boasts fantastic engineering and research science departments. In order to qualify for the honors program at Wyoming, high school students must have a minimum 3.7 GPA, at least a 1240 combined score on the SAT, or composite ACT scores of at least 28. Honor students are required to take five honors courses throughout their time at

UW, two freshman year and one each of the three remaining years. One student at UW commented that the courseload was "pretty manageable, but continued to get more difficult as you go. The honors classes and the science courses are amongst the most challenging."

A Little Too Small

Similar to many campuses, most students at Wyoming usually move off campus after freshman year. For those students still on campus, their housing options include Wyoming's six dorm buildings located at the center of campus, "Prexy's Pasture." With the ability to move off campus, approximately 50 percent of sophomores do so along with almost all the juniors and seniors. "It's sort of a rite of passage to be able to live off campus. Although it's nice to live close to classes, living off campus is really liberating: no restrictions and no RAs," commented one Wyoming senior. As far as the architectural style of the University is concerned, students find it somewhat uninviting. The cement facades seem to emphasize the barren winter months. However, the University is undergoing "a lot of renovation and is committed to modernizing all of campus."

For those students still living on campus, the dining halls are one of Wyoming's best features: "The dining halls are all renovated and the food offered by UW is actually really good. There's a lot of variety and the food is pretty fresh," one freshman noted. Open until 10:30 p.m., the dining halls resemble more of a food court than a dining hall. Off-campus students don't have to miss out. Local businesses are able to serve Wyoming students through the use of their WyoOne ID cards. Thus, all students can take advantage of a late-night slice of pizza or cup of coffee with the swipe of a card.

A Separate Place

Students can feel a true sense of community in Laramie. With only 25,000 people occupying the small town, more than half are students. As great as a small-town community may feel, it can be a bit restricting, "Laramie is about a two-hour drive from anywhere. Most students will usually stay on campus," one sophomore said. But most students do have cars, so the possibility for escape is always there. When on campus, upperclassmen mostly hit the bar scene, with Lovejoy's Bar and Grill and Altitude Chophouse & Brewery being two favorites. Underclassmen usually either attend the usual frat parties or

make their way to the athletes' houses. Because many upperclassmen live off campus, the underclassmen "don't really intermingle regularly with juniors and seniors unless they are a part of the same team or organization," one junior said. The University of Wyoming has a strict policy against alcohol in the dorms and really tries to curb underage drinking, but "alcohol is very accessible" nonetheless. The big event all students can look forward to is the annual Beach Party that one on-campus frat puts on. "The frat actually drags sand in and transforms the entire house into a beach. It's pretty fun; everyone goes," one sophomore said.

> "I think the fact that the entire state of Wyoming is behind the university and all of its programs means a lot to the students here."

Although it is hard for some students to feel so isolated, Laramie has many other kinds of attractions, including its breathtaking scenery. The surrounding areas include everything from grassy plains to rocky climbing areas. With a mountainous landscape in the background, many students rock climb, hike, or even ski at Snowy Range or Happy Jack. On weekends, many students set aside a day to head up to the mountains and get some fresh air.

Saddle Up for the Gold and Brown

With an overall student body of over 12,000, many students find their niches in diverse activities. Varsity athletics are valued highly. With football and basketball bringing in the biggest crowds, other sports draw supportive crowds as well. "As a swimmer at Wyoming, I am proud to say that we bring in more spectators at home meets than any other school in our conference," remarked one junior. Wyoming also emphasizes an active lifestyle by providing 18 different club sports, involving nearly 6,000 students, faculty, and staff. UW's Half Acre Gym is a "hot spot to hang out and one of the most noteworthy buildings on campus." Life at UW is one of comfort. Many students will show up to class in sweats and sometimes pajamas. The general feel is that the atmosphere is easygoing and laid-back, but where school spirit is concerned, the Cowboys and Cowgirls find themselves very well supported.

Nowhere Else

Students across the nation have school pride; that's a given. But for students at the University of Wyoming, it's deeper than that. The community involvement is really treasured, and the people are friendly. "First and foremost, I go to the University of Wyoming. I think the fact that the entire state of Wyoming is behind the university and all of its programs means a lot to the students here. Also, I think that the small community brings the students here closer together."—*Taylor Ritzel*

FYI

If you come to the University of Wyoming, you'd better bring a "big winter coat and anything that protects you from the wind."

What is the typical weekend schedule? "Party Fridays, sleep and climb Saturdays, party Saturday nights, and study on Sundays."

If I could change one thing about the University of Wyoming, I'd "get rid of the wind. The weather can be really nice on any given day, but the wind ruins the day."

Three things every student at the University of Wyoming should do before graduating are "ski at Snowy Range, attend a home UW football game, and hike Vedauwoo."

Canada

Despite Canada's image as a country of winter storms and glaciers, thousands of American students cross the border every year to seek an education from their country's northern neighbor. The reasons for this northbound move range from low tuition to beautiful landscape to high educational standards. Given the numerous advantages of attending Canadian universities, it is certainly worthwhile for American students to take a close look.

Money Matters

One important factor in choosing which college to attend is money. In that respect, Canadian universities, which are all public, have significant advantages over their American counterparts. The tuition rates at the most expensive schools are generally below $8,000 for Canadians. Even for American citizens, the average rate hovers below $20,000, much cheaper than the price tags of many universities in the United States, which are rapidly approaching $40,000.

Another major expense that students will face, the cost of living, depends greatly on location—living in Toronto is certainly more expensive than, say, Wolfville, Nova Scotia, but it is still cheaper than a number of cities in the United States. American students in need of financial aid can apply for Stafford loans from the federal government, even if they study in Canada. Both merit- and need-based scholarships are also available.

The low fees, however, come with a disadvantage. Funding for universities in Canada depends on the government. This means that they tend to have fewer resources than many private institutions in the United States. In general, however, the overall impact of tight government funding on the quality of education is minimal, especially for undergraduates.

A Whole Different Country

Each Canadian province maintains its own system of higher education. For example, in Quebec, most students attend a post-secondary program called a College of General and Vocational Education (CEGEP) prior to enrollment in universities, making the academic programs more specialized. In fact, unlike many American universities, which encourage students to study in a wide range of subjects, Canadian schools tend to place greater emphasis on career preparation.

Most American students studying in Canada choose to attend one of the major research universities, creating the perception that undergraduate education in Canada is always within large, impersonal institutions located in urban centers. While it is true that the better-known universities, such as McGill University and the University of Toronto, enroll tens of thousands of undergraduate and graduate students, there are plenty of smaller, predominantly undergraduate schools housing only a few thousand students, very similar to liberal arts colleges in the United States. Choices abound for those who would like to escape the noises of bustling cities and settle in the countryside.

One aspect of college life that Canada fails to offer is school spirit. Although students wear their college gear and cheer for their sports teams, their attachment to their schools is not as strong as in the United States, many students say. This is in part because intercollegiate sports are not as important in Canada. Youngsters who aspire to become professional athletes mostly rise through junior leagues instead of collegiate competitions. Furthermore, the large number of students in off-campus housing diminishes the sense of community in many universities.

Getting in

The admissions process in Canada places greater emphasis on grades and standardized test scores than do American universities. Although extracurricular activities and achievements outside of school are also considered, academic performance significantly outweighs everything else. Many schools even set cutoff limits for SAT scores and high school GPAs. Of course, this is not universal, and different schools have different policies regarding admissions.

Studying in Canada for non–Canadian citizens requires a student visa, which is easy to obtain once the student is admitted. Just like those in the United States, Canadian universities attract thousands of students from around the world every year. The cold weather and the differences in college life may turn away many American students, but given its quality of education and affordability, Canada is certainly a great destination for college students and deserves strong consideration.—*Xiaohang Liu*

Carleton University

Address: 1125 Colonel BY Drive, 315 Robertson Hall Ottawa, ON K1S5B6
Phone Number(s): 613-520-3663
E-mail address: liaison@admissions.carleton.ca
Web site URL: www.carleton.ca
Year Founded: 1945
Private or Public: Private
Religious affiliation: None
Location: Urban
Number of Applicants: Unreported
Percent Accepted: 73%
Percent Accepted who enroll: Varies by Program
Number Entering: 5,000
Number of Transfers Accepted each Year: 830
Middle 50% SAT range: Unreported
Middle 50% ACT range: Unreported
Early admission program (EA/ED/None): None

Percentage accepted through EA or ED: NA
EA/ED deadline: NA
Regular Deadline: Rolling
Application Fee: CA$85
Full time Undergraduate enrollment: 20,746
Total enrollment: 23,161
Percent Male: 50%
Percent Female: 50%
Total Percent Minority or Unreported: Unreported
Percent African-American: Unreported
Percent Asian/Pacific Islander: Unreported
Percent Hispanic: Unreported
Percent Native-American: Unreported
Percent International: Unreported
Percent in-province/out of province: 85%/15%
Percent from Public HS: Unreported
Retention Rate: Varies by Program

Graduation Rate (4-year): Unreported
Graduation Rate (6-year): Unreported
Percent in On-campus housing: 15%
Number of official organized extracurricular organizations: 78
3 Most popular majors: Varies by Program
Student/Faculty ratio: 26:1
Average Class Size: 2 to 9
Percent of students going to grad school: Unreported
Tuition and Fees: CA$14,936
In Province Tuition and Fees (if different): CA$4,794
Cost for Room and Board: CA$7,247
Percent receiving Financial aid, first-year (out of those who apply): Unreported
Percent of Undergraduates Receiving Financial Aid: Unreported

Located in Ottawa, Ontario, Carleton University combines the splendor of Canada's English-speaking capital city with the French-Canadian culture of nearby Québec. In addition to a treasure trove of national museums, government buildings, memorials, and celebrations of heritage, safe and scenic Ottawa offers trendy night spots, sidewalk cafés, hiking trails, the beautiful Rideau Canal that turns into the world's largest skating rink, and world-class research and development facilities in technology and medicine. Carleton students benefit from abundant opportunities for co-ops, internships, and real-world field experience as well as their school's challenging academic programs in a variety of areas.

Pre-Professionalism

Carleton is best known for its challenging professional programs in journalism, architecture, engineering, and public affairs. The school is one of only two universities in Canada to offer a degree in aerospace engineering, and the program has been growing quickly in recent years. Students within this major choose to focus on aerodynamics, propulsion and vehicle performance; aerospace structures, systems, and vehicle design; aerospace electronics and systems; or space systems design, and everyone must complete a final independent project before graduation. Many students take advantage of the option to take an aerospace engineering co-op internship instead of classes during their fourth year of enrollment, although this decision stretches the time required for graduation to five years. Carleton's program in criminology and criminal justice is also quite popular, and the proximity of the Parliamentary and other governmental buildings in Canada's capital city allows for a unique experience in field placement for internships. Criminology majors can choose to intern with attorneys, policy analysts, police, or victim counselors, to name a few of the options that present an exceptional opportunity to learn about the discipline from a front-line, hands-on perspective. The University's College of the Humanities offers a four-year, interdisciplinary Bachelor of Humanities degree focusing on the great Western canon. There students read a veritable "who's who" list of the most well-known historical works in Western civilization, including selections by Plato, Homer, Virgil, Shakespeare, Molière, and Kant. Although well-rounded, this major does not necessarily come with the best reputation, as one non-humanities student admitted to hearing that the program is "easy" and "basically for people who have less of a clue about what they want to do with themselves than people studying the arts." Carleton also boasts one of the "best journalism programs in Canada," which prepares students to become premiere journalists with an understanding of the responsibility of the press and which incorporates short apprenticeships as well as the possibility of specializing in print or broadcast media.

Carleton offers a program called ArtsOne for first-year students who have not yet chosen a major and who are undecided about which courses they should take when they arrive. This program, which offers several different sets, or "clusters," of four courses revolving around a particular theme, contributes to the eventual awarding of a Bachelor of Arts degree. One hundred students enroll in each cluster and thus take all of the same classes, providing a smaller peer group within the larger university and a way to establish a home base of friends.

Professors at Carleton can be "eccentric," "enthusiastic," and "witty," and students generally find them to be easily accessible and very helpful. The most popular professors understandably tend to be the most dynamic and engaging: Professor Matthew Yeager of the sociology and anthropology department, for example, asks his students to call him "Thunder" as a reflection of his unique, theatrical lecturing style (although as one student warned, "do not sit in the front rows, or even at the edge of any row, because he THUNDERS around the class!").

Students at Carleton are known for being welcoming and sociable and, according to one student, "it's easy to meet people because everyone at school is very friendly and willing to talk to people they don't know. Most people are in the same situation: they're in a new city where they don't know anyone and they are looking for friends to fill the loneliness of missing home." The school also prides itself on the carefully cultivated diversity within its student body and boasts a high rate of international enrollment with more than 140 different countries represented.

Tunnel Moles and Party Rats

Carleton offers underground, well-lit, heated tunnels that connect every building on campus and allow students to travel between their dorm rooms and classrooms in warmth and comfort as the outside temperatures drop to an average high of 21°F in January. The tunnels are appreciated by under- and upperclassmen alike, but as one student notes, this method of travel can become a way of life: "Some students living in the residence halls can go for months without actually seeing daylight! We call them tunnel-rats or tunnel-moles. But the tunnels do make going to school in one of the coldest cities (in this part of Canada) a lot easier." Luckily, the campus is fairly compact, and walking from one class to another takes only a few minutes.

"You don't mess with the R.A.s."

Housed in "institutional, modern and artsy style buildings," undergraduates at Carleton can choose between two major options for dorm life: "Suite Style" residence halls such as Leeds and Prescott come equipped with various kitchen appliances in each room, while "Traditional Style" dorms do not permit in-room cooking and instead require students to buy a meal plan and eat in the Residence Dining Hall or in the various additional on-campus food outlets. The resident advisors in each dorm can be pretty strict about upholding the rules; as one of their undergraduate charges put it, "you don't mess with the R.A.s." Most students move out of the residence halls, or "res," after their first year and relocate to apartments off campus. However, "there are a few lifers who love res too much to ever leave and go on to be Residence Advisors or just live in upper-year residences for the duration of their schooling."

The drinking age in Ontario is 19, and students who have reached this birthday milestone are permitted to bring alcohol into their rooms within the residence halls but must refrain from carrying it outside or into shared dorm spaces such as stairways, lobbies, and elevators. Binge drinking exists as at any other college, but it is not especially prevalent; marijuana use, on the other hand, is "a big thing," and students "see people smoking weed pretty much every day."

The weeknight social scene revolves around Carleton's on-campus pub, Oliver's. Oliver's tends to be extremely popular on Tuesdays and particularly Thursdays, when "everyone from different social circles attends and intermingles," providing an excellent opportunity for meeting new people. In contrast, weekends are "usually left for parties and other clubbing and bar experiences throughout the city." Because Carleton is located in the suburbs of Ottawa rather than in the middle of the city, "the social scene right around the school is a little lacking," but students can reach the downtown area very quickly thanks to the city's efficient transit system. Students also like to hang out in the food court in the recently renovated University Centre, particularly in the student-run Rooster's Coffeehouse, which offers an assortment of coffees and teas as well as a seating area in front of a wide-screen TV. Underclassmen who have not yet reached Ontario's drinking age often journey into Hull, Québec, about 15 to 20 minutes away by car, where the legal age of imbibing is only 18 and where "the bars are all scuzzy but promise a good time."

No Football? No Problem

Carleton does not have a varsity football team—it was disbanded in 1999—and instead, school pride rests with the successes of the "best men's basketball team in Canada," according to one enthusiastic student. Indeed, the Ravens seldom disappoint and have won many championships and titles, including the Canadian Interuniversity Sport (CIS) National Championship Tournament for five consecutive years between 2002 and 2007. The school's rivalry with the nearby University of Ottawa keeps the competition heated when the two basketball teams meet on the court. Carleton also hosts varsity fencing, golf, hockey, rugby, and water polo, among many other sports, as well as a variety of intramurals, including flag football for the pigskin enthusiasts who bemoan the loss of the varsity team. The Physical Recreation Centre, the largest facility of its kind in Canada, features two gymnasiums, a 50-meter indoor pool, a cardio center, a fitness testing lab, squash and tennis courts, a yoga room, and the Ice House skating and hockey rink, and serves the student body with training programs and services to accommodate everyone from beginner athletes to professionals.

As with many universities located in colder climates, the CU Ski and Snowboard Club is a popular organization on campus. Every fall, this organization generally sponsors a big hip-hop show accompanied by ski and snowboard movie premieres that caters to "the hip-hop community, the ski and snowboard community, and the drinking community (party people)." Carleton also offers over 150 student-run organizations, including the sexagenarian weekly campus newspaper *The Charlatan*, the Sock 'n' Buskin Theatre Company, the community radio station CKCU-FM, and the Rideau River Residence Association (RRRA), which oversees students living on campus in the dorms. Generally, Carleton "frowns on frats and sororities," but they do exist off campus, and all Greek activities operate without University support.

Undergraduates at Carleton University generally exhibit enthusiasm and pride when discussing their alma mater and appreciate their school's efforts to keep them happy, from the underground tunnel system to the dedicated professors, from the friendly rivalry with the University of Ottawa to the co-op opportunities sponsored and arranged by the various academic departments. As one student summed up, "the atmosphere at Carleton is very positive. Everyone seems to really enjoy being at school and everyone is proud to be a student here."—*Kristin Knox*

FYI
If you come to Carleton, you'd better bring "a good supply of winter clothing."
What is the typical weekend schedule? "Attempt to do work on Saturday but instead choose to go
  to Ottawa and have fun. Then on Sunday you really try to get work done."
If I could change one thing about Carleton, I'd "take away dry frosh week (no drinking events)."
Three things every student at Carleton should do before graduating are "climb all the stairs in
  Dunton Tower (if you don't, you're doomed to be jobless forever!), jump in the Alumni Park
  fountain during convocation, and hang out at Oliver's."

McGill University

Address: 845 Sherbrooke Street West Montreal, Canada H3A 2T5
Phone Number(s): 514-398-3910
E-mail address: admissions@mcgill.ca
Web site URL: www.mcgill.ca
Year Founded: 1821
Private or Public: Public
Religious affiliation: None
Location: Urban
Number of Applicants: 20,391
Percent Accepted: 54%
Percent Accepted who enroll: 43%
Number Entering: 4,781
Number of Transfers Accepted each Year: 933
Middle 50% SAT range: M: 640-720, CR: 640-740, Wr: 650-720
Middle 50% ACT range: 29-31
Early admission program (EA/ED/None): None
Percentage accepted through EA or ED: NA

EA/ED deadline: NA
Regular Deadline: 15-Jan
Application Fee: CA$80
Full time Undergraduate enrollment: 20,459
Total enrollment: 29,585
Percent Male: 40%
Percent Female: 60%
Total Percent Minority or Unreported: Unreported
Percent African-American: Unreported
Percent Asian/Pacific Islander: Unreported
Percent Hispanic: Unreported
Percent Native-American: Unreported
Percent International: Unreported
Percent in-province/out of province: 61% /39%
Percent from Public HS: Unreported
Retention Rate: 92%
Graduation Rate (4-year): 68%

Graduation Rate (6-year): 83%
Percent in On-campus housing: 11%
Number of official organized extracurricular organizations: Unreported
3 Most popular majors: Business/Commerce, Political Science, Psychology
Student/Faculty ratio: 16:1
Average Class Size: 10 to 19
Percent of students going to grad school: Unreported
Tuition and Fees: CA$13,965 to CA$15,420
In Province Tuition and Fees (if different): Unreported
Cost for Room and Board: CA$7,694
Percent receiving Financial aid, first-year (out of those who apply): Unreported
Percent of Undergraduates Receiving Financial Aid: Unreported

I f you're looking for a truly international college experience, look no further than McGill University in Montreal, Quebec. While the Canadian university system is not well known in the United States, the caliber of students that McGill attracts from all over the world and its emphasis on undergraduate studies make it a top-tier international institution. Founded in 1821 by James McGill, a prominent Montreal merchant, this publicly funded university boasts a diverse student body, a cosmopolitan setting, and, as a result of recent efforts, top research facilities.

Parlez-vous français?
Located in Montreal, the second-largest French speaking city in the world, McGill is one of only three English-language universities in the province of Quebec. Most students do not consider McGill to be a "bilingual school." "If you want to immerse yourself in French, Montreal is a great place to start, but if you don't want to learn a word, it's not a problem," said a junior political science major. With the exception of the Faculty of Law, students are not required to speak or learn French. However, the influence and presence

of French and francophone culture is integral to the McGill experience. As one senior said, "It's wonderful to hear a mix of French and English being spoken on campus since it truly gives the cultural experience I was looking for." Since 1964, students in all faculties have had the option to write exams and papers in either English or French. While less-than-perfect *français* is not a problem in the classroom, don't attempt to use developing language skills in the streets of Montreal: "If you try to speak French the Montreal-ers will respond in English—they know a fakie when they hear one."

Eleven Faculties

Given McGill's international campus culture, it is only fitting that McGill has a very diverse student body where international students are a significant presence. Close to 20 percent of McGill's student body is comprised of international students, a third of which are American. These students are attracted to McGill for its European feel, diverse culture, and the relatively reasonable tuition. Since 1996, McGill has been following the Ministry of Education, Leisure and Sports guidelines by exempting qualified international students from paying certain tuition fees. Due to this financial policy, more American students are expressing an interest in McGill and other Canadian schools close to the border.

In order to meet the interests of this diverse, multilingual student body, McGill has 13 different departments called faculties. Unlike most American universities, prospective students apply to each faculty, rather than applying to the university as a whole. Some of these faculties include the Schulich School of Music, the Faculty of Dentistry, and the Desautels Faculty of Management. A third of all students are enrolled in the Faculty of Arts, while the Centre for Continuing Education, the Faculty of Science, and the Faculty of Engineering all enroll around 10 percent each. Some students complain that the mandatory introductory classes in each of these faculties can result in 500-person lectures that are "impersonal" and "intimidating." However, one upperclassman claimed that "it gets better after those entry-level courses." Once students are done with the requirements, there are many thought-provoking and unique electives to choose from.

The "Rez"

McGill's main campus is situated in downtown Montreal by Mount Royal, a beautiful park enjoyed by students and denizens of Montreal for its walking trails. It is close to the metro stations of McGill and Peel, often filled with off-campus students. Once you enter through the Roddick Gates, you are surrounded by a refreshing mix of gray limestone architecture and trees, where it is easy to forget that you are in the bustling business district of Montreal.

The second campus, the Macdonald Campus, is home to the natural sciences such as the Faculty of Agricultural and Environmental Science and the School of Dietetics and Human Nutrition. The Macdonald Campus has a hands-on approach to learning and focuses on preparing students for careers in science and technology.

> "If you want to immerse yourself in French, Montreal is a great place to start, but if you don't want to learn a word, it's not a problem."

Unlike those at many American colleges, after their first year, McGill students do not stay in residence halls, colloquially known as "rez." Although accepted first-year students are guaranteed on-campus housing, due to the limited space, upperclassmen are expected to find housing off campus. A freshman at McGill reports that living in residence "is definitely a great way to meet people, but it can get pretty loud in the hallways sometimes." There are four main rezzes you can live in. Most freshmen live in Upper Rez (officially Bishop Mountain Residences). Royal Victoria College was a women's university turned women's-only residence hall. Solin Hall is an apartment-style residence four metro stops away from central campus. The most coveted residence is New Residence Hall. New Rez was originally a four-star hotel, and students describe it as being superior in décor, space, and food. "They have sushi, steak, whatever you want, basically," says one former inhabitant of New Rez.

Beware of the McGill Bubble

Finding off-campus housing can be a bit of a hassle for McGill students. Although there are many university-owned apartments, some students have trouble finding off-campus housing due to strict housing markets and rising rents in the areas near campus. The section of Montreal dubbed McGill Ghetto, an area east of the campus, seems to be growing in popularity among McGill students. Despite the complications of living off campus, most upperclassmen like living on their own:

"Unlike a lot of U.S. schools, McGill really lets you be an adult. I am 21; I can make my own food."

Another reason why students love living off campus is because they can explore the city of Montreal. "There is really no shortage of things to do in Montreal!" gushed one literature major. The city provides something different for every taste. For those who enjoy bar- and club-hopping, the streets of St. Laurent, St. Denis, and Ste. Catherine are lively with students on the weekends. For those who prefer a more relaxing scene, there are many jazz venues and lounges to be discovered. Students describe the people of Montreal and McGill as very accepting and tolerant, and the city as very gay-friendly. Because the city and the university are so integrated, many students warn of getting caught in the "McGill Bubble." One senior said, "Since I am always surrounded by students, I don't have a sense of living in a 'real-world' community."

Because so many students live off campus, most of the weekend activities take place off campus as well. The drinking age in Quebec is 18, so throughout their McGill career, students have easy access to bars, pubs, and alcohol. There are also several on-campus events that are not to be missed. In the warmer month of September, students flock to the lower field to partake in the outdoor open-air pub commonly known as OAP. Another event fondly looked back on is Frosh, the first week of freshman year. "Basically a week of non-stop drinking and debauchery," reminisced one sophomore.

A Society of Students

If McGill students mostly reside off campus, what do they do on campus? In a school with over 20,000 undergraduates, one of the ways in which McGill students form communities amongst themselves is through clubs. There are over 150 student clubs and organizations to choose from. Students can be involved in everything from performance art to political action. Through some of these clubs, McGill students contribute to the community as well. Healthy Minds is an organization devoted to visiting children in hospitals, and Santropol Roulant is a student-run organization that delivers over 100 hot meals a day to housebound senior citizens.

The core of all of these student activities is the University Centre on the main campus. The William Shatner University Centre is a place for students to hang out with their friends, watch TV, play foosball, and hold club meetings. Named after William Shatner, alumnus and actor on *Star Trek*, the facility includes a food court, a legal clinic, a pub, and a lounge, all run by the Students' Society of McGill University. The SSMU is a student union that not only serves as an umbrella organization for many student activities but also serves as the voice of the student body. "I appreciate the efforts that SSMU goes through to makes sure our needs and voices are heard by the administration," said one senior. "It definitely brings the McGill student body together."—*Lee Komeda*

FYI

If you come to McGill, "you'd better bring a Canadian phone, a strong liver, and a good work ethic."

What's the typical weekend schedule? "A lot of reading and essay writing but also a lot of fun! On Saturdays you can head down to St. Laurent, St. Denis, or Ste. Catherine streets to have dinner with friends, then go to a bar, club, or a relaxing lounge. On Sundays you can take in a gallery show, go to a concert, or stroll down to the Old Port for a glass of wine."

If I could change one thing about McGill, I'd "make the final examination dates part of the syllabus (we wait until November, which makes booking a ticket home for Christmas costly)."

Three things every student at McGill should do before graduating are "get trashed during Frosh Week, go to Winter Carnival, enjoy OAP in September."

McMaster University

Address: Gilmour Hall Room
108, 1280 Main Street
W. Hamilton, Ontario,
Canada L8S4L8
Phone Number(s):
905-525-9140
E-mail address:
macadmit@mcmaster.ca
Web site URL:
www.mcmaster.ca
Year Founded: 1887
Private or Public: Public
Religious affiliation: None
Location: Suburban
Number of Applicants:
Unreported
Percent Accepted: Varies by
Program
**Percent Accepted who
enroll:** Varies by Program
Number Entering: Unreported
**Number of Transfers
Accepted each Year:**
Unreported
Middle 50% SAT range:
Minimum score of 580 for
Critical Reading and 520 for
Math
Middle 50% ACT range:
Minimum score of 27

**Early admission program
(EA/ED/None):** None
**Percentage accepted
through EA or ED:** NA
EA/ED deadline: NA
Regular Deadline: 9-Feb
Application Fee: Varies by
Program
**Full time Undergraduate
enrollment:** 20,600
Total enrollment: 27,337
Percent Male: Unreported
Percent Female: Unreported
**Total Percent Minority or
Unreported:** Unreported
Percent African-American:
Unreported
**Percent Asian/Pacific
Islander:** Unreported
Percent Hispanic: Unreported
Percent Native-American:
Unreported
Percent International:
Unreported
**Percent in-province/out of
province:** Unreported
Percent from Public HS:
Unreported
Retention Rate: Varies by
Program

Graduation Rate (4-year):
Unreported
Graduation Rate (6-year):
Unreported
**Percent in On-campus
housing:** Unreported
**Number of official organized
extracurricular
organizations:** Unreported
3 Most popular majors:
Vaires by Program
Student/Faculty ratio: Varies
by Program
Average Class Size: Varies by
Program
**Percent of students going to
grad school:** Unreported
Tuition and Fees: CA$13,693 -
$20,611 for visa students
**In Province Tuition and Fees
(if different):** Unreported
Cost for Room and Board:
Dependent on residence and
meal plan
**Percent receiving Financial
aid, first-year (out of those
who apply):** Unreported
**Percent of Undergraduates
Receiving Financial Aid:**
Unreported

Sprawling over 300 green acres and studded with ivy-covered Gothic buildings, McMaster is regarded as one of the top universities in Canada. The University is named after Senator William McMaster, who in 1887 bequeathed a large sum of money to found a "Christian school of learning." Today, the affectionately named "Mac" is home to around 20,600 students and stands as an undisputed center for ground-breaking research and innovation.

Bring on the Innovation!

If there is one thing that students agree on, it's the breathtaking variety of programs that McMaster offers, with majors ranging from anthropology and women's studies to software engineering and Italian. Both basic three-year programs and four-year "Honors Programs" are available. The Honors Programs usually require a higher GPA than

their three-year counterparts, as well as an application.

McMaster is especially well-known for its health sciences, business, natural sciences, and engineering departments. Not surprisingly, these are also some of the most difficult programs. "Math is ridiculously hard," said one fourth-year behavioral science major. "Sometimes the introductory classes become very difficult because they are designed to weed out students." But most science majors agree that it's worth it. Kinesiology, the study of human bodily movement, is especially acclaimed among undergrads.

Even if you're not into the hard-core sciences, McMaster still offers a great range of humanities courses. The limited-enrollment Arts & Science program is touted by current students as a great way to get a broad-based liberal arts education. "The Arts & Science program offers a carefully constructed program drawing from both the sciences and humanities," explained one student. Approximately 60 students enroll in this program each year, and its small class sizes guarantee that the students get plenty of attention from their professors.

Outside of the Arts & Science program, McMaster's classes tend to be quite large, especially freshman year. "First year, 300 in a lecture, easily," said one fourth-year. "But when you get into upper-level classes, they become more and more specialized. One of my current classes has 10 students." Another student agreed, advising newcomers not to be intimidated by larger lectures. "First year is full of lectures, but we have tutorials once a week with a TA. One of my favorite classes was Intro to Psych, which is a huge, impersonal class in most colleges. At Mac, we had the professor on video lecture, and when it was done, the TA's there to answer questions for us. It was really interactive and cool." Indeed, for a large research university, students agreed that professors and TAs are readily available and easy to approach, often giving McMaster the feeling of a small liberal arts college.

> **"What defines McMaster really is the diversity of its students . . . [And we're] always on the cutting edge of teaching methods."**

One of the more peculiar things about a McMaster education is its grading scale. Classes at McMaster grade on a zero to 12 scale, zero being fail, one being pass, and 12 being an A+. Students are required to have an average of seven (or a B in most colleges) in order to move up to the next level. In general, students seem to enjoy this method of grading, because it is more specific than simple letter grades. However, some lament that this results in a stricter curve, the disadvantages of which are especially felt within the science sectors.

McMaster is renowned, above all, for its innovative teaching. One of the most interesting facets is the "Inquiry" program, in which a student can form an inquiry problem and explore his or her chosen problem with the help of an instructor, called a "facilitator." The "Inquiry" program has been expanded to most disciplines at McMaster. While it's inventive, there are downsides. One student complained that "Inquiry" projects are more like "giant independent study projects that most students put on the back burner until a few weeks before they're due." Others disagreed:

"My two to three years of Inquiry have taught me an entirely different skill set compared to my traditional lecture-based courses," said one third-year health student. "It really depends on what kind of facilitator you have," explained another.

Just Like John Belushi

The stress of a McMaster education shakes off pretty quickly during the weekends. After all, this is the school that graduated Ivan Reitman, one of the producers of *National Lampoon's Animal House*. In fact, a popular campus tale is that Reitman actually based some of the wild antics in the movie on actual events that occurred on the McMaster campus. One science student reported, "The Engs (engineers) work hard, but they party pretty hard too!" Indeed, that seems to be the social attitude of this friendly college.

The "weekend" starts on Thursday night, even though most students have class on Friday. A big component of the McMaster social life is the lack of Greek societies, which are prohibited under college rules. Thursday nights usually consist of clubbing or bar-hopping. Most students head over to either Quarters, a popular all-ages-allowed on-campus bar and club, or Hess Village in Hamilton, home to places like Elixir and Funky Munky. Those who are not yet 19 frequent "keggers," even though kegs are technically not allowed in dormitories. Off-campus house parties are also popular. Friday is described by most students as "off day," but once Saturday rolls around, the McMaster students are back in true collegiate-partying form.

Since the legal drinking age is 19 in Ontario, drinking is a popular activity on campus. The students agree that the administration is very reasonable about the alcohol policy. Alcohol is allowed in dorm rooms, provided that the occupants are not under 19, and the alcohol doesn't come in the form of glass bottles or kegs. At Quarters, the alcohol policy is said to be strictly enforced. Beyond alcohol, pot is the drug of choice for students, but very few actually partake in the so-called "heavier" drugs.

Not all of the partying needs to involve alcohol, though. The McMaster Students Union holds a Charity Ball every single year, which draws hundreds of students in formal attire. Nearby downtown Hamilton is also home to great live music venues, malls, and movie theaters. In addition to all of this, annual faculty formals, Homecoming, and Frost Week (the first week back after Winter Break) are yearly events conducive to an exciting campus life. Incoming freshmen can expect to get their first taste of the McMaster social scene at Welcome Week (also known as Frosh Week), which is, according to one student, "just really one whole month of partying. I don't think there was one night my entire freshman year in which I didn't have fun." One notable Frosh Week tradition is the "Pajama Parade." The new first-years don their best sleepwear and walk five or six blocks in broad daylight. Upperclassmen take their lawn chairs out and sit right at the street, greeting them and shaking their hands as they go past. Some upperclassmen get a little more affectionate, bestowing kisses on the new members of Mac.

Marauding Through Student Life

McMaster offers a host of extracurricular activities for its students. Recent success in sports has made athletic activities very popular at Mac. "The whole college comes out for the football games!" one student enthused. "It seems like *everybody* knows somebody on the team." Beyond football, basketball, volleyball, and men's rugby are all highly regarded varsity teams. In addition to varsity, students can also participate in a range of intramural sports such as water polo. "Ultimate Frisbee is *huge* here," a third-year political science major said. However, be prepared for a bit of dedication. "Athletics can be a little cultish at Mac," one student admitted. "Be aware that if you're going out on your own, and you run into your team, they might very well ostracize you."

If sports are not your thing, though, there are a host of other extracurricular activities in which to participate. A glance down the sprawling list of clubs yields the Chinese Commerce Association, the Jane Austen Society, the Trampoline and Power Tumbling Club, the Ismaili Students Association, and Students for Literacy. The major student-run organization is the McMaster Students Union (MSU), which does everything from running the design and copy center to publishing *The Silhouette*, McMaster's weekly newspaper. However, the MSU's biggest job is to regulate all campus clubs. "The MSU is really meant to be the connection between the students and the McMaster administration," said one student. And to that extent, "They get the job done."

One of the most distinguishing features of McMaster is the diversity. "Mac is very culturally diverse," said one second-year. "It was a culture shock coming from a mostly white high school. Diversity is really pro-moted during Welcome Week in September. Mac does a good job of accepting everyone." Indeed, one of the biggest events on campus is Pangaea, a multicultural performance housed in a pavilion in which the campus groups get to showcase the food, beverages, history, and traditions of their cultures.

Home, Home in Westdale

McMaster students who apply for residence choose from apartment-style or traditional-style dorms (in the latter, you can choose a single, double, or triple). Mac has one female-only residence, and students can opt for substance-free floors or international-themed residences. Brandon Hall has a reputation for being the party dorm, but that is as far as the stereotypes go. "It really depends on who gets assigned to which dorm," one student explained.

About 4,500 undergraduate students live on campus every year, and 65 percent of dorm space is reserved for freshmen. Students often gush about their "residence." "It's a great experience. I lived on a French floor, and I met most of my friends through residence."

Freshman year, rooms are randomly assigned. McMaster's two apartment-style residence halls often go to the upperclassmen, international students, or students with medical issues. Priority for upperclassmen housing is given to those who make the Dean's Honor List (average of 9.5 or above) and students who show exemplary leadership in extracurricular activities. "However, even if you get DHL, you may not get your first pick of residence—for most, their first choice is Mary E. Keyes."

At McMaster, Community Advisors (CAs) are assigned to each dorm. One of their biggest responsibilities is holding the "Connections" program, in which new students are able to air grievances, agree on overnight guest policies, and generally communicate with their roommates. How large a role a CA has in a first-year's life varies. "Are there residential advisors?" one student asked half-jokingly. "Probably. But if we did [have one], I didn't have much contact with her." A second-year commerce major, on the other hand, cited a "very good experiences with my CA. We are still friends and talk all the time."

Even though many students enjoy their time in residence, many others choose to live off-campus. Rents around campus are pretty inexpensive, and to some, it seems like a natural transition to share a house with several other classmates after their first year. All full-time students receive an eight-month bus pass free, which makes getting around a whole lot easier. A large number of students also commute from nearby Toronto and London.

But regardless of whether you live on campus or off, dining is an important aspect of campus life. McMaster offers 10 meal plans for students, and they operate on a debit-card (that is, à la carte) system. Students on a meal plan can use their plans in any of 18 locations, including Commons Marketplace, which offers a host of healthy-food options, and the East Meets West Bistro in the Mary E. Keyes Residence. Few individuals, if any, complain about the quality of food at this university. McMaster features the only completely vegetarian college cafeteria in Canada, the Bridges Café. "Food at McMaster is perhaps one of the best among Canadian universities," boasted one student.

If there is one area to complain about, however, it is perhaps the price of food on campus. Students who live in campus dorms are required to subscribe to a minimum meal plan. Those who live off can choose from two meal plans. "Sometimes, however, it's just easier and cheaper to bring a sandwich from home," said a commuting student.

A Little Bit of Green

Despite the fact that McMaster is commonly listed as a part of Hamilton, Ontario, students are more likely to identify with upper-class Westdale, the village in which McMaster is located. "Nobody says it, but Westdale really is a university town," explained one McMaster student. "Hamilton? There are some people who have spent four years here but have never gone into downtown Hamilton." Other students agreed, one third-year stating that "Hamilton's gotten a bad rap over the years, so I was actually a little bit apprehensive about coming to McMaster. But McMaster is pretty isolated—it's easy for it to become your entire life." Some argue that Hamilton has its charms, however. Surely it supplies McMaster with plenty of things to do in the form of bars, pubs, clubs and music venues. "Everybody should get out of Westdale at least once and hang out in downtown Hamilton. No, you will not get shot or robbed, and you'll find very interesting places to hang out or eat," advised one student.

Of course, some will need that little bit of encouragement to leave campus. Current students rave about McMaster's grounds: "McMaster's campus is really beautiful, with lots of greenery and pathways, a rock garden, and picnic tables." It also doesn't hurt that it's surrounded by a conservation area known as Cootes Paradise. McMaster's pedestrian-friendly atmosphere extends even well into the night, since safety does not really rate as a concern for students living on campus and in Westdale.

There is one complaint about McMaster's grounds, though. "Parking is a disaster!" exclaimed one commuter. Agreed another, "My advice to first-years—definitely don't bring a car if you're living on campus."—*Janet Xu*

FYI

If you come to McMaster, you'd better bring "a healthy liver! You're going to be working it to death."

What's the typical weekend schedule? "Going to clubs or bars on Thursdays, just hanging out with friends on Fridays, then going out again Saturday night. On Sundays, you wake up, hit yourself on the head, and then go straight to work."

If I could change one thing about McMaster, I'd change "the corporate atmosphere. They're cutting back on the humanities programs because they don't make enough money, which I don't think is fair."

Three things every student at McMaster should do before graduating are "live in residence, go to Quarters, and get involved in a sport."

Queen's University

Address: Gordon Hall, 74 Union Street Kingston, ON K7L 3N6	**Percentage accepted through EA or ED:** NA	**Graduation Rate (4-year):** Unreported
Phone Number(s): 613-533-2218	**EA/ED deadline:** NA	**Graduation Rate (6-year):** Unreported
E-mail address: NA	**Regular Deadline:** 16-Feb	**Percent in On-campus housing:** Unreported
Web site URL: www.queensu.ca	**Application Fee:** CA$135	
	Full time Undergraduate enrollment: 16,038	**Number of official organized extracurricular organizations:** Unreported
Year Founded: 1841	**Total enrollment:** Unreported	
Private or Public: Public	**Percent Male:** 40%	**2 Most popular majors:** Business/Commerce, General Sport and Fitness Administration/Management
Religious affiliation: None	**Percent Female:** 60%	
Location: Urban	**Total Percent Minority or Unreported:** Unreported	
Number of Applicants: 25,403	**Percent African-American:** Unreported	**Student/Faculty ratio:** 16:1
Percent Accepted: Varies by Program	**Percent Asian/Pacific Islander:** Unreported	**Average Class Size:** 20 to 29
Percent Accepted who enroll: Varies by Program	**Percent Hispanic:** Unreported	**Percent of students going to grad school:** Unreported
Number Entering: 3,246	**Percent Native-American:** Unreported	**Tuition and Fees:** CA$3,551
Number of Transfers Accepted each Year: Unreported	**Percent International:** Unreported	**In Province Tuition and Fees (if different):** No difference
Middle 50% SAT range: Unreported	**Percent in-province/out of province:** 82%/18%	**Cost for Room and Board:** CA$7,600
Middle 50% ACT range: Unreported	**Percent from Public HS:** Unreported	**Percent receiving Financial aid, first-year (out of those who apply):** Unreported
Early admission program (EA/ED/None): None	**Retention Rate:** Varies by Program	**Percent of Undergraduates Receiving Financial Aid:** Unreported

Situated on the rustic northwestern shores of Lake Ontario, Queen's University is known for its beautiful location as well as its solid reputation for providing students with an unparalleled undergraduate experience. One of Canada's smaller institutions, with approximately 13,500 undergrads, Queen's University has the atmosphere of an Ivy League institution without the Ivy League costs.

Slackers Need Not Apply

Academic requirements at Queen's are quite stringent. "Lazy students will not succeed academically at Queen's," one undergraduate explained. The "Freshman 15" at Queen's does not refer to weight gain, but to the expected grade deflation of 15 percent from one's high school GPA. However, students report that those who are not aiming for an honors B.S. degree tend to have an easier time with their workloads. Getting into desired classes is also generally not a problem, as long as you register early enough.

Queen's uses a grading system unlike the system in the United States. In most Canadian schools, including Queen's, 90 to 100 percent is an A+, 80 to 89 percent is an A, 65 to 79 percent is a B, 55 to 64 percent is a C, and, as a senior at Queen's reported, "if you get any grade below a 55 percent, you are pretty much boned."

With such distinguished graduates as John Roth, the current CEO of networking giant Nortel, the commerce, or business, program at Queen's is considered one of the best in Canada. The program's rigorous entry requirements also mark it as one of the most competitive. Queen's also offers programs in nursing, engineering, and physical education.

Despite its relatively small overall student population, freshman classes tend to be quite large, often numbering in the hundreds. Students, however, report that the student-to-teacher ratio falls dramatically after the first year as students move beyond the necessary prerequisites. Upper-level courses and seminars tend to have no more than 20 to 30 students.

Students are generally happy with their professors, and some even go so far as to describe their professors as "cool." "My Classics 101 professor gave me a 10 percent bonus on a midterm because I could think up five references to Greek or Roman civilization from *The Simpsons*, one student said.

Queen's University offers a wide range of study-abroad opportunities. These programs are strongly encouraged, and most students participate in at least one of such programs in their four years at Queen's. Study abroad usually lasts a semester or a year. However, students also have the option of taking single classes for two to three weeks in different countries. The University even owns a castle in England, which students are encouraged to visit.

Drink to the Queen (or Don't)

Although Kingston, Ontario, is widely perceived as an affluent retirement community, there exists a vibrant social life both on and off campus. Alcohol is a big part of the social environment, but non-drinkers do not feel isolated. "There is always something to do for everyone," one student said. Even though the drinking age in Ontario is 19, freshmen typically take their parties off campus, as they are not permitted to bring beer bottles or kegs into the residences.

Queen's is proud of the fact that it does not have fraternities or sororities. Instead, most students enjoy barhopping and clubbing on weekends at local hotspots including The Alehouse, Stages, and the campus bar, Queen's Pub. Smidgie's is the most popular bar for fourth-year students. Drug use among students is not conspicuous, nor is it seen by students as a major issue on campus.

However, the administration *is* strict in its alcohol policies. For example, it does not tolerate alcohol at university events unless it is in a licensed, fenced-off area. Furthermore, getting caught with a fake ID will get you banned from campus pubs for the rest of your academic career.

Besides the bars and clubs, campus events are generally well attended. Movie nights, concerts, dances, and boat cruises are some of the most popular events. The student center, or the JDUC (John Deutsche University Centre), is well used by many different student organizations—including the central student governing council, the Alma Mater Society.

Beautiful People Abound

"There are many attractive guys and girls around," one undergraduate said. "There's always someone pleasant to adore." That said, some students complained that the student population is too homogeneous, with the majority of the students hailing from white, upper-middle-class backgrounds. As one student explained, "We have a stereotype of the Gap-wearing, khaki-donning preppie school." Geographically, the majority of the students hail from various metropolitan areas of Ontario such as Toronto and Ottawa. Nevertheless, there is a sizeable international student population from countries such as Barbados, Jamaica, Trinidad, New Guinea, Saudi Arabia, China, and India. Meeting people at Queen's is not a concern. "It's really easy," one junior said. "People here are really friendly." However, that being said, another sophomore complained, "The school could use some more diversity."

Crammed Like Sardines in a Tin Can

Some students report being disappointed with the living arrangements. "I got an economy double that crammed two beds, two desks, and two metal hutches into a single-sized room my freshman year," one student lamented. "It was more than a little cramped." Despite the disappointing quality of the living arrangements, many students find that the residence system is amenable to a great social life. "I've met my closest friends through the residence system."

> "If I could choose my university all over again, I would not even waste my time considering another institution—it would be Queen's all the way!"

Each residence has "Floor Seniors" who are typically second-year students, as well as "Floor Dons," who are fourth-year students. The Floor Seniors tend to be strict, enforcing quiet hours during the weekdays, as well as guest and alcohol policies. "They just have bugs up their butts for the most part," one freshman complained.

Some of the dorms reportedly have different personalities. "For example, the McNeil girls are nuns, the Vic Hall kids party all the time, and the Leonard Hall boys are all rowdy and obnoxious," one undergraduate explained. After first year, most students move out of the residence system into houses with four to six friends. There are many student houses in the area, as well as in an area affectionately known as the "Student Ghetto." Rent is reasonable, generally amounting to about $450 per month, and most student houses are within five minutes of campus.

The campus itself is fairly compact, only taking up three to four square blocks. The buildings tend to be a mix of modern and old, with the older buildings being based around designs from the University of Edinburgh. "The buildings are modern inside, yet historical on the outside—so it creates a nice contrast," one student said. The Queen's Learning Commons, which opened in 2005, unites the library with other student academic services such as the Writing Centre and ITS support.

As a result of being located in quiet Kingston, students reported feeling very safe at Queen's. Nevertheless, there exist various safety measures, such as the nighttime escort service, that bolster campus safety.

As for dining on campus, students considered the plan to be well-organized and flexible, though many complain that the offerings tend to be repetitive and bland. "The food is edible, but it's lower than prison quality," one hungry undergrad explained. There are vegetarian options available at all times, but it is "nothing spectacular." "I'm getting very sick of eating pasta all the time." Luckily, dinner times tend to be social hours, and students reported feeling very comfortable just sitting down with anyone and striking up a conversation. Of course, much finer dining options can be found off campus at one of Kingston's numerous upscale restaurants.

Tams and Gaels

Virtually all students tend to engage in a least one extracurricular activity during their academic career at Queen's. From debating to sports to writing for publications, Queen's has it all. "It depends on your personality," one undergraduate said. "If you like arguing, you hit the debate team. If you're athletic, you get in with the sports teams."

Tension regarding sexuality and gender is not as big a problem at Queen's University as it is at other colleges. Queen's boasts a Queerientation Week, groups and publications for transgendered and gay students, women-friendly spaces, and a gender neutral bathroom that many students use.

The Golden Gaels, Queen's popular football team, draw in large student crowds to all their football games. "There is tons of school spirit with lots of traditions, including many songs and chants," one junior said. Homecoming is an especially festive occasion, as is the big annual game, which is usually against archrival McGill University. For those not skilled enough to hit the varsity ranks, there are numerous on-campus athletic facilities to satisfy students' desires to remain fit and active throughout college. Students can also join low-cost recreational clubs to learn a whole spectrum of sports, from break dancing to scuba diving. Scuba, in particular, benefits from Queen's proximity to the freshwaters of Lake Ontario.

Scottish traditions run deep at Queen's. All students are given Scottish berets called tams and are taught how to sing the school song, the "Oil Thigh." Furthermore, Queen's is also known as the Canadian university with the best orientation week. "Other places have a paltry two or three days," an undergraduate explained. "We have a full week!"

All the different faculties also have their own traditions. The engineers, for example, are known to dye themselves purple and slam their leather jackets on the ground at certain times. Every year, the engineering freshmen have to climb a 24-foot-high greased pole and grab a hat off the top of it. "We have a lot of special and fun traditions around here," one student said. "It's what makes Queen's great!"

With its proud Scottish traditions, talented student body, and ideal location, it is no wonder that Queen's students are proud to announce, "I go to Queen's!"—*Christine Geiser*

FYI
If you come to Queen's University, you'd better bring "a lot of spirit and enthusiasm."
What is the typical weekend schedule? "Attending a Golden Gaels football game wearing your Queen's coveralls and tams, going to a post-game party at Stages or The Alehouse, going down to the lake and reading a book under a tree, and going out to dinner at a restaurant with friends."
If I could change one thing about Queen's I would "change the sport's team name—Golden Gaels just sounds sissy!"
Three things every student should do before graduating are "watch a homecoming football game, join the Queen's band, and jump into the lake wearing your Queen's coveralls."

University of British Columbia

Address: Room 2016, 1874 East Mall Vancouver, BC V6T 1Z1, Canada

Phone Number(s): 604-822-3014

E-mail address: NA

Web site URL: www.welcome.ubc.ca

Year Founded: 1908

Private or Public: Public

Religious affiliation: None

Location: Urban

Number of Applicants: 18,773

Percent Accepted: 60%

Percent Accepted who enroll: 44%

Number Entering: 5,017

Number of Transfers Accepted each Year: 889

Middle 50% SAT range: Unreported

Middle 50% ACT range: Unreported

Early admission program (EA/ED/None): None

Percentage accepted through EA or ED: NA

EA/ED deadline: NA

Regular Deadline: 28-Feb

Application Fee: CA$60

Full time Undergraduate enrollment: 30,170

Total enrollment: 38,811

Percent Male: 47%

Percent Female: 53%

Total Percent Minority or Unreported: Unreported

Percent African-American: Unreported

Percent Asian/Pacific Islander: Unreported

Percent Hispanic: Unreported

Percent Native-American: Unreported

Percent International: Unreported

Percent in-province/out of province: Unreported

Percent from Public HS: Unreported

Retention Rate: 92%

Graduation Rate (4-year): 78%

Graduation Rate (6-year): Unreported

Percent in On-campus housing: 20%

Number of official organized extracurricular organizations: 250

3 Most popular majors: Biological and Physical Sciences, Computer and Information Sciences, Psychology

Student/Faculty ratio: 15:1

Average Class Size: 2 to 9

Percent of students going to grad school: 50%

Tuition and Fees: CA$144.75 per credit, plus CA$692.15 fees

In Province Tuition and Fees (if different): Unreported

Cost for Room and Board: CA$3,362 for shared room, CA$3,898 for single room

Percent receiving Financial aid, first-year (out of those who apply): Unreported

Percent of Undergraduates Receiving Financial Aid: Unreported

Students at the University of British Columbia will strongly urge you not to overlook the benefits of spending four years in a foreign country—even if it's only across the border in Canada. UBC's blend of stunning natural surroundings, thriving city life, and comprehensive academic offerings gives the Thunderbirds good reason to be proud of their global school.

Studying: Canadian Style

UBC is divided into several schools, or faculties, within which students may choose their majors. Some of the most popular are the Faculty of Arts, which encompasses much of the university's liberal arts programs, and the Faculty of Applied Sciences, which houses the Engineering departments and the School of Nursing. Other options include the Faculty of Forestry, the School of Human Kinetics, and the School of Journalism. "UBC really requires more of you than many other Canadian universities," one sophomore said. And although the general requirements are considered to be a nuisance, most students recognize the value of taking these core classes. In the Faculty of Arts, students must enroll in English, Literature, Science, and Language courses, although some of the requirements may be fulfilled by scores on standardized tests.

It may not be surprising that nearly all of the introductory-level courses at UBC consist of large lectures averaging 200 students a class, but students take comfort in the knowledge that these classes also feature small 15-person weekly discussion groups to go over the material. In addition, upper-level courses go down in size, and after their first years, most students can find themselves in classes of 50 or fewer people. Although students lamented that "it's easy with such big classes to get overlooked," professors generally make themselves very available through e-mail and office hours. For freshmen looking for a gentler transition to the large university scene, UBC offers the Coordinated Arts Program, in which 100 first years have three of their five classes with the same group of people. Signing up for classes can pose a problem, particularly for first and second years, who get last pick, but one student reassuringly said that "if you really want to take a course, just go to the professor and they'll sign you up." For all years, the order of course signups is determined by grade point average.

The sciences, particularly engineering, are generally considered to be more difficult, and students described them as requiring more of a continuous workload than liberal arts courses. Within the arts departments, the International Relations major has a competitive application process. Highly recommended courses include History 103, a comprehensive general history class starting in 1800, and Economics 101 and 102, taught by Robert Gateman, who writes his own textbook. Political Science professor Bruce Baum also gets high marks for "dressing up as Marx" during a lecture. Overall, UBC's position as a highly regarded research community makes its students proud—one sophomore observed that the serious discoveries that her professors are making "really trickle down to the undergraduates they teach, and we benefit from their work."

No Need for a Fake ID

In this large of a university, which has an undergraduate population of 30,000, making friends as a first year might seem like an overwhelming task. However, students meet the majority of their friends in their residence halls through a variety of residence-sponsored activities and simple proximity to a large number of varied and interesting personalities hailing from all over the globe. Events hosted in the dorms include Totem Park's annual "Meat Market," where scantily clad first years are the norm, and an assortment of theme parties such as "Graffiti Night," which features a black light and the opportunity to use highlighters to create fluorescent works of art on other students' shirts.

One of the advantages of going to school in Canada, as many students will inform you, is that the legal drinking age is only 19. This increased access to alcohol contributes to UBC's extensive bar and pub culture, a feature of the University's social life that is all the more exciting because of the city of Vancouver's renowned nightlife. However, under-graduates need not stray far to drink, since the school itself has a number of drinking establishments on campus. The most-frequented of these is the Pit Pub, which hosts "Pit Night" every Wednesday, an event that students describe as an opportunity to "get really drunk, fall over, and stumble home." A lot of drinking occurs in the residences, where the more lenient RA's "don't crack down on underage drinking, but they can be hard on drugs," at least in the dorms. One girl claimed that "the best pot comes from British Columbia" and that this is reflected in the student body's affinities, but other students countered that "while [marijuana use] is a definite part of the UBC culture for many students, it's not over the top." The importance of having events and activities close to the dorms comes into play when it's raining, which "can get very dreary and usually lasts for several months at a time."

The social scene at UBC is characterized as being "generally very friendly," although students commented on certain cliques that form, particularly around ethnic groups and substance users. Not surprisingly, the campus is "extremely liberal" politically, although conservative students said that the atmosphere is "not repressive." Even though it is a public school, many students are perceived to be upper middle class and relatively affluent, which a girl speculated may stem from the fact that "tuition fees are higher for international students." Over 5,000 international undergraduate and graduate students from over 140 countries attend UBC, which creates a unique campus atmosphere. One sophomore even stated that she "can walk all the way across campus and not hear any English," an experience that she attributed to UBC's extensive international recruiting programs.

An International City

UBC is unique in that it does not require first years to live on campus. Those freshmen who do choose to live in the residence complexes settle in either Totem Park or Place Vanier, living situations that are described as "incredibly convenient." Each dorm features an assortment of singles, doubles, triples, and quads, as well as a lounge, study area, small gym, cafeteria and mini-mart. Totem has a reputation for being the party dorm, while Vanier is seen as "nicer and more sedate." There is a wider variety of residences available to upperclassmen, including Walter Gage, featuring suites of six bedrooms and shared living space, and Fairview Crescent, which consists of townhouses. The distinct Ritsumeikan-UBC House, or "Rits," was built as a symbol of UBC's academic partnership with Ritsumeikan University in Japan, and offers not only four-bedroom suites with shared kitchen and living room, but also a Japanese tatami room for "relaxing and meditation."

> **"I can walk all the way across campus and not hear any English."**

There is one RA on each floor in Totem and Vanier, each overseeing about 50 students. How strict they are depends on the person, but general consensus is that people get away with a lot in the dorms. Students say UBC does not make its substance policies clear, but the residences do have clear policies that forbid drinking in the hallway but allow it in the rooms. Drugs are not allowed in the dorms, although a single offense will not get you removed. When outside the residences, one junior girl claimed that "you can walk around campus with a joint and rarely get in trouble, and if you're drinking outside, campus security will just tell you to dump it out."

A large number of students choose to forgo UBC's provided housing, which only accommodates one-fifth of the undergraduate population, and instead look to off-campus options. Students who take this option claim that the advantages of these living situations, which vary in distance from campus and can be as far away as the other side of Vancouver, far outweigh the drawbacks, since the many attractions of the greater city are even more accessible, especially with the convenience of local public transportation. Students can purchase "U-Passes," which give them unlimited access to the Vancouver bus system, which runs until four in the morning.

Thunderbirds find plenty to do on and around campus. The Student Union Building, also known as the SUB, houses a food court, the Pit, a number of small food vendors and restaurants, the Norm Theatre, and even clothing vendors on its multiple levels. The availability of these alternate eating opportunities can be a relief for students who find the cafeteria fare everything from "monotonous and unhealthy" to "disgusting." Meal plan money may be redeemed at other on-campus eateries besides those in Totem and Vanier, but many students choose to cook their own food.

While campus architecture is described as "eclectic but not very attractive at times," the scenic area surrounding UBC more than makes up for it. A junior gushed that "you're surrounded by forest, looking out on the water, with mountains on the other side—it's incredibly picturesque." Right next to campus, down a flight of stairs, is the famous Wreck Beach, where clothing is optional. Many students spend their wintry weekends at the famous Whistler resort skiing or snowboarding. The city of Vancouver, however, is one of the main reasons students choose UBC. According to a senior: "You could manage by staying strictly on campus all four years, but you'd be missing out on a whole world out there." From clubs and bars to pubs and restaurants, Vancouver seems to have everything in the way of culture and entertainment. Students' favorite joints to frequent include the Blarney Stone and the King's Head Pub for drinks, Numero Uno Pizza for cheap late-night slices, and the many ethnic cuisine restaurants, since "you name a country and you can probably find a restaurant that serves its food somewhere in Vancouver."

Thunderbirds Are Go!

UBC's varsity sports are apparently played down since, as a sophomore commented, "I'm not sure anyone attends many of the games at all." While they may not be following their fellow Thunderbirds closely, the rest of campus is reported to be pretty active, with students running outside whenever it isn't raining, or using the Birdcoop Fitness Centre. Intramural sports are popular, as well. With over 300 student-run organizations, UBC students have plenty of choices. Many take advantage of nearby Whistler by joining the extremely popular "Ski and Board Club," which offers discount season passes to the slopes. Clubs centered around celebration of ethnic and cultural heritage are ubiquitous, due largely to the number of international students, as well as to the significant population of recent immigrants to Canada. These groups "put on a lot of events, like beer gardens and mixers."

A much-appreciated aspect of student life at UBC is the University's fun annual events. These include Day of the Longboat, when students gather in teams of 10 to participate in a frantic canoe race, and Arts County Fair, which is held on the last day of classes and offers a chance for students to unwind, listen to famous bands, and "basically start drinking around breakfast and keep it going all day." Daily surprises can include sightings of the many celebrities who film their projects in the Vancouver area, ranging from Jessica Alba to Al Pacino.

UBC offers its students the opportunity to live and study in a renowned research university setting bordered by a "wealth of natural beauty" and one of the most exciting cities on the West Coast, Vancouver. It may be large, but "everyone finds their place here in this laid-back community," which is made even more attractive by its affordability. Students described UBC as a "completely comprehensive university," promising that "no matter what program you go into, you're going to get a great education out of it." Those looking for a truly international university in the top tier of Canadian education might want to consider giving border-hopping a try.—*Kimberly Chow*

FYI

If you come to the **University of British Columbia**, you'd better bring: "a George Foreman Grill for when you get tired of the cafeteria food, and rain boots."

What's the typical weekend schedule? "Friday night, go to a residence party or a beer garden on campus. Saturday play IM sports, go to Granville Island for its shopping market; at night go to downtown Vancouver for its pubs, bars, and clubs. Sunday, play some sports and cram in the studying."

If I could change one thing about UBC, I'd "increase school spirit and promote clubs and organizations more."

Three things every student at UBC should do before graduating are: "Jump off the 10-meter high dive in your underwear or naked, gather your friends and race on Day of the Longboat, and go up the clock tower and appreciate the stunning view."

University of Toronto

Address: 25 King's College Circle Toronto, Canada M5S 1A1

Phone Number(s): 416-978-2190

E-mail address: NA

Web site URL: www.utoronto.ca

Year Founded: 1827

Private or Public: Public

Religious affiliation: None

Location: Suburban

Number of Applicants: 59,541

Percent Accepted: 67%

Percent Accepted who enroll: 33%

Number Entering: 12,771

Number of Transfers Accepted each Year: Unreported

Middle 50% SAT range: Unreported

Middle 50% ACT range: Unreported

Early admission program (EA/ED/None): None

Percentage accepted through EA or ED: NA

EA/ED deadline: NA

Regular Deadline: 1-Mar

Application Fee: CA$80

Full time Undergraduate enrollment: 58,182

Total enrollment: 69,711

Percent Male: 45%

Percent Female: 55%

Total Percent Minority or Unreported: Unreported

Percent African-American: Unreported

Percent Asian/Pacific Islander: Unreported

Percent Hispanic: Unreported

Percent Native-American: Unreported

Percent International: Unreported

Percent in-province/out of province: Unreported

Percent from Public HS: Unreported

Retention Rate: 95%

Graduation Rate (4-year): 76%

Graduation Rate (6-year): Unreported

Percent in On-campus housing: 10%

Number of official organized extracurricular organizations: 200+

3 Most popular majors: Arts, Sciences, Engineering

Student/Faculty ratio: 20:1

Average Class Size: Varies by Program

Percent of students going to grad school: Unreported

Tuition and Fees: Dependent on major

In Province Tuition and Fees (if different): NA

Cost for Room and Board: CA$7,000

Percent receiving Financial aid, first-year (out of those who apply): Unreported

Percent of Undergraduates Receiving Financial Aid: Unreported

A prestigious institution with three picturesque campuses spread around Canada's most vivacious and culturally diverse city, the University of Toronto has a wide selection of academic, athletic, and entertainment resources both on and off campus. The school is well known for its innovative research and academic prowess and has the best course selection in the nation. While most students are generally proud of the school and pleased with their choice, the intense workload and academic pressure can be overwhelming for many.

Competition in the Classroom

The professors at the University of Toronto are some of the most respected academics and experts in their respective fields. Past and present faculty members have made major contributions to academia and research, including Sir Frederick Banting and J.J.R. Macleod, who won the Nobel Prize in 1923 for their discovery that insulin could control diabetes, as well as geneticist Tak Mak, who was the first person to clone a T-cell gene.

A senior noted, however, that one of the drawbacks of having world-class professors is that the class sizes are usually extremely large with limited student-faculty interaction. With over 50,000 undergraduate students, "it's hard to avoid feeling like a number," a freshman said. Courses at Toronto are extremely challenging, with professors who are noted to have higher standards than those at most other Canadian universities. Some students feel lost in the large classes and find the competitive nature among students and the overall academic intensity to be stifling.

One student expressed a desire to have professors "grade on academic achievement rather than academic achievement as compared to the rest of a class." But despite the high stress that comes with the academic prestige of the University, students don't regret the choice of attending; one student called his experience "an unparalleled educational opportunity," and said that the hard work is always worth it. Students are also encouraged to utilize on-campus resources such as counseling, writing centers, and tutorials designed to help with rigorous course loads.

With the new waitlist feature that allows students to sign up for a maximum of six courses, including waitlisted courses, U of T students are finding it more difficult to enroll in their classes of choice. But prospects become brighter as students delve deeper into their majors. Class size diminishes and student-faculty interaction increases with each year.

Out of 16 total faculties, there are four main faculties at the U of T: applied science and engineering, music, arts and science, and physical education and health. Applicants to the University apply directly to the faculty of their choice. Co-op programs within faculties incorporate classroom teaching with real-world working experience, as students switch between university work and co-op jobs each semester. There are also specified tracks offered for students interested in science, as well as research opportunities that allow students to work side by side with their highly regarded professors.

The Toronto Triad

The University of Toronto is broken down into three campuses: the St. George Campus, the Mississauga Campus, and the Scarborough Campus. The St. George Campus is the oldest of the three, established in 1827, and is nestled in a park-like setting in the downtown area. This, the primary campus, hosts about 50,000 undergraduate and graduate students. The approximately 10,000 students at Mississauga are located west of downtown in a more modern environment, while the comparably sized student body of the Scarborough campus is part of a small, friendly academic community east of Toronto. Each regional section has its own student culture and campus pride, but a freshman expressed frustration with this division. "I'd have the three separate campuses together," she said. "There are rivalries between the campuses and I think U of T would be stronger as one."

Students explain that the buildings of all three campuses are aesthetically beautiful. One student said, "The buildings downtown are exquisite, old and new ones. The old ones are all so unique and detailed, and have such a history. The newer buildings also offer a modern type of uniqueness to the campus." The University has created a residential college system in order to create smaller communities within the overwhelmingly large student body. Seven of the nine colleges are located in the downtown campus, with the other residences located within the two smaller campuses.

A senior explained that the dorm situation is largely traditional, with students housed in doubles their first year and singles in the following years; some students, however, live in suites or townhouses. One student explained that Toronto "does have a large commuter community, with many upper year students opting to live off campus in houses or apartments in the downtown core." He added that some students live at home with their parents, which takes away from the student life aspect of the Toronto experience.

Opportunities for Involvement

The University of Toronto has over 380 officially recognized student clubs, and opportunities for involvement are endless. Each of Toronto's three campuses has its own radio station, and there are over fifteen student publications, including two main newspapers. Campus groups are an integral part of the student experience, from the Aeronautics team to Women in Life Learning. Hart House is a social, cultural, and recreational facility centered on cultural programming such as arts and music, and is a popular hangout for students.

First-rate athletic facilities include courts, pools, tracks, dance studios, beach volleyball courts, a sports medicine clinic, and facilities for weight training, aerobics and martial arts. There are free instructional classes each week as well as intramural sports leagues.

> **"It is an urban metropolis that allows for anyone to explore culture, passions, or interests."**

Students embrace the vast size of the campus and the opportunities available there, although it can be intimidating at first. "It is an urban metropolis that allows for anyone to explore culture, passions, or interests," one senior said. "However, it can be alienating and overwhelming for newcomers." The cultural diversity and social acceptance at U of T is a perk for many. One student explained, "Social groups are really very non-cliquey, with many students open to meeting friends that they normally would not have associated with in high school."

The student body is diverse, with a multitude of international students and cultural events that expose students to different foods, traditions, and beliefs. One sophomore explained that he's met students from all over the map. "You really feel like you are part of the global village," he said.

In Search of a Social Scene

Students say that while there are a multitude of on-campus parties and events, the city is the best place for nightlife and week-end parties. "There's a lot to do in Toronto City," a student explained. "There are loads of activities going on all the time—parties, plays, shows, musicals, concerts . . ." Popular downtown clubs for the university crowd include Tonic and Joe. The Duke of Gloucester, on Yonge Street, is often regarded as the best student hangout close to campus.

The drinking age in Canada is 19, a perk for students who can legally drink two years earlier than they would have been able to in the States. "Clubs and bars are spread out all over downtown Toronto," one student said. "That's what life is here!" One student said that "for a break from campus, U of T students generally go to one of the many nearby pubs to down a pint." Students explain that the general trend is pubs on Thursdays, clubs on Saturdays.

The Greek scene and sports scene are not central to student life at Toronto, falling far below the emphasis placed on academics. One student explained, "Toronto school spirit is generally lacking. Although students are proud of their academic and extracurricular life, generally that isn't parlayed into a strong school spirit." A senior said that many students at U of T spend much of their weekends studying, but there are opportunities for fun if schedules allow. Typical hangouts are Diablo's at University College, the UnderStudy Café in the central campus area, and The Cat's Eye at Victoria College.

The city of Toronto is the largest in Canada and offers a plethora of resources for food, fun, and entertainment beyond those available to students at the University. Toronto has a wide variety of ballet, dance, opera, music, and theater companies. The world's first permanent IMAX movie theater is in Toronto, as well as an open-air venue for music concerts, a popular pedestrian village, and a theater district. The yearly outdoor Shakespeare performances and international film festivals draw people from around the world, and sports fans will not be disappointed, as Toronto is the only Canadian city with teams in the NHL, NBA, and MLB.

The city is brimming with clubs, restaurants, sporting events, festivals, theaters, and shops, and students don't run out of things to do in this multicultural and cosmopolitan city. Toronto's subway, bus, and streetcar systems are speedy and efficient, allowing students to get around town with general ease, and Toronto students have discounted rates to many events.

Despite student complaints about the "mountains of work," Toronto is said to hold the torch for education in Canada. With superior academics, distinguished professors, a wide range of on-campus organizations, and a city with endless opportunity for exploration and enjoyment, the Toronto experience is hard to compete with as long as you're willing to work.—*Catherine Cheney*

FYI

What is the typical weekend schedule? "It involves studying and essay writing. But when schedules are clear, pubs on Thursdays and clubs on Saturdays are popular social events, and allow for the much-needed blowing off of steam."

If I could change one thing about Toronto, I'd "combine the three campuses."

Three things every student at the University of Toronto should do before graduating are: "Attend a toga party at St. Michael's college, visit the U of T art gallery, and attend the special lectures offered, particularly those offered by visiting academics."

University of Waterloo

Address: 200 University Avenue West Waterloo, Ontario, Canada N2L 3G1

Phone Number(s): 519-888-4567

E-mail address: admissions@uwaterloo.ca

Web site URL: www.uwaterloo.ca

Year Founded: 1957

Private or Public: Public

Religious affiliation: None

Location: Urban

Number of Applicants: 31,741

Percent Accepted: 61%

Percent Accepted who enroll: 0

Number Entering: 6,390

Number of Transfers Accepted each Year: Unreported

Middle 50% SAT range: Minimum score of 1100 for combined Critical Reading and Math

Middle 50% ACT range: Minimum score of 26

Early admission program (EA/ED/None): None

Percentage accepted through EA or ED: NA

EA/ED deadline: NA

Regular Deadline: Varies by Program

Application Fee: Varies by Program

Full time Undergraduate enrollment: 22,368

Total enrollment: 28,845

Percent Male: 49%

Percent Female: 51%

Total Percent Minority or Unreported: Unreported

Percent African-American: Unreported

Percent Asian/Pacific Islander: Unreported

Percent Hispanic: Unreported

Percent Native-American: Unreported

Percent International: Unreported

Percent in-province/out of province: 98%/2%

Percent from Public HS: Unreported

Retention Rate: 98%

Graduation Rate (4-year): Unreported

Graduation Rate (6-year): Unreported

Percent in On-campus housing: Unreported

Number of official organized extracurricular organizations: 160

3 Most popular majors: Computer Science, Kinesiology and Exercise Science, Mathematics

Student/Faculty ratio: 15:1

Average Class Size: Varies by Program

Percent of students going to grad school: Unreported

Tuition and Fees: Varies by program

In Province Tuition and Fees (if different): Varies by Nationality

Cost for Room and Board: CA$5,950

Percent receiving Financial aid, first-year (out of those who apply): Unreported

Percent of Undergraduates Receiving Financial Aid: Unreported

W here else can you get great academics, great work experience, and great bratwurst, all at Canadian prices? According to students at the University of Waterloo, all are within close reach.

A Taste of the Real World

The University of Waterloo is well-known for its rigorous academic programs. Students keep busy fulfilling the minimum 40 classes required for graduation (10 per year), while double majors are even more demanding. Academic programs are structured around Waterloo's six faculties: applied health sciences, arts, engineering, environmental studies, mathematics, and science; each has its own set of requirements and expectations. In addition, there is also an Independent Studies Program for those looking for something more specialized. While math and engineering have an especially strong reputation (Waterloo has more students enrolled in math than any other school in the world), the other departments are equally demanding. There is little reported grade inflation, and professors are fairly accessible. One arts student, discussing the personal attention students receive, commented that he could not remember taking any English classes with more than 40 students per class, even freshman year.

One of Waterloo's biggest highlights is its well-developed, prestigious co-op program, where students divide the school year by alternating terms of school and employment. The co-op program is the largest of its kind in the world, with over half of the student body participating. As a result, Waterloo operates on a trimester system, with classes in session all year long to allow students in the co-op program to graduate within five years. Current undergrads highly recommend the program, saying, "not only can you get some much-needed cash, but you also get work experience, which is great for future employment." Being a part of the co-op system means having the opportunity to travel—not just to nearby Toronto, but to places outside of Canada as well. Students also report that coming back to school from the "real world" after working for a term provides a better perspective on classes and university life in general. One undergraduate said that "sometimes it's nice just to get away for a change of scenery and to refocus my energies."

Building Friendships
Waterloo has no on-campus housing requirements, but almost all first-year students live in the dorms. Many second-years also try to stay on campus, but a recent housing shortage has made this difficult. The university's eight on-campus residences (primarily for first-year students) can be categorized into two main communities—the "UW residences" and the "University college residences." Each dorm has a resident advisor, nicknamed a "don," who is an upperclassman. The UW residences consist of

Village 1, Mackenzie King Village, UW Place, and Ron Eydt Village. The University college residences are Conrad Grebel, Renison, St. Jerome's, and St. Paul's. They are small religiously affiliated colleges with ties to the University. Many students are very enthusiastic about living within a residential college system. Offering both separate classes and housing spaces, the church colleges reportedly offer a "homier" atmosphere. Although each church college has a specific religious affiliation, students of any creed may apply for residence. Students say the church colleges have the most "spirit," and according to some, they also have better food—try Conrad Grebel for Mennonite cooking. Most students live in doubles, and on the whole, dorm rooms are small, but are the place where "we start to build lasting friendships so it isn't so bad—in a sense, we are all in it together."

> "We really know how to go after what we want."

Upperclassmen tend to live off campus—there is plenty of available housing conveniently near the school, and the cost of living is more affordable. By living off campus, students are able to avoid the meal plan, which freshmen are quick to call "a total rip-off." Many find tasty food off campus at popular places like East Side Mario's, Subway, and Campus Pizza, all located at University Plaza, which is open 24 hours a day.

Friendly, Outdoorsy Atmosphere
Students find the town of Waterloo, Ontario, a quiet kind of university town and are quick to differentiate it from nearby "gross, industrial, abandoned-factory-like" Kitchener. For the outdoorsy types, the area around Laurel Creek provides the perfect opportunity to jog, swim, and bike. For those eager to explore the social scene, the Student Life Centre organizes free movies and other recreational activities on campus and around Waterloo. The area is also famous for its great Oktoberfest celebration every year: people come from all over to sample the bratwurst, take in the dancing, and absorb the unique atmosphere of the festival. Students enthusiastically recommend the event, even if it means just taking a tour of the local breweries.

As for the night life, students often head to Bombshelter. The student-run bar and club, also known as "Bomber," features popular

Wednesday night parties, concerts, and infamous hot wings ("Our wings are so hot you need to sign a waiver!"). Other than that, there are the usual weekend parties with plenty of alcohol available. Waterloo may have a reputation for being a studious school, but as one student commented, "even the engineering students know how to relax once in a while." Some students leave town on the weekends and head for Toronto, about an hour away, but most stay on campus, preferring to hang out with friends there.

Though not sanctioned by the University, fraternities and sororities do exist and are growing in size and number. Besides providing a social outlet, the groups organize a number of philanthropic events throughout the year. "Joining Kappa Kappa Gamma not only gave me the opportunity to do charity work, but it was also a great way to meet a fantastic group of smart, talented women," raved one fourth-year.

As a co-op school, the Waterloo campus is active year-round. Students on campus over the summer can attend the "huge" Canada Day party held on the first of July at Columbia Lake. The event features concerts, carnival games, and fireworks, giving students a chance to enjoy the warm summer weather.

IMs and More

Due to the co-op system, many students do not have a lot of time to pursue other extracurricular activities. However, clubs and organizations number over 160, and include an active student government, the Federation Orientation Committee (which runs frosh week) and *Imprint*, the main student newspaper. Intramurals are also strong, with a number of fine facilities available. Any student with interest can play, and the lack of pressure on the field makes the experience enjoyable. By comparison, varsity sports are more on the periphery of students' interest. One senior had "never even thought about going to a sporting event!"

Quest for the Pink Tie

Waterloo, like all universities, has its own colorful traditions. Among them is the quest for the pink tie, which occurs during freshman week at the start of the school year. Math students, or "mathies" as they are called, enjoy the week-long activities and get the coveted pink tie. Later, a huge pink tie is hung over the side of the math building, and this often adds to the touch of rivalry between the math and engineering departments. During frosh week, engineering students try to steal the giant pink tie, while mathies try to sneak out the "tool," the engineering faculty's prized possession. As one student said, "we love to scheme and plot, but it is really just fun and games."

A Place to Grow

Waterloo students take their academic demands very seriously. "There are lots of smart people, especially in the sciences and engineering," said one undergrad. Students head to the Dana Porter Library to study, and computer clusters are readily available on campus. While the academic atmosphere may not be cutthroat, some complain that there are people who study compulsively. One student remarked that there exists a clear separation—"half the students study like crazy, and half have a life." Students at Waterloo can be cliquish, so school unity has room for improvement. However, the University of Waterloo still remains one of Canada's foremost educational institutions for engineering, math, and the arts, and those who attend do take note of the formidable job placement rate after graduation. Above all, Waterloo students in general agree about the number of academic and social opportunities available. If there is one thing to remember about the people at Waterloo, it is that "we really know how to go after what we want." It is just that passion that keeps Waterloo growing and its students succeeding.—*Laura Sullivan*

FYI

If you're coming to Waterloo, you'd better bring "cleats and shin guards so you can play in the intramurals."

What is the typical weekend schedule? "Eat, play sports, party, STUDY."

If I could change one thing about Waterloo, I'd "improve the architecture."

Three things that every Waterloo student should do before graduating are "go tubing in Laurel Creek, go out for a team (competitive or intramurals), and check out Oktoberfest."

University of Western Ontario

Address: 1151 Richmond
Street London, Ontario,
Canada, N6A 3K7
Phone Number(s):
519-661-2111
E-mail address: NA
Web site URL: www.uwo.ca
Year Founded: 1878
Private or Public: Public
Religious affiliation: None
Location: Suburban
Number of Applicants: 27,652
Percent Accepted: 59%
**Percent Accepted who
enroll:** 36%
Number Entering: 5,871
**Number of Transfers
Accepted each Year:**
Unreported
Middle 50% SAT range:
Unreported
Middle 50% ACT range:
Unreported
**Early admission program
(EA/ED/None):** None
**Percentage accepted
through EA or ED:** NA

EA/ED deadline: NA
Regular Deadline: 1-Jun
Application Fee: CA$105
**Full time Undergraduate
enrollment:** 25,287
Total enrollment: 5,871
Percent Male: 41%
Percent Female: 59%
**Total Percent Minority or
Unreported:** Unreported
Percent African-American:
Unreported
**Percent Asian/Pacific
Islander:** Unreported
Percent Hispanic:
Unreported
Percent Native-American:
Unreported
Percent International:
Unreported
**Percent in-province/out of
province:** 96%/4%
Percent from Public HS:
Unreported
Retention Rate: 95%
Graduation Rate (4-year):
Unreported

Graduation Rate (6-year):
Unreported
**Percent in On-campus
housing:** Unreported
**Number of official organized
extracurricular
organizations:** 171
3 Most popular majors:
Digital Comminications and
Media/Multimedia, Medicine
Student/Faculty ratio: 12:1
Average Class Size: Varies by
Program
**Percent of students
going to grad school:**
Unreported
Tuition and Fees: CA$13,050
**In Province Tuition and Fees
(if different):** No difference
Cost for Room and Board:
CA$6,941
**Percent receiving Financial
aid, first-year (out of those
who apply):** Unreported
**Percent of Undergraduates
Receiving Financial Aid:**
Unreported

L ocated just under two hours from Toronto, Canada's largest city, which styles itself as "the center of the universe," the University of Western Ontario is one of the nation's most prestigious universities and a mecca in its own right. Outstanding professors, a beautiful campus, a world-renowned business school, and high-quality undergraduate programs. draw many of Canada's top students to London, Ontario. The students here benefit not only from a highly respected degree but also from four years of "unparalleled fun."

Advancing Academics

The quality of the undergraduate academic experience at Western is, by most accounts, "steadily improving" as the administration tries to strengthen the school's academic credentials in order to attract top students. But though it is undeniably a "challenging" academic environment, for some students Western is "rightly known as a laid-back party school."

In general, classes are huge for most first-year students. Good professors are often found teaching underclassmen, but usually "there are about 500 of them crammed into a room at one time." Upper-level classes, however, tend to be a lot smaller. Says one student: "Western is not exactly well-known for its graduate and doctorate programs, so you definitely get the sense in third- and fourth-year classes that the professors are trying to woo you over to their discipline to build up the school's postgraduate reputation."

Of course, a student's impression of Western's academic experience depends greatly on which program he or she pursues. Western offers a competitive BA/HBA program in conjunction with its Richard Ivey School of Business, an internationally ranked management school. One student in the joint degree program described it as "very elite and 10 times harder than the rest of Western's undergraduate program." The University also boasts smaller, affiliate colleges, such as Huron College, which set their own academic programs and offer smaller classes. Students in other majors report varying degrees of overall satisfaction. A social science major would give Western academic experience a "five or six of ten," saying that there are "only a handful of amazing profs," and that "it's hard to get individual attention." An actuarial science major, on the other hand, reported receiving a lot of academic guidance during her first year.

Other students complain about a lack of grade inflation in certain departments. Many frustrated students find themselves with 67–75 percent when they feel that their work deserves better. However, one proactive student noted that approaching the professor and complaining about the TA's ineptitude often can result in a higher grade. Like many other big schools, Western is "a haven for finding loopholes."

A typical day at Western can stretch from early in the morning to late at night—one student reports having class from "9:00 a.m. to 10:00 p.m. with only a couple of hours of breaks in between." Engineering students sometimes have up to 35 hours of class a week. Ultimately, your schedule, your academic program, and your time at Western will be products of your ability to make the most of what the enormous school offers.

A Good Deal—Unless You're Hungry

Despite its sprawling size, Western retains a "tight, close-knit feel, even though it's a huge school," perhaps because London is so "tiny" and "in the middle of nowhere." Many say that London is "beautiful and cheap to live in" although "like elsewhere in Canada, the weather is pretty shitty."

All first-year, full-time students are guaranteed housing. There are two main kinds of residences, "suite-style" and "traditional." The suites are generally quite spacious, often featuring two bedrooms, two bathrooms, and a kitchen for four occupants. Rooms freshman year, says one student, are very clean. "We had cleaning service every day and our own bathroom."

Residential life is extremely social. The largest dorm, Saugeen-Maitland Hall, nicknamed "The Zoo," made it onto David Letterman's top 10 list of best places to get laid in North America. Both guys and girls can be "pretty skanky," says one student. Though not everyone shares that sentiment, many find that the dorms are the center of the campus social scene.

Food on campus is purchased on a pay-per-item basis, and though it is "generally pretty healthy," it can also be prohibitively expensive. Students living in residences get a sub-

stantial discount on the dining hall food. The meal plan allows students to purchase a debit card for use anywhere on campus and even in some London restaurants. Students praise the variety of offerings, including sundae and salad bars and pizza in some dining halls, but complain about the cost. Students living off campus—including most upperclassmen—more often take advantage of London's numerous eateries. There are many sushi places, and Starbucks shops abound. Says one student smugly, "the food around here is much better than at Queen's [University]," Western's chief rival and sport nemesis.

Students mainly describe the overall financial burden of attending Western as "reasonable," although "this school will nail you on expensive books—but you don't have to actually buy them unless you're a science major!" When the vast majority of upperclassmen move off campus, there is a wide variety of high-quality, relatively low-cost housing. As one student said, "$500 a month can get you a pretty nice place." And despite the higher tuition charges for international students and the current exchange rate, Western is still a bargain for Americans compared to U.S. schools of similar quality.

Primped and Primed

Students generally report that Western hosts a wide variety of people, and that every student can find their niche. Nevertheless, Western has a well-earned reputation as "Canada's private school" where many are the "children of wealthy families." There are "a lot of legacies," and "networking is really important here," says one student.

> "I thought that everyone would go to class in their pajamas, but people really dress up here!"

Another common observation about Western's student body is the *GQ*- and *Vogue*-worthy people who attend the University. There are some "very, very attractive women" who go here, and many students dress to impress. "I thought that everyone would go to class in their pajamas, but people really dress up here!" laments one student.

Like many other colleges, Western boasts an eccentric and resourceful group of engineering students. Recently a group of adept pranksters replicated a famous MIT stunt by dissembling a campus police car and reassembling it on the roof of a tall building. Each year several engineering students show their school colors by dyeing themselves purple for Homecoming Week. For one unfortunate student, however, the ink proved indelible for months. Students can join many extracurricular activities during their time away from class. Charity fashion shows are quite popular. One student says that her sorority was "a great way to meet people and become involved early on." Improv groups, student media organizations, and pre-professional clubs are also abundant on campus.

Nightlife at Western revolves mainly around campus bars and clubs. Though some city natives complain that all the bars "resemble Cheers," most students report satisfaction with a bustling downtown scene. One bar even has a terrace that overlooks the library. Greek organizations can offer an important socializing venue for first-years, many of whom are not yet 19 and cannot drink in London unless they have a fake ID. The Greek community, however, is not affiliated with the University, and some students lament the hostile attitude on the part of the administration towards fraternities and sororities, which has inhibited their presence on campus from becoming more widespread.

In general, a "very collegial atmosphere" prevails on campus. For the motivated students willing to seek them out, Western offers many wonderful academic and social possibilities that, for many, verify its reputation as one of Canada's top schools.—*Sara Schlemm*

FYI

If you come to Western, you'd better bring an "ironing board," "fancy clothes," and "independence."

What's the typical weekend schedule? "Go to bars on Richmond Street or frat parties. There may even be a toga party!"

If I could change one thing about Western I'd change "the expensive on-campus food."

Three things every Western student should do before graduating are "climb to the top of University College tower, follow the football team to Queen's, go to Jack's (the only on-campus bar where 'everyone' goes)."

Index